CONTROLS

USING DOCUMENTS AND FORMS

CONTROLLING COMPUTERS

Handbook of
EDP
Auditing

STANLEY D. HALPER, CPA, CISA (Certified Information Systems Auditor), is a Partner of Coopers & Lybrand and National Director of Auditing, the Computer Audit Assistance Group and National EDP, which develops software for client services. He has been an officer of the EDP Auditors Foundation and has served on the AICPA Computer Services Executive Committee.

GLENN C. DAVIS, CPA, CISA, is a Partner of Coopers & Lybrand and Director, Special Services for the National Computer Audit Assistance Group. He has had responsibility for developing computer audit policy, procedures, training and education programs, marketing, publications, and field standards.

P. JARLATH O'NEIL-DUNNE, CPA, CISA, FCA (Fellow of the Institute of Chartered Accountants in England and Wales), is a Partner of Coopers & Lybrand, directs computer audit policy, and is in charge of the "Audit of the Future" project at Coopers & Lybrand. He is a member of the AICPA Subcommittee on EDP Auditing Standards.

PAMELA R. PFAU is a Manager in the National Computer Audit Assistance Group of Coopers & Lybrand and has written several guidebooks on the use of computer software in the audit environment. She has taught computer concepts and programming at the college level and has been instrumental in developing and presenting the New York University diploma program for Information Systems Auditing.

Handbook of
EDP
Auditing

Stanley D. Halper

Glenn C. Davis

P. Jarlath O'Neil-Dunne

Pamela R. Pfau

COOPERS & LYBRAND

Simonoff Accounting Series

WARREN, GORHAM & LAMONT
Boston • New York

ISBN 0-88712-267-1

Library of Congress Catalog Card No. 85-51038

Published by

WARREN, GORHAM & LAMONT, INC.

210 SOUTH STREET, BOSTON, MASSACHUSETTS 02111

PREFACE

THIS BOOK REPRESENTS a consolidation of materials produced since 1974, the year that Coopers & Lybrand (C&L) established its Computer Audit Assistance Group (CAAG). The group was created to lend computer-related assistance on audits and to provide a large variety of services in relation to reviewing controls, performed primarily by EDP professionals trained in auditing who are highly experienced in automated environments. This book represents an overview of proven plans and procedures that have been developed and used successfully over those years. The detail reports, analyses, and other materials, given here in a necessarily brief form due to the requirements of a book format, exist in their entirety in the over 100 C&L offices in the United States.

In 1978, an earlier version of this book became the basis for the course, *Auditing in the Contemporary Computer Environment*, presented by Coopers & Lybrand and cosponsored by the EDP Auditors Association. Since then, we have presented more than 300 sessions of this course; it has also been customized for specific industries. The version developed for the banking industry has been cosponsored by the Bank Administration Institute. In 1983, Manufacturers Hanover Trust Company worked with C&L to further customize the course to make it specific to their environment and is now offering it to MHT's over 3,000 correspondent banks.

Since 1982, the basic course has been given as the basis of the New York University School of Continuing Education's diploma program in Information Systems Auditing.

This book contains many industry-specific concerns that are a result of our working with a diverse array of clients. The information presented throughout the book is therefore tried and tested and continues to evolve in practice and theory as the profession of EDP auditing grows and changes to meet the needs and challenges of the future.

Starting as an oddity that filled an entire room, and growing as it shrank into a small piece of equipment found in offices everywhere, the computer has evolved into an everyday presence. The daily use of computers, both to provide the kind of management information needed by organizations and to help audit financial systems, has become commonplace.

Our body of audit tools has likewise grown. During these years, over 400 publications of all kinds have been created by CAAG. Some have appeared in other forms in other places. Yet, this book is the result of our desire to compile and extract the kind of relevant information that can be used by those interested in the ever-changing world of EDP auditing. Aside from the hundreds of publications already cited, our practice materials include a 12-volume set of *Audit Software Reference Manuals* and a similar size *Field Standards Reference Manual* that give us constant guidance in the conduct of our practice.

Our own use of computers has grown as well. Not only do we audit computers, we use computers to audit. In 1975, we developed a generalized audit software package with a language we designed specifically for auditors, called AUDITPAK II. This package generates programs automatically, based on the auditor's selection of criteria that will meet specific audit objectives. It has been particularly helpful and has been used to generate over 100,000 AUDITPAK II programs that are reperformed periodically at our clients as an integral part of our audits of large systems. Application-specific packages have also been created to meet objectives in numerous audit situations. These packages have become so useful to us and our clients that we have made them available through local C&L offices throughout the country.

With the advent of microcomputers, we became able to use computer power at all of our clients, not just those that had their own machines. We have developed suitable audit-related software tools for microcomputers that are most useful to the CPA performing the broad range of work known as external auditing.

To serve our diverse client organizations, which range in size from the largest corporations in the United States to local businesses implementing their first computer-based systems, a remarkable group of people from all over have made it possible to provide this kind of individualized, competent service.

Acknowledgments

It was only through the efforts of numerous individuals that this written material could be developed. It would be impossible to list them all here. However, there are people whose special insight, unswerving devotion, and functional assistance in the formulation of new policies, practical working procedures, and overall strengthening of our team deserve special mention. We would like to thank them for their contributions to areas of concern to us all: Richard Barth, Frederick Beal, Jr., Douglas R. Bean, Stewart A. Berman, Vincent A. Campitelli, John W. Cassella, Robert M. DePalma, Allan W. Doe, Raymond W. Elliott, Thomas Farrell, Leonard Gilbert, Lynford E. Graham, Jr., Paul Heit, James E. Homet, Martin D. Jaslow, John E. Koretz, David B. Morrison, Michael A. Murphy, William R. Robinson, Thomas Y. Rush, John F. Shoosmith, Richard M. Steinberg, Jerry D. Sullivan, Kenneth A. Tucker, Arnold Wasserman, William Warrick, Henry R. Jaenicke, Myra D. Cleary, Joseph J. DiMuro, Thomas J. Flanagan, Eamon McMahon Glynn, Maureen McCarthy, Daniel J. Nealis, and William H. Wilson. James Keane and Mary Dempsey, in litigation support, also provided assistance.

One of the things that makes C&L such a dynamic organization is the truly international scope of the firm. Our group has had the benefit of the fresh point of view and different perspective provided by talented people from all parts of the globe. In particular, we would like to mention Darryl Ogden, Great Britain; Michael Stoneham, Canada; Willem Boshoff, South Africa; Nigel Ampherlaw, John Bruce, Elizabeth Kelly, and Catherine Stafford, Australia; and Teck Soon Chew, Singapore. As they came to our national office in New York, and continued their assignments in CAAG offices throughout the United States, we found that we learned much from those who had originally come to learn from us.

Special thanks are due to Coopers & Lybrand (International) and Coopers & Lybrand (United Kingdom) for permitting us to make use of selected portions of "An Audit Approach to Computers," by Brian Jenkins and Anthony Pinkney (both partners of Coopers & Lybrand, United Kingdom); and also to John Wiley & Sons, publishers, for use of selected portions of "Evaluating Internal Control" by Kenneth P. Johnson and Henry R. Jaenicke.

We acknowledge with thanks the permission granted to us by the American Institute of Certified Public Accountants, the Institute of Internal Auditors, and the EDP Auditors Association to quote or paraphrase passages from their publications. Copies of the complete documents can be obtained from those organizations.

For their help in providing an independent perspective of the book, we would like to thank Michael Cangemi, a Vice President at Phelps Dodge Corporation, responsible for auditing, data processing, and other areas; Dan C. Kneer, Assistant Professor of Accounting at Arizona State University; Walter N. Coleman, Staff Vice President of Auditing for RCA Corp.; and John M. Schnappauf, Director of MIS Auditing for RCA Corp.

To gather in all of the diverse C&L materials and publications to form this work and to bring it into reality, the role of project manager and senior editor was established here: Xenia Ley Parker had this responsibility and, with it, the monumental task of editing and rewriting all of this material to create a logical, uniform structure and stylistically consistent book.

Eugene Simonoff, Senior Vice President of Warren, Gorham & Lamont, was the driving force behind that firm's decision to publish the book and has been of special assistance. We also appreciate the efforts of their editorial staff and their editor.

We think that you will find the information here as useful as it has been to us, as you face the challenge of EDP auditing in the constantly evolving computer environment.

STANLEY D. HALPER

GLENN C. DAVIS

P. JARLATH O'NEIL-DUNNE

PAMELA R. PFAU

New York
March 1985

SUMMARY OF CONTENTS

PART V — USING DOCUMENTS AND FORMS

PART VI — CONTROLLING COMPUTERS

TABLE OF CONTENTS

xii TABLE OF CONTENTS

2 The Auditor and EDP Auditing

3 The EDP Auditing Profession

4 Systems Audit Approach

6 The Data Processing Department

7 The System Development Life Cycle

8 *On-Line Systems*

9 System Software

10 Data Base

11 Introduction to Accounting Systems

12 Revenue Systems

13 Disbursement Systems

14 Production Systems

15 *General Ledger Systems*

PART IV

Controls

16 Introduction to Controls

17 Controls for Completeness and Accuracy of Input

18 Controls for Completeness and Accuracy of Update

19 Controls for Validity, Maintenance and Operations

20 General or Integrity Controls

21 Control Reviews and Compliance Tests

22 Substantive or Validation Procedures

PART V

Using Documents and Forms

23 How to Document Systems and Use Flowcharts

24 _Interviews and Transaction Reviews in an Audit_

25 The Evaluation Process and How to Use Documents

26 Internal Control Reference Manual—General Controls

27 Internal Control Reference Manual — Application Controls

PART VI

Controlling Computers

28 Testing Techniques for Computer-Based Systems

29 Implementation Reviews

30 Microcomputers and How to Audit Them

31 Computer Abuse

32 Security

APPENDIX
Questionnaires, Forms and Charts

PART I

Audit Needs, Roles and Management

CHAPTER 1

EDP Auditing

WHY THERE IS A NEED FOR EDP AUDITING

Data processing technology has made great strides since its inception. Things that could only be thought of as engineer's dreams 30 years ago are a reality today. Improvements in hardware are matched by those in software. This evolution has ushered in teleprocessing, data base management systems, software security systems, distributed processing, minicomputers, and micro-computers.

Since computers have become an integral part of many organizations, management has come to rely on computers for efficient processing of the information needed to run an organization. Even small businesses, which until recently had been limited to using manual systems, can now afford computers.

Management rightly sees electronic data processing (EDP) as a powerful business tool. Yet its ever-increasing capabilities have raised some issues:

- The highly technical language of EDP sometimes impedes management's ability to communicate its needs, as well as to understand, use, and control computers.

- Distorted information produced by inefficient or improperly controlled systems can threaten the soundness of corporate decisions.

- The concentration of previously scattered information-gathering, record-keeping, and accounting functions has made organizations more vulnerable to error, malfunction, and fraud.

- The very nature of computer processing has spawned a trend toward less visual evidence of records being processed, increasing the need for stronger controls to protect records from intentional unauthorized changes and inadvertent errors.

The preceding items are some of the more pressing issues created by rapidly advancing computer technology and are of great concern to financial management and auditors who must cope with these changes.

Throughout industry, government, financial service organizations, and the public sector, there is a growing involvement with computers. Computerized accounting systems, for one, tend to be the rule, rather than the exception. At the same time, not only is the responsibility for controls changing, but the controls themselves are changing as well. The auditing profession needs to make a commitment to developing the computer skills of an already competent audit staff, while continuing to develop new procedures for the auditing of computer-based systems.

KEY ISSUES FOR THE AUDITING PROFESSION

Today's auditors must confront the issues raised by technology. Among these concerns, addressed throughout this book, are the following:

- Has the profession responded appropriately to the challenge of technical developments?

- Have organizations built up their EDP audit expertise?

- Is there a communications gap between internal auditors and EDP auditors?
- Are internal departments structured to suit the needs of their organizations?
- Is policy clear, well-defined, and in existence?
- Does planning take place early in the audit process and in the proper context?
- Is there consistent documentation to describe systems, their implementation, and their controls?
- Can auditors rely on controls within and over systems; do they need to check data and systems independently (substantive procedures)?
- Is the audit structure flexible enough to adapt to changing requirements?

The answers to many of these questions will become apparent as EDP auditors and their function within any organization evolve to meet the challenge of the future.

EDP Auditing in the Future

General trends and future concerns are being addressed by meetings of internal auditors and other forums for such discussions. The function of EDP auditing in the 1980s and into the 1990s will be developed, to a large extent, by people from across the country representing internal auditing, public accountancy, management, EDP professionals, and academia.

In one recent meeting, discussions yielded the following points, which will continue to affect the profession:

In system development, the auditor will increasingly take on the role of active controls consultant to management. As such, the EDP auditor will become an integral part of new systems by advising system development groups on controls. Of course, management is responsible for providing a quality assurance function as part of operations; the EDP auditor will not be part of the quality assurance function, but will continue to monitor it.

Auditing will occur on a much more timely basis. Interactive monitoring of systems should come into its own in the 1980s and 1990s. The building of software and the imbedding of software routines into new systems should be an important part of the EDP auditor's work.

Many people recognize that future non-EDP auditors will, of necessity, have some of the skills of the EDP auditor of today. The EDP auditor will be much more involved on a technical level in the auditing of general controls and providing software for the audit team. Security will be a key issue; to address it, the EDP auditor must be an integral part of auditing the general controls.

Audits will be much more operational controls-oriented than they are today. Both internal and external audit departments will have to concentrate on the operational or administrative controls, as well as on financial controls.

The external auditor will have to place more reliance on the internal auditor, since systems and general controls will be monitored on a continuing basis.

Distributed processing will accelerate in the 1980s and will have to be audited. This will require additional technical skills, which can be provided by the EDP auditor.

Regulatory reporting by internal and external auditors will increase over the next decade. Any possible occurrences of major fraud cases will tend to accelerate this reporting. (Controls may have to be reported on by companies in the future.)

Packaged software will start replacing customized software. Standards for controls are needed and should be set for packaged software. There will be a need to evaluate controls over packaged software and make evaluations available to internal auditors.

An audit decision support system is needed and should be developed. Such a system would be driven by a computer and would enable the auditor to create models, for example, of financial audit problems, and come to alternative decisions.

Third parties will be an integral part of systems in the future. For example, increasing information requirements will necessitate third-party organizations such as videotex service providers. These will have to be reviewed by external and/or internal auditors.

Pressures on internal audit management for increased productivity will be felt over the next 10 years. Productivity can be increased by developing new software to monitor systems, which will require less human resources, as well as new tools, such as decision support systems.

Microcomputers will have a place, primarily in decision support systems. The larger computers will continue to be the major "number crunchers" of the corporations and will have to perform much of the audit work. There probably will be more local problem-solving through distributed systems. Eventually the mainframes will be used as a source of computer power and for retention of data bases. No one expects microcomputers to replace large mainframes; however, microcomputers will complement the mainframes when appropriate.

There will be an increasing need to go into outside data bases to aid in the decision support systems. The microcomputer will be an important tool used to access such public data bases for analytical reviews and the like.

Standards for audit documentation as well as controls must come from the internal audit community. If auditors request that certain levels be standardized to create meaningful documentation, the organization concerned should comply. Documentation should be automated.

There is a need for development of good analytical software, for functions not currently available.

Statistical sampling may play an increased role in the future. (However, use of audit software may allow the need for sampling to be reduced or eliminated in many areas. Since audit software allows interrogation of all data held on computer files, many people believe that sampling could actually decrease.)

Audit software in the future must be "auditor friendly." Hardware and software vendors should be asked to build audit capabilities into their systems. Audit software should include quantitative and analytical methods, as well as easy access to external data bases.

Existing tools and knowledge may be under-used by many auditors. Future EDP auditors will take on additional roles, requiring interpersonal as well as technical skills:

- *As a business consultant* — To understand the business functions, risks, and opportunities of the systems of their companies.

- *As an information systems professional* — Technical demands on the EDP auditor will increase significantly.

In addition to audit software, many currently believe that audit hardware is necessary. In a distributed network, audit hardware could interface with, and monitor, the system.

A universal audit information system would be a valuable resource. An organization that would evaluate software packages for control purposes and provide an information link to internal auditors would likely be a real help.

The EDP auditor of the future will probably have to be expert in data communications and data base. The emphasis on technical proficiency of the EDP auditor will be stressed.

Many companies are now obtaining their EDP auditors through their data processing departments, and this trend should continue because of the technical requirements of EDP auditing. The EDP professional, once he or she becomes part of the audit team, must continue to get sufficient exposure to new technical aspects on an ongoing basis.

Potential for fraud will become an even more critical issue in the future. Monitoring of systems and general controls will be crucial in preventing fraud or detecting it on a timely basis.

External auditors are viewed as a resource. Therefore, external auditors may provide technical resources to internal audit staff to educate and assist management in setting up the necessary programs.

Internal and external audit staff must become more involved in security and contingency planning, with guidance from the Institute of Internal

Auditors (IIA), the American Institute of Certified Public Accountants (AICPA), and the EDP Auditors Association (EDPAA).

The EDP auditing profession is in a good position to meet these and other related challenges of the future. In order to do so, it becomes all the more important for current EDP audit departments to be well-structured and logically situated within the organization.

Factors in the Development of EDP Auditing

From management's viewpoint, internal auditing is concerned with minimizing risk, as is EDP auditing. EDP auditing developed in part because of management's need to face the undesirable consequences of malfunctioning controls. Failures can lead to these possibilities:

- Financial risks (such as misstatements of assets)
- Management risks (such as inappropriate decisions)
- Noncompliance violations (such as with the Foreign Corrupt Practices Act of 1977 or the Right to Financial Privacy Act of 1978)
- Other legal liabilities (such as stockholder's suits)
- Fraud (such as entry of unauthorized transactions)
- Business interruption or closure (due to inability to issue bills or payments, fulfill orders, and so forth)
- Adverse publicity

In the early days of EDP auditing, the primary concern was to ensure that the data was accurate by checking input, output, and user controls. This approach, sometimes called auditing *around* the computer, became ineffective as the volume of transactions to be checked became prohibitive and processing became more complex, often leaving no paper trail. Today's EDP audit function has evolved from testing only the results of processing to testing results and processing, plus performing evaluations and reviews of controls. Particularly when performed using audit software, this is sometimes called auditing *through* the computer.

Considerations in Implementing an EDP Audit Function

To implement sound EDP audit capability, management needs to consider the costs and benefits involved. The tangible costs include salaries, fringe benefits, office maintenance, training, development of audit programs, and computer usage. A major benefit can be cost savings, resulting from improved controls that minimize the potential for error or fraud. Another benefit is the operational improvement of the internal audit department due to effective EDP auditing: increased audit efficiency through the use of automated audit tools.

EDP Audit Activities

The EDP audit function's activities usually include the following:

- General (integrity) controls reviews
- Application controls reviews
- Tests of controls
- Software development support to internal auditors
- Data security/privacy reviews
- Risk analysis/contingency and disaster planning
- Training and education to maintain "state-of-the-art" knowledge

To perform these tasks, software can be implemented by the EDP auditor to produce audit reports and improve testing.

Audit Reports. The EDP auditor has a responsibility to provide information to the director of internal audit or the general auditor. By organizing and extracting data through the use of software, the EDP auditor can present information to assist the understanding of the other auditors.

Testing. To test the results of processing, the EDP auditor organizes data in order to cross-reference files, for example, comparing payroll to personnel. Tests are not always easy comparisons of data: Searching the files for unmatched comparisons may be needed.

In addition to software, the EDP auditor may use manual techniques. Traditional manual techniques involve processing individual accounts, vouching, reperformance, and tracking, among others. Specialized manual techniques require more extensive knowledge of EDP and include program reviews, examination of computer logs, and test data.

ENVIRONMENTAL AUDIT CONSIDERATIONS

Many of the situations encountered in developing EDP auditing functions are fairly commonplace. Figure 1-1 is an overview of various situations and their implications.

COORDINATION BETWEEN INTERNAL, EDP, AND EXTERNAL AUDITORS

Internal and external auditors frequently audit the same systems. The systems audit approach provides a suitable framework to share and divide audit tasks

(continued on page 1-10)

Situation	Audit Implications
☐ Auditors may assume that small computers mean simple systems, which is often not the case. This may mean that the EDP auditor is not involved to a sufficient degree in determining audit strategy and planning audit procedures.	☐ If the EDP auditor is not involved in setting audit strategy and planning the audit procedures, the budgeted hours for the job may be substantially underestimated. Also, there may not be sufficient time available before the audit deadline in which to develop any required audit software.
☐ The organization may have little or no EDP knowledge or experience and little or no knowledge of how to control computers and computer systems in operation.	☐ Lack of EDP knowledge and experience may ■ Cause high audit set-up time (in gaining an understanding, implementing software, and so forth). ■ Increase chance of undetected errors. ■ Result in the organization or the auditor placing reliance on programmed procedures whose failure may not be detected. ■ Require more EDP skill from the auditor when the users cannot be expected to supply technical support. ■ Cause significant problems in budgeting, since total audit costs may be underestimated.
☐ It may not be possible to use standard file interrogation programs (audit software) due to the diversity of equipment, storage methods, and programming languages.	☐ Customized audit software is expensive to develop, requiring knowledge of the language and equipment; this situation is further aggravated if the users have no programming skills. ☐ Allowance must be made for an environmental learning curve. ☐ The use of computer query or command language will probably be a viable alternative, if available.
☐ There may be a cost or time constraint.	☐ The auditor still must proceed with understanding and auditing complex systems.

FIG. 1-1   Environmental audit considerations

Situation	Audit Implications
	☐ Use of automated techniques is costly. The smaller the audit budget, the less likely that it will support automated techniques. However, this depends on the auditor's skill and the audit objectives, so it may still be possible to use software.
☐ Packaged or turnkey systems may be low in cost, but at the same time may be very complex. For packaged or turnkey systems also consider the impact of:	☐ If the systems are complex, the cost of the audit may tend to be disproportionate to the amount of time required to gain an adequate understanding and the extra time needed to implement EDP audit techniques (such as audit software).
■ How well the package is known	■ If the package is well known and has a good track record, then it is unlikely that the programmed procedures will be in error.
■ How well it is documented	■ The lack of adequate documentation may — Restrict the auditor's ability to gain an adequate understanding of the processing, resulting in the need for heavy analytical research. — Result in the user's inability to control the operation of the system effectively due to a lack of knowledge.
■ Whether the package has been modified	■ If the system has been modified substantially by the user, then there may be a greater risk of errors occurring within programmed procedures.
■ Whether the package provides adequate information so that basic user controls can be established	■ If the system does not provide adequate information (such as printout of control totals) the auditor may be precluded from making control recommendations which will be inexpensive to implement.
☐ There may be a loss of audit or information trail due to: ■ A lack of history files ■ A potential lack of complete output	☐ A loss of audit or information trail may result in: ■ The inability of the auditor to substantiate data simply because it is not available.

(continued)

Situation	Audit Implications
■ Destructive program updates ■ Limited retention of data files	■ A significant effect on the timing and spread of audit tests. ■ Automated/manual reperformance of financial updates becoming difficult or impossible.
☐ The supplier of the hardware and/or application software may not give reliable and adequate support.	☐ The users may find that they have a lot of unsupported, unmaintainable software and equipment, with resulting difficulties in processing.
☐ Timing execution of audit software may be critical due to: ■ Limited data retention ■ Systems unavailable	☐ Early planning of run times for audit software is essential to ensure that the data files and computer time required are available.

FIG. 1-1 *(continued)*

in order to increase the efficiency and effectiveness of the combined effort. The work can be shared between internal, EDP, and external auditors in many ways. Following are some possibilities:

- Internal auditors and management should discuss ways in which the work can be split with external auditors to reduce audit costs.
- Internal EDP auditors can draw the flowcharts.
- Internal EDP auditors can obtain record layouts.
- Internal auditors can assist external auditors with working papers, to give the external auditor what is needed.
- Internal auditors can follow up on the external auditor's management letter comments from the previous year to determine which recommendations were implemented.
- Internal EDP auditors can develop software that both internal and external auditors can use. For example, the EDP auditor might develop software to test accounts receivable at year-end. The internal auditor can run the same programs quarterly.
- External EDP auditors can develop software that both external and internal auditors can use. For example, external EDP auditors may develop software for fluctuation analysis of various accounts to test whether the fluctuation represents the valid climate of the business.
- Internal EDP auditors can act as liaisons between EDP, management, users, and others to determine what systems have changed before software is to be run by the external auditor.
- Internal EDP auditors can use flowcharts to train their staff in how the systems work.

RELIANCE ON INTERNAL AUDITORS

A recent article in a major accounting journal discussed the results of a survey of almost 100 public accountants and internal auditors (split about equally). The purpose of the survey was to determine (1) the extent and manner in which external auditors are relying upon the internal audit function; (2) whether both groups believe the extent and manner of reliance is sufficient; and (3) how that reliance may change in the future. Since EDP auditors are found in both internal audit departments and in external auditor teams, this can affect their function.

The survey showed that virtually all external auditors rely on internal auditors to some extent, while about half of both groups indicated that reliance on internal auditors could be increased. Reasons reliance is not greater included the following:

- Lack of understanding on both sides
- Insufficient cross-training in methods and procedures
- The limits of reliance on each other
- External auditors' perception of internal auditors' unwillingness to participate in the financial audit

About three fourths of those surveyed agreed that internal auditors should be relied on in many audit areas. A majority seem to want to strengthen and extend the reliance relationship under the proper conditions.

Statement of Auditing Standards (SAS) No. 9, *The Effect of an Internal Audit Function on the Scope of the Independent Auditor's Examination*, in AU Sections 322.05–322.07, "Reviewing the Competence and Objectivity of Internal Auditors," and Section 322.08, "Evaluating the Work of Internal Auditors," requires the independent auditor to consider the competence and objectivity of internal auditors and to evaluate their work. (See Chapter 2, "The Auditor and EDP Auditing.") Although somewhat more than half of the internal auditors surveyed agreed that the external auditors were qualified to determine their competence and three fourths agreed that external auditors are qualified to determine their objectivity, all of the external auditors thought themselves qualified. These reviews sometimes create resentment on the part of the internal auditors. Of course, the terms competence and objectivity are not subject to precise definition; to make such a determination, the external auditors must show perception and tact.

External auditors seem to believe that internal auditors need be only as competent and objective as their work requires, while two thirds of internal auditors thought their competence was comparable to that of the external auditors in a reliance relationship. Some internal auditors cited the relatively inexperienced external audit staff people sent on some audits and believe their own competence may exceed that of many external auditors. In all respects, internal auditors believe that they are technical equals of the external auditors.

To test internal auditor's work, SAS No. 9 in AU Section 322.08 suggests the external auditor may examine a portion of details audited by the internal auditors to confirm the internal auditor's findings. Survey responses suggest that external auditor's tests can be based on both reperformance and an examination of evidence of internal auditors' work, such as initials on a document. Some internal auditors thought that there is a tendency for external auditors to review and test internal auditors' work more extensively than similar work performed by their own staff members; about a third of external auditors surveyed said they probably would apply stricter standards to supervising and testing internal auditors' work.

The survey indicated that a little more than one half of the external auditors surveyed have a firm-wide policy statement regarding reliance on internal auditors. Less than one half of the internal audit organizations have adopted a formal policy statement concerning cooperation with external auditors. Although many technical areas of external auditing have produced detailed policy statements, programs, manuals, questionnaires, and training functions to provide general guidance in official statements on auditing, this has not happened in the reliance area. Survey results seem to indicate that external auditors are relatively satisfied, but internal auditors seek improvement.

Cost savings and better audit coverage by cooperative audit performance were among the benefits identified. Other benefits include:

- External auditors can obtain better insight into the client's operations, especially in specialized areas, through the experience and knowledge of internal auditors.

- Improved relations can result from cooperation in a coordinated effort.

- External auditors would be able to concentrate on more significant areas.

- There can be a rotation of audit emphasis.

- A small internal audit department can make use of the resources and specialization available in a large public accounting firm.

In the next decade, reliance on internal auditors and their work is likely to increase due to increasing legal responsibilities, audit committees requirements, increased governmental regulation, and other factors. External auditors will need to rely on internal auditors who have a good knowledge of their own company systems. This is already taking place at present, as seen by the use of a permanent set of files used by both the internal and external auditors. Management letter comments, recommendations, flowcharts, questionnaires, and such can be located in the "common user file" of working papers.

SELECTING A VIABLE EDP AUDIT ORGANIZATIONAL STRUCTURE

In their pursuit of increased audit effectiveness, a growing number of organizations expect internal and EDP auditors to make a more significant contribution. One method of structuring EDP auditing within an organization is to view the function as an integral part of internal audit. Thus, its primary purpose is to generate audit reports through the use of software. Another method views the function as independent, reviewing the processing and other general controls, together with independent reviews of EDP systems. In the latter structure, the EDP audit function does not fit easily into the general auditing function.

Between these two extremes is a range of choices open to management. Whether the EDP auditing group reports to internal audit or is a separate entity, open lines of communication must be maintained. Key elements are that EDP auditors know internal and operational auditing, know practical auditing techniques, and have in-depth knowledge of data processing.

The size of an organization has a significant impact on the structure and function of EDP auditing. In a smaller company with limited staff, the EDP auditor is frequently active in many areas, performing reviews as well as implementing and executing software. In larger organizations, the process of reviewing data processing is often a function in itself, due to the increasingly specialized knowledge required to audit a large EDP system. In a large-scale environment, reviewing controls in data processing is usually distinct from reviewing controls over the user functions, such as bill processing or other applications.

The internal audit department's own operations can be either helped or hindered by its organizational structure. To operate effectively, internal and EDP auditors should communicate directly and routinely with the audit committee. This results in closer working relations, which tend to strengthen the objectivity of both. Simultaneously, the auditors gain greater independence from operating personnel, and the audit committee receives a regular stream of accurate and timely information. The internal audit function (including EDP audit) should be headed by a senior executive, reporting administratively to the highest levels of the organization (such as the president) to obtain serious consideration of the auditors' findings and recommendations. Of course, this executive should also report regularly to the audit committee.

Internal and EDP auditors can function successfully only when they have the ability to respond promptly to changing legal, regulatory, and professional requirements. It is understood that they need a high level of professionalism, expertise, and understanding of the business. Unrestricted access to company activities, records, property, and personnel is essential. Annual audits should include visits to important locations and regular reviews of functions exerting a substantial influence on profits.

The audit committee can participate in approving audit schedules, setting audit policy, reviewing major findings, and monitoring the operations of, and coordination between, internal auditors, EDP auditors, and external auditors or public accountants. In addition to the relationship of the internal audit function with the audit committee and the president, effective departmental organization is needed. This can be achieved on a centralized, decentralized, or hybrid basis.

Centralized Organization

In a centralized organization, the internal and EDP auditors report directly to headquarters. The advantages of this type of organization include independence from local management and a resultant measure of objectivity. The auditors have close ties with corporate management, whose support can be expected to bring quick action on recommendations. There should be flexibility in making audit staff available to meet requests for service and improved coordination with external auditors.

One of the disadvantages of a centralized organization, however, is the potential for the development of an adversary relationship between the internal auditors and local management. This type of situation can lead to less than complete cooperation — if not actual resistance — on the part of local management, who may perceive the audit function as a control rather than a service.

Decentralized Organization

In a decentralized organization, each division has its own internal and EDP auditors who report to local management. The positive aspects of this arrangement include close ties at the local level which could facilitate management's acceptance of the auditors' recommendations. Cooperation at the local level also may be enhanced by management's perception of the benefits it receives. Further, reduced travel expenses and lessened personal strains should promote economy and efficiency.

A disadvantage is that auditors may come to identify with local interests to the detriment of their objectivity. Further, uneven performance may stem from difficulties in standardizing audit approaches and setting standards for evaluations.

Hybrid Organization

A hybrid organization melds both headquarters auditors and divisional auditors. A smaller group of auditors are assigned to headquarters under the general auditor to oversee guidance and coordination. Each division has internal and EDP auditors of its own, who report to the division president. These field auditors are rotated among the divisions often enough to maintain their independence and objectivity. Although they report on a divisional basis, in effect they also report to the general auditor.

The advantages of the hybrid organization are that it is based on a combination of the best features of centralization and decentralization. In this way, corporate headquarters can furnish expert guidance to the local auditors and, at the same time, acquire detailed knowledge of local operations at the site.

Audit Control Group

The hybrid arrangement sometimes works well with a headquarters audit control group, which operates under the aegis of the president or the audit committee. This group can be of significant help; it can evaluate audit findings and disseminate to all divisions pertinent ideas for lowering costs or augmenting revenues. An audit control group can monitor the response of different divisions to audit findings and recommendations, and can control the quality of audits by auditing the auditors to ensure that professional standards are maintained at all units.

An audit control group should also contribute by researching advanced auditing techniques to enhance audit effectiveness and by coordinating all the activities of internal and EDP auditors and external auditors or public accountants. It can also integrate the work of the internal, EDP auditing, and EDP departments to make certain that audit findings are accorded the attention they deserve when existing systems are modified or new ones are designed. An audit may indicate that modification is needed.

THE AUDIT COMMITTEE

Audit committees have become an integral part of most major organizations in the United States. Since they were first proposed as a preventive measure by the New York Stock Exchange in 1939 and the Securities and Exchange Commission (SEC) in 1940 in response to the McKesson-Robbins scandal, they have clearly shown their worth.

As the business community has come to see how helpful audit committees can be in meeting obligations to shareholders, while at the same time providing the board of directors with a different perspective on corporate operations than that provided by management, their strength and effectiveness has grown.

Audit committees were created to establish the independence of auditing functions from the managements they were auditing. Although there are general guidelines from the New York Stock Exchange, the SEC, and AICPA, their activities vary from company to company. Most audit committees have several basic functions; due to EDP inclusion in much of the processing of today's organizations, it is an implicit part of these concerns:

- Monitoring external audit plans and procedures
- Reviewing the internal and EDP audit departments
- Checking audit results
- Reviewing financial statements
- Reviewing the selection of external auditors
- Conducting investigations and other board-related tasks
- Facilitating communication between the board of directors and internal/external auditors

To determine the range of responsibilities the audit committee should take on in a particular organization, certain factors should be considered. These include size and complexity of the organization, the number of locations (including computer centers), its external environment and response to its financial accounting and auditing functions, special industry needs, the extent of computerization, the function of other corporate committees, the need to develop or enhance EDP systems that affect financial and other management information, special interests and concerns of audit committee members, the number of meetings held per year, and the ability of members to participate.

Concurrently, the committee can help meet the perceived needs of top management for strengthening of organizational internal controls, enhancement of management information systems, further development of enforceable standards, computerized processing and practices for financial recordkeeping and statement generation, and maintenance of competent, knowledgeable internal, EDP, and external auditors. To assist management in addressing these concerns, the audit committee has taken on a larger role in the highest levels of planning and development. This role frequently includes taking part in EDP steering committees.

Reporting to the board of directors, an effective audit committee has become truly useful to both sides of the corporate coin. On one side, it aids the board, whose directives include setting policy, to ensure that management performance meets these expectations and fulfills corporate responsibilities to the shareholders. On the other, it assists the management in charge of controlling operations and systems to ensure performance according to top management's intentions.

Establishing an Audit Committee

Careful planning and thought should go into creating an audit committee so that it can provide an organization with functional service. Usually the board of directors establishes an audit committee by a resolution.

Once the mandate for an audit committee is clear, the board of directors must coordinate its actions according to state laws, the organization's charter, and any existing policies regarding the formation of committees. The board should make important decisions about assembling an audit committee, including the committee's objectives, its size and composition, its membership, the term of office of members, the frequency of meetings, and the mechanism for reporting to the board.

The Audit Committee's Objectives

The first step in creating an audit committee is for the board of directors to define clearly what it wants the committee to achieve. The board should also outline the extent of the committee's authority, and its specific tasks and responsibilities, in writing. Any subcommittees, such as an EDP steering committee, should be described. Relevant external and internal personnel should receive the statement to understand the function and purpose of the audit committee.

Determining Its Size and Composition

The board should create a committee to afford maximum balance in perspective, experience, and wisdom. In many cases, there are about five members, selected from outside the company. Generally, it is most effective to select external members with diverse background who provide an objective point of view. Due to the increasing importance of EDP, if possible at least one member should have sound working knowledge of the area.

The audit committee should meet immediately prior to the board of directors meeting to provide current information about their activities. The number of meetings per year is influenced by the scope of the committee's responsibilities; most audit committees meet between two and four times a year. Special meetings, such as on EDP concerns, can be set up when required. Typical audit committee meetings include preaudit, postaudit, and periodic meetings.

Preaudit Meeting. Conducted with the external auditors, the preaudit meeting familiarizes the audit committee with the basic approach of the external auditors, the accounting procedures and policies of the organization, new developments in regulations or accounting practices that may affect the organization, internal controls, the impact of EDP on the audit, or other areas that require the attention of the committee.

Postaudit Meeting. Held after the audit but before a financial report is released to the public, the postaudit meeting is used for discussion of findings and recommendations. Members of management and the external auditors should be present, as well as the entire audit committee.

Periodic Meetings. These meetings can be held with management, external auditors, and internal auditors to discuss topics such as more effective controls, regular operations, special assignments (for example, fraud investigations), or general management concerns (for example enhancing existing EDP systems or handling conflict-of-interest situations).

Reporting to the Board

Reports to the board of directors should detail activities of the audit committee. Written reports can include the minutes of the audit committee meetings taken by a member or recording secretary. Oral reports can be supplemented with the agendas and meeting minutes. The audit committee should submit suggestions that require board action in writing.

Areas of Concern

Developments in three areas have become important concerns of many audit committees: compliance with the Foreign Corrupt Practices Act, organizational codes of conduct, and corporate filing in accordance with the SEC's integrated disclosure system.

The Foreign Corrupt Practices Act. One of the many concerns of audit committees is corporate compliance with the Foreign Corrupt Practices Act of 1977, which requires that all publicly held companies maintain records of transactions and that internal accounting controls be in place. (See Chapter 3, "The EDP Auditing Profession.") The proper function of EDP systems that process those records and transactions becomes essential for their accurate maintenance. Relevant to the Act, the audit committee may

- Meet with the internal auditors and EDP auditors to receive assurance that the internal control system is adequate.
- Review reports of internal, EDP, and external auditors to assess internal controls over financial reporting and protection of assets.
- Suggest possible improvement of controls.

- Ensure the effectiveness of the corporate policies on conflict of interest and code of conduct.

Codes of Conduct. Many organizations have instituted formal codes of conduct that let their personnel know exactly what is expected of them when conducting business. Although a code of ethics does not always deter illegal practices without concomitant effective internal controls, it helps establish an environment conducive to acceptable behavior. Internal and EDP auditors are usually expected to follow the professional standards and codes of ethics set by the IIA and the EDPAA, and any other applicable standards.

Organizations often require certain employees to sign statements that they understand company policies and have not violated them. When there are questions, they are referred to a conflict-of-interest committee, legal counsel, or management; the audit committee may sit in on the proceedings. Since conflicts of interest are an area of particular concern, it is important to ensure that internal policies specify conditions that may serve as deterrents.

Securities and Exchange Commission's Integrated Disclosure System. In recent years, the SEC has substantially altered its reporting requirements. It now requires that Form 10-K be endorsed by the board of directors, the chief executive officer of the company, and its main financial and accounting officers. The audit committee can be particularly helpful in review of the Form 10-K because the committee members understand both the principles involved and the company's financial information included in the document.

The Audit Committee and the Internal Audit Department

The rise of the audit committee has occurred during a parallel boom in internal and EDP audit activities. With increasing frequency, audit committee members seek out the internal auditors for appraisal of internal accounting and operational controls (including controls over EDP systems) and special investigations.

Defining the exact role of the audit committee is complicated by the fact that individual internal audit departments differ greatly in their approach. Some have extensive EDP audit staff; others have none. Some internal audit departments adhere closely to supporting the system of internal control. They focus on matters such as surprise cash accounts and inventory verifications. Some support the external audit by focusing on evaluations of internal accounting controls and validation of account balances. Others concentrate on the effectiveness of management and are broadly responsible for judging the degree of compliance with company policy and practices. Certain internal audit departments are interested primarily in operational audits and have well-developed strength in EDP, sophisticated software, and techniques that are valuable in themselves. Internal and EDP audit departments frequently serve as management training for rising executives.

Audit Committee Influences on EDP and Internal Audit Development

The differences in approach can be attributed in part to the diverse routes that internal audit departments have followed in their development. The concept of a strong audit committee itself is sponsored in many places; audit committees have been assuming an increasingly active role in guiding the internal and EDP audit function. Early on in many industries, notably banking, audit committees established a close working relationship with the internal audit function. For example, the New York Stock Exchange has shifted from just encouraging audit committees to requiring them for listing on the exchange. The direction that internal and EDP auditing takes in the future will be influenced strongly by the attitudes of audit committees and the directors who sit on them.

Since the approaches to internal and EDP auditing vary so widely, the benefits of divergent approaches should be explored by audit committees. They can determine how the internal and EDP audit function can best help them to fulfill their objectives and how they can bring about coordination of the internal audit and the external audit. Some audit committees have selected either a financial or an operational audit approach. Many encourage a combination of methods, the rationale for which is that the external auditor's tests, observations, and evaluations are aimed at expressing an opinion on the financial statements, while the internal and EDP auditors provide the audit committee with valuable additional information from an operational point of view.

Operational Auditing

Some internal audit departments concentrate on and scrutinize documents and records that external auditors test in more limited fashion. The internal and EDP audit functions can be especially valuable to management when they also identify operational problems and recommend possible solutions that may not be of major concern to the external public accountants in their annual audit.

The IIA's *Statement of Responsibilities of the Internal Auditor* opens with the following explanation: "Internal auditing is the review of operations as a service to management. It is a managerial control which functions by measuring and evaluating the effectiveness of other controls." Operational auditing goes "beyond the accounting and financial records to obtain a full understanding of the operations under review."

Internal Audit Charter

From time to time the audit committee should review and revise the internal audit charter. The revision should provide the ability to cope with information technology and state the department's responsibilities. Possible areas include the following:

- Setting policies for the audit function, including EDP audit policies
- Developing a comprehensive long-range audit program, including the role of computerized auditing
- Evaluating management's stewardship at all levels for effectiveness in complying with company policies and procedures, beginning with customary financial auditing
- Assessing internal accounting and administrative or operational controls and their relation to achievement of corporate objectives
- Recommending improvements to administrative or operational controls to safeguard assets, secure EDP systems, promote corporate growth, and increase profits
- Issuing audit reports, including findings and recommendations that point out deficiencies and areas for improvement
- Appraising the effectiveness of actions taken to correct deficiencies (until they are resolved satisfactorily)
- Conducting special investigations into sensitive areas, such as incidences of computer abuse or conflict-of-interest situations, at the request of management, the external auditors, or the audit committee
- Investigating defalcations to determine cause and extent of loss and to recommend appropriate action
- Assisting the chief financial officer in facilitating and coordinating the work of the external auditors
- Giving assistance to the audit committee

Communication Between the Audit Committee and the Internal Audit Department

In practice, an audit committee can bring a number of specific benefits to the internal auditor's relationship with an organization. An audit committee can help assess the alertness and energy of the internal and EDP auditors, the scope and limitations of their work, and the quality of their contribution to the organization.

Through working with the auditors, the audit committee gains insight into the audit function. Knowing what the auditor does, or can do, enables the committee to use that function more effectively. Through enhanced communication with external, internal, and EDP auditors, the members of the audit committee can develop a better perception of sensitive areas and potential trouble spots in the company's financial affairs. This may prepare the committee to cope with trouble, should it develop. As a result of obtaining input from the internal auditors, the audit committee is in a better position to weigh the quality and sufficiency of the information given them by management. In general, a strongly motivated and effective audit committee, aided by an internal audit charter strengthens the performance of the internal and EDP auditors and thereby increases protection for shareholders, directors, and management.

The audit committee needs to have clearly defined lines of communication with the internal auditors to strengthen its effectiveness and objectivity. To maintain a smooth flow of communication, these general conditions should be met: the internal audit function should be able to respond to changing requirements quickly and efficiently; the audit staff must possess a high level of professional and technical expertise and an understanding of the businesses they will review; the audit staff must also have unrestricted access to all company functions, records, property, and personnel. As mentioned previously, the general auditor should report to a high-level executive to ensure that deficiencies are considered promptly and corrective actions are monitored. To maintain effective communications, the audit committee must understand and be involved in the annual internal audit program. Naturally, the audit committee should maintain a close working relationship with the general auditor and the internal and EDP audit staff.

Annual Audit Program

An annual program defines and establishes an audit schedule and the workload for the internal audit department that is consistent with the department's charter. The annual audit program should provide an appropriate plan to track the company's operations, financial records, and EDP systems in order to detect variances from procedures or goals, uncontrolled situations, and exposure to risk. Use of risk analysis can help planning.

For an annual audit program to succeed, the general auditor must communicate with operating units and obtain local management cooperation. There should be coordination with the organization's external auditors to assist them without duplicating efforts, review of previous management letters from the external auditors to check follow-up on their comments, and visits to the major corporate and divisional departments and, possibly, computer centers or plants to gain information. All this is done to determine which areas to audit and how to proceed. For each activity, this information should help prescribe an audit scope, audit frequency, time requirements, use of audit software and computer processing time, areas of potential improvement (such as dollars spent or income generated), special problems, EDP processing capabilities, number of people working in the area, key people to contact, and proposals for modifications to systems.

General Auditor

The general auditor is responsible for carrying out the annual program, managing the internal auditing department, and conveying the results of audit operations to the appropriate levels of management. The general auditor helps ensure that a company is protected against dissipation of its assets or loss of profit opportunities through noncompliance with authorized policies and practices, uneconomical use of resources, or inefficient EDP systems and methods of operation. The general auditor should further the company's interests with comments and suggestions for extension, modification, or additions to established policies and practices. It goes without saying that the general auditor should bring significant deficiencies (such as fraud, computer crime, or other illegal acts) to the immediate attention of senior management and the audit committee.

To conform with the established audit charter, policies, and budgets, the general auditor has responsibility to

- Schedule and direct reviews at all locations to evaluate the effectiveness of internal accounting and operational controls (including general controls over computer processing departments).
- Install an appropriate system to monitor responses to audit findings and recommendations, and determine the adequacy of any remedial actions taken.
- Furnish audit committee members with schedules of internal audits, and other reports, data, computer-generated summaries, and commentary they need to conduct their duties.
- Provide professional development and training opportunities for the internal audit staff (including strengthening of EDP audit and technical computer skills).
- Develop modern auditing techniques and programs for audit staff use (including use of audit software).
- Maintain and/or recruit for sound EDP audit strength (including adding personnel or retraining staff as required).
- Establish a quality control program to review audit plans, programs, documentation, and methods that safeguard the independence, scope, technical proficiency, and efficient performance of audits throughout the organization (including use of computer processing, audit software, and other techniques).
- Institute a system of cost control over audit programs.

- Review audit findings with staff at all management levels, especially with those responsible for the functions examined, to motivate corrective measures and action when needed.

- Ensure that staff is technically proficient and kept up to date in the latest techniques, including use of audit software and related skills.

- Make internal audit findings and supporting working papers, reports, and commentary available to the external auditors.

- Integrate results of auditing components of an EDP system, especially when spanning departments, locations, and computers.

- Integrate results of general and application control audits to determine overall risks.

- Inform the external accountants of past and projected internal audit schedules and computer processing capabilities, to avoid duplication of effort.

- Maintain appropriate communications with the audit committee, the corporate EDP department, and other staff departments and functions.

Internal Audit Staff

The general auditor manages staff members, sometimes considered junior executives in a training assignment. Their work background is often in other departments or public accounting firms. College training in accounting, including internal auditing or management and EDP systems, is important. Staff members should be willing to participate in professional development and self-improvement programs and be interested in qualifying as certified internal auditors (CIAs); EDP auditors should want to qualify as certified information systems auditors (CISAs). In addition, they should follow the IIA's code of ethics and the EDPAA's code of ethics, as appropriate.

Internal auditors should not be burdened with routine tasks that divert them from their primary duty of reviewing and evaluating internal accounting and operating controls. Additionally, they should be aware of others in the company who perform audit functions, even though they may carry titles relating to marketing, purchasing, or other functions. The general auditor should assess the extent to which the work of personnel in other departments may be relied on by the audit staff.

Internal Audit Function Checklist

The internal audit function is assuming ever-increasing importance as corporations expand and their accounting systems become more complex and computerized. Pressures continue to mount on executives and boards of directors to maintain vigilance over all aspects of their organization's operations, including audit procedures. Equally important, a properly functioning internal audit system can help pinpoint areas of potential revenue improvement and cost reduction. Recommendations to streamline information processing frequently include evaluation of EDP systems in use.

Many external auditors have developed checklists to aid in assessing internal auditors. Management can use such lists to evaluate the internal audit function. Following is a sample checklist of this nature.

	Yes	*No*
1. Organization		
a. Does the board of directors' audit committee participate in approving the audit schedule, guiding the work of the internal audit staff in a broad sense, and overseeing the coordination of internal, EDP, and external audit operations?	☐	☐
b. Does the manager in charge of the internal audit function report to a high-level executive who can ensure that deficiencies are considered promptly and that corrective action is monitored?	☐	☐
2. Qualifications:		
a. Do personnel appointed to the internal audit staff have the capacity to advance to higher positions?	☐	☐
b. Do internal auditors engage in continuous training and self-development?	☐	☐
c. Are internal auditors in a position to maintain independence in matters they review?	☐	☐
d. Does the staff possess sufficient EDP skill to deal with computerized systems?	☐	☐
3. Performance Guide:		
a. Are internal and EDP auditors overly burdened with routine tasks?	☐	☐
b. Do internal and EDP auditors have full access to all areas of the company that their work requires?	☐	☐
c. Does the internal audit schedule provide coverage of all physical facilities within a reasonable time cycle?	☐	☐
d. Do internal and EDP auditors submit periodic reports, which permit management to evaluate progress in terms of the established schedule?	☐	☐
e. Is the audit team's work guided by written programs?	☐	☐
f. Are audit programs flexible enough to respond to changing control conditions?	☐	☐

	Yes	No
g. Do the audit staff's working papers include comprehensive documentation of all tests, stating what was examined, procedures that were followed, and the results obtained?	☐	☐
h. Are all audit programs signed off to indicate completion of steps?	☐	☐
i. Are the results of each examination stated in a written report to management and expressed in terms that are suitable for follow-up?	☐	☐
j. Does the follow-up include a way to ensure that all control deficiencies pointed out by the internal audit are corrected as soon as possible?	☐	☐
k. Does the internal audit staff review operational (administrative) and general EDP controls on a cyclical basis, with special attention to areas of potential revenue improvement and cost reduction?	☐	☐
l. Has the internal audit function been independently reviewed?	☐	☐

SUMMARY

The increasing importance of EDP auditing to the auditing profession as a whole is due not only to the growing number of installed computer systems but also to the new capabilities and user applications that are constantly being developed for computer systems.

Already, in the short period of its existence, the manner in which EDP auditing is performed has undergone a change. The auditor's emphasis has shifted from the direct evaluation and verification of normal processing results, such as data files, records, and reports, to the evaluation and verification of the controls that ensure the continuing accuracy, usefulness, and reliability of processing results. (The shift has been from auditing *around* the computer to auditing *through* the computer.) This shift has been necessary because many of the procedures that process data have been automated and can no longer be reviewed and tested through direct observation.

Over the past couple of decades, the growing importance of data processing in today's workplace brought about the emergence of this new specialization within the audit function. Most EDP auditors have a background in either general auditing or data processing and decide to learn the skills of the other profession. The work involved in EDP auditing requires extensive preparation not only at the outset: Even experienced EDP auditors require ongoing training to keep abreast of the new technologies and frequent modifications to audit policies and methods. As EDP auditing faces the future, this continuing commitment to development of skills will ensure that there are qualified people to meet the challenges to come.

CHAPTER **2**

The Auditor and
EDP Auditing

INTRODUCTION TO EDP AUDITING

Auditing has changed considerably over the years as electronic data processing (EDP) techniques have had an enormous impact on the way in which management information is processed. Although fundamentals of the profession remain the same, the need to develop and maintain current knowledge of computer systems is growing. To provide special skills and expertise, the EDP auditor has come into the organizational picture. Although many of the same control questions are involved, the EDP auditor is a specialist in computer-based systems who can provide invaluable assistance to the organization and to other auditors regarding controls over those systems. In this way, the audit functions are naturally intertwined.

Many of the professional ethics and requirements for internal, external, and EDP auditors are the same. Some differ only because of the specific job-related activities that each type of auditor performs. This chapter discusses some of the major pronouncements of the Institute of Internal Auditors (IIA), the American Institute of Certified Public Accountants (AICPA), the EDP Auditors Association (EDPAA), and other organizations relevant to the internal auditor or, in some cases, to external and internal auditors. For more about the EDP auditing profession itself, see Chapter 3, "The EDP Auditing Profession."

PROFESSIONAL STANDARDS FOR THE PRACTICE OF INTERNAL AUDITING

Statement of Responsibilities of Internal Auditors

Internal auditing is an independent appraisal activity within an organization that reviews operations as a service to management. It is a managerial control which functions by measuring and evaluating the effectiveness of other controls. Particularly in today's computerized environment, controls over EDP systems can be essential to an organization's conduct of business.

Objectives and Scope

The basic objective of internal auditing is to assist all members of management in the effective discharge of their responsibilities. The internal audit department provides this assistance by furnishing management with analyses, appraisals, recommendations, and pertinent comments concerning the activities reviewed. Internal auditors may be concerned with any phase of business activity in which they can be of service to management. This frequently involves going beyond the accounting and financial records to obtain a full understanding of the operations under review. As well as reviewing EDP systems that process financial data, frequently EDP auditors are called on to monitor computer systems of all kinds within an organization. To attain this overall objective, activities include the following:

- Reviewing and appraising the soundness, adequacy, and application of accounting, financial, and other administrative controls, and promoting effective control at reasonable cost, including controls over EDP
- Ascertaining the extent of compliance with established policies, plans, and procedures
- Ascertaining the extent to which company assets are accounted for and safeguarded from losses of all kinds, including security of EDP systems
- Ascertaining the reliability of management data developed and systems producing that information within the organization
- Reviewing EDP systems that record and process financial or management data
- Appraising the quality of performance in carrying out assigned responsibilities

Responsibility and Authority

Management policy should clearly establish the responsibilities of the internal auditor within the organization. Management's express authority should provide the internal auditor with full access to all of the organization's records, properties, and personnel that could be relevant to the subject under review. The internal auditor should be free to review and appraise policies, plans, procedures, and records.

Responsibilities of the internal auditor include:

- Informing and advising management and discharging this responsibility in a manner that is consistent with the code of ethics of the IIA
- Coordinating internal audit activities with others to best achieve both the audit objectives and the objectives of the organization

In performing their functions, internal auditors have no direct responsibility or authority over any of the activities reviewed. Therefore, the internal audit review and appraisal does not in any way relieve other people in the organization of the responsibilities that have been assigned to them. For example, if internal EDP auditors review the phases of the system development life cycle (SDLC), the responsibility for following the steps required still rests with the EDP department and others designated as users or systems developers. (See Chapter 7, "The System Development Life Cycle.")

Independence

Independence is essential to the effectiveness of internal auditing. This independence is obtained primarily through organizational status and objectivity:

- The status of the internal audit function within the organization and the support accorded to it by management are major determinants of its range and value. The head of the internal audit function, therefore, should be responsible to an officer whose authority is sufficient to assure both a broad range of audit coverage and the adequate consideration of, and effective action on, the audit findings and recommendations.

- Objectivity is essential to the audit function. Therefore, an internal auditor should not develop and install procedures, prepare records, or engage in any other activity that he or she would normally review and appraise and that could reasonably be construed to compromise the independence of the internal auditor. The internal auditor's objectivity need not be adversely affected, however, by determining and recommending standards of control to be applied in the development of the systems and procedures being reviewed.

The "Statement of Responsibilities of the Internal Auditor" was originally issued by the IIA in 1947. The continuing development of the profession has resulted in three revisions of that statement, in 1957, 1971, and 1976. The current statement embodies the concepts established previously and includes such changes as are deemed advisable in light of the present status of the profession. Standards for the practice of internal auditing, as shown in Figure 2-1, have been developed and, with their final adoption, changes may occur in both the statement of responsibilities and the code of ethics. EDP auditors, as part of internal audit, operate under the same code of ethics.

CODE OF ETHICS OF THE INSTITUTE OF INTERNAL AUDITORS

Interpretation of Principles

The provisions of the IIA's code of ethics cover basic principles in the various disciplines of internal auditing practice. Members should realize that individual judgment is required in the application of these principles. Members have a responsibility to conduct themselves so that their good faith and integrity should not be open to question. While having due regard for the limit of their technical skills, they should promote the highest possible internal auditing standards to the end of advancing the interest of their company or organization.

INDEPENDENCE — Internal auditors should be independent of the activities they audit.

- **Organizational Status —** The organizational status of the internal auditing department should be sufficient to permit the accomplishment of its audit responsibilities.

- **Objectivity —** Internal auditors should be objective in performing audits.

PROFESSIONAL PROFICIENCY — Internal audits should be performed with proficiency and due professional care.

The Internal Auditing Department

- **Staffing —** The internal auditing department should provide assurance that the technical proficiency and educational background of internal auditors are appropriate for the audits to be performed.

- **Knowledge, Skills, and Disciplines —** The internal auditing department should possess or should obtain the knowledge, skills, and disciplines needed to carry out its audit responsibilities.

- **Supervision —** The internal auditing department should provide assurance that internal audits are properly supervised.

The Internal Auditor

- **Compliance With Standards of Conduct —** Internal auditors should comply with professional standards of conduct.

- **Knowledge, Skills, and Disciplines —** Internal auditors should possess the knowledge, skills, and disciplines essential to the performance of internal audits.

- **Human Relations and Communications —** Internal auditors should be skilled in dealing with people and in communicating effectively.

- **Continuing Education —** Internal auditors should maintain their technical competence through continuing education.

- **Due Professional Care —** Internal auditors should exercise due professional care in performing internal audits.

SCOPE OF WORK — The scope of the internal audit should encompass the examination and evaluation of the adequacy and effectiveness of the organization's system of internal control, and the quality of performance in carrying out assigned responsibilities.

- **Reliability and Integrity of Information —** Internal auditors should review the reliability and integrity of financial and operating information and the means used to identify, measure, classify, and report such information.

- **Compliance With Policies, Plans, Procedures, Laws, and Regulations —** Internal auditors should review the systems established to ensure compliance with those policies, plans, procedures, laws, and regulations which could have a significant impact on operations and reports, and should determine whether the organization is in compliance.

(continued)

FIG. 2-1 **Professional standards for the practice of internal auditing, adapted from** *Standards for the Professional Practice of Internal Auditing* **(Institute of Internal Auditors: Altamonte Springs, Fla., June 1978)**

- **Safeguarding of Assets** — Internal auditors should review the means of safeguarding assets and, as appropriate, verify the existence of such assets.

- **Economical and Efficient Use of Resources** — Internal auditors should appriase the economy and efficiency with which resources are employed.

- **Accomplishment of Established Objectives and Goals for Operations or Programs** — Internal auditors should review operations or programs to ascertain whether results are consistent with established objectives and goals and whether the operations or programs are being carried out as planned.

PERFORMANCE OF AUDIT WORK — Audit work should include planning the audit, examining and evaluating information, communicating results, and following up.

- **Planning the Audit** — Internal auditors should plan each audit.

- **Examining and Evaluating Information** — Internal auditors should collect, analyze, interpret, and document information to support audit results.

- **Communicating Results** — Internal auditors should report the results of their audit work.

- **Following Up** — Internal auditors should follow up to ascertain that appropriate action is taken on reported audit findings.

MANAGEMENT OF THE INTERNAL AUDITING DEPARTMENT — The director of internal auditing should properly manage the internal auditing department.

- **Purpose, Authority, and Responsibility** — The director of Internal auditing should have a statement of purpose, authority, and responsibility for the internal auditing department.

- **Planning** — The director of internal auditing should establish plans to carry out the responsibilities of the internal auditing department.

- **Policies and Procedures** — The director of internal auditing should provide written policies and procedures to guide the audit staff.

- **Personnel Management and Development** — The director of internal auditing should establish a program for selecting and developing the human resources of the internal auditing department.

- **External Auditors** — The director of internal auditing should coordinate internal and external audit efforts.

- **Quality Assurance** — The director of internal auditing should establish and maintain a quality assurance program to evaluate the operations of the internal auditing department.

FIG. 2-1 *(continued)*

I. Members shall have an obligation to exercise honesty, objectivity, and diligence in the performance of their duties and responsibilities.

II. Members, in holding the trust of their employers, shall exhibit loyalty in all matters pertaining to the affairs of the employer or to whomever they may be rendering a service. However, members shall not knowingly be a party to any illegal or improper activity.

III. Members shall refrain from entering into any activity which may be in conflict with the interest of their employers or which would prejudice their ability to carry out objectively their duties and responsibilities.

IV. Members shall not accept a fee or a gift from an employee, a client, a customer, or a business associate of their employer without the knowledge and consent of their senior management.

V. Members shall be prudent in the use of information acquired in the course of their duties. They shall not use confidential information for any personal gain nor in a manner which would be detrimental to the welfare of their employer.

VI. Members, in expressing an opinion, shall use all reasonable care to obtain sufficient factual evidence to warrant such expression. In their reporting, members shall reveal such material facts known to them, which, if not revealed, could either distort the report of the results of operations under review or conceal unlawful practice.

VII. Members shall continually strive for improvement in the proficiency and effectiveness of their service.

VIII. Members shall abide by the bylaws and uphold the objectives of The Institute of Internal Auditors, Inc. In the practice of their profession, they shall be ever mindful of their obligation to maintain the high standard of competence, morality, and dignity which The Institute of Internal Auditors, Inc., and its members have established.

FIG. 2-2   Articles of the code of ethics of the Insitute of Internal Auditors

Articles

The IIA's code of ethics consists of eight articles, presented in Figure 2-2.

AICPA PRONOUNCEMENTS RELEVANT TO THE EDP AUDITOR

Over the years, the AICPA has become increasingly specific in its statements about the external auditor's responsibilities in the audit of EDP systems. Particularly important are Statement on Auditing Standards (SAS) No. 1, *Codification of Auditing Standards and Procedures*, and SAS No. 48, *The Effects of Computer Processing on the Examination of Financial Statements*, which superseded SAS No. 3, *The Effects of EDP on the Auditor's Study and Evaluation of Internal Control*. SAS No. 48 was effective for examinations of financial statements for periods beginning after August 31, 1984, and earlier application of the SAS was encouraged.

SAS No. 48, *The Effects of Computer Processing on the Examination of Financial Statements*

SAS No. 48 integrates guidance on auditing in an EDP environment into other existing professional standards: SAS No. 22, *Planning and Supervision*, at AU Sections 311.03, .09, and .10; SAS No. 23, *Analytical Review Procedures*, at AU Section 318.07; SAS No. 1, at AU Sections 320.03, .33, .34, .37, .57, .58, and .65−.68; and SAS No. 31, *Evidential Matter*, at AU Section 326.12. The portions of the SASs that are relevant to the EDP auditor are outlined in the following sections.

Other statements that are relevant to internal EDP auditors are summarized in the following sections.

SAS No. 1, *Codification of Auditing Standards and Procedures*

SAS No. 1 represents a broad codification of auditing standards and procedures. It contains the following statement in AU Sections 320.33, .34, .37, .57, .58, .65, .66, .67, and .68, "Methods of Data Processing," regarding the auditor's basic responsibility in the audit of the EDP systems:

> .33 The methods an entity uses to process significant accounting applications may influence the control procedures designed to achieve the objectives of internal accounting control. Those characteristics that distinguish computer processing from manual processing include —
>
> a. *Transaction trails.*[1] Some computer systems are designed so that a complete transaction trail that is useful for audit purposes might exist for only a short period of time or only in computer-readable form.
>
> b. *Uniform processing of transactions.* Computer processing uniformly subjects like transactions to the same processing instructions. Consequently, computer processing virtually eliminates the occurrence of clerical error normally associated with manual processing. Conversely, programming errors (or other similar systematic errors in either the computer hardware or software) will result in all like transactions being processed incorrectly when those transactions are processed under the same conditions.
>
> c. *Segregation of functions.* Many internal accounting control procedures once performed by separate individuals in manual systems may be concentrated in systems that use computer processing. Therefore, an individual who has access to the computer may be in a position to perform incompatible functions. As a result, other control procedures may be necessary in computer systems to achieve the control objectives

---

[1] A transaction trail is a chain of evidence provided through coding, cross references, and documentation connecting account balances and other summary results with original transactions and calculations.

ordinarily accomplished by segregation of functions in manual systems. Other controls may include, for example, adequate segregation of incompatible functions within the computer processing activities, establishment of a control group to prevent or detect processing errors or irregularities, or use of password control procedures to prevent incompatible functions from being performed by individuals who have access to assets and access to records through an on-line terminal.

d. *Potential for errors and irregularities.* The potential for individuals, including those performing control procedures, to gain unauthorized access to data or alter data without visible evidence, as well as to gain access (direct or indirect) to assets, may be greater in computerized accounting systems than in manual systems. Decreased human involvement in handling transactions processed by computers can reduce the potential for observing errors and irregularities. Errors or irregularities occurring during the design or changing of application programs can remain undetected for long periods of time.

e. *Potential for increased management supervision.* Computer systems offer management a wide variety of analytical tools that may be used to review and supervise the operations of the company. The availability of these additional controls may serve to enhance the entire system of internal accounting control on which the auditor may wish to place reliance. For example, traditional comparisons of actual operating ratios with those budgeted, as well as reconciliation on a more timely basis if such information is computerized. Additionally, some programmed applications provide statistics regarding computer operations that may be used to monitor the actual processing transactions.

f. *Initiation or subsequent execution of transactions by computer.* Certain transactions may be automatically initiated or certain procedures required to execute a transaction may be automatically performed by a computer system. The authorization of these transactions or procedures may not be documented in the same way as those initiated in a manual accounting system, and management's authorization of those transactions may be implicit in its acceptance of the design of the computer system.[2]

g. *Dependence of other controls on controls over computer processing.* Computer processing may produce reports and other output that are used in performing manual control procedures. The effectiveness of these manual control procedures can be dependent on the effectiveness of controls over the completeness and accuracy of computer processing.

---

[2] To the extent that the computer is used to initiate transactions or execute procedures, the application program usually includes procedures designed to assure that the steps are executed in conformity with specific or general authorizations issued by management acting within the scope of its authority. Those procedures might include checks to recognize data that fall outside predetermined limits and tests for overall reasonableness.

For example, the effectiveness of a control procedures that includes a manual review of a computer-produced exception listing is dependent on the controls over the production of the listing.

.34 Where computer processing is used in significant accounting applications, internal accounting control procedures are sometimes defined by classifying control procedures into two types: general and application control procedures.[3] Whether the control procedures are classified by the auditor into general and application controls, the objective of the system of internal accounting control remains the same: to provide reasonable, but not absolute, assurance that assets are safeguarded from unauthorized use or disposition and that financial records are reliable to permit the preparation of financial statements.

*   *   *   *

.37 Incompatible functions for accounting control purposes are those that place any person in a position to both perpetrate and conceal errors or irregularities in the normal course of his duties. Anyone who records transactions or has access to assets ordinarily is in a position to perpetrate errors or irregularities. Accordingly, accounting control necessarily depends largely on the elimination of opportunities for concealment.

For example, anyone who records disbursements could omit the recording of a check, either unintentionally or intentionally. If the same person also reconciles the bank account, the failure to record the check could be concealed through an improper reconciliation. In an accounting system using a computer to print checks and record disbursements, the computer may also generate information used to reconcile the account balance. If the same person entering information into the computer to execute the payment process also receives the output for the reconciliation process, a similar failure could be concealed. These examples illustrate the concept that procedures designed to detect errors and irregularities should be performed by persons other than those who are in a position to perpetrate them; that is, these procedures should be performed by persons having no incompatible functions. Procedures performed by such persons are described hereinafter as being performed independently.

*   *   *   *

.57 Control procedures that achieve or contribute to the achievement of one or more specific control objectives are often interdependent. Some control procedures may be essential to the operation of other control procedures that meet specific control objectives (that is, they need to be functioning adequately for the achievement of those specific control objectives). In an accounting system that uses computer processing, the auditor's concern over the interdependence of control procedures may be

---

[3] General controls are those controls that relate to all or many computerized accounting activities and often include control over the development, modification, and maintenance of computer programs and control over the use of and changes to data maintained on computer files. Application controls relate to individual computerized accounting applications, for example, programmed edit controls for verifying customers' account numbers and credit limits.

greater than in a manual system because of the increased concentration of functions within the operations of computer processing.

.58 Control procedures that are designed to contribute to the achievement of specific control objectives, through their interdependence with specific control procedures, may be classified as general control procedures. Control procedures that are designed to achieve specific control objectives may be classified as application control procedures. Application controls are often dependent on general controls. For example, if an application control procedure, such as matching shipping information with billing information, were to be performed by a customer-billing computer program, the auditor might review the controls over the access to and changing of computer programs before reviewing this programmed control procedure or other programmed application control procedures. The adequacy of this programmed application control procedure is dependent on the adequacy of control procedures that ensure unauthorized changes have not been made to the computer program performing those procedures during the period under review. Accordingly, it may be more efficient to review the design of internal accounting control procedures that are essential to the operation of several specific control procedures before reviewing those specific control procedures.

*   *   *   *

.65 Some aspects of accounting control require procedures that are not necessarily required for the execution of transactions. This class of procedures includes the approval or independent review of documents evidencing transactions. In a manual processing system the evidence of performing those procedures may be supported by those transaction documents because the individual assigned to perform that control procedure is normally required to indicate approval (for example, by initialing the document). If an accounting application is processed by computer, however, those procedures performed by an application program frequently will not provide visible evidence of those procedures and may not be performed independently of the original processing of transactions.

.66 Tests of such procedures performed manually require inspection of the related documents (a) to obtain evidence in the form of signatures, initials, audit stamps, and the like; (b) to indicate whether the procedures were performed, and by whom; and (c) to permit an evaluation of the propriety of their performance. Tests of such procedures performed by a computer may be made in a similar manner, provided that the computer produces visible evidence (a) to verify that the procedures were in operation and (b) to evaluate the propriety of their performance. For example, a computer-generated error list may provide such evidence if the list is tested by comparison to a list of the transaction file used by the same application program. If such evidence is not generated by the computer, those control procedures may be tested by using computer-assisted audit techniques to reperform the processing of the relevant information and then comparing the results of reperformance with the actual results. Another method may be submission of test data to the same computer process. It is important to understand that tests designed to verify the operation of programmed control procedures can be effective only if the auditor can obtain reasonable assurance of the consistency of their operation throughout the period under examination. Reasonable assurance may be obtained by testing controls over the maintenance and processing of those programs or from alternative procedures such as testing the programmed control procedures throughout the period.

.67 Other aspects of accounting control require a segregation of duties so that certain procedures are performed independently, as discussed in paragraph .37 (as amended above). The performance of these procedures is largely self-evident from the operation of the business or the existence of its essential records; consequently, tests of compliance with such procedures are primarily to determine whether the procedures were performed by persons having no incompatible functions. This is true for both manual and computerized accounting systems. Examples of this class of procedures may include (*a*) the receiving, depositing, and disbursing of cash; (*b*) the recording of transactions, and (*c*) the posting of customers' accounts. Since such procedures frequently leave no audit trail of who performed them, tests of compliance in these situations are necessarily limited to inquiries of different personnel and observation of office personnel and routines to corroborate the information obtained during the review of the system. While reconciliations, confirmations, or other audit tests performed in accordance with the auditing standards relating to evidential matter may substantiate the accuracy of the underlying records, these tests frequently provide no affirmative evidence of segregation of duties because the records may be accurate even though maintained by persons having incompatible functions.

.68 In a computerized accounting system, functions that would be incompatible in a manual system are often performed by computer. Individuals who have access to computer operations may then be in a position to perpetrate or conceal errors or irregularities. This need not be a weakness if there are control procedures that prevent such an individual from performing incompatible functions within the accounting system. These control procedures might include (*a*) adequate segregation of incompatible functions within the data processing department, (*b*) segregation between data processing and user department personnel performing review procedures, and (*c*) adequate control over access to data and computer programs.

This statement is more a citation of a basic responsibility of the auditor than a procedure to be followed. (Special considerations in EDP systems are found integrated in specific SASs as a result of issuance of SAS No. 48.)

More specific recommendations regarding the implementation of the standards set forth in SAS No. 1 are covered in the audit and accounting guide entitled *The Auditor's Study and Evaluation of Internal Control in EDP Systems*, prepared by the Computer Services Committee of the AICPA. A summary of the guide is included in this chapter.

SAS No. 9, *The Effect of an Internal Audit Function on the Scope of the Independent Auditor's Examination*

Although the work of internal audit cannot be substituted for the work of the external (independent) auditor, particularly as to judgments on audit matters, the external auditor can, and indeed should, consider the procedures performed by the internal auditors. If the external auditor decides that the internal auditors' work may have a bearing on his or her own procedures, the standard set forth in SAS No. 9 (AU Section 322) requires that he or she also review the competence and objectivity of the internal auditors and evaluate their work. To review competence, the external auditor is required by the standard to inquire about the qualifications of the internal audit staff, including, for example, consideration of the practices for hiring, training, and supervising the internal audit staff, especially in relation to their technical EDP capabilities. Regarding the objectivity of internal auditors, the external auditor considers the organizational level to which internal auditors report the results of their work and the organizational level to which they report administratively. One suggested method for judging internal auditors' objectivity is to review the recommendations made in their reports.

To evaluate the work of internal auditors, the external auditor examines, on a test basis, documentary evidence of the work performed by internal auditors and considers such factors as whether

- The scope of the work is appropriate.
- Audit programs are adequate.
- Working papers adequately document work performed.
- Conclusions reached are appropriate in the circumstances.
- Any reports prepared are consistent with the results of the work performed.

The external auditor also performs tests of some of the work of internal auditors, and may make use of internal auditors to provide direct assistance in performing an examination in accordance with generally accepted auditing standards (GAAS). Internal auditors may assist in performing audit tests or, for example, getting computer processing time for tests to be run using audit software, when testing has been automated. When the external auditor makes use of internal auditors in these ways, the competence and objectivity of the internal auditors must be considered and their work supervised and examined to the extent appropriate under the circumstances.

Many internal auditors have derived benefits from collaborating with external auditors. Particularly in EDP, many companies find auditing resources scarce. Cooperation can lead to a more effective and efficient use of these scarce resources. From the internal auditor's view, the first step to an effective relationship is often establishing a properly trained professional department that produces working papers that document their work adequately. Two common areas of cooperation are audit documentation and audit testing techniques (particularly when using software). Sharing the audit documentation of systems and control evaluations can help avoid unnecessary repetition of work. When using software, cooperation permits the internal auditor to get on-the-job training while the external audit specialist installs and executes these more sophisticated audit tests. The internal auditor is then better placed to re-execute the software (run it again) on a periodic or surprise basis. The knowledge gained can also be used to install and execute the software for other purposes whenever necessary.

SAS No. 20, *Required Communication of Material Weaknesses in Internal Accounting Control*

SAS No. 20 (AU Section 323) requires that the external auditor communicate material weaknesses in internal accounting control to senior management and the board of directors or its audit committee. This statement also indicates that the auditor should follow up on any action taken to correct previously communicated control weaknesses in internal accounting controls to the extent such weaknesses and corrective action affect the study and evaluation of internal controls in connection with his or her current examinations.

The current communication of control weaknesses may include corrective action taken or in process. In AU Section 320.71 a material weakness is described as a

> condition in which the specific control procedures or the degree of compliance with them do not reduce to a relatively low level the risk that errors or irregularities in amounts that would be material in relation to the financial statements being audited may occur and not be detected within a timely period by employees in the normal course of performing their assigned functions. These criteria may be broader than those that may be appropriate for evaluating weaknesses in accounting control for management or other purposes.

SAS No. 20 notes that the auditor may become aware of the existence of weaknesses in internal accounting control through an initial review of the system, tests of compliance, and/or substantive tests. The nature, extent, and timing of the audit tests is affected by the existence of a material weakness in internal accounting control. Since the auditor normally tests only selected items, it is possible that all material weaknesses in internal accounting control may not be disclosed. (See also SAS No. 30, *Reporting on Internal Accounting Control*, AU Section 642.)

SAS No. 22, *Planning and Supervision*

SAS No. 22 (AU Section 311.03), with SAS No. 48 integrated, has the required planning consideration expanded.

.03c The methods used by the entity to process significant accounting information (see paragraph .09), including the use of service organizations, such as outside service centers.

[c through g are redesignated d through h]

Additional paragraphs (AU Sections .09 and .10) summarize those aspects of computer processing that may have an effect on planning and examination of financial statements. They also describe how the auditor might consider the need for using a professional possessing specialized skills to determine the effect of computer processing on the examination.

.09 The auditor should consider the methods the entity uses to process accounting information in planning the audit because such methods influence the design of the accounting system and the nature of the internal accounting control procedures. The extent to which computer processing is used in significant accounting applications,[2] as well as the complexity of that processing, may also influence the nature, timing, and extent of audit procedures. Accordingly, in evaluating the effect of an entity's computer processing on an examination of financial statements, the auditor should consider matters such as —

a. The extent to which the computer is used in each significant accounting application.

b. The complexity of the entity's computer operations, including the use of an outside service center.[3]

c. The organizational structure of the computer processing activities.

d. The availability of data. Documents that are used to enter information into the computer for processing, certain computer files, and other evidential matter that may be required by the auditor may exist only for a short period or only in computer-readable form. In some computer systems, input documents may not exist at all because information is directly entered into the system. An entity's data retention policies may require the auditor to request retention of some information for his review or to perform audit procedures at a time when the information is available. In addition, certain information generated by the computer for management's internal purposes may be useful in performing substantive tests (particularly analytical review procedures).[4]

---

[2] Significant accounting applications are those that relate to accounting information that can materially affect the financial statements the auditor is examining.

[3] See SAS No. 44, *Special-Purpose Reports on Internal Accounting Control at Service Organizations*, and the related AICPA Audit Guide *Audits of Service-Center-Produced Records* for guidance concerning the use of a service center for computer processing of significant accounting applications.

[4] SAS No. 23, *Analytical Review Procedures*, describes the usefulness of and guidance pertaining to such procedures.

e. The use of computer-assisted audit techniques to increase the efficiency of performing audit procedures.[5] Using computer-assisted audit techniques may also provide the auditor with an opportunity to apply certain procedures to an entire population of accounts or transactions. In addition, in some accounting systems, it may be difficult or impossible for the auditor to analyze certain data or test specific control procedures without computer assistance.

.10 The auditor should consider whether specialized skills are needed to consider the effect of computer processing on the audit, to understand the flow of transactions, to understand the nature of internal accounting control procedures, or to design and perform audit procedures. If specialized skills are needed, the auditor should seek the assistance of a professional possessing such skills, who may be either on the auditor's staff or an outside professional. If the use of such a professional is planned, the auditor should have sufficient computer-related knowledge to communicate the objectives of the other professional's work; to evaluate whether the specified procedures will meet the auditor's objectives; and to evaluate the results of the procedures applied as they relate to the nature, timing, and extent of other planned audit procedures. The auditor's responsibilities with respect to using such a professional are equivalent to those for other assistants.[6]

SAS No. 23, *Analytical Review Procedures*

SAS No. 23 (AU Section 318.07), as amended by SAS No. 48, is expanded to include features that the auditor should consider when planning and performing analytical review procedures.

07*e. The increased availability of data prepared for management's use when computer processing is used.* Computer systems have created an ability (which may not be practical in manual systems) to store, retrieve, and analyze data for use in achieving broader management objectives. These data and analyses, although not necessarily part of the basic accounting records, may be valuable sources of information for the auditor to use in applying analytical review procedures, other substantive tests, or compliance testing.

[*e* and *f* are redesignated *f* and *g*]

---

[5] See the AICPA Audit and Accounting Guide *Computer-Assisted Audit Techniques* for guidance relating to this specialized area.

[6] Since the use of a specialist who is effectively functioning as a member of the audit team is not covered by SAS No. 11, *Using the Work of a Specialist*, a computer audit specialist requires the same supervision and review as any assistant.

SAS No. 31, *Evidential Matter*

SAS No. 31 (AU Section 326.12), as amended by SAS No. 48, makes it clear that audit evidence is not affected by the use of computer processing. Only the method by which the auditor gathers that evidence can be affected.

> .12 The auditor's specific audit objectives do not change whether accounting data is processed manually or by computer. However, the methods of applying audit procedures to gather evidence may be influenced by the method of data processing. The auditor can use either manual audit procedures, computer-assisted audit techniques, or a combination of both to obtain sufficient, competent evidential matter. However, in some accounting systems that use a computer for processing significant accounting applications, it may be difficult or impossible for the auditor to obtain certain data for inspection, inquiry, or confirmation without computer assistance.

AUDIT AND ACCOUNTING GUIDE

The accounting and auditing guide entitled *The Auditor's Study and Evaluation of Internal Control in EDP Systems* was issued by the AICPA to provide the external auditor with guidance in the implementation of SAS No. 3, by illustration and description of various control techniques and related audit procedures. Although SAS No. 3 has been superseded by SAS No. 48, the audit study and evaluation of internal control remains unaffected. In its overview, the guide presents the following qualifications:

- There are no existing standards for the specific combination of controls that should be used in a given system, and the guide does not attempt to establish such standards.
- The guide relates to batch-oriented EDP systems.
- Although more experience with advanced systems is required before consensus about accounting controls for such systems develops, many of the control objectives, techniques, and compliance testing procedures described in the guide are applicable to advanced systems (here meaning systems other than batch, such as on-line systems).

The auditor's study and evaluation of the EDP controls is broken down into, and described in detail within, the following stages:

1. Preliminary phase of review
2. Preliminary phase of reivew — assessment
3. Completion of review — general controls
4. Completion of review — application controls

5. Completion of review — assessment

6. Tests of compliance

7. Evaluation

The guide summarizes its presentation of the auditor's study and evaluation of EDP controls in a logic diagram format. There discussion of general and application controls is expanded considerably compared to the corresponding coverage in the SASs. Each control included under the two general classifications is described in detail, with methods of review and examples of tests of compliance.

In all, 19 general controls are defined, as follows:

1. A segregation of functions should exist between the EDP department and users.

2. Provision should exist for general authorization over the execution of transactions (prohibiting the EDP department from initiating or authorizing transactions).

3. Segregation of functions should exist within the EDP department.

4. The procedures for system design, including the acquisition of software packages, should require active participation by representatives of the users and, as appropriate, the accounting department and internal auditors.

5. Each system should have written specifications that are reviewed and approved by an appropriate level of management and applicable user departments.

6. System testing should be a joint effort of users and EDP personnel, and should include both the manual and computerized phases of the system.

7. Final approval should be obtained prior to placing a new system into operation.

8. All master file and transaction file conversions should be controlled to prevent unauthorized changes and to provide accurate and complete results.

9. After a new system has been placed into operation, all program changes should be approved before implementation to determine whether they have been authorized, tested, and documented.

10. Management should require various levels of documentation and establish formal procedures to define the system at appropriate levels of detail.

11. The control features inherent in the computer hardware, operating system and other supporting software should be used to the maximum possible extent to provide control over operations and to detect and report hardware malfunctions.

12. System software should be subjected to the same control procedures as those applied to installation of, and changes in, application programs.

13. Access to program documentation should be limited to those persons who require it in the performance of their duties.

14. Access to data files and programs should be limited to those individuals authorized to process or maintain particular systems.

15. Access to computer hardware should be limited to authorized individuals.

16. A control function should be responsible for receiving all data to be processed, ensuring that all data is recorded, following up on errors detected during processing to see that they are corrected and then resubmitted by the proper party, and verifying the proper distribution of output.

17. A written manual of systems and procedures should be prepared for all computer operations and should provide for management's general or specific authorization to process transactions.

18. Internal auditors or some other independent group within an organization should review and evaluate proposed systems at critical stages of development.

19. On a continuing basis, internal auditors or some other independent group within the organization should review and test computer processing activities.

An argument can be made for classifying control 16 as an application control rather than a general control, since, for a given situation, the existence of this type of control could vary within its individual applications.

Controls related to specific applications are identified as follows:

- Only properly authorized and approved input, prepared in accordance with management's general or specific authorization, should be accepted for processing by EDP.
- The system should verify all significant codes used to record data.
- Conversion of data into machine-sensible form should be controlled.
- Movement of data between one processing step and another, or between departments, should be controlled.
- The correction and resubmission of all errors detected by the application system should be reviewed and controlled.
- Control totals should be produced and reconciled with input control totals.
- Controls should prevent processing the wrong file, detect errors in file manipulation, and highlight operator-caused errors.

- Limit and reasonableness checks should be incorporated within programs.
- Run-to-run controls should be verified at appropriate points in the processing cycle.
- Output control totals should be reconciled with input and processing controls.
- Output should be scanned and tested by comparison with original source documents.
- Systems output should be distributed only to authorized users.

OTHER PUBLICATIONS

Among AICPA publications relevant to the EDP auditor are:

- *Computer Assisted Audit Techniques* (Audit Guide)
- *Audits of Service-Center-Produced Records* (Audit Guide)
- *Guidelines for General Systems Specifications for a Computer System* (Guidelines Series)
- *Audit Considerations in Electronic Funds Transfer Systems* (Guidelines Series)
- *Audit and Control Considerations in a Minicomputer Environment* (Guideline Series)
- *Audit and Control Considerations in an On-Line Environment* (Guidelines Series).

Copies of these publications are available from the American Institute of Certified Public Accountants, 1211 Avenue of the Americas, New York, N.Y. 10036.

REPORT OF THE SPECIAL ADVISORY COMMITTEE ON INTERNAL CONTROL (THE MINAHAN REPORT)

In 1977, the AICPA established a committee to provide guidance to management on internal accounting control. The committee comprised representatives from industry and public accounting under the chairmanship of Gene Minahan, former controller of Atlantic Richfield Co. (ARCO). The committee issued its report in 1979.

The report is valuable because it adapts existing auditing literature to the broader needs of management. The concept of internal accounting control in existing literature (and in the Foreign Corrupt Practices Act of 1977) was originally developed to meet the specialized needs of external auditors. The main points of the report are summarized in the following sections.

Need for Guidance

Management's interest in evaluating internal accounting control is increasing, probably because of the following developments:

- The suggestions of the Independent Commission on Auditor's Responsibility that management reports on financial statements, presenting management's assessment of the company's accounting system and related controls, be prepared. This suggestion is supported by the Financial Executives Institute.

- The internal accounting control provisions of the Foreign Corrupt Practices Act. The Securities and Exchange Commission (SEC) has made it clear that companies subject to the Act should review control systems and business practices and take any actions necessary to comply with the Act. (Note that at one point the SEC suggested that management publish the results of its review and that the external auditors should issue an opinion of this review. This suggestion was withdrawn, but the SEC is continuing to monitor this area.)

Scope of Internal Accounting Control

Management is concerned with the effectiveness of all of the organization's controls. Obviously, not all of these internal accounting controls (which the special advisory committee on internal control defined as being concerned with the reliability of the financial statements; the broad control objectives of authorization; accounting and asset safeguarding; and accounting controls) should extend to external reports of historical financial information.

The Internal Accounting Control Environment

The special advisory committee found the term "internal accounting control environment" to be a convenient catchall to describe the various factors (structure, policies, delegation of authority, communication of responsibility, budgets and financial reports, organizational checks and balances, and EDP considerations) that contribute to an appropriate atmosphere of control-consciousness. A poor control environment allows some procedures to become relatively inoperative when, for example, local management overrides specific senior management control procedures. Even in a strong control environment there is not absolute assurance that controls cannot be circumvented by employee collusion or management override.

The committee concluded that an overall evaluation is a necessary prelude to the evaluation of specific control procedures and techniques.

EDP Considerations

The special advisory committee noted the following effects of EDP on internal accounting controls:

- There is less documentary evidence of the performance of control procedures.
- Files and records are held in machine-sensible form and often cannot be read without a computer.
- Concentration of data, multiple users and multiple access all may increase the vulnerability of information to physical disaster, human error, unauthorized manipulation, or mechanical malfunction.
- Computer processing of individual transactions may require better planning to deal with potential problems.
- Various functions may be concentrated in an EDP system, thus reducing traditional segregation of duties. A single individual may be able to make unauthorized changes, modifying programs or data that negate internal accounting controls or permit improper access to assets. Segregation of functions within EDP may help overcome this weakness.
- Additional specialized knowledge may be required to evaluate controls.
- Changes to the system are often more difficult to implement.
- With proper controls in place, EDP systems can provide greater consistency because they uniformly subject all transactions to the same controls.

EDP systems make it all the more important for management to understand the exposures and controls. The degree of reliance that can be placed on controls exercised by the EDP system depends on the degree of control exercised by management over the development, installation, maintenance, and use of the computer equipment and software. The development of modern EDP systems requires a substantially higher level of coordination within the organization and among technical disciplines, which management should recognize.

Evaluating Internal Accounting Controls

The Minahan report provides some specific guidance in the design and evaluation of internal accounting controls, including the following steps:

1. Preliminary assessment
2. Evaluating specific control procedures and techniques
3. Monitoring compliance

4. Documentation

5. Cost/benefit considerations

6. Limitations on internal accounting controls

Preliminary Assessment. A preliminary assessment of the internal accounting control environment, and existing accounting control procedures and techniques, is based on management's overall knowledge of the company. The degree to which compliance with accounting control procedures is enforced by the control environment should be considered. Important corporate and accounting policies and procedures should have been formalized. The use of internal audits or supervisory reviews, control weaknesses identified in the normal course of business or by audit findings, and the corrective action taken all should be considered.

Evaluating Specific Control Procedures and Techniques. On the basis of its preliminary assessment, management can evaluate specific control procedures and techniques including:

- Deciding on the appropriate approach
- Obtaining an understanding of the flow of transactions and of the accounting control procedures in place
- Concluding whether those controls provide reasonable assurance that the broad objectives of authorization, accounting, and asset safeguarding have been met

The special advisory committee proposed that management can evaluate control procedures effectively in the following manner:

- Classify transactions by function, operating units, cycles, or other logical classification
- Convert the broad objectives of internal accounting control into specific objectives, appropriate to transaction classifications
- Identify and evaluate the control procedures in place to determine whether they meet the specific objectives, giving appropriate consideration to the internal accounting control environment

An appendix to the Minahan report illustrates specific objectives, with examples of selected control procedures and techniques. (The method is similar to that used in the various internal control questionnaires discussed in this book.)

Monitoring Compliance. Management should monitor compliance with established accounting control procedures to obtain reasonable assurance that controls in place continue to be appropriate and function properly. Monitoring includes management supervision, representations, audits or compliance tests, and approval and control of changes in procedures. Monitoring is an integral part of the continuing process of evaluating the control environment.

Documentation. Management should consider ensuring an appropriate level of documentation for its evaluations, providing both an important support for representations about the company's internal accounting control and the usual benefits of good documentation. (The audit approach discussed throughout this book provides audit documentation that is effective for diverse management purposes.)

Cost/Benefit Considerations. The Foreign Corrupt Practices Act and related literature include the concept of "reasonable assurance": that the costs of specific controls should not exceed their anticipated benefits. However, almost all cost/benefit decisions involve subjective business judgment: final decisions on internal control requirements in areas where exposure could be material should be reviewed carefully by an appropriate level of management. The committee considered this an important area for future research.

Limitations on Internal Accounting Controls. Inherent limitations on a system of internal accounting controls include the possibility of circumvention or changes in the degree of compliance due to changing conditions within a company. Relationships between operating efficiency and increasingly complex control procedures necessary to reduce exposures, become a trade-off. The materiality limit, below which it is impractical to institute control procedures, is another factor for management consideration.

The implications of the Foreign Corrupt Practices Act of 1977 and the possibility of public representations on internal accounting control must be considered; a careful balance between those concerns and the wider range of management's business concerns is needed. The special advisory committee emphasized that having effective internal accounting controls should not prevent management from taking prudent business risks.

Conclusions

The special advisory committee concluded its report by pointing out that

- There is insufficient knowledge of how extensively control procedures are employed, in what combinations, in which industries, in companies of what size, and so forth. A lack of knowledge about current practices in a majority of companies for purposes of effective internal accounting control may complicate the task of evaluation.

- Companies do not have a theoretical model to use in making informed, supportable judgments on the cost/benefit decisions implicit in developing their accounting control procedures and techniques.

Copies of the Minahan report are available from the American Institute of Certified Public Accountants, 1211 Avenue of the Americas, New York, N.Y. 10036.

MANAGEMENT'S NEED TO DEVELOP EDP AUDITORS

More than ever, today's management needs assurance about controls operating within its automated information systems. The complexity of nearly all business systems makes the loss of these controls more likely than ever before. One of the largest scandals in the history of advertising is a recent case in point. A leading agency, through fictitious account entries to a computer over four years, overstated its revenues by $30 million. This example points up the need for special attention to controls within EDP systems.

To resolve these concerns, EDP auditors have entered the organizational picture. To best serve the needs of management, EDP auditors are part of the internal audit department. Their job fuses many of the skills of both internal auditing and EDP, including programming, system design, data base management, hardware, communications, security, implementation, and more. This special combination of skills is in short supply because the function has expanded far faster than the supply of professionals available to staff it. When management's need to audit hundreds of thousands of computer installations around the world is considered, the demand for EDP auditors becomes clear.

Even as recently as 1977, the *Systems Auditability and Control Report* commissioned by the IIA, showed that only 15 percent of the corporations polled had an EDP audit function. By 1980, estimates put that figure at 50 percent. A study sponsored by the Financial Executives Research Foundation (FERF) in 1980 disclosed that of the 49 companies responding, 21 had no specifically trained EDP auditors, and this was not for lack of trying or funding.

The study sponsored by FERF, *Internal Control in U.S. Corporations: The State of the Art*, was based on interviews with 350 corporate executives in 50 randomly selected U.S. corporations: chief financial officers, controllers, representatives of legal counsel's offices, internal auditors, data processing managers, and various staff and operating executives. The companies surveyed had an average data processing budget of $20 million for computer hardware, software, and personnel (ranging from $70,000 to $94 million). The managements of almost all the companies recognized the need to devote more resources to EDP auditing. The market is extremely competitive, so much so that in some geographical regions the supply of EDP auditors is almost nonexistent.

Although job descriptions vary from company to company, according to management definition, the EDP auditor's duties have several common factors. Requirements include a familiarity with systems and systems design and analysis; a good understanding of several programming languages, such as COBOL; and experience or training in accounting and auditing.

In the future, management should be able to staff EDP audit functions with people who are attending college now. Auditing students are better off than their predecessors: Several schools have melded EDP, accounting, and auditing into one course of study, so the student is not confronted with an either/or choice.

Since colleges and universities are just beginning to design courses for EDP auditing, where does management find people to staff EDP audit functions today? From among data processing (EDP) personnel such as systems analysts? From other companies? From internal audit departments? From CPA firms (a very common source)? Once likely candidates are located, how does management train them? In-house training is an ideal route, but many organizations do not have the time or capabilities for such an undertaking. And, once an EDP audit staff has been developed, how does an organization keep them when other companies try to recruit them? The answers to these questions are different in different places.

To find one company's answers to some of the questions just raised, the manager of a major corporation's EDP audit function (which he started in July 1979) provides its response. He reports to the general auditor. He believes that the best way to find and/or train EDP auditors is to hire people who are technically sound and have had experience in data processing, accounting, and auditing, although this combination may be hard to find. He has a somewhat controversial view that it is better to train an EDP professional in auditing techniques than to train auditors in technical EDP areas. He emphasizes that EDP auditing requires a logical mind and that elusive, hard-to-test-for quality, creativity. This corporate computer audit group uses three sources or approaches to develop EDP auditors. It locates within the company or hires

- People with prior EDP audit experience (from one to four years, preferably) and a good understanding of computer languages. Although a professional accounting degree is not essential, experience and/or training in accounting is necessary. Operational auditing experience is desirable. (Some companies require a knowledge of specific hardware.)

- Systems analysts with solid experience who have specialized in designing accounting systems. These people are then trained in auditing techniques.

- Financial auditors who can become EDP auditors. The company gives them the equivalent of six months of training spread over a period of time. They use on-the-job training combined with outside courses in the technical aspects of EDP. For example, their EDP audit staff recently transferred an employee from internal audits to EDP audits. (While basically sound, this approach may not work when highly technical EDP skills are required.)

Because there are differences between the two types of auditors, the internal auditor's functions will never be wholly taken over by the EDP auditor or vice versa. (See Figure 2-3 comparing the two functions as they exist at this company.) The need exists for both types of expertise. Each group must remain in constant communication if optimum use of staff resources is to result in greater audit effectiveness.

This EDP audit manager feels that one of the most critical factors in the effective function of the EDP auditing group is the understanding and support of the total internal audit department, and that is a team undertaking.

In the future, the number of EDP auditors will increase much more rapidly than the number of internal audit staff members because EDP audit is still in its formative stages. In addition, the growth of businesses in general, the newer and more versatile hardware, and the development of more intricate applications will require expanded EDP audit coverage.

Obviously, there is no one solution for all organizations, but management awareness of several factors is increasing:

- Computerization at all levels is accelerating.
- EDP-generated information must be reviewed for audit significance.
- A special combination of data processing skills and internal auditing capabilities is needed to produce an EDP auditor.
- The internal auditing department will probably never consist only of EDP auditors.

According to this company's general auditor, the introduction of more sophisticated and more powerful computer hardware at reasonable costs means that not only the larger industrial companies, divisions, and profit centers are leasing or procuring this equipment. As the costs of computer power decline, many organizations are acquiring complex systems. As a result, the need for EDP auditing is expanding so rapidly that the audit staff mix will continue to change, making the recruitment, training, and development of EDP auditors a top management priority.

Training EDP Auditors

Many companies use professional EDP auditing courses and materials to train their EDP auditors. In 1981, Coopers & Lybrand's National Computer Audit Assistance Group joined with New York University to establish a new diploma program in information systems auditing for the University's School of Continuing Education, thus providing another training resource.

Internal Auditors	EDP Auditors
1. Business degree.	**1.** Same and/or computer science degree.
2. Entry position requires knowledge of accounting theory and practice. Advanced position requires, in addition, prior auditing/financial experience.	**2.** Same, except emphasis is on data processing knowledge. Programming capability desired.
3. Separated into regional teams responsible for certain geographical areas of the world.	**3.** Corporate-based; responsible for worldwide coverage.
4. Moderate travel.	**4.** More extensive travel.
5. Auditing and financial technical training and personal development training.	**5.** Similar training, except EDP technical aspects are emphasized to keep people abreast of the state of the art.
6. CPA and/or MBA desirable; CIA also acceptable (certified internal auditor, given by Institute of Internal Auditors).	**6.** MBA (preferably in computer science), CDP (certified data programmer), CCP (certified computer programmer), or CISA (certified information systems auditor, given by EDP Auditors Foundation) preferred.

FIG. 2-3   A comparison of the internal auditors and EDP auditors in one large corporation

Another major corporation has taken a different approach to training its EDP auditors. The training program, described subsequently, is based on a different philosophy than the previously described corporate approach. Both of these examples show the need for flexibility in order to respond effectively to different situations.

This corporation is involved in primary metals production, manufacturing, and energy. It operates utility, railroad, mercantile, and agricultural activities in the southwestern United States, and has offices and plants located throughout the United States and overseas. While the corporation uses professional EDP auditing courses to train their auditors, there is a major difference. No separate EDP audit department exists, since the objective is for everyone in the audit department to learn EDP auditing.

The director of corporate audit has directed staff training in a new way, toward what he believes is the professional approach to EDP auditing. This approach centers on the need to keep EDP audit as an integral, rather than separate, function of internal audit, since the auditing objectives are the same.

The 22 members of the company's internal audit staff are divided between two major locations. Among them only six individuals, primarily managers and seniors, have an extensive background in EDP auditing. Entry-level auditors are not hired on the basis of EDP skills but because of their strong financial backgrounds. (Most have MBA degrees.) They are also required to have a basic knowledge of EDP and must understand the significance of EDP in business.

Entry-level auditors review application controls in simple EDP systems and internal accounting controls in manual systems. They receive intensive on-the-job training by more experienced staff, who write the software and perform reviews of more sophisticated systems. It is planned that through training, entry-level personnel will gradually become skilled auditors. The audit director's goal is for everyone in the internal audit department to be able to audit simple systems in simple environments, with an eventual migration toward being able to audit more complex systems in increasingly complex environments.

One element in this company's auditing education program is a course developed and presented by Coopers & Lybrand (C&L), "Auditing in the Contemporary Computer Environment," a comprehensive approach to controls in EDP systems.

An important consideration in choosing among the firms that offer EDP auditing courses is that instructors have computer experience beyond the classroom; they all should have had active involvement in EDP auditing. Another important consideration is that the audit approach presented in the course is a comprehensive methodology for auditing computerized business systems. Class presentations should be amplified by case studies, so that participants can apply their knowledge to practical audit situations. Courses should be tailored to the specific educational objectives of management.

At the corporation under discussion, along with formal courses, intensive on-the-job training, and seminars sponsored by professional organizations, entry-level internal audit staff may also be offered participation in the corporation's unique financial management development training program. The goal is to be able to fill key financial and general management positions throughout the corporation. (Many larger companies regularly use their internal audit departments to develop future management.)

Professional education for EDP auditors becomes more of a problem than training in EDP, since both the auditing and EDP disciplines are involved. Developments, new technology, and regulations are important reasons to keep knowledge and education up to date.

The continuing importance of EDP audit education to management is to

- Minimize the impact of shortages of qualified EDP audit personnel; develop and retain key staff.
- Improve working relationships between internal and external auditors.
- Assist EDP management and staff in meeting management's control requirements.

- Improve auditors' efforts (such as in compliance with existing and projected regulations).
- Maintain a unified body of knowledge and approach toward solving EDP control and audit problems.
- Assure that both internal and external auditors possess state-of-the-art knowledge and practical auditing techniques that can be applied on the job.

The development of an EDP audit education function can be seen in the example of C&L. In 1974, the firm was one of the first to establish a computer audit assistance group staffed by EDP professionals.

The group maintains the high level of computer audit expertise required to design and implement appropriate computer audit procedures, including creating the wide array of both generalized and customized software needed. Research to keep up with developments in EDP technology and the cross-training of general auditors in EDP auditing and EDP auditors in general auditing are other aspects of the computer audit functions.

Until about five years ago, all staff members had heavy data processing backgrounds, averaging about seven years of systems analysis and programming experience (typically in financial systems work) and two years of other business experience. There now are about 350 of these professionals working at the firm. With solid middle and senior management in place, junior staff can reprocess the existing audit software programs and execute the firms' generalized audit software. Recent college graduates who majored in computer science and information systems and, generally, who had participated in work-study programs, can be hired, due to the existence of a large cadre of seasoned EDP auditors. The group's director believes that staff members hired right out of college require extensive supervision and training to be able to function in complex EDP environments.

During the first 18 months, junior staff members take courses in computer auditing, internal controls, and technical subjects, both in-house and at vendors' training schools, to be brought up to audit proficiency. They learn how to use generalized audit software packages and begin writing their own custom programs, and they have access to a series of instructional materials about auditing different industries and reporting systems. Because their backgrounds vary, training is tailored to each individual. The most practical training they receive is on the job, from their supervisors.

Firm instructors have in-depth experience in EDP auditing; many have helped design and implement the courses. "Hands on" experience and the transmission of practical methods to be applied in a working environment are key elements.

The EDP audit education program includes instruction on a broad range of software packages and developments in EDP, such as data base management systems, communications networks, distributed processing, and mini-computers and microcomputers.

Courses developed by C&L have been sponsored by the EDP Auditors Association, the IIA, and the Association of Systems Management, among others. EDP audit education is given for federal and other government entities and corporations. Developed for the firm's own staff, the courses now reach internal, general, and EDP auditors and informations systems specialists throughout the country. In some cases, organizations are trained in use of the material to teach the courses themselves.

This firm's experience demonstrates how knowledge of EDP and internal and external auditing are blended to develop an EDP audit education program. Comprehensive training and development methods are essential to minimize the impact of the personnel shortage; to maintain a unified body of knowledge that will strengthen the links between internal and external auditors, as well as between EDP and non-EDP auditors; and to ensure that the audit function keeps pace with technological developments.

CHAPTER 3

The EDP Auditing Profession

EDP AUDITING — ROLES OF PARTICIPANTS

Role of the Internal Auditor

Internal auditing is an independent appraisal function established within an organization under management sanction to examine and evaluate its activities. The internal auditor is almost always concerned with the adequacy of the controls over the management information system and, in most cases, with the cost-effectiveness of the procedures used. A systems audit approach provides the internal auditor with a methodology for reviewing the controls in today's systems.

Although the audit environment as a whole is changing, the overall objectives of the internal auditor remain constant. The primary function of the internal auditor is still to assist management in meeting its responsibilities to ensure the following:

- Safeguarding of company assets
- Accuracy and reliability of accounting records
- Promotion of operational efficiency
- Adherence to company policies and legal obligations (such as the Foreign Corrupt Practices Act of 1977, summarized later in this chapter)

Role of the EDP Auditor

To ensure that management and the internal audit function can meet the preceding requirements, EDP skill is becoming more important all the time. The EDP auditor assists the internal auditor by supplying technical skills and EDP expertise to the audit function.

One of the main reasons for this increasing need is technological advances in computer systems which affect the procedures and techniques used to accomplish the objectives of the internal EDP auditor. In many cases it is not possible to verify the procedures used to summarize, calculate, and categorize data through manual testing, as they were verified in the past. Audit software and other computer-assisted techniques must be used. At the same time, the EDP auditor's emphasis has shifted from evaluating and testing processing results (such as data files, records, and reports) to evaluating and testing system controls. This new methodology ensures that continuing completeness, accuracy, authorization, maintenance, usefulness, and reliability of processing results can be achieved.

Role of the External Auditor

The principal objective of an external audit is to be able to express an opinion about the quality of an organization's financial statements. Therefore, the external auditor is concerned primarily with the reliability of financial information. Because so much of this information is computer-based, the external auditor needs computer-assisted tools and EDP-trained staff to perform the audit in accordance with today's professional requirements. (See Chapter 2, "The Auditor and EDP Auditing.") The only economical way to perform adequate substantive tests may be with audit software; in some systems it may be the only way. The auditor must also consider controls as a basis for determining the nature, extent, and timing of the substantive tests. Many of these controls are incorporated in computer programs or are exercised in the EDP function. To achieve results in an increasingly computerized environment, external audit staff today usually includes EDP audit specialists. Their role is to develop and apply computerized audit techniques, including the use of audit software, to evaluate and test the more technically complex EDP controls.

RESPONSIBILITIES OF THE EDP AUDITOR

EDP audit tasks can be grouped into four main categories:

1. Reviews of systems under development
2. Data center reviews
3. Application system reviews, often supporting non-EDP auditors
4. Support for non-EDP auditors, such as execution of audit software

Reviews of Systems Under Development

Pre-implementation reviews of systems under development, or reviews of planned improvements and enhancements to existing systems, are increasingly performed by non-EDP auditors as well as EDP auditors. They should include an examination of the systems' design in order to ensure the presence of adequate controls within the new applications.

Early auditor participation helps eliminate the need to retrofit controls after a system has been implemented, which is difficult and expensive, perhaps even impossible. The EDP auditor, however, should maintain objectivity and independence during development participation. In this role as consultant, recommendations for control improvements can be made, while the operational responsibility for the new system remains outside of the audit department.

A review must include proper testing and compliance with the development plan and procedures. Whether this is done or not often depends on management requirements and how they are met in a particular organization. In addition, the EDP auditor can monitor project management for efficiency and effectiveness.

Data Center Reviews

Data center audits are an increasingly important function, almost always performed by EDP auditors. This type of review incorporates evaluation of the data processing organizational structure, staffing practices, systems development standards, operating procedures, security, program and data library control procedures (the general controls), communications network, and backup and disaster recovery procedures. The effectiveness of these basic procedures and controls has an impact on the accuracy and completeness of processing results. Additionally, the EDP auditor may review administrative or operational efficiency and the effectiveness of the procedures in place at the computer center. In part, the scope of this type of review is up to management; an EDP auditor may suggest broader review when necessary.

Application System Reviews

Application system reviews are usually performed by non-EDP auditors with advice and assistance from EDP auditors. Two primary areas are usually addressed by the EDP auditor in an application system review:

1. *Programmed procedures* — These are the parts of processing that are automated within the computer. Programmed control procedures, such as input edit checks and exception report production, are of particular significance.

2. *User control procedures* — These include segregation of duties within the EDP and user departments, existence of proper management approval procedures, and timely performance of job responsibilities. Many of these control procedures depend on the proper action taken on computer output, such as the investigation and correction of exceptions produced by the programs.

Audit procedures applied to these areas include the following:

- Evaluating computer system controls to determine if they are adequate to
  a. Ensure the accuracy and completeness of processing results and the proper maintenance of programs and data files.
  b. Prevent errors and omissions from going undetected.
  c. Ensure the continuing reliability of data processing results.
  d. Ensure that only properly authorized transactions are processed.

- Testing to determine that the controls are properly and consistently applied, which will provide evidence of compliance with established control procedures and assurance of continued reliability.

- Testing to ascertain that the results of processing data files and reports are accurate and complete.

- Evaluating the effectiveness of the system in achieving the objectives of the users and management.

THE EDP AUDITING PROFESSION

3-5

Support for Non-EDP Auditors

An EDP auditor may provide audit assistance to either traditional internal auditors within the organization or to external auditors who come into the organization to perform a review.

Assistance to Internal Auditors. The internal audit staff of most corporations has varying areas of knowledge and levels of experience. As a result, an EDP auditor may assist the non-EDP auditor in technical areas or, for example, in arriving at a judgment or performing an evaluation of some phase of operations related to computer processing. In this regard, the EDP auditor functions as an in-house adviser. This in turn can make the best use of time in conducting an audit, and the most efficient use of software and processing. The following are among the types of assistance normally provided:

- Gathering and analyzing data
- Creating report formats and analyzing reports
- Testing a computer system's internal controls
- Extracting data from existing files, by using audit software
- Investigating inconsistencies or omissions in output generated by the computer system

Assistance to External Auditors. Most enterprises, either voluntarily or according to regulations such as those for corporations that are registrants of the Securities and Exchange Commission (SEC), have an annual audit of the financial statements conducted by an independent certified public accountant (CPA). In this context, the independent CPA is an external auditor. The procedures used and the results obtained by the internal EDP auditors can assist the external auditor in determining the nature, timing, and extent of required audit procedures. Coordination of efforts between the two areas results in increased audit efficiency. External auditors often coordinate their activities with the activities outlined in the organization's annual audit program, including the use of computer time and processing capabilities. When appropriate, the external auditors examine the related working papers, audit scope, and conclusions drawn in the internal auditor's report.

Additional Responsibilities. Due to their skills and experience, EDP auditors are often called on to take on other responsibilities, including:

- Training EDP and non-EDP auditors in EDP and EDP audit methods to meet continuing education requirements. EDP auditors can develop, coordinate, or teach such courses.

- Coordinating audit department's own EDP use for administration and performance of work (e.g., staff scheduling, report writing, working paper processing). Many EDP auditors manage the hardware and software used for such processing.

Problems Confronting the EDP Auditing Profession

The problems confronting the EDP auditing profession are found in several areas.

Lack of Trained, Experienced EDP Auditors. Currently, the EDP auditing profession enjoys the seemingly enviable position that the demand for EDP auditors exceeds the supply. There are not enough qualified personnel who have both audit and data processing skills. Combined with organizational budget constraints, this situation frequently leads to inadequate staffing and high turnover. These factors have had an impact on the ability of EDP audit groups to satisfy their objectives. Alternatives that could help mitigate this problem are

- The establishment of good training programs, that both provide an incentive for people to stay in an organization and solve the problems of inexperienced, untrained staff.
- Rotation of staff, such as with the data processing department, to develop skills in both areas.
- Preparation of standardized working papers, which is particularly important where there is high turnover.

Insufficient Support and Cooperation From Upper Management. Because EDP auditing is a relatively new function, it is rarely as well understood as the more traditional areas of the organization. This lack of understanding sometimes leads to a dearth of meaningful communication from upper management and audit committees. A large gap is often found between what management says EDP audit is doing and what EDP audit says — and knows — it is doing. In some locations, management resists implementing EDP audit recommendations until it feels convinced that the EDP auditors have proven their worth. Good communication skills are a particular asset for an EDP auditor when interacting with management. The EDP auditor needs these skills to explain clearly the ramifications of control deficiencies and the inherent usefulness of the EDP audit effort in correcting them. A goal should be to bridge the communication gaps that sometimes exist between EDP audit, EDP in general, and management.

Keeping Up With Rapid Technological and Auditing Developments. Continuing technical training and reading, such as review of technical journals, are necessary for the EDP auditor to remain current in the profession. Unique problems are emerging in relation to distributed data processing, microcomputers, teleprocessing, and data base systems. These must be addressed by people who understand the concepts and business impact. Most EDP audit groups expend a considerable effort on basic training and keeping the skills of experienced auditors up to date. Continuing education is a professional requirement. A systems specialist trained in auditing still needs to maintain current systems knowledge, and vice versa. A survey of 145 companies conducted by the Conference Board noted that the companies surveyed provided EDP auditors with a median of 11 days of training per year. This training was evenly split between available internal and external sources. (These statistics excluded training time spent actually working in other departments within the company.) The survey results still apply, and they also note that the major problems encountered in training were the following:

- Availability (or lack thereof) of quality external courses
- Amount of time required to train staff
- Difficulty of training auditors to be data processing specialists and vice versa
- Lack of accepted EDP audit standards and procedures

Addressing the Problem Areas

The problems facing the profession can be addressed in several ways. Careful review of the content and practicality of available external courses is one answer. The reputation of the organization presenting the course, as well as its practical EDP audit skills and educational skills, should be considered. In addition, where possible, the course materials should be reviewed prior to enrolling in the course. Using training available in the data processing department (such as manufacturers' training courses) is another workable solution for keeping up to date. Organizing in-house seminars is a possibility, especially when there are none available currently. Joining professional associations (such as the EDP Auditors Association (EDPAA), the Bank Administration Institute (BAI), and the Institute of Internal Auditors (IIA)) is an excellent way to keep in touch with professional people working in the same areas. These organizations are also an excellent resource for course information, publications, and the like.

GUIDELINES FOR THE PROFESSION

Among the basic guidelines for the profession as a whole are the materials prepared by the American Institute of Certified Public Accountants (AICPA). The AICPA has published technical literature to be used as guidance in the accounting and auditing profession since 1917. Currently, the Auditing Standards Board of the AICPA furnishes this guidance to the external auditing profession through the issuance of Statements on Auditing Standards (SAS). These statements define the nature and extent of the auditor's responsibility, and provide a course of action to follow in carrying out professional duties. An outline of statements particularly relevant to EDP auditing is presented in Chapter 2.

Summary of the Foreign Corrupt Practices Act of 1977

The Foreign Corrupt Practices Act has had major impact on the profession of auditing. The Act is divided into three sections. One section deals with illegal foreign payments. Another section deals with books and records and internal accounting control. A third section, regulating disclosure of information when a significant beneficial ownership interest is acquired, is not discussed here since it does not relate directly to EDP audit considerations.

Foreign Corrupt Payments. The Act prohibits any domestic company — or its officers, directors, employees, agents, or stockholders — from using any means of interstate commerce in furtherance of an offer, payment, promise, or authorization of payment of money (or anything of value) to a foreign official to act on its behalf. Specifically, the law proscribes payments to foreign officials, political parties, and candidates for the purpose of obtaining or retaining business by

- Influencing any act or decision of such foreign officials, political parties, or candidates, in an official capacity (including a decision to fail to perform that official function), or
- Inducing such foreign officials, political parties, or candidates to use their influence with a foreign government (or instrumentality) to sway any act or decision of such government.

If convicted of violating the law, a company can be fined up to $1 million; an officer, director, employee, agent, or stockholder can be personally fined up to $10,000 and imprisoned for up to five years. Fines levied on individuals cannot be paid, directly or indirectly, by the company.

The term "foreign official" is defined broadly to include officers or employees of a foreign government (or department, agency, or instrumentality, or anyone acting in an official capacity on behalf of such a government). However, the term does not include employees "whose duties are essentially ministerial or clerical."

The section of the Act dealing with foreign payments applies not only to publicly held companies but also to other entities termed "domestic concerns," which, defined broadly, include any citizen, national, or resident of the United

States, or any corporation, partnership, association, or sole propietorship that has its principal place of business in the United States, or that is organized under the laws of a state, territory, or other entity of the United States.

Internal Accounting Control. The part of the Foreign Corrupt Practices Act that deals with internal accounting control has had a much greater impact on American business than the section on foreign payments, and it has simultaneously had greater impact on auditors and auditing. The Act requires all publicly held corporations to keep adequate records and to be properly controlled. The Act applies even if the corporation does not trade outside the United States.

Specifically, the law provides that publicly held companies must

- Keep books and records that, in reasonable detail, accurately and fairly reflect their transactions, and
- Maintain appropriate systems of internal accounting control.

These requirements, which amend the Securities Exchange Act of 1934, relate only to publicly held companies, not to "domestic concerns." The subject companies are primarily those whose securities are traded on the national stock exchanges or in the over-the-counter market.

The system of internal accounting control must be adequate to provide reasonable assurances that

- Transactions are executed in accordance with management's general or specific authorization.
- Transactions are recorded as necessary to permit preparation of financial statements in conformity with generally accepted accounting principles (GAAP) or any other criteria applicable to such statements, and to maintain accountability for assets.
- Access to assets is permitted only in accordance with management's general or specific authorization.
- The recorded accountability for assets is compared with the existing assets at reasonable intervals, and appropriate action is taken with respect to any differences.

Although the penalties for illegal payments do not apply here, failure to maintain appropriate books and records and systems of internal control would violate the Securities Exchange Act of 1934. Liability for failure to comply will not be imposed, however, when a person acts pursuant to a directive of a federal department or agency for national security purposes.

Action Plan. Companies are advised to adopt a comprehensive action plan to meet the requirements of the Foreign Corrupt Practices Act. This plan should contain a program for evaluating internal accounting controls. The program should include the controls over the company's significant EDP accounting systems.

The Institute of Internal Auditors — Systems Auditability and Control Report

International Business Machines Corporation (IBM) provided a grant to the IIA to fund a project on the audit and control of EDP systems. The study was conducted by Stanford Research Institute, now called SRI International. The results were published as a set of three reports:

1. Executive Report
2. Control Practices Report
3. Audit Practices Report

Although published in 1977, many of the findings are still relevant to the auditing and control of today's EDP systems. Copies of these reports are available from the Institute of Internal Auditors, 249 Maitland Avenue, Altamonte Springs, Fla. 32701.

The Executive Report. This report represents an overview of the audit of EDP systems. Some of the major topics covered are listed here:

- Hazards of inadequate audit and control
- Project methodology
- Management responsibility
- Need for improved controls
- Participation by internal audit in systems development
- Verification of controls
- Need for improved internal audit involvement
- EDP audit staff development
- Need for improved EDP audit tools and techniques
- Need for audit and control assessment
- Cost implications of systems auditability and controls

The general conclusion of the study is that, although data processing systems and internal audit techniques are continuing to evolve, there has been little coordination between the two disciplines. The study found that EDP managers do not have a clear understanding of the internal auditors' mandate and scope of activities, while most internal auditors are investigating an environment in which they may have limited experience, knowledge, and tools.

Compounding these conditions is the fact that top management in many organizations has been insufficiently informed and may not give adequate attention to the potential repercussions of inadequate EDP audit and control procedures. These findings confirm perceptions throughout the profession.

The Control Practices Report. This report states that EDP auditing is a rapidly developing field, in many respects just beginning to fulfill many of the requirements for an effective level of control and proper evaluation of data processing systems. While discussing the general subject of controls within an EDP environment, the study arrives at the following conclusions:

- The primary responsibility for overall internal control resides with top management, while the operational responsibility for the accuracy and completeness of computer-based information systems should reside with users.

- There is a need for improved controls, because inadequate attention has been given to the importance of internal controls in the data processing environment.

- Internal auditors must participate in the systems development process to ensure that appropriate audit and control procedures are designed and built into new computer-based information systems.

- Verification of controls must occur both before and after installation of computer-based information systems.

- As a result of the growth in complexity and use of computer-based information systems, the need exists for greater internal audit involvement relative to auditing in the data processing environment.

- An important need exists for EDP audit staff development, because few internal audit staffs have enough data processing knowledge and experience to audit the data processing environment effectively.

- Few current EDP audit tools and techniques are adequate to serve the needs of the EDP auditors as they approach the task of testing the accuracy and completeness of data processing activities and results. New tools and techniques are needed.

- Many organizations are not adequately evaluating their audit and control functions in the data processing environment. Top management should initiate a periodic assessment of its audit and control programs.

The control practices report discusses specific control techniques, classifying them under computer application controls and general controls. (These are the types of controls that have been incorporated into the systematic audit approach discussed in this book.)

The report emphasizes that controls tend to evolve in a relatively irregular manner as the system is used. In most companies, both users and internal auditors have tended to refrain from commenting on the incorporation of controls until after the system has been installed and is running. (Sometimes this is because they do not realize beforehand why controls are needed.) Any suggestions implemented thereafter are invariably more expensive than when they are considered at the time of systems design. Furthermore, systems analysts and programmers are generally reluctant to incorporate revisions to a system after it has been launched. Auditors should encourage the pre-installation review recommendations of the report. When someone who understands why controls should be built in (the EDP auditor) participates in the process, better systems result.

The Audit Practices Report. This report contains a list of 28 data processing audit tools and techniques, discussed in further detail in the balance of the report.

The section entitled "Audit Management Tools and Techniques" provides audit management with four overall approaches to take when applying EDP audit techniques.

1. *Multisite audit software.* This approach can be used by auditors involved with centralized systems development and decentralized computer data centers. For this environment, the computer audit software programs are written centrally and run on a multisite basis. Presumably, only minimal variations are required from site to site; the computer centers are usually sufficiently similar in equipment configurations and applications systems for the audit programs to work with minor modifications.

2. *Competency center.* This concept can also apply to multisite locations. In this case, the competency center receives data from outlying locations and executes the computer audit software programs centrally. The resulting reports are then distributed to the auditors responsible for auditing the individual sites.

3. *Audit area selection.* This approach recommends applying computerized techniques to organizations with multiple locations in order to determine which locations to audit. Central to its use is the development of location profile material, providing key indicator information for each location. The key indicators are evaluated by the computer in order to determine the points at which audit emphasis is required. This method could be applied manually for situations in which the profile pattern or key indicator development is relatively simple.

4. *Scoring.* The scoring technique requires that a number of attributes be assigned to a computer application, with appropriate point values, from a risk analysis standpoint. The weighted characteristics of a system are combined to develop its total score.

The applications that contain the greatest number of points are those to which the auditor would give the most attention to during the course of examination.

The audit practices report also describes a variety of specific techniques that auditors can use when examining ongoing EDP systems. In some cases, the techniques require that the auditor make direct use of the computer as an audit tool. In other cases, the technique is concerned with review and/or manual testing of the system. Some of these techniques have stood the tests of time and practicality better than others, but they are all known to EDP auditors. They are as follows:

- *Test data method.* The auditor creates special test input data, passes it through the computer programs that have been determined to be of audit significance, and compares the output to predetermined results.

- *Base case system evaluation.* This technique employs a standardized body of data for testing purposes, normally established by user personnel. It is used to validate production computer application systems. The data can be used to test the ongoing accurate operation of the system throughout its lifetime.

- *Integrated test facility.* The Integrated Test Facility (ITF) processes test data in the actual system. It usually represents a set of fictitious entities such as departments, customers, and products. The auditor can process any variety of transactions against the ITF in a live operating environment, and call for printed reports to confirm the correctness of the processing. This method is especially useful when it is not considered practical to test the system on a separate processing cycle basis, and does not have an effect on processing of valid, existing entities.

- *Parallel simulation.* In many cases, it is possible to confirm the accuracy of records of accounting significance by performing a process that is equivalent, but not identical, to the one employed by management. This normally requires a smaller number of programs, since it limits the logic and calculations necessary to secure the equivalent results in the areas of auditor interest. A variety of program types can be used for this type of simulation, such as generalized audit software, manufacturer's utility programs, custom-coded programs, and programs written by the EDP function under audit control.

- *Transaction selection.* The auditor uses a separate computer program to select transactions for further review and testing. Transaction selections can be made on a random or a statistical sampling basis, or by stratification using auditor-established criteria, such as dollar value and age.

- *Embedded audit data collection.* A screening process can be incorporated into regular production programs. Items that fulfill certain criteria established by the auditor then can be selected during regular production runs. This requires that screening routines be specially coded and inserted within the production programs at those logic points where the selection is to occur. (It also requires that the programs be designed that way to begin with, which means including EDP audit participation in their development.)

- *Extended records.* Sometimes it is necessary to take various different elements relating to an item from a number of different files and then combine these elements into a single record. This new record contains the total set of elements required, thus forming a work record that can be processed. The computer is then able to review the relationships of various elements in the new record to determine if any conditions of audit significance exist.

- *Generalized audit software.* This technique employs computer software that has been written to apply certain generalized processes in order to make selections, summarizations, reports, and the like. The user of generalized software must prepare specification sheets, describing the contents of the file and the specific computer processes to be employed against those files. Whichever selections are to be made, or other processes applied, can be supplemented by further actions directed by parameters that the auditor prepares at the time the program is run.

- *Snapshot.* It is sometimes desirable to determine precisely which elements of information were available to the computer at a given moment in time while performing a logic or decision-making process. Through special coding, a triggering process can take place whereby all data that is pertinent to analysis of the specific situation is printed. This is a "snapshot" of that processing instant. Usually this technique is employed to help determine why a computer has produced questionable results when the reasons are not readily apparent and cannot be determined otherwise.

- *Tracing.* This method is, in effect, a walk-through of a given transaction or other record through the computer process. It usually generates computer-printed output, used to determine exactly which computer instructions have been executed by the computer program upon the transaction or record, as well as the sequence in which they were executed.

- *Mapping.* Ordinarily, mapping is used to confirm the thoroughness with which test or production data has been applied against a given computer program. From an audit standpoint, it can be used to determine if there is any unexecuted code within a computer program. This can represent routines that are dormant at the moment, but which might have been added to permit improper computer use. Any unexecuted code should be examined.

- *Control flowcharting.* In many cases, the auditor wants to gain a general understanding of a system while providing specific consideration to the individual controls. This can be achieved by flowcharting the process, placing narrative emphasis on the control points. (The system of flowcharting described in this book has been designed to meet this objective; see Chapter 23, "How to Document Systems and Use Flowcharts.")

- *Job accounting data analysis.* Many computer systems create a log of system use in magnetic media form. Software can be employed to analyze this system use. The auditor can review the results of that analysis to determine the appropriateness of the action that was performed during a given scheduled working day or other period.

- *Audit guide.* An audit guide provides the internal auditor with an outline of the steps to perform when conducting an audit of an area or application system. (The questionnaires and programs described in this book for use during the audit process provide similar guidance.)

- *Disaster testing.* This technique makes use of a simulated disaster in the computer service center to test the adequacy of the center's contingency planning and response to the disaster.

- *Code comparison.* An auditor is often concerned with whether a program being executed in the production environment corresponds to a controlled, authorized copy of the program. To establish the validity of the production program, the auditor uses the computer version maintained under audit control and makes comparison tests of the two versions.

The audit practices report also discusses the internal auditor's increasing role in the development and life of EDP systems. This involvement is covered under the following topics:

- System development life cycle
- Control guidelines for use during system development
- System acceptance and control group
- Post-installation audit

The report particularly emphasizes the internal auditor's involvement during the development process, which helps ensure that

- User requirements are properly satisfied.
- Adequate application controls are installed and maintained.
- Anticipated cost/benefit or procedural improvements are realized.
- Adequate acceptance testing occurs.

- Projects are completed as scheduled and within costs as budgeted.
- Administrative or operational controls are adequate to ensure a methodical and disciplined development process.
- Adequate application controls are incorporated into new or revised application systems to prevent undetected errors and omissions.
- Predictability is improved in system development.

Perhaps in part as a result of this report, and other similar developments, management is becoming more aware of the advantages of audit participation in systems development.

CERTIFIED INFORMATION SYSTEMS AUDITOR PROGRAM

Objectives of the EDP Auditors Foundation

The EDP Auditors Foundation, Inc. (see page 3-21 for a discussion of the EDP Auditors Association) was founded in 1976 to pursue the following objectives:

- Develop, improve, and implement EDP auditing education
- Engage in research in the field of EDP auditing
- Assist qualified individuals in the study of EDP auditing

Certified Information Systems Auditor Program

On June 21, 1978, the EDP Auditors Foundation established a certification program to

- Evaluate the competence of individuals to conduct EDP audits;
- Provide a mechanism for motivating and monitoring EDP auditors' maintenance of that competence; and
- Aid top management in developing a sound EDP audit function by providing criteria for personnel selection and development.

Anyone can sit for the certified information systems auditor (CISA) examination; however, a minimum of five years' professional information systems auditing work experience, as outlined in the following sections, is required for certification. However, the auditor can substitute the following:

- One year of EDP experience or auditing experience for one year of information systems auditing experience

- 60 or 120 college semester credit hours for one or two years, respectively, of information systems auditing experience

The general content of the examination is taken from work routinely performed by information systems auditors in the following areas:

- Application Systems Controls Review
- Data Integrity Review
- Systems Development Life Cycle Review
- Application Development Review
- General Operational Procedures Controls Review
- Security Review
- Systems Software Review
- Maintenance Review
- Acquisition Review
- Data Processing Resource Management Review
- Information Systems Audit Management

Recertification/Continuing Education Units

The recertification requirement of the certification program was established to

- Keep the CISA up to date in the knowledge and skills that were required for original certification, such as accounting, auditing, management, and data processing.
- Help the CISA attain new knowledge and skills to keep abreast of the continually changing technologies in data processing.
- Provide a process whereby continued certification is based upon maintenance, through education, of the information systems auditor's professional competence.

Continuing education units (CEUs) will be assigned by the EDP Auditors Foundation Education Board to seminars, meetings, lectures, and the like that contribute to the professional competence of the CISA.

Recertification is required every three years, by amassing 120 contact hours of continuing education (or 12 CEUs, when a CEU consists of ten 50-minute contact hours) over the three-year period or by retaking the current examination.

Code of Professional Conduct

The EDP Auditors Foundation has established the following Code of Professional Conduct for CISAs:

- CISAs shall promote the establishment of and compliance with appropriate standards, procedures, and controls for data processing systems and operations, consistent with generally accepted professional practices.
- CISAs shall promote the need for adequate data processing controls to senior management and to the general public.
- CISAs shall perform their assigned responsibilities in a loyal and honest manner and not knowingly be a party to any illegal or improper activity.
- CISAs shall promote the education and understanding of the interrelationship between data processing and auditing.
- CISAs shall develop and communicate their opinions in an objective manner. Sufficient documentation and evidence should support their professional judgments.
- CISAs shall maintain the confidentiality of privileged information obtained during their normal duties.
- CISAs shall maintain their competencies in data processing and auditing through participation in professional development activities.
- CISAs shall uphold high standards of conduct, character, and morality in both their professional and their personal activities.
- CISAs shall not participate in activities that may be, or appear to be, in conflict with policies of their employers or clients. Activities that threaten the independence or perceived independence of the CISA also should be avoided.

THE GROWTH OF THE EDP AUDITING PROFESSION

A decade or so ago, many large firms were confronted with the question of performing effective reviews of EDP activities. As accounting information was increasingly massaged and manipulated by computers before it appeared in financial reports, EDP auditors had to interact all the more with the EDP department, and their external auditors and their own audit group. The response of the profession to these needs has been described throughout this chapter.

Today, as in the late 1960s and early 1970s, management's needs in relation to EDP demand a sophisticated response from their EDP support people. Given the rapid development of computer technology, management's control and auditing needs have become more complicated. Automated systems involve hidden languages, interrelated files, high speed transactions, concealed information, difficulties in obtaining data, and a cost/price labor spiral, all of which have changed the way an audit can be conducted. These considerations are especially important in relation to data base management systems, communication networks, distributed processing systems, mini-computers, and microcomputers. As a result, key management needs in this area and ways EDP auditors have met — and continue to meet — them have developed.

Some of the areas management can consider in its effort to develop EDP audit capabilities are summarized in the following checklist:

1. Controlling and Auditing Systems:

☐ *Control assurance* — Assuring that resources and assets are effectively controlled; assisting with problems that can occur as a result of auditing "around the computer," or seeing what goes in and what comes out of the computer, without considering what happens within the computer system during processing.

☐ *EDP audit recommendations* — Making practical recommendations about adequately meeting EDP audit needs within budget constraints.

☐ *Regulatory compliance* — Assisting in complying with the increasing complexity of EDP-related law and regulations; assessing management's responsibility to establish and document controls in the data processing department.

☐ *Installation recommendations* — Examining the audit alternatives and effects involved in implementing new equipment and systems.

☐ *Interruption of processing* — Helping in EDP disasters or interruptions that can have a severe impact on an organization.

☐ *Security consulting* — Establishing control, since EDP systems can be the target of abuse by highly technical staff who look upon the complex organization as a puzzle, or a challenge to be met. Since most systems allow multiple access — a benefit to users — this is a potential control trouble spot for management.

2. Software Needs:

☐ *Current software requirements* — Assuring that both internal and external auditors apply the most advanced and effective software technology.

☐ *Analysis of future trends* — Examining future and available alternatives for developing computerized audit software to assist management in meeting its audit objectives.

3. Staff Training:

☐ *EDP audit staffing* — Establishing EDP training programs, since at present, there is a great shortage of qualified EDP audit personnel, and the operation of EDP systems requires specialized technical knowledge in order that the systems be audited effectively.

4. Computer Audit Advisory Services:

☐ *Systems control review* — After EDP auditors analyze, evaluate, and review computerized systems, this process includes documenting existing controls and generating practical recommendations for improvements where weaknesses and deficiencies exist.

☐ *EDP audit assistance* — EDP audit specialists can be useful in assisting external and internal audit teams by providing an objective evaluation of automated systems and documenting recommendations for improvement.

☐ *Implementation reviews* — Assessing the controls involved in the implementation of new equipment and systems, and performing cost/benefit analyses.

☐ *Risk analysis/contingency planning/disaster planning* — Helping analyze the audit implications involved in planning ahead for interruptions to processing.

☐ *Data security assistance* — Giving management advice on areas such as maintaining, developing, and strengthening controls to minimize the impact or possibility of computer fraud.

5. Advanced Software Capability:

☐ *Application of audit software* — Using generalized audit software to interrogate financial data maintained on the computer, thereby assisting computer auditors and organizations in testing controls, substantiating account balances, and documenting regulatory compliance.

☐ *Research and development effort* — Ongoing research and development efforts to produce audit software for today's systems and those of the future.

6. Professional Education and Development:

☐ *Ongoing professional education* — Developing and maintaining the EDP auditors' state-of-the-art knowledge, providing practical auditing techniques that can be applied on the job.

The management response to modern developments in EDP technology will continue to change as needs change. One frequent goal is to establish a staff or group of full-time EDP auditors. EDP auditors' ongoing efforts to maintain, develop, and apply advanced methodologies in EDP auditing have important implications for the accounting profession and financial management, internal auditors, and EDP specialists in both the public and private sectors.

THE EDP AUDITORS ASSOCIATION

The EDP Auditors Association, Inc. (EDPAA) is the only professional membership association dedicated to EDP auditing. Derived from many disciplines — data processing, accounting, management, and security — EDP auditing is leading the way toward the controlled and manageable use of information systems. The EDPAA was founded in 1969; today it has members in 48 countries. The Association fosters professionalism through:

- *Information Transfer* — Facilitating the free exchange of audit techniques, practices, and problem-solving methods.

- *Communication* — Supplying current information on the latest developments in the field of information systems auditing.

- *Education* — Providing the finest in seminars, conferences, and professional forums.

The EDPAA Code of Ethics follows.

CODE OF ETHICS

BE IT THEREFORE RESOLVED:

The EDP Auditors Association, Inc. sets forth the following CODE OF ETHICS to guide the conduct of its members in their professional and personal activities:

1. MEMBERS shall promote the establishment of appropriate standards, procedures, and systems of control commensurate with the application and/or operation under review and with generally accepted professional practice.

2. MEMBERS shall serve in the interest of members' employers, their stockholders, clients, and the general public in a diligent, loyal, and honest manner, and shall not knowingly be a party to any illegal or improper activity.

3. MEMBERS shall hold privileged information obtained in the normal course of their duties confidential. Confidential information shall not be used for personal benefit or released to other parties without proper authorization.

4. MEMBERS shall perform their duties in an independent and objective manner, setting aside personal biases.

5. MEMBERS shall use prudent care to obtain and document sufficient factual material on which to base conclusions and recommendations.

6. MEMBERS shall strive to improve their competence in the interrelated fields of auditing and electronic data processing.

7. MEMBERS shall promote the education and understanding of the fields of auditing and electronic data processing to management, clients, and the general public, and shall promote a better understanding between data processing personnel and users of computers and automated systems.

(continued)

8. MEMBERS shall maintain high standards of conduct, character, and honor at all times in their professional and personal activities. Members shall refrain from participating in activities that may be, or appear to be, in conflict with policies or goals of their employers or clients. They shall not accept fees or gifts from employees, clients, or any business associate without the prior knowledge and consent of their management.

9. ALL MEMBERS of the EDP Auditors Association, Inc. shall abide by the By-Laws of the Association and shall subscribe to this CODE OF ETHICS.

10. MEMBERS found in violation of any CODE OF ETHICS provision are subject to revocation of Association membership.

CHAPTER 4

Systems Audit Approach

OVERVIEW OF THE SYSTEMS AUDIT APPROACH

Organizations that rely on computer-based information systems need to have appropriate control over their systems. To review and test the effectiveness of these control systems, the auditor needs an approach that is both thorough and easy to use. One successful approach divides the audit into manageable component phases so that each phase can be handled using standardized techniques and documents. A similar approach is followed by many auditors.

The auditor can apply this systems approach to all audits regardless of the way data is processed, including manual systems and automated systems of varying degrees of technological complexity.

One example of this type of an approach is presented here, in terms appropriate to systems that are in place and operating. The audit approach can also guide audit involvement in new systems development and administrative or operational audits.

Using this approach, the auditor should first determine the objectives or purposes of the audit, then plan the audit and secure the requisite resources. This process is more than scoping, although it is based on scoping information. Adequate planning involves determining an adequate auditing procedure to be applied and an allocation of the needed resources.

Gathering information about the systems is the next step. To do so, the auditor should first gain an understanding of the management information system and its controls through inquiry, analysis, and careful documentation. Use of flowcharts and questionnaires is employed when the auditor plans to rely on controls, as appropriate to the circumstances. The auditor evaluates the understanding to identify likely control strengths and weaknesses and their effects on the system.

Next the auditor tests the controls to establish that they are actually operating properly; to determine whether controls, initially assessed as apparently reliable, can be relied on in practice. Based on the results of these compliance tests, the auditor determines the requisite level for testing system procedures, and then executes and evaluates those tests. The auditor simultaneously evaluates the extent to which the organization's procedures and standards are actually being followed; he or she may then want to test the underlying data and organizational procedures. This is not an automatic step but depends on the audit objective and on the extent to which controls can be relied on.

The preceding steps in this approach should give the auditor all the information needed to reach certain conclusions, including the level of reliance that can be placed on the system and decisions about whether the audit objectives have been satisfied. This is the central activity of the audit, to which all the activities described contribute. Finally, the conclusions are communicated to all concerned in an audit report of Findings and Recommendations.

The process just described consists of the following sequence of activities:

1. Planning, based on audit objectives

2. Obtaining, recording, and confirming an understanding of the system and its controls

3. Making a preliminary evaluation of controls

4. Performing compliance tests on the controls

5. Performing substantive tests and procedures

6. Determining and reporting findings and recommendations

At certain points in the audit, the results of previous steps need to be assessed and the audit plan reconsidered. Some procedures may need to be modified in light of this process. For example, while confirming the understanding, matters may come to light that make it necessary to amend the recorded understanding.

This approach involves a number of different tasks; at each stage, auditors may refer to guides, reference manuals, questionnaires, and forms. These standardized documents are useful in maintaining the consistency, thoroughness, and quality of audits. (See Part V, "Using Documents and Forms.")

This chapter presents an overview of the approach, as well as explanations of planning and audit reports, both of which can have an impact on audit strategy.

Applying the Approach to Other Audit Functions

The audit approach described previously is applied primarily in the evaluation of internal controls. It is equally suitable for an external auditor performing a controls-based audit of a client's financial statements or for an internal auditor whose responsibility is to audit controls. However, internal EDP auditors (and, in some cases, external EDP auditors) may also be involved in other functions such as security reviews, operational audits, pre-implementation reviews of systems, and participation in the system development life cycle. The same approach can be applied, in whole or in part, to these audit functions.

PLANNING

Planning the overall audit strategy is an integral part of any audit. Plans can cover the long range (three to five years), the short range (annual), the audit plan for the audit unit, and the work plan for individual areas to be reviewed. During the planning process the auditor should perform the following steps:

1. Develop an annual plan.

2. Obtain and document a preliminary current understanding of each system to be audited.

| Audit Techniques | Study and Evaluation of Internal Control | | Substantive Audit Procedures | |
	Understand the System	Compliance Tests	Tests on Transactions and Balances	Analytical Review
Substantive Testing Techniques				
General audit software	X	X	X	X
Specialized audit software	X	X	X	X
Utility software	X	X	X	
Program Testing Techniques				
Test data, including use of an Integrated Test Facility	X	X		
Program code review	X			
Program comparisons		X		
Integrity Testing Techniques				
System log analysis			X	X
Data base analysis			X	
Microcomputer programs	X	X	X	X
Time-Sharing Programs	X	X	X	
Additional Techniques	X	X	X	X

FIG. 4-1   Audit techniques to evaluate internal controls

3. Determine risks, set audit objectives, and determine resources.
4. Determine the audit strategy that yields the best mix of effectiveness and efficiency. (See Figure 4-1.)
5. Document and communicate the planned audit strategy.
6. Monitor the plan and react to changing circumstances and findings.

(See Figure 4-2 and the section entitled "Audit Planning" for further discussion.)

OBTAINING, RECORDING, AND CONFIRMING THE UNDERSTANDING

Before the auditor can evaluate controls or a decision can be made about the audit procedures to be applied, an understanding of the system under review must be developed. The auditor normally obtains this understanding by interviewing personnel, reviewing previous audits, and reading system descriptions, such as flowcharts and system narratives.

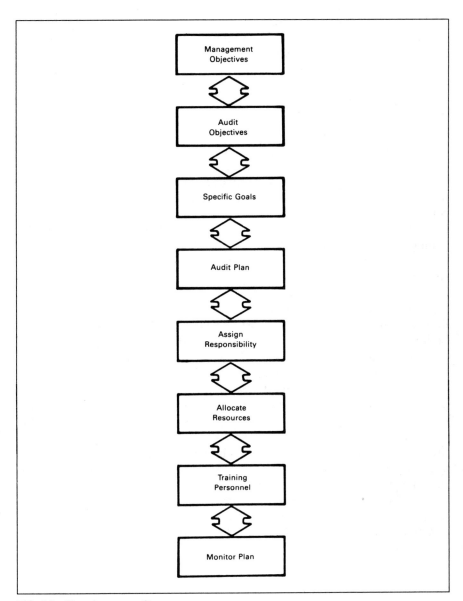

FIG. 4-2 Planning an audit

The auditor needs to prepare an adequate record of the system's procedures and controls. Parts of this recording may be obtained from system users. This type of record is a prerequisite of the audit. It makes both supervisory review and on-the-job training more effective and it saves time on subsequent audits. A formal requirement to prepare or obtain such a record also imposes its own discipline on the auditor, since it helps him or her to understand the system as the control procedures are recorded. Thus, the understanding itself is made more comprehensive and precise.

An understanding of the system can be recorded either through the use of flowcharts or through the use of narrative notes.

As a preliminary step in recording an understanding of a system, it is usually necessary to prepare a computer overview flowchart for each important computer application. Overview flowcharts should summarize all significant input items, files, and output or reports. These flowcharts are also useful for planning purposes and supervisory review of audit work.

Detailed flowcharting is a common means of recording an understanding when the auditor plans to rely on controls. It is a graphic way to document the internal control procedures established for the processing of each transaction type. The auditor then uses this recorded understanding as the basis for evaluating the system. The flowchart or other record should always integrate both manual and automated procedures, in order to show the flow of transactions through the whole system.

After the flowcharts or narrative notes have been prepared or updated, the auditor should confirm that the system has been understood and recorded properly. One way to obtain this confirmation is by tracing one transaction of each type through the system. This process is referred to as a transaction review. The transaction review enhances subsequent audit efficiency by ensuring, as far as possible, that the auditor's understanding of the system is correct and that it has been recorded accurately. In computer-based business systems, the auditor must confirm the understanding of the manual procedures, programmed procedures, and general controls. Even though transaction reviews in computer-based systems are carried out for the same purpose as in non-computer systems, the characteristics of computer-based systems may change the methods the auditor uses to confirm the understanding.

EVALUATING THE INTERNAL CONTROLS

The Nature of Controls

The phrase "internal control" covers the methods, procedures, and organizational arrangements adopted within the organization to ensure, to the greatest possible degree,

- The safeguarding of resources,

- The accuracy and reliability of records,
- The promotion of operational efficiency, and
- The adherence of employees to organization policies.

Other internal controls are concerned with nonfinancial records, qualitative measures, and administrative or operational controls. In practice, although relationships can be found between the different types of controls, they are usually considered separately for clarity. Within the systems audit approach, the word "control" is defined by dividing it into its two necessary parts:

1. *Basic controls*—Those procedures and actions that are applied directly to the data, programs, output, or manual processing steps.
2. *Disciplines over the basic controls*—Those procedures and actions that confirm or assure that the basic control has been performed. This is accomplished by
   - Supervision,
   - Separation of duties, and
   - Controls over physical access.

The evaluation of internal controls is directed toward determining the adequacy of the control system. For any weaknesses or control deficiencies discovered during the evaluation, the auditor must determine if there are controls that compensate for those weaknesses. If there is no compensating control, the auditor must then determine whether that weakness can have a significant impact on the reliability of the information produced by the system.

Controls in Computer-Based Systems

The introduction of computerized processing methods for accounting and management decision support usually results in significant changes in the methods of processing and controlling transactions. Since different control techniques are available, changes in the manner of both applying and evaluating controls may result. The extent of change depends on the scope of computer processing in each system. The principal changes are

- Many accounting and control procedures, which previously were carried out manually, are replaced by precise steps in the computer programs. These steps are referred to as programmed procedures.
- Data is held on computer files instead of manual records. This usually means that greater reliance is placed on the general controls over the integrity of the programmed procedures.

User reliance on programmed procedures usually results in reduced examination of the output from processing. Therefore it requires increased controls over the continued correctness of data held on computer files.

Holding data on computer files may affect the manner in which controls are applied to prevent unauthorized changes to that data, or to assure the continued and proper operation of computer software.

To aid in the audit of computer-based systems, it is useful to review controls according to whether the controls are specific to a given application performed by the system or whether they are applicable to the general performance of computer processing.

Controls specific to a given application performed by the system are called "application controls." Controls relating to the general performance of computer processing and the computer environment are called "general controls" or "integrity controls." Both application controls and general controls consist of two parts, basic controls and disciplines over those controls.

Application Controls

Application controls are the specific controls over each separate computer application system (such as inventory management, accounts payable, general ledger). They should ensure that only authorized data is completely and accurately processed by that system. Application controls can be exercised by a combination of programmed procedures and the manual procedures conducted in the system's user departments. For example, a programmed procedure might consist of an edit program that flags invalid data and prints a report. The report is then the basis on which the user can investigate and manually correct the erroneous data.

If programmed procedures are complex, and especially if their proper functioning is not assured by the manual procedures, the auditor should first ascertain the significance of the programmed procedures. Then the auditor needs to ensure that related general controls, implemented within the EDP environment, are adequate.

General Controls

An application control may depend on the proper functioning of a particular program. The proper functioning of that program may depend on the EDP department's appropriate compliance with certain general or integrity controls. To meet this objective, these general controls should include controls over the design, implementation, security, and use of computer programs and data files.

The main function of general controls is to ensure that key programmed functions operate consistently and properly, and that data and programs stored in the system are adequately secured. General controls are implemented by those responsible for the computer environment. They work by manual procedures, procedures conducted by the system software, or a combination of both. System software consists of computer programs of a general nature that control the computer itself, such as operating systems, compilers, utility and librarian programs, data base management systems, and teleprocessing systems.

Evaluation of Application Controls

As part of the audit approach, the auditor can use methods employing the following documents and explanatory manual to evaluate internal controls in computer applications:

- Control Matrix
- Internal Control Questionnaire (ICQ) and Control Matrix
- Computer Internal Control Questionnaire (CICQ)
- Record of Control Weaknesses (RCW)
- *Internal Control Reference Manual* (ICRM)

These documents were developed and are used by Coopers & Lybrand. Other audit approaches use similar documents. Throughout this book the specific names of documents, when used, refer to the ones listed here. (For a detailed discussion of these, see Chapter 25, "The Evaluation Process and How to Use Documents," Chapter 26, "*Internal Control Reference Manual*—General Controls," and Chapter 27, "*Internal Control Reference Manual*—Application Controls.")

Control Matrix. The Computer Application Control Matrix provides a one-page summary of the completeness, accuracy, authorization, and maintenance controls applied to each transaction type. It can be used in two ways to evaluate existing computer applications:

1. It can be the principal recording document on which application controls are identified.
2. It can be used in conjunction with the ICQ (described in the following section)
   - As a scoping tool in the initial evaluation of the system before using the ICQ; the information contained on the matrix is subsequently transferred to the questionnaire.
   - As a summary of the ICQ results.

For each transaction type of audit significance (the proper identification of which is essential), the auditor records the following information on the Control Matrix:

- The particular input types processed. These may be documents or records on a computer file.

- The techniques used to achieve control for each transaction type. Control is applied to the following areas:
  a. Completeness of input and update
  b. Accuracy of input and update
  c. Validity or authorization of data
  d. Continuity or maintenance of data on computer files
- For administrative or operational reviews:
  a. The additional techniques, if any, needed to ensure timely detection of errors and the timeliness of reports needed by management.
  b. An assessment of the efficiency of the controls, and if appropriate, of the other aspects of the system.

Internal Control Questionnaire. For a detailed evaluation of internal controls in computer-based systems, the auditor can use a set of questionnaires. As a group, in the format presented in this book, they are called the "Internal Control Questionnaire."

The manual ICQ contains questions for manual systems and for controls that do not vary significantly when they are computer-based. The ICQ is organized by control objectives.

If a control objective requires a different control procedure in a computer-based system than in a manual one, then the auditor can use the Computer Internal Control Questionnaire.

Computer Internal Control Questionnaire. The CICQ consists of two parts. The first covers application controls and is organized by control objectives to correspond to the control objective structure of the ICQ. At the end of this document, a separate section covers controls over master file data specifically. The other part of the CICQ covers the general or integrity controls over stored data and programs.

Record of Control Weaknesses. The RCW form is used to list and summarize all control weaknesses identified by using the questionnaire or the Control Matrix. The purpose of the RCW is to bring together in one document:

- All control weaknesses identified during the evaluation
- Evaluation of possible effects, including potential errors of a substantial nature
- Amendments required to the audit program, due to the existence of weaknesses
- The results of discussing those weaknesses with local management
- Any reporting to senior management or corrective action taken

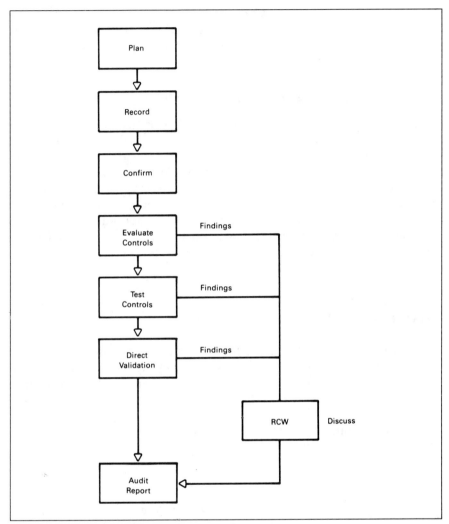

FIG. 4-3 Systems audit approach (also called Coopers & Lybrand Audit Approach because of similarities to some audit procedures used by Coopers & Lybrand)

The RCW also provides a way to review the possible effects of weaknesses on the organization's management information. The RCW can be used throughout the later phases of the audit cycle. (See Figure 4-3.)

Internal Control Reference Manual. The ICRM is designed to assist the auditor in completing the CICQ, the Control Matrix, and the RCW. It identifies internal control questions, outlines procedures that might be effective for performing each task, and gives examples of how these procedures might operate in practice. The ICRM helps bring greater uniformity to subjective judgments about the controls of the systems. It is in two parts, general controls and application controls. (See Chapters 26 and 27.)

Evaluation of Management-Defined Procedures

Other aspects of the audit include review and assurance that organizational procedures instituted by management are being followed. Since well-defined procedures should indicate specific actions to be taken and the areas of responsibility, these become the basis for review, testing, and evaluation. There should be a clear relationship between the established corporate procedures and the actual transaction-centered activities. When the relationship is not obvious, the audit approach provides a way to suggest warranted changes in the procedures. (See the following section entitled "Determining and Recording Findings and Recommendations.")

COMPLIANCE TESTS

Compliance or functional testing is the process of testing controls (identified on a matrix or questionnaire) to determine if they are operating as planned. Testing consists of inquiries, examining evidence, reperforming procedures, and observation to see whether the planned controls are in fact being performed. These tests are usually recorded on an audit program. (See the following section entitled "Audit Program.")

Specimen Tests

A schedule of specimen compliance testing procedures and other guidelines is useful to assist the auditor in designing tests. (Additional information is given in Chapter 21, "Control Reviews and Compliance Tests," and Chapter 22, "Substantive or Validation Procedures.")

Audit Program

It is a good idea to record the tests to be performed on a standardized audit program form. One such form is called the Program and Record of Compliance Tests and Administrative Reviews (PRT). (See Chapter 25.) The form is designed to record the actual execution of each test step. The same PRT can be followed in subsequent audits as long as the system does not change.

Tests of Management-Defined Procedures

Consideration and review of each organizational procedure often provides the auditor with a parallel test of the important controls. It also can yield extensive insight into how and whether management expectations are being fulfilled. Tests of compliance applied to organizational procedures may overlap the compliance tests of internal controls.

SUBSTANTIVE TESTS

Auditors, or other internal organization personnel, frequently perform tests of account balances and other record summaries. These are referred to as substantive procedures or tests. They are performed as regular duties, in conjunction with work performed for external auditors, or by external auditors.

Computer Audit Software Tools

In computer-based systems, the auditor may use audit software programs to perform a number of functions leading up to and/or including the generation of reports used for audit examination. These reports may be useful in performing a number of different audit functions. Neither the data files accessed nor the production programs need to be modified for, nor should they be affected by, these audit software programs. The functions performed may include the automated reading and analysis of information in files, selecting and summarizing data, totaling and performing comparative calculations, formatting output, comparing different versions of program code, and analyzing access paths and security.

Two of the more significant features of using computer audit programs are: (1) more information can be and normally is examined (unlike manual tests, in which only a portion of the data normally is examined), and (2) additional information that would not otherwise be available to the auditor often can be produced. These factors usually enable the auditor to carry out more effective tests on computer-based systems using audit software. In paperless systems where there is a lack of audit trail, computer-assisted techniques may be the only way to perform effective tests. (See Chapter 28, "Testing Techniques for Computer-Based Systems.")

DETERMINING AND RECORDING FINDINGS AND RECOMMENDATIONS

The purpose of control reviews, compliance testing, analytical reviews, and substantive testing is to provide the auditor with the information needed to make an informed audit judgment. Indeed, in the context of the audit objectives, the auditor is called upon to give conclusions on the extent to which the audit objectives have been satisfied. For the external auditor the audit objectives, standards, and regulations should relate to the generally accepted auditing standards (GAAS) followed to provide the basis of an audit opinion. For the internal auditor, this audit approach leads systematically to the determination of audit conclusions and indicates the findings of the audit. If recommendations to correct control deficiencies are possible, they are included as well.

At the conclusion of the audit, the auditor should report internal control deficiencies that have been identified to senior management. The form and content of these reports is usually dictated by the needs of each organization. The internal auditor normally prepares a formal report, which includes assessments of the system or area reviewed and comments on internal controls. When deficiencies are noted, the auditor sometimes makes a recommendation that outlines the possible corrective action to be taken to ensure that adequate controls are implemented.

Merely identifying and reporting weaknesses and recommending corrective action to management is not enough. Follow-up procedures should be adequate to ensure that corrective action on control deficiencies has been taken on a timely, cost-effective basis, resulting in the implementation of an adequate system of internal control. This is part of the auditor's responsibilities and duties. Recent court decisions have also had legal ramifications for the auditor's duty and resultant liability in certain areas.

AUDIT PLANNING

Since an effective planning process is essential to the proper management of any business activity, it is also so in developing overall audit strategies and conducting audits.

Effective development of an audit or audit procedures requires that the audit department understand the objectives of management before developing an audit strategy. In this way, planning becomes one of the most important aspects of an efficient audit, for both internal and external auditors.

To devise a workable audit plan, the audit department should perform the following tasks:

- Develop audit objectives from management objectives.
- Translate audit objectives into specific goals and develop a plan for implementation.
- Assign responsibility for implementing the various facets of the plan.
- Ensure adequate resources, especially time and manpower, for the plan to succeed.

- Schedule EDP audit training for staff to ensure availability of needed expertise.
- Monitor the plan to detect any needed changes.

Within the framework just described, the planning process for work done by an internal audit department can be managed within its two basic components:

1. Preparation of an annual audit program
2. Development of detailed audit strategies or a program for each audit contained in the annual program (see Figure 4-4)

Preparing the Annual Audit Program

In many organizations, time and people are limited resources. Availability of computer time for auditors' use may also be limited. To allocate these resources effectively and efficiently, a systematic evaluation procedure should be employed. It is important to establish the priority of the audits included in the annual audit program. Initially, the auditors can develop a comprehensive list of all possible audit areas. Once each of these audit areas has been evaluated, priorities can be assigned. Some factors to consider when evaluating the areas to be audited are:

- Financial statement impact. Areas that would have a significant impact on the financial statements should almost always have high priority.
- Previous audit history. Areas where previous audits showed deficiencies may require follow-up.
- Length of time since the last audit was conducted. All areas should be audited on a cyclical basis within a reasonable period of time.
- Changes in policies or procedures. When these have occurred, assurance that there was proper implementation of any substantial changes in company policies or procedures since the last audit should be a high-priority item.
- Changes in government regulations, legal requirements, or federal or state tax laws affecting the industry. These may require special audit attention.
- Implementation of new systems. This includes computerization of a formerly all manual system or modifications to a computerized system. The level of involvement is based on:
  a. Accounting significance of the system
  b. Operational exposure
  c. Need to determine compliance with established methodologies for implementing the new systems or maintaining current systems

Task	Procedure
1. Plan the audit.	Determine the audit objectives. Obtain an overall understanding of the application through preliminary interviews. Record the preliminary understanding on the overview flowchart and other planning aids. Define and document audit strategy.
2. Obtain an overall understanding of the conditions of control.	Become familiar with organizational and site operations, using the Internal Control Questionnaire. Conduct preliminary site interviews.
3. Obtain and record understanding of the internal control system.	Conduct site interviews, review documentation, and prepare flowcharts.
4. Confirm understanding of the system.	Inquire, and examine available evidence, trace transactions, and modify flowcharts if necessary.
5. Evaluate the system to determine if there are any inherent weaknesses.	Complete Internal Control Questionnaire and/or Control Matrix, using *Internal Control Reference Manual*.
6. Assess control weaknesses and determine their potential significance.	Complete Record of Control Weaknesses, using *Internal Control Reference Manual*.
7. Test controls that are in place to determine if they are operating effectively.	Prepare Program and Record of Compliance Tests and Administrative Reviews. Perform compliance tests to gain reasonable assurance that procedures are being applied as prescribed.
8. Perform substantive tests in areas of significant control deficiency.	Analyze the extent and effect of the control deficiency.
9. Report findings.	Write an evaluation on the adequacy of controls and the system in question. If weaknesses are found, determine their potential effects and offer realistic and quantifiable solutions.
10. Follow up with subsequent audit.	Schedule a review or subsequent audit to determine if appropriate steps have been taken to eliminate weaknesses in the control system.

FIG. 4-4   Overall audit approach for an audit of an existing system

- Establishment of new contracts for computer hardware or software, or proposals planned or outstanding for new contracts.
- Use of a service bureau for data processing.
- Requests from external auditors for assistance in their annual audit of the financial statements.
- Specific requests from the audit committee.

- Requests from management. Operational managers may be aware of particular concerns in their departments that should be addressed; the internal audit staff should solicit these requests through suitable procedures, such as the distribution of form letters.
- The resources available versus requirements for involvement in special projects, based on past experience.

Once these factors have been evaluated, the auditors can prepare the annual audit program based on that evaluation and the amount of audit time available. Individual auditors should be assigned specific responsibilities for each audit within the annual program.

Upon completion, the annual audit program should be reviewed and approved by management and the audit committee. In most cases the auditees should be notified when the audit is to be conducted in their area. The status of the annual audit program should be updated continually by the auditors so that amendments can be made whenever necessary. Management involvement with the planning process is a key to its success. For internal auditors, interactive planning with the external auditors is an important element.

Developing Individual Audit Strategies

The second component of planning an audit is the development of an audit strategy for each of the individual audits within the annual program. (See Figure 4-5.) When the audit is being done on a system currently in place, this planning process can be divided into the following four major steps:

1. Review the latest audit reports and identify factors and related risks that may significantly affect the audit strategy.
2. Obtain and document a current preliminary understanding of the systems to be audited.
3. Determine the most effective and efficient audit strategy.
4. Document the planned audit strategy.

When the audit relates to the implementation of a new system, the planning process should include

- Establishing ongoing communication with the data processing department.
- Establishing control standards that require internal audit sign-off at the completion of each step of the implementation process.
- Scheduling training for EDP auditors to bring them up to date on the new system, when appropriate. Then they will be able to evaluate the new, possibly more complex systems and participate constructively in the systems development process.

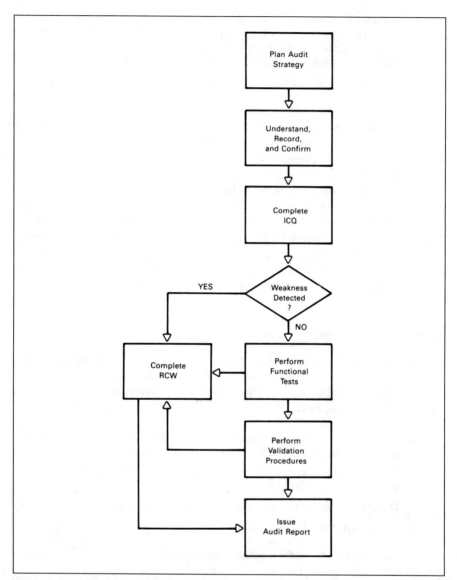

FIG. 4-5   An audit approach

The following sections provide specific information about these steps. The planning procedures described illustrate an effective planning process that

- Integrates manual and computerized audit approach procedures and
- Uses existing documentation that describes the systems.

Gathering Information

When conducting an audit of a particular area, the auditor may wish to obtain a general understanding of the characteristics of the auditee. If the audit emphasis is financial, then the auditor should examine the particular transactions and balances reflected in the financial statements related to the area under review. Of special interest would be:

- Significant changes in account balances, deviations from budget, or unusual relationships with other account balances
- The composition and relative size of account balances, including an approximation of the number of transactions reflected in such balances

The preceding information may be available in prior audit working papers or located through inquiry. Other significant factors that may have an impact on the audit scope include:

- New or unresolved accounting and reporting issues that affect the areas encompassed by the audit. This information may be obtained by reviewing pronouncements issued by the American Insititute of Certified Public Accountants (AICPA), the Financial Accounting Standards Board (FASB), and the Securities and Exchange Commission (SEC) since the last audit. Summary interpretations of these pronouncements may be available internally through the company's accounting or reporting departments.
- Changes in matters affecting the nature of the organization and its operating environment, such as:
  a. General and industry economic conditions
  b. Level of governmental regulation
  c. Technological improvements
  d. Warranties, unusual contracting practices, related party transactions, and other contractual requirements or constraints
  e. Significant acquisitions and disposals
  f. Changes in corporate structure, personnel, policies, or procedures
- Potential for use of audit software for compliance testing or substantive procedures.
- Results of similar audits conducted at other locations or subsidiaries of a corporation with multiple locations or subsidiaries. The appropriate internal audit departments should be contacted and copies of their audit reports should be obtained. This is particularly relevant when standardized procedures are in effect at the parent and all subsidiary locations.

The Preliminary Understanding

The auditor should obtain and document a current preliminary understanding of the systems to be audited. The examples here relate to financial audits.

Certain accounts in the financial statements usually are audited by relying principally on substantive procedures. The following are examples of these accounts:

- Long-term debt and interest expense
- Property, plant, and equipment
- Depreciation of property, plant, and equipment
- Intangible assets and amortization
- Income tax liability, deferred income taxes, and income tax expense
- Capital stock and other stockholder's equity transactions

If the auditor can identify these accounts initially, there may be no need to obtain a preliminary understanding for the purpose of selecting an audit strategy.

If there is any initial doubt about the appropriate strategy, the auditor should obtain and document the preliminary understanding in order to select the most effective and efficient audit strategy. Examples of accounts or groups of accounts for which this is usually done are:

- Accounts receivable and sales
- Accounts payable and purchases
- Inventory and cost of goods sold

In some recurring audits, the auditor may be able to determine initially that certain significant accounts, groups of accounts, or other groups of data on which management relies, will be audited by relying on controls. In this situation, the purpose of the preliminary understanding is to

- Enable the auditor to plan the appropriate review and evaluation of internal control and limited substantive procedures.
- Encourage the auditor to re-evaluate the audit strategy to ensure that it is the most effective and efficient possible.

On most recurring audits where there are no significant systems changes, the information the auditor needs for the preliminary understanding, including the systems documentation, probably exists already. In this case, a simple review of existing systems documentation and an inquiry about major changes in the systems are usually sufficient.

Procedures for Obtaining a Preliminary Understanding

Before the auditor can obtain an overview understanding of the EDP systems that affect the audit, he or she needs background information on the computer systems, including new audit areas, new systems, or major systems revisions. There are established methods available to record significant features of computer hardware, system software, and EDP departmental organization. On recurring audits just an update can be done, since the basic information should already be contained in the prior audit working papers.

There are various ways in which an auditor can obtain the preliminary understanding. For manual systems the alternatives include:

- Inquiring about major changes in the systems or controls and performing an overall review of existing detailed flowcharts or narratives from prior years
- Preparing an overview flowchart showing the significant controls
- Preparing a brief narrative of the systems showing the significant controls

For computer systems, the alternatives include:

- Inquiring about major changes in the systems or controls and performing an overall review of existing overview flowcharts, detailed flowcharts, and existing Control Matrix or CICQ from prior audits
- Completing a Control Matrix with overview flowcharts
- Preparing an overview flowchart that shows significant controls either on the flowchart or on an attached brief narrative

The first alternative under both manual and computer systems would be used for recurring audits where there are no major new systems or systems revisions. The other alternatives can be used in new audit areas, new systems, or major systems revisions. Under all the alternatives listed for computer systems, the documentation of the preliminary understanding should include identifying and classifying significant programmed procedures. Although the auditor may use the preliminary understanding of the systems of internal controls to determine audit strategy, technical assistance from EDP auditors may be needed to reach conclusions and decide on audit strategy when computer systems are involved.

Preparation of the overview flowchart, narrative, and Control Matrix is described in detail elsewhere and is not repeated here. (See Chapter 23, "How to Document Systems and Use Flowcharts," Chapter 24, "Interviews and Transaction Reviews in an Audit," and Chapter 25, "The Evaluation Process and How to Use Documents.") A method for identifying and classifying significant programmed procedures follows.

The types of significant output reports and programmed procedures that the auditor should identify are

- Reports used for internal accounting or administrative control such as exception reports, or reports used for control account reconciliation.
- Reports that the auditor can use for substantive testing purposes such as a detail listing of extended inventories.
- Programmed procedures that perform important accounting functions, such as evaluations, updates, and distributions to the general ledger. These significant programmed procedures should be described briefly.

The auditor should classify significant programmed procedures as follows:

- *User-controlled.* If the user controls significant programmed procedures by reperforming them, or by other effective means, the system is known as user-controlled. For example, users may check that exception reports produced list exceptions properly, and then users follow up on those exceptions.
- *Non-user-controlled.* If the user does not control the programmed procedures by reperforming them, the system is known as non-user-controlled. In this case there may be insufficient evidence of what steps the computer performed for either the user or the auditor to reperform the programmed procedures. In some cases, the evidence exists but the user does not reperform the programmed procedures. General controls are usually relied on in these situations.

A preliminary understanding of general controls should be obtained and documented where the systems are not user-controlled. Frequently, the programmed procedures in these systems are tested using audit software or other computer-assisted methods.

Determining the Audit Strategy

Considering all the relevant factors and related risks identified in previous steps that may significantly affect the audit strategy, the auditor should now determine the most effective and efficient audit strategy for each important area to be audited. This decision requires a high degree of professional judgment and has a significant impact on audit effectiveness and efficiency.

Once an audit strategy has been developed, the auditor should discuss the audit plan with the audit manager and obtain appropriate approval prior to implementation.

Documenting the Audit Strategy

The audit strategy should be documented. This documentation should include:

- A brief explanation of the reasoning behind the key decisions in selecting the audit strategy
- The method to be used for detailed systems documentation and the questionnaire to be used, where appropriate

The basic concept of a systems audit approach is that the planned audit strategy should be

- Reviewed continually as the audit progresses and
- Revised as necessary throughout the audit.

These required strategy changes should also be documented appropriately.

AUDIT REPORTS

The audit report is the auditor's formal written communication with the auditee and management. It is the focal point for an auditor and for all those who rely on the auditor's work, since it provides a concise statement of what was found.

The report should be designed to help management. Since management must meet its responsibility to establish and maintain an adequate system of internal control, a well-written report of deficiencies in control identified during the course of an audit is of great help. In addition, due to a general knowledge of the auditee's affairs and an independent viewpoint, the auditor is often able to make constructive suggestions regarding the operations of the organization. Therefore, careful consideration should be given to the development of the report. It should ensure that management's attention is directed to the more significant weaknesses and that the information can be understood readily.

Auditors should make clear distinction between those items reported as weaknesses or deficiencies and those that are reported for other reasons. The degree of detail supplied is largely a matter of judgment, influenced greatly by management preference. Some managements prefer to have all audit findings reported, no matter how minor they are; others prefer to receive a general description of significant findings. Auditors must bear in mind that their ultimate accountability demands that findings of major significance be brought to the attention of executive management and the board of directors.

Purpose of Audit Reports

Among the general purposes of audit reports are to:

- Inform management of the current state of the operations in the area being reviewed. Without this information, management can only assume that the area's day-to-day operations are in accordance with their prescribed standards. This entire concept supports the premise that the audit function is the eyes and ears of management.

- Comply with current internal audit professional standards. Both the Institute of Internal Auditors (IIA) and the Bank Administration Institute (BAI) have adopted formal reporting requirements as part of their professional standards that should be met.

- Provide the auditor with the flexibility of communicating technical audit findings through the use of basic summary comments. These comments should be easy to understand. The details of the finding can be given in an addendum for the more technical reviewer.

- Inform management of the scope or limits of the review. Without this information it is difficult for management to determine whether the findings are related to the entire function or are concentrated in a particular area. The statement of scope also helps management determine whether the findings pertain to a limited period or remain applicable over an extended period of time.

- Provide a mechanism for the auditees to state their position as it relates to the findings. This assists senior management, since it presents the situation from the viewpoint of both the auditor and the auditee. Then management is in a better position to develop a response and to determine the corrective actions necessary to eliminate control deficiencies.

- Provide a formal record of recommendations for correcting the deficiencies, to which management should respond. The response should outline the corrective action management will take, or the reasons that it chooses not to act at this time.

- Provide motivation to act on control deficiencies.

Audit Report Structure

The report structure is critical to effective communication of audit results. Without an established structure it is very difficult for management to evaluate the reports it receives from year to year consistently. The report should include some common elements to assist in evaluating the report findings. One way to present these common elements includes statements that

- Identify the scope of audit work,
- Identify the functions or accounts that have been reviewed,
- Provide background or an introductory statement,
- Provide management with an opinion of the system reviewed,
- Provide an executive summary for findings that require either technical expertise or a detailed knowledge of the operation, and
- Present the audit findings in a clear and concise manner.

Scope of Audit Work

Part of the report is a statement of the scope of audit work performed. The date of the audit, as well as the time span subject to review, are essential to inform the reader of the period that was the focal point for the auditor.

To evaluate each element in the scope of audit work separately, the following topics are considered:

- Adequacy
- Efficiency
- Effectiveness
- Quality of ongoing operations

Adequacy. A system is adequate if it contains key control procedures that are designed to prevent or detect significant errors or irregularities. The auditor determines adequacy by obtaining an understanding of the system through discussions with the appropriate personnel and referring to documentation such as procedure manuals, job descriptions, and flowcharts, as well as observation of key activities and documentation thereof. The auditor then determines whether key control procedures are in place to satisfy control objectives. This determination can be made after completing either an ICQ or a Control Matrix.

Efficiency. Efficiency is concerned with the fact that the cost of internal controls should not exceed the value of expected benefits. The auditor uses general experience and expertise to judge the practicality of controls in terms of their cost in relation to their benefits.

Effectiveness. The auditor determines the effectiveness of the degree of compliance with the system by performing tests. These compliance tests are designed to provide reasonable assurance that key control procedures are being applied. Compliance tests of internal control procedures require inspection of internal documents to obtain evidence in the form of signatures, initials, and so forth. They also include observation of certain principles of control, such as segregation of duties, to permit an evaluation of the performance of such duties.

Quality of Ongoing Operations. Operations are the routine steps, procedures, or processes that are designed to satisfy predetermined organizational and control objectives. Management is responsible for ongoing operations and must be confident that the system is actually in process and is meeting operational needs. The auditor should review the system and should evaluate and report on the quality of ongoing operations.

The auditor's evaluation generally assesses and confirms what was discovered during examination. If the auditor determines that the system is adequate and effective, the report should state that the quality of ongoing operations is satisfactory. If the system is inadequate or the degree of compliance with the system is ineffective, the quality of ongoing operations is unsatisfactory.

Audit Findings

Audit findings begin to emerge by a process of comparing what is with what should be. When a difference between what is and what should be is identified, the auditor has begun to develop an audit finding. The "what is" is the statement of condition and the "what should be" is a statement of criteria for what could be.

When an auditor determines that there is a difference between the real and the ideal, the impact must be weighed. If the impact is significant, it should be worth reporting. If the deviation is of little practical consequence, the auditor should consider discussing it orally with the auditee. If an audit report is to be useful, the auditor must determine the cause of the deviation. An audit finding is not really complete unless it includes information detailing the causes of the problem. The next step, after identifying the cause, is to consider what type of action is necessary to eliminate or minimize recurrence of the situation. This is presented in the form of a recommendation.

When writing audit findings, the auditor should make certain that explanations of reasons for qualification include the following:

- Statement of condition
- Impact
- Cause
- Recommendation

A well-developed audit finding includes these points and clearly distinguishes each from the others. The reader of the report should have no difficulty understanding what was found, what is thought about what was found, what the effect is, why it happened, and how the auditor thinks it should be corrected.

Using the Record of Control Weaknesses. The auditor should refer to the RCW for the weaknesses that were identified through the audit. The RCW should contain the results of any discussions with management regarding the finding, as well as any corrective actions taken.

The RCW is also useful in reviewing the possible effects of the weaknesses on the organization's financial statements. It can also be used to weigh the effect the weakness might have on the nature and timing of subsequent audit procedures.

As a rule, the RCW is compiled during the completion of an ICQ or a Control Matrix. Weaknesses may also be encountered during the compliance and/or substantive testing stages. Evidence of these weaknesses would emerge as a result of the failure to exercise certain controls during some stage of the system processes.

Oral Reports

Although written reports are the most common way of presenting findings, oral presentation may be more appropriate at times. Oral presentations are very effective for minor findings that do not require senior management's attention. In addition, oral presentations provide immediate feedback, which is necessary for findings requiring immediate attention.

Oral reports can also promote better relations between the auditors and the auditees, as they are given an opportunity to present their view of the findings. In fact, these discussions may disclose areas requiring additional audit effort.

In any event, all oral discussions with management regarding audit findings should be recorded on the RCW.

Technical Findings

The manner of presentation of technical EDP findings depends on who is going to receive the report. Senior management in many organizations may not be sufficiently familiar with the control requirements in computer-based systems and the systems themselves. Management should be able to understand the impact of a particular finding. Therefore, many auditors choose to prepare an executive summary to begin the report. This summary addresses the effect of the control weakness in essentially nontechnical terms. The technically worded finding can be placed in an appendix to the main report or be issued as a separate report.

The criteria and recommendation elements of a finding may be affected in an EDP environment by the auditor's inability to obtain sufficient information on each element. For example, management may not have established an adequate system development life cycle. This lack of established criteria may lead the auditor to comment on the desirability of adopting specific standards. The recommendation section, on the other hand, may be complicated by the amount of time the auditor needs to research the most efficient means of correcting the weakness. This is compounded in an EDP environment by the time required to analyze the various options. In these situations, where it is not practical to recommend a specific or best way to achieve corrective action, a more general recommendation or suggested approach to the problem is appropriate.

Report Distribution and Follow-Up

It is a good idea to have a quality control review of the audit report itself, since it is the culmination of the entire audit effort. This review should ensure the high quality of the final audit report released by the audit department. At the very least, this review should polish the language in the report and eliminate typographic errors. A final step in distribution is to make sure that all individuals on the distribution list actually receive a copy.

Prior to final distribution of the report, a draft copy should be reviewed with the auditee. The review of report drafts with auditees is both a courtesy and a form of insurance for the auditor. In complex systems, it is easy for the auditor to miss a point or report it incorrectly. Reviewing the report with the department concerned can bring out any inaccuracies of this kind for correction before the final report is issued.

Once the report is released, the auditee should be requested to respond to the auditors' findings in writing. This contributes to the effectiveness of the audit function and helps to ensure that the findings receive appropriate attention. In rare circumstances, responses to audit recommendations will not be in writing. If the audit reply to the findings and recommendations is verbal, a write-up of that response should be made. A mechanism should be established to ensure that all audit replies are received in a timely manner. A copy of the written response, or write-up of verbal responses, should be included in the audit working papers.

On receipt of the reply, the auditor should evaluate the response. This evaluation should determine that corrective action was taken and that the corrective action is achieving the desired results. To ensure this corrective action, the auditor should maintain ongoing contact with the auditee management. The auditor may determine that interim audit work is necessary to review the corrective action taken by auditee management.

In most cases it is a good idea to communicate the recommendations for improvements in control to the audit committee and the board of directors simultaneously.

PART II

Computer Processing

CHAPTER 5

Computer Concepts

UNDERSTANDING COMPUTER SYSTEMS

One may think that it is not necessary for an internal or non-EDP auditor to have extensive knowledge of computer concepts. While this may have been true in the past, today all auditors need an understanding of how data is processed in a computerized information system. Of course, an EDP auditor is expected to have a thorough understanding not only of how computers work but also of how computerized applications and processing are integrated into business systems. For those without any EDP experience or training, this chapter provides an overview of computer concepts. (See Chapter 9, "System Software," for a detailed discussion of auditing system software.)

The basic features in computer systems that an auditor needs to know in order to understand the fundamentals of computer processing discussed in this section include:

- Basic units of a computer configuration and their interrelationship and common EDP terminology
- Process of creating EDP systems
- Functions of the operating system and other standard software
- Nature of computer processing steps and controls from input through output

IMPACT OF COMPUTERS ON BUSINESS

As computers began to be prevalent in business, early EDP systems were mainly used to computerize various clerical functions. EDP personnel did not always have formal EDP education; in fact, many were kept on and retrained in the new technology once their old jobs were performed by a computer. Others were EDP technicians with engineering or mathematical backgrounds. Today, however, a large computer installation often involves dozens of highly trained specialists with a variety of skills.

Applications, too, have changed. Beyond the development and evolution of the mainframe centralized computer system there have been significant, indeed revolutionary, changes that affect computer availability and use for business applications in multiple settings. Systems that encompass a wide variety of business functions and incorporate decision-oriented analytical and forecasting techniques have been implemented. (See Figure 5-1 for a sample financial information and budgeting system.) The trend toward fully integrated financial and management information systems has accelerated and is continuing to do so. As a result, in-house computer availability is practically a necessity for all but the smallest businesses.

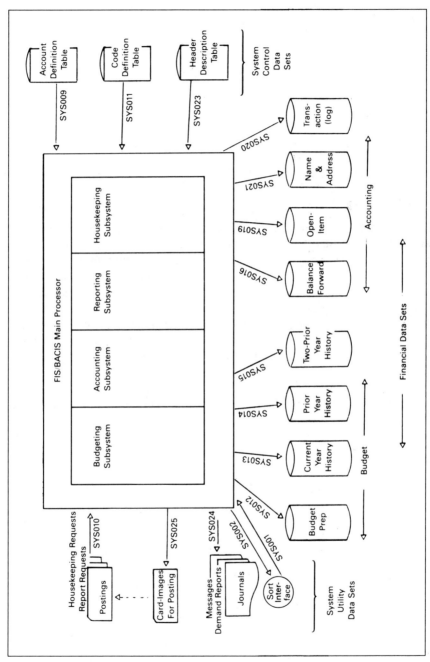

FIG. 5-1 Main processor system design (courtesy of International Business Machines Corporation)

Three developments in particular have brought computing tools and capabilities to an extraordinary range of organizations and tasks. These changes are:

1. Microcomputers and related developments
2. Packaged computer software
3. Computer time-sharing arrangements

COMPUTER CLASSIFICATIONS

Mainframe Computers

The development of computers was pioneered by a generation of computer manufacturers whose original work was in the scientific and educational fields using mainframe computers and concepts. The term "mainframe" refers to both the central processing unit of a computer (peripheral or remote devices are classified separately) and to the traditional computer that is used for commercial or scientific processing. As a rule, the core size, measured by kilobytes (K) (one K = 1,024 bytes; see page 5-15), and physical dimensions of a mainframe computer are likely to be much larger than those of minicomputers or microcomputers. Mainframe computers may be employed by individual organizations through time-sharing systems, which access and use the capacities and power of that system's mainframe. Organizations with huge processing needs maintain their own mainframe operations. Mainframe computers continue to offer the greatest variety of system software.

Minicomputers

In response to perceived needs, companies such as Digital Equipment Corporation, Hewlett-Packard, and Data General developed a range of lower-cost processors. These were geared to multiple users working via terminals that were simple to operate and program and did not require special environmental conditions. These computers became known as minicomputers to differentiate them from the large mainframes, which could fill a room. Their apparent usefulness for commercial data processing resulted in versions of the basic models being repackaged for the commercial market. About the size of a refrigerator, they surpassed the early mainframes in speed and memory. Still referred to as minicomputers, they commonly

- Incorporate the virtue of simplicity in systems development and operation.
- Are designed for the direct entry and checking of data and for the immediate updating of files and inquiries to files.

- Are designed for operation in an office with user staff entering data and controlling the operation rather then requiring special computer operations staff.
- Can form part of a computer network that communicates with remote terminals and a large central computer.

A typical configuration for a minicomputer is a processor with 512K characters of memory, four keyboards and screens, 40 million characters of disk storage, and a line printer operating at 600 lines per minute.

This minicomputer configuration is capable of supporting an operation where a sales clerk can enter orders, an accounts clerk can post cash to sales ledgers, a third clerk can make a stock position inquiry, and a fourth clerk can initiate a batch payroll system, all at the same time.

Microcomputers

The microcomputer is easily the fastest-growing segment of the computer marketplace and the area of the most exciting technological development. Numerous surveys in the United States have plotted the rapid growth of installations, the dramatic improvements in cost/performance ratios, the variety of new entries to the market, and the ever-broadening base of applications. In many respects this growth parallels the earlier expansion of sophisticated electronic calculators, except that the scale and capability of microcomputers is, of course, much more extensive than calculators. Yet, development has followed a similar path of technological advances, miniaturization, and falling costs.

Microprocessors having more and more powerful microchips are among the latest developments in the electronics industry. They are rapidly being introduced into computing equipment of all types. When packaged with the necesary supporting peripheral devices, they are known as microcomputers. A typical microcomputer for business use consists of:

- A microprocessor with 256K characters of memory
- Dual diskette drives giving immediate access to 0.5 million characters of information (equivalent to 8,000 stock records)
- A printer operating at 60 characters per second
- A monitor or display screen and keyboard

Microcomputers are suitable for a wide variety of tasks. A typical system covering order entry, stock control, sales analysis, and ledger accounting could be implemented for a distributor with 5,000 stock items, 500 customers, and 200 order lines a day on the equipment just described. The equipment can also be used as a terminal providing local processing capability and linked via a modem and telephone lines to a larger central computer. Microcomputers can be linked together in local area networks (LANs). They are available in many varieties, including briefcase-size portables.

Microcomputers are limited at present by the volumes of work they can process. For instance, the maximum number of transactions that can be entered and handled via one keyboard is approximately 500 per day, given the amount of disk storage that is possible, which is about 1 to 2 million characters. However, the newer hard disks for microcomputers allow 10 to 30 million characters of storage. Increasing capacity or upgrading can be achieved by acquiring a second microcomputer, by using hard disk drives that allow multi-user configurations, or by moving up to a minicomputer. If such expansion is expected in the short term, it is usually more sensible to start with a machine at the low end of the minicomputer range. Such a machine, with similar capabilities, can be enhanced by adding multiple keyboards, display screens, and larger-capacity disks.

The attraction of microcomputers and minicomputers is that they bring the facilities of powerful computers into daily use. At a remote office location, instead of user staff completing input forms, sending them to a central computer department for processing, and receiving an error report listing data errors many hours later, the user can control the computer by entering data on a keyboard and checking for errors immediately. Once the data has been checked, the processing of individual transactions can take place and can elicit an immediate response. Thus, systems can be designed in which, for example, an order for goods entered by a sales clerk causes packing and dispatch instructions to be printed immediately on a remote printer in a separate storage area. Other systems allow bank customers to use coded cards for entry into the system to check account balances, transfer funds from one account to another, or get cash 24 hours a day.

A comparison of the three computer classifications follows:

Type of Computer	Features
Mainframe	Large-capacity professional computer offering comprehensive data processing capacities and a variety of storage and output capabilities. Offers time-sharing function.
Minicomputer	Disk-based computer usually with multiple keyboards, display screens, a printer, and mass storage, often on magnetic tape.
Microcomputer	Desk-sized processor usually equipped with a single keyboard and display screen, a printer, and magnetic diskette storage.

INPUT, OUTPUT, AND PROCESSING CONCEPTS

Data Flow and Processing Concepts

It is extremely helpful for an auditor to be able to identify the processing features that are common to computer systems and to define terms that are used frequently. When dealing with computer applications, one should be able to distinguish between:

- *Input*—The initial recording of a transaction and the subsequent activity until the transaction is written to a file in the computer.
- *Processing*—All the work carried on within the computer.
- *Output*—The printing, or presentation on a screen, of information processed by the computer.

Input

The flow of data can be divided into three stages:

1. Recording transactions
2. Converting the data into input media
3. Writing the input to a magnetic file

Recording Transactions. In many cases, the methods of recording transactions are the same as in noncomputer systems. All the information for a transaction has to be obtained prior to the transaction being processed. For example, a customer purchase requires recording the transaction quantity, product number, description, price, customer name, date, and any terms. A computer can also be programmed to initiate or generate data for a transaction. This happens, for example, when a computer program reaches a condition that indicates it will call on another program to produce a report or other document.

There are a number of methods that can be used to convert data such as transactions into the form in which data is acceptable to the computer. In general use, those methods include the use of display screen terminals (cathode ray tube — CRTs) and devices for entering data directly onto magnetic tape or disk. The latter are often arranged as a number of operator stations using terminals that are linked to a small computer. (See Figure 5-2.) The computer can be programmed to check the data to some extent before submission to the main computer. This can be a great advantage in detecting errors and identifying queries at an early stage. (See Figure 5-3 for a sample screen format for data entry through CRTs.)

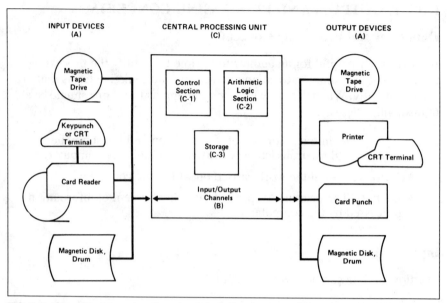

FIG. 5-2   Simplified overview flowchart depicting basic configuration of a computer

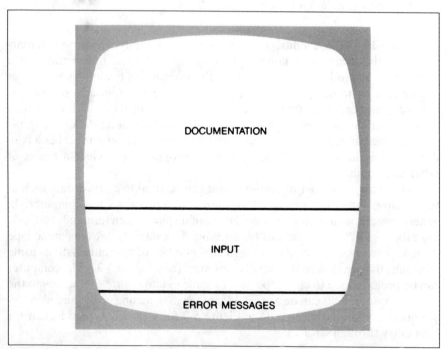

FIG. 5-3   Display screen for direct data entry (courtesy of International Business Machines Corporation)

In older systems, punched cards are the prevalent input media, and some systems that use paper-punched cards or tape for data entry are still in use today.

Data Conversion for Input. In addition, there are a number of devices that can input data to the computer by reading source documents and thus avoid manual keying or entry of this information. Magnetic ink character readers (MICRs) read special characters preprinted or keyed into the document by a special machine. These characters can be seen on checks, where the account and check number are preprinted along the bottom to be read later as the check is processed. These documents can also be used as physical or hard copies, so that documents prepared in this way do not need to be rekeyed.

Optical character readers (OCRs) read special characters preprinted or typed on documents. An example of a document prepared this way is a telephone bill. This is also called a turnaround document, since it can be sent back with payment and reentered into the system. Mark-sensing devices or optical mark readers (OMRs) read special marks preprinted on documents. These characters can be seen in the universal product code that is read by OMRs at supermarket checkout counters. Some of these devices even provide an audio response that states what the product is as it runs over the sensing device.

Input devices can be operated at a distance from the main computer using telecommunications. In this context, "telecommunications" is used to describe the process of transmitting data over telephone lines or via microwaves (which may be sent via satellites). Data entered at a remote terminal is converted into a form suitable for transmission, transmitted, and reconverted.

Writing Input to a File. The third stage of flow of input data, writing input to a file, results when the data that is being, or has been, converted into some form of input medium is made available to the computer along with appropriate instructions for creating a file.

Processing

Processing may be defined as including all of the functions carried on within the computer. Although by no means all-inclusive, the following is a synopsis of significant processing stages.

Editing. Editing is the checking of data that has been entered by programs in the computer. Editing usually consists of a mixture of validity, accuracy, and reasonableness checks. These checks can include tests such as whether alphabetic data is acceptable in a particular field, or whether a code number is within a predefined range. Editing can also include matching input with data

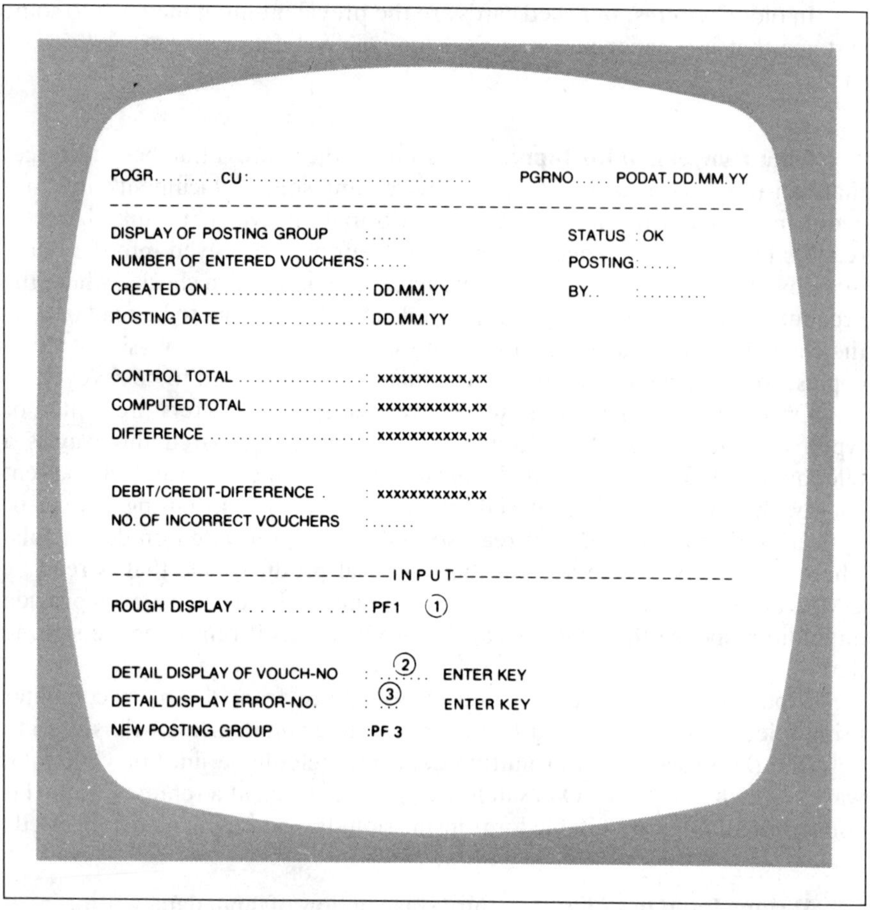

```
POGR.........CU:.............................        PGRNO..... PODAT.DD.MM.YY
----------------------------------------------------------------------------
DISPLAY OF POSTING GROUP      :.....               STATUS  : OK
NUMBER OF ENTERED VOUCHERS:.....                   POSTING:.....
CREATED ON...................: DD.MM.YY            BY..      :.........
POSTING DATE.................: DD.MM.YY


CONTROL TOTAL ...............: xxxxxxxxxxx,xx
COMPUTED TOTAL ..............: xxxxxxxxxxx,xx
DIFFERENCE ..................: xxxxxxxxxxx,xx


DEBIT/CREDIT-DIFFERENCE .    : xxxxxxxxxxx,xx
NO. OF INCORRECT VOUCHERS    :......


-------------------------INPUT----------------------
ROUGH DISPLAY ...........:PF1  (1)


DETAIL DISPLAY OF VOUCH-NO   : (2)..  ENTER KEY
DETAIL DISPLAY ERROR-NO.     : (3)    ENTER KEY
NEW POSTING GROUP           :PF 3
```

FIG. 5-4 **Display screen for writing input to a file in an on-line environment (courtesy of International Business Machines Corporation)**

already held on files. When terminals are used in an on-line processing system, editing functions are usually carried out at the time data is being input to the system. (See Figure 5-4 for a sample screen used to enter data in an on-line system.)

Calculating. Calculating is defined as using an arithmetic computation on the data, such as multiplying hours by rate to produce pay. The process typically consists of matching standing data, in this example the wage rate that is stored on a master file, with transaction data, here the hours worked, which is input and processed only once.

Summarizing. Summarizing is the process of accumulating all transactions (often after calculation, as explained previously) and generating a total. Using the previous example, the amount of the weekly payroll is the total.

Categorizing. Categorizing consists of analyzing and grouping individual components of a summarized total. For example, categorization would occur to analyze payroll expense by department. Categorizing is usually achieved by reference to a code included in the data input for each transaction.

Updating. Updating is the process of adding, changing, or deleting data in the system.

Initiating Transactions

Computer systems can be programmed to generate transactions and reports automatically. Computer initiation of transactions can be done in a number of ways, two of which are

1. The processing of one transaction may trigger initiation of another transaction. This occurs when, for example, the processing of a sales order that reduces inventory below the minimum triggers a replacement purchase order. In such cases, the trigger condition is recognized through a comparison with master file data. In this example, the trigger would be the predefined minimum stock level.
2. A request to initiate transactions may be input. For example, a requisition code to generate a parts listing can be input.

Files

Computer files are similar to the files in any manual system. Their organization can be compared to the folders in a well-organized cabinet. They can hold financial and reference data of importance to more than one processing run (such as sales and stock ledgers or price files). These are called master files. Suspense files are similar to suspense accounts in a manual system and normally hold only transaction data (such as outstanding orders or records of goods received). Records are individual groups of data, somewhat like a page in a manual file system. Individual items within the records are called fields or data elements. (See Figures 5-5 and 5-6 for sample transactions that maintain data fields and records in a financial information system.)

Files are updated by adding, changing, or deleting data (e.g., in the case of accounts receivable, adding invoices and recording cash receipts to the open invoice file or deleting dormant customer accounts from the customer master file). The method of updating depends on the file organization. Tape

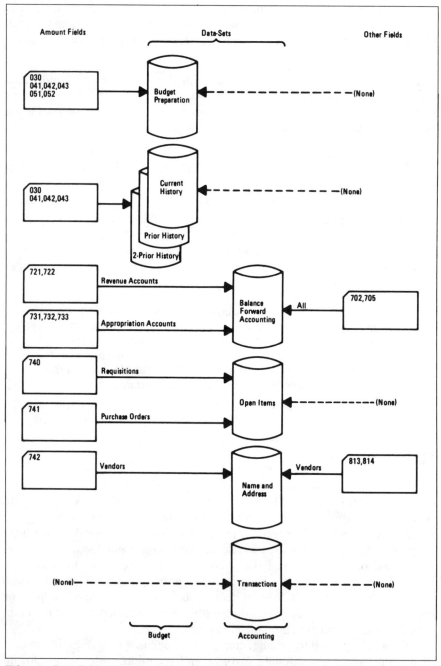

FIG. 5-5   Data field transactions (courtesy of International Business Machines Corporation)

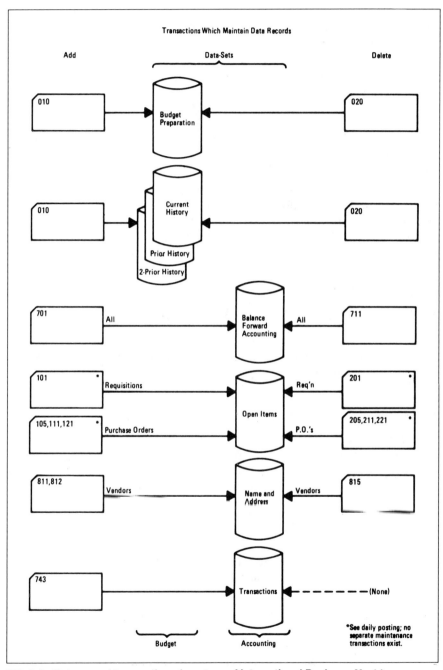

FIG. 5-6 Data record transactions (courtesy of International Business Machines Corporation)

files are updated by sequentially reading the old master file and the current transaction file to create a new master file (merging). Disk files can also be processed in this manner. However, direct access on an item-by-item basis, as in disks, is faster than reading the whole file, as is required in tape, when only the records affected by current transactions need changing.

Output

The most important output of a computer program is often the updated master file, which may or may not be printed out. Generally, information from the updated master file is printed only when it is requested or updated and may consist of listings, analyses, exception reports, or accounting documents, such as invoices and checks. Information for third parties is sometimes transferred directly to magnetic tape or disk (e.g., transfer of credit details from a bank to its customer or sales statistics from branches to head office for consolidation). Output may also take the form of display on a terminal screen.

COMPONENTS OF A COMPUTER SYSTEM

Computer system components are similar whether in microcomputers, mini-computers, or mainframe computers. Since microcomputers are familiar to so many, their components are described here.

Central Processing Unit

The central processing unit (CPU) is the brain of any computer configuration. Within the processor, in addition to the input/output (I/O) control channels, the CPU is composed of three sections: (1) the control section, (2) the arithmetic-logic section, and (3) storage.

1. The control section directs all operations in the computer system, including:
   - Execution of program instructions in the proper sequence.
   - Transfer of data between storage and the arithmetic-logic section and between storage and I/O devices.
   - Control of I/O devices.
2. The arithmetic-logic section (also called the arithmetic logic unit or ALU) performs:
   - Mathematical operations, such as addition, subtraction, division, multiplication, rounding, and so forth. Esentially the ALU does all of the operations by adding and/or subtracting the 0's and 1's of binary digits as many times as required to reach an answer. It

can do thousands or millions of these per second, so that even when handling large numbers the answer is given very quickly.

- Logical operations, such as comparisons and the resulting decisions as to the sequence of operations.

3. Storage or memory is the place where the computer keeps the information it is going to use, saves the results of its work, and keeps the programs that tell it what to do.

The microprocessor can be contained on a single integrated circuit chip in the CPU of a microcomputer. To perform the actual processing, system software programs tell the computer what to do and when (discussed in the section entitled "System Software.")

Internal Memory

The microprocessor has a very limited number of places to store information at any one time. In order to execute useful programs or process large amounts of data, the CPU must have a place to store instructions and data. Memory (also called internal storage, as distinct from external storage on a recording device) consists of microchips on an integrated circuit board or card that can store a certain number of bits, maintaining each bit as an electrical signal. The memory size is the number of discrete, uniquely addressable memory locations, and the unit of measurement is the byte, made up of 8 bits or binary digits. However, memory size is measured by kilobytes. A kilobyte is not 1,000 bytes, as the Greek prefix would suggest, but 1,024 bytes (2 to the tenth power); likewise, 8K equals 8,192 bytes of storage, 16K equals 16,384, 64K equals 65,536, and so forth. The amount of memory available depends on the microcomputer's architecture: the construction, interconnection, and organization of the internal circuitry in the computer.

Basically, all internal memory is random access, which means that any bit can usually be accessed in the same amount of time, no matter where it is physically located in the memory. There are three classifications of storage:

1. Random access memory (RAM) is read/write memory. RAM can have data stored in it and extracted from it; data can be written to and read from it. RAM can have its contents altered, and new data can be stored, overwriting what was previously there. RAM is volatile: It loses its contents when the power is turned off. (Some computers have batteries to maintain the contents intact).

2. Read-only memory (ROM) can have its contents read, but data cannot be written to it, except once during manufacture. ROM cannot have its contents altered; once data is stored there, it is permanent. ROM is nonvolatile: When the power is off, its contents remain intact. ROM is used to give the CPU initial start-up

instructions, to hold a specific computer language, or to store frequently used routines.

3. To store large quantities of data, external storage is used, since the
   RAM is volatile and limited in size.

   • While magnetic tape drives are used in minicomputers to store
     large amounts of data inexpensively, smaller tape drives are used
     in microcomputers. Standard audio cassettes are used in sim-
     ple microcomputer systems. All tape drives have sequential
     access, which means the machine has to search through the en-
     tire sequence of data on the tape to find the data requested.

   • Disk storage:
     a. Disk drives are the most popular medium used to store data
        files — on floppy diskettes, which are of 8 inches, 5¼ inches,
        or 3 inches, with single or double density, and single or double
        sides.
     b. Disks record information in a direct access format. The ma-
        chine goes right to the data requested.
     c. Floppy diskettes store much less data than hard disks and are
        slower to process. Hard disks have much greater capacity than
        floppy diskettes and provide faster access. Backup facilities
        (such as tape) are often used together with disk drives.

Keyboards

There is a keyboard to enter data into the system. Most keyboards have keys
similar to a typewriter; some have additional numeric keypads like an adding
machine. Programmable function keys are found on many keyboards and
simplify using menu-driven software. Key touch and arrangement varies.

Monitors

The monitor, which is similar to a television screen, displays the data typed in
and the computer's output. The quality of the image depends on the resolution,
or number of pixels or tiny dots that create the images on the monitor screen.
The monitor can display different numbers of characters in columns across the
screen (e.g., 80 characters equals a normal business letter size of 8½ × 11
inches). The display monitor can be one color (monochrome), but a black
background with green characters is thought to be easiest to read. Black and
white or sometimes amber on black are also used. Color monitors for graphics
are available, which look even more like a television screen.

   To indicate where data will be entered, the screen displays a cursor,
usually a rectangle or an underline that blinks on and off. As data is entered,
the character is displayed at the cursor position, which moves with the entry.

Terminals

Terminals are used when several users share a microcomputer or for access to the systems of minicomputers or mainframe computers.

Terminals are differentiated in terms of their "intelligence." Intelligence in a terminal allows changes to be made in the data that was keyed in before sending it to the processor. These facilities are called editing functions, such as tabulation, clearing or erasing the screen, deleting a line or character, or inserting a line or character.

"Dumb" terminals use conversational operation, where data travels from the terminal to the processor one character at a time. Editing functions may be limited to only deleting a line or a character.

"Smart" terminals use message operation, where data generally travels to the processor one line at a time. Smart terminals have a full complement of editing functions, located on separate keys, that allow cursor control functions (arrow keys) to move the cursor up and down, left and right, and HOME (the top lefthand corner of the screen). Smart terminals have several visual attributes, such as inverse video (the color of the characters can be reversed with the color of the background), highlighting (designating portions of the screen in different intensities of light), and scrolling, which is the ability to move the display up or down (and sometimes left or right).

"Intelligent" terminals, which have a built-in microprocessor, use page operation, where data is generally transmitted to the processor a screenful or page at a time. They may include graphics, which enable simple block or line drawings to be produced; special character sets, such as mathematical symbols or foreign alphabets; protected fields or the facility to "freeze" a given area of the screen so that no changes can be made to the data in that area; built-in memory, which provides storage of data before transmission to the processor; and soft keys, also known as user-definable keys or function keys (often labeled F0, F1, F2, and so on), which can be assigned a particular task or sequence of other keystrokes. (For example, using a soft key, the steps needed to request that a program be loaded can be activated using one keystroke.)

Peripherals

For actual use, a processor must be connected to peripherals, which are the I/O devices (such as magnetic tapes, disks, card reader, and printers) that provide the means of getting data into the processor and also for seeing or recording the results of processing.

Interfaces. The connection or channel between a processor and a peripheral is called an interface, which takes binary data from the processor and arranges it for the peripheral device to accept and act on, and vice versa.

Interfaces may sometimes be built into the processor itself; if not, they are usually available in the form of a small printed-circuit board or card that plugs into the processor and is connected to the peripheral via a cable. Interfaces have been standardized to a large extent, so that various types of equipment from different manufacturers can be used together. These standards govern the way the data is transmitted and received, the signal types and levels, and the way sockets, plugs, and wires are interconnected. Each standard is known by the name of the governing body that set the standard and by a number, such as EIA RS232 (Electronics Institute of America) and IEEE 488 (Institute of Electrical and Electronic Engineers).

Some peripherals also have a built-in buffer or a temporary storage area for data. It is used to hold data being passed between the processor and other devices, such as a printer, which operate at much slower speeds. The buffer compensates for a difference in the rate of data flow.

There are two widely used interfaces: Serial and parallel. Serial interfaces, like the RS232, allow data to flow along a wire as a sequence of bits, one after the other. Parallel interfaces, like the IEEE 488, enable data to flow along several wires, with bits parallel to each other, at the same time. The channel path along which the data flows from one or more sources to one or more destinations is referred to as a "bus," which is a circuit of parallel wires. A computer with one of the common bus standards has more growth potential than one without. Additional peripherals with the appropriate interfaces can enhance the computer's abilities. Each interface requires a port or an entrance and exit for data from the processor. The more ports a processor has (determined by the bus structure) the more peripherals that can be connected to it.

Emulators. Some peripherals have built-in emulators, which eliminates the need to obtain a separate attachment. Emulators are, in effect, translators that convert data presentation as defined by one of the international standards such as Extended Binary Coded Decimal Interchange Code (EBCDIC) or American Standard Code for Information Interchange (ASCII) into the presentation of a specific manufacturer, or vice versa, so that the peripheral imitates and behaves like another peripheral from a different manufacturer.

Printers. The peripherals that are used most often include a printer that produces hard copy output similar to that produced by a typewriter.

Some points about printers are:

- Dot matrix printers create characters that are composed of many dots. They are sometimes called utility printers, since they are used for printing documents that do not need a finished appearance. Some dot matrix printers have a double-strike feature that makes the print almost letter quality.

- Letter-quality printers use type elements such as a daisy wheel, thimble, or ball-type. They are expensive but produce finished-looking documents.

- Printers print different numbers of characters per line (80 for letters, 132 for printouts) and are available in various price ranges and sizes. They must be compatible with the interface for a system.

- Plotters are graphics output devices used to print charts and graphics. They are also available in a wide range of prices and styles and must also be compatible with system interface.

SYSTEM SOFTWARE AND OPERATING SYSTEMS

Each CPU uses a certain operating system that is part of the system software. System software works with the computer, not the user: It controls and coordinates the running of the computer and its many functions. The operating system is the most important component of this software category. It is a set of programs, usually written in machine code or assembly language, that acts as an intermediary between the user, the processor, and the applications software. The operating system informs the user of any errors that occur with the processor, I/O devices, or programs. It also provides a repertoire of simple commands for otherwise complicated functions. The operating system (or portions of it) may come installed in ROM and is therefore permanently stored. This software, unalterable by the user, is often referred to as "firmware." In microcomputers there is more user interaction with the system software than in larger computers, where system software is usually "off limits" to all but the EDP personnel who run the system.

Operating Systems

Most microcomputers use a disk operating system (DOS), although it may not be called DOS but could be called CP/M, MP/M, or PC DOS, depending on the manufacturer. The DOS is responsible for reading and writing data from and to the disk; it tells the disk drive's read/write head to move to the appropriate track/sector on the disk and reports any errors that may occur during access. The DOS is also responsible for program and file management. It creates files on the disk by allocating space, giving file names, erasing or deleting files from the disk, and keeping a directory, or catalog, of the disk's contents. To find a file on disk, the DOS refers to the directory in the same way one would look at the index of a book. The DOS also initializes and formats the disks and moves programs into memory so that they can be used.

One popular operating system for small computers is CP/M (Control Program/Microprocessor) of which there are several versions. Other examples of popular operating systems are PC DOS, UNIX, and Apple DOS. A program written on one computer can usually be used on or adapted to another, provided that both use the same version of the same operating system and the same disk format.

Utility Programs

Another type of system software is the utility program. Utility programs are used for maintenance and other functions only when needed and are not an integral part of the operating system. Two common utilities are the copy program (which is used to make duplicate copies of disks for back-up purposes) and the sort program (which uses a key or a field within a record to sequence the contents of a file; e.g., putting names in alphabetical order).

SOFTWARE

Software enables the microcomputer to perform the work. The term "software" applies to the programs used as instructions for the operation of general and specific tasks and applications performed by the computer. Three types of software perform the overall programming functions that are needed for the operation of a computer system: (1) system software, (2) utility software, and (3) applications software. (Both system and utility software have already been discussed.)

The availability of inexpensive, high-quality software that is designed to handle most standard business applications has contributed to the rapid growth in the use of microcomputers. However, software that works on one machine does not always work on another. When implementing a system, it may be advisable first to choose the software that meets application needs and then choose the hardware that is compatible with that software.

Applications Software

The most critical type of software for the accounting profession, as with any highly specialized profession, is the applications software. There are two types of applications software:

1. Generic programs
2. Application packages

Generic programs perform general tasks, such as data base management (organizing, searching, and retrieving records), word processing (preparing text), and electronic spreadsheets and graphics. Application packages, on the other hand, perform specific functions, such as general ledger, payroll, and inventory management.

Software Packages

Applications software is often called packaged software, providing the computer user with prewritten programs for generic or specific applications. The package comes with software and instruction manuals, which are designed to help users work with and tailor the package to particular system needs. Many software vendors provide implementation assistance along with their package sales. Among the most widely used software packages are accounting applications, word processing, data base management and other file and data storage and manipulation packages, graphics packages, and programs for preparing spreadsheets and spreadsheet analysis.

As the variety of potential uses of applications software grows, the number of vendors increases dramatically. Once software is selected and purchased for use in a business application, the data contained within the system that uses it becomes a reflection of the organization. It is important to ensure that it be treated like any asset purchase, suited as specifically and accurately as possible to organizational needs.

COMPUTER SHARING, TIME-SHARING, AND DATA BASES

Service Bureaus

The computer-sharing arrangement most widely used is the service bureau, which usually has one or more large computers and its own programming and operations staff. A computer user who cannot justify the expense of an in-house computer, or who needs additional capacity, can go to a service bureau and buy the use of the computer and the assistance of bureau support staff for operations. Service bureaus frequently make the same programming services available as do software vendors, tailoring applications software packages to the specific needs of the customer.

One such specialized service provides a specific application, namely payroll processing. When a business subscribes to such a service, its data processing for payroll can be externally maintained. This is helpful, since payroll applications always require annual maintenance, or updating, to keep abreast of changes in the tax laws. This kind of service provides an additional level of security by removing the payroll functions from the EDP department. When an application with such potential for abuse as this one is physically removed from an organization's general user computer, there is far less opportunity for unauthorized access from within. Naturally, there is a need to ensure the safety and integrity of data at the service bureau itself. To this end, a third-party review of the processing services can be done. (For further discussion of third-party reviews, see Chapter 29, "Implementation Reviews.")

Time-Sharing

Computer time-sharing is a concept that permits many users to access the same large-scale computer simultaneously. This access is most often via a time-sharing terminal and a local telephone call. This permits users, whether small companies or departments within large companies, to have access to the facilities of a large-scale computer. In this way they do not have to make the required investment in computer hardware and associated costs for a computer center. Such requirements can include special air conditioning, power supply security, and even physical plant requirements, such as floor or joist reinforcement to support the weight of the computer. Subscribers pay only for the time and resources they actually use.

A continuing trend is the development of libraries of standard programs written by technical experts in the field. These are available to users throughout the country (or the world) through the use of widespread telephone networks. This approach avoids the constant reinventing of the wheel and permits the spreading of development costs among many users. It also allows for timely reaction to changing conditions, such as new tax laws.

Public Data Bases

There is an ever-growing number of public data bases accessible to users via telephone and modem or, soon, through cable or satellite distribution. These include videotex, an interactive information service that provides transaction services as well (e.g., banking and shopping), and information-only services, which may have abstracts or full text of newspapers, magazines, and books, or other business information, such as stock prices.

SOFTWARE PROGRAM DEVELOPMENT

The steps involved in developing the software instructions or programs are:

- *Request for system design* — Analysis and possible solution of situations that the system program will address.
- *Detailed system specifications* — Written requirements in detail.
- *Program development* — Using computer language to express program instructions and source program logic. High-level languages

like COBOL and FORTRAN are frequently used and require subsequent conversion to machine-readable form.

- *Testing* — Running the program with test data to compare output results with predetermined results. This allows verification of the proper operation of the program and correction of any errors found as a result of this procedure.

- *Storing the program* — Maintaining the final authorized version of the program for production.

Only those steps that relate to the execution of a program are discussed here. (See Chapter 7, "System Development Life Cycle," for a detailed discussion of the creation of programs.)

Preparing the Program for Processing

To code a program, it must be entered in a form, or language, the computer can read. The program is usually printed out to make human interpretation and handling possible.

A set of instructions written in a high-level language comprises what is referred to as a source language program. In a business-oriented environment, COBOL (Common Business-Oriented Language) is the usual source language used. FORTRAN (formula translation), RPG (report program generator), and PL/1 (a programming language developed by IBM), among others, are also used. Other forms of programming include BAL (Basic Assembler Language) and fourth and fifth generation languages still in development.

Compilers

Compilers are actually language translator programs because they translate a source language program into an object language program meaningful to the computer. Separate compilers are used for each source language.

The compiler edits the source program for syntax errors, which are any errors in spelling, errors in sequencing the commands that tell the computer what to do, or errors in applying the rules of the language.

Some of the basic rules or syntax for using the languages are the following:

- All data fields must be defined.
- Only valid commands can be used.
- Correct format and sequence of instructions must be followed.
- Spelling of data fields must be consistent in all instructions.

Once the compiler has made sure that there are no syntax errors, it converts the source program to an object program. This is accomplished by

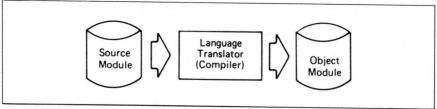

FIG. 5-7   Language flow using a compiler

translating the high-level statements into the bits of machine code. Then the program is in machine language that the computer can understand. (See Figure 5-7.)

Source Statement Conversion

MACRO commands can also be included in programs. They are then included in the machine-language instructions. A MACRO is a single word or mnemonic instruction that refers to previously written set of instructions for frequently used operations that is stored. The compiler converts all the required source statements into machine-language instructions. This means that the compiler can convert either single-source statements or MACRO-source statements. DIVIDE is one example of a MACRO command; in machine or assembly language, division is carried out by repetitive subtraction, using a number of commands. MACRO commands make it possible to use such commonly required functions without having to write their steps into a program each time they are needed.

To perform the conversion of source statements to machine-readable language, the compiler also carries out two related functions:

1. The compiler assigns a storage location (address) to each of the commands in the program so that when the program runs, the commands and data items will be available in the specified location.

2. The compiler assigns a storage location (address) to each data name created in the program. Collectively this is known as a name table and is referred to throughout the processing of the program.

Testing

After the program has been written, syntax errors have been corrected, and the program has been compiled, it should be tested. Sometimes the results of the test data have been predetermined manually. If the processing results in different output, the programmer must investigate to discover the cause of each error and make any necessary corrections. This process is sometimes called debugging. There are programming aids that can be used, but often the programmer must make a painstaking search for such logic errors.

Storing the Program

After the program has been tested and all errors are corrected, it must be stored in machine-readable form for future use.

The computer stores the program in the medium specified by the user, depending on the system's I/O devices. Generally, the user retains three copies of each program as follows:

1. A working copy on magnetic tape or disk, from which it can be loaded or executed.

2. Additional copies of the source and object language programs on tape or disk, kept in case of problems with the working copy; also used to make subsequent changes to the programs.

3. A printed copy of the source program for future reference, or as an aid in planning later revisions.

Loading and Running the Program

Before a computer can use a program, it must be entered into the storage area of the CPU. As part of the compilation process, each command is assigned to a specific location or address in a specific part of the storage area.

To start, the address of the first command is entered into the control section. After the CPU is instructed to process the program, the first command is executed and the address of the second command is entered into the control section. When the first command has been fully executed, the second command is performed and the address of the third command enters the control section. This process, which is handled automatically by software, is repeated until all steps have been carried out for all data involved. Production programs are run repeatedly to process the organization's data.

CONTROL PROCEDURES

A computer system cannot be effective unless control procedures ensure the accuracy, completeness, and validity of information stored in the system. Other controls ensure the security and integrity of the system and its operation. Controls help identify and investigate errors and unusual situations. An auditor can identify, understand, record, and test the controls over and processing

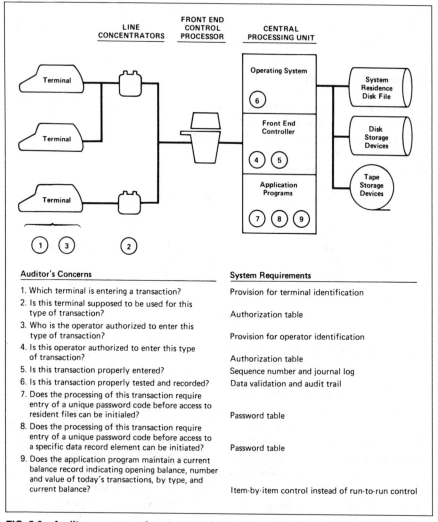

FIG. 5-8 Audit concerns and system requirements in an on-line environment

of data throughout the system and perform substantive procedures on computer data. (See Figure 5-8 for an overview of audit concerns in on-line systems.) Controls are discussed in Chapter 16, "Introduction to Controls," and Chapter 20, "General or Integrity Controls."

Management or Information Trail

It is obviously important that there be adequate information available to manage a company and to provide a basis for investigating any errors and unusual situations that arise. This important control feature can be called a "management trail" or "information trail." However, many computer systems are adequately controlled without detailed supportive listings of totals and analyses. Conversely, exception reports showing only exceptional items may provide no visible means of checking that these were the only items of this nature. The existence of supporting information is also called the "audit trail."

For example, an exception report for a wire funds transfer system that is designed to require that all transactions over $25 million be reported for examination would not report a transaction for a $10 million wire transfer that might have required closer scrutiny. Exception reports are designed to pinpoint problems and bring them to the attention of management. However, the program procedure for exception reports must be evaluated carefully to make sure that the appropriate levels of exceptions are being reported. For another example, when the failure to print data constitutes a weakness in control (such as the contents of suspense files are not regularly printed), then the system may be deficient. An internal or external auditor is correct to draw this to the attention of the organization. But if the failure to print does not represent a weakness in and of itself, due to compensating controls, then an auditor needs to devise alternate techniques to test the controls.

Loss of Audit Trail

In computer systems data is frequently stored only as long as it is in use, or to meet government requirements for financial data. The problems of lack of visible evidence and destruction of data are sometimes referred to as "loss of audit trail." The term "audit" or "information trail," in this context, implies the existence of information at every stage of the processing cycle that can be used to check on the exact nature of the operations that are carried out. However, the term "audit trail" is also used to refer to the existence of visible evidence (as when every programmed operation on every transaction is recorded on a computer report). It can also refer to systems designed in such a way that the auditor can continue to use conventional audit tests without considering the computer. For these reasons, the term "loss of audit trail" can be replaced with the more specific term "loss of visible evidence" when talking about computerized operations. The growing use of paperless systems, in which transactions are recorded directly into the system, has increased the need for computer-assisted audit techniques.

SUMMARY

The basic concepts help in using and incorporating computer technology into professional operations. The technology of computers and computer-related work is, however, constantly changing. To keep up with this constantly evolving field, it is a good idea to talk to EDP personnel and find out how they are moving with the changing tide. Have they installed terminals or microprocessors with new capabilities? Have they been experimenting with new equipment and systems, seeking appropriate reaction and feedback from users along the chain of command? The specifics of a data center operation are described in Chapter 6, "The Data Processing Department." Auditing system software is discussed in Chapter 9, "System Software." The issues involved in controlling minicomputer and microcomputer operations are presented in Chapter 30, "Microcomputers and How to Audit Them."

The Data Processing Department

ORGANIZATION OF THE EDP FUNCTION

As computer use became widespread, organizations sometimes discovered that they needed more processing capability than the one EDP department that was the central processing area. In effect, lots of tiny EDP departments developed wherever user departments needed processing capability. This decentralization of processing was basically a sound concept, since many of the smaller processing tasks could be accomplished locally, where the source of transactions was located. One of the difficulties in this approach was that the various small systems, because of ever-decreasing hardware costs, could be easily purchased without any thought about the larger organizational picture (e.g., whether the various systems were compatible). Their installation and use were similarly uncontrolled in many instances.

This proliferation of computer use without a concomitant plan for acquisition and subsequent implementation caused more than minor concern in many organizations. A similar situation developed as local managers discovered microcomputers, which were frequently purchased without following EDP standards and procedures.

In one major corporation, probably representative of many all over the country, the number of different microcomputer and minicomputer systems being used in various locations started to cause real problems in the early 1980s. At this time, senior management began to learn of the problems developing as a result of the number of systems they had in use. Throughout the company, managers had bought the system they thought best for their area, without considering whether the information they processed could be accessed by another system within the company. To solve this problem, the company organized a central department that had responsibility for the development of a sound, overall corporate plan for the management of all information systems. It also had final approval over all systems — no matter how small — to be bought for the company. As local management learned to follow the new procedures developed for implementation and maintenance of systems and data, the new EDP planning area had to make every computer in the company compatible, and then ensure the integrity of programs and data in use in many locations. Eventually it all worked, and the reports from business planning could be run on the financial department's computers, but time, money, and energy had been wasted.

Problems such as this are becoming less and less common as organizations realize how important it is to have a sound, written policy to control computer system purchase, use, and maintenance. At the same time, having a well-organized EDP department that can handle all of the major processing for the organization and can help implement the policy for all users, no matter where they are located, is essential to the effectiveness of management information systems.

Another invaluable, and sometimes overlooked, source of assistance in planning and controlling computer use in any organization is the internal audit department. This is particularly true when one or more of its members are EDP audit specialists. Their participation in the system development life cycle can assure that the computers and software implemented in an organization will be the ones that fulfill the requirements.

In the past, EDP strategy often developed on a "catch-as-catch-can" basis, with new computers being purchased because old ones had simply collapsed under the strain, or new programs being written in the middle of a crisis to meet present needs. Often there was no time to investigate and plan for the future. In today's rapidly moving world of computer technology, this kind of approach simply will not work.

There are many different ways to develop a sound EDP strategy. Their names are based on their methods, such as the "bottom-up" or "top-down" approach to planning, yet it can be said that there is a common thread in all of them. They all involve the implementation of policy and procedures through the talents of people in the department most directly concerned: the EDP department. Data processing has become so important to the success of the organization itself that a well-structured, well-running EDP department should be high on the list of priorities for any organization.

Since organizational needs fluctuate according to seasons and economic conditions, the EDP department must be flexible enough to meet the changing demands for its services. To function successfully, the structure should take into consideration the peaks and valleys in demand for processing so that when there is a lot of work to be done, the system is able to do it without becoming overloaded and slowing down. For many organizations, these needs are predictable enough that expected volume requirements can be designed into the system.

The EDP department and its systems also must be adaptable, in order to integrate new software and hardware as needed. As technological advances naturally occur, the system should be able to incorporate them, to grow and develop, rather than requiring replacement of entire systems in order for such advances to be implemented.

This chapter discusses various aspects of department structure, operating procedures, and organization that can apply to any EDP department. This information can be used to ensure that an existing EDP department meets basic standards. Simultaneously, the checklist of EDP department functions, structure, and controls in the second half of the chapter can be used to ensure that an EDP department has appropriate procedures and controls in place.

DATA PROCESSING ENVIRONMENT, ORGANIZATION, AND CONTROLS

The Computer Department

Computer departments vary considerably from one organization to the next. The structure of the computer or EDP department obviously depends on physical constraints such as size and workload, but the structure reflects two basic divisions:

1. System development — Designing and programming computer systems (see Chapter 7, "The System Development Life Cycle")
2. Operations — Controlling and processing data

It is becoming increasingly common in medium to large installations for other support groups, in addition to these basic areas, to exist.

An organizational chart of a typical medium-size installation is shown in Figure 6-1. This chart indicates the broad functional divisions that exist within a computer department. The extent of formalization, or lack of it, within these divisions depends largely on the size of the department. However, in any structure the operational aspects of the computer department, the role of the data base section, and the role of the software support group are similar. What may differ is the number of people available to do these jobs. Figure 6-2 shows some of the areas in a company where EDP support is required.

Computer Operations

A typical medium-size computer used for batch and on-line applications, such as an IBM 4341, might have a data center manager in charge of operations, with the following functions reporting:

- Operations manager responsible for computer operations
- Chief operator (responsible for senior operators in charge of each shift and other computer operators on staff)
- Security administrator
- Data base administrator (if a data base management system is used)
- Technical support
- Control section
- Data preparation
- Scheduling
- Job assembly
- Library
- Output distribution

Control Section. The control section is responsible for monitoring information passing into, through, and out of the computer operations area. However, these duties vary according to the demands of the type of system in operation.

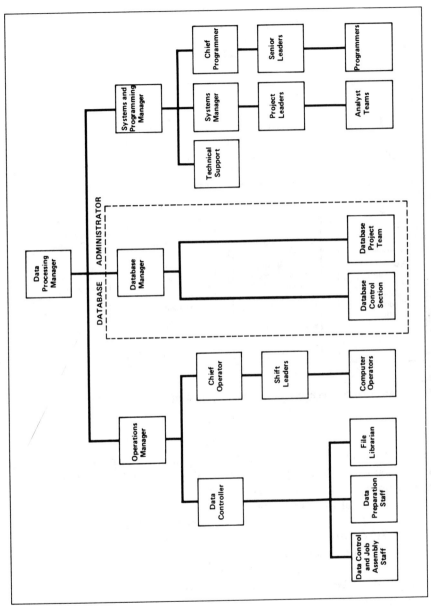

FIG. 6-1 An organization chart for a data processing department

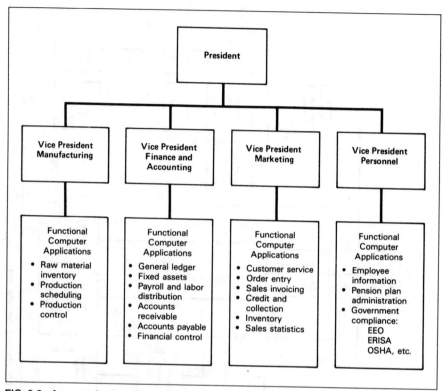

FIG. 6-2   An organization chart for a company, showing EDP support functions

The "central batch environment" is still fairly common. In this situation, batches of documents are received for entry to operational procedures. They are accompanied by batch control data that contains identifying information and user approval for processing, such as batch totals, document count, and date. Other information often includes document counts and control totals (see Chapter 17, "Controls for Completeness and Accuracy of Input" and Chapter 18, "Controls for Completeness and Accuracy of Update") for each batch. These details should be recorded in a register. The subsequent progress of each batch should also be recorded (such as date of processing, details of output, and date of distribution) in the same log.

Where data is input at a location remote from the computer, control over transmitted data may be established at the central location by software. (See Chapter 8, "On-Line Systems.") The physical control of source documents, which is otherwise part of the central control section's function, will be carried out at the outlying (remote) location. Controls should be in place to ensure that only authorized personnel can gain access to the computer programs and files through remote terminals. These can consist of software checks, such as passwords or account codes, or hardware features, such as terminal locks.

Upon completion of each scheduled job, the control section should check, for each program or series of programs run, that

- Data specified as input was fully processed.
- Required output was produced in the correct form.
- Correct computer programs and control records were used.
- Correct tape, disk, and other files were used at every stage.
- Data files were correctly read or written.
- Correct action was taken by the computer operator following program halts, both scheduled and unscheduled.
- There is no evidence of unauthorized alteration of data or programs.
- Computer and associated procedures were completed without undue delay.

Data Preparation. Although considerable progress has been made in automating methods of preparing data for input (light pens, magnetic ink, and the like), the most common form of off-line data conversion is still through a keyboard to a terminal with a display and magnetic tape or disk. For older systems, keypunched cards are still used. The staff involved in keying data in central locations is normally a section within the computer operations group. Where data entry is done at outlying points, it is likely that the staff will be responsible to local management for administrative reasons. On-line systems typically use terminals and direct keying, often by the user departments.

Keyed data should be verified. If possible, data should not be keyed and verified by the same operator. A separate subsection is often set up for verification by the more experienced operators.

A record is normally maintained in the data preparation area to monitor the progress of documents through the various stages of preparation and verification. Sufficient information should be recorded to indicate the present whereabouts of each batch of documents, together with the date and, if necessary, time of completion of processing for each stage.

Scheduling. For every job run on the computer, there should be a detailed schedule that sets the total time for the job to run, the sequence of events within the job, and the various peripherals and files involved. These schedules are used to determine each day's work for the computer. There should be a work scheduler, who has responsibility for preparing:

- A detailed schedule, divided if necessary into a schedule for each operating shift. (This is usually reviewed by the data control supervisor or operations manager.)
- Detailed schedules for the week or month ahead.
- Outlines of long-term forecasts of computer time requirements and other operating workloads, which may cover periods of 6, 12, or more months. The periods selected for long-term forecasts should extend far enough in advance for effective action to be taken to recruit and train additional operating staff if needed. Cases where work volumes are expected to increase significantly may require the increase of computer or other equipment's capacity.

The daily schedule provides each shift of computer operators with the work to be done, the sequence in which programs are to be run, and, where possible, lower-priority work that can be introduced if time becomes available. At the end of a shift, each operator should pass to the work scheduler or to the next shift of operators (when the work scheduler is not on duty) a statement of the work completed and the reasons any scheduled work was not completed.

It is necessary to revise the detailed schedules if there are errors or failures that substantially delay the completion of the computer procedures or make it necessary for them to be repeated. The work scheduler should be kept informed of the progress of work and, in the event of delays or failures, should amend the schedules. The detailed schedules should also be revised when delays occur in the submission, to the operations group, of input documents or other media, or in input media preparation by operations group staff. As the relative importance of scheduled procedures may change because of the delay, the work scheduler may need to consult users before making these revisions. If it is necessary to repeat entire jobs or procedures, it is likely that there will be a conflict over the job priority between several users who expect their jobs to be completed. Such situations must be handled with care and might require the computer operations manager to step in to decide the sequence of jobs to be run and make the necessary arrangements with users. The EDP manager should be informed whenever significant delays occur or when extensive rerunning is necessary.

Job Assembly. Job assembly or job set-up is the physical assembly of the material necessary for processing. This material may include the tapes or other devices that hold the relevant programs and data, the job control statements, the run instructions, and the parameters. In more advanced systems, system software takes over some of these functions and the programs and data files are often available in the on-line program library.

Job control statements contain the instructions for programs to execute in a particular sequence. Job control statements also define system resources (such as data sets, tape and disk drives, printers, and terminals). In more advanced systems they are stored on disk and are usually called into operation via terminal entry.

Run instructions contain the program operating instructions. They give details of the action to be taken by operators before, during, and at the completion of the operation of the program. Run instructions also provide the current processing instructions, which give details of the programs and files to be used and the stationery requirements. These run instructions are specific to a job and complement the standard operating instructions that apply to all processing.

Some applications use parameters which contain run information that a program needs but which is variable in nature. The most common parameters are dates, which are used, for example, in the generation of data and the aging of accounts receivable and inventory balances. Parameters may also be used to indicate whether program steps used only periodically, such as production of customer statements, should be activated. Parameters are often stored as table files or can be entered as part of the job control statements.

The job set-up personnel are responsible for the maintenance of the job set-up instructions and ensuring the use of the proper instructions during processing. It is usual for the control section to match the job set-up instructions with the details of job control statements and the parameters that are actually used. Once the programs, files, run instructions, job control statements, and parameters requested on the daily, or shift, schedule have been assembled, they are passed to the computer operators for processing.

Library. Programs and data files in use include tapes and disks that have been loaded for a specific processing run but are otherwise stored off-line in the production library, for batch systems. They are permanently loaded on disk or tape and available for inquiry or updating in on-line and real-time systems. (See Chapter 8, "On-Line Systems.") Files organized as a data base (see Chapter 10, "Data Base") would normally be in the latter category. Off-line files and programs are held in a physical library and require an operator to mount or place them on the tape drive or other device, or the librarian may be able to mount them mechanically.

The physical library should be a lockable storage area, separate from the computer room. Preferably, the library should be supervised by a full-time librarian responsible for the issue, receipt, and security of all files. Where the installation is not large enough to warrant a full-time librarian, a member of the control section should have similar specific duties. Access to the library should be restricted to staff authorized to obtain and deliver programs and data files; even then such activities should be in accordance with the authorized processing schedules prepared by the work scheduler.

The librarian should follow up on all issued tapes and disks in order to ensure their prompt return. The librarian is responsible for maintaining adequate records of all tapes and disks, either manually (in the form of a register or index card file) or through an automated library system run on the computer. Other routine functions include the transfer of files and programs to "back up" for storage as a safeguard against destruction or loss of operational copies.

Output Distribution. The printed output from computer processing is usually voluminous. Its decollation (i.e., separation into units and removal of carbon paper, if any) and distribution are normally the responsibilities of personnel within the control section. Output should be distributed only in accordance with current processing instructions and only after the control section is satisfied that processing was properly completed in accordance with those instructions.

Computer Operators. Computer operators are responsible for the accurate and efficient operation of the scheduled jobs on the computer. The computer operators report directly to the chief operator or, where shifts are worked, to the shift supervisor.

Operator procedures should be based on standing instructions. These instructions deal with the operation of the computer and its peripheral equipment, the actions to be taken in the event of machine or program failure, and the records to be kept. The standing instructions, when combined with the run instructions, provide rules for each step that may need to be taken by operators. A responsible official, such as the operations manager, should review the operating instructions periodically and confirm that they are up-to-date. Except in the smallest computer installations, operators should not carry out work associated with:

- Job set-up
- Control procedures
- Writing operational programs

After processing has been completed, the computer operators should distribute the files used and any printed or punched output according to the current processing instructions. Tape and disk files should either be retained for a subsequent operation or returned to the file library. Before being forwarded to the control section, printed output should be labeled to indicate the computer program that produced it, the processing cycle reference number (which may be the creation date or a unique reference number), and the time it was produced.

The computer operator should record the start and stop times of computer runs and report any delay times. Although most computers have software capabilities that provide for this information to be logged and displayed on the console or master terminal by the supervisory program, it is sometimes necessary for a separate manual report to be compiled by the operator. This report should provide the details of delays and problems, together with any actions taken to correct them. Where the delay occurred as the result of a machine failure, a copy of any report prepared by the vendor's customer engineer should be filed with the chief operator's copy of the delay report.

Technical Support

In large operations it is not unusual to find that the computer operations department has developed a specialist software support service, staffed by systems programmers. These programmers are responsible for such activities as

- Obtaining detailed knowledge of the operating system and other system software.
- Using their software knowledge to resolve inquiries from development and operating staff.
- Controlling the incorporation of software amendments provided by manufacturer or software house.
- If necessary, devising and incorporating additional amendments to the system software, usually to improve its efficiency and to tailor it to the organization's requirements and computer configuration.

Although considerable improvements to operating efficiency can sometimes be obtained from local amendments to generalized software, there is a risk to security, especially when the amendments are devised and controlled entirely within the computer operations department.

The size and complexity of data bases often lead to the appointment of specific personnel responsible for all aspects of data base administration. These personnel are collectively called the data base administrator (DBA). Their tasks include the design and maintenance of the schemas (description of all data in the data base) and subschemas (description of all data available to a particular program); the maintenance of the data base management system (DBMS) and related software; and liaison with users, other computer department staff, and outside suppliers. The DBA may thus combine responsibility for procedures and controls that would normally be carried out by separate people in conventional computer systems. (See Chapter 10 for a discussion of data base concepts.)

REVIEWING THE EDP DEPARTMENT

As organizations of all sizes seek to control costs, they often focus on their EDP operations. Basically, they want to know how successful their EDP function is in supporting overall organizational objectives. But how does an organization go about determining the effectiveness, efficiency, and reliability of its EDP function?

One approach is an EDP operational review, which is frequently performed by an outside organization such as an accounting firm with EDP audit capabilities. The review encompasses user services, EDP management, technical development, operations, facilities, and contingency plans. This is a good way for management to get an independent assessment of its EDP function. (The chart in Figure 6-3 shows some of the questions in relation to access that would be assessed during such a review.)

Obviously, each entity's EDP needs are different, but there are general questions that all types of organizations should ask themselves. An EDP operational review can supply management with answers to such questions as:

- Is the organization getting a dollar payback on its EDP expenditures?
- Are users getting the processing results they need?
- Is the entire function managed effectively?
- Is the EDP function responsive to overall organizational objectives and plans?
- Are EDP resources being applied to the appropriate needs?
- Is the total EDP function performing productively?

Determining When a Review Is Needed

Quite apart from the broad questions above, how does an organization know it needs a review? If an organization exhibits some of the following symptoms, it may be time to investigate the feasibility of an EDP operational review:

- Unfavorable user attitude toward the EDP department
- Excessive costs
- History of aborted or suspended development projects
- Budget overruns on development projects
- Excessive staff turnover
- Unsupported hardware/software procurement requests
- Frequent computer errors or omitted processes
- Insufficient processing abilities due to organizational growing pains
- New requirements due to external growth or organization expansion

The objectives and outcome of an EDP operational review can differ according to the organization's needs and even the industry it is in.

Indicate who is responsible, or normally has access to, the following records, equipment, and files.

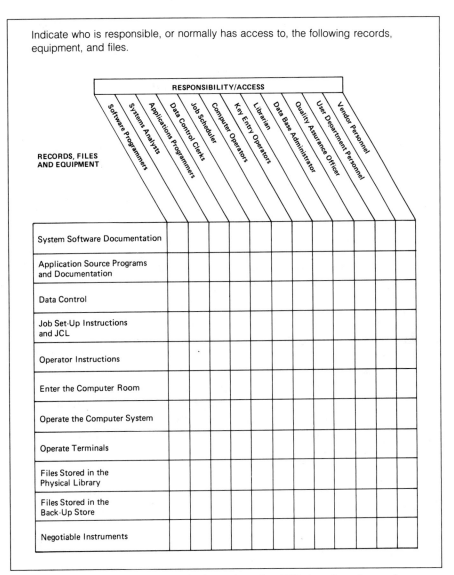

FIG. 6-3 Specimen form to be used in the review of an EDP department regarding access to records, equipment, and files

Internal Growing Pains. A pharmaceutical research and manufacturing company was concerned with the rapid growth of both staff and functions in its EDP operation. They wanted a review to evaluate EDP strengths and weaknesses, develop a corporatewide definition of future EDP requirements, establish a basis for developing an action program to deal with deficiencies, and formulate a long-range EDP plan, among other things. The review resulted in recommendations, with accompanying detailed work plans, that

- Senior management become more deeply involved in directing, planning, and funding EDP operations to better achieve corporate goals.
- EDP organization, standards, and procedures be examined.
- Existing technical expertise be enhanced.
- Security and contingency plans be developed.

If implemented, the recommendations would lead to a more effective EDP operation with increased productivity.

External Growth. A major utility wanted to assess how the merger of three subsidiaries would effect the EDP function. The review focused on organizational requirements, existing EDP plans, EDP planning process, equipment, data communications, applications consolidation, data base consolidation, and staffing.

A short-range action program was suggested, concentrating on the consolidation. A financial forecast projected program cost and the ultimate possible savings. (Note that operational reviews are not necessarily made with cost-cutting in mind.)

REVIEWING AN EDP FUNCTION — CHECKLIST

The following checklist shows some of the issues to be considered during an internal or external review of an EDP department.

1. **Applications.** Develop a list of the major computer-based applications that are both in production and proposed for the future. (See Figure 6-4 for a sample questionnaire used to review applications.)

2. **Equipment:**

   ☐ Create a list or diagram of EDP equipment at each location, including service bureaus.

   ☐ Describe plans for equipment purchases or enhancements and their intended use. (Figure 6-5 shows a sample chart used to assess equipment during a review.)

APPLICATIONS

Client_____   Date_____

Engagement #_____   Prepared by_____

Location_____   Review_____

Fiscal Year-End_____   Review_____

APPLICATION (Enter actual name)	FOR APPLICATION IN USE: Is documentation up-to-date and in accordance with current standards	FOR PROPOSED APPLICATIONS: Approximate Implementation Date	PROGRAMMING LANGUAGE	Batch	On-line	Data base
Order Entry						
Billing/Invoicing						
Accounts Receivable						
Cash Receipts						
Sales Analysis						
Raw Material Inventory						
Work in Progress						
Bill of Materials						
Finished Goods						
Cost Accounting						
Purchase Orders						
Goods Received						
Accounts Payable						
General Ledger/ Budgets						
Fixed Assets						
Investments						
Payroll						
Labor Distribution						
Pensions						
Cash and Bank						

FIG. 6-4 Specimen chart to be used in review of application programs run by the EDP department

INSTALLED EQUIPMENT

This schedule may be used if the client does not already have an equipment inventory or diagram.

Location: _____   Type_____

CPUs: Quantity_____   Memory: Real _____

                                                    Virtual _____

Peripheral Devices	Quantity	Type
Magnetic Tape Drives		
Disk Storage Drives		
Card Reader		
Card Punch		
Printer		
Typewriter Console		
Display Console		
Other: (List) including terminals, RJE stations, Point-of-sale devices, optical scanner, etc.		

Operating System Employed Version Name _____

    Version No._____ Release Date_____ Memory Req._____

FIG. 6-5 Specimen chart to be used to record the equipment in the EDP department as part of a review

---

SYSTEM SOFTWARE

(include both vendor supplied and specially developed software)

Location(s) or System(s)_____

System Program, software product, or utility	Titles of manuals describing the software	Describe the documentation setting out the options and adaptions of the software actually in use	Group responsible for software support
Operating System_____ Version #_____ Release Data_____			

FIG. 6-6   Specimen chart to be used in review of system software

3. System Software:

☐ Make a list of the software products and packages in use, including vendor-supplied and specially developed system software.

☐ Specify the type of documentation available which records the particular software features and any adaptations. (Figure 6-6 is a sample chart used to evaluate system software during a review.)

Note: System software is software not particular to any one application (e.g., the operating system, utilities, sorts, compilers, file management systems, librarian packages, time-sharing software, communications software, job accounting software, DBMS, and security software).

4. Personnel:

☐ Obtain an organization chart of the EDP function.

☐ Attach job descriptions of computer department functions.

☐ Do any EDP personnel have responsibilities outside the computer department? If so, list the individuals, their functions, and their external responsibilities. (See the section entitled "Disciplines over Basic Controls: Segregation of Duties" in Chapter 16, "Introduction to Controls.")

☐ Develop a list of those personnel who have access to particular documentation, files, and equipment.

☐ Describe special procedures, if any, for segregating and reviewing EDP personnel's own records and accounts (e.g., payroll data, retail sales account, bank account).

5. Personnel Policies:

☐ What are the computer department policies with respect to delegation of duties when staff are absent because of illness, vacation, or other reason?

☐ What are the computer department policies for obtaining references before hiring new employees?

☐ What are the computer department policies for continuous assessment of personnel performance and provision of necessary training?

☐ What are the termination procedures for relieving personnel of sensitive duties and retrieving keys and invalidating their passwords?

☐ Who is responsible for reviewing and approving organization charts, job descriptions, and policies to determine that they are up-to-date?

6. Installation Standards:

☐ Is there an installation standards manual (attach a summary or table of contents) for the following?
- Selection of purchased hardware, software, and other computer services
  a. System development
  b. Program modifications
  c. System and program testing
  d. Computer operations
  e. System programming
- Quality assurance
- Security of software and data stored on computer media
- Privacy and confidentiality of documentation, output, and information stored in computer files
- Physical safeguarding of equipment, documentation, and computer files
- Procedures for DBA and DBMS support
- Development and maintenance of the processing systems and networks
- Procedures for teleprocessing support

☐ Is conformity to standards mandatory, or are they considered to be guidelines that can be varied in individual cases?

☐ Describe procedures for developing and changing installation standards and who is responsible for preparing the standards.

☐ What functions or procedures are not presently covered by the standards manual?

☐ What areas of the standards manual are out-of-date and what plans are there for bringing the manual up-to-date?

7. Backup:

☐ Describe the procedures for determining the need for backup and rerun arrangements (such as by estimating the mean time between failures).

☐ Describe the backup arrangements, both on-site and off-site, for:
- Data processing and transmission equipment
- Data, programs, and systems information stored on computer media
- Documentation instructions and source data

☐ Describe arrangements for alternative processing facilities in the event of equipment failure (contingency plans).

☐ Describe the procedures for periodically testing and reviewing the effectiveness of the backup arrangements for the following:
- Data processing and transmission equipment
- Data, programs, and systems information stored on computer media
- Documentation, instructions, and source data

8. Insurance:

☐ Describe the insurance coverage for hardware and software, and for recreating data and files.

☐ Describe the fidelity bond coverage for EDP personnel.

9. Contracts:

☐ Describe the procedures for reviewing contracts for computer services, hardware, and software before they are signed.

☐ Attach a copy or a summary of any significant current contracts (such as for service bureau services).

10. **Forms Design.** Describe the procedures for reviewing input forms, output formats, and terminal screen formats before implementation to ensure that they are understandable and easy to use.

REVIEWING IMPLEMENTATION AND MAINTENANCE OF SYSTEMS — CHECKLIST

1. System and Program Documentation:

☐ Does documentation in accordance with the installation standards exist for all applications and programs developed or modified:
  • In the current financial year?
  • In previous years?

☐ Describe any system and program documentation aids or documentation software products in use.

☐ Do the source programs conform to the installation programming standards for all programs written:
  • In the current financial year?
  • In previous years?

☐ How and where are the documentation and source listings filed?

☐ Where modifications have to be made to old programs that have not been developed in accordance with the current standards, what procedures are followed to bring the documentation of the applications up-to-date?

2. Access to System and Program Documentation:

☐ Describe how and where source statement listings, flowcharts, file layouts, sign-on procedures, passwords, and other system documentation are held.

☐ Who is responsible for the custody and issue of documentation?

☐ Who has access to the documentation?

☐ How are unauthorized persons prevented from gaining access to the documentation?

☐ Describe the procedures for the issue and return of documentation.

3. Approval of System Specifications:

☐ Who has the authority to approve system specifications for proposed new applications in the following?

- User department(s)
- System development function
- Computer operations function
- Quality assurance function

☐ What documentation is presented to the above for approval?

☐ How are the approvals evidenced?

☐ When the system specifications are modified during the development process, how are the approvals for the change documented?

☐ How and where are system specifications and approvals filed?

☐ Describe any variation in the above procedures for new systems implemented or under development in the past year.

4. Testing New Applications:

☐ For new applications, describe the involvement in program and system testing of:
- Analyst(s) who specified the programs
- Programmer(s) who wrote the programs
- Computer operations function
- Users
- Quality assurance function
- Others (such as a separate testing group or the internal audit department)

☐ Describe the use made of system and program documentation in designing the tests.

☐ What documentation is produced in the process of program and system testing?

☐ What is the policy for the retention of testing documentation and test data files?

☐ When system software (such as utilities, interrogation packages, sorts or routines incorporated by the linkage editor) is incorporated into applications, is its proper functioning always covered by the normal application testing?

☐ Describe any variations in the above procedures for new systems that were tested in the past year.

5. Approval of Modifications to Production Programs:

☐ How are modifications to production programs requested?

☐ How is the nature of the required change documented?

☐ Who has the authority to approve program modifications in the following:

- User department(s)
- Systems maintenance function
- Computer operations function (if appropriate)
- Quality assurance function

☐ How are the approvals evidenced?

☐ How and where are the records of program modifications filed?

☐ Describe any variations in the above procedures (such as for minor modifications or as a result of changes in standards during the year).

6. Control of Approved Program Modifications:

☐ How are all approved modifications controlled to ensure that they are subsequently implemented as authorized?

☐ What are the procedures for reviewing modification requests to ensure that they are implemented within the required time frame?

☐ How are the results of this review documented?

7. Testing Program Modifications:

☐ What documentation is produced in the process of program and system testing?

☐ What is the policy for the retention of testing documentation and test data files?

☐ When program modifications are tested, what procedures are used to ensure that the modification does not affect unchanged parts of the programs or system (e.g., when retained system test data is rerun)?

☐ When system software (e.g., utilities, interrogation packages, sorts or routines incorporated by the linkage editor) is incorporated into applications, is its proper functioning always covered by the normal application testing?

☐ Have all modifications made during the current financial year been tested in accordance with the installation standards?

☐ Under what circumstances, if any, may the normal testing procedures be waived?

☐ When the normal testing procedures are waived, what alternate steps are taken to ensure the proper operation of the modified systems?

☐ Who may approve the waiving of testing, and how is this approval evidenced?

8. Urgent Modifications:

☐ Under what circumstances may urgent modifications that bypass the normal procedures be made to production programs or job control language (JCL) procedure libraries?

☐ Describe the procedures for making such modifications and recording their occurrence.

☐ What procedures are in force, either at the time the modification is made or at a subsequent time, to ensure that the modification is properly documented, tested, and approved?

9. Acceptance by Users of New Applications and Program Modifications:

☐ How are users notified of the effective date when new systems and modifications to systems are to become operational?

☐ Who in the user department(s) is responsible for giving the final approval of new systems and modifications for production use? How is this approval evidenced?

☐ Are there any types of program modification to which the users are not required to give approval?

☐ When users give their approval, how do they ensure that
  • Programs and systems have been adequately tested with respect to the methods used and scope of testing?
  • Satisfactory results were achieved from testing?
  • Instructions for user procedures have been appropriately prepared or amended?

10. Final Approval for New Applications and Program Modifications by the EDP Function:

☐ Prior to implementation of a new application, who is responsible for checking that the following are complete, up-to-date, and in accordance with the installation standards?
  • System and program documentation
  • Job set-up and operating instructions

☐ How are the results of this check documented?

☐ In the case of program modifications, who is responsible for checking that the following have been amended to be brought up-to-date and in accordance with the current standards?
  • System and program documentation
  • Operating instructions

☐ How are the results of this check documented?

☐ Who is responsible for checking that system and program testing of new applications and program modifications has been properly carried out before programs are made operational, and how are the results of this check documented?

☐ Who is responsible for checking that user approvals have been received, and how are the results of this check documented?

☐ Who is responsible for giving the final approval to make new applications and program modifications operational, and how is this approval evidenced?

11. Cataloging Approved New Applications and Program Modifications:

☐ Describe the procedures for segregating programs being amended from normal production programs.

☐ Describe the procedures that ensure that only authorized changes are made during programming (such as program comparison software being run on the before-and-after versions to identify all code that has been changed, or accumulations of changes, in a file that updates the previous version in the library in batch mode and that can be reviewed through an update utility or supervisory review of the source code after programming).

☐ Describe the procedures that ensure that
  • The correct version of the program is transferred to production status.
  • Unauthorized changes are not made to approved programs between the time they are approved for implementation and the time they are taken into production libraries.
  • Changes made to source statement libraries are also made to executable program libraries or vice versa.

☐ Who is responsible for carrying out the work?

☐ How is this work evidenced?

☐ How is the work supervised, reviewed, and approved?

REVIEWING JOB SET-UP, SCHEDULING, AND DATA CONTROL — CHECKLIST

1. Scheduling:

☐ Describe the procedures for scheduling production work.

☐ Who authorizes the schedule, and where are the authorized schedules filed?

2. Data Control and Job Set-Up Instructions:

☐ Have data control and job set-up instructions (including job control statements, parameters, sequence of operations, and control over file generations) been prepared for all applications in accordance with the installation standards?

☐ How are the instructions for controlling and setting up jobs kept correct and up-to-date?

☐ Who has access to the instructions? How does the company ensure that only authorized personnel have access to the instructions?

3. Data Control (Application Controls):

☐ Describe the responsibilities of data control and associated personnel for preparing and correcting input data (such as a result of rejections).

☐ What procedures are in force to ensure that no unauthorized changes are made to input data?

☐ Who has access to the data control records?

☐ How is control over access to the data control records enforced?

☐ Who is responsible for supervising, reviewing, and approving data control activities?

4. Job Set-Up:

☐ What procedures are followed to ensure that job control variables and program parameters are prepared in accordance with approved instructions?

☐ When departures from normal job set-up procedures occur (e.g., the use of programs from the test library for production), how are such departures authorized?

5. Use of Correct Files:

☐ What controls are there to ensure that correct data files are used in production processing (e.g., use of generation data sets, manual review of system logs, or reliance on an automated tape management system)?

☐ When these controls rely on automated procedures, can such procedures be overridden (e.g., overriding label checks)?

☐ What procedures are in effect to report any incorrect use of data files?

☐ Are the results of the action taken on reported, incorrect use of files reviewed and approved and, if so, by whom?

☐ How are the results of the reviews and approvals documented?

6. Review of Processing:

☐ To what extent are the results of processing (such as the job execution log or production output) reviewed to ensure that
- The established production schedule is adhered to and no unauthorized processing has occurred?
- No unauthorized changes were made to production JCL and parameters after job set-up?
- The output appears reasonable?

☐ How is the review of processing documented?

7. Variations in Normal Procedures:

☐ Describe any variation in the job set-up and review of processing procedures during the following periods:
- Second and third shifts (if any)
- Weekends and holidays (if applicable)
- Periods of nonproduction processing (such as program testing)

REVIEWING COMPUTER OPERATIONS — CHECKLIST

1. Computer Room Access:

☐ Who is normally permitted access to the computer room?

☐ Under what circumstances may others be permitted access?

☐ How is control over computer room access enforced?

☐ How does this control operate during the following periods?
- Second and third shifts (if any)
- Weekends and holidays (if applicable)
- Periods of nonproduction processing (such as application and system software testing)

2. Operation of Computer Equipment:

☐ Who is normally permitted to operate computer equipment for the following?
- Production processing

- Application testing
- System software development and testing
- Third-party processing (Is there processing for outsiders?)

☐ Under what circumstances may others be permitted to operate computer equipment?
- How is control over the operation of computer equipment enforced?
- How does this control operate during the following periods?
  a. Second and third shifts (if any)
  b. Weekends and holidays (if applicable)
  c. Periods of nonproduction processing (such as hardware maintenance)

3. **Operator Duties.** What, if any, transactions of a financial or accounting nature can be initiated within the operations department?

4. **Operating Instructions:**

☐ Do the installation standards require the operating instructions to contain the following?
- Operating instructions for system software (where applicable)
- Operating procedures for applications
- Restart and recovery procedures
- Procedures for labeling and disposition of input and output tapes
- An application system flowchart or run instructions for each run
- An identification of all input and output forms and media

☐ Have operating instructions been prepared for all applications in accordance with these standards?

☐ Who has the authority to approve operating instructions (or changes thereto) in the following?
- Applications development and maintenance functions
- Computer operations function
- Quality assurance function

☐ How are the approvals documented?

☐ What procedures are adopted to ensure that the operating instructions remain correct and up-to-date?

5. **Program and Data File Security:**

☐ What are the procedures (such as librarian packages and password access systems) for preventing unauthorized access to the following files?

- Source statement libraries
- Object program modules
- Executable program libraries
- Procedure libraries (job control language)
- Sign-on procedures and passwords
- Production data
- System files (such as those containing system software programs and utilities)
- Log files (such as SMF)

☐ Who is authorized to access these files, and what level of access is permitted (such as read-only or write access)?

☐ In the event that an unauthorized access occurs, are control procedures exercised to detect such an access?

☐ When password protection is used to prevent unauthorized access to program and data files:
- Describe the procedures adopted, including maintaining secrecy.
- Who is responsible for setting and distributing passwords?
- Are passwords periodically changed and, if so, how often?
- Are accurate records kept of authorized user access levels?

☐ When comparison of independently controlled copies of authorized programs to those in the production library is used to detect any unauthorized access:
- How often and by whom are such comparisons made?
- Describe the software used to make the comparison.
- Are comparisons made on a surprise basis?
- Where are records of the results of the comparisons filed?

☐ Who supervises, reviews, and approves the work described above?

☐ How are the results of the reviews and approvals documented?

6. Logs of System and Operations Activity:

☐ What manual and automated logs are produced that provide the following information? (Note: include job accounting information, control logs, DBMS logs, or other)
- Operator commands entered on the system console
- Jobs and programs executed
- Abnormal termination of jobs and programs
- Jobs and programs rerun
- Program and data files accessed

- Utilities used
- Operating problems encountered and action taken

☐ In the case of any automated logs, what software was used to generate them? Indicate the information recorded in each log (such as by attaching a copy of the output or record layout or by referring to the relevant sections of the software manuals).

☐ When vendor-supplied software is used (such as SMF), what amendments, options, or user exits have been used and for what purpose?

☐ How is the completeness and accuracy of the manual and automated logs ensured? By whom and to what extent are these logs reviewed and approved? How are the results of the review documented?

☐ If, for any reason, this review was not properly carried out, how would the lack of review be detected?

7. Emergency Program Modifications:

☐ Under what circumstances may urgent modifications be made to production programs or JCL procedure libraries that bypass the normal procedures?

☐ Describe the procedures for making emergency modifications and recording their occurrence.

☐ What records are kept of emergency modifications that have been made?

☐ What procedures are in force, either at the time the modification is made or at a subsequent time, to ensure that the modification has been properly documented, tested, and approved?

8. Utilities:

☐ What records are kept over the use of utilities and other similar programs that can do the following?
- Dump data
- Change production programs, data files, or memory at execution time

☐ What controls are in effect over the use of these utilities?

☐ Who must authorize the use of utilities?

☐ What procedures are in effect to ensure that only duly authorized use occurs?

9. Supervision of Operators:

☐ Who is responsible for reviewing and supervising the action of operators?

☐ If, for any reason, operators do not adhere to installation operating procedures, how would this fact be detected?

REVIEWING STORAGE OF PROGRAMS, DATA FILES, AND FORMS — CHECKLIST

1. Access to Files:

☐ When program and data files are not being used for processing, where are they held (on-site and off-site)?

☐ Who is normally permitted access to these files?

☐ Under what circumstances may others be permitted access?

☐ How is control over access to files enforced?

☐ How does this control operate during the following periods?
  • Second and third shifts (if any)
  • Weekends and holidays (if applicable)
  • Periods of nonproduction processing (such as application and system software testing)

2. Issue and Return of Files:

☐ Who is responsible for the custody and issue of files?

☐ Describe the procedures for the external labeling of files and for organizing the storage of files (such as through the use of labeled racks) in the:
  • Computer room
  • Main file libraries
  • Backup or disaster storage

☐ Describe the procedures for requesting, recording, and authorizing issue and prompt return of files (including files containing software).

☐ Who is responsible for supervising, reviewing, and approving the activities of librarians and the security and issuing procedures?

☐ Describe any variation in the procedures during the following periods:
  • Second and third shifts (if any)

- Weekends and holidays (if applicable)
- Periods of nonproduction processing (such as application and system software testing)

3. Storage and Issue of Forms (Application Controls):

☐ Develop a list of computer forms that require special security. (Normally these will only include checks or other potentially negotiable instruments.)

☐ Where are stocks of these forms stored?

☐ Who is normally permitted access to these stocks?

☐ How is access to the stocks restricted?

☐ Is the restriction effective outside the normal working period during the following periods?
- Second and third shifts (if any)
- Weekends and holidays (if applicable)

☐ Who authorizes the use of such forms?

☐ Describe the procedures for controlling the inventory of forms.
- What are the procedures for issuing forms from, and returning forms to, stock?
- Are inventory records maintained?
- Is actual form usage reconciled to inventory issues?

☐ Describe the procedures for controlling spoiled and canceled forms.

REVIEWING SYSTEM SOFTWARE PROGRAMMING — CHECKLIST

1. System Software Documentation:

☐ Has documentation in accordance with the installation standards been prepared for all system software implemented or modified:
- In the current financial year?
- In previous years?

☐ Does the documentation describe the functions, options selected, user exit changes, and specially designed routines?

☐ When reliance is placed on documentation provided by the software supplier, what records are kept of the particular options, versions,

software reviews or fixes, and changes implemented by the
company?

☐ When enhancements have to be made to old system software that
has not been developed in accordance with the current standards,
what procedures are adopted to bring the documentation up-to-date?

2. Access to System Software Documentation:

☐ Describe how and where documentation of the functions of the
system software, including system generation reports, suppliers'
manuals, documentation of options selected, fixes applied,
descriptions of security features, and documentation of system
software designed or modified by the company, are held.

☐ Who is responsible for the custody and issue of system software
documentation?

☐ Who is authorized to have access to the documentation?

3. Approval of System Software Enhancements:

☐ Describe the procedures for selecting new system software,
evaluating the different options provided by the software, and
designing the operating procedures for its use.

☐ How are necessary enhancements to existing system software
identified?

☐ How are repairs to software (fixes) provided by the software supplier
reviewed for applicability?

☐ Who has the authority to approve new system software,
enhancements, and fixes in the following?
  • Department(s) that will make use of the software (unless covered
    by computer operations below)
  • Computer operations function
  • Quality assurance function

☐ What documentation is presented to the above functions for
approval?

☐ How are the approvals evidenced?

☐ How are the records of enhancements controlled to ensure that all
required enhancements are made within the required time frame?

4. Review of Vendor-Supplied System Software Enhancements:

☐ What procedures are used to review or test enhancements and
ensure that the enhancement does not affect other system software?

☐ Describe the involvement in system software review or testing of:

- System programmer(s) who implemented the software enhancement
- Computer operations function
- Department(s) that will use the software (if not covered by computer operations above)
- Quality assurance function
- Others (such as a separate review or testing group or the internal audit department)

☐ What documentation is produced in the process of supervising, reviewing, or testing the enhancement?

☐ What is the policy for the retention of testing documentation and test data files?

☐ When enhancements are made to system software (such as utilities, interrogation packages, sorts, or routines incorporated by the linkage editor) that are incorporated into applications, what procedures are used to ensure that the enhancements do not adversely affect the results produced by the application programs?

☐ Have all enhancements made during the current financial year been reviewed or tested in accordance with the installation standards?

5. Testing of System Software Designed or Modified by the Company:

☐ What procedures are used to test the system software and ensure that the enhancement does not affect other system software?

☐ Describe the involvement in system software testing of:

- System programmer(s) who implemented the software enhancement
- Computer operations function
- Department(s) that will use the software
- Quality assurance function
- Others (such as a separate review or testing group, the internal audit department)

☐ What documentation is produced in the process of testing the enhancements?

☐ What is the policy for the retention of testing documentation and test data files?

☐ When enhancements are made to system software (such as utilities, interrogation packages, sorts, or routines incorporated by the linkage editor) that are incorporated into applications, what procedures are used to ensure that the enhancements do not adversely affect the results produced by the application programs?

☐ Have all enhancements made during the current financial year been tested in accordance with the standards?

6. Unauthorized Enhancements. How are unauthorized amendments made to system software detected?

7. Urgent Modifications:

☐ Under what circumstances may urgent modifications, which bypass the normal procedures, be made to system software?

☐ Describe the procedures for making such modifications and recording their occurrence.

☐ What procedures are in force, either at the time the modification is made or at a subsequent time, to ensure that the modification is properly documented, reviewed or tested, and approved?

8. Acceptance of System Software:

☐ Who in the department(s) that will use the system software (usually the computer operations department in the case of system software) is responsible for giving the final approval to software enhancements for production use?

☐ How is this approval documented?

☐ Are there any software enhancements for which the users of the software are not required to give approval?

☐ When users give their approval, how do they ensure that
- The methods and scope of the reviews or tests are adequate?
- The results of the reviews or tests are satisfactory?
- Instructions for using the software have been appropriately prepared or amended?

☐ How are users notified of the effective date when the system software enhancements are to become operational?

9. Final Review and Approval of System Software Enhancements by the Data Processing Function:

☐ Prior to implementation of a system software enhancement, who is responsible for checking that the following are complete, up-to-date, and in accordance with the installation standards?
- System software documentation
- Job set-up and operating instructions

☐ How is this check documented?

☐ In the case of vendor-supplied software enhancements:
  - Who is responsible for checking that proper review or testing of the enhancement has taken place?
  - How is this check documented?

☐ In the case of system software designed or modified by the company:
  - Who is responsible for checking that testing has been properly carried out?
  - How is this check documented?
  - Who is responsible for checking that the department(s) that will make use of the software has approved it?
  - How is this check documented?

REVIEWING QUALITY ASSURANCE — CHECKLIST

The following relates to areas of the EDP review where a quality assurance (QA) function might be involved. When a separate review of the QA function is undertaken, the EDP review checklist can be completed using the areas of QA involvement. QA can be included in an EDP review by making a separate entry when QA is involved in the activities.

1. Organization of the EDP Function:

☐ Which personnel are involved in QA?

☐ What personnel policies are in place for this function?

☐ Are there written installation standards?

☐ Are there contracts?

2. Implementation and Maintenance of Systems:

☐ Are system and program documentation subject to QA?

☐ Is approval of system specifications subject to QA?

☐ Does testing of new applications meet QA requirements?

☐ Is approval of modifications to production programs involved?

☐ Is there control of approved program modifications from a QA standpoint?

☐ Is there testing of program modifications to meet QA standards?

☐ Are urgent modifications subject to the same requirements?

☐ Is final approval of applications and program modifications by the EDP function involved?

☐ Does cataloging of approved new applications and program modifications fall under QA?

3. **Job Set-Up, Scheduling, and Data Control.** Is QA concerned with data control and job set-up instructions?

4. **Computer Operations:**

☐ Are operating instructions in conformance with QA standards?

☐ Does update of production program libraries fall under this area?

5. **System Software Programming:**

☐ Does system software documentation have to be submitted to QA?

☐ Is there QA approval of system software enhancements?

☐ Does control of approved system software enhancements include QA?

☐ Does review of vendor-supplied system software enhancements include QA?

☐ Is testing of system software designed or modified by the company subject to QA?

☐ Do urgent modifications have to meet the same QA standards?

☐ Does acceptance of system software come into this category?

☐ Does final approval of system software enhancements by the EDP function have to meet QA requirements?

REVIEWING TELEPROCESSING SUPPORT — CHECKLIST

1. **Implementation and Maintenance of Teleprocessing (TP) Applications.** TP systems and applications should be subject to the same types of procedures for implementation and maintenance as are batch or other systems. Describe any differences in the authorization and control of TP application program development and maintenance compared with the rest of the EDP department (see above). In particular, what are the procedures for the following?

☐ Authorization of changes to the TP network or terminals.

☐ Authorization of changes to the TP system software.

☐ Authorization of changes to any password or security software.

☐ Notification to users of any changes affecting their applications.

☐ Describe how TP application programs are tested and how test results are reviewed.

☐ Describe any differences in the procedures for updating TP program libraries.

☐ Are TP application programs maintained on a separate program library?

2. TP Applications:

☐ List and describe the use of TP for financial accounting applications. For each application, record the following:
- TP software used (such as CICS)
- Types of communication lines used (such as leased or dial-up)
- Data base software used
- Numbers and type of terminals used (such as remote job entry (RJE))
- Use made of terminals (such as for inquiry or input)
- Location of the host computer
- Whether any edits, conversions, or other processing is carried out at the terminal

☐ List and describe the use of TP for program development and maintenance. Note especially:
- Type of software used (such as TSO, CMS)
- Number and location of terminals used

☐ Are there any master or administrative terminals that can modify controls or data that regular terminals cannot access?

☐ How is the use of the terminals controlled?

☐ Is there an approved schedule of transactions and applications that may use the TP system?

☐ Describe the procedures for ensuring that only authorized transactions and applications are processed.

3. Error Detection and Recovery Procedures:

☐ Describe the procedures for error detection and error recovery during transmissions to and from the host computer.

☐ How do the terminals and TP network account for all messages sent to and from the host computer?

☐ Does the TP network provide for a way to inform the terminal operator and/or the master terminal operator of possible lost messages?

☐ Do the terminals provide for a way to store messages from the terminal in the event of TP network or host computer failure?

☐ Is there a method of retransmitting these messages when the TP network is restarted?

☐ Is there a log of all messages sent to and from the terminals and the host computer?

☐ Are there adequate restart and recovery procedures in the event of the TP network or the host computer failure?

☐ Are the users notified of a network failure so they may re-enter any messages lost by the failure?

4. Use of Terminals:

☐ Are terminals and other communication equipment located in one area to prevent access by unauthorized individuals?

☐ Are terminals equipped with locks or other protective devices to prevent their use by unauthorized individuals?

☐ Are terminals equipped with multiple locks to control the transactions that may be authorized (such as master keys)?

☐ Describe the controls within the software that prevent unauthorized users from accessing the system.

☐ Are all terminals given a unique identification that is recognized by the system as the authorization for that terminal to access the network?

☐ Describe the procedures for setting or changing the definition of which terminals are authorized for use in each TP application. Where is that definition maintained? How is the definition protected against access by unauthorized persons?

☐ Are passwords or other authorization codes used to limit access to the TP system?

☐ Describe the procedures for adding, changing, and deleting passwords and/or other authorization codes enabling access to an application from a terminal.

☐ Where is the computer file of passwords maintained?

☐ How is the file protected?

☐ Is the password or other authorization code printed out or displayed when used?

☐ Who has access to the list of valid passwords?

☐ How often are passwords changed?

☐ Describe any special or additional passwords required for updating critical data elements or gaining access after normal business hours.

☐ How are passwords constructed?

☐ What controls exist within the software to prevent one authorized user from accessing the data files and programs of another authorized user?

☐ What action is taken when unauthorized users attempt to gain access to the system or when other violations are attempted/committed?

☐ Are terminals disabled if they are inactive for a predetermined period of time?

☐ Is the authority of the user periodically reverified?

☐ Where passwords are not used, describe the controls that
  • Restrict file access to authorized users, terminals, or jobs.
  • Restrict users, terminals, or jobs to the functions they are authorized to perform.

☐ How is access to important files restricted during periods when they are not under the control of the terminal or security software?

☐ If dial-up lines are used:
  • Are phone numbers periodically changed?
  • Are phone numbers listed on the terminals?
  • Are special "restricted" telephone numbers used to limit allowable terminal functions?
  • Is "call back" used to verify origination of calls?

☐ In relation to programmer terminals:
  • Can the terminals be used to obtain access to live programs or data files, either via interactive processing or by submission of batch jobs through the terminal?
  • Describe the procedures used to prevent programmer terminals from accessing live programs or data files.

5. Logging and Review of TP Activities:

☐ Is all significant network activity recorded in a log?

☐ Are the following significant activities recorded?
  • Successful and unsuccessful attempts to access the network
  • Disabling or disconnection of terminals
  • Reverification of user authorization

☐ Is a responsible official, outside the EDP department, responsible for the security of the TP network?

☐ Does this official periodically change passwords and other authorization codes?

☐ Does the same official ensure that the list of valid passwords is protected from disclosure to unauthorized individuals?

☐ Does this official periodically review the log of TP network activity to ensure that

- Unauthorized attempts to access the network are investigated?
- Successful attempts were by authorized users?
- Other unusual activity is properly investigated?

6. Distributed Processing:

☐ Obtain or prepare a description of the distributed processing network showing sites at which

- Remote processing may be performed.
- Data files are maintained.

☐ Regarding each remote processing site and the central processing facility, obtain or prepare a list of

- System software and application software in use at the site.
- Data files maintained and the transactions/applications processed.

☐ How does the system determine the site at which a particular transaction and/or application is to be processed?

☐ If data redundancy exists, how does the system or the user ensure that data is synchronized and reported only once in consolidated financial reports?

☐ In relation to processing carried out at remote sites, are application programs the same at each site?

- If so, describe the procedures to ensure that programs at different sites are and remain identical (such as distribution of load modules only or no remote compiler facilities).
- If not, describe the procedures to ensure that local programs interface properly with other processing sites in the network and operate in accordance with management's intentions.

☐ From an audit planning viewpoint, do either of the following require special arrangements?

- Ownership of remote processors by other than the organization
- Location of any processing facilities across international boundaries

REVIEWING DATA BASE ADMINISTRATION — CHECKLIST

1. Organization of the Data Base Function:

☐ Indicate which major computer-based applications use a data base system (such as IMS from IBM — examples here relate to the IMS system).

☐ Indicate the data base support products and packages in use.

☐ Include the particular features and adaptations in use of:
- Information Management System/Virtual Storage (IMS/VS)
- Application Development Facility (IMS/ADF)
- Data dictionary facilities
- Report generators and inquiry facilities

☐ Describe the organization of the data base support function.

☐ Include organization chart, job descriptions, and the division of responsibilities.

☐ Show who is responsible for the following:
- Data base administration and control
- Maintenance of the data base data dictionary
- Maintenance of the data base system or IMS libraries
- Maintenance of the data base or IMS systems
- Coding of program specification blocks (PSBs) and data base definitions (DBDs)

☐ Indicate any differences in the personnel policies relating to the data base support function.

☐ Indicate the installation standards regarding data base administration and support.

☐ Indicate the specific backup and recovery procedures applied to the following:
- System libraries
- Data bases

2. Data Base Documentation:

☐ Does documentation exist in accordance with the installation standards for all data bases, components, generating (GEN) options, dictionaries, and other DBA and system support functions?

☐ Describe any IMS documentation aids or documentation software products in use.

☐ Indicate whether there are any differences in the procedures for controlling the access to this documentation.

3. **Implementation and Maintenance of Data Base Applications.** Describe the following:

☐ Any differences in the authorization and control of data base application program development and maintenance

☐ The role of the data base support function in the maintenance of those applications

☐ How the applications are tested, and how the results of the tests are reviewed

☐ Any differences for updating these application program libraries

☐ The data base generation (IMS GEN) options in use

4. **Controls:**

☐ Describe the DBA's participation in the development of program specification blocks (PSBs) and data base definitions (DBDs) for data base (IMS) applications.

☐ Does the DBA approve all the processing options (PROCOPTs) for the various segments and fields within the data bases?

☐ When logical relationships are used, does the DBA explain to all affected user departments the effects of the various processing options (such as PROCOPTs) on the physical data involved in the logical relationship?

☐ Are separate production and test libraries maintained for DBD and PSB (and ACB — access method control block — when used) libraries?

☐ List the names of the libraries used for the following:
 • PSB
 • DBD
 • ACB (when used)

☐ Who has access to the above libraries?

☐ Who has access to the data base system (IMS) macro library?

☐ Are application programmers permitted access only to the PSBs required for testing their programs?

☐ Are there adequate procedures to ensure that only authorized programs, with authorized PSBs, are used to access production data bases?

5. Cataloging:

☐ Describe the procedures for segregating PSBs and DBDs in a test status from those being used by production programs.

☐ Describe the procedures that ensure that
- Correct PSBs and DBDs are transferred to production status.
- Unauthorized changes are not made to approved PSBs and DBDs between the time they are approved for implementation and the time they are placed in production libraries.

☐ Is a log maintained of all production PSBs and DBDs?

☐ Does this log include details about:
- Which data bases the PSBs use?
- Which program uses which PSBs?
- Program communications blocks (PCBs) contained in the PSB?
- PSB sensitivity to segments and fields in the data base?

☐ Are the PSB and DBD (and ACB when used) libraries periodically reviewed in order to ensure that no unauthorized changes have been made?

6. Standards:

☐ Describe the standards for the use of data language (DL/1) to access the data bases.

☐ Describe the procedures for handling the DL/1 status codes for application programs accessing the data bases.

7. Log:

☐ Are there any log records (IMS or SMF) maintained that record accesses to the data bases
- By programs not executing under the control of the data base (IMS) system?
- By programs executing under the control of the data base (IMS) system?

☐ Are there procedures to prevent or detect unauthorized accesses to the data bases?

☐ Are the system logs (IMS or SMF) controlled to prevent unauthorized access?

8. Utilities:

☐ What records are kept on the use of utilities and other similar programs such as the following?
- DL/1 test program

- Data base system file select and formatting programs
- Data base system (IMS) reorganization/load utilities
- Data base system (IMS) recovery utilities
- System log recovery program
- Data base mapping program
- The program that builds DBDs (DBDGEN)

☐ What controls are in effect over the use of these utilities?

☐ Who must authorize such use?

☐ What procedures are in effect to ensure that only duly authorized use occurs?

9. Libraries:

☐ Who is authorized to access the data base system (IMS) production libraries and what level of access is permitted to the following?
- PSB library
- DBD library
- Data base (IMS) macro library
- Data base system (IMS) library

☐ What are the procedures for preventing unauthorized accesses to the above libraries?

☐ Are there control procedures to detect unauthorized access?

☐ When password protection is used to prevent unauthorized access to programs and data files:
- Describe the procedures adopted.
- Who is responsible for the establishing and distributing of passwords?
- How is password security maintained?
- Are passwords periodically changed and, if so, how often?

☐ Who supervises, reviews, and approves the above? How are the results of the reviews and approvals documented?

SUMMARY

The EDP function is usually a major cost center, with an effect on most operating groups and management areas of an organization. Yet it is still often possible to improve controls over EDP operations, which is important for the organization as a whole. As a result of weak or improper controls over EDP, financial, computer, human, and physical resources can be misapplied. An inadequate response by the EDP department to user needs is another possible outcome. Using the information obtained from an operational review, management can allocate and redirect resources to build on the strengths of its EDP operation, instead of permitting control weaknesses to continue.

CHAPTER 7

The System Development Life Cycle

THE NEED FOR A SYSTEM DEVELOPMENT LIFE CYCLE

Whenever the need arises for a new system or for modifications to an existing one, the system development life cycle (SDLC) is a methodology that can be initiated and followed through each of its phases. This cycle starts with a perceived need and extends throughout the installation, evaluation, maintenance, and periodic review of the system. Following the steps in the cycle can be particularly helpful because they can be applied to the modification of existing systems or programs as well as to developing new computer applications. There are many SDLC models; a widely used and effective methodology is presented in this chapter. Following each phase of this cycle ensures that the new or revised system meets the organization's needs and is properly implemented.

As an example, one company spent a year and a half developing a new billing system without following a set methodology for system development. By the time it was complete, the company had hired a new controller. After reviewing the system, the controller found it produced an insufficient information trail, had no way to balance key reports to input documents, and had inadequate controls over the data being entered. Since the system was designed without following established procedures, there had been no real analysis of controls and information requirements. The electronic data processing (EDP) department had created what they thought the old controller requested, but it was not what the organization needed. There was little documentation of the request and no way to be sure what had happened. The system was scrapped and the project had to be started all over again; the results were inadequate information, a lack of control, and large expenditures of time and money.

This kind of situation occurs more often than might be expected. However, the problems and frustrations that arise may be avoided if system developers follow proper procedures and document their work. These standards are maintained by following the phases of the SDLC. There are many ways to describe the SDLC, and the steps taken may differ to meet the various requirements of different organizations. The SDLC given here is a model. The methodology is a guide but may be changed and modified as necessary to meet the needs of a particular environment.

This chapter describes the organizational arrangements and SDLC procedures that are beneficial in developing new computer applications or modifying existing systems or programs.

WHO SHOULD PARTICIPATE IN THE SYSTEM DEVELOPMENT LIFE CYCLE?

Today's EDP systems are increasingly complex. As a result, particular attention must be paid to the roles of individuals in the user and the EDP departments, such as the system support and operations people. Which personnel will authorize and review both the system or program descriptions and the results of testing the finished programs, or the entire system, is an important consideration. Equally important to the success of a system are the final acceptance, testing, and implementation procedures and determining who will perform these procedures. An SDLC methodology addresses these concerns.

To support the need for a clear definition of system design methodology, observe what happened when the XYZ Company decided to automate the purchasing accounts payable system. This function had been performed manually but its volume and complexity now warranted a computerized process.

The controller, who had been with the company only a few months and had little experience with computers, assumed that systems were designed by data processing. When it came time to design the system, the EDP manager, as the predominant member of the team, specified a system that fit easily into the EDP operation and met most of the needs of the accounting department. The purchasing department did not have time to get involved in the design of a system; they asked data processing to show it to them when they could use it.

The resulting system was tested and implemented. The user departments all signed off on the system. During the parallel conversion from the existing manual system to the new computerized system, the user departments got so much paperwork that they were not as careful in their review as they should have been and simply agreed that it was acceptable. As they signed off, they assumed that the EDP manager could make any changes that they might want after using the new system for a while.

Thus, the system became operational with the following problems: a lack of adequate user controls, lack of easy access to information, and difficulty in producing reports. During the course of the next year, the EDP manager fixed all of the problems as they arose. Unfortunately, this required so much of the department's resources that other new systems work was delayed. The existing system had more and more patches in it, and some of the system still had to be reworked.

The operations manual, written for the system as it was originally designed, was never rewritten; handwritten amendments were merely added to it. These notes from the user departments were sometimes accurate and sometimes legible, but not always both. And, of course, no one was sure who had written what, so no one could go back and ask about a particular note.

The inevitable consequence was that the user departments were not happy with the new system. The system did not work exactly as the instructions said it would, and they began to think it was not as easy to use as their old manual system had been.

This example demonstrates the need for an adequate system plan and the need to check on participant roles, properly control the system, and provide full documentation.

To fully understand and address the concerns of everyone involved in

EDP systems, there should be companywide representatives participating in systems planning and development. This involvement frequently takes the form of a company-established high-level strategy and policymaking "EDP Steering Committee." To work best, such a committee typically includes user department officials (such as the controller), senior EDP officials, and the internal auditor (with EDP audit support). With the support of a staff of specialists, the steering committee helps set company policy. Then an implementation group or project team participates in the selection of computer hardware, assigns priorities to system development projects, and performs reviews at various stages in the system development and implementation life cycle.

The role of the internal auditor in the SDLC is that of a monitor and an adviser. The SDLC can be viewed as a natural part of the overall EDP management.

Figure 7-1 shows the cycle in the EDP framework. This figure depicts a typical system planning management structure, segmented into the concerns of the EDP department as a whole and the fact that the department must fit into the overall corporate plan.

The EDP department's functions should be clarified in order for a systems plan to work. The auditor's role in relation to this department is effective in the project organization area as monitor and adviser to new systems development, as mentioned previously. However, this does not mean that the auditor may not be called on to provide advice, counsel, or to monitor system activities whenever such support is required.

The SDLC can be thought of as a methodology that comes into play whenever it is needed. It is a tool to aid management in controlling progress on systems projects. The cycle is closely related to the other elements of EDP project management: planning, organization, and control. The SDLC can help provide a way to divide these tasks into manageable steps.

THE SYSTEM DEVELOPMENT LIFE CYCLE AS A COST-EFFICIENT MANAGEMENT TOOL

Once an awareness is gained of the different phases of the SDLC, it is possible to understand why following such a methodology is one of the most cost-effective procedures in data processing. It has been estimated that a major portion of the cost of a system over its useful life is incurred for maintenance after the system becomes operational. If the system is well-developed and fully functional as a result of following the steps in the SDLC, the maintenance costs should be lower. On the other hand, if little attention is given to the SDLC in the creation of a system, excessive maintenance costs can be incurred in a couple of months if the reworking of major features is necessary. For example, if a system is built without adequate controls, it is very costly to put the controls in after the system is already in production.

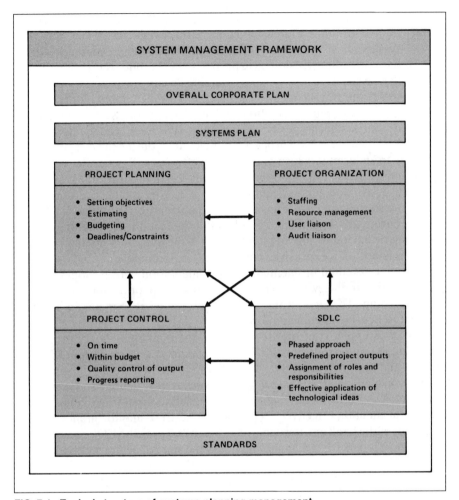

FIG. 7-1 Typical structure of systems planning management

Where controls are inadequate, the results can be expensive in other ways as well. For example, where controls over individual transactions in applications are missing, a seemingly minor error can have major ramifications. In a recent case, a major city's budget was sent into total disarray by a single wrong entry: The value of a home was entered as $510,035,500 instead of $35,500. It is thought that this happened when a computer terminal operator entered both the transaction code and the dollar amount in the dollar amount field. Using this assumed income from a multimillion dollar property, the city and its schools' administrators planned to spend $2 million they would not receive. It took so long to discover this that it was too late to change some of the spending decisions. In addition to having to depart from the school board's position of not requiring a state loan to balance the budget for the first time in five years, the city administration suffered public embarrassment, lack of income, the need to review all of its existing information for a similar occurence, and a perceived loss of millions of dollars in property tax revenue. A problem such as this could have easily been avoided by building an edit check into the program that processes the transactions.

During the pre-implementation review phase of the SDLC, an auditor can monitor the system at specific checkpoints to ensure that adequate controls are in place and will function properly. For example, during the design phase it is critical to determine which reports the software will generate, since the reports must provide the right kind of information in order for the controls to be effective. An adequate system of controls can be established during the system's design phase. It is much more economical to establish a system of controls during this stage than to build it after the fact; this helps eliminate the possibility of having to provide controls after the system is up and running. Redesign is not only expensive, but difficult to accomplish.

Another potential problem area is documentation, which should be adequate to maintain the system. The consequences of poor documentation may be far-reaching. Throughout the SDLC, it is important to maintain accurate and comprehensive documentation.

As an example, controls are needed in the banking industry over ever-increasing computerized operations. The adequate documentation of these controls and their assessment has become essential. In general, to help assess controls, an EDP audit manual can specify policies, procedures, and standards. The manual can describe all the activities needed to monitor and manage the EDP audit function effectively. The role of the EDP auditor in meeting the objectives of the bank and the department as specified in the EDP audit charter can be included. Such a manual might contain the following sections:

- Internal audit objectives
- EDP audit management
- Planning
- Reporting
- Standards and management policies
- Staffing policies
- Procedures and work programs for computer-assisted audit techniques
- Guidelines for audit software evaluation and selection

Once in use, such a manual can help a bank meet regulatory requirements through standardized audit procedures that test the controls in place over its EDP environment.

AUDITOR'S ROLE IN THE SYSTEM DEVELOPMENT LIFE CYCLE

A consideration of the auditor is that management has both a plan and allocated resources for each phase of the system development life cycle. Everything should be done according to a logical plan. There should be a full definition of the phases, including both the organization required and the resources available to accomplish it. Then, the internal auditor ensures the phase is carried out as defined. As each phase is completed, it can be properly signed off as proof of completion before proceeding to the next step.

The internal auditor should be aware of the danger of overinvolvement. Sometimes the auditor is asked to actually do the work instead of monitoring and advising. A good working knowledge of the development function and its proper management helps prevent this from happening. For example, when it is stated who should approve each step, there can and should be authorized sign-off on new systems. Systems are basically management's responsibility; management enforces system standards, and the internal auditor monitors adherence to those standards.

During the course of the SDLC, an auditor should, or may

- Review the feasibility study.
- Review the process used to select any new hardware or software.
- Monitor compliance with system development standards.
- Review the controls being designed into the new system.
- Evaluate the reporting, input, and processing features to ensure the adequacy of controls over completeness, accuracy, and authorization.
- Review the system design to ensure an adequate audit or information trail.
- Review and possibly reperform the testing plans and procedures.
- Evaluate the system at a test site or during parallel processing.
- Review and possibly test the conversion procedures.
- Review the adequacy of documentation.
- Perform a post-implementation review to help identify areas for future improvement.

PHASES OF THE SYSTEM DEVELOPMENT LIFE CYCLE

With the support and involvement of the people whose work will affect, or be affected by, the system development, the phases of the SDLC can proceed properly. Requirements for the system should be clearly defined. They are

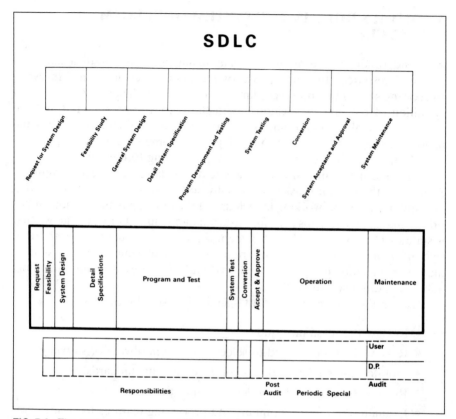

FIG. 7-2   The system development life cycle phases

based on the perceived needs of the people who will use the system and on the job the system must accomplish. At this point, the system is completely flexible, since nothing has actually been done.

After defining the requirements, system building can take place. In this area, some limited changes may be made after the actual work has started if it is realized that something has not been included or certain controls are not in place. Once this phase is complete, system implementation begins. At this point, it is essentially too late to make extensive amendments.

Once the system is implemented, amendments for control or to rectify problems that arise in the day-to-day operation can be made, once they have been approved and authorized. If such changes are to be made, they can follow the steps in the cycle, starting at the beginning with defining the requirements.

The phases of the cycle fit into the broad definition in the preceding paragraphs, but in the approach presented here they are further broken down into more concrete, specific steps. (See Figure 7-2 for an illustration of these steps within their environment.) These steps are clearly separated and can be defined both in terms of what needs to be done and who should be involved in doing it; they include a request for system design, a feasibility study, the general systems design, the detailed system specifications, program development and testing, system testing, conversion, system acceptance and approval, and operations and maintenance.

Request for System Design

User departments, such as the payroll department, general accounting department, or the treasurer's office, are the most frequent source of requests for system design, but they are not the only source of requests. New application projects are often initiated by the EDP staff to provide greater efficiency or cost-effective use of processing time. An application in current use may need to be enhanced or modified.

System design requests may be based on a real need, a change in a law, a regulatory requirement, or even a dream or fantasy. However it originates, and whomever it originates with, the request should be in writing so that it can be considered and properly examined by the organization. Normally, the EDP department designates one person to receive these requests. The idea can be processed and recorded and, if warranted, prepared for the next phase. It is a good idea to find out how such requests are initiated and tracked in an organization. A common problem in many organizations is the lack of a set methodology for requesting a system design, which can lead to haphazard handling of requests.

Regardless of how the request arises, authorization and approval by a responsible official of the user department should be required, not only at initiation of the process but also at the completion of stages or important checkpoints during the SDLC.

As each checkpoint is reached, approval is based on whether the evolving system truly meets the needs of the user organization. Another important consideration in giving or withholding approval is whether the system includes adequate internal controls that are consistent with management's objectives.

Important points where approval is warranted are:

- At the completion of the feasibility study stage
- After developing the general system design
- After preparing the detailed system specifications
- As each program is "final tested"
- After system testing
- After conversion
- At system acceptance

Feasibility Study

Careful and logical planning should be emphasized in development of EDP systems. Attention should be focused on the information needs of the entire organization prior to developing computerized systems. A feasibility study can be used to establish whether the user department and the systems analyst can reconcile the perceived needs in terms of the worth of the proposed system versus the contribution it will make toward the achievement of the organization's objectives. Sometimes a system request cannot be justified within the overall objectives, no matter how useful it would be to one part of the organization. Typically, a cost/benefit analysis is prepared as part of the feasibility study, which measures the suitability and economic realities of the proposed system.

Through the mechanism of the feasibility study performed by appropriate personnel designated by the EDP steering committee, considerations about whether or not the application is workable can be made. For example, does the existing hardware have sufficient capacity for the new application to run? Are there enough personnel to run it, or will more people be required? Will the new program or application require that hardware be purchased? If so, is the organization ready to do so and how much will it cost? Finally, how does the new system request fit into the organization's long-term plan, and how does it relate to existing priorities? All of these questions should be addressed by a feasibility study in order for the responsible parties in user, EDP, and other concerned departments to have enough information to decide on the appropriate action to take.

In short, a feasibility study should

- Analyze the current system, identifying specific problems and needs.
- Provide an overall, simple analysis of what is involved.
- Determine costs and benefits, times, schedules, and resources.
- Determine the practicality of the basic idea.
- Determine whether the request warrants further consideration.
- Have user and EDP departments sign off to approve or authorize its findings.

As a final step after the feasibility study, the auditors should be informed about any potential changes to existing systems or any new systems that may be created as a result of the study.

The study should be retained, even if the project request is rejected. Then future requests for the same project will not incur additional costs to reevaluate it, since the decision will already have been documented and can be referred to and brought up to date.

General System Design

Once the system request has gone through a feasibility study and there has been sign-off and agreement that the project should proceed, it must be proved that the idea, concept, or change can be accomplished. At this stage, audit, data processing, and users should be involved.

In most cases, the implementation of a requested idea can be accomplished in many different ways. It is always a good idea to prepare a number of alternate designs so that the benefits and disadvantages of each can be compared.

The auditor should ensure that a procedure for this phase exists, that competent EDP and user representatives are assigned to work on this phase, and that the end result is understood and signed off by the system's users.

The question of whether a system is feasible is addressed, in part, by a systems analyst. The duties of the systems analyst are to

- Fully define the user's need, translating it into system terms.
- Review the present methods of meeting that need.
- Determine the effects on the user environment of installing a new or modified system.
- Determine a time frame and plan to accomplish the system design.
- Set forth functional specifications for the system designer to use in creating the system.

As a rule, a good general system design provides a basis for the parties involved (user, auditor, analyst, programmer, computer operator) to understand their respective responsibilities during the system's development and subsequent operation.

The information flow should be clearly depicted, with control points and processes identified. The input, cutoff, output, processing, and reporting should be addressed. The analysis should go to each user department. The users should then sign off when certain the system will do what was requested.

Conversion techniques (see section entitled "Conversion," later in this chapter) and parallel processing considerations should be focused on at this stage, since they will have an effect on the overall project timing. The major checkpoints, providing the steering committee with the necessary milestones for measuring the project's progress, are often established at this stage.

Detailed System Specifications

Detailed system design involves translating the approved general system design into a set of specifications for programming and implementing the system. It includes the actual programming information that tells what each program will do, which sequence the programs will follow, which files are used, which reports are generated, and which controls are built into the system.

The detailed system specification is probably the most important phase in the cycle. Viewed as a contract, it describes the entire request, how it will be accomplished, and who, in addition to programmers, has responsibility. These specifications encompass the total system, from origin through final use, including testing and training.

The system specifications normally include the following documents:

- A system narrative of the objectives, the major functions to be performed, and the relationship of the major functions (see Figure 7-3).
- A system flowchart showing the programs, data files, and reports of the system (see Figure 7-4).
- Data record layouts showing the contents planned for each data record (card, tape, disk) and file in the system (see Figure 7-5).
- Screen formats showing which fields are fixed, which are taken from the data base, and which are entered by the user. For user-modified fields, the edit and control functions to be applied are described.
- Data element definitions describing the content of each data field in each record, its characteristics (alphabetic, numeric, alphanumeric), its code structure or value, its source, and its intended use (see Figure 7-6).
- Report layouts showing the formats and data content of each report produced.
- Detailed specifications for each program in the system (see Figure 7-7).
- Procedures for gathering and preparing data, establishing controls and reconciling differences, and converting data to machine-sensible form.
- Definition and documentation of procedures for equipment operation, data file backup, and retention.
- A test plan identifying methodologies and responsibilities for test data creation, execution, and approval. The plan should include the steps necessary to ensure that programs function correctly, both individually and in combination with each other.
- Cost/benefit analysis.
- Time schedule.

Detailed system design specifications should be reviewed and approved before programming is started. This approval should come from a responsible official of the user department(s) and from the steering committee.

BK01CAAG - System Editor

Objectives

This program processes all client converted files (i.e., Savings Transaction, Loan Transaction, Savings Master and Mortgage Loan Master), and validates each field of the input record.

The edit program generates 2 severity level errors: Warning and Fatal. Records containing warning errors are accepted by the editor, i.e., passed to subsequent processing. Fatal error records are purged.

As a result of executing BK01CAAG the Specialist is:

. aware of any errors or possible data problems in the converting of the client's file prior to execution of other system programs. This avoids subsequent abnormal terminations due to incorrect field values and definitions as well as wasted computer time.

. alleviated of identifying a file as "Savings" or "Loan" in subsequent program processing.

. aware of the exact number of records contained in each file. This aids in the determination of work file and sort space calculations.

. provided with an additional detail report of records contained on the transaction files.

Files used:

The input files to the BK01CAAG program are as follows:

. Converted Client Savings Transaction File (SYS011): client savings transactions converted into the Banking format.

. Converted Client Loan Transaction File (SYS012): client loan trans-actions converted into the Banking format.

. Converted Client Savings Master File (SYS013): beginning or ending period client savings master converted into the Banking format.

. Converted Client Mortgage Loan Master File or Installment Loan Master File (SYS014): beginning or ending period client loan master converted into the Banking format. The Payment Code (Inactive Interest) in position 254 determines the file type. If the code is "Y" or "N", the Installment Loan Master File is assumed. If the code is "S", "M", "Q", "A" or blank, the Mortgage Loan Master File is assumed and a slightly different output file is produced.

FIG. 7-3 Specimen of a typical system narrative, describing a banking audit system package

In detailed system specifications work, the auditor should ensure that this phase has been accomplished as planned. This includes checking all of the documentation listed previously.

The auditor can be thought of as an impartial liaison between users and data processing to ensure that users get the system they both want and need. This is especially important when users must check technical documentation they cannot understand. The auditor can help interpret the specifications so that the user knows what the system will and will not do.

(text continues on 7-18)

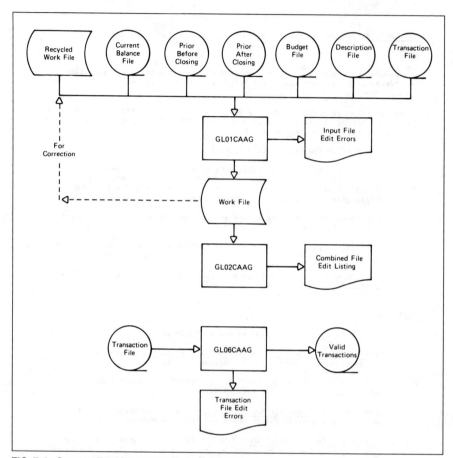

FIG. 7-4   System flowchart for a general ledger program package, depicting the programs, data files (input), and reports (output)

```
File Layouts
                                                                        Data
       Field      Field              Position        Data    Dec.    Element
       No.        Description        From  To  Length  Type    Pos.    Def. No.

Work file - WRKFILE, RWRKFILE, WRKFILE2, WRKFILE3

                  Label records are standard,
                  Block contains 6 records (3168 characters),
                  Records and blocks are fixed length.

       1          Company number        1    3    3     X       -         1
       2          Subsidiary number     4    6    3     X       -         2
       3          Financial line number 7    9    3     X       -         3
       4          Account number:                                         4
                  a) Primary           10   12    3     X       -
                  b) Intermediate      13   15    3     X       -
                  c) Basic             16   20    5     X       -
       5          Description:
                  a) Company           21   35   15     X       -         5
                  b) Subsidiary        36   50   15     X       -         6
                  c) Financial line    51   65   15     X       -         7
                  d) Account           66   95   30     X       -         8
       6          Balance:
                  a) Current           96  108   13     S       2         9
                  b) Prior after closing 109 121 13     S       2
                  c) Prior before closing 122 134 13    S       2
                  d) Total transactions 135 147  13     S       2
       7          Totals by month:                                       10
                  a) Current (1)      148  160   13     S       2
                  b) Month -   2      161  173   13     S       2
                  c) Month -   3      174  186   13     S       2
                  d) Month -   4      187  199   13     S       2
                  e) Month -   5      200  212   13     S       2
                  f) Month -   6      213  225   13     S       2
                  g) Month -   7      226  238   13     S       2
                  h) Month -   8      239  251   13     S       2
                  i) Month -   9      252  264   13     S       2
                  j) Month - 10      265  277   13     S       2
                  k) Month - 11      278  290   13     S       2
                  l) Month - 12      291  303   13     S       2
                  m) Month - 13      304  316   13     S       2
                  n) All other       317  329   13     S       2
       8          Budget total current 330 342  13     S       2        11
       9          Budget by month:                                      12
                  a) Current (1)      343  355   13     S       2
                  b) Month -   2      356  368   13     S       2
                  c) Month -   3      369  381   13     S       2
                  d) Month -   4      382  394   13     S       2
                  e) Month -   5      395  407   13     S       2
                  f) Month -   6      408  420   13     S       2
                  g) Month -   7      421  433   13     S       2
                  h) Month -   8      434  446   13     S       2
                  i) Month -   9      447  459   13     S       2
```

FIG. 7-5 Specimen data record (file) layout

Data Element Definitions

    General

Data element definitions for each of the elements on the nine possible types of
files used by the general ledger package are described in sequence of the file
layouts. Many data element definitions can occur on different files, but
they are only described once. Editing of each field is carried out by GL01CAAG
or GL06CAAG. The data element definitions for the ADJOURN file are described
under the parameter card section dealing with GP09, consolidating journal
entries.

In general, the contents of alphanumeric fields should be left justified and
consist of at least one non-space character (e.g., company number). Numeric
fields must be right justified with correct decimal alignment. Numeric fields
have leading spaces transformed to zero prior to any edit. Fields are edited in
GL01CAAG in accordance with the presence indicators. Fields occurring on a
file not designated as the origin of the particular element by the presence
indicators will be ignored.

Editing of the transaction file elements differs between GL01CAAG and GL06CAAG.
These differences are referred to in the individual data element definitions.

    1 - Company Number

The General Ledger Package envisages that the client's file will contain records
for multiple companies and perhaps multiple subsidiaries. The sum of the
balances for all records for a particular company should be zero. Single
companies may still use the package except for the consolidation portion. In
this case, the company number should be filled at the time of reformatting with
any valid constant character. It could be an unprintable character. The field
is the first part of the match key with other files in the package. It is
edited to ensure that it is not all spaces, else,

        E 0008 Company number is all spaces

will issue and the program will prematurely terminate.

In GL06CAAG, this field is also edited to ensure it is not all spaces, but
instead of E 0008,

        W 0171 - Company number is all spaces - rec dropped

is issued. The program prints the first fify records having this error. After
fifty, the program ceases to print the errors but does not prematurely terminate.
The record in error will not be written to the output file.

FIG. 7-6   Partial data element definition

Objectives

The major objective of GL01CAAG is to produce a work file in a syntactically and logically correct format containing all required information from the reformatted client's files, plus supplemental information supplied by the specialist. The file produced will be used by subsequent programs for the production of reports which are useful to the auditor. The detailed functions of the program are as follows:

. Read and edit the parameter cards.

. Read the six reformatted client files and, depending on presence indicator information, match records of these files to produce an output workfile.

. Analyze each of the fields on the client files for syntactical correctness and report on violations.

. Use parameter card information (e.g. financial line attribution) to add information not provided on the original files.

. Provide the possibility at a later time to recycle the work file and either correct originally erroneous information inserted in a previous run of GL01CAAG, or add information not available on the original running of GL01CAAG.

. Provide record totals for run to run controls with the reformatting program and subsequent General Ledger Package programs.

In any given application of the package it is possible, but not recommended, to by-pass GL01CAAG entirely. Information as to the record layout and data element definitions of fields in the work file is provided in the file description section. If the specialist elects not to run GL01CAAG, other programs, which rely on a valid work file, may abnormally terminate or produce incorrect information.

Files Used

The program uses a maximum of six reformatted client files (CURBAL, PREBECL, PREAFCL, BUDGET, DESFILE, TRANFILE), a recycled work file that has been previously produced by GL01CAAG (RWRKFILE), three temporary work files (TWORK1, TWORK2, TWORK3) and an output work file (WRKFILE). The record layouts of these files, except for the TWORK files, is set out in the file description section of this guide. The TWORK files are temporary work files used for the duration of the job. Space considerations for the output and TWORK files are set out in the operating instructions section of this guide. In addition to these disk or tape files, the program also uses a parameter card file and the printer.

Only a minimum of one reformatted client file is necessary to run the program. The file descriptions of the client files have been constructed in such a manner than information is repeated in a fixed position on different files. For example, the budget amounts can be found on either the current balance file or the budget file.

FIG. 7-7   Specimen detailed specifications for a program

Some problems to watch for are the following:

- Substitution of a vague narrative in place of actual detailed specifications.
- Dragging detailed system specifications out while data processing is already programming. (Without specifications to follow, they may write the wrong programs, or write the programs wrong.) Program writing before detailed specifications may be done when implementation is phased.
- Ignoring purchased programs and program packages from other sources that can be just as useful as, and sometimes cheaper than, assuming that programs must all be coded internally.
- Neglect of non-EDP elements in the specifications, stemming from the pervasive assumption that everything of importance is done by data processing. For example, specification of controls on user input are just as significant as what is in the programs.
- A plan that asks the user to sign off when documentation does not exist. This can lead to untold complications, since the user has agreed to specifications that have not been written. The user has no control over the results.

The auditor can work to ensure that these problems will not occur. More specific roles in the creation of detailed system specifications are described later in this chapter.

The auditor can review this phase in order to

- Provide advice with respect to the control methodologies envisaged.
- Document the audit understanding, evaluate the controls, and design the audit tests to be performed on the system.
- Establish the planning and timing of the implementation control review.
- Evaluate the impact of the audit function on the implementation of the proposed system.

The EDP department may not appreciate the significance of computerized audit routines. Yet, if these audit routines are built into a system, the routines to produce the audit reports will be available when needed. Data processing may assume these reports can be created easily be reprocessing the original data for a particular period under review, but they may not realize that this frequently cannot be done in the time that is available.

If an external auditor asks to review selected materially significant transactions, then a program — already in place — that produces these transactions in report form is especially helpful. With the internal auditor's suggestion during development that these reports will be needed at some time in the future, the system design will include them from the outset. Having built such audit routines into the system will be helpful to everyone in the long run. One such audit report is the accounts receivable confirmation letter, which is frequently requested. As an accounts receivable function is being developed, planning ahead will include this as an optional report.

Program Development and Testing

This phase deals with both the development and testing of the individual programs, whether they are purchased packages or written by internal programmers. For the actual coding, or program writing, details of each program and the interrelationship of the programs within the system are on the specifications from the systems analyst. Then the actual coding can take place according to the system design.

The overall program development plan is frequently created by a programmer analyst in the EDP department. If any existing or purchased programs are to be used, they must be placed in their proper sequence and linked or joined to the rest, usually by code written for the purpose. Then individual programs are written by the programmers.

Program writing involves the translation of program specifications, which are provided by the systems and programmer analysts, into a machine-readable format. The computer's instructions are the programs. A variety of high-level computer languages are used for this purpose, among which are Common Business Oriented Language (COBOL), BASIC, and FORTRAN. The actual machine instructions are produced, usually, by a compiler or interpreter in the computer that translates these languages into the bits or binary digits, 0's and 1's, of machine-understandable code.

Programs are tested in accordance with the plan set forth in the detailed design specifications. These tests are usually split into program tests and system tests. Test data to be used is developed by the system design team, most often the user and the systems analyst. Program testing should not be left to programmers alone because they tend to create data that tests only their understanding of how the program or system is intended to function and, at that, only the EDP portion of the system. If the programmer has misunderstood any of the specifications, the tests may not meet system requirements. They will only show that the program does what the programmer expected it to do.

For the preceding reason, the user department should be involved in the tests, and user department approval after testing should be required. Test data and results should be retained and used to test future modifications of the system. This retention of information provides the auditor with a tool to determine the integrity of the programs or system in the future, when test data can be reused with known results.

The data to be tested is developed, along with the "right" or expected responses to each test, by the team, which generally includes both EDP personnel and users. The users may be in the best position to design the test data. (How can I make the system do what it should? How can I make the system fail?) The users know what they want the system to do and can help create tests accordingly.

Any purchased programs or program packages should be tested in a similar manner, according to the particular situation.

A side benefit of user involvement at this stage is that it will take these users less time to learn to run or use the system when it becomes operational. Proper documentation must be prepared and maintained at this stage. Once all programs work and are linked together, the next phase of the SDLC can begin.

System Testing

System testing is the next phase in the cycle. The purpose of system testing is to determine if the system will perform as expected. This is the final effort of warranting that all previous work has been done and the anticipated results have been achieved.

Test data of many types are usually used. These include checks that the logic of various individual programs link together to form the integrated system described in the detailed specification requirements.

System testing should be a joint effort of the user and the EDP departments. Once adequate system testing has been done, there is assurance that the programs and data files operate in concert with each other, are in conformity with design specifications, and satisfy the requirements of the user departments.

The test plan should include testing of both the manual and computerized phases of the total system. In effect, the design and completion of an adequate system test is a project in itself. This is sometimes called end-to-end testing, in which the conditions of production are simulated.

If there is an existing system, parallel testing may be done. The same data is used to see whether the results are essentially the same. They may be in a different format or have fewer features than the new or enhanced system, but the results should be the same. In addition to the valid transactions and common situations the system is designed to handle, such tests should also take into account the effects of invalid transactions and unusual conditions.

Conversion

Since most new systems are replacements of older systems and/or extensions of current systems, great care must be taken to ensure that the files are converted accurately and completely. The EDP auditor can make a major contribution to the conversion phase of the cycle. This is an important area, in which audit involvement can be a crucial factor. The integrity of data files is essential and should be maintained during the conversion process.

Conversion may involve converting manual accounting records into machine-readable data files, or converting one set of data files into another. Since errors can occur during the conversion process, strict control procedures should be established. These are designed to prevent inaccurate or unauthorized changes, and they ensure accurate and complete results. Sample controls are record counts, one-for-one checking, edit checks, hash totals, amount totals, and independent program comparison; all these controls can be used to reconcile data on the converted file with the original manual records or data files.

At minimum, correct conversion, as assured by auditing tests, should assure that all data is retained and that the records remain exactly equivalent.

An example of conversion, and an unexpected problem that arose, can be found at a company that installed a new purchasing system. This new system analyzed 24 months of prior sales per product to determine an economic order quantity to restock inventory. The old system only used 12 months of data for this analysis. To create the new system files, two years of data were merged. The auditor reviewed the program that converted the data and found that the record count control totals matched and a hash total of all units balanced. The system was signed off for production.

Seven months later, the purchasing department was called in to explain what looked like inefficient ordering, after the internal audit department had reviewed the number of stockouts and items with low inventory turnover. The purchasing department pointed to the computer reports which showed what to order and had been used for their decisions.

As it turned out, the system testing had not uncovered a logic error in the conversion program. Although all of the total files added up correctly, the actual merging of data was out of sync by one record. The sales of 12 months of apples had been merged with 12 prior months of apricots. Thus, the totals proved out consistently, but the wrong items had been merged.

Frequently, program logic errors such as this are the hardest to detect. They can create the most damage while providing a false sense of security. Since the totals seemed correct, all the parties approved the conversion and signed off on it. In reality there was a serious flaw in the system.

System Acceptance and Approval

System acceptance and approval is the final step before a system is put into operation. Now the question is whether the system does exactly what the user agreed it should do, as described in the detailed system specifications. When the user agrees that the system does what was wanted, it should be signed off as the system is accepted. However, sometimes the new system may not be approved for operation. For example, the operations staff may not approve of actually running the new system because processing takes too long.

For this reason, before a system is used in daily operations, it should receive final approval from everyone who was involved in the system design and development; this includes the user department, the EDP department, steering committee, and appropriate levels of management. Typically, at this stage, reviews have been conducted of the final test results, conversion procedures, parallel processing, documentation, and changes from the design specifications.

Now the final system test should detect any processing errors within the system and correct them before the system is placed into production. This is called acceptance or system testing, which should be user-supervised but, as stated before, is a joint effort of the user and EDP departments and possibly of management.

The final system test should be an exhaustive test of the entire system. It ensures the readiness of the departments involved to absorb the system's input, processing, and output requirements. It is extremely important that all phases are tested item-by-item at this stage of the SDLC. Often, only daily operations are tested, without giving due recognition to different periods' processing requirements. For example, testing the production of the weekly payroll and failing to adequately test the quarterly and annual processing should not be allowed. All processing should be tested during this phase.

Parallel processing for a selected time period is recommended, whether the system is replacing a manual system or an existing automated system. Data gathering, preparation, control, processing, and reconciliation procedures should be carried out by the same individuals and under the same conditions that will exist when the new system is installed. If the system is replacing an existing automated version, it may be feasible to process actual data through both systems for the parallel time period. Then the results can be compared and reconciled to determine the reliability of the new system.

System Maintenance

System maintenance is usually the longest phase in a system's life. It is a major function of both data processing and users. Changing requirements and the need for improvements to the system can consume a major portion of the EDP programming budget. As discussed at the beginning of this chapter, these costs can be kept in line by proper controls over system development.

Maintenance takes place when new requirements arise after the system is up and running. However, procedures to control the maintenance phase should be in effect and operating before any new needs arise. There should also be standardized procedures and controls over the cataloging of production programs.

Maintenance can be considered a minicycle of the entire SDLC, although a feasibility study is not necessary for minor changes such as a new report title or heading.

Of course, needed and approved changes must take place. During the course of system development, and later during use, changes to some of the programs may be inevitable. Reasons for such modifications and enhancements might be changes in policy, business environment, regulatory agency reporting requirements, computer processing considerations, or the discovery of programming errors. Some changes are essential; others are desirable and subject to regular evaluation criteria.

In any event, implementation of modifications requires specific identification and written documentation of the modification request, which is usually made by the user. In some instances a request of modification is initiated by the EDP department. Regardless of the source, written approval and authorization of the modification request should be obtained from the user and EDP departments and from the steering committee.

Appropriate procedures regarding program and system testing, approval of test results, maintenance of documentation, and implementation should be followed, just as they are in the initial SDLC. If system modifications are not adequately controlled, the integrity of the system may be compromised by unauthorized changes in programs, procedures, or data.

For example, one such unauthorized change was made with all the best intentions. A programmer was making an authorized change to a program and noticed some code that was causing an operational inefficiency. It did not seem to relate directly to the program in question. Without checking further, the programmer decided on immediate corrective actions, and so, two changes were made instead of one. The authorized change was duly tested and accepted. The performance change was so minimal that the programmer did not even bother to write it up.

At the quarter end, the quarter-to-date totals came out with unreadable garbage records included. What the programmer had excised was the imbedded program switch that handled quarterly processing. All the quarterly data had to be recreated. Luckily, the original documentation permitted restoration of the missing code.

Naturally, all system modifications and enhancements should be tested prior to being implemented. As previously mentioned, test data created during the design phase should be retained for just this purpose. The user departments should compare the new test results with the originally approved test results and make any necessary reconciliations. Logically, the user is an integral part of the system maintenance function.

DOCUMENTATION

Throughout all the phases of the cycle, a common thread is the need for proper documentation. Documentation is necessary for any kind of system. In systems

involving computers, it is extremely important to management, user departments, the EDP department, and the auditor that documentation be in conformity with well-defined written standards. Ideally, documentation is initially
developed during the programming, testing, and implementation phases. Then
it is reviewed and approved as part of the system acceptance function. Documentation should provide the following:

- An understanding of the objectives of the system, the concepts and
  methodologies employed, and the output of the system
- A source of information for all personnel responsible for
  maintaining and enhancing the system
- Information necessary for supervisory review
- A basis for training new personnel
- A source of information about the controls in the system
- Adequate user manuals and information needed to use the system
- Information needed by computer operators to run the system

Documentation, along with interviews of key personnel, provides the
auditor with a basis for gaining an accurate understanding of the computer
processing phases of the system. It also serves as a source of information for the
study and evaluation of controls.

Documentation should include all of the following:

1. System Documentation:

☐ System narrative

☐ Flowcharts of:
  - System architecture
  - Organization of programs
  - Procedures and usage (audit-oriented)

☐ Input descriptions (e.g., source documents, parameters)

☐ Output descriptions (printed reports, data files, turnaround
  documents)

☐ File descriptions

☐ Data capture instructions

☐ Descriptions of controls (batch, manual, and computer) embodied in
  the system

☐ Report distribution and data file retention requirements

☐ Copies of written change requests showing authorization for each
  change, the programs and files involved in the modification or
  enhancement, approvals of the test results and the effective date the
  change is to be implemented

2. Program Documentation:

☐ Detailed program narratives

☐ Decision tables and flowcharts

☐ Detailed file formats and record layouts

☐ Data element descriptions

☐ Report layouts

☐ Operation flowcharts showing input and output of the programs

☐ A listing of program processing parameters

☐ Source program compilation listings

☐ Record of changes, their authorizations, and effective dates

3. Operations Documentation:

☐ Operations flowchart

☐ Operating instructions, including:
  - Frequency, operating system requirements, job set-up instructions, sequence of input files, listing of program messages and responses, program halts and remedial action, restart and recovery procedures
  - Estimated normal and maximum running times per program
  - Emergency procedures

4. User Documentation:

☐ Description of the system

☐ Graphic representations of the system structure and of the sequential order of activities involving both the system and manual operations

☐ Description of the source documents for the system and procedures for their preparation

☐ Description of the output of the system and the procedures governing its use, security, review, disposition, and retention

☐ Control procedures, including cutoff requirements, controls to be established and maintained, reconciliation procedures, error correction, and resubmission

☐ Titles of individuals responsible for all control functions

USER DEPARTMENT INVOLVEMENT

Throughout the cycle, user involvement has been stressed. There is a good reason for this emphasis. User involvement is the most efficient way to develop

automated systems that contain adequate controls and reconciliation procedures to provide the user with accurate, timely, and meaningful information.
This involvement includes step-by-step authorization. The most extensive user
involvement should occur during the system analysis, design specifications,
system testing, conversion, and final system acceptance stages.

User involvement throughout the SDLC helps to avoid developing systems that:

- Do not meet the user's need
- Are inefficient
- Are not adequately controlled
- Are not acceptable to, or understandable by, operating-level
  personnel

An example of how users should speak up and make their desires known
occurred when a new accounts payable system was implemented. The user
department head felt uncomfortable while attending the obligatory steering
committee meetings. The computer buzzwords made him wish for the days
when he knew exactly what people in meetings were saying. Once or twice he
tried to bring up the way he actually did the work, in the hope that the computer
people could make the machine work the same way. The answer always
seemed to be, "Of course, the new system will do all that and more, and faster
than you can." When he asked for particulars, someone suggested that he take
a computer course "just to understand the new technologies a little better." He
decided to go along with their decisions without any further comments.

When the new system was installed, he discovered that it made his day
longer, not shorter as he had hoped. His staff was enlarged to compensate, but
the information just did not seem as easy to come by as it used to be. He found
that they had to write a lot of checks by hand to avoid missing vendor discounts
for timely payment. When internal audit reviewed his operation, he received
unfavorable comments for the first time. He explained to internal audit that it
was the unresponsive system that created all of his department's headaches.
The auditor agreed, and they went back to the steering committee. This time,
the user spoke up and got the modifications he needed. Eventually, the
department head even began to like the revised system. It finally did just
what he wanted, and faster too!

QUALITY ASSURANCE

Quality assurance is an ongoing effort, throughout the cycle and system use.
When it is implemented in an organization, quality assurance should consist
of the following activities:

- Formulation of systems and programming standards
- Examination of system design documentation to ensure that it has been prepared in accordance with standards and that the new system has incorporated adequate functions for effective control
- Review of program testing, system testing, and parallel or pilot runs to ensure adequacy and compliance with standards
- Review of data conversion procedures for adequacy and compliance with standards
- Affirmation that systems and programming practice is in accordance with standards

AUDIT INVOLVEMENT

As has been discussed, in the system development life cycle, whether a system development project involves one person or a team, an adequate evaluation of the system and its documentation and controls should be made at critical stages. Internal auditors, whether participating as members of the steering committee or acting as independent reviewers, can perform this important function. They must be sufficiently trained in EDP concepts and controls to do this job.

It is usually more difficult and expensive to build adequate controls into a system once it has been implemented. The auditors should perform a thorough analysis of the proposed controls of the system at the general and detailed system design stages. Appropriate corrective action can then be taken before programming is started, as discussed at the beginning of this chapter.

Of course, the users are generally responsible for designing controls. This responsibility should not be delegated to internal auditors. However, internal auditors do bear responsibility for making sure that proper controls have been built into the system. If the controls are not adequate, the auditor should recommend controls that suit the particular situation.

Some organizations even have the separate function of manager of internal control to educate users on controls and their use. Other organizations have the auditor sign off the system during development to make sure controls have been included.

By evaluating these critical stages of system development, an auditor can include programs or computerized audit routines that will help in testing and evaluating the applications programs. This is a direct benefit to the user and also provides facilitation of audits of existing application systems.

An important responsibility and contribution of an internal auditor is to ensure that the SDLC is based on procedures and standards. The internal auditor can also review the resulting system to determine whether it does exactly (and only) what was specified by the user. A post-implementation review or audit of a system development project can include a report comparing the cost of developing and implementing the system with the benefits derived. Such a report is based on an analysis made at the time the specifications are approved by the user.

Ideally, a report would work like this: A major system was developed for a company. During the second year it was in production the internal auditor scheduled it for review. The new system had cost $200,000 to develop. It had met all of its original objectives, including the following benefits:

- *Prolonging the life of the current computer hardware.* A hardware upgrade with associated costs was delayed 18 months. This savings alone paid for the development of the system.
- *More accurate information.* Clerks who handled customer complaints were reduced in number because there were fewer complaints.
- *More timely information.* Questions that needed to be answered to make important decisions were speedily addressed.

The costs of developing new systems should be treated as any other type of investment, since the resulting system is an asset to the organization.

The SDLC is much like any other tool. The auditor should know the environment, determine the critical decision points, and then get involved. In this way, the auditor can determine that the work has been done according to the standards established for effective performance. That is why the SDLC may be one of the most cost-effective areas for internal audit involvement.

A SYSTEMS AUDIT APPROACH TO THE SYSTEM DEVELOPMENT LIFE CYCLE

To relate the basic techniques of one audit approach to the phases of the SDLC, refer to the chart shown in Figure 7-8. The key points shown in this chart are:

- The audit approach and the SDLC stand on their own as approaches to data processing and auditing and can be coordinated.
- With the SDLC there is also the internal auditor's viewpoint.
- Where both approaches are coordinated, the internal auditor can be productive in the organization's EDP environment.
- A systems audit approach can be applied throughout the SDLC (as new systems are developed and brought on-line).

Figure 7-8 also shows the phases of the systems audit approach as it relates to the SDLC, as follows:

AUDIT APPROACH	SYSTEM DEVELOPMENT LIFE CYCLE								
	Request	Feasibility	Design	Specifications	Program and Test	System Test	Conversion	Accept and Approve	Operation
Planning	X	X	X	X	X	X	X	X	
Gaining			X	X	X	X			X
Recording			X	X	X	X			X
Confirming			X	X	X	X			X
Evaluation	X	X	X	X	X	X	X	X	
Testing					X	X	X	X	X
Comments			X	X	X	X	X		X
Substantive Tests							X	X	X
Findings/Recommendations	X	X	X	X	X	X			X
Assurances				X	X	X	X	X	X

FIG. 7-8　Using the systems audit approach

- *Request phase*
  a. Requires a controlled method of handling the requests.
  b. Describes the work that has been requested.
  c. The auditor is usually not involved at this point.
- *Feasibility phase* — Audit may evaluate the feasibility study for a new system or change during this phase. It might be appropriate at this time to provide recommendations for controls, security, and information trails.
- *Design* — At this phase the auditor should:
  a. Gain, record, and confirm an understanding of the system as designed.
  b. Where appropriate, provide comments for guidance on the adequacy of the design of controls, security, and information trails.

- *Specifications* — At this level, the auditor should:
  a. Gain assurance that design considerations have been appropriately incorporated into detailed specifications.
  b. Confirm and, where necessary, enhance the recorded understanding of the system gained during the design phase.
- *Program and test* — Audit usually reviews and evaluates the program testing performed by EDP. In addition, some reperformance testing may be conducted.
- *System test* — As for program testing, audit generally evaluates and monitors the results of system testing.
- *Conversion* — By auditing the conversion of data, assurance can be gained as to its completeness and accuracy.
- *Acceptance and approval* — This is generally the responsibility of the user and data processing. As such, auditing plays a lesser part.
- *Operations phase* (the phase of the cycle at which the audit approach is most often applied) — The auditor should:
  a. Plan the audit on the system currently in operation.
  b. Gain, record, and confirm an understanding of the system currently in operation.
  c. Evaluate and test the controls in the system currently in operation.
  d. Perform substantive tests on the data produced by the current system.

The end result is a system in which controls have been considered continuously during the construction. They are in place and useful for system test conversion and operations.

In this way, the audit approach can be applied to the SDLC.

OTHER SYSTEM DESIGN METHODOLOGIES

There are many ways in which to design a system. Some other methods are:

- *Prototyping* — Building a smaller, simpler model of a complex system.
- *Model-by-model approach* — Creation of an evolving series of models, each more closely realizing the desired objective.
- *Bottom-up synthetic approach* — Identification and creation of an appropriate set of functional building blocks that can later be integrated into a complex system.
- *Simulation* — Using a general purpose simulation language, like GPSS (General Purpose Systems Simulation, from IBM), one can

simulate the proposed system's function in order to optimize design parameters.

- *Top-down approach* — Specification and creation of overall interface modules prior to the creation of the functional system subparts or individual programs.
- *Program Evaluation Review Techniques (PERT)* — A two-dimensional SDLC, where tasks are broken up into a hierarchy to accomplish a large project. Completed tasks are called events and are arranged in a network.
- *Critical Path Method (CPM)* — Critical path through the network according to the time required (essentially like PERT).

The method used depends on the personnel, the complexity of a project, and needs of the organization.

CHAPTER 8

On-Line Systems

INTRODUCTION TO TELEPROCESSING CONCEPTS

Early computer systems typically consisted of a mainframe with a small number of peripheral devices. Due to the size of this equipment, it was located in one large computer room and direct electrical wiring allowed transfer of data between the mainframe and peripherals. An operator controlled all computer operations from a console in the computer room. Jobs submitted for processing were entered through a peripheral device, usually a card reader, in "batch" mode. Each job ran in sequence. Things were done this way in part because, by current standards, the first mainframes had limited capacity. These early machines, despite their size, had as little as 4K (kilobytes) of memory. (See Figure 8-1.)

A number of major technical developments, combined with changing user requirements, have made today's computer systems and configurations vastly different from the early systems. To be able to cope with ever-increasing organization-wide demands on computer resources, the design of central processing systems that could handle a number of applications simultaneously was a major priority. A faster rate of data capture and transmission to the processing unit was also needed.

These needs, coupled with technological advances designed to meet them, resulted in the introduction of new kinds of systems. For example, when a company's commercial activities were concentrated in a relatively small area, such as a warehouse, transporting data to another location so that it could be processed was difficult. With the new systems, transactions could be captured at a number of terminals located throughout the warehouse. Terminals could be placed where they were needed, such as at the sales desk or in the receiving area. These terminals could be connected directly to the mainframe, providing on-line capability. This configuration is called a local network. (See Figure 8-2 for an illustration.)

Alternately, for companies with a number of remote warehouses, systems became available that gave each warehouse on-line access to a central process-

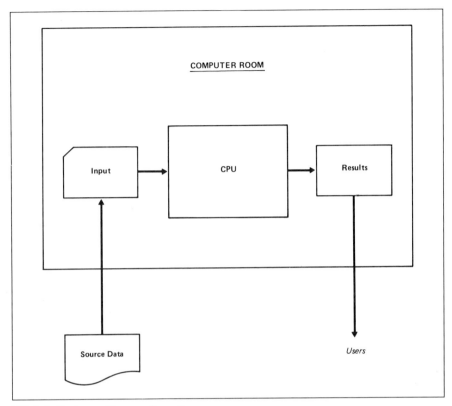

FIG. 8-1 Early machine configuration

ing unit (CPU). Because of the distances involved, communication of data between the remote sites and the CPU required special handling. For every organization to set up direct electrical wiring links between the CPU and remote locations would have involved enormous and unjustifiable costs. In many cases it was physically impossible. The logical answer was to find a way to transmit data through a widespread communication network already in existence: the telephone system. Technology made this kind of data transfer possible in configurations called remote networks. (See Figure 8-3 for an example of a remote network.)

Interactive, or time-sharing, systems developed as well. In these systems, remote users gained direct access to computer processing capabilities via a communications channel. This channel allowed access to the processing capabilities of large-scale computers without the expense of owning them, since users paid only for their actual system usage.

As technological developments continued at a rapid pace in the electronics industry, new system concepts began to emerge. A major advance was the idea

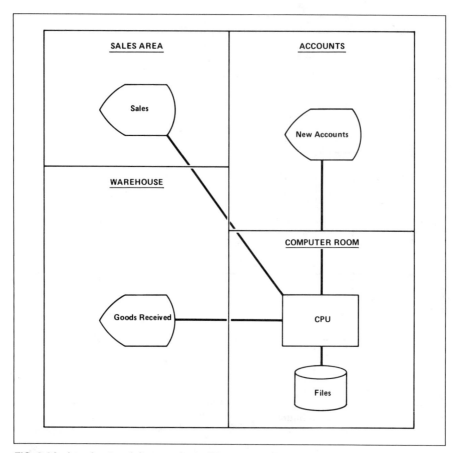

FIG. 8-2A Local network in manufacturing

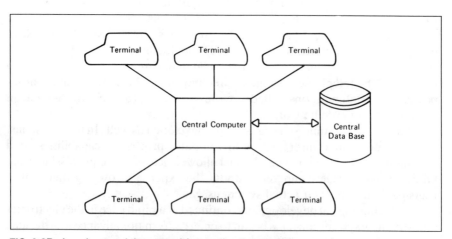

FIG. 8-2B Local network in general (centralized) processing

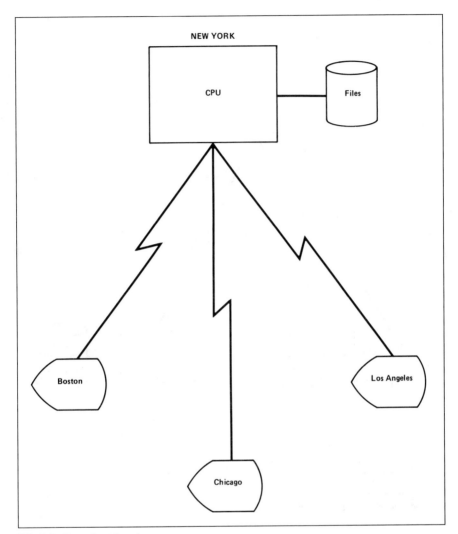

FIG. 8-3   Remote network

of creating areas of intelligent computer processing within a network, performing certain functions locally that previously were carried out by the central computer. This configuration makes it possible to locate certain data processing activities, such as data validation procedures or maintenance of local inventory data bases, where they can be carried out most efficiently. This type of configuration is known as a distributed processing network and requires terminals that have their own processing capabilities, as contrasted with "dumb" terminals that can only communicate with a central CPU. (See Figure 8-4 for an example of a distributed processing network.)

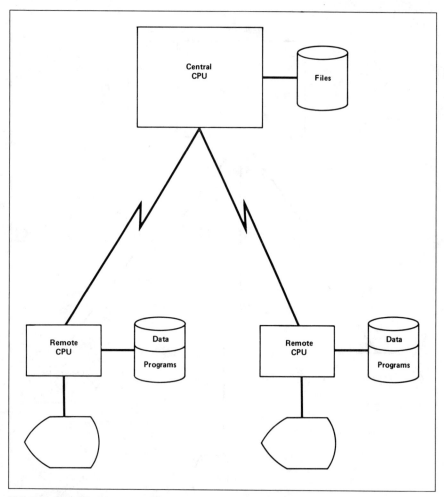

FIG. 8-4 Distributed processing network

Even more advanced methods of data communication are needed. New methods now being commercially developed and used include satellite linkups and microwave transmission.

TELEPROCESSING IN COMPUTER NETWORKS

Data Transmission

Data characters in computer systems are represented by strings of bits or binary digits, the 0's and 1's of machine code. To represent characters, these conform to coding conventions developed for consistency within the industry, such as EBCDIC and ASCII. These codes were developed to achieve compatibility in the transfer of data between different data devices. Information in this format is known as digital data, which consist of off and on signals that represent the 0's and 1's.

Digital transmission is used to send data between devices in a computer room, such as from the computer to the line printer, or between terminals and the computer in a local network. When the terminal and the computer are connected in a remote network (as in Figure 8-3), the method of transmitting data depends on the type of communication channel being used and the protocols in existence. Extensive public digital transmission systems are being planned and are already in use in some areas.

However, present telephone systems use analog transmission, as opposed to digital transmission, for most communications. Analog transmission is the modulation of electromagnetic waves (the sine or carrier waves) sent over the transmission line. There are three forms of modulation: amplitude, frequency, and phase. In all three forms the wave is continuous, which makes the method ideally suited to transmitting voice over the phone, or sound over a radio.

Messages are indicated by varying the amplitude (height) of the signal (amplitude modulation), varying the frequency of occurrence of the signal (frequency modulation), or varying the direction of the cycle (phase modulation).

Amplitude modulation is generally used for slower speed data transmission due to its high distortion factor. Frequency modulation is used for lower bit rate transfers. Phase modulation over different amplitudes is used for higher rates of data transfer.

For a remote terminal to communicate with a central computer, its digital signals must be converted to analog form in order to be transmitted through existing telephone lines. The communication must then be converted back to digital signals before it can be processed by the computer. A modem (which stands for modulator-demodulator) at each end of the transmission line translates the data from digital form to analog form (and vice versa) to allow sending data over the phone lines.

Transmission Modes

Following is a definition by example of the different modes of transmission:

- *Full- and half-duplex.* Transmission lines can be used to transmit data along a given channel in
  a. One direction only (simplex),
  b. Both directions, but not at the same time (half-duplex), or
  c. Both directions at the same time (full-duplex).

Full-duplex transmission allows the transmission of data in both directions or the sending of data in one direction and control signals in the other. Full-duplex transmission can be achieved on lines that have four wires or on a two-wire line by splitting the band width of the line into two separate frequency bands.

- *Parallel and serial transmission.* In parallel transmission, multiple wires simultaneously transmit the component bits that make up a data character, and the control bits that indicate various things, such as the end of a particular message. In this method, there is one bit sent on each wire. Parallel wire transmission is often used to transmit digital data over short distances (e.g., in a local network to connect terminals to a central computer). Serial transmission is the transmission of a series of data characters as strings of bits sent along the same wire. Serial transmission is used on analog lines, since only one bit can travel over the line at a time.

- *Asynchronous and synchronous transmission*
  a. With asynchronous transmission, start and stop bits are used to signal the beginning and end of a character. This form of transmission is usually slow and is normally used when characters are transmitted irregularly, such as for teletypes. It is also used by many microcomputers.
  b. With synchronous transmission, characters are transmitted in blocks. Typically, the bit string starts with a unique synchronization bit pattern that the receiving machine understands. The block ends with an end-of-message character, followed by an error-checking character that is compared against the error-checking pattern accumulated by the receiving device. This is widely used for terminals that transmit large quantities of data at one time, such as those in distributed processing networks or computers communicating with other computers.

In practice, there are a variety of protocols used to regulate the transfer of data. This tends to limit the possibility of system interchanges among different manufacturers' products. Recent developments include devices that can automatically translate the information from one system so that it can be understood by another system.

Transfer Rates

The capacity of a communication channel is measured in terms of the bit rate, which is the number of bits transmitted per second (bps). The speed of a transmission line is measured by the baud rate, which is the number of times the line condition (on or off) changes per second. In a series of binary signals, 1 baud is 1 bit per second; for two-state signaling (where 2 signals are sent simultaneously), the baud rate will equal the bit rate.

The bit rate is equal to the baud rate multiplied by the number of bits per state. For example, on a 1600 baud-carrier line, eight-state modulation will achieve a data transfer rate of 4800 bits per second.

COMPONENTS OF A TELEPROCESSING NETWORK

The relationship of terminals and computers to each other when they communicate in a network is called the topology. This describes the different configurations that are possible; some of the widely used topologies are the star, tree, ring, and bus. These names loosely define the structure employed.

Terminals

Terminals are the input and output devices in a teleprocessing network. These include teletype terminals, video terminals, remote job entry terminals, transaction terminals, and intelligent terminals. The features of each of these terminal categories are shown in Figure 8-5.

Modems

As discussed previously, when analog transmission is used, a modem is needed to encode digital signals from sources in the computer network into the range of frequencies required to transmit data along the communication channel. When the modem receives incoming analog signals, they are decoded back into digital signals so that the data can be processed by the receiving point in the computer network. There are different varieties of modems: Some require a telephone, others take the place of a phone, and some terminals have modems built in. The use of a basic modem is shown in Figure 8-6.

Multiplexers and Concentrators

A multiplexer is a hardware device that connects several communications devices to the same communications channel. A multiplexer typically links several low-speed lines to one high-speed line in order to enhance transmission capabilities. In time-division, or time slot, multiplexing there are successive scans of the connected transmission lines; messages that were found as a result of the scanning are retransmitted. For example, one message might be a block of data composed of one character that is scanned from each terminal for

Type	Characteristics
1. Low-speed teleprinter	■ 0−1,200 bits/second ■ Generally unbuffered ■ Asynchronous transmission ■ Limited intelligence ■ Mostly dial-up lines used ■ Examples: a. TI Silent 700 (acoustic coupler) b. TTY−Texas 745
2. Visual display terminals (VDTs, also called CRTs)	■ 100−9,600 bits/second ■ Generally unbuffered, linked to cluster controller ■ Limited intelligence ■ Synchronous or asynchronous transmission ■ Dedicated, dial, or lease lines ■ Example: a. IBM 3278's linked to IBM 3274 buffered controller
3. Remote job entry (RJE) terminals	■ 2,400−9,600 bits/second ■ Card reader, printer, operator console (CRT and diskette options in configuration) ■ Buffered, often programmable ■ Normally synchronous transmission ■ Dial or lease lines ■ Examples: a. IBM 3770 b. IBM 3780
4. Transaction terminals	■ 2,400−9,600 bits/second ■ Buffered ■ Dial or lease lines ■ Examples—Special industry application: a. IBM 3600 series (banking) b. IBM 3650 series (retail) c. Diebold Tabs ATM (banking)
5. Intelligent terminals	■ 2,400−9,600 bits/second ■ Buffered ■ Programmable; can control a number of peripherals; can handle data entry, editing ■ Often used as cluster controllers ■ Dial or lease lines ■ Examples: a. Four-Phase System IV b. IBM 8100

FIG. 8-5 Features of various terminal categories

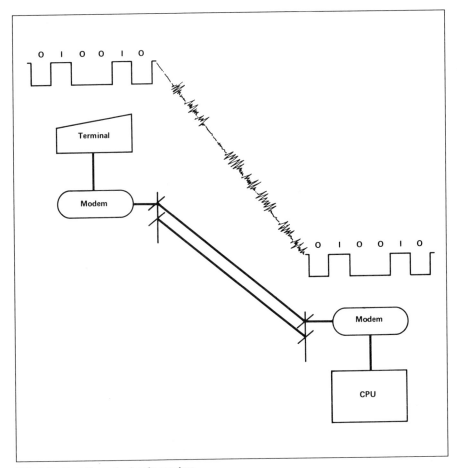

FIG. 8-6 Function of a basic modem

transmission to a host computer. Frequency division multiplexing involves the assignment of a separate frequency range, on a high-speed line, for each low-speed line. Thus, each terminal has its own frequency range on its line. In these methods the time slots or frequencies are fixed.

A concentrator is used to group several low-speed lines to a high-speed line in much the same way as a multiplexer. In addition, it is capable of certain processing functions. The shared channels can be used by terminals on a demand basis. For example, terminals may transmit to the concentrator in asynchronous mode; the concentrator stores and formats the message into a block or segment, adds the necessary address and control characters, and retransmits the data on a higher speed line in synchronous mode. The concentrator can be programmed to handle devices transmitting at different speeds automatically, while a multiplexer can only handle a preset speed or

	Carrier (Examples)	Bits per Second	Full (F) or Half (H) Duplex
Public Switched Network (dial-up)			
Low-speed (such as teletypewriter)	Western Union	0–150	Generally H
Voice-grade (public telephone network)	AT&T (DDD) (WATS)	0–9,600	F or H
Wide band (limited)	Graphnet (VAN)	0–56,000	F
Private Line (leased)			
Low-speed	AT&T Communications, Western Union; others	0–150	F or H
Voice-grade	AT&T Communications	300–9,600	F or H
Wide band	AT&T Communications	> 10,000	F
T1	AT&T Communications	1.544 million	F
T2	AT&T Communications	6.3 million	F
WT4	AT&T Communications	274.0 million	F

FIG. 8-7   Various types of communication lines

preset group of speeds. On the whole, the concentrator is more flexible and can deal with a variety of circumstances.

Communication Lines

Computer networks can be linked by the public telephone system, although for larger networks private lines can be leased. The choice of communication links depends on the cost and performance of the available lines and the requirements of the applications using the network. (See Figure 8-7 for a description of some communication lines.)

Front-End Communications Processor

A front-end communications processor is a hardware device that connects all of the network data communication lines to a central computer. It is used to relieve the central computer of the overhead of network control and message handling. In an IBM system, for example, the hardware unit might be a 3705 communications controller, directed by the Network Control Program. The IBM 3705 is a key component of IBM's System Network Architecture (SNA), which connects devices using their Synchronous Data Link Control (SDLC) protocol. Typical functions of such devices are:

- Polling and addressing of remote units
- Dialing and answering stations on a switched network

- Determining to which remote station a block is to be sent
- Character code translation
- Dynamic buffering
- Transmission rate selection
- Control character recognition and error checking
- Error recovery and diagnostics
- Activating and deactivating communication lines

Central Processing Unit

The CPU carries out the major processing tasks of the computer and is the heart of any system. Binary data from the front-end communications controller is accepted via a designated channel. The access method (such as VTAM, or Virtual Telecommunications Access Method, and TCAM, or Telecommunications Access Method) is used to manage the allocation of resources and the flow of data within the central system. Communications software, such as Customer Information Control System (CICS) or Information Management System/Data Communication (IMS/DC), provides the interface between users and applications.

Teleprocessing Equipment in Data Communication Networks

Typical uses of teleprocessing equipment in networks include:

- *Cluster controller.* Figure 8-8 illustrates a cluster control mode, which is a communications terminal controlling a number of CRTs. In such a system, all messages are buffered by the controller and forwarded. The communications terminal can be partitioned, so that the first partition controls the cluster and the second acts as a concentrator.

- *Multiplexer.* Figure 8-9 illustrates a multiplexer linking several terminals. It can also be used to link several cluster controllers. The outward-bound line is generally a high-speed line. If the linked terminals are in remote locations, modems are required to convert analog signals to digital form before multiplexing. (This is a dial-up line, since the modem is used to call into the host computer.)

- *Multidrop or multipoint connection.* Figure 8-10 illustrates a number of terminals linked to a multidrop line, which is a line wired directly into the terminals. Only one message can be transmitted or received on the line at any one time, since it is a single line with multiple connections. Multidrop connections are only used on dedicated lines (lines reserved for a single device, terminal, or user). In a switched network, the lines are not dedicated.

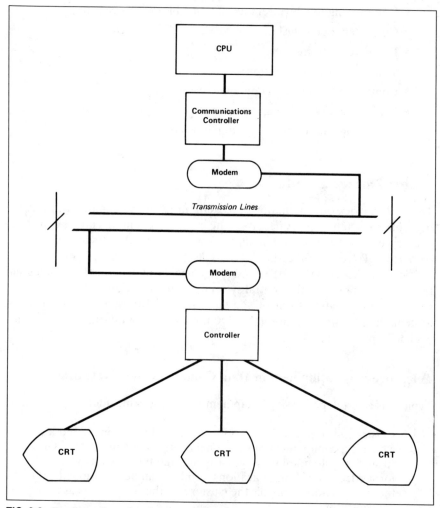

FIG. 8-8   Configuration of a cluster controller

TRANSMISSION CONTROL TECHNIQUES

Accuracy of Data Transmission

Errors in data transmission are different from those caused by erroneous data or errors in data input. Transmission errors often occur as a result of line noise or erratic impulses of sufficient magnitude to damage or garble the data being sent. They also occur when equipment controlling the transmission fails.

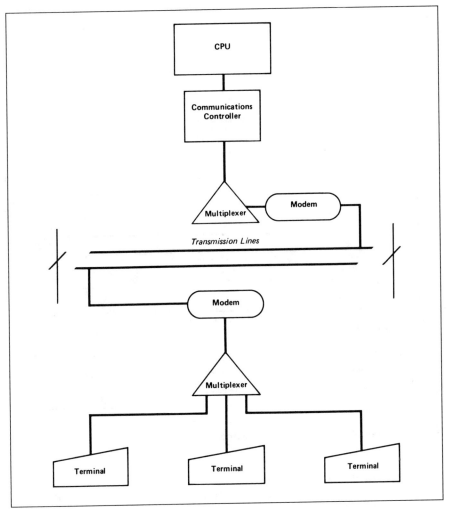

FIG. 8-9   Example ot a multiplexer configuration

A number of control techniques can be used to help detect transmission errors. Some of these are:

- *Redundancy bits/characters*. These bits or characters are additional information included in a message by the sending unit. They enable the receiving unit to perform an error check on the data received. Examples are:
  a. Parity bits (less reliable at high transmission rates)

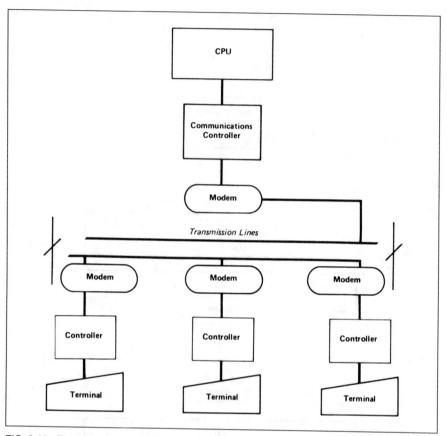

FIG. 8-10 Example of a multidrop line connection

    b. Polynomial checking
    c. Cyclic redundancy check (CRC) (a check character calculated using polynomial cyclic code on the bits in a block of data)

- *Loop checks (echo check).* The receiving unit sends messages back to the sending unit to make it possible to check the transmission against the stored message.

If an error is detected, the following techniques can be used to correct it:

- *Automatic retransmission.* The most common method in transmission systems, automatic retransmission uses special characters that are defined by the transmission protocol in effect. An example is IBM's Binary Synchronous Communication protocol. The sending unit waits for an acknowledgment (ACK) or negative acknowledgment (NAK) from the receiving unit. If ACK is received, the next block is sent; if NAK, the last block is retransmitted.

- *Forward error correction.* As well as enabling the receiving unit to detect errors, sufficient redundant data is included to allow the receiving unit to reconstruct the correct message using special codes. Thus, the sender does not need to retransmit the data.

- *Operator retransmission.* The terminal operator is informed of the error, and the message is either retransmitted (if held in a buffer) or reentered.

Completeness of Data Transmission

There is always a possibility that messages will be lost in transmission. When the data being transmitted is significant, as in an on-line transaction, it is particularly important to be able to detect the loss of messages. If there is no method to check on whether a message is lost, there is no way to know for sure that all messages sent were received.

In some systems messages are numbered so that their sequence can be checked. For example, in IBM's Synchronous Data Link Control protocol, each message frame or unit forwarded by a secondary station is numbered sequentially. Then the primary station can check that all messages were received in the correct sequence.

Audit Significance of Transmission Controls

In situations where specific application controls are lacking, the auditor may need to consider the effect on the adequacy of data transmission control procedures. In any case, it is important to be sure that there are adequate controls over data transmission that function properly.

SWITCHING SYSTEMS

Line Switching

Line switching involves the creation of a physical path or circuit between incoming and outgoing lines (e.g., the switched public telephone system) in order to provide linking for distant locations. Private line-switching systems are not common; private organizations use message-switching systems, which may use the public switched networks.

Message Switching

Message switching involves the storing of messages from remote terminals or concentrators by another concentrator or minicomputer in the network. Each message is subsequently routed to the destination address on the message header as soon as a line becomes available. Incoming messages are always accepted, even if they cannot immediately be transmitted to their destinations (e.g., messages for terminals on a multidrop line or for terminals that are busy).

Packet Switching

Packet switching is designed to transfer data through a network. Data from terminals or other computers in the network is formed into "packets" (often blocks of fixed length) by an interface computer (node) and sent to its destination via a high transmission (wide band) communication line. Alternate communication paths are designed into the system to provide different paths that can be used in the event of line congestion or failure. A particular message may be broken up into a number of packets, and each packet may be transmitted via a different path.

KINDS OF TELEPROCESSING SYSTEMS

All teleprocessing systems include some form of remote computer activity. For example, a simple activity might be the remote logging of transactions and subsequent transmission of a batch to a central computer for processing. On the other hand, fairly complex processing capabilities may be distributed to centers remote from a host computer. When this is done, the maintenance of data files, and possibly program libraries, at remote locations becomes necessary.

To audit computer systems with teleprocessing features, the auditor must understand those systems and their features. This knowledge enables the auditor both to classify accounting systems in use throughout an organization and to perform preliminary surveys of general or integrity controls.

Remote Job Entry

A remote job entry (RJE) configuration is illustrated in Figure 8-11. RJE systems normally include the following features:

- In batch-oriented systems, data capture is usually through key-to-disk or key-to-tape at remote locations; the data is transmitted in a batch mode to the host computer.
- Data is spooled to disk or tape at the host computer to await processing.
- A remote user initiates jobs (via terminal, card reader, or diskette reader), which are entered into the job queue by the host computer.
- Job requires little operator intervention other than loading required files.

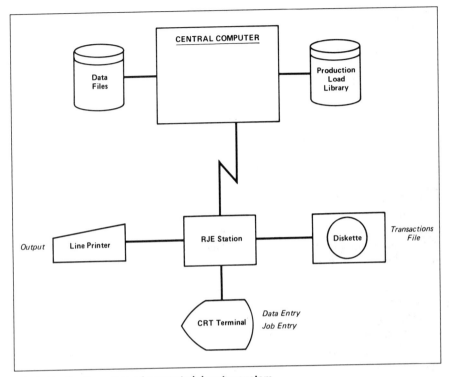

FIG. 8-11   Configuration of a remote job entry system

- Output is returned to the remote user and printed on the remote printer when the job is finished, unless it is specifically routed to another printer or screen.

The method of data capture may vary from system to system. Essentially, RJE gives remote users access to a central computer in a remote batch-entry mode.

An example of an RJE application is a divisional payroll system where time sheets and other data are keyed to diskette on a daily basis and accumulated for each week. At the end of the period, the RJE operator initiates the weekly edit runs. After the edit report is received and all errors are corrected, the divisional paymaster authorizes the payroll production run. This run is done in the remote batch-entry mode.

On-Line Systems Capabilities

An on-line system accepts data from the source, where it is created, and may involve immediate processing of the data. An on-line system may have the following capabilities:

- On-line inquiry
- On-line data entry
- On-line update (add, change, or delete)

However, a given application may not use all of the above capabilities.

On-Line Inquiry. On-line inquiry, which is a common feature of computer systems in a teleprocessing environment, enables a remote user to retrieve data directly from the computer files. Since this access may create problems if it is unrestricted, the system software should control what data is available to be read by remote terminals. Access to data should be regulated rather than unlimited.

On-line inquiry situations are common in banks. A bank teller can confirm that a customer has sufficient funds to cover a check via a terminal at the teller's station. No transaction actually takes place at the terminal, but the use of the inquiry feature provides an important control step.

On-Line Data Entry. With on-line data entry, a terminal is used to enter data for transmission to a host computer. The data can be held for intermediate storage (batch processing mode) or sent for immediate processing (transaction processing mode). In transaction processing mode, a number of transactions may be processed concurrently on different remote terminals. These transactions may be the same type or of different types. For example, several sales orders and cash receipts can be processed concurrently. In order for this to work, the computer must be programmed to

- Recognize the transaction type and select the appropriate program (including programmed format) for that type.
- Queue the messages received concurrently from different terminals and handle situations where different terminals wish to access (or update) the same data files at the same time.

In transaction processing mode, on-line processing normally includes

- Matching to master files to check the existence of data on which the transaction will act (e.g., customers, suppliers, or products) or matching to related transaction data (e.g., as purchase invoices to records of goods received). This matching may include interactive checks and controls. For example, the computer may retrieve the full customer name based on the reference field input; visual verification by the terminal operator ensures that the correct customer name has been entered.
- Temporary storage of data keyed in on a work file during the edit and validation stages. Then, if the data is accepted, it is written to a transaction file for subsequent batch updating.

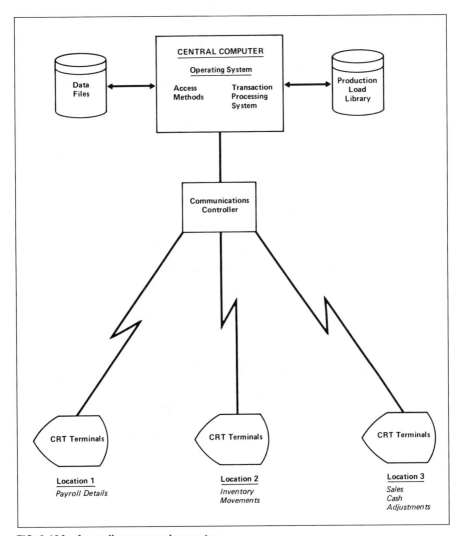

FIG. 8-12A   An on-line processing system

On-Line Update.   Transaction processing systems may perform on-line updating of relevant master files or data bases (to add, change, or delete data) on a transaction-by-transaction basis. An on-line transaction processing system is illustrated in Figure 8-12. In Figure 8-12A, Location No. 1 is processing all the payroll details based on daily employee time records. A limited amount of validation is performed on-line so that the operator can make immediate corrections. Transactions are written to a transaction file. The actual payroll production is run in batch mode each week using the relevant data on the transaction file.

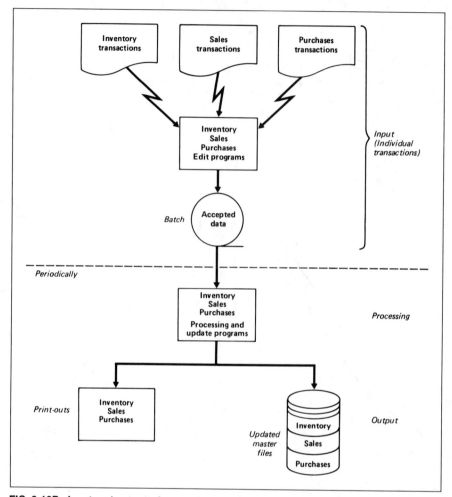

FIG. 8-12B Input and output of an on-line processing system

At Location No. 2, various inventory movement transactions, such as stock count adjustments, are being entered and updated to the inventory master file, which is always on-line.

At Location No. 3, sales orders are processed on-line. At the time of input, each order is compared to information on the updated inventory file to ensure that sufficient inventory is on hand to fill the orders. Accounts receivable balances are updated overnight from a file of invoices and adjustments created during the day's processing of accepted sales orders. Figure 8-12B shows the input and output of an on-line sales and inventory system.

Time-Sharing Systems and Public Data Bases

Time-sharing systems are terminal-oriented. They are designed to handle the processing requirements of a number of different users at the same time. Each user acts independently using individual data files stored by the time-sharing system and the programs available on that system. Time-sharing systems are interactive: They are designed for conversational situations where the application system and terminal operator send instructions and data back and forth. Use of computer resources is controlled by the time-sharing system, which limits the time that any one program may control processing on a time-slice basis (i.e., the amount of time the computer resources can be used for a particular process). Once the slice is used up, the computer goes to the next task. For this reason, time-sharing systems are not suited to running large batch jobs, which may take too long to execute efficiently. In such a situation, processing would be constantly interrupted each time a time slice was completed.

Time-sharing services to process application data are provided by a large variety of time-sharing bureaus; one of the largest is the General Electric Time-Sharing System (GEISCO). From the user's viewpoint, time-sharing has many of the characteristics of an RJE system.

In-house time-sharing systems, such as TSO (Time-Sharing Option) and CMS (Conversational Monitor System), are normally used for on-line program development and maintenance rather than for application processing.

Public data bases are an expanding area of on-line system use. These systems permit business and individual use, for a fee, of the data base of information maintained by the service provider. Users access the computer, usually through the telephone lines using a modem, to receive text-only or text and graphics information (videotex). Text-only videotex is popular for business use, such as the legal data provided by LEXIS or news provided by NEXIS. Text and graphics videotex, a growing area, provides information and, frequently, transaction services, such as banking and ordering capabilities.

Distributed Data Processing

The term "distributed data processing" (DDP) refers to the decentralization of computerized data processing functions through the interconnection of computers and terminals. These are arranged in a network designed to meet the user's processing and information needs.

Unlike most of the preceding types of systems, in DDP certain functions are off-loaded or sent from the central computer to the remote processing sites. This improves the overall information and processing system, since some of the demands on the central computer are reduced. Obviously, the economic assumption underlying such a transfer is that it can be done relatively cheaply,

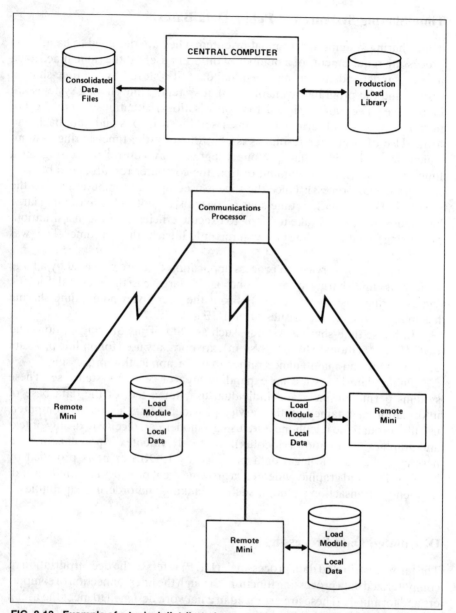

FIG. 8-13   Example of a typical distributed processing system in manufacturing

which is now possible due to technological developments and decreasing hardware costs.

DDP refers to the existence or creation of a teleprocessing network structure. The following functions may be scattered throughout the system:

- Data collection
- Data editing and correction
- File creation and maintenance
- Transaction processing
- Data base management

These functions are located at remote sites and are performed and controlled by a local processor. This differentiates distributed processing systems from terminal networks, which are under the control of a central processor.

Any number of different DDP network structures can exist in practice. A typical network structure in a manufacturing company with large divisional offices is illustrated in Figure 8-13. In this example, each division is responsible for processing and maintaining its own data. Certain information is transmitted to the central computer for further processing, such as sales details, costing, and so forth. New versions of application programs and systems software are sent to the divisions as load modules.

Sometimes, DDP is structured so that a node (usually a mainframe or a minicomputer) performs a certain type of processing for the other nodes. This is called centralized distribution.

More complex network structures are used by organizations that adopt an even more decentralized approach. In these systems, multiple communication paths might exist with work nodes linked to various other work nodes in the network. In many organizations, microcomputers are linked together and into networks that communicate with mainframes or minicomputers. When the microcomputers are linked locally, it is called a local area network (LAN). When they are also linked to remote sites, it is called a wide area network (WAN).

CONTROL ASPECTS OF ON-LINE TELEPROCESSING SYSTEMS

The term "teleprocessing" applies to any computer system that has terminals connected to it via communications channels. Teleprocessing systems can be divided into three functional subsystems:

1. Terminals
2. Communications
3. Computers

Thinking in terms of these subsystems reduces the complexity of analyzing a vast variety of possible hardware/software configurations to simple common denominators. The overall system can be evaluated more easily by first considering the subsystems. This applies to DDP environments as well as to on-line and time-sharing systems.

The large number of possible different teleprocessing system configurations creates a broad spectrum of security and other control considerations. There are, however, certain basic control features that are important in any teleprocessing environment, and are of particular concern to auditors, including:

- Security of terminals and access
- Control over data
- Backup and recovery of the system
- General control considerations
- Communications controls

Security of Terminals and Access

The principal objective in securing the terminals in a system is to control access via terminals to the computer. It is desirable to restrict or monitor physical access to terminals wherever possible. Software access controls are more effective. In addition, access controls should require authorized users to identify themselves to the control software. This is normally done using security software. Where dial-up lines are used, the correct destination telephone number must also be known to the user. A dial-back feature provides better security, so that numbers uncovered through trial and error then call back; if the caller's phone number is not that of an authorized user, the system will not provide access.

Controls over terminal access should ideally include the following procedures:

1. Passwords and transaction authorization codes that are validated by the access control software should be used to ensure that only authorized users are allowed access to the system.

2. Access to the computer system by authorized users should be logged. Conversely, attempted access by unauthorized users should also be logged. On-line notification of unauthorized access attempts makes it possible to take action.

3. The access control software should disable or disconnect a terminal after a predetermined number of invalid attempts (use of wrong password) to access the network.

4. The access control software should disable a terminal if the terminal has been inactive for more than a predetermined amount of time.

5. The access control software should periodically request a password or other identification to verify that the authorized operator (the person who originally signed on) is the same person still using the terminal.

6. A control log should record all of the above activity. It should be periodically reviewed by EDP management and the auditor when required, and exception items should be investigated.

7. Critical information, such as passwords and other authorization codes, should not be displayed on the terminal. (Password software is part of security software that is part of, or can be added to, system software.)

8. Lists of valid passwords should be secured against unauthorized access, with additional password protection or data encryption.

9. Passwords should be easy to change, should be changed periodically, and should be disabled immediately for separated users.

10. When dial-up lines are used, phone numbers should be changed periodically. Phone numbers should not be listed on the terminals.

11. Entry of system commands that effect the status of terminals should be restricted to master terminals.

12. System commands should be logged, reviewed, and restricted.

Where possible, terminal security control procedures should enforce an adequate separation of duties. Operators and terminals should be restricted to the particular functions that should be performed within each application and only as required for the particular job responsibility. For example, a terminal in a warehouse, used to track inventory, should not have access to the customer master files.

Many of the terminal control procedures described above will not necessarily detect successful attempts to use terminals in an unauthorized manner. Rather, they are intended to prevent such unauthorized attempts from succeeding in the first place. The presence of terminal security controls in itself does not provide conclusive evidence that unauthorized use of terminals did not, in fact, occur. Their actual use must be reviewed for the auditor to place reliance on these controls.

Control Over Data

Application controls are defined as those controls built into each application to ensure the complete and accurate input, update, validity, and maintenance of the application data.

On-line teleprocessing systems differ from document-oriented batch processing systems because transactions may be originated at a terminal instead of on a controllable document. If source documents are available, user controls similar to those commonly used in batch systems may also be present. If, however, the initial transaction record is on the terminal screen, such user controls may not be feasible. The correct operation of the system will depend largely on the appropriateness of programmed procedures built into the application programs and system software. The key concerns in control of data are discussed in the following sections.

Transaction Authorization. In an on-line system, transaction authorization is largely a function of security software. Terminals can be limited to certain types of transactions, and codes required to enter transactions. If an operator is allowed unlimited access to the system, unauthorized browsing through the files can occur; it may even be possible to create a transaction that will update the data files. That is why it is so important to make sure that only authorized use is permitted. Access to the system must be controlled, as previously discussed under "Security of Terminals and Access."

Transaction Accuracy and Validity. In on-line systems it is possible and helpful to check the validity of data fields before a transaction is accepted. Tests for transaction validity should ensure that

- Data is in the correct format, through on-line prompting or questioning of the user and format checks.
- Account or reference keys are accurate and valid. In particular:
  a. The operator should be notified of invalid keys so corrections can be made. An invalid account number, for example, may mean that the account does not exist and could mean that the transaction is unauthorized.
  b. The selected key should be correct. By introducing an interactive check that provides the operator with the description of each account key entered, it becomes possible to visually check that the correct key or information was entered.
- Transaction data is reasonable and within defined limits, such as a sales order should not exceed the available credit limit or balance for an account.

To reduce the likelihood of updating files with erroneous data, a transaction should not be accepted until the required operator and computer subsystem message exchanges (such as responses to the prompts) have been completed. Suspense files may hold unaccepted transactions or, alternately, the transaction can be terminated. The follow-up action taken will depend on the nature of each application.

In situations where incoming data is validated by reference to data fields that will themselves be updated once the incoming data is accepted, it is important to ensure that other, subsequent incoming data is not validated until the previous transaction has been completed. For example, incoming sales orders are often subject to a credit availability check: The credit limit must exceed all unpaid sales transactions for that account by at least the value of the new order. If the order is accepted, it increases the amount of unpaid sales and decreases the credit availability by an equal amount. If the system allows a second order for the same customer to be validated before the update of the previous order has been completed, the credit check becomes invalid, since it will not take the first order into account.

Completeness of Transactions. Ensuring completeness of input can be a problem in on-line systems whenever accountable documents are not used as a basis for entering transactions. In some applications, such as on-line banking systems, transactions are logged and/or totaled at each terminal. Transaction totals can be subsequently reconciled to cash balances to provide a completeness of input control.

In other applications, where transactions are created on-line, an interactive feedback check may be relied on. For example, a sales clerk taking orders over the telephone enters a transaction without having a physical document on hand. The application program sends an acknowledgment that the order has been accepted and permits the next sales order to be entered. It is critical that the application program logs the accepted transaction on a transaction history file and adds it to a control total as part of the acknowledgment routine. The allocation of sequence numbers by the application program is not in itself a control over completeness of input. It may, however, facilitate subsequent control procedures, such as computer matching or control over completeness of update.

File Updating. Control over file or data base updates in full on-line update applications is usually achieved by reconciling the control totals of the transaction history file to the totals from the updated files. This reconciliation is normally performed at the end of the day's on-line processing. In this way, the day's transactions are grouped for processing and reconciliation in a manner similar to one batch. If the reconciliation process finds that the totals disagree, further processing is required to find the errors.

Another technique involves taking copies of the master file at selected checkpoints in processing. These copies are subsequently updated in batch mode by the transactions recorded on the history file. Such updates are often processed using a technique called "memo updates," in which the system issues a memo to temporarily update a copy of the file (important so that, for example, cash withdrawals from an automated teller machine do not exceed the available balance) and then actual update is performed in batches overnight. Matching the updated copy file against the master file used during actual on-line processing then provides assurance of both the completeness and the accuracy of the update process.

Backup and Recovery of the System

Adequate procedures should be built into the system to handle either a complete system failure or the failure of a system component. The purpose of recovery procedures is to allow normal operations to resume as quickly as possible, without the introduction of errors.

Recovery procedures should include the following:

- The ability to identify the status of all processing in the computer subsystem so that a cutoff can be established. A checkpoint facility may be incorporated where before-and-after images of the master file fields being updated are written to the transaction file, allowing the computer to reinstate the records it held prior to the failure.

- The ability to status check and account for all messages in transit, such as numbering, time/date identification, and logging of messages at switching centers and communication controllers. This is important to ensure that messages are neither lost nor processed twice as a result of system failure.

- Provision for maintaining security copies of transaction history files and other log files needed for restarts or reruns.

- The safe storage of critical system information, such as current network configurations.

- Dynamic back-out of partially processed transactions.

Cutoff procedures following system recovery are simplified if the user terminals can be advised of the last transaction accepted. Then the users can resume processing by entering the next transaction in sequence. If users do not know the last transaction accepted, they may reprocess accepted transactions.

For long delays caused by major failures, alternate processing facilities may be required to permit normal business to continue. The alternatives may include manual processing or use of backup computer facilities for situations where manual processing is not practical or possible. In a large-scale network, it is possible to designate one of the remote sites to take over processing on an interim basis.

Depending on the nature of the system and the adequacy of its application controls, many backup and recovery procedures may be essentially administrative or operational in nature. This possibility should be taken into consideration when reviewing the controls.

General Control Considerations

On-line teleprocessing systems often involve programmed procedures that cannot be checked in detail by the user. Consequently, these systems are often classified as non-user controlled. Such systems cannot be readily controlled or audited solely by examining output. Therefore, all aspects of general controls over such processing environments are likely to be important.

Implementation Controls. System design and implementation procedures are critical in on-line teleprocessing systems. This is due to the operational and control complexities involved and the high level of reliability required. Auditors should be involved in the design stages to ensure that appropriate control procedures are incorporated. (See Chapter 7, "System Development Life Cycle.")

Program and Data File Security Controls. Some of the major data file security considerations were addressed earlier in the section entitled "Security of Terminals and Access." Adequate data file security within the computer system itself is also essential. On-line programming facilities available via telecommunications and other links require that program files be protected by the same sort of terminal security controls that have been discussed for use with data files. Principally, the production, source, and load libraries should be protected against unauthorized access either through the on-line programming system or through jobs entered from the programmers' terminals.

Computer Operations Controls. There are various considerations that need to be made regarding adequacy of operations controls:

- To the extent that processing (either batch or on-line) can be initiated from locations outside the computer room, there should be procedures to ensure that only authorized processing occurs. (See Part IV, "Controls.") Procedures should ensure that only authorized jobs are processed using the correct data files and programs.
- In a centralized processing environment, one security technique is limiting access to the computer. When computer operations hardware or software, such as the master terminals, are located outside the environment, similar restrictions should be placed on access as would normally be enforced in a centralized processing environment.
- When possible, development systems should be segregated from production systems by electronic separation (separate systems).

System Software. Controls over system software (including communications software and security software) are necessary to ensure the correct operation of the system, its software, and the controls that rely on that software. (See Chapter 9, "System Software.")

Communications Controls

To consider the significance of the communications controls, it may be useful to limit the examination to the following areas of concern to an auditor:

- A message may be lost from the system
- A message may be routed to the wrong address in the system
- A message may contain errors
- An unauthorized message may be introduced into the system
- Messages may be monitored by unauthorized methods

One technique used to provide error control in transmission links is the automatic request for repetition (ARQ) technique. This technique is a feature of almost all data transmission systems that provide for error control and involves attaching an additional sequence of bits, called "check bits," to a block of data. This sequence of bits is computed from the contents of the block. Then, at the receiving terminal, the check sequence is recomputed. If the computed sequence does not match the check bits that were received, a request to retransmit the data block is automatically sent to the transmitting terminal.

IBM's Synchronous Data Link Control (SDLC) and Binary Synchronous Communication (BSC) protocols provide this capability. This type of line-error protocol detects transmission errors between a sending and a receiving point that employ the protocol.

Routing verification procedures, such as checks of message addresses in headers, are also necessary to ensure that

- The message destination is valid and is authorized to receive data.
- Unbroken message sequences are received.

The communications network makes it difficult to control physical access to transmission lines. This creates a risk of unauthorized monitoring, unauthorized modifications to messages, or both. As a result, security software often provides alternate methods to restrict access. Encryption of messages reduces the chances that unauthorized intervention will produce any useable information, but this is not generally employed in accounting applications. Multiplexing messages with others increases the difficulty of understanding messages through monitoring.

As discussed previously, full end-to-end control includes the use of acknowledgments between the terminal and the application program. When this level of control is built into application programs, it may provide assurance that transmission is complete and accurate. Controls over the system of communications, however, may be viewed as helping to ensure the reliability of the communications environment rather than the accuracy of the application data, so that even where controls over communications are adequate, the application data controls must still be reviewed, evaluated, and tested.

CONTROL ASPECTS OF DISTRIBUTED DATA PROCESSING SYSTEMS

Impact of Distributed Data Processing

Computer resources are decentralized to varying degrees in distributed data processing systems, as was described previously. This decentralization can include:

- Distributed data
- Distributed software
- Distributed system development and maintenance

Distributed Data. In distributed processing systems, the creation and maintenance of data by remote network users results in distributed data. Since these users are not in the central location, particular data may be collected and processed only at their remote location. It may be retrieved from, and transmitted to, other points in the network. Data may be stored locally, either in standard file structures or as a data base.

Distributed Software. In order to permit processing at sites outside the central computer facility, the system software and application programs required to process the data must be located at the remote site. In many cases this occurs as part of a computer configuration that includes microcomputers or minicomputers, or both, with local processing abilities.

Distributed System Development and Maintenance. Software located at remote sites may be developed centrally. In other cases, the remote users are responsible for the design, implementation, and maintenance of the systems running at their location. When this is true, it is necessary to make sure that there are standards and controls over these procedures. The same types of controls over program maintenance and development, such as procedures to ensure that only authorized changes are made to programs and that those changes are properly tested and implemented, are required.

Audit Considerations in Distributed Processing

For the purpose of an audit, distributed processing is usually viewed as a configuration where application systems are processed in whole or in part at locations other than the central computer. This frequently includes the use of financially significant data files and programs at sites outside the central computer facility. Important considerations in understanding and evaluating such systems are

- Extent to which application systems are processed outside the central computer facility.
- Extent to which program and data files are located outside the central facility.
- Means by which the systems are controlled; in particular, the effectiveness of general controls at the various points in the network where significant processing is performed and significant computer files are used.

Areas of Concern in Distributed Data Processing Environments — Checklist

Evaluation of controls in a distributed data processing environment involves similar audit concerns and control objectives as in a centralized processing environment. However, there are frequently many more exposures. Ideally, application controls should be implemented to ensure the complete and accurate input and update of data, its validity, and the proper maintenance of data held on computer files. Also, programmed procedures are usually not controlled by the user, so that general controls should exist. Problems arise because the controls that are typically found in centralized computing systems may not be implemented in smaller remote sites associated with DDP environments. Another concern is that when microcomputers are used in such systems, it is rare to find adequate general controls. Similar difficulties arise in installations that use minicomputers, since the staff is usually too small to implement an adequate division of duties, for one example. Some factors that have resulted in unfavorable control characteristics in distributed systems are outlined below.

1. Access to Microcomputers and Other Intelligent Nodes:

☐ Security software adequate to prevent unauthorized access to computer files or to the network may not be implemented at the microcomputer or minicomputer levels.

☐ The size of main storage may preclude the use of available security software that requires a substantial memory area for installation and takes up much of the processing capability.

☐ Use of security software may degrade the performance of the microcomputer or minicomputer systems so much that the overall performance of the distributed system is no longer acceptable. In this case, it is often decided not to employ the security software.

☐ In the absence of adequate security software, physical security procedures (e.g., locks, voice-activated mechanisms, etc.) may be the only means of protecting access both to the network and to files maintained at the remote site. The local user may be unwilling or unable to implement such physical security procedures, when they are expensive or impossible due to space constraints and such.

2. Application Controls at Local Sites:

☐ The local user may not understand the need to implement application controls, or they may be inadequate even when understood.

☐ Depending on the nature of the system, strong central supervision of locally operated controls may be necessary to ensure that controls are properly coordinated throughout the remote sites.

☐ If there are redundancies in the distributed data, centrally monitored controls may be necessary to ensure that data is not included more than once in any financial information prepared from the distributed data. The data must also be synchronized so that it does not become out of date and/or vary from one remote site to the next.

3. Local System Development:

☐ This usually suffers from lack of enforceable standards, such as controls to ensure that programs are satisfactorily tested.

☐ Documentation of locally developed systems is often insufficient or nonexistent.

☐ Documentation of program changes is often insufficient or inadequate.

☐ Small numbers of local staff may result in an inadequate separation of duties at the remote site.

☐ It is less likely that adequate controls will be included when systems are developed. Provision for audit information and control reports are two items that are frequently overlooked.

Ways to Achieve a Controlled Environment — Checklist

There are many ways to control remote and distributed data processing, including:

1. Centralization of System Development:

☐ All new systems and enhancements should be developed by a central software support function.

☐ Only the load modules should be distributed to remote user locations. Those locations should not be permitted to have compiler facilities. Unique version numbers should be used that will identify the copies of the same programs when they are distributed to different locations.

2. When Remote Users Are Directly Responsible for the Development of Accounting Applications:

☐ A centrally controlled quality assurance function should be established to ensure adherence to minimum control standards.

☐ The actual network configuration and communications system should be controlled by a central teleprocessing software administrator.

3. Access to the System via Remote Terminals:

☐ Software controls over access to the computer, data files, and remote access to the network should be implemented.

☐ The physical control environment should be as secure as possible, such as having lockable terminals and computer room.

☐ Supervisory controls should be established over terminal and computer operations at the remote locations.

☐ Opportunities for unauthorized people to gain a knowledge of the system should be limited, such as by implementing controls over access to system documentation and manuals.

4. Applications Controls:

☐ Controls should exist over data transmitted between locations, such as sales in one location that update accounts receivable files at another location. The sending location should transmit control information, such as transaction control totals, to enable the receiving location to control the update of its files. When practical, central monitoring of controls should ensure that all remotely processed data is correct.

☐ When replicated files exist at multiple locations, controls should ensure that all files used are correct and current and, when data is used to produce financial information, that no duplication arises.

On the whole, teleprocessing has made the efficient processing of data from remote locations possible for many organizations. When the proper controls are built in, the benefits of computer networks far outweigh any negative aspects such as security risks. In a well-designed and controlled environment, such risks can be kept to a minimum.

System Software

SYSTEM SOFTWARE CONCEPTS

The widespread use of computers has brought about the concentration of data within the EDP department, which has resulted in a greater need for control. A single individual is now in a position to obtain far more knowledge about the organization, its data, and its procedures and controls, particularly someone in the system programming and operations areas. Consequently, management and the auditor have placed greater emphasis on ensuring that the controls operating within an EDP environment are sufficient to provide security over the computer, its programs, data, and the distribution of reports.

In addition to the security arrangements associated with computerized operations, it is increasingly possible to optimize the use of computer processing power. One sensitive area that affects this use is control over the system software. System software can be defined as any software that is not specifically related to an application program; it is the software that controls the computer itself. This chapter presents functions of the EDP auditor in relation to general controls over system software, its operation and maintenance, and the relationship to operation of application systems.

System software includes:

- Operating systems
- Operations support software
- Telecommunications support software
- Security software
- Data base management software
- Compilers
- Utilities

System software is supplied by hardware/software vendors, who maintain and upgrade the software through new releases and problem/program temporary fixes (PTFs). The software is distributed via "PUT" or installation tapes. System software is generally nonspecific when it arrives at an installation; it has generalized processing capabilities. When required, the system programmer customizes it to describe a particular environment. Programming and computer operations control the method used to "customize" generalized system software to meet the needs of a specific environment, by defining and implementing the required parameters. Figure 9-1 shows the system genera-

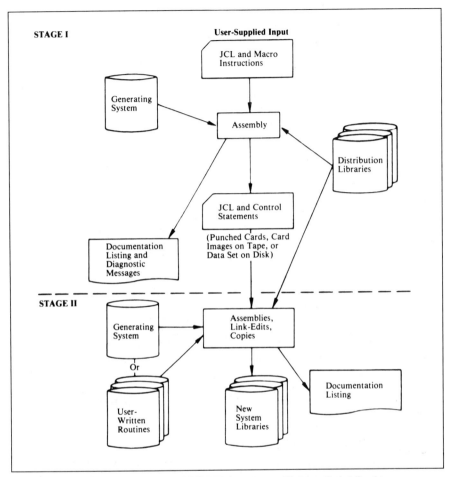

FIG. 9-1 The SYSGEN process for MVS/370 (courtesy of International Business Machines Corporation)

tion (SYSGEN) process for MVS/370, an operating system for IBM mainframe computers, where the software can be modified by the user.

The two general areas of EDP operations most concerned with system software are:

1. System programming
   - Software selection
   - System software installation and maintenance
   - Teleprocessing support
   - Hardware and software tuning for performance
   - Problem resolution
   - Backup and recovery procedures

Group	Macro Instruction	Complete System Generation	I/O Device Generation	Eligible Device Table Generation
Generation	DATASET[1]	Required	Required	
	EDTGEN			Required
	GENERATE	Required	Required	
Machine Configuration	CHANNEL[1,2]	Required	Required	Required[3]
	CONSOLE[1]	Required	Required	
	IODEVICE[1,4]	Required	Required	Required[3]
	UNITNAME[1]	Required	Required	Required
Control Program	AFFINITY	Optional	Optional[5]	
	CKPTREST	Optional	Optional	
	CTRLPROG	Optional	Optional[6]	
	EDIT	Optional	Optional	
	JES	Optional[7]		
	SCHEDULR	Optional	Optional	Required
	TSO	Optional	Optional[5]	
Data Management	DATAMGT	Optional	Optional[5]	
User-Written SVC Routines	SVCTABLE[1]	Optional	Optional[5]	

FIG. 9-2 MVS/370 required and optional SYSGEN macro instructions (footnote numbers refer to information in the IBM manual) (courtesy of International Business Machines Corporation)

2. Operations support
- Operations support software, such as file space management
- System measurement
- Job control language (JCL) support

In this example, there are two stages: The first stage assembles the SYSGEN macros prepared by the system programmer and expands them into job control statements and utility control statements; the second stage uses the data created in the first to build the new or updated operating system libraries. Figure 9-2 shows the required and optional SYSGEN macro instructions. Figure 9-3 is an example of the detailed parameters that the system programmer would prepare. For example, the system programmer determines what the input/output (I/O) device type is in each case (such as an on-line disk drive) and enters the required parameters. The configuration of a system (e.g., hardware, such as number of disk drives) varies in different environments, and the system programmer does the mapping of the operating system to correspond to the actual hardware in use.

[symbol]	IODEVICE	ADDRESS={address| (address,number of units)}
		UNIT={device|DUMMY}
		[ADAPTER=adapter][1]
		[AP={YES|NO}]
		[CUNUMBR=(number[,number]...)][2]
		[DEVTYPE=type]
		[ERRTAB=nnn]
		[EXPBFR={number|4096}][1]
		[FEATURE=(feature[,feature]...)][1]
		[GCU={2848-1|2848-2|2848-21|2848-22}][1]
		[MODEL=model][1]
		[NUMSECT={number|16}][1]
		[OBRCNT=number][1]
		[OFFLINE={YES|NO}]
		[OPTCHAN=number]
		[PATH=chpid][3]
		[PCU=n][1]
		[SETADDR=value][1]
		[TCU={2701|2702|2703}][1]
		[TIMEOUT={Y|N}][3]

FIG. 9-3 MVS/370 input/output device macro instructions (footnote numbers refer to information in the IBM manual) (courtesy of International Business Machines Corporation)

Supervision of System Programming

System programmers have assigned tasks and procedures. Although many vendor software installation guides spell out in detailed step-by-step instructions exactly how to install software and how to customize it to an organization's specific needs, there is sometimes a tendency for system programmers to make some changes without following established procedures. Management of this function should employ the same disciplines that are used to manage any technical function, whether it is performed by engineers or by scientists, including:

- Team walk-through
- Testing of systems and machines
- Documentation of procedures

- Documentation of activities
- Change control procedures

It is essential for the system programmer to make notes and keep track of what point has been reached in the implementation or maintenance of the system software. In any location with one or more system programmers, logs are a necessity.

To control system software and system programming, it is important to consider some management controls:

- Work review
- Time analysis
- Software
  a. Log analyzers or job accounting
  b. Maintenance journals
  c. Functioning of software
  d. Independent testing by quality assurance staff
- Organizational controls
- Separation of duties

Procedural Controls

These controls are designed to ensure that procedures already in place are actually followed, including restart and recovery procedures. The following questions should be asked regarding procedures for the system programs:

- What are the specific procedures?
- What documentation exists?
- What are the processes?

Once the answers to these questions are known, it is possible to ascertain whether the authorized steps are followed as described.

A main area of concern is the ability of the system programs, and programmers, to access such "restricted resources" as files and programs for production. Other control tools include:

- Review of system log reports
- Job accounting reports
- Software controls, such as
  a. Passwords
  b. Data file protection
  c. Security software

AUDITING SYSTEM SOFTWARE

Prior to audit, it is necessary to evaluate the following:

- Manual controls over computer processing
- Controls over application programming and computer operations
- Controls over system programming

When auditing system software programming, there must be a review of the following:

- System software documentation
- Access to system software documentation
- Approval of system software enhancement
- Control of approved system software enhancements
- Vendor-supplied system software enhancements
- Testing of system software designed or modified by the company
- Unauthorized enhancements
- Urgent modifications
- Acceptance of system software
- Final review and approval of system software enhancements by the EDP function

The usual approach concentrates on having the auditor evaluate adherence to established production schedules and the unauthorized execution of production programs. It is important to realize that this approach produces information to help analyze the controls over unscheduled access to authorized programs—not the completeness, accuracy, or validity of the data being processed.

It may appear that adherence to authorized processing schedules is of no immediate concern to the auditor, but without it computer programs could be executed to process financially significant or highly sensitive data without adequate control. Authorized programs could be run in the wrong sequence, at the wrong time, or with uncontrolled parameters. This problem becomes particularly important in a multiprogramming environment, where several programs may be executed simultaneously and job scheduling becomes difficult to follow.

The system console operator cannot be expected to detect all possible unauthorized use of data files. If, in fact, a proper segregation of duties is in force, the computer operator will not even know which data files are considered to be proprietary in nature. Unless there is a detailed, independent review of programs executed, the auditor may not be able to rely on the controls over

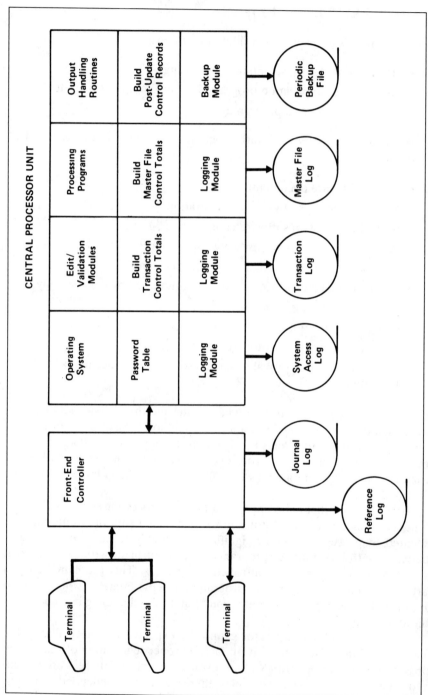

FIG. 9-4   Control procedures for on-line systems

production, scheduling, and/or unauthorized program processing of financial data.

Substantive testing of computer operations controls usually involves the tedious and time-consuming task of reviewing computer-generated logs as an audit or information trail of processing. (See Figure 9-4.) The sheer volume and technical content of the logs, however, increases chances of human oversight or error. Also, this information may not even be printed or retained, so that manual review may not be possible.

Audit software, such as Coopers & Lybrand's SMF Analyzer, addresses these problems by organizing the information in a readable format for analysis and manual reconciliation to the processing schedules.

AUDIT APPROACH TO COMPUTER OPERATIONS CONTROLS

When a systems audit approach has been adopted, and significant programmed accounting procedures are not enforced by user controls, it is necessary for the auditor to consider the procedures exercised within the EDP department to ensure the continued and proper operation of the programs.

These procedures should control the development and maintenance of system software and application programs, program security, computer operations, and data file security. When these controls are to be relied on, there should be a formal evaluation of them using a general controls questionnaire. Then their operation should be tested.

The auditor examines the controls over computer operations to determine whether significant programmed accounting procedures are applied consistently and to ensure that correct data files are used. Computer operations controls include controls over operator actions, job preparation and submission procedures, file control, and recovery procedures following a processing failure. These controls often depend on the system software for their effectiveness.

Weaknesses in computer operations controls may adversely affect program and data file security as well as having a direct effect on accounting information (e.g., through inappropriate use of programmed procedures). If authorized processing schedules are not strictly followed, programmed procedures may not be applied in the correct sequence or may not be applied at all, which could result in accounting errors. Similarly, unauthorized jobs and programs could be executed to process accounting data.

OPERATING SYSTEM CONCEPTS

Operating system concepts, terminology, and techniques are essential to understanding system software, since the operating system is a central feature of all system software. This chapter's discussion of operating systems relates to auditing mainframe computer environments; minicomputer and micro-computer operating systems are discussed in Chapter 5, "Computer Concepts," and auditing microcomputers in Chapter 30, "How to Audit Microcomputers."

It is important for the auditor to understand the concept of operating systems and be able to communicate, using accurate terminology, with the people to be interviewed. Without knowing a common language, the auditor is unlikely to be able to analyze the computer environment effectively to deter-mine potential exposures.

In very small computer systems, such as microcomputers, there is little need for a complex operating system. Equipment sharing can be handled on a manual basis. For example, a user may sign up to use the system between 10:00 and 11:00 A.M. It is the user's responsibility to provide all software to run the system. At the end of the allocated time, the user relinquishes the machine to the next person on the list. In a complex environment, the operating system handles some of these tasks.

Automatic Job Scheduling

The problem with manual scheduling is that the equipment may be idle for long periods between the time one user finishes work and the next user sets up the machine. For larger computer systems, operating systems can provide software that automatically begins running the next job as soon as necessary resources are available.

Introducing an automated scheduling system can more than double the amount of data processed simply by eliminating idle time between jobs. The obvious disadvantages of such a system over manual scheduling are the ex-pense of the software that does the sequencing and the need to provide memory and disk space to store the operating system.

Logging of System Activity

Operating systems commonly keep a log of the activity of the computer system. The log may record the time each job is started and finished, as well as the resources (central processing unit (CPU) time, I/O time, and so forth) con-sumed by the job. This information is the basis for charging users for the resources they consume while running their jobs. The log may also record the usage of the various equipment components in the computer system, which can be used to adjust the system and improve its efficiency. Failures in the com-puter equipment or software can be recorded in the log; these entries can be used for maintenance of the equipment and to improve the system's reliability. Within IBM's MVS, logging is performed by the System Management Facility (SMF). The information retained can be very helpful to the EDP auditor. Figure 9-5 is a flowchart for SMF audit software; details are given in the later section entitled "SMF Concepts."

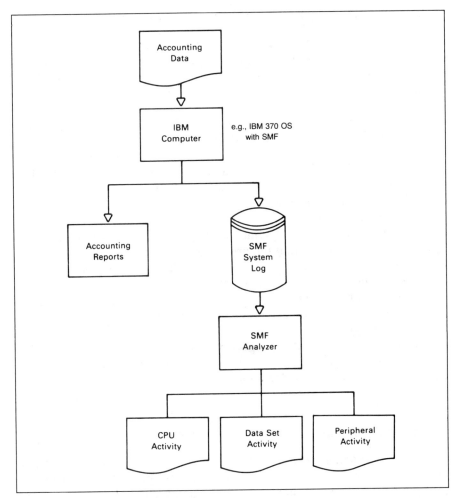

FIG. 9-5 Flowchart for the SMF Analyzer

Command or Job Control Language

Some computer systems provide their users with a variety of services, such as several computer language translators, file-managing programs, and applications programs. The user of a computer system can specify which services a job requires by using control statements, which the operating system reads and follows. The control statements accepted by a particular computer system are the JCL or a command language. In many systems, this information is entered through a terminal or via files that are part of automatic job scheduling systems.

Multiple Programs in Memory (Multiprogramming)

In computer systems where there is a lot of concurrent I/O activity, especially on a large number of devices, it may be advantageous to load more than one user's program into memory at a given time. This technique is called multiprogramming.

Consider a large business EDP job that uses little CPU time but a lot of disk time to update a file of customers' accounts. Except for the disk, such a job will leave most of the system's resources idle. This not only wastes resources, but also means that users with small jobs must wait a long time while the large EDP job ties up the system. Multiprogramming can solve these problems. In a multiprogramming operating system, more than one job can be active at a time. When the CPU is idle while waiting for an I/O operation to finish, the operating system can start the CPU working on another job. Similarly, if one job is not using part of the system's resources (such as the magnetic-tape drives), then another program requiring the idle resources can be activated. For this to work, the main memory is divided into partitions, segments, or pages, depending on the particular operating system, to allow jobs to run at the same time. Multiprogramming can also solve the problem of poor turnaround time for small jobs by allowing them to be started and completed while a large job is in progress.

In computer systems that support interactive terminals, many user programs are active at one time. The operating system automatically switches CPU attention from one user to another as needed, giving each user the impression that the CPU is doing only their job.

Using Multiprogramming to Implement Spooling

Once multiprogramming is available in a system, it can use special programs at the same time as user programs. For example, one special program can read cards from the card reader onto magnetic disk or tape. The cards representing a user's job are stored until the system is ready to process the job. Similarly, when a user job produces lines to be printed, these lines are temporarily stored on a disk or tape. Later, a special program reads the stored lines and sends them to the printer. This technique is called spooling (Simultaneous Peripheral Operations On-Line).

When user jobs are stored on a disk, spooling provides a scheduling advantage. If there are several jobs on the disk waiting to be run, the operating system can choose those high-priority jobs that require fast turnaround to run first.

The use of multiprogramming is advantageous because it can improve CPU and I/O resource utilization, improve turnaround time for small jobs, and provide good response for interactive terminals. Unfortunately, such a complex operating system is expensive to produce, and, therefore, may not always be available for the computer that is being used.

An example of a program like this is the IBM licensed program, DOS/POWER, a spooling program that provides the user with automatic staging of input and output and priority scheduling of all programs executed under its control. DOS/POWER resides in one partition, or area, of the main memory and is able to serve all remaining partitions of the DOS (disk operating system) environment placed under its control, provided these have a lower system dispatching priority than that of the DOS/POWER partition.

DOS/POWER maintains input and output queues, or waiting lines, for jobs to be processed on direct access storage (disk) for the card readers, tape drives, diskette I/O drives (input only), card punches, and printers associated with the partitions under its control. These queues are filled or emptied as jobs are created and executed by the appropriate physical devices. When a program under DOS/POWER control makes an input or output request to one of these devices, POWER dynamically moves the next record from the appropriate input queue for a job waiting or collects the record and places it in the appropriate output queue for a job completed.

The queues are under operator control. The system operator can modify the order in which programs are executed by manipulating the queues with DOS/POWER operator commands. When DOS/POWER is generated, the system programmer may select features to include or exclude job accounting information. When these options are selected, job and program execution data is written to a job accounting file via an interface support to all partitions.

AUDIT IMPLICATIONS OF THE DISK OPERATING SYSTEM

IBM's DOS has had a major impact on computer operations procedures, especially when the DOS/POWER spooling facility is used. DOS controls the use of multiprogramming by providing the partitions, maintaining the job queues, scheduling job processing, routing output, and providing job accounting information. DOS maintains a log of programs executed and files used and can be used to control the files accessed.

Like any automated system, DOS can only control operations adequately when appropriate manual procedures exist. DOS is, however, the major tool used by the operations staff and can provide useful information to the auditor. A major audit problem may be the sheer volume of information produced by the system, or that reports produced are simply not printed and retained. This is where an audit software analyzer, such as the Coopers & Lybrand DOS/POWER audit software analyzer, can come into use.

The analyzer helps the auditor perform a review and tests of job scheduling procedures. Using the reports generated, the auditor can test for the execution of proprietary software and assess whether the software is executed only in accordance with authorized schedules. The following information is usually reported:

- Jobs executed by partition
- Programs executed by date and time

The analyzer may be used as part of the compliance testing of general controls when these are to be relied on as a tool to improve understanding of job scheduling procedures, and to support the management report or to aid substantive testing of computer operations where scheduling controls are found to be deficient.

In a DOS environment the auditor obtains an understanding of the procedures in the DP department in the normal way, by interviewing personnel, observation, and reviewing the relevant documentation. A general controls questionnaire can be used to deal with computer operations. When assembling the information necessary to evaluate the controls over operations, the auditor should consider:

- How does the organization identify jobs or programs? It is useful to obtain an understanding of the job or program-naming conventions and to examine how rigorously the personnel observe these conventions.
- What are the most sensitive or critical programs or data files? How are they identified?
- When a job fails or when the operators intervene to alter the automatic scheduling system, how are these events recorded?
- Has the organization installed anything over and above the standard cancellation records?
- Has the organization installed any special system software that could affect the standard records?
- How many partitions are in use, and what are the differences between them?

All this information can help the auditor to decide whether the audit software analyzer should be used and, if so, to interpret the analyzer results.

The auditor should also determine (1) which jobs were executed and that they were executed in accordance with an authorized schedule; (2) that all tasks are scheduled to promote efficient use of the facilities and to meet user requirements; and (3) whether correct class assignments or priorities have been established to allow for prompt processing.

Audit Program — Sequence of Events

The following program of events shows how DOS/POWER audit software can be implemented.

Events	Auditor's Actions
Planning	• Develop an audit plan and budget. • Collect the information concerning scheduling procedures for the computer. • Prepare planning working papers. • Determine period to be tested. • Agree to provide management reports within the time requirements. Keep audit staff informed as to progress and any causes for additional time. • Before the due date, install the package and execute a test run.

Audit review	• Identify job streams and programs that process sensitive or financially significant data.
	• Obtain the following documentation:
	  a. List of all regularly scheduled applications
	  b. List of all applications scheduled on an irregular basis
	  c. Job rerun report indicating reasons for reruns
	• Prepare a memo specifying required system programmer assistance, computer resources, and authorization.
	• Perform procedure to confirm production programs and job streams.
	• Execute audit software package with required test period parameters.
	• Compare output results with the processing schedule obtained from computer operations department.
	• Help analyze and evaluate the adequacy of controls over production scheduling and prepare management report where appropriate.

Completion	• Summarize time, costs, and expenses. Document any reasons for changes from original budget. Provide suggestions for the coming audit period.

Using the Report

Two typical reports produced using audit software procedures are shown in Figure 9-6. Standard follow-up audit procedures are to select the period and the programs to be examined. This depends on the assessment of the controls over operations and program security. The auditor needs to understand the organization's program-naming conventions and be able to identify the most significant programs. These could be application programs incorporating important programmed accounting procedures or powerful system utility pro-

REPORT NO. DOSREP01-1
REPORT DATE 03/25/82

COOPERS & LYBRAND (CAAG) DOS ANALYZER
JOBS EXECUTED BY PARTITION

PAGE NO. 8
PERIOD ENDED 03/16/82

PRTN	JOB DATE	JOB TIME	POWER JOB NAME	JOB NO	DOS JOB NAME	STEP NUMBER	PROGRAM NAME	CNCL DOS	CNCL PWR	RJE I/O	OBS NUMBER	REMARKS	ID
EG	01-05-82	18-40-52	DFMAINT	6.008	LIBMOVE	2	CORGZ				197		
BG	01-05-82	18-40-58	DFMAINT	6.008	LIBMOVE	3	MAINT				198		
BG	01-05-82	18-49-43	ZBA-DAT	6.015	ZBA-DAT	1	FCOBOL				199		
EG	01-05-82	18-50-36	ZBA-DAT	6.015	CATAL	1	MAINT	0F			200		
BG	01-05-82	18-50-47	ZBA-DAT	6.015	CATAL	2	LISTLOG	FF			201		
BG	01-05-82	18-50-50	ZBA-DAT	6.015	RESET	1					202		
BG	01-05-82	18-54-52	DELPVT	6.017	DELPVT	1	MAINT				203		
EG	01-05-82	18-56-54	DELPVT	6.018	DELPVT	1	MAINT	23			204		
BG	01-05-82	18-57-19	DELPVT	6.018	DELPVT	2	LISTLOG	FF			205		
BG	01-05-82	18-57-21	DELPVT	6.019	DELPVT	1	MAINT				206		
BG	01-05-82	18-57-51	DELPVT	6.020	DELPVT	1	MAINT				207		
BG	01-05-82	18-59-44	ZBA-DAT1	6.021	ZBA-DAT1	1	FCOBOL				208		
BG	01-05-82	19-00-16	ZBA-DAT1	6.021	CATAL	1	MAINT	0F			209		
DS	01-05-82	19-00-29	ZDA-DAT1	6.021	CATAL	2	LISTLOG	FF			210		
DG	01-05-82	19-00-32	ZBA-DAT1	6.021	RESET	1					211		

REPORT NO. DOSREP01-5
REPORT DATE 03/25/82

COOPERS & LYBRAND (CAAG) DOS ANALYZER
PROGRAMS EXECUTED

PAGE NO. 5
PERIOD ENDED 03/16/82

PROGRAM NAME	PRTN	JOB DATE	JOB TIME	POWER JOB NAME	JOB NO	DOS JOB NAME	STEP NUMBER	CNCL DOS	CNCL PWR	RJE I/O	OBS NUMBER	REMARKS	ID
CORGZ	BG	01-06-82	08-29-27	DFMAINT	6.046	LIBMOVE	2				183		
DITTO	F4	01-04-82	11-54-23	PACDITTO	2.034	PACDITTO	1				184		
DITTO	F4	01-04-82	14-30-06	PACDITTO	2.034	PACDITTO	1				185		
DITTO	F4	01-04-82	15-04-28	PACDITTO	2.034	PACDITTO	1				186		
DITTO	F4	01-04-82	15-51-17	PACDITTO	2.034	PACDITTO	1	24			187		
DITTO	F4	01-04-82	15-55-23	PACDITTO	2.034	PACDITTO	1				188		
DITTO	F4	01-05-82	11-52-03	PACDITTO	2.034	PACDITTO	1				189		
DITTO	BG	01-05-82	13-55-18	DPDITTO	5.937	DITTO	1				190		
DITTO	F4	01-06-82	10-21-49	PACDITTO	2.034	PACDITTO	1				191		
DITTO	F4	01-07-82	12-21-27	PACDITTO	2.034	PACDITTO	1				192		
DITTO	F4	01-07-82	14-30-44	PACDITTO	2.034	PACDITTO	1				193		
DITTO	F4	01-07-82	15-24-58	PACDITTO	2.034	PACDITTO	1	24	40		194		
DITTO	BG	01-07-82	15-32-54	BANKTCPY	4.244	BANKTCPY	1				195		
DITTO	EG	01-07-82	15-35-22	PACDITTO	2.034	PACDITTO	1	24	40		196		
DITTO	EG	01-07-82	15-37-39	PACDITTO	2.034	PACDITTO	1	1A			197		
DITTO	EG	01-07-82	16-05-51	PACDITTO	2.034	PACDITTO	1	24	40		198		
DPCDDISK	F3	01-04-82	11-17-29	V4ACTABL	5.857	V4ACTABL	1				199		
DPCDDISK	F3	01-04-82	12-07-28	V4ACTABL	5.661	V4ACTABL	1				200		
DPCDDISK	F3	01-05-82	08-41-27	V4ACTABL	5.907	V4ACTABL	1				201		
DPCDDISK	F3	01-07-82	14-55-17	V4ACTABL	6.447	V4ACTABL	1				202		
DPCDDISK	F3	01-07-82	16-09-01	V4ACTABL	6.476	V4ACTABL	1				203		
DSERV	BG	01-05-82	14-34-41	DISPLAY4	3.617	DISPLAY4	1				204		
DSERV	BG	01-05-82	14-34-49	DISPLAY3	3.619	DISPLAY3	1				205		

FIG. 9-6   Audit software reports: Jobs executed by partition (top) and programs executed (bottom)

grams. The auditor should remember to include compilations and other such regular but important functions, as well as software utilities that bypass normal controls (see page 9-18), and should be alert for programs that have not been named in accordance with the naming conventions. To test this, the auditor can include some apparently insignificant programs in the audit sample, particularly where there is a suspicion that programs are being named incorrectly. Of course, the auditor should tailor the tests to suit the assignment.

Checking Normal Use of Application Programs

For the selected application programs, the auditor traces the entry on the audit software analyzer report to the authorized job schedule for the period and confirms that it was run at the right period and in the right sequence.

Checking Use of System Software

For the selected nonapplication programs, the auditor should

- Trace the entry on the audit software analyzer report to the authorized job schedule, the authorized run request, or whatever authorization is appropriate for the installation, to ensure that proper authorization was issued.
- Using the console log, or whatever other records may be maintained in the installation. Determine which data files were accessed (these could be application data files or other programs, depending on the nature of the utility) and confirm that this access was covered by the related authorization.

Audit Report Comments

The auditor should include any control weakness noted as a result of the follow-up procedures in the audit report. For example, a weakness exists when it is possible to execute sensitive production payroll programs outside of normal processing schedules with no supporting authorization or information trails to document the reasons for the execution.

AUDIT APPROACH TO PROGRAMMED PROCEDURES

Programmed procedures are procedures incorporated in programs. They are of interest to the auditor because they perform such functions as comparisons, calculations, summarizations, and generation of data. The results of programmed procedures will not normally be checked to the extent required in a noncomputerized system. This is because these procedures function consistently without error, provided the relevant programmed procedures are properly designed and implemented and controls exist to prevent their unauthorized alteration and ensure their proper use.

Any errors in programs can produce disastrous results because they have the potential of affecting all data processed by the program and may not be detected by manual procedures. Therefore, program implementation and security controls are the cornerstones of a well-controlled EDP environment.

Control

Proper control over program implementation and change includes:

- Authorization prior to the program implementation and change (see Chapter 7, "The System Development Life Cycle")

- Review and approval of the new program or change of an existing program

- Proper and controlled conversion of the program into executable form (compile and link-edit)

To translate a source program (written in a high-level language) into machine-readable form (object), the computer uses a compiler, which is another type of program. Once a compile occurs (after no errors in program format or syntax have been detected by the compiler), the computer executes a link-edit. The link-edit combines object programs with the standard functions necessary to produce a machine-executable (load) program. (See Figure 9-7.)

Programs must be secured from utility programs that can alter a program during or after the controlled compile and link-edit. Programs should only be changed at source level, but they may also be changed directly at the object or executable level. "ZAP" is the name of a program that can change an executable program. The ZAP bypasses the controls created by the compile and link-edit procedure, which makes ZAP a difficult tool to control.

To evaluate these areas, audit software can be used. Coopers & Lybrand's Special Link Library Analysis Package (SLAPS) assists in achieving program implementation and security audit objectives (see Figure 9-8) as follows:

- *Finds program changes.* It provides the COMPILE/LINKEDIT Report, which lists, in working paper format, the program name, compiler name, date of compile, and the link-edit data. With this information, the auditor can trace all changes and new program implementations for the examination period. By comparing reported dates with authorization dates, the auditor can also ensure that changes were not made without management's authorization. Examination periods can be limited to a few days, a month, or even years.

- *Reports ZAPs.* It generates the ZAP report that furnishes the program name, the link-edit date, ZAP date, any ZAP comments, and the control section where the ZAP occurred (a standard function, a subprogram, or a main program). This report can be used as a working paper to trace the changes to proper authorization.

- *Compares program maintenance.* Effective general controls ensure that all programs implemented or deleted since the last audit test were properly authorized. To achieve this objective, the program can perform a comparison between two examination periods and report changed and new programs or programs not changed during the period.

Figure 9-9 shows reports generated by this software. The first report generated by SLAPS, the LINK/ZAP Date Report, lists by date all programs found in date sequence. The user may want the list of older programs to

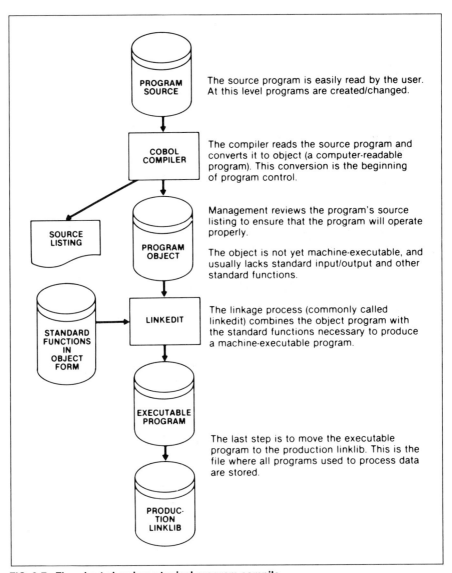

The source program is easily read by the user. At this level programs are created/changed.

The compiler reads the source program and converts it to object (a computer-readable program). This conversion is the beginning of program control.

Management reviews the program's source listing to ensure that the program will operate properly.

The object is not yet machine-executable, and usually lacks standard input/output and other standard functions.

The linkage process (commonly called linkedit) combines the object program with the standard functions necessary to produce a machine-executable program.

The last step is to move the executable program to the production linklib. This is the file where all programs used to process data are stored.

FIG. 9-7 Flowchart showing a typical program compile

determine if they are still in use and, occasionally, to see if they are compatible with the current computer system.

Audit Reliance

Programmed procedures are those steps in the computer system designed to ensure that data is recorded and processed completely and accurately. Audit

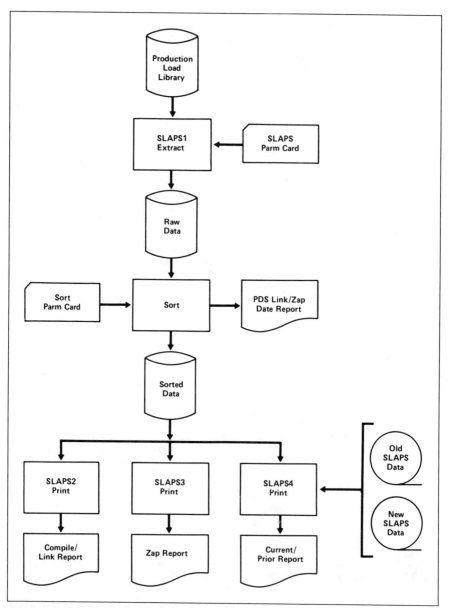

FIG. 9-8 Flowchart for the SLAPS audit software

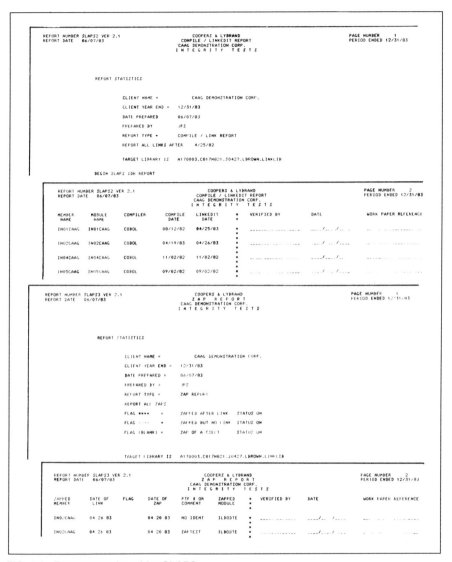

FIG. 9-9 Reports produced by SLAPS

software can also be used when the auditor needs to rely on programmed procedures in a specific application program or a series of programs. The auditor can continue to rely on programmed procedures once they have been examined, expending a minimum amount of time in subsequent audits by using an analysis program with two-period comparison ability, in conjunction with other audit software.

Limitations. The quality of the information received from any audit software that analyzes the system use depends on the quality and reliability of the data in the target load library. The load module library contains a record (known as a ZAP record) with information about all changes made to each load module in the library. The auditor should be aware that the information in this record can be changed by the use of a ZAP. The ZAP record relates to uses of ZAP on a load module. ZAPs can also be made on physical memory locations to alter whatever data is in that location. There is no means of recording such uses of ZAPs.

Audit Objectives. As a result of the aforementioned limitations, the audit objectives here are to

- Confirm that ZAP is only used on the production load libraries on the basis of appropriate authorization.
- Confirm that production load modules are only compiled and linked following appropriate authorization.
- Ensure that all deletions from the production load library in the period under review were performed on the basis of appropriate authorization.
- Confirm that all production load modules follow the standard naming conventions in the installation (where appropriate).

When using an audit software analyzer as an application review tool, the auditor can help determine what key programs have changed since the last review period. Other audit software can then be used to analyze the changes and determine whether reliance is still appropriate. This can greatly reduce the amount of work when application reviews are needed.

AUDITING SYSTEM USAGE

To optimize the use of computer processing power, one of the most efficient methods is the analysis of information on computer usage. In response to desires to increase efficiency in use of computerized resources, computer hardware manufacturers have developed and automated methods for recording, for subsequent analysis, details of all computer usage.

System Management Facility (SMF) is a feature of the IBM OS System Control Programs (OS/MFT, OS/MVT, OS/VS1, OS/VS2, SVS, MVS, MVS/XA). It provides a way to gather and record information that can be used to evaluate system use.

Coopers & Lybrand has developed the SMF Analyzer to use the information recorded by the IBM SMF. As an audit tool, the SMF Analyzer extracts and reports SMF data to assist the auditor in evaluating and testing general controls.

When using this software, the audit approach includes evaluation of internal controls in computer systems. A subset of the internal controls is the application controls and the programmed procedures, which are defined to include the following:

- *Application controls* — Controls over the completeness, accuracy, and validity of the data being input, processed, and maintained on file. These normally consist of edit tests, accumulation of totals, reconciliations, and the identification and reporting of incorrect, exception, or missing data. These functions are normally effective only if combined with related manual procedures. As an example, identifying and reporting exception data is ineffective unless there is a subsequent manual investigation of the exceptions.

- *Programmed procedures* — Calculation, summarization, and categorization procedures applied to the data. These are significant in that the results are not normally checked to the extent required in a noncomputerized system. The results are not checked because these procedures function consistently without error, provided the relevant programmed procedures are properly implemented and controls exist to prevent their unauthorized alteration and to ensure their proper use.

Controls over the design, implementation, security, and use of computer programs and the security of data files are collectively known as general or integrity controls. These controls, performed mainly within the EDP function, are a combination of manual controls and system software. Basically, the same general controls are applied to all systems being developed or processed at a computer installation. In this respect, the SMF Analyzer does not affect the auditor's approach to the completeness, accuracy, or validity of data but merely provides certain information as to how data of financial significance was processed.

Audit Approach

Where analyzing general controls, the auditor should perform the following functions:

- Obtain and confirm an understanding of the internal accounting control system.
- Evaluate the effectiveness of the internal accounting control system.
- Perform audit testing of compliance or substantive nature, or both.

Audit Objectives

The main areas of general controls in which audit software analyzers may be used to assist the auditor are:

- Program security controls
- Computer operations controls
- Data file security controls

Control Objectives

Adequate steps should be taken to ensure the security of programs. (See Chapter 32, "Security.") Computer operations procedures should be adequate to ensure that

- Authorized programmed procedures are consistently applied.
- The correct data files are used.

SMF Concepts

As an example of how the audit can be done in a mainframe computer environment, this section provides an understanding of IBM's SMF, the information it gathers, and how Coopers & Lybrand's SMF Analyzer is designed to use the information recorded by SMF. (See Figure 9-10.)

As was mentioned previously, SMF is a feature of IBM's OS System Control Program operating system. Some subsystems, such as ACF2 (a security software package), also generate SMF data. SMF collects and stores data that reflects the activity that takes place within the computer. The primary purpose of SMF is to provide accounting and system performance data for an installation to help manage it. (See Figure 9-11.) Data from SMF can be used for billing processing costs to users and for adjusting hardware and system software configurations for better performance. This same data can also be quite useful in supporting a number of audit applications.

SMF collects its data by writing various records to disk storage during computer operations. SMF records its data in one of two data files and keeps track of which file it is using. When one data file is full, SMF issues a message to the operator to dump that data to tape, and SMF starts writing to the other. If the second file data fills up before the operator dumps the first data file (both are full), SMF stops recording data until one of the data files becomes available. Recent releases of SMF allow the installation to define more than two data files, but the processing is essentially the same. In other systems, this data sometimes automatically over-writes itself once a data file is full.

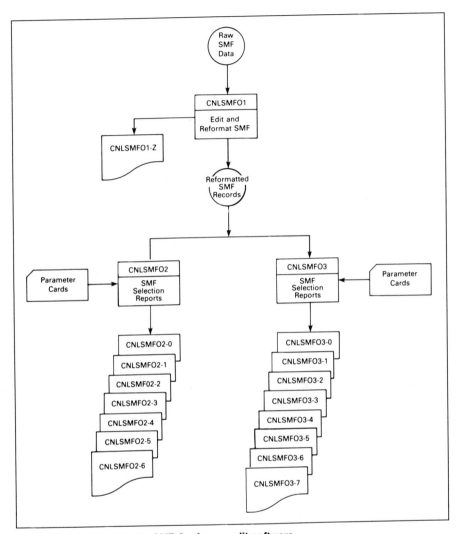

FIG. 9-10 Flowchart for the SMF Analyzer audit software

The types of SMF records that are recorded are determined by the options selected by the installation. SMF records can be divided into five types:

1. Accounting records
2. Data set records
3. Volume records
4. System records
5. Subsystem records

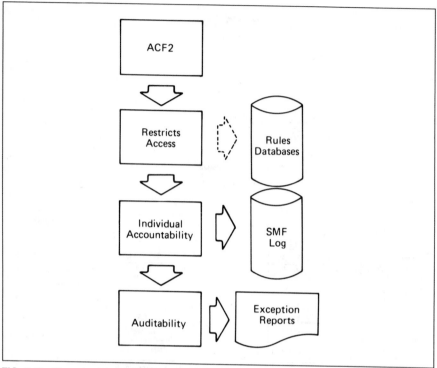

FIG. 9-11   Flowchart for the ACF2 audit software program, which also analyzes the SMF log

Accounting Records. Accounting records describe the computer re-sources (programs, data, and so forth) used, the user, and how long the resources were used. SMF generally writes accounting records at the end of jobs and job steps. The following are tracked:

- Job log and user identification
- Problem program name and start time
- Step name and number
- Job and step start and end times
- Job and step completion codes

Data File Records. Data file, also known as data set, records describe the characteristics, activity, and users of data files. Information includes user, job, and characteristics of the data file. SMF generally writes data file records when a data file is scratched, renamed, closed, or accessed. These records include such data as:

- Data file name
- Number of volumes
- Volume serial number
- Record formats and lengths

Volume Records. Volume records describe the space available on direct access tape volumes, provide error statistics for tape volumes, and describe data spaces in a VSAM (virtual storage access method) catalog. SMF generally writes volume records when the computer system is started and stopped and when a tape volume is demounted. They include such data as:

- Volume number
- Number of read and write errors
- Number of unallocated cylinders and tracks

System Records. System records describe the system configuration and SMF options in effect, provide system statistics, and record the occurrence of specific events. SMF generally writes system records at 10 minute intervals of CPU processing time and at the time of certain operator commands. They include such data as:

- SMF options
- System wait time
- Count of SMF records generated but not written during periods when SMF data files were not available for writing
- Start and end time of periods without SMF recording

Subsystem Records. Subsystem records describe the activities and events of the various subsystem components in use. Examples are Time-Sharing Option (TSO), Job Entry Subsystem (JES2 or JES3), and security software. Subsystem records are generally written at the time the activity or event takes place and include such data as:

- TSO step termination
- JES2 options
- Length and text of SIGN-ON messages

In addition to the records generated by SMF, the installation has the option of writing additional information to the SMF data files. These user records are not processed by SMF but are merely recorded along with data produced by SMF.

An installation has the option of performing additional processing requirements not otherwise available under SMF. At specified points in the SMF processing cycle, control passes to user-written code for predefined actions to be performed. These exit points are called SMF User Exits. This information includes:

- Volume of SMF data to be analyzed (SMF generates considerable data on systems usage)
- Period(s) for which SMF data should be analyzed
- Completeness of SMF data
- Integrity of SMF data

Analysis of SMF Data

Audit Concern	*Audit Response*
SMF generates large amounts of data. How much data must be analyzed?	• Depends on extent to which the results of the SMF Analyzer are being relied on. Existence of and reliance on general controls would probably result in less analysis. • Value of test needs to be considered. Substantive testing would probably result in the analysis of greater amounts of data than with compliance testing.

How should data to be analyzed be selected?	• Depends on approach adopted (e.g., substantive or compliance testing of general controls).
	  a. Substantive techniques would involve spreading testing over the period being audited.
	  b. Compliance tests may result in testing SMF data for the same period that basic controls and disciplines over basic controls have been tested.

All SMF data is generated.	• Review SMF parameters and user exits to ensure that information required by the SMF Analyzer is not being suppressed. • The installation controls the use of SMF through parameters. At initial program load (IPL), the

Audit Concern	*Audit Response*
	operator may advise the system as to which set of SMF parameters is to be used. These parameters, if used, enable the operator to modify options. The auditor should determine whether parameters have suppressed any data necessary for the effective use of the SMF Analyzer.
	• SMF writes records to one of two disk files (SYS1.MANY and SYS1.MANX). As one file fills up, SMF begins writing records to the next. The system advises the operator to dump the data from disk to tape. In the event that the operator fails to purge a disk file and both files are full, the system generates a message to that effect and SMF stops writing records until space is made available. The auditor should ensure that such an occurrence has not caused a loss of data for the period being tested.
	• Review controls over SYS1.PARMLIB to ensure that access is restricted and that SMF options are appropriate.
SMF data generated is secure.	• Review access controls of SMF data files (SYS1.MANY and SYS1.MANX) to ensure that access is restricted.
	• Ensure that the procedures for copying SMF data to tape, and the subsequent storage of those tape files, are adequate to prevent the unauthorized manipulation of data.

In addition to the preceding audit concerns, there are several limitations inherent in SMF of which the auditor should be aware. The major limitations are described below.

• SMF does not collect or record data for system tasks, only for problem programs.

- SMF data may be lost in the event of a machine failure or if the operator fails to enter the appropriate HALT command before performing an IPL or powering off the machine, or if the operator fails to dump one of the SMF record files before the other file is full.

- SMF recording may not be performed for jobs started by the operator from the console.

- Timing is not performed for jobs or job steps with certain parameters, so the SMF timing exits would not be entered for those particular jobs.

- Program names are not recorded when programs are executed with a refer-back feature (usually used for program testing).

- Programs executed as subroutines or subsystems, such as IMS (Information Management System) or CICS (Customer Information Control System) application programs, are not identified by program names. For example, if an on-line IMS system is operating, only one-step execution is recorded in SMF along with all of the files accessed during the period of operation. In the case of a batch IMS system, each execution of IMS may be shown, but the specific application program executions will not be identified because they are not recorded in SMF. Such subsystems may create their own logs that can be used to monitor program executions and file access.

- Data file activity records will not be created if the files are not allocated through data definition (DD) statements. System products such as the Structured Program Facility (SPF) under TSO access data files without using DD statements.

- Data activity records may not contain all of the data elements on the record. Data file characteristics such as creation date, expiration date, and label type are only collected by SMF when the file is created.

- SMF data is recorded for the first load library when load libraries are concatenated.

- The member name of a partitioned data set (a particular data file) is not always available. For example, the linkage editor does not provide SMF with the name of the program being added or replaced in a load library.

Audit Program — Sequence of Events

The following audit procedure can be used to analyze SMF data with audit software:

Event	Auditor's Actions
Planning	• Develop a plan and budget.
	• Collect the preliminary information concerning the EDP operations. This may include reviewing the recorded understanding of the system for any change in data processing. Prepare planning working papers.
	• Agree to provide the review of the general controls within the audit time requirements. Keep audit staff informed as to progress and any reasons for additional time.
Audit review	• Identify programs or data that have financial statement significance.
	• Obtain the following documentation:
	a. Programs authorized for production
	b. Production schedule
	c. Data files and authorized users
	• Prepare a memo specifying required system programmer assistance, computer resources, and authorization to access SMF log files and libraries.
	• Perform procedure to confirm production libraries.
	• Install the audit software package. Execute the software package.
	• Complete the working paper analysis (i.e., record the understanding in the working papers). The extent of analysis is determined by the auditor's identification of significant data.
	• Assist in the analysis and evaluation of the principal internal controls of the system from the working papers, and prepare a management report where appropriate.
Completion	• Summarize audit time, costs, and expenses. Document any reasons for changes from original budget. Provide suggestions for the coming audit period.

AUDITING PROGRAM SECURITY, IMPLEMENTATION, COMPUTER OPERATIONS, AND SYSTEM SOFTWARE CONTROLS

Source programs must be controlled to ensure that unauthorized changes are not made at the source level to the production program that processes data. Program security controls relate to source programs, but they also ensure that the appropriate load modules are executed. Audit software packages are designed to assist the auditor with audit concerns for program security, implementation, computer operations, and system software controls.

The auditor can use various methods in the evaluation of the program security, implementation, computer operations, and system software controls. It is important to realize that the packages produce the information to analyze these controls over programs, but not the information to analyze the completeness, accuracy, or validity of the data being processed, nor the appropriateness of the programmed procedures.

An important aspect to remember when auditing data processed by programmed procedures is that the information that may be processed is no different from that available in a noncomputerized system. The auditor's ultimate purpose in examining the data remains unchanged.

Thus, auditors must concern themselves with the accounting and control functions that occur within the computer environment. This concern has focused on two aspects of the use of computers in accounting applications: (1) the inclusion of accounting procedures and internal control procedures in computer programs and (2) the maintenance and security of accounting data in the computer environment.

The following are examples of accounting procedures that take place within computer programs:

- Calculation of gross pay, deductions, and net pay
- Calculation of sales invoice amount
- Automatic selection of invoices for payment

These procedures would ordinarily be subject to manual checking in a noncomputerized system.

The following are examples of internal control procedures that take place within computerized programs:

- Verification of proper vendor account codes
- Credit check for customer orders
- Preparation of lists of missing inventory counts

These procedures would be considered control functions if they were carried out manually and, therefore, should be considered control functions within the computer. These programmed procedures constitute one aspect of an auditor's concern with respect to computers.

The second aspect of an auditor's concern is the maintenance and security of accounting data in the computer environment, since they relate directly to the reliability of the accounting data. This data is in a form that can be accessed only by programs. Thus, like automated accounting procedures and controls, the maintenance and security of accounting data depends on programs.

Therefore, consistently proper operation of programmed procedures is an issue within the audit of every business or service organization that uses a computer to process data. Audit assurance for programmed procedures may be obtained by checking the results of processing. As the volume of data that is processed grows, however, such audit procedures become less and less efficient. To supplement audit reliance in large-volume situations, auditors often place reliance on the design, implementation, security, and use of programmed procedures and on the security of data within the computer environment. Controls over this design, implementation, security, and use of programmed procedures and over the security of data are the general or integrity controls.

Testing of General Controls

A major concern within general controls is the control over changes to programs. Two aspects of this control are to

1. Ensure that authorized changes are applied correctly.
2. Prevent unauthorized changes.

Compliance testing of general controls often addresses the procedures of the controls. For example, to test that a program change is authorized, the auditor verifies that specified authorized individuals signed the program change forms. To test that unauthorized changes are prevented, the auditor tests the computerized password system.

The ultimate test for authorized and unauthorized changes to programs is to compare the programs used in actual production processing with retained copies of the programs. The meticulous work required to do such a comparison can be performed routinely by computer software. Computer audit software tools automate the program comparison task. Two examples of such software are Coopers & Lybrand's Source Compare Program and Core Image Compare Program, which provide the tools to aid in compliance or functional testing of general or integrity controls.

Technical Concepts for Program Comparison Software

This section discusses technical concepts that are a basis for understanding and using the reports from program comparison software. The concepts (and terminology) apply specifically to IBM computers operating under the DOS or OS operation systems, or the various derivatives of these systems. They provide an idea of the overall concepts in a mainframe environment.

Language Translators (Compilers). Computer hardware is designed to perform a relatively small number of different operations. These "wired-in" operations correspond, one-to-one, to the relatively small number of instructions that comprise its machine language. Computers obtain their flexibility by being able to perform large numbers of these operations at great speed. When programs "run" on computers, they are directing the computer's activities through a series of instructions coded in machine language.

Machine language consists of various strings of the binary digits 0 and 1. Thus, the term "digital computer" is derived from the use of these two digits. This machine language directs the operation of a computer. However, it is an unnatural, error-prone, and inefficient process for a human to use machine language. Therefore, a number of programming languages have been developed that are more like English and are therefore more appropriate for programming the computer to perform the desired tasks. These languages are known as high-level languages (e.g., COBOL). When these are used, the results are called source programs. (See Chapter 5.)

A program written in a high-level language must be converted to machine language before it can be run on a computer. This conversion is accomplished by a compiler, which acts as a language translator. A language translator is itself a computer program that is able to change statements from a high-level language into instructions in machine code or language. The input to the language translator, called a source module, is a program written in a high-level language. The compiler first checks the program for syntax errors or mistakes in using the language. When these are present, no compile occurs. The output, called an object module, contains instructions in machine language.

The object program, as written in machine code, is very difficult for a person to analyze or interpret. It is clearly important that the object modules used to process information should correspond with the source version of the program. Should this not be the case, processing results may be unpredictable and program maintenance may become hazardous, not to mention the possibility of hidden, unauthorized instructions or routines being included in the object version.

An object module can be changed in various ways. Normally this is done by recompiling the source version of the program and replacing the previous version of the object program in the program library with a completely new version. However, object modules are maintained on disk files and may be changed directly using utility programs such as ZAP.

Other divergences may arise between the two versions:

- A modified or even unrelated program can be compiled using the same name and library as an existing authorized production program.
- Members of program libraries can be transformed or renamed.
- Modifications can be made to the source version of a program without being reflected in the object version.

Most installations have procedures to prevent the aforementioned occurrences that are a part of implementation and program security controls, including software protection of production libraries and rigorous cataloging procedures.

In addition to the machine language instructions, the object module contains certain information that provides flexibility in programming and execution. The flexibility derives from the programs' ability to be divided into subprograms and to be relocated within the computer for execution.

Programs written for IBM computers running on DOS or OS (or their derivatives) may be divided into subprograms or subroutines, as can programs for many systems. Such a division is desirable for the following reasons:

- Each subprogram may be written in the source language most suitable to the program's purpose (e.g., COBOL for business applications or FORTRAN for scientific work).
- Different programmers may work on different subprograms.
- Subprograms can be tested independently.
- Common routines may be written once, then stored and incorporated into all programs that need the routines.

In order for subprograms to be combined into a composite program, communication between the subprograms is necessary. One program has to be able to transfer execution to another subprogram and to define data for the subprogram. This communication is accomplished by defining external symbols, or values reference by various subprograms.

A portion of the object module known as the external symbol dictionary contains a list of all external symbols in the object module. The external symbol dictionary contains entries for:

- Symbols referenced in this module but defined in another module
- Symbols defined in this module and available for reference by other modules

Programs process data by referencing the memory location, or address, of the data stored in the computer. Additionally, a program transfers execution to other parts of the program by referencing locations within the computer.

If the language translator assigned a fixed value to the referenced addresses within a program, the program would have to occupy the same memory area of the computer every time it was executed. This is undesirable, since computers can usually have more than one program loaded and ready to execute at a time. To use computer resources efficiently, programs must be able to be relocated to addresses other than those assigned to the program by the language translator.

For the most part, the language translator defines locations in a program relative to the beginning of the program. Therefore, actual physical addresses are usually not required. For those situations where actual addresses are required, the language translator defines address constants. An address constant is a location in a program that must contain the actual physical address when the program is executing. Language translators make note of the location of each address constant in the section of the object module known as the relocation dictionary. The relocation dictionary contains an entry for each address constant; each entry contains the address of the address constant and describes how the value of the address constant will be determined when the program is eventually loaded for execution. Thus, the relocation dictionary can be thought of as a "road map" for relocating programs.

The following represents the structure of an object module:

- External symbol dictionary
- Text (code) of one program
- Relocation dictionary
- End

The text is the machine language of the translated source module. An object module always contains an END record, which marks the termination of the module. It also contains the address within the program to indicate when execution will begin.

The Linkage Editor

The concept of combining subprograms into a composite program is so useful, and so pervasive, that language translators do not generate modules that can be executed directly. Instead, they generate object modules to be combined with other object modules by the linkage editor, before direct execution. An object module is in relocatable format but is not in a format that can be executed. For example, it is common for language translators to omit routines for performing common procedures, such as reading and writing files, from object modules. These routines are combined with the object module before execution.

When a language translator creates object modules, the modules are segmented into one or more control sections, which is a unit of coding that is considered an entity. A control section is the smallest separately relocatable unit of a program. In the last example, the object module would contain one or more control sections (e.g., each routine is a control section).

It is the function of a program called the linkage editor to combine object modules into a single module that can be executed. The output module from the linkage editor is called a load module. The linkage editor can accept multiple input object (and load) modules. The following illustrates the functioning of the linkage editor with two input modules.

The linkage editor processes the modules in a two-pass operation. The first pass merges the three components of the input modules (the external symbol dictionary, the text, and the relocation dictionary) and assigns address values relative to the beginning of the merged module. The second pass uses the address values to update the composite external symbol dictionary. Specifically, for each section of the load module, the linkage editor does the following:

- *Composite external symbol dictionary.* The linkage editor merges the external symbol dictionaries of the input modules and matches external symbols that were referenced but not defined with the definition entered for the external symbol. This matching process is called resolving external references.

- *Text.* Each input module contains one or more control sections. The linkage editor assigns relative addresses to each control section by assigning an origin to the first control section encountered. It then assigns addresses, relative to the origin, to all other control sections to be included in the output module. The linkage editor minimally reformats the machine language to make it executable.

- *Relocation dictionary.* The linkage editor merges the relocation dictionaries of the input modules and updates each entry with the revised relative addresses.

Audit Review of Programs

Because programmed procedures are important to the functioning of accounting systems, auditors often perform reviews of key programs. In this review, an auditor closely scrutinizes the programs to ensure that they function as represented. As part of the review, the auditor should verify that the version of the program reviewed is identical to the version of the program used in production. For example, the Coopers & Lybrand Source Compare Program compares two source modules, and the Core Image Compare Program compares the machine language object versions to aid this verification.

It is important to note that these software programs cannot determine if a program is functioning correctly and in conformity with management's objectives; the packages can only compare two versions of a program. For example, if two identical versions had the same error in a calculation, the software would not detect a difference in the programs (since there is none) and it would not detect the error.

Audit Approach

Audit areas where program comparison audit software could be useful are:

- Compliance testing of general controls
- Audit review of computer systems
- Audit review of computer programs

This section provides specific examples of how the auditor may use program comparison software to address specific audit concerns.

Compliance Testing of General Controls. Most of the following illustrative examples of specific uses of program comparison software require that the auditor capture and retain copies of modules for subsequent comparison. This capture procedure can be repeated at regular (or random) intervals for ongoing testing. The frequency of capture will vary depending on the number of program changes that take place at an installation and on the scope of the audit testing. The frequency should increase when the number of changes is high and/or the scope of the testing is large.

Example 1. To identify and control changes to source programs. Using the source program comparison software, compare a retained copy of a source module to the copy of the source module in the production source library. Any differences should be supported by authorized change forms.

Example 2. To ensure that no changes have been made to tested programs. Using the core image comparison software, compare the tested program to a retained copy of the load module in the production load library. Any differences should be supported by authorized change forms.

Example 3. To ensure that the object version of a program corresponds with the current source version. From a current source module, generate an object module and then, using the core image comparison program, compare the object module to the corresponding current load module being used in production. This comparison should show no significant (unexplainable) differences.

Example 4. To test job control statements and parameters. The comparison software may not be strictly limited to source modules. It may be used to compare JCL or parameter files in the same manner as Example 1.

Example 5. To test vendor-supplied software. Vendors of application system software often supply their products in object module form. Using the comparison program, compare the vendor-supplied modules with those used in production. Any material differences should have resulted from authorized changes to the vendor's software.

Example 6. To control distributed copies of programs. When software is run at more than one data center, use comparison program software to verify that the version in use at each data center is identical to the authorized master version. This comparison should show no significant differences.

Any exceptions found in the above tests should be communicated to management and considered when deciding whether to rely on general controls.

Audit Review of Computer Systems. These examples show some of the situations where program comparison software can be used:

Example 1. To ensure that the reviewed program corresponds to current production executable program. From the source module under review, generate an object module and then, using comparison program software, compare the object module generated with the object module being used in production. If this comparison shows no significant differences, then the auditor is assured that the source module under review is identical to the version of the program being used in production.

Example 2. To follow up in subsequent audits. Retain a copy of both object and source versions of the program reviewed, and, in subsequent audits:

- If no changes have been authorized for the program, use the core image comparison program to ensure that the production version of the program is unchanged.
- If changes have been authorized, use source comparison software to identify changes made, review only those changes, and then run the core image comparison software to ensure that only these changes have been made to the object version.

Audit Review of Computer Programs. Program comparison software can be used in the following situations:

Example 1. From the source module under review, generate an object module and then, using the core image comparison software, compare the object module generated to the corresponding current load module being used in production. If this comparison shows no significant differences, then the auditor is assured that the source module under review is identical to the version of the program being used in production.

Example 2. Retain a copy of the program reviewed, and in subsequent audits use the source comparison software to determine if the program had any changes. If no changes occurred, no further review is necessary. If changes did occur, review only the changes.

Audit Program — Sequence of Events

The following audit program describes steps in gaining and confirming an understanding of the controls over programmed procedures through the use of the program comparison audit software packages. The EDP auditor is responsible for generating and interpreting the reports. The audit program involves the completion of a general control questionnaire. (See Chapter 24, "Interviews and Transaction Reviews in an Audit," Chapter 25, "The Evaluation Process and How to Use Documents," and Chapter 26, "*Internal Control Reference Manual* — General Controls.")

Event	*Auditor's Actions*
Planning	• Develop a plan and budget.
	• Collect the preliminary information concerning the programmed procedures. This may include reviewing the recorded understanding of the system for any change in data processing. Prepare planning working papers.
Audit review	• Identify programmed procedures that have financial statement significance.
	• Obtain documentation identifying source and production libraries.
	• Specify required system programmer assistance, computer resources, and authorization to access libraries.
	• Assist in preparing a detailed program of tests designed to address the significant programmed procedures identified, taking into account the principal internal controls of the system.
	• Identify the corresponding source and load libraries and perform tests to confirm their use for production.
	• Install the software packages and take control copies of the programs concerned.
	• In later periods, identify authorized amendments to the programs and execute the software.
	• Analyze the results of the software executions and compare these results with the appropriate documentation.

Event	*Auditor's Actions*
Audit review *(cont'd)*	• Prepare report, evaluate conclusions with the head auditor, and prepare the management report where appropriate.
Completion	• Summarize audit time, costs, and expenses. Document any reasons for changes from original budget. Provide suggestions for the coming audit period.

Data Base

DATA BASE CONCEPTS

The data base is a collection of structured data elements with a particular organization; this physical structure is the way data is stored by the data base management system (DBMS). A data base is a collection of logically similar records; those records contain data elements, which are collected and stored in the data base. In a data base, elements for an application are defined as needed, giving more flexibility than the standard file structure. Access to the data base can be made according to the data base structure and is controlled by the DBMS.

The data base system is comprised of three components: (1) the data, (2) the schema that describes the arrangement of the data, and (3) the programs that perform operations on the data. A structural component of the schema (a view of the entire data base) (see Figure 10-1) is the subschema; each subschema describes the data base as seen and accessed by one particular user or application.

Each request for data made by an application program must be analyzed by the DBMS program. The request is stated in terms of the logical name of the data (used in the application). It is converted by the DBMS into a set of physical file addresses, so that the physical data can be retrieved and transmitted by the DBMS to the application program.

Data Independence

Prior to the development of data bases, data files were designed for, and viewed as belonging to, one or more closely related application programs. The data was stored in the logical and physical relationship required by the application. (See Figure 10-2.) When new applications were developed, it was more practical to create new data files containing the specific data and format requirements. This made it possible to avoid program amendments in existing applications, since generally any change in data structure required a program amendment. Data could only be obtained from existing files in inflexible formats, unless extraction and reformatting programs were written. This data-

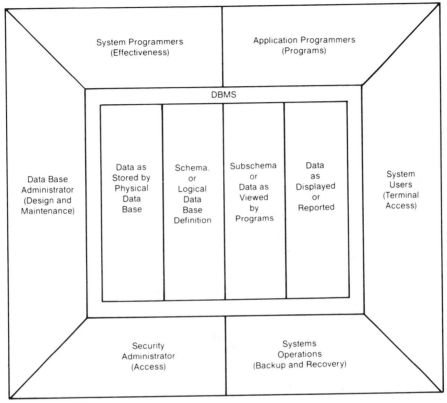

FIG. 10-1   Four viewpoints of the schema

dependent style of processing resulted in program maintenance problems, piecemeal development efforts, and duplication of data.

The data base concept separates the data requirements from the application requirements. Both requirements are evolving processes that are not necessarily compatible. A data base provides for the integration and sharing of common data among different programs. (See Figure 10-3.) In a data base approach, the data elements (fields and segments) are stored with little or no redundancy, and the physical (or real) file structure(s) may bear little resemblance to the logical records and files being processed by application programs. From a data processing point of view, a data base is a means of gaining flexibility by creating independent data and application programs.

Data Base Management Systems

The data that an organization generates, manipulates, and stores for the continuing operation of the organization is one of its most important tangible

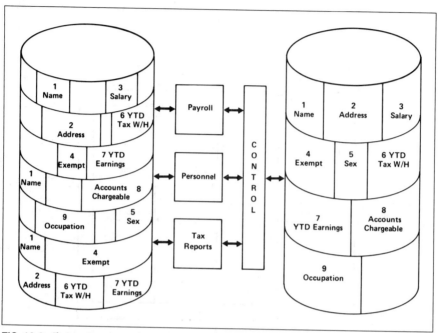

FIG. 10-2 Before the data base, data was stored logically by application requirements; creating a data base satisfies data requirements

assets. A shared collection of information that best satisfies the organization's needs is often a data base. Various EDP systems have been developed to build and manipulate data bases, for example, the Information Management System (IMS) developed and marketed by IBM. (See Figures 10-4 and 10-5 for examples of IBM's financial application programs, the Interactive Financial System 1-4 (IFS 1-4), which use a data base.) Most data base systems employ similar data base concepts, although the names used within each system vary. IMS is widely used, so its descriptions and terminology are used in this chapter to provide an example. While many different data base structures are possible, IMS is one of the most frequently implemented DBMSs. IMS uses hierarchical architecture and concepts; other widely used architectures are relational and network.

The DBMS translates data requirements of application programs and executes data management functions (store, update, delete, retrieve) on behalf of that program.

When an application program using a DBMS requests data, the DBMS looks up the description of the data. This description is defined when the data base is implemented. If there is an index, the DBMS uses it to find the data. The DBMS also determines whether the program has permission to access or update the data, information that is defined when the data base is constructed.

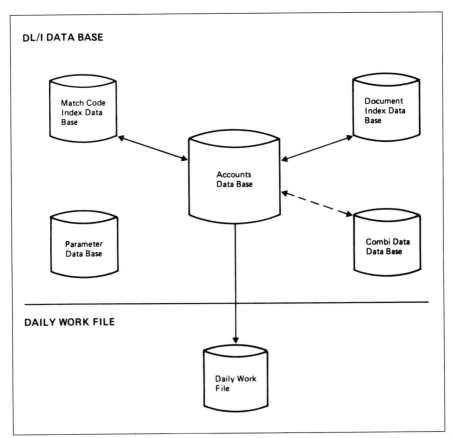

FIG. 10-3 Relationship between data bases within the data base organization (courtesy of International Business Machines Corporation)

   If the application program is used to update a record, additional instructions from the application program return the modified data to storage.

Role of the Data Base Administrator

The data base administrator (DBA) is the manager of the data base. (See Figure 10-6.) One responsibility is security and information classification — not everyone has access to all the information. This duty may be shared with a data security administrator in a large data base environment. (In fact, the access to information is the primary audit concern.)

   The DBA is responsible for the data base design, definition, and maintenance. Other functions include setting policies and procedures for backup and recovery, determining appropriate access permissions for applications programs and users, and resolving any conflicts among users of the data.

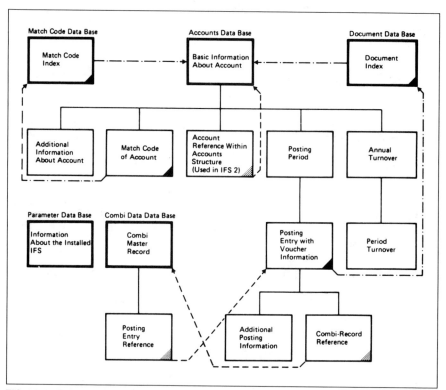

FIG. 10-4   Relationship between the data bases and their segments (courtesy of International Business Machines Corporation)

Data Organization

A data base system can be described as being information-oriented, then user-oriented or data-oriented. Information-oriented data is meaningful to the organization as a whole; user-oriented relates to how a user of the information wishes to manipulate or retrieve the information; and data-oriented means storing the data only once and being able to access and retrieve it easily.

The data in a data base is stored in fields that represent units of information (e.g., the number "4891100" is seven digits which, taken as a whole, could be the telephone number 489-1100 or an invoice amount of $48,911.00). Interpretation of the data depends on the user and the computer application program processing the data.

Perhaps the easiest way to describe the data base concepts as implemented is to describe how a hospital may create, manipulate, retrieve, and store data. Figure 10-7 illustrates the concept of data in this environment.

The patient information shown can be used to identify patients for billing, treatment, insurance reporting, and such, each of which is an application

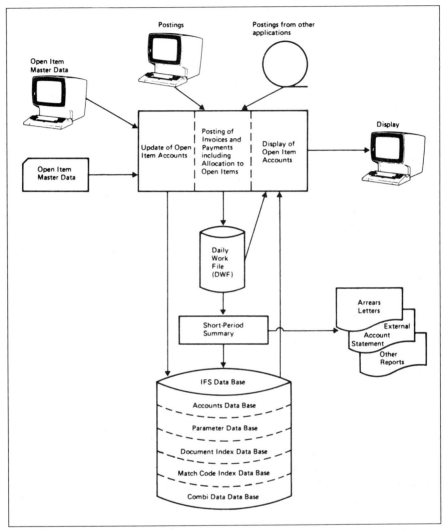

FIG. 10-5 Data flow from user to data bases in a DBMS (courtesy of International Business Machines Corporation)

system in the data base. One application program in the billing system is the invoicing of patients for treatment received. In this case, the invoice is triggered by treatment, which may have been triggered by an appointment register. All of these activities represent different data base applications. The receptionist making appointments in a doctor's office does not need access to the patient's entire file, only to the information necessary to make the appointment. When the receptionist enters the appointment in the appointment register, it may be done via a terminal that allows only appointment transactions to

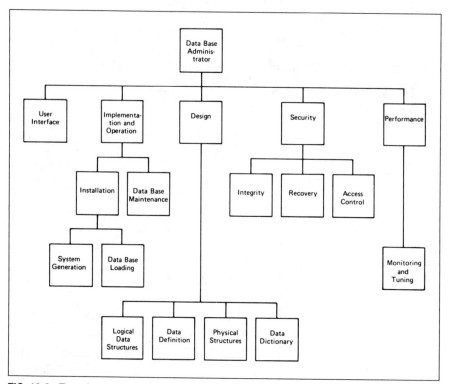

FIG. 10-6 Functions of a data base administrator

be entered. This transaction simultaneously causes the scheduling of a doctor and an examination room for the day and time of the appointment.

Figure 10-8 presents the data elements (fields) in a physical relationship that describe their location as stored on disk versus the logical relationship. This is a very simple description of a system, but it suggests how important it is to have a DBA design the logical relationships of data, control the access to the data via terminals, and determine how the data is to be maintained.

In an IMS system, the process of describing both the physical and the logical data base is done in the data base definition generation (DBDGEN). The generating process is accomplished by defining, with key words and parameters, the specific information that describes and relates to the data base environment.

Logical Data Bases

IMS has the capability to describe logical data bases (those that use the data for a specific application) that may be composed of already defined physical data bases. Logical data bases do not have a separate existence. Instead, segments

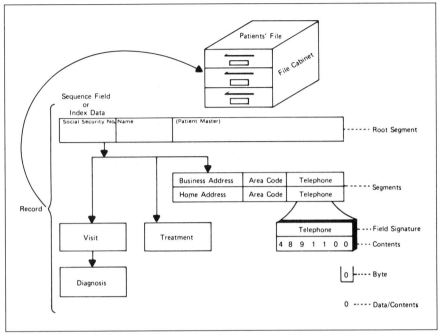

FIG. 10-7   Data base concepts illustrated using a hospital's data requirements

comprising the logical data bases are defined as required from the underlying physical data bases. They are passed to the application program on request after the DBMS has determined that the program as defined can access the data elements requested. Conversely, logical data base segments are accepted from the application program and inserted, replaced, or deleted as appropriate.

To optimize processing, an indexed data base can allow alternate keys to access data elements; in the earlier example, the patient's name relates to the patient's files and can be used as a key to accessing that data. The receptionist making appointments can enter the patient's name and the insurance clerk can enter the patient's social security number; both gain access to the same set of patient information. The index also allows access using a key other than the one used to store the data.

Data Structures

A data base environment is a structure with data elements that are accessible according to the definition of the data base. In IMS, program specification blocks (PSBs) define how any particular application program can use the data. A PSB is always required in IMS.

PSBs are composed of program communications blocks (PCBs) that per-

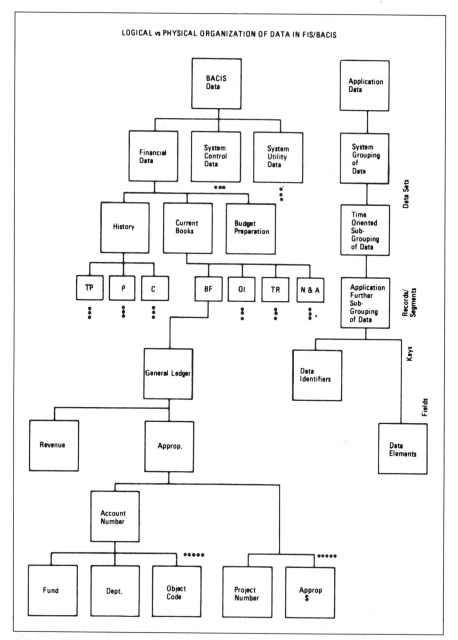

FIG. 10-8   Data structure based on the logical relationship of data versus the physical organization of data elements in their hierarchy (courtesy of International Business Machines Corporation)

mit viewing the data (reading the data without changing it), or changing, updating, deleting, or adding to the data, according to the permissions included in the definition of PSBs and PCBs.

The design of the structure is called the schema (in IMS, the PSB), governed by the DBA. How applications use the data is the subschema (in IMS, the PCBs), of which there can be several. A data base should be planned as an entity. Figure 10-9 illustrates how the application program may view a data base via the defined PSBs and PCBs.

The data base dictionary (DBD) is analogous to a blueprint. There are many types of DBDs. Their use depends on the DBMS employed. In IMS, a DBD is not required for the system to function. In IDMS (Cullinet Software, Inc.'s data base management system) or IDMS/R, (Cullinet Software, Inc.'s relational data base management system) the data dictionary is a required part of the DBMS. The Integrated Data Dictionary in IDMS is a data base in itself. The structure is built according to the DBD documentation and should reflect that documentation in every detail.

Audit software programs can be used to perform the data base inspection and inventory. The auditor still must analyze whether the data base environment is suitable to the organization's informational needs and whether it needs additional security.

Processing the Data

Viewing a data base is only one part of processing the data; other operations include modifying, adding, or deleting. In an IMS system, predefined processing codes are used during the generation process (PSBGEN) to define the PSB. The PSB definition allows application programs to access or change data. A PSB is composed of one or more PCBs. The processing codes or options are entered on the PCB statements with the keyword "PROCOPT." For example, a G code is used to retrieve or view data. To delete data, a D code retrieves the appropriate data and flags it for deletion. These processing option codes are important because they are the mechanism that enables an application program to manipulate the contents of the data base. For another example, a PSB that has a PROCOPT code of A allows any program using the PSB to retrieve a segment, insert a segment, replace a segment, and delete a segment. Simply stated, an A code is extremely powerful . An auditor should know who has the ability to use this and other commands that can alter data.

The processing options determine which, and to what extent, segments may be manipulated. The logical insert, replace, and delete rules have to do with how physical data bases are changed when a segment is inserted, replaced, or deleted. These rules are used for logical relationships when no sequence field or a nonunique sequence field has been defined. The nonunique sequence field usually has key information that allows multiple occurrences of a trans-

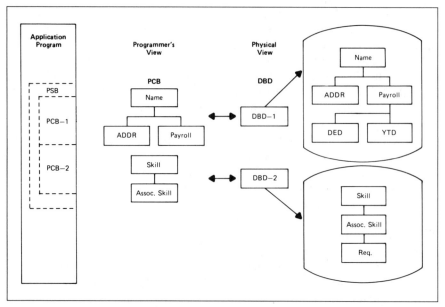

**FIG. 10-9   Two views of the data base through the PSBs and PCBs (courtesy of
International Business Machines Corporation)**

action. For example, in the hospital application already described, it is possible
that the same patient will make several visits in one day. Therefore, a key
field of date would be nonunique.

SYSTEM COMPONENTS

The data base and how it is accessed in a batch environment has been described. This information also applies to the on-line environment, except that
more concepts are involved.

One on-line environment implemented under the IBM program product is
IMS Data Communication (DC). With IMS/DC, remote terminals can be used
to access the data base. The IMS load library contains an on-line nucleus
member; when IMS is executed in an OS/VS region, IMS control regions are
created. Within this nucleus are control blocks that define the teleprocessing
network, control blocks that define which transactions/applications can be
used, and control blocks that define which data base(s) can be accessed.

The IMS/VS (virtual storage) control program region contains the data
base, data telecommunications, and control facilities for IMS. Once the
IMS/VS control region is operative, the IMS/VS message and batch processing regions can be initiated. Figure 10-10 illustrates the interrelationships of the
components.

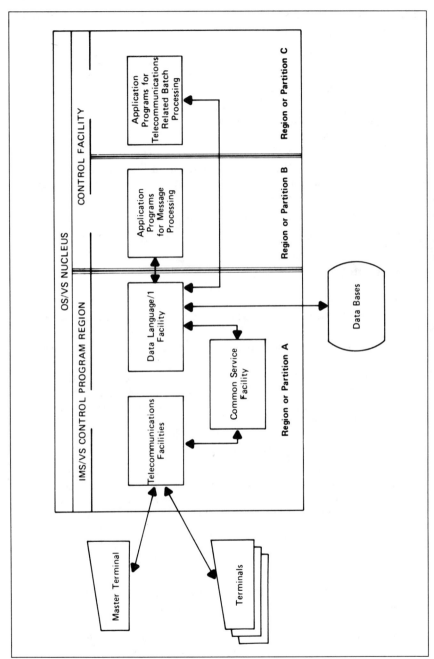

FIG. 10-10 IMS/VS system flow (courtesy of International Business Machines Corporation)

Defining the type of system for a particular organization's computer processing is accomplished by the following:

- *OS/VS SYSGEN.* This is the operating system generation that results in the nucleus. It is usually performed by the operating system programmer.

- *IMS/VS SYSGEN.* This is the IMS system generation that provides the computer with the logical names and the definition of the IMS/VS system, the application programs that use IMS/VS, the transactions processed by each application program, the data bases to be controlled by IMS/VS, communication lines, terminals, processing classes, and regions. This task is usually accomplished by the IMS systems programmer.

- *IMS DBDGEN.* The data base definition generation describes the data base. This task is usually done by the DBA, as is the PSBGEN.

Security Features

After the IMS/VS SYSGEN, mechanisms for adding to the security of data by terminal, password, resource access, transaction command, and user identification may be employed.

Terminals are classified as physical, logical, and master as follows:

- Physical terminals are the hardware devices as defined in the OS/VS SYSGEN via data definition statements in the IMS start-up. Physical terminals are defined in OS/VS SYSGEN so that the operating system knows they exist and in IMS SYSGEN so that IMS knows they exist. Without such definition they cannot interact with the system. They are protected by restricting access.

- Logical terminals are the names related or assigned to a physical terminal so that IMS/VS can construct and transmit messages. One physical terminal can have one or more logical terminals associated with it. Logical terminals exist so that if one particular physical terminal breaks down, another physical terminal can be substituted to receive data that might be queued for processing. Logical terminal security is established by defining which transactions and commands can be entered via the logical terminal.

- The master terminal is a logical terminal that acts as the operational hub of IMS/VS. This terminal has complete control over IMS/VS communication facilities, message scheduling, and data base operations. Note that because the master terminal is a logical terminal, it can be dynamically reassigned to another physical terminal. The operating system console can be used as an alternate master terminal. Often the master terminal is named "CTRL" and the operating system console is named "WTOR." However, they may be assigned any name (of one to eight alphanumeric characters) that relates to the physical devices defined during the OS/VS SYSGEN. Obviously, the master terminal requires the greatest security protection, since it is capable of entering all commands.

Passwords provide another level of security that identifies a user, thereby enabling him or her to access the data. The problem with passwords is that they must be controlled (e.g., through frequent changes) and users must be educated to ensure that the passwords remain secret. Passwords can be used to limit or restrict access to physical terminals, logical terminals, transactions, commands, and data bases. Passwords do not accomplish their purpose if they are posted on the physical terminal for easy reference.

Command security determines which users are permitted to issue IMS/VS commands. The command language is designed to provide for interrogating or altering the processing functions. Figure 10-11 indicates the need to audit the commands associated with logical terminals. The organization's commands to the data base are identified by a unique name (from one to eight alphanumeric characters in length). Functions are defined by the user and can be named appropriately according to naming conventions. The commands are predetermined by IMS/VS. If terminal security is not defined to the system, then the default allows all IMS/VS commands to be entered from any terminal. Furthermore, the default allows transactions to be entered from any terminal.

The final mechanism for security within IMS/VS is the user identification verification, which defines which physical terminals require sign-on processing. Sign-on processing is accomplished through the use of the SIGN command, which requires entering up to eight characters of user identification and user data. Thus, the SIGN ON/OFF command is designed to safeguard physical terminals.

The application programs that process transactions are called transaction processing programs. On-line transactions are processed by message processing programs. Batch message processing programs (BMPs) generate transactions to access on-line data bases. A transaction entered at a terminal may result in more than one message being processed. An example is a transaction that permits information to be entered for updating a data base. The transaction is edited on-line and, when all processing is complete, a message is generated for later batch message program processing. This means that once a batch of transactions is processed, the master file will actually be updated.

General Controls in a Data Base Environment

Because general or integrity controls are concerned with preventing unauthorized access and changes to data stored on computer media, they have been affected by advances in data base technology. The concept of data shared by many users is essential to understanding a DBMS. The fact that data elements

IMS/VS COMMANDS	MASTER TERMINAL	REMOTE TERMINAL	ELIGIBLE AS TRANSACTION	AUDIT CONCERN	DESCRIPTION
ASSIGN	X		X	*	This command alters the relationships between various IMS/VS system resources and resets certain values specified during IMS/VS system definition. The relationships that can be changed that cause audit concern are: The logical terminals can be assigned to a non-switched physical terminal for output and input purposes. Consequently, logical terminals can be moved from one physical terminal to another physical terminal.
BROADCAST	X	X	X		A command used to send a message to terminals in one or more IMS/VS systems.
CANCEL		X			Cancels all segments of an input message. Usually used to correct input errors.
/CHANGE	X		X	*	Changes one password to another password. Password protection is subject to breakdown if non-authorized terminal users have access to this command.
CHECKPOINT	X		X		Records control and status information on the system log tape and restart data set.
CLSDST	X		X		Causes IMS/VS to disconnect a VTAM terminal.
COMPT	X		X	*	Sets a particular terminal component to an operable (ready) or inoperable (not ready) state. Output messages queued for a particular component will not be sent unless the component is operable. A terminal could be turned off, thereby eliminating control messages.
DBDUMP	X		X	*	Is used to stop the scheduling of transactions that can update IMS/VS data bases. Impacts the updating of data bases, so should only be entered by authorized terminals.
DBRECOVERY	X		X	*	Used to stop the scheduling of transactions that update or read IMS/VS data bases. Impacts the data bases so should only be entered by authorized terminals.

FIG. 10-11 IMS/VS terminal commands

can be accessed by many users makes it necessary to control access to specific data elements. In a data base, the application programs no longer access data or perform data management functions directly; rather, the DBMS acts as an interface to all the programs accessing the data base. This access mechanism is the technique whereby data independence, sharing, and manipulation are controlled.

- *Data independence.* The organization's data is integrated and available to all application programs using the data base. This alters the traditional relationship between application programs and data, where specific data files were created for each program.

- *Data sharing.* The organization's data elements are no longer application-owned. Individual data elements may be used by many applications, and the users and providers of data may be different. For example, certain users may only retrieve data elements, while others may have the authority to add, delete, or modify the data elements. Finally, certain users may have no reason to access the data element because it is not relevant to their tasks.

- *Data manipulation.* The processing requirements (read, update, insert, delete) of the programs are carried out by data manipulation routines that are a part of the DBMS.

Establishing who can access data elements and who can perform manipulation (add, change, and delete) functions is an important audit consideration. The relationship between functions, transactions, programs, and data may not be as easily established as in the case of traditional file systems. The use of a DBMS makes the task of gaining and confirming an understanding of the internal control system more complex.

DISTRIBUTED DATA BASE SYSTEMS

In a centralized system the data files, programs, and directories reside in the same processing system. In a distributed system, the programs, directories, and files associated with a particular request are spread among different processors. (See Figure 10-12.) It is this separation that creates the unique audit and other problems associated with distributed data base systems (DDBs).

A DDB exists when an information network has two or more computers, each of which has permanent files attached. The set of permanent files forms the DDB.

DDBs provide certain potential advantages not offered by centralized data bases. The DDB allows files to be located at the point of need in a geographically dispersed organization and thus offers the potential for reduced communications costs and reduced response time.

The designer of a DDB system is faced with several design factors that do not exist in a centralized data base system. These factors must be considered carefully if performance is to be satisfactory to the system's users. The designer must decide how to split the files, how to split the directories, where to locate the programs, and how to design the communications network to support the message flow between nodes or parts of the system created by splitting the components of the data base. (See Figure 10-13.)

File Splitting

The typical DDB system splits its files according to geography or function. For example, an organization may be geographically distributed, with each branch serving a reasonably unique set of customers. It would be logical to place all records and files relevant to that segment of the customer base at the local branch. The branch computer would process all requests pertaining to its data base without requiring any assistance from other processors. If a customer account requires data that is stored elsewhere, the local processor can issue a request to the appropriate branch processor to retrieve the desired record. (See Figure 10-14.)

Another way to split a data base is by function. A typical business operation may have personnel data, accounts receivable data, accounts payable data, inventory data, and order data. This information can reside in one or more data bases, which are similarly split (for the personnel department, inventory department, and so on). Each department can be assigned its own processor and, if warranted, its own data base. Interdepartment transactions are handled via intercomputer communications. (See Figure 10-15.)

Directory Location

Directory location techniques can be divided into three major categories:

1. *Centralized.* The directories in the entire data base are located at one processing location or node. Subdirectories associated with local data bases may or may not be located at the local nodes.
2. *Distributed/Total.* A copy of the entire directory is located at each node.
3. *Local.* A copy of that portion of the directory pertaining to the local node is located only at that node.

The selection of the appropriate technique depends on various tradeoffs between the costs of storage, processing, communication, the time required to respond to a data request, and the need to keep all data current.

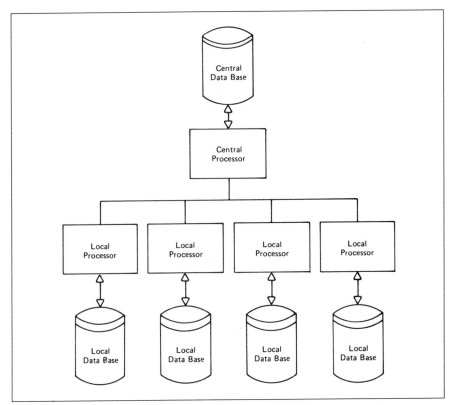

FIG. 10-12 **Structured overview of how the DDB spreads processing from the central data base to separate local processing units**

Program Distribution

There are situations in which a program must operate on an entire file, rather than on a small set of records. It is desirable to locate these programs at the nodes where their supporting files reside. This can be done where there is ample storage at each node for the programs. In many systems, the data base is large relative to total program size, so that room is readily available for program storage on the physical devices that store the data. However, if storage space is at a premium, it may not always be possible to associate programs with files.

If programs are to be moved, the question becomes how and where to store the programs and how to control their movement. The programs can be centralized at a master node and dispatched as needed to requesting nodes. Copies of heavily used programs can be stored at local nodes to reduce the program data flow. Alternately, the programs could be locally distributed according to use, with no central node. This would reduce the overall amount

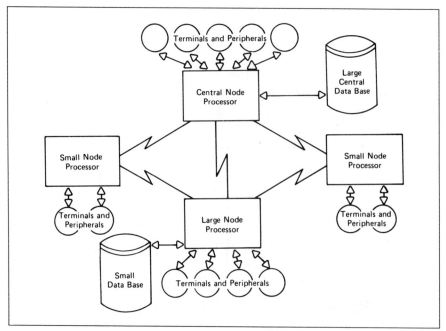

FIG. 10-13 Distributed processing in a loop network structure

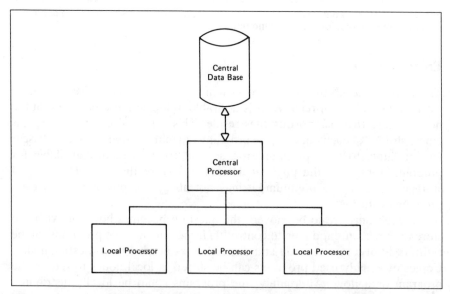

FIG. 10-14 Distributed processing with a limited sharing of local data bases

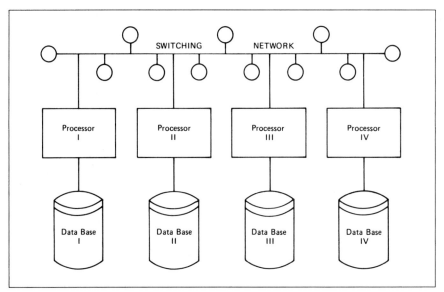

FIG. 10-15 A fully distributed system

of program storage. However, each node would then need a directory of program locations so that nonlocal programs could be requested. It may be possible for the directory to be located at one or several nodes through which all program requests would be directed.

Communications

The DDB system closely interrelates data base software with communications. The network characteristics must be designed to support the data transfers necessitated by the distributed data base.

File Consistency

Problems of data consistency arise when an application updates files at more than one node and when files at one node are updated by more than one application. Although these problems exist in conventional centralized data base systems, they are potentially more critical in a remote system because of update time delays.

A simple way to avoid inconsistencies is to lock out a record from further use while it is being updated. This can be done by the DDB in the node receiving the request. However, to avoid unnecessary lockouts, the request-or should inform the node whether an update is to be performed. If the file action is read-only, there is no need for the file to be locked out.

Another approach is to allow files to be updated only by processes located at the node where the file resides. The update request is then transmitted from the processing node to the resident file node. The update is carried out at the resident file node. The record has to be locked out only for the duration of the update.

Deadlock

A deadlock occurs if two or more processes bid for the same resources in a mutually exclusive manner. Consider the following: Process *A* starts and seizes and locks out File A while Process *B* starts and seizes and locks out File B. Process *A* then requests File B while Process *B* requests File A. Both files are locked out. Hence, neither process can complete and release its file, causing an indefinite impasse. Most DBMSs provide facilities to identify this situation and control it.

Error Recovery/Reliability

The DBMS DDB systems must provide a mechanism for recovery of lost files and for operation while certain nodes are unavailable. The responsibility for recovery could be left to each node. Local data base and directory updates could be logged. In case of a file failure, the start-of-day file is reloaded and the day's activities restored by processing the log tape. The failed node is unavailable until the restoration is complete. A way to inform the other nodes of the failed node's condition must be developed, so that processes do not stop while awaiting responses. For example, this mechanism can be a time-out function (that ends a request after a certain period of nonprocessing time) associated with each request, or an explicit message sent from a monitoring node indicating the unavailability of the failed node.

Files that are crucial to system operation must be duplicated to ensure continuous availability. This can be accomplished by placing redundant physical files and processors at the critical node. Another approach is to place copies of critical files at more than one node, which in turn brings up the problem of keeping these files consistent. A third approach is to log the file updates to a neighboring node, so that if the original node fails, the file can be reconstructed at the neighboring node. The other nodes in the network will then be informed of the change in location of the critical file.

Application Areas

The general characteristics of applications suitable for DDB systems include a clear, logical split of data needs according to either a functional or a geographical basis; a low (less than 20 percent) probability that a user at one node will need data from another node on any particular transaction; a low probability of file transfer or, stated another way, a low volume of data transferred per request; and a dedicated application that can be built around relatively homogeneous systems.

The following is a list of some application areas in which DDBs have been used successfully:

- *Retail point-of-sale.* Each store is a node with terminals, a local processor, and a store-wide data base. The nodes communicate with a central system-wide data base.

- *Large banks.* In one type of system, each branch has its own customer data base, which contains partial files. Detailed history files are stored in a central data base.

- *Airlines reservation systems.* These tend to be heterogeneous. Each airline has its own reservations data base but can access each other's data bases through well-structured message requests and data transfer formats.

- *Distribution systems.* A manufacturing organization has installed a computer at each major distribution center. Each node has its own customer file and inventory file. A central node retains a complete inventory file for the entire system.

AUDIT APPROACH IN A DATA BASE ENVIRONMENT

The existence of data base technology may affect the auditor's approach in the areas of obtaining and confirming an understanding of the accounting system and audit testing.

The evaluation of internal control is based on the auditor's understanding of the system and the results of compliance testing. In a data base environment, the evaluation of control and assessment of risk may be more difficult to make. However, the traditional processes that an auditor must follow to arrive at a judgment are unchanged.

Obtaining and Confirming an Understanding

The auditor obtains an understanding of the accounting system through discussions with personnel and through observation and review of existing procedures and policy manuals. The auditor must identify the data elements of accounting significance and determine their relationship within the accounting structure. The auditor should clearly recognize the logical relationships between data elements, programs, and transaction types. The DBA should be able to supply this information from the data dictionary.

Documentation can include narratives, flowcharts, and listings. The documentation to be audited should clearly show the following:

- Physical structure of the data base
- The elements of each data base (fields, keys, segments), or the schema
- The programs using each logical view of the data bases, or the subschema
- The transactions processed by each program
- The terminal and/or users entitled to enter each transaction or command

The auditor should document the relationships for only those data elements that have accounting significance. This documentation is necessary for the auditor to understand the processing flow. In an audit of the system itself, the EDP auditor may need a broader understanding, since the audit will be concerned with the system and not just the elements of accounting significance.

Data File vs. Data Base

Any EDP installation that uses a DBMS is likely to introduce audit concerns that can vary from control objectives for traditional file systems. The use of DBMS means a different method of creating, processing, and retrieving data. Yet, the auditor must still determine whether general controls are reliable and adequate.

In an environment that uses traditional data file structures, the data is maintained by applications that are usually designed to meet the needs of a single user. Each user is responsible for creating and maintaining individual data files. These traditional files are usually associated with one specific application, which results in each user thinking of the data used as "my file." For example, the payroll file belongs to the payroll clerk, who is responsible for the completeness, accuracy, and validity of the data. Furthermore, there is limited access to the file, ensuring its security.

The auditor should understand that the data base, as a minimally redundant collection of data elements integrated to meet the needs of many users in an organization, is a community of data for a community of users. In a data base environment, data elements are usually organized in a structure that retains their relationship for processing by different applications. For example, a purchasing department orders merchandise, thus creating an open purchase order. The receiving department accepts the goods upon delivery, updates the open purchase order, and creates a voucher for payment. The accounts payable department receives a vendor invoice and authorizes payment based on the receipts voucher. The data elements, if maintained as separate files, will be redundant; that is, each file will have the vendor number, goods covered, and so on. In a data base the redundancy of data is minimized by combining the data elements. Since data is application independent, it becomes a resource that must be available to the authorized community of users. Figures 10-16 and 10-17 illustrate the difference between traditional file autonomy and the possible interrelationship of an organization's data in the data base environment.

The data base must be protected from access by unauthorized people in the user community. Establishing that the proper access controls are in place is of major concern to the auditor. The integrity concern deals with the accidental or erroneous destruction of data by authorized users. The security concern relates to the intentional or deliberate destruction of data by authorized or unauthorized users. Although these concerns apply to all information systems, they are especially important in a DBMS environment because of the concentration of data in the EDP department, the diversity of the user population, and the processes that access and distribute data.

If a DBMS integrates the payroll data with the organization's other business operating data, it may no longer be possible or practical to physically lock up the payroll data in a vault. Instead, the DBMS must be responsible for ensuring the security of all data. The auditor must then decide if the controls over the access to data are proper and effective.

Batch Processing vs. On-Line Processing

Batch processing is the processing of transactions at given time intervals or after a certain number of transactions have been accumulated. A data base provides facilities for running batch applications. It is possible to extend the data base with a data communications feature to develop on-line applications (i.e., applications that support access to the data base from a remote terminal). Such an application may use the same facilities as a batch application to actually access the data base. The IMS/DC data communications feature provides the facilities required for the terminal to access the application, not the data base.

Many environments have both batch and on-line applications. The on-line applications are often data base inquiry or on-line data capture. Updating or maintenance is often handled as a batch application, since it is easier to control batch processing. Since one of the reasons for a DBMS is to have timely, current data, on-line updating is used in systems that require it, such as airline reservations or credit approval systems.

The audit concerns in an on-line environment are an extension of those in a batch data base environment. The introduction of on-line processing means that security must include adequate controls over access to the on-line teleprocessing (TP) network. (See Chapter 8, "On-Line Systems.") In a data base environment, access is often controlled by user passwords, transaction passwords, and terminal commands, managed by a data security administrator.

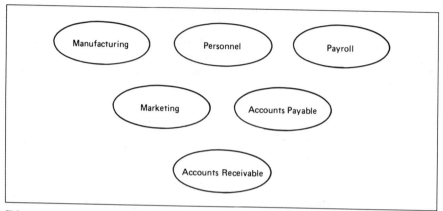

FIG. 10-16 Traditional files are audited according to application

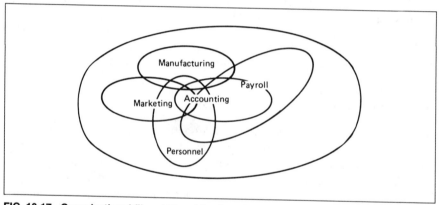

FIG. 10-17 Organizational file relationships in a data base environment

Understanding DBMS

Most business data base systems are implemented and maintained by highly
trained individuals in the EDP department. When an auditor understands the
concepts, he or she can proceed with the audit without having to rely heavily on
these technically trained people. The concentration of functions in a complex
system and the time/cost problems associated with understanding such systems
may result in a less than satisfactory audit of a data base environment, unless
the auditor has developed the requisite understanding.

- *Concentration of functions.* The introduction of a DBMS adds to
  the responsibilities of the EDP department in maintaining its ability
  to process data. The highly technical work of those individuals in

the EDP department who are responsible for using and maintaining the data base may make their activities difficult to supervise and monitor, except on a very general level.

- *Time/costs.* The complex software of a DBMS requires that the auditor spend more time gaining and confirming an understanding of the data relationships. The external auditor must become involved in data base analysis when a DBMS is used for applications that are significant to the financial statements.

Organizational Change

Establishing a DBMS, means that an organization must change to cope with the system's many technical complexities and control coordination of the activities and communications between the many applications and departments that share the data base resources. These functions are usually undertaken by a DBA and a data security administrator. The DBA plans and manages the overall needs for data resources and may handle discipline and set standards for the data bases. The security administrator is usually responsible for determining and monitoring the controls over access to the data.

The DBA is an important factor in the auditor's review and evaluation of controls. The auditor obtains much of the understanding about how the data base is used and which controls are employed from talking to the DBA and reviewing his or her activities. Confirmation of that understanding is accomplished by using software and techniques that relate to the system.

The DBA and the security administrator may not exist in an organization; individuals should be assigned the functions they would normally perform. The absence of coordinated structure to fulfill these responsibilities may constitute a control weakness in itself.

The DBA uses tools to assist in carrying out his or her responsibilities, and some of these tools can also be used by the auditor. The most important and useful tool for the auditor may be the data dictionary. It organizes and maintains information concerning the relationships, attributes, and definitions of the data elements within the data bases. There are two types — integrated and nonintegrated — which may present different audit concerns. The dictionary may be maintained manually or it may be computerized. For example, IMS has a computerized dictionary that is maintained separately from IMS. The dictionary may or may not reflect the actual data bases in IMS. In IDMS/R (and others), the only way to use the DBMS is to use the dictionary. The auditor may use it to gain an understanding but must realize that the dictionary does not necessarily represent the actual situation. Therefore, the auditor needs to conduct a sufficient number of tests to establish the validity of the dictionary. (See "Audit Program" on page 10-33.)

Control Over Access

The implementation objectives of a DBMS — to eliminate redundant data and integrate the data of many users into a common pool — make it necessary to establish controls over who may access which elements of data. For example, an accounts receivable system can share a customer data base with a customer service system. The customer's accounts are updated with invoices and payments entered by the accounts receivable department and transactions that result when returned merchandise is entered by the customer service department. The control over access for this example means that only these two departments may adjust the customer's balances. The sales department also has access to the data base. Although they may write sales orders, they cannot enter payments or invoices. The audit concern is that proper controls have been implemented to ensure that the sales department does not have access to information reflecting accounts receivable or have the ability to enter unauthorized transactions.

An important aspect of auditing a data base is identifying authorized users and their EDP capabilities. The audit concern for controlling access to data residing in a data base system can be further divided into the following:

- Data element access
- Password systems
- Terminal security

Data Element Access. Authorized programs should access only those data elements required to execute their processing tasks. The control objective for this concern is that the data base description should be adequate to minimize unnecessary access. The data base is designed to aid in providing the appropriate control over access to pertinent data elements. The design of data base structures and the translation of user requirements for data access to a data base are complicated tasks. Therefore, the auditor is likely to encounter data bases that do not have the appropriate access controls. For example, in IMS a PSB may access all the data requested for all the programs in an application system, or the same PSB may be used for more than one program in a batch environment.

Controlling access to data during normal production is a major concern, but control over access during testing of application programs and systems is just as important. Testing should be done using a test data base to ensure that production data is not distorted and that sensitive data is not vulnerable to exposure. Therefore, the auditor should determine that test data bases, not production data bases, are used during applications development.

Password Systems. Unauthorized access can be prevented by passwords. The control requirement for this concern is whether the password system is adequate to prevent unauthorized access.

Password security is provided in the on-line environment at two levels:

1. *Sign-on verification security* — Identifies a particular user as being present at the physical terminal.

2. *Transaction entry and command functions* — When a transaction is defined as requiring a password, the system should not allow the user to execute the transaction unless the password is specified with the transaction code.

Command functions can be protected against unauthorized use in three ways:

1. Permit the command verb to be entered only from certain logical terminals.

2. Require that a password be entered with the command verb.

3. Use a combination of both.

If a data base has been implemented without defining passwords, then no passwords are required to access the data. The control is nonexistent. When passwords have been implemented, the auditor must ensure that they are controlled on an ongoing basis, such as maintaining accurate, secured records of users and their permissions, and promptly removing separated employees from the system.

Terminal Security. The control requirement for terminal security is that it be adequate to prevent unauthorized access. The security of the physical location of the terminal and of the physical/logical terminal link are both important, as is security over the telecommunications network. One physical terminal may have more than one logical terminal associated with it. Terminal security restricts the entry of transactions and commands to specified terminals. When a terminal security feature is not used, all terminals may enter all transactions and commands, thereby negating the control.

The effectiveness of the controls over access is determined by how the environment is implemented and what standards are enforced to maintain the established controls. The impact of DBMS on general controls varies depending on the data base functions, the complexity and extent of data base usage, the use of telecommunications, and to what extent source/user and application program procedures ensure the reliability of data.

Audit Testing

The auditor should identify those control procedures on which reliance will be placed and conduct tests to ensure that the procedures are proper and ongoing. If the auditor has identified programmed procedures to rely on, and the continued proper operation of those procedures is not assured by manual controls conducted at the source or user level, control procedures exercised within the EDP department to ensure the continued and proper operation of the programs must be studied. Procedures over application program development and maintenance, system software development and maintenance, computer operations, and program security should be tested.

The auditor should also test controls over the DBMS and data access. Testing related to the DBMS should be designed to ensure that the DBA's responsibilities are performed and supervised. The auditor should also be required to reperform certain procedures and ensure that the exercise of control is evident. Data base definitions and logical relationships existing in the system must remain in accordance with established standards and data dictionary representation.

Various audit software programs exist to help the auditor review and test the control requirements for the DBMS without having to access data residing in the data base. One example is Coopers & Lybrand's IMS analyzer software.

Using the reports generated, the auditor can test the validity of the DBA's documentation and determine that the control standards appear to be operating properly. The following information is reported:

- Contents and structure of each data base
- On-line programs that can access each data base
- On-line transactions that may be processed by each program
- Data base segments accessed by each PSB
- Data manipulation functions that may be performed on each segment by programs using the identified PSBs
- Transactions a terminal can issue
- Commands a terminal can issue
- Transactions a password can authorize
- Commands a password can authorize

Defining a Data Base

In an IMS environment, data bases (physical, logical, or secondary index, which permits the specification of an alternate entry to an existing data base) are defined to IMS by a process called data base definition generation

(DBDGEN). All data bases must be defined through a DBDGEN before the data may be loaded into the data base and prior to use by an application program. Input to a DBDGEN consists of parameters defining the data base characteristics, organization (structure), access method, and physical and logical relationships among data. Output, a data base definition (DBD) control block, is stored in the DBD library for use during data base creation, recovery, reorganization operations, and in processing data base access by application programs.

The DBD library is one of the libraries analyzed by the IMS PSB/DBD Analyzer package, an audit software package from Coopers & Lybrand. Before the program is executed, a DBD must be provided for each data base that will be used by an application program. How the user implements the DBD determines which data elements are associated with specific segments. The logical relationship defined gives the user access to the data elements contained in the various segments. If a user defines all of an application's data as being contained in one data base, then the audit approach is simplified because only that one data base has to be investigated. However, if a user defines an application's data as being in more than one data base, it is critically important for the auditor to understand the relationship among the data bases. The audit software is especially useful for this purpose.

Batch Processing of a Data Base

Batch processing programs are application programs that access the data base. An application program (e.g., payroll transaction edit) may be written in any one of several languages, such as assembler language or COBOL or PL/1. An application program accesses the data via PCBs that are part of a PSB that has been stored in the PSB library. Among other functions, the PSB control block defines the data bases used by the application program. In addition, it defines the manner in which the data bases are used (i.e., retrieval only, retrieval and update, or data base create), and the segments and fields within each data base to which the application program is sensitive. A PSB is a collection of PCBs. In its simplest form, a PSB is identical to a PCB. The PSB generation parameters identify and describe the data base resource characteristic being used. One of the keyword parameters of the PCB control statements is PROCOPT, which describes the processing options associated with an application program. Typically, a DBA will have established naming convention standards so that the PSBs are readily identifiable to the application program and to the data base. The PSB library can be analyzed by the same audit software analyzer discussed in relation to the DBD library.

When a data base is defined and processed for a batch environment, the audit software is useful in gaining and confirming an understanding of the user data base(s).

On-Line Data Bases

On-line capabilities for IMS are provided through the Data Communication (DC) feature, which allows users on-line execution of the IMS system with user access via terminals. Two or more IMS systems can transmit transactions to each other through the capabilities of the Multiple Systems Coupling (MSC) feature.

The transaction-processing facilities of IMS/VS permit the messages entered via terminals to be processed by application programs. Application programs may communicate via transactions that are messages. There are two general categories of transactions:

1. Data Communication (DC) transactions processed by the DC feature
2. Fast Path (FP) transactions processed by the FP feature

The primary difference between the two features, from an audit viewpoint, is that FP transactions can originate only from terminals, whereas non-FP transactions can originate from a terminal or from an application program.

When an application program is scheduled for execution, IMS/VS must first have available the DBD and the PSB control blocks previously created by the DBDGEN and PSBGEN procedures. These control blocks are merged and expanded into an IMS/VS internal format called application control blocks (ACB). The ACBs must be created before the on-line system is started in a process called ACBGEN.

The DC feature provides two types of transaction processing: (1) message processing programs (MPP) and (2) batch message processing (BMP). A batch program may use an ACB or a PSB; DC must have an ACB.

The IMS/DC Analyzer is an audit software package designed by Coopers & Lybrand to provide information for gaining and confirming an understanding of the interaction of transactions, applications, teleprocessing (TP), PCBs, and the data bases. The software enables the auditor to identify the following:

- Transactions that may be entered from terminals
- Application programs that will be invoked to process the transactions
- PCBs that control access to a data base
- Control program (nucleus) that is controlling the execution of the IMS system

User Authorization

A user may view the IMS system as resources to which passwords provide access. These resources include terminals, commands, transactions, and data.

User-defined security requirements may be implemented to control the transmission of transaction and command messages. Two types of security verification may be designated: terminal security and password security. If passwords and terminal controls are used, then the auditor may wish to use the audit software security analyzer to verify that standards for passwords and terminal use are being enforced.

The IMS/VS product is packaged in two major parts: the data base system, which is implemented with Data Language/1 (DL/1) and the DC feature. Implementation of the DC feature requires the data base system. The following chart summarizes the possible use of the Coopers & Lybrand IMS audit software analyzers:

	IMS	
Package	*DL/1*	*DC*
IMS PSB/DBD Analyzer	X	X
IMS DC Analyzer		X
IMS Security Analyzer		X

AUDIT PROGRAM — SEQUENCE OF EVENTS

This section describes an audit program for gaining and confirming an understanding of a data base environment by using the audit software analyzer packages. The EDP auditor is responsible for generating and interpreting the reports.

Event	*Auditor's Actions*
Planning	• Develop plans and budget.
	• Collect the preliminary information concerning the user's data base environment. This may include reviewing the recorded understanding of the system for any change in data processing. Prepare planning working papers.
	• Agree to provide the review of the general controls within the time requirements. Keep audit staff informed as to progress and any reasons for additional time.
Audit review	• Identify transactions or data that have audit significance.
	• Obtain the following documentation from user:
	a. I/O configuration chart

(continued)

Event	Auditor's Actions

Audit review
(cont'd)

b. Identification of the production IMS libraries

c. Data dictionary reports (if used; data dictionary is not required in IMS)

• Request system programmer assistance, computer resources, and authorization to access PSB, DBD, and RES libraries.

• Perform procedure to confirm production libraries.

• Install and execute the audit software packages.

• Complete the working paper analysis (e.g., record the understanding in a working document such as the Data Base Analysis Matrix, which is described in this section). This step may be done by starting with a transaction, a data base, or a data field. The method of analysis is determined by the auditor's identification of financially significant data. If the auditor specifies transactions, then that would be the method.

• Compare the analyzed results with the DBA's documentation (data dictionary).

• Analyze and evaluate the principal internal controls of the system from the working papers and prepare management letter comments where appropriate.

Completion

• Summarize time, costs, and expenses. Document any reasons for changes from original budget. Provide suggestions for the coming audit year.

The audit program for these packages has been expanded to include some suggested techniques for aiding in the overall analysis of the data base environment. The reports generated by the audit software analyzer packages are detail reports. (See Figure 10-18.) They contain wide-ranging information that must be carefully studied to determine whether the results indicate either weaknesses or breakdowns in internal control. A Data Base Analysis Matrix can be used to assist in analyzing these reports. An example of a Data Base Analysis Matrix is shown in Figure 10-19. It shows how the columns of information can be completed and gives sample entries. Some auditors may find they do not need to use the matrix to organize their thoughts and arrive at evaluations, but the concept is a useful guide.

Once the matrix is completed and the reports are reviewed, the data base may be analyzed. There are three starting points for analyzing the access controls:

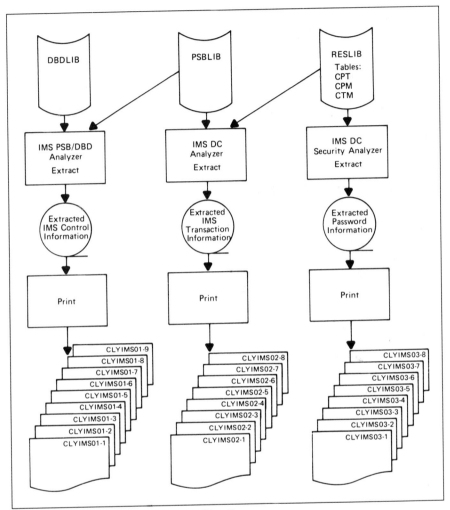

FIG. 10-18 Flowchart for data base audit software

1. Transaction
2. Data base
3. Data element (field)

The auditor determines which information is significant in order to determine which starting point should be used. For example, the auditor is reviewing a payroll application; the transaction PAYTIME is used to enter the number of hours and the job class from which gross pay is calculated. The auditor then

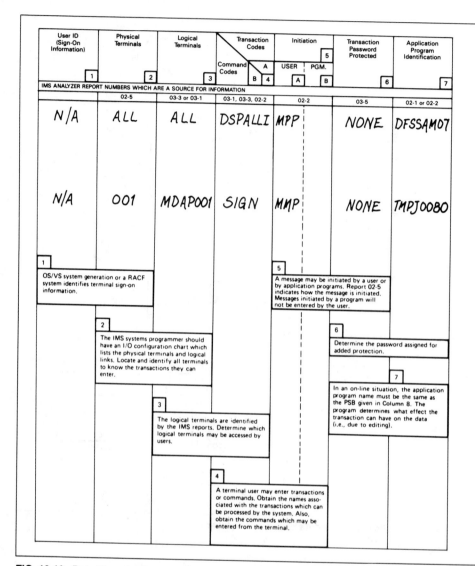

FIG. 10-19 Data Base Analysis Matrix

wants to identify the application program that processes the transaction and verify that the PAYTIME transaction cannot modify the pay rate data element in the data base. The auditor would want to know which terminals can enter the transaction "PAYTIME," which data bases are accessed, and whether or not unauthorized access to data (such as the pay rate data element) is possible.

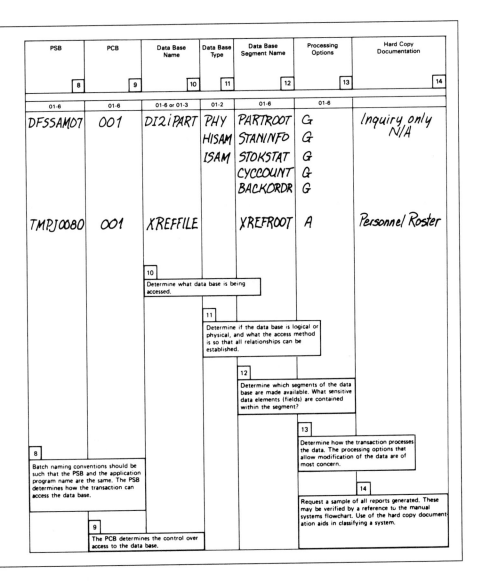

PSB	PCB	Data Base Name	Data Base Type	Data Base Segment Name	Processing Options	Hard Copy Documentation
[8]	[9]	[10]	[11]	[12]	[13]	[14]
01-6	01-6	01-6 or 01-3	01-2	01-6	01-6	
DFSSAM07	001	DI2iPART	PHY	PARTROOT	G	*Inquiry only N/A*
			HISAM	STANINFO	G	
			ISAM	STOKSTAT	G	
				CYCCOUNT	G	
				BACKORDR	G	
TMPJ0080	001	XREFFILE		XREFROOT	A	Personnel Roster

[10] Determine what data base is being accessed.

[11] Determine if the data base is logical or physical, and what the access method is so that all relationships can be established.

[12] Determine which segments of the data base are made available. What sensitive data elements (fields) are contained within the segment?

[13] Determine how the transaction processes the data. The processing options that allow modification of the data are of most concern.

[8] Batch naming conventions should be such that the PSB and the application program name are the same. The PSB determines how the transaction can access the data base.

[14] Request a sample of all reports generated. These may be verified by a reference to the manual systems flowchart. Use of the hard copy documentation aids in classifying a system.

[9] The PCB determines the control over access to the data base.

Starting With a Transaction Type

Traditionally, the auditor obtains an understanding of the internal control system by identifying transactions of particular significance and following the processing of transactions, in detail, to identify control procedures. Generally, this review extends from the origination of the transaction to its final summarization in the financial statement or other report. This process is complicated in computer systems by the fact that, after the transaction is entered into the system, evidence may be lost until it emerges later as output. In many computer systems there is a lack of visible evidence for detailed results of processing and the data stored in the data base. Such systems cannot readily be controlled or audited solely by examining output. Sometimes, even though the information is available, it may be too voluminous or in a form too inconvenient to check within a reasonable time. During processing, the transaction may be vulnerable to unauthorized modification by other users. This is particularly true in an on-line data base environment.

Using a Data Base Analysis Matrix or similar document, the auditor can assemble all the pertinent information for gaining, recording, and confirming an understanding of a system in an on-line environment that accesses a data base(s). The matrix can be used to

- Record and identify all the transactions that are of concern to the audit.
- Determine how transactions can affect the data base.
- Determine the capability of the transaction to access the data base.
- Locate and identify all physical and logical terminals and the transactions they may enter or process.

Starting With a Data Base

Analysis of data bases is often another possible starting point for the data base audit. For example, the auditor may determine that the application system uses a data base. The auditor may request that the data base be analyzed. (Remember that a data base environment does not require that all data be stored in the data base. Traditional files may be used concurrently in data base applications.) Starting with the data base eliminates the need for the auditor to determine which transactions access a particular data base. Again, a Data Base Analysis Matrix is helpful. Use the matrix to

- Record and identify the data bases of concern to the auditor.
- Record the segment name in which the data element resides and determine which data bases or applications (PSBs) have access to that segment (physical and/or logical).
- Determine how the data base can be manipulated by transactions.
- Identify the application programs and transactions that may access the data base and segment.
- Identify and locate all physical and logical terminals that may enter a transaction that can access the data element.

Starting With a Data Element

Sometimes only a few data elements are determined to be of audit significance. For example, in an accounts receivable system, perhaps the auditor only wishes to substantiate the balance due. The auditor is concerned with determining what general controls exist for that one field of data. Again, a Data Base Analysis Matrix is helpful. The auditor can use the matrix to

- Record the segment name in which the data element resides and determine which data bases or applications (PSBs) have access to that segment (physical and/or logical).
- Identify the application programs and transactions that may access the data base and segment.
- Identify and locate all physical and logical terminals that may enter a transaction that can access the data element.

Analyzing the Data Base Analysis Matrix

The interpretation of the reports and the process of recording information in the Data Base Analysis Matrix assist in evaluating the appropriateness of the access controls. All accesses to the data base with processing options that allow the data to be modified (add, delete, replace) should be investigated to determine which transactions use the PSBs and which terminals can enter the transactions.

The matrix, read from left to right, provides a way to determine how the data base can be accessed and what controls are in place (e.g., passwords, nonglobal transactions, and processing options).

It is entirely possible that once the matrix has been completed, a visual inspection will reveal gaps in the information. For example, it is possible for a transaction to be defined without a PSB. This occurs when a new transaction is being implemented. Transactions are implemented by a nucleus generation, whereas PSBs are implemented with a PSBGEN. These are two different processes that do not have to occur simultaneously.

Transactions or application programs with processing options that permit the modification of data should have hard-copy documentation to support the transaction. This not only provides an audit trail but also makes backup and recovery possible if the data base is lost.

Analyzing the matrix, which is really a condensation of the report information, will indicate potential areas of exposure that should be reported to management. Below are examples of concerns that might be raised to management:

- Software controls should be implemented to restrict unauthorized access to data and unauthorized program execution.

- Lack of security means that unauthorized persons may gain access to the system and initiate unauthorized transactions.

- All transactions updating the data base should subsequently be reported in a hard-copy document (such as a master listing). Documentation makes it possible to ascertain that transactions are complete and have been properly authorized.

PART III

Accounting Systems

CHAPTER 11

Introduction to Accounting Systems

INTRODUCTION

When considering the kinds of things that computers do best, it almost seems that they were invented to allow business to automate accounting systems. The business community was fast to embrace the new technology when it saw how well computers could keep track of the vast quantity of data required to run a business on a day-to-day basis. Seemingly endless streams of numbers, details, and transactions that once were recorded painstakingly in longhand can be tracked on an up-to-the-minute basis if that is what a business requires.

Of course, the people involved in a making sure that all that data was not only on hand, but accurate and complete at the same time, were quick to appreciate the obvious. To have a machine that not only followed orders to the letter, but could rapidly calculate to a precision beyond that of the finest mathematicians, is something that an organization could only dream about a few short decades ago. Some of the most repetitious and tedious work — footing and refooting sets of numbers, backtracking of transactions from first order through getting paid for same, performing "what if" calculations — can be done in seconds. It is not surprising that the value of computers to business was recognized at the outset. The first business data processing on a computer occurred in the mid-1950s when General Electric acquired the UNIVAC-1, the first commercially marketed computer.

Accounting's manual procedures have not changed much since people figured out why they needed debits and credits to make a system of book-keeping work. The only difference is that over time they have become increasingly complex. More descriptive names have been developed for the same procedures. The data processing (DP) department has become management information systems (MIS). These new titles have even amused the uninitiated, as a recent newspaper article demonstrated when it did not know what to make of a trade paper's advertisement for a MISManager.

Whatever it is called, data processing is still responsible in part for the same number-crunching, sorting, and reporting of information from accounting. Even after "accounting" has become "financial information systems," it still has to make sure that its trial balances balance.

ACCOUNTING PROCEDURE'S RELATIONSHIP TO SYSTEMS

To apply the principles of accounting to organizations, there is a standard set of systems and procedures to be followed. These systems consist of a set of records that are filled out in a specific series of steps. These records are the basis of all accounting systems, regardless of whether they are manual or computerized, and include ledgers, journals, and registers. All the financial activity in an organization is recorded in these records so that there is a physical place where the information is available for reference, the actual numbers can be reconciled, and the material is available for use in the creation of reports and financial statements.

To enter this data, or "keep the books," the following procedures are generally the same, both for computer and for manual recordkeeping:

- Creating and processing documents, the basis of business transactions, such as invoices or purchase orders, and ensuring the accuracy of those documents and transactions.

- Keeping records of all transactions in the appropriate place, such as sales orders in the sales journal or payroll data in the payroll register. These primary sources are usually called books of original entry or subsidiary ledgers.

- Posting all transactions to a subsidiary ledger and to the general ledger.

- Preparing general ledger balances and making sure that they agree with the subsidiary ledgers.

- Preparing the trial balance from the general ledger.

- Preparing financial statements using the trial balance. These statements include the balance sheet, income statement, statement of cash flow, statement of changes in financial position (source and allocation of funds), and any other statements that may be required to depict an organization's position or operating results. (Figure 11-1 shows the financial reports created by the IBM Interactive Financial System 1-4 (IFS 1-4).)

- Creating reports and projections for management, based on existing financial data. (Figure 11-2 shows the financial data processed by the IBM Financial Information System/Budget Accounting Information Subsystem (FIS/BACIS).)

FINANCIAL INFORMATION SYSTEMS

The significance of computer systems in providing financial information may be best understood in terms of three elements that can be ranked according to their potential impact on financial statements. Usually they are ranked under the following headings:

- Transaction data
- Master file data
- Programmed procedures

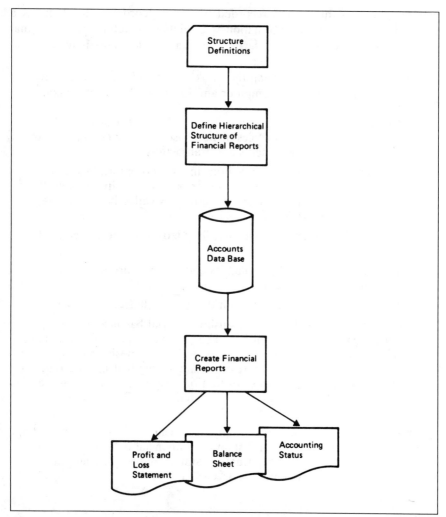

FIG. 11-1 Main data flow of Interactive Financial System 2 (IFS-2) showing reports produced (courtesy of International Business Machines Corporation)

Transaction Data

Transaction data is the data that is specific to each transaction. It may be held in its original form (such as by invoice number, invoice date, or invoice amount) or in a summary form (such as current inventory stock on hand). Figures 11-3 and 11-4 present an overview and details of financial transactions processed by IBM's FIS/BACIS.

Errors in transaction data have a limited impact. Errors are limited to one transaction at a time and often are detected by subsequent manual or pro-

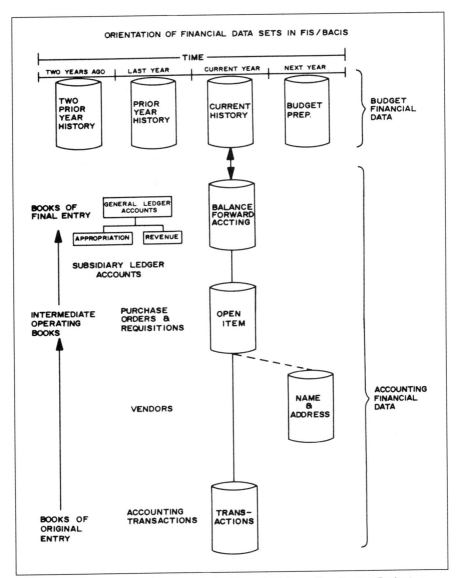

FIG. 11-2 Financial data processed by the Financial Information System/Budget Accounting Information Subsystem (FIS/BACIS) (courtesy of International Business Machines Corporation)

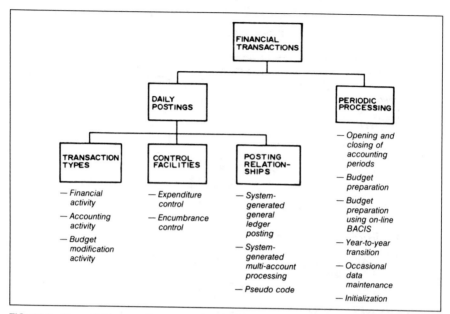

FIG. 11-3 Financial transactions overview flowchart for FIS/BACIS (courtesy of International Business Machines Corporation)

grammed procedures. However, a significant error may result from a single wrong transaction. There is also a danger that bogus transactions will be entered into a poorly controlled system.

Master File Data

Master file data is data of a permanent or semipermanent nature, such as customer number, sales price, employee name, and depreciation rate. Frequently, master file data operates on transaction data for purposes of control, such as customer credit limits on orders, or bookkeeping, as when inventory cost prices are used to calculate inventory value. (This master file reference data is sometimes called standing data.)

Errors in master file data may affect many transactions or all transactions for a particular account, such as the customer, employee, product line, vendor, and so forth. Furthermore, the error may not be detected by manual procedures, since master file data is not frequently printed out and checked. Programs are less likely to be designed to detect errors in low-volume master file data (such as a customer credit limit entered once) than in high-volume transaction data (such as sales to that customer). As an example of such an error, imagine what the repercussions would be if a customer credit limit was entered as $1,000,000 instead of as $1,000.

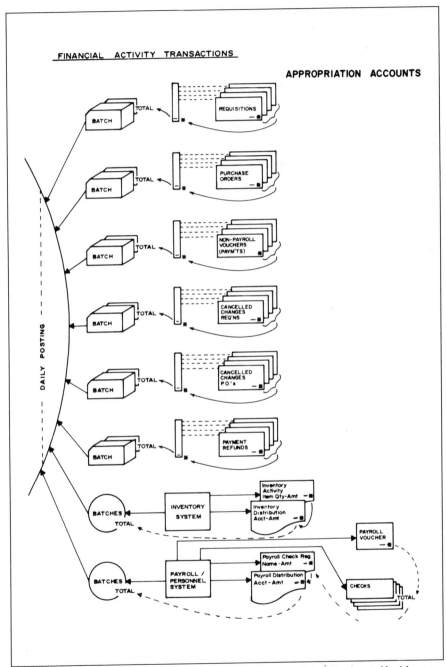

FIG. 11-4 Transaction posting details (courtesy of International Business Machines Corporation)

Programmed Procedures

Program errors have the potential to affect all transaction and master file data that is processed. The errors may not be detected by manual procedures because of a lack of visible evidence and user assumptions that the system is functioning properly. Programmed procedures that do not function properly and other related errors have a way of mounting up over time. They may not be noticeable at first, but eventually they can cause a major difference in the financial records. For example, an erroneous calculation of interest on savings accounts at a large bank of only one cent per account could mean a difference of thousands of dollars over a long period.

FINANCIAL SYSTEMS PROCEDURES

Manual Procedures

Manual procedures in a computerized financial systems environment are sometimes similar to those used in noncomputer systems. They differ in the following ways:

- Specific procedures are required both to prepare data for computer processing and to act on the results of computer processing, as shown by printed reports or by displays on a terminal screen. As an example, to prepare an item for an inventory system there must be a special inventory number scheme that is related to the item descriptions. Those numbers have a specific meaning to the computer and are the key to how it stores the information.

- There is a decrease in the number of manual procedures, with the result that data receives less manual scrutiny and review. For example, invoice extension and calculation are done by the computer, not by hand.

Note that manual procedures are frequently described in written instructions, similar to written procedures of the programs. However, manual procedures are not usually followed as closely as the computer follows the programmed procedures.

Programmed Procedures

Programmed procedures can be used to perform many of the routine calculations, information storage, and decision functions of an accounting system. For convenience, these procedures may be divided into the following categories:

- Bookkeeping functions such as calculation, summarization, categorization, and updating procedures that are applied to the data.

For example, an upgrade in an employee's salary requires an update of the payroll master file to arrive at an accurate calculation of the paycheck. (Figure 11-5 shows the balancing of financial data in IBM's FIS/BACIS.)

- Procedures relating to control over the completeness, accuracy, validity, and maintenance of data. These normally consist of edit tests, accumulation of totals, reconciliations, and the identification and reporting of incorrect, exceptional, or missing data. Just as automated teller machine customers must use valid transaction codes for cash withdrawal and all inventory items in a retail establishment require inventory numbers, procedures must ensure an accurate, complete, and effective data control system.

- The automatic generation of accounting data or paperwork following the occurrence of another transaction, such as the automatic creation of purchase orders when inventory is reduced below prescribed levels.

Obviously, these programs must contain, in specific detail, all the processing steps required for the computer to be able to accomplish the desired results.

The relative mix and importance of manual and programmed procedures varies, depending on the complexity and type of system in use.

Nature of Data

Traditionally, accounting information is recorded on visible accounting documents (such as invoices, purchase orders, and checks) and in the ledgers and journals of the company. Even when techniques such as microfilm and microfiche are used, the nature of the data and its accessibility do not change.

Lack of Visible Evidence

In a computer system, data is recorded and held in machine-readable form; as such, it is an "invisible" record. Furthermore, not all data held in the computer is printed; summaries and exception reports may be all that is output until the data is required for a particular function. The data that makes up the financial records may not be fully available. Intermediate results of computer processing may be unavailable as well.

For example, detail transactions may be available for a certain period (such as a month). Then, at the end of the period, a total figure summarizes all the detail transactions that occurred within that period. Sales history by product is often maintained in detail for one month and then totaled to sales for the month. This technique is used as an effective way to save on the cost of computer storage. However, this may also mean that a detailed analysis beyond the stored totals may not be readily available.

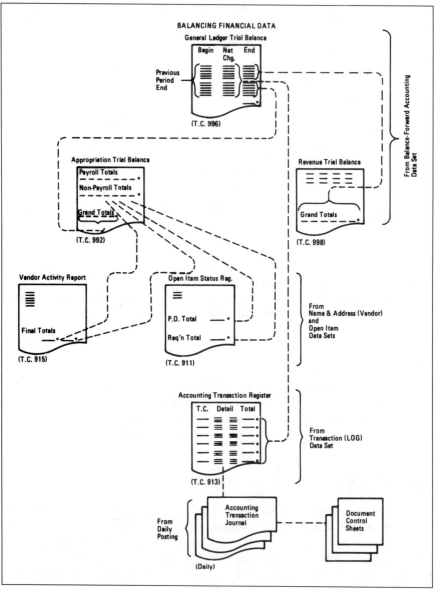

FIG. 11-5 Balancing financial data, showing interaction of system data sets (courtesy of International Business Machines Corporation)

Data Storage

Data is stored in computer files or data bases. Files are organized sets of data, each with a common subject. Five types of files are generally used:

1. *Temporary files.* These files hold transactions during job processing. They are not usually of major concern to an auditor when considering controls, since the transaction data ends up on master files (see item 3) at the completion of each job. An example of a temporary file is the open invoices file from accounts receivable, often sorted in sequence by date. In the master file, the same information is probably stored in sequence by invoice number. Normally, the open invoice file is stored in sequence of customer number, account number, and invoice number.

2. *Suspense files.* These files contain transactions held in suspense, pending some further action. Examples of these are erroneous transactions held back from further processing and awaiting correction, such as an invoice with an invalid customer number, or orders awaiting shipment.

3. *Master files.* These files represent the subledgers or books of account. They contain all permanent information for each account as well as the current balances (such as accounts receivable master with customers and balances, payroll master with employees and payroll history, general ledger chart of accounts with account descriptions and current month's activity). Master files contain both transaction data and more permanent reference data (also called standing data):
   - *Transaction data.* This is the data unique to each transaction (such as invoice number, invoice date, invoice amount), held in its original form or in a summary form. It represents the current balance, status, or cumulative history of each account.
   - *Reference data.* This is data of a permanent or semipermanent nature such as customer number, sales price, employee name, depreciation rate. Frequently, this master file data is referenced for purposes of control (such as customer credit limit on orders) or accounting computations (such as inventory cost price used to calculate inventory value).

4. *Table files.* These are files of reference data, often used to convert codes and indicators to values. Common table files are a stock price table and a currency conversion rate table.

5. *System files.* These files are used by the system. They can contain system software, application programs, tables that control processing, and activity logs.

The most sophisticated type of file is a data base. Data base concepts are discussed further in Chapter 10, "Data Base."

Data Parameters

Parameters (values that restrict or determine the specific form of the instructions) are entered for a job each time it is to be run on the computer. These values may change each time the program is executed (such as date, file generation number, batch number, batch control total). Parameters may also be variable data that could otherwise be coded into the program but is entered separately to allow for flexibility in modifying the system. Examples are a code indicating whether the program is executed daily or monthly, and the dollar value above which sales credit memoranda are reported as exceptional.

Data Retention

In noncomputer systems, there is normally complete retention of all financial records, at least for the period being audited and for the period required by government regulation. Nothing is destroyed until after year-end, and many files are retained for five to seven years.

In computer systems, the cost of storage on magnetic tape or magnetic disk is high. Thus, it is economically impractical to retain all versions of all data files ever created. Older copies of computer files are destroyed as data is summarized and updated into current versions.

Although the cost of computer storage has dropped dramatically and this trend is expected to continue, it is still not economically feasible to store all financial records. However, government requirements force many companies to retain data related to tax reporting, personnel, safety, and so forth for prolonged periods. For example, the Internal Revenue Service's Revenue Ruling 71-20 concerns retention of machine-sensible data for five to seven years. Such retention periods for important files are standard in many organizations.

Transaction Processing Systems

Accounting systems relate to business transactions. The systems exist to record and analyze these transactions within a set of defined categories. They are used to record the past activity or history of an organization, portray the current state of its financial affairs, and make forecasts of its future.

One of the best ways to think about these systems is to consider the related transaction groups that are usually found together in an organization. These sets of transactions occur cyclically and in reaction to each other, in a chain of cause and effect. As a result, there are specific procedures to be followed in specific sequences. (Figure 11-6 shows the possible sequence of functions for IBM's IFS 1-4.)

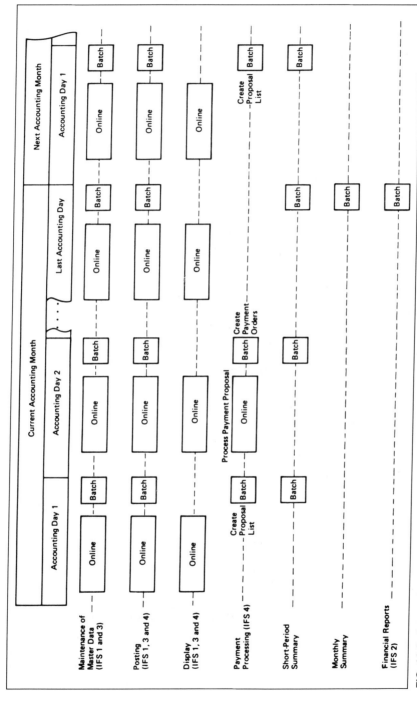

FIG. 11-6 Interactive Financial System 1-4 (IFS 1-4): Possible sequence of functions (courtesy of International Business Machines Corporation)

Some typical transactions for various industries are:

- Financial services industry
  a. Securities, bought and sold
  b. Loans, billing and accounts receivable
  c. Mortgages, billing and accounts receivable
  d. Lease accounting
  e. Insurance premiums and claims
- Wholesale and retail businesses
  a. Purchases and cash disbursements
  b. Billing and cash collections
- Manufacturing companies
  a. Purchases and payments
     — Purchase orders and receiving reports
     — Purchase and expense distribution
     — Accounts payable
     — Cash disbursements
  b. Sales and collections
     — Sales orders
     — Customer credit control
     — Shipping
     — Billing and accounts receivable
     — Cash receipts
  c. Production and costs
     — Production orders
     — Inventory control
     — Cost accounting
  d. Payroll
     — Employee recordkeeping
     — Timekeeping
     — Distribution of labor
     — Payroll disbursements

Often a monthly operating statement is produced for each set of transactions. It should be completed within a few days of the close of the month and contain the information required to run the organization. These statements yield a picture of how the business is doing from a financial standpoint. They are created by using the data from various transaction processing systems, so the systems must be able to produce this material on a timely basis and in a format that is readily usable. Naturally, these reports and statements are created to fit the needs of a particular organization. Some organizations also create projected results and/or budgets, which are then compared with the actual figures after each period.

Transaction Size and Volume. Individual transactions are rarely significant to a business, but when a transaction is spectacular, everyone concerned takes notice. The sale or purchase of a major asset is an example. For instance, when MGM/UA sold its music publishing division to CBS Inc. for a reported $68 million in 1983, it was news. Yet, this one transaction was probably not subject to the daily MGM/UA accounting system. It is likely a safe assumption that to process a transaction of this size is not a daily occurrence in most business accounting systems.

Routine accounting systems are designed to handle the usual transactions, not the exceptions; common, everyday items are the ones these systems handle best. In fact, one of the guidelines in determining whether a manual procedure is ready for automation is whether there is a sufficient volume of routine transactions. Another consideration is whether these transactions have become so complex that it is really no longer cost-effective to process them by hand.

Other accounting systems are created for routine transactions that are regularly in the millions of dollars. In the banking community, certain large banks handle millions of dollars worth of transactions daily; a $68 million transaction in such a system might not be large enough to generate an exception report. It is what the system was created to do that makes a difference here.

Accounting Transactions. Transactions are categorized into major groups, which are commonly found in many organizations. These are also accounting systems categories:

- Sales accounting
- Inventory control
- Purchase accounting
- Payroll
- Fixed asset
- General ledger

To understand a general overview of the systems most often used in large organizations, remember that the various transactions drive their particular system. The transactions can affect more than one system, but not necessarily at the same level of detail. For example, the payroll check created for work done by an employee this week is processed initially in the payroll system and eventually becomes part of a summary total posted to the general ledger system.

Another point worth emphasizing about accounting systems in general is that, almost without exception, an organization's business flow has peaks and valleys. As a result, its systems must be able to deal with inconsistent volume. Many businesses are cyclical in nature, and this is reflected in the number and volume of transactions on record for each cycle.

One industry with clearly defined cycles is toy manufacturing. Its busy season is during the summer, when it fills orders taken at spring buyers' shows for delivery to retailers in early fall. If toy manufacturers miss any part of this cycle, their merchandise will not be available when shoppers start to flood the stores right after Thanksgiving Day, traditionally the start of the Christmas shopping season.

It is essential that department store retailers have systems that can absorb the volume created by the Christmas rush, when they capture a large percentage of their total annual sales. Their sales processing systems have become more complicated over the years, and are often set up to handle the growing use of a variety of credit cards. The system must be able to process the sale while verifying that the customer's credit limit covers all purchases made. If the system cannot do this, it can cost the organization a lot in terms of lost sales or sales over credit limit that should not have taken place.

It can also cost a store dearly if its system appears slow or inefficient, causing a customer perception of inordinate time spent making a purchase. If customers have to wait for a prolonged period for a sale to go through, they may consider shopping where purchases are easier and faster. This perceived speed and ease is one factor that has kept more expensive stores in business, since many people tend to think of long lines and slow service in connection with discount operations. The degree to which these perceptions — whether true or false — affect customer decisions is something a retailer must consider when choosing a system.

For example, a retailer had a new system that recorded inventory at point of sale. It also processed the customer credit limit check at the same time. This point-of-sale system was implemented during the slow summer season. The sales people, who used to write up an order and ring it up on the cash register (for later processing by data processing), now had to enter over thirty characters into an interactive terminal connected to a cash drawer. The numbers included the codes for customer's account number, sales clerk number, transaction type, merchandise code, item quantity, and price. Each register automatically added the date, store number, register number, and transaction number. The line item extensions and totaling of transactions were automatic. Sales tax was automatically calculated and added to the total or could be overriden when necessary. The system then checked all credit card sales to see whether the total was acceptable and within the customer's limit.

As an example of an extremely interactive system, this one also performed edit checks and syntax checks of each code entered. While all this was happening, the customer stood and waited. During the summer this was not a problem, since there were not that many customers and the few who were there were happy to be in a cool store rather than outdoors in the heat. When the Christmas rush began, the lines seemed longer than ever and management thought that the store had more customers than usual. Once the system printed volume comparisons with the prior year, however, the message filtered through: There were not more customers, there were just more lines. The system was too slow. In such a short season there was no time to add sales stations; hiring and training sales staff, even if it could be done, was not the answer, there were no more stations for them to use. The industry reported the best season in years while this particular retailer was looking at unsold inventory and disappointing sales figures.

There were many similar stories throughout the 1960s and 1970s. When automated accounting systems did not perform properly in the time required, some organizations were brought to the brink of disaster. This is still applicable when systems are not properly designed and developed to suit the organization. There are other stories of systems that never got past the design and approval phases because the process took too long. By the time acceptable systems designs were completed, management had changed, business needs had changed, and the proposed systems were out of date before they could even be programmed.

Management Influence on Systems

Another factor complicating the selection and design of accounting systems is the general volatility of the business climate. Giant companies that did not even exist 40 years ago have become national presences, like McDonald's, Xerox, and, more recently, Apple Computer. Others that seemed like institutions have gone, such as W.T. Grant. Mergers created new conglomerates, as Coca-Cola bought Columbia Pictures and Allied merged with Bendix, to name only two. Divestitures also changed the face of corporate America, as shown by the breakup of the world's largest corporation, AT&T. All these changes reveal the need for new accounting systems and a fast response to changing conditions.

The particular focus or management style of any organization is often the key factor in determining which systems are chosen and automated for use. As a result, accounting systems are strongly influenced by management and by its perception of the needs of that organization. For example, an organization that stresses the control and careful negotiation of purchases is likely to have an excellent purchasing system. One that is service-oriented, based on a labor-intensive operation, will have a well-run payroll system that relates closely to the billing system.

Addressing Management Concerns

Although accounting systems are mainly used to record transactions, they are usually designed with the capacity to answer other kinds of management questions. One such response to management's need for information is the production of monthly financial reports. These usually take the form of a balance sheet, an income statement, and a statement of cash flow or position. Since these reports are an overview of the organization's entire financial picture, more specific management concerns are addressed by specialized reports, which are created on request. When systems are designed to provide the right kind of information, such information can be obtained without having to develop additional programs. In well-designed systems, the basic data for reports is there when it is needed.

For the most part, special management reports focus on particular areas of concern. Among these are:

- *Profit by area.* These reports analyze potential problem areas where profits may not match expectations, and can also detect areas where profits are large and can be used to finance new products or expansion. Such reports can cover one product or an entire line. Production issues may be indirectly involved, for example, if a product is not making money due to difficulties in producing it. The report can also help management pinpoint ways to make more money. Changes in demand, competition from other manufacturers, and general softness in the market can all be included as a part of a profitability analysis. Management can use such an analysis to find ways to improve production, change marketing strategy, increase prices, or perhaps decide to expand or drop a particular line.

- *Production reports.* These focus specifically on production issues, such as identifying unfinished jobs and determining how far behind schedule they are. Production reports can be used to help manage resources more efficiently and to address the demands of the organization.

- *Cost variance reports.* These reports show the difference between projected costs and actual costs. They reveal whether a product or project is being handled efficiently or inefficiently.

- *Payroll analysis reports.* These can range from reports on projected versus actual payroll, to comparisons of payroll within the industry or at different locations within the geographic area. They can also analyze the efficiency of a workforce by comparing cost of productivity and are widely used to do internal trend analysis.

- *Inventory reports.* These are critical to the success of an organization, since management of inventory can have widespread implications for a company. Rather than trying to analyze all inventory in one report, this kind of analysis is often broken down into smaller segments for ease of understanding. For example, aging of inventories yields reports that distinguish between fast- and slow-moving items or back-ordered items and can be analyzed to set effective production schedules, purchase materials, and control inventory. An inventory analysis usually includes a balance of inventory levels, to help management decide whether to increase, decrease, or maintain the current levels of inventory.

- *Accounts receivable analysis.* This is also a critical area for management, because long-outstanding receivables can indicate other, potentially greater problems. Aging of receivables to analyze patterns and trends can provide management with the information it needs to decide whether the problem is with the product itself, as indicated by a general trend toward late or nonpayment for goods received, or with a specific customer.

- *Cash flow.* Consistent reporting on the cash position of any organization is another critical area. Future cash needs should be analyzed, as well as the availability of surplus cash for which an investment strategy should be planned.

- *Sales reports.* These reports analyze sales trends and sales by grouping (area, product line, division, salesperson, etc.). These reports can help to ensure that production schedules are being met and that purchasing required to be able to produce the goods takes place on schedule.

- *Employee reports.* These reports can include the degree of turnover in the organization as a whole or in only one department. Since high turnover rates can have a negative impact on productivity, reports comparing turnover with past years, and possibly with the industry as a whole, can be significant.

- *Projection reports.* These reports try to predict how the business will do in coming months, based on the months just past and on seasonal fluctuations. They may also analyze what would happen if certain changes were made. The production of projection reports has been greatly accelerated by the use of "what if" financial modeling software packages. Microcomputers with this software can provide spreadsheet analysis of changes in different variables in seconds, as opposed to the days it used to take to create them by hand.

All the reports just listed can compare historical data with current data. Additionally, certain information can be used to evaluate the effect or performance of management itself. For example, assume that one management goal is to reduce by 25 percent the total value of accounts receivable balances more than 30 days past due. Reports can easily measure whether this goal is achieved.

Another goal might be to raise the average value of each invoice by 5 percent and reduce the number of line items by 10 percent. This means a bigger dollar volume for less paperwork, thereby reducing operating expenses. The goal might be accomplished by creating a more aggressive sales force that takes full advantage of access to data on the customer's historical buying patterns.

For example, Customer *A* places four orders a month, one each week. Suggesting to the customer that it place the order twice a month in order to save time and take advantage of a volume discount would increase the transaction size and reduce the number of transactions.

Whatever purpose these reports serve, it is critical that the data be complete and accurate so that it maintains its integrity. Otherwise management can easily be misled, which can impair the functioning of the organization and even affect its shareholders, vendors, customers, and other third parties.

Sometimes the information presented to management has such broad implications that to react to it precipitously can hurt the business. For example, a security and casualty company recently decided that due to losses of its direct insurance business, mostly automobile insurance, it should increase rates. Lacking adequate data to determine which groups of policyholders were causing the losses, an across-the-board rate increase was made. Policyholders with a good risk profile, who could obtain lower-cost insurance, went elsewhere. The insurance company was left with the poor risks who could not obtain insurance otherwise. The system should have been able to provide the information necessary for determining an appropriate rate increase structure.

Reporting requirements often help determine how data will be organized and accessed. Complex or changing reporting requirements can be met most often by using special data base structures, which allow information to be readily retrieved as needed. A data base can help answer questions for management in the most efficient way. In other system structures, it can be much more difficult to get the information quickly, if at all.

Another issue that arises in systems design, due to management's information requirements, is how the controls are put into a system. The system must be able to reflect the actual business conditions and record data on a timely basis. A data file not only has to be maintained by transactions, but it has to store the data correctly. It also needs to provide continuity of stored data and have proper security to guard against unauthorized changes to that data. When the data relates to physical assets, there must be control over those assets.

Another issue is the transaction flow through various systems. One type of transaction is rarely sufficient to build the kind of system that is needed to provide useful management information. Certainly, if the management of an organization is focused on its inventory, its particular system will be fairly elaborate. The system will probably process things like returned sales (think of the number of items that return to inventory after Christmas at a department store) that form a transaction type in themselves. The system would also be likely to process other transaction types, which handle records of shrinkage (as determined by physical inventory counts); damaged goods (things broken or found to be unsalable); and received merchandise or materials. A general inventory system contains many programs in itself. Their use ensures that management has all the information it needs to keep an accurate record of what is on hand.

As an example, in one organization there was a particular desire to make sure that there were no stock-outage situations. To avoid them, there was aggressive purchasing, often by railcar lots. Somehow the paperwork for an entire railcar full of plastic dinnerware was not processed on a timely basis. The goods were received in the warehouse and began to be disbursed to the stores to meet the demands of the summer season. As shown by the computer reports, the inventory quantity was substantially below the reorder point. Without checking further, the purchasing department placed a rush order for another railcar's worth. As a result, that second lot sat in the warehouse for a full year as the company waited for the picnic season to roll around again. Management had relied completely on the reports in its ordering. Although there could have been several reasons for the problem, such as operator error, it may also have been indicative of a pervasive defect in the system itself. Even though this happened only once, it should have been a warning signal for management to look for a possible flaw in the system.

Timeliness of System Response

Management frequently worries about the availability, timeliness, and accuracy of the information on which important decisions are based. The rapid development and implementation of the immediacy of response from on-line, interactive systems was stimulated by management's desire to have faster results than those provided by the older batch processing. Since batch processing was done either at set intervals or when there was a sufficient quantity of work to be processed, results were simply not available fast enough. In response to these needs, second and third DP shifts began to do overnight batch processing. Even this was not timely enough, since the data was only current first thing in the morning, at the start of the business day. In a high-volume transaction system, three hours worth of transactions can make quite a difference. During the early 1970s, the New York Stock Exchange discovered that its systems could not handle the volume of trading. The maximum volume projected during the design phase was rapidly exceeded, years before the projections had indicated. Until the system was enlarged and updated, the exchange actually had to close early to catch up on its transactions.

Interaction Between Accounting Systems

When transactions are processed, they frequently go through more than one system. The department store example in the preceding section shows how a sale is first processed in the sales accounting system, then processed by the accounts receivable system (if the purchase was by credit card), and for either cash or credit sales, through the inventory system (when they are linked). In yet another system, that same sale might trigger the purchase accounting system to

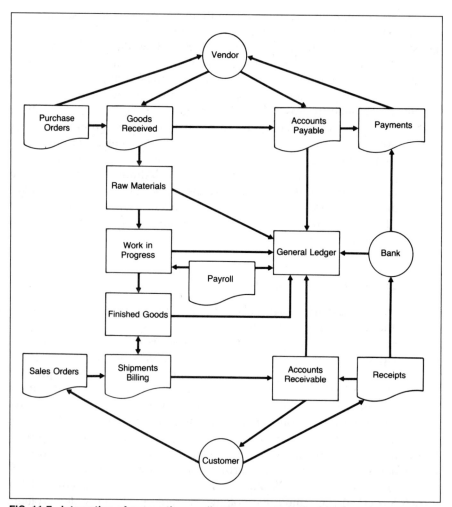

FIG. 11-7 Integration of accounting applications overview flowchart

replace depleted inventory. Eventually the transactions become part of the general ledger system, as all transactions are recorded somewhere in that system. For the integration of systems to be effective, processing of transactions must be complete, accurate, and timely. If it is not, a ripple effect impairs the integrity of the data.

A view of the transaction flow, in relation to all the accounting applications in a manufacturing system, is shown in Figure 11-7. This flowchart depicts how transactions proceed from vendor (the manufacturer, in this case) to customer. In reviewing this system, remember that the order could just as well have been shown in reverse (from customer through vendor).

The system should be designed to cope with the peaks and valleys in a processing cycle. In service-related businesses where there are a number of repeat customers, processing loads can be evened out by staggering the billing — a technique used by the telephone company or any large department store with a large volume of charge account customers.

From the manufacturer's point of view, the customer is involved directly with three of their systems: the one that processes sales orders, the sales accounting system; the accounts receivable system, which processes invoices for payment by the customer; and the system in which receipts are processed. The other accounting systems shown in this chart are internal to the manufacturer: the purchase accounting system; the inventory system (including goods received, and those on hand, as well as work-in-progress systems); the accounts payable system, which includes payments made; the general ledger system, into which all transactions involving dollar amounts are entered eventually; and a payroll system, which processes pay for all the people who work for the manufacturer.

System Accuracy

Management is also concerned about the accuracy of the system response and data on which important decisions are based. Data may be inaccurate due to weaknesses in control or flaws in the system's ability to catch erroneous transactions, but it can also be in error due to a lack of security over the data. If anyone can access data, then there is nothing to stop someone from changing the information. This can be equated to the idea of leaving files of data open for anyone to look through. Systems should demonstrate that they restrict access to data to only authorized users of the data. This means that the data elements processed by the systems have to be categorized by:

- *Data independence* — How the organization's data is structured so that it can be made available to the various accounting applications.

- *Data sharing* — The organization's data elements are no longer owned by specific applications. Individual data elements may be used by many applications, and the users and providers of the data may be different. For example, certain users may only retrieve data elements, while others may have the authority to add, delete, or modify the data elements. Finally, certain users may have no reason, or permission, to access the data element at all, simply because it has no relationship to their tasks. For example, the order entry clerk has no need to see the employee pay rates.

- *Data manipulation* — The processing requirements of the programs that process the transactions through to the data base.

Certainly these systems can be controlled. However, the opportunity for possible fraud in accounting systems should not be overlooked. This can range from theft or embezzlement concealed by changing the records intentionally to the deliberate manipulation of information in the records, or "cooked books." One example of system misuse is the Equity Funding case where approximately 65 percent of the insurance policies recorded in the insurance policy master file were nonexistent. The bogus transactions had entered the system with some management approval, since this particular situation was created by certain members of management acting against the organization. (The issue of security over data is discussed in more detail in Chapter 32, "Security.")

Industry Commonality

Accounting systems are strongly influenced by the industry in which the organization functions. Broad, general categories that can be used are agriculture, banking, construction, education, utilities, energy, forestry and paper products, health care, high technology (computers and so forth), entertainment, financial services, communications/information, insurance, mining, real estate, retailing, government (city, state, federal), and transportation.

The needs of different industries place specific demands on the people who run these organizations. One organization may be involved in many aspects of a particular industry. The unique business practices and accounting procedures of each industry necessitate different types of systems. It is common for different businesses in an industry category to have very similar processing methods. As system vendors concentrate on particular industries, the trend toward similarities increases.

Geographic Influence

As one might expect, the physical location of an organization has a strong influence on both what it does and how it does it. According to just where an organization is, it will need accounting systems that can conform to the local regulations as well as the reporting requirements of any state or federal government agencies that might be involved.

Within the United States, the accounting system most affected by geographic location is probably payroll, due to different local, state, and federal tax requirements. Other kinds of taxes are handled by sales accounting systems in many areas.

Multinational organizations need systems that can deal with currency conversions and possibly with the tax requirements of several different countries. Routines that perform currency conversion and can be adapted for changes in rates are built into the systems that need them.

Influence of Growth

An organization that has set a goal to achieve a certain level of growth each period needs systems that measure the growth and provide quick feedback as to whether the growth was achieved in the last or prior period. American management, and some multinationals, stress and strive for growth. Since growth usually implies power and a measure of success, many fail to realize that with growth often comes chaos and lack of control over transactions.

A growth-oriented organization must have systems that can grow as rapidly and be as flexible as required for expansion. Furthermore, the systems must have appropriate controls to ensure that the growth is real, according to generally accepted accounting principles (GAAP), and not merely creative bookkeeping, derived from management's need to achieve. The need to build in the kinds of controls that can prevent this distortion of information deserves special emphasis.

PACKAGED ACCOUNTING SYSTEM SOFTWARE

Whether an organization is for profit or nonprofit, wherever it obtains its supplies, and whoever the buyers of its goods or services may be, management needs certain basic accounting functions to make it possible for those goods or services to be available. Accounting systems, although they may be tailored to suit an industry's specialized functions, apply to many industries. This is the reason that packaged accounting software systems have been developed and are so popular: They are flexible enough to meet many needs.

The DATAPRO* Directory of Software lists and describes the kinds of accounting system software packages under the following headings:

- Accounts Payable
- Accounts Receivable
- Fixed Assets
- Contractor/Construction Accounting
- General Accounting
- Professional Accounting/Billing Systems
- Tax Accounting Systems
- Utility Billing/Municipal Accounting Systems
- Special Application Accounting Systems

---

*DATAPRO Research Corp., Delran, N.J., February 1983.

Other major headings describing available packaged software are:

- Banking and Finance
- Education
- Engineering and Scientific
- Finance
- Health Care
- Insurance
- Management Services
- Manufacturing
- Payroll and Personnel
- Sales and Distribution
- Utilities

In over two decades of software development, the accounting function software has, for the most part, been developed to be generic and usable in a variety of industries, often by making the packages flexible with options to satisfy the different users' needs.

THE SYSTEM AND DATA AS AN ASSET

Most organizations realize the value of their computer systems and resident software simply because they know how much they cost to buy and put in place. Like other assets, they need to be maintained and are updated as organizational requirements change. Many organizations are beginning to realize that the data within the system is itself an asset. This realization has spawned vaults that guard backup tapes of data for businesses.

Some kinds of data have been recognized as an asset for a long time, such as customer master lists, which can be used as an excellent source of mailing lists for special-interest groups. In some industries, the data itself is made all the more valuable by lack of source documents. For example, electronic funds transfers — hailed by some as the beginning of a cashless society — are independent of paperwork. The funds transfer systems, as a group, have been subjected to very strict controls, since the data itself literally represents an asset. As systems of this sort become widespread, the need for controls and proper authorization procedures is also becoming more apparent.

Sometimes the controls over authorization procedures are not followed, occasionally with far-reaching results. As reported in November 1983, a major bank was involved in a serious dispute with the government of Colombia over unauthorized funds transfers of $13.5 million. This transfer was made by telexes, which turned out not to have been sent by the Colombian government official whose name appeared on them. The formal procedures for transfer were detailed and had six different steps to be followed before any monies were disbursed. The government of Colombia alleges that these procedures were not followed by the bank. The telexes themselves did not contain the required code or "test keys" that are used in bank communications for normal verification of transactions. Since the money was transferred anyway and its whereabouts were still unknown when the story was written, the ramifications of these unauthorized transactions are international in scope. One way in which such transactions can be controlled is to build the authorization requirements into a system, as is described in Statement on Auditing Standards No. 48, *The Effects of Computer Processing on the Examination of Financial Statements.* (See Chapter 2, "The Auditor and EDP Auditing.")

ASSESSING FINANCIAL SYSTEMS

The accounting systems that are in widespread use range from relatively simple and straightforward to complex and integrated. Simplicity is actually a desirable feature, since the more complex a system becomes, the more difficult it is to catch errors, follow the transaction logic, and detect operational weaknesses. When a system is unnecessarily complex, it can even be hard to detect unauthorized activities. Following the proper evaluation procedures to select and implement an accounting system produces a basic system that does just what it needs to, with the appropriate degree of control over its use.

When a system is up and running, it is still possible to make sure that it is performing in the way it should be and to make any corrective measures that are required. The following questions raise issues that are basic to the functioning of a financial information system. They can be used to make a broad assessment of a system that is already running (or, for that matter, to assess one that is to be purchased or designed):

- Does the system provide the kind of reports and information the organization needs from the data that is available?
- Is the information available within a reasonable time frame?
- When the information is obtained, is it accurate?
- Can the system provide the kind of information needed to make forecasts and projections?
- Can the system provide information needed to make analyses of components (such as product performance by region)?
- If a system handles billing, are the transactions taking place on a timely basis? Does it provide adequate information on outstanding and past-due items? Can these be analyzed by time period?
- If a system handles inventories, does it provide an accurate picture of what is on hand? Can it do aging analyses? Can it track work-

in-progress information or track merchandise and stock transfer between warehouses?

- If the system handles payables, does it establish priorities for them? Does it ensure that it processes items on time for vendor discounts? Are payments made on a timely basis?
- Are erroneous transactions flagged or rejected and shown on exception reports?
- Are there controls to ensure the integrity of data?
- Can income statements and other financial statements be generated on a timely basis, feeding off data already in the system?
- Can the cash position of the organization be readily discerned whenever this information is necessary?
- Is a lot of manual work required to complete tasks that the system does not finish on time?
- Are there any major reports that still have to be created from scratch whenever the financial information they contain is required?

Of course, this is a brief overview of the functions and controls in computerized financial systems, but it provides some of the basics to consider when working with these systems.

CHAPTER *12*

Revenue Systems

INTRODUCTION

Revenue systems are those systems that process transactions that bring money into an organization. As such, they are obviously vital to the financial health of the organization. There are several different systems that fall into this category.

The development of a suitable system for any organization depends on the computer processing facilities and technology available. It is important to spend some time reviewing typical computerized accounting systems in order to become familiar with their operation. In the sales accounting systems and the purchase accounting systems discussed in this chapter, the complexity of the computerized accounting system depends on the number of different applications incorporated in the system. When systems such as this were developed in-house, they frequently started with one application and were built on as the need arose. Now that software packages are so widely available, it is more common for an organization to acquire a system that does the applications required.

SALES ACCOUNTING SYSTEMS

Applications

Most sales accounting systems perform three basic accounting functions:

1. *Accounts receivable processing* — Recording transactions in the accounts receivable records or ledgers.
2. *Billing* — Calculation of invoices from shipping notes in order to bill customers, and processing details of goods shipped to generate sales figures.
3. *Order entry* — Processing customer orders resulting in the shipment of goods and generation of shipping documentation.

Some aspects of the system may be computerized, while some can remain manual. The following list of the systems described here is presented in the usual sequence in which computerization takes place as a growing business evolves:

- Accounts receivable systems
- Billing systems
- Order entry systems

ACCOUNTS RECEIVABLE SYSTEMS

In the simplest accounts receivable systems, the computer processes the accounts receivable records while order entry and billing functions remain man-

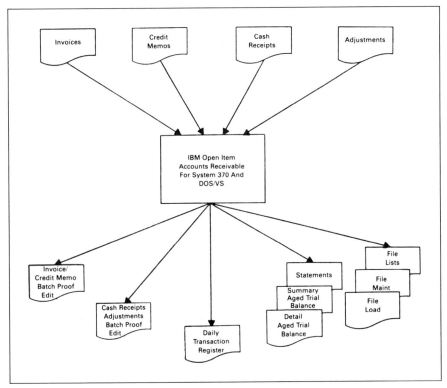

FIG. 12-1A   Accounts receivable system flowchart (courtesy of International Business Machines Corporation)

ual operations. This type of system is illustrated in the overview flowchart in Figure 12-1A. Figures 12-1B and 12-1C detail the input documents' data flow illustrated in the overview in Figure 12-1A.

Accounts Receivable Master File

Records are maintained on the accounts receivable master file for each customer with which the company has business. The accounts receivable records hold both:

- *Master file data* — The permanent reference data required to be held (e.g., customer's name, address, and credit limit).
- *Transaction data* — Information about the transactions processed against that account (e.g., outstanding transactions).

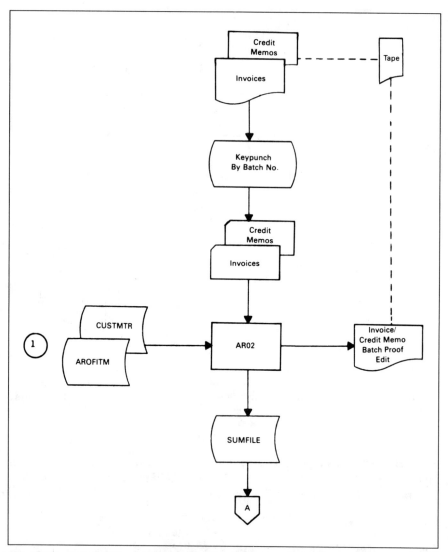

FIG. 12-1B   Data flow for invoice/credit memo entry and balancing (courtesy of International Business Machines Corporation)

Information on the accounts receivable files is used for financial accounting purposes and also for other uses, such as credit control and marketing. Examples of this information are:

- *Financial accounting* — Outstanding balance; unmatched cash and adjustments; goods on consignment; back orders; contract details;

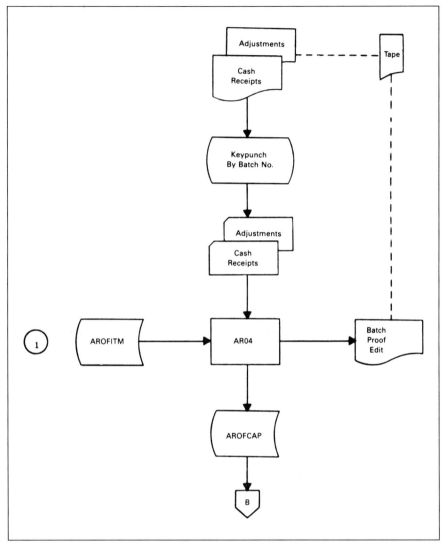

FIG. 12-1C   Data flow for cash receipts/adjustments entry and balancing (courtesy of International Business Machines Corporation)

special terms, prices, or discounts; prepayments; standing charges such as rents, dues, and subscriptions; and salespeople's and agents' commissions.

- *Credit control and collections* — Name and address, reports of credit investigations, and reports by credit agencies, bankers, and employers, often converted into a credit limit or other summary form; doubtful debt, stop shipment, and delinquent indicators; an analysis of amounts due by age; a history of previous late payments and any dunning notices sent.

- *Marketing* — Sales region; delivery/shipment information; sales history; main product interest; statistical information.

An example of an accounts receivable master file layout is illustrated in Figure 12-2.

Accounts Receivable Functions

The main types of transactions processed in accounts receivable functions are:

- Sales invoices
- Adjustments
- Cash received from customers
- Master file data amendments

Charges to Customers. Sales invoices are prepared manually from details of goods shipped or services rendered, and are then entered into the system.

The invoices are updated to the customers' accounts on the accounts receivable file, and the total value of transactions is summarized for posting to the general ledger. The total may be categorized for financial reasons (e.g., providing a basis for the payment of commissions), or for operational reasons (e.g., classification of sales by geographic region). Exception reports may also be produced, such as balances over credit limits as a result of updating invoices.

The summaries of transactions may be printed on a report or written to a file for direct input into a computerized general ledger application. In more advanced applications, the updating of the accounting receivable records and general ledger records may take place simultaneously.

Adjustments. Adjustments will always be necessary to account for returns, cash discounts allowed, allowances for defective products or partial shipments, reversals of mispostings and other errors, and writeoffs of bad debts. Different input codes are often used to indicate the type of adjustment.

Adjustments are usually processed in the same way as the invoices. In more advanced systems, certain adjustments, for which the entry of documents is required in simpler systems, may be initiated by a computer program. For example, the program may identify and write off small balances outstanding for longer than a certain specified time.

Adjustments are updated to the accounts receivable records and are summarized and categorized for posting to the general ledger in the same way as for invoices.

CUSTOMER MASTER FILE

Record:	Customer Master	File Organization:	Index Sequential
Disk File:	CUSTMTR	Key Length:	6
Record Length:	160	Key Location:	4

Field	Description	From	To	Length	A/N/P	Decimal Position
RECCD	* Record Code (CM)	1	2	2	A	
DELCD	* Delete Code Blank-active,'D'-deleted	3	3	1	A	
CUSNO	* Customer Number	4	9	6	N	0
CUSNM	* Customer Name	10	34	25	A	
CUSA1	* Customer Address	35	59	25	A	
CUSA2	* Customer City and State	60	79	20	A	
ZIPCD	* Zip Code	80	84	5	N	0
SLSNO	Salesman Number	85	89	5	N	0
STCDE	State Code	90	91	2	N	0
CUSCL	Customer Class/Status	92	96	5	A	
TXCDE	Customer Tax Code - user defined	97	97	1	A	
TRDCT	Customer Trade Discount Percent	98	99	2	P	3
TERMS	Cash Discount Terms - user defined	100	100	1	A	
PHNER	* Customer Phone Number	101	110	10	N	0
SMTCD	* Statement Code - N=No Statement	111	111	1	A	
CRLAM	* Credit Limit Amount	112	114	3	P	0
DLTPM	* Date of Last Payment	115	118	4	P	0
DUEOO	* Amount Due - Current	119	122	4	P	2
DUE30	* Amount Due - Over 30	123	126	4	P	2
DUE60	* Amount Due - Over 60	127	130	4	P	2
DUE90	* Amount Due - Over 90	131	134	4	P	2
CURSL	$ Sales Current Month	135	139	5	P	2
YTDSL	$ Sales Year-to-Date	140	144	5	P	2
CURCT	$ Cost Current Month	145	149	5	P	2
YTDCT	$ Cost Year-to-Date	150	154	5	P	2
	Not Used	155	160	6	-	-

* Required For Accounts Receivable

FIG. 12-2 An accounts receivable master file layout (courtesy of International Business Machines Corporation)

Cash Receipts. The method of updating details of cash received usually depends on the way in which the transaction data is stored in the accounts receivable file.

In a balance forward system, details of individual invoices are not retained. The amount outstanding is summarized into either a single balance or a series of balances for various age categories. Cash receipts may be applied against the outstanding balance or may be allocated against specific age categories, such as the oldest. The true aging of the file may be distorted if specific invoices are in dispute or otherwise remain unpaid.

In an open item system, the file contains a separate record of each uncleared transaction. Individual invoices are cleared by matching them with the relevant cash receipt. Unmatched cash receipts are posted as new open items. The matching operation may be performed either by manual allocation prior to processing or by programming the computer to allocate cash receipts to the relevant items. The second method is especially useful when only one periodic charge arises, as in the case of utilities and insurance companies, since separate records can be matched and cleared. Cash received that cannot be matched is normally reported for investigation.

Master File Data Amendments. Amendments to master file data are processed to alter the data held on the customer's accounts receivable record. Such amendments are needed to:

- Open new accounts.
- Change master file data on an existing account.
- Close accounts.

Master file data amendments may be entered on documents in batch mode or by using entries into terminals.

In some systems, the computer programs may initiate amendments to master file data. Examples of this are discounts based on historical records of sales, or increased credit limits, based on payment history and sales volume. A listing of master file data amendments is normally produced.

Transaction Codes. When data is entered, it is common to use a single document format, or layout for the data, for a variety of purposes. Different transactions can then be processed in the same way by the computer system. For example, the same document format may be used to enter invoices, credit memos, and cash, depending on entries for that information. In such systems, it is necessary to indicate the type of transaction being processed, usually by means of an appropriate code, so that each transaction can be recognized by the programs and processed as required. This transaction code entry makes it possible to use one input document format for several transaction types.

Periodic Output. Apart from the reports resulting from the processing of transactions, it is usual for the accounts receivable master file to be read periodically to:

- Produce statements.
- Categorize open items or balances by age, and summarize these categories to provide an age analysis.
- Summarize balances and provide a listing of balances.
- Provide information for control purposes, such as summarized details of movements on the accounts receivable records.

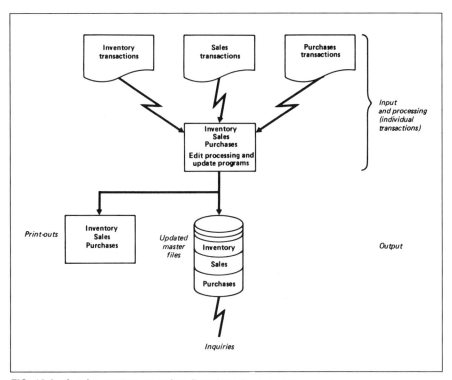

FIG. 12-3 A sales system overview flowchart for a real-time system

- Produce exception reports, such as lists of credit balances or balances over the customer's credit limit.

Figure 12-3 is a flowchart for an on-line sales accounting system. When only the accounts receivables processing is computerized,

- Accounts receivable master file is updated by transaction data and master file data amendment.
- Transaction data includes sales invoices to customers, cash received, and adjustments.
  a. Charges are entered in the form of invoices.
  b. Cash received is entered depending on the manner in which transaction data is stored on the accounts receivable file (balance forward or open item).
- Master file data amendments are necessary to open new accounts, to change data on file, and to close old accounts.

- Accounts receivable master file information includes reference data and transaction data for financial accounting, credit control and collections, and marketing.
- Output from the sales accounting system with one application — accounts receivable processing — would typically include the following:
  a. Statements for customers, showing the monthly activity for each account
  b. Age listing, reporting the current status of the accounts
  c. Sales analysis, detailing sales results by region, salesperson, product, and so forth
  d. Master file movements summary, showing changes to the master file data
  e. Reference data amendments, showing the change to the data

In a system with just the one application — accounts receivable processing — billing and order entry are manual operations or are performed by a separate computerized system.

BILLING SYSTEMS

The purpose of the billing and invoicing function is to calculate and print customers' invoices. In these systems, the computer is usually also involved in maintaining the accounts receivable records. Order entry may remain a manual operation. It is common for billing systems to be integrated with the processing of inventory records for finished goods. The shipping notes are used not only to process sales but also to update the inventory records. An application of this nature may be run as part of a data base system, as can the other applications discussed.

Billing Function

The billing function is illustrated in Figure 12-4. The initial documents to be entered are the recorded details of goods shipped. Upon entry of these documents, the following processing takes place:

- The items shipped are matched with the relevant prices (cost and selling) held as reference data on a master file, usually the inventory master file or a separate prices master file.
- The value of each transaction is calculated. It is common for the computer program to report unusual sales invoices, such as where the invoice value or discount allowed is abnormally high. This may be displayed in the form of a report produced as part of the invoice

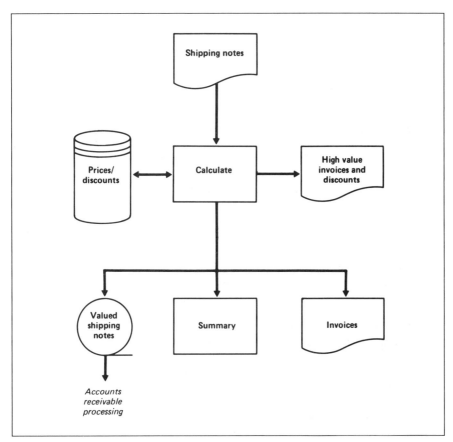

FIG. 12-4 A billing system that processes shipping notes

processing. Alternately, in on-line systems, such transactions may be identified by the program at the data entry stage, when the shipment details are entered through the terminal. This gives the operator a chance to check the details entered.

- Discounts and surcharges are calculated and applied. For this purpose, it may be necessary to simultaneously access the accounts receivable records or other customer records to obtain data for calculating terms that apply to specific customers.

- The total values of sales and cost of sales are accumulated. In batch input systems, these totals are accumulated during the run in which the sales invoices are extended, and are reported at the end of that process. In on-line systems, transactions are normally entered individually and the relevant totals are accumulated during the processing of transactions.

- Sales invoices are produced. In batch systems, the printing of sales invoices is done by one program in the system through which batches are passed. Even when transactions are entered on-line, it is unusual to print out sales invoices immediately. Instead, the details required to enter the invoices are accumulated on a file and the invoice print program is run against this file at a later stage.

Integration of Billing and Accounts Receivable Functions

As well as carrying out the new function of billing, an integrated system of billing and accounts receivable also carries out the same functions as an accounts receivable system. However, the integration of the billing function results in certain differences:

- The details of invoices entered in an accounts receivable system are replaced by the details of extended shipping notes.
- Many of the details for posting to the general ledger are output at the billing stage rather than as part of the accounts receivable processing.

Figure 12-5 shows a system of this type. In this installation, the billing or invoicing applications are part of the system. In the configuration:

- Quantities are matched with the relevant selling prices held on the inventory master file in order to calculate the invoice amounts.
- Quantity discounts, taxes, freight charges, and special prices are calculated as necessary.
- Special term/prices may require that the accounts receivable master file be accessed for that information.
- Individual customer accounts may be updated at the same time that the invoices are prepared.
- Or, the system may produce a file of evaluated shipping notes that would be used later to update the accounts receivable file.
- Additional output might include invoices and possibly inventory issues

ORDER ENTRY SYSTEMS

In an order entry system, the computer is involved in the processing of all components of sales accounting: accounts receivable, billing, and order entry. It is common for such systems to be integrated with the processing of inventory records for finished goods. Systems of this nature are logically developed as a

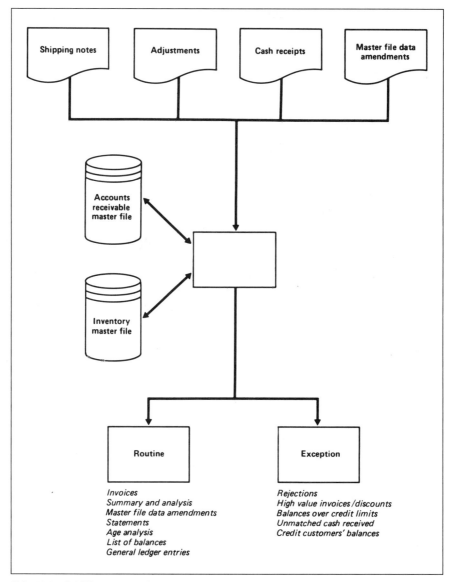

FIG. 12-5   A billing system integrated with accounts receivable and inventory

data base in order to eliminate data redundancy and make the information readily available.

Order Entry Function

Figure 12-6 is a flowchart for a basic order entry system. The initial entry in this application is the sales order. Two important control checks may be carried out during editing.

First, and most likely, the finished goods inventory records may be referenced to establish that there is sufficient stock available to satisfy the order. Second, the accounts receivable records may be referred to in order to assess the credit status of the customer. The customer's record contains the necessary information as master file reference data (such as credit limit, stop shipment indicator, bad-debt indicator) and transaction data (such as history of previous largest order, payment history, oldest balance still outstanding).

The check on credit status often involves a calculation. For example, the order is extended, using prices held on the inventory master, and is added to the customer's outstanding balance. The resulting new balance is then compared with the credit limit. In integrated systems, this is done automatically.

An order failing any of these tests is frequently rejected or held in suspense as an open order until

- The inventory is sufficient to satisfy the order (a "back order"); or
- The customer's credit status improves; or
- The shipment is authorized by the credit manager despite the customer's poor credit status.

Accepted orders are written to an accepted orders file, which usually shows both quantity and value. Then picking tickets and shipping notes are produced. The production of shipping notes may be carried out in real time as each order is accepted, or in batch mode at a later stage. A summary of all orders processed and their shipping notes produced is printed out periodically. Subsequent processing varies according to the type of order entry system in operation. The two types of order entry systems are referred to as postbilling and prebilling.

Postbilling Systems. In postbilling systems, customer charges are prepared from shipping notes returned from the warehouse after the goods have been shipped. The shipment details are reentered and matched with the accepted orders file. Matched items are either deleted and written to a goods-shipped file, or their status on the order record is changed to indicate that they are now matched. In either case, a summary of the matching process is normally accumulated and printed for control purposes. Duplicate or mismatched items are normally either reported or rejected for investigation. In on-line systems, a duplicate or mismatched item usually cannot be accepted.

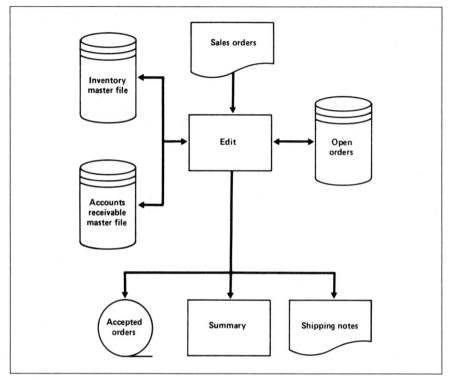

FIG. 12-6 Basic order entry system processing

The accepted order record, at any time, contains details of shipping notes produced but not yet reentered. These records are read periodically, and records remaining unmatched for a given period are printed, providing details of outstanding shipping notes. It is necessary to be able to process adjustments to the accepted order records so that entries on the records can be amended (e.g., if the goods actually shipped differ from those ordered) or eliminated (e.g., when the order is canceled by the customer).

Matched shipping records are passed through to the billing function and, when integrated, to inventory applications, as described for billing systems.

Prebilling Systems. In prebilling systems, accepted sales orders are treated as matched shipping records and passed directly into the billing and accounts receivable functions. Invoices are printed and a picking ticket sent to the warehouse to initiate shipment. A shipping note is produced and the goods are shipped. The customer is therefore charged before actual shipment.

Prebilling systems depend on an accurate system of inventory control. Unexpected lack of stock in the warehouse when attempting to pack the shipment can cause major problems. It is difficult to reverse the chain of accounting entries; therefore, only companies with few stock lines or with vigorous systems of inventory control can operate effective prebilling systems. This point is sometimes overlooked by designers of such systems.

To ensure that all amounts billed to customers reflect shipments actually made, it is necessary to establish methods of control. This may be accomplished by reentering the shipping note and matching it against the order record. This matching operation determines the need for adjustments for incomplete deliveries and provides a control over the dispatching of orders.

Integration of Order Entry and Billing

As well as carrying out the new function of ordering, an order entry system also carries out the same functions as a billing system. However, the integration of the ordering function results in certain differences:

- The shipment details entered in a billing system are replaced by the details of matched shipping notes (in a postbilling system) or orders (in a prebilling system).

- The calculation of the sales and cost-of-sales values of transactions may be carried out as part of the processing of the original order and not as part of the processing of invoices.

An integrated order entry system is illustrated in the overview flowchart in Figure 12-7.

When the order processing application is present, the system can do the following:

- Sales orders become the initial input. Two important checks may be performed during editing:
  a. The inventory master file may be referred to in order to determine that the goods are available.
  b. The accounts receivable master file may be referred to in order to establish credit status.

- Orders failing these tests are either rejected or held in a suspense file until the reason for the rejection has been cleared, as by manual checking ending in improved credit status.

- Accepted orders are written to an outstanding orders file and the shipping notes are produced.

- Order entry applications are often combined with invoicing and accounts receivable applications in one of two ways: either as a prebilling system or as a postbilling system, depending on whether the invoice is produced before or after shipment of goods.

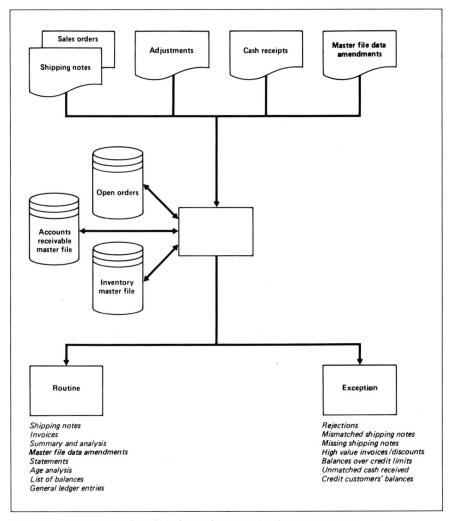

FIG. 12-7 An overview flowchart for an integrated order entry system

To reiterate, in a prebilling system, the entry of accepted orders results in the preparation of an invoice, the updating of the accounts receivable master file, and the preparation of the shipping note — in effect, invoicing the customer before the goods are shipped. Prebilling systems are dependent on the following:

- The shipping notes result in the order being shipped promptly.
- There is an accurate system of inventory control.

In a postbilling system, invoicing is not done until the system receives notification of actual shipment:

- Shipping notes are reentered, matched with and deleted from the accepted orders file, and passed through to invoicing and accounts receivable.

- The accepted orders file contains details of shipping notes produced but not yet reentered.

- Posting summaries may be printed out for a manual journal entry into either a manual or computer general ledger application.

- When the general ledger itself is on the computer, the journal entries may be passed across to the general ledger in the form of a data file. This file directly updates the general ledger master file.

Industry Variations

Variations peculiar to a particular industry are often found in these systems, as discussed in the following paragraphs.

Service Industries.   These do not have a shipping transaction to initiate invoicing; instead, a completion report or order may start the billing cycle. Billing in service-related industries is often more complex, since the services rendered can vary from month to month and may require documentation to prove accuracy of charges. A billing file may be used to accumulate costs in the same way as a work-in-process inventory file. Payroll costs, purchase costs, and other costs may be recorded, at their selling price, on the file. Such invoicing files are used, for example, by hospitals, advertising and public relations agencies, lawyers, accountants, and temporary employment agencies. At a suitable time, the accumulated costs are invoiced to the customer and the charges are transferred to the accounts receivable file. These applications do not always use a separate computer accounts receivable file, in which case cash received may be recorded directly on the billing file.

Subscriptions, Dues, and Rentals.   Systems where revenues are related to subscriptions, dues, or rentals have no input to initiate the billing cycle. The cycle starts processing automatically on an anniversary date, which is usually held as reference data on the master file. With some of these applications (such as rents or magazine subscriptions) sales must be prepaid and the actual sale does not take place (the goods or service are not provided) until payment is received. The computer therefore ensures that benefits are not received by nonpayers (rental applications may automatically issue an eviction or repossession notice, or magazine applications may stop issuing shipping labels so that no more magazines are sent). Many book and record clubs ship and invoice the goods automatically unless a "no order" notice is returned by the customer before a certain date.

Utilities. In utilities such as gas and electric companies, the date on which a meter-reading sheet should be initiated is held as master file reference data. Current dates are entered as parameters, and the computer produces the relevant meter-reading sheets or renewal notices. Details of documents produced are written to a suspense file awaiting reentry of the meter-reading sheets or renewal notices. This file operates like an order suspense file in a postbilling system, which awaits details of goods shipped. Sometimes billing combines transaction data (meter reading), master file reference data (rental or minimum charge), and transactions from other sources (sales of appliances or repairs).

Banking. In customer service financial institutions, transactions involving checking, savings, or credit card data are initiated by individual customer activities (such as by writing a check). Periodic processing through an update program can match or adjust master file records according to this input. Final processing of updated master files creates output that accurately reflects transactions and permits customer inquiries as well as cyclical record output for customer references. This process can often access information from the reference field for visual checking by the terminal operator, providing effective control over accuracy of input and master file data.

System Description: A Sample Accounts Receivable Data Base

Cash flow is important for any organization, and control over the accounts receivable contributes to this end. The amount of money owed to a company by its customers for merchandise sold or services rendered can be tracked and used to provide management information. When it runs efficiently, this process can increase the flow of cash back into the company. Prompt and accurate accounts receivable recordkeeping and processing are essential to any organization.

The IBM Accounts Receivable System software described in this section facilitates recordkeeping for customer invoices from data entry to receipt of total payment. In the sample system described here, transactions, including charges, cash receipts, credits, and adjustments, are recorded and posted to the customer accounts, as would be expected.

Customer invoices and credit memos must be coded with the correct customer number and invoice number so that they can be entered into the system. The system edits each transaction as it is entered and flags error situations. An invoice/credit memo batch edit listing is produced with batch totals, error messages, and cumulative totals. Data that passes the edit checks is saved in a temporary disk file. Cash receipts and adjustments are input separately and subjected to the same controls.

The two temporary files (invoice/credit memos and cash receipts/adjustments) are then merged and combined into a single input. A proof totals listing is produced, showing totals that include any discounts taken.

The combined input is then sorted in sequence by customer number. This combined input is used to update the open item master file.

The transactions are applied to the open item master file and, as a result of the update, a new open item master file is created. A report is produced that shows open item previous totals and then the new open item totals resulting from this run.

Customer statements can be produced either selectively or for all customers on demand. Final totals are printed after the last statement for control purposes. At the top of each statement, provision is made for the addition of a printed message. The actual text of messages is entered through the input device and can be changed. It is possible to produce statements selectively or for all customers, without updating the customer master file.

An aged trial balance can be produced on demand in either a detailed or summary format. It offers information about a customer such as:

- Date of last payment
- Credit limit, flagging any customer who exceeds the limit
- Total outstanding amount due
- Amounts due (current, 30, 60, and 90 days and over)
- Totals for this information (outstanding amounts due — total and by age) for all customers

Having this information on a timely basis assists a sales or credit manager to make suitable business decisions. It can help answer such questions as:

- Should we not sell anything more to this customer until the outstanding invoices are paid?
- Should we increase a customer's credit limit?
- Should we change our discount policies to encourage earlier payment?
- Should we investigate why a customer has not purchased anything recently?

The customer master file can be printed on demand, either in total or for selected customers by inquiry, to show pertinent information about each customer.

Invoice summary and credit memos are entered with two-digit preassigned batch numbers. As each enters the system, totals are accumulated for each field in the record. These totals are printed on the batch edit report for each batch. They should be balanced against totals accumulated on an adding machine. For invoices, the customer number is checked against the customer master file for validity.

The open item master file is checked for duplicate records. Credit memos are also checked against the open item master file for duplicate records.

Cash receipts and adjustments are processed in a similar manner as invoices and credit memos. They are grouped together in batches, batches are printed on the batch edit report, and the report is balanced against totals. The system also matches each transaction against the open item file to verify that it is being processed against a valid open item.

One or more times a day, the invoice/credit memo file and cash receipt/adjustment file are combined to form a daily activity file. This file is used to print the daily transaction report and to update the open item master file and customer master file.

One of the most important products of the system is the customer statement. The statements are a valuable communication with the customer because they show the details of all account activity until an invoice is cleared. The statements show the customer the age of any overdue amounts, which should help stimulate prompt payments. The statement form designed for this particular system includes a remittance stub. When this is returned with the payment, it should help apply cash to the correct account.

Two forms of aged reports provide information and control. One aged trial balance report summarizes each customer with an outstanding balance onto one printed line. This shows the name, telephone number, credit limit, the total outstanding, and the amounts due by age. This form of the aged trial balance should be run at least monthly to provide the credit manager with a document that indicates where collection follow-up is required. This report provides information current through the last posting of activity. The other aged report provides a detailed listing of all items in the open item file, spread by the age of the original invoice entry.

AUDITING REVENUE SYSTEMS

To audit revenue systems, an understanding of the system can be obtained using the following methods:

- Create or obtain overview flowcharts, often so useful that they may become a required piece of documentation in many EDP audits.
- Review audit or user documentation and/or procedure manuals.
- Analyze detailed flowcharts for a more thorough understanding of the system.

- Follow processing through both computer and manual portions of the system.
- Interview management and staff.
- Observe system operations.

Testing Accounts Receivable

Generalized accounts receivable audit software packages were developed to increase audit efficiency by automating some of the common substantive testing procedures. When these functions are precoded into the software, it can be installed quickly. The auditor should retain flexibility in choosing parameters and in the generation of computer reports. Audit software can be used to assist in the audit of most open item and balance forward accounts receivable systems. Software is particularly effective when there are a large number of open items or balances.

Many common accounts receivable substantive testing procedures, such as the following, should be performed by an audit software package:

- Adding, aging, and stratifying account balances
- Selecting accounts for positive and/or negative confirmations
- Producing confirmation letters and control working papers
- Identifying cash received after audit testing date
- Testing transactions dated after audit testing date

Thus, the accounts receivable audit software can assist the auditor in achieving the following substantive testing objectives:

- Determining whether recorded accounts receivable represents amounts due to the company
- Determining whether material amounts due to the company have been omitted from the books of account
- Determining whether shipping cutoffs have been performed satisfactorily
- Determining whether the allowance for doubtful accounts is adequate

Use of the software may also reveal breakdowns and weaknesses in internal controls requiring management report comments. Figure 12-8 illustrates how audit software can be used to meet some of the important objectives.

Audit Objectives	Software Capabilities
Determine whether recorded accounts receivable represents amounts due to the company at year-end or early substantive testing date.	■ Performs additions of account balances. ■ Produces a stratification of account balances to assist in selecting accounts for confirmation or other audit tests. ■ Selects accounts for positive and negative confirmations. ■ Produces confirmation control working papers. ■ Produces positive and negative confirmation letters using format and wording designed by the auditor. ■ Identifies and lists subsequent payments for accounts selected for confirmation.
Determine whether material amounts due to the company at year-end or early substantive testing date have been omitted from the books of account.	■ Performs a second aging of accounts receivables at a date subsequent to year-end or early substantive testing date. ■ Selects accounts with credit balances or unapplied credits for confirmation. ■ Identifies and reports transactions after the audit date.
Determine whether shipping cutoffs have been performed satisfactorily.	■ Selects accounts based on date of last debit or last credit. ■ Identifies and reports transactions after the audit date.
Determine whether the allowance for doubtful accounts is adequate.	■ Performs an aging of accounts receivable at year-end, early testing date, or any other date. ■ Identifies and lists accounts with irregular customer information. ■ Identifies and lists subsequent payments of accounts selected for confirmation.

FIG. 12-8 Accounts receivable audit objectives

Audit Program — Sequence of Events

The following sample audit program illustrates the use of the Coopers & Lybrand Accounts Receivable Audit Software package. Software reports generated by this audit software package are listed as events.

Events	*Auditor's Actions*
Planning	• Develop plan and budget.
	• Decide on confirmation strategy.
	• Collect the information concerning the accounts receivable system. Prepare planning working papers.
	• Determine desired report options.
	• Agree to create reports within the audit time requirements. Keep audit staff informed as to progress and any reasons for additional time.
	• Inform audit staff of the following dates:
	a. Year-end or audit date
	b. Aging categories
	c. Confirmation mailing date
	d. Subsequent payments period
	• Before the due date, install the package, execute the edit program, and review the results for exceptions.
Report	
List of Open Transactions After Closing Date	• Review the accounts receivable file total.
	• Edit the accounts receivable file and agree the totals.
Audit review	• Reconcile totals to books of account. Select the stratification method and supply the necessary parameters.
Reports	• Prepare reports and agree the totals.
Aged Open Transactions File — Summary	
Aged Accounts Receivable Listing	• Use aging reports for audit tests.
Stratification Histogram	• Determine selection criteria for confirmation.
Selection Criteria Total — Accounts Receivable	• Check that the correct number and value of accounts have been selected.
	• Code selection criteria onto parameter cards and prepare reports. Review results of selection.

Events	Auditor's Actions
List of Customers Confirmed	• Provide wording for positive and negative confirmation letters.
Confirmation Letters	• Arrange for controlled mailing of letters and follow-up responses.
List of Transactions After Closing Date	• Confirm the period for examining subsequent payments. Select the required report detail option.
Accounts Confirmed With Subsequent Payments	• Use the report to update the list of customers selected for confirmation but for which a reply was not received.
Second Aging After Validation	• Use reports to determine the effect of subsequent transactions on long overdue amounts.
Completion	• Summarize time costs and expenses. Document any reasons for changes from original budget. Provide suggestions for the coming audit year.

Implementing Revenue Systems

Auditors often participate in the design, selection, and implementation of new systems. One function that is important is to ensure that controls are built in and that proper procedures for purchasing, programming, testing, and installing the new system are followed. (See Chapter 7, "The System Development Life Cycle.") The following checklists can be helpful in determining the initial requirements for such systems.

ORDER ENTRY

Location _____

1. How many customers do you do business with? _____
2. How many of these customers are considered active? _____
3. What is your customer's file growth rate? _____
4. How many orders are processed on the average day? _____
   Peak day? _____
5. What is the average number of line items on each order? _____
6. Do you use back order processing? ☐ Yes ☐ No

7. If so, how many individual back order entries are written per day?

   _____

8. How long (in days) before a back order is filled? _____

9. On what basis do you fill back orders? _____

10. Do you have a customer number scheme? (Describe) _____

    _____

11. How many invoices are processed on the average day? _____
    Peak day? _____

12. Do you handle over-the-counter sales?   ☐ Yes   ☐ No
    Number daily _____

13. Do you require separate ship-to information?   ☐ Yes   ☐ No

14. Do you have multiple ship-to addresses for each sold-to address?
    ☐ Yes   ☐ No

15. If so, how many additional ship-to addresses in total? _____

16. Do you have a commission plan for your sales people?
    ☐ Yes   ☐ No

17. Briefly explain sales commission processing. _____

    _____

18. What is the largest quantity sold? _____

19. How many prices do you use per product? _____

20. Do you use any special pricing formulas?   ☐ Yes   ☐ No

21. What is the largest unit price? _____

22. Do you give discounts (e.g., quantity discounts, item discounts, or
    chain discounts)?   ☐ Yes   ☐ No
    Explain. _____

23. Do you distinguish between exempt or nonexempt sales for
    tax purposes?   ☐ Yes   ☐ No

24. Is freight included on invoices?   ☐ Yes   ☐ No

25. If yes, how is it determined? _____

    _____

26. Are there any other miscellaneous charges included (labor, deposits,
    handling, etc.)?   ☐ Yes   ☐ No

27. What type of sales analysis reports are now being maintained from your order-writing and/or invoice systems? _____

_____

28. Is there any other information that you feel is pertinent to your system?

_____

SALES ANALYSIS

Location _____

1. Are you currently compiling sales analysis information?

    ☐ Yes   ☐ Manual
    ☐ No   ☐ Automated

2. How are your sales analysis reports compiled?

Category	Yes	No	Frequency
By customer	☐	☐	_____
By customer class	☐	☐	_____
By product	☐	☐	_____
By product class	☐	☐	_____
By state or region	☐	☐	_____
By supplier	☐	☐	_____
Other	☐	☐	_____

3. Indicate if information is compiled in:
    ☐ Detail (by line item), or
    ☐ Summary only (total of detail items)

4. Do you perform comparison to prior statistics?

    ☐ Yes   ☐ Last month   ☐ Year to date
    ☐ No   ☐ Last quarter   ☐ Last year (by month)

5. Please indicate the number of:

   Customer classes   _____

   Product classes   _____

   Active states or regions   _____

   Salespeople   _____

6. Indicate any other sales analysis information that may be helpful to us.

   _____

   _____

   _____

SUMMARY

In practice, computerized revenue systems may begin with one simple computer-based application, gradually adding and linking others to provide the total system. The principal control considerations are that reliable software is used and that manual procedures do not, by error or otherwise, interfere with or affect normal processing.

A sound, practical knowledge of these types of computer systems is an important factor that enables the auditor to use, evaluate, and test the revenue systems developments discussed in this chapter. Although computer systems differ depending on the system requirements and design, their features are often similar enough to provide a knowledge base.

Disbursement Systems

INTRODUCTION

Disbursement systems are those systems where goods and services are purchased and paid for. They lend themselves to misuse, since use of these systems results in payments. It is important to ensure that their use and that the results — payments — are controlled, accurate, and timely. There are several systems that can be categorized as disbursement systems, including:

- Payroll
- Purchase accounting
- Accounts payable

- Goods received processing
- Order processing

PAYROLL SYSTEMS

Overview

The payroll system processes the cost of the labor force that supplies the products and services an organization produces. Just about everyone in an organization sees the results of the system in the form of its output — paychecks — and knows that input is necessary, often in the form of time sheets and time cards. The payroll system is thus highly visible and fairly easy to understand. It is important that it is always accurate, since there is no better way for an electronic data processing (EDP) department to lose credibility than by not being able to get the payroll done, both on time and correctly.

Payroll systems are sometimes developed by an in-house programming staff. If a system is not already in place, it is usually faster to implement one by buying a package. Packaged payroll systems have been available for a number of years, since they are common to all industries. An outside service bureau that does the entire payroll processing can also be used.

Whatever type of payroll processing system is in place, it should be audited to ensure control over it and its input. For example, the larger the organization, the more likely it is to find employees who are not recording their time accurately. But even more important, the payroll system is the way to track how much the labor force is costing a business. This information is especially valuable to sales analysis, profit analysis, and forecasting.

Payroll systems often process checks for expenses incurred by the employee for the company for which the employee is reimbursed. Since many organizations have their employees prepare expense reports concurrently with time reports, they become part of the payroll system. (Separate employee expense report systems also exist and are usually considered part of accounts payable.)

While it is not always critical from an overall financial statement perspective, payroll is one of the most important computer applications for an organization. Anyone who has worked in EDP knows that, whatever else happens, payroll has to get out on time. Good employee relations depend on an accurate and timely payroll system.

Because checks are frequently printed automatically, authorization and data security are also needed to provide adequate protection against potential fraud. The processing flow for part of a typical payroll system and the disk files used are illustrated in Figure 13-1.

There are two major kinds of payroll systems:

1. Salary systems, where employees are paid a fixed amount each pay period.
2. Hourly pay systems, where employees are paid on the basis of hours worked. Similar systems exist for piece work (where employees are paid for work done) or commission systems (where employees are paid according to a certain percentage of sales made).

In practice, most systems combine the two types, because salaried employees may still be paid for overtime, or the organization may employ both types of worker. At the same time, it is also common for organizations to run separate payroll systems for different classes of employee. Unionized shop employees, perhaps paid under the terms of a negotiated union contract, may be separate from salaried clerical and managerial staff. The requirement for confidentiality often means that executives are handled by a different system. The special system of executive incentives, bonuses, and stock option plans also argues for such a split.

The Payroll Master File. The main file is the payroll master, which is sometimes integrated with the personnel data base. The latter contains profiles of employees, including qualifications, employment history, training completed, and employment health records.

The payroll master file itself contains:

- *Master file data* — Pay rates, deduction rates, and the necessary minimum of personnel data needed for payroll purposes (social security number, employee number, name, address, department, job classification, etc.).

- *Transaction data* — Most of which is held for tax or other reporting purposes, this includes year-to-date figures for pay and deductions.

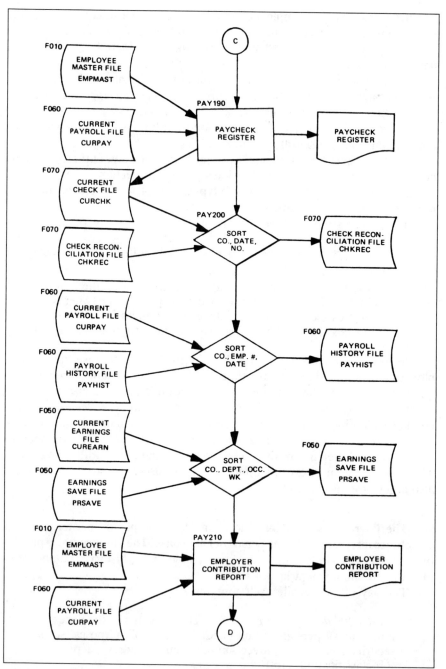

FIG. 13-1A   Payroll system overview flowchart (courtesy of International Business Machines Corporation)

File Name	File ID	File Orgn.	Record Size	Block Size	Format No.
EMPMAST	Employee Master File	VSAM	384	1152	F010
EMPLOAD	Load File	SAM	96	960	F020
TIMEWRK	Time Card Work File	SAM	38	380	F030
TIMECRD	Time Card File	VSAM	38	380	F030
TIMDATA	Time Card Data File	SAM	96	960	F040
CUREARN	Current Earnings File	SAM	120	960	F050
CURPAY	Current Payroll File	SAM	175	875	F060
CURCHK	Current Check File	SAM	18	504	F070
CHKREC	Check Reconciliation File	SAM	18	504	F070
PAYHIST	Payroll History File	SAM	175	875	F060
PRSAVE	Earnings Save File	SAM	120	960	F050
DEDREC	Deduction File	SAM	24	480	F090
CANCHK	Cancelled Check File	SAM	14	280	F080
TCHECK	Temporary Check File	SAM	18	360	F070
HISTREQ	History Request File	SAM	80	80	F120
WKCOMP	Workmans Comp. File	SAM	16	320	F100
UNION	Union File	SAM	120	960	F050
UNPREM	Union Premium File	SAM	28	560	F110
SUNION	Selected Union File	SAM	120	960	F050
NEWMAST	New Employee Master File	VSAM	384	1152	F010
JOBCLAS	Job Class Table	SAM	80	80	F130
FEDTAX	Federal Tax Table	SAM	80	80	F140
CALTAX	State Tax Table-California	SAM	80	80	F150
OCCGRP	Occupation Group Table	SAM	80	80	F160
UNRATE	Union Premium Rate Table	SAM	80	80	F170
EMPMASB	Double Definition of EMPMAST				
BEMPMAS	Backup Employee Master File	VSAM	384	1152	F010
BCURPAY	Backup Current Payroll File	SAM	175	875	F060
BPRSAVE	Backup Current Earnings File	SAM	120	960	F050
BPAYHIS	Backup Payroll History File	SAM	175	875	F060
BCHKREC	Backup Check Reconciliation File	SAM	18	504	F070

FIG. 13-1B   Payroll system disk files (courtesy of International Business Machines Corporation)

Some systems also hold current, month-to-date, monthly, quarterly-to-date, or quarterly historical figures as well.

An example of the data elements as shown by a payroll master file card record layout is shown in Figure 13-2 on pages 13-8 and 13-9. Most payroll systems use the employee number as a key to the information, keeping the employee number separate from the social security number. However, other systems rely on the social security number as the key control field. The reason the social security number is not always used is that the employee number rarely exceeds five digits, whereas the social security number is nine digits — considerably more key entry to record transactions. As a result, the social security number becomes master file data, since it will never change.

Input and Output. The most important input to a payroll system is the master file data changes. For example, a change in pay rate could affect employee salary paid every pay period. Where necessary, the time cards, time sheets, or other records of work performed are also input. Vacation pay, bonuses, manually processed checks, and other unusual events are handled by special adjusting transactions.

The main output is the payment to employees, usually by check. Regular and exception reports provide required information trails and the appropriate basis for control. Another important output is the distribution of expense to the appropriate general ledger code.

Master File Data. Amendments to master file data are processed to

- Record new employees, terminations, and employees on leave on the employee master file.
- Alter rates of pay, pay status, or details of allowances.
- Change deductions or other data (such as change in tax status or department number).

A part of a file layout for the employee master file, illustrating the variety of data that such files can hold, and for which amendment routines may be necessary, is shown in Figure 13-3 on page 13-10.

In some systems the computer may be programmed to:

- Calculate changes to master file data on the basis of input, such as increments to rates of pay as a result of changes in personnel details (such as the passing of examinations).
- Initiate amendments to master file data, such as increases in rates of pay on anniversary of starting date.

Payroll Production

In hourly payroll systems, it is usually necessary to enter details of time worked. The input can be all hours worked or variances from the standard hours held as master file data. Variances include overtime, holidays, and absences. The computer is often programmed to report cases where the hours entered exceed a defined norm.

For the system to act on the payroll input, it has to reference other files of standard information. Among these are:

- Overtime rate multiple
- Premium rate multiple
- Report options selected
- Pay rate table
- Valid bank code table
- Valid state code table
- Valid local code table
- FICA rate table
- FUTA rate table
- Vacation entitlement table
- Sick pay entitlement table
- Bank number and name table

These provide the rest of the data needed to calculate meaningful output.

The system matches transaction data with the relevant employee details on the master file. Unmatched input or erroneous data is usually rejected (such as duplicate input) or reported (such as no time report received), whichever is appropriate to the system.

The computer then

- Calculates the pay details for each employee.
- Updates the transaction data on the master file.
- Summarizes the accounting total for posting to the general ledger.

The totals are often categorized. This is done as a basis for posting work-in-process or cost accounts. These summaries may be produced for noncomputer processing or for subsequent input to the general and cost ledger computer applications; this input may be by document or by the file created during payroll production.

In salary systems it is normal for the monthly or annual salary to be held as master file data. The only transaction data entered is any adjustments or

(text continues on 13-11)

CARD RECORD LAYOUTS

Card No.	Card Name	Input to Program(s)
C010	Employee Master Name and Address Card "A"	PAY810
C011	Employee Master Name and Address Card "B"	PAY810
C012	Employee Master Payroll Status Card "A"	PAY810
C013	Employee Master Payroll Status Card "B"	PAY810
C014	Employee Master Quarterly Accumulation Card "A"	PAY810
C015	Employee Master Annual Accumulation Card "A"	PAY810
C016	Employee Master Annual Accumulation Card "B"	PAY810
C017	Employee Master Deduction Card "A"	PAY810
C020	Company Data Card 1	PAY820
C021	Company Data Card 2	PAY820
C022	Company Data Card 3	PAY820
C023	Company Data Card 4	PAY820
C024	Company Data Card 5	PAY820
C030	Job Class Table Cards	PAY800
C031	Federal Tax Table Cards	PAY800
C032	California Tax Table Cards	PAY800
C033	Occupation Group Table Cards	PAY800
C034	Union Premium Rate Table Cards	PAY800
C040	Select Time Cards Limits Card	PAY110
C050	Earnings Card "A"	PAY115
C051	Voucher Earnings Card "B"	PAY115
C052	Voucher Earnings Card "C"	PAY115
C060	Paycheck Control Card	PAY180
C070	Cancelled Check Card	PAY575
C080	Personnel Inquiry Limits Card Personnel Listing Limits Card History Request Limits Card Employee W-2 Limits Card	PAY563 PAY570 PAY573 PAY760
C090	Effective Date Card	PAY510
C100	Alpha/Numeric Date Card	PAY530 PAY560 PAY710 PAY720 PAY770

FIG. 13-2A   Payroll master file card records (courtesy of International Business Machines Corporation)

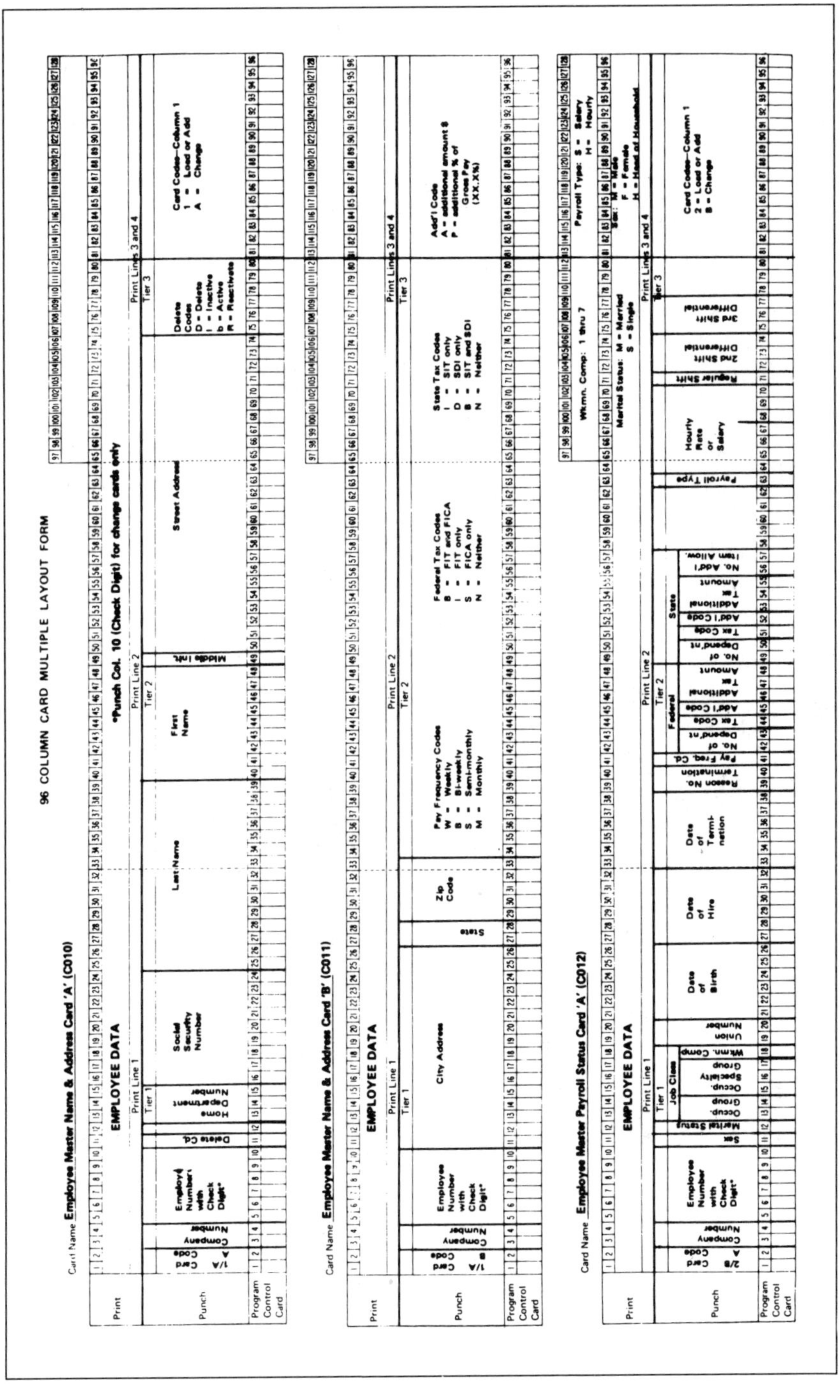

FIG. 13-2B Sample column card layout (courtesy of International Business Machines Corporation)

EMPLOYEE MASTER FILE - EMPLOYEE RECORD

Format: FØ1Ø

Field Description	Field Name	Field Length	Dec Pos	Format	Positions	Comments
RECORD CODE	MRECCD	2		A	1-2	'EM' in all cases
DELETE CODE	MDELCD	1		A	3	'D' = Deleted 'I' = Inactive/Terminated Blank = Active Employee
COMPANY CODE	MCOMPY	2	Ø	N	4-5	Two digit designator for each unique company
EMPLOYEE NO.	MEMPNO	6	Ø	N	6-11	Includes five digit employee number with check digit (modulus 10)
UNUSED		2			12-13	
DEPARTMENT NO.	MHDEPT	3	Ø	N	14-16	
SOCIAL SECURITY NO.	MSOSEC	9	Ø	N	17-25	
EMPLOYEE LAST NAME	MLSTNM	15		A	26-40	Employee last name, if JR, SR, III etc place after last name
EMPLOYEE FIRST NAME	MFSTNM	9		A	41-49	
EMPLOYEE MIDDLE INITIAL	MMINIT	1		A	50	
STREET ADDRESS	MSTRAD	25		A	51-75	
CITY ADDRESS	MCITY	16		A	76-91	
STATE ADDRESS	MSTATE	2		A	92-93	

FIG. 13-3 Payroll master file layout (courtesy of International Business Machines Corporation)

overtime details. The computer is programmed to select or calculate the salary and take account of any additional input.

Sample System Overview

A software aid for payroll systems is IBM's COBOL Payroll Management System. It includes a basic payroll system and additional subsystems, which may or may not be implemented. The basic system provides employee file loading and maintenance, tax and other table loading, time and attendance processing, payroll processing, file backup, personnel reporting, quarterly statements (941s), and year-end W-2 Forms. The additional subsystems, not interrelated, are the check reconciliation system, time card preparation, employer contributions report, vacation/sick pay report, labor distribution, payroll history, deduction report, union reporting, and worker's compensation report. Implementation of all components of the payroll management system makes comprehensive reporting to management — with strict controls, edits, and information or audit trails — possible.

Time Card Preparation System

A time card preparation system produces employees' time cards on the computer's printing device. The system prints employee details on card-stock continuous forms. Time cards are usually printed in company number, home department, and employee name sequence. Upper and lower limits are input to the time card printing program so that groups may be printed selectively. Programs included in this optional system are:

- Select time card data
- Load time card file
- Print time cards
- Build deduction file
- Deduction report
- Pay period vacation/sick pay report

Upon completion of this processing, the payroll cycle associated with the pay period is complete except for backing up critical files.

AUDITING PAYROLL SYSTEMS

Among the procedures for auditing payroll systems are common payroll substantive procedures such as:

- Identifying duplicate social security numbers
- Comparing current period's payroll figures with a previous period's payroll figures
- Identifying employees with "unusual" payroll records (such as those with excessive overtime)
- Identifying possible excessive increases in an employee's salary

As a result, an auditor can achieve the following substantive objectives:

- Determining whether the net income for the year and the individual items of income and expenses that are disclosed in the income statement are fairly stated
- Determining whether production in relation to cost is appropriate, where pay is related to production
- Determining whether liabilities for accrued liabilities and other accounts payable have been recorded and fairly stated

Using Audit Software to Analyze Payroll

Audit software packages exist to assist the auditor by automating many of the tasks associated with payroll substantiation. Additional audit work required is sometimes beyond the scope of most payroll audit packages. For example:

- Recalculation of federal, state, and local taxes
- Verification of accruals for vacation pay

Many common payroll substantive tests or procedures can be performed using audit software. Since the data is maintained on computer files, it was natural to develop audit software that analyzes this information. The auditor can thus be assisted in analysis of data and controls.

A number of data elements can be analyzed to determine whether there are any weaknesses in the controls and whether there has been any breakdown.

Duplicated Data. Whenever there is a possibility of duplicated data (inappropriate for processing), there is usually a way for the computer to deal with it. For example, using the master file, the program can sort by social security number to locate any duplicate social security numbers. This may raise a few more questions to be answered via software, because there are situations where more than one master record with the same social security number will exist. For example, in a company where employees change departments and receive new employee numbers, both master records may be kept on file for a certain period (although one should be coded as inactive). (See Figure 13-4 for an example of a report from the Coopers & Lybrand package.) Once the report

SOCIAL SECURITY	EMPLOYEE NUMBER	DEPT. NO.	EMPLOYEE NAME	START DATE	STOP DATE	PAY TYPE	PAY RATE	DEP.	GROSS PAY	TOTAL DEDUCTIONS	NET PAY
011-21-8765	416	1017	HARDY, KENNETH	01/21/75		A	15,000.00	2	15,000.00	4,000.00	11,000.00
011-21-8765	416	1122	HARDY, KENNETH	01/21/75		H	5.25	1	10,920.00	3,920.00	7,000.00

REPORT NO. PRO5CAAG-1
REPORT DATE 02/28/81

COMPUTER MFG CO
DUPLICATE SOCIAL SECURITY NO.

PAGE NO. 1
PERIOD ENDED 01/31/81

*** TOTAL RECORDS PROCESSED   22,000 ***

RECORDS PRINTED ABOVE   2

EMPLOYEES WITH DUPLICATE SS NO.   1

FIG. 13-4 Duplicated data report

has been obtained, the reasons for the duplicate numbers should be investigated to ensure that they represent valid employees.

No Match and Excessive Increases. Another technique to analyze the data is to obtain the payroll master file from two periods (usually two calendar years). Then each employee's current information can be compared with the corresponding historical information to identify excessive increases in pay rates, changes to number of dependents, date of birth, and date of hire. It is also possible to determine who has been hired and terminated during the period. (See Figure 13-5 for a sample report.)

The report totals are subsequently agreed to payroll master file report totals, highlighting any unusual or unsubstantiated results. All reasons for employee information that does not match the previous period data can then be investigated.

Large Increases. An organization may have a standard guideline for pay increases. Using this as a guide, employees can be reviewed to determine how many received pay increases that were above the guideline. Once selected, the pay increases can be checked to see that they agree with authorized documents. It is possible that such an increase is warranted and was duly authorized.

Operational Audits. This last analysis might also be very effective for operational audits. To evaluate a particular department, this type of payroll information gives a perspective of how well the department is functioning. Analysis can be made of:

• Number and frequency of pay increases.

• Department turnover. Excessive new hires and terminations reflects on the department business. Too many terminations may indicate an overzealous "mean and lean" operation that could affect future production. A combination of too many new hires and terminations

```
REPORT NO. PR07CAAG-1                                    COMPUTER MFG CO                                    PAGE NO. 1
REPORT DATE 02/28/81                            NO MATCH AND EXCESSIVE INCREASES                     PERIOD ENDED 01/31/81

 SOCIAL     DEPT    EMPLOYEE    PERIOD   BIRTH    DATE    STOP   DEP   PAY      TYPE   GROSS     TOTAL        NET      REASON
 SECURITY   NO.     NAME                 DATE     HIRED   DATE         RATE            PAY       DEDUCTIONS   PAY

 101-25-1011 1211  JONES, THOMAS  CURR  012245   050180     0  60,000.00   A  45,000.00  13,950.00  31,050.00  NEW
 121-16-8011 1212  SMITH, FRANK   CURR  061354   021578     2  30,000.00   A  30,000.00   8,500.00  21,500.00  TYPE CHG.
                                  PREV  061354   021578     2   2,000.00   M  24,000.00   6,000.00  18,000.00
```

```
REPORT NO. PR07CAAG-1                                    COMPUTER MFG CO                                    PAGE NO. 212
REPORT DATE 02/28/81                      NO MATCH AND EXCESSIVE INCREASES STATISTICS               PERIOD ENDED 01/31/81

DESCRIPTION:                     EMPLOYEES       RECORDS       GROSS PAY       DEDUCTIONS        NET PAY

NEW EMPLOYEES                      2,000          2,000        30,000,000      7,500,000        22,500,000

TERMINATED EMPLOYEES                 500            500         7,500,000      1,875,000         5,625,000

EXCESSIVE PAYRATE                    100            100         5,000,000      1,000,000         4,000,000

PAYTYPE CHANGE                       200            200        10,000,000      2,000,000         8,000,000

BIRTHDATE CHANGE                      10             10           100,000         25,000            75,000

DATE OF HIRE CHANGE                   20             20           100,000         35,000            65,000

NO. OF DEPENDENTS CHANGE             600            600        20,000,000      5,000,000        15,000,000

TOTAL PRINTED - CURRENT FILE       2,930          2,930        65,200,000     15,560,000        49,640,000

TOTAL NOT PRINTED -CURRENT FILE   20,194         20,194       275,316,711     14,555,000       260,761,711

*** GRAND TOTALS - CURRENT FILE   23,124         23,124       340,516,711     30,115,036       310,401,685

TOTAL PRINTED - PREVIOUS FILE      1,330          1,330        42,000,000      9,935,000        32,065,000

TOTAL NOT PRINTED - PREVIOUS FILE 20,270         20,270       288,425,675     20,174,804       268,250,000

*** GRAND TOTALS - PREVIOUS FILE  22,000         22,000       330,425,675     30,109,804       300,315,871
```

FIG. 13-5 No match/excessive increases report

indicates heavy employee turnover, which could have a serious impact on the department's ability to achieve its business objectives.

Along these lines, a report such as the one in Figure 13-6, can be produced showing a comparison of current-year information to previous-year information.

Department hours, overtime hours, regular pay, gross pay, and number of people with percentage of change in gross pay can be analyzed. Where there are large changes in percentages, the auditor ensures that they are valid and that they are properly reflected in the costing of products and services.

High and Sample Reporting. An analysis based on gross pay can be made by sorting master file year-to-date gross pay in descending sequence. The ranking by pay is then shown. Of course, sample data should be taken in different ranges. (See Figure 13-7 for a report example.)

Analyzing the Effectiveness of the Controls

Using the software and the data stored in the files, it is possible to obtain the results of system processing and determine how effectively it was controlled by seeing what was recorded.

| REPORT NO. PR10CAAG-1 | | | | | | | | | COMPUTER MFG CO | | | | | PAGE NO. 1 |
| REPORT DATE 02/28/81 | | | | | | | | | ANNUAL COMPARISON BY DEPARTMENT | | | | | PERIOD ENDED 01/31/81 |

	CURRENT YEAR INFORMATION									PREVIOUS YEAR INFORMATION			
REGULAR HOURS	OVERTIME HOURS	REGULAR PAY	GROSS PAY	NO. OF PEOPLE	I DEPT I I NO. I I	NO. OF PEOPLE	GROSS PAY	REGULAR PAY	OVERTIME HOURS	REGULAR HOURS	PERCENT CHANGE
10,400	500	104,000	114,000	5	I 211 I	4	89,880	74,880	1,000	8,320	27 ***
				23,124	*TOTALS*	22,000					
		RECORDS IN CURRENT FILE		23,124		22,000	RECORDS IN PREVIOUS FILE				

FIG. 13-6   Annual comparison by department report

| REPORT NO. PR04CAAG-1 | | | | COMPUTER MFG CO | | | | | | PAGE NO. 1 |
| REPORT DATE 02/28/81 | | | | HIGH AND SAMPLE REPORT | | | | | | PERIOD ENDED 01/31/81 |

SOCIAL SECURITY	EMPLOYEE NUMBER	DEPT. NO.	EMPLOYEE NAME	START DATE	STOP DATE	PAY TYPE	PAY RATE	DEP.	GROSS PAY	TOTAL DEDUCTIONS	NET PAY
101-25-1011	1211	1016	JONES, THOMAS	05/01/80		A	60,000.00	0	45,000.00	13,950.00	31,050.00
127-44-5601	843	1016	SMITH, GEORGE	02/16/78		M	1,014.50	1	12,174.00	3,165.24	9,008.76
079-46-6403	844	1017	KNIGHT, JR., CARLTON	01/10/78		H	5.25	2	10,920.00	2,948.40	7,971.60
111-16-6021	1016	211	RUSH, ANNE	02/01/80	02/15/80	H	4.00	0	8,320.00	1,913.60	6,407.00

| REPORT NO. PR04CAAG-1 | | | COMPUTER MFG CO | | | PAGE NO. 27 |
| REPORT DATE 02/28/81 | | | HIGH AND SAMPLE STATISTICS | | | PERIOD ENDED 01/31/81 |

CRITERIA	RECORDS	EMPLOYEES	GROSS PAY	NET PAY	DEDUCTIONS
SELECTED BY GT-TEST	15	15	175,000.00	127,750.00	47,250.00
TOTAL ABOVE CUTOFF VALUE	10	10	385,612.00	285,353.00	100,259.00
SELECTED BY LT-TEST	40	40	120,000.00	90,000.00	30,000.00
TOTAL BELOW CUTOFF VALUE	500	500	282,614.42	209,134.68	73,479.75
SELECTED BY BT-TEST	22	22	1,621,817.16	1,216,362.89	405,454.27
TOTAL BETWEEN RANGE VALUES	618	618	2,112,819.80	1,593,230.26	519,589.54
TOTAL SELECTED	215	215	3,225,000.00	2,418,750.00	806,250.00
TOTAL NOT SELECTED	21,785	21,785	327,200,675.12	297,102,879.00	30,029,179.00
*** TOTAL IN FILE ***	22,000	22,000	330,425,675.12	300,315,871.00	30,109,804.12

FIG. 13-7   High and sample report display

Garbage, or garbled transactions or data, may mean that the computer system does not operate properly. There may be undetected errors in the programs. For example, FICA deductions that exceed the limit may indicate that the program did not know when to stop deducting. FICA deductions that stop before the specified gross is reached may indicate that a required change probably was not made to the system. Possibly the payroll department may not have notified data processing of a new rate, or EDP did not make the change properly. This usually means that there is poor control over programmed procedures.

These are not all the analyses that can be performed on payroll data, because different organizations have different needs, but they give an understanding of how many ways this data processed by the computer can be analyzed. Many payroll audit procedures currently performed manually can be automated in this way.

Audit Program — Sequence of Events

The effective use of an audit software package requires cooperation between the auditor and an EDP auditor. The EDP auditor can explain the package capabilities and can implement and execute the package. However, the auditor has overall responsibility for properly performing the audit.

This section describes the typical sequence of tasks to use the Coopers & Lybrand Payroll Audit Software package; the title of each report is listed as an event.

Events	*Auditor's Actions*
Planning	• Develop plan and budget.
	• Collect the information concerning the payroll system. Prepare planning working papers.
	• Determine desired report options and assist in preparing the appropriate parameters (e.g., what is the maximum acceptable pay rate).
	• Agree to provide reports within the audit time requirements. Keep audit staff informed about progress and any reasons for additional time.
	• Inform audit staff of the following:
	a. Year-end or test date
	b. The exception profile applicable to the edit report
	• Before the due date, install the package, execute the edit program, and review the results for exceptions.
Report	
Payroll Master File Edit and Exceptions and Statistics	• Obtain the relevant payroll totals.
	• Edit the payroll file (edit current-period file as well as prior-period file as two processing steps), resolve error messages, and agree the totals.
Audit review	• Review any error messages to determine significance and make any adjustments that may be required. Check records printed as exceptions against employee personnel records. Decide, based on errors, whether the "Employee Master File Printout" is required. Provide information on the high and low values and the sample rate to be used for producing the "High and Sample Report."

Events	*Auditor's Actions*

Report

High and
Sample Report

- Assist in determining significance of error messages.
- Review the report and agree the totals.

Audit review

- Review the report for unusual pay. Check sample to personnel records to verify accuracy of data.

Report

Duplicate
Social Security
Numbers

- Use the report to identify duplicate social security numbers.

Audit review

- Follow up any duplicates, determine audit significance, and make any adjustments required.

Report

Employee
Master File
Printout

- Use this report in place of "Payroll Master File Edit" when that report discloses significant errors.
- Prepare report and agree the totals.

Audit review

- Compare selected employees with personnel information.

Report

No Match and
Excessive
Increases and
Statistics

- Prepare report and agree the totals.

Audit review

- Check new hires, terminations, amendments, and increases to appropriate authorizations.

Report

Annual
Comparison by
Department

- Prepare report and agree the totals.

Audit review

- Agree the totals to departmental cost figures. Consider whether movements in period indicate that further audit testing is required.

(continued)

Events	*Auditor's Actions*
Completion	• Summarize time and expenses. Document any reasons for changes from original budget. Provide suggestions for the coming audit year.

Implementing Payroll Systems

The following material provides an example of documentation for questions that can be answered to develop a payroll system when an auditor participates in the system development. (Figure 13-8 provides a completed matrix to analyze this application.)

PAYROLL

Location _____

1. How many employees are on your payroll? _____
2. What is your yearly turnover? _____
3. How many companies do you process payroll for? _____
4. What type of payroll do you have?
   ☐ Hourly and salaried
   ☐ Piecework
   ☐ Special distribution to job cost
   ☐ Manufacturing (other)
   ☐ Special (explain)
   Special: _____
   _____
   _____
5. What is your employee numbering scheme? _____
   _____
6. By what method are they paid?
   ☐ Weekly
   ☐ Biweekly
   ☐ Semimonthly
   ☐ Other (specify) _____
7. What factors are used in calculating gross pay (salary, hourly rate(s)), overtime (O.T.), bonus, commission, sickpay, expense reimbursement, piecework performance, etc.)?

_____

_____

8. Is there more than one state involved in calculating state taxes? _____

_____

9. Do you process city taxes?   ☐ Yes   ☐ No

10. If so, what cities? _____

11. What types of deductions are used in your payroll and in what frequency are these deductions taken (medical insurance, life insurance, union bonds, credit union, stock purchase, etc.)?

_____

12. If union deductions are taken, how many are involved and how are they calculated? _____

13. How many union reports are processed? _____

14. Do you generate any special reports (insurance deductions, etc.)? _____

_____

15. Do you produce a departmental expense report?   ☐ Yes   ☐ No

16. Is your payroll system going to be interfaced with any other applications (job cost, manual checks, wage accrual)?

_____

_____

17. What control totals do you keep on your present payroll?

_____

_____

18. Is there any other information that you feel is pertinent?

_____

_____

PURCHASE ACCOUNTING SYSTEMS

Purchase accounting systems process the data for purchases and payments. Since purchases automatically lead to payments, if purchases are properly contracted, control over payment should be effected, but not entirely. Controls over payments are still needed to ensure that every payment was made for goods and services received, that the same purchases were not paid for twice, and that they were indeed paid. Analysis of how purchases and payments were

Transaction	Completeness	Accuracy	Authorization	Maintenance	Programmed Procedures
Time cards Daily Weekly Pay Period	Manual: Review and reconciliation of total hours to Transmission Control and Error (TCE) Report and Labor Distribution Report. Programmed: Based on salary status code on employee master file.	Manual: Review of pay detail on Payroll Register. Programmed: Edit numerics, pay date, and status codes. Validity check of employee number.	Manual: Authorization of vacation, holiday, and sick time based on earned accrual by supervisory personnel. Programmed: Based on employee master file data.	Manual: Review and reconciliation of Quarter-to-Date and Year-to-Date Listings to previous Quarter-to-Date and Year-to-Date Listings and current pay period Payroll Register. Programmed: Employee master file crossfoot.	Calculation of overtime based on overtime data and method in employee master file. Calculation of pay based on time card hours and master file data elements.
Supplemental time cards	Manual: Review and reconciliation to TCE and Labor Distribution Reports. Programmed: Exception code reported. Batching on hours.	Manual: Review of pay detail on Payroll Register. Programmed: Same as regular time cards.	Manual: Authorization of vacation and other advances based on earned accruals by supervisory personnel. Programmed: Valid pay period check performed.	Manual: Same as maintenance of regular time cards. Programmed: Employee master file crossfoot.	Calculation of pay based on time card hours and master file data elements.
Deduction refunds	Manual: Review and reconciliation of gross deduction refund from payroll register to manual log of deduction refunds.	Manual: Same as completeness.	Manual: Determination of validity of refund and amount to be refunded by supervisory personnel.	Manual: None.	

FIG. 13-8 Information systems Control Matrix — payroll application

made can be done as well; for example, were they timely so that the benefit of discounts was received?

Purchase accounting systems can handle various types of purchases, including:

- *Trade* — Those that are bought to sell or convert before reselling.
- *Other* — Expense-type items such as supplies, assets, and equipment.

Applications

Most purchase accounting systems perform three basic accounting functions:

1. *Accounts payable processing* — Recording of transactions in the accounts payable records.
2. *Goods received processing* — Recording of details of goods received, but not yet invoiced.
3. *Order processing* — Recording of goods ordered, but not yet received.

The computer may be involved in each of these activities, and the extent to which they are computerized determines the complexity of the purchase accounting system. The various types of systems are described under the following headings:

- Accounts payable systems
- Goods received processing systems
- Order processing systems

Payment of creditors can also be carried out by the computer. This is considered a separate function, which can be integrated with any of these systems.

ACCOUNTS PAYABLE SYSTEMS

Accounts payable systems are appropriate systems for the auditor to review. When the system is computerized, the auditor's task can be that much easier: The data can be analyzed more quickly and effectively to find the exceptions that could be unauthorized payments.

The larger the volume of transactions being processed by the system, the greater the opportunity for bogus transactions to be entered, processed, and easily paid. A faulty accounts payable system can also result in poor vendor relations and loss of favorable payment terms. Likewise, if the accounts pay-

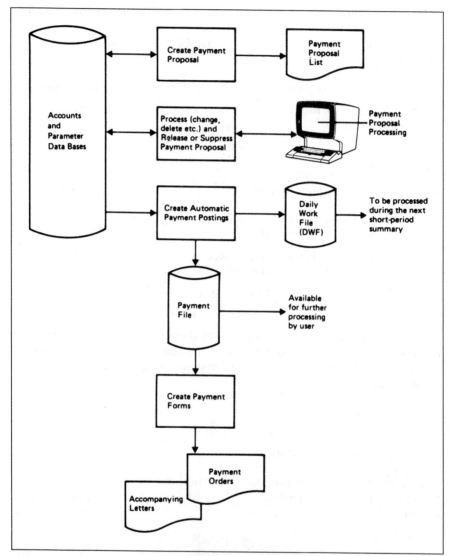

FIG. 13-9 Accounts payable data base system overview flowchart (courtesy of International Business Machines Corporation)

able transactions are not properly posted to the cost of doing business, this can be easily misstated, making the organization appear to be either more or less profitable, depending on how the error has occurred.

In these systems, the computer processes the accounts payable records. Order processing and goods received functions are manual operations. An example of this type of system is illustrated in the overview flowchart in Figure 13-9.

Accounts Payable Master File

Records are maintained for each of the vendors whose transactions are processed by the system. The accounts payable records for each vendor hold the following information:

- *Master file* — Vendor's name and address, payment terms, vendor's bank account details, special terms.
- *Transaction details* — Outstanding transactions, invoice history, payment history.

An example of an accounts payable file layout and invoice record is given in Figure 13-10.

Accounts Payable Function

The main types of transactions processed are:

- Vendors' invoices and credit notes
- Adjustments
- Cash payments
- Master file data amendments

Vendors' Invoices and Credit Memos

Details of vendors' invoices and credit memos are input. These details include:

- Vendor's account number
- Cost ledger expense codes
- Gross, tax, and net amounts of each invoice or credit memo, together with any discounts (either as a separate figure or as a percentage)
- Date used to identify the due date for payment (this may be the invoice date, if payment is due a set time after invoicing, or the actual due date)

Purchase invoices and credit memos can be entered and then processed in batch mode or processed through interactive terminal entry in on-line systems with immediate update.

The invoices and credit memos are updated to the vendor's accounts on the accounts payable master file. The total value of transactions is summarized and categorized for posting to the general/cost ledgers.

The Accounts Payable Package uses three permanent files and thirteen
temporary work files. The records in each file contain a unique Record
Code as the first two characters of the record. They also contain a Delete
Code as the third character of the record; a blank means a valid record,
a "D" means a deleted record.

WHERE USED LIST

FILE NAME	RECORD CODE	DESCRIPTION	WHERE USED
VENDOR - SYS010	01	Vendor Master File	AP30, AP01, AP02, AP05, AP07, AP10, AP17, AP20, AP21, AP31, AP40, AP41
PAYABL - SYS012	02	Payables File	AP31, AP02, AP03, AP04S AP06, AP12, AP20, AP22, AP42, AP43
CHECKS - SYS014	03	Check File	AP31, AP09, AP10, AP13, AP15, AP16, AP23, AP44, AP45
DETAIL	20	Distribution File	AP03, AP17S
CASHED	21	Cashed Checks	AP13, AP13S
OCHECKS	03	Outstanding Checks	AP16
WORKA	20,02	20 Invoice Line Item 02 Invoice Total	AP02, AP02S

**FIG. 13-10A   Accounts payable files (courtesy of International Business
Machines Corporation)**

Summaries may be printed to form the basis for a manual journal entry
into a manual or computerized general ledger or may be written to a file for
input into a general/cost ledger application. When the processing of the
general/cost ledger is integrated with accounts payable processing, updating
may be simultaneous.

During updating of the accounts payable records, the computer normally
summarizes the items or balances and produces information for control
purposes. Lists of balances and exception reports (such as debit balances) may
also be produced.

```
                    Check Work File   (WORKF1)

                Invoice Record - Record Code 23

                       Sequential File


    Record      Field     Field     Dec      Decimal
    Position    Name      Size      Pos      Format    Contents

    1-2         RCDCD     2                            Record Code is "23"

    3           DELET     1                            Blank

    4-8         VNDNR     5         0                  Vendor Number

    9-14        INVNR     6         0                  Invoice Number

    15-20       INVDT     6         0                  Invoice Date

    21-24       DISGR     7         2        packed    Invoice Gross

    25-28       DISDS     7         2        packed    Invoice Trade Discount
                                                       Allowed

    29-32       DISCS     7         2        packed    Cash Discount Taken

    33-36       DISCS1    7         2        packed    Cash Discount Not
                                                       Taken

    37-114                                             Unused
```

FIG. 13-10B   Accounts payable invoice record (courtesy of International
Business Machines Corporation)

Adjustments

Adjustments will always be necessary to input corrections to entries in the accounts payable records. The principal purpose of adjustments is to correct mispostings or change invoice values. Adjustments may also be needed for other purposes, such as to adjust for a payment discount after processing a "quick" payment to take advantage of cash discount terms offered by a vendor. Adjustments are summarized and categorized in a similar manner to invoices and credit memos.

Cash Payments

Cash payments are normally dealt with separately. This is discussed later in this chapter in the section entitled "Payment of Creditors."

Amendments to Master File Data

Amendments to master file data are needed to open and close vendors' accounts and alter the various data fields. A listing of master file data amendments made is normally produced.

USING AUDIT SOFTWARE TO ANALYZE ACCOUNTS PAYABLE

A major concern for the auditor is the potential for understatement of liabilities and overstatement of assets. In this regard, four specific areas of accounts payable merit special attention: (1) cutoffs, (2) debit balances, (3) duplicate payments, and (4) confirmations. Inaccuracies in any of these areas can significantly affect the financial statements. Therefore, it is especially important that they are examined comprehensively. There are various ways in which this can be done.

Generalized accounts payable audit software helps the auditor to analyze the data for these vital areas, as well as automating many of the common substantive procedures encountered in the audit of accounts payable. An overview flowchart of accounts payable audit software is shown in Figure 13-11.

To determine whether receiving cutoffs have been performed satisfactorily, the Coopers & Lybrand Accounts Payable Audit Software package can furnish the following different reports:

- *Last five days of period* — Lists transactions in vendor sequence that were processed during the last five calendar days of the validation period.

- *New items before closing date* — Lists those transactions that were recorded after the test date but should have been recorded on or before the closing date.

- *First five days after closing* — Lists all transactions dated in the first five days following the test date.

In the area of debit balances, there are other reports:

- *Debit accounts payable balances* — Lists those accounts that have a debit balance and quantifies the total for possible reclassification as receivables.

- *Detailed debit accounts payable balances* — Lists the individual transactions that make up each vendor account having a debit balance.

Another report, possible duplicate payables, identifies possible duplicate payment transactions based on the same vendor number and the same amount.

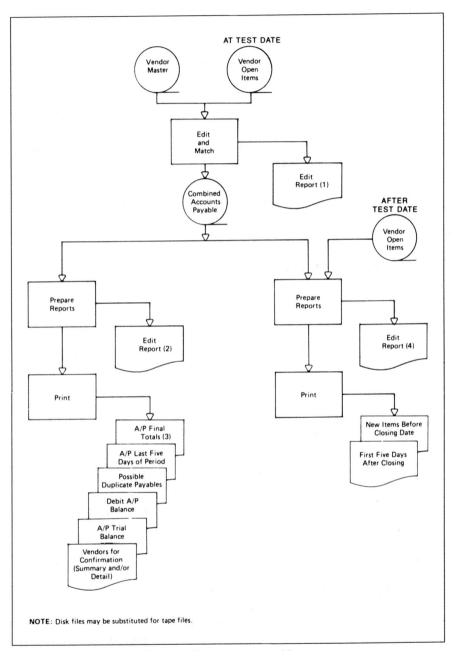

FIG. 13-11 Audit software flowchart for accounts payable

To facilitate an efficient confirmation process, the software usually furnishes two levels for confirmation reports (one summary and one detailed). These reports list vendors selected for confirmation, with totals and reasons for selection. The selection criteria are provided by the auditor. Therefore, the auditor can be assured that all accounts meeting the specified criteria will be selected for confirmation.

The following are other reports produced by this audit software:

- *Edit report* — Lists data errors encountered on vendor master and transaction files.

- *Trial balance* — Represents summarization of year-to-date purchases and accounts payable outstanding for each vendor.

- *Detailed trial balance* — Lists the individual open item transaction amounts for each vendor, as well as totals by vendor.

Use of audit software can assist the auditor in achieving the following substantive objectives:

- Determining whether all material liabilities for trade accounts payable existing at the balance sheet date have been recorded.

- Determining whether recorded liabilities for trade accounts payable represent valid liabilities and are fairly stated.

- Determining whether receiving cutoffs have been performed satisfactorily.

In addition, an analysis of the reports generated by the software may reveal breakdowns and weaknesses in internal controls. The auditor can communicate these problems to management for follow-up.

Two distinct phases are included in the software. First, there is the analysis and reporting of the accounts payable at the test date. Second, there is the optional analysis and reporting of relevant transactions subsequent to the audit date. There is also flexibility in the ability to vary guidelines (parameters) on the processing of data and selecting those reports that satisfy the audit objectives for a particular situation.

Audit software is particularly effective where there are a large number of accounts payable transactions or balances.

An example of this software in use occurred when a large discount retail company found that it did not have adequate controls within its accounts payable system to detect debit balances with sufficient accuracy. Accounts payable audit software was implemented during a recent year-end audit of the company. The debit accounts payable balances report indicated over $1 million in debit balances. Nearly $3 million in unrecorded liabilities were detected during the same audit, using the software report on new items before closing date.

Many common accounts payable substantive tests or procedures, such as the following, can be performed by the Coopers & Lybrand Accounts Payable Audit Software package:

- Adding and listing transactions and account balances
- Selecting accounts for confirmation or statement reconciliation
- Identifying transactions pertaining to the audit period but recorded after the test date
- Identifying transactions with a date immediately before or after the test date
- Identifying possible duplicate payments
- Identifying transactions not pertaining to valid vendors

Accounts Payable Audit Objectives

An accounts payable audit software package can help the auditor meet the following audit objectives.

Audit Objectives	*Package Capabilities*
Determine whether all material liabilities for trade accounts payable existing at the balance sheet date have been recorded.	• Identifies and reports transactions processed after the test date that should have been processed before. • Selects accounts for confirmation or statement reconciliation. • Selects accounts with debit balances for confirmation or statement reconciliation.
Determine whether recorded liabilities for trade accounts payable represent valid liabilities and are fairly stated.	• Performs additions of account balances. • Identifies and reports accounts with irregular vendor information. • Lists accounts payable balances in optional sequence and at various levels of detail to assist in review for unusual accounts. • Identifies and reports possible duplicate transactions. • Reports all vendors with a debit balance and optionally includes all open file items for these vendors.
Determine whether receiving cutoffs have been performed satisfactorily.	• Identifies and reports transactions with a date after the test date.

(continued)

Audit Objectives	*Package Capabilities*
	• Reports all transactions processed during the five days preceding the test date.
	• Reports all transactions processed during the first five days after the test date.

Audit Program — Sequence of Events

The effective use of audit software packages requires cooperation between the auditor and the EDP auditor. An EDP auditor who knows the software can explain the package capabilities to the audit staff and can implement and execute the package. Overall responsibility for properly performing the audit belongs to the auditor, as usual.

This section describes a typical sequence of tasks necessary to use such software. The title of each report from the Coopers & Lybrand package is listed as an event.

Events	*Auditor's Actions*
Planning	• Develop plan and budget.
	• Collect the information concerning the accounts payable system. Prepare planning working papers.
	• Determine desired report options.
	• Obtain the following dates:
	a. Test date of accounts payable
	b. Subsequent transaction examination period
	• Complete reports within the time requirements. Keep audit staff informed as to progress and any reasons for additional time.
	• Before the due date, install the package, execute the edit program, and review the results for exceptions.
Report	
Accounts Payable — Edit Report	• Obtain the accounts payable total.
	• Edit the vendor master file and accounts payable open item file and agree the totals.
Audit review	• Reconcile report totals to books of accounts.

Events	Auditor's Actions
Audit review *(cont'd)*	• Confirm the reports to be produced and supply the necessary confirmation selection parameters.

Reports

Events	Auditor's Actions
Accounts Payable — Edit Report	• Examine report for records identified as unusual. Compare items with hard-copy documentation to ensure that no further audit response is required. • Ensure that report requirements and confirmation selection parameters have been confirmed. Agree processing totals to totals from planning report.
Vendors for Confirmation	• Examine the report and agree calculated balance for each selected vendor to the detailed accounts payable records. Perform appropriate confirmation procedures. • Ensure that all reports required have been printed.
Accounts Payable Trial Balance	• Use the report to indicate the accounts tested and the procedures used.
Accounts Payable — Last Five Days of Period	• Review accounts listed to ensure that activity levels are not unusual. Test cut-off procedures.
Debit Accounts Payable Balances	• Review accounts listed to determine reclassification or to ensure that there are no unrecorded liabilities.
Possible Duplicate Payables	• Review transactions listed to determine possibility of duplicate transactions.
Accounts Payable — Edit Report	• Examine report for records identified as unusual. Compare items with hard-copy documentation to ensure that no further audit response is required.
New Items Before Closing Date	• Check reported results by comparing items to hard-copy documentation and ensuring that cutoff was adequate.
First Five Days After Closing	• Use selected items on the report to test cutoff procedures.
Completion	• Summarize time, costs, and expenses. Document any reasons for changes from original budget. Provide suggestions for the coming audit year.

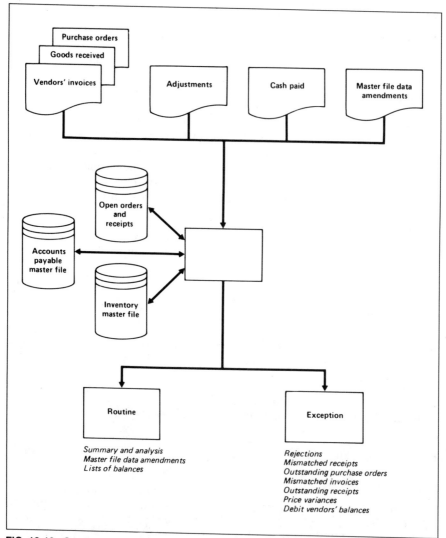

FIG. 13-12 Goods received processing system integrated with purchase order processing flowchart

GOODS RECEIVED PROCESSING SYSTEMS

In these systems, the computer is involved in goods received processing, but the order processing and accounts payable may remain a separate manual operation. It is common for such systems to be integrated, such as with the processing of the raw material inventory records. The goods received details are used not only to process purchases but also to update the inventory records for raw materials at the same time or in a subsequent run.

Goods Received Function

The goods received function is illustrated in Figure 13-12. Goods received details are prepared and entered, and the following processing is carried out:

- *Valuation of goods received.* The value of goods received is calculated by reference to costs (such as standard costs) held as master file data.

- *Recording of outstanding invoices.* Goods received details are entered and stored as suspense records of goods received but not invoiced. A summary of movements in the suspense records is normally produced for control purposes.

Amendments to Master File Data

Amendments to master file data are needed to open and close vendors' accounts and alter the various data elements or fields. A listing of master file data amendments is usually produced.

The main effect of computerization on the accounts payable system is that the manual matching of purchase invoices with goods received details is replaced by a programmed matching with the suspense records of details of goods received. The goods received processing is illustrated in Figure 13-13. The following procedures are performed:

- *Invoice matching.* Goods received records remain in suspense until matched with the vendors' invoice details; invoices may be matched on quantities and/or price. Matched items are deleted.

- *Calculation of price variances.* Performed at the time of matching, provided the goods received details are held at standard cost value. The computer may calculate the cost variances.

- *Follow-up of invoices not received.* Periodically, the suspense records are read, and the goods received that have not been matched with vendors' invoices for a given period are printed.

- *Liability for goods received not invoiced.* Where the goods received records are held in dollar amounts or can be valued by reference to a costs file, the total accrued liability with respect to goods received can be periodically summarized and printed.

A capability must be incorporated in the system to ensure that invoices relating to items other than inventory can be processed. This may be achieved by the entry of dummy goods received details. Another method is to include an indicator on the relevant invoices that the program recognizes as an instruction to bypass the matching of that item with the goods received suspense file.

Audit procedures are similar to those for an accounts payable system, as discussed previously in this chapter.

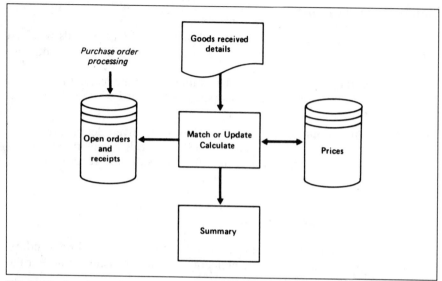

FIG. 13-13 Goods received and purchase order processing system flowchart

ORDER PROCESSING SYSTEMS

In these systems, the computer may be involved in processing all components of purchase accounting — accounts payable processing, goods received processing, and ordering. As with goods received processing, systems of this type may be integrated with the processing of raw materials inventory records.

Order Processing Function

The order processing function is illustrated in Figure 13-14. The initial processing in this application relates to purchase orders: Purchase orders are either entered or initiated by the computer.

When orders are entered manually, on-line data entry techniques are often used. The computer then produces the order document to send to the supplier.

The computer initiation of orders may be triggered by

- Comparing current stock balance with minimum stock levels held as data on the master file.
- Using more complex modeling programs, taking into account historical usage, current orders, marketing forecasts, seasonal trends, carrying cost, safety factors, future scheduled deliveries, lead times, and economic order quantities.

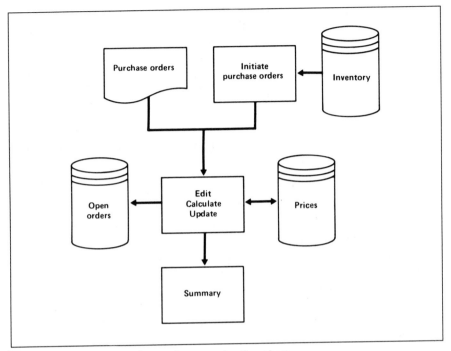

FIG. 13-14 Order processing system overview flowchart

Computer-produced orders are often manually scrutinized prior to being sent to the vendor.

Once purchase orders are manually entered or generated by the computer, they are written to an open order suspense file to await the receipt of the goods and the processing of the goods received note. Open orders may be recorded in terms of both quantity and estimated purchase value of each order.

In some systems, when the order is written to the open orders file, the computer produces a goods received note that is used later to enter details of the goods actually received.

Integration of Order Processing and Goods Received Functions

The effect of this integration is illustrated in Figures 13-12 and 13-13. When the goods are received, the order of processing is as follows:

- The goods received note is entered and matched with the appropriate open order record. In addition to matching on the order number field, the computer may also be programmed to match on the inventory reference field, quantity field, and/or value field.

- Matched items are either deleted from the open orders file and written to a new suspense file of goods received awaiting invoices, or their status on the order record is changed to indicate that they are matched. In either case, a summary of the matching process is normally accumulated and printed for control purposes. Mismatched items are usually reported or rejected. In on-line systems, mismatched items usually cannot be accepted by the computer.

The open order suspense records, at any given time, contain details of orders placed for which a goods received note has not been processed. These records are read periodically and those remaining unmatched for a given period are printed. The printed records may be used to follow up on old orders and to ensure that goods received notes are being processed upon receipt of goods. Totals of the open order suspense records, where they are maintained in dollar amounts, may also be produced, and these figures provide details of the purchase commitments not yet fulfilled.

A capability is usually necessary to process adjustments to the open order suspense records so that entries can be amended. Examples of these adjustments might be amendments to orders or canceled orders.

Once goods received notes have been matched against outstanding orders, the receipt and the related invoice are processed in the same manner as described for the accounts payable processing and goods received processing systems.

PAYMENT OF CREDITORS

The method used to process details of cash paid to creditors depends on whether items are selected for payment manually or by the computer, as described in the following paragraphs.

Manual Selection

When items are selected manually, the details of items paid should be entered and updated in the same manner as vendors' invoices. The computer usually matches on either the account number alone, or the account number, invoice number, and value.

Computer Selection

A purchase accounting system may include computer selection of items for payment. Normally the computer updates the account for payment details and prints remittance advices showing the makeup of the payments. As a result of the selection, the computer may produce the following:

- Details from which checks are prepared
- Checks for manual or mechanical signature
- Presigned checks

The normal selection criteria are date and, less frequently, the discount indicator. The computer may be programmed to recognize an indicator on invoices for which a discount is available if payment is prompt. The computer may also be programmed to calculate the discount by reference to discount terms held as master file data. However, the processing of invoices of this nature is often diverted for separate manual payment.

Manually produced checks may also be required for other purposes. Details of such manual payments would be entered as adjustments.

Some systems can also produce cash requirement forecast reports to assist in the management of the company's cash flow. If so, there may be a capability to delay payments when funds are low and to speed up payments (such as to take advantage of discounts) when excess funds are available.

Production Systems

INTRODUCTION

The pressure of a competitive business environment underscores the need for comprehensive controls over the organization, its product, and its production systems. Internal conflicts or communication problems may persist in an organization when the needs of sales, production, and finance collide. Monitoring systems that are not linked together can unintentionally cause conflict with internal and overall management goals, as when they track only a single department. Ideally, production system monitoring must be part of an integrated, comprehensive control approach.

The framework to prepare such a comprehensive monitoring plan includes the following elements of production systems planning:

- Inventory control system
- Raw materials movements and balances
- Fixed assets systems

These components are discussed in this chapter, including production controls, cost and sales auditing, operational controls, and overall audit objectives.

INVENTORY CONTROL SYSTEMS

Applications

Inventory control systems are designed to record the purchase, manufacture, and sale of a company's inventory. Such systems may vary substantially in operation, but they can be divided into three main applications:

1. Raw materials
2. Work-in-process
3. Finished goods

Each application can be considered in the context of the following functions: inventory recording, inventory valuation, and inventory counting.

Inventory Recording Function

The raw materials, work-in-process, and finished goods inventory records are updated by entering updates or adjustments to master file data and transaction data, such as inventory movements. Adjustments are also made to correct mispostings and inventory differences when these are discovered. Summaries and analyses of movements and adjustments are produced from these updates.

Amendments to master file data are also made in order to open and close records of stock items and to alter the various master file data fields. In most systems a list is normally produced of all master file data amendments that have been made.

An example of an inventory file layout, depicting the data elements included follows:

Inventory Details	Number of Characters
1. Part number	14
2. Product group	6
3. Stock description	30
4. Unit of measure code	1
5. Made in/bought out indicator	2
6. Store location	5
7. Latest purchase price	9
8. Reorder level indicator	1
9. Reorder level	7
10. Reorder quantity	7
11. Safety (minimum) stock	7
12. Maximum stock	7
13. Production reserve	7
14. Lead time	3
15. Average weekly demand	7
16. Standard cost	9
17. Current selling price	11
18. Price-effective date	6
19. New price increase percentage	5
20. New selling price	11
21. Stock on hand	7
22. Allocated stock	7
23. Shipping stock	7
24. Outstanding sales orders	7
25. Outstanding purchase orders	7

CURRENT WEEK DETAILS

26. Transfers	7
27. Receipts	7
28. Outstanding orders	7
29. Shipments	7

(continued)

Inventory Details	*Number of Characters*
30. Adjustments	7
CURRENT MONTH DETAILS	
31. Transfers	7
32. Receipts	7
33. Outstanding orders	7
34. Shipments	7
35. Adjustments	7
WEEKLY AVERAGES	
36. Transfers	7
37. Receipts	7
38. Outstanding orders	7
39. Shipments	7
40. Stock on hand	7
41. Last year's standard cost	9
42. Physical inventory check count	3
43. Physical inventory check frequency	2
44. Beginning inventory this year	7
45. Outstanding purchase requisition indicator	1
46. Outstanding purchase requisition quantity	7
47. Latest purchase quantity	7
48. Latest issue date	6
49. Date of latest purchases	6
50. Forecast total demand	7

Raw Materials

The main transaction types that are entered for raw materials records are:

- Receipts of inventory (or materials coming into the warehouse or store that increase inventory). Data entered from goods received records will also be processed for purchase accounting if the systems are integrated.

- Issues to production (or materials required for production to start that reduce or decrease inventory) — usually made before computer processing details are entered from production schedules or requisitions. (Details are listed on a bill of materials.)

In more advanced systems, materials issued to production from the warehouse or store may be generated by the programs in the following ways:

- The computer generates issues to production on the basis of low finished-goods stock or the receipt of sales orders.

- The computer generates issues to production based on entries in the work-in-process application, of a production number or stage in processing reached. This is common with bill-of-materials or list of materials issued processing systems.

In the preceding cases, information about the material necessary for the relevant job is held as master file data. The computer prints out the issue documentation, including the production schedule, and updates the raw materials file. Occasionally computer processing is carried out prior to the actual issues from the stores. The details generated are sometimes held in suspense until they can be matched with details of the actual quantities issued to production. Raw materials recording is illustrated in Figure 14-1.

Work-in-Process. Work-in-process recording is often the most complex part of the inventory system. Figure 14-2 is an overview flowchart for inventory control work-in-process recording. The main transaction types of input for this category of records are:

- *Issues to production.* As described previously, the computer can generate issues based on production schedules or requisitions. Work-in-process records are often updated at the same time as the raw materials file.

- *Labor charges.* These are usually entered from manually prepared input documents or from details produced during the payroll production. The computer categorizes labor charged by referring to an input code. In some cases, standard labor charges are held as master file data and the computer may be programmed to calculate variances.

- *Overheads.* Overhead rates are normally held as master file data, and the computer calculates how much to charge the appropriate jobs.

- *Transfers to finished goods.* These are usually entered from manually prepared documentation. In advanced systems, the computer may be programmed to initiate details of the transfer when a completion request is entered, while transfer details are held on the inventory file as master file data. Variances between actual and standard quantities produced may be reported.

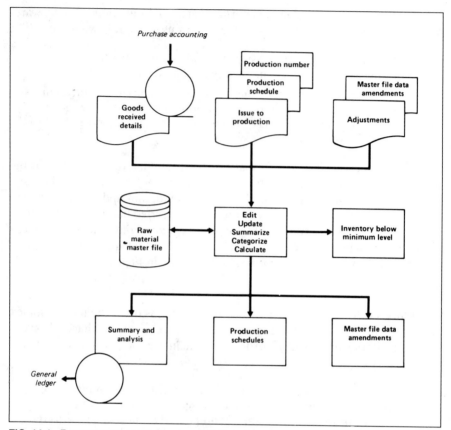

FIG. 14-1 Raw materials inventory control flowchart

Finished Goods. The main transaction types entered for this category of records are as follows:

- *Receipts.* As described previously, this input includes details of completed work prepared manually for processing or initiated by the computer. The finished goods file is often updated simultaneously with the work-in-process file.

- *Issues.* Details of shipments made are entered. Updating of the finished goods file is often integrated with billing and sales accounting. If the cost of finished goods is recorded, the cost of sales will be summarized.

Finished goods recording is illustrated in the overview flowchart in Figure 14-3.

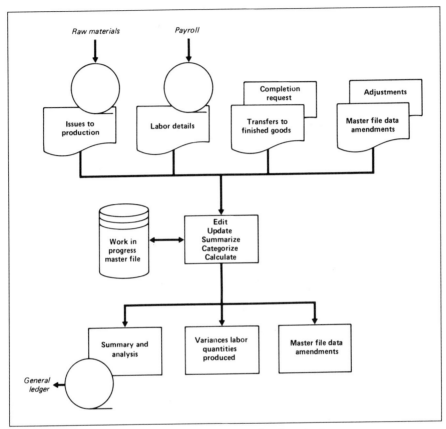

FIG. 14-2 Inventory control work-in-process overview flowchart

Inventory Valuation Function

Although it is common for the inventory movements and balances to be recorded in item quantities, costs are normally available in the form of master file data. In this way, the value of inventory can be calculated regularly.

Computer systems also offer the ability of holding several costs of inventory, used for different purposes. Examples of this are average cost for accounting, standard cost for determining variance, and replacement cost sometimes used for calculating future sales prices.

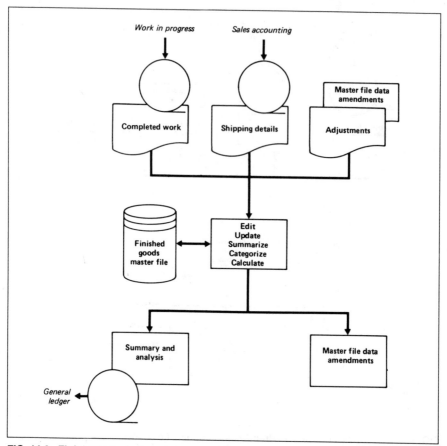

FIG. 14-3 Finished goods inventory control flowchart

Raw Materials Movements and Balances. It is common for the computer to calculate the value of raw materials movements and balances by one of the methods listed here:

- *Reference to a standard cost price.* The computer is also programmed to report variances if actual costs are entered in this method.

- *Reference to the ordered price.* If goods received reports are matched manually to orders before entry, the price may be recorded manually on the goods received report. If matching is done by computer, the price can be picked up by the matching program.

- *Reference to actual invoiced costs.* There is usually a need to book receipts into inventory immediately, for operational reasons. To maintain an accurate inventory, the booking cannot wait for the arrival of the invoice to be processed. Therefore, many systems based on actual cost use one of the two preceding methods as an approximation until the invoice is received. Then the approximate cost is replaced by the actual invoiced cost; this temporary approximation seldom distorts the value of inventory materially.

When determining actual costs, most computer systems calculate an average figure. The computer can easily be programmed to compute the changes to the average cost price each time a purchase is made.

The booking of movements under FIFO (first-in, first-out) or LIFO (last-in, first-out) is more complicated to program, since each shipment may have a different cost price. (Therefore, they are used less frequently.) One obvious exception to this rule is the inventory systems that treat each purchase as a separate inventory item (such as automobile sales).

Most systems using actual costs (FIFO, LIFO, or average) are programmed to identify and report receipts whose cost price is significantly different from that of previous receipts, or whose actual cost is different from the standard or normal values.

Work-in-Process Movements and Balances. Materials used in production are charged out at the rates at which they are held as raw materials. Labor and overhead may be charged at standard predetermined rates, at actual rates, or at a combination of the two (e.g., labor hours at actual rates with predetermined overhead charges). Predetermined rates are held as master file data.

Labor Hours. Labor hours may be charged at standard or actual hours. If standard hours are used, the hours are normally taken from the bill of materials or otherwise held as master file data.

Actual hours may be charged by manually prepared documents or may be produced as output from the payroll application. The payroll application would then include some means of identifying the cost centers to be charged, either from employees' time reports or from information permanently kept as master file data on the payroll master file. If standard hours are also held, the computer may be programmed to report variances.

Labor and Overhead Rates. Hourly labor rates are usually held as master file data within the payroll or inventory records. The labor costs are calculated by multiplying hours (at actual or standard) by the rate.

Overhead may be included in the labor rate. It may also be held in another way, such as a separate charge on each bill of materials. Whatever method is used, the overhead rate is effectively held by the computer as master file data and is applied automatically to each production job.

Finished Goods Movements and Balances. Finished goods may be held at actual cost (such as the costs transferred from the work-in-process application), average actual cost, or standard cost price. Variances or abnormal price changes are normally identified and reported.

Inventory Provisions. The computer may be programmed to periodically calculate and report other information relevant to the value of inventory. Depending on the system, this may include details of excess stock, obsolete stock, and slow-moving stock. Excess stock is usually calculated by comparing inventory on hand with past usage or future requirements. Obsolete stock may be calculated by referring to usage or by setting an indicator (e.g., a component of a finished product that is no longer in production). Slow-moving stock may be calculated by referring to the date of last movement. The scope of reports of this nature is governed mainly by the range of information held on the file.

Inventory Counting Function

Procedures will always be needed to adjust any differences between what is shown in the books and the actual inventory by count. The differences may result from a periodic count of all inventory. However, if records are processed by computer it is easier to ensure their reliability, so that continuous cycle counts are more likely. If a continuous inventory count is carried out, one of the following three methods is normally used:

1. The inventory is counted and compared with the most recent report of the balance on the file adjusted for outstanding issues and receipts. The adjustments can be made manually or by the computer. A manual record is kept of items to be counted.

2. Inventory is counted and compared, and adjustments are processed as above. At the same time as the adjustments are processed, the date of the inventory count is entered. The computer records the date and produces a regular report of items that have not been counted for a specified period.

3. Inventory is counted and the details of the physical balances are entered. The computer calculates any differences between the physical and book inventory.

Integrated Systems

The applications described can be combined to form a wide variety of computer systems that process inventory activity. The activities may vary from the simple recording of raw materials or finished goods to the integrated recording of materials, work-in-process, and finished goods in computer-controlled production.

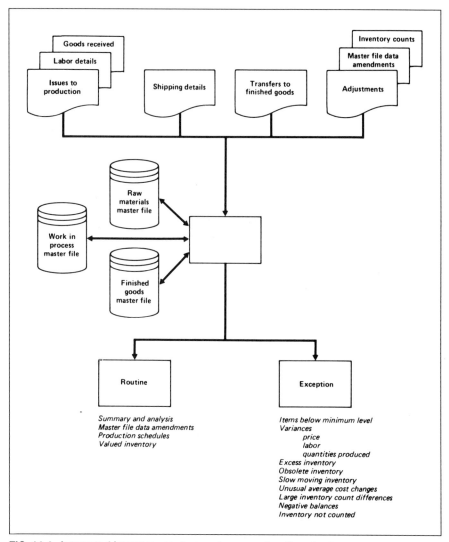

FIG. 14-4   Integrated inventory control system overview flowchart

Chapter 12, "Revenue Systems," and Chapter 13, "Disbursement Systems," discuss how inventory recording systems may be integrated with purchases and sales accounting and how replenishment of materials may be initiated by the computer. As a result of these variations, the systems that include inventory in groupings of applications can vary widely.

An integrated inventory recording system is illustrated in the overview flowchart in Figure 14-4. Although not shown on the flowchart, it would be quite common for purchases and sales to be integrated in such a system. Some inventory systems are used in conjunction with manual accounts receivable and

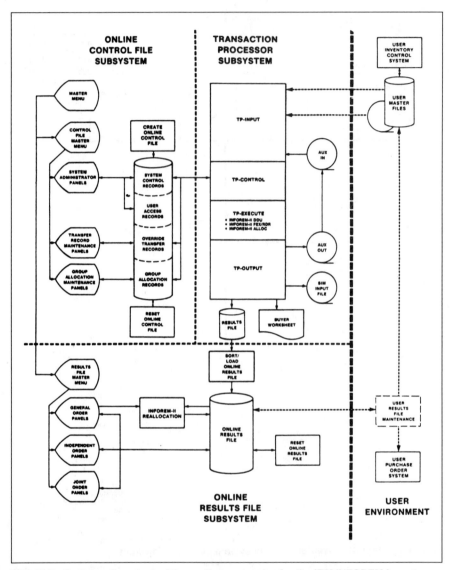

FIG. 14-5 Overview flowchart of the on-line processor for the IBM INFOREM inventory system (courtesy of International Business Machines Corporation)

accounts payable systems. Inventory systems without computerized accounts payable may still account for purchase orders and goods received — including the matching of orders, goods received, and invoices. Similarly, computerized inventory systems with noncomputerized accounts receivable may still account for sales orders and shipments; such manual systems are common when the number of suppliers or customers is small. The manual systems rely heavily on reports of goods received and shipments made produced by the inventory systems.

Obviously, wholesalers, retailers, and other nonmanufacturing companies without work-in-process may have only one type of inventory. In these circumstances, the systems combine the characteristics of raw materials and finished goods applications.

For example, IBM offers a field-developed software package, the INFOREM-II system, that provides solutions for a wide variety of inventory management problems that exist in many business operations. Grocery, wholesale distribution, retail, drug, manufacturing, utilities, and other industries all have large investments in merchandise, spare parts, maintenance materials, and other types of inventories. The IBM package is designed to aid in maintaining the proper quantities of inventory items while balancing the two basic conflicting goals: to provide the maximum level of service with the minimum investment in inventory. The system is designed to be used with an existing or planned customer or internal stock status system, which is responsible for maintaining on-hand and on-order balances plus historical data. Figure 14-5 is an overview of the on-line processor INFOREM system from IBM.

IMPLEMENTING INVENTORY SYSTEMS

Auditors often participate in the design, selection, and implementation of new systems. One function that is important is to ensure that controls are built in and that proper procedures for purchasing, programming, testing, and installing the new system are followed. (See Chapter 7, "The System Development Life Cycle.") The following checklist can be helpful in determining the requirements for an inventory system.

INVENTORY

Location _____

1. How many individual inventory items do you stock? _____
2. Do you sell nonstocked items?   □ Yes   □ No
3. What is your inventory file growth? _____

4. What is the largest quantity (individual units) of inventory units on hand? _____

.5. Do you have multiple warehouses?   ☐ Yes   ☐ No

6. How many product classes do you have? _____

7. Do you have an existing inventory numbering system?
   ☐ Yes   ☐ No

8. If yes, what is the maximum length of your inventory code number?

   _____

9. How comprehensive is the description of your products? _____

10. Is more than one vendor involved when purchasing any particular inventory items?   ☐ Yes   ☐ No

11. Do you give quantity discounts or price breaks to particular types of buyers (price matrix)?   ☐ Yes   ☐ No

12. Do your prices change frequently?   ☐ Yes   ☐ No

13. How are your pricing changes made? _____

	Yes	No
On a percentage basis	☐	☐
Individual items only	☐	☐
By product class	☐	☐

Other _____

14. What is the costing method of your inventory? _____

   _____

15. What types of reports are being produced from your inventory? _____

   _____

16. Is there any other information that you feel is pertinent? _____

   _____

OPERATIONAL AUDITING

Slow economic growth and high interest rates can force management to focus on controlling operational expenditures. In today's manufacturing environment, effective management of inventory, financing, carrying costs, purchase material costs, direct labor efficiency, overhead, human resources, and office systems has never been more important.

To meet these concerns, operational auditing for manufacturing helps auditors and consultants to identify management problems, as well as the financial and general control weaknesses.

To assist in operational audits, diagnostic software helps provide necessary technical, audit management, and supporting documentation to conduct a comprehensive operational audit of a company's manufacturing function and related organizational activities. Important considerations are manufacturing's direct responsibilities and interrelationships with other organizations within the company.

The objectives of such a diagnostic approach are to

- Review the manufacturing executive's direct and related responsibilities.
- Develop key findings and analyze the manufacturing operation's strengths and weaknesses.
- Identify and set priorities for key problem areas.
- Report the diagnostic results in a well-organized summary and detailed format.
- Establish a transition between current procedures and an improved operating environment.

Such an approach is usually based on interviews and reviews of reports, systems, the decision-making process, and the policies and organizations that have guided manufacturing.

Methods for applying diagnostic software in an operational audit vary widely, depending on the audit's scope, complexity, and purpose. In general, all such efforts require a set of standardized audit tasks, which can be preplanned and integrated to use audit software, as for any audit. Overall audit management and control are essential to perform a diagnostic review. As a result of a diagnostic or operational review, an audit report is issued to management. The final report may include these components:

- Performance profile for each function and area, indicating areas of risk and the significance of problems
- Description of each problem area, further detailing and supporting the performance profile
- Definition of corrective action and alternatives
- Documentation of the approach for corrective actions, supported by conceptual systems design where appropriate
- An action program structured by priority for management consideration
- A work program indicating the specific tasks, resource requirements, and schedule for implementing a corrective action program

Inventory Analysis Software

Inventory analysis software is a system of computer audit software programs that can quickly and economically diagnose how well a company is managing its inventory. Most such software can be used with manual and computerized recordkeeping systems, in a time-sharing mode, or on the organization's computer.

The objectives of inventory analysis are to

- Provide the auditor with a quantitative diagnosis of inventory performance.
- Identify and quantify performance problems that indicate inadequate planning and control.
- Measure the potential for improvement.
- Provide a technique to establish and monitor inventory performance goals, in aggregate and in detail.
- Quantify the need for reserves for inventory obsolescence.

Inventory analysis software can produce various reports. The following reports are produced by the Coopers & Lybrand (C&L) package:

- *Usage Distribution Report* — Classifies inventory items by dollar value of usage and corresponding levels of inventory.
- *Inventory Turnover Report* — Shows the investment in slow-moving stock, a quantification of shortages, and a stratified analysis of turnover.
- *Management Report* — Synthesizes the software output reports into a management summary.

Recently, using inventory analysis software at a $1 billion multi-industry manufacturing firm, auditors found $16 million of slow-moving inventory that had not been identified as such; two thirds of the inventory was concentrated in five slow-moving product groups, and a correlation of high stock outs and excess inventories.

Applying the Manufacturing Diagnostic, another C&L software package that helps assess operational concerns, auditors discovered, at the same company, that responsibility for inventory and customer service functions were not identified, sales forecasting was inadequate, and inventory decisions were not supported by economic evaluations.

A program of reorganization was recommended that would lead conservatively to a reduction in inventory of $30 million, about 15 percent. The entire program was financed on a cash-flow basis after six months, and a discounted cash-flow analysis showed a return in excesss of 200 percent.

INVENTORY AUDITING

Facing a rapid rise of interest rates and other expenses, management strives to keep costs at a minimum. This means making sure that inventory is maintained at normal, or even reduced, levels. Consequently, the information developed from the internal auditor's examination of inventory takes on renewed importance. If inventory has crept up substantially, it is a more significant factor on the balance sheet and, hence, an increasing concern for the external auditor.

Auditing inventory may be particularly time-consuming where there is an unusually large number of items in the inventory. Coopers & Lybrand's Inventory Audit Software package is an example of the kind of generalized audit software designed to increase audit efficiency by automating some of the common validation procedures. It is especially effective for a large inventory.

Counting the Inventory

Audit software for testing the counting of inventory often includes reports, such as the following, furnishing data that assists the auditor in performing an accurate physical count:

- Stratification histogram furnishes a stratification of inventory values (extended cost). With this data, the auditor is able to specify the most appropriate selection criteria, thereby facilitating a scientific selection of items for physical count. (See Figure 14-6.)

- Selection for physical count is a worksheet showing the parts selected for the auditor's independent count.

- Selection by part shows the parts selected for the auditor's further testing procedures.

- Auditor's physical comparison compares the auditor's independent count with the company's physical count. (See Figure 14-7.)

- Physical comparison with book or inventory as recorded compares the company's physical count with the book or recorded quantity. The auditor uses this data to investigate discrepancies and to determine their effect on the total inventory valuation. (See Figure 14-8.)

- Missing tag report lists all possible tag numbers, distinguishing those present from those missing. Duplicate tags are also identified. (See Figure 14-9.)

- Physical inventory lists the company's physical counts, either in part number sequence or in tag number sequence.

- Cyclical count procedure lists each item not counted within a specified period, together with the current book quantity and the calculated value.

```
REPORT NO. IN02CAAG-2                        COMPUTER MFG CO                              PAGE NO.    1
REPORT DATE 12/04/79               STRATIFICATION HISTOGRAM  PLANT 00200          PERIOD ENDED 12/31/79

                                            ARITHMETIC METHOD

SEQ     INTERVAL----BOUNDARIES        # ITEMS      VALUE      % OF   CUM      MEAN      STANDARD    DISTRIBUTION
 #                                                           TOTAL    %                DEVIATION   SCALED 1 FOR    6,192

 1          41.40 TO     10,000.99      26       41,674.42    8.89   8.89   1,602.86   2,568.16  ******
 2      10,001.00 TO     20,000.99       0            0.00    0.00   8.89       0.00       0.00 *
 3      20,001.00 TO     30,000.99       0            0.00    0.00   8.89       0.00       0.00 *
 4      30,001.00 TO     40,000.99       0            0.00    0.00   8.89       0.00       0.00 *
 5      40,001.00 TO     50,000.99       1       50,000.00   10.66  19.55  50,000.00       0.00 ********
 6      50,001.00 TO     60,000.99       2      120,000.00   25.58  45.13  60,000.00       0.00 ********************
 7      60,001.00 TO     70,000.99       0            0.00    0.00  45.13       0.00       0.00 *
 8      70,001.00 TO     80,000.99       2      154,815.56   33.01  78.14  77,407.78   2,592.21 ***************************
 9      80,001.00 TO     90,000.99       0            0.00    0.00  78.14       0.00       0.00 *
10      90,001.00 TO    100,000.99       0            0.00    0.00  78.14       0.00       0.00 *
11     100,001.00 TO    102,543.02       1      102,543.02   21.86 100.00 102,543.02       0.00 ****************

       ** TOTALS **                     32      469,033.00                  14,657.28  28,270.99

       CREDITS                           0            0.00

       LOWEST VALUE ON FILE                            41.40
       HIGHEST VALUE ON FILE                      102,543.02


REPORT NO. IN02CAAG-2                        COMPUTER MFG CO                              PAGE NO.    1
REPORT DATE 12/04/79               STRATIFICATION HISTOGRAM  PLANT 00300          PERIOD ENDED 12/31/79

                                            FIXED INTERVAL

SEQ     INTERVAL----BOUNDARIES        # ITEMS      VALUE      % OF   CUM      MEAN      STANDARD    DISTRIBUTION
 #                                                           TOTAL    %                DEVIATION   SCALED 1 FOR     636

 1          0.00 TO         99.99      14          690.09    2.58   2.58      49.29      26.85 *
 2        100.00 TO        499.99      13        3,047.63   11.39  13.97     234.43     118.76 ****
 3        500.00 TO        999.99       0            0.00    0.00  13.97       0.00       0.00 *
 4      1,000.00 TO      1,999.99       5        7,085.78   26.49  40.46   1,417.15     245.83 ***********
 5      2,000.00 TO      4,515.00       5       15,924.33   59.54 100.00   3,184.86     868.19 *************************

       ** TOTALS **                     37       26,747.83                     722.91   1,120.26

       CREDITS                           0            0.00

       LOWEST VALUE ON FILE                             0.00
       HIGHEST VALUE ON FILE                        4,515.00
```

FIG. 14-6   Stratification histogram

```
REPORT NO. IN04CAAG-1                        COMPUTER MFG CO                              PAGE NO.    1
REPORT DATE 12/04/79              AUDITORS PHYSICAL COMPARISON                    PERIOD ENDED 12/31/79

PART NO    PLANT  LOCATION/TAG    C&L COUNT   CLIENT COUNT  BOOK QTY  UNIT COST  CALC VALUE  CLIENT PHYS VAL DIF

MTF3601    00100 001105104A330130  101.0200    101.0000    101.0000   2.5000      252.55      252.50 ***
MTW3601    00100 0010000A330135    190.0000    190.0000    190.0000   2.6666      506.65      506.65
MTW3603    00100 0010000A330137    120.0000    125.0000    125.0000   1.5000    3,096.00    3,225.00 ***
MT3601     00100 001105001A330125  200.0000    200.0000    200.0000  25.8000    3,096.00    3,225.00 ***
MT3602     00100 001105001A330126  2,000.0000  210.0000    210.0000   3.0000   18,000.00    1,890.00 ***
MT3603     00300 0010500188        301.0000                                                        ***
MT3604     00100 0010500198        120.0000    150.0000    150.0000   0.8500    1,020.00    1,275.00 ***
                                    30.0000                                                         ***
RB1212     00100 001100101A330101  305.0000    300.0000    300.0000   1.5000      457.50      450.00 ***
RD810      00100 001100101A330106   30.0000-   105.0000    105.0000   1.2000       36.00-     126.00 ***
WB22       00100 00100000A330119    30.0000-   125.0000-   125.0000   1.5000       45.00-     187.50-***

                                          TOTALS

                       SELECTED ITEMS       VALUE      NUMBER
                          CALC VALUE:     24,851.70        9
                          CLIENT PHYS:     9,137.65        9
                          DIFFERENCE:     15,714.05        9
                       NON SELECTED ITEMS
                          CLIENT PHYS:  1,423,195.22     149
                       TOTAL FILE       1,432,332.87     158  (CLIENT PHYS)
```

FIG. 14-7   Auditor's physical comparison report

PART NO	PLANT LOCATION/ TAG	PHYS COUNT	BOOK QTY	UNIT COST	PHYS VALUE	BOOK VALUE	DIFFERENCE
CMP6000	00200 0020040B9130241	1.0000	1.0000				
	00500 005003000		1.0000				
	TOTAL PART	1.0000	2.0000	60,000.0000	60,000.00	120,000.00	60,000.00
FBF1212	00200 0020000B9130216	65.0000					
	TOTAL PART	65.0000	0.0000	55.0000	3,575.00	0.00	3,575.00-
FB810	00100 00100300A330114	10.0000					
	00200 0020030B9130205	25.0000	25.0000				
	00300 00302300C772513	9.0000	9.0000				
	TOTAL PART	44.0000	34.0000	5.0100	220.44	170.34	50.10-
FB816	00100 00100300A330115	15.0000	15.0000-				
	00200 0020030B9130206	71.0000	71.0000				
	00300 00302300C772514	15.0000	15.0000				
	TOTAL PART	101.0000	71.0000	4.0367	407.71	286.61	121.10-
MT3601	00100 00105001A330125	200.0000	200.0000				
	00300 0030700001B		220.0000				
	00500 0050600010934713	500.0000	500.0000				
	TOTAL PART	700.0000	920.0000	4.0000	5,600.00	7,360.00	1,760.00

REPORT NO. IH04CAAG-2 — REPORT DATE 12/04/79 — COMPUTER MFG CO — PHYSICAL COMPARISON WITH BOOK — PAGE NO. 2 — PERIOD ENDED 12/31/79

	PHYSICAL RECORD COUNT	BOOK QTY RECORD COUNT	COST RECORD COUNT	PHYSICAL VALUE	BOOK VALUE	DIFFERENCES
*** T O T A L F I L E ***	158	159	75	1,432,332.89	1,491,255.69	67,925.20
NO DIFFERENCES	118	118	62	1,356,754.18	1,356,754.18	
DIFFERENCES LESS THAN $1	0	0	0	0.00	0.00	0.00
DIFFERENCES LESS THAN $10	0	0	0	0.00	0.00	0.00
DIFFERENCES LESS THAN $100	5	5	2	326.00	306.90	81.10
DIFFERENCES LESS THAN $1000	9	7	4	1,615.21	1,114.11	1,251.10
OTHER DIFFERENCES	6	8	4	73,637.50	133,080.50	66,593.00
PHYSICAL RECS W/O COST RECS	19					
QTY RECS WITH NO COST RECS		21				
DUPLICATE PHYSICAL RECORDS	1					
DUPLICATE COST RECORDS			0			
COST RECORDS ONLY			3			
* * * * * * * * * * * * *						
BOOK RECS. WITH NO PHYS REC		35				
PHYS REC WITH NO BOOK RECS.	34					
ABSENT COST RECORDS			18			

FIG. 14-8 Physical comparison with book or inventory as recorded report

Evaluating Costs

Evaluation of cost is another key concern in the audit of inventory. It is often addressed by reports, such as the following, that are produced by this software:

- Cost compared with selling price reports items that are overvalued based on a comparison of calculated cost and sales values. This report assists the auditor in ensuring that the cost values of the parts in inventory do not exceed their net realizable values. (See Figure 14-10.)

- Individual invoice price comparison compares the sales value recorded on the current book cost file with selling prices used on sales invoices. The report prints the difference between the standard unit selling price (USP) and the invoice USP.

```
REPORT NO. IN05CAAG-1                              COMPUTER MFG CO                              PAGE NO.      1
REPORT DATE 12/04/79                            MISSING TAG REPORT                          PERIOD ENDED 12/31/79

        PRESENT                       MISSING                          AUDITORS FOLLOW-UP
     FROM          TO            FROM           TO

 A   330101
                                A   330102
 A   330138                                           *DUPLICATE*
 A   330103     A   330138
                                A   330139     B  9130199
 B  9130211                                           *DUPLICATE*
 B  9130200     B  9130242
                                B  9130243     C   772499
 C   772503                                           *DUPLICATE*
 C   772500     C   772538
                                C   772539     D   934700
 D   934701     D   934702
                                D   934703     D   934704
 D   934705     D   934722
                                D   934723     X  7900499
 X  7900500     X  7900515


                                              TOTALS

                                    TOTAL RECORDS PROCESSED    158

                                    DUPLICATES                  3
```

Interpretation of sample report:

- The starting tag number is A 330101.
- Tag number A 33102 is missing.
- Tag number A 330138 is duplicated.
- Tag numbers A 330139 through B 9130199 are missing.
- The last tag number is X 7900515.

FIG. 14-9 Missing tag report

- Current costs compared with previous costs shows the percentage of cost increase from one period to another. (See Figure 14-11.)

Reporting on Sales

Sales history is important, not only to verify revenue from sales, but to use as a basis for judging whether items are valued correctly. Four software reports in the C&L Inventory Audit Software package furnish information that assists the auditor in determining inventory usage and possible obsolescence:

1. *Sales history edit listing* — Designed to detect and report various types of errors in sales history data. (See Figure 14-12.)

2. *Inventory aging* — Presents an aging of the current book quantity sold. The report indicates slow-moving merchandise and inventory turnover by part number, based on historical sales. (See Figure 14-13.)

3. *Sales by month by item* — Sales summary report by part number. This report is useful in identifying whether the company's explanations of apparently slow-moving items are correct and can also be used to verify the total turnover for a month. (See Figure 14-14.)

REPORT NO. IN06CAAG-1 REPORT DATE 12/04/79			COMPUTER MFG CO COST COMPARED TO SELLING PRICE							PAGE NO. 1 PERIOD ENDED 12/31/79	
PART NO	DESCRIPTION	CLASS	CUMUL QUANTITY	U/M	UNIT COST	COST VALUE	MAR	CALC SALES VAL	UNIT SELL PRICE	SALES VALUE	OVERVAL %Z
CAB0500	COMP'T CABINETS	FN500	112.0000	1.0000	80.0000	8,960	1.00	8,960	0.0000	0	8,960
FB1212	MFG 12X12 COP-BRD	FN500	212.0000	1.0000	5.0000	1,060	1.00	1,060	0.0000	0	1,060
FB1416	MFG 14X16 COP-BRD	FN500	55.0000	1.0000	4.9560	272	1.00	272	0.0000	0	272

REPORT NO. IN06CAAG-1 REPORT DATE 12/04/79		COMPUTER MFG CO COST COMPARED TO SELLING PRICE							PAGE NO. 3 PERIOD ENDED 12/31/79	
PART NO	DESCRIPTION	CLASS	CUMUL QUANTITY	U/M	UNIT COST	COST VALUE	MAR	CALC SALES VAL	UNIT SELL PRICE	SALES VALUE OVERVAL %Z

RECORDS

		COST VALUE	CALC SALES VAL	SALES VALUE	OVERVAL %Z
24	TOTAL PRINTED ABOVE	67,939.00	115,669.88	28,497.35	87,172.53
14	NOT PRINTED NEGATIVE	-,131,976.39	1,133,776.39	2,500,730.50	1,366,954.11-
0	POSITIVE	0.00	0.00	0.00	0.00
38	TOTAL TESTED	1,199,915.39	1,249,446.27	2,529,227.85	1,279,781.58-
0	DUPLICATE COST RECORD				
34	EXCLUDED RECORDS				
3	RECORDS WITH NO COST				

FIG. 14-10 Cost compared with selling price report

REPORT NO. IN07CAAG-1 REPORT DATE 12/04/79		COMPUTER MFG CO CURRENT COSTS COMPARED TO PREVIOUS COSTS						PAGE NO. 1 PERIOD ENDED 12/31/79	
PART NO	DESCRIPTION	QUANTITY	U/M	CURRENT UNIT COST	CURRENT VALUE	PREVIOUS UNIT COST	PREVIOUS VALUE	PERCENT INC	
CAB0400	WIP CABINETS	30.0000	1.0000	40.0000	1,200.00	40.0000	1,200.00	0.00	
CAB0500	COMP'T CABINETS	112.0000	1.0000	80.0000	8,960.00	80.0000	8,960.00	0.00	
CD96	96 COLUMN CARDS	60.0000	1,000.0000	0.0075	450.00	0.0075	450.00	0.00	
CMP4000	COMP'T 4000	4.0000	1.0000	40,000.0000	160,000.00	40,000.0000	160,000.00	0.00	
CMP4100	WIP 4000 COMPUTER	6.0000	1.0000	17,090.5025	102,543.01	17,090.5025	102,543.01	0.00	
CMP5000	COMP'T 5000 COMPUTE	2.0000	1.0000	50,000.0000	100,000.00	50,000.0000	100,000.00	0.00	
CMP5100	WIP 5000 COMPUTER	3.0000	1.0000	24,938.5192	74,815.55	24,938.5192	74,815.55	0.00	
CMP6000	COMP'T 6000 COMPUTE	2.0000	1.0000	60,000.0000	120,000.00	60,000.0000	120,000.00	0.00	
CMP6100	WIP 6000 COMPUTER	2.0000	1.0000	30,000.0000	60,000.00	30,000.0000	60,000.00	0.00	
DDF100	DISK DRIVES	15.0000	1.0000	20,100.0000	301,500.00	20,100.0000	301,500.00	0.00	
DDM100	MINI PACK DISK DRI	23.0000	1.0000	19,000.0000	437,000.00	0.0000	0.00	*NEW*	
EL2001	GAGE1 WIRE	25,000.5750	0.8900	0.0032	71.20	0.0031	68.97	3.12	
EL2002	GAGE2 WIRE	20,500.0250	0.9000	0.0040	73.80	0.0039	71.95	2.49	
EL2003	GAGE3 WIRE	12,875.0000	0.8150	0.0069	72.40	0.0068	71.35	1.44	
EL2004	LIGHT CABLE	8,901.0750	0.9250	0.1950	1,605.53	0.1949	1,604.70	0.05	
FBF1416	COMP'T 14X16 BRD	28.0000	1.0000	4.6120	129.13	44.2753	1,239.70	*DEC*	
FBF35	COMT' 3X5 BRD	15.0000	1.0000	34.5055	517.58	0.0000	0.00	*NEW*	
FBF46	COMP'T 4X6 BRD	26.0000	1.0000	32.2203	837.72	0.0000	0.00	*NEW*	

REPORT NO. IN07CAAG-1 REPORT DATE 12/04/79		COMPUTER MFG CO CURRENT COSTS COMPARED TO PREVIOUS COSTS						PAGE NO. 2 PERIOD ENDED 12/31/79	
PART NO	DESCRIPTION	QUANTITY	U/M	CURRENT UNIT COST	CURRENT VALUE	PREVIOUS UNIT COST	PREVIOUS VALUE	PERCENT INC	

ITEMS

		CURRENT VALUE	PREVIOUS VALUE
11	NEW ITEMS	443,242.53	
0	INCREASES ABOVE 5 PERCENT	0.00	0.00
4	DECREASES	1,861.30	9,809.56
25	SAME PRICE	947,274.90	947,249.98
31	ITEMS NOT PRINTED	98,818.46	94,824.86
71	TOTAL ITEMS	1,491,197.19	1,051,884.40
159	CURRENT BOOK QTY RECORDS		
75	CURRENT BOOK COST RECORDS		
72	PREVIOUS BOOK COST RECORDS		

FIG. 14-11 Current costs compared with previous costs report

```
REPORT NO. IN08CAAG-1                          COMPUTER MFG CO                              PAGE NO.      1
REPORT DATE 12/04/79                      SALES HISTORY EDIT LISTING                    PERIOD ENDED 12/31/79

INVOICE   DATE    PART NO    DESCRIPTION            QUANTITY        UNIT          TOTAL      ERROR
NO                                                                 PRICE         VALUE      DIAGNOSTIC

  6677500 01-02-79 CAB0400   WIP CABINET              2.0000       0.0000          0.00 SLSDTE OUT RANGE
  7744401 01-19-79 CD80      80COLUMN CARDS          25.0000       9.7500        243.75 SLSDTE OUT RANGE
  7744402 06-28-79 CD80      80COLUMN CARDS         100.0000       9.7500        975.00 SLSDTE OUT RANGE
  7750211 04-01-79 CD80      80 COLUMN CARDS         10.0000       9.7500         97.50 SLSDTE OUT RANGE
  7744405 06-21-79 CD96      96 COLUMN CARDS        150.0000       9.5000      1,425.00 SLSDTE OUT RANGE
  7744406 04-19-79 CD96      96 COLUMN CARDS         15.0000       9.5000        142.50 SLSDTE OUT RANGE
  7750200 01-02-79 CD96      96 COLUMN CARDS        110.0000       9.5000      1,045.00 SLSDTE OUT RANGE
  7750200 01-02-79 CD96      96 COLUMN CARDS        110.0000       9.5000      1,045.00 SLSDTE OUT RANGE
  3999103 01-30-79 CMP4000   SERIES 4000 COMPUTER     1.0000  80,000.0000     80,000.00 SLSDTE OUT RANGE
  3999162 07-07-79 CMP4000   SERIES J/// COMPUTER     1.0000  80,000.0000     80,000.00 SLSDTE OUT RANGE
  7744400 01-13-79 CMP4000   SERIES 4000 COMPUTER     1.0000  80,000.0000     80,000.00 SLSDTE OUT RANGE
  7744407 08-08-79 CMP4000   SERIES 4000 COMPUTER     1.0000  80,000.0000     80,000.00 SLSDTE OUT RANGE
  7750202 02-28-79 CMP4000   COMPUTER SERIES 4000     1.0000  80,000.0000     80,000.00 SLSDTE OUT RANGE
  3999107 07-04-78 CMP5000   5000 SERIES COMPUTER     1.0000  90,000.0000     90,000.00 SLSDTE OUT RANGE
  7744400 01-13-79 CMP5000   COMPUTER SERIES 5000     1.0000  90,000.0000     90,000.00 SLSDTE OUT RANGE
  7744409 01-13-79 CMP5000   COMPUTER SERIES 5000     2.0000  90,000.0030    180,000.00 SLSDTE OUT RANGE
  3999108 03-03-79 CMP6000   6000 SERIES COMPUTER     1.0000  95,000.0000     95,000.00 SLSDTE OUT RANGE
  7744411 05-25-79 CMP6000   COMPUTER 6000 SERIES     2.0000  95,000.0000    190,000.00 SLSDTE OUT RANGE
  7750300 06-21-79 CMP6000   COMPUTER SERIES 6000     2.0000  95,000.0000    190,000.00 SLSDTE OUT RANGE
  7750303 03-09-79 CMP6000   COMPUTER SERIES 6000     1.0000  95,000.0000     95,000.00 SLSDTE OUT RANGE
  7750304 00-00-00 CMP6000   6000 SERIES COMPUTER     1.0000  0095000    9    5000 090179 INVLD SELL PRICE
                                                                                      INVLD SLS VALUE
                                                                                      INVLD SLS DATE
  3999109 02-15-79 DDF100    DISK DRIVES              1.0000  35,000.0000     35,000.00 SLSDTE OUT RANGE
  7744400 01-13-79 DDF100    DISK DRIVES              1.0000  35,000.0000     35,000.00 SLSDTE OUT RANGE
  7744413 02-15-79 DDF100    DISK DRIVES              1.0000  35,000.0000     35,000.00 SLSDTE OUT RANGE
```

```
REPORT NO. IN08CAAG-1                          COMPUTER MFG CO                              PAGE NO.      2
REPORT DATE 12/04/79                      SALES HISTORY EDIT LISTING                    PERIOD ENDED 12/31/79

INVOICE   DATE    PART NO    DESCRIPTION            QUANTITY        UNIT          TOTAL      ERROR
NO                                                                 PRICE         VALUE      DIAGNOSTIC

  7750350 07-18-79 FBF35     3X5 MEMORY BOARD         1.0000     120.0000        120.00 SLSDTE OUT RANGE
  3999118 06-01-79 FBF44     4"X4" MEMORY BOARD       2.0000     120.0000        240.00 SLSDTE OUT RANGE
  7760210 01-30-79 FBF44     MEMORY BOARD 4X4         1.0000     120.0000        120.00 SLSDTE OUT RANGE
  7760220 03-23-79 FBF44     MEMORY BOARD 4X4         2.0000     120.0000        240.00 SLSDTE OUT RANGE
  7760220 08-10-79 FDF44     MEMORY BOARD             1.0000     120.0000        120.00 SLSDTE OUT RANGE
  7760230 07-24-79 FBF44     4X4 INCH MEMORY BOARD    1.0000     120.0000        120.00 SLSDTE OUT RANGE
  3999120 08-10-79 FBF46     LOGIC BOARD              3.0000      64.5330        193.50 SLSDTE OUT RANGE
  3999121 06-05-79 FBF810    I-O CONTROL BOARD        3.0000  000060 0000        120.00 INVLD SELL PRICE
  3999123 05-05-79 FBF810    I-O CONTROL BOARD        1.0000      60.0000   0000000060 00 INVLD SLS VALUE
  7744400 06-14-79 FDD12     DUAL DISK PACK           2.0000  0000000 350        700.00 INVLD SELL PRICE
  3999133 06-20-79 FDD92     DUAL DISK PACK           3.0000  0000000 350      1,050.00 INVLD SELL PRICE
  5543003 06-10-79 FDD92     DUAL DISK PACK           2.0000  0000000 350        700.00 INVLD SELL PRICE
  5543004 01-19-79 FDD92     DUAL DISK PACK           1.0000  0000000 350        350.00 INVLD SELL PRICE
  3999134 10-10-80 FSD46     SINGLE DISK PACK         2.0000  0000000 300        600.00 INVLD SELL PRICE
  3999135 12-13-79 FSD46     SINGLE DISK PACK         3.0000  0000000 300        900.00 INVLD SELL PRICE
  5543005 09-10-79 FSD46     SINGLE DISK PACK         2.0000  0000000 300        600.00 INVLD SELL PRICE
  5543006 09-09-79 FSD46     SINGLE DISK PACK         2.0000  0000000 300        600.00 INVLD SELL PRICE
  5543007 02-13-79 FSD46     SINGLE DISK PACK         4.0000  0000000 300      1,200.00 INVLD SELL PRICE
  5543008 04-01-79 FSD46     SINGLE DISK PACK         2.0000  0000000 300        600.00 INVLD SELL PRICE
  5543009 05-12-79 FSD46     SINGLE DISK PACK         2.0000  0000000 300        600.00 INVLD SELL PRICE
  5543010 06-14-79 MDD23     MINI DISK PACK           2.0000  0000000 240        480.00 INVLD SELL PRICE
  9111007 01-10-79 TD824     800 BPI TAPE 2400'       1.0000  000055 0000         55.00 INVLD SELL PRICE

           RECORDS                       --- TOTALS ---

                 0                                                                 0.00 INVLD PART NUMBER
                 0                                                                 0.00 INVLD QUANTITY
                15                                                             8,555.00 INVLD SELL PRICE
                 2                                                                      INVLD SLS VALUE
                 1                                                                 0.00 INVLD SLS DATE
               120                                                         1,825,739.65 SLSDTE OUT RANGE
                69                                                           855,547.55 NO ERRORS DETECTED
                 0                                                                 0.00 SAMPLED ITEMS
               193                                                         2,683,387.20 GRAND TOTAL

                          *** PROCESSING CONTINUES ***
```

FIG. 14-12 Sales history edit listing

4. *Sales by month by product class* — Produces sales totals for each
   product class (or group).

The C&L audit software may be implemented in the organization's EDP
environment or at a service bureau. Three distinct phases are involved: (1) the
company's inventory-related files are edited and combined; (2) the information is analyzed and selections made based on the criteria specified by the
auditor; and (3) the various reports are produced. The software has been
designed so that the first phase is required but the other two phases are
optional, depending on the requirements of the auditor. Flexibility is usually
provided by the report options or alternatives available.

REPORT NO. IN08CAAG-2 REPORT DATE 12/04/79			COMPUTER MFG CO INVENTORY AGEING							PAGE NO. 1 PERIOD ENDED 12/31/79
PART NO	DESCRIPTION	QUANTITY SOLD	QUANTITY ON HAND	VALUE	NOT AGED	UP TO 1 MTHS	2 TO 2 MONTHS	3 TO 3 MONTHS	4 TO 4 MONTHS	5 TO 5 MONTHS	OVER 5 MTHS
CAB0500	COMP'T CABINETS	0	112	8,960		0	0	0	0	0	8,960
CD96	96 COLUMN CARDS	1,000	60	450		450	0	0	0	0	0
CMP4000	COMP'T 4000	2	4	160,000		20,000	20,000	20,000	20,000	20,000	60,000
CMP5000	COMP'T 5000 COM	4	2	100,000		50,000	50,000	0	0	0	0
CMP6000	COMP'T 6000 COM	2	2	120,000		30,000	30,000	30,000	30,000	0	0
DDF100	DISK DRIVES	0	15	301,500		0	0	0	0	0	301,500
DDM100	MINI PACK DISK	4	23	437,000		19,000	19,000	19,000	19,000	19,000	342,000
FBF1416	COMP'T 14X16 B	14	28	129		16	16	16	16	16	49
FBF22	COMP'T 2X2 BRD	9	30	1,155		89	89	89	89	89	710
FBF35	COMT' 3X5 BRD	2	15	518		17	17	17	17	17	433
FBF44	COMP'T 4X4 BRD	2	40	1,560		20	20	20	20	20	1,460
FBF46	COMP'T 4X6 BRD	11	26	838		93	93	93	93	93	373
FBF810	COMP'T 8X10 BRD	0	20	600		0	0	0	0	0	600
FBF816	COMP'T 8X16 BRD	5	45	1,440		40	40	40	40	0	1,240
FB1212	MFG 12X12 COP-B	0	212	1,060		0	0	0	0	0	1,060
FB1416	MFG 14X16 COP-B	0	55	273		0	0	0	0	0	273
FBC2	MFG 2X2 COP-BRD	0	52	154		0	0	0	0	0	154
FB35	MFG 3X5 COPPER	5	46	315		9	9	9	9	9	270
FB44	MFG 4X4 COPPER-	0	103	671		0	0	0	0	0	671
FB46	MFG 4X6 COP-BRD	0	51	247		0	0	0	0	0	247
FB810	MFG 8X10 COP-BR	0	34	170		0	0	0	0	0	170
FB816	MFG 8X16 COPPER	0	71	287		0	0	0	0	0	287
FDD92	DUAL DENSITY PA	4	19	2,850		150	150	150	150	150	2,100
FSD46	SINGLE DENSITY	0	23	2,990		0	0	0	0	0	2,990
MDD23	MINI-DUAL DENSI	3	15	1,800		90	90	90	90	90	1,350
MSD18	MINI-SINGLE DEN	2	18	1,260		35	35	35	35	35	1,085
MTF3601	METAL SIDING	0	564	1,410		0	0	0	0	0	1,410
MTF3602	FRAME AND BASE	0	238	14,597		0	0	0	0	0	14,597
MTF3603	LOGIC SUPPORT C	0	273	13,726		0	0	0	0	0	13,726
MTF3604	INTERIOR FRAME	0	397	13,950		0	0	0	0	0	13,950
MTF3605	BRASS SCREWS	0	470	186		0	0	0	0	0	186
TD100	TAPE DRIVE	7	12	6,786		969	969	969	969	969	1,941
TD81	800BPI TAPE 100	10	50	661		33	33	33	33	33	496
TD815	800BPI TAPE 150	7	30	419		25	25	25	25	25	294
TD818	800BPI TAPE 180	2	40	582		7	7	7	7	7	547
TD824	800BPI TAPE 24	6	50	863		26	26	26	26	26	733
TD918	900BPT TAPE 18	11	18	264		38	38	38	38	38	74
TD924	900BPT TAPE 24	15	13	244		81	81	81	1	0	0

REPORT NO. IN08CAAG-2 REPORT DATE 12/04/79			COMPUTER MFG CO INVENTORY AGEING							PAGE NO. 2 PERIOD ENDED 12/31/79
PART NO	DESCRIPTION	QUANTITY SOLD	QUANTITY ON HAND	VALUE	NOT AGED	UP TO 1 MTHS	2 TO 2 MONTHS	3 TO 3 MONTHS	4 TO 4 MONTHS	5 TO 5 MONTHS	OVER 5 MTHS
015	TOTALS DO NOT EXCEED LIMIT			0.00	0.00	0.00	0.00	0.00	0.00	0.00	0.00
000	TOTALS NEW ITEMS			0.00	0.00	0.00	0.00	0.00	0.00	0.00	0.00
038	TOTALS PRINTED			1,199,915.28	4.00	121,187.92	120,737.92	70,737.92	70,656.66	40,656.65	775,938.21
053	TOTALS FILE			1,199,915.28	0.00	121,187.92	120,737.92	70,737.92	70,656.66	40,656.65	775,938.21

FIG. 14-13 Inventory aging report

For most efficient use, an inventory audit software package should provide the information required for implementation, such as a technical guide or user manual, and the magnetic media containing the software itself.

In the recent audit of inventory at a major retailer in the Southwest, an automated package was needed to process data for an exceptionally high volume of inventory items. Consequently, the C&L inventory audit software package was implemented. Using data generated by the package's stratification histogram, the auditors were able to identify that, out of an inventory of over 30,000 items, 1,500 represented 80 percent of the inventory's dollar value. This finding was invaluable in ensuring the proper and efficient selection of items for substantive testing.

The computer manufacturing division of a large company had an inventory count of 17 million items, valued at approximately $42 million. The inventory audit software package assisted in identifying several discrepancies

REPORT NO. IN08CAAG-3   COMPUTER MFG CO   PAGE NO. 1
REPORT DATE 12/04/79   SALES BY MONTH BY ITEM   PERIOD ENDED 12/31/79

PART NO	DESCRIPTION	TOTAL SALES	MTH 79-12	MTH 79-11	MTH 79-10	MTH 79-09	MTH 79-08	MTH 79-07	MTH 79-06	MTH 79-05	MTH 79-04	MTH 79-03	MTH 79-02	MTH 79-01	OTHER
CD80	80 COLUMN CAR*	2,243	146	146	1,951	0	0	0	0	0	0	0	0	0	0
CD96	96 COLUMN CAR	9,500	3,800	2,850	2,850	0	0	0	0	0	0	0	0	0	0
CMP4000	COMP'T 4000	160,000	80,000	80,000	0	0	0	0	0	0	0	0	0	0	0
CMP5000	COMP'T 5000 C	360,000	180,000	90,000	90,000	0	0	0	0	0	0	0	0	0	0
CMP6000	COMP'T 6000 C	190,000	0	95,000	95,000	0	0	0	0	0	0	0	0	0	0
DOM100	MINI PACK DIS	120,000	60,000	30,000	30,000	0	0	0	0	0	0	0	0	0	0
FBF1212	COMP'T 12X12	500	300	0	200	0	0	0	0	0	0	0	0	0	0
FBF1416	COMP'T 14X16	1,125	663	0	462	0	0	0	0	0	0	0	0	0	0
FBF22	COMP'T 2X2 BR	702	312	78	156	156	0	0	0	0	0	0	0	0	0
FBF35	COMT' 3X5 BRD	240	0	120	120	0	0	0	0	0	0	0	0	0	0
FBF44	COMP'T 4X4 B	240	120	0	120	0	0	0	0	0	0	0	0	0	0
FBF46	COMP'T 4X6 BR	710	0	452	258	0	0	0	0	0	0	0	0	0	0
FBF816	COMP'T 8X16 B	325	130	0	195	0	0	0	0	0	0	0	0	0	0
FB35	MFG 3X5 COPP	0	0	0	0	0	0	0	0	0	0	0	0	0	0
FDD92	DUAL DENSITY	1,400	0	700	700	0	0	0	0	0	0	0	0	0	0
MDD23	MINI-DUAL DEN	640	240	400	0	0	0	0	0	0	0	0	0	0	0

REPORT NO. IN08CAAG-3   COMPUTER MFG CO   PAGE NO. 2
REPORT DATE 12/04/79   SALES BY MONTH BY ITEM   PERIOD ENDED 12/31/79

PART NO	DESCRIPTION	TOTAL SALES	MTH 79-12	MTH 79-11	MTH 79-10	MTH 79-09	MTH 79-08	MTH 79-07	MTH 79-06	MTH 79-05	MTH 79-04	MTH 79-03	MTH 79-02	MTH 79-01	OTHER
MSD18	MINI-SINGLE D	240	0	240	0	0	0	0	0	0	0	0	0	0	0
TD100	TAPE DRIVE	4,900	1,400	1,400	2,100	0	0	0	0	0	0	0	0	0	0
TD81	800BPI TAPE 1	350	140	210	0	0	0	0	0	0	0	0	0	0	0
TD815	800BPI TAPE 1	287	0	0	208	79	0	0	0	0	0	0	0	0	0
TD818	800BPI TAPE 1	89	89	0	0	0	0	0	0	0	0	0	0	0	0
TD824	800BPI TAPE	330	0	0	220	110	0	0	0	0	0	0	0	0	0
TD915	900 BPI TAPE*	225	0	90	135	0	0	0	0	0	0	0	0	0	0
TD918	900BPT TAPE	545	99	50	396	0	0	0	0	0	0	0	0	0	0
TD924	900BPT TAPE	959	512	447	0	0	0	0	0	0	0	0	0	0	0
25	TOTALS	855,547.55	327,950.15	189,610.75	296,731.25	131,255.40	0.00	0.00	0.00	0.00	0.00	0.00	0.00	0.00	0.00

FIG. 14-14 Sales by month by item report

within the division's financial reporting system. The information listed in the missing tag report helped highlight items that were included in one of the reports but missing in another. The physical comparison with book report assisted the auditors in determining that several items in inventory had been incorrectly valued. Adjustments were subsequently made to the division's records.

Inventory Audit Objectives

Many common inventory substantive test procedures, such as the following, can be performed by the use of appropriately selected inventory audit software:

- Adding and stratifying inventory valuations
- Recalculating extended costs
- Selecting items for an independent count of inventories
- Selecting items for detailed substantive tests, including verification of costs
- Identifying uncounted items where cyclical counts are used
- Comparing audit counts with organization's physical counts
- Identifying missing or duplicate inventory tags
- Comparing organization's physical inventory with perpetual inventory records
- Comparing current period's cost prices with a previous period's cost prices
- Comparing selling prices with cost prices
- Detecting decreasing cost prices
- Identifying items sold at other than standard selling price
- Identifying slow-moving inventory items
- Identifying unusual inventory items
- Determining whether the inventory quantities are reasonably stated
- Determining whether slow-moving, damaged, or obsolete inventories have been appropriately identified and valued
- Determining whether the inventory summaries are arithmetically accurate
- Determining whether pricing of inventory quantities as to cost is appropriate
- Determining whether appropriate net realizable values have been used in making any required inventory writedowns
- Determining whether the net income for the year and the individual items of income and expense that are disclosed in the income statement are fairly stated

Figure 14-15 is the overview processing flowchart for the C&L package.

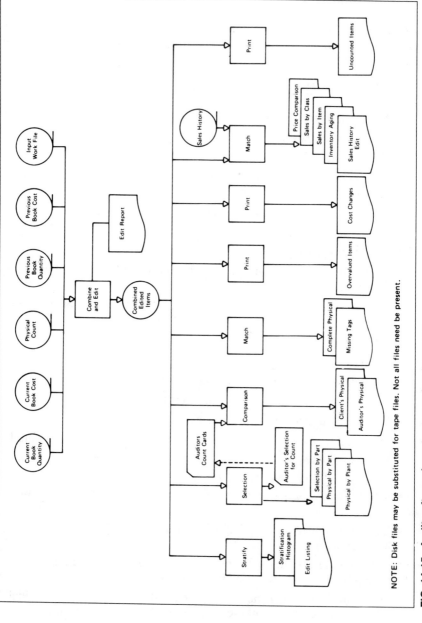

FIG. 14-15 Audit software inventory overview flowchart

NOTE: Disk files may be substituted for tape files. Not all files need be present.

Sequence of Events

The effective use of the packaged audit software in an inventory audit requires cooperation between the non-EDP auditor and EDP auditor. An EDP auditor who knows the software can explain the package capabilities, implement, and execute the package. However, the auditor naturally has overall responsibility for properly performing the audit tests.

This section describes a typical sequence of tasks that can be followed to use an audit software package of this kind. The column headed "Auditor's Actions" includes actions that the auditor should perform and assumes the inclusion of the EDP auditor. The title of each report from the C&L package is listed as an event.

Events	*Auditor's Actions*
Planning	• Develop plan and budget.
	• Collect the information concerning the inventory system. Prepare planning working papers.
	• Determine desired report options and prepare the appropriate parameters (such as margin for net realizable value tests).
	• Complete reports within the audit time requirements. Keep audit staff informed of progress and any reasons for additional time.
	• Inform audit staff of the following:
	a. Year-end or test date
	b. Aging categories
	c. Sales history periods
	d. Physical count date
	e. File date for stratification
	• Before the due date, install the package, execute the edit program, and review the results for exceptions.
Report	
Input File Edit Errors	• Edit the inventory files, resolve error messages, and agree the totals.
Audit review	• Review any error messages to determine significance and corrections.
	• Assist in determining significance of error messages.

Events	*Auditor's Actions*

Report

Work File Edit Listing	• Obtain the inventory valuation total. Review the edit report for accuracy of data. • Review the edit report and agree the totals.
Audit review	• Reconcile report totals to books of account. Select the stratification method and supply the necessary parameters. • Determine stratification method.

Reports

Stratification Histogram	• Use the report to determine selection criteria for auditor's count. • Prepare reports and agree the totals.
Selection for Physical Count	• Check that the correct number and value of items have been selected. • Code selection criteria onto parameters and prepare report. Review results of selection.
Selection by Part	• Check that the correct number and value of items have been selected. • Code selection criteria onto parameters and prepare report. Review results of selection. • Perform independent count.
Auditor's Physical Comparison	• Use the report to investigate discrepancies and to review inventory valuations. Use report to determine the effect of discrepancies on total inventory valuation.
Physical Comparison With Book	• Use the report to investigate discrepancies and to determine their effect on the total inventory valuation.
Missing Tag Report	• Use the report to identify missing or duplicate tags.
Physical Inventory	• Use the report for audit tests.
Cost Compared to Selling Price	• Use the report to detect inventory overvaluation.
Current Costs Compared to Previous Costs	• Use the report to identify unusual cost increases and/or items where the cost did not increase.

Events	*Auditor's Actions*
Reports *(cont'd)*	
Sales History Edit Listing	• Review any error messages to determine significance and corrections.
	• Assist in determining significance of error messages.
Inventory Aging	• Use aging report for audit tests.
Sales by Month by Item	• Use the report to review seasonal fluctuation of parts. Agree to sales figures for the period.
Sales by Month by Product Class	• Confirm product mix and slow-moving product analysis.
Individual Invoice Price Comparison	• Review transactions listed to determine possibility of erroneous recording.
Uncounted Items	• Check that all items have been counted during the period.
Completion	• Summarize audit time costs and expenses. Document any reasons for changes from original budget. Provide suggestions for the coming audit year.

SUMMARY

Ultimately, the steady, clear stream of information presented by a comprehensive computerized monitoring system can start to approach the ideal of "continual audit." Recent implementation plans for monitoring systems are recognizing this fact, as seen in one plan developed for a major telecommunications corporation. Auditors involved in the system development recognized that this booming industry, along with other high-technology sectors, is extremely vulnerable to constantly and rapidly changing markets and economies. Industries in the high-tech market must be able to rely on a comprehensive, competent audit approach to inventory control and overall systems management.

The auditors supported the need for comprehensive audit systems by providing examples of manufacturers whose systems were unable to match control capabilities with the needs of high-volume sales environments. More than one of the companies cited used inventory control systems that were unable to distinguish between sales to distributors' inventories and those to end users. The results in a highly competitive market were, of course, disastrous.

The auditors proposed a comprehensive production system and monitoring plan that would ultimately provide an overall "management system." Such a system relies on the integration of information from the entire range of sectors responsible for development, production, marketing, and sales. This type of development in audit procedure — comprehensive system of inventory control, auditing, and analysis — provides an integrated tool to meet the demands of a constantly shifting economic and marketing picture.

CHAPTER **15**

General Ledger Systems

INTRODUCTION

In a rapidly changing economic environment, it is necessary for an organization to have accurate and comprehensive financial information and to have ready access to it. The accounting department should be able to deliver up-to-date information to help management in organizational decision making whenever it is required. The exchange of information between different departments should be fast and complete. Financial accounting is the foundation of an information system for the entire financial and accounting area. Conducted efficiently, according to generally accepted accounting principles (GAAP), financial accounting can be a great asset in producing timely, useful reports of an organization's transactions, whether they are needed for the annual summary, for financial statements, for tax accounting, or for other informational purposes.

Organizations depend on the general ledger to keep track of all financial transactions. Every transaction, no matter how small, is eventually entered into the general ledger, either directly or via a subsidiary ledger. In automated general ledger systems, many of the time-consuming manual processes are replaced by faster computerized techniques.

General ledger systems depend for their functioning on the generation of separate records for each debit and credit posted. In a computerized general ledger, the debits and credits are then grouped and printed in accordance with the general ledger account codes.

Other computer functions may be carried out according to requirements set out in the master file data held within the system (e.g., accounts may be grouped together and summarized for financial statement purposes; special programs can then group all similar accounts to print a monthly financial statement).

Major functions of a general ledger system are shown in the overview flowchart in Figure 15-1.

Simple Ledger Systems

The simplest computerized general ledger systems duplicate the manual functions of posting journal vouchers: Journal vouchers showing the account code and amount to be posted are entered. At the end of each month, the debits and credits are separately sorted by account code and printed out with a new balancing total. The balancing total is carried forward to the next month, together with a permanent header record for each account. The header record generally contains the account description, the format in which it will be printed, and perhaps certain summary information from previous months.

Journal entries arise from many sources, some of which are other com-

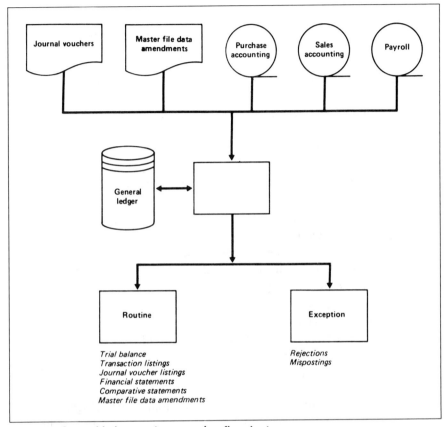

FIG. 15-1   **General ledger system overview flowchart**

puter applications (such as sales, payroll, or accounts payable systems). These other applications will, when necessary, summarize the journal entries required. When designed that way, they can feed the general ledger system directly.

Of course, it is also possible to reenter the summary, as a journal voucher, into the general ledger application. This approach is not necessarily inefficient if the number of accounts affected is small. However, it is also common for the other applications to prepare a computer file of journal entries that can be entered into the general ledger application.

Following is an example of a general ledger file layout, illustrating the kind of data elements that make up a general ledger record, including data elements and the number of characters each element uses in this particular format.

Detqils	Number of Characters
1. Transaction type "5"	1
2. Company	4
3. Account number	5
4. Department number	4
5. Subsidiary account number	4
6. Budget code	5
7. Account code	1
8. Account title	30
9. Print control characters and various flags	10
10. Balance — beginning of year	5
11. Balance — end of last period	5
12. Current amount for last period	5
13. Balance — after processing this period	5
14. Current amount for this period	5
15. Last period end date	4
16. Current period and base amount	5
17. Year-to-date and base amount	5
18. Comparative data this year, periods 1–12	60
19. Comparative data last year, periods 1–12	60
20. Budget data periods	60

Purchase invoices normally affect many different general ledger accounts. It is rare to see a company's general ledger application that is not linked to accounts payable in this same way. In fact, the ability to analyze invoices by general ledger expenditure account is often one of the major reasons for using a computer to do accounts payable work.

Advanced Ledger Systems

Many general ledger applications are of the simple sort, total, and print type described in the preceding section. However, the speed and versatility of a computer can be used when systems provide enhancements such as:

- *Automatic reversing entries.* These are entries, such as prepayments and accruals, that are entered at the end of a period. At the beginning of the next period, they must be reversed out; the journal voucher input can be coded so that the reversal takes place automatically at the beginning of the next period.

- *Automatic repeating entries.* Some entries must be made each period (e.g., to allocate 1/12 of the yearly rent to each month). These journal entries are held as master file data, carried forward and repeated each period.

- *Budget figures.* Budget figures are often incorporated into general ledger systems for actual versus budget comparison purposes. The computer will print exception reports of large variances. The system can also be used to perform variance and fluctuation analysis. Budget figures do not form part of the accounts proper but are used for management control. In some cases, budget figures are used by the programs to set up accrued expenses and prepayments. Figure 15-2 is a system overview of IBM's Financial Information System/Budget Accounting Information Subsystem (FIS/BACIS).

- *Standard costs.* These costs can be used in the same way as budget figures but actually form part of the accounts. They are especially used to accrue expenses and prepayments, to normalize fluctuations from one period to another, and to allocate expenses among departments. The actual figures, when entered, are matched to standard costs to generate the posting of a variance.

- *Other statements.* General ledger figures may also form part of other financial statements, such as cash flow projections, departmental budgets, cost ledgers, consolidations, and financial statements themselves. Therefore, one set of financial records can serve many purposes. The use, or uses, to which each separate account can be applied is usually indicated by master file data included in the header for the account. (See Figure 15-3 for a system overview of financial processing by IBM's FIS/BACIS.)

The account code from the chart of accounts is often entered manually on journal vouchers, then entered to a general ledger system. When the transactions are entered to a previous application, such as an accounts payable system, the same principle applies: The invoice or other transaction is coded with the general ledger account code so that the system can identify the account throughout processing.

However, in certain circumstances, the account code may be generated from master file data held within the general ledger or another application. For example, sales to associated companies are identified by a code held on the customer's account in the accounts receivable file. This is then translated into the appropriate general ledger account code by a conversion table in the invoicing, accounts receivable, or general ledger application program.

Occasionally, the debits and credits on a journal voucher do not balance. Such vouchers may be

- Rejected.
- Held in suspense within the computer.
- Posted, despite the error, along with a balancing figure to force the whole ledger into balance.

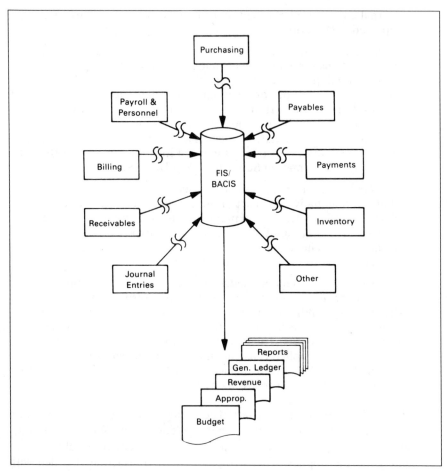

FIG. 15-2   Financial Information System/Budget Accounting Information Subsystem (FIS/BACIS) overview (courtesy of International Business Machines Corporation)

Obviously, users must correct such errors as soon as possible, especially when they are posted despite the errors.

INTERACTIVE FINANCIAL SYSTEM SOFTWARE

Facilitating access to timely and accurate financial accounting information is one goal of appropriately designed and developed computer software. Two such packages are IBM's FIS/BACIS and the same company's Interactive Financial System 1-4 (IFS 1-4), which is a planning and control data base

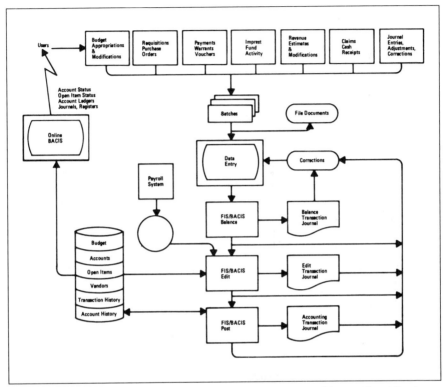

FIG. 15-3   Flowchart of FIS/BACIS daily processing (courtesy of International Business Machines Corporation)

system. See Figure 15-4 for an illustration of programs included in this system, which are:

IFS 1 — Postings and General Ledger

IFS 2 — Profit and Loss Statement, Balance Sheets, Financial Status Report

IFS 3 — Open-Item Accounting

IFS 4 — Payment Processing

The system provides financial processing, including a general ledger function, with the following capabilities, as described by IBM:

• The accounting data base organization and management functions

• Posting in conversational or batch mode

• Creation of the journal and the general ledger

• System documentation and restart functions

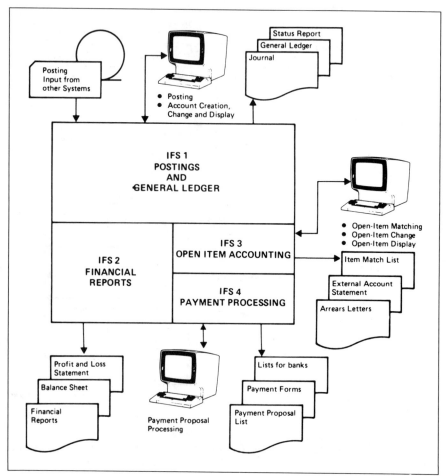

FIG. 15-4   Interactive Financial System 1-4 (IFS 1-4) overview (courtesy of International Business Machines Corporation)

The Interactive Financial System's programs make it possible to do accounting functions in conversational mode. This means that any account and any voucher can be entered, displayed and, if necessary, processed at CRT terminals, using a question-and-answer format. Such interactive, on-line processing helps the accounting department do financial processing independent of lists and account cards. (See Figure 15-5.) Advantages to such computerized processing, as described by IBM, include:

- Transactions on prime documents can be entered directly at the terminal, avoiding the need to transfer documents to intermediate recording media (magnetic tape, diskette, or punched card). Transactions are immediately validated or verified, corrected, and then entered.

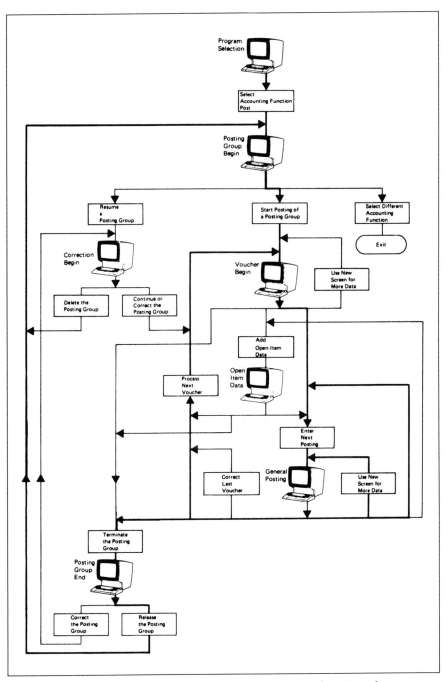

FIG. 15-5 Screen form sequence for posting in posting groups (courtesy of International Business Machines Corporation)

- The storage and processing capacities of the computer can be accessed directly by the terminal. Operating procedures and daily processing can be controlled in the department as a result. (There is no need to work through the EDP department.)
- Posting is performed from the transaction's prime document, directly into the system.
- The system labels postings that are entered incorrectly and stores them in a suspense file for later correction, eliminating the need to reenter postings after correction.
- Transaction entry and its subsequent posting time span is considerably reduced. Transactions posted immediately update the master files, which are then available for any other accounting activity, so that little processing time is lost.
- Special reports can be created and printed on short notice.

There are other advantages to an integrated accounting system; in IFS these include the following:

- Open-item allocation and matching, including discount posting and sales tax adjustment, is possible.
- Specific open-item information can be displayed and updated.
- An automatic arrears letter procedure writes individually worded reminder notices.
- Automatic account payment control can be performed at variable intervals.
- Payment proposals can be updated in conversational mode at the terminal.
- The allocation of open invoices to payment processing and banks is done in conversational mode.
- The match code can be used to search for account numbers based on fragmentary data about the account holder; possible matches are presented.
- The permanent link with the computer via the terminal enables the users (such as accounting department) to work with the computer as required.
- Business transactions can be processed as soon as they become evident, to optimize working cycle efficiency.

Payment Option

The Interactive Financial System makes it possible to avoid excessive manual processing of exceptions, such as unvalidated or unverified invoices, since each vendor can be given a "payment option." This option distinguishes vendors whose unverified invoices may be entered from those whose unverified invoices are to be investigated and paid manually. The payment option characteristic is entered into the system by an entry in the account master file record for each creditor.

Suspense Accounts

In an interactive financial system, suspense accounts (or accounts that hold items requiring further investigation and/or processing) are often used to process unverified invoices. In IFS 1-4, the qualifier that identifies an account as a suspense account is contained in the account master record. The suspense account operates in an open-item mode.

SECURITY ASPECTS AND DATA INTEGRITY

Financial data base systems contain financial accounting data of great significance to an organization. Accessing and updating this data, especially in an interactive or conversational mode, requires that controls protect the data base from unauthorized access, from unintentional changes or errors, and from destruction. This is particularly important in such a system because the master files are updated immediately by transactions entered at terminals. An unauthorized user could create much damage in a short period of time.

Following is an overview of the security measures provided by the application programs of IBM's IFS 1-4. They are presented here to depict how such systems can be controlled by programmed procedures. They provide four types of security:

1. Preventing posting errors
2. Protecting updating or posting data
3. Protecting account master file data
4. Preventing unauthorized access

Preventing Posting Errors

Two main procedures serve to prevent updating or posting errors: (1) validation of posting data and (2) rejection of posting groups containing unvalidated data.

Validation of Posting Data. The IBM programs, like other systems of this kind, provide comprehensive edit checks and validation tests of posting data as it is entered. In this case, entered data does not actually update the file until the items of the posting group have been successfully balanced. The following balance checks can be carried out as an option for each voucher and are mandatory for the total number of vouchers collected as a posting group:

- *Voucher balancing.* Before entering a group of transactions, the user can specify whether the system should check the debit/credit equality of each voucher within the group. An incorrect voucher can be corrected either immediately or later during the correction phase of the posting program.

- *Posting group balancing.* Two checks are always carried out on the vouchers of the posting group as a whole: (1) that there is an overall debit/credit balance and (2) that the total posted agrees with a previously entered control total. Entered data can be finally posted only if these two checks are satisfactory.

Rejection of Unvalidated Data. The program ensures that entered transaction groups are not posted if they contain unvalidated data or data that for some reason is subject to correction. It also ensures that once a posting group is posted, it cannot be changed. To effect this, entered posting groups here are classified into two subgroups:

- *In progress (HOLD status).* Posting groups with HOLD status may be changed, completed, and corrected. They are not posted during short-period summary (processing completed to a certain time or date), but are retained until they have OK status.

- *Posted (OK status).* Posting groups with OK status are assumed posted; that is, their data is final and cannot be changed. The actual posting of the data occurs during the next short-period summary.

A posting group cannot be given OK status unless the posting group balance check is satisfactory. If voucher balancing was also to be carried out, the posting group can be given OK status only if all vouchers in this posting group are balanced. Posting groups with OK status will be entered in the data base and in journals during the next short-period summary.

Protecting Posted Data

In addition to the checks described previously, further checks are carried out during and after storage of the postings in the data base. These checks are carried out during short-period summary, monthly summary, and when account statements are requested.

To prevent falsification of stored data, the accounting date (determined only by selected personnel) accompanies all entries. Deletion of stored data is always accompanied by a report of the stored data (which shows the data as it was just before deletion).

Short-Period Summary. Posting groups with OK status are transferred to the data base during short-period summary for storage. During short-period summary all postings are printed in the general journal of the organization. At the time the postings are transferred to the data base, a further debit/credit equality check is made. (At this point, discrepancies can have been caused only by a program defect or by unauthorized manipulation of posting data.)

Journal discrepancies or exceptions are reported in a special printout that indicates whether program errors or unauthorized attempts at data manipulation have occurred between the time the postings were entered and the printing of the journal.

Account Statements. When account statements are produced as nonperiodic reports, they are checked by the system. Differences between the total stored in the individual account and the sum of the separate items are shown in the statements, with an indication that the difference was due to a program error or unauthorized data manipulation.

Monthly Summary. The monthly summary is carried out for each account. IFS 1-4 ensures that no further postings can be made for a particular month, once it has been subject to the monthly summary.

The checks carried out during monthly summary are:

- Debit/credit balance checks of monthly and annual turnovers for all the accounts.
- The amount shown in the journal must match the accumulated monthly turnovers of all appropriate accounts.

Discrepancies are indicated so that they can be investigated. Only if the summary balances can the month be finally closed. (Figure 15-6 shows period closing reports from IBM's FIS/BACIS.)

Accounting Date. The accounting date is entered at the beginning of a session by selected personnel. Usually only one person with authority can enter the date, to prevent the falsification of accounts by the entry of data under an incorrect date. (Note that this authorization should be checked as part of controls.)

Controlled Manipulation of Stored Data. To limit the amount of posted data stored in the system, the user must decide for how many closed months posting data should be retained in the data base. Data for the preceding months is deleted and the program provides a report of all of the deleted posting data. The deleted data can be stored on magnetic tape, according to the require-

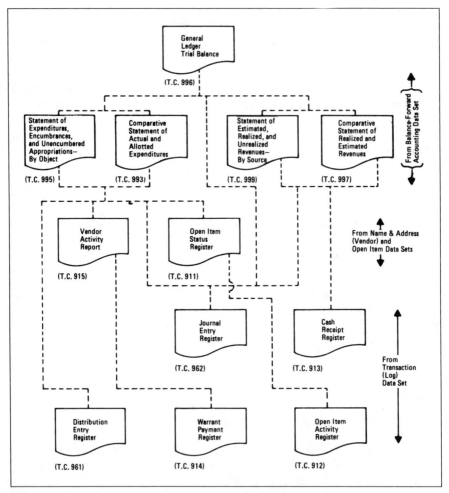

FIG. 15-6 Financial reports (period closing reports) based on general ledger from FIS/BACIS (courtesy of International Business Machines Corporation)

ments of the organization. In this way, past data is retained for auditing purposes and later analysis. To delete data from the data base, the following conditions must be fulfilled:

- The posting month must have been closed.
- In the case of open-item accounting, items must be balanced and printed on an item matching list.
- Postings must have the status "verified," meaning that they have been appropriately checked and are ready for deletion.

Protecting Account Master File Data

When account master file data is created, changed, or deleted, the system verifies that the user is authorized and that the data is reasonable. A report of the data concerned is then produced.

Creating and Changing Account Master File Data. In order to create or change account master file data, users must first identify themselves to the system. In addition, the system allows the user to carry out only those functions for which that user is authorized. Plausibility checks are carried out by the system on all changes to master file data, and the changes are recorded. Similar plausibility checks are carried out for data entered by batch processing.

Deleting Account Master File Data. Accounts that are no longer in use may be deleted from the data base to release storage capacity for other purposes. It is possible to delete master file data created before a certain selection date for a given account. In order to delete master file data, the following conditions must be met:

- No subaccounts may exist for a main account being deleted.
- The amount balanced from the account brought forward, the turnovers of the previous and the current year, as well as the turnovers of posting months 1 and 2, must be zero.
- The turnovers for posting months 1 and 2 and for the thirteenth month of the previous year must all be zero on both the debit and credit sides of the account.
- In the case of an account being used more than once, the debit and credit turnovers for the current year must be zero, and no accounts may have been posted after the selection date.

Deleted accounts are printed and can also be stored on magnetic tape. Users can write programs that extract or combine data for statistical or financial reports. In this format, deletion of account master file data can be executed only in batch mode.

Preventing Unauthorized Access

A well-designed financial data base system ensures that unauthorized users are denied access to the system; authorized users are permitted to carry out only predetermined authorized functions. In general, the system first checks the identity of the user for authorization. Authorized users are then checked for the accounts they can access and whether they have authorization to change (post) or only to view or display data.

User Identification. IFS 1-4 is programmed to respond to users who identify themselves by means of an authorized name and password; unauthorized users are denied access to the system. So that the password cannot be observed by onlookers, it does not appear on the screen when it is entered. Three unsuccessful attempts at identification by a user causes the terminal to be deactivated. It can be reactivated only by the master terminal.

User Authorization. The user name (or USERID) is designed and implemented to indicate and permit a predetermined level of authorization. Only certain users can carry out master terminal functions, such as initiating or terminating sessions or activating or deactivating terminals. For bookkeeping functions, the user name has two categories of authorization: (1) the accounts to which access is allowed and (2) the functions that can be processed using those accounts.

As an example, the accountant responsible for creditors may be authorized to have access to all creditor accounts and expenditure accounts to post items: This is the "update" or "write" permission. For information only, the "read" or "inquiry" permission allows display of debtor accounts. An attempt by a user with only read or inquiry permission to enter new debtor account postings would be unsuccessful and would cause an error message to be displayed.

The various levels of authorization should be determined by a person with appropriate authority in the organization.

USING AUDIT SOFTWARE FOR GENERAL LEDGER AUDITS

General ledger audit software is designed to increase audit efficiency by automating some of the common substantive procedures. Because many functions are precoded into the software, it can be installed relatively quickly. The auditor has flexibility in choosing parameters and in the generation of computer reports. Audit software can be used to assist in the audit of most computerized general ledger systems. Such a package is particularly effective where there are a large number of transactions and accounts comprising the general ledger. Some financial information systems have their own built-in report capabilities that can be useful to the auditor. (See Figure 15-7.)

Testing Facilities

Many common audit substantive procedures can be performed by an audit software package:

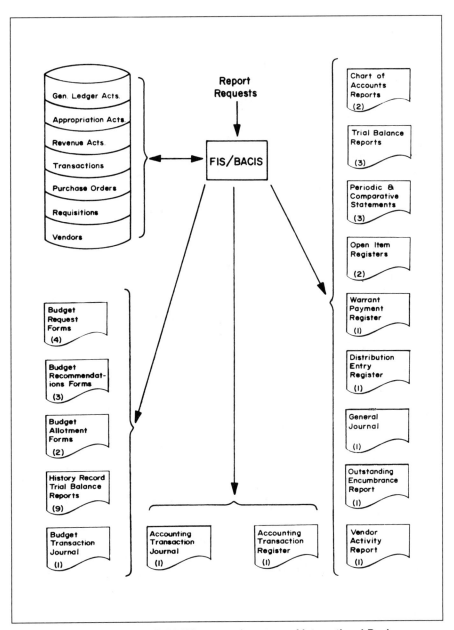

FIG. 15-7   Fifteen types of FIS/BACIS reports (courtesy of International Business Machines Corporation)

- Analyzing data for consistency and accuracy of information
- Identifying new accounts (see Figure 15-8)
- Identifying closed accounts
- Identifying abnormal account conditions
- Comparing current, prior, and budget figures for all accounts in the trial balance
- Identifying transactions comprising the account balances
- Identifying accounts comprising the financial line
- Preparing financial line analysis, including current- and prior-year balances (see Figure 15-9)
- Selecting transactions for detailed validation tests
- Detecting different transaction dates within the same journal entry (see Figure 15-10)
- Checking journal entries to ensure that debit and credit entries balance
- Checking that transaction details correctly sum to the account total
- Selecting journal entries for detailed validation tests
- Comparing current, prior period, and budget account totals for selected accounts on financial lines
- Comparing financial line totals over a five-year period (see Figure 15-11)
- Plotting movements in selected accounts or financial lines in graphic form (see Figure 15-12)
- Calculating financial ratios for two to five accounting periods
- Calculating a vertical consolidation or a consolidation worksheet of multicompany and/or multisubsidiary accounts (see Figure 15-13)
- Reprinting the general ledger trial balance and preparing a trial balance worksheet (see Figures 15-14 and 15-15)

Many audit objectives are achieved more easily as a result of using general ledger audit software. Figure 15-16 is an overview of processing by the Coopers & Lybrand (C&L) package. The extent of the assistance obtained from use of the package is affected by:

- The capabilities of the package in use
- The nature of the organization's general ledger system — in particular, the extent of the information relating to individual transactions
- The audit approach adopted for a particular situation

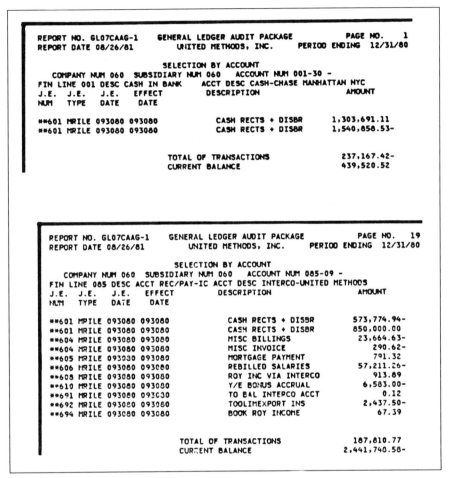

```
REPORT NO. GL07CAAG-1    GENERAL LEDGER AUDIT PACKAGE         PAGE NO.    1
REPORT DATE 08/26/81          UNITED METHODS, INC.    PERIOD ENDING  12/31/80

                          SELECTION BY ACCOUNT
       COMPANY NUM 060  SUBSIDIARY NUM 060    ACCOUNT NUM 001-30 -
   FIN LINE 001 DESC CASH IN BANK     ACCT DESC CASH-CHASE MANHATTAN NYC
   J.E.   J.E.   J.E.   EFFECT        DESCRIPTION               AMOUNT
   NUM    TYPE   DATE   DATE


   **601 MRILE 093080 093080          CASH RECTS + DISBR     1,303,691.11
   **601 MRILE 093080 093080          CASH RECTS + DISBR     1,540,858.53-


                        TOTAL OF TRANSACTIONS               237,167.42-
                        CURRENT BALANCE                     439,520.52




   REPORT NO. GL07CAAG-1    GENERAL LEDGER AUDIT PACKAGE         PAGE NO.   19
   REPORT DATE 08/26/81          UNITED METHODS, INC.    PERIOD ENDING  12/31/80

                          SELECTION BY ACCOUNT
       COMPANY NUM 060  SUBSIDIARY NUM 060    ACCOUNT NUM 085-09 -
   FIN LINE 085 DESC ACCT REC/PAY-IC ACCT DESC INTERCO-UNITED METHODS
   J.E.   J.E.   J.E.   EFFECT        DESCRIPTION               AMOUNT
   NUM    TYPE   DATE   DATE


   **601 MPILE 093080 093080          CASH RECTS + DISBR       573,774.94-
   **601 MRILE 093080 093080          CASH RECTS + DISBR       850,000.00
   **604 MRILE 093080 093080          MISC BILLINGS             23,664.63-
   **604 MRILE 093080 093080          MISC INVOICE                 290.62-
   **605 MRILE 093030 093080          MORTGAGE PAYMENT             791.32
   **606 MRILE 093080 093080          REBILLED SALARIES         57,211.26-
   **608 MRILE 093080 093080          ROY INC VIA INTERCO          913.89
   **610 MRILE 093080 093080          Y/E BONUS ACCRUAL          6,583.00-
   **691 MRILE 093080 093030          TO BAL INTERCO ACCT            0.12
   **692 MRILE 093080 093080          TOOLIMEXPORT INS           2,437.50-
   **694 MRILE 093080 093080          BOOK ROY INCOME               67.39


                        TOTAL OF TRANSACTIONS               187,810.77
                        CURRENT BALANCE                   2,441,740.58-
```

FIG. 15-8 Selection by account report

The results obtained from using the package when a system is particularly well-suited for it may be sufficient to warrant an extended substantive approach when it would be otherwise impractical or unwarranted.

Substantive audit objectives are typically split up according to major balance sheet headings. The general ledger, by its nature, contains information relating to all of these headings and also to the income statement itself. Thus, a general ledger audit software package can assist the auditor in many of the different substantive audit objectives. For example, the procedures usually include, as a minimum, the requirement to prepare a detailed analysis on a comparative basis or to obtain these from the user. A good general ledger software package prepares these analyses automatically.

REPORT NO. GL11CAAG-1   GENERAL LEDGER AUDIT PACKAGE   PAGE NO. 1
REPORT DATE 08/27/81   UNITED METHODS, INC.   PERIOD ENDED 12/31/80

CO. NUM: 020 DESCRIPT: UNITED METH.INC CHANGE BY FINANCIAL LINE NUMBER (FULL) SUB NUM:020 DESCRIPT: UNITED METHODS

LIN NUM	DESCRIPTION	CURRENT BALANCE	PERCEN CHANGE	PRIOR BEFORE CLOSE	PERCEN CHANGE	BUDGET	PERCEN CHANGE	PRIOR AFTER CLOSE
001	CASH IN BANK	4,971,477.89	53.51+	3,238,468.48	11.95-	5,646,831.61	53.51+	3,238,468.48
002	CASH ON HAND	12,494.60	46.13+	8,550.00	7.78-	13,548.80	46.13+	8,550.00
003	MARKETABLE SEC.	489,000.00-	0.00+	0.00	77.54-	2,177,016.72-	0.00+	0.00
007	ACCT.REC.-OTHER	790,343.32	370.88+	167,842.19	6.01-	840,926.40	370.88+	167,842.19
010	NOTES RECEIVABL	12,387,767.06	598.93+	1,772,369.00	1.44+	12,211,368.53	598.93+	1,772,369.00
030	PREPAID INS.	322,100.57	289.67+	82,659.70	7.03-	346,457.64	289.67+	82,659.70
032	PREPAID ROYLTS.	750,844.05	66.59+	450,701.44	6.60-	803,984.52	66.59+	450,701.44
033	PREPD.FIN.CHGS.	75.70	0.00+	75.70	9.09-	83.27	0.00+	75.70
034	PREPD.ADVACATLG	307,483.74	284.37+	79,995.40	7.06-	330,863.39	284.37+	79,995.40
036	PREPAID WAGES	120,987.85-	0.00+	0.00	35.60-	167,879.20-	0.00+	0.00
037	SUSPENSE	224,336.57	256.44+	16,538.55	9.57-	248,090.63	256.44+	16,538.55
038	PREPAID OTHER	42,305.96	21.49+	34,885.88	54.41-	92,990.19	21.49+	34,885.88
040	LAND	884,521.85	0.00+	884,521.85	9.09+	972,974.03	0.00+	884,521.85
044	LAND IMPROVMNTS	936,480.29	3.31+	906,471.02	8.90-	1,027,985.81	3.31+	906,471.02
045	RESV-LAND IMPRV	597,343.67-	10.40+	541,027.98-	8.44-	652,458.21-	10.40+	541,027.98-
048	BUILDINGS	11,791,341.12	0.00+	11,791,341.12	9.09+	12,970,475.23	0.00+	11,791,341.12
049	RESRV-BUILDINGS	3,241,609.77-	10.44+	2,934,919.67-	8.45-	3,541,135.32-	10.44+	2,934,919.67-
052	BLDG.IMPROVMNTS	1,166,477.39	7.91+	1,080,914.03	8.56-	1,275,676.55	7.91+	1,080,914.03
053	RESV-BLDG.IMPRV	337,150.33-	49.91+	224,901.83-	6.78-	361,701.85-	49.91+	224,901.83-
056	LEASEHOLD IMPRV	689,283.48	20.68+	571,120.67	8.37-	750,313.02	20.68+	571,120.67
057	RESV-LSHOLD IMP	412,916.81-	23.92+	333,196.95-	7.74-	447,558.68-	23.92+	333,196.95-

REPORT NO. GL11CAAG-1   GENERAL LEDGER AUDIT PACKAGE   PAGE NO. 3
REPORT DATE 08/27/81   UNITED METHODS, INC.   PERIOD ENDED 12/31/80

CO. NUM: 020 DESCRIPT: UNITED METH.INC CHANGE BY FINANCIAL LINE NUMBER (FULL) SUB NUM:020 DESCRIPT: UNITED METHODS

- TOTALS -

RECORDS					
77	TOTAL PRINTED:				
	DEBIT	198,600,932.15	140,407,642.13	212,472,873.86	152,676,629.00
	CREDIT	385,446,640.43-	175,505,452.75-	410,082,981.71-	219,547,504.07-
8	NOT PRINTED:				
	DEBIT	0.00	0.00		0.00
	CREDIT	0.13-	21,730,312.00-	2,812.72-	0.00
85	GRAND TOTAL:				
	DEBIT	198,600,932.15	140,407,642.13	212,472,873.86	152,676,629.00
	CREDIT	305,446,640.56-	197,235,764.75-	410,085,794.43-	219,547,504.87-

REPORT NO. GL11CAAG-2   GENERAL LEDGER AUDIT PACKAGE   PAGE NO. 1
REPORT DATE 08/25/81   UNITED METHODS, INC.   PERIOD ENDED 12/31/80

CO. NUM: 020 DESCRIPT:UNITED METH.INC CHANGE BY FINANCIAL LINE NUMBER (BUDGET) SUB NUM:020 DESCRIPT: UNITED METHODS

LIN NUM	DESCRIPTION	CURRENT BALANCE	BUDGET	DIFFERENCE	PERCEN CHANGE
001	CASH IN BANK	3,238,468.48	5,646,831.61	2,408,363.13-	42.64-
002	CASH ON HAND	8,550.00	13,548.80	4,998.80-	36.89-
007	ACCT.REC.-OTHER	167,842.19	840,926.40	673,084.21-	80.04-
010	NOTES RECEIVABL	1,772,369.00	12,211,368.53	10,439,999.53-	85.49-
030	PREPAID INS.	82,659.70	346,457.64	263,797.94-	76.14-
032	PREPAID ROYLTS.	450,701.44	803,984.52	353,283.08-	43.94-
033	PREPD.FIN.CHGS.	75.70	83.27	7.57-	9.09-
034	PREPD.ADVACATLG	79,995.40	330,863.39	250,867.99-	75.82-
037	SUSPENSE	16,538.55	248,090.63	231,552.09-	93.33-
038	PREPAID OTHER	34,885.88	92,990.19	58,104.31-	62.49-
040	LAND	884,521.85	972,974.03	88,452.18-	9.09-
044	LAND IMPROVMNTS	906,471.02	1,027,985.81	121,514.79-	11.82-
045	RESV-LAND IMPRV	541,027.98-	652,458.21-	111,430.23	17.07-
048	BUILDINGS	11,791,341.12	12,970,475.23	1,179,134.11-	9.09-
049	RESRV-BUILDINGS	2,934,919.67-	3,541,135.32-	606,215.65	17.11-
052	BLDG.IMPROVMNTS	1,080,914.03	1,275,676.55	194,762.52-	15.26-
053	RESV-BLDG.IMPRV	224,901.83-	361,701.85-	136,800.02	37.82-
056	LEASEHOLD IMPRV	571,120.67	750,313.02	181,192.35-	24.08-

REPORT NO. GL11CAAG-2   GENERAL LEDGER AUDIT PACKAGE   PAGE NO. 22
REPORT DATE 08/25/81   UNITED METHODS, INC.   PERIOD ENDED 12/31/80

- GRAND TOTALS -

RECORDS				
252	TOTAL PRINTED:			
	DEBIT	664,670,081.60	630,587,296.41	483,768,805.41
	CREDIT	664,670,081.60-	591,360,416.0-	522,935,765.78-
68	NOT PRINTED:			
	DEBIT	0.00	123,774,154.27	163,001,034.64
	CREDIT	0.00	163,001,034.64-	123,774,154.27-
320	GRAND TOTAL:			
	DEBIT	664,670,081.60	754,361,453.68	646,769,920.05
	CREDIT	664,670,081.60-	754,361,450.68-	646,769,920.05-

FIG. 15-9 Change by financial line number (full or limited) report

REPORT NO. GL09CAAG-1   GENERAL LEDGER AUDIT PACKAGE   PAGE NO.   2
REPORT DATE 08/10/81   UNITED METHODS, INC.   PERIOD ENDED 12/31/80
                                 JOURNAL ENTRY SELECTION
CO. SUB   ACCOUNT   J.E. J.E. J.E. EFFECT   DESCRIPTION   AMOUNT   REASON
NUM NUM   NUM   NUM   TYPE DATE DATE

060 060 001-30 -   **601 MTILE 093030 093030   CASH RECTS + DISBR   1.353.691.11 ALL SUBSID
060 060 001-30 -   **601 MTILE 093030 093030   CASH RECTS + DISBR   1.540.253.95-
060 060 001-31 -   **601 MTILE 093030 093030   CASH RECTS + DISBR   206.601.91
063 060 007-03 -   **601 MTILE 093030 093030   CASH RECTS + DISBR   51.854.34-
060 060 005-09 -   **601 MTILE 093030 093030   CASH RECTS + DISBR   573.774.94-
060 060 005-09 -   **601 MTILE 093030 093030   CASH RECTS + DISBR   250.000.00
060 060 035-15 -   **601 MTILE 093030 093030   CASH RECTS + DISBR   664.249.19-
060 050 201-000-00000 **601 MTILE 093030 093030   CASH RECTS + DISBR   15.709.29-
060 060 608-112-00000 **601 MTILE 093030 093030   CASH RECTS + DISBR   411.012.44
060 060 901-939-00000 **601 MTILE 093030 093030   CASH RECTS + DISBR   5.034.64
060 060 901-959-01000 **601 MTILE 093030 093030   CASH RECTS + DISBR   73.93
060 060 901-959-01000 **601 MTILE 093030 093030   CASH RECTS + DISBR   1.012.09
060 060 901-959-01000 **601 MTILE 093030 093030   CASH RECTS + DISBR   4.05
060 060 909-079-01000 **601 MTILE 093030 093030   CASH RECTS + DISBR   1.916.65
060 060 909-249-01000 **601 MTILE 093030 093030   CASH RECTS + DISBR   16.879.50
          TOTAL JOURNAL ENTRY DEBIT =   2.846.366.29   CREDIT =   2.846.366.29-

060 060 001-31 -   **602 MTILE 093030 093030   LONDON OFFICE ACTVY   223.009.90- ALL SUBSID
060 060 007-00 -   **602 MTILE 093030 093030   LONDON OFFICE ACTVY   165.80
060 060 007-99 -   **602 MTILE 093030 093030   LONDON OFFICE ACTVY   3.917.15-
060 060 035-01 -   **602 MTILE 093030 093030   LONDON OFFICE ACTVY   101.97.75

REPORT NO. GL09CAAG-1   GENERAL LEDGER AUDIT PACKAGE   PAGE NO.   6
REPORT DATE 08/10/81   UNITED METHODS, INC.   PERIOD ENDED 12/31/80
                                 JOURNAL ENTRY SELECTION
                                     - TOTALS -

          RECORDS ENTRIES   DEBIT   CREDIT   REASON
             0   0   0.00   0.00   BAD DATE
           124   26   8.502.969.80   8.502.969.80-   ALL SUBSID
           124   26   8.502.969.80   8.502.969.80-   TOTAL SELECTED
             0   0   0.00   0.00   NOT SELECTED
           124   26   8.502.969.80   8.502.969.80-   FILE TOTAL

             0   0   0.00   0.00   W0129 DIFFERING EFFECTIVE DATES
             0   0   0.00   0.00   W0130 DIFFERING TYPES
             0   0   0.00   0.00   W0131 NON-BALANCING ENTRIES

FIG. 15-10   Journal entry selection report

REPORT NO. GL11CAAG-3   GENERAL LEDGER AUDIT PACKAGE   PAGE NO.   1
REPORT DATE 08/27/81   UNITED METHODS, INC.   PERIOD ENDED 12/31/80

CO. NUM: 020 DESCRIPT: UNITED METH.INC   SUB NUM: 020 DESCRIPT: UNITED METHODS
                                          FIVE YEAR CHANGE REPORT
LIN DESCRIPTION   CURRENT   PERCEN   PRIOR   PERCEN   CURRENT   PERCEN   CURRENT   PERCEN   CURRENT
NUM   BALANCE   CHANGE   BEFORE CLOSE CHANGE   -3   CHANGE   -4   CHANGE   -5

001 CASH IN BANK   4.971.477.09 53.51+ 3.238.468.45 33.50- 4.872.047.54 3.10+ 4.722.903.23 4.30+ 4.524.044.15
002 CASH ON HAND   12.494.60 46.13+   8.550.00 30.10-   12.244.70 3.10+   11.869.87 4.30+   11.370.08
003 MARKETABLE SEC.   459.000.00- 0.00+   0.00 100.00-   479.220.00- 3.10+   444.550.00- 4.30+   444.990.00-
007 ACCT.REC.-OTHER   790.343.32 370.85+   167.842.19 78.30-   774.536.45 3.10+   750.826.15 4.30+   719.212.42
010 NOTES RECEIVABL 12.387.767.06 598.93+ 1.772.369.00 85.40- 12.140.011.71 3.10+ 11.768.378.70 4.30+ 11.272.666.02
026 INVENTORY-OTHER   0.00   0.00+   0.00   0.00+   0.00 0.00+   0.00 0.00+   0.00
030 PREPAID INS.   322.100.57 289.67+   82.659.73 73.80-   315.656.55 3.10+   305.995.54 4.30+   293.111.51
031 PREPAID INTRST.   0.00   0.00+   0.00   0.00+   0.00 0.00+   0.00 0.00+   0.00
032 PREPAID ROYLTS.   750.844.05 66.59+   450.701.44 38.70-   735.827.16 3.10+   713.301.84 4.30+   693.268.08
033 PREPD.FIN.CHGS.   75.70   0.00+   75.70   2.00+   74.18 3.10+   71.91 4.30+   68.88
034 PREPD.ADV&CATLG   307.483.74 284.37+   79.995.40 73.40-   301.334.06 3.10+   292.109.55 4.30+   279.810.20
035 PREPAID TAXES   0.00   0.00+   0.00   0.00+   0.00 0.00+   0.00 0.00+   0.00
036 PREPAID WAGES   120.957.85- 0.00+   16.538.55 92.40-   219.849.83 3.10+   213.119.74 4.30+   204.145.27
037 SUSPENSE   224.336.57 256.44+   34.885.88 16.00-   41.538.26 3.10+   40.266.68 4.30+   38.571.24
038 PREPAID OTHER   42.355.95 21.44+   34.885.88 16.00-   41.538.26 3.10+   40.266.68 4.30+   38.571.24
049 FURN.INSTL.COST   0.13- 0.00+   0.00 100.00-   0.13- 0.00+   0.12- 0.00+   0.11-
040 LAND   884.521.85   0.00+   884.521.85   2.00+   866.831.41 3.10+   840.295.75 4.30+   804.914.88
044 LAND IMPROVMNTS   936.439.29   3.31+   904.471.02   1.20-   917.750.68 3.10+   889.656.27 4.30+   852.197.06
045 RESV-LAND IMPRV   597.343.67- 10.40+   541.027.93- 7.50-   555.374.79- 3.10+   567.476.48- 4.30+   543.582.73-
048 BUILDINGS   11.791.341.12 0.00+ 11.791.341.12 2.00+ 11.555.514.29 3.10+ 11.201.774.06 4.30+ 10.730.120.41

REPORT NO. GL11CAAG-3   GENERAL LEDGER AUDIT PACKAGE   PAGE NO.   3
REPORT DATE 08/27/81   UNITED METHODS, INC.   PERIOD ENDED 12/31/80

CO. NUM: 020 DESCRIPT: UNITED METH.INC   FIVE YEAR CHANGE REPORT   SUB NUM: 020 DESCRIPT: UNITED METHODS

                                          - TOTALS -

RECORDS
   42   DEBIT   198.600.932.15   140.407.642.13   194.628.913.74   188.670.885.69   180.726.848.42
   43   CREDIT 385.446.640.56-   197.235.764.75-   377.737.707.59-   366.174.308.35-   350.756.442.69-

FIG. 15-11   Five-year change report

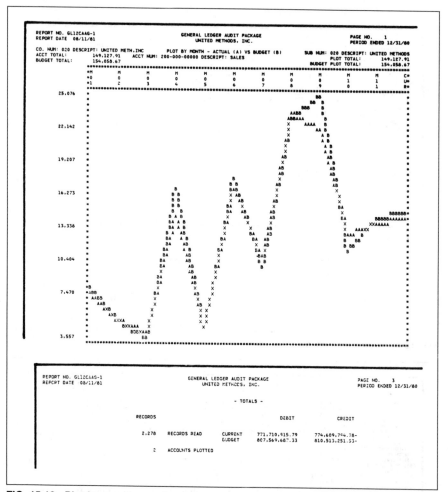

FIG. 15-12   Plot by month report

Capabilities and Limitations

Where substantive testing has been performed prior to year-end, the auditor is usually obliged to perform an examination of the transactions between the early test date and balance sheet dates. The component analysis of each account, as performed by a general ledger audit software package, provides the auditor with the raw data for this task.

The component analysis, fluctuation analysis, and ratio capabilities of the software package can, however, be related to a particular auditing procedure.

REPORT NO. GL16CAAG-2
REPORT DATE 08/26/81

GENERAL LEDGER AUDIT PACKAGE
UNITED METHODS, INC.

PAGE NO. 1
PERIOD ENDING 12/31/80

VERTICAL CONSOLIDATION

	CURRENT PERIOD	PRIOR PERIOD
001 CASH IN BANK		
020 UNITED METH,INC		
020 UNITED METHODS	4,971,477.09	3,238,468.48
TOTAL COMPANY	4,971,477.09	3,238,463.48
050 UNITED COMM,INC		
050 UNITED COMM,INC	404,804.88	259,102.00-
TOTAL COMPANY	404,804.88	259,102.00-
060 UNITED METH.INT		
060 UNITED METH.INT	618,604.89	103,967.39
TOTAL COMPANY	618,604.89	103,967.39
- SUBTOTAL -	5,994,885.86	3,033,333.87
TOTAL FINANCIAL LINE	5,994,886.86	3,083,333.87
002 CASH ON HAND		
020 UNITED METH,INC		
020 UNITED METHODS	12,494.60	8,550.00
TOTAL COMPANY	12,494.60	8,550.00
060 UNITED METH.INT		
060 UNITED METH.INT	558.00	558.00
TOTAL COMPANY	558.00	558.00
- SUBTOTAL -	13,052.60	9,108.00
TOTAL FINANCIAL LINE	13,052.60	9,108.00
003 MARKETABLE SEC.		
020 UNITED METH,INC		
020 UNITED METHODS	489,000.00-	0.00
TOTAL COMPANY	489,000.00-	0.00
- SUBTOTAL -	439,000.00-	0.00
TOTAL FINANCIAL LINE	489,000.00-	0.00

REPORT NO. GL16CAAG-2
REPORT DATE 08/26/81

GENERAL LEDGER AUDIT PACKAGE
UNITED METHODS, INC.

PAGE NO. 26
PERIOD ENDING 12/31/80

VERTICAL CONSOLIDATION
- TOTALS -

RECORDS		--- CURRENT PERIOD ---		--- PRIOR PERIOD ---	
		DEBIT	CREDIT	DEBIT	CREDIT
258	020 UNITED METH,INC	666,286,327.32	666,286,327.32-	571,843,299.41	571,843,299.41-
24	050 UNITED COMM,INC	9,793,738.48	9,798,738.48-	47,979,264.01	47,979,264.01-
39	060 UNITED METH.INT	44,209,730.22	44,209,730.22-	44,647,518.18	44,847,518.18-
321	ALL COMPANIES	720,294,796.02	720,294,796.02-	664,670,081.60	664,670,081.60-
85	020 UNITED METHODS	198,600,932.15	385,446,640.56-	140,407,642.13	197,235,764.75-
24	021 UNITED COMM,INC	9,798,738.48	9,798,738.48-	47,979,264.01	47,979,264.01-
39	022 UNITED METH.INT	44,209,730.22	44,209,730.22-	44,847,518.18	44,847,518.18-
52	023 NUTS DIVISION	323,481,199.14	131,136,740.98-	379,087,931.11	322,101,729.39-
22	024 N.E.M.S.	22,410,048.99	14,269,348.64-	22,529,132.76	18,620,509.72-
18	025 MILLING DIV.	0.00	0.00	126,722.49	87,399.41-
2	026 LATHE DIVISION	0.00	0.00	0.00	0.00
27	027 EDUCATIONAL DIV	3,930,581.36	4,211,473.64-	7,944,296.90	8,469,163.40-
28	050 BOLT DIVISION	12,535,744.01	14,533,691.67-	21,747,574.02	25,328,732.74-
24	060 U.M.ELECTR. DIV	105,327,821.67	116,688,431.63-	0.00	0.00
321	ALL SUBSIDIARIES	720,294,796.02	720,294,796.02-	664,670,081.60	664,670,081.60-
14	CONSOLIDATING JES	39,974,000.13	39,974,000.13-		
335	GRAND TOTAL	760,268,796.15	760,268,796.15-	664,670,081.60	664,670,081.60-

FIG. 15-13 Vertical consolidation report

This procedure is determined as follows:

- All significant items of income and expense have been recorded.
- Costs and expenses have been appropriately matched with income or the net income for the year, and the items of income and expense that are disclosed in the income statement are fairly stated.
- All items of income and expense necessary to give a proper understanding of the operating results have been identified, and all required disclosures have been made.

```
REPORT NO. GL05CAAG-1                                                                    PAGE NO.   1
REPORT DATE 07/30/81            UNITED METHODS, INC.                            PERIOD ENDED  12/31/80

       COMPANY NO 020 DESCRIPTION UNITED METH.INC       TRIAL BALANCE    SUBSIDIARY NO 020 DESCRIPTION UNITED METHODS
  ACCOUNT         DESCRIPTION         FIN    LINE         CURRENT            PRIOR          PRIOR          BUDGET
  NUMBER                              LIN  DESCRIPTION    BALANCE        BEFORE CLOSE    AFTER CLOSE

 001-01   CASH-NEWARK BANK            001 CASH IN BANK     121,163.11        83,425.29-      83,425.29-     159,505.14-
 001-02   CASH-FIRST BANK-REGULAR     001 CASH IN BANK   1,168,473.94     1,289,169.35    1,289,169.35   1,464,312.81
 001-03   CASH-FIRST BANK-PAYROLL     001 CASH IN BANK       5,000.00        5,000.00        5,000.00      18,528.29-
 001-04   CASH-CONN BANK-FREIGHT      001 CASH IN BANK      61,506.48      171,798.13-     171,798.18-     98,234.72
 001-05   CASH-CHASE MANHATTAN        031 CASH IN BANK   1,652,695.61      768,339.53      768,339.53   1,947,108.70
 001-06   CASH-CONTINENTAL ILLINOIS   001 CASH IN BANK      40,999.99        2,833.33        2,833.33      44,237.85
 001-07   CASH-FIRST NATIONAL CITY    001 CASH IN BANK   1,574,557.12    1,247,697.74    1,247,697.74   1,866,617.69
 001-08   CASH-N E MERCHANTS          001 CASH IN BANK     327,107.12      155,457.03      155,457.03     344,593.36
 001-14   CASH-CHASE-AG MUNICH        001 CASH IN BANK      15,026.04       11,769.38       11,789.38      16,707.31
 001-15   CASH-CONT ILL-MUNICH        001 CASH IN BANK      15,970.98       10,227.43       10,227.48      15,273.74
 001-16   CASH-CONT ILL-LONDON        001 CASH IN BANK       2,528.57        1,656.95        1,656.95       2,870.67
 001-17   FIRST BANK-NE-NJC/VISA      001 CASH IN BANK      11,139.66        6,163.87        6,163.87      11,559.08
 001-18   CASH-CITIBANK FRANKFORT     001 CASH IN BANK         590.36            0.00            0.00         644.95
 001-98   TRAVELETTER CLEARING        001 CASH IN BANK       5,412.89-       4,692.76-       4,692.76-      7,810.67-
 001-99   CASH-INTERBANK TRANSFER     001 CASH IN BANK           0.00            0.00            0.00           0.00
 002-01   CASH-OFFICE-E WASHINGTON    002 CASH ON HAND       5,000.00        5,000.00        5,000.00       5,500.00
 002-02   CASH-OFFICE-BAYSTATE        032 CASH ON HAND       4,607.50        2,000.00        2,000.00       4,997.65
 002-03   CASH OFFICE-DALLAS          002 CASH ON HAND          50.00           50.00           50.00          55.00
 002-04   CASH-EXPEDITING-E LONG      002 CASH ON HAND         200.00          200.00          200.00         220.00
 002-05   CASH-OFFICE-FEDERAL SQ      002 CASH ON HAND         351.85            0.00            0.00         349.38
 002-06   CASH-OFFICE-NY-NUTS/SOLE    002 CASH ON HAND       1,000.00        1,000.00        1,000.00       1,100.00
 002-07   CASH-OFFICE-FALL RIVER      002 CASH ON HAND         703.74            0.00            0.00         713.80
 002-03   CASH-MAINT-E WASHINGTON     032 CASH ON HAND         581.53          300.00          300.00         587.52
 002-99   CASH-CHECKS EXCHANGED       002 CASH ON HAND           0.00            0.00            0.00          25.45
 003-00   MARKETABLE SECURITIES       003 MARKETABLE SEC     489,000.00-          0.00            0.00   2,177,814.72-
```

```
REPORT NO. GL05CAAG-1                                                                    PAGE NO.   49
REPORT DATE 07/30/81            UNITED METHODS, INC.                            PERIOD ENDED  12/31/80

       COMPANY NO 020 DESCRIPTION UNITED METH.INC       TRIAL BALANCE    SUBSIDIARY NO 027 DESCRIPTION U.M.ELECTR. DIV
  ACCOUNT         DESCRIPTION         FIN    LINE         CURRENT            PRIOR          PRIOR          BUDGET
  NUMBER                              LIN  DESCRIPTION    BALANCE        BEFORE CLOSE    AFTER CLOSE

901-959-92000 REBILLED EXPENSES       901 G&A-COMMON EXP       0.00            0.00            0.00           0.00
901-989-92000 MISCELLANEOUS           901 G&A-COMMON EXP   7,342.69            0.00            0.00       7,596.95
901-999-92000 ALLOCATION              901 G&A-COMMON EXP  212,365.46-           0.00            0.00     234,496.07-
909-039-91000 BAD DEBTS               909 G&A-UNIQUE EXP  672,315.17            0.00            0.00     707,812.12
909-119-91000 PUBLICITY & GOODWILL    909 G&A-UNIQUE EXP     297.55            0.00            0.00         319.85
909-129-91000 MANAGEMENT FEE          909 G&A-UNIQUE EXP 3,013,765.16           0.00            0.00   3,067,443.61
909-269-91000 EMPLOYMENT-ADVERTISING  909 G&A-UNIQUE EXP  30,478.88            0.00            0.00      29,814.73
909-389-91000 DIVISIONAL MANAGEMENT FEE 909 G&A-UNIQUE EXP 735,909.98          0.00            0.00     743,878.09
929-129-91000 INT - NUTS DIVISION     929 NON-OPER.EXP&S 11,313,874.09          0.00            0.00   1,337,325.46
939-019-91000 PROVISION-CURRENT       939 FED. INCOME TA 11,360,643.77          0.00            0.00  11,783,918.04
939-019       *** SUB-TOTAL ***                          11,360,609.96-          0.00            0.00  11,733,833.08-

   SUBSIDIARY    TOTAL    RECORDS =    202         DEBIT   106,655,337.61         0.00            0.00  109,591,317.88
                                                  CREDIT   118,015,947.57-        0.00            0.00  121,375,156.96-

   COMPANY       TOTAL    RECORDS =  2,120         DEBIT   720,107,037.11   592,874,771.93  220,414,220.47  752,477,452.32
                                                  CREDIT   720,107,037.11-  592,874,771.93-  220,414,220.47-  752,477,452.32-
```

FIG. 15-14 Trial balance

Although the software package assists the auditor by automating many of the tasks associated with general ledger auditing, there is usually additional audit work that is outside the scope of the package.

The C&L general ledger audit software is not designed to be run in its entirety each time it is used. There are several distinct phases, each of which may be used alone or in combination with other phases, in a particular situation. Some phases, such as the component analysis, may be run only once; others, such as the trial balance production, can be run as many times as required during the audit period. These phases include:

- Input file verification and analysis
- Trial balance production
- Component analysis for financial line or account
- Selection of journal entries and reperformance of posting

FIG. 15-15 Trial balance work sheet

It is, therefore, particularly important for the auditor to understand the capabilities of a general ledger audit software package before using it.

The following descriptions of the package and the reports it produces will help provide an auditor with an understanding of the kinds of tasks that can be automated by using software. Additional information is also given to aid the auditor in becoming aware of options and reports that can be selected.

Audit Procedures

Using C&L general ledger audit software, the following audit tasks can be accomplished. The names of reports generated are shown in parentheses.

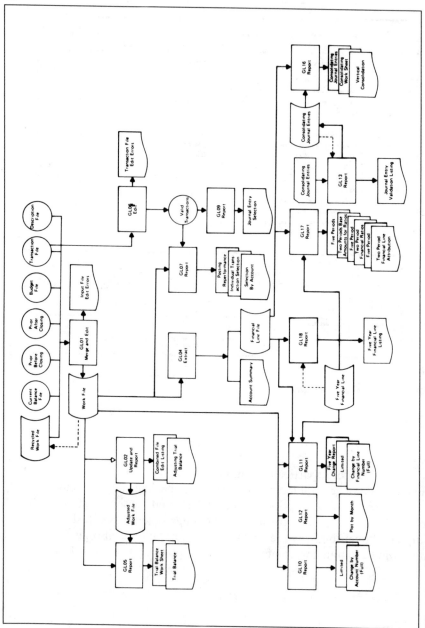

FIG. 15-16   General ledger audit software processing flowchart

Audit Procedures	*Package Capabilities*
Review of general ledger trial balance	
Determine that the general ledger trial balance contains all necessary accounts.	• Provide a comparative trial balance showing current, prior, and budget figures (Trial Balance).
Determine that all of the accounts in the general ledger trial balance are valid.	• Provide a comparative trial balance showing current, prior, and budget figures (Trial Balance).
	• Select transactions from the cumulative transaction file on the basis of their deviation from a predefined norm or on a random basis for manual follow-up (Individual Transaction Selection).
Determine that all necessary entries, reclassifications, or adjustments are reflected in the trial balance, and that all necessary consolidating journal entries are reflected in the consolidated balances.	• Prepare a trial balance showing current figures with columns for auditor's adjustments (Trial Balance Work Sheet).
	• Provide a mechanism for the auditor to adjust the trial balance amounts and produce a new trial balance. This process can be performed many times (Adjusting Trial Balance).
	• Prepare a schedule of all transactions making up an account balance (Selection by Account).
	• Select transactions from the cumulative transaction file on the basis of their deviation from a predefined norm or on a random basis for manual follow-up (Individual Transaction Selection).

Audit Procedures	*Package Capabilities*
Review of general ledger trial balance *(cont'd)*	• Provide a mechanism for the auditor to process consolidating journal entries to the financial lines and produce either a vertical consolidation or a traditional horizontal worksheet. This process can be performed many times.
Determine that all entries in the general ledger are proper and valid.	• Prepare a trial balance showing current figures with columns for auditor's adjustments (Trial Balance Work Sheet).
	• Provide a mechanism for the auditor to adjust the trial balance amounts and produce a new trial balance. This process can be performed many times (Adjusting Trial Balance).
	• Prepare a schedule of all transactions making up an account balance (Selection by Account).
	• Select transactions from the cumulative transaction file on the basis of their deviation from a predefined norm or on a random basis for manual follow-up (Individual Transaction Selection).
	• Ensure that, in a multiple company file, the component debits and credits of each journal entry stay within one company (Journal Entry Selection).
	• Ensure that within journal entries the effective dates of application of transactions are identical for all transactions (Journal Entry Selection).
	• Ensure that all journal entries balance to zero (Journal Entry Selection).

Audit Procedures	*Package Capabilities*
Review of general ledger trial balance *(cont'd)*	• Provide for selection of total journal entries based either on their total magnitude, or on some exceptional characteristic applicable to the entire journal entry (Journal Entry Selection).
Determine that the classifications of accounts are proper and consistent with prior years.	• Analyze the input files for consistency and accuracy of information (Input File Edit Errors). • List new accounts (new; not on old file) (Combined File Edit Listing). • Provide a comparative trial balance showing current prior and budget figures (Trial Balance). • Prepare a schedule of all transactions making up an account balance (Selection by Account). • Select transactions from the cumulative transaction file on the basis of their deviation from a predefined norm or on a random basis for manual follow-up (Individual Transaction Selection). • Compare account totals for current period, prior period, and budget for selected accounts; provide differences between periods in both amount and percentage (Change by Account Number).
Determine that the general ledger and the trial balance are mathematically accurate.	• List abnormal account conditions, such as bad footings within records (Combined File Edit Listing). • Verify the mathematical accuracy of the general ledger trial balance (all reports, but in particular Trial Balance).

Audit Procedures	*Package Capabilities*

Review of financial statements (external auditor)

Identify areas that, as a result of unusual activity, unexpected fluctuations, or ratios, appear to involve a higher audit risk and therefore warrant detailed validation.

Determine that the financial statements contain all of the proper accounts.

- Provide a mechanism to attribute a financial statement line number to each account for financial line correspondence (Input File Edit Errors).
- Summarize accounts into a financial line and provide the lead schedule showing each account with the comparative prior year for figures (Account Summary).
- Compare financial line totals between current, prior, and budget; provide difference between amounts in dollar value and percentage (Change by Financial Line).

Determine that the accounts listed on the financial statements are valid and properly classified.

- Provide a mechanism to attribute a financial statement line number to each account for financial line correspondence (Input File Edit Errors).
- Summarize accounts into a financial line and provide the lead schedule showing each with the comparative prior-year figures for financial line analysis (Account by Summary).
- Select transactions from the cumulative transaction file on the basis of their deviation from a predefined norm or on a random basis for manual follow-up (Individual Transaction Selection).

Audit Procedures	*Package Capabilities*
Review of financial statements (external auditor) *(cont'd)*	• Compare financial line totals between current period, prior period, and budget; provide difference between amounts in dollar value and percentage (Change by Financial Line Number).
	• Calculate the 24 ratios commonly used for financial statement analysis for current period, prior period, and budget (Two-Period Financial Ratios).
Determine that the grouping of accounts included in the financial statements is proper and consistent with prior years. Furthermore, an important part of "analytical review" is to determine those areas of audit risk by identifying large or unusual activity in particular areas.	• Summarize accounts into a financial line and provide the lead schedule showing each amount with comparative prior-year figures for financial line analysis (Account Summary).
	• Select transactions from the cumulative transaction file on the basis of their deviation from a predefined norm or on a random basis for manual follow-up (Individual Transaction Selection).
	• Compare financial line totals between current period, prior period and budget; provide difference between amounts in dollar value and percentage (Change by Financial Line Number).
	• Calculate the ending balance for each financial line amount for five-year period showing movement between each period in percentage (Five-Year Change Report).

Audit Procedures	*Package Capabilities*
Review of financial statements (external auditor) *(cont'd)*	• Calculate the 24 commonly used ratios for financial statement analysis for current period, prior period, and budget (Two-Period Financial Ratios). • Select accounts and plot movement in graphic form with comparative budget amounts (Plot by Month). • Summarize financial line amounts in the base amounts used for calculating the ratios (Five-Period Financial Line Attribution).
Determine that consolidated journal entries are correctly processed and that the consolidating process is accurate and proper (both internal and external auditors).	• Within a multicompany or multisubsidiary file, summarize company and subsidiary amounts by financial line to provide a traditional horizontal consolidation worksheet (Consolidation Work Sheet). • Within a multicompany or multisubsidiary file, summarize all accounts by financial line to produce a vertical consolidation (Vertical Consolidation).
Additional audit information	• Provide totals of each amount used within the ratio calculations for subsequent analysis. Reference information required if any ratios need more detailed analysis (Five-Period Base Amount for Ratios).

Audit Program — Sequence of Events

The effective use of the C&L general ledger audit software package requires cooperation between the non-EDP auditor and the EDP auditor. An EDP auditor who knows the software can explain the package capabilities and can implement and execute the package. However, as usual, the auditor has overall responsibility for analyzing results and properly performing the audit tests.

This section describes the use of the C&L package. Because the events involved in using the package vary depending on the extent and timing of the auditor's substantive tests, an assumption has been made for convenience that a substantive audit approach has been adopted and that early testing is not being performed. The title of each report is listed as an event to show relative timing of procedures.

Events	*Auditor's Actions*
Planning	• Develop audit plan and budget.
	• Collect the information concerning the general ledger system. Prepare planning working papers.
	• Determine desired report options and prepare the appropriate parameters (e.g., validation date, five-year comparison option).
	• Create reports within the time requirements. Keep audit staff informed as to progress and any reasons for additional time.
	• Finalize the following:
	a. Audit date.
	b. Exception profile applicable to the edit report.
	c. Any other information needed in respect to those phases of the package to be executed. (This package has numerous options available for the auditor to specify.)
	• Before the due date, install the package, execute the edit program, and review the results for exceptions.

PHASE 1 — INPUT FILE VERIFICATION AND ANALYSIS (RECOMMENDED)

Reports	
Input File Edit Errors	• Ascertain relevant general ledger details.
Combined File Edit Listing	• Edit the general ledger files, agree the totals, and create reports.
Transaction File Edit Errors	

Events	*Auditor's Actions*
Audit review	• Review any error messages to determine significance and corrections.
	• Review new accounts and old accounts that existed in prior periods for reasonableness or for justification.

PHASE 2 — REPERFORMANCE OF THE TRIAL BALANCE PRODUCTION (OPTIONAL)

Reports

Trial Balance	• If the trial balance does not have comparative figures, produce the reports prior to starting the audit.
Trial Balance Work Sheet	• If adjusting journal entries are required, prepare entries.
Adjusting Trial Balance	• Prepare reports and agree the totals.
Audit review	• Agree totals and selected details to the trial balance. Use reports as a basis for audit tests including the general ledger. Identify unusual accounts for later extraction for audit review.

PHASE 2A — TRIAL BALANCE PRODUCTION (RERUN) (REITERATED AS REQUIRED)

Reports

Adjusting Trial Balance	• Discover any adjusting journal entries required as a result of audit tests.
Trial Balance	• Prepare reports and agree the totals.

PHASE 3 — COMPONENT ANALYSIS FOR FINANCIAL LINE OR ACCOUNT (OPTIONAL)

Reports

Selection by Account	• Review the accounts that require details of all the period's transactions.
Account Summary	• Prepare reports and agree the totals.
Audit review	• Agree the totals and selected details to the trial balance. Review for unusual account classification. Identify unusual variations from budget for further follow-up. Use reports as lead schedules.

Events	*Auditor's Actions*
Audit review *(cont'd)*	• Use information for detailed audit tests, including checking to source documentation.

PHASE 3A — COMPONENT ANALYSIS FOR FINANCIAL LINES (RERUN)

Report	
Account Summary	• If adjusting journal entries have been processed as a result of Phase 2, request rerun of this report.
	• Prepare reports and agree the totals.
Audit review	• Ensure all journal entries appear to be taken up in final lead schedules.

PHASE 4 — SELECTION OF JOURNAL ENTRIES AND REPERFORMANCE OF POSTING (OPTIONAL)

Reports	
Selection by Account	• Choose dates and accounts for selection.
	• Prepare report and agree the totals.
Individual Transaction Selection	• If auditor prefers selection by transaction, decide characteristics of transactions to be selected, and whether transactions are to be selected using a random start and interval sampling.
Posting Reperformance	• Select dates and accounts for reperformance posting.
Journal Entry Selection	• Select characteristics for journal entry and decide whether journal entries are to be selected using a random start and interval sampling.
Audit review	• Review any posting errors to determine significance and corrections. Use information in detailed audit tests of transactions.

PHASE 5 — FLUCTUATION ANALYSIS (OPTIONAL)

Reports	
Change by Account Number (Full or Limited)	• Make the special selection criteria for comparing accounts: Current-period balance to prior periods or current-period balance to budget (monetary or percentage).

Events	*Auditor's Actions*
Reports *(cont'd)*	• Prepare report and agree the totals.
Change by Financial Number (Full or Limited)	• Formulate special selection criteria for comparing financial lines: Current-period balance to prior periods or current-period balance to budget (monetary or percentage).
Five-Year Change Report	• Decide that the five-year comparison report is to be produced.
Plot by Month	• Choose accounts or ranges of accounts to be plotted. If no accounts are specified, then all financial lines will be plotted.
Audit review	• Use reports as basis of analytical review procedures to identify those areas requiring detailed audit tests.

PHASE 6 — RATIOS FOR FINANCIAL STATEMENT ANALYSIS
            (OPTIONAL)

Reports

Two periods

Financial Line Attribution	• Obtain any extra information required for report production.
Financial Ratios	• Prepare reports and agree the totals.
Base Amounts for Ratio Calculations	

Five periods

Financial Line Attribution (Five Years)	• Obtain any extra information required for report production (e.g., extract years for producing five-year reports).
Financial Ratios (Five Years)	
Base Amounts for Ratio Calculations (Five Years)	
Audit review	• Use reports as part of analytical review procedures to determine areas for detailed audit test and investigation.

Events	*Auditor's Actions*
Audit review *(cont'd)*	• Review financial line attributions and base amounts used to produce ratios. Review ratios for trends and unusual changes. Where necessary, specify individual transactions for follow-up.

PHASE 7 — CONSOLIDATIONS (REITERATED AS REQUIRED)

Reports	• Prepare consolidating journal entries needed.
	• Arrange for journal entries to be key entered, prepare report. Assist in determining significance of error messages.
Consolidating Journal Entries	• Resolve any journal entries not properly processed.
Vertical Consolidation	• Prepare report and agree the totals.
Consolidation Work Sheet	
Audit review	• Agree or reconcile to the organization's totals. Review for reasonableness and possibly omitted eliminations. Use consolidation report in preparing consolidated financial statements.

PHASE 8 — CONSTRUCTION (OPTIONAL)

Reports	
Five-Year Financial Line Listing	• Provide information for combining prior periods with current-period data to create five-year data.
	• Input the prior year's file to construct a new updated five-year financial line file.
	• Prepare report and agree the totals.
	• Check report to ensure that data appears to be correct. Give clearance for data to be filed for next year's use.

COMPLETION

	• Provide brief written comments on use of package (e.g., effect on audit, user acceptance, ease of use, suggested enhancements, staff evaluation).

Events	*Auditor's Actions*
Reports *(cont'd)*	• Summarize time, costs, and expenses. Document any reasons for changes from original budget, provide suggestions for the coming audit year.

OPERATIONAL CONSIDERATIONS

The C&L general ledger audit software package consists of many separate programs designed to provide an easy-to-use tool to assist in auditing a computerized general ledger. The programs are written in COBOL and are often used in an IBM environment. The package can be used in the organization's EDP environment or at a service bureau.

Total Transaction System

Automated general ledgers generally fall within the range between a total transaction system and a master file balance-forward system. A total transaction system is one where each transaction is added to a cumulative file that is kept for a period of time. Each journal entry is made up of multiple transactions, since under this system it is necessary to add up all transactions on the file to determine an account balance at any point in time. The opening balance at the beginning of the period is usually shown as a dummy transaction. Some systems maintain only the transactions for the current month, and all prior transactions are summarized into one brought-forward entry. This type of system may be modified to create a separate file containing account numbers, descriptions, and budget amounts.

Master File Balance-Forward

In a master file balance-forward system, one record is kept for each account, and this record is updated by any transactions that occur during the period. In most such systems, a total by month of all transactions is kept within the record for a minimum of 12 months and often for up to five years. Transactions are applied to each account (record) as their effective date falls due. These transactions are archived to a historical file either on a cumulative or monthly basis. The C&L General Ledger Audit Software package was built to correspond to this widely used technique. (IBM, MSA, Software International, and Informatics have all adopted a master file concept.)

Journal Entries

Regardless of the method used to maintain an account balance, there are differences in the way in which journal entries originate, depending on the computerization of the system. In the highly developed data processing system, movements in the subsidiary applications, such as sales, accounts payable, and inventory, may result in automatic journal entries at month-end that summarize the movement for the period and debit and credit the correct accounts. Journal entries that do not originate in an automated system may be of two types: (1) a standing journal entry or (2) an adjusting journal entry. Standing journal entries typically relate to such items as depreciation and are set up either as a semiautomated procedure or as their effective date falls due. Adjusting journal entries are prepared manually and generally relate to the correction of errors and year-end movements. In a more basic EDP system, all journal entries may be manually prepared and entered. The characteristics of a particular general ledger system therefore affect the way in which the C&L general ledger audit software package is used.

IMPLEMENTING GENERAL LEDGER SYSTEMS

Auditors frequently participate in system development. (See Chapter 7, "The System Development Life Cycle.") The following is a sample of the kinds of questions an auditor may ask when assisting in the planning, design, selection, and implementation of a general ledger system. These questions can help the auditor to determine initial requirements for such a system.

GENERAL LEDGER SYSTEM

Location _____

1. How many ledgers (separate companies) do you have? _____
2. How many divisions/profit centers do you have on each ledger? _____
3. Are the following reports produced by divisions/profit centers?

	Yes	No
a. General Ledger	☐	☐
b. Trial Balance	☐	☐
c. Profit and Loss	☐	☐
d. Balance Sheet	☐	☐

4. If there is more than one ledger, are consolidated reports produced?
☐ Yes ☐ No

5. Is your accounting period other than monthly? ☐ Yes ☐ No
If yes, give details. _____

6. Do your fiscal year and calendar year coincide? ☐ Yes ☐ No
If no, give details. _____

7. Is a comparison of this year versus last year made?

	Yes	*No*
a. Month-to-date	☐	☐
b. Year-to-date	☐	☐

Does your consolidated report also reflect this? ☐ Yes ☐ No

8. Do you do budgeting on your income and expenses?
☐ Yes ☐ No
If so, is it a:

a. Monthly budget ☐

b. Quarterly budget ☐

c. Yearly budget ☐

9. What is the total number of accounts in your chart of accounts? (real and nominal accounts) _____

10. Do you have subaccount numbers to identify your profit center's operations? ☐ Yes ☐ No
If yes, how many? _____

11. How many of the account numbers indicated in Question 9 are affected by profit centers? (total number) _____

12. What is the length of your account number (taking into consideration subnumbers for profit centers)? _____

13. What is the approximate number of transactions? (sum total of transactions from different journals) _____

14. Are quarterly and yearly ledgers prepared? ☐ Yes ☐ No

15. Is there additional information that may be of use? _____
_____

CORPORATE REPORTING SYSTEMS

A corporation often needs a reporting system that will accumulate, retain, and consolidate large amounts of financial data. Ideally, management should have ready access to this information to enhance reporting and financial analysis. When a company has multiple locations but lacks an established automated communications network, it may be difficult to access data, in the desired format, on an accurate and timely basis.

System Flexibility

Coopers & Lybrand has developed a highly flexible, efficient, interactive system of programs (known as CLIFFORD), which performs financial data retention, consolidation, and reporting. The system is available through a time-sharing network, so financial data from subsidiaries in remote locations — either domestic or foreign — can easily be sent to the corporate financial center.

The system is described here to show how such systems can be adapted to a broad range of accounting and reporting functions. This particular one was designed with the knowledge that, although there is a great deal of similarity in general accounting functions, there can be a significant variation in the way they are performed in a particular business. The system easily accommodates the addition of data bases, consolidations, and reports to a CLIFFORD-based system, even after it is implemented for particular corporate requirements.

The user is able to record actual and/or budget information for up to 72 periods. The system can handle up to 3,000 financial accounts and statistical classifications per data base. Any number of reports can be generated at one time, and there is no limit on the number of units that can be consolidated. The user maintains total flexibility in designing reports, data base structure, and development of application systems.

Business Segment Reporting

In the corporate environment, systems such as this are especially useful where the organization must report financial data by business segment. It is possible to set up an actual and budget data base — containing income statement, balance sheet, cash flow, and statistical data — for each business segment.

The system can be used to

- Prepare monthly, quarterly, and annual financial reports.
- Perform multidivisional financial consolidations.
- Analyze financial data for trends, fluctuations, and exceptions.

- Develop short-range information and track performance against budget.
- Translate foreign subsidiary financial data into U.S. dollars (or any other currency).
- Prepare special-purpose financial analysis.

Used in conjunction with a complementary planning system, the system can be used to

- Prepare regular financial statements and management reports.
- Generate multidivisional consolidated statements for audit or tax purposes.
- Perform reviews of financial statements and detailed examination of selected components as a part of the external or the internal audit function.
- Prepare or validate forecasts, budgets, or any projections, and do comparative analysis with actual financial data.
- Perform multicompany/industry analysis in a financial analysis environment.
- Evaluate financial strategies, such as merger and acquisition, and project financing, comparing the consequences of different alternatives.
- Analyze a foreign currency exposure and related risks on a daily, weekly, or monthly basis, for multinational operations.
- Analyze commercial loan credit (for banking and other financial institutions).

Applications Modules

The system is composed of seven modules that interact to perform the various applications:

- The data base module creates the initial data base, updates it on a regular basis, changes various elements, and lists the data in various formats. There is no fixed account structure, so the system will accept any kind of financial or statistical data in any chart of accounts.
- Two reporting modules allow the user to specify format and contents for virtually any kind of financial and/or statistical report. Information drawn from any number of data bases may be combined and presented in tabular form.
- The consolidation module combines any number of data bases for purposes of financial consolidation. Multiple levels of consolidation

can be performed. Adjustments may be applied to accomplish the desired accounting consistency, and the consolidated data bases can then be used for reporting analysis or further consolidation.

- The foreign currency module translates any data base into another currency for reporting or consolidation purposes. Rates of exchange for 40 countries are available on an on-line data base.

- The planning module links with planning system and allows data to be selected from the data base for planning or budgeting, and projections to be transferred back into the data base.

- The file creation and plotting module permits information to be extracted from any data base and stored in files formatted according to requirements of other financial or statistical analysis programs available.

The Systems in Use

The financial reporting and consolidation system just described was implemented at a major transport corporation. The company collects approximately $5 billion annually in revenues, and contains numerous subsidiaries in the areas of air freight, forest management, forest products, oil and gas, coal and minerals, railroad land and real estate, trucking, and corporate financial services. These subsidiaries, located throughout the Midwest and the West, were linked through a time-sharing network, so each subsidiary was able to enter its own data directly.

The consolidation and reporting features enabled the user to produce business segment income statements with comparison to budget, business segment balance sheet reports, and several different levels of consolidated financial and operating reports.

The project was begun in late December and was completed in just a few weeks for a January closing. A two-day training course about the time-sharing and the reporting system was provided for employees from each business segment who were responsible for entering the information. A separate three-day training program on the use of the system was conducted for the analysts responsible for performing the consolidations and producing the reports. An operations manual was prepared specifically for users to enable them to run the system independently, although field support is available.

By using the time-sharing network and reporting system, the company has significantly reduced the time and effort required to produce management reports. They are now developing additional types of reports. For the first time, the organization has an efficient method for data collection, consolidation, and reporting without having to hire employees with programming experience.

Another example of effective use of the C&L general ledger audit software package is its application in a recent annual hospital audit. The audit task was complicated by the existence of nine separate major account groupings, embracing approximately 1,000 accounts and 1,000 account subgroupings. The problem was minimized by using the general ledger audit software package.

The package was used to facilitate the preparation of lead schedules. The following reports were generated:

- Input File Errors, which examines items that cannot be processed further due to irregularities
- Combined File Edit Listing, which reports any abnormal conditions detected after files have been combined
- Adjusting Trial Balance, which lists and edits accounts affected by the auditor's adjustments
- Account Summary, which summarizes (1) financial line information and (2) accounts comprising each financial line, that can be used as the auditor's lead schedules

In the past it had taken two weeks to prepare lead schedules during the course of an audit. When the programs were implemented, this phase of preparation took less than three days. Substantial time savings will increase as the programs continue to be used. Furthermore, the package was used to prepare consolidated statements required for a recent bond issue.

Since general ledger systems track all of an organization's transactions, they are particularly important to implement and control for the best possible results.

PART IV

Controls

CHAPTER *16*

Introduction to Controls

NATURE OF CONTROLS

Internal Control

Internal control refers to all the methods, policies, and procedures adopted within an organization to ensure the safeguarding of assets, the accuracy and reliability of management information and financial records, the promotion of administrative efficiency, and adherence to management standards.

Internal control deals with the processes and practices by which management attempts to ensure that approved and appropriate decisions and activities are made and carried out. These decisions and activities can be governed by external forces: federal regulation, professional ethics, and accounting standards. Internal factors also influence how controls may be implemented to assure management that their business operates the way they expect.

Internal control is also aimed at preventing officers, employees, and those external to an organization from engaging in prohibited and inappropriate activities. In this way, control provides the mechanism for preventing chaos, crisis management, and other abnormal events that interfere with the smooth running of an organization. Controls make organizational life easier when everyone learns how to make them work for the good of all. As with any standardized procedure, controls must be reviewed and maintained to be effective; when they are, controls work to business' benefit. They should not be so stifling that they make it hard to get anything done, but they cannot be so lax that nothing works well. Without proper controls, every decision becomes a guess.

Modern information systems, spurred by technological change, have undergone significant advances in recent years. As a result, traditional controls are often not applicable to new electronic data processing (EDP) methods.

To an extent, certain controls exist within the EDP department, but they are often particular to that department. The more mature the EDP department is within a business environment, the more likely it is that standard controls will have been implemented. But for EDP, as for most new departments, becoming operational takes priority over controlling the departments that are already operational.

The uncontrolled computer can have serious financial repercussions for an organization. It can also have a devastating effect on employee morale when the staff has to work long hours to recreate data that is destroyed or mangled because of a lack of control. Few things are more disheartening than having to do the same work over and over again. While most companies experience some problems created by computer support systems, an out-of-control system could ruin a business. It is not usually a one-time-only or big mistake that causes the greatest difficulties, but many related minor mistakes. Employees normally pitch in and help in a crisis, but they may not respond well to the day-to-day crisis management that an uncontrolled environment requires.

In one fast-growing computer company, orders for the product were pouring in faster than they could be processed. The division had done $5 million worth of business the year before. This year they had received so much publicity from one major sale that their orders had risen to $37 million. Employees put in long hours and went home exhausted, but pleased to be getting the work done. Although merchandise was going out the door at a rapid pace, customers were not paying on time. Billing was running almost two weeks behind shipping because of the overload. After running 24 hours a day, the computer broke down; it took two days to get it working again. At that point it was discovered that the data files had been destroyed in the breakdown and no one had taken the time to properly prepare backup files every day. The company had to return to the last month-end copies; the paperwork and processing delay put them a total of five weeks behind billing. Because customers were not getting invoices, they were not paying. Because employees were overworked, they were not scrutinizing every transaction. When everyone finally caught up and the division took stock of its status, they found that the profit margin had been whittled away by errors and operating inefficiencies. Working with vendors on duplicate payments and nonpayments, and with customers on lost invoices and shipping papers took its toll. The few controls that existed simply helped them realize that they had lost control. Like the shoemaker's children, this high-tech computer company had neglected to provide itself with a system that could take care of its own needs.

CATEGORIES OF INTERNAL CONTROL

Internal controls can be separated into two overall categories:

1. Internal accounting controls
2. Operational or administrative controls

Definition of Internal Accounting Control

Internal accounting control is the organizational plan, procedures, and methods of keeping records that ensure the reliability of financial data and records. It is responsible for safeguarding assets through an awareness of what they are, where they are, and what is being done to control them.

These internal accounting controls are designed to provide reasonable assurance that

- Transactions are executed in accordance with management's general or specific authorization.

- Transactions are recorded as necessary to
  a. Permit the preparation of financial statements in conformity with generally accepted regulatory or statutory accounting principles.
  b. Maintain accountability for assets.
- Access to assets is permitted only as authorized by management.
- The recorded assets are compared with the existing assets at reasonable intervals; appropriate action is taken with respect to any differences.

Internal accounting controls consist of basic controls and disciplines over basic controls. Basic controls are necessary to maintain the accuracy of the accounting records. The disciplines over basic controls ensure the continued and proper operation of basic controls.

The accounting or financial department usually has main responsibility for installation and maintenance of internal accounting controls. Data processing and other departments are responsible for conforming to control requirements, and internal audit is there to check that the controls are being followed. Coordination among these and other departments is also necessary for an efficient system.

Definition of Administrative Control

Administrative, or operational, control is distinguished from internal accounting control by its primary operating purpose. It is usually exercised by the operating management over all departments and includes management control over the financial and accounting departments. Administrative controls are the procedures necessary to ensure that the resources of an organization are used efficiently to keep it running according to management's intentions.

These types of control may not concern internal accounting controls at all. For example, quality control over production may include a policy of producing and selling only first-grade merchandise. This is a strict control of administrative procedures that does not have anything to do with safeguarding assets or maintaining reliable financial records, the concerns of an external auditor.

In other cases, administrative controls and internal accounting controls are not mutually exclusive. Procedures and records used to ensure that administrative controls are operating effectively can simultaneously ensure that internal accounting controls are adequate. For example, a failure to calculate economic order quantities for repetitively purchased articles could result in overstocking and related inventory problems. This situation involves both kinds of control. Management should make sure that the accounting implications of all such administrative operating control weaknesses are evaluated by the auditors. The evaluation should be acted on properly by management.

The main reason for the distinction between administrative controls and internal accounting controls is that they may be two entirely different concerns.

Controls over records and accounting procedures directly affect the reliability of the organization's financial statements. As a result, internal accounting controls are often of special concern to external auditors. For organizations to maintain and evidence compliance with the Foreign Corrupt Practices Act of 1977, internal accounting controls can be particularly significant.

CONDITIONS OF CONTROL

In order to be able to exercise control, first there must be

- Some degree of systemization (a system).
- Documentation of transactions and their disposition.
- Competent, honest people to operate the system.
- Sufficient resources to keep it going.

These conditions, necessary for the functioning of controls, are described in the following sections.

Systemization

A detailed, established plan is needed for the control of any operation. For example, it is not possible to design appropriate controls over an accounting system when the system itself has not been adequately defined. When all of the procedures in an operation are described clearly and completely, it is easier to perform those procedures and keep them under control.

Under ideal circumstances, all personnel concerned with an operation would have knowledge of how to perform under every possible condition. In reality this is unlikely. The next best thing is knowing these specifications for one's own job. An example is someone who knows how to handle unauthorized, incomplete, or erroneous transactions, as well as normal transactions ready for complete processing.

Without a clearly defined system, control is next to impossible. At best, it is difficult and time-consuming. There is also a greater chance that things will get out of control when there is no definition of what "under control" is in that system. Thus, the system itself is perhaps the most fundamental control. The more clear-cut and better understood it is, the more effective the other controls are likely to be.

Documentation

Documentation is inherent in and implicit to a system. It is a separate condition of control because it is so essential to creating adequate controls. Without a complete and accurate description of what should happen in a transaction, exercise of control over that transaction is not possible. Documentation enhances communications between departments and permits analysis, accountability, and proper control.

Documentation may be used for several purposes simultaneously. In some cases, it is required solely for the purpose of control. For example, the performance of specific tasks is documented usually by initialing or some other means of identifying the person who did them. This affixes personal responsibility to those tasks and permits their supervision. It also serves as a control to check on who did what when things go wrong.

Some documentation required primarily for control purposes contributes to other useful functions. For example, the numbering of documents is mainly a way to make sure that all authorized transactions are fully processed. At the same time, it serves to identify and locate documents when they are needed for other purposes.

Competence and Integrity

Systems and all other control procedures are useless unless the people assigned to carry them out do so consistently and conscientiously. Each person must have a level of competence adequate to the task and enough personal integrity to take responsibility for doing it as well as possible. The competence and integrity of the individuals found in an organization can be influenced by many factors. The most important of these are:

- The organization's reputation and geographic location (availability of experienced personnel)
- Its personnel selection and retention policies
- Training policies and practices
- Difficulty of the work
- Amount and quality of supervision
- Degree of systemization

People should be selected for their ability to do the tasks required by a specific job or be trained to do them. If this is not possible, the system and its supervision must be modified so that they are appropriate to the staff's level of competence (rather than finding people appropriate to the system), while still ensuring maintenance of the established level of controls needed to keep the organization running.

Ordinarily, competence and integrity are not directly tested because there is no practical way to do so before hiring. Once someone is in an organization, his or her competence is fairly easy to judge. Integrity, such as compliance with company policy, may be harder to assess immediately. In the long run, the presence of effective disciplinary controls, such as supervision, normally provides the needed assurance that employees are competent, that their integrity meets organizational standards, and that conditions of control are adequate.

INTERNAL ACCOUNTING CONTROLS

Factors affecting the internal accounting control system can be classified on three levels:

1. The conditions under which control can take place
2. The basic controls performed directly on transactions and assets, either individually or in groups
3. Disciplinary controls that serve to enforce, supervise, and maintain discipline over the operations and their results

Under different conditions, one control activity may be more important than another. As a general rule, the conditions permitting control and the disciplines over them are just as important as the specific control operations themselves. The latter are unlikely to function well without the former.

Basic Internal Accounting Controls

Basic controls are those controls designed to ensure that only valid transactions are recorded and processed completely and accurately. For purposes of internal accounting control, the control system should include steps to reasonably ensure that

- All transactions are initiated, executed, and recorded once and only once. (There are few things worse than discovering that the same bill was paid twice, unless it is discovering that an invoice was never sent and, as a result, never paid.)
- Data for a transaction is recorded and transcribed accurately. (This is especially important for decision making.)
- Transactions and their data are executed and recorded in accordance with management's intentions. (The Equity Funding scandal is an example of how they were not. This episode is discussed in Chapter 19, "Controls for Validity, Maintenance, and Operation.")
- Recorded information remains correct and up-to-date (such as a change in vendor payment terms).

The system should either prevent or detect errors in execution or recording on a timely basis in order to achieve the preceding objective. Although internal accounting control aims at preventing and/or discouraging unauthorized transactions and errors, absolute prevention is impossible. Instead, controls should provide a way to detect both types of errors if and when they occur.

BASIC INTERNAL ACCOUNTING CONTROLS IN THE COMPUTER ENVIRONMENT

It is just as important to have basic controls in the computer environment as it is in manual circumstances. It may be even more important when the methods of implementing these controls are different. Some of the steps in the process can be programmed to take place within the computer. For the operation of the computer — independent of specific application programs — this programming of controls is embedded in the system software and its operating system, which tells the computer what to do and when to do it. The system software actually controls the computer and provides the information needed to process application programs. For application programs, the programmed control steps are referred to as programmed procedures.

Certain aspects of EDP systems are of great advantage to management when the systems are properly controlled. These are shown in Figure 16-1. Conversely, EDP systems, because of their nature, can sometimes cause great concern to management. Some of these particular areas of concern are also shown in the figure.

For the convenience of analysis and review, controls for the computer-supported environment are described here in two overall groups:

1. Application controls
2. General or integrity controls

Application Controls

Application controls are defined as the controls particular to a specific application. These applications are usually defined by which task they accomplish. Controls can consist of procedures applied by EDP users both before and after data is processed. Other controls are the procedures performed by the computer application programs. In this context, users are defined as all those who work with the computer but are not involved in systems development, systems maintenance, or computer operations.

Some application controls in computer systems are unrelated to computer processing itself. Examples include checking the quality and condition of goods received or ensuring that all transactions are initially recorded. Other application controls consist of clerical procedures to check the results of computerized procedures. An example is checking the extensions and additions of invoices

---

Advantages of Properly Controlled EDP Systems

When EDP systems are properly controlled:

- They are more consistent than manual systems.
- They can process more information faster.
- They can generate new, complex reports not easily available otherwise.
- They produce complete results much more quickly than manual processing.
- The cost of processing is usually lower, since it is less labor-intensive.

Many of the functions for processing transactions can be programmed into the EDP system in advance of the transactions themselves.

In EDP systems, data records and processing are often centralized in one computer. Consequently, disaster planning and adequate segregation of data and duties are imperative.

Areas of Concern to Management

- A complex EDP system cannot be re-created manually. Most information is either not printed or is too voluminous.
- Many computer records can be read only by the computer (usually no visible trace of changes exists).
- Most EDP systems allow multiple access. This is an advantage to users, but can cause security risks.
- There tends to be less manual scrutiny in the EDP system environment than in the manual environment.
- Unusual items not foreseen in systems design may be treated incorrectly and may even go undetected.
- EDP systems require specialized technical knowledge and language, which can interfere with clear communication.
- Changes in EDP systems are more costly than in manual systems.
- The effects of disasters can be very great (although the chances of disaster are probably no greater than they are for manual systems).

FIG. 16-1 Characteristics of EDP systems

produced by the computer. Still other application controls rely on programmed procedures, since they involve examining and acting on computer-produced reports. The objectives of these manual procedures can be met only if the related computer processing is appropriate. For example, investigation of items reported by the computer as missing or exceptional is effective only if all missing or exceptional items are reported.

When application controls are actually conducted by the computer itself, they are called "programmed procedures."

Programmed Procedures. These can be described as:

- Procedures relating to control over the completeness, accuracy, validity, and maintenance of data. These normally consist of edit tests, accumulation of totals, reconciliations, and the identification and reporting of incorrect, exceptional, or missing data.

- Accounting or record processing functions such as calculation, summarization, categorization, and updating procedures applied to the data.

- The automatic generation of new accounting data or transactions following the occurrence of another transaction, such as the production of purchase orders once inventory has fallen below specified levels.

Effective and consistent operation of programmed procedures can usually be ensured by controlling the design, implementation, security, and use of the programmed procedures within the EDP function. The same assurance can be achieved by checking the results of processing manually.

The relative mix and importance of manual and programmed procedures varies, depending on the complexity of the system.

Conditions Required for Effective Programmed Procedures. In order for programmed procedures to be considered appropriate, the following conditions must be met:

- The method used in the program must be consistent with the prescribed accounting principles, such as the first-in, first-out (FIFO) method of determining cost of goods sold.

- The method used in the program must be authorized by management, which must understand the methods used so that its approval is meaningful.

- The method used in the program must be understood by the user departments who prepare input and take action on output. Although programmed procedures are often kept confidential, users must understand the nature of processing well enough to carry out their assigned tasks.

- The programs must be set up to handle all types and volumes of data that could occur, including all possible combinations of correct and incorrect data, in the right way. For control purposes, it is sufficient to terminate or issue a report for all unusual situations and for errors that cannot be processed. These can then be handled in a specified manner.

Programmed procedures can operate only in the circumstances and on the type of data envisioned when they were written. The results in unforeseen circumstances are not predictable. Many unusual circumstances may cause a termination of processing or an obvious error in the output. However, this should not be expected, since it may not always happen.

Data Security and Access Controls. When data is held on computer files, it affects the manner in which controls intended to prevent unauthorized changes to the data are applied. These access controls include the use of passwords, encryption of data, and setting up limited access paths into the system. (See the next section and Chapter 20, "General or Integrity Controls.")

GENERAL OR INTEGRITY CONTROLS

Controls over the design, security, and use of computer programs, and the security of data files, are collectively known as general or integrity controls. These controls consist of a combination of system software and manual procedures and usually cover all applications. General controls can be divided into five main areas, designed to ensure that corresponding procedures are performed:

1. *Implementation controls* — Appropriate procedures are most effective when they are included in the program, both when the system originally becomes operational and when changes are subsequently made.

2. *Program security controls* — To prevent unauthorized changes to computer programs.

3. *Computer operations or administration controls* — To ensure that procedures in computer operation are consistently applied.

4. *Data file security controls* — To prevent unauthorized access or changes to data files. These protect data from destruction, theft, or disclosure. They can also protect assets, since the theft of assets is possible through the manipulation of records.

5. *System software controls* — To ensure general controls as components of the system software for the computer, system software (which consists of programs that are not specific to any particular application) must be controlled, since it is used in the design, processing, and control of all applications. (System software includes operating systems, compilers, library packages, security programs, and others.) For example, programs may be protected against unauthorized change by the program library software. System software may also perform tasks such as software label checks to ensure use of correct files. The proper processing of jobs is controlled by procedures included in the operating system and related software. Obviously, controls are required over the implementation and security of the system software.

DISCIPLINES OVER BASIC CONTROLS

Disciplinary controls are those parts of a system designed to ensure two things. They are concerned with making sure that the basic controls continue to operate properly and that assets are safeguarded.

Disciplines over basic controls monitor and enforce basic control tasks in EDP as in all other departments. A system without disciplinary controls is conceivable, but it would be error-prone at best. Disciplines are important because their presence gives an organization reasonable assurance that the basic EDP and clerical control operations are functioning as designed. They allow procedures to continue to operate efficiently on a day-to-day basis and help assure that any errors that do occur are detected on a timely basis.

The value of disciplinary controls has been implicitly recognized for many years. However, they deserve much more explicit consideration than they have received. As with basic controls, disciplinary controls are tasks that must be done if control objectives are to be met. Those tasks can be accomplished in many different ways.

Three disciplines are necessary features of an adequate system of control: (1) segregation of duties, (2) custodial arrangements, and (3) supervision. Segregation of duties allows the work of one person to act as a check on the work of another. Custodial controls prevent access to data and programs not specifically required to do a particular job; they are necessary to prevent unauthorized activity of all sorts: from loss or misuse of assets to loss or misuse of the general ledger. Supervisory controls may be considered the most important group of controls, since they permit the detection and correction of errors caused by weaknesses in other, basic controls.

Supervisory controls can be part of a system's programmed procedures. Since the computer system can be a consistent and fair supervisor, these can be very effective. On the other hand, it is possible to have too much reliance on this aspect. Reviews are, and should be, conducted to ensure that all is actually going as well as hoped.

Segregation of Duties

The separation of one activity from another serves several purposes. Aside from other control objectives, it is usually more efficient to specialize tasks and people to do them, whenever the volume of activity is sufficient. For example, it is usually better to train one person to handle cash exclusively and another to keep the records of those assets. To try to find, train, and supervise someone versatile enough to both handle the assets and keep the records is unnecessarily time-consuming. When evaluating the costs and benefits of segregating duties, management should realize that the benefits can often include operating efficiencies.

Segregation of Duties and Administrative Efficiency. The control features of segregation of duties may be so important that this disciplinary control should be adopted regardless of whether it actually creates administrative efficiencies. In fact, it is often worth doing, even when it results in inefficiencies. An analysis of the potential risk of mistakes and even possible fraud can justify the segregation of duties, even when it is inefficient. For example, the dollar amounts passing through electronic funds transfer (EFT) systems in banks may justify having one person prepare and enter the transfer data, including authorization codes, and another re-enter the authorization codes on a duplicate screen with the code fields left blank.

If two parts of a single transaction are handled by different people, each serves as a check on the other. For example, one person can process a day's payments for credit card accounts received through the mail while another posts those receipts to the computerized payment processing system. Checking the total of the postings to the total receipts gives assurance that each operation was accurately performed.

Segregation of Duties as a Deterrent to Fraud. Segregation of duties can also serve as a deterrent to fraud or concealment of gross incompetence, since it is necessary to get another individual's cooperation. Collusion may be less likely than the possibility of fraud where one person is acting alone. Separation of responsibility for the physical security of assets and related recordkeeping is in itself a significant custodial control. An official such as the controller who signs checks cannot hide an unauthorized disbursement by making a false entry in the disbursements records if he or she has no access to the corresponding computer records. Only the authorized recordkeeper or bookkeeper should have access to the records. Custodial control is even further enhanced if neither the treasurer nor the bookkeeper, for example, is responsible for periodically comparing the cash on hand and in the bank with the cash records. Someone else should make this comparison and take appropriate action if there are any differences.

Since a computer can perform many of these tasks, it is always important for the system to be designed to assure that it is possible to create a meaningful and proper segregation of duties.

Custodial Arrangements

To prevent unauthorized transactions, whether they constitute theft or simply well-intentioned activity inconsistent with the system, it is necessary to restrict access to information that can be used to initiate or process transactions. Such arrangements are most commonly thought of in connection with the physical security of negotiable assets. Cash, securities, inventory, and other items that are easily convertible to cash or to personal use are most likely to be protected. The need for protective measures applies equally to access to the data, computer files, books and records, and to the means of altering them — unused forms, unissued checks, check signature plates, files, computer tapes, computer programs, ledgers — in short, everything important to the process.

Custodial Controls in an Internal Accounting System. An internal accounting control system should deal with two kinds of situations:

1. The separation of responsibilities for the physical security of assets, data, and the related recordkeeping
2. Physical arrangements that prevent unauthorized access to assets, data, and accounting records

Not all physical safeguards are related to accounting controls. If the absence of a custodial control cannot cause accounting errors, the control is administrative rather than accounting in nature. For example, management may consciously risk some degree of pilferage of computer supplies in preference to installing supply room procedures. As long as any losses are honestly accounted for, the books and financial statements can accurately reflect what has taken place.

Physical Security Controls. In its simplest form, physical security consists of such things as a safe, a vault, a locked door, a storeroom with a custodian, or a guarded fence. However, physical safeguards are useless without a discipline that prevents unauthorized people from coming and going at will. The discipline can be automated to some degree. Issuing a special card that unlocks the door and can often identify the cardholder to the physical security system is an elementary form of automated authorization to enter a locked area. Physical security measures also protect assets and records from physical harm, such as accidental destruction, deterioration, or the results of simple carelessness.

Supervision

Procedures used to perform the basic control tasks are important. The amalgam that holds the entire system together is a disciplinary control: namely, supervision. Effective supervision of personnel performing the work has numerous benefits. It leads to necessary modifications of the system when new types of transactions occur, corrective action when the system reveals errors, and follow-up action when weaknesses in the system become evident. A control cannot be regarded as effective in the absence of adequate supervision. Supervision is any other control that monitors the performance of a basic control.

Supervisory Control Weaknesses. Together with systemization, supervision is essential to control operations. If supervision exists, it provides the means for correcting other weaknesses. Without adequate supervision, the best of systems and control operations run the risk of becoming erratic or undependable in short order. Under pressure, systems and disciplines may be cut short or bypassed, reconciliations may be omitted, errors and exceptions may be left unattended, and documents may be lost, mislaid, or simply not journalized or posted to the appropriate ledgers. Supervisory and administrative personnel may be drawn into the day-to-day work of processing data and correcting errors. When this happens, they will be less able to perform their supervisory control duties.

Even in a well-designed system, problems in the accounts may signal a lack of supervisory controls. If there are an inordinate number of errors and exceptions, backlogs and bottlenecks, and instances of prescribed procedures that are not followed, they should serve as a warning. If problems proliferate and it appears that supervisors are bogged down with details or have inadequate knowledge of their responsibilities, management should be made aware that it cannot rely on other control procedures, no matter how well-designed.

Supervisory Control Routines. Many of these controls are specific, observable routines. They are designed to assure supervisors that the specified conditions of control and the required basic control operations are maintained. The performance of these administrative routines must be documented by:

- Checklists
- Exception reports
- Initials evidencing review of controls
- Reconciliation procedures
- Vouchers and other authorizations for spending
- Log books for review routines
- Written reports

When this kind of documentation exists, it can be used to determine the quality of the supervisory controls.

ADMINISTRATIVE CONTROLS

Administrative or operational controls are concerned with the overall business perspective of management: increasing efficiency, increasing revenues, and the effectiveness of the management decision-making process. Administrative control concerns include:

- Reliability of management information — a wider concern than the reliability of financial information

- Timeliness of management information
- Speed with which errors and exceptions are detected and corrected
- Efficiency of administration in general and of control procedures in particular
- Nature and type of information available to management
- Response of operating units and whether management's intentions are carried out
- Appropriateness of serious decisions made by management or those with delegated authority from management

Administrative controls represent the wider concerns of management. As a result they are not subject to the same boundaries as are internal accounting controls.

Establishing effective and efficient administrative or operational procedures usually requires a high level of technical skill. It requires awareness, a knowledge of alternate operating methods, and a sound business sense, in order to judge which option is the most efficient or appropriate.

INTRODUCTION TO APPLICATION CONTROLS

There are several kinds of control techniques commonly found in computer-based systems. They usually include techniques covering the basic controls carried out by the users and the programmed procedures carried out by the computer that are associated with each technique. These are controls of applications or specific programs that accomplish specific tasks, such as a payroll system.

Scope of Application Controls

The control structure adopted for each application should take into account the application's whole sequence of manual and computer processing. The sequence runs from the first record of the transaction through the use of the management report or other output. A system of control should extend as far as the final destination of data or output. It should include work that has to be carried out as a result of the information shown on the output, such as the investigation and disposition of items listed on exception reports.

Within the preceding framework, it is convenient to consider application controls under the following headings:

- Completeness of input
- Accuracy of input

- Completeness of update
- Accuracy of update
- Validity of data processed
- Maintenance of data on files
- Calculating, summarizing, and categorizing procedures
- Computer-generated data
- File creation and conversion

Types of Data to Be Controlled

There are different types of data within computer systems: Transaction data consists of single transaction items, whereas master file data consists of the basic information and reference data (also called standing data) required by the program to process a number of transactions. It is therefore usual to require higher standards of control for master file data than for transaction data, since the latter generally affects only certain individual accounts or records. Computerized controls or programmed procedures require an even higher standard of control than master file data, since programmed procedures can affect all data when a program is run. (See Chapter 5, "Computer Concepts," for a more detailed discussion.)

The different data fields within a record can also vary in the degree to which standards of accuracy and extent of checking are important. Transactions normally contain some data that requires conversion into financial terms (such as the quantity of an item sold) and some that is included only for reference purposes (such as a customer name and address). Although a higher standard of accuracy may be more appropriate for the financial data than for the data included for reference purposes only, reference data can also be of major significance. As in all systems, transactions that deal with liquid assets (such as cash) often require a much higher standard of control.

Controls and Standards of Accuracy

When designing a system of control, one should ensure that no vital control has been omitted, while avoiding the inclusion of unnecessary controls. These can become controls for their own sake. In particular, the real purpose of each control must be considered. A balanced judgment should be made, weighing the cost of operating the control against the losses that might result if it were omitted.

Controls adopted for each application can be chosen from the wide range of control techniques available, taking into consideration the differences in complexity, efficiency, and expense. It is often possible to compensate for a control weakness at one point by including an appropriate control at another stage. The object is to establish an effective overall system of control.

Different transaction and data types require different standards of accuracy and methods of checking. The strength of the control requirements depends on how data is used, the extent to which subsequent processing can be relied on to detect an error, management use of the data, and its possible effect on reports and financial statements.

PRINCIPAL CONTROLS

Selection of Controls for Testing

When examining how controls have been implemented in existing systems, several control techniques, all satisfying the same control concern, are often found in place. This happens because of the operational requirements of computer systems. Systems must be constantly monitored and controlled so that computer processing need not be inefficiently repeated or corrected.

For testing, auditors choose only those techniques that satisfy internal control concerns. The auditor normally selects, as a principal control, the technique that is most effective and whose functioning can be tested most efficiently. These techniques are controls that

- Provide more conclusive evidence of control. For example, a cumulative report of missing sequence numbers, with evidence that appropriate corrective action has been taken, provides more conclusive evidence of completeness than the manual reconciliation of batch totals.

- Are stronger alternatives. For example, a one-for-one check usually provides greater certainty as to the accuracy of input and update than a format edit check. The strength of a control depends on both the effectiveness of the user controls and the propriety of the programmed procedures.

- Cover several areas. For example, a control account covering completeness of input and update, as well as maintenance, of the dollar total is more efficient to test than a combination of individual alternate controls.

- Provide evidence about the consistent and proper operation of programmed procedures.

Interrelationship of Controls

Different control techniques are effective for different portions of the processing cycle. The interrelationship of control techniques is particularly important to ensure completeness and accuracy over the whole processing cycle. It also ensures that authorization is effective and is not circumvented by subsequent amendments to the authorized data. The auditor must establish a suitable combination of principal controls that cover the entire processing cycle without any gaps. The span of control encompassed by the different control techniques is illustrated in Figures 16-2A and 16-2B.

Noncomputer Control Techniques

The application control techniques discussed so far are designed to cover computer processing. They may also cover all or part of the manual processing prior to entry, as well as all or part of the action on the output. Any manual procedures not covered by computer application control techniques must be covered by manual control techniques and are therefore not relevant to a discussion of controlling computerized processing.

AUDIT CONSIDERATIONS IN COMPUTERIZED SYSTEMS

Many readers are familiar with accounting controls and how the concepts of control affect audit work. Basic controls and disciplines over controls function differently in different locations in various organizations.

Controls in a computerized accounting system are a direct concern of EDP auditing. An overview of the relationship between procedures and controls in a computerized accounting system is presented in this chapter in terms of the categories of controls in such a system and through the applicable terminology explained in the chapter. Specifics are discussed in the next four chapters. To get an idea, however, of what these controls mean to an auditor of computerized systems, an accounts payable system is an example. To see how controls are implemented from an audit standpoint, a case in point is converting part of this imaginary system from a manual to a computerized system.

A manual accounts payable system consists of a string of procedures, some of which are designed to ensure the accuracy of the accounting information and to protect the assets of the organization.

To look at one part of the hypothetical system, the first step is the physical delivery of the invoices received on any given day. These are taken to the accounts payable department or to whichever department handles them.

Next, the invoice arithmetic is checked by the accounts payable clerk. If any math errors are found, the third step is the correction of those errors. Once these three things have been done, the clerk usually signs or initials the invoices to show that they were in fact received and checked.

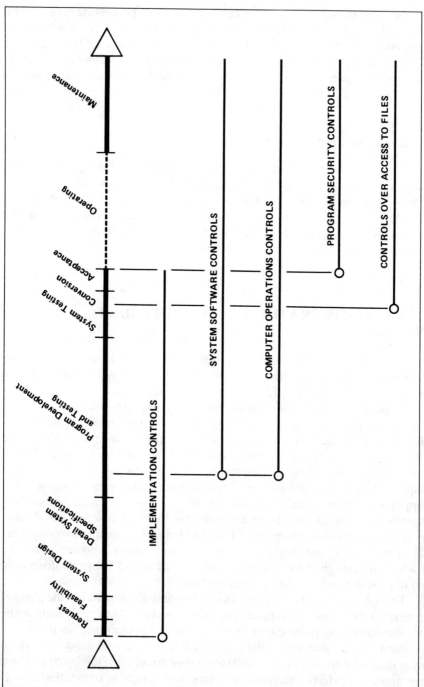

FIG. 16-2A   Span of general controls in the system development life cycle

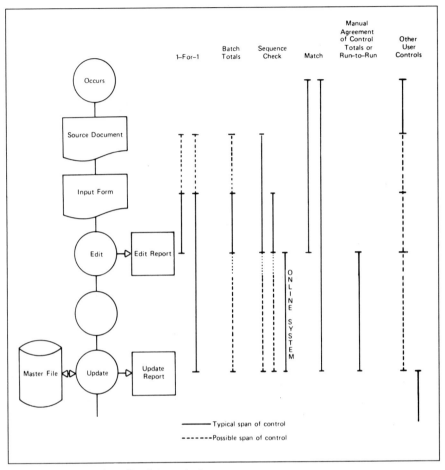

FIG. 16-2B Span of application controls

These three steps taken together form a basic procedure or control that ensures both the receipt and the arithmetical accuracy of all invoices that arrive each day.

A basic control can consist of a combination of steps or procedures, as it does in this case. It can also be one procedure by itself. This example also shows how some procedures in a system are not accounting controls. In this example, the delivery of invoices to the accounts payable department is not an accounting control.

The next level in controls as presented here is the discipline over basic controls. To provide that discipline in this system, the accounts payable supervisor gives final approval of each invoice. In this step, approval is shown by initialing the invoice.

The disciplines over basic controls are designed to ensure that the related basic controls continue to operate and that assets are safeguarded. In this case, the supervisor's approval procedure serves both purposes. It guarantees that the clerk is following the procedures for arithmetical accuracy and will continue to do so. It safeguards the company's assets, since it is also authorization for the invoice payment or spending of company cash. Disciplinary controls, including division of duties, custodial controls, physical controls, and supervisory controls, cover many areas.

Some of these types of controls are found in operation in this imaginary manual system. After a computerized system that accomplishes the same processing tasks is introduced, these concepts of basic controls and disciplines over them continue to operate.

Assume that the manual accounts payable system is fully computerized. The second step — the checking of additions and calculations — is now done by the computer. This is a programmed procedure, since this procedure is performed by a computer program. As part of the program, the calculations and additions for each invoice are checked and the computer produces a listing of invoices with arithmetical errors.

This list is the exception report. It is used in the third procedure to investigate errors and to ensure that they have been properly corrected and cleared. Essentially, this step — the correction of errors — and the fourth step — the evidence of error follow-up — remain unchanged from the manual system.

The basic control to ensure the arithmetical accuracy of the invoice still consists of the group of three procedures. The only thing that has changed by computerizing the application is that the arithmetic in step two is now handled by the computer and is called a programmed procedure. Note that, just as in a manual system, this is only one procedure out of three that make up the basic control. This is important. A programmed procedure by itself does not constitute a basic control. The manual procedures done in the third and fourth steps are still parts of the control. The basic control will be inadequate if the manual procedures are lacking, even if the computer functions properly.

One thing that does change in a computerized system under the terminology presented here is the name for both basic controls and disciplines; in a computerized application, the basic controls and disciplines are referred to together as the application controls.

In this computerized accounts payable application, the fourth procedure still constitutes a discipline over the basic controls. Since the procedures that constitute the basic control include a programmed procedure, some questions arise: How do the people who review the report of exceptions know that all exceptions are on the report? Or, to look at it another way, how do they know that the programmed procedures operate correctly?

In a computerized accounts payable system, as just described, two procedures involve checks based on the computer exception report. Therefore, they both rely on the correct operation of programmed procedures for their effectiveness. To justify this kind of reliance, two accepted methods can be used to ensure that computer programmed procedures operate correctly. The first is to manually reperform the programmed procedure. In this case, the computer would have to print out all the required information to make this reperformance possible. Then the results can be compared.

The second way to ensure that the programmed procedures operate correctly is by relying on the procedures and controls exercised in the EDP department. These procedures, which reside and operate in the EDP department, are the general or integrity controls, a string of procedures in the EDP department that, either individually or in combination, are identified as controls. They consist of both basic controls and disciplines over basic controls.

Essentially, general controls must operate over all applications, such as payroll, accounts receivable, or general ledger, to ensure that the accounting applications are processed correctly. And, since the same general controls operate for the most part over all applications, a single weakness in those controls may affect every system that uses the computer. This makes the evaluation and testing of general controls a particularly important part of an audit, especially when reliance is placed on these controls.

Overview Structure of Controls

The relationship between controls (see Figure 16-3) can be seen in the following steps:

- Procedures
  a. Data is gathered
  b. Data is entered or transmitted
  c. Records are maintained
- Basic control
  a. Someone checks, compares, and balances
  b. Someone reconciles and investigates

SUMMARY

For the most part, the same basic controls and disciplines that work in a manual system also work in a computerized system, but some of them are performed by the computer in the programmed procedures.

Application controls, including programmed procedures, are designated separately from the other controls that work in the EDP department as a whole. In the following chapters, the interrelationship between controls, which

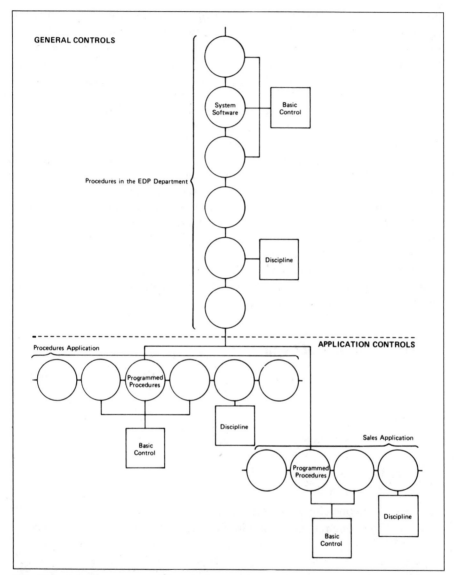

FIG. 16-3 Overview structure of controls

becomes more complex as a result of exceptions, can be seen. But at this point it is important that the basic concepts and distinctions between kinds of control are understood.

One might think that everyone would have the same interest in controls, knowing how important they are to the smooth, efficient functioning of an organization. But frequently the controls themselves are most important to the auditor, while accurate recordkeeping is most important to the accountant, technology is important to the EDP department, and profits are of critical interest to the financial department. As a knowledge of controls and their application in an organization is developed, it is important to realize that controls may not be everyone's priorities. To many, controls seem restrictive or even stifling. Yet, without them, businesses and other organizations would have a hard time sustaining growth and progress.

CHAPTER 17

Controls for Completeness and Accuracy of Input

COMPLETENESS OF INPUT

Introduction

A well-designed computer system has built-in controls for all of its functions
and for all aspects of its operation. One of the most fundamental of these
application controls is completeness of input. This is the control designed to
ensure that every transaction to be processed is recorded and then entered for
processing.

This control is concerned with the actual number of documents and items
to be processed. Control is created to meet the following criteria:

- Is every transaction recorded?
- Is every recorded transaction entered into the computer?
- Is every transaction accepted?
- Which items are rejected by the computer?
- Is every transaction entered once and only once?
- Are duplicate items identified?

Those are the objectives. To help achieve them, various control techniques exist that can be used either in batch or on-line systems. These techniques accomplish essentially the same thing, but the way they do it, and their
effectiveness, varies.

Controls for completeness are not concerned with the correctness of any
details of a transaction, but merely with the act of recording and entering the
transaction. Completeness simply means that all of the transactions arrived and
were processed as specified. Accuracy relates to the control of the individual
data elements that make up each transaction. The reason for the distinction is
that the techniques used to control completeness are often different from those
used to ensure accuracy, which is also discussed in this chapter.

As an example of how this distinction operates in a payroll system,
completeness of input means that every employee who was supposed to be paid
was paid, and accuracy of input means that every employee who was paid
received the right amount.

The larger problems that can result due to inadequate controls over
completeness and accuracy surfaced when a company acquired a new division
with a data processing (DP) center from another firm. The new management

was impressed by the seemingly comprehensive reports of computerized accounting systems. As staff left, new people were trained in computer operations. Management continued to rely on the information in reports produced by the center to make major decisions. As time passed, the reports were neither as complete nor as accurate as management assumed. An investigation revealed that the previous staff had been highly trained and had followed their own system of controls. They understood the system and could make up for its deficiencies. Also, they simply did not make as many errors as the new staff. The previous staff had not formalized any of their procedures by writing them into the procedures manual or by requesting that they be programmed into the system. To correct this situation, the new management had to redesign the system, both manual and computerized, to ensure that it functioned efficiently and according to standardized procedures, independent of staff turnover.

Completeness Controls

There are two parts to these controls. The first is to make sure that all transactions are

- Recorded initially.
- Entered into the computer.
- Accepted by the computer.

Once the transactions are in the computer, the second part of the controls should check the following aspects of completeness:

- All rejected transactions should be reported.
- Each transaction should be processed only once.
- Duplicate transactions should be reported.

All Rejected Transactions Should Be Reported. For example, if a payroll system rejects an employee's time sheet from further processing because the employee number is invalid, the program has discovered and rejected an invalid number, as it should. There are several possibilities why this might occur: The number could be recorded incorrectly on this particular time sheet (which can happen if the numbers are entered by hand each time); the program doing the edit check of valid numbers may be in error; the master file data being matched may be incorrect; or, least likely, the employee does not exist and has been entered on the payroll fraudulently. Whatever the answer, the situation must be resolved and the time sheet reentered. If this is not reported as an exception, it could be that erroneous employee numbers are paid automatically and, as a result, employees could be paid twice, enter false time sheets, and so forth.

Each Transaction Should Be Processed Only Once. The importance of transactions being processed only once is somewhat obvious on consideration of the problems a company could experience if, for example, vendor invoices are paid twice. And, of course, the difficulties that can result from duplicate billings may have an adverse effect on customer relations. They can also distort the picture created in the entire system by showing more income potential than actually exists and also by indicating that twice as much material was sold, thereby prompting the purchase of more inventory when it is not warranted.

Duplicate Transactions Should Be Reported. If there is a weakness in the reporting of duplicate transactions, they may recur. Once the system properly identifies duplicates, it is important to discover how the duplicates made it that far in processing and to strengthen the controls to ensure that duplicates are not processed in the first place.

Controls for completeness should also include controls designed to ensure that rejected data is resubmitted after the problem has been resolved.

CONTROL TECHNIQUES FOR COMPLETENESS OF INPUT

Various techniques are available to control the completeness of input. The most commonly encountered techniques are:

- Computer sequence check of serially numbered documents
- Computer matching with previously processed data
- Agreement of manually established batch controls
- One-for-one checking of reports

These techniques, together with tasks that need to be done in the case of rejections, are discussed in the following sections.

Computer Sequence Check

In computer sequence checking, the computer checks the preassigned serial numbers of input transactions and reports missing or duplicate numbers for manual investigation. Ideally, transactions should be recorded on serially prenumbered documents. They can also be sequenced after preparation. The first method is preferred, but is not possible if a document originates outside the organization (e.g., a supplier's invoice).

Computers also record transactions on serially prenumbered documents. For example, when checks have been preprinted with serial numbers, it is necessary to record the actual use of these otherwise blank preprinted checks. The numbers are used by the bank and by the issuer, but they are also entered in a control register in the organization as they are actually used. Before the checks can be filled out by the computer's printer, the check forms must be aligned within the printer, and this almost always means that at least the first, and maybe the second, check is voided because the operator has to set up the top-of-form. The operator then enters the preprinted number of the first check actually used into the check-writing program via the operator's console. As each check is printed, it contains both the preprinted number and the number printed by the computer (if any), which helps control the use of blank check forms. These two should be the same (in some systems they are not) to make control easier. When the computer operator returns any unused forms to the control point, those voided for form alignment also should be returned so that they can be accounted for. In many systems, all of the check numbers are recorded in the computer's check register file by the computer. It can easily tell whether a number has been skipped, which indicates an unrecorded check, or, perhaps less likely in a modern system, whether a number has been used twice. Handwritten checks can also be entered into the system by using a check number sequence. The program must have this routine built in as a way of tracking manually processed checks. In this way both manually prepared and computer-printed checks have an appropriate serial number to enable the checks processed at the bank reconciliation stage to be controlled for completeness of input.

In an on-line system, the transaction may be assigned a sequence number by the edit program upon entry. Computer-assigned sequence numbers can be highly effective in tracing the exact point of cutoff after a processing failure. If such a failure necessitates a restart further back in the processing cycle, it is easier to locate the right place for the restart.

There are different ways to carry out a sequence check. Two of the most widely used are described in the following sections.

Cumulative Sequence Check. A cumulative sequence check, shown in Figure 17-1, typically operates in this way:

- A file is created containing a table of all document numbers that have been issued. This file may be created by entering the numbers of the documents to be issued, or it may have been generated by the computer as a product of a previous accounting process.

- Transactions are recorded on standard, serially numbered documents, or are serially numbered on receipt.

- The transactions are entered and items on the file are flagged to indicate that the transaction has been processed. Any arriving transactions that have already been flagged as processed are rejected and reported as "duplicates."

- Periodically, reports of missing numbers are produced for manual follow-up.

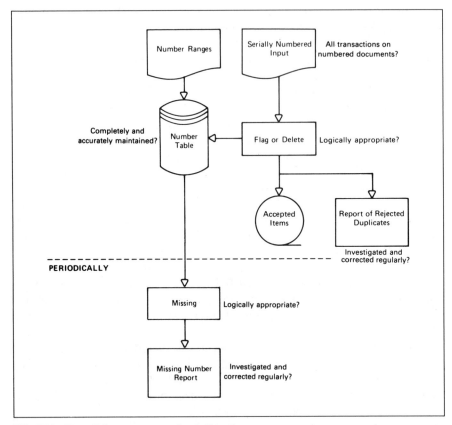

FIG. 17-1 Cumulative sequence check (input)

Batch Sequence Check. In a batch sequence check, shown in Figure 17-2, the sequence of transactions within a batch or file is checked as follows:

- The serially numbered transactions are entered together with the range of the numbers to be checked. (The range is the first and last numbers in the particular sequence.)
- The computer program first sorts the transactions into numerical order, then checks the documents against the sequence number range and reports missing, duplicate, and out-of-range transactions.

Control Requirements

For computer sequence checking to be effective as a control technique, the following user controls and programmed procedures must be present:

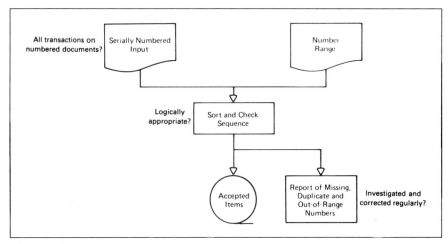

FIG. 17-2 **Sequence check on batches (input)**

- There must be adequate procedures to ensure that all forms are indeed numbered after completion or, if practical, that all transactions are recorded on serially prenumbered forms.

- The method used in the program for checking the numerical sequence must be logically appropriate and understood by the user department. In this context, procedures are required to deal with:
  a. Changes or breaks in sequence
  b. More than one sequence running concurrently (such as when different locations use different blocks of numbers)
  c. Identification and reporting of duplicate numbers

- When a suspense file of missing numbers is maintained, there should be adequate controls to ensure that unauthorized adjustments are not made to this file.

- Reports of missing and duplicate numbers must be produced frequently to allow for prompt follow-up action to correct the error.

- There must be adequate manual procedures to investigate missing numbers. Any rejected duplicates must be manually checked. Then they are canceled or reentered, depending on the outcome of the investigation.

- A cumulative sequence check is easier to operate, since it rejects all duplicates and keeps reporting overdue items. If the sequence check is not cumulative, then specific manual procedures are needed to check for duplicates in different runs and to ensure that each item reported as missing is followed up.
  a. Changes or breaks in sequence for the batch-type sequence check ranges should also be verified, manually or by a computer program, to ensure that sequence continuity is maintained from computer run to run, subject only to new sequences issued.

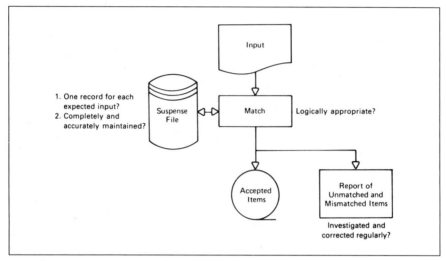

FIG. 17-3 Computer matching (input)

Computer Matching

The computer matching technique is shown in Figure 17-3. It consists of the computer matching of input data with information held on master or suspense files. Unmatched items are reported for manual investigation.

As an example, the computer might match an employee's time sheet details, as entered, against a payroll master file. Then it would identify and report missing or duplicate time sheets. Or, the computer might match suppliers' invoices with a file of goods received details and report invoices for which goods have not been received. In these examples, the matching process is an effective control over the completeness of input. As a result of the first, all time sheets and employees will be accounted for, and in the second, invoices for goods not received will not be processed for payment until the goods have been located.

Computer matching is especially useful in on-line systems because the system has the ability to match with up-to-date master or suspense files during editing.

For this control technique to be effective, the following user controls and programmed procedures must be present:

- There must be adequate controls over the file holding details of items to be matched. This is usually achieved by a regular agreement of file totals with an independent control account.

- All adjustments to the data on file should be properly authorized. For example, partial shipments in an accounts payable system need special authorization.

- The method used in the program for matching must be logically appropriate and approved by the system users. The number of data elements matched must be sufficient to make the transaction unique. For example, matching a date is usually inappropriate, since many transactions can have the same date. Matching an invoice number may also be inappropriate if there are many branches, all of which use the same range of invoice numbers. In this case, to make them unique, a possible solution is to add the branch number to the invoice number, creating a unique transaction number.

- The matched items must be appropriately indicated on the reference file to permit production of a report listing unmatched items.

- Manual procedures must be adequate to follow up outstanding and mismatched items. If reports contain a cumulative list of outstanding items, control over investigation is easier.

- The current generation of the file holding details of items to be matched must be used. If an older file were used, many mismatches would turn up, merely because the file would be out of date.

Batch Controls

The batch control technique involves manually grouping transactions at the input stage and establishing a control total over the group. This control total can be based on document count, item count, dollar totals, or hash totals.

For totals of transactions, the methods used may be one or more of the following:

- *Document counts* — A simple count of the number of documents entered, which is agreed to the number of documents processed. This is normally the minimum level required to control completeness of input. It is not sufficient if more than one transaction can appear on a document.

- *Item or line counts* — A count of the number of items or lines of data entered (such as a count of the number of items or lines on a sales invoice). The number of items or lines is agreed to the number processed.

- *Dollar totals* — An addition of the dollar value of items in the batch, which is agreed to the dollar value of items processed.

- *Hash totals* — An addition of any numeric data existing for all documents in the batch, which can be checked against the total of the same numeric data fields for items processed (such as total of quantities, total of part numbers, total of all numeric fields entered).

The use of batch totals is a common control technique in batch processing systems. It has also proven effective in on-line systems where documents are entered as received. A batch concept is created by choosing a time frame in which transactions are entered and treating it as a batch. There are a number of different ways batch totaling may be carried out.

Manual Agreement of a Batch Register. This technique, illustrated in Figure 17-4, is used in the following manner:

- The batch total is established manually and recorded in a register or batch control book.
- The batch is entered to the computer, accumulated, and the batch total printed.
- The total printed is manually agreed to the total recorded in the register or control book.
- Procedures are required for adjusting the batch totals in the register or control book for rejected items.

Computer Agreement of Batch Totals. This technique, illustrated in Figure 17-5, is used in the following manner:

- The batch total is established manually and entered on a batch header slip with the batch.
- The application program accumulates the batch total and compares it with the total entered. (This technique is sometimes referred to as zero-batch balancing, since the total of the batch minus the total on the batch header should be zero.)
- A report is produced that normally contains details of each batch, together with an indication of whether the totals agreed or disagreed.
- Batches that do not balance are normally rejected. Some applications write the batch to a suspense file pending the reentry of corrected items.

Manual Agreement of a Control Account. This method, which is illustrated in Figure 17-6, is a variation on the use of a batch register and works in the following manner:

- Totals of all types of transactions that update the master file (such as invoices, credit notes, cash, and adjustments) are established during an initial edit program prior to the program that would update the master file. These totals are established in the same way as for manual agreement of a batch register.
- The totals are recorded in a control account.

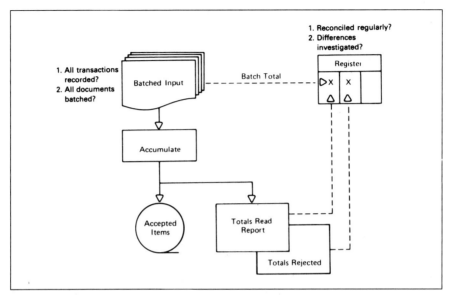

FIG. 17-4   Batch totals and batch register — Manual reconciliation (input)

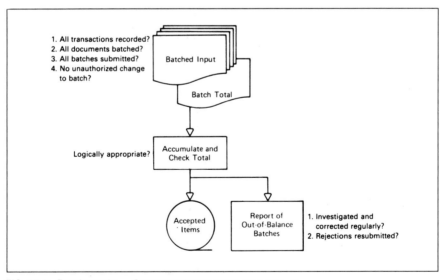

FIG. 17-5   Batch totals — Computer batch balancing (input)

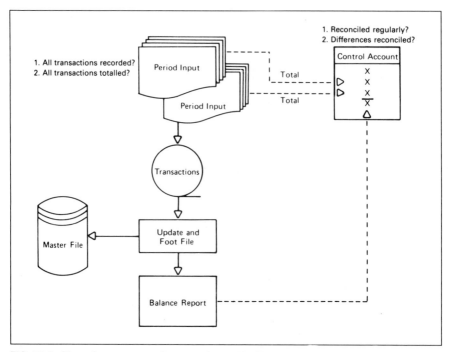

FIG. 17-6 Manual agreement of a control account (input and update)

- Transactions are entered and processed in the master file.
- Periodically, the balance on the control account is agreed manually to an accumulation of all individual balances on the master file. For example, in an accounts payable system, each vendor on the vendor master file might have a data element designated as month-to-date payments. A total of all the vendor month-to-date payments should agree to the total paid to all vendors, calculated from each batch of checks written during that month.

This method, as well as ensuring completeness of input, also ensures completeness of update (discussed in Chapter 18, "Controls for Completeness and Accuracy of Update," under the heading "Completeness of Update").

Batch totaling is effective as a technique when the following user controls and programmed procedures are present:

- There should be adequate controls to ensure that a document is created for each transaction.
- There should be adequate controls to ensure that all documents are batched.

- There should be adequate controls to ensure that all batches are submitted for processing (such as a manual or computer sequence check on batch numbers).
- The user should determine that all batches have been accepted by the computer.
- When computer agreement of batch totals is used, there should be adequate evidence printed that the checking was carried out.
- There should be adequate procedures for the investigation and correction of differences disclosed by the input reconciliations. These procedures must be performed on a timely basis.
- There should be adequate procedures for the resubmission of all rejections.

One-for-One Checking

This technique, illustrated in Figure 17-7, consists of checking each individual document or source document with a detailed listing of items processed by the computer. To rely on this technique, it is necessary to ensure that all documents are submitted for processing. This is usually achieved by one of the following methods:

- Retaining a copy in the originating department of all documents sent for processing. The report is then checked with the retained copy, and missing items are followed up. Checking against copies returned from data processing does not guard against forms being mislaid before they are entered, and therefore cannot be considered a satisfactory control for completeness.
- Reconciling the number of documents sent for processing with the number actually processed, and accounting for differences

In Figure 17-8, the report produced and checked contains items that have updated the files. This provides control over completeness of both input and update. Alternately, the report may be produced at the edit stage and contain items that have been accepted but not updated. This provides adequate control only over completeness of input.

If carried out effectively, checking of detail reports is a powerful control; it is, however, time-consuming and costly. Checking of detail reports is normally used as a technique to control important low-volume transactions, which might include:

- Master file data amendments
- Adjustments

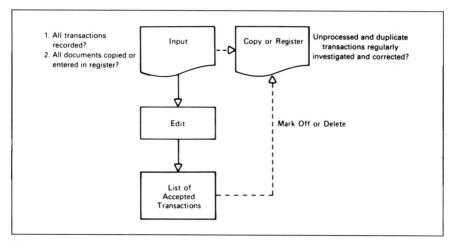

FIG. 17-7   One-for-one check (input)

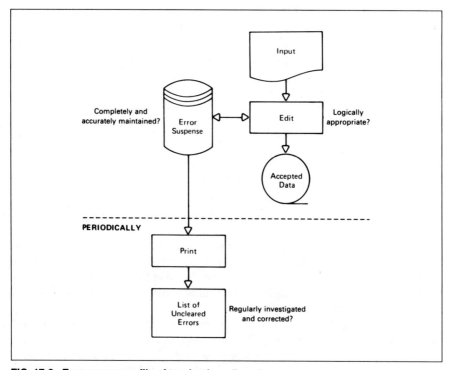

FIG. 17-8   Error suspense files for rejections (input)

For checking of reports to be effective as a control technique, the following user controls and programmed procedures should be present:

- There should be adequate controls to ensure that all documents are submitted for processing (such as checking output with retained copies by sequence checking or by document counts).
- There should be regular review of source documents to detect unprocessed items.
- Missing or duplicate items disclosed by the checking process should be identified and followed up promptly.

Rejections

The data entered for processing in a computer system often contains incorrect items. Particularly in batch processing, it is not possible or practical to investigate and adjust each incorrect item as it occurs during processing. It is usually faster to have the computer continue processing the batches on hand as it handles input errors. This is frequently done in two ways:

1. The computer rejects the items or particular batch from further processing, with no record other than a report of the rejections.
2. The computer rejects the items or particular batch from further processing, but maintains error suspense files within the computer system of items awaiting correction. It then produces cumulative reports of all uncleared items on the error files. This is illustrated in Figure 17-8.

Detailed procedures are required to ensure that

- Rejection reports and items held on error files are promptly investigated, and rejections are corrected and resubmitted.
- Previously established control totals are adjusted in relation to the rejected data.

The timely correction of rejections is important in real-time systems where input data is matched with master files for validity. If rejections were left uncorrected, the master files would not be up-to-date when the validity of subsequent input is checked. This would be of particular importance where, for example, a bank recording a withdrawal would match the information entered with a customer's balance. The timeliness of correction procedures may also be important when data base organization is used, since several users may depend on common input and other users are not likely to be kept aware of outstanding rejections from a particular user's area.

Rejections in an On-Line System. When an on-line system is used and the data is edited as it is entered, it is possible for the terminal operator to correct rejections as they occur by amending the entered data on the terminal screen.

Specific procedures to deal with rejections are normally needed where a suspense file is not used to control rejections in computer sequence and matching techniques, or where batch totals form the input control. Checking of detail reports, computer sequence checking, or computer matching techniques that use a suspense file of accumulated rejections serve as adequate controls over rejections because these techniques usually continue to identify items that are unprocessed, missing, or unmatched. This may not be the case when other techniques form the control, because the computer may not store, and continue to report, details of rejected items or batches.

Monitoring Rejection Procedures. How rejection procedures are monitored depends on whether the batch totals are checked manually or by the computer as follows:

- *Manual checking of totals.* There is a register or batch control book. Rejections should be recorded when the control totals are adjusted.

- *Computer checking of totals.* There is no predetermined record of the batch totals and no record of the adjustment. There is less visible evidence of the volume of rejections and a greater reliance on exercising and supervising the detailed procedures for dealing with any rejections that are reported by the computer program.

ACCURACY OF INPUT

There is a difference between controls designed to ensure completeness of input and those designed to ensure the accuracy of that data. Controls for accuracy of data are concerned with the data on the transactions being processed. Controls for completeness are mainly concerned with whether a transaction is processed at all.

Controls over accuracy of input, shown in Figure 17-9, are designed to ensure that

- The initial recording of data is correct.
- Where applicable, the data from source documents to input documents is transcribed accurately and the data is converted accurately into machine-readable form.

The requirement to control accuracy is greater at the data entry stage than during processing and updating, since data typically does not become cor-

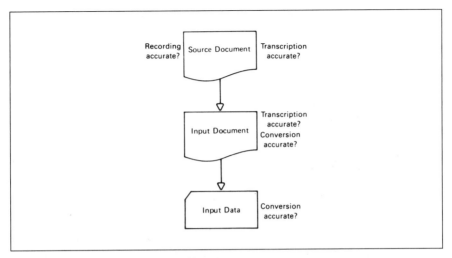

FIG. 17-9 Controls over accuracy of input

rupted or unintentionally changed during processing. For example, during key entry, an employee number might be erroneously recorded. It would be rejected during subsequent edit checks because it fails to match any employee number on file, or for syntax error. Another example might be the inclusion of an alpha character in an all-numeric employee number. Or perhaps a keystroke error transposes two digits in an employee number, inadvertently matching it to another number in the master file. This type of error, which might be caught by an edit program looking for duplicate time sheets, might escape detection if one of the employees had not worked that week. A review by the payroll clerk to ensure that each time sheet processed produced a paycheck is one manual control that would catch such a compounded type of error that the computer might not catch.

Data to Be Controlled

All important data elements or fields should be controlled to effect real accuracy. Initially, therefore, it is necessary to decide which data elements are the important ones.

After that has been done, the degree of control necessary for each element must also be established. It may not be practical to achieve an exhaustive degree of control over all data.

Which elements are the important ones and the degree of control necessary for each element are not necessarily obvious. To find out, use the following guidelines:

- All financial data elements are usually important (such as values or elements that enter into a calculation of value, such as hours, quantities, and discount codes).

- Less obvious but still important is reference data, such as account numbers, dates, and indicators. Examples of the importance of reference data fields are:
  a. Reference numbers. The accuracy of reference numbers such as those for personal accounts, inventory lines, and general ledger codings is important to ensure that the correct accounts are updated. The accuracy of inventory line numbers is likely to be particularly important to ensure that pricing is carried out on correct balances, incorrect orders are not automatically generated, and unnecessary physical count adjustments are not created.
  b. Dates. The accuracy of dates can obviously be important. Dates held as master file data may initiate a computer accounting process. For example, the discount date may trigger a check to be produced as payment for a bill prior to the time the discount would be lost. Failure to enter dates accurately may lead to loss of revenue or inability to successfully carry out control procedures. Dates entered as part of transactions may also be important. For example, in the case of sales or inventory transactions, computer aging of customers and inventory balances is an essential part of controlling the revenue flow.
  c. Indicators. The accurate entry of indicators (such as special codes to indicate transaction types to the program) can also be important. The type of transaction is often identified by an indicator. An error could lead to an effect that is the opposite of the one intended. For example, in wage and salary or payroll systems it is common for the same form to be used for new hires and for terminated employees. A different indicator shows whether the person is a new hire or a termination. Indicators can also be important from a control point of view. For example, where an inventory item is defined as a high-risk or high-security item, it is entered with an indicator, so that the program will select it to be counted more frequently than low-security items.

  Unless a system is specifically designed with default options (which provide an answer if none is supplied), specific decision checks should be built into the program for each allowable value. For example, suppose transaction types 1 and 2 are treated in different ways. The system should be designed to identify and process type 1, identify and process type 2, and reject all other transaction types.

CONTROL TECHNIQUES FOR ACCURACY OF INPUT

Various techniques are used to control the accuracy of data input. The most widely used are as follows:

- Completeness control techniques used for accuracy

- Programmed edit checks
- Prerecorded input
- Key verification

Completeness Control Techniques

Although the objective of controlling accuracy of input is different from controlling completeness of input, some of the techniques used are identical. The applicable completeness of input controls described earlier are listed here, together with a description of the circumstances in which they can control accuracy.

- *Computer matching.* Computer matching can be effective as a control for accuracy, but it establishes the accuracy of only those elements matched by the program. Often several fields are matched by the program, each of which is therefore controlled in this way.

- *Batch totals.* The agreement of manually established batch totals can control the accuracy of those data fields that are totaled and agreed. This does not, however, guard against the possibility of compensating errors in one or more individual items. It is unusual, because of the time that would be involved, to establish batch totals over a large number of fields. Batch totals of numbers of documents or line items do not control for accuracy.

- *Checking of detail reports.* The checking of detail reports can control the accuracy of those fields covered in the detailed checking. Often several data fields are covered by the checking and can be controlled in this way. Data should be checked with the original input documents retained by the user department. This provides the only adequate control over accuracy of input and/or update.

Programmed Edit Checks

As seen in the preceding list, it is unusual for completeness control techniques to cover all important data elements. Programmed procedures are often used to check the accuracy of other data.

Programmed procedures of this kind are usually called edit checks. Edit programs often include several checks, which can be ingenious and powerful. At the program specification stage, it is important to ensure that all appropriate checks are included in the program and that the logic of the checks is correct. Powerful editing is usually easier to achieve in on-line systems, since a variety of data is available for reference at the data entry stage.

In many cases, edit checks cannot provide conclusive proof that only accurate data is accepted. However, a suitable combination of edit checks may be very helpful in reducing the likelihood of error.

Sometimes data may be entered on-line by an operator who is not from the originating department. Under these circumstances, there is a danger that the operator may incorrectly adjust a transaction that fails an edit check, so close supervision is required.

It may also be possible to override edit checks. In such cases, the system should be designed to ensure that all instances of override are suitably reported for investigation by users. The reasons an override was used should be included in the system's documentation.

The most common types of programmed edit checks are the following:

- Reasonableness checks
- Dependency checks
- Existence checks
- Format checks
- Mathematical accuracy checks
- Range checks
- Check digit verification
- Document reconciliation
- Prior data matching

Reasonableness Checks. These are checks to test whether the contents of the data entered fall within predetermined limits. The limits may describe a standard range or may be determined in relation to previous input. Data that fails such a check is not necessarily wrong but is considered sufficiently suspicious to require further investigation.

Reasonableness checks can often be applied to data fields (such as dates and indicators) that are difficult or impractical to control in any other manner.

An example of the use of a standard range is frequently encountered in payroll applications where the input is number of hours worked. The computer program identifies and reports employees who have worked more than a given number of hours and, less frequently, fewer than a given number of hours.

Following is an example of a reasonableness check by reference to previous input. A computer program identifies new items taken into stock in instances where the price of the stock item is unusually high or low in relation to previous prices. The data referred to for the reasonableness check may be held on a file (as with the price example discussed previously), included in the computer program (as in the range limits possibly used in the preceding wages example), or input at run time (the more likely approach in the wages example).

For reasonableness checks to be effective as a control for accuracy, the following user controls and programmed procedures should be present:

- The method used in the program for identifying exceptional items should be logically sound and should ensure that neither too few nor too many items are identified. This requires care in setting ranges.
- Periodically, the parameters used should be reviewed by the user department. This is particularly true when the parameters are variables.
- Where data referred to in the reasonableness check is entered by means of parameters, adequate controls are required to ensure that the correct parameter data is used each time.
- Reports of transactions failing the edit should be produced at regular intervals. Positive reporting methods should be employed so that the user knows that all such reports are received.
- There should be adequate procedures for the investigation of the exceptional items reported.

Reasonableness checks are illustrated in Figure 17-10.

	Input Data	Reasons for Failing Validity Check	Stored Data
REASONABLENESS CHECK	Date received: 021183 (MMDDYY)	Must be received today or before.	System date: 021282
	Hours worked: 72	Hours exceed normal maximum.	Maximum hours: 55
	Stock cost $/unit: 010.25	New inventory cost exceeds previous price by more than 10%.	Previous cost $/unit: 001.25
DEPENDENCY CHECK	Date received: 81067 (YYDDD)	Expiration date exceeds date received by more than the shelf life of 4 months.	Shelf life: 00120 (YYDDD)
	Expiration date: 83159 (YYDDD)		
EXISTENCE CHECK	Department numbers:		Valid department numbers:
(Matching)	169		169
	224	Department 224 is invalid.	214
	598		598
	624		624

Note: 1. Stored data must be correct.
2. Program must be logically correct and must report all failures.

FIG. 17-10 Examples of programmed validity and edit checks: Reasonableness, dependency, and existence checks

Dependency Checks. These are checks to test whether the contents of two or more data elements or fields on a transaction bear the correct logical relationship. Considerable ingenuity can be required in devising checks of this nature. They can provide a strong control over the accuracy of the fields concerned when properly designed and implemented.

As an example, when entering details of a loan agreement, there should be a logical relationship between the amount advanced, the number of repayments to be made, and the repayment installments. As with reasonableness checks, dependency checks are often applied to dates and indicators.

For dependency checks to be effective as an accuracy control, the following user controls and programmed procedures should be present:

- The method used in the program for relating the data concerned should be logically appropriate.

- There should be adequate procedures for the investigation of items reported as failing the checks.

Dependency checks are also illustrated in Figure 17-10.

Existence Checks. These are checks to test that the data codes entered agree with valid codes held on the file or in the program.

As an example, when purchase invoices are processed, they require the allocation of a general ledger code and an accounts payable code. On input, the program checks that the codes allocated exist as valid account numbers in the general and accounts payable ledgers. Items that do not match are reported.

Existence checking is usually limited to the control of reference numbers or, occasionally, indicators. It is not, on its own, a complete control, since it does not detect the entry of an incorrect but valid code. Further controls are required. Careful construction of codes can reduce the possibility of erroneous but valid codes being entered. The code should be sufficiently complex. The use of check digits (see the section entitled "Check Digit Verification") or alphanumeric codes can assist in adding the needed complexity. The use of check digits often occurs in conjunction with existence checks. In this case, the use of the check digit complements the existence check by making the number more complex. It is therefore more likely that an incorrect number will be identified, especially when the error is a transposition of numbers.

For existence checks to be effective as a control, the following user controls and programmed procedures should be present:

- The allocation of codes to transactions should be checked.
- The method used in the program for validating the input data should be logically appropriate.
- The file holding the code table should itself be adequately controlled.

- There should be adequate procedures for the investigation of items reported as a result of the check.

Existence checks are also illustrated in Figure 17-10.

Format Checks. These check the format (existence of expected numeric or alphabetic characters) of a transaction. They ensure that all required data is present. Checks of this nature are often included for operational reasons and may assist in ensuring that reference data, such as dates and indicators, is present.

All numeric data should be properly subjected to format checks. However, since format checks usually only determine that data complies with certain wide general rules, it is unlikely that they will be of much help in the control of the accuracy of data. Format checks are illustrated in Figure 17-11.

Mathematical Accuracy Checks. These check the calculations performed, as shown in Figure 17-11.

Range Checks. These check to see whether a number falls within a predefined set of numbers or the range, as shown in Figure 17-11.

Check Digit Verification. This technique is used to control the accuracy of input of reference numbers. A check digit is designed to prevent an incorrect, but valid, match. The numbers are constructed in such a way that the last digit bears a mathematical relationship to the preceding digits. As transactions are entered, the computer checks that the reference number contains this relationship. This is especially useful if the table of valid codes, against which existence is checked, is not available on-line.

For check digit verification to be effective as a control, the following user controls and programmed procedures should be present:

- The method used in the program for the calculation of the check digit should be logically appropriate.
- There should be adequate procedures for the investigation of items reported because the check digit is incorrect.

Check digit verification is also illustrated in Figure 17-11.

Alphanumeric codes, which are combinations of letters and digits, can function in a manner similar to check digits, since alphabetic characters have a numeric value in the system. When these, or numbers edited with existence checks as described previously, are constructed with check digits, it avoids the possibility of a number in error matching with a valid code. If existence can be checked on input, it is not necessary to also apply these computational checks.

		Input Data	Reasons for Failing Edit Check
FORMAT CHECK	Reference number: Dollar value: Name:	122 476 00013A4 _____	Embedded blank. Nonnumeric. Must enter (cannot be blank).
MATHEMATICAL ACCURACY CHECK	Invoice:	$ Value Goods 2000.00 Tax 10.00 Total 2100.00	 Does not foot.
RANGE CHECK	Date:	131381	Month 13 is illegal (out of range).
CHECK DIGIT VERIFICATION	Employee numbers:	046176	Modulus 11 check digit $6 \times 1 = 6$ $7 \times 2 = 14$ $1 \times 3 = 3$ $6 \times 4 = 24$ $4 \times 5 = 20$ $0 \times 6 = 0$ Total is 67, not divisible by 11. Should be 046167.
DOCUMENT RECONCILIATION	Document number: Code: Value: Hash total:	1394 17 1732.59 2144.59	 Hash total does not foot.

Note: Program must be logically correct and must report all failures.

FIG. 17-11 Examples of programmed edit checks: Format check, mathematical accuracy check, range check, check digit verification, and document reconciliation

Document Reconciliation. This technique, which is common in on-line systems, involves checking the mathematical accuracy of the entry of the numeric data on transactions.

In effect, each transaction is treated as a batch. Prior to entry, a hash total is established of all, or all important, numeric data elements on the document. The total is recorded on the document and the document entered, usually through a terminal.

Then, the program totals the data and checks the result with the hash total. Transactions that do not balance are not accepted. The terminal operator can see on the terminal screen if an input error was made and, if so, correct it. If the error is the result of an incorrect hash total, the document should be returned to the originating department for correction. Document reconciliation is illustrated in Figure 17-11.

Prior Data Matching. Neither existence checks nor check digit verification can tell when an incorrect but valid reference number has been entered. To overcome this drawback, prior data matching is used. This technique is commonly used for the control of master file data amendments and works in the following way:

- The new data to be processed is entered, together with the old data, which is to be superseded. For example, if the price of an inventory item is to be amended, the product reference number is entered with both the new price and the price to be replaced.
- The computer matches the product number and the old price as entered with those held on the file. If a match is obtained, the new data is updated to the file.
- If a match is not obtained, the item is reported for investigation.

This technique ensures that the correct product number is updated. It controls the accuracy of which reference field is entered, but not the accuracy of the new information being put on the file. For example, in this case it cannot ensure that the new price is accurate, only that the correct item received a new price.

For prior data matching to be effective as a control technique, the following user controls and programmed procedures should be present:

- The method used in the program to match the prior data should be logically sound. In general, the more prior fields that are matched, the stronger the control. The possibility of a chance match of an incorrect record with identical prior data is reduced as more fields are matched.
- There should be adequate manual procedures to follow up mismatched items.

Prior data matching is illustrated in Figure 17-12.

Prerecorded Input

Errors frequently arise during the initial recording of a transaction. By preprinting certain information fields on blank document forms, these errors can be reduced. Of course, there should be strict control over the accuracy of the initial design of prerecorded data included on the documents.

It is even possible to use optical character recognition (OCR), mark sensitive (OMR), or magnetic ink character (MICR) forms. These make the input form itself machine-readable and avoid the errors inherent in keying.

Control over both initial recording and conversion to machine-readable form will be adequate for the above types of prerecorded input, as long as

- The particular edit software used is appropriate to identify, report, and reject any incorrect input forms from further processing.

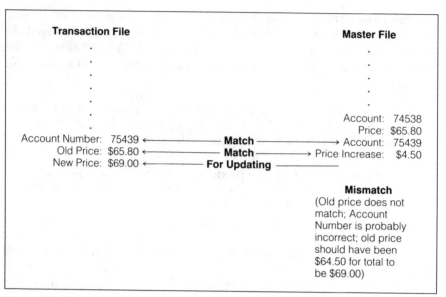

FIG. 17-12 Prior data matching

- User procedures include the investigation, correction, and reentry of rejected data. If documents are damaged, which precludes use of the original input technique, there must be alternate procedures readily available to ensure the accuracy of such input.

Examples of prerecorded information include:

- Preprinted serial numbers used in a computer sequence check.
- Preprinted MICR customer numbers on bank checks.
- Preprinted transaction-type indicators, identifying different document types.
- Preprinted department, branch, depot, division indicators, and so on, on all documents used by that department.
- Magnetically encoded credit cards used to identify customers at bank terminals or retail point-of-sale (POS) terminals.
- Preprinted payment advice forms, which are sent to customers with the request that they return the form with the payment. When the payment amount is preprinted, the payment requires special handling if a different amount is in fact paid.

The payment advice form sent to customers is a familiar example of what is often called a turnaround document. This is a document that is produced by the computer for subsequent entry to its own or to a related system.

Turnaround documents can also be used to amend master file data. When the master file data is first set up, the complete contents of the record are printed, and the output document is filed. Once an amendment is necessary, the data that needs to be changed is crossed out and the new values are entered next to it. This process reduces the chances that incorrect values will be written down and increases the effectiveness of supervisory approval of the document. The changed fields are keyed for entry to the computer. The new output document is checked back one-for-one with the input and filed for use next time. It is also possible for the program to indicate on the report which data was changed, thus increasing the effectiveness of the one-for-one check. The use of turnaround documents is illustrated in Figure 17-13.

Key Verification

Key verification is a common technique for controlling the conversion of information from input documents into machine-readable form. It is normally used for key entry, and involves a repetition of the keying-in process by a separate individual using a machine that checks the results of the keystrokes with what was originally keyed. (In some on-line systems, the equivalent of key verification is performed on-screen.) The technique usually is of limited use in the absence of the other techniques discussed previously because

- The technique checks only the actual keying process. Errors at other stages of the input cycle are not covered (such as errors in preparing the input form).
- All fields are not usually key verified.

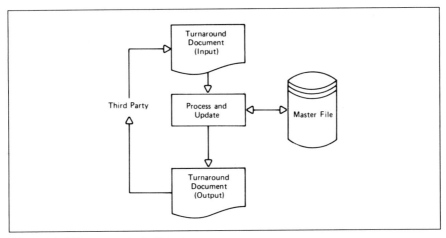

FIG. 17-13 Using prerecorded input

- Errors that result from poor interpretation of handwritten figures often remain undisclosed.

- Possibly fraudulent changes to the input document are not detected.

- There are difficulties in supervising verification personnel to ensure that the process is carried out effectively. Experience shows, for example, that the existence of the verification indicator does not always provide adequate evidence that the keying-in process was correctly performed.

Verification on key-to-tape or key-to-disk machines can be more reliable than key-to-card because the supervision of the verification process is a programmed procedure, which can be more effectively controlled.

ACTION TAKEN ON ERRONEOUS DATA

Edit checks identify erroneous or suspect data. In batch systems, it is printed out on a report for manual action. Data failing edit checks may be handled in any one, or a combination, of the following ways:

- When data is rejected and dropped from subsequent processing, it requires correction and reentry.

- When data is rejected and held in suspense, it requires either an amendment to the suspense file for any errors or a manual override of the edit check if the transaction is correct.

- When data is not rejected but is identified, reported, and carried through processing in the normal way, the report must be investigated. Corrective action is necessary only if the transaction was in fact wrong. However, this method is not preferred. It is usually not good system design to identify problems and continue processing unless the problems are minor in nature. If there is a real problem, then another transaction has to be entered to back out the transaction in error before reentering the correct transaction.

In on-line systems, edit checks are usually applied as data is entered. Erroneous data may be highlighted on the terminal screen to allow the operator to take corrective action.

Many on-line systems permit the terminal operator to override edit checks. For example, an item may fail a reasonableness check. The operator, after scrutinizing the data input and deciding that it is correct, can override to process the data in the normal way. Operator overrides should be more selective than this to afford better control. The operator should be allowed to override only by using a password or supervisor's key. In systems where the terminal operator does have the discretion to override edit checks, it is important that a record of every override is maintained and printed for subsequent approval. When no record of overrides is provided, checks that can be overriden should not be relied on to provide adequate control.

CHAPTER *18*

Controls for Completeness and Accuracy of Update

COMPLETENESS AND ACCURACY OF UPDATE

A major concern of any organization is ensuring that data already in the computer is completely and accurately updated. Chapter 17 describes how important it is to make sure that all data is complete and accurate when it is entered; that is the beginning of the processing of data by the computer. Inside the computer, the data is handed off to the next processing stage.

The data may go through a series of processing steps, such as:

- Sorting and calculation by programmed procedures
- Analysis and accumulation
- Updating a master file

Several things can go wrong with the data once it has been entered into the computer for processing. Problems can result from the following:

- *Programming errors.* Program procedures do not perform as expected or desired. For the most part, programs are designed, written, tested, and then put into production to handle common types of transactions in a particular system. Consequently, these procedures are usually well tested. It is when unforeseen errors or exceptions occur that the programmed procedures may not be able to process the data correctly. And it is possible for programs to have logic errors that escape detection in testing. A program can be accurate when implemented, but errors may be introduced when new procedures are added. Since such errors may occur in the way the data is processed, the errors can go undetected for long periods of time.

- *Operational errors.* During the operation of standard computer procedures, the operator may do something wrong, such as selecting an out-of-date master file for processing current transactions. Computer operating manuals may become out-of-date or erroneous; computer operators may have to be re-trained; and, of course, they can — and do — simply make mistakes. Equipment failure is another possible cause of error.

Some examples of problems that can occur due to both types of errors are:

- *Wrong record updated.* A transaction to update information on the vendor record for one company instead updates the next record, which is for another company. Such an error occurs when the program selects the wrong record for updating, and it happens because the programmer did not build in a check to see which record was selected for updating. A control for completeness would not necessarily catch an error of this sort, but a control over accuracy, such as one-for-one checking, should show the error in processing.

- *Wrong calculations.* Either the formula for the calculations is in error or the variable and table data used in the calculation are incorrect. Calculations that include the date commonly fail to consider that in a leap year transactions can be dated "2/29." A program may disregard the fact that payroll is variable; errors in table data can result when the payroll department forgets to have the program that handles payroll calculations updated with the most current information on withholding deductions.

- *Analysis and accumulation errors.* Incorrect programmed procedures can produce these errors. If data analysis is based on matching data to another file and the wrong file is selected, then the resulting analysis would be incorrect. For example, if purchases are recommended by analyzing year-to-date information and the operator is running purchase recommendations for December, he or she should use the file containing year-to-date for November but instead uses year-to-date for October. The analysis has been performed correctly, but the wrong data has been used.

    Accumulation errors do not usually occur when columns can be added to a total. They usually take place when the numbers are selected and categorized into accumulations that are not easily footed.

These are some of the examples of how things can go wrong even when the data is complete and accurate at the input stage.

A well-controlled system ensures that data is complete and accurate when it is entered and updates files with equal completeness and accuracy. Completeness and accuracy of update is the way that data is controlled through every stage, including the internal computer processes carried out by programmed procedures. Only when these steps are followed can all data entered into the computer be processed without being garbled or lost during its passage though the computer.

COMPLETENESS OF UPDATE

Completeness of update controls are designed to make sure that all data entered into, and accepted by, the computer is updated to the proper master file. Not just the actual act of updating but all stages of processing must be controlled, from acceptance of items through to the updated master file. (See Figure 18-1.)

Essential to ensuring the completeness of update are the controls over the correction and resubmission of items that are rejected at the update stage. When these items are reprocessed after being corrected, they become new update items in the next round of updating.

	Completeness of Input	Completeness of Update	Accuracy of Input	Accuracy of Update	Validity	Maintenance
One-for-One Checking	X	X	X	X	X	X
Batch/Control Totals	X	X	X	X		X
Computer Sequence Check	X	X				
Computer Matching	X	X	X	X		
Programmed Checks			X	X	X	X
Prerecorded Input			X			

FIG. 18-1   A comparison of the appropriateness of application

CONTROL TECHNIQUES EMPLOYED

There are two basic ways to assure that files are updated completely:

1. Introduce controls for completeness of input that can also apply to update.
2. Institute specific update controls.

Sometimes controls over the completeness of input also control the completeness of update. When controls can do both, the input controls described earlier are reviewed, with a description of the circumstances in which they can be used to control updating.

Computer Sequence Check

Normally, a computer sequence check is performed when data is entered; however, it does not ensure completeness of update. The following situations are found in some systems, particularly in on-line and real-time environments:

- A sequence check and identification of missing and/or duplicate transactions is carried out on the updated master file after the transactions have updated the file.

- The file that maintains the sequence numbers is not flagged until after the master file has been updated.

As a result, in the cases described previously, computer sequence checking provides a control over the completeness of update.

In on-line systems, the sequence check often operates along with procedures to update the master file. This ensures the completeness of input and update. No duplicates can be entered; they would probably be rejected at the input stage, as the computer does not allow the terminal operator to reuse a previously entered number.

Some systems carry out the sequence check by flagging the sequence number file, as the last step prior to actually updating the master file. This does not normally provide sufficient control over updating of the master file, so it is important to know how the particular system operates before deciding to rely on this control. The use of a computer sequence check to control completeness of update is illustrated in Figure 18-2.

Computer Matching

As with sequence checking, computer matching is normally carried out as data is entered. In certain circumstances the matching process also provides a control over the completeness of update. Matching is then conducted against:

- A master file (as opposed to a suspense file). The missing data report is produced by reading the master file after the matching process has been completed.
- A suspense file that is not updated until after the master file has been updated. As with sequence checking, care is required, since some systems update the suspense file immmediately before updating the master file. In the latter case, the matching does not normally provide control over updating of the master file.

The use of computer matching to control completeness of update is illustrated in Figure 18-3.

Batch Totals

The computer agreement of batch totals never ensures completeness of update, since the technique can only check totals at the input stage. If this is the technique used to control input, specific update controls are required.

The manual agreement of a batch register sometimes ensures completeness of update, depending on what sort of report is checked to the register. Checking a report that lists items that have been written to the file ensures completeness of update; checking batch totals against reports produced at the edit stage, however, does not, so specific update controls are required. The use

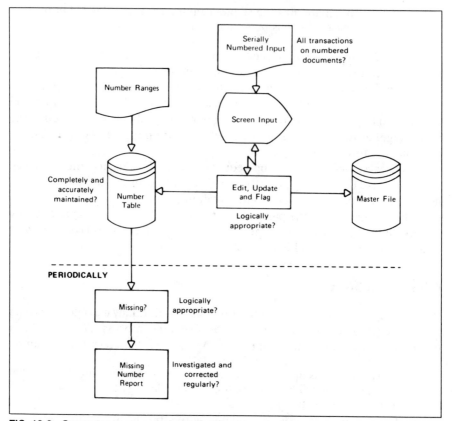

FIG. 18-2 Computer sequence check (input and update)

of a batch register to control input and update is shown in Figures 18-4A and 18-4B.

Manual agreement of a control account usually ensures completeness of update, because the control account is checked against an accumulation of the balances on file.

Manual agreement of a batch register and of a control account can usually be applied only where there is little or no intermediate processing and the data updating the file is identical in form with the data originally entered (such as processing details of cash received).

More often, the data entered is subject to further processing before updating. During this time the form of the data may change (e.g., figures for quantities shipped are converted to sales invoice values). When this happens, batch totals cannot be checked manually against the updated totals, so specific updating controls are required.

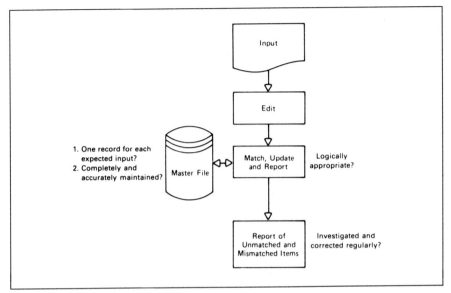

FIG. 18-3   Computer matching (input and update)

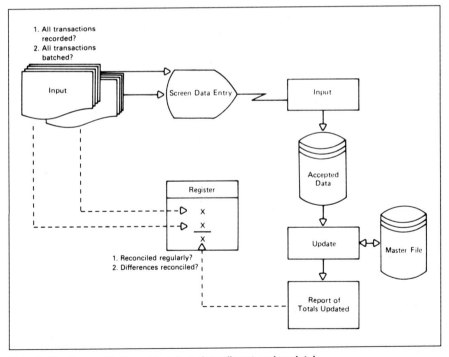

FIG. 18-4A   Reconciliation of batch register (input and update)

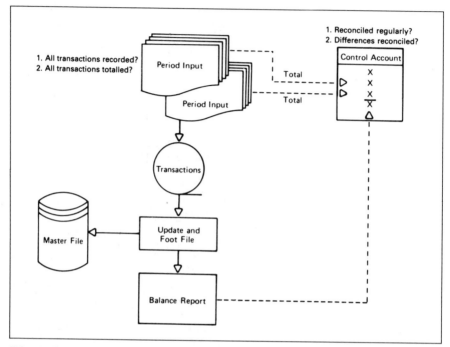

FIG. 18-4B   Using a control account (input and update)

One-for-One Checking of Detail Reports

This technique ensures completeness of update in cases where the report checked contains items that have been used to update the file. If such reports are produced only at the edit stage, they will not control updating.

Checking of reports is not an effective control technique unless the appropriate method is used in the program that updates transactions to a master file. If the user checks the source documents for a report that shows the record after update, this check will also control the reliability and logic of the programmed procedure. The user must clearly understand this method for it to work effectively. The use of this technique to control updating is illustrated in Figure 18-5.

SPECIFIC UPDATE CONTROLS

Whenever an input control does not also apply to completeness of update, updating is usually controlled by the agreement of control totals. These control totals are generated by the computer programs during, or prior to, applying the input control. This control uses the totals of items that have updated the file.

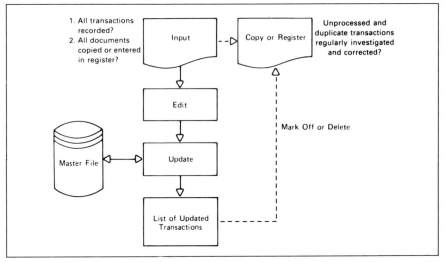

FIG. 18-5 One-for-one check (update)

Totals cannot always be checked directly to see that they agree. To rely instead on reconciliation procedures, consider the following:

- Control totals may be summarized (such as when several input batches are combined for subsequent processing).
- The type of control total used may change as a result of a particular intermediate processing step (e.g., a hash total of quantities may change to an invoice currency value total as a result of pricing).
- Items may be, or may have been, rejected at an intermediate step.

The totals of accepted items can be reconciled either manually or by the computer.

Techniques that can be used to control updating are described in the following sections, and different methods for accumulating the totals of accepted items are explained.

Manual Reconciliation of Accepted-Item Totals

The manual reconciliation of accepted-item totals is illustrated in Figure 18-6A. This method works as follows:

- The computer program accumulates and reports the total of items accepted when the input control was exercised.
- The computer then processes items onward through a series of programs. Reports that include the relevant control totals are produced, usually at the conclusion of each program in a series.

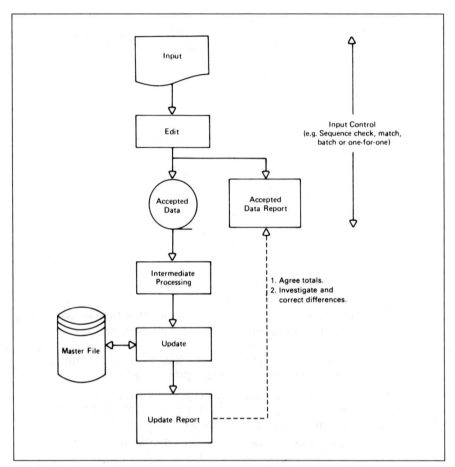

FIG. 18-6A   Accepted-item totals — Manual reconciliation (update only)

- When totals are summarized or changed, the new control totals are printed at the end of the computer run. The old totals are usually printed and may be carried through all later processing.
- After updating, the totals of items updated to the master file are reported.
- The totals of accepted items are manually reconciled to the updated totals, using any summarization or change in totals that has taken place. Any rejections are also taken into account.

When there is no change in the totals, the accepted-item totals may be recorded in a manual control account or cumulative register. The balance on the control account or register can then be periodically agreed to an accumulation of the total balances on file to prove completeness of update.

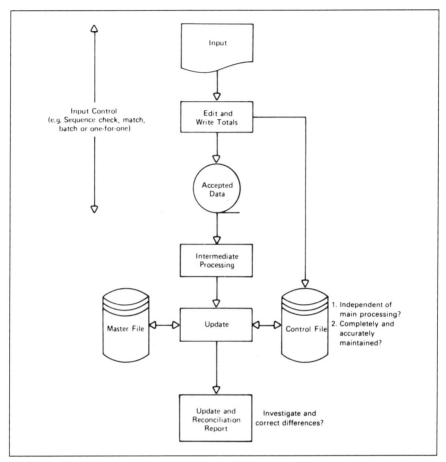

FIG. 18-6B   Accepted-item totals — Computer reconciliation (update only)

Computer Reconciliation of Accepted-Item Totals

Computer reconciliation of accepted-item totals is illustrated in Figure 18-6B. This method of control works as follows:

- The computer program accumulates the totals of accepted items in the same way these totals are accumulated in manual reconciliation. After all data has been entered and processed, the control totals are recorded on a control record in the file of accepted items. In sequential tape files, the totals are added to the trailer label; in disk files that are indexed-sequential, or can be accessed randomly, the control record information is usually contained as a header record or as the first record of the file. The opening control total on the file should be checked to the previous closing total to determine that the correct generation of the file was used.

- During each subsequent program run in the series, the computer accumulates the totals of transactions that have been processed and reconciles them with the total forwarded from the previous program run. This technique is often called run-to-run control totals.

- At each stage in the reconciliation process, the program produces evidence that the reconciliation has taken place — usually the totals themselves — and a message stating whether the totals agree or disagree.

- The computer-produced reconciliations are then manually checked and any differences are investigated.

Another method of control that uses computer reconciliation of accepted-item totals works as follows:

- In computer systems where all transactions are first summarized on independent control files, the totals are balanced by a set of programs. In some cases these are independent programs. This set of programs makes certain that the correct files have been used and that all transaction files have been combined for processing.

- Manual intervention ensures that programmed reconciliations are not bypassed as a result of unusual events, such as system failure. It is also necessary to make sure that control totals are brought forward each time the system is closed down and restarted.

Establishment of Totals of Accepted Items

The way the total of accepted items is established depends on whether transactions are entered and processed in batches or individually, as is the case in many on-line systems. Depending on the method used, the following procedures are employed:

- *Batch systems* — The total of accepted items should be accumulated during or prior to the program run in which the computer sequence check, computer matching, or other input control is carried out.

- *On-line systems* — The concept of a program run or the complete processing of a batch of transactions does not exist. Transactions are entered one by one and trigger whichever programs are required to process them. Transaction totals are progressively accumulated at intervals during processing and are periodically reported or reconciled by the computer. These totals can be done daily or more frequently when there are many transactions. It is important that accepted-item totals are accumulated during or prior to applying the input control for the input control to be effective.

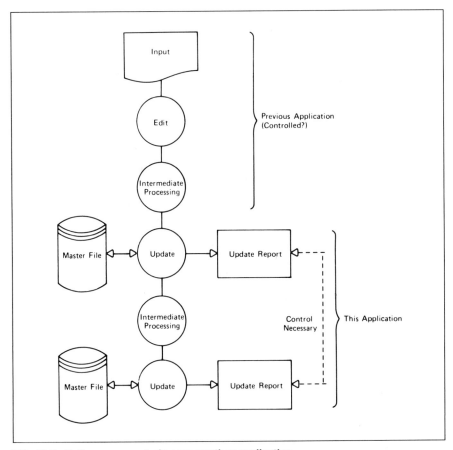

FIG. 18-7 Reliance on controls over another application

Reliance on Controls Over a Previous Application

As systems become more integrated, a file produced by one application is often used for another application. When this happens, the completeness of input to the first application should be controlled to ensure completeness of input to the next application.

Specific update controls, described in this section, are necessary to ensure that all transactions accepted by the first application are passed through to the second. This is illustrated in Figures 18-7 and 18-8. In addition, if two or more files are updated at the same point in the processing cycle, the same input and update controls may be effective over each file.

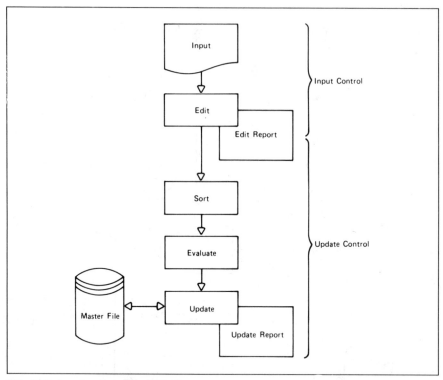

FIG. 18-8 Input and update controls

On-Line Sequence

Another method of control, the on-line sequence check, is illustrated in Figure 18-9. It is organized as follows:

- Transactions are assigned a sequence number as they are entered.
- A report of missing and duplicate numbers is produced after all transactions have updated the master file.

On-line sequence control is similar to a batch sequence check. This type of control also helps to prevent unusual events such as the possible loss of transactions when the system fails to operate, since transactions can be identified and recovered at the proper point in processing.

Duplicate Processing

Duplicate processing is common in an on-line data base environment. When transactions are entered in this type of operation, a memo update is usually

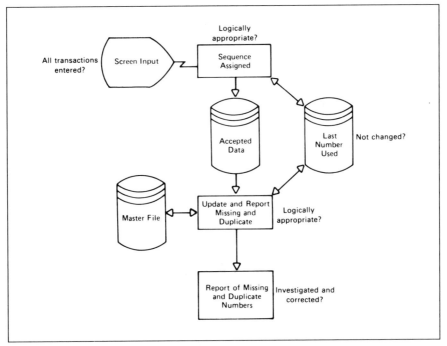

FIG. 18-9   On-line sequence check (update only)

made to the data base. This memo update enables the current updated status to be checked at any time. The data base, however, is not actually updated until overnight processing is done. At the time the actual updating occurs, the transactions are rechecked against the memo update and a report is produced. This report lists the differences between the memo update and the overnight update. Duplicate processing is illustrated in Figure 18-10.

Rejections

Rejections may arise at the update stage as well as on input. Rejections at the update stage usually occur because a transaction cannot find a matching master file record.

In on-line systems such rejections are much less common, because the system can match the transaction against a master file record on entry and establish that a matching record exists.

The procedures and techniques required to control rejections arising at the update stage are similar to those required for rejections produced at the data entry stage.

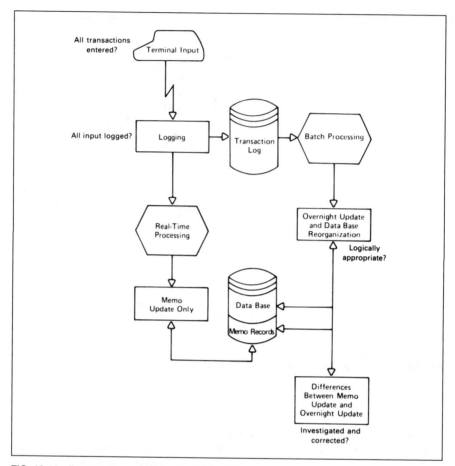

FIG. 18-10   Duplicate processing (update only)

ACCURACY OF UPDATE

When computer files are updated, controls are needed to ensure that the new input is accurately carried through intermediate processing and accurately updated to the correct data on the correct generation of the master file. This is illustrated in Figure 18-11.

As with the control of input, both master file data and reference data must be accurately updated.

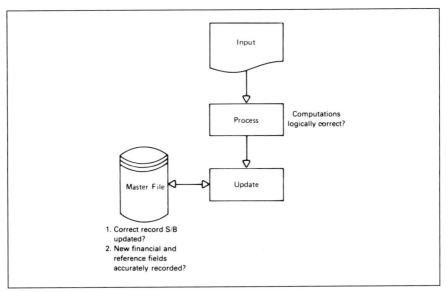

FIG. 18-11 Accuracy of update

Financial Data

Control techniques previously described can ensure the accurate updating of financial data. Control techniques that do this are:

- *One-for-one checking of detail reports.* Checking a report of items that have updated the file ensures that financial data covered by the checking is accurate.

- *Manual reconciliation of accepted-item totals and computer reconciliation of accepted-item totals.* Both of these techniques ensure the accuracy of the data covered by the reconciliation.

- *Programmed edit checks.* Normally these checks are applied to data as it is entered and do not ensure accuracy of update. Occasionally a variation of the reasonableness and dependency checks may be encountered where the programmed editing is carried out on the master file after updating. In such cases, the reasonableness and dependency checks may also control accuracy of updating of the data involved.

In practice, it is likely that one or more of the above techniques will be used in batch or on-line systems. When this is the case, they serve as a control for accuracy of update.

Not all significant financial data fields may be controlled in one of these ways. Often, only the primary financial data fields (such as the invoice value) are so controlled.

Prior Data Matching

This method controls accuracy of update as well as accuracy of input. It is commonly used for the control of master file data amendments and works in the following way:

- The new data that is to be processed is entered together with the old data to be superseded. For example, if the price of an inventory item is to be amended, the product reference number is entered with both the new price and the price to be replaced.
- The computer matches the product number and the old price entered to those held on the file. If a match is obtained, the new data updates the file.
- If a match is not obtained, the item is reported for investigation.

This technique ensures that the correct product number is updated. It controls the accuracy of the reference data entered but not the accuracy of the new information being put on the file. In this case, it does not ensure the accuracy of the new price.

For prior matching to be effective as a control technique, the following user controls and programmed procedures should be present:

- The method used in the program to match the prior data must be logically sound. In general, the more prior data that is matched the stronger the control, since the possibility is reduced that the new data will be accidentally matched with an incorrect record bearing identical prior data.
- Adequate manual procedures should be used to follow up mismatched transactions.

An example of prior data matching is shown in Figure 17-12 (Chapter 17, "Controls for Completeness and Accuracy of Input").

Sequential Updates

When performing sequential updates, the sequence of both files, but especially the transaction file, should be specifically checked. Out-of-sequence records should be rejected. If duplicates are found, they also should be rejected and investigated.

Reference Data

The accurate updating of reference data means ensuring that

- Correct accounts are updated.
- Dates and indicators are accurately updated.

Control techniques that may ensure that reference data is updated accurately are one-for-one checking of detail reports and programmed edit checks.

In practice, it is likely that reliance is placed on a combination of the following to ensure the accurate updating of reference data: the proper operation of the computer programs; the controls over accuracy of input; and other procedures (such as checking of suppliers' statements and the dispatch of statements to customers).

These procedures do not cover all accuracy requirements. Generally, the accuracy of the programmed procedures is relied on to ensure that some or even all of the significant data fields are accurately updated.

Correct Master File Generations

Master files are processed according to generations. The previous master file is run with the input transactions to create a new master file. In subsequent runs, the new master file will become the old master file, and so on. If the most recent file is not used, all transactions processed since the last correctly updated master file will be lost.

Controls Over Master File Generations

When a control account technique is used at input, no additional control is necessary to ensure that updating has been performed on the correct generation of the master file. The control account technique records all types of transactions that should eventually reach the master file in a control account; the cumulative totals of these transactions are carried forward from period to period. The balance of the control account is compared at intervals with the accumulated individual balances on the master file to see if they are the same. If the wrong generation of the master file is used for an update, the control account and master file balance will disagree.

CALCULATING, SUMMARIZING, AND CATEGORIZING PROCEDURES

Calculating

Calculating consists of two sets of data being used to produce a third. For example, a program multiplies the quantity shipped by the sales price to produce the sales value. Matching typically consists of marrying:

- Master file data (such as the price), which is held permanently on a master file, with
- Transaction data (such as the quantity), which is entered and used only once.

For computer calculating to be effective (see Figure 18-12), the following conditions are necessary:

- The master file data must be reliable. This involves all controls over amending and maintaining the data on the file.
- There should be controls to ensure that the correct generation of the file containing the data is used.
- The transaction data must be entered completely and accurately.
- The method used in the program to carry out the calculation must be logically sound and approved by management.
- There should be some check on the accuracy of the calculations. This is usually a manual review of exceptions (such as excessive wages produced and reported by the computer or comparison with budgets). A manual review of the results of the calculations can also be done, in the form of an overall reconciliation.
- Computations that could result in an overflow condition in the data field, or in an intermediate field, should be checked for the potential overflow condition and a report produced, or other appropriate action taken.

Summarizing and Categorizing

Summarizing is accumulating all transactions, often after calculating, and producing a total (such as the total value of sales for the day).

Categorizing consists of analyzing a summarized total, such as purchases analyzed by general ledger account classification. Categorizing is normally performed by referring to a code that is included in the details entered for each transaction.

For summarizing and categorizing to be effective, the following user controls and programmed procedures are necessary:

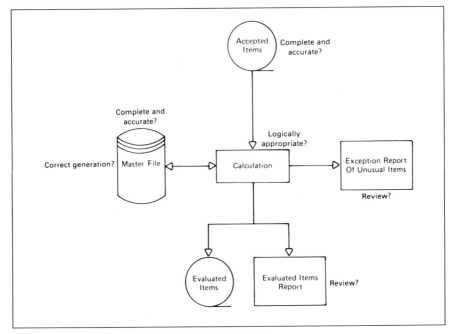

FIG. 18-12 Computer calculation

- The codes on which summarization and categorization are based must be accurately determined and entered.
- There must be adequate controls over the completeness of summarization.
- The basis on which the program carries out categorization must be sound.

COMPUTER-GENERATED DATA

Method of Data Generation

The previous sections have dealt with data that is entered for processing. A computer can also be programmed to initiate data, as illustrated in Figure 18-13.

Data can be generated in the following ways:

- The processing of a transaction may create the condition that triggers generation of data. For example, processing a stock issue reduces stock below minimum level and a purchase order is

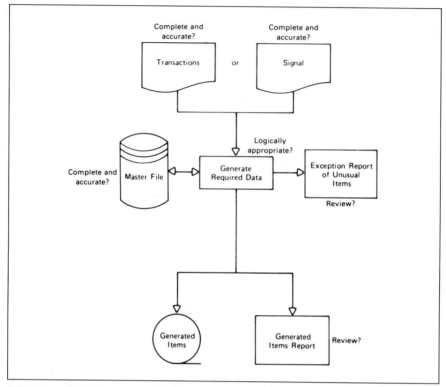

FIG. 18-13 Computer-generated data

produced. In these cases, the conditions that cause the new data to be generated are normally identified by a comparison with master file data: in this instance, the minimum stock level.

- A signal to initiate transactions may be entered. For example, the entry of a certain date initiates the production of checks for all suppliers' invoices prior to that date; entering a particular stage of production that has been reached generates the appropriate charges to work-in-process; the entry of a requisition code generates a list of the components to be issued.

Controls Over Generated Data

Generated data requires controls over completeness and accuracy. These controls should cover the generation process and, at times, the updating of the data produced. All generated data does not update a file. For example, a computer can generate premium renewal notices that are sent to customers. If data is to be produced by the computer completely and accurately, the following user controls and programmed procedures are necessary:

- The data (such as dates or stages of production reached) that triggers the generation of other data must be entered completely and accurately.

- The steps carried out by the program in generating the data must be logically sound.

- The master file data that is referred to (such as the minimum stock level) or used as the basis for generating the new data (such as reorder quantity) must be reliable. This involves all the controls over the amendment and maintenance of master file data on the file because the master file data may not be manually checked on the documents as it is in manual systems.

- The generated data should be controlled for accuracy, either by a manual review (such as a scrutiny of purchase orders before dispatch) or by programmed procedures (such as reporting all checks over a certain dollar amount so that they can be investigated).

After the data is produced by the computer, it may need to be subjected to update controls. These are similar to the controls already outlined for entered data. They are based on the control totals accumulated while the data is being generated. In practice, updating often takes place prior to, or at the time of, production of the data.

CHAPTER **19**

Controls for Validity, Maintenance and Operations

VALIDITY OF DATA PROCESSED

It is essential that only valid data, authorized by management and representing economic events that actually occurred, be written to master files, printed on reports, or incorporated in records. Thus, all data should be appropriately authorized or checked.

Validity Controls

It is the controls over validity that are so important in preventing fraud that could occur because of unauthorized transactions being entered into the system. These transactions include any transaction that is not properly authorized, never occurred, or is otherwise not genuine. Certainly, with a computer system that does not question the validity of transactions, it is simple to enter unauthorized transactions. The possibility also exists for the computer to be used to create fictitious transactions that, when processed, look very real.

Possibly the largest detected computer fraud involved the Equity Funding Corporation of America, where millions of dollars worth of false transactions were entered into the system. More than 20 officers of the company were involved in the case, in which invented insurance policies with fictitious documentation were entered into the regular system as if they were real and then sold to reinsurers. Claims for "deaths" were entered to collect cash. As any premiums came due, more policies were invented and sold. This pyramid grew to incredible proportions; in the 1973 annual report, Equity claimed almost 100,000 policyholders and over $730 million in assets. Only a third of the policies were real. Yet, these transactions were processed as valid because many company people were involved and whatever controls existed were circumvented.

A validity control can be built into a computer application system to test transactions against predetermined conditions, often established as a result of reviewing historical data. For example, an insurance company may decide to monitor the premiums for all policies falling into a certain category. It is important to ensure that they are valid by matching them with the expected increase for the policy type. If it is not within the expected range, the policy should be rejected.

Sometimes validity of transactions can be ensured by matching an organization's data to other data. An example of this technique is when a store that accepts bank credit cards checks a transaction with the bank systems.

The most difficult transaction to detect is the transaction that appears genuine and passes all of the checks and controls. Historical information can assist in determining whether transactions are really valid.

Another example is a last-in, first-out (LIFO) inventory system, where inventory is costed out at the most recent purchase price. The inventory application programs can compare the current cost to previous cost, looking for stock with an abnormal increase or decrease in purchase prices. Depending on the organization's costing procedures, costs may be expected to increase by a certain percentage during the period. Items showing unusual change should be reported and investigated. This type of exception report is helpful in detecting unauthorized transactions, or if inventory is overvalued, this method detects any abnormal increases.

An example occurred when an inventory system was designed for a company by its data processing department, which was unfamiliar with costing techniques. The accounting department arrived at a procedure to value inventory that did not use the computer records. The inventory system basically kept track of stock quantities and not their cost. Cost updates to the inventory valuation data were entered when they were announced by vendors (not when stock was actually purchased). Every day the computer option generated an inventory value of stock-on-hand that bore no relation to what the stock had actually cost, since the stock was not actually purchased at the new cost.

This system was used effectively for several years until the company was sold. The new owner brought in new staff who reviewed the computer reports and accepted the numbers. At first they thought they had made a great deal, because they had paid much less for the inventory than the book value. Then they realized that the computer figure was incorrect, throwing doubt on the book figure. When these doubts were investigated, both figures proved inaccurate; the book value was less so than the computer figures, but the potential for a claim based on overvaluation of inventory against the previous owners existed.

Validity controls can also help ensure that all assets are fairly represented. Although a transaction may be valid, sometimes the computer programs, due to established criteria, conclude that a transaction is invalid. A familiar example is that an inventory system may refuse to allow the balance-on-hand (BOH) to go to a negative quantity. This is based on the fact that a quantity that does not exist cannot be shipped. Logically, this is not possible; however, if the paperwork is in error or out of date, then it is entirely possible that the stock indeed exists and the transaction is indeed valid.

Consider a situation in which there are two very similar products, so similar in appearance that one is constantly mistaken for the other. These products differ by number; for example, an item with the product number 300 is stored near product number 800. Illegible carton markings might cause the 300 to be mistaken for an 800, causing subsequent recording of inventory and pricing to be significantly erroneous. The warehouse office shows a negative BOH for the 300 unit (which sells for far less than an 800). Investigation should uncover the error and result in an authorized transaction to adjust the inventory balances to reflect what is actually in stock. Of course, it is important that an adjustment of this type take into consideration that all paperwork prior to the physical inventory has been processed.

In many cases, the authorization procedures are similar to those used in a noncomputer system. There are, however, the following important differences in authorizing data in computer systems:

- Data is often authorized at the time it is entered into the computer system rather than at the time the resulting output is used.
- Instead of authorizing data manually prior to processing, the computer may be programmed, in accordance with management's specifications, to identify and report defined items for manual

authorization (e.g., in a payroll system, excessive overtime). This focuses attention on important items likely to be incorrect, making manual checking more efficient and effective.

- In some cases the ability of the program to test an item's validity is so precise that manual authorization is no longer required.

The significance of these differences is discussed in the following paragraphs.

Timing of Authorization

The authorization of data at the time of entry, rather than when the resulting output is produced, occurs both with master file data and with transaction data. For example, sales prices may be authorized when they are written to the file. Thereafter, the price is not normally authorized again when sales invoices are produced. Another example is that credit given to customers may be authorized at the time the claim is input and not when the credit note is produced.

When data is authorized at the time of input, it is important to ensure that the authorization remains effective and that changes cannot be made after authorization, during the subsequent processing.

In some cases the controls for completeness and accuracy of input and update indicate the presence of unauthorized data. For example, processed output is sometimes checked in detail with authorized input using one-for-one checking of master file data amendments. Input is matched with authorized data held on file, such as goods received details being matched with a file of purchase orders.

In other cases, specific procedures are required. These normally consist of either authorizing the data after controls for completeness and accuracy of input and update have been established (such as authorizing items in batches after batch totals have been established and recorded) or checking that all items have been authorized after control has been established (such as checking that all items on serially numbered documents have been authorized). These procedures are illustrated in Figure 19-1.

Selective Manual Authorization

Selective manual authorization is used when the computer is programmed to identify and report defined items for manual authorization. This involves the program matching the input with criteria stored as master file data or tables (e.g., matching hours worked with a standard, and reporting excessive overtime). For this form of authorization to be effective, the criteria must be correct and reasonable, the matching process must be logically sound, and all items reported as exceptional must be checked.

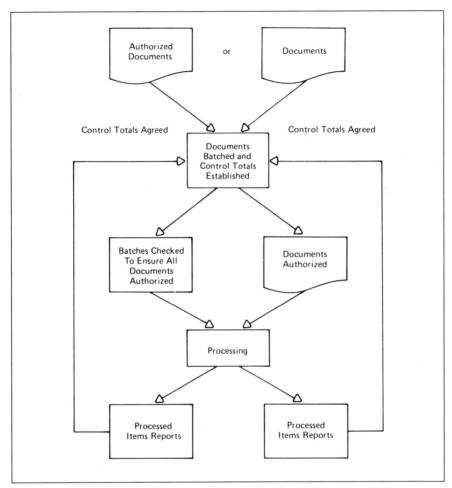

FIG. 19-1 Authorization and validity of data processed flowchart

- The criteria should be reasonably set; otherwise, too few or too many exceptions will be reported. Too many exceptions are just as bad as too few, since unnecessary follow-up on exceptions is an expensive procedure.

- The matching process must be logically sound. Current transaction data must be matched to the appropriate master file data; otherwise, an erroneous exception report can be generated.

- Items reported as exceptions must be checked. There is no sense in preparing a report of exceptions if no one follows up to determine why the exceptions exist. Likewise, exceptions should be investigated and reviewed in detail rather than receiving global approval.

An example of the preceding procedure occurred when an EDP system for sales orders was developed. All sales orders over $10,000 had to be approved and signed off by the sales manager before the order was sent to the warehouse. Every day, all the sales orders over $10,000 were extracted from standard processing and placed in a suspense file for approval. The sales manager believed that all sales were good and would authorize the entire batch with his signature at the end of the day. In this case, the control procedure existed, but was being improperly used. It appeared that the procedure was being followed, since the routine of having the sales authorized was acted out. The authorization function was taken away from the sales manager after the controller reported difficulty in collecting for these large sales. The authorization function was given to the accounts receivable department manager, who actually checked up on every exception.

The concept of authorization criteria is not so rigid that it must apply to all transactions. For example, in a payroll system the criterion might be that since a 40-hour work week is the norm, no employee should ever work more than 60 hours a week. This would be the standard criterion for all payroll transactions. Rigid application might result in frequent exception reports for a particular department. Due to an excessive workload, that department might warrant a more valid criterion of 72 hours. To avoid unnecessary exceptions, it is important to decide how many criteria there should be and where they should be set.

Criteria can also be set for vendor purchase orders, such as amount per vendor, maximum sales tied to credit limits, and so forth. Examples are found in the authorization of credit card transactions:

- Many stores require a $10 minimum sale for use of a credit card, and the system will not accept credit card sales under that figure.

- Any purchase under $25 is processed without manual approval beyond the programmed procedures (discussed in the following section).

- A sale over $25 requires a telephone credit check to ensure that the transaction is valid. This manual procedure is evidenced when store clerks are given authorization reference numbers to record on the sales slip.

Programmed Checking of Validity

As an extension of selective manual authorization, the computer can be programmed to make a precise test of an item's validity. This can be accomplished in various ways. The computer can accept, reject, or report the item for follow-up based on the predetermined authorization criteria. This occurs when the program matches input with a master file. An example is that sales orders are usually tested against a predetermined credit limit held on the customer's master file. It is important that items reported for follow-up are in fact reviewed by a responsible individual and that appropriate action is taken. All exception reports should be investigated by the user department on a timely basis.

Another example of authorization occurs in the matching of transactions to another file. An open purchase order is often authorization for a receipt of merchandise. The validity control might be the existence of a valid purchase order number. If a particular order does not exist as an open purchase order, it can be for one of the following reasons:

- Merchandise was shipped without a valid purchase order number.

- Duplicate shipments of merchandise took place against one purchase order. In times of low inventory turnover, this might be a deliberate "error" on the part of the supplier to help clear out excess stock. The supplier can then claim a clerical error and subsequently ask the organization that received the overshipment to keep it for a reduced price.

It is not enough for the system to match the purchase orders. It must also ensure that individual items received match individual items ordered. Vendors sometimes make substitutions for higher-priced merchandise, claiming stock outage, without adjusting the price.

Output is generated under certain conditions. For example, it is common to find inventory systems that generate reports of recommended economic buying quantities, or even the purchase orders themselves, based on pre-defined order quantities, when a minimum stock level is reached. This represents a standard management decision, activated according to management design when the computer establishes that a particular set of circumstances exists. Controls should exist over this output to determine that reports are distributed to the appropriate management personnel for checking and that the reports are useful to management in their current format.

When minimum stock level quantities control whether a purchase order is issued, the minimum stock level quantities have to be reviewed periodically. This review ensures that correct quantity figures are being used, by analyzing inventory turnover. A low inventory turnover may indicate that the minimum stock level should be changed. This analysis can be performed by a computer program, with authorization for a change being made by management.

In both these methods, the programmed procedures are based on predetermined management criteria, leaving people out of the day-to-day decision-making process for these items. Even more control, however, is required over the original authorization used as the criteria in the system. It is very important that adequate controls exist over the amendment and maintenance of master file data used by the program (such as credit limits or minimum stock levels). These procedures are illustrated in Figure 19-2.

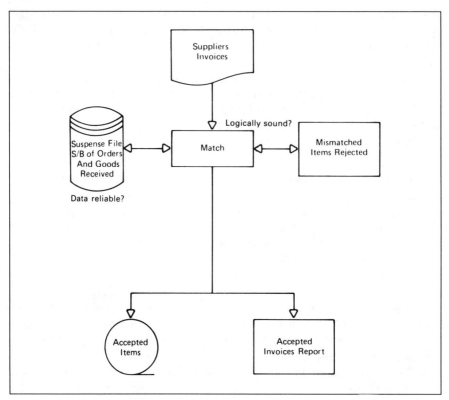

FIG. 19-2   Programmed checking of validity flowchart

Rejected Transaction Reports

Rejected transactions usually require the investigation and correction of all transactions reported as in error. This may mean that previously authorized data can be subject to authorized or unauthorized changes.

For example, a sales order is processed and falls within the credit limit for the customer. The customer sends in a check to pay the previous balance and the check is returned marked "insufficient funds." The accounts receivable clerk immediately updates the customer's record, putting a hold on future shipments and sales. Meanwhile, the previously authorized sales order is being processed in the warehouse for shipment. As a control, the organization runs a prebilling program after staging the merchandise but prior to its delivery. During the prebilling processing, that customer's order would be rejected. This is an example of an authorized change.

An unauthorized change can also occur. For example, a customer's original sales order can be processed within the credit limit and properly prebilled.

Then the customer can come to pick up the merchandise, at the same time requesting that additional merchandise be added on. If the add-ons are fairly small, the organization might have no procedures for credit checking of add-on information. The customer might notice that the add-ons are not processed in the usual way and make this a regular practice, to get past the established credit limit per shipment, thus bypassing the authorization procedures.

Of course, a transaction can be in error, subsequently corrected, and sent for processing. Depending on the type of error (if in fact rejected for validity), any additional change would have to be authorized.

For example, in a payroll validity error, an employee's time sheet may be rejected because it shows 80 hours of overtime when the standard is 20 hours of overtime. The transaction is investigated and found to be in error. Since all overtime went into an overtime bank that was paid quarterly, there was no real need to report the overtime in a timely fashion. The employee had recorded overtime for two periods into one period, and had also been late turning in the time sheets. The employee was automatically paid for 45 hours every week unless otherwise reported. The records were adjusted, and a call made to the employee about the error; the supervisor was asked to authorize the change after correction. To prevent such situations, adjustments should be authorized by the supervisor after review, and corrective action taken.

The extent to which authorizations need to be repeated or checked after correction of errors is an important consideration. The sequence of events is also significant. The presence of an authorizing signature on a source document may not in itself be sufficient, since people frequently sign things out of habit.

MAINTENANCE OF DATA ON FILE

Once an organization ensures that data is completely and accurately processed onto the file, the stored data must remain properly on the file until amended, deleted, or added to during subsequent authorized processing.

This may not seem to present any special problems, yet it can. Remember that unless action is taken against the data, it will remain on file, untouched, and possibly unreviewed until something unusual happens.

Usually, every master data record should have a date mark to indicate when the record was first entered or last amended. Then guidelines can be set for review of any data not amended for a certain period of time (such as one year). It is easy to overlook reviewing data, forgetting that the data can be seriously out of date and create repercussions for the organization. Recently, an insurance company discovered that it was using a 1945 actuarial table to calculate the life expectancy and the reserves on hand. The life expectancy of Americans has increased since 1945, and coverage will be required for longer periods.

Not only is it important to ensure that the data remains accurate, but it must also remain complete. When data is untouched for long periods, it is important to make sure that records are not lost in the interim.

Controls that ensure that data remains correct are called controls for the maintenance of data. Maintenance controls are required for both transaction data and master file data. They are designed to provide controls over the following:

- *Currency of data* — To ensure that data is kept up-to-date and that unusual data requiring action is identified.

- *Correctness of data* — To ensure that the data stored on the file cannot be changed other than through the normal, controlled processing cycle.

Currency of Data

A date mark is the best way to indicate when the data was last amended. However, if the system does not create date marks, master file data from a prior period can be matched to the master file data of the current period. Records that are identical for both periods may be the exceptions that require investigation.

In addition, maintenance controls should provide assurance that the correct generation of the file has been used each time it is updated.

Correctness of Data

Data can be changed by one-time fix-it programs, often called quick-and-dirty programs, written and processed to change data due to other program errors or operational errors.

For example, in a particular billing system, the invoice date was entered on a batch parameter for the day. At the start of the new year, the computer operator kept entering the month and date correctly but forgot to change the year. No one caught the error; they were not used to seeing the new year either.

The first aging for the year showed that accounts receivable over 90 days had increased dramatically. The clerk could not believe it, and an investigation uncovered the error. To have the invoices aged properly, the date had to be changed for all the invoices processed during the first four days of the year. The invoices themselves had already been mailed. To issue credits and reprocess all the invoices seemed like too much work, so the EDP manager suggested a quick-and-dirty program that would change only the last digit of the year. It seemed to be such a simple solution that the program was not even tested. Unfortunately, it had a logic error that is quite common in programming. The program forgot to write the last record read, dropping the last invoice on the file while still adding it to the totals. The invoice was deleted from the records.

When the customer received a statement, only the amount shown was paid.

An EDP operation may use a utility program to change data already on file. Such an example could occur at year-end when the year-to-date balances are not set to zero. It is simple to use a utility to do this, but the utility must operate correctly, or it can zero out other valuable data by accident.

In both of the preceding cases, the examples are found in operations that were not daily occurrences. What a staff does every day, it usually does well; it is the procedures done infrequently in which errors often occur.

CONTROL TECHNIQUES EMPLOYED FOR MAINTENANCE

The main techniques to control the maintenance of data stored on file are the following:

- Reconciliations of file totals
- Exception reports
- Detailed checking of data on file
- Data file security controls

Reconciliations of File Totals

A very effective maintenance control is the regular reconciliation of an accumulation of the records on a file with an independently maintained control total. The control total used may take one of the following forms:

- Manually maintained control account
- Control record maintained as part of the file
- Control record maintained as part of another file within the system (such as a receivables control account in the general ledger to control the detailed items on the outstanding receivables ledger)

Manually Maintained Control Account. The manual reconciliation of file balances with control accounts involves regular agreement of the accumulation of individual balances on the computer file to a manual control account. It is usually applied to transaction data but can also be used for master file data if a hash total control account is maintained. The most common example is the use of batch logs, in which the value of the batch and the total of all batches processed is recorded in order to check the accuracy of the data. For example, in a batch billing system, all invoices for all batches would be added to open accounts receivable, all receipts would be subtracted, and the new total then reconciled to the new weekly accounts receivable trial balance.

An example of applying this technique to master file data is frequently found in payroll applications. Often there is a data field on each record of the hourly rate of pay, which is used in the program to calculate gross pay. The payroll clerk maintains a manual record of the total of all pay rates. Periodically, this hash total of pay rates is agreed to the total of individual pay rates on the payroll master file. This technique helps to ensure that data in the fields totaled remains complete and accurate on the file. It does not guard against compensating errors between accounts (e.g., if the pay rates for two individuals were inadvertently transposed). The use of a manually maintained control account is illustrated in Figure 19-3.

File Control Record. Using this technique, a control record on file (usually the last record in a sequential tape file, or often the first record in an indexed-sequential disk file) contains a total, or totals, of items held on the file. Every time the file is updated, the control record is altered. Periodically, the relevant data fields on each record are accumulated and agreed to the control record. Out-of-balance conditions are reported and corrected.

An imbalance in the control record can normally be attributed to either operational or programming errors. One common program error is the deletion of a record with a balance. For example, in some inventory systems, inventory items can only be deleted when no balance on hand exists. If there is obsolete stock, it must then be taken out of inventory for scrap on a shipping document. Since this procedure is designed into the system, no one would expect an item, when finally deleted, to still have a value in balance on hand.

The frequency of the reconciliation procedures should be sufficient to ensure that errors do not accumulate to the point that it is difficult to investigate and correct them. Because the total is stored in the same record as the data it controls, this technique would not detect the use of the wrong file. Each time the file is updated, a report should be printed showing the opening balance, transaction balance added, deleted, or changed, and closing balance on the file. The opening balance can then be agreed manually to the closing balance on the previous report.

The use of a file control record as a maintenance control is often encountered in data base and on-line systems where programmed reconciliations are relied on for updating purposes. (See Chapter 18, "Controls for Completeness and Accuracy of Update," the section entitled "Completeness of Update.") A file control record used in this way is illustrated in Figure 19-4.

Independent Control File. This method of control, less frequently encountered, is similar to the reconciliation of a manually maintained control

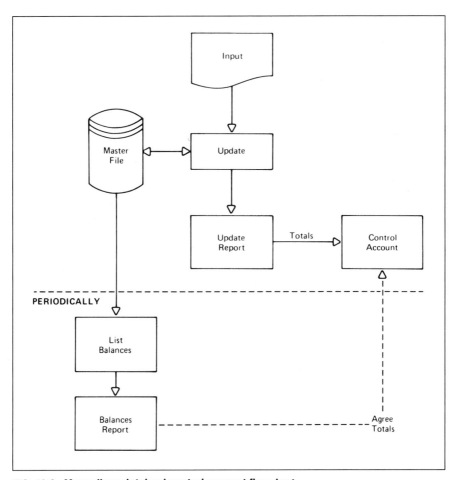

FIG. 19-3 Manually maintained control account flowchart

account. A typical case is when the general ledger system is integrated with the processing of subsidiary ledgers (such as receivables or payables).

The control technique consists of the maintenance of control totals in a separate file, which is updated each time transactions are processed to the master file. The control total is agreed to the total of individual items on the master file each time the file is updated. This agreement may be carried out manually or by computer program.

The technique can also occur when total balances for one file are kept as part of another file. For example, consider an accounts receivable open invoice file and a separate customer master file. The customer master file contains one record for each customer, while the open invoice file has one record for each invoice — and there may be many invoices per customer. Therefore, the

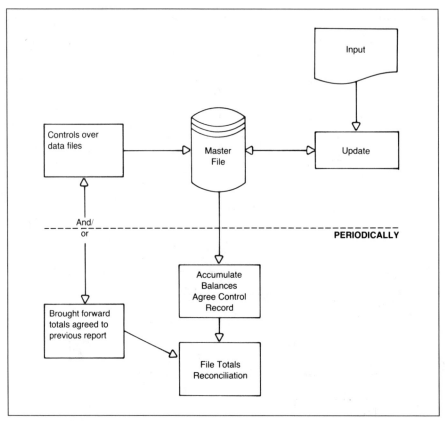

FIG. 19-4   File control record flowchart

customer master usually has a total balance outstanding for the customer. This total acts as a control between the two files if it is reconciled regularly.

This method provides greater assurance as to the maintenance of data than the file control record method discussed previously, since the comparison of totals is from two separate files, not two records on the same file. For this control technique to be effective, there must be

- Adequate controls over the file containing the control total, both to prevent unauthorized alteration and to ensure the use of the correct generation of that file.
- A reconciliation of the opening balance to the previous closing balance each time the system is stopped and restarted.
- Adequate procedures to identify and follow up differences arising from the reconciliation.

The use of an independent control file is illustrated in Figure 19-5.

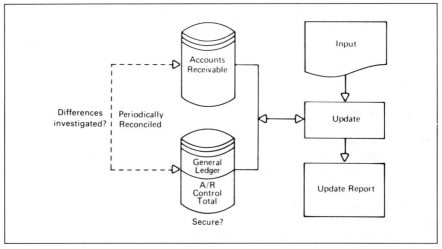

FIG. 19-5   Independent control file flowchart

Exception Reports

This technique involves using a computer program to examine the data on file and report items that appear incorrect or out-of-date. It is valid for both master file and transaction data. For example, with respect to master file data, this technique can be used to control the correctness and timeliness of inventory prices held on the file by periodically producing exception reports of

- Prices that have not been amended for a certain period.
- Prices with an abnormal relationship between the cost and selling price.
- Prices showing an abnormally high or low fluctuation.

For transaction data, exception reports can be produced of old or slow-moving items (such as past-due accounts receivable or slow-moving inventory). For the exception reports to be relied on:

- The method used in the program for identifying exceptional items must be logically sound. This requires that careful consideration be given to the setting of parameters used.
- When parameters are used, adequate controls are required to ensure that the correct parameter data is used. For example, who authorizes and determines that all records that have not been accrued for a year should be reviewed? Or, during such a review the operator enters a parameter date of 365 days or a year (010183) one year prior to the current year (010184). If the operator enters 010182 by mistake, then the data selected would be two years old. Few people

would notice an error of this type, since they would assume that all items selected were really old and that no records were found in the one- to two-year category.

• There should be adequate procedures for the investigation of the exceptional items reported.

Detailed Checking of Data on File

Controls for the maintenance of master file data can also be exercised by regularly checking data on the file against authorized source documentation. When this checking is done, it is usual to check only a portion of the file at a time. Thus, the whole file is regularly checked in cycles. As a result, the control technique is often referred to as "cyclical checking." The frequency of checking depends largely on the importance of the data and the existence and strength of other controls (such as the checking of suppliers' statements).

If checking is carried out on a cyclical basis, the selection of items for checking should preferably be made at random. It should not be predictable, which might inspire a manipulation of data just prior to the check.

Data File Security Controls

Data file security controls are required within the EDP department to prevent unauthorized access to, and use of, data files. The control provided relates only to the correctness of data, providing no assurance as to the currency of data. (These procedures are discussed in Chapter 20, "General or Integrity Controls.")

Application of Control Techniques

Adequate maintenance controls require the application of the relevant control techniques, described earlier, to both master file data and transaction data. Separate control techniques may be required to satisfy correctness and currency. Sometimes more than one technique is required to provide adequate control. Figure 19-6 illustrates the likely techniques that may be encountered.

	Correctness	Currency
MASTER FILE	■ Detailed checking ■ Data file security ■ Exception reports	■ Detailed checking ■ Exception reports
TRANSACTION DATA	■ Total reconciliation ■ Data file security ■ Exception reports	■ Exception reports

FIG. 19-6 Control techniques for master file and transaction data

CONTROLS OVER FILE CREATION AND CONVERSION FOR NEW SYSTEMS

Whenever new systems are ready to be implemented, it is necessary to convert the old master files and suspense files to the new formats so that the system can be put into use. The conversion process, because it is a one-time occurrence and often takes place in a hurry, is susceptible to errors and mistakes. These can have a far-reaching impact, particularly if they occur in converting the master file data. As a result, the conversion process needs to be controlled. In fact, it can be thought of as a mini-application. The normal application control techniques can be applied to ensure the completeness, accuracy, and validity of converted data.

When implementing a new EDP system, the master file data can be entered for the first time using the future system's normal data input procedures. The new system, of course, should have adequate application controls built into the data change process. Providing that these controls are adequate, the main problem is that the controls are being operated by inexperienced people for the first time and in volumes that are higher than normal. Therefore, the entire procedure is more susceptible to mistakes. The control procedures should be carefully monitored to ensure the correct conversion of the data. When existing EDP systems are changed for new ones, it may also be necessary to enter new master file data. The same considerations apply when the new master file data amendment procedures are used.

It may not be practical to convert all the data using the new manual data amendment procedures, whether converting an existing manual or EDP system. Account balances and other cumulative transaction data, as well as master file data from existing computer system, are usually converted by computer programs that are written especially for this purpose. These programs may not always be developed and tested with the same care as the new system as a whole. Therefore, there is a particular need to ensure that the conversion process takes place correctly. It is always advisable to test the conversion programs thoroughly. Proper application controls over the conversion process are necessary; they are significant whenever, for any reason, the conversion programs have not been tested.

One-for-one checking is a common technique for data entered manually to the new files. It is also commonly applied to data transferred from one file to another, particularly when the data is sensitive and the volume is not too large.

As a minimum, when information is transferred from one file to another, control totals should be used on all significant fields. A program should read the existing applications file and establish hash totals for each field on the file. After conversion, these totals should be independently reconciled to similar totals taken from the new file.

Programmed edit checks are valuable control techniques, particularly for controlling the accuracy and the validity of data. Their disadvantage for controlling conversions lies in their complexity and the time necessary to program and test them. However, it is sometimes possible to pass the newly converted data through the edit programs in the new system. This technique should be applied wherever it is feasible. It is not possible to treat all data fields in this way, since the edits in the new system are usually designed to handle input transactions, whereas the conversion process is trying to convert existing master file data and balances. The use of edits is particularly valuable for data that is being collected and used for the first time; data coming from existing manual systems, which tend to be less accurate than well-controlled computer systems; or data that comes from an existing EDP system that is known to be inaccurate in some respects.

Whichever techniques are used, it is always desirable to manually review the data after conversion to ensure that it is valid. This process is similar to the authorization of transactions and should be carried out by someone with sufficient knowledge of the company's operations to be able to notice any substantial errors.

Parallel running can be used to test the operation of the new system. The comparison of the results produced by the new system with the results produced by the old system from the same input may expose some errors on the new master files. The longer the parallel tests are run, the more likely it is that errors on the new file will be picked up. Maintenance controls (those controls over the continued correctness and currency of stored data) may also detect errors on the new file. Although valuable in helping to detect errors, these controls cannot be used as a complete substitute for the types of detailed application controls described previously.

Because of the high risk of error and the potentially significant consequences of those errors, the conversion process is often checked or audited by supervisory personnel, the EDP auditor, a quality assurance group, or a similar function.

Techniques used to check the conversion process include:

- Test checking individual data and records on the new file to the source records
- The use of audit software or verification programs to look for exceptional or unusual data on the new file
- The use of audit software or specially developed programs to compare information on the new application files with that on the existing application files and to report differences

File conversions are very rarely simple when, for every record in the existing format, the record will be reformated for the new system. Often, conversions are no more than making the change from a 9-digit identifying number to a 10-digit number (such a change means that the entire organization will have to implement it at the same time). A more difficult conversion occurs when the data for the new application will be derived from the old data through the use of logic in programmed procedures. The programs, obviously, must be accurate.

ADMINISTRATIVE CONTROLS

Administrative or operational controls are designed to ensure that an organization's information structure functions as management intended. The application controls deal mainly with internal controls. Management's concerns are, of course, much wider in scope.

Administrative controls relate to the effectiveness of operations within an organization. They can be considered as the controls that ensure the timeliness of information and the efficiency of the control procedures and of the processing in general. They also relate to the effectiveness of management decisions. The reliability of the information on which management decisions are based and the procedures for implementing management decisions are inextricably linked. A review of administrative controls might also consider the appropriateness of management's decisions in relation to the objectives of the organization.

Efficiency

Efficiency relates to the cost incurred in processing and controlling the system. A review of administrative controls typically includes the efficiency of internal accounting control procedures as well as a consideration of efficiencies in all parts of the system. A knowledge of the most cost-efficient techniques is particularly valuable when designing or modifying systems. In some cases the more effective control procedures are also less costly. An example is when time-consuming, detailed clerical checks are replaced with accurate EDP reporting procedures. These are usually more precise and less costly to operate, making a twofold contribution to efficiency.

Timeliness

A company can operate more effectively if its information is up-to-date. Some delays are inevitable, but timeliness can be enhanced.

Figure 19-7 illustrates the age of information in three typical circumstances. Generally, the easiest ways to reduce the age of the information are to shorten the period involved, increase the frequency of the reports, or switch from batch processing to an on-line system.

The speed with which errors, exceptions, and control failures are detected

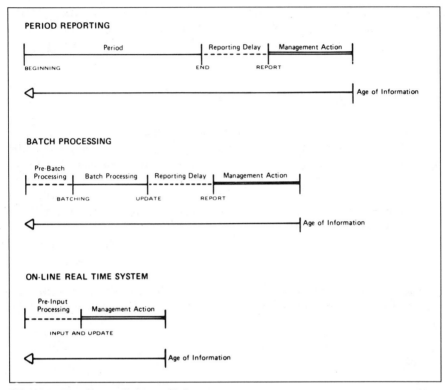

FIG. 19-7 Timeliness: The age of information

should be considered. The timely detection of errors has the following advantages:

- Further errors, or a repetition of the same mistake, can be prevented by changing the procedures that allowed the error to take place.
- The investigation of the cause of an error is easier when checking transactions recently completed.
- Reversing the effect of an error is easier earlier in the transaction cycle before the error has had a chance to affect other information within the system.
- If the error is caught early in the transaction processing cycle, it will pass through only the early stages twice, avoiding duplicate processing at the later stages (once for the erroneous transaction, once for the correct one).

Management Information

Management needs far more than financial information. For this reason, many accounting information systems are part of management information systems. In such systems, accounting procedures are just one of the systems that exist within the overall system.

Much management information is derived from processing that is very similar to that occurring in a financial information system. One major difference is in the required precision of the results. Information accurate to within 5 percent may be sufficient for many management purposes. This is particularly true when more accurate information is more costly to prepare or would take more time. Other features of management information systems include:

- Need for up-to-date information.
- Greater need for specialized inquiry and reports, as opposed to the routine reports of financial information systems.
- Need to produce summary reports, exception reports, or graphic representations of information in a form that is easily used by management.
- Power of senior management to request special information, which may take priority over much of the normal processing.
- Possible unfamiliarity of senior management with the capabilities of the management information system. This is particularly true when the EDP system is technologically advanced. Management may not realize, and therefore not specify, the detailed nature of the information available from the systems that would be of greatest assistance.

Management information systems naturally include many nonfinancial transactions and data. Control techniques for these are similar to those used in financial systems. They cover the same concerns of completeness, accuracy, authorization, and maintenance of data. In addition, the efficiency of processing, as well as the timeliness, quality, and usefulness of the management information should be considered.

Quality of Information

Due to background and experience, the operational or EDP auditor is able to make suggestions that will improve the information received by management. This is particularly valuable when senior management is not intimately familiar with details of the management information system or the capabilities of EDP systems. Common suggestions could include:

- Adding information to a report that would make it more useful to management

- Resequencing a report so that the most significant items appear at the front

- Restructuring reports for clarity and ease of use

- Producing better summaries and subtotals so that management can review information at an overview level

- Greater use of exception reports, thereby decreasing the cost of producing the reports and making management more effective by concentrating attention on those items that require action

- Suggesting additional reports that can be readily produced for management, since the data already exists within the system

CHAPTER **20**

General or
Integrity Controls

INTRODUCTION

In a computer system, there is heavy reliance on processing by programs and much data stored in EDP. The logical question is then: How are these programmed procedures controlled and the stored data protected?

In a simple computer system, the details of all application data processed are printed. As a result, the programmed procedures performed by the computer can be controlled by manually checking the computer's operations.

In more complex systems it becomes impractical, and is sometimes impossible, to manually reperform the programmed procedures for applications performed by the computer. For example, when the computer checks the sequence of prenumbered shipping documents, it may be programmed to print only an exception report. There is no logical way that the user can reperform all of the intermediate steps that the computer has taken to account for all prenumbered documents. This is where the second level of computer controls comes into play. An alternate set of controls must be established over programmed procedures to ensure their consistent and proper operation. These controls, normally known as general or integrity controls, are actually controls over the data processing as a whole. Figure 20-1 illustrates the data stored by the computer for both applications and the processing of applications (the programs).

Some of the differences between general controls and controls over specific applications are:

- General controls are controls over the EDP environment as a whole.
- Application controls are controls over specific applications; general controls apply to all applications.
- Application controls are made up of both manual procedures and programmed procedures.
- General controls regulate the EDP environment to ensure that programmed procedures continue to work properly.
- If there are weaknesses in the general controls, there is no assurance that programmed procedures will continue to work properly, even though they have not been changed.
- General controls secure programs and data, protecting them from unauthorized change.

GENERAL CONTROLS

General controls are the procedures within the EDP department that ensure that programs operate properly and that unauthorized changes are prevented. They include controls over the design, implementation, security, and use of computer programs and files.

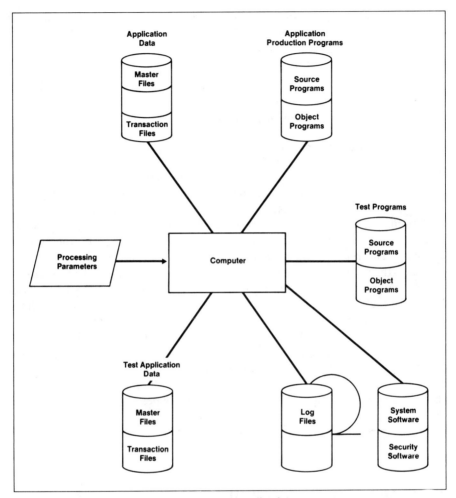

FIG. 20-1 Programs and data required to run application programs

The same general controls normally pertain to all applications. As with application controls, they consist of basic controls and disciplines over basic controls. Their effective operation may, in some cases, depend on computer software procedures, such as software generation of the operations log.

The Five Primary General or Integrity Controls

General controls can be divided into the following five major areas:

1. Implementation controls, designed to ensure that programmed procedures are suitable and that they are effectively implemented in the computer programs. These controls apply to new systems and to subsequent changes made in existing systems.

2. Program security controls, designed to ensure that unauthorized changes cannot be made to programmed procedures.

3. Computer operations controls, designed to ensure that programmed procedures are consistently applied during all processing of data.

4. Data file security controls, designed to ensure that unauthorized changes cannot be made to data files.

5. System software controls, designed to ensure that suitable system software is effectively implemented and protected against unauthorized changes.

The first three areas relate to controls over the programmed procedures; the fourth area, data file security, relates to the maintenance of data; the fifth area, system software controls, can relate either to programmed procedures or to data files. Since the system software controls the computer, many general control procedures rely on the functions that are performed by the system software. The relationship between general controls and system software is similar to the relationship between user controls and programmed procedures.

One important factor that influences the nature of general controls in a location is the structure of the computer department. How the department staff should be organized depends largely on the extent of computer processing, the number of people employed in the department, and the control techniques used. The larger the department, the greater the opportunity to install a satisfactory system of general controls. Such a system can make use of the software features that are available in a large installation and provide better disciplines over the basic controls. These disciplines are actually easier to create and enforce when there is a larger staff, since an appropriate division of tasks can be arranged.

IMPLEMENTATION CONTROLS

Implementation controls are designed to ensure that the proposed programmed procedures are both suitable and effectively implemented. These controls apply to new systems and to subsequent changes to the existing systems.

The work undertaken by an organization between the time it completes a feasibility study for a proposed computer system (see Chapter 7, "The System Development Life Cycle") and the time it successfully implements that system is usually significant. It may take a considerable amount of time to translate the user's requirements from an overall statement into a series of detailed production programs and related instructions for both the computer and the user departments.

The Auditor's Role

The role of the auditor is usually to ensure that adequate controls are incorporated into the new or changed system; that development or change procedures follow standards or are otherwise appropriate; that adequate testing is performed; and that file conversion is controlled. In addition, the auditor plans future audit activity for the system.

Controls Over New Systems

The procedures concerned with the development of new systems are the following:

- System design and program preparation
- Program and system testing
- Cataloging

It is important to monitor the timetable for implementation to ensure that the implementation is proceeding as planned. To do so, an implementation committee is often established. This technique can provide a way to ensure user involvement at the appropriate stages in development by including relevant user personnel on the committee.

System Design and Program Preparation

System design and program preparation should ensure that the programmed procedures are appropriately designed and properly written into the programs. Effective design requires thorough preparation and the use of system specifications. Detailed programming should start once the detailed system descriptions have been reviewed and approved by both the user and computer departments.

In this stage, an auditor should confirm both the existence of good system description documentation and the written evidence of approval by appropriate parties.

The quality of system description is also of major importance when it becomes necessary later on to make program changes. It is difficult to make effective changes unless a reliable, detailed record of the original system exists.

Program and System Testing

Program and system testing is normally carried out in three distinct stages: (1) program testing, (2) system testing, and (3) parallel running.

1. *Program testing* consists of checking the logic of individual programs. The principal methods used are desk checking and test data. Desk checking consists of analyzing the various logical paths in the program and confirms that the program code meets the program specifications. Wherever practical, desk checking should be carried out by a programmer other than the one who designed and wrote the program. The original programmer might be likely to think the logic is correct and try to prove it rather than really check it. Desk checking is normally performed in conjunction with the use of test data. Test data is fictitious data prepared according to the system specification for entry into the system and should be designed to cover all possible processing and/or error conditions. Formal procedures should be set up to identify and correct any errors discovered during testing. All results of running the test data should be documented and retained as evidence that the tests were performed. The same data can also be used to test future changes to the system.

2. *System testing* consists of checking that the logic of the various individual programs is consistent and links together to form a complete system that meets the requirements of the detailed system specifications. The principal technique used is test data. The test results should be carefully scrutinized. The test data should be rerun, and redesigned if necessary, until all failures in logic are detected. In addition to common situations that the system is designed to handle, the tests should also try out the effect of unusual conditions on the system. Wherever possible, system testing should be performed or checked by people other than those responsible for the detailed programming.

3. *Parallel running* means operating the new system at the same time as, or in parallel with, the existing system. Then the results obtained from the dual processing can be checked to identify and investigate any differences. Parallel or pilot running is a means of testing the complete system in operation, including all user procedures. Unlike system testing, the purpose of parallel or pilot running is to test the system's ability to cope with real, rather than test, data and to deal with actual volumes, rather than individual transactions. The new system should not be fully accepted by the relevant user departments, nor should the existing system be dropped, until the full processing cycle has been successfully run, as far as practical, on the new system. In addition, recovery procedures — the ability of the system to recover from an abnormal termination — should be tested and documented. The results should be reviewed by people other than those responsible for the detailed programming, if possible.

Cataloging

Cataloging is the set of procedures necessary to transfer the tested programs into operation. Important procedures are those that ensure that testing and documentation have been satisfactorily completed before the programs go into production, and that the manual procedures for the new or changed system are already in place in both the user and the computer departments. This includes the preparation of written operating and user instructions, reviewed and approved by responsible officials from the departments involved. There should be a procedure for the transfer of the new or changed programs, when appropriate, from a test to a production status, including instructing the staff in the new procedures. When programs are held on-line, transferring the accepted programs from a test status on the program library file to a production or operational status is a software procedure.

Cataloging procedures should include checks to ensure that all required changes, and only those, have been made to the programs. Proper testing can provide much of this assurance. Even stronger control can be provided by using software to compare the changed program with the original and then reviewing the changes. This technique acts as a good discipline over programming staff and can be used to detect attempts to introduce fraudulent code. Another concern is that changes may be made to programs between the time of testing and their cataloging to secured program libraries. A solution is to use a test library, separate from the production and programming libraries, which can be kept secure because programmers do not need access to it. Programs ready for checking are first cataloged to the secure test library; after testing, they can be transferred to the production library with the assurance that the tested version has not been modified.

Naturally, the executable form of a program is tested and used for production. The source version must also be kept because any subsequent authorized changes are made to this version. With all these versions available, it is important to check that the source program retained coincides with the executable version placed in production. Program library software packages can help control versions and track changes that are made. Another good practice is to re-compile programs before the final acceptance tests, essential if the source-to-source comparison described previously is to be relied on; software is available to check that a re-compiled program is identical to an executable version.

Program Changes

A significant amount of work is usually involved in making a change to a program from the time that the initial request is made until the revised program is put into production use. The controls required for the development of authorized program changes are similar to those for new systems. The request for a change must be properly defined to form an adequate basis for decision about its acceptance and design. The changed program must be tested, following the same standards as those used for new systems. There must be suitable approvals of the work done before implementation.

Another important practical consideration when making program changes is one that is not relevant to new systems. There should be a procedure to ensure that all valid requests for changes are accounted for and promptly acted on. This is important to an organization for operational and control reasons, since other controls will not necessarily identify an ongoing deficiency that the change was designed to eliminate. All system and program changes should be supported by appropriate written authorization.

Occasionally it may be necessary to amend production programs without adhering to standard procedures. This might happen, for example, in an emergency where a processing deadline has to be met, or at night when the staff is minimal. In such cases, there should be controls to ensure that these amendments are subjected to the normal authorization, testing, and implementation procedures on an after-the-fact basis.

PROGRAM SECURITY CONTROLS

Program security controls are designed to ensure that unauthorized changes cannot be made to the production programs that process data. They ensure that the only changes are those made through the normal program change procedures. Program security is of special concern to an auditor when an unauthorized change in a particular program might benefit the person making the change (e.g., a change made in systems processing wages and cash payments that could result in unauthorized payments being made).

Program security controls are necessary for programs both while they are in use and while they are held off-line. Programs in use are defined as programs that can be accessed through the system, either by operators processing jobs or through terminals. Off-line programs are held away from the computer, in a separate storage area sometimes called a tape library, and must be retrieved for use. In addition to the basic controls over program security, disciplinary controls should also be installed to further reduce the possibility of unauthorized changes to the production programs.

Programs in Use

The principal method of securing programs in use is a comprehensive access security system that limits the ability to change programs to authorized programmers. Others may execute programs, but not change, delete, or replace them. It is also good practice to secure the "reading" of programs so that they cannot be copied for unauthorized purposes.

Other possible techniques include:

- Review of a comprehensive computer report of jobs processed. By comparing this report with the authorized job schedules, any unauthorized accesses of production programs can be identified and investigated. This report should be reviewed and approved by a responsible official.

- Authorization of jobs at the time they are set up, and prior to passing them to operators for processing. However, in the latter case it is necessary to ensure that unauthorized changes cannot be made to the jobs after set-up, and that unauthorized jobs are not added to the approved jobs.
- Comparison of the production programs with independently controlled copies on a regular basis. These copies, and the software executing the comparison, are normally held in either a permanent, supervised physical library, or off-site at a remote location.
- The periodic running of test data by responsible officials.

Off-Line Programs

When programs are held off-line they should be subject to physical library controls; that is, they should be securely held, issued only on appropriate authority, and promptly returned. Backup copies and program documentation should be protected to prevent unauthorized personnel from obtaining a detailed knowledge of the contents of the programs.

Disciplines Over Program Security Controls

With sufficient technical skill and detailed knowledge of their contents, users could circumvent security and make changes in production programs. Protection against this possibility is normally enhanced by a suitable segregation of duties. When duties are separated, the users cannot obtain a detailed knowledge of the programs; on the other hand, those responsible for the development and maintenance of the programs cannot gain unsupervised access to production programs. It is important to maintain this segregation of duties at all times, even outside of normal working hours.

COMPUTER OPERATIONS CONTROLS

Computer operations controls are designed to ensure that systems continue to function consistently, as planned. They include controls over the use of the correct data, programs, and other resources, and the proper performance of this function by operators, particularly when a problem occurs. These controls are described in the following sections:

- Job Set-Up
- Operations Software and Computer Operating
- Disciplines Over Computer Operations Controls
- Backup and Recovery Procedures

Job Set-Up

Job set-up is the name normally given to the preparation of an application for processing. Programs and data sets must be defined and loaded onto the system, the sequence of events must be specified, and the devices must be allocated. In many advanced systems, there is less need to complete some of the steps because the job control commands defining such procedures are held in a procedure library and many data files are on-line.

Job set-up is important for computer operations controls primarily because it helps to ensure that the job control statements and parameters are properly prepared and that the correct data files are used.

The normal way to ensure that valid job control statements and parameters are being used is to maintain approved written set-up instructions. There is also a need to check that the statements and parameters actually used correspond with those instructions. This should be reviewed and approved by a responsible official. The set-up instructions should cover all applications and system software. They should include, where appropriate, processing flowcharts, information regarding set-up of peripherals and files, job control language (JCL) requirements, and run parameters.

In many cases, the normal updating and maintenance controls described as application controls ensure that the correct data files are being used. However, specific controls over the use of the correct files are still necessary. This is particularly true for files that contain tables referred to in processing (for example, the lists of numbers when sequence checks are used).

There may be manual controls over the data files from the time they are issued from the physical library until job set-up, or system software may ensure that the correct files are loaded. When system software is used as a control technique, each file held on a device includes a header containing information such as the file name and the version number. When the file is loaded for processing, the details of the header are checked. Any operator override of these controls should be reviewed and approved.

Operations Software and Computer Operating

Computer processing and operations are usually controlled by manual and programmed procedures. In more advanced systems, the procedures are increasingly carried out by software. The manual functions are usually restricted to actions required or requested by the software. The principal control considerations are that the system software used is reliable and that the manual procedures do not, because of error or for other reasons, interfere with or affect normal processing.

Controls over the manual procedures depend largely on the nature of the system software and the size of the installation. They normally comprise a combination of procedures, designed both to prevent and to detect errors. These preventive procedures usually include providing operating instructions for system software, application procedures, restart and recovery procedures, procedures for labeling, disposition of input and output tapes, and the establishment, where practical, of a suitable segregation of duties. Measures employed to detect error are based on reviews of operator activity.

Disciplines Over Computer Operations Controls

A review of operator actions is usually based on a computer-produced report or a manual report, such as a problem log. The system software usually records, on a file, details of all activity during processing. The details on this file, called the system log, can be interrogated for review. Unusual activity such as hardware malfunction, reruns, abnormal endings (abends), and the resulting operator actions can thus be investigated. However, the information recorded on these logs is voluminous and technical in nature, so that a full review is often impractical. Packaged audit software is available, or audit software can be created, which analyzes the entries as an aid to audit investigation.

Backup and Recovery Procedures

Backup procedures and arrangements should exist. In the event of a computer failure, the recovery process for production programs, system software, and data files should not introduce any erroneous changes into the system. Principal techniques that may be used are:

- A facility for restarting at an intermediate stage of processing. This is applicable to programs terminated before their normal ending and avoids the need to reprocess the whole run.
- A system to copy and independently store master files and associated transactions. This makes it possible to restore any files lost or damaged during the disruption.
- Similar procedures to ensure that copies of operating instructions, run instructions, and other essential documentation are available if the originals are lost.
- Formal instructions for the restoration of processing or its transfer to other locations.

(See the section entitled "Disaster Recovery and Contingency Planning" in Chapter 32, "Security.")

DATA FILE SECURITY CONTROLS

Data file security controls are controls to ensure that unauthorized changes cannot be made to data files. The need for data file security controls is likely to be greater for the master file data than for transaction data. This is because not all significant master file data elements are subject to regular reconciliation procedures. Any cyclical checking of data on files may not be done often enough to provide timely identification of unauthorized changes.

Data file security controls are also important from an operational standpoint. Operational considerations include protecting data from destruction or erasure, both accidental and intentional, and from theft or other misuse.

Controls are required for data files both while they are on-line and while they are being held off-line. On-line data thus includes both tapes and disks that have been loaded for a specific processing run but are otherwise stored off-line, as in batch systems. They may also be disks permanently loaded and available for inquiry or updating, as in on-line and real-time systems. Off-line data files are those held in a separate library.

Access Controls

A particular threat to data is unrestricted access, allowing data to be changed in an unauthorized manner. In batch systems, where data files have been loaded for a specific processing run, the problem is limited to controlling the action of operators during that particular run. On-line and real-time systems require a combination of control techniques, including restricting the access paths into the system and the range of activities permitted to users. Dial-up systems require particularly high levels of security due to the dangers of access by hackers. The appropriate level of access control is determined by the sensitivity of the data, the division of duties of users, and the resources available.

Access by Users. The control procedures designed to protect data files from unauthorized access by users during processing are similar to those already described for programs. These procedures, which can usually be carried out at the same time as those for programs, include system software functions such as library packages, security software, passwords, communications software, and data base management systems.

Access to On-Line Data. In situations where data is entered through a terminal, as it is in on-line and real-time systems, it is essential to protect against the entry of unauthorized information that will subsequently update the data.

The entry of invalid data might be made to either transaction data or master file data. Invalid transaction data is normally entered into the system to alter the effect of a transaction already on file. For example, a fictitious credit note to match a sales invoice on file would alter the status of the invoice. Invalid master file data might consist of a complete record, such as a fictitious supplier's account, or a data element, such as the rate of pay or an interest rate.

When data files are on-line to terminals, there should be a suitable combination of system software, such as restricting terminals to particular transactions, programs, or files. Only authorized personnel should be able to access the files, either to obtain information or to enter alterations.

Access by Production Programs. In addition to user and terminal access controls, procedures should be established to restrict access to data by the various programs. These accesses to data can be restricted through the use of software, including which data elements a program can access and whether it can read or update this data. Reports, generated by the software, of all accesses of the programs, can be produced. They should be reviewed and investigated as necessary.

Off-Line Files. Files held off-line are protected against change as long as they are not mounted on a computer, but they can be removed, possibly for unauthorized purposes. This can occur when files are not physically protected or properly monitored and their release is not controlled. The control features should protect against the unauthorized removal or destruction of files, including those stored off-site for use in disaster recovery.

Physical Security. To secure off-line files from unauthorized access, there should be a lockable storage area. It should be separate from the computer room and, preferably, supervised by a librarian responsible for the issue, receipt, and security of all files. Access to the library should be restricted to only the staff authorized to obtain and deliver files.

Procedures are needed to ensure that files are issued only for authorized processing. This means that processing schedules should be prepared that specify in detail which files are required for processing. Schedules should be prepared for all applications and be approved by a responsible official. Specific authorization should be required to move files off-site or to another computer.

Library Records. Each removable storage device, such as a tape, should be given a unique identity number, and this number should be permanently recorded on the device. A record of devices can then be maintained as a way to account for and control both the files issued from the library and those created during processing. Records of devices and files can be maintained either manually or by the system software.

SYSTEM SOFTWARE CONTROLS

System software is the set of computer programs that control the functions of the computer itself and make possible the use of application programs. System software consists of programs that are not specific to any particular application but may be used in the design, processing, and control of all applications. It includes operating systems, librarian packages, security packages, data base management systems, and communications software. System software is important to the auditor because it assists in control of both the programs that process data and the data files. Although controls over system software do not directly affect the programs and data, they affect the extent to which the auditor can rely on the other general controls.

The system software that may be relevant to control includes the programs that relate to:

- Cataloging
- Reporting of jobs processed
- File handling
- Data communications
- Reporting of operations
- File set-up
- Security protection
- Library records
- Data bases

The Auditor's Interest in System Software

The auditor must ensure that the system software procedures listed previously have been properly implemented and are kept secure. The controls over the implementation and security of system software procedures are discussed in the following sections.

Implementation and Use. The controls required for the successful implementation of system software are essentially similar to those required for the implementation of application programs. Specific considerations relating to system software are discussed here.

All vendor-supplied system software should be subject to review and approval by a person with sufficient knowledge to be able to determine the software's impact on existing systems and operating procedures. He or she should also be able to determine that the software will meet the company's needs and objectives. This review should encompass both basic software packages and available options.

When new system software interfaces directly with existing application programs, it is imperative to test this software using proven application programs. If anomalies occur, they can then be identified as resulting from the system software.

Instructions and other documentation for system software and options that are supplied by an outside vendor should be reviewed by technically competent personnel. They should make sure that the documentation properly describes the procedures necessary to use and operate the software correctly.

Use of system software should be restricted to authorized users. For example, the technical support group may need to use some utilities and service aids, which should not be available to operators or dial-up users.

Security. Controls similar to those described earlier (see section entitled "Program Security Controls") should be applied to ensure that unauthorized changes are not made to system software. Password and security tables, and the means by which they can be changed, require the highest possible level of protection on the system.

THE EFFECT OF GENERAL CONTROL WEAKNESSES

In order to determine whether or not significant errors can arise, an auditor must consider the effect of the weakness on the programmed procedures or data elements at risk. "At risk" are any programmed procedures and data identified as not being checked in detail by the user. Weaknesses in the different areas of general controls have different effects on the programmed procedures and data as follows:

- Weaknesses in the implementation controls generally cause new systems, or systems that have been modified, to function incorrectly. Often such errors are embedded in the system, and the erroneous processing continues until the error is identified and corrected.

- Weaknesses in the program security controls generally mean that unauthorized changes can be made to the systems. These are changes that are not subject to the normal implementation controls. The organization may not be sure which systems have been changed and which have not. Opportunities for the misappropriation of assets are also increased.

- Weaknesses in the computer operations controls generally mean that random errors may occur in the system. Some errors, such as those in master file data, have lasting consequences. The main effect of such weaknesses is similar to the effect of weaknesses in a noncomputer system: Most processing is correct, but occasionally it is not. This contrasts with the continuous errors arising from implementation control weaknesses.

- Weaknesses in the data file security controls generally mean that unauthorized changes can be made to stored data. How long it takes to discover these unauthorized changes depends largely on the structure of the application controls. Some errors in transaction data may be discovered fairly quickly through the operation of control accounts, the mailing of statements, and so forth. If it is a payment system, the error may never be noticed — particularly if it is an incorrect overpayment of pensions or suppliers. Errors in master file data usually take longer to detect. Weaknesses in data file security controls combined with weaknesses in program security controls provide particular opportunities for almost undetectable misappropriation of assets. Weaknesses in data file security controls coupled with weaknesses in the application controls over the continuity of the data increase the likelihood that undetected errors will occur.

- Weaknesses in system software controls do not usually have a direct effect on the applications. Such weaknesses may, however, mean that system software, which is relied on for the proper functioning of the other general controls, is not appropriate. As a result, one or more of the control areas described previously may be weak.

Reporting General Control Weaknesses

When control weaknesses or deficiencies exist in a system, they may fall into some of the categories described in Figure 20-2. They are grouped according to the type of control, possible deficiency, possible audit comments, and recommended audit procedures.

AUDITING GENERAL CONTROLS IN USE

When half a million customers depend on a company for electric power, advanced computer systems can help deliver that power more efficiently. Such a system is in use at a public utility that serves 28,000 square miles in the southern United States. In addition to its half million electricity customers, the company also provides gas and steam to customers in a major city. In February 1982, the utility moved into a new building that also houses their computer center. They recently converted to a new IBM computer that supports over 800 terminals within the building and throughout the service area.

In the past few years, the utility has installed many new and advanced computerized applications. As a result, its management and external auditors have become increasingly dependent on the computer hardware, software, and data processing. The utility management has recognized the need for a high

(text continues on page 20-20)

Description	Possible Audit Comments	Recommended Audit Procedures
Limited size of staff means that there may be: ■ No segregation between EDP and users. ■ Poor segregation between user departments. ■ Limited number of technical EDP personnel so that there is a poor segregation of duties within EDP. ■ Lack of disciplines over basic controls.	■ For all deficiencies noted evaluate risk areas and design or modify to improve compensating user controls. In addition: a. Implement segregation of duties where possible. b. Review user and operation logs where possible. c. Rotate duties.	■ Extended testing of data with more emphasis on cash systems (such as controls over cash receipts and payments). ■ Evaluate control procedures. ■ Spread tests through year.
A lack of experience in computerized environments may result in a lack of adequate completeness and accuracy controls being built into the system or considered when purchasing package systems.	■ Institute controls over completeness and accuracy. ■ Modify systems to create edit check processing at input time (such as comparison of counts, totals, etc.), range tests, verification of part numbers, display of vendor/part name in response to input of number. ■ Screen design could include use of menus, prompts for missing data, and production of meaningful diagnostics.	■ Extended testing of data to include manual reconciliation of input and update totals and to ensure that data files are footed. ■ Reperformance of input and update transactions.
■ Poor systems, programs, and operations documentation.	■ The organization should review requirements for standards and then develop and adhere to those documentation standards. standards.	■ Gain understanding by discussion with EDP and user departments and, if necessary, with vendor.

(continued)

FIG. 20-2 Control deficiencies

Description	Possible Audit Comments	Recommended Audit Procedures
■ Program and system development may be undertaken on an ad hoc basis with few development standards — or none at all.	■ Ensure that vendor-supplied systems are documented in accordance with contract terms. ■ Establish controls over program development, which will include: a. Review the need for controls. b. Ensure that users are involved. c. Ensure that responsible officials have no conflicting duties.	■ Extended testing of data can include direct tests of significant programmed procedures.
Controls over program data and data file security may be weak due to: ■ A lack of system software controls over program libraries.	■ Develop and implement controls over program libraries so that all program changes are logged and approved.	■ Copy programs at beginning of year and do comparison with programs at the end of year; investigate differences. ■ Testing of data on data files can be spread throughout the year.
■ Where interpretive languages are used (such as BASIC), the source code is available to the user on execution.	■ Replace interpreters with compilers if possible and restrict use of compilers to authorized program development.	■ Increase tests of data.
■ No notification of unsuccessful log-on attempts; only one level of use.	■ Employ physical security over terminals, such as use of terminal key locks. ■ Change passwords regularly. ■ Review and make full use of the security features available for the particular machine.	

FIG. 20-2 *(continued)*

Description	Possible Audit Comments	Recommended Audit Procedures
	■ Restrict terminals as to functions.	
	■ Inactivate or otherwise restrict special keys.	
	■ Log access to files and assign file passwords.	
	■ If secure password system does not exist, program or obtain one.	
■ No restrictions on users entering data and making inquiries using screens.	■ Restrict access to computer and data files.	
■ Utilities are available for entering, changing, and interrogating data, bypassing application controls.	■ Remove data alteration utilities from the system (may be easier said than done) or disable the functions or log their use if the utility cannot be removed.	
■ Destructive program updates so that no program history exists (very common).	■ Manually document program amendments.	
■ Vendor-supplied utilities that may be used to make program patches.	■ Disable functions or restrict their use to exceptional authorized circumstances.	
There may be: ■ Few system software controls to ensure only authorized use.	■ Restrict access to computer.	■ Testing of data can include reperformance of any significant programmed procedures.
■ No controls to ensure that only tested and approved programs are executed against data files.	■ Catalog only tested and approved programs (manual control). ■ Data librarian should not be same individual as operator, and duty may be rotated periodically.	

(continued)

Description	Possible Audit Comments	Recommended Audit Procedures
Typically, the console log is either nonexistent or too voluminous.	■ Develop adequate system log procedures.	■ Audit software can be used to examine voluminous systems logs.
Inadequate backup and contingency planning.	■ Develop and test backup and contingency plans including design of good recovery method. ■ Performance of backup should be logged (including date of performance, as-of date, and use of file labels). ■ The adequacy of backup and contingency plans should be regularly reviewed.	■ However, this may affect "going concern" consideration.
There may be little or no control over amendments made to vendor-supplied system software.	■ Develop controls over modifications to system software. ■ If possible, ensure that system software programmers are not allowed access to application programs or documentation.	■ Assess risk (there may be none) and increase levels of tests, or extend testing if appropriate.

FIG. 20-2 *(continued)*

level of control over the computer environment. Their computer applications department, with support from upper management and their auditors, began establishing a system of controls over the design, implementation, security, and use of computer programs and files. These general control procedures encompass all applications and help ensure that the computer area is processing the financial data according to management's intentions.

As part of this effort, their auditors have monitored this process and noted the improvement in the level of general control over the last several years. While planning for the audit, they determined that testing the general or integrity controls would be important in the audit procedures.

These improvements in general controls were implemented by:

- The implementation of a software security package to control access to resources such as program libraries and data files.

- The development of formalized procedures by the computer applications department to control the implementation of and modifications to computer programs.
- Use of a variety of general control audit software by the utility's internal EDP audit staff to test general controls on an ongoing basis.

One objective of the audit team was to increase overall audit coverage and quality without increasing audit time. The improvements in general controls helped the audit team achieve this objective. These enhancements provided an effective framework for the consistent and proper operation of programmed procedures and the security of programs and data files.

Increased audit coverage and reduced audit time were achieved through

- Testing the implementation of and use of the security software package. It ensures that only authorized personnel have access to the appropriate data sets. Therefore, audit testing of this software resulted in a reduction of the manual and automated testing that is normally performed to ensure that only authorized accesses are made to programs and data files.
- Testing of procedures in the computer applications department, governing the implementation and modification of all computer programs, provided assurance that the programs were operating as management intended.
- Using the information generated by the general control software, which was processed by the utility's internal auditors.

After a preliminary scoping of the controls was performed, tests were developed. To assist in identifying specific controls to be tested, the external audit staff developed a general control summary, specifically for this organization. The summary identified specific controls and areas where limited or no controls existed. In areas where there were no controls, other integrity control software packages were used to ensure that no irregularities occurred during processing of certain application programs.

The summary identifies controls for six areas:

1. Data file security
2. Program security
3. Operations
4. Implementation/change procedures
5. System software
6. Data base security

Primary and secondary preventive and detective controls were identified for each of the six areas listed. In addition, the summary highlighted specific systems and how general controls affect them. With this in mind, an efficient approach of testing only key controls in the data base area could be justified. They were complemented by tests of manual application controls over specific application systems. Applied in this manner, the general control summary integrated general testing with more efficient testing of application controls.

The summary also provided the director of the computer applications department with clear, concise documentation of key controls that could be tested and relied on. It was also used to keep EDP personnel informed about areas that needed improved control.

After identification of critical controls over the utility's system and selection of appropriate testing procedures, procedures were applied throughout the year. These included manual tests, as well as use of integrity control software. Analysis program software was used to extract a sample of changes to programmed procedures to ensure compliance with the change/implementation and testing controls. Analysis programs for the information management system and communications system were used to confirm the level of security in the data base and on-line communication systems.

The increased reliance on computers, the consolidation of many previously manual operations into computer systems, and the sharing of data by different departments for control procedures, all combined to increase management's concerns about their system. This concern was addressed by a high level of computerized controls to meet the demands of a changing environment. Now, new capabilities exist to restrict both EDP personnel and other staff to only the information that is required for their respective jobs.

In all, an increased level of awareness of the need for general controls has created an efficient system that benefits all concerned.

INTRODUCTION

An auditor performs a control review to make a professional risk assessment of a system and its controls. The objective may be to write an audit report (a common objective of the internal auditor) or to determine what substantive tests are required (the normal objective of the external auditor).

The audit conclusions resulting from the review often concentrate on the deficiencies or weaknesses in the control system. These deficiencies are featured in the internal auditor's report as items requiring management attention. They are also communicated to management by the external auditor and, more important, are used as a basis for determining the additional substantive tests and other auditing procedures required. In spite of this apparent concentration on deficiencies in the results of the review, the control review in fact focuses mainly on control strengths. The auditor applies procedures designed to determine what risks the system might be subject to, what controls are in place that would reduce these risks, whether the controls are properly designed, and whether the controls continue to function through time. The auditor normally applies a variety of auditing procedures in performing these tasks, including:

- Interviews and inquiries
- Documentation and analysis
- Examination of evidence
- Reperformance of manual or computer processes
- Observation and physical inspection

These audit procedures are clearly interrelated; the typical control review includes most of these techniques, performed in appropriate sequences. The systems audit approach divides the control review into a number of steps, which are covered in different sections of this book:

- The documenting and analysis of the processing system is covered in Chapter 23, "How to Document Systems and Use Flowcharts."
- Inquiry techniques are covered in Chapter 24, "Interviews and Transaction Reviews in an Audit," along with the audit procedures that can be used to confirm the documented understanding of the system.
- The documenting and analysis of control points are covered in Chapter 25, "The Evaluation Process and How to Use Documents," with further guidance for general controls in Chapter 26, "*Internal Control Reference Manual* — General Controls," and for application controls in Chapter 27, "*Internal Control Reference Manual* — Application Controls."

Control Reviews and Compliance Tests

This chapter focuses on the next step of the systems audit approach, those audit procedures called compliance tests, the main purpose of which is to ensure that the controls operate as planned.

Scope of Compliance Tests

Auditors may compliance test some of the controls but rarely test them all. Which controls are selected for testing depends on the objectives of the audit. External auditors typically restrict their review, and therefore their tests, to internal accounting controls. Additionally, internal auditors sometimes test the operational or administrative controls to identify opportunities for system improvements that do not affect internal accounting controls. Internal auditors sometimes omit compliance testing altogether, preferring to rely on other control review procedures. They do this to best use scarce internal audit resources and get the maximum coverage from the resources available. Internal auditors may restrict the compliance tests they perform to a single point in time. The external auditor more frequently extends the scope of the tests to a part or all of the period under review. The internal auditor concentrates on testing those controls that are of most importance to management; the external auditor, on controls that cover a significant risk of error or irregularity and have an effect on the nature, extent, or timing of the substantive tests. Other factors that may affect the decision of whether or not to test specific controls include:

Materiality considerations

- The approximate volume or number of transactions that pass (or should pass) through the control point. An auditor can use a number of techniques to make a reasonable estimate of volume, such as inquiries of knowledgeable personnel, review of statistical records maintained by personnel operating the system, and review of use of serially numbered documents.

- The estimated monetary value of the transactions that pass (or should pass) through the control point and the approximate range of individual transactions. An auditor can use a number of techniques to make a reasonable estimate of the monetary value, such as inquiries of knowledgeable personnel, review of records maintained by personnel operating the system, and relating recorded monetary values to the company's known operating levels.

- The effect of an error resulting from a control weakness. An internal auditor may concentrate tests on areas where errors or late processing could have a significant effect on operations. An external auditor may apply a lower materiality threshhold for items such as net income, working capital, and restrictions on retained earnings than for items that affect only classification in financial statements.

For example, a control weakness that can lead to an overstatement of inventory is more likely to be material if the offsetting erroneous credit is to income than if it is to accounts payable.

Risk factors, that is, the susceptibility of particular accounts and transactions to material errors

- The amount of accounting judgment involved in the measurement and classification process.
- The susceptibility of an account to misappropriation.
- The extent to which account balances are derived from estimates.

Other considerations

- The risk that error may not be detected in later stages of processing.
- Any other indications of potentially significant errors.

Types of Compliance Tests

Compliance or functional testing normally includes the following procedures:

- *Examination of evidence* — Inspection of records, documents, reconciliations, reports, and the like for evidence that a specific control appears to have been applied properly. An example is the inspection of signatures or initials on a purchase invoice for evidence that the invoice was matched with a purchase order and record of goods received. Another method is by inspection of exception reports.

- *Reperformance* — The repeating, either in whole or in part, of the work processes performed by people or computers. For example, the matching of a purchase invoice with the corresponding purchase order and record of goods received.

In some situations, observation or inquiry is the principal compliance test that can be performed. For example, control over counting and examining incoming goods and the physical security of inventory are tested by observation of the procedures used. Where observation is employed, an auditor should bear in mind the possibility that the observed control may not be performed when the auditor is not present. In addition, it is important to see evidence of the action taken as a result of the application of the observed control (such as follow up on exception reports).

These tests should not be confined solely to the inspection of signatures, references, and the like. An auditor should review the nature and reasonableness of the transaction recorded, make a general observation of the circumstances in which the operations are being carried out, and be alert to anything that appears to be out of the ordinary.

Tests of operational controls normally consist of examination of evidence and, to a lesser extent, observation of procedure. Unless there has been a specific decision by management, operational controls generally may not be reperformed.

CATEGORIES OF CONTROLS TO BE TESTED OR REVIEWED

As discussed in Chapter 16, "Introduction to Controls," internal controls can be divided into two categories:

1. Internal accounting controls, which may be further divided into
   - Basic controls: those controls that are necessary for the completeness and accuracy of the accounting records
   - Disciplines over basic controls: those controls designed to ensure the continued and proper operation of basic controls and to safeguard assets
2. Administrative or operational controls, which may also be divided, as above

Internal Accounting Controls

Basic controls cover a wide range of checks and procedures. Typical examples are

- Checks on completeness (such as by means of sequential numbering of transactions)
- Matching or comparison of documents or files
- Checks of addition, calculation, and extensions
- Electronic monitoring and reporting of exceptions
- Controls over groups of transactions (frequently by means of control totals)
- Controls over the recording of physical movements of goods

Compliance testing of basic controls generally includes examination of evidence, reperformance (when appropriate), and observation.

Disciplines over basic controls comprise the following:

- Custodial controls
- Segregation of duties so that the work of one person adequately checks that of another

- Supervisory control or adequate supervision of the work of people involved in the operation of the basic controls

Testing of custodial controls and segregation of duties usually involves observation and inquiry and/or examination of signatures and initials on documents and records. These tests are normally carried out as part of the tests of the related basic controls, rather than as a separate operation.

Compliance testing of the supervisory controls, on the other hand, is based largely on the examination of evidence. The primary evidence examined is the signature or initials of the person exercising the control on the relevant document or record. Particular attention should be given to other evidence (such as evidence that computer-produced exception reports have been investigated and follow-up action taken) that has been produced as a result of the supervisory control. In addition, the application of the supervisory control to current transactions can be observed.

Complete reperformance of a supervisory control is usually not possible. The auditor rarely has knowledge and experience of the supervisor concerned; the nature and extent of the checks carried out at the supervisor's discretion may not be evidenced clearly. Reperformance is limited to the tasks that are expected to be undertaken in the exercise of the supervisory control. It normally includes inspection of the supporting documentation that should have been seen by the person exercising the supervisory control, together with evidence of prior checks as required by entity procedures. Using the same items for examination of evidence of basic controls provides increased efficiency. The existence of errors in the application of the basic controls that were not detected by the supervisor may indicate that the related supervisory control is not being applied effectively.

Administrative Controls

Administrative or operational controls deal with the efficient use of resources. Tests of operational controls are based largely on the examination of evidence. Such evidence may consist of the items that form the basis for the control, including an organization chart or policy manual; a report or worksheet, such as technical performance specifications for goods to be purchased; a document, such as a purchase order containing routing, delivery date required, and other instructions; or exception reports or internal memoranda indicating that the control is being applied. Tests of some administrative controls may involve observation.

Reperformance of an administrative control is often not practical, primarily because of the large amount of time that may be required to reperform those controls. For example, an auditor does not normally take the time to recalculate economic order quantities or to check the accuracy of routing instructions for purchased goods. On the other hand, the auditor ordinarily examines evidence that economic order quantities are used and that routing instructions are provided to purchasing personnel.

Sometimes, however, the auditor can reperform an administrative control procedure with a limited expenditure of time. For example, the auditor may wish to reperform a calculation to determine whether a cash discount on a purchase invoice was performed correctly by a programmed procedure. Applying this test to a sample of the invoices permits the task to be done efficiently.

Controls in EDP Systems

In a computer environment, internal controls are categorized as follows:

- *Application controls* — Those controls that are unique to individual user systems or applications
- *General or integrity controls* — Those controls that ensure the effective operation of programmed procedures, including controls over design, implementation, security, and use and amendment of computer programs and files

Both application and integrity controls consist of basic and disciplinary controls.

Compliance tests of application controls are similar to compliance or functional tests of controls in a manual system. The types of tests carried out are the same. However, the documentation being examined and the manual operations being reperformed may differ. Compliance tests of user controls are sufficient in computer systems where the user checks all output and no reliance is placed on programmed procedures or data held on computer files. In most computer systems, the output is too voluminous and/or there is not adequate visible evidence to be checked manually. In these circumstances, it is necessary to rely on, and therefore perform compliance tests on, the general controls. (See Chapter 20, "General or Integrity Controls.")

It is often best to test the general controls before testing the related application controls. Even when application controls are adequate, the auditor may not be able to rely on them if they are related to undependable general controls. For example, there is little point in testing the action taken on computer reports if the programs creating those reports cannot be relied on.

Sometimes the auditor does not believe that the results of testing application controls and general controls provide sufficient assurance as to the consistent and proper operation of programmed procedures. At that point, the use of other testing techniques should be considered. These techniques, such as the use of audit software, can ensure that the programs are appropriate and operating consistently. Normally, these are considered substantive tests, not compliance tests, because the auditor is attempting to gain satisfaction with the programmed procedures by direct tests, rather than by evaluating and testing the general controls. Nevertheless, management may wish to consider such testing as a possible alternative to compliance tests in the situation described.

Compliance tests of general controls consist of examination of evidence, reperformance, and observation. These tests are performed on implementation controls, computer operations controls, data file security controls, and system software controls.

Tests are prepared for many common internal control techniques (see examples in Figure 21-3 later in this chapter). These tests can be segregated into types: tests of user controls in computer systems, tests of general controls, tests of programmed procedures, and tests of manual systems.

NATURE OF TESTS AND REVIEWS

It is not possible to prescribe hard and fast rules for determining levels of tests (such as the number of items to be tested). The level to be selected in each case is a matter for judgment in light of all relevant factors including risk, tolerable error, expected error, and considerations related to the coordination of work with other auditors. The objective, however, should always be to obtain reasonable assurance that a control is functioning properly, while testing to the minimum extent necessary. To make a judgment about an appropriate level of tests, all relevant factors should be taken into account, including the complexity of the transactions and experience of previous evaluations.

In many instances where the examination of evidence or reperformance is involved, the level of testing to be performed involves decisions about audit sampling. As defined in Statement on Auditing Standards (SAS) No. 39, *Audit Sampling*, sampling is "the application of an audit procedure to less than 100 percent of the items within an account balance or class of transactions for the purpose of evaluating some characteristic of the balance or class." (See the later section entitled "Applying Sampling.")

The nature of compliance tests is affected by:

- *The type of compliance test performed.* The levels of reperformance tests should be lower than the levels for examination of evidence.

- *Whether the control involves groups of transactions.* For example, in the case of a monthly control over the completeness of sequentially prenumbered documents, compliance testing might typically take the form of:
  a. Examination of monthly exception reports of missing numbers to confirm that, apparently, missing numbers are being identified and investigated.
  b. Reperformance based on such reports. This involves selecting a number of batches of documents, seeing that any missing numbers were listed, and reviewing the results of the investigations.

Thus, the auditor may choose to test the primary evidence of control, rather than the underlying individual transactions.

- *The risk that errors may not be detected.* In an effective system of internal control, a breakdown in one control is often detected by the operation of another (normally later) control. The following circumstances need to be considered in determining the extent of risk that an error may not be detected:

  a. *Disciplines over basic controls.* The auditor may consider whether it is more efficient to test supervisory controls rather than testing the basic controls exclusively. Effective supervisory controls should identify any breakdown in the operation of underlying basic controls. However, when underlying basic controls must be tested in order to conclude that the supervisory controls are operating, testing the basic controls directly may result in less testing.

  b. *Interrelated basic controls.* Many basic controls are interrelated. For example, if the controls over the completeness of purchase invoices break down, this should be detected as a result of the investigation of unmatched records of goods received or by the agreement of suppliers' statements with the accounts payable records. Therefore, the auditor may choose not to test the completeness of purchase invoices directly, but to rely on the results of other tests.

  c. *Overall reconciliations.* If it is possible as part of the regular control procedures to carry out overall reconciliations (such as of quantities of sales, purchases, and inventories), the auditor may feel justified in testing the operation of those reconciliations.

As with tests of controls, there are no hard-and-fast rules for determining the levels of reviews. (The number of items selected for review is the level of review.) In each case, the level chosen is a matter for judgment by management in light of all relevant factors. The objective should be to review to the minimum extent necessary to determine the apparent existence and effective operation of the controls.

The levels of tests of administrative controls should consider the effort involved in performing a particular review procedure. When the additional time to review a control is small and the potential impact of a control breakdown is large, the level of test of the administrative control should be relatively high. This is normally the case when an administrative control is reviewed in conjunction with the testing of a related internal accounting control. On the other hand, where the effort to review an administrative control is great and the potential impact of a control breakdown is small, it may not be necessary to perform any tests of administrative controls.

Selection of Representative Samples

When an audit performed by an external auditor requires use of sampling, SAS No. 39 requires that items in the sample be selected from the population in a manner that allows them to be representative of that population. Although they are not required to do so, internal auditors will find that following the auditing standards of the American Institute of Certified Public Accountants (AICPA) improves their ability to coordinate their work with the work of external auditors.

In order for the sample items to be representative of a population, all items in the population should have a chance of being selected. When this is so, the sample actually chosen is more likely to be representative of the characteristics of the population as a whole. If a sample is selected from less than the entire population, or is composed only of items found in a particular area or unit (such as from one page in a report of a computerized ledger or from one period of time), it cannot be relied on to be truly representative.

When there are several attributes in a population, they may not all be represented in a particular sample. When selecting a sample, the auditor may determine which attribute is of major concern (such as the size of error) and make a sample selection designed to be representative of that concern.

Representative samples for nonstatistical sampling can be attained using various methods, including dollar-weighted (or value-weighted), unsystematic, and systematic selection. When an auditor makes sample selections based on "dollar weight," items are chosen according to the auditor's judgment, assigning more weight to items that have larger recorded values. Such dollar-weighted sampling is not the same as examining all items over a certain dollar limit and a sample of the rest of the items.

Unsystematic or haphazard sample selection is used to achieve a sample that is as random as possible from the population as a whole, avoiding the normal human tendency to favor particular items (such as never choosing the first or last item on a report from a computerized ledger). Once the auditor is assured that the complete population is available for selection (e.g., being satisfied that the report from the computerized ledger completely lists all items), a number of items can be selected unsystematically from the entire population. This selection should be as unbiased as possible under the circumstances, although there is always some possibility that bias in selection will exist without the auditor's awareness.

When an auditor is using statistical sampling, a random sample must be selected, no matter what impediments to doing so exist. Random number selection and systematic selection with a random starting point are two techniques that may be used. Computer-assisted techniques are particularly useful in using random number selection samples, since the machine can use random number generators and tables that are completely free from human bias and save time in the selection process. A random sample is not required in nonstatistical sampling, but an understanding of random sampling techniques can help an auditor select a representative sample.

Systematic sample selection is choosing items at an interval, based on a formula that divides population size by sample size. The answer is the interval used for item selection, starting at a single random point between the first item in the population and the interval size. The sample may also be selected using multiple random starting points to minimize the chance that an unexpected pattern in the population will be reflected in the sample. For example, in a sample designed for two random starting points, the computed interval would be twice the size of the interval computed for the single random starting point sample, and two random points within the enlarged interval would be chosen to begin the selection process. Using software, computerized selection can be used to select items at intervals specified from computerized ledgers, saving a lot of time and manual effort.

The main difference between using systematic sample selection in statistical and nonstatistical applications is that nonstatistical techniques do not require that the starting point be random.

Compliance tests and administrative reviews are designed to both test the operations and review the apparent existence and effective operation of specific controls. They are concerned primarily with the flow of transactions through individual control points, rather than the flow of transactions through the entire system. Accordingly, different documents within the same transaction processing system may be selected for examination to verify different control points. It is not necessary, although in some cases it may be more efficient, to test or review related controls using the same documents.

Obviously, in computer systems many programs and data files do not have accounting significance. When carrying out reperformance tests of general controls, the auditor should select control procedures carried out on programs and files that have accounting control significance when this is what is being tested. For example, the auditor normally selects procedures relating to changes in programs in the inventory system rather than changes in programs in the personnel scheduling system. The auditor can identify appropriate programs and data when obtaining and confirming an understanding of the accounting system and completing or updating an evaluation of internal controls. On the other hand, when an auditor is reviewing a system itself or administrative controls, then controls that apply to all significant programs and files are covered.

If implementation controls vary from system to system, the auditor should test the different sets of controls separately.

Although there are two separate types of general controls dealing with program security and data file security, the same controls may apply to both programs and data files. For example, both may be stored in the same physical library or both may be protected by the same software while on-line. When this is so, only one set of compliance tests is required.

Order of Performing Tests and Reviews

Internal controls need not be tested in the same order in which they appear in the control questionnaires used. Supervisory controls are often tested before the related basic controls. Controls over groups of transactions are tested because the results of tests of supervisory or group controls can help determine the levels of tests needed for underlying controls. It is equally acceptable to test the basic controls first, or the basic controls and the supervisory controls at the same time, if this is more efficient.

Administrative controls should be reviewed in the most efficient order. Review of an administrative control should be carried out in conjunction with the compliance test of a related internal control procedure whenever efficiency is enhanced by doing so. For example, in testing controls over the matching of purchase orders with receiving reports and purchase invoices, the auditor usually determines at the same time whether routing and other instructions are on the purchase order and whether a cash discount was taken. Since these tests can be done simultaneously, it would be less efficient to make them separate tests.

APPLYING SAMPLING

To apply sampling, the auditor considers the sampling risk (the risk of incorrect acceptance or risk of over-reliance on a control); the tolerable deviation rate or error rate; and the attributes of the population, such as the deviation rate or error amount that might be expected (or the fact that items themselves may vary*).

When using nonstatistical sampling, also referred to as judgment sampling, such factors need not be quantified; the auditor can express the criteria used in qualitative terms.

Sampling Risk

Sampling risk is defined as the risk the auditor can accept that the results of a sampling application might be less than accurate. The test may indicate that a control can be relied on (or that an account balance is not significantly misstated*) when there is a chance that the control is unreliable (or the account is significantly misstated*). This risk can be seen as the complement of the desired level of assurance that the auditor seeks from a particular sample. When the auditor desires a test to provide a high degree of assurance, a low degree of sampling risk is required. Sampling risk also has a relationship to the

*Refers to substantive tests.

size of the sample. The larger the sample is, the smaller the sampling risk, as long as other factors do not change.

The tolerable deviation rate (or error amount*) is the rate that management has specified as acceptable for a given control situation. When accepting a sample that is designed with an extremely high tolerable error rate, however, the auditor's procedures may become too imprecise to draw meaningful conclusions at a low level of risk.

The Attributes of the Population

The expected deviation rate (or error amount*) in a sample is based on the auditor's best estimate of the actual deviation rate (or error amount*) in the population as a whole. To make such an estimate, information from prior audits can be used, as long as any change in the controls or the circumstances of a particular test are considered. The characteristics of the population in this regard can affect sample size.

The sample size required to meet an auditor's acceptable degree of sampling risk for a given tolerable deviation rate (or error amount*) increases as the population's expected deviation rate (or error amount*) increases. When using statistical sampling, this relationship — the increase in expected deviation rate or error amount and the increase in sample size — is not directly proportionate. (If an expected error amount comes close to the tolerable error amount, it may be necessary to use very large sample sizes.)

COMPLIANCE TESTS AND PROGRAMMED PROCEDURES

To perform compliance tests in an EDP environment, the auditor can follow three basic strategy approaches. These can provide the auditor assurance as to the continued and proper operation of significant programmed procedures:

1. Testing user controls over programmed procedures.
2. Testing the general or integrity controls.
3. Testing significant programmed procedures themselves through computerized or manual techniques:
   - Using computer-assisted techniques, such as audit software, is required for programmed procedures that are not user-controlled. It is often more efficient to test programmed procedures that can be tested manually (since they are user-controlled) using computerized techniques such as audit software.
   - Manual reperformance of programmed procedures that are user-controlled.

---

*Refers to substantive tests.

Testing user controls does not raise sampling issues that are different from those already discussed, as is also so when testing general controls. However, due to the pervasive effect that can result from breakdowns in general controls, the auditor should be especially careful to set the tolerable error rate to a meaningfully low rate. Programmed procedures that function improperly, or are inadequate, may have an adverse effect for prolonged periods. Since computer processing usually includes far greater use of summary level reports and exception reports requiring follow-up, there is far less manual review of details of processing. In fact, it may not be possible to review or even know what the details are. As a result, any errors in programs or data files are not likely to be detected by users, since the controls may rely on the availability of those details. Controls over master file data are similarly affected, and similarly important, since incorrect master file data has a wide-ranging effect on numerous transactions.

To plan general controls testing, consideration should be given to the detailed tests that may require the use of sampling or, alternately, examination of 100 percent of the items. It may be necessary in some of these planned tests to employ other audit procedures. These include observation or inquiry procedures. Some general control procedures are less critical to the audit objectives than others. For example, controls over security of the financial system access methods are more significant to the audit than controls over access to the personnel system (exclusive of payroll). For less critical procedures, other audit procedures not involving sampling can often be used. Audit software and other computerized techniques may make it efficient and cost-effective to examine 100 percent of a class of transactions.

AUDIT APPROACH CONSIDERATIONS

Basic and Supervisory Controls

The systems audit approach includes consideration of the structure of a system of controls within an organization. This hierarchy of controls can affect the extent and method of testing. For example, basic controls may be monitored by supervisory controls.

To test basic and supervisory controls that are exercised over the same function, the auditor usually selects a sample that is representative of the period for which he or she wishes to place reliance on the system. There may be no need to spread the tests of the basic controls in this way when supervisory level control tests are selected to represent the entire period. When limiting the period over which the basic controls are tested, the auditor makes the assumption that the supervisory controls and their testing will provide evidence that operation of the basic control during a restricted period is much the same as its operation during the entire period. Such an assumption, when made, needs to be supported by documentation; for example, when results of inquiries about the internal control system do not uncover any changes during the year. When there are inadequate supervisory controls, tests of basic controls should be spread over the entire period of reliance.

Some additional assurance can be obtained about the continued and proper operation of a basic control by observation of the supervisory control, without testing. For example, when a representative sample of 40 items has been examined for the proper operation of the basic control, and no errors found, a degree of assurance that the system of controls is operating properly exists. If observation shows that supervisory controls are also in place and are operating, more comfort can be drawn from the system of controls than in the absence of evidence that a supervisory control was in place.

DEPARTURES AND BREAKDOWNS

To perform compliance tests of controls and assess whether there have been departures or breakdowns, the auditor needs to know management's desired level of compliance for each control. This can vary according to many factors, including the risk of errors that management is willing to accept, the environment, and the requirements of external auditors planning to rely on a control. For a particular control, management may require few deviations, as is the case when a tolerable rate of errors is set close to zero. To determine the extent of compliance tests that include sampling, the expected deviation rate for a sample selected from a population is based on an estimate of the true deviation rate within the population as a whole. Whether or not sampling is being used, knowledge of management's requirements is necessary for proper evaluation.

To evaluate the effect of possible breakdowns in control uncovered during compliance testing (using sampling or nonsampling procedures), the auditor needs to determine the reasons behind the departure. The breakdown may be an isolated incident (such as a processing delay due to computer downtime) or it may indicate a breakdown, requiring the auditor to recommend different corrective actions.

To find out whether the exception is an isolated incident, the auditor should determine why the exception arose. This can be done by inquiry and examination of the circumstances of the exception. Alternately, it may be necessary to extend the testing. If so, care should be taken to ensure that extending the sample of items tested actually helps determine the nature and extent of the exception. If the exception is isolated, the implications of the quantity of exceptions needs to be assessed. If the auditor is not then concerned about the quantity of exceptions found relative to the tolerable level of exceptions for that control, then no further audit procedures to assess the effectiveness of this control are generally necessary. If, however, it is discovered that there is a departure from or breakdown in the prescribed systems that has not been corrected, it should be recorded on the Record of Control Weaknesses (RCW) and the flowcharts; the questionnaires (ICQ or Computer Internal Control Questionnaire (CICQ)) or Control Matrix should be amended, or annotated, accordingly. (See Chapter 25 for discussion of the RCW, ICQ, CICQ, and Control Matrix; see Chapter 23 regarding the use of flowcharts.) Often additional procedures, including a report to management, are employed when a breakdown in controls has been determined.

If a departure or a breakdown has been corrected, this should be noted on the Program and Record of Compliance Tests and Operational Reviews (PRT). (See section entitled "Program and Record of Compliance Tests and Operational Reviews.") If no exceptions are found as a result of the compliance tests, this also should be noted on the PRT.

DOCUMENTATION

The documentation for compliance tests and administrative reviews should include, as a minimum, the following:

- A description of the tests and/or reviews performed (see examples in Figure 21-3, later in this chapter)
- A cross-reference from each compliance test and/or administrative review to the related question numbers on the ICQ
- Identification of levels of tests and/or reviews
- Indication of periods tested and/or reviewed
- Identification of the evidence examined
- Identification of exceptions noted, if any, during the performance of the tests and/or reviews and their disposition
- Indication that the work has been completed, usually the initials of the person completing the work, and the date of its performance

When used in conjunction with external audits, sample documentation should conform to the requirements of SAS No. 41, *Working Papers*, considering the requirements of SAS No. 39.

All this information should be included on the PRT and on any related working papers. Instructions regarding the use of forms such as the PRT and related working papers are found in the next section. The use of the compliance test and administrative review documentation, including schedules of specimen tests, illustrates how these procedures can be implemented. The documentation for compliance tests and administrative reviews usually consists of the following:

- The Program and Record of Functional (Compliance) Tests and Operational Reviews or PRT (see Figures 21-1A, 21-1B, and 21-1C)
- Summary sheet to the PRT (see Figure 21-2)

In addition, tests and procedures exist for many common internal accounting control techniques. (See Figure 21-3 later in this chapter.) These can be used, when appropriate, in the manner described subsequently.

PROGRAM AND RECORD OF COMPLIANCE TESTS AND OPERATIONAL REVIEWS

The PRT, like the ICQ and Control Matrix, is designed to be used for more than one period. In the period of its first introduction, the program can be prepared in the manner described subsequently. When the program of proposed tests and reviews has been reviewed and approved by management, photocopies can be made for use in subsequent periods. In each of these subsequent periods, the auditor should consider the continued appropriateness of the program in the light of

- Experience in carrying out the tests or reviews in previous periods.
- Any changes in control procedures, as identified during the repreparation or updating of the questionnaire or matrix, for the current period.

When a proposed compliance test or administrative review is no longer appropriate, or when different or additional tests are necessary, the program should be amended accordingly. If the proposed compliance test or administrative review is intended to be performed on a cyclical basis (such as twice a year), that should be written down as well. When substantial changes are required, for example, as a result of a fundamental change in the system, it is probably preferable to prepare a new PRT.

The compliance tests and administrative reviews should be included on the PRT sheet(s) in the most efficient order. This should also permit the auditor to conduct the reviews most easily. In most cases, this means ordering tests and reviews in accordance with the control objectives in the ICQ and the Control Matrix; frequently used forms such as these are arranged in this order. However, other arrangements also are possible depending on the format the auditor is using.

For example, tests and reviews of controls relating to payroll activity might be listed together on one page. Those relating to fixed assets can be listed on another page. Other alternatives for grouping tests and reviews include groupings by transaction type or by activity as shown on the procedural flowcharts.

Location _____

Control Objective No. 6 – Payroll

June 30, 198X

(1) ICQ Ref.	(2) Details of Test or Reason for Omitting Test	(3) Level of Test	(4) Program Update (√)	(5) Evidence Seen, Period(s) Selected (or Workpaper Reference)	EXCEPTIONS			(9) Signature and Date
					(6) Yes/No	(7) Cleared	(8) W.P.Ref.	
6.2a c,d 6.7b	1A. Examine daily time sheets for evidence that they are approved and dated by supervisors.			106 116	No No			FC 4/8X FC 7/8X
	1B. Reperform control by selecting a sample of approved daily time sheets and ensuring that they are reasonable.			106	No			FC 4/8X
6.11b 6.12 6.14b 6.15b 6.16 6.17a 6.18a 6.19a	2A. Examine the batch control book for evidence that numerically-sequenced batch totals for hours worked and payroll dollar value are recorded in the control book.			107	No			FC 4/8X
6.21 6.22 6.23 6.25a 6.26a	2B. Examine the batch control book for evidence that the totals are being regularly agreed by payroll clerk to Edit Reports and by the controller to Weekly Total Recap			107 116	No No			FC 4/8X FC 7/8X
	2C. Reperform control by: i) Testing agreement of Batch Control Book with the total printed on the Edit Reports and Weekly Total Recap.			107	No			FC 4/8X

FIG. 21-1A Program and Record of Tests (functional = compliance) and Operational Reviews (PRT)

```
                    FUNCTIONAL TESTS - PAYROLL

                    June, 198X


Interim Testing                                March, 198X
Control Objective 6                            FC
```

2D. I have examined the edit reports and selected those
     that contained error messages as follows:

2E.

2F.

Date	Nature of Error	2D Initialed by payroll clerk	Initialed by dept. head	2E Agreed to time cards; followed up for reason-ableness	2F Edit Report initialed by accountant
8/ 9/8W	Data Conv.	✓	✓	✓	✓
10/ 2/8W	Data Conv.	✓	✓	✓	✓
12/11/8W	Non-Data Conv.	✓	✓	✓	✓
1/21/8X	Data Conv.	✓	✓	✓	✓
2/ 7/8X	Non-Data Conv.	✓	✓	✓	✓
3/11/8X	Non-Data Conv.	✓	✓	✓	✓

2G. I have examined the Missing and Duplicate Reports and verified
     that the items are cleared on a regular basis, and that there
     was evidence of the accountant's review.

2H.

Date	Empl. No.	Nature of Error	Reason	Initialed by accountant	Correctly cleared
1/9/8X	121	Missing	Terminated 1.	✓	✓
8/9/8X	254	Duplicated	Retro. Increase 1.	✓	✓
3/2/8X	842	Duplicated	Worker's Comp. and Wages	✓	✓

   1. Payroll clerk on vacation, PMDI's not processed in time.

FIG. 21-1B Test reference on the PRT: Interim testing

```
                    FUNCTIONAL TESTS - PAYROLL

                         June, 198X


      Final Update                                    July 10, 198X
      Control Objective 6                             FC


        1A.    Date           Employee No.      Approved by supervisor

               4/ 7/8X           183                    ✓
               4/28/8X           279                    ✓
               5/15/8X           341                    ✓
               6/ 1/8X           452                    ✓
               6/20/8x           660                    ✓

        2B.    I reviewed the Batch Control Book and verified that the
               controller initials the Control Book as evidence of
               approval.

        2F.    I examined the following edit reports and verified that
               they were reviewed and approved by the accountant:

               Date of reports:    4/11/8X
                                   6/20/8X
```

FIG. 21-1C   Test reference on the PRT: Final update

The activity or other classification to which the compliance tests and administrative reviews, included on a particular PRT, relate should be entered on the PRT summary sheet. They are usually listed under the heading of "Control Objective Number ___ ."

Preparation of Program (Period of Introduction)

Generally, a PRT sheet as shown in Figures 21-1A, 21-1B, and 21-1C should be used as follows:

- Use a separate sheet for each control objective for which compliance testing or an administrative review is proposed.
- Enter the ICQ/Control Matrix reference for each question in column 1 (ICQ Ref.). At the same time, the PRT page reference number should be entered on the ICQ/Matrix.
- Enter complete details of tests or reviews to be performed in column 2 (Details of Test). The specimen tests in the last section of this chapter can be used as a guide to understand preparation of the detailed compliance tests. A mere cross-reference to the specimen tests that does not contain details of the work performed does not ordinarily constitute a satisfactory description of the compliance test performed.

Location __Payroll_____   Year-End June 30, 198X

COMPLETION OF PRT

INDEX		COMPLETION OF PROGRAM	
Control Objective No.	File Reference	SIGNATURE	DATE
6 (Incl.	101 to 110	FC	7/8X
S.D.)	114 to 116		
9 (Part)	112 to 114	FC	7/8X
13 (Part)	111	FC	7/8X

REVIEW AND APPROVAL

Preparation/updating of program	J. Terwiliger	7/8X
Completion of program	D. Brighteyes	7/8X

FIG. 21-2 A summary sheet encompassing the tests and reviews covered on individual PRTs in Figure 21-1

- If any internal control questions that were noted in the ICQ will not be compliance tested, reasons for not performing the test should be recorded in column 2. Management may also decide that it wants the reasons for the omission of reviews of administrative controls listed as well. Thus, no control for which questions were answered in the ICQ will be overlooked.

- Tests or reviews are normally omitted because
  - a. There is a "no" answer to a question.
  - b. The control cannot be relied on because of other "no" answers related to the same control objective.
  - c. Management has decided for its own reasons, which can include efficiency considerations, that testing or review is unnecessary.
- Enter proposed levels of test or review in column 3 (Level of Test).
- Review the PRT column in the ICQ/Matrix to gain the necessary assurance that all control procedures that should be considered for compliance testing or administrative review are included in the program.
- The program should be reviewed and approved by responsible supervisory management before the compliance tests or reviews are performed.
- The work described in the preceding paragraphs should be carried out at the same time as, or immediately following, completion of the ICQ/Matrix, preferably by the same person who recorded and confirmed the understanding and who evaluated the related controls.

Updating of Program (Subsequent Period)

The relevant column (here, column 4, Program Update) of the PRT should be marked to indicate the continued appropriateness of the proposed compliance tests or administrative reviews. If column 2 was completed for administrative controls during preparation of the program, and if those controls are not to be reviewed in the current period, no mark should be placed in column 4. Enter the letter "a" (for administrative control) in column 4 to indicate that the review will not be performed in the current period. If the administrative controls were not reviewed in the period the program was prepared but are to be reviewed in the current period, columns 1, 2, and 3 should be completed as described previously.

Completion of Program

When the compliance tests or administrative reviews have been carried out, the evidence seen and period(s) selected are entered in column 5 (Evidence Seen, Period(s) Selected (or Workpaper Reference)). If space is insufficient, a separate working paper should be prepared and cross-referenced in column 5.

- The existence or absence of exceptions found by carrying out compliance tests or operational reviews is indicated by a "yes" or "no" answer in column 6 (Exceptions — Yes/No). This indicates exceptions and eases subsequent review and reporting. Details of exceptions and the action taken are recorded on a working paper, which should be cross-referenced in column 8 (Exceptions — W.P. Ref.). The clearance of exceptions is evidenced by a mark placed in column 7 (Exceptions — Cleared).

- The PRT should be signed and dated in column 9 (Signature and Date) by the person carrying out the tests or reviews.

PRT SUMMARY SHEET

A PRT summary sheet should be completed in each period for each cycle of the ICQ/Matrix. (See Figure 21-2.) This provides a means of evidencing the following:

- Approval by responsible supervisory management of the preparation or updating of the program of compliance tests and administrative reviews
- Completion by the auditor of the compliance tests and administrative reviews
- Review by a responsible supervisor of the work performed

The PRT summary sheet also serves as an index to the individual PRTs. Detailed instructions for the completion of this document are given in the following paragraphs.

Preparation of Program

The index, which comprises the first two columns of the summary sheet, is completed with respect to each control objective in each period. If some other activity or grouping is used, the entry in the column should agree with the identification used in individual PRTs.

Review and Approval

The proposed tests and reviews, or in subsequent periods proposed changes, should be reviewed and approved by management. Approval should be evidenced by signing and dating the appropriate box. If there have been any changes in the system, management should ensure that the program has also been suitably amended.

Completion of Program

On completion of the compliance tests and administrative reviews relevant to each individual PRT, the auditor should sign and date the column under the heading "Completion of Program." This shows that

- The compliance tests and administrative reviews have been carried out to the auditor's satisfaction.
- Any amendments or additions to the program have been clearly recorded on the PRT or on a working paper cross-referenced thereto.
- Any exceptions noted in the course of compliance tests and administrative reviews have been identified as isolated instances (or temporary breakdowns that have been corrected) or as control breakdowns and properly recorded on the RCW or subjected to other appropriate action.

Review and Approval

The auditing supervisor should review the completed PRT and supporting working papers (including any amendments to the flowcharts, ICQ, and RCW) and sign and date the appropriate box to indicate that

- The program of tests and reviews appears to have been completed properly.
- All exceptions that are noted have been disposed of correctly.
- Any departures or breakdowns have been recorded, where and as appropriate, on the right documents — flowcharts, ICQ/Matrix, and RCW.
- Senior management is advised immediately of any significant weaknesses in internal control.

Evidence of Work Performed

Sufficient detail should be recorded, either on the PRT or on a separate work paper, to identify the particular record, document, or other evidence that was examined. When complete reperformance of an internal accounting control is not appropriate, it is normally necessary to prepare a working paper recording the extent of reperformance carried out. For example, when the reconciliation of a control account is reperformed, it is desirable to summarize the reconciliation on a working paper. The auditor can indicate the specific balances checked from the ledgers, the extent to which additions were reperformed, and any other tests performed on the working paper. If sampling has been employed in the testing process, supporting working papers should include information that was necessary for planning the sampling application, as well as information related to performing and evaluating the results of the sample.

For the disciplines over basic controls and administrative controls, supporting working papers are prepared to record the specific evidence examined, the procedures reperformed, or the nature and circumstances of the observations.

EXAMPLES OF COMPLIANCE TESTS

The specimen compliance tests in Figure 21-3 here are used in conjunction with the CICQ. (See Chapter 25.)

The Coopers & Lybrand CICQ contains cross-references to internal specimen compliance tests. Each detailed question in the CICQ contains a specimen test reference and a list of all related questions in the same document that can be tested by the same specimen test. This approach aids the auditor in designing a single test for all related questions. Obviously, not all such tests or all details of the CICQ can be presented here. A sample is given to illustrate this questionnaire and related tests. When testing is required, it is the auditor's responsibility to construct or locate suitable tests.

The specimen test references used in the CICQ are alphabetic to correspond to compliance tests for user controls in computer systems as performed by Coopers & Lybrand.

Specimen tests for programmed procedures are not part of this group, since the need to test programmed procedures depends on the strength of the general controls and the relative importance of the program function. (See Chapter 27, *"Internal Control Reference Manual* — Application Controls.") Tests of programmed procedures vary, depending on their nature. Frequently, the tests are performed using audit software. This software either reperforms the programmed function (sometimes called parallel simulation) or examines the results produced by the program for erroneous or unusual data. Other techniques for testing programs include the following:

- Audit test data
- Program code analysis
- Manual reperformance (provided that sufficient output is available)

(text continues on page 21-28)

Computer Systems — User Controls

Nature of Control	Specimen Test
A. Review of computer-produced exception or rejection reports: ■ Completeness of input and updating ■ Accuracy of input and updating ■ Continuity (maintenance) of data	**1.** When a computer sequence check or computer comparison of batch totals is relied on for the completeness and accuracy of input, test the initial recording on the input form as follows: **a.** When the information is transcribed from another source document, one of the tests suitable for manual systems may be applicable. **b.** When the first record of the transaction is the input form, or the transaction is first entered through a terminal, visit the appropriate departments and observe that there are adequate procedures to ensure that transactions are completely and accurately recorded. **2.** Review computer reports for evidence that items or batches reported (such as outstanding, mismatched, or missing) are checked and investigated regularly by people with no conflicting duties. **3.** When appropriate, determine that the results of the procedures in (2) have been reviewed and approved by a responsible official. **4.** If necessary, reperform the control by selecting a sample of reported items or batches and seeing that they have been properly cleared.
B. Manual agreement of predetermined batch totals: ■ Completeness of input and updating ■ Accuracy of input and updating	**1.** Test the initial recording of transactions on the input form as follows: **a.** When the information is transcribed from another source document, one of the tests suitable for manual systems may be applicable. **b.** When the first record of the transaction is the input form, or the transaction is first entered through a terminal, visit the appropriate departments and observe that there are adequate procedures to ensure that transactions are completely and accurately recorded.

FIG. 21-3   Specimen compliance tests

Nature of Control	Specimen Test
B. Manual agreement of predetermined batch totals *(continued)*	**2.** Review computer reports, control registers, or other documentation for evidence that the predetermined batch totals have been regularly agreed with the totals printed on the computer report by people with no conflicting duties.
	3. Determine that differences have been investigated by people with no incompatible duties.
	4. When appropriate, determine that the results of the procedures in (2) and (3) have been reviewed and approved by a responsible official.
	5. If necessary, reperform the control by selecting batches of source documents and
	a. Test the additions of the predetermined batch totals.
	b. Test the agreement of the predetermined batch totals with the computer report.
	c. Inspect the control register to ensure that all batches have been processed.
	d. Obtain satisfactory explanation for any discrepancies.
	6. When appropriate, determine that there are controls that ensure that rejections are properly corrected and then completely and accurately resubmitted. Reperform the control if necessary. The exact nature of the test will depend on the user department procedures and should be specified on the PRT.
	7. When appropriate (such as in the case of batches of payments and credit memoranda), see that the input documents and supporting documentation have been effectively cancelled to prevent subsequent reuse.
C. Manual agreement of computer-established totals (run-to-run control): ■ Completeness of updating ■ Accuracy of updating	**1.** Review computer reports, control registers, or other documentation for evidence that the computer-produced totals have been regularly agreed with the totals printed out on the update report by people with no incompatible duties. (*Note:* Take into account any summarization of totals or any changes in the totals used.)

(continued)

Nature of Control	Specimen Test

C. Manual agreement of computer-established totals (run-to-run control) *(continued)*	**2.** Determine that differences have been investigated by people with no conflicting duties. (See ICQ.)
	
	3. When appropriate, examine evidence indicating that the results of the procedures in (1) and (2) have been reviewed and approved by a responsible official.
	
	4. Reperform the reconciliation by selecting reports of computer-established totals:
	  a. Check the total against that shown on the subsequent report.
	  b. Obtain satisfactory explanation for any discrepancies.

FIG. 21-3 *(continued)*

COMPLIANCE TESTS OF GENERAL OR INTEGRITY CONTROLS

The types of compliance tests that may be performed on general or integrity controls, and areas to be tested, are addressed under the five main components of general controls. These include: implementation controls, computer operations controls, programs security controls, data file security controls, and system software controls.

Implementation Controls

Implementation controls are exercised over the development of new systems and the maintenance of present systems. They ensure that appropriate programmed procedures are properly implemented and adequately maintained. The auditor tests these controls for new systems and for changes to ongoing systems. The tests of implementation controls may include

- Examination of evidence to determine that system specifications and documentation are adequately prepared, reviewed, and approved.
- Examination of evidence and reperformance of system and program testing to establish that testing procedures are adequate to ensure the appropriateness of the programmed procedures.
- Examination of evidence to verify that tested programs or changes thereto are brought into use without subsequent alteration.
- Determination that users are sufficiently involved in system development.

If implementation controls vary from system to system because different development groups are involved, the auditor should test each different type of control.

Computer Operations Controls

Controls over the consistency of computer operations ensure that jobs are set up properly and run in accordance with authorized instructions and procedures. The tests of control over the consistency of operations may include

- Determination that adequate separation of duties exists (e.g., that computer operations personnel do not have programming responsibilities).
- Examination of processing schedules, operating instructions, and job control language (JCL) to determine if jobs were properly scheduled and set up in accordance with written instructions.
- Examination of job processing sheets, console log reports, problem log reports, and the like, reperforming the control procedures to verify that jobs were properly run in accordance with established procedures and that any problems that arose did not adversely affect the results.
- Observation of controls over the restriction of access and exercise of supervision.

Program Security and Data File Security Controls

Program security and data file security controls are designed to prevent unauthorized changes to programmed procedures and data files. Separate tests should be carried out for each of the following:

- Off-line programs protected by physical custody controls (such as supervised storage areas)
- On-line program libraries protected by software controls (such as passwords)
- Off-line data files protected by physical custody controls
- On-line data files and other files protected by software controls

The tests of program security controls may include:

- Examination of evidence to determine that production program libraries are maintained separately from test libraries.
- Examination of execution JCL listings, librarian listings of source program modifications, and standards manuals to determine that

adequate procedures exist to ensure the correct version of the program is transferred to the production program library.

• Examination of evidence to determine adequate procedures are in place to monitor consistency between source and object programs.

• Examination of evidence to determine that production program libraries are password-protected and that access violations are investigated.

• Examination of computer-generated output resulting from the production program library updating process for evidence of authorization and supervisory review.

• Observation of off-site backup storage area and examination of operations schedule listing backup jobs run to ensure adequacy of program file recovery procedures.

The tests of file security may include

• Examination and reperformance of the log of physical movements to determine if they are recorded and whether files are returned promptly to the library.

• Observation to see whether overdue files remain in the computer room (they should not) and, further, that access to data files is restricted.

• Examination of the console log, or other report, of password protection messages to find evidence of the company's investigation of unauthorized attempts to access password-protected files.

• Determination by observation and examination of evidence that adequate backup files and recovery procedures exist.

• Examination of evidence of password changes to verify that they take place regularly and that the passwords of separated employees are removed promptly.

• Examination of evidence of supervisory review of output from tape and disk library management systems.

System Software Controls

System software assists in the control of both the programs that process data and the data files themselves. Therefore, although controls over system software do not affect the programs and data directly, they affect the auditor's ability to rely on the other general controls. The auditor tests the controls over the implementation and security of the system software. The compliance tests performed are discussed in the preceding sections, "Implementation Controls" and "Program Security and Data File Security Controls." Security considerations are discussed in Chapter 32, "Security."

SPECIMEN COMPLIANCE TESTS OF GENERAL CONTROLS: IMPLEMENTATION AND MAINTENANCE OF APPLICATIONS

1. **System and Program Documentation (Specimen Test):**

   ☐ Examine system development and maintenance records for evidence that up-to-date system and programming documentation has been prepared for all programs and systems.

   ☐ Reperform control by reviewing system and programming documentation and source listings to confirm that
   - The applications conform to generally accepted accounting principles and to the company's own requirements.
   - The documentation appears to be up-to-date.
   - The documentation contains sufficient detail to form a suitable basis for making subsequent program modifications.
   - The documentation agrees with source listing. (*Note:* The use of a flowcharting package, to help document and understand the source listing, may assist in carrying out this step.)
   - The programs have been coded in accordance with generally accepted EDP standards.

   ☐ When modifications have been made to programs that were not developed or maintained in accordance with generally accepted EDP standards, examine evidence that the documentation has been brought up to date as part of the process of making the modification.

2. **Access to System and Program Documentation (Specimen Test):**

   ☐ Observe that source statement listings, flowcharts, file layouts, and other system documentation of application programs are held securely and are restricted from access by computer operators, job controllers, and system programmers.

   ☐ Observe the access-granting procedures for the above documentation when it is given to applications programmers and programmer analysts in the course of their jobs.

   ☐ By observation and inquiry, ensure that operators, job controllers, and system programmers do not borrow application program documentation or write application programs.

   ☐ Observe that manually maintained records of the means of access to programs and data files (such as password listings) are held securely and restricted from access by unauthorized people.

3. **Approval of System Specifications (Specimen Test):**

   ☐ Examine system development records or other documentation for evidence that system specifications have been prepared for all new applications that have been implemented and for any new applications still under development.

☐ Examine system specifications for evidence that
- They have been reviewed and approved by a responsible official in the user department(s).
- They have been reviewed and approved by responsible officials in the data processing function (such as the operations manager, applications programming manager, system programming manager, quality assurance manager).
- Subsequent changes to the approved system specifications are properly approved.

4. Testing New Applications (Specimen Test):

☐ Examine the documentation and results of testing of new applications implemented to confirm that
- A test plan was prepared and executed for program and system testing.
- The methods used in testing were appropriate to test the proper functioning of both the individual programs and complete systems.
- The volume and variety of transactions used to test the program was adequate to ensure the proper operation of programmed procedures for all transactions types, both individually and in combination.
- System software that is incorporated into the application programs has been adequately tested.
- The programmers who wrote the program being tested either were not involved in the testing or were involved but their work was subject to review.

☐ Reperform control, as appropriate for the control techniques used, by
- Tracing dummy transactions through the source statement listing.
- Checking test data results with predicted results.
- Selecting a period from the parallel running and testing the results with the output from the previous system.
- Selecting a part of the pilot run and checking the results.

5. Approval of Modifications to Production Programs (Specimen Test):

☐ Examine program change records for evidence that they have been approved by responsible officials in:
- The user department(s);
- The system maintenance function;

- The computer operations function (if appropriate); and
- The quality assurance function.

☐ Reperform control by checking program change records against the program change requests.

6. Control of Approved Program Modifications (Specimen Test):

☐ Examine the register of program changes for
- Evidence that entries therein appear to be up-to-date.
- Evidence that outstanding program changes are being reviewed regularly and investigated when appropriate.

☐ Reperform control by testing entries in the register with program change records to establish that the change has either been implemented or is a valid outstanding item.

7. Testing Program Modifications (Specimen Test):

☐ Examine the documentation and results of testing program modifications to confirm that
- A test plan was prepared and executed for programs and system testing.
- The methods used in testing were appropriate to test the proper functioning of:
  a. The program modification;
  b. Other, unchanged, parts of the changed programs; and
  c. Other related programs in the system.
- The volume and variety of transactions used to test the modification was adequate to test the proper operation of programmed procedures for all affected transaction types, both individually and in combination.
- System software that is incorporated into the application program has been adequately tested.
- The programmers who made the modifications being tested either were not involved in testing or were involved but their work was subject to review.

☐ Reperform control, as appropriate for the control techniques used, by
- Tracing dummy transactions through the source statement listings.
- Checking test data results with predicted results.

8. Urgent Modifications (Specimen Test):

☐ Examine the records of urgent program modifications that bypass the normal control procedures for evidence that

- The modifications made were properly documented and tested.
- The action taken was reviewed and approved by a responsible official in the data processing function. (*Note:* When the controls over the documentation and testing of urgent modifications consist of the retroactive application of the standard procedures for the documentation and testing of non-urgent modifications, in most cases further tests are not necessary.)

☐ When the controls over the documentation and testing of urgent modifications do not consist of the retroactive application of standard procedures, reperform the controls designed to ensure that

- The modification made is logically valid.
- The system and program documentation is brought up to date.
- The modification is properly tested.

9. Acceptance by Users of New Applications and Program Modifications (Specimen Test):

☐ Examine evidence of user approval of new applications and modifications for production use.

☐ Reperform control by confirming that the documentation supporting the approval has been prepared, including

- Results of testing;
- Computer department approvals; and
- User instruction.

☐ Examine documentary evidence of the notification from the computer department to the user department of the effective date that the new system or modification is to become operational.

10. Final Approval of New Applications and Program Modifications by the Data Processing Function (Specimen Test):

☐ Examine evidence of computer department approvals of new systems and modifications for production use.

☐ Reperform control by confirming that the documentation supporting the approval has been prepared, including

- System documentation;
- Program documentation;
- Operating instructions; and
- Results of testing.

11. **Cataloging of Approved New Applications and Program Modifications (Specimen Test):**

☐ Examine evidence that the cataloged changes to the production libraries are being checked to ensure that

- All authorized programs are being cataloged.
- The correct version of the authorized programs are being cataloged.
- Suitable action is being taken when the cataloging process fails.

☐ Select a number of new or modified programs and reperform the controls over cataloging.

CHAPTER 22

Substantive or Validation Procedures

INTRODUCTION

When internal controls cannot be relied on, substantive procedures are normally used to test computer systems. The main objective of substantive or validation procedures is to determine whether errors exist in account balances. Using these procedures, the auditor can determine whether the computerized and manual accounting treatment of the related transactions (application controls) was appropriate. When this is so, the processing and account balances produced should not contain errors or irregularities. For example, substantive procedures (and related controls) check that:

- Assets and liabilities exist at a given date and recorded transactions have occurred during a specified period (existence/occurrence);
- Transactions are recorded in the proper accounts at the correct amounts (accuracy);
- Transactions are properly authorized in accordance with management intentions (authorization and validity);
- All transactions and accounts that should be presented in the financial statements or management reports are included (completeness);
- Assets and liabilities that appear on the balance sheet represent rights and obligations of the organization (rights and obligations); and
- Components of financial statements or management reports are properly classified, described, and disclosed (presentation and disclosure).

Substantive procedures also include identifying and evaluating the accounting principles used and evaluating judgments used by management that affect valuation estimates. In addition, these procedures complement compliance tests, since they provide further evidence as to whether the internal accounting controls have continued to operate.

When Substantive Procedures Are Performed by an Internal Auditor

The internal auditor may find it necessary to perform substantive procedures under the following circumstances:

- When there are no relevant internal controls
- When the internal auditor may be required to assist the external auditor in a cooperative effort during the annual examination of the financial statements
- When required by regulatory agencies

This section addresses the nature, extent, and timing of substantive procedures and how they constitute an integral part of a systems audit approach.

Substantive Procedures and a Systems Audit Approach by an External Auditor

A systems audit approach can be flexible; it allows the external auditor to rely on controls and limit substantive testing. It also permits the auditor to rely principally on substantive techniques for all or part of an audit when reliance on controls appears impractical or less efficient.

There is a direct correlation between the level of internal controls and the amount of substantive testing required. If the results of compliance testing reveal the presence of adequate internal controls, the auditor is justified in minimizing the substantive procedures. Conversely, if the compliance testing reveals weaknesses in control that may raise doubts about the completeness, accuracy, or validity of the accounts, substantive testing can alleviate these doubts.

In any decision on the extent of substantive procedures required by computer-based accounting systems, the following two general factors might justify a reduction in the levels that would be applied in noncomputer systems:

1. The increased satisfaction that usually can be obtained from the other auditing procedures, based on improved account analyses produced by computer

2. The potential in computer systems for relying on and testing improved internal controls over the updating and maintenance of details of account balances and master file data held on computer files

In computer systems where the auditor cannot, or prefers not to, rely on or compliance test the internal controls, it is necessary to perform extended substantive procedures. These extended substantive procedures include additional work on data or tests to confirm that programmed procedures are operating properly. The additional work on data may include the following:

- Additional use of procedures already planned, such as verifying a greater proportion of the items that make up an account balance

- Greater depth in the procedures already planned, such as seeking more complete documentary evidence in support of payments made

- Using procedures not previously considered, such as confirming accounts payable with suppliers where this has not already been done

The auditor is free to choose whatever methodology provides the most effective and efficient approach. However, relying principally on substantive procedure techniques does not supply assurances that internal controls are adequate, although it may result in the identification of some control weaknesses.

Generally, the results of the various substantive tests can provide some insight into the system of internal accounting controls. For example, if the system is operating properly,

- Subsidiary records should agree with, or be easy to reconcile with, control accounts.

- Confirmation exceptions should be few.

- Cutoff tests should indicate that transactions are recorded in the proper period.
- Book-to-physical inventory variances should be relatively small.
- Depreciation expense per the analysis of fixed assets should agree with the related expense accounts and so forth.

Audit Software Advantages

To perform substantive tests in a computerized environment, the use of audit software offers advantages not found in the traditional manual techniques because computer files usually hold large volumes of accounting data. Each record may contain a great deal of information, such as the history of debtors' payments or the details of stock issues. In addition, detailed records of transactions processed during the year are often held on transaction files. This concentration of data allows the auditor to use audit software to carry out extensive substantive tests on the records with relative speed and ease.

The principal advantages of the use of computer audit software programs are as follows:

- Test results are more conclusive when all data on a file is examined consistently and accurately, rather than only a sample. Reperformance can be much more extensive when computer programs are used, since it is relatively simple and less time-consuming to have the software subject all items in an account balance to the calculation and accumulation procedures.
- The ability to quantify precisely data that meets a particular condition is improved. For example, the software can quickly and accurately produce a total of all customer balances larger than twice their credit limits.
- The performance of sampling procedures, whether statistical or nonstatistical, are more cost-effective when software is employed, providing a time-saving alternative to work that would otherwise have to be done manually.
- It is only necessary for the program to print the results of tests on items that are selected for investigation. Clerical audit work can then be devoted to examining items defined by the auditor as significant. Again, this is less time-consuming than the equivalent manual procedures.
- Because the programs can examine large volumes of data, in some cases it may be more efficient to carry out extended substantive tests rather than to evaluate and test the system of internal control.

Although the purpose of the substantive tests remains unchanged when an audit software program is used, the facilities the program provides make it possible to approach the work in a different way. In conventional audit work, conclusions are drawn from a thorough examination of a limited number of transactions. When an audit software program is used, every transaction can be examined thoroughly with a specific purpose in mind, and the results can be quantified. An example is producing analyzed totals of obsolete inventory.

Samples of the kinds of tasks performed by audit software programs are outlined in the sections dealing with the specific applications.

NATURE OF SUBSTANTIVE PROCEDURES

Substantive procedures can be divided into two categories: substantive tests that are direct tests of the account balances and their components, and other auditing procedures, such as analytical reviews, which are also used for planning.

The nature of the substantive procedures varies depending on the account balance being examined. Examples of these procedures include:

- Confirmation
- Inspection
- Reperformance
- Cutoff testing
- Vouching

- Analysis of fluctuations
- Analysis of financial trends and ratios
- Reconciliation
- Account analysis
- Observation

These procedures can be performed manually or with the assistance of computer programs (audit software). They are described in greater detail in the following sections.

Confirmation

Confirmation consists of obtaining verification of a fact or condition, such as account balances, through correspondence with a third party. This independent verification strongly supports the existence of the account balance. Confirmation often serves as the principal substantive test for accounts receivable and cash account balances. Audit software may be used to assist in the selection of items for confirmation; it also may be used to print confirmation letters and to identify missing returns, where a second request may be needed.

Inspection

Inspection involves physically counting and/or examining the items represented by the dollar balance in an account. Management normally has the count performed by staff people, while the auditor observes and tests the procedures used. At times, the auditor may actually perform the physical count. This substantive procedure is typically applied to inventory; less often, it is applied to fixed asset account balances. EDP audit assistance may be used for the following:

- Selecting the items for physical inspection
- Providing lists of duplicate or missing tags
- Performing book-to-physical comparisons
- Isolating differences

All of these tasks are time-consuming when performed manually.

Reperformance

In many instances, an account balance may represent the result of a computation or an accumulation of computations. Examples of this are the allowance for depreciation, and the provision for doubtful accounts. Reperformance of the computation is the principal substantive procedure applied to those account balances. When judgment is the basis of a computation, reperformance of the computation should also include an evaluation of the reasoning behind the judgment.

Cutoff Testing

Cutoff testing consists of examining documentation to determine that transactions were recorded in the proper period. It is usually easier to carry out effective cutoff tests in computer systems, particularly in batch systems. The discussion that follows is limited to cutoff tests of sales and purchases. Cutoff tests should also be applied to cash receipts and disbursements to determine that those transactions have also been recorded in the proper period.

The principal requirements are to identify the last processing run for sales, purchases, and inventory movements in the period being audited. Then, by reference to batches of input around that time, the auditor needs to confirm that data was entered in the correct period and that rejections were dealt with properly. Note that the nominal date of the last processing run may differ from the actual date on which that run occurs, since the files may be held open after the end of the accounting period in order to process outstanding transactions.

Cutoff tests are made even easier when sales or purchases processing is integrated with the related inventory processing. In this case, no cutoff difference between sales and inventory or purchases and inventory is likely to arise, since the updating of accounts receivable or accounts payable and inventories becomes concurrent. In all cases, it remains necessary to test that the sales and purchases documentation reflects actual shipments and receipts on the dates recorded.

Vouching

Vouching is the examination of evidence supporting a transaction or item in order to determine its validity. Vouching includes:

- A review of company procedures for supporting documentation
- The examination of supporting documentation
- A review for unusual items

Vouching is typically used to validate the accounts payable balance and additions to or retirements from the fixed-asset accounts. Computer programs can be used to assist in the selection of items to be vouched. In many cases, the isolation of unusual items for review consists of sifting through extensive selection criteria; the use of audit software can ease this process greatly.

Analysis of Fluctuations

Analysis of fluctuations in account balances includes obtaining explanations for unusual changes (or a lack of expected changes) in recorded amounts, as compared to budgeted amounts or amounts for prior periods. The explanations are evaluated for reasonableness in relation to other financial information and the auditor's knowledge of the company's affairs. This procedure is normally a necessary supplement to the substantive tests of details. It may reveal audit areas that require particular attention, such as inappropriate entries in the accounts, or items that should receive little or no audit emphasis. Audit software can be used effectively to calculate absolute dollar and percentage changes and to indicate account balances that show significant fluctuations. Manual effort can then be concentrated on evaluating the differences.

Analysis of Financial Trends and Ratios

Analysis of financial trends and ratios involves reviewing the financial position and performance of the company. This is expressed by significant performance indicators, such as:

- Gross profit percentages
- Working capital ratios
- Ratios of receivables to sales
- Ratios of inventories to sales
- Ratios of expenses to sales

Analysis includes ascertaining whether these indicators have a logical relationship, obtaining reasonable explanations for unusual relationships, and considering whether the findings indicate that changes should be made in the nature, extent, or timing of substantive tests. For example, increases in inventories in relation to sales or reductions in gross profit percentages might cause the auditor to extend tests with respect to realization (market value) of inventories. Analysis of financial trends and ratios usually is performed in conjunction with the analysis of balance sheet and profit-and-loss account fluctuations.

Reconciliation

Reconciliation consists of identifying and accounting for any difference between two amounts that should agree (one of the amounts is usually an account balance). For example, the auditor compares the general ledger balance for accounts receivable with the total of the detailed accounts receivable records by customer, or the book balance for a bank account with the balance shown by the related bank statement. When differences are found, the auditor then performs substantive tests to determine whether adjustments are required to the account balance.

Reconciliations usually are carried out more frequently in computer systems. The individual balances on computer files (for example, accounts receivable files) are usually reconciled either to an independent control account or to a control record on the file every time the file is updated or reorganized. As a result of these regular reconciliations, the auditor can carry out compliance tests of these reconciliation procedures more easily than in a noncomputerized system. This should reduce the audit effort required for reconciliations during the substantive procedures.

Account Analysis

Account analysis involves categorizing and summarizing the details of an account to provide an enhanced understanding of the items that constitute the balance. There are two principal forms that an account analysis can take:

1. A summary of the activity for the period under examination
2. An analysis of the composition of the closing balance to determine the major items or categories of items included therein

The first type is useful in dealing with accounts such as property, plant, and equipment, where major elements of the account balance at the beginning of the period remain in the account at the end of the period. The second type is useful in analyzing accounts such as accounts receivable where there is significant activity and the year-end balance consists largely of transactions that occurred during the period covered by the examination.

A greater number of account analyses, often in the form of exception reports, are normally produced in a computerized environment. Also, more complex analyses, which make use of data that is not part of the account balance (such as an analysis of accounts receivable in relation to credit limits), can be produced by computer systems. This type of information, if used properly by the auditor, can provide a better understanding of the nature of the items that constitute an account balance than is normally possible in manual systems.

EXTENT OF SUBSTANTIVE PROCEDURES

Many substantive tests of details of transactions and account balances involve sampling. If they do, the guidance for determining the level of compliance testing that is presented in Chapter 21, "Control Reviews and Compliance Tests," is applicable.

In considering sampling risk, tolerable error, and expected error in a sampling application, the auditor should be cognizant of the following factors:

- The materiality or significance of the items and their relative risk
- The nature, number and size of the items that comprise the particular account balance
- The extent to which an account balance can be correlated with other accounts and with other information obtained in the course of the audit
- The extent to which exceptions have previously been identified in the course of applying substantive procedures
- The degree of reliance that can be placed on the organization's system of internal control based on the results of compliance tests
- The possibility that someone has taken advantage of control deficiencies (fraud) or that errors have arisen, and their extent
- The effect of factors and conditions on sample size in performing substantive tests of details, as described in Statement on Auditing Standards (SAS) No. 39, *Audit Sampling*, and shown in the following table taken from AU Section 350.47

| | Conditions Leading to | | Related Factor |
| | Smaller | Larger | for Substantive |
Factor	Sample Size	Sample Size	Sample Planning
a. Reliance on internal accounting controls	Greater reliance on internal accounting controls	Lesser reliance on internal accounting controls	Allowable risk of incorrect acceptance

(continued)

	Conditions Leading to		Related Factor
Factor	Smaller Sample Size	Larger Sample Size	for Substantive Sample Planning
b. Reliance on other substantive tests related to same account balance or class of transactions (including analytical review procedures and other relevant substantive tests)	Substantial reliance to be placed on other relevant substantive tests	Little or no reliance to be placed on other relevant substantive tests	Allowable risk of incorrect acceptance
c. Measure of tolerable error for a specific account	Larger measure of tolerable error	Smaller measure of tolerable error	Tolerable error
d. Expected size and frequency of errors	Smaller errors or lower frequency	Larger errors or higher frequency	Assessment of population characteristics
e. Number of items in population	Virtually no effect on sample size unless population is very small		—

Materiality of Account Balances and Relative Risk

The essence of the materiality concept is that insignificant differences do not matter. In relation to substantive testing, it is a well-accepted practice that items that are not material in the aggregate are generally ignored in the audit process. Thus, the audit effort is related to the significance of the subject matter.

A critical element that must be considered is relative risk. The allocation of audit efforts is also affected by the relative risk of error or misstatement in a particular environment. For example, inventory is likely to present more of a problem than fixed assets in terms of control, valuation, and application of accounting principles, although both accounts may be material. Thus, inventory has a greater relative risk than fixed assets, from an audit standpoint.

The greater the risk and relative materiality of the account balance, the greater the need for extensive substantive procedures.

Account Balance Composition

The extent of substantive procedures performed is also affected by the composition of the account balances, in terms of quantity and value of items and the amount of human judgment required to arrive at the balance. The auditor normally should examine a greater proportion of items in an account balance where judgment is an important consideration, such as inventory valuation of slow moving items. The use of audit software or computer programs that make the examination of all items possible, and then provide useful account analyses, can be of benefit in these areas.

In a manual environment, there is a tendency to rely on the results of compliance testing and limited substantive testing when an account balance consists of a large number of items with relatively low individual balances. The use of audit software provides the alternative of performing extensive, even 100 percent, substantive testing in preference to compliance testing. When an account balance consists of a small number of items with relatively high individual values, the auditor is likely to subject all (or a substantial portion) of the individual items in the account to direct substantive tests. The use of computer programs in this situation is less advantageous unless the high-value items themselves represent the accumulation of a large number of relatively small individual entries (for example, in the charges to long-term construction contracts over a period of months or years).

Correlation With Other Accounts and Information

Information obtained from tests that were performed on related accounts (for example, correlating the interest charge with the related debt after allowing for any variations in the amount outstanding during the period) may reduce the need for extensive substantive procedures. However, other information obtained during the course of the audit may indicate the need for expanded levels of substantive tests. For example, a review of performance indicators may reveal unexplained changes in the ratio of cost of raw materials used to total cost of production. This may indicate an error in cutoff procedures. At this point, the auditor may wish to expand cutoff tests to see if this is the case.

As a result of analytical review procedures, such as comparison of current financial information with information from comparable prior periods, anticipated results, or similar industry averages, the auditor may decide to limit or expand substantive testing. These considerations are made according to the auditor's related experience and professional knowledge.

The auditor should be aware that information relevant to the audit may be available in the form of existing reports generated by the system. In addition, information can be extracted from the system through the use of audit software. Before it is possible to rely on information produced by audit software, an auditor must establish by other audit tests that the data on the file being examined is complete and accurate. It should be remembered that computer programs can examine only the data actually on the file. If that data is inaccurate or incomplete, the results will be also.

Exceptions

When exceptions, such as errors and deviations from established procedures, are found as a result of substantive procedures, the auditor should determine the reason for each type of exception. It is also important to determine the effect of exceptions on the system. This should be done in terms of their implications both for the functioning of the internal control system and for the account balance under examination. The effect on related account balances also should be investigated.

Bear in mind that even a single, seemingly isolated exception can be an indication of a serious weakness in a control procedure. This is particularly true if the breakdown is in a programmed procedure, or if there is a possibly significant misstatement of an account balance, or both. On the other hand, care should be taken to avoid extending substantive procedures because of an exception before its potential significance is ascertained.

All significant exceptions should be investigated, and the auditor should inform management immediately of any significant exceptions noted during substantive testing.

The auditor may need to rely on certain programmed procedures that either form part of the system of internal control or produce additional information at the test date, such as account analyses or exception reports. The auditor must be satisfied that these programmed procedures are functioning properly and that the information produced is complete and accurate. This can be done by testing the programmed procedures as part of the substantive work. Another method is testing the operation of the disciplines for the period until year-end.

The auditor may not wish to do compliance tests on the general controls, either because they are weak or because it is more efficient to perform extended substantive tests on the programmed procedures. Testing programmed procedures usually involves reperformance of the programmed procedure through the use of audit software or the use of test data. It might also involve examination of the program instructions to confirm that the program functions properly. If this technique is used, it is also necessary for the auditor to follow certain procedures when running the program to ensure that the correct version of the program is used and is run against the correct data file without any unauthorized intervention. The tests should be spread over the period under review, to obtain assurance that the programmed procedures operated properly throughout the period. Tests of programmed procedures often are not straightforward. There is often a lack of visible evidence to indicate exactly how the program has performed its work. Sometimes this visible evidence can be created, so that simple manual tests can be carried out. In other cases, specialized testing techniques are required. A range of testing techniques is available for programmed procedures. (See Chapter 21, "Control Reviews and Compliance Tests," Chapter 26, "*Internal Control Reference Manual — General Controls,*" and Chapter 27, "*Internal Control Reference Manual — Application Controls.*")

COMMON TASKS FOR COMPUTER AUDIT SOFTWARE PROGRAMS

There are a growing number of audit software packages available that are capable of performing the kinds of tasks described in the following checklist under each type of application.

1. Accounts Payable:

☐ Matching subsequent period payments against earlier period items and balances, and identifying unmatched payments.

☐ Identifying old invoices or goods received documentation unmatched on the file.

☐ Identifying unusual transactions; for example, large nonstock purchases for particular account codes.

☐ Identifying unusual master file data; for example, accounts for inactive suppliers.

☐ Identifying accounts not reconciled to suppliers' statements for a significant period of time.

2. Accounts Receivable:

☐ Stratifying the balances or transactions into age categories. Often a more detailed analysis than the one prepared by the company is required; analyzing by transaction type may produce useful information regarding payments on account and unmatched adjustments.

☐ Identifying balances in excess of credit limits, segregating them into strata by reference to the amount by which the credit limit is exceeded, and computing the amount of excess over credit limits.

☐ Identifying accounts with unusual credit limits or no credit limits.

☐ Identifying unusual transactions, for example, large sales near year-end or transfers between accounts.

☐ Identifying unmatched transactions; for example, payments on account.

☐ Identifying unusual master file data; for example, high discount rates.

☐ Selecting items for confirmation and printing appropriate confirmation requests. These items can be written to a file and replies can be matched.

3. Work-in-Process:

☐ Analyzing the balances into age categories.

☐ Identifying items where the full value of work done may not be recoverable. This can be achieved by
  • Identifying items whose actual costs exceeded authorized or budgeted costs.
  • Identifying items whose costs to date exceed fixed selling prices.
  • Identifying items whose costs are not rechargeable to customers (such as warranty work).
  • Selecting items for comparison of realizable value with total expected cost to complete.

☐ Identifying balances that include unusual items; for example, adjustments.

☐ Identifying closed work-in-process items not invoiced within a reasonable period of time.

☐ Identifying items that have been open for an unreasonable period of time.

4. Fixed Assets:

☐ Calculating depreciation and checking the company's figure.

☐ Identifying fully depreciated assets and calculating depreciation on them.

☐ Identifying unusual depreciation rates.

☐ Classifying items according to age categories since last physically inspected.

☐ Identifying properties with no title deed reference.

5. General Ledger:

☐ Identifying items that appear unusual in relation to budgets or past periods.

Specialized Applications

Similar tasks can be carried out with respect to applications in specialized businesses, as in audit software tailored to the portfolios in a financial services organization.

TIMING OF SUBSTANTIVE PROCEDURES

When assisting an external auditor in the annual examination of the financial statements, it may be desirable to perform substantive procedures as of a date prior to year-end. This may be done to increase audit effectiveness, detect problem areas early, and satisfy stringent audit report deadlines. However, early substantive procedures are not appropriate in all cases. SAS No. 45, *Omnibus Statement on Auditing Standards — 1983*, provides guidance on performing substantive tests prior to the balance sheet date.

When the auditor decides to carry out his or her substantive procedures on account balances mainly as of the balance sheet date, it still may be desirable to carry out certain substantive work prior to the year-end. Substantive procedures that involve the examination or review of transactions during the year (for example, purchases and disposals of fixed assets) can be performed prior to the year-end with respect to transactions for part of the year. Transactions for the remainder of the year would then be examined in the course of the substantive work that is carried out as of the balance sheet date. This is particularly relevant when these examinations and reviews are performed by computer programs, since it is usually relatively easy to run the program regularly throughout the period being audited.

SPECIMEN TESTING PROCEDURES

Various kinds of substantive procedures are applied to typical testing situations. The following procedures suggest possible substantive audit procedures for certain applications, particularly when the audit strategy is not to rely on controls. The procedures are designed to assist in

- Developing substantive audit procedures for when the audit strategy is not to rely on controls.
- Reviewing existing substantive audit programs.

Figures 22-1 and 22-2 present specimen substantive audit procedures. These figures are not intended to be a maximum, minimum, or all-inclusive list of substantive audit procedures. They are provided here as examples of one approach that can be used.

Possible substantive procedures, both manual and computerized, for specified audit situations, including use of audit software, are shown in Figure 22-1 for trade accounts receivable and sales and in Figure 22-2 for property, plant, and equipment.

If the audit strategy decision is to test and rely on controls, the auditor's objective should be to take this into account in setting the nature and extent of substantive procedures according to management's objectives. The nature of many substantive procedures may not vary greatly whether or not controls are in place, since controls may not address all substantive audit assertions. However, when the controls are relied on

- The planned extent of the substantive procedures should consider this.
- The timing should be appropriately evaluated giving consideration to early substantiation.

When the auditor does not plan to rely on control tests, procedures such as those described in the figures could be considered. To assist the auditor in locations with significant computer systems, procedures include indication of where computer audit software can be used efficiently.

Substantive audit procedures should always be tailored to the specific audit objectives. In doing this, the auditor should

- Select the steps applicable to the audit strategy. Many steps may not be applicable in particular circumstances.
- Modify the steps selected to:
  a. Describe clearly the program steps as tailored for particular circumstances.
  b. Indicate the extent of testing to be performed.
  c. Identify the timing and period to be covered by the tests including any effects of early validation.
- Add any additional steps necessary to meet the needs of the situation or to achieve the audit strategy or audit objectives.

Whether or not controls are relied on for all, some, or parts of the system processing cycles, the auditor should consider all of the factors in an audit approach when deciding which tests to administer.

Substantive Audit Objectives

Obtain audit evidence that

A. Recorded trade accounts receivable exist and represent amounts due to the company at the balance sheet date.

B. Material amounts due to the company at the balance sheet date have been recorded.

C. Trade accounts receivable are carried at net collectible amounts (i.e., the allowances for doubtful accounts, discounts, returns, and similar items are appropriate).

D. Trade accounts receivable pledged as collateral are identified and disclosed.

E. Sales transactions recorded during the period are valid transactions, properly computed and recorded.

Summary of Trade Accounts Receivable

1. Obtain or prepare a comparative summary of year-end trade accounts receivable balances. Verify the mathematical accuracy of the summary and agree totals to the general ledger trial balance and the previous year's working papers. Trace significant reconciling items to supporting documentation.

Analytical Review

Note: Analytical review procedures may be performed during the initial planning stages, during the conduct of the examination, or near the conclusion of the examination, depending on the auditor's objectives. Some of these procedures may be performed in connection with income statement substantive procedures.

2. Review performance indicators relevant to trade accounts receivable and sales; such a review could include some of the following comparisons with budget and/or equivalent ratios or other indicators at periodic accounting dates during the year or at previous year-ends:

  a. Average receivables (opening balance plus closing balance divided by 2)
  b. Receivables turnover ratio (sales divided by average receivables)
  c. Average daily sales (sales divided by 365)
  d. Days sales outstanding (average receivables divided by average daily sales)
  e. Sales mix (percentage breakdown of sales by product line or other classification)
  f. Receivables mix (percentage breakdown of receivables by aging category)
  g. Bad-debt ratios (bad-debt allowance dividend by gross receivables; bad-debt expense divided by gross sales)
  h. Discount ratios (discounts divided by gross sales)
  i. Commission ratios (commmissions divided by gross sales)
  j. Interest/finance charge as a percentage of receivables
  k. Selling expense as a percentage of sales
  l. Advertising as a percentage of sales
  m. Account balances for major customers
  n. Unmatched cash as a percentage of receivables

Identify and obtain explanations for major fluctuations from expected results and consider their impact on nature, extent, or timing of other audit procedures.

Audit Software: Most of the calculations required above can be economically achieved by manual means, but some of the base figures may not be available in an appropriate format. The sales mix may be obtained through an inventory audit software package, the receivables mix and the unmatched cash by an

(continued)

FIG. 22-1   Specimen substantive procedures for trade accounts receivable and sales

accounts receivable audit software package, and account balances for major customers by using generalized audit software, such as AUDITPAK II.

Detailed Trade Accounts Receivable

3. Obtain a detailed list of trade accounts receivable balances aged by customer. Verify the mathematical accuracy and trace totals to the summary obtained in step 1. Determine the propriety of significant reconciling items through inquiry and examination of supporting documentation.

   Audit Software: The aging by customer can be reperformed and the mathematical accuracy verified by using an accounts receivable audit software package.

4. For a sample of receivables, trace amounts to subsidiary ledgers (see step 23f for testing of ledgers) or to supporting documentation to determine the reliability of the aging.

Cutoff

Note: In most cases, the cutoff substantive steps for sales can best be carried out in conjunction with the cutoff substantive steps for inventories.

5. Review the cutoff at the time of inventory taking and at year-end (if different):
   a. For a sample of sales, determine that the sales invoices are recorded as sales in the proper period by examining the related records of goods shipped and services performed.
   b. For a sample of credit (debit) memoranda, determine that the credit (debit) memoranda are recorded in the proper period by examining the related records of returns and claims from customers.
   c. Inquire into the processing of returned goods (a large backlog of unprocessed returned goods may be indicative of future credits for which provisions have not been made).
   d. Where practicable and where shipping and return documents are prenumbered, account for the numerical sequence of unused shipping and return documents.

   Audit Software: An accounts receivable audit software package can be used to determine and report on items incorrectly included in the current period. Additionally, generalized audit software could be used to select items outside the correct period and produce lists of items for confirmation with customers.

6. Where the volume of direct shipments from suppliers to customers is significant, determine that there has been a proper cutoff by confirming shipping information for such sales for a period around year-end directly with the supplier.

7. Investigate significant credit balances to determine cause and consider whether reclassification is necessary.

   Audit Software: Either generalized audit software or an accounts receivable audit software package could be used to disclose significant credit balances included in accounts receivable.

8. In conjunction with inventory testing, determine whether sales have been recorded for inventory that is still on the company's premises. Consider any adjustment that may be appropriate.

Direct Confirmation

9. Select customers' accounts for confirmation and the method of confirmation (positive, negative, or a combination). Confirmation requests should be sent under the auditor's control and, where appropriate, itemized statements should be sent to customers to facilitate responses. Second requests should be mailed when

FIG. 22-1 *(continued)*

responses to positive confirmations have not been received within a reasonable time period.

Audit Software: An accounts receivable audit software package may assist in determining the criteria for selecting accounts for confirmation by using a stratification option to select accounts based on a wide range of criteria, to prepare the confirmation worksheet, and to print the positive and negative confirmation letters.

10. Investigate any discrepancies reported or questions raised by customers and determine whether any adjustments are necessary. Consider whether adjustments required indicate weaknesses in control and whether the scope of the examination should be appropriately revised.

11. For positive confirmations unanswered after second requests or where it is not possible or desirable to confirm a selected account

  a. Compare subsequent remittances credited to these accounts with remittance advices or other receipt records to ascertain that payments relate to the account balance (in some cases it may be advisable to examine other related documentation such as sales invoices, etc.).

  b. For items not paid since the validation date, examine documentation such as shipping documents, copies of sales invoices, and relevant correspondence supporting the unpaid portion of the account balances.

Audit Software: By using a transaction file subsequent to confirmation date, an accounts receivable audit software package can be used to extract subsequent payments on accounts for which confirmation has been requested.

12. Summarize confirmations and alternative procedure coverage.

Audit Software: An accounts receivable audit software package produces a report and summary of the confirmations.

13. Review the aged trial balance and identify significant old receivables and receivables in dispute based on confirmation replies or other factors and

  a. Review subsequent cash collections, examine related remittance advices or other supporting documentation to ascertain that payments relate to the account balance (in some cases it may be advisable to examine other related documentation such as sales invoices, etc.);

  b. Determine the adequacy of collateral, if any;

  c. Discuss all significant potentially doubtful accounts with management;

  d. Review relevant credit file information, such as customer financial data and correspondence.

Audit Software: An accounts receivable audit software package could be used to prepare an aged trial balance of the accounts receivable. Subsequent cash collections for old outstanding balances could be extracted by using generalized audit software.

14. Obtain a summary of the activity in the allowance account during the year and examine authorizations and other documentation supporting significant write-offs. Agree opening balance to prior year's working papers, current year's provision to the income statement, write-offs to the receivables records, and the closing balance to the general ledger trial balance.

15. Determine whether any formulas used are

  a. Consistent with past years;

  b. Appropriate to the circumstances of the business;

(continued)

    c. Indicative of actual bad-debt experience or estimated bad-debt experience if the company has not been in business long enough for actual experience to be meaningful.

16. Based on procedures described in steps 13–15, determine whether the allowance for doubtful accounts is adequate.

Other Allowances

17. Consider whether other allowances are required relating to Accounts Receivable or Sales (e.g., trade allowances, rebates, claims, and warranties).

Interest and Service Charges

18. Test to see if interest or service charges on accounts receivable have been properly computed and recorded. (Software is sometimes used.)

Commissions

19. Test the reasonableness of sales commissions (software is sometimes used):
    a. Determine the methods (e.g., percent of sales) and bases (e.g., net sales, net collections) of computing commissions by inquiry, reviews of policy, and/or examination of agreements with salespeople.
    b. Where practicable, perform an analysis of the reasonableness of total commissions as a percent of sales.
    c. Test the propriety of the computation of sales commissions and summarization in the general ledger.

Sale of Consigned Items

20. Where client is consignor, examine the consignment agreement and test the recording of sales and related commissions of consigned items to reports of sales from consignee. In conjunction with the work being performed on the inventory balances, either obtain confirmation directly from the consignee or observe physical count of inventory.

21. Where the company is consignee, examine the consignment agreement, compare consignment reports sent to consignor with accounting records, and test computation of consignee's commission. Obtain direct confirmation from consignor of
    a. Merchandise for which the consignee is responsible as at the balance sheet date, if appropriate;
    b. Amounts owed to consignors for consignment sales; and
    c. Any commissions or compensation due from consignor.
    Where significant amounts of consigned inventory are held, observe the physical count of inventory, ascertain that such inventory is not included in the financial statements, and ascertain that the appropriate liability is provided for amounts due consignor.

Sales Commitments

22. Where material losses could arise from unfulfilled sales commitments, assess whether a provision should be made for such potential losses by
    a. Examining open sales commitments (such records, if maintained, are generally presumed not to be under accounting control);
    b. Inquiring of employees who make sales commitments as to any significant unfulfilled commitments at year-end;
    c. Reviewing shipping records and related sales invoices for a period after the balance sheet date for evidence of sales commitments outstanding at the balance sheet date;

FIG. 22-1 *(continued)*

    d. Requesting selected major customers to advise of details of any sales commitments outstanding at the balance sheet date when it is considered necessary in the company's circumstances.

Audit Software: By accessing the open order file, generalized audit software could be used to analyze open commitments and, depending on the company's system, disclose possible potential losses.

Annual Sales, Related Discounts, Returns and Allowances, and Credit Memoranda

23. For a sample of sales (and related discounts, returns and allowances, and credit memoranda) recorded during the period (the sample should include both sales reflected in receivables and collected sales)

    a. Trace to supporting documentation (e.g., sales orders, shipping documents, sales receipts, invoices).
    Audit Software: Can be used to extract a sample of items for comparison with supporting documentation. It could also be used to compare the records in independent transaction files, such as comparison of sales with invoices.

    b. Verify the mathematical accuracy (software can be used).

    c. Determine that sales have been properly authorized or are in compliance with policy.

    d. Compare the prices to authorized catalogs, other official company sources, or approval by an authorized official (software can be used).

    e. Determine that discounts and allowances are in compliance with company policy and/or approved by an authorized official; where authorization is not required or there is no formal policy, ascertain that discounts and allowances are reasonable and/or in line with industry practices, etc.

    f. Trace posting to the accounts receivable subsidiary ledger.

    g. Trace to receipt of cash, if appropriate, by examining the cash receipts book entry, posting to the accounts receivable ledger, the deposit ticket, and entry on the bank statement.

24. For a sample of months during the year, verify the mathematical accuracy of the sales journal and trace the proper posting to the general ledger. (Summarization and posting of the cash receipts book should be performed in connection with the cash accounts.) (Software can be used.)

25. Determine that all sales for a selected period(s) have been posted to the sales journal by accounting for the numerical sequence of invoices and shipping documents. Trace all appropriate information on the shipping documents to the sales invoice and investigate differences. (Software can be used.)

26. Review postings to the general ledger to determine that all material types of transactions have been covered by audit testing. Devise and perform additional procedures, as necessary, to test the completeness, propriety, and validity of transaction types not previously tested, such as:

    a. Sales previously recorded as deferred revenue

    b. Amounts recorded as advances on sales

    c. Sales of scrap

    d. Sales of byproducts

    e. Cash sales

Accounts Receivable Pledge as Collateral

27. Identify assets pledged as collateral for company indebtedness by reviewing debt and lease agreements, confirmation replies, and minutes of directors' meetings; inspecting public records; and inquiring of management.

(continued)

Early Substantiation

28. If early substantiation of Trade Accounts Receivable is contemplated, additional audit work will be required.

Other Matters

29. If, based on knowledge of the company's business and industry and the results of audit tests, there is a possibility of notes being received in settlement of trade accounts receivable, inquire as to whether such notes have been separately disclosed. Consider whether reclassification is appropriate.

    Note: If the existence of such notes is discovered from other audit tests (e.g., confirmation, tests of subsequent cash receipts), decide if the scope of tests should be expanded.

30. Determine if there were any transactions during the year or balances at year-end denominated in foreign currency and whether they have been translated at appropriate rates.

31. Determine that all appropriate matters to be included in the management letter have been noted.

32. Devise and perform any additional steps deemed necessary for this particular client.

Note: At this point, the auditor should consider whether the results of the audit steps performed satisfy the substantive audit objectives for Trade Accounts Receivable and Sales and whether all appropriate comments have been prepared.

FIG. 22-1 *(continued)*

Substantive Audit Objectives

A. The cost or other basis of property, plant, and equipment is appropriate and has been consistently applied.

B. Additions to property, plant, and equipment accounts are appropriate.

C. There are no material items charged to expense that should have been capitalized.

D. All retirements of property, plant, and equipment have been appropriately recorded.

E. Property, plant, and equipment recorded in the financial statements exist and are owned or leased under capital leases.

F. Appropriate methods of depreciation have been properly applied to property, plant, and equipment and are consistent with the previous year.

G. Property, plant, and equipment pledged as collateral is identified and disclosed.

Summary of Property, Plant, and Equipment

1. Obtain or prepare a comparative summary of year-end property, plant, and equipment balances. Verify the mathematical accuracy of the summary and agree the totals to the general ledger trial balance and the previous year's working papers. Trace significant reconciling items to supporting documentation. (Software is sometimes used.)

Individual Balances

2. Obtain or prepare a detailed analysis of property, plant, and equipment cost and accumulated depreciation (software is sometimes used) including details of

a. Total amounts, by classification, at the beginning of the year;

b. Purchases, including a description of the assets acquired, and investment tax credit;

c. Assets sold, abandoned, or written off, including a description of the assets, gain or loss on sale, cost, accumulated depreciation, and investment tax credit recapture;

d. Depreciation charges by classification, including the range of useful lives;

e. Other adjustments during the period (e.g., abandonments, fully depreciated assets retired);

f. Total amounts, by classification, at the balance sheet date.

Note: Amounts of minor significance may be grouped.

3. Verify the mathematical accuracy of the analysis, tracing beginning balances and ending balances to the summary obtained in step 1. Trace significant reconciling items to supporting documentation.

Audit Software: Could be used to verify the mathematical accuracy of the detailed property, plant, and equipment records (including selection and recalculation of details of additions, disposals, and depreciation) and compare opening balances to prior period closing balances.

4. Review the analysis for reasonableness, consistency of amounts between years, and any obvious omissions.

Additions

5. Examine suppliers' invoices, title deeds, capital lease agreements, purchase agreements, construction contracts, progress billings, work orders, and other data supporting major additions. (Software can be used.)

(continued)

FIG. 22-2   Specimen substantive procedures for property, plant, and equipment

6. Obtain or prepare an analysis of repair and maintenance accounts. Examine supporting documentation (e.g., suppliers' invoices) for significant charges to determine whether they should be capitalized. (Software is sometimes used.)

7. Review the minutes of meetings of the board of directors or other authorizing committees for appropriate authorizations for major additions, sales, abandonments, etc.

8. Examine supporting documentation (e.g., bills of sale) for significant sales and trade-ins, and test the computations of accumulated depreciation and the calculation of gain or loss recorded on the sales.

9. Consider the following, which indicate unrecorded retirements or questionable carrying values:
   a. Additions that replace existing property
   b. Major changes to plant layout or product design
   c. Changes in insurance coverage
   d. Idle property, plant, or equipment
   e. Property held for sale

10. Trace significant adjustments made to property, plant, and equipment accounts during the period to supporting documentation.

Existence

11. Review the company's procedures for verifying the existence and ownership of recorded assets and consider the necessity of independently verifying the physical existence of and, if appropriate, the title to property, plant, and equipment, including construction in process. Consider performing physical inspection of major additions during the period under review. (Software is sometimes used.)

Depreciation

12. Determine whether the depreciation practices followed by the company are reasonable in the company's circumstances and consistent with the prior year. These practices may include estimates of useful lives and salvage values, procedures for the depreciation of additions and retirements, and accounting for fully depreciated assets. (Software can be used.)

13. Compare for reasonableness, current and prior year depreciation amounts for each significant category of property, plant, and equipment, obtaining explanations and supporting documentation for any significant fluctuations. Test depreciation calculations to the extent considered necessary. (Software is sometimes used.)

    Audit Software: Could be used to recompute accumulated depreciation and gain or loss on sale. Additionally, it could be used to select significant sales from the detailed fixed assets records.

Recoverability

14. Consider whether adjustments should be made to the carrying value of assets to reflect a permanent diminution in value (step 9).

Leases

15. Examine records of leased assets, lease agreements, and other relevant data for leases capitalized during the period to determine if they were properly capitalized in accordance with Statement of Financial Accounting Standards (SFAS) No. 13 (as amended).

FIG. 22-2 *(continued)*

Audit Software: Time-sharing audit software could be used to recalculate capitalization of the leases in accordance with SFAS No. 13 (as amended).

16. Examine support for rentals under operating leases to determine if any leases should be capitalized in accordance with SFAS No. 13 (as amended).

Interest Capitalization

17. Examine supporting documentation for interest capitalized during the period in accordance with SFAS No. 34.

18. Inquire of management as to the existence of any capital projects that require a period of preparation before they are ready for their intended use for which interest has not been capitalized. Examine project authorizations, progress payments, and other supporting data (including notes payable and long-term debt) to determine if interest should be capitalized in accordance with SFAS No. 34.

Property, Plant, and Equipment Pledged as Collateral

19. Identify assets pledged as collateral for company indebtedness by reviewing debt and lease agreements, confirmation replies, and minutes of directors' meetings; inspecting public records; and inquiring of management.

Other Matters

20. Determine whether profit or interdepartmental transfers or intercompany sales of assets is eliminated from property, plant, and equipment accounts.

21. Determine if there were any transactions during the year or balances at year-end denominated in foreign currency and whether they have been translated at appropriate rates.

22. Determine that all appropriate matters to be included in the management letter have been noted.

23. Devise and perform any additional steps deemed necessary for the company.

Note: At this point, the auditor should consider whether the results of the audit steps performed satisfy the substantive audit objectives for Property, Plant, and Equipment and whether all appropriate comments have been prepared.

PART V

Using Documents and Forms

CHAPTER **23**

How to Document Systems and Use Flowcharts

OBTAINING, RECORDING, AND CONFIRMING THE UNDERSTANDING

An auditor has to obtain an understanding of any system under review in order to plan a logical audit strategy. Obtaining an understanding means learning about the system. To do so, the auditor may review correspondence files, key business statistics, organization charts, internal audit reports, consultants' reports, procedural manuals, and external audit reports, including previous comments to management. Furthermore, the auditor may interview personnel at the location to be reviewed or tour the site to get first-hand knowledge of the operations under review. An important part of the audit is the documenting, or flowcharting, of systems under consideration.

It is also helpful for an auditor to review working papers from prior years. These reveal the type of work that was done in the past and the kinds of problems that were encountered. Finally, whenever possible, it is a good idea to interview the auditor who performed the review in the past. This can provide valuable insight into problem areas.

In short, obtaining an understanding is a research process the auditor performs in order to become familiar with the operation of the system.

FLOWCHARTING TECHNIQUES

There are several popular methods of flowcharting that are used to document, or clearly put down on paper, just what happens in a system. Flowcharts have become popular because their users find this special illustrative technique particularly effective.

Some of the major system-oriented flowcharting techniques and their principal characteristics are

- *ANSI (American National Standards Institute)* — Uses standardized flowchart symbols and techniques.

- *PERT (Program Evaluation Review Technique) and CPM (Critical Path Method)* — Show precedence of activity, the relationships between events, and relative time sequence.

- *HIPO (Hierarchy: Input-Processing-Output)* — Depicts program or system elements in a hierarchical format, similar to a tree structure. This presentation can be quite helpful to an auditor in achieving an understanding of the purpose of the programs or systems. It subdivides systems into parts, and those parts are further subdivided into appropriate subparts.

- *Circuit diagrams* — Relate the electronic circuit elements and provide a technical explanation of the circuit behavior (rarely used by auditors).

- *Transaction flow diagrams* — Emphasize each transaction type and the procedures that affect each transaction. These are used frequently by auditors.

There are a number of different graphic flowcharting techniques auditors use to structure their presentation of system information. The way the transaction flow itself is set out on the flowchart varies. Some of the more common techniques are:

- *Horizontal.* The transaction flow is shown from left to right on each page, with the far right of a page connecting with the far left of the following page.

- *Horizontal by organization.* The flow is depicted from left to right by organizational subunit. Within each subunit the sequential procedures or operations are shown vertically. The flowchart generally proceeds from top left to bottom right of a page.

- *Vertical.* A transaction flows down a single line, which shows the sequential operations that affect each transaction and the files or records that are needed at each operation. A key characteristic of this type of flowchart is that it shows final disposition of each transaction, file, or record on the flowline.

Each of these types of flowchart may employ its own set of unique symbols, as well as some fairly standard ones. The connecting line is the only universal feature of all flowcharting techniques.

An auditor interested in controls requires flowcharts that clearly define the point at which a control begins to exist and the range of operations or procedures covered by the control. In purely system-oriented flowcharts, the controls may not even be depicted. A single flowline flowcharting technique (with a minimum of parallel functions) is very effective in documenting controls in both manual and automated systems. One such technique is presented here.

RECORDING THE UNDERSTANDING — FLOWCHARTING

Objective

Auditors flowchart systems to achieve the specific goals of recording and documenting the system and its controls. To meet these objectives, the following topics need to be reviewed:

- Summary of flowcharting principles and techniques to be used in documenting accounting systems of management information systems.

- Specific symbols and methods used in an audit-oriented flowcharting technique. The Coopers & Lybrand method is shown here to illustrate one such functional flowchart system.

- Presentation of the flowcharting considerations unique to a computer-based system.

- Some of the more common errors encountered in flowcharts of computer systems.

Recording the Understanding

An understanding of the processing system for each transaction type and the controls incorporated is fundamental to an effective system evaluation. This understanding is the basis for evaluating internal controls and should be properly documented. Many auditors and system analysts use flowcharts for this purpose.

Advantages of Flowcharting

A flowchart serves two functions: comprehension and communication. By showing procedures in graphic form, flowcharts improve comprehension and provide a superior means for communicating information. Flowcharts enable the auditor to readily identify particular control features in the system. The significance of those features can then be evaluated to see whether they are meeting the objectives of the internal control system. Flowcharting promotes efficiency and uniformity in the preparation of working papers. For these criteria to be met, the charts must be prepared logically, concisely, and clearly.

When the right kind of flowchart is prepared, it also improves communication among those involved in the administration and evaluation of the internal control system, such as management, systems development, and users.

Criteria for Flowcharting

The flowcharting technique used by Coopers & Lybrand was designed specifically to depict control procedures. An auditor or system analyst can determine which procedures are significant for purposes of meeting the internal control objectives of a system from these charts. This technique is shown here because it has worked well for a number of reviews and types of systems.

The flowcharts should meet the following criteria:

- Procedures should be shown in sequence.
- All copies of pertinent documents should be explained and accounted for.
- The maintenance of files and preparation of reports with control significance should be shown.
- The flow of transactions among the various departments of the business should be shown.
- Both manual and EDP operations should be shown.
- The title or position and, where practical, the name of the persons performing the procedures should be shown.

One Flowcharting Technique

The flowcharting technique designed by Coopers & Lybrand meets the preceding criteria. Moreover, it provides a suitable basis for carrying out transaction reviews. The technique adapts standard flowcharting approaches to the special needs of the auditor (although it has also been found useful by others). Specifically, it

- Identifies records, files, and reports.
- Provides descriptions of operations and related documents in the sequence of processing.
- Guides the auditor through all the processing steps leading to the disposition of copies of documents with internal accounting control significance.

Main Flowline. The Coopers & Lybrand flowcharting technique features a "main flowline" illustrating the flow of processing and the documents involved. The flowline runs from the beginning to the end of each system. It starts with the inception of transactions and ends with their recording in the financial or management records. It includes both manual and computer procedures. To depict a complete flow of transactions to their termination, flowcharts and/or narratives should show the posting to the general ledger. This helps to trace the flow of transactions into the accounting records and ensures that all principal documents in the system have been covered in the charts. Particular attention should be given to showing the steps in the flow of principal documents through the entire system and thus providing a suitable basis for carrying out transaction reviews. Figure 23-1 illustrates this concept of flowcharting.

Preparation of Flowcharts. The preparation or updating of flowcharts is an integral part of the internal control evaluation process. The same individual who obtains (or updates) the understanding of the system and related controls should record the understanding. The help of EDP auditors may be required in flowcharting computer systems. Flowcharts should be reviewed by supervisory personnel after they have been prepared.

Updating Flowcharts. Flowcharts or narratives should be reviewed and updated at scheduled intervals, preferably annually. When changes are necessary, the auditor may either draw new charts or correct the old charts. A complete redrawing of flowcharts is not usually required unless they have been entirely superseded or they are no longer legible due to the number of changes. If the flowcharts require a few changes, photocopies of the old charts should be made beforehand so that there is a record of the procedures in force at a particular date.

Knowledge Required. Apart from providing the auditor with a general idea of how the procedures operate, the main audit use of flowcharts is to document controls. The evaluation of a system and the subsequent compliance

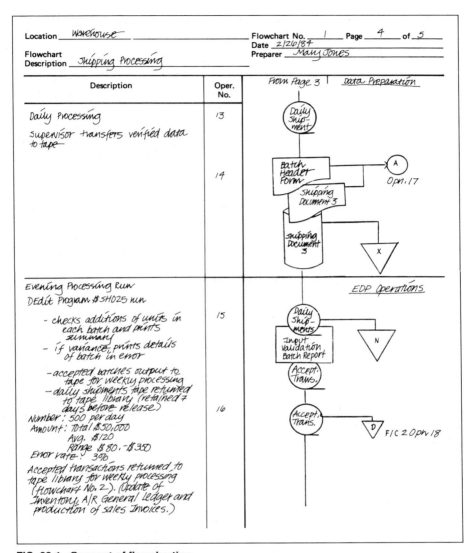

FIG. 23-1 Concept of flowcharting

testing of that system is based on the Internal Control Questionnaire (ICQ) and/or Control Matrix (see Chapter 25, "The Evaluation Process and How to Use Documents") and the flowcharts that are used to document and illustrate the controls identified. It is therefore important that before preparing detailed flowcharts of a system the auditor has

- A clear understanding of documents used to evaluate the system (such as the ICQ or matrix), and

- A general idea of the nature of the procedures and controls in the system itself.

Unless this is done, the auditor will have some difficulty in cross-referencing a control identified in the ICQ or matrix with a flowchart operation. The ICQ in particular, with its detailed questions, acts to some extent as a check on the flowcharts. On the other hand, the Control Matrix is in a shortened format and provides less specific guidance. Therefore, more care is needed when preparing the flowcharts that accompany it. The person preparing the flowcharts should also complete the ICQ or matrix, in most cases.

Interviews. The auditor usually obtains information necessary for preparing or updating flowcharts by interviewing personnel at each site about procedures followed, and by reviewing procedure manuals and other system documentation. Inquiries can be made concurrently with the performance of transaction reviews, particularly when flowcharts are being updated.

Gaining an understanding typically involves extensive interviewing. See Chapter 24, "Interviews and Transaction Reviews in an Audit," for a discussion of conducting an effective internal control inquiry.

Flowcharts Prepared by Others. In light of the special emphasis of this flowcharting technique, flowcharts previously prepared by management may not be acceptable. If they were prepared by a systems area, they may not contain all the information needed for an audit. However, certain previously prepared flowcharts may be acceptable if they meet the criteria discussed previously.

In computerized systems, the quality of documentation tends to be good. The auditor should be aware of opportunities to make use of it. The company's computer personnel often use flowcharts and other documentation to describe the sequence of computer runs, inputs, outputs, and certain processing details. This information may be particularly useful to the auditor in obtaining an initial understanding of the computer applications and in documenting programmed procedures. It is unlikely, however, that the material available will meet all the auditor's needs, particularly in relation to controls. Consequently, it usually cannot substitute for the kind of flowcharting described here. Nevertheless, the existing material may provide a useful supplement to the auditor's own flowcharts. The parts describing programmed procedures can be integrated with flowcharts of the manual procedures where possible.

The auditor must fully understand flowcharts prepared by others, when they are used. They must be suitable for the intended audit purposes and also be adequately cross-referenced to other flowcharts that are being prepared.

Copies for Site Personnel. Copies of flowcharts prepared by the auditor can be given to the site personnel, who may find them useful for their own purposes. Since those who use a system should know it best, the auditor may find it helpful to ask site personnel to comment on and confirm the accuracy of the flowcharts.

Internal Accounting and Operational Controls

Flowcharting is considered appropriate for most of the procedures that have significant accounting implications. The flowcharts should reflect all operations having accounting control significance. The phrase "accounting control" refers not only to the accounting control objectives and procedures set out in the ICQ, but also to any compensating controls. The flowcharting technique shown here makes it possible to integrate administrative controls. For example, the part of the payments cycle flowchart describing control procedures in the purchasing function may describe such administrative control procedures as the calculation of minimum economic order quantities, lead times, and buffer stocks, or the solicitation of competitive bids from vendors and the maintenance of vendor evaluation files. If it is more efficient, these controls can be discussed in the narratives that supplement the flowcharts. Decisions about review of administrative controls and the extent of documentation to be done for such a review must be made before the system review starts.

Ordinarily, an auditor flowcharts procedures relating to document handling and retention only to the extent that they are relevant to internal accounting (or certain administrative) controls. However, when management so desires, flowcharts can detail the handling and retention of all copies of documents as part of an evaluation of the effectiveness and efficiency of company documentation procedures.

Flowcharts in Nonfinancial Systems

The flowcharting technique also can be used to depict nonfinancial management information systems. The auditor can then evaluate the quality and reliability of the management information produced, and the efficiency of the procedures involved.

Amount of Detail

Flowcharts should not be elaborate; they should show only what is needed for understanding. Preparation time should be commensurate with the expected benefits. Accordingly, a lot of time should not be spent on charts with only limited usefulness. It is rarely necessary to flowchart every process applied to every copy of every document in detail. The information should be confined to what is essential for an understanding of significant aspects of the system and related controls. Flowcharts used to evaluate internal accounting controls alone can be less detailed than those used to assess administrative controls.

Properly prepared, detailed flowcharts are particularly helpful to people who subsequently perform the compliance testing of controls. When the person responsible for documenting the system is not the one to carry out the tests, the control procedures should be described in some detail. Then, the location of documents and the names by which they are known to site personnel will be readily available to the auditor actually performing the tests.

Using Narratives

This approach to flowcharting can be applied to most businesses, regardless of size. Nonetheless, there are situations — such as when major changes will be made in the system or when control procedures seem to be nonexistent — when it may be more efficient for the auditor to prepare a succinct narrative explanation of his or her acquired understanding of the system. When narratives are used, the auditor should make sure that they contain the same information concerning the system that would have been shown in flowcharts. The reasons why narratives were used instead of flowcharts should be explained in the working papers.

Overview Flowcharts

Overview flowcharts are useful for outlining computer-based systems. They can also show the broad flow between departments. When flowcharting an application for the first time, it is often helpful to sketch a brief outline of the system as a prelude to preparing detailed flowcharts. Instructions for overview flowcharts are discussed later in this chapter.

Computer Overview Flowcharts

In computer-based systems, the auditor should prepare an overview flowchart for each important computer application. Normally these charts are prepared before detailed flowcharting to convey the scope of computer processing, which may best be done by an EDP auditor. The information depicted is often useful in planning an evaluation.

The computer overview flowchart indicates significant input, master files, and output, in terms of both routine and exception reports. (See Figure 23-2.) In more complex systems, it is helpful to show the flow of data through the separate subsystems within the overall system, indicating the points in the process at which the various reports and files are generated. (See Figure 23-3.) The disposal of reports can be indicated on the computer overview flowchart.

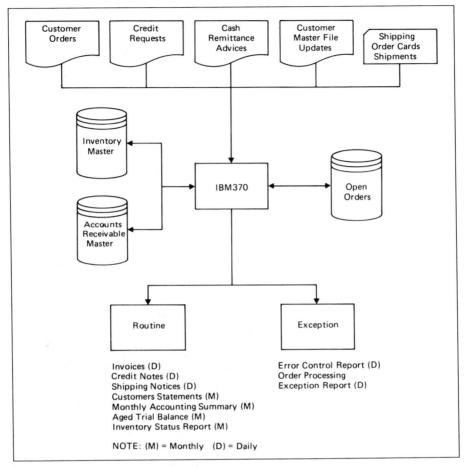

FIG. 23-2 **Computer overview flowchart**

Departmental Overview Flowcharts

When a system is especially complex, it is important for someone other than the original preparer of the detailed flowcharts to be able to obtain a broad view of the flow among the various departments of the organization. In this case, it is useful to prepare a departmental overview flowchart to serve as a summary or index to the detailed flowcharts. In noncomputerized systems, the overview flowchart is often prepared after the preparation or updating of detailed flowcharts. It is done mainly for convenience and its use is optional. (For an example and its narrative, see Figures 23-4A and 23-4B.)

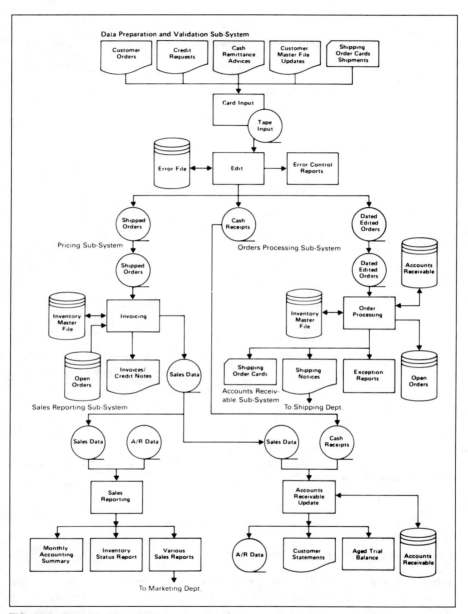

FIG. 23-3 Flow of subsystems

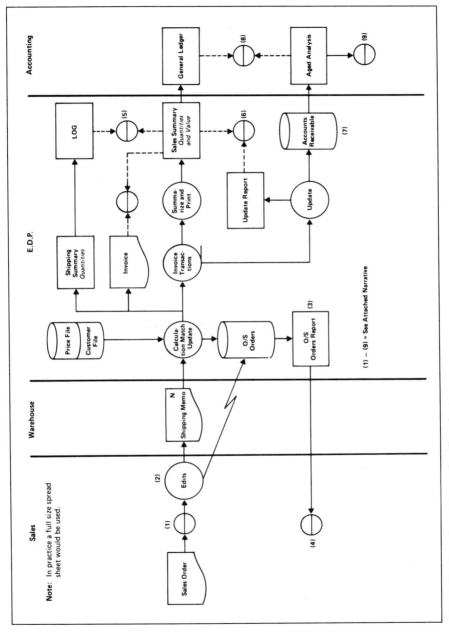

FIG. 23-4A   Departmental overview flowchart

1. Sales order approved by the sales manager for all orders over $500.

2. On-line edits for - valid customer number
                      - valid product number

3. Weekly report prepared of all orders not matched to shipping memo that are over one week past shipping date.

4. The sales manager reviews the outstanding orders report and has his assistant investigate reasons for no shipment.

5. Daily shipping quantities accumulated in a log and the monthly total reconciled to total quantities per the sales summary by the input/output clerk.

6. Monthly sales per sales summary balanced to update report from A/R update by the input/output clerk.

7. Accounts receivable file is fixed-length, balance-forward record with fields for current, 30, 60, and over 90 days. Cash is deducted from the oldest category.

8. Accounts receivable analysis balanced to general ledger control by an Accounting Department clerk.

9. Aged accounts receivable analysis reviewed and followed up by the credit manager.

FIG. 23-4B   Departmental overview narrative

Preliminary Review

Sometimes an auditor starts with a preliminary review and evaluation of controls. This type of review obviously does not provide the same depth of knowledge and quality of evaluation as a detailed review. Yet, this method may be useful in some circumstances, for example, when it would not otherwise be possible for the auditors to evaluate all the systems or as a means of identifying those systems with major problems which therefore require a detailed review as soon as possible. For these purposes, the departmental overview flow-charting may be modified to show the major control points.

Size and Volume of Transactions and Balances

Many auditors record information about the size and volume of account balances and transactions flows. This information is useful in evaluating the potential existence of identified accounting control weaknesses or administrative control exceptions. It can also help assess the costs and benefits of making changes in the system.

Information about the extent of balance records or accounts includes the number of accounts or balances in the files and ledgers and the total net dollar amount split between positive and negative balances.

Information on transaction flows includes the following:

- The number of transactions flowing through a transaction processing system in a certain time period
- The total dollar amount
- The range of amounts
- The average amount of transactions flowing through a transaction processing system in a certain time period
- If available, error rates in transaction processing

Since this information may not be immediately available at sites, it is a good idea to give prior notification to the site personnel to allow time to develop the data. In addition, the auditor may find it useful to use structured interview techniques to obtain data when visiting the site. Chapter 24 gives examples of useful interview techniques, including interview procedures for obtaining estimates of error rates.

BASIC PRINCIPLES OF THE FLOWCHARTING TECHNIQUE

Preparing Flowcharts

Three major points should be kept in mind when preparing flowcharts.

1. The flow of transactions through a system must be charted step by step.
2. All relevant information relating to the transactions, such as completeness of documentation, establishment of control totals, and review of open files, should be recorded so that the controls can be properly evaluated.
3. Clarity and simplicity in presentation are the key.

Transaction Processing Systems

Flowcharts should follow the main flowline of transactions from their inception to their termination. Then a separate flowchart is prepared for each transaction processing subsystem or major part of the overall system.

Transactions Defined

A transaction is defined as a series of business activities related to an exchange involving money, goods, or services, or to any other change in an asset or liability that should result in an accounting entry. For example, all the activities that result in recording a purchase of raw materials in the accounts are part of a transaction. Those activities normally include:

- Preparing a purchase order.
- Recording the receipt of the goods.
- Matching the supplier's invoice with the record of goods received and the purchase order.
- Approving the supplier's invoice for payment.
- Paying the supplier (including, where applicable, preparing, signing, and mailing checks).
- Recording the purchase in the appropriate asset or expense account.
- Controlling the foregoing documents before and during the related processing activities. Controls over unmatched receiving reports and controls to ensure that all approved suppliers' invoices are recorded properly are examples.

Types of Transactions

Different types of transactions arise when the procedures followed and the controls applied to one transaction vary from the procedures followed and the controls applied to another. For example, if purchases of raw materials are processed and controlled in the same manner as purchases of office supplies, then both purchases represent only one type of transaction. On the other hand, if purchases of raw materials are processed and controlled in a manner different from that followed for purchases of office supplies, then the purchases represent two different types of transactions.

To distinguish types of transactions, emphasis should be placed on differences in control. The fact that otherwise similar transactions are processed by different people, or in different locations, does not in itself mean that they are different types of transactions. If the control procedures are uniform and there is reason to believe that they are adequately supervised, the transactions can be considered to be the same type.

Template

To go along with the basic technique, Coopers & Lybrand developed a standard plastic flowcharting template with the set of flowcharting symbols, as shown in Figure 23-5. Most of these symbols are familiar to people who use

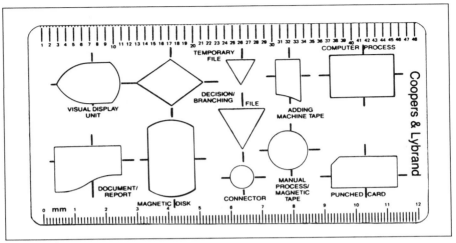

FIG. 23-5   Flowcharting template with symbols

flowcharts, although they may vary slightly. Commercially sold templates are available.

Standard Format

For consistency, it is a good idea to work with a standard format for flowcharting working papers. One possible format is illustrated in a specimen form in Figure 23-6.

Sign-Offs

It is important to know who prepared or updated a flowchart, and when. A standard form that provides space for signing off to show who prepared or updated the flowcharts and who performed the related transaction reviews can be used. Dates should always be included with sign-offs. Space can be allowed to show that the flowcharts were reviewed. The specimen form in Figure 23-6 includes these spaces with appropriate titles.

Exhibits

Copies of all relevant documents (such as copies of, or extracts from, pertinent procedure manuals; examples of filled-in forms; sample reports; computer file layouts; and descriptions of programmed procedures) should be cross-referenced to and filed with the flowcharts. These are particularly useful in explaining how a control operates, how a control is evidenced, what the

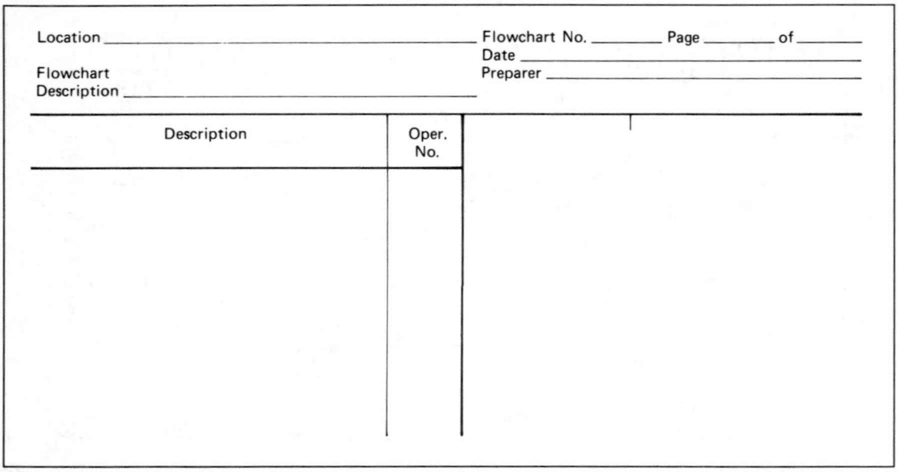

Location _____		Flowchart No. _____ Page _____ of _____
Flowchart		Date _____
Description _____		Preparer _____

Description	Oper. No.	

FIG. 23-6   Standard format for flowcharting working papers

document or form looks like, and where the relevant details of the control are located on a complex report.

Extent of Balances

It is often useful to collect information about the extent of balance records or accounts. This information can help place specific control procedures in a proper perspective. It includes:

- The number of accounts or balances in the files and ledgers
- The total net amount of the file or ledger split between positive and negative balances

Figure 23-7 depicts the extent of balances in flowchart format.

Extent of Transaction Flows

Many flowcharts also record information about the extent of transaction flows. This information is useful in evaluating the potential existence of identified accounting control weaknesses or administrative control exceptions. It should include

- The number of transactions being processed. The period involved should be specified, such as 1,000 per week.
- The value of transactions being processed. The total amount, the range of amounts, and/or the average amounts can be used.

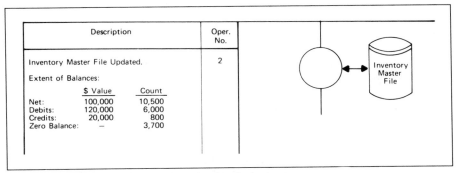

FIG. 23-7   Extent of balances in flowcharting format

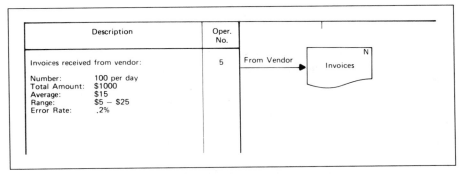

FIG. 23-8   Extent of transaction flows in transaction processing

- If available, error rates in transaction processing. This information is particularly useful for evaluating the efficiency of the system. For an example, see Figure 23-8.

More extensive statistics may be available in a computerized system, either from regular management reports or as a result of running audit software.

The preparer may find it useful to use structured interview techniques to obtain this data when visiting the site. (See Chapter 24.)

SYMBOLS AND DEFINITIONS

Form Heading

The location and a description of the transaction flow being recorded should be entered at the top of the form. Each flowchart should be given a separate flowchart number, and the individual pages within that flowchart should be

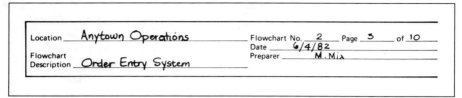

FIG. 23-9 Flowcharting form heading

numbered sequentially. The form usually provides space to record the name of the person who prepared or updated the flowchart and the date this was done. (See Figure 23-9.)

Organizational Units

The area of responsibility should be shown when the flow of transactions passes from one organizational unit to another, for example, from the purchasing department to the accounting department. Use a horizontal line or a separate page to indicate this motion. At this point, the name of the new organizational unit, the title, and, if desired, the name of the person in charge is placed on the right side of the flowchart. Repeat this information at the top of each subsequent page dealing with the same department. For flowcharting purposes, an organizational unit may vary from a large department, such as a sales department, to one individual, such as the credit manager. (See Figure 23-10.)

A choice must be made between starting a separate page or using a horizontal line on the same page to indicate when the processing flow enters a new department. If relatively few operations are performed, more than one department can be shown on a page, in line with the flow of processing. In other cases, the use of separate pages may be advantageous: The pages can be sorted by department and all activities within a particular department brought into perspective. The pages should be re-sorted into the actual processing sequence before being filed.

Operation or Process

The symbol that indicates processing is a circle. A process is an action performed by either a person or a programmed procedure. Examples of a process include recording batch totals in a control log and updating a transaction or master file.

Description	Oper. No.	Accounting Department Chief Accountant

FIG. 23-10 Organizational unit

A horizontal line in the circle processing symbol indicates an approval, comparison, verification, or checking routine. It includes edit and validation

checks performed by programmed procedures. If errors that are detected are cleared by the person performing the step, this need not be mentioned in the narrative and the correction process need not be charted. If correction involves re-routing of the documentation, the correction routine should be flowcharted or narrated, as appropriate. (See later section entitled "Rejections.")

Descriptions

For each operation that appears on the right of the flowchart, a brief narrative description should appear at the corresponding location on the left. When applicable, the narrative includes authority limits, explanations of how controls are evidenced, and the frequency of operation of the control. These descriptions should enable a reader to understand the nature of processing and related controls. (See Figure 23-11.)

Operation Numbers

One operation number should be used for each process. The numbers should appear in a separate column between the narrative description on the left and the main flowline on the right.

If the process produces a document or other information medium, only the medium symbol (as discussed subsequently) should be placed on the main flowline; it is not necessary to show it with an operation symbol. However, the operation is assigned its own number. If the activity involves a yes/no decision, the special diamond symbol (described subsequently in the section entitled "Decision and Branching") is used in lieu of the operation symbol. Again, a separate operation number is assigned.

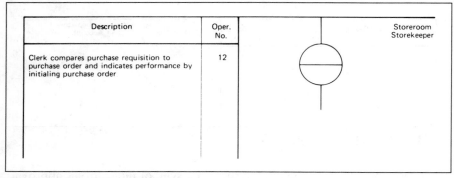

FIG. 23-11   Descriptions of operations

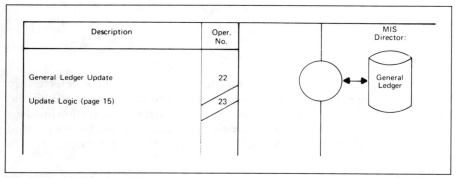

FIG. 23-12   Attached narratives

Attached Narratives

If a separate flowchart is used to show the details of a particular operation, or if the narrative required is so long that it will not fit on the page, the operation shown on the main flowchart should be referenced to the detail by a single numbered operation set off by oblique lines. This method is particularly useful for cross-referencing flowchart operations to attached copies of programmed procedures extracted from the system documentation. (See Figure 23-12.)

Main Flowline

Processing within an organizational unit moves along a vertical line on the chart, its main flowline. (See Figure 23-13.) Symbols for documents or other information media needed for processing appear on the main flowline, as described subsequently, at the point those documents or media are created or received. The media are then presumed to flow along with the processing, from

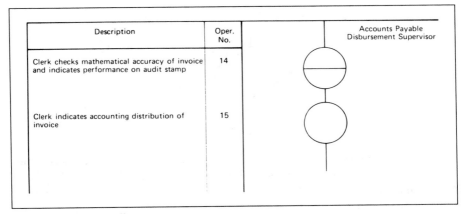

FIG. 23-13   Main flowline

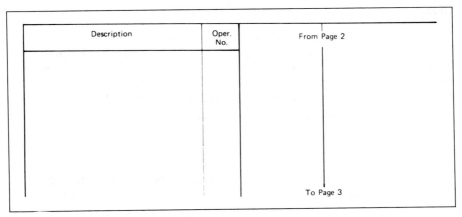

FIG. 23-14   Continuation main flowline

department to department, until their disposition is indicated. File/storage symbols and connector symbols, discussed subsequently, provide a simple means for indicating the permanent or temporary removal of media from processing. Only documents and media that are directly related to the function being described normally remain on the main flowline.

When the flowline is continued on another page, appropriate references should be entered at the bottom of the first page and at the top of the second page. (See Figure 23-14.)

Decision and Branching

The decision and branching symbol is a diamond. This symbol represents a point at which alternate procedures come onto the flowchart. Processing along

the main flowline is suspended until the branch condition has been accommodated. If alternative processing is significant and/or extensive, a separate flowchart can be made. (For an example of the decision/branching symbol used in a
flowchart, see Figure 23-15.)

Media

A symbol for information media of the type concerned appears on the main
flowline when the media are prepared or received and reappears when they are
distributed, filed, or disposed of. They are assumed to continue in process
in the interim. If their origin coincides with their disposition in a single
(numbered) operation, the symbol appears only once. Individual media
symbols used are described in the following paragraphs.

Document

The symbol for documents is used to designate items such as a purchase order,
requisition, invoice, or voucher. The name of the document is inserted in the
symbol.

    When more than one copy of a document is prepared and distributed, the
multiple-copy overlapping symbols may be used or the number of copies may

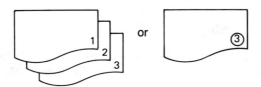

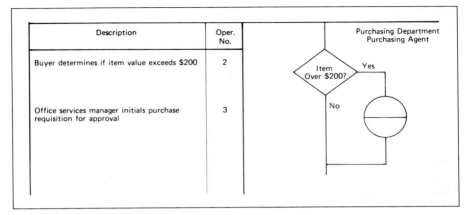

FIG. 23-15   Decision and branching symbol in flowchart

be indicated by a circled numeral placed within the single document symbol. Each copy that has accounting significance should be followed through from its origin to its disposition.

If a document, whether single or multiple copy, is numbered serially for accounting control purposes, the letter N is placed in the upper right corner of

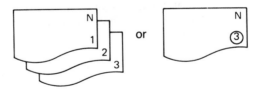

the document symbol. This treatment is useful in alerting the auditor to numerical control aspects. The disposition of the documents is flowcharted by showing the copy (or copies) with the identifying number.

Report/Book

A rectangle is used to represent a report, journal, book, register, computer listing, or similar document, which may be machine-printed or completed by manual entry. Its title is inserted in the symbol. The symbol usually represents an output medium that is self-contained (such as a complete listing of selling prices) and that may be used as input for other processing (such as pricing customers' invoices).

Adding Machine Tape

This symbol is used to depict a continuous machine-printed paper tape, such as control or proof tapes from adding or posting machines.

EDP Media

Electronic data processing systems also make use of machine-readable media. In batch processing systems, the conversion of source or input documents into machine-readable input media should be shown on the flowchart. The EDP media symbols are discussed in the following paragraphs.

Punched Card

This symbol is used to represent one or more punched cards containing a single data file. It can also be used to indicate general data entry.

Paper Tape

This symbol represents a single data file contained on a strip or coil of perforated paper tape used in conjunction with electronic data processing. (This is not very common in modern systems.)

Magnetic Tape

This symbol represents one or more reels or cassettes of tape containing a single data file.

Magnetic Disk

This symbol is used in conjunction with electronic data processing to represent a single data file contained on one or more disk packs. As illustrated, this symbol may be used to represent more than one file.

Diskette

This symbol represents a magnetic diskette that is used as a computer storage device. It is also called a floppy disk.

Terminal or CRT

This type of symbol is used, instead of an operations symbol, where data is entered through a terminal or CRT. The narrative should indicate whether the terminal is operating in an on-line or real-time (immediate update) mode. The narrative should include enough detail to make evaluation of the related control procedures possible. This is shown in Figure 23-16.

Communications Link

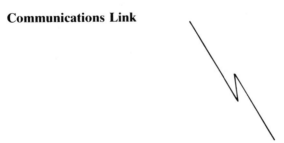

This symbol is used to represent the transmission of information by a telecommunications link, most typically via telephone lines. It is not used to show transmission through a hardwired terminal or device. Communications links between departments can either be depicted with this symbol or explained in the narrative. (An example is shown in Figure 23-17.)

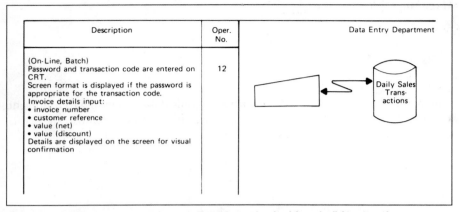

FIG. 23-16   Illustrative narrative to indicate how terminal (symbol) is operating

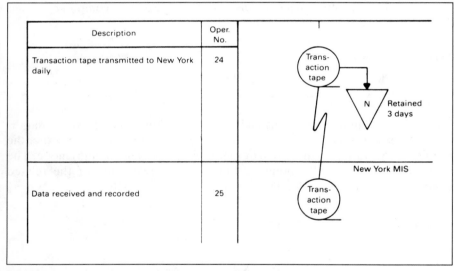

FIG. 23-17   Communications link between departments

INFORMATION FLOW AND DISPOSITION

Referral Line

The symbol for referral line, is a broken line. It is used when referring to information, for example, when reviewing a file to obtain information or when

— — — — — — — — — — — — — — — —

posting information. The referral line leads to a symbol depicting the media and content of the reference source. That source does not travel with the main flowline but remains in physical custody of, or is accessible to, the organizational unit indicated. A tape or file that simply supplies data, and is not superseded, should be shown with a referral line. (An example is shown in Figure 23-18.)

Media Distribution Line

A solid line is used to indicate the media distribution line. The movement of all documents and other information media follows the main flowline from one

————————————————————————

organizational unit and process to the next. The movement of information media to or from the main flowline is indicated by a horizontal distribution line attached to the document or other media symbol.

Information media leaving or entering the system from outside or from an organizational unit and not charted with the origin or disposition explained are shown on a horizontal line. The line is marked with an arrowhead to show movement. Media may be brought onto the main flowline from either the left or the right. Normally, document disposition is shown moving to the right. (See Figure 23-19.)

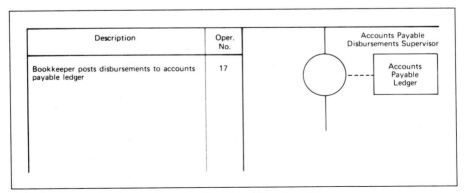

FIG. 23-18 Nonsuperseded tape showing data with referral line

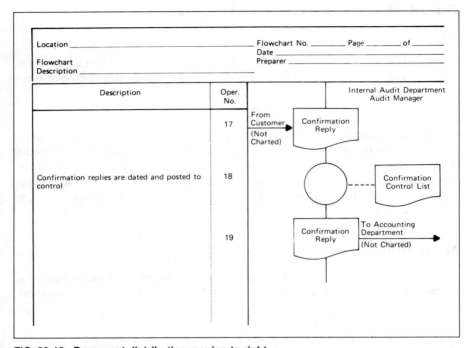

FIG. 23-19   Document distribution moving to right

Connector

The connector symbol, a small circle, is used in sets of two, one at each point that is being indexed. Each of the pair of symbols contains the same unique

identification letter of the document distribution line. Connector symbols are used to cross-reference the continuation of a horizontal document distribution line. The horizontal distribution line joins the connector and the document or other media symbol. Note the operation number or page reference next to corresponding connectors, particularly those that do not appear on adjacent pages. If the reference is to another flowchart, that chart number should also be shown. The name of the organizational unit of destination or of origin should be written above the horizontal distribution line. (See Figure 23-20.)

   If a document or other media come from or are sent to another organizational unit, the media symbols appear on the main flowline at the point at

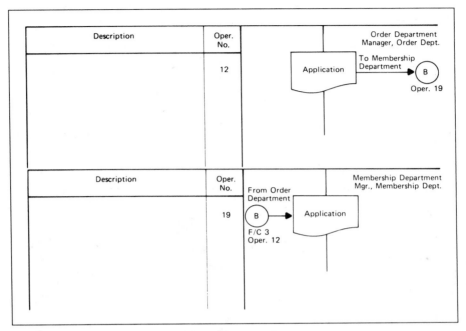

FIG. 23-20 Reference to another chart with connector

which the media enter or leave the processing. Connector symbols, cross-referenced as described subsequently, are drawn at the end of the document distribution line (with arrowheads) to or from the media symbols on the main flowline. If the media are stored without immediate or further processing, the symbol on the main flowline carries a document distribution line connected with a file/storage symbol, to indicate that disposition. (An example is shown in Figure 23-21.)

References between narratives or other working papers and flowchart pages may cite the flowchart operation number in addition to the page.

Match and Update

The symbol for match and update is used in conjunction with electronic data processing. It represents the matching on a specified record key and the update

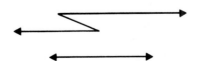

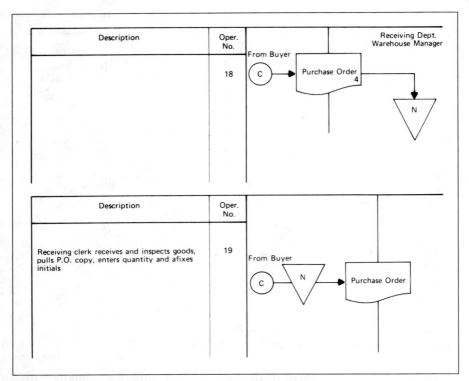

FIG. 23-21   Document distribution with file/storage symbol

of one or more data elements on the master file. The match and update logic should be explained, either in the narrative or as an additional item attached to the flowchart. The communications version of this symbol indicates that the file is in a remote department and accessed via a communications link. The straight line indicates an update within EDP. Figure 23-22 shows an example.

Note that a tape on the flowline must be removed after use in match or update to provide a visual indication that the tape will not be used for further processing. Also, it is not necessary to show both generations, old and new, in a sequential update process.

The techniques for updating or referring to tapes or disks that are not shown on the flowline but are to be included in the flowchart are shown in Figure 23-23.

Ghosting

If the nature of documents or media remaining on the main flowline might not be evident to the potential flowchart reader, the symbols are shown surrounded by brackets on the main flowline as a reminder. This technique is referred to as ghosting. (See Figure 23-24.)

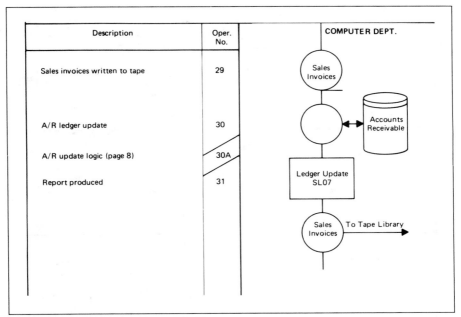

FIG. 23-22   Match and update symbol in use

File/Storage

The file/storage symbol takes several forms. A large triangle *(a)* indicates a permanent file, while a small triangle *(b)* indicates a temporary file. A

(a)   *(b)*   *(c)*   *(d)*

document, or equivalent recording media, that has temporarily been taken off the flowline for convenience in flowcharting may be indicated by a small triangle placed within a larger one *(c)*. (Use of this symbol is optional.) An "X" in a triangle *(d)* indicates a file that is to be destroyed. A letter designation is used to indicate the manner of filing:

A — Alphabetic
N — Numeric
D — Date
S — Sundry (to be specified)

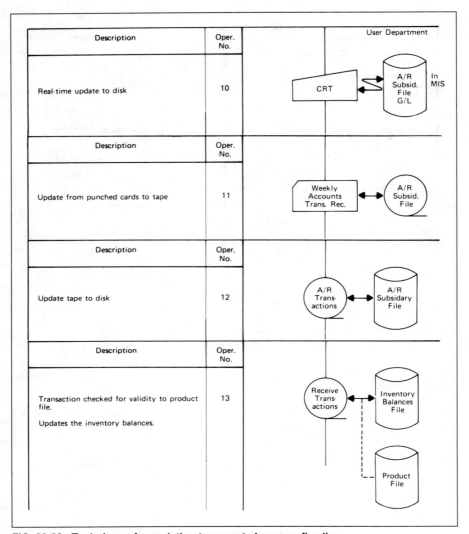

FIG. 23-23 Techniques for updating tapes not shown on flowline

The file/storage symbol is used to indicate that a document or other information medium that has left the main flowline (via a horizontal document distribution line) is being held in the organizational unit under which the symbol appears.

The filing of information media is shown by placing the appropriate file symbols at the end of the horizontal document distribution line, drawn from the media symbols on a main flowline. The retrieval and restoration of a

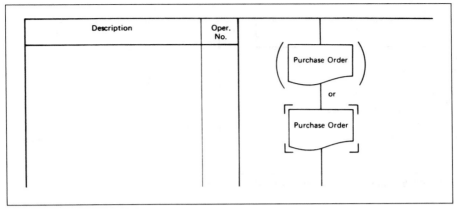

FIG. 23-24   Ghosting

document or other media to the main flow of processing are shown in the same way. The direction of movement is indicated by arrowheads on the document distribution line. Or, the file/storage symbol can be entered at the top and exited at the bottom.

It is not usually necessary to show the tape library as a separate organizational unit. Library procedures are documented as part of the general control review. The filing of information stored on a magnetic tape is shown by either a permanent file or by a file to be destroyed, with an indication of its retention period. (An example is shown in Figure 23-25.)

METHODS

Number of Flowcharts

It is often impractical, except in very simple systems, to prepare a flowchart covering an entire transaction processing system or systems cycle. For example, separate flowcharts may be required for the purchase of goods, the purchase of services, and the computation and payment of wages, when the control procedures are different for each. In these cases, separate flowcharts should be prepared for each process. If, at a point, common procedures are applied to these transactions, they are shown together. For example, a system that involves sales of finished goods and a procedure for leasing goods may both conclude with the same cash receipts procedures.

In computerized systems, it is usually most efficient to prepare a separate flowchart for each input-processing-output cycle.

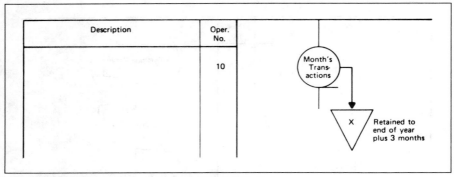

FIG. 23-25   Filing of information stored on magnetic tape

Computer-Generated Data Flowcharts

Computer-generated data, transactions, or reports can be

- Shown on the same flowchart when they are stimulated by input, for example, the generation of general ledger entries.
- Recorded on a separate flowchart when they are produced at the end of a period, for example, a monthly report.
- Divided into other convenient flowchart units according to processing.

An example is shown in Figure 23-26.

Overview Flowcharts

The detailed flowcharts of computer systems should always be prepared after completing the overview flowchart. Unless a clear general understanding of the system is first obtained from the overview flowchart, it is almost impossible to ensure that the detailed flowcharts will be relevant to the entire system.

Minor Deviations

Minor deviations from the system should be explained in the space provided in the flowcharts for narrative. If necessary, deviations can be explained in separate notes, thereby avoiding needless complications on the flowchart. This is true even when different transaction types are involved. For example, if purchases of goods and purchases of services are processed similarly except with respect to the initial authorization, both types of transactions can be covered in the same flowchart if the deviation is explained in the narrative column.

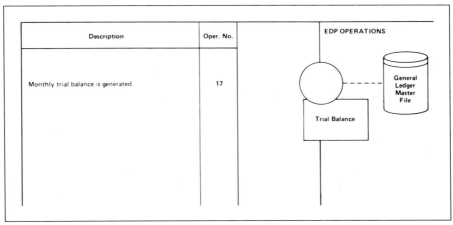

FIG. 23-26   Computer-generated report

Periodic Processing

To avoid clutter, overall controls that operate on a periodic basis may be described in a separate narrative or flowchart form. Examples of such periodic processing are the monthly reconciliation of control accounts and the weekly production of a report that lists exception items on the file requiring action.

Data Conversion and Key Verification

The conversion of documents into machine-readable information media or the conversion of one form of machine-readable information media to another is shown on the flowchart. The creation of the new form of information media is indicated using the appropriate symbol on the main flowline. The old form of information media should be removed from the flowline and its disposition should be shown.

When an off-line keyboard device is used for key verification, the verification is shown as a separate step. It is indicated as a process involving approval, comparison, verification, or checking (a circle with a horizontal line).

Similarly, when data is input by terminal, this is shown on the flowchart with an operation symbol. A narrative is included to indicate whether the terminal is operating in on-line or real-time mode. This narrative should be sufficiently detailed to make possible evaluation of the related control procedures.

Once the input medium has been written to a file, the input medium is removed from the flowline and its disposition is shown.

Data conversion and key verification are illustrated in Figure 23-27.

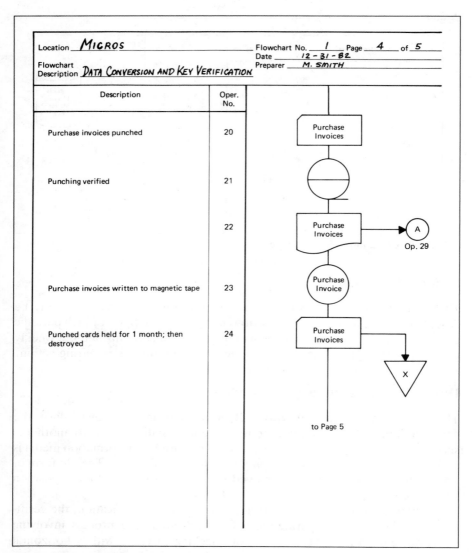

FIG. 23-27   Data conversion and key verification

Rejections

In a batch processing system, rejections normally arise at the edit and update stages. The system usually includes standard procedures for investigating, correcting, and resubmitting rejections, either with the next original input run or as a separate run. Accordingly, these procedures are normally flowcharted or described in narrative form only once. Thereafter, when rejections arise, a reference to the rejection flowchart or narrative is made on the main flowchart.

In the case of on-line data entry where data validation is carried out on input, rejections arise on an individual item basis. Rejections that are the result of keying errors are usually corrected by the operator and re-entered immediately. Sufficient narrative should be incorporated in the flowchart to allow evaluation of these procedures.

Rejections arising for other reasons require clearance by the originating department. In this event, the rejection flowcharting procedures for batch processing, discussed previously, are appropriate.

Programmed Procedures

Where operations are performed by a computer program, such as edit tests, calculations, matching checks, or exception reporting, the method used in the program should be described in sufficient detail to enable it to be evaluated properly. EDP system documentation, if available, should be attached and cross-referenced to the flowchart for this purpose.

EDP Library Procedures

The physical movement of tape or disk master files to and from an EDP library is not usually shown. Controls of this nature can be better assessed as part of a review of the general controls in the computer department. However, when a transaction tape finally leaves the system, its destination should be recorded on the flowchart to provide a visual indication that the tape will not be used for further processing. (See the section entitled "File/Storage.")

Master File Data Amendments

A flowchart of a computer system should show the procedures relating to the amendment of master file data for each master file used in the system. Experience has shown that these procedures are difficult to incorporate within the body of the main flowcharts. These procedures should be flowcharted separately or recorded in narrative form.

General Controls

The general or integrity controls within EDP, while relevant to the consistency of processing, generally operate separately from the flow of data through the application systems. Accordingly, EDP department procedures should be flowcharted separately or recorded in narrative form.

Common Errors

Some of the more common faults encountered in flowcharts, particularly those of computer systems, include the following:

- Overview flowcharts have not been prepared for computer-based applications.

- When overview flowcharts have been prepared in advance, the overview and detailed flowcharts differ (for example, different master files may be shown).

- Computer procedures are not flowcharted. Thus the flowchart shows documents sent to the computer department and a printout or report returned, without any indication that the master files have been updated. This is particularly common when processing is done at a service bureau or another remote location.

- Controls are shown on the flowcharts but evidence that they are operating is not described or explained.

- Programmed procedures are not described in sufficient detail.

- Master file data and transaction data are documented on a single flowchart. This error is common in payroll system flowcharts.

- Insufficient thought is given to planning the overall structure of the flowchart in relation to different transactions. A particularly common error is to flowchart computer processing procedures only once, covering all transaction types, so that a conglomeration of resulting output is shown at the same point on the flowline. The result is that procedures relating to a specific document type become difficult to follow, to say the least. This in turn makes it difficult to identify principal controls when these differ for various transactions. In order to maintain the general clarity of the flowchart and to assist in identifying the control procedures relevant to each transaction type, flowcharts should be structured chronologically in order of processing, and logically according to the sequence in which each transaction type occurs. For example, invoices that are processed weekly and adjustments that are processed monthly should be treated separately.

- Flowcharts are prepared without regard to the control questions to be answered. As a result there are gaps in the transaction flow, superfluous procedures are flowcharted, and critical control procedures are not shown.

- Attempts are made to flowchart procedures that either do not fit into the general movement of the flowchart processing or operate on a periodic basis. For example, a chart might show the maintenance of master files and data together with the reprocessing of rejections arising at the input stage. The resulting flowchart becomes confusing and difficult to understand. Where it is necessary to record controls of this nature, it is often clearer to record them in narrative form on a separate sheet to be filed behind the flowcharts.

USING FLOWCHARTS AS PART OF AN AUDIT

Since overview flowcharts provide a summary view of systems, they are useful to outline and understand the overall flow in EDP systems. As already discussed, they can also show the broad flow between departments and indicate major control points. Thus, they are valuable to an efficient audit.

Computer overview flowcharts show the major input, output, and files used in a particular application. They can also be used to show how the different parts of the system are linked. (See Figures 23-1, 23-2, and 23-3.)

Computer overview flowcharts illustrate the following:

- All relevant source documents that are entered to the computerized part of the system.

- All computer master files and suspense files that hold data of accounting significance and are used in the system under review. When recording systems that use related data element file structures (such as a data base), it is necessary to indicate clearly the particular data within the data base that is affected by noting the input processed. For clarity, the data usually should be described according to the same system employed by the user.

- The type of computer used.

- A summary of computer-produced output or reports, dividing them into routine and exception. Routine reports are for transactions that were processed normally. Exception reports are the reports generated by the computer when data that does not fit into the routine is encountered. Examples are differences in stock count or abnormality reports, such as stock not counted within specific time limits and sales of products at abnormal gross profit (or loss) margins. Exception reports are also produced for transactions that cannot be processed further for any of a number of reasons.

Although it is unlikely that specific control techniques can be identified from a computer overview flowchart, the flowchart can provide sufficient information for the following considerations to become apparent:

- The nature and type of the application, such as accounts receivable processing, invoicing, or sales order processing systems.

- The relevant control objectives.

- Whether the detailed questions should be for computer or for manual systems. It is common to use a combination of control objectives and detailed questions to evaluate a computer system. There are usually some manual aspects in computerized systems. For example, the preparation and authorization of sales invoices in a computerized accounts receivable processing system is almost always a manual procedure. Therefore, detailed questions about manual procedures are also required.

- It is usually possible to obtain a good idea of the principal controls operating in the system from the types of input, the master files used, and the various routine or exception reports. For example, a file of unused goods-received note numbers suggests that a numerical sequence check can be used as the completeness of input control for goods-received note numbers; batch reports indicate that batching can be used as a completeness control, or as an accuracy control, or both.

Computer overview flowcharts do not necessarily provide a summary of all the accounting procedures for a given application. While an overview flowchart for a sales order processing system often covers the entire revenue cycle — from sales orders, invoicing to debtors ledger, finished goods stock ledgers, and preparation of general ledger entires — the overview flowchart for an accounts receivable processing system includes only the debtors ledger. The computer overview flowchart covers only that part of the system processed by the computer.

Especially in complex situations, it may be better to break the total system down into a number of subsystems to make the complete system easier to understand. The relationship between different parts of the system can then be described. A form of computer overview flowchart that can be used to depict such situations is illustrated in Figure 23-4.

The auditor should prepare computer overview flowcharts for all significant computerized applications before beginning detailed flowcharting. Along with the overview charts, a narrative describing what happens is usually an essential aid to others' understanding of the completed flowcharts.

Interviews and Transaction Reviews in an Audit

CONDUCTING AN EFFECTIVE INTERNAL CONTROL INQUIRY

Introduction

In order to flowchart a system, the auditor must understand it. To obtain that understanding, gathering information from site personnel regarding the accounting systems in use is an important and time-consuming part of the evaluation of internal control. Things the auditor can do to increase the reliability of this information and reduce the time required to obtain it are discussed in the following order:

1. Prepare adequately in advance
2. Learn how to conduct interviews
3. Become familiar with the different types of questions

Advance Preparation

Before discussing internal control matters with site personnel, the auditor should

- Be as familiar as possible with the matters to be discussed. For example, any previously prepared flowcharts and transaction review working papers, the Internal Control Questionnaire (ICQ), and the like should be studied. Interviews always go better when the auditor is prepared and knowledgeable about the topic being discussed.

- Try to ensure meeting the appropriate individual, or the person best able to answer questions. For example, the management information systems director may be the appropriate person to interview for an overall understanding of the system, while the programmer/analyst may be the appropriate person if a detailed knowledge of the inventory management system is required. The auditor should try to figure out who is most likely to have the information that is needed.

- Formulate the questions to ask beforehand. The interview will proceed more smoothly and quickly, and the need for follow-up interviews should be reduced. When questions are not adequately prepared, relevant information that was overlooked in the initial interview may have to be obtained in a second meeting.

- Obtain as much information as possible from other company personnel about the personal characteristics of the individual to be interviewed. Knowing in advance that the person to be interviewed is quite busy can increase the likelihood of establishing rapport by getting right down to business. A busy person being interviewed may appreciate a no-nonsense approach.

- Consider scheduling carefully. The person to be interviewed should have sufficient time to answer questions and should know in advance how much time will be required.
- Consider the management level of the person to be interviewed. If he or she is a member of senior management, a senior audit staff person should do the interview whenever possible.

The Interview

An auditor does not need professional training as an interviewer to be effective in obtaining information during a meeting with site personnel. The methods described in the following paragraphs are useful in interview situations. The steps include

1. Telling the person about the purpose of the interview.
2. Attempting to establish a basic rapport.
3. Emphasizing positive behavioral factors.
4. Choosing vocabulary carefully during the interview.

Most people being interviewed want to know the following:

- The reason for the interview
- Why they were selected
- How the information or data will be used
- Whether they will be informed about any outcome

These questions should be anticipated and dealt with early in the interview. The answers can provide positive motivation and make it easier to get the desired responses. If the relevance of the interview is unclear or the questions asked do not seem to relate to the stated purpose, unnecessary barriers may be created.

As interviewer, the auditor should provide the necessary motivation to continue the interview. If the interviewee identifies with the interviewer and enjoys the interaction, or sees the interviewer as someone who may help to effect some desired change in procedures, the interviewee will be more likely to respond. On the other hand, the interviewee may be unwilling to provide certain information because it seems to be potentially threatening or embarrassing. Sometimes information is forgotten or overlooked. An inability to respond may also result from repressed envy or hostility. An inability to ask meaningful questions may indicate the same.

The better the psychological forces at work during an interview are understood, the easier it is to minimize or control any negative forces. The interviewer should try to see the world as the interviewee sees it, through his or her particular set of experiences and background, to develop greater understanding on both sides.

The behavior of both parties in an interview can act as a positive or negative influence. The interviewer's role is to maximize the forces that enhance communication and minimize or eliminate the negative forces or barriers. Behavioral factors include physical, vocal, listening, and feedback behavior.

Physical Behavior. Physical behavior includes eye contact, facial expressions, and mannerisms. A pleasant and relaxed appearance creates a relaxed and comfortable atmosphere. The initial impressions, conveyed in the first 30 or 60 seconds, can seriously affect the remainder of the interview. As an expert in the field puts it, "You can't make a first impression a second time." Therefore, in most interviews it is important to try to establish rapport immediately. Taking notes during the interview, to some people, is a sign that the interviewer is listening and that what they are saying is important; to others, it seems threatening. Physical factors are somehow magnified during an interview. An interviewer must be particularly aware of any personal characteristics and mannerisms that can create a positive or a negative effect, as well as of other potentially distorting environmental influences.

Vocal Communication. Good vocal communication skills entail the following aspects:

- Pleasant voice
- Audibility
- Articulation
- Naturalness and spontaneity

Negative vocal factors, which can create barriers, include

- Speaking too fast or too slowly
- A brisk or impersonal speaking manner, in which little interest or enthusiasm is projected
- Mumbling or "over-articulate" speech

Physical and vocal communication are important. But what is most important and can overcome both physical and vocal limitations is conveying a feeling of genuine and personal interest in the interviewee.

Listening and Responding. Listening and responding concerns both the sensitivity and the willingness of the interviewer to behave according to different cues from the interviewee. The interviewer should listen and try to understand the interviewee, not simply conduct a monologue.

Restating the interviewee's response in his or her own words is an effective technique. This creates the impression that the interviewer is really listening. It can also increase the accuracy of the interchange, since people sometimes need help expressing their thoughts. A good interviewer should make certain to allow ample time for a response to his or her questions and always encourage the interviewee to express things in the most natural way. The interviewer should be quick to sense when the interviewee wants to express or elaborate on a particular point but is unable to do so without some prodding or help. Some areas may be difficult to discuss, or there may be some question about their perceived appropriateness. The good interviewer senses these difficulties and tries to create an atmosphere where the interviewee feels free to discuss sensitive areas.

As interviewer, the auditor should have the flexibility to adjust and modify the interview in light of the responses, while making sure that the objectives of the interview are met.

Vocabulary

The vocabulary or choice of words used in an interview can be a major help or a major problem in the communication process. Words must be understood by both parties in the interview. This is very important for the EDP auditor, who must understand EDP terms well enough to be able to use them. (The glossary provides definitions of many EDP terms and acronyms.) If the interviewee is unfamiliar with certain terms or concepts, the interviewer should notice this and try to establish a frame of reference; this could be called educating the interviewee.

Sometimes the interviewer may have to vary his or her vocabulary to include words chosen by the interviewee. For example, if the interviewer refers to the process of accounting for the numerical sequence of prenumbered documents as a completeness control, while the interviewee refers to it as "the number control," then the interviewer should remember to refer to the process as the number control. Using words chosen this way motivates the interviewee to communicate. However, chosen words should not be beyond the vocabulary level easily understood by the interviewee, nor should they appear to be deliberately oversimplified.

Another aspect of word choice is making sure that an appropriate verbal setting is established and followed. For example, if the interviewee is responsible for both on-line and data base systems, the interviewer should ensure that questions and answers deal with the same aspect of the system under discussion, such as system security. When discussing on-line systems, this aspect of system security should be referred to specifically or the words that are particular to the process should be used.

Sometimes, including a question referring to possible extenuating circumstances indicates a nonjudgmental attitude and increases the likelihood of getting an accurate response. For example, assume that the person who receives exception or rejection reports does not follow up on all missing items or batches. To which of the following questions is that person likely to give an accurate answer: "Why don't you follow up on all the missing items or batches?" or "I can see that you're very busy. Do you always have a chance to follow up on all the missing items or batches?" Ordinarily, most people are more likely to answer the second question accurately.

Types of Questions

The basic types of questions, discussed in more detail in the following paragraphs, are

- Open-ended   • Closed   • Probes
- Direct   • Yes/No   • Restatement

Open-Ended Questions. These questions are broad and basically unstructured; they simply establish the topic and allow the interviewee to structure the answer. They let the person know that the interviewer is interested in their feelings, frame of reference, attitudes, and value system.

Open-ended questions establish good rapport and can often help maintain good communication. The degree of openness varies. Some examples are

- Tell me about the organization's EDP systems.
- What are the procedures to ensure that only authorized users access your system?
- How do you process program changes?
- How do you process transactions for the accounts payable system?

Although these questions are all open-ended, they are successively more specific, and therefore more limited in their degree of openness. Open-ended questions cannot be answered with a "yes" or "no"; they force the interviewee to really think about the answer, thereby giving the interviewer an insight into the interviewee's frame of reference.

Direct Questions. Many interviewing situations require that, once rapport has been established, certain questions be asked directly. Direct questions ask for explanations or further expansion on a particular point; they call for a specific reply on a specific topic. The following are examples of direct questions:

- How do you make sure that all transactions are processed?
- How do you ensure that programs in production have been properly tested and approved by management?

The advantage of asking direct questions indirectly is that they do not sound as much like questions, but it is obvious that a response is sought. They also leave a broader area for response.

Closed Questions. These are a form of direct question that greatly narrows the range of possible responses. The closed question is appropriate when the objective is to lead the interviewee to identify with a certain attitude or perspective, or to express agreement or disagreement with a stated viewpoint. For example:

- Do you restrict access to the system using system software security, physical security, or specific password identification method?
- Why don't you account for all users who have access to the system?

If the question does not seem threatening, it is usually answered easily (as in the first question). If, however, it is perceived as threatening, it may not be answered directly and can create barriers (as in the second question). The use of closed questions assumes that

- The interviewer has substantial knowledge of the interviewee's information level;
- There are a limited number of known frames of reference, which are clearly presented in the question;
- The interviewer has information or an opinion on the matter.

Since closed questions assume considerable knowledge about the situation, they should be used with caution. When the interviewer's objective is to force the interviewee to consider or think through several factors or alternatives before coming to a conclusion, a series of closed questions can be effective. In this case, the interviewer should determine that all the conditions for use of closed questions are met.

Yes/No Questions. These are the most extreme form of closed questioning. They allow the interviewee virtually no latitude or response except "yes" or "no," or possibly "I don't know." This sort of question is most often used by an inexperienced interviewer. While it is useful for the purpose of filling out forms and obtaining specific facts, it also tends to limit the amount of information obtained. Since the "law of least effort" usually operates, the interviewee answers only what is asked. Even if some additional information is volunteered, interviewers who ask such questions are apt to pay little attention, since they are likely to be too busy formulating more questions and not really listening.

A major problem with yes/no questions is that they tend to turn the interview into an interrogation. The tendency to ask questions in rapid order often causes the interviewee to react defensively rather than to give frank, honest answers. Short-answer questions should be used to get needed factual data. They should be interspersed within the interview as needed, and a long list of yes/no questions should generally be avoided.

The Computer Internal Control Questionnaire (CICQ) shown in the Appendix includes a yes/no format for the questions to ask. This does not mean that they must be asked in this manner, but rather that the answers are to be recorded in this format.

Probes. Probes are used to stimulate discussion and obtain more information. They motivate the interviewee to expand on, clarify, or explain reasons for information already given. Probes are ways of following up on partial or superficial responses. When done well, they direct the interviewee's thinking toward further aspects of the topic under discussion. Some examples of probes are

- Why do you think this happens?
- Is there some way you would change the situation?
- Can you give me a reason for that?

Probing is one way to obtain specific, complete responses. Some interviewees have difficulty putting their thoughts into words, so that their answers are unclear or incomplete. Others may want to hide information they feel would be unacceptable to the interviewer. Probes can be used after any question to encourage the interviewee to think further about the topic. For example:

INTERVIEWER: How does your organization process program amendments?
DATA PROCESSING MANAGER: Haphazardly.
INTERVIEWER: What makes you feel that way?
DATA PROCESSING MANAGER: There are no established procedures in place so that some changes are put into production without proper testing.

As a result of this exchange, an inconclusive answer is turned into a useful piece of information.

Restatement. The purpose of restatement is to verify the interviewer's understanding of what the interviewee has said. It also allows the person being interviewed to hear what has been said as encouragement to go on speaking, examining, or looking deeper into the question. Good use of restatement communicates this impression to the interviewee: "I am listening to you very carefully. So carefully, in fact, that I can restate what you have said. I am doing so now to help you to hear yourself through me so that you may absorb your statement and consider its impact, if any, on you. For the time being, I am keeping my thoughts out of it." The most effective method of restating seems to be to restate that part of what has been said that the interviewer feels is most significant and worth having the interviewee hear again. To continue with the example from the previous paragraph:

> INTERVIEWER: What do you mean?
>
> DATA PROCESSING MANAGER: Joe has no control over those guys and they never fill out the control sheets anymore.
>
> INTERVIEWER: The programmers never make out control sheets and the program changes are processed for production without them?
>
> DATA PROCESSING MANAGER: Yes, that's right. We have to make so many changes and our programmers are so familiar with the system we rely on them to test the changes.
>
> INTERVIEWER: There are numerous changes made to programs and some of the general controls are not being implemented properly?

To use the restatement technique, interviewers should not state their own views. Instead, without making a commitment or evaluation, the restatement technique shows that the interviewer understands the interviewee's point of view. It also enables the interviewee to hear his or her own logic, possible biases, and assumptions that may be based on false fears and doubts. Restatement should have a positive effect on the interviewee because it demonstrates that the interviewer is listening and trying to understand what is being said. Like all good things, however, restatement can also be overdone, resulting in an artificial and affected situation.

PROCEDURES ON ERROR RATES

Finding out about rates of error can be tricky, since people tend to be defensive about any discussion of errors. In general, the auditor should take the position that what is going on is an attempt to gain information that might help to make the interviewee's job easier and better. It is important to avoid giving the impression that as interviewer, an auditor is looking for something wrong. If possible, it is helpful to take the position that all parties concerned are engaged in a mutual learning process.

Possible Questions to Ask About Error Rates

There are many questions that might be asked of an interviewee to try to get complete information about the rate of errors for a given process. Several assumptions should underlie these questions.

- It is desirable to avoid the use of terms such as "error rate," since these frequently put the interviewee on the defensive.

- In many cases, information about error rates may not be very precise because company procedures may not routinely produce that information. Accordingly, the auditor should realize that the information may be incomplete.

- The auditor should consider the types of errors as well as the rate of errors. Frequently the only information available relates to types of errors. However, it typically is useful in evaluating weaknesses or exceptions and may also point to appropriate corrective action.

- It is usually preferable to determine rates of error per error type. Information about the composite rate of all errors is also useful and should be documented if it is the only information available.

- Frequently, questions about error rates in a control process performed prior to the processes performed by the person being interviewed are more readily answered.

Possible questions to use in investigating error rates include:

- "How could the task be done more easily or better?" There are two aspects to this question. First, responses frequently help to identify ways to improve efficiency and control. Second, responses often indicate whether errors are frequent and the type of errors involved. This information can then be pursued further.

- "What kinds of things cause you to take extra time in processing documents?" This question can elicit information about errors from two possible sources: first, errors that come up through the system to the interviewee and, second, errors that are identified later in the system and are sent back to the interviewee to be rectified.

- "What is the most common mistake that you see in documents you process?" While this question can usually identify types of errors, it is a more general question designed to get the interviewee to consider errors that are routinely encountered. The auditor should not stop here, but should use any response as a basis for pursuing further information. A follow-up question might be: "Do any others come to mind?"

- "Who tells you when you've made a mistake?" This question can be used to initiate a discussion of what kinds of errors are returned to the interviewee for correction. It also identifies personnel farther along in the system who can be queried about errors.
- "Why do you think people keep making the same mistake?" This may identify possible improvements and may also provide a better understanding of why the error happens so often.
- "Do you keep track of errors that you correct?" This may provide information about the type and quantity of errors and logging procedures for them.
- "Do you refer mistakes that you find back to the user departments?" Even if the person does not initiate such communications, he or she can often identify who does, and that person may be a useful source of information. If there is no communication of errors, the auditor may have uncovered a major problem area.

Other Ways to Detect Errors

When asking the preceding questions, an auditor should try to identify procedures that are in effect and that might be useful in detecting error rates. Some typical examples follow:

- *Computer rejects.* If error runs are made, or if input is frequently kicked back from computer processing there may be a record of error rates. There may also be some indication of error types.
- *Manual listings.* In addition to the errors corrected by the interviewee, there may be listings of documents returned for additional information or correction, or listings of types of errors typically encountered. For example, there may be a list of program change requisitions returned to the users because there was no indication of proper approval.
- *Budget variance analysis.* A form of control over errors may exist as part of the investigation of budget variances. Whoever performs these investigations may be a useful source of information about the type and extent of errors found.

Recording of Information

As described previously, a great deal of information the auditor receives is imprecise, and it may consist of rather subjective impressions. Whenever possible, the person being questioned should be encouraged to give a percentage estimate. This helps the auditor to understand the order of magnitude. For example, if somebody says there is "probably only a 2 to 5 percent error rate," the auditor gains a different appreciation of the range of the problem than if the interviewee says there is "a good chance that the stuff will be wrong." When personnel do not feel that they can give a percentage estimate, the auditor might try to get a better overall impression of the extent of error, for example, "appears to be low frequency of error" or "may be frequent errors." There is no set procedure for recording this kind of feedback; auditors are encouraged to use any means that they feel communicates the necessary information and can be accomplished reasonably. The objective is to help senior management identify trouble spots so they can reorder their priorities when necessary.

Types of Errors

An auditor will probably find that some errors are more important that others. As a result, it is likely that he or she will spend more time identifying the error rate for certain types of errors. For example, if the error type would permit the conversion of corporate assets or would not be caught and corrected at a subsequent point in the internal control system, further inquiry is warranted. Factors considered important enough to warrant a greater degree of inquiry should be noted, since feedback might be used to develop a questionnaire or other procedures designed to improve controls in these areas.

Questions About Irregularities

The preceding discussion focuses on errors, unintentional acts or failures to act that lead to mistakes. Auditors are also concerned about intentional acts, such as irregularities that may be fraudulent. When this is the subject being investigated, the auditor must know how interview procedures can elicit information about these acts.

This is an extremely delicate area. Any questions should be framed carefully and cautiously. One possible question is: "How do you know that everything that you are approving is OK?" A frequent answer is that the interviewee has confidence in the integrity of his or her personnel. There may also be occasional spot-checks. In most instances such interview responses taken alone provide very little assurance that irregularities do not exist.

Organizations normally employ a variety of other procedures for dealing with irregularities or possible frauds. For example, one general approach is establishing a code of corporate conduct, monitoring compliance, and taking necessary corrective action. These procedures are usually outside the scope of an internal accounting control system evaluation. Accordingly, separate consideration should usually be given to reviewing and evaluating such procedures.

Conclusion

Whenever frequent errors are found, the auditor should consider whether other controls compensate for or correct these errors. This is helpful in completing the ICQ or other documents and in reporting to senior management.

CONFIRMING THE UNDERSTANDING — TRANSACTION REVIEWS

Having completed the interviews and flowchart or narrative of the system, the auditor should trace one transaction of each type through the company's accounting system in order to confirm the recorded understanding of the system.

In this regard, a transaction is defined as a series of business activities related to an exchange involving money, goods, or services, or to any other change in an asset or liability that should result in an accounting entry.

Normally, transaction reviews are performed after the flowcharts have been prepared or updated. However, it may be more efficient to perform the transaction reviews and prepare the related documentation at the same time an understanding of the system is obtained or updated. The auditor who prepares or updates the flowcharts should generally perform the transaction reviews.

Selection of Transactions

Each type of transaction identified at the time the understanding was obtained and the flowcharts were prepared should be subjected to a transaction review. A transaction review should also be performed annually to update the understanding.

Nature of Transaction Review

The transaction review should cover each operation shown on the flowchart. The specific way in which this is done depends on the circumstances. When carrying out a transaction review, the auditor should be aware of the possibility that operations with internal accounting control significance have been omitted from the flowcharts. This is particularly true when using flowcharts prepared by others. If that is the case, the necessary additions should be made to the flowcharts. The starting point of a transaction review may be any stage in the flow where the type of transaction is readily identifiable. Normally, a transaction is traced all the way from its inception to its termination as an entry in the general ledger. However, the transaction review may begin in the middle of the flow or at the end, providing all steps in the process are covered at some time.

If individual types of transactions are combined during processing and subjected to common procedural and reporting controls from that point forward, only one example of the combined type need be traced through subsequent procedures.

Documentation

Transaction review working papers should document the work performed. To minimize the time required in preparing these working papers, use of the following techniques is recommended:

- A worksheet should be prepared in a form that will accommodate several years' evaluations, whenever this is possible.
- A worksheet should be set up in columnar form, with the numbers of the operations from the flowchart and supporting narratives listed on the left. The operation numbers listed on the worksheet indicate the procedures performed as outlined on the flowchart or narrative. When there are numerous or complex procedures indicated by a single operation number, it may be necessary to provide an explanatory note on the worksheet.
- The specific transactions reviewed should be identified in a column of the worksheet.

If the work performed is evident from the flowchart, and the document reference is shown on the transaction review working papers, no further documentation is required. (See Figure 24-1 for a sample transaction review worksheet.)

Results of Transaction Reviews

If the transaction reviews confirm the understanding of the system and that understanding has been correctly recorded in the flowcharts or narratives, no further work with regard to transaction reviews is necessary. If the transaction reviews indicate that the auditor's initial understanding of the system was incorrect, the next step is to find out the procedures actually in effect, revise the documentation of the system accordingly, and note this on the working papers.

If management contends that an exception revealed by the transaction review is an isolated instance, the auditor should perform a few additional reviews of the procedures that gave rise to the exception. This is done to determine whether the exception really is an isolated event before any revisions are made to the flowcharts or narratives.

Completion of the transaction reviews should be indicated in the space provided on the Record of Flowchart Preparation and Transaction Reviews (PRT) or another document being used for this purpose.

Location _____

Preparation/updating of flowcharts (F) and performance of transaction reviews (TR)

FLOWCHART		19				19				19			
		Prepared/Updated*				Prepared/Updated*				Prepared/Updated*			
NO.	DESCRIPTION OF SYSTEM	F	TR	Done By	Reviewed By	F	TR	Done By	Reviewed By	F	TR	Done By	Reviewed By

*Place ticks (√) in columns provided.

FIG. 24-1   Flowchart preparation and transaction review worksheet

TRANSACTION REVIEWS IN COMPUTER SYSTEMS

Transaction reviews are carried out in computerized systems for much the same reasons as in noncomputerized systems. However, the characteristics of a computerized system may change the methods the auditor uses to confirm an understanding.

The application of transaction reviews to computer systems is dealt with in the following sections:

- *Manual accounting procedures* — Accounting procedures carried out manually both prior to and subsequent to the processing of data by the computer.

- *Programmed procedures* — Procedures carried out by the computer programs that relate to:
  a. The completeness, accuracy, validity, or maintenance of data, and
  b. The calculation, summarization, categorization, updating, or generation of data.
- *General or integrity controls* — Procedures within the EDP department that ensure the effective operation of programmed procedures. These include controls over the design, implementation, security, and use of computer programs and files, and subsequent amendments.

Manual Accounting Procedures Within Computerized Systems

A transaction review of manual accounting procedures within computerized systems is carried out in a manner similar to one in a totally noncomputerized system, except

- It may not be practical to trace the same transaction through both input and output procedures because
  a. The computer system may hold items for considerable periods of time on suspense or on master files before the data is used, such as orders awaiting shipment; or
  b. There may not be sufficient evidence to easily trace input to output or vice versa.
- When input transactions are batched or posted to a computer file, the batch, file, or total should be traced, rather than the individual transaction.
- The output reviewed may consist primarily of exception reports, since this is the type of information that is most commonly generated.

Programmed Procedures

Transaction reviews of manual accounting procedures are not adequate to confirm the auditor's understanding of a computerized system; the programmed procedures should also be confirmed.

Ideally, the auditor should carry out a transaction review to confirm an understanding of the programmed procedures. However, in practice it is not easy (or sometimes even possible) to confirm the program logic adequately by tracing transactions through the system. The following problems are encountered:

- Transactions are generally grouped into batches or files for computer processing. A summary of the procedures applied to the group is usually reported, but complete evidence about the effect of processing on each individual transaction may not be.

- A particular programmed procedure may consist of one or more complex programs and may involve several computer files. Each program may encompass many different logical paths (a hundred or so is not uncommon). Not all these paths are of accounting significance, so an overall review may be necessary to first identify those that are.

As in manual systems, the auditor looks for evidence that may be used to confirm an understanding. Some methods to follow in performing transaction reviews of programmed procedures are discussed subsequently.

An auditor should bear in mind that these methods involve reperforming programmed procedures, reviewing program documentation, and performing limited reviews of actual source code.

- If the computer prints out all the details of the transaction, such as quantity, unit price, and total, the auditor may reperform the procedures manually. Here, the auditor would compare the quantity and unit price to the source data and reperform the calculation. This would confirm the results of the operation of the programmed procedures. The technique generally provides sufficient confirmation only in the simplest computer systems, because the information reported is frequently incomplete.

- Programmed procedures are often described in the system and program documentation. If the documentation is adequate, the auditor may review it to confirm the understanding. If program documentation is to be used, the auditor must be satisfied that
  a. The program documentation reflects the logic incorporated in the source programs, and
  b. The documentation corresponds to the production programs currently in use.

- The transaction review may also include a limited review of relevant portions of the source code.

- The auditor may sometimes find that the documentation does not adequately describe the programmed procedures. It may be incomplete, out-of-date, or badly prepared, and thus cannot be used in confirming an understanding of the programmed procedures. In these circumstances, the auditor should
  a. Be sure that the program listing is current and up-to-date before performing reviews of program code;
  b. Interview key data processing personnel to determine the accuracy of the recorded programmed procedures; and
  c. Reperform the programmed procedures, as stated previously.

General Controls

The auditor should confirm an understanding of general, or integrity, controls (general computer procedures) by tracing the various types of activity through the procedures that were documented. Methods of confirmation vary from the one used in an application system review due to the following factors:

- General control procedures are usually not flowcharted, but appear in narrative form
- Less documentation may be available for review
- There may be no transaction to follow through the system

In many cases there are various manual procedures carried out by EDP staff. Consideration should also be given to confirmation of system software procedures whenever these are relied on.

In general, the methods used to confirm the understanding include:

- Examination of evidence, which may be either manually prepared, such as system specification change forms, or prepared by computer, such as the console log
- Checking the functioning of system software, using procedures similar to those described for the confirmation of application programmed procedures (described previously)
- Observation of, or inquiry into, procedures followed

Types of General Controls

The different types of general controls encompassed by a review are discussed in the following paragraphs.

Implementation Controls. The auditor normally needs to select separate activities with respect to system development and system maintenance. If implementation controls over new systems vary from system to system, as they would when separate groups are responsible for the various systems, the auditor should review each type of control. This may entail a review of procedures incorporated into software, such as program library maintenance packages. Much of the evidence is prepared manually, such as a system specification change notice or a program flowchart. Some is prepared by computer, such as a source listing.

Program Security Controls. The activities confirmed in this area should include procedures over program libraries and security of both system-resident files (files that reside in the system) and off-line files. The procedures may include both software and physical controls over files. In this situation, it may be sufficient to review only one type of procedure, provided the auditor is satisfied that this type by itself can be relied on to provide effective control over all program files. Evidence is usually limited to library issue records, console log reports of incorrect uses of passwords, and the like. In addition, the auditor should try to inquire about the actual procedures that are followed, since they can differ from the ideal procedures that management wants followed.

Computer Operations Controls. The auditor should confirm an understanding of activities such as the following:

- Job set-up procedures
- Operator activities
- Investigation of entries on the operations log
- Review of job accounting reports

The job selected for review may conveniently be one of those involved in the review of applications. In a situation where one job does not encompass all activities, it may be necessary to select several jobs to be reviewed. This ensures that all activities are reviewed. Software procedures requiring review include certain aspects of the operating system functions, such as the generation of the console log. Evidence is usually limited to items such as processing schedules, problem reports, job accounting reports, and console logs. The auditor should also consider whether the same procedures are applied at all times, for example, if there are night shifts and weekend work.

Data File Security Controls. The procedures involved in confirming activities that relate to data file security are similar to those discussed for assuring the security of program files. To the extent that procedures or controls are the same for both program and data files, only one of these types of control needs to be verified during the confirmation.

System Software Controls. The auditor must ensure that software procedures are functioning properly. This "assurance" makes it possible to rely on the software's output, such as a job processing log, as part of other general control review procedures. Review procedures should include a review for adequate technical supervision over the maintenance of operations software. However, it is also necessary to confirm those procedures that ensure the correct implementation and security of system software. This can be done in a manner similar to the one described previously for implementation controls.

Effects of Transaction Reviews

The effects of the transaction review of a computer system on the audit, and on the audit documentation, are as follows:

- It is important to time the transaction review carefully to obtain the maximum advantage. The work schedule should allow sufficient time for the controls to be evaluated before audit tests are begun.

- Much of the work of the transaction review, in particular parts relating to how the programs treat individual items, can be done at the time an understanding of the system is obtained, for example, by reviewing program documentation.

- For the preceding reason, and also because of the complexity of the work, it is especially desirable that the person who obtains the understanding also carries out the transaction review.

- Transaction review working papers for computer application systems are similar to those for noncomputer systems. They show flowchart operation numbers down the page and transaction types across the page, and should be referenced to the transactions reviewed. Where the same transaction has not been traced through the system, this should be made clear on the transaction review working papers.

- It is apparent from the preceding discussion that the time spent on procedures included in the transaction review of a computer system is likely to exceed the time spent on a transaction review of a manual system. This should be considered when planning for the evaluation.

Special skills and experience are necessary to carry out transaction reviews of programmed procedures and general controls in an EDP system. The EDP auditor should have sufficient expertise in this area to be able to carry out the task.

CHAPTER **25**

The Evaluation Process and How to Use Documents

EVALUATING INTERNAL CONTROLS

To evaluate the internal controls in a system, it is helpful to use a methodical process. This process can include the use of flowcharts, forms, questionnaires, and guides. The discipline of the process and the tools used are integral parts of an evaluative approach. This kind of approach has been adopted by management and by external and internal auditors in business, industry, and government. This chapter provides an overview of one such process, and of the documents that can be used. The questionnaire documents are shown in detail in the Appendix.

THE FOUR PHASES IN EVALUATING INTERNAL CONTROLS

There are essentially four phases to the process of evaluating internal controls in a structured audit approach.

- *Phase I* — Establishing the scope of the evaluation, the audit objectives, and how they will be attained.
- *Phase II* — Establishing the overall conditions, both environmental and regulatory, of the organization within which the controls operate. The auditor needs to know what the organization itself is like before documenting or flowcharting can begin. Once this is accomplished, the auditor should have acquired a clear understanding of the system. Then the documentation of the system of controls can be done.
- *Phase III* — Defining the control objectives required, finding out whether the required system of controls exists, and testing the controls to determine whether they are operating as planned.
- *Phase IV* — Determining the importance of any control weaknesses uncovered during Phase III, making appropriate recommendations, and following up on subsequent audits of the system.

Phase I — Scope of Evaluation

Before evaluating a system, the auditor needs to establish the objectives of the audit review. This often includes determining the objectives of the functional unit being audited. At the same time, the auditor considers the ways in which these audit goals will be met.

Phase II — Conditions of Control

After establishing audit objectives, the auditor defines the conditions under which the overall system of the organization's controls operate. These conditions include both environmental and regulatory matters that may affect the nature and scope of the controls in use. The Conditions of Control Questionnaire is one of the documents that can be used to arrive at this definition. The questionnaire can be completed early in the audit (before the flowcharting process) or just before the process of determining control objectives and reviewing the controls in use (Phase III).

Establishing what the control conditions are is part of the larger objective of obtaining and recording an understanding of the system. In conjunction with completing a Conditions of Control Questionnaire or similar document, other tasks should be performed. These can include interviewing key personnel, obtaining data file descriptions and other documentation of the system, and drafting a detailed flowchart of the system based on transaction types.

Conditions of Control Questionnaire. The internal auditor should have a general understanding of the operations being evaluated and the conditions of control, or the control environment, in the organization. The Conditions of Control Questionnaire was designed by Coopers & Lybrand for internal use to improve the auditor's awareness of the organization and its control environment. Although it does not cover all the possible conditions that might be found in a business organization, it does cover many of those that are likely to be of the greatest interest to the auditor. (See Figure 25-1 for a page from this questionnaire.)

The conditions dealt with in the questionnaire are organizational arrangements and control procedures that

- Provide general conditions that make it possible for the system of accounting and administrative controls to operate efficiently, such as the use of organizational charts and procedural manuals.
- In part, monitor performance of the accounting system through report routines and analytical follow-up activities, such as budget preparation and variance analysis.

Completing the questionnaire assists the auditor in understanding

- The nature of the work or business of an organization.
- The way that the work or business is conducted.
- Any special legal or commercial requirements relevant to the organization.
- The accounting principles and policies followed in the organization that are particular to its industry.
- The sequence of processing within the work or business cycle. In a computer-based system this sequence may be different than the procedures followed in an otherwise similar manual system.

Questionnaire	Reference	Yes	No	"No" Answers Reported to Senior Management Yes (Date) No
(b) has the policy been distributed to all corporate persons; (c) are there adequate procedures for monitoring compliance with the policy?				
B. Organization of the Accounting Department 5. Are the duties, lines of responsibility, and accountability of the accounting department staff adequately defined in: (a) organization charts; (b) written job descriptions?				
6. Are the organization charts and written job descriptions: (a) reviewed periodically to determine whether they are appropriate and up-to-date; (b) approved by appropriate levels of management? (S)				
7. Are there written policies in respect of accounting department staff relating to: (a) delegation of duties when staff are absent; (b) annual vacations for all staff; (c) obtaining references for new staff?				
C. Accounting Policies and Procedures 8. Has the company written policies relating to:				

FIG. 25-1   A page from the Conditions of Control Questionnaire

Phase III — Determination of Control Objectives and Controls-in-Use Review

Phase III is the focal point of the evaluation of controls. The Control Matrix, and optionally the Internal Control Questionnaire (ICQ), guide the auditor through the process of defining the controls required and determining which required controls are functioning and adequately in place. (See the Appendix for samples of the Control Matrix and parts of the ICQ.)

Control Matrix. The Control Matrix (Figure 25-2) can be used as the principal document to determine if controls are in place. For the experienced auditor who is well-versed in detailed control objectives, the matrix is a convenient form that provides a shorthand format for organizing the review of controls.

For someone who requires more detailed guidance or step-by-step formatting, the sample Control Matrix can be reviewed as a summary tool to help complete the ICQ (discussed subsequently).

A matrix is used to evaluate whether the control objectives (such as completeness, accuracy, maintenance, and validity) are being achieved for a particular transaction type. To do so, the auditor must first identify the transaction types of audit concern to be evaluated on the matrix.

Transaction Type. A transaction, for these purposes, is any change to the computerized records. A transaction can be a manually created document that is entered and recorded by the computerized system. It can be a computer-created document, such as an invoice, which is later re-entered when the payment is made. The transaction can be computer-generated, without any entry. For example, the interest calculation on a charge card account is typically computer-generated. This means that the program was written so that it initiates the calculation automatically.

When selecting transactions to follow, the auditor should consider how the control procedures over one transaction vary from the control procedures applied to another transaction. For example, if employee sales are processed and controlled in the same manner as regular sales, then both sales represent only one type of transaction. On the other hand, if they are processed and controlled in two different ways, then each type of sale should be handled as a separate transaction.

It is important to emphasize differences in control when distinguishing types of transactions. The fact that otherwise similar transactions are processed by different people, or in different locations, does not in itself mean that these transactions are of different types. If the control procedures are uniform and there is reason to believe that they are adequately supervised, the transactions can be considered to be of the same type. Each transaction type should be entered on the matrix.

Application Payroll

Location

Date 3/10/8X

Prepared By T. Horgan Reviewed By

Transaction (Document)	COMPLETENESS		ACCURACY*		Validity (Authorization)	Maintenance†	Timing (Establishment and Exercise)	Effectiveness and Efficiency	Programmed Procedures
	Input	Update†	Input	Update†					
Daily Time Card	Batch totals	Manual agreement of totals	Hours Batch totals Employee Number Computer matching		Authorized by supervisor prior to batch totals being established	Transaction Data: Year-to-date balances on payroll master file No controls			1. Calculation of gross pay. 2. Application of standard deductions and calculations of net pay. 3. Update of individual employees' master file records. 4. Edit procedures (accumulation of batch totals).

†Specify file or data base. *Specify significant fields.

FIG. 25-2 A Computer Application Control Matrix, as filled out for a payroll application

After the auditor has defined the various transaction types involved, the next step is to identify specific files and/or data elements of concern. This can be accomplished by interviewing systems and programming personnel as well as by reviewing design specifications. The files and/or elements are recorded on the matrix under the applicable control objective.

Control Technique. Next the auditor enters the control technique that accomplishes the specific control objective for each transaction type listed on the matrix. In many systems, more than one control technique may be used to achieve a particular objective (such as computer matching, computer sequence checking, or batch totals). In these situations, it is necessary for the auditor to select the principal control. This is usually the technique that is most effective and whose functioning can be tested most efficiently. The selection process should also take into consideration the span of control of a particular technique, since a technique may accomplish several control objectives.

After deciding on the most appropriate control technique, the auditor should state exactly how it is implemented (such as computer batch on amount, reconciled by branch clerk). In addition, the processing steps should be identified and listed by technique, and should be cross-referenced to the flowcharts and narratives. These documents should define the steps required to

- Establish the control, such as initial recording on a serially numbered document or creation of the control total.
- Operate the control, or the procedure that detects the error, such as edit checks or computer matching, as well as the batch-balancing, reconciliation, and checking of documents.
- Investigate and correct any of the errors, such as the action taken on an edit report.
- Ensure the control is functioning (discipline):
  a. Segregation of duties so that the work of one person checks that of another (for division of duties).
  b. Supervision of the work of people involved in the operation of the system of basic controls (for supervision).
  c. Separation of responsibilities for custody of assets and the related recordkeeping, and for security arrangements that prevent unauthorized access to assets or accounting records (for custodial controls).
- Alternate controls that compensate for the lack of any specific procedure.

If a particular control objective is not covered by a control technique, the words "None RCW" should be entered on the matrix under that column, indicating that there is a control deficiency which has been recorded on the Record of Control Weaknesses (RCW).

The condition should be noted on the RCW along with the possible effect and the extent of modifications to audit procedures that will be required as a result of discovering the weakness.

The extent of audit procedures depends on the control structure adopted for each application. The auditor should take into account the whole sequence of processing, manual and computer, from the time when the initial events occur to the time when the management report or other output is used.

Application Controls and the Matrix. Within the preceding framework, application controls on the matrix should be analyzed according to the following control objectives (a column is provided for each objective):

- *Completeness controls.* These are designed to ensure that all transactions are processed and that they are processed only once.

- *Accuracy controls.* These are related to specific data elements. Each input/update element is entered with its significance and the corresponding accuracy control (such as, for data, a reasonableness test within the previous month; for account number, a check digit verification).

- *Maintenance controls.* These should ensure the continued propriety of stored data elements. Both aspects of this control are entered:
  a. Correctness, to ensure that stored data remains complete and accurate and that no unauthorized changes are made (such as for correctness, general controls plus a manual control account);
  b. Timeliness, to ensure that stored data is up-to-date and examined to identify items requiring action (such as the suspense file is reviewed daily).

- *Validity/authorization.* These controls ensure that only appropriate transactions are allowed. The authorization procedure is entered, as are the controls that protect against subsequent unauthorized changes (such as a computer check of a customer's credit limit or general controls over subsequent access to those files).

- *Programmed procedures.* These should include all significant accounting processes carried out by a computer (such as categorizations and updates) as well as those relied on for control purposes (such as production of control totals and exception reports). Those controlled by the user are marked "U" and those for which general controls are relied on are marked "G."

For system-generated transaction, the report or file name is entered in the left-hand column under "Transaction/Input." Completeness applies to the completeness of the file(s) entered. The programmed procedures include the generation of the transaction as well as calculation and the like, such as accounts payable general ledger distribution.

All weaknesses, as previously stated, should be identified on the matrix by the notation "None RCW" and then recorded on the RCW.

It is advisable to check the matrix by following each significant data element on reports back to the point where the data originated, to ensure that all control aspects of the system have been considered.

Computer Internal Control Questionnaire

The Computer Internal Control Questionnaire (CICQ) is one of the documents that may be used for the evaluation of internal controls in computer-based systems. It provides a detailed method for analyzing controls. Use of the CICQ requires the complementary use of the Control Matrix.

The CICQ should be completed by referring to the flowcharts or narratives that record the understanding of the system and procedures. It is structured in different parts that correspond to the types of controls in place. Use of the manual ICQ may also be required.

- *Application controls.* The questions on application controls are divided into those relating to manual controls (manual ICQ) and to computer application controls (discussed in the following section).

- *Controls over master file data.* For convenience, this section is printed at the end of the section on application controls in the CICQ.

- *General or integrity controls.* General control questions of the CICQ are printed as a separate document.

CICQ — Application Controls Section. In general, application control techniques apply to the controls over

- Completeness and accuracy of input and updating;
- Authorization or validity; and
- Maintenance of transaction data on a master file.

The application controls comprise a mixture of controls, either carried out manually or included in the computer programs. The manual controls are sometimes referred to as user controls; the others are called programmed procedures.

Although the control objectives remain the same, regardless of how transactions are processed, alternate sets of questions are available to evaluate control techniques used in both computerized and noncomputerized systems. The manual ICQ should be used to evaluate control techniques found in all systems, regardless of processing method. The CICQ should be used for all procedures, manual or automated, specific to computer-based processing.

PAYMENT CYCLE

1. Orders   Purchases should be initiated only on the basis of appro-
                  priate authorizations and records of commitments should be
                  maintained as a basis for:

                  o Determining that transactions are executed in accordance
                     with authorizations

                  o Establishing the amount of any provision required for
                     losses arising from unfulfilled commitments

2. Receipts   Control should be established over goods and services
                  received as a basis for:

                  o Determining and recording the liability for goods and
                     services received but not entered as accounts payable

                  o Where required, posting the items to detailed inventory
                     records

3.c/m Returns   Control should be established over goods returned to, and
                  claims on, suppliers as a basis for:

                  o Obtaining credit for all such items

                  o Where required, posting the items to detailed inventory
                     records

4. Approval   Invoices and related documentation should be properly
                  checked and approved as being valid before being entered
                  as accounts payable.

5. Posting   All valid accounts payable transactions, and only those
                  transactions, should be accurately recorded as accounts
                  payable.

Note: c/m = Control objective common to both computer and manual based
       accounting systems.

FIG. 25-3A   Answers to CICQ questions: Payment cycle

The questions under each control objective vary according to whether

- Data is being entered to a computerized system and either a master file updated or a suspense file updated, or
- Data is being produced or checked by a computerized system.

When evaluating controls over data that is entered into a computerized system, and the update of a file, use detailed questions structured as follows:

- *Completeness of input and updating.* Alternate control techniques are set out, followed by detailed questions examining each technique. Questions are also asked relating to the disciplines over the relevant manual procedures.

- *Timing of authorization of input.* A single question is included to identify controls that prevent the alteration of authorized data. The answer normally requires a reference to the questions (under a prior control objective) dealing with the authorization of transactions.

- *Generation of data.* When appropriate, questions are asked about the writing of generated data to the master file.

- *Maintenance of data on the master file.* Questions are asked for each maintenance control and the disciplines over the manual procedures.

When data is being produced or checked by a computerized system, the structure of the detailed questions, including the existence of likely alternate techniques, varies somewhat. The questions normally seek to identify controls over

- The master file data used (authorization, amendments and maintenance). This is a trigger question that directs attention to the master file data controls section.
- The validity, completeness, and accuracy of input of any transaction data involved, where appropriate.
- The completeness and accuracy of processing of the data, where appropriate.
- The clerical or programmed checking and approval of the processing of data, where appropriate.

In many systems, more than one control technique may be used to achieve any particular objective (such as computer matching, computer sequence checking, or batch totals). In these situations, the CICQ refers to the various alternate control techniques that are likely to be met in actual practice. Only the questions relating to the operation of the principal control should be answered. (See Figures 25-3A, 25-3B, and 25-3C for some answers to CICQ questions for various applications.)

```
PRODUCTION CYCLE

20.c/m  Approval      Control should be established over:

                      o  Issues from inventories of materials and supplies
                         to production, and returns

                      o  Charges to production for labor and overheads

                      o  Transfers from production to inventories of parts
                         and finished products; as a basis, where required,
                         for making the entries in the inventory records.

                      This control objective does not cover the controls over
                      the receipt of materials and supplies from suppliers which
                      are put directly into production or the shipment of
                      finished products directly from production to customers,
                      which are included within the scope of control objectives
                      2 and 3 and 31, 32 and 33 respectively.


21.     Posting       Accurate inventory records should be maintained of work
                      in progress.


22.     A/C           General ledger entries arising from the production cycle
        Distri-       should be accurately determined. (This control objective
        bution        does not cover the general ledger entries for the receipt
                      of raw materials and supplies which are put directly
                      into production, and the shipment to customers of
                      finished products directly from production, which are
                      included within the scope of control objectives 13
                      and 38 respectively.)
```

FIG. 25-3B   Answers to CICQ questions: Production cycle

CICQ — Master File Data Controls Section. Since master file data controls do not vary markedly from application to application, it is possible to use a generic or common master file data controls section that incorporates both application and general control concerns. This section covers the following:

- The identification of all master file data elements that have accounting significance
- Controls over:
  a. File creation
  b. Authorization of amendments
  c. Completeness and accuracy of written amendments to the file
  d. Computer-generated amendments to the file
  e. Maintenance of the data on the file

CICQ — General Controls Section. In EDP systems where significant programmed procedures have been identified, or where principal controls are

REVENUE CYCLE

30.   Orders   Records should be maintained of unfulfilled sales commitments as a basis for determining any provision required for losses arising therefrom.

31.   Shipments   Control should be established over goods shipped and services performed as a basis for:

o Making charges to customers for all such sales

o Determining the amount of the related revenues which have not been entered as accounts receivable

o Where required, making the related entries in the detailed inventory records.

(This control objective is not intended to cover sales in retail and similar businesses where the invoices or similar documents are issued to customers at the time the goods are supplied (see control objective 32).)

32.c/m Cash Sales   Control should be established over cash sales of goods and services as a basis for:

o Accounting for all such sales

o Where required, making the related entries in the detailed inventory records.

(For this purpose "cash sales" should be regarded as including credit sales made under similar conditions, i.e., where the customer receives the goods or services on the vendor's premises and the sales invoice or similar document is issued to the customer at the same time.)

33.c/m Returns   Control should be established over goods returned by, and claims received from, customers as a basis for:

o Determining and recording the liability for goods returned and claims received but not entered in the accounts receivable records

FIG. 25-3C Answers to CICQ questions: Revenue cycle

located within the data processing department, it is necessary to evaluate the relevant general controls. Those controls will be identified by means of the trigger questions included at the end of each control objective in the general controls section of the CICQ. The last question of each and every computer-based control objective requires the auditor to list those programmed procedures whose continued and proper operation is not assured by user controls (such as manual procedures that constitute either a form of application or general control). When the auditor relies on programmed procedures, the general controls section of the CICQ must be completed.

Reference to general controls is triggered whenever the maintenance of master files is a programmed procedure that is not subject to manual reperformance or review. Again, the general controls section of the CICQ must be completed whenever the programmed procedure is to be relied on.

Review of Controls in Use

Determining the Controls on Which to Place Reliance. In a computer system, determining the controls on which to place reliance involves identifying the controls that have been established to ensure the completeness, accuracy, and validity of the data processed. This involves an evaluation of the application controls and the general controls. The following sections discuss these controls and how they affect the appropriateness and continued proper operation of the programmed procedures.

Controls Over Programs. In some cases, the application controls alone may be adequate to ensure that the programmed procedures operate consistently and correctly. Reliance may be placed on the application controls if the evaluation and compliance testing produce satisfactory results.

Usually, however, the general controls are relied on to ensure the appropriateness and continued proper operation of the programmed procedures. If the results of this evaluation and compliance tests of the general controls are satisfactory, it may not be necessary to test all the procedures included in the computer programs on which reliance is placed. The auditor may have already tested some of these procedures — when they were included in some of the programs — while conducting compliance tests of the general controls.

Interdependence of Control Assessment. In some circumstances a control objective can only be assessed by considering the conditions that relate to another control objective. These are

- *Reliance on controls over another application.* Where two or more applications are integrated or where files are updated simultaneously, the controls over input will be identified under the earlier control objective.

- *Computer matching.* Where the principal control is matching, the controls over the input, updating, and maintenance of the original items to be matched are important, but they may have been dealt with under an earlier control objective.

Questions on Program Logic. A number of computer-related questions seek to establish whether the logic of a programmed procedure is valid. These are specific to a particular program. The following question is a typical example: "Is the method used in the program for the calculation of value appropriate?"

In order to answer questions of this nature, it is necessary for the auditor to have gained and confirmed an understanding of the logic of programmed procedures and to have determined whether the method used is sound. This may require an examination of the program documentation or even of the program source listing.

Phase IV — Reporting, Rectifying, and Recording Weaknesses

All control weaknesses should be properly recorded and reported, and their effects should be evaluated. Recommendations for action should be presented in the audit report. To accomplish this important objective, the auditor can make use of the RCW. The *Internal Control Reference Manual* (ICRM) can be useful in completing the RCW and as a guide.

Internal Control Reference Manual. The ICRM is used to determine the effects of weaknesses in controls. It may also be used to assist in establishing special questions not found in the standard CICQ. It can be thought of as a guide, which presents the control evaluation possibilities in a clear format. (For a presentation of the ICRM, see Chapter 26, "*Internal Control Reference Manual* — General Controls," and Chapter 27, "*Internal Control Reference Manual* — Application Controls.")

The ICRM is principally designed to assist in answering the internal control questions in the CICQ and to aid in completing the RCW. It explains the purpose of each internal control question and also describes possible procedures to use in performing each task. Then it gives examples of how these procedures might operate in practice. The ICRM is useful in evaluating the answers to questions in the CICQ. The first part of each manual contains instructions for its use.

The ICRM helps bring greater uniformity to subjective judgments about the control system. It covers both application and general controls in computerized systems and was developed by Coopers & Lybrand to assist its auditors in evaluating such systems. It has been used successfully by the firm for many years.

Record of Control Weaknesses. The RCW is the principal form used to integrate the work performed in relation to any weaknesses found in the control system. Figure 25-4 illustrates an RCW.

The purpose of the RCW is to bring together in one document

- All control weaknesses that were identified during the evaluation,

Function __Payroll__   Date __3/10/8X__

Location _____   Prepared By _____   Reviewed By _____

Workpaper Reference #	Nature of weakness and possible effect on internal accounting control and/or on efficiency of operations	COULD SUBSTANTIAL ERROR ARISE?		Audit Program Reference #	EFFECT ON NATURE, EXTENT AND/OR TIMING OF AUDIT PROCEDURES	NOTIFICATION OF WEAKNESS TO RESPONSIBLE MANAGEMENT		
		Yes/No	Justification		Nature of Amendment Required	Informal discussion with Site Management (Date)	Formal Report to Senior Management Yes (Date) / No	Management Response/Comments (If Applicable)
(1)	(2)	(3)	(4)	(5)	(3)	(7)	(8)	(9)
	Completeness of Input There is no control to ensure that all time sheets are delivered to the payroll department. This could result in a cut-off problem at year-end for payroll expense.	No	Employee who does not receive a check will complain. It is unlikely that the error will not be corrected immediately.		NTL.	3/8X		Disagree. Employee complaint is an adequate control. Cost of new controls does not justify possible benefits.
	Authorization of Time Sheets Although daily time sheets are authorized by supervisors, there is no control to ensure that the time sheets are not being changed during subsequent processing. This could result in excess payments to employees and to over-statement of payroll expense.	No	Weekly Payroll Expense Reports are reviewed by supervisors. Significant variance in reported time will be revealed.		NTL.	3/8X		Disagree. The supervisors review the Payroll Expense. Any "unusual" hours reported will be detected.

FIG. 25-4 A Record of Control Weaknesses, as filled out in a review of a payroll application

- The results of discussing those weaknesses with appropriate management,
- Any reporting to senior management, and
- Any corrective action taken.

The RCW also provides a ready means of reviewing the possible effects of weaknesses in the organization's internal accounting controls.

Thus, all weaknesses found when completing the Control Matrix or CICQ should be recorded on the RCW. How these weaknesses affect the nature, timing, and extent of substantive testing work should also be identified (unless there are compensating controls).

The nature of the weakness, its possible effect on the financial statements, and its effect on management reports are not always easy to determine in computer-based systems. Making this determination is difficult, and EDP auditors should be of assistance in identifying compensating controls. Following are general observations that can be made regarding the effects of a weakness:

- *Manual application controls procedure.* Generally, the nature and effects of the weakness are obvious. However, when the control is acting as a control over a programmed procedure (such as follow-up action taken on an exception report or scrutiny of computer-generated data) the effect of the weakness on that programmed procedure should also be considered.

- *Programmed procedures.* Again, the direct effects of the failure are usually obvious. However, the existence of the failure may, in itself, cast doubt on the effectiveness of the general controls.

- *General controls.* There may not be a direct effect, but the failure may cast doubt on the continued and proper operation of all, or some, of the programmed procedures.

Identifying Weaknesses. In order for the auditor to place reliance on a system of internal control, he or she needs to both identify weaknesses and consider the effect those weaknesses may have on subsequent audit procedures. Weaknesses may arise from the absence of a required control or from the failure to exercise a control. The auditor should identify the absence of required controls when completing the CICQ (or matrix, if used alone). A failure to exercise controls is often uncovered during the review of compliance test results.

One important feature of a systems audit approach is that the auditor must make a judgment about each weakness that has been identified, its possible effects (accidental or intentional), and what changes should therefore be made in the audit work.

Depending on its nature, a weakness in the internal controls might lead to error in the following ways:

- Assets or liabilities may be understated or overstated, with a corresponding effect on the profit statement.

- Losses may occur or a possible fraud may go undetected.

- Management information may be distorted and incorrect decisions made as a result.

If the auditor decides that an error could occur, further tests may be necessary to determine if this has already happened and, if so, the extent of the error. In order to reach a satisfactory conclusion, alterations may have to be made to the audit procedures that would otherwise have been carried out.

Factors the auditor must consider in deciding whether a control weakness could lead to error depend on the particular circumstances of each weakness. However, certain factors are usually common to each assessment.

The common factors auditors find in relation to internal accounting controls are

- The assets and liabilities involved are themselves significant in relation to the financial statements.

- Any related control procedures might show that a significant error arose.

- The effects of weaknesses in controls over master file data are likely to have greater consequence than the effects of weaknesses in controls over transaction data.

- Weaknesses in controls over completeness are likely to have a more serious effect than weaknesses in controls over the accuracy or validity of individual transactions.

- Weaknesses in programmed procedures are more likely to be significant than weaknesses in user controls, particularly if a high volume of data passes through the programmed procedure and/or the results of that programmed procedure are not subject to manual scrutiny or checking.

- A breakdown has been corrected before the audit, and this is confirmed by appropriate audit tests. It may, however, be necessary to carry out further audit tests if the weakness could have presented an opportunity for major irregularities during the period before it was corrected.

When the auditor has decided that the overall adequacy of implementation, program security, or computer operations controls is deficient, each programmed procedure at risk must be reviewed. A decision must then be made whether a significant error could arise if the procedure is not operating properly.

If the tests of programmed procedures disclose that a programmed procedure is not functioning properly, the auditor should find out the reasons behind the malfunction. Often the procedure was not properly included in the program to begin with (stemming from a weakness in implementation or program security controls) or the program was not properly used (a weakness in computer operations controls). Once the cause has been identified, the auditor needs to assess its effect on both the programmed procedure at fault and other programmed procedures. This assessment usually entails further tests on the programmed procedures, or on the relevant general controls, to determine the extent of weaknesses in those controls.

If the auditor has decided that the data file security control as a whole is deficient, then each data element at risk must be reviewed. For example, the rates of interest or the sales prices might need review. Then it will be possible to decide whether the lack of control over such elements could lead to error.

If the overall review confirms that an error could be present in an account balance, the auditor usually has to extend the tests carried out on the individual items that make up that account balance. The tests may also be extended to the specific part of the account balance in question. When the concern has arisen that unauthorized transactions may have occurred relating to cash and wages, the auditor may also wish to examine more transactions during the period under audit. The nature of these extended substantive procedures is discussed further in the detailed description of substantive procedures in Chapter 22, "Substantive or Validation Procedures."

Common Weaknesses in Computer Systems. Weaknesses often occur because of a failure to plan controls adequately during the early stages of system development. As a result, controls are developed on an ad hoc or unstructured basis. Consideration of the entire system, both computer and noncomputer, during the planning of controls is essential. However, this integrated approach is often overlooked. Manual controls frequently are not decided on until after the system has become operational. The need to restructure existing manual controls when computer processing is introduced also may be overlooked.

The more common weaknesses, in relation to user controls and programmed procedures, include

- Failure to establish controls over the maintenance of master file data
- Failure to recognize the need to control reference data
- Ineffective authorization procedures, particularly in relation to irregular entries, such as adjustments
- Failure to recognize the importance of supervisory controls
- Failure to check the accuracy of computer-generated data (for example, interest charges) by either reasonableness checks or manual reviews of the generated data

- Unrealistic criteria in programmed reasonableness and dependency checks, with the result that either too few or too many exceptional items are rejected or reported

The more common weaknesses in relation to general controls include the following:

- Failure to establish a proper segregation of duties within the EDP department in order to clearly distinguish the functions of systems analysts, programmers, and computer operators
- Failure to produce easy-to-understand reports of computer use so that a meaningful review of computer operations can be carried out
- Absence of control over modifications made to program libraries, particularly to ensure that only properly authorized amendments can be made to existing programs
- Failure to safeguard data files against access by unauthorized personnel
- Failure to ensure that restrictions over the operation of a computer and access to data files are enforced at all times, particularly during evening and weekend shifts

The more common breakdowns that are encountered during compliance testing include the following:

- Failure to act promptly on exception reports
- Build-up of uninvestigated rejections
- Build-up of suspense items on files
- Delays in the follow-up of outstanding and overdue items, such as follow-up letters for overdue bills
- Failure to carry out reconciliation procedures due to time pressures resulting from processing delays
- The low priority often given to cyclical checking of master file data
- Inadequate enforcement of restrictions on the operation of the computer, in particular, permitting unsupervised programmers to operate the machine or to test programs
- Amendments made to operational program libraries that bypass the normal control procedures and authorization requirements

To assess the effect of breakdowns in controls over computer systems, the auditor should realize that an exception relating to the failure of a programmed procedure is unlikely to be an isolated incident. At best, it indicates a breakdown in the general controls. At worst, it points to a fault in the program itself. In the latter case, the situation should be reported to management immediately, since the fault will remain until it is corrected.

The Effect of Control Weaknesses on Audit Procedures. It is not possible to state precisely the effect of control weaknesses that could lead to errors in audit procedures. For the auditor, much depends on the nature and significance of the assets and liabilities involved and the likelihood that a substantial error will arise.

When a chance for error exists, an overall review may confirm its existence or nonexistence. For example, the auditor can study such summary information as month-to-month totals of processed transactions, comparisons with budgets and previous periods, and performance indicators such as gross profit percentages or budget variances. When the records of relevant assests, liabilities, or transactions are held on computer files, it may be possible to use computer audit programs to help confirm whether an error exists. Audit software programs can generate reports that can be used to assess the extent of error in either user controls or programmed procedures.

Errors in application controls can be handled in the same manner as in the following example: In a medium-size warehouse, continuous stock-taking procedures are found to be in arrears. It may be possible to use a computer audit program to age the inventory by the date of last count (for example, 6 months, 12 months, 18 months, and over 18 months). This information will show if a significant part of the total inventory has gone uncounted for long periods. This type of software use can be very helpful because it simulates events, such as aging of inventories.

Errors in programmed procedures can be handled in a manner similar to the following example: The program for reporting uncleared items on the outstanding accounts receivable file produces only partial reports. A computer audit program can be used to examine the accounts receivable files to produce a report of outstanding items, analyzed by date of entry to the suspense file. This information shows whether a significant volume or value of shipments remain outstanding for an unreasonable period of time. This type of testing can be done for many different kinds of programmed procedures.

ADDITIONAL EVALUATIVE CONSIDERATIONS

Management Reporting

After internal controls have been evaluated, compliance or functional tests can be conducted. Subsequently, when the audit is completed, a formal report is required which includes an assessment of the system or area reviewed. This report should also discuss the internal controls. In addition, where deficiencies are noted, recommendations should outline whatever corrective action is needed to ensure that adequate controls are implemented.

With the passage of the Foreign Corrupt Practices Act, corporate officers can be held accountable for the adequacy of internal controls that affect an organization's financial statements. Thus, merely identifying and reporting weaknesses and recommending corrective action to management is not sufficient. Adequate follow-up procedures should exist to ensure that corrective action is taken on a timely, cost-effective basis, so that an adequate system of internal control results.

Alternatives to Reliance on Controls

When the auditor cannot, or for reasons of efficiency chooses not to, rely on the general and/or application controls to ensure the operation of the programmed procedures, suitable alternate procedures should be adopted. For example, it may be appropriate to test the operation of the programmed procedures to a significant extent.

Controls in New Systems

When new systems are introduced, the auditor may decide that it is more efficient not to rely extensively on the implementation controls over new systems, especially if there are weaknesses. Instead, the auditor may choose to make sure that the programmed procedures are operating properly. The remaining general controls should then be evaluated and tested to ensure the consistent and proper operation of the programmed procedures during the entire period under review.

It can be useful to evaluate the adequacy of the controls in an application system before the application becomes operational, for the following reasons:

- It is difficult to make changes in a computerized system once it is operational. The auditor should therefore make any suggestions or recommendations at the relevant stage of development so that they can be incorporated without problems. Indeed, users often encourage or specifically request the auditor's evaluation and comments prior to system implementation.

- The auditor needs to know the nature and extent of programmed procedures in order to decide whether to rely on and test the implementation controls. Without adequate lead time before implementation, it may be impossible to plan and perform tests.

- The auditor may be able to arrange for additional features to be included in the system that will assist in subsequent audit tests. For example, facilities may be arranged to obtain printouts or reports on request, or to include additional data elements on the master files so that the subsequent examination by a computer audit program will be easier (such as date of last interest bill).

- If, in exceptional circumstances, a weakness cannot be covered by substantive procedures, the auditor may want to reconsider the extent to which the findings properly describe the control situations.

In these circumstances, the auditor should ensure that subsequent auditing procedures give appropriate consideration to the weaknesses.

If it is necessary to amend the nature, extent, or timing of substantive procedures, the audit program reference and the amendments made should be recorded on the appropriate document. On the RCW, the changes should be noted in column 5 (Informal Discussion) and column 6 (Letter to Senior Management), both under "Notification of Weakness to Responsible Management." If no amendment is considered necessary, "none" should be entered in column 6, together with an appropriate explanation and a cross-reference to the audit program schedule where applicable.

Administrative Control Weaknesses

When administrative control questions are addressed, the RCW is prepared in the following manner. When practical, the auditor should quantify the effect of a weakness (for example, in terms of revenue losses or cost increases) in order to make the related control comments as meaningful as possible. Putting these effects in pragmatic dollars-and-cents terms helps readers of the report to understand it. If this is not practical, an effort should be made to determine the order of magnitude of the transactions, or of the operations affected by the control weakness. For example, if a failure to calculate economic order quantities leads to lost revenue or additional costs, the auditor may be unable to quantify the loss precisely. When this happens, the auditor should comment instead on the total volume of purchases, or purchased-goods inventory, or other amount that can be quantified.

The auditor should consider whether the identified weakness could have financial or nonfinancial audit implications. If the weakness could result in an error that would be important to management, this possibility, together with the justification for the decision, should be recorded in column 2 (Nature of Weakness) and column 4 (Could Material Error Arise?) of the RCW.

The overall purpose is to be able to provide management with useful, meaningful reports in specific terms that can be understood and acted on.

Internal Control Reference Manual — General Controls

INTRODUCTION

The *Internal Control Reference Manual* (ICRM) was developed by Coopers & Lybrand to assist the auditor in reviewing general, or integrity, controls. The relevant section of the standard Internal Control Questionnaire (ICQ) is normally completed by an EDP auditor. It can be reviewed using the ICRM, which is also helpful in completing the Record of Control Weaknesses (RCW).

The ICRM consists of two volumes, one of which is presented here in an edited format to show how general control questions can be addressed. (The other volume is presented in Chapter 27, "*Internal Control Reference Manual* — Application Controls.") It depicts differences in audit procedures as a result of answers to control questions. The material discussed can be summarized as follows:

- The nature of general controls
- Appropriateness of evaluation of control procedures
- Evaluation of "no" answers
- Organization of the ICRM

THE NATURE OF GENERAL CONTROLS

Two important features of computer systems are

1. The inclusion of procedures relating to internal control and accounting in computer programs and, as a result, their concentration in the computer department. These procedures are referred to as "programmed procedures."
2. The maintenance of data in the form of computer files in the data processing department that can normally be read only by the computer.

Therefore, the auditor is concerned with the consistent and proper operation of the programmed procedures and the protection of data stored on files.

Controls Over Programmed Procedures

Computer systems use computer programs that incorporate precise instructions for processing. The programmed procedures are of concern to the auditor when they relate to

- Procedures that would be considered control functions if they were carried out manually; for example, a programmed sequence check and preparation of a list of missing numbers.
- Accounting procedures that ordinarily would be subjected to checking in a noncomputer system; for example, the calculation and

preparation of sales invoices or the automatic generation of insurance premium renewals.

Usually, the effective and consistent operation of programmed procedures can be assured by controlling the design, implementation, security, and use of the programmed procedures within the EDP function. The same assurance might, of course, be achieved by checking the results of processing in the user department. However, the latter method is generally less efficient because of the large volume of data that would have to be checked; indeed this method can be carried out only when the results of each processing step are reported, as they are in the simplest computer systems.

Controls Over Data Files

Information of several types is stored on computer files. The information of particular concern to the auditor includes the following:

- *Transaction data* — Representing individual transactions and the cumulative effect of these transactions (such as the invoice number, invoice date and amount, and the total amount due)
- *Master file data* — Permanent or semi-permanent reference information applicable to many transactions (also called standing data, this includes information such as sales prices, customer name, and account number)
- *Programs* — As discussed previously, programs can serve many purposes and are normally stored in several different forms (such as in a source statement form written by the programmer and in object form as executable programs)

Information stored on computer files can normally be read only through the use of programs designed to print out the contents of a file. The information stored on a file might therefore be changed without visible evidence of the change. The files are normally kept in the custody of computer operations, which is also responsible for their correct use.

Application controls are designed to ensure that authorized data is completely and accurately processed, and that the stored data continues to remain correct. However, unless the results of processing are checked in detail, some reliance must be placed on the security controls within the EDP department to ensure that unauthorized changes are not made to data files.

General Controls

The controls over the design, implementation, security, and use of computer programs and the security of data files are known as general, or integrity, controls. These controls, performed mainly within the EDP function, are a combination of manual controls and system software. Like other controls, they consist of basic controls and disciplines over basic controls. Generally they are performed manually by EDP department personnel. When effective general controls exist,

- Appropriate procedures are effectively included in the programs, both when the system originally becomes operational and when changes are subsequently made. These are defined as "implementation controls."

- Unauthorized changes cannot be made to computer programs. These are defined as "program security controls."

- Procedures in computer programs are consistently applied. These are defined as "computer operations controls."

- Unauthorized changes cannot be made to data files. These are defined as "data file security controls."

- System software is properly selected and implemented, and unauthorized changes cannot be made. These are defined as "system software controls."

System Software

System software comprises programs that are not specific to any particular application but that may be used in the design, processing, and control of all applications. It includes operating systems, librarian packages, security packages, data base management systems, and communications software. For example, programs may be protected against unauthorized change by program library software; use of the correct files can be assured by software label checks; and the proper processing of jobs depends on procedures included in the operating system and related software. Just as application controls may depend on the consistent and proper operation of application programs, many general controls may depend on the consistent and proper operation of system software. Controls over system software do not affect the application programs and data directly, but rather affect the auditor's ability to rely on the other general controls.

Materiality of Programmed Procedures and Data Files

As part of the review of each application control objective, the auditor should identify significant programmed procedures and data elements. General controls are important insofar as they control the integrity of these programs and data. The auditor should consider at all times the materiality of the programs and data in relation to the control objectives involved.

User-Controlled Simple Systems

The effective operation of manual application controls can provide assurance as to the consistent and proper operation of programmed procedures or protection of data files. For example, if a computer-produced listing of missing prenumbered documents includes the numbers of all documents that should have been processed, together with an indication of those documents that are missing, and the manual application controls include an investigation of missing numbers and a review to determine that all documents sent for processing appear on the listing, then no reliance need be placed on the general controls. This option is usually limited to simple computer systems.

In simple computer systems, detailed printed reports are available at each stage of processing. All output is directly identifiable with corresponding input. Calculations, summarizations, and categorizations are printed out with supporting detailed information. Exception and rejection reports show accepted and unaccepted items. Master file data is printed out each time it is used. Accordingly, an individual can reperform the processing functions carried out by the computer and can check that data stored on computer files is correct (for example, by performing a one-for-one check of output to input or by manually reperforming calculations). Control over the consistent and proper operation of the programmed procedures therefore can be exercised manually.

If, in a simple system, manual application controls are to be relied on rather than general controls, the following elements must be present:

- The manual checking of output must actually be carried out; it is not enough to have the information available for checking.
- The actual checking must cover all significant programmed procedures and data.
- The output that is checked must be produced at an appropriate stage of processing. For example, an edit report cannot be used to check that the update took place properly.
- The manual application controls must be designed to detect significant errors and irregularities that might occur through unauthorized changes in programs, data files, software, or operating procedures.

Most computer systems, even simple systems, are not user-controlled but rely on a suitable combination of user controls and general controls. While the consequences of weak user controls are fairly obvious, the consequences of weak general controls are less so. Therefore, there may be a tendency to dismiss such weaknesses without considering their impact. A weakness in general controls can affect all programmed procedures and data files that are not user controlled. As the general controls are common to all applications, a weakness can have a significant impact on the overall audit plan by affecting many applications.

TECHNICAL COMPUTER KNOWLEDGE REQUIRED

The auditor needs a knowledge of the techniques of computer system development and computer operations in order to understand and audit general controls, just as a knowledge of accounting and manual accounting procedures is necessary to audit manual systems. While auditors cannot be expected to have the technical knowledge and experience required of an EDP auditor or computer audit specialist, those members of the audit team involved in the planning and audit decisions must have an understanding of the audit implications of EDP controls and should be able to recognize the need for technical assistance.

APPROPRIATENESS OF EVALUATION OF CONTROL PROCEDURES

As with other portions of the ICQ, the auditor completes the general controls section after recording and confirming an understanding of the system. This understanding is frequently recorded following a data processing interview guide, or using a narrative form, rather than flowcharts. The confirmation process does not involve a transaction review, as in a manual system, since accounting transactions are not usually involved. Instead, similar review procedures are followed to confirm the understanding of EDP department procedures.

Before evaluating general controls, the auditor should consider whether

- The programmed procedures and data files involved are material in terms of the control objectives involved.
- The computer systems are "simple" and, if so, whether the company relies on user department checks of the system output, general controls, or both.
- Extended substantive or validation testing of the programmed procedures, the data stored on computer files, and/or the final results of processing would be more efficient than evaluating the general and application control procedures, performing compliance tests, and maintaining normal levels of substantive procedures.
- Questions related specifically to the company's particular data processing methods are needed in addition to those in the standard ICQ.

These determinations must be made for all applications covered by the general controls.

Efficiency of Extended Substantive Procedures

In some cases, it may be more efficient for the auditor to apply extended substantive procedures, rather than to evaluate the control procedures, perform the necessary compliance tests, and carry out normal levels of substantive tests. The factors to be taken into account (usually by external auditors) are

- The extent to which there appear to be weaknesses in the general controls or the application controls.
- The nature and significance of the programmed procedures and the data stored on computer files.
- The number of significant programmed procedures and data elements involved.
- The volume of data that needs to be substantiated. This need not be a problem when audit software is used to assist in the substantiation procedures.
- The extent to which important data, which might be used for audit purposes, has been destroyed because the company's normal retention period has expired.
- The relative effectiveness, efficiency, and coverage of substantive procedures, including the use of audit software and other computer-assisted audit techniques.
- The possibility of carrying out substantive tests on programmed procedures to ensure that any breakdown in controls has not had an adverse effect on programs and data. The effect of using audit software in this area should be considered.
- The extent to which audit software and other tests can be, or have to be, set up or carried out before year-end.
- The extent to which it is more difficult to perform substantive tests to ensure the completeness of the accounting records as opposed to relying on, and testing, the application controls over completeness.

Supplementary Considerations

An organization may employ unusual or advanced data processing methods. In this case, the auditor may find it appropriate to devise additional questions to supplement the standard questions. The format and style of the questions should be similar to the standard questions and should be drafted by someone with experience in the particular processing methods involved.

Evaluation of "No" Answers

The auditor should consider carefully the audit response to a "no" answer in the ICQ. It may be helpful to follow these steps:

- Determine whether there is a compensating control.
- Determine whether the effect of the "no" answer is inconsequential.
- If the effect is not inconsequential, determine whether the organization is willing to correct the weakness.
- If the organization will not correct the weakness, consider whether the weakness could give rise to a material error in the financial statements (an external auditor's concern).
- Consider, based on knowledge of the system as a whole, whether other control procedures reduce or eliminate the significance of the "no" answer.
- If the significance is not reduced or eliminated, decide what specific substantive procedures will enable the auditor to determine whether or not the financial statements are materially in error.

Compensating Controls

Because the questions in the ICQ generally ask whether a particular control is present, rather than about the details of the procedure (those details should be included in the general control checklist, narratives, or flowcharts), compensating controls are not likely to exist in practice. However, an example of a compensating control is presented here for illustrative purposes.

Example. A company's system does not require that for new systems, formal systems specifications be prepared and approved in writing. However, both user departments and EDP supervisory personnel are heavily involved in the design and particularly the testing of a new system, to the extent that they devise appropriate tests and check the results.

Inconsequential Weaknesses

In some cases, the effect of "no" answers to the questions in the general controls section of the ICQ may be so minor that no errors in the programs or data files are likely to occur as a result. For example, this can occur in relation to weaknesses in the system software controls when the system software in use is relatively unsophisticated and the weaknesses are not that widespread. In this circumstance, the auditor may conclude that the most likely result is a failure of the computer system to function at all, rather than for it to produce results containing undetectable errors. As with compensating controls, the circumstances should be explained on the general control questionnaire in the space provided. The assessment of the adequacy of the general controls would then disregard such "no" answers.

Corrected Weaknesses

If the auditor concludes that there is no compensating control and that the effect is not inconsequential, the possibility of corrective action should be discussed with the organization. If the organization is willing to correct the control weakness, the auditor may be able to reduce the overall audit time by delaying compliance tests until the corrective action has been taken. For example, if the organization has not properly retested the unchanged portions of modified systems but agrees to carry out the testing before the end of the year (to include assurance that any errors discovered have not distorted previous processing results), the auditor can delay testing in this area until the control has been installed.

Possibility of Significant Errors or Irregularities

If the organization does not take corrective action, the auditor should consider carefully whether significant error can arise. For this purpose, the word "error" refers to unintentional mistakes made in processing. It includes mathematical or clerical mistakes in, and omissions from, the underlying records and data. The word "error" does not refer to mistakes in financial statements arising from misappropriations of assets related to internal control weaknesses. The word "error" also does not refer to intentional distortions of financial statements, such as deliberate misrepresentations by management or misappropriation of assets arising from circumvention of the company's system of internal control. The latter kinds of misstatements are referred to as "irregularities."

Thus, errors arise because of the absence of or weaknesses in internal control procedures, while irregularities arise from a circumvention or overriding of the system of internal control. Accordingly, the auditor's evaluation of internal control and reperformance of compliance tests may help to reveal errors that may be present. Substantive procedures, including those procedures carried out on programmed procedures and other data available within the EDP function, are more likely to identify irregularities that may have occurred.

To determine whether or not material error can arise, the auditor must first consider the effect of the weakness on the programmed procedures or data elements at risk. These are the same programmed procedures and data identified in each application control objective as not being checked in detail by the user.

Weaknesses in the different areas of general controls have different effects on the programmed procedures and data as follows:

- Weaknesses in the implementation controls may cause new systems or systems that have been modified to function incorrectly. Often such errors are imbedded in the system, and erroneous processing will continue until the error is identified and corrected.

- Weaknesses in the program security controls generally mean that unauthorized changes can be made to the system, so that changes can be made that are not subject to the normal implementation controls just discussed. Since the organization may not be sure which systems have been changed and which have not, opportunities for misappropriation of assets are increased.

- Weaknesses in the computer operations controls generally mean that random errors may occur in the system. While some errors, such as those in master file data, may have a lasting effect, the main effect of these weaknesses is similar to that of weaknesses in a noncomputer system: Most processing is correct but occasionally it is not. This contrasts with the continuous errors arising from implementation control weaknesses, as discussed previously.

- Weaknesses in the data file security controls generally mean that unauthorized changes can be made to data stored in EDP. The time taken to discover these unauthorized changes depends largely on the structure of the application controls. Some errors in transaction data may be discovered fairly quickly through the operation of control accounts or through the mailing of statements. If the system is a payment one, however, the error may never be picked up (for example, incorrect overpayment of pensions or suppliers). Errors in master file data usually take longer to detect. Weaknesses in data file security controls combined with weaknesses in program security controls provide a particular opportunity for undetectable misappropriation of assets. Weaknesses in data file security controls coupled with weaknesses in the application controls over the continuity of the data increase the chances of undetected errors occurring.

- Weaknesses in system software controls do not have a direct effect on the applications. Such weaknesses may mean, however, that system software that is relied on for the proper functioning of the controls described previously is not appropriate. As a result, one or more of those control areas may be weak.

Having identified the general control weaknesses as well as the programmed procedures and data elements at risk, the auditor should then determine whether or not significant errors or irregularities could arise. These factors, among others, should be considered for each programmed procedure or data element at risk:

- The approximate volume or number of transactions that pass (or should pass) through a programmed procedure or data file. The auditor can use a number of techniques to make a reasonable estimate of volume. Examples might include inquiries of knowledgeable organization personnel, review of statistical records maintained by personnel operating the system, review of usage of serially numbered documents, use of audit software, or review of record counts printed on reports.

- The estimated monetary value of the transactions that pass (or should pass) through the programmed procedure or data file and the approximate range of individual transactions. The auditor can use a number of techniques to make a reasonable estimate of the monetary value, such as inquiries of knowledgeable organization personnel, review of records maintained by personnel operating the system, review of the organization's internal financial operating statements, use of audit software, or review of report totals.

- The effect of errors on management information.

- Whether the organization applies special control procedures to certain kinds of transactions. An example might be the review of exception reports of transactions that have a relatively high monetary value or fail to conform with established norms. In this case, however, the auditor will be concerned with the correctness of the exception reporting programs.

- The specific effect that a program or data error would have on the financial statements. Ordinarily, the materiality threshold is lower for items such as net income, working capital, and restrictions on retained earnings than it is for items that affect only classification in financial statements. For example, a control weakness that can lead to an overstatement of inventory is more likely to be material if the offsetting erroneous credit is to income than if it is to accounts payable. Errors in master file data are likely to have a greater cumulative effect than errors in transaction data.

The external auditor should consider these factors, among others, in answering the RCW question, "Could material error arise?" After making a judgment that there is only a remote possibility that a material error could arise, the auditor should answer the question "no."

Other Controls

If the auditor concludes that significant error can arise from a control weakness, consideration should be given to whether other controls can be relied on to ensure that material errors do not, in fact, arise. (Since the ICQ does not include redundant questions, this situation also does not occur frequently in practice.)

Modification of the Substantive Procedures

If an external auditor concludes that material error can arise, it is necessary to modify the substantive procedures to determine whether the financial statements are materially misstated as a result of the control weakness. The auditor should ensure that the modification is relevant to the specific control weakness.

Ordinarily the auditor performs the procedures related to balance sheet accounts as of the year-end date. The extent, if any, to which substantive procedures should be applied to transactions, data files, or programs processed during the year depends on the need to see whether material losses have occurred as a result of the control weakness. Those losses need to be disclosed in the financial statements or as a service to the organization. In some cases, the results of the auditor's review of relevant performance indicators may be of some assistance in determining the required extent of substantive procedures on transactions processed during the year.

As mentioned subsequently, the ICRM includes a discussion of the effect of a "no" answer on the audit procedures. In practice, the auditor should consider all the relevant "no" answers before finalizing the substantive procedures. Whether the organization has other controls that would mitigate the audit significance of the control weakness should be considered.

Organization of the ICRM for General Controls

The ICRM for general controls in computer systems is organized under headings that correspond to the control objectives dealing with the different types of general controls. The explanation of the questions within the control objectives is structured as follows:

- *Group* — A heading describes the type of controls considered in the group in relation to particular questions in the ICQ.

- *Purpose* — Appears immediately following the question and explains the purpose of the control procedures covered by the question.

- *What constitutes adequate control procedures?* — Sets forth in general terms the procedures usually necessary to ensure adequate internal controls. The procedures described assume a familiarity with computer processing, EDP department procedures, and system software, but do not deal with procedures specific to particular processing environments or systems.

- *Possible errors and audit effect* — Describes the usual effect of "no" answers on the application systems or other general controls and on the audit procedures. This section describes the general effect when one or more of the questions is answered "no." The information is set out in three parts, as follows:

a. *Possible errors in application systems* — Explains the types of errors that could be present in the application systems or other general controls as a result of the control weakness described. The actual errors can be determined only by analyzing the systems to identify the programmed procedures and data at risk.

b. *Example* — Illustrates some of the errors that may be present as a result of the control weakness.

c. *Effect on audit procedures* — Describes the changes that usually would be made in audit procedures as a result of the control weakness. This assumes that if the control were present, the audit procedures would have been based on reliance on that control. That is, compliance tests would have been emphasized and substantive tests restricted to the maximum extent possible. In this context, substantive tests include direct tests of programs and data carried out separately from the tests of control procedures.

Other points to keep in mind while using this section include the following:

• The paragraph on the effect on audit procedures often refers to audit software and other computer audit testing techniques. It is assumed that the reader is familiar with these techniques and with the circumstances in which they can be used. The actual tests applied are usually a suitable combination of the audit procedures suggested. This depends on many factors, such as the nature and number of application programs and data files at risk; the applicability, effectiveness, and efficiency of the technique in the actual environment involved; and the compounding effect of other weaknesses. References to Coopers & Lybrand's AUDITPAK II should be taken to include other generalized audit software packages, specially written programs, or any other method of achieving the same purpose (such as utility programs or use of an on-site report generator program).

• The auditor should consider whether the procedures set out under the heading "Effect on Audit Procedures" can be performed by organization personnel, subject to review and testing of results.

• The effects on audit procedures are discussed only in general terms. The auditor, in fact, performs specific audit procedures determined by the nature of the programmed procedures and data elements at risk. References to the use of AUDITPAK II and other techniques do not imply that use of the technique in isolation is a sufficient test. For example, audit software must be properly set up and applied to the correct data; the resulting reports must then be reviewed and tested by the auditor as required to complete the test.

IMPLEMENTATION CONTROLS — APPLICATION SYSTEMS DEVELOPMENT

PURPOSE:

To determine whether new application systems are suitably designed, authorized, and tested.

ADEQUATE CONTROL PROCEDURES:

All new systems descriptions, as revised during the design stages, are written down in appropriate detail and used as a basis for recording the mutual understanding and approval of both the non-EDP user organization and the EDP systems design and programming staff.

Comprehensive program and system testing is carried out or checked by EDP personnel independent of the programmers who wrote the programs being tested to confirm the compliance of the system in accordance with the approved system specifications.

POSSIBLE ERRORS. If system specifications are not prepared, not approved, or not properly tested, new applications may not function in accordance with management's intentions.

EXAMPLES. Programmed pricing or costing is performed accurately and consistently but contrary to company policy regarding rate classifications and discounts.

Due to a misunderstanding, the total inventory figure includes goods in transit which have already been sold to customers and therefore are included in accounts receivable.

EFFECT ON AUDIT PROCEDURES. If no system descriptions exist, the auditor should obtain oral representations of significant programmed procedures. The auditor reviews oral representations or system specifications to ensure that the applications appear to conform with generally accepted accounting principles (GAAP) and the organization's requirements. If necessary, the auditor discusses the procedures with users and EDP supervisory staff to ensure that the programmed procedures are appropriate.

To confirm oral representations or to check on unapproved or untested systems specifications, the auditor should consider

- Checking specifications or oral representations to source code, then independently confirming that the source code is actually in use (for example, by recompiling the source and carrying out an audit software program comparison). (See the section entitled "Program Security Controls.")
- Reprocessing data manually or with audit software and comparing the audit result with the organization's result.
- Using test data or an Integrated Test Facility (ITF).
- Using AUDITPAK II or other audit software to analyze processed data for unusual or unlikely results.

IMPLEMENTATION CONTROLS — APPLICATION SYSTEMS MAINTENANCE

PURPOSE:

To determine whether program modifications are authorized, and are implemented completely and accurately.

ADEQUATE CONTROL PROCEDURES:

- Modifications are recorded and approved.
- All programs and systems are adequately documented so that when changes have to be made they can be made accurately.
- Changed program procedures are tested together with the effects of the modification on unchanged parts of the system.
- Program modifications are controlled for completeness and implementation.

POSSIBLE ERRORS. If program modifications are not documented, not approved, or not properly tested, the possible errors and the effect on audit procedures are the same for changed systems as for new systems, described previously under "Systems Development." The auditor should also consider the use of program comparison software to check the accuracy of changes made. (See the section entitled "Program Security Controls.")

If program modifications are not controlled for completeness, the organization may not know which systems have been changed, and critical changes or changes due on a certain date may become overdue.

EXAMPLE. Legislation required changes to a payroll system in relation to withholding and payroll taxes. Because the change was not made, the company has an undisclosed liability for back taxes and penalties.

EFFECT ON AUDIT PROCEDURES. By reviewing documentation and by discussions with users and data processing staff, the auditor should determine changes that should have been made and confirm that these changes have been made.

The auditor should consider using program comparison software or other techniques to identify unchanged programs that should have been changed.

IMPLEMENTATION CONTROLS — APPLICATION SYSTEMS FINAL ACCEPTANCE

PURPOSE:

To determine whether the necessary supervisory reviews have been performed before new and changed systems are accepted into production. The review helps to ensure adherence to standards of documentation, testing, and approval.

ADEQUATE CONTROL PROCEDURES:

Adequate procedures deal with controls for supervisory review and approval.

POSSIBLE ERRORS. If final reviews by responsible officials in user departments and the data processing functions are not carried out, refer to application system development and maintenance for procedures to follow. In the absence of a supervisory control, these procedures may not be performed. Accordingly, the possible errors are the same as when the control procedures do not exist.

EXAMPLE. The personnel performing the procedures observe that their work is not reviewed by anyone and they start to omit some of the important control steps.

EFFECT ON AUDIT PROCEDURES. To determine whether the related basic and division of duties controls have continued to operate properly, the auditor should perform the supervisory review for selected periods during the year. (Refer to the common control procedure for "Supervision.")

IMPLEMENTATION CONTROLS — CATALOGING

PURPOSE:

To determine whether procedures are adequate to ensure that only authorized and tested programs are properly taken into production.

ADEQUATE CONTROL PROCEDURES:

- An appropriate combination of manual and software procedures ensures that programs are properly tested and authorized prior to being taken into production.
- Procedures are adequate to ensure that no unauthorized changes can be made to programs after final testing and authorization but prior to their being taken into production.
- All forms of a program (such as source listing, source library, object program, executable program) are checked as being accurate and derived from the same source.

POSSIBLE ERRORS. If unauthorized or untested programs can be taken into production, the possible errors and effects on audit procedures are the same as those described under "Application Systems Development" and "Program Security Controls." Refer to tests indicated there.

If all forms of a program are not the same — specifically, if source versions differ from executable forms — subsequent modification and recompilation of the source version will introduce any deficiencies present in the source program into the executable program.

EXAMPLE. A utility program has been used to modify an object program without altering the source library program, which, as a consequence, is out of date. A subsequent modification is required and achieved by amending and recompiling the source library program. However, this produces an executable program that lacks the modification originally introduced using the utility, and consequently the processing using the program is incorrect.

EFFECT ON AUDIT PROCEDURES. The auditor should consider using program comparison software to ensure that source and executable forms of programs are the same. If there is a possibility that an error has already been introduced (as in the preceding example), the following procedures can help identify it:

- Reprocessing actual data using AUDITPAK II or other audit software, and comparing the results with those obtained using the organization's program.
- Using test data or ITF to test the correctness of the important programmed procedures, taking care to ensure that the program tested is the one actually in use.
- Using linkage analysis software to determine potential mismatches due to the use of utility programs. (See Chapter 28, "Testing Techniques for Computer-Based Systems.")

IMPLEMENTATION CONTROLS — SUPERVISION OF CATALOGING

PURPOSE:

To determine whether cataloging procedures are reviewed, thereby ensuring that the basic and disciplinary controls have continued to operate.

ADEQUATE CONTROL PROCEDURES:

These questions deal with the controls for supervisory review and approval.

POSSIBLE ERRORS. If the supervisory control is absent, refer to "Implementation Controls — Cataloging." In the absence of a supervisory control, these procedures may not be performed. Accordingly, the possible errors are the same as when these control procedures are not performed.

EXAMPLE. The people performing the cataloging procedures observe that their work is not reviewed by anyone and they start to omit some of the important control steps.

EFFECT ON AUDIT PROCEDURES. To determine whether the related basic division of duties and custodial controls have continued to operate properly, the auditor should perform the supervisory review for selected periods during the year. Refer to the common control procedure for "Supervision."

PROGRAM SECURITY CONTROLS

PURPOSE:

To determine whether all changes to production programs are authorized.

ADEQUATE CONTROL PROCEDURES:

- Access to originals or copies of production program and system documentation is restricted, on a need-to-know basis, to computer programmers and systems analysts, librarians, custodians, EDP officials, and auditors and "user" organization officials.
- All changes to programs loaded or resident on the computer system are authorized either before or after the change takes place.
- Access to back-up copies and other copies of programs stored on computer media is restricted to authorized users.
- Unsupervised access to the computer room and libraries is properly restricted.

POSSIBLE ERRORS. If changes can be made to production programs, bypassing the normal controls over program modifications, then

- Unauthorized or incorrectly made changes may cause the programs to cease functioning in accordance with management's intentions.
- Users may not be aware of changes made; as a result user procedures on the output may no longer be appropriate.
- Opportunities for the misappropriation of assets through changes to programs are increased.

EXAMPLES

- A programmer believes a program can be made more efficient and makes a change. Because the change is not tested, the program now produces incorrect results.
- A change is made to the inventory system to show "inventory in transit" as a separate figure. However, the control account procedures are not changed and the company's inventory figure in the general ledger is understated by the amount of goods in transit.

- A change is made to a payments system to make fictitious payments. The control total balancing programs are also adjusted to disguise the difference.

EFFECT ON AUDIT PROCEDURES. The auditor should consider

- Using program comparison software or other techniques to identify changed programs and ensure that the changes made were properly documented, approved, and tested.
- Reviewing the source code for unusual or inappropriate code then independently confirming that the source code is actually in use. For example, an auditor might recompile the source code and reprocess actual data using the recompiled programs to ensure that the result is the same as the organization's result.
- Reprocessing actual data manually or with AUDITPAK II or other audit software, and comparing the audit result with the organization's result.
- Using test data or ITF to test the correctness of the programs. If the user retains test data and results, consider reprocessing this test data to ensure that the programs are still functioning properly. Precautions must be taken to ensure that the programs tested are those in use.
- Reviewing records of processing activities for evidence of unauthorized changes to production libraries, such as the use of an SMF (IBM's System Management Facility) analyzer audit software program.
- Taking inventories of documentation and back-up copies of program files to identify any unauthorized withdrawals.
- Using AUDITPAK II or other audit software to analyze processed data for unusual or unlikely results. Software can also assist in ensuring that control accounts are made up of individual items by footing the file and printing a selection of detailed records.

Note that most of the preceding techniques do not always detect deliberate irregularities when the evidence of changes has been removed (such as a program that is changed and then changed back). The auditor should therefore consider performing tests on a surprise basis.

PROGRAM SECURITY CONTROLS — SUPERVISION

PURPOSE:

To determine whether the procedures that control the security of programs are reviewed. This review helps to ensure that the basic controls continue to operate.

ADEQUATE CONTROL PROCEDURES:

These questions deal with the controls for supervisory review and approval.

POSSIBLE ERRORS. If the supervisory control is absent, these procedures may not be performed. Accordingly, the possible errors are the same as when these control procedures are not performed.

EXAMPLE. The people performing the procedures observe that their work is not reviewed by anyone and they start to omit some of the important control steps.

EFFECT ON AUDIT PROCEDURES. To determine whether the related basic division of duties and custodial controls have continued to operate properly, the auditor should perform the supervisory review for selected periods during the year. (Refer to the common control procedure for "Supervision.")

COMPUTER OPERATIONS CONTROLS — JOB SET-UP

PURPOSE:

To determine whether jobs are set up in accordance with authorized instructions.

ADEQUATE CONTROL PROCEDURES:

There should be authorized standing instructions for each production job. All variations to parameters and departures from the instructions should be checked and authorized.

POSSIBLE ERRORS. If jobs are not set up in accordance with authorized procedures, the results of processing may be incorrect. The incorrect results could occur at any time.

EXAMPLE. The cycle billing calendar requires two cycles to be run on a particular day. Because the calendar was not referred to, or checked, the job was set up to bill only one cycle. Statements for the other cycle were not sent and amounts due were not shown as past due.

EFFECT ON AUDIT PROCEDURES. The auditor should determine for each production job what could go wrong and whether or not the error would be detected. The audit procedures used depend on the type of error discovered. The auditor should consider

- Using AUDITPAK II or other audit software to analyze files (particularly cumulative transaction files and master file or standing data) for unusual or erroneous conditions.

- Using AUDITPAK II or other audit software to reprocess user data and compare results to user's results.
- Spreading substantive tests throughout the year to search for the effects of inconsistent processing.
- Extending cutoff tests.
- Searching for significant errors, particularly in payment systems and other systems where people might also have some access to assets, by
  a. Use of AUDITPAK II or other audit software to search for erroneous or exceptional transactions.
  b. Surprise visit to interrogate files and compare programs.
  c. Surprise manual audit of assets at risk, such as surprise securities count.
- Carrying out extended tests on account balances. Consider use of AUDITPAK II, as indicated previously.

COMPUTER OPERATIONS CONTROLS — SUPERVISION OF JOB SET-UP

PURPOSE:

To determine whether job set-up procedures are reviewed, thereby ensuring that the basic and disciplinary controls have continued to operate.

ADEQUATE CONTROL PROCEDURES:

This question deals with the controls for supervisory review and approval.

POSSIBLE ERRORS. If the supervisory control is absent, refer to questions under "Job Set-Up." In the absence of a supervisory control, these procedures may not be performed. Accordingly, the possible errors are the same as when these control procedures are not performed.

EXAMPLE. The people performing the procedures observe that their work is not reviewed by anyone and they start to omit some of the important control steps.

EFFECT ON AUDIT PROCEDURES. To determine whether the related basic division of duties and custodial controls have continued to operate properly, the auditor should perform the supervisory review for selected periods during the year. Refer to the common control procedure for "Supervision."

COMPUTER OPERATIONS CONTROLS — OPERATOR ACTIONS

PURPOSE:

To determine whether the activities of operating the computer system are performed properly.

ADEQUATE CONTROL PROCEDURES:

- Up-to-date operating instructions exist.
- The activities of operators are supervised. Unusual situations and resulting operator actions are reviewed and approved.

POSSIBLE ERRORS. If up-to-date operating instructions do not exist, required operating procedures may not be followed.

EXAMPLE. An external person telephoned the operator to say he had forgotten the password. Because there were no instructions stating that passwords were not to be given out, the operator gave this person the password. As a result the person was able to fraudulently read and amend data through a telephone connection in the system.

EFFECT ON AUDIT PROCEDURES. Refer to the procedures set out under "Job Set-Up."

POSSIBLE ERRORS. If operator actions are not supervised, unusual situations are not investigated, and recoveries from system failures not controlled, unauthorized or incorrect operator actions may remain undetected.

EXAMPLE. As a result of a disk head crash, the file containing the inventory costs was destroyed. The operator mistakenly loaded the previous year's costs file from backup data. Through lack of supervision, no entry was recorded in the problem log and thus no check was performed to ensure that the correct action was taken. Inventory was understated.

EFFECT ON AUDIT PROCEDURES. Refer to procedures set out under "Job Set-Up."

DATA FILE SECURITY CONTROLS

PURPOSE:

To determine whether data files are protected against unauthorized change or access.

ADEQUATE CONTROL PROCEDURES:

If user controls are adequate to detect unauthorized use of data files, general controls need not be relied on in this respect. However, it is unlikely that this will be so, except in the simplest computer systems and in any case, general controls may still be important for operational reasons.

- A comprehensive security plan is in existence to identify all access paths into the system and to restrict access to resources and data on a need-to-know basis.
- Access to all documentation that provides details of file layouts or contents is restricted to authorized staff. In particular, computer operations personnel are not allowed access to this type of information.
- Physical security of files not in use (including backup copies) ensures that these are only issued for authorized processing.
- All access to loaded or resident data files is authorized either before or after it occurs.

POSSIBLE ERRORS. If unauthorized changes or access to data files can occur, opportunities will exist for the fraudulent or mischievous manipulation of data and missappropriation of assets.

The concentration of data in the EDP department means that changes can be made to all types of data records including individual transaction details, control data, and master file data. If controls over program file security are also weak, the possibilities for undetected manipulation of both data and processing are essentially limitless.

Changes to data may be used to cover up errors in processing arising from inadequate program procedures.

EXAMPLES.

- Fictitious employee data is written to the payroll master file. Payments are made automatically each period to the bank account so indicated.
- Fictitious supplier records are written to the accounts payable master file. Fictitious invoices are then written to the accounts payable detail file; checks are generated automatically each month for these items and sent to the address indicated in the master file data. Program procedures are amended to ensure that the fictitious information is never printed out or included in control totals, except in the case of checks, which are included in the detail check listing used for bank reconciliation procedures.
- Programmed reconciliation of file totals to a separate control file is relied on to ensure completeness and accuracy of update. The

program has not been completely debugged and occasionally differences arise. Control records are amended to force a balance, and the user is not aware that the reconciliation is in error.

EFFECT ON AUDIT PROCEDURES. Detailed audit procedures depend on the application controls over data files and the auditor's assessment of the likelihood that material error could arise. The auditor should consider

- Using AUDITPAK II or other audit software to analyze files (particularly cumulative transaction files) for unusual or erroneous conditions.
- Using AUDITPAK II or other audit software to reprocess user data and compare the audit results to the user results. This may indicate whether fictitious transactions have been inserted and then deleted from the history files.
- Spreading substantive tests throughout the year to search for unauthorized transactions.
- Searching particularly sensitive systems (such as payment systems and those involving liquid assets) for unauthorized processing. Methods might include
  a. Use of AUDITPAK II to search for errors or to assist in carrying out extended substantiation of account balances.
  b. Surprise interrogations of data files or manual audits of assets at risk.
- Reviewing records of processing activities for evidence of unauthorized changes or access to data files such as the use of SMF analyzer audit software.
- It should be noted that, depending on the extent of the weakness, deliberate irregularities could have occurred and all evidence subsequently removed. Carrying out tests on a surprise basis should be considered in an attempt to identify such situations.

DATA FILE SECURITY CONTROLS — SUPERVISION

PURPOSE:

To determine whether the procedures that control the security of data files are reviewed, thereby assuring that the basic controls continue to operate.

ADEQUATE CONTROL PROCEDURES:

These questions deal with the controls for supervisory review and approval.

POSSIBLE ERRORS. If the supervisory control is absent, refer to questions about data file security controls. In the absence of a supervisory control, these procedures may not be performed. Accordingly, the possible errors are the same as when these control procedures are not performed.

EXAMPLE. The people performing the procedures observe that their work is not reviewed by anyone and they start to omit some of the important control steps.

EFFECT ON AUDIT PROCEDURES. To determine whether the related basic division of duties and custodial controls have continued to operate properly, the auditor should perform the supervisory review for selected periods during the year. Refer to the common control procedure for "Supervision" for guidance on procedures to follow.

SYSTEM SOFTWARE CONTROLS

PURPOSE:

To ensure that system software that is relied on for the purpose of the general controls is appropriate.

ADEQUATE CONTROL PROCEDURES:

- The system software is appropriate to control the functions desired by the organization.
- The controls over system software are adequate to ensure that the software is properly implemented and kept secure.
- All appropriate action is taken with respect to system software output.

Just as application controls may depend on the proper functioning of programmed procedures, so general controls may depend on the proper functioning of system software. The relationship between the controls over system software and the rest of general controls is similar to the relationship between general controls and application controls.

POSSIBLE ERRORS. If system software procedures are not appropriate for the purposes intended or controls over system software are weak, the relevant portion of the general controls may be ineffective. Refer to the section of the general controls involved.

EXAMPLE. Management authorized the purchase of a well-known program library maintenance software product to control changes to production libraries. In order to enable the system to work more efficiently and to increase flexibility, the software programmer who installed the product did not also install its security features.

EFFECT ON AUDIT PROCEDURES. Refer to the section of the general controls involved.

POSSIBLE ERRORS. If system software output is not properly reviewed and acted on, the general control that depends on the action will be ineffective.

EXAMPLE. All changes to system-resident production program libraries are reported. However, the report is sent to the programmer who makes the change and not to an independent reviewer.

EFFECT ON AUDIT PROCEDURES. To determine if the review would have disclosed problems, the auditor should reperform the review spreading the tests throughout the year. Also, refer to the section of the general controls involved.

SYSTEM SOFTWARE CONTROLS — IMPLEMENTATION

PURPOSE:

To determine whether new system software and software changes are properly designed, authorized, tested, and implemented, and whether security of system software is adequate.

ADEQUATE CONTROL PROCEDURES:

- Specifications for new system software and software changes are recorded and approved.
- Changes to system software are controlled for completeness.
- System software designed or modified by the company is adequately tested.
- System software programmers are supervised.
- The security of the software is protected.

POSSIBLE ERRORS. If controls over system software are inadequate, the general controls that depend on the system software may not function correctly. Refer to the section of the general controls involved.

EXAMPLE. Management authorized the development of comprehensive software to protect its data files. However, management claimed that system software programmers were too difficult to control. The new software was designed, written, and installed to provide password protection to all data files. Because the work was not documented and supervised, no one noticed that the password file, all program files, and all system software files (including the protecting software itself) were not controlled. In addition, the data bases, which remained open all day, were unprotected.

EFFECT ON AUDIT PROCEDURES. The detailed audit procedures often depend on the general controls at risk. However, the auditor may be able to examine records of system software implemented to ensure that the proper procedures have been adopted. Some systems provide internal records of system software change activity which can be examined by the auditor. Refer also to the relevant section for the general controls at risk.

Internal Control Reference Manual — Application Controls

INTRODUCTION

The *Internal Control Reference Manual* (ICRM) for computer systems was designed by Coopers & Lybrand to assist the auditor in evaluating internal control in computer-based systems and in completing the Record of Control Weaknesses (RCW). The evaluation of internal control is based on consideration of control objectives as described in the standard Internal Control Questionnaire (ICQ) and may be achieved either by completing the Computer Internal Control Questionnaire (CICQ) or by using the Computer Control Matrix. The material that is discussed can be summarized as follows:

- Internal control in computer systems
- Structure of control in computer systems
- Design of the ICQ
- Structure of the CICQ
- Organization of the ICRM for computer systems

Reference should also be made to Chapter 26, "*Internal Control Reference Manual*—General Controls." The following points are relevant to both manual and computer systems:

- Appropriateness of evaluation of control procedures
- Evaluation of "no" answers

INTERNAL CONTROL IN COMPUTER SYSTEMS

The definition and related basic concepts of control are expressed in terms of control objectives that are independent of the method used to process data. Consequently, they apply equally to manual or computer-based data processing systems. However, the nature of computer processing creates significant changes in methods of processing and controlling data. The availability of different control techniques therefore results in changes in the manner of applying and evaluating control in computer systems. The extent of change depends on the scope of computer processing in each system. The principal features of control in computer systems are

- Many accounting and control procedures that had previously been carried out manually are replaced by steps in the computer programs. These steps are called "programmed procedures."
- Data is held on computer files as well as in manual records. This may affect the way controls are applied to prevent unauthorized changes to data. In particular, consideration should be given to those controls within the EDP department that are designed to prevent unauthorized access to data files. These controls may be particularly important when reliance on programmed procedures results in reduced checking of the output from processing. Therefore, the need for controls over the continued correctness of data on computer files is increased.

Programmed Procedures

Programmed procedures consist of precise processing instructions embedded in the computer programs. Good control requires that these instructions are correct and function consistently. Then the organization and the control designer/reviewer can place reliance on the programmed procedures in their contribution to an adequate system of internal control. Usually, the effective operation of programmed procedures is achieved by controlling the design, implementation, security, and use of computer programs. Although the same assurance might be obtained by checking the results of processing, this method is usually less efficient because of the volume of data that would have to be reported and checked.

Programmed procedures are of concern when they relate to

- Procedures identified as control functions when carried out manually, such as a programmed sequence check that produces a list of missing or duplicate numbers.
- Procedures of an accounting nature that would be subject to checking in a noncomputer system, such as the automatic generation of insurance premium renewals.

In many cases, programmed procedures are an important part of the common control procedures. The appropriateness of the programmed procedures is therefore relevant to the adequacy of a particular control technique. For this reason, comments on adequacy of control should include, where applicable, a note of what would be an acceptable programmed procedure.

General Controls

The controls over the design, implementation, security, and use of computer programs, and the security of data files, are referred to as general, or integrity, controls. These controls usually apply equally to all applications, operate within the EDP department, and are a combination of manual and system software procedures. System software is computer programs of a general nature and includes operating systems, compilers, librarian and utility programs, and data base management systems. General controls should also ensure the correct implementation and security of system software. Adequacy of general controls is discussed in Chapter 20, "General or Integrity Controls," and in Chapter 26.

User Controls

User controls refer to those manual controls carried out by a user department on the data being processed. Here, a user is defined as a person, other than those in systems development, systems maintenance, and computer operations, who is involved with computer processing. Users are those who prepare input, take action on output, or otherwise use the system for business functions. User controls often depend on programmed control procedures, as when users follow up on exception reports.

STRUCTURE OF CONTROL IN COMPUTER SYSTEMS

Overall control of computer systems is achieved by a suitable combination of application controls and general controls.

Application Controls

Application controls are the specific controls over each separate computer system which should ensure that only authorized data is completely and accurately processed. They consist of a combination of programmed procedures and user controls. Application controls are the subject of this chapter.

Application controls, as they relate to a computer system, may be considered under the following headings:

- *Completeness of input and update*—All transactions must reach the computer and subsequently be recorded on the computer files, once and once only.

- *Accuracy of input and update*—Data reaches the computer accurately and is recorded correctly on the computer files.

- *Validity (authorization)*—Data is authorized or otherwise checked as to the appropriateness of the transaction.

- *Maintenance (continuity)*—Data on computer files continues to remain correct and current.

If adequate overall control of a computer system is to be achieved, the combination of user controls and programmed procedures must ensure that all the aspects of control listed previously are satisfactory.

The control structure adopted for each application should take the whole sequence of processing—from the time transactions occur to the time the relevant output is used—into account. A wide variety of control techniques may be applied to ensure that the overall system of control is effective. Consideration should be given to the fact that a control weakness at one point can often be compensated for by the operation of a strong control at another stage of processing. For instance, certain types of controls over the maintenance of master file data, such as a manual check of all items reported on a full printout of the file, may compensate for weaknesses in the areas of input and update.

Since different controls are likely to be applied to the different stages of processing, it is necessary to be satisfied that there is no break in the control sequence and that overall control is achieved. When considering the effectiveness of a series of controls, it is important to identify two stages in the exercise of a control technique:

1. The stage of processing at which control is established, such as the recording of transactions on sequentially prenumbered documents
2. The stage of processing at which the control operates, such as the identification and reporting of missing and duplicate numbers for investigation.

In order to achieve an unbroken line of control, each control technique used in a sequence of controls must establish control at or before the stage at which the previous control operates. For example, if completeness of input is ensured by a computer sequence check of sequentially prenumbered documents, and completeness of update is ensured by run-to-run control totals, then a total of accepted items must be accumulated during or before the run in which the sequence check operates and must subsequently be agreed to the total of items updated to the master file. This ensures that transactions are not lost between input and update stages. The use of a series of different controls and the associated possibilities for uncontrolled gaps are particularly important when evaluating controls over the completeness of transaction processing.

Standards of Control

Establishing an adequate overall control system may involve a variety of control techniques. The decision whether to control or not includes consideration of the cost/benefit relationship of the control. Two factors that can be expected to influence the decision are

1. Different control techniques have different levels of complexity, efficiency, and expense; and
2. Different transaction and data types require different standards of accuracy and checking; the strength of control required depends on the ultimate use of the data, the existence of compensating controls during later stages of processing, and the effect of errors on the financial statements.

Common standards of control required are:

- Master file data usually requires a higher standard of control than transaction data. In general, an individual error in transaction data affects only that one transaction, whereas an error in master file data, which may be used each time the file is processed, may affect many or even all transactions processed.

- Programmed procedures require a high standard of control, since they can affect all data processed each time a program is run.

- Different data fields within a transaction or record may also vary in the standard of control required. Financial data is usually significant, but the standard of control necessary for reference data (such as codes, indicators, and dates) depends on the ultimate use of that data.

- Transactions that deal with liquid assets (such as cash, payroll, accounts payable, credits, or receivables) may require a higher standard of control.

- Data processed manually generally requires greater checking for accuracy and completeness due to the inconsistent performance of people. Data processed by programmed procedures generally requires greater manual scrutiny for unusual situations or errors that may not have been foreseen when the system was designed and therefore may be treated incorrectly by the programs.

Principal Controls

In many situations, several control techniques that satisfy the same control objective are in use. This happens due to the operational requirements of computer systems. Errors must be continually monitored and controlled so that subsequent computer processing is not inefficiently repeated or corrected. Principal control techniques are those that

- Give more conclusive evidence of control. For example, a cumulative report of missing sequence numbers, with evidence of the taking of appropriate corrective action, provides more conclusive evidence of completeness than the manual reconciliation of batch totals.
- Are stronger alternatives. For example, a one-for-one check usually provides greater certainty as to the accuracy of input than does an edit check that the data is within a range. The strength of a control depends both on the effectiveness of the clerical action and on the function of the appropriate programmed procedures.
- Cover several areas of control. For example, a control account that covers completeness of input and update, accurate input and update of the dollar total, and maintenance of the dollar total is more efficient to test than a combination of alternate controls.
- Provide evidence as to the consistent and proper operation of programmed procedures.
- Detect the error earlier in the processing cycle.
- Automate the control process.

DESIGN OF THE INTERNAL CONTROL QUESTIONNAIRE

Although the control objectives remain the same whether processing is manual or computerized, two sets of detailed questions in the ICQ have been designed to recognize the differences in methods of processing and control techniques between computer and manual systems. The group of control objectives for which detailed computer questions have been prepared is found collectively within the CICQ. If there are insufficient differences in control techniques to warrant separate questions, or it is considered that relevant procedures are unlikely to involve computer processing, computer-related questions are not prepared. A Control Matrix has also been designed as an alternative to the use of the computer-related questionnaire. The matrix is a form used to record the control designer/reviewer's evaluation of controls in a computer-based system. It may be employed, instead of detailed computer questions, for any of the control objectives in the CICQ.

For each relevant control objective, the control designer/reviewer should select either the manual questions or the computer questions/matrix. The complete ICQ for any system where computer processing is involved is, consequently, a combination of computer and noncomputer control objectives. Because computer systems differ in complexity, the extent to which the different documents are used varies from system to system.

The general rule is that computer questions or the Control Matrix should be selected when any of the processing relating to a particular control objective is performed by computer. Since most such control objectives incorporate both manual and computer procedures, questions to evaluate the associated manual controls are included in the computer-related questions. Therefore it is not necessary to complete both computer and manual forms of a control objective (unless two separate systems, one manual and one computer, exist and both are relevant).

The ICQ is designed so that any combination of manual and computer control objectives can be assembled to form the complete ICQ.

STRUCTURE OF THE COMPUTER INTERNAL CONTROL QUESTIONNAIRE

The CICQ refers to those control objectives for which detailed computer questions have been prepared. In addition, there are two separate sections:

1. Master file data controls
2. General controls

These sections are completed in response to "trigger" questions included in the control objectives.

Master File Data Controls

The section of the CICQ dealing with master file data controls evaluates controls over amendments to and maintenance of master file data held on computer files. Within each control objective to which these controls apply, there is a trigger question that refers to the master file data controls section and asks that consideration be given to the adequacy of the relevant data controls. As a general rule, this section of the CICQ need not be completed unless there is a trigger question in the transaction portion of the questionnaire.

General Controls

General controls are controls in the EDP department that provide assurance as to the reliability and consistent functioning of programmed procedures and the security of data files. In certain simple computer systems, management may not need to place reliance on general controls because the concerns are adequately satisfied by user procedures. Situations of this kind are becoming so unusual, however, that it may be more efficient to place reliance on general controls.

At the end of each computer control objective there is a "trigger" question that

- Requires a listing of all the programmed procedures that are relevant to the control objective and are not adequately controlled by user procedures.
- Refers the control designer/reviewer to the general controls section of the ICQ to determine whether the requisite procedures exist to ensure the continued reliability of the programmed procedures identified.

For those computer control objectives that include questions on data file security, the control designer/reviewer is first asked whether there are adequate user controls. If user controls are not adequate, the section on general controls helps determine whether these general controls provide the necessary data security.

Organization of Detailed Questions

Within each control objective, detailed questions are organized under headings corresponding to those aspects of control that have been listed. When several different control objectives may be met, a preliminary question lists the techniques that are likely to be encountered. The control designer/reviewer is asked to identify the principal control on which reliance will be placed. When answering this question, the following points should be borne in mind:

- A single principal control must be identified for each of the transaction types processed by the system.
- The control technique used may be different for different transaction types.
- The identification of a principal control points to the particular group of detailed questions that assesses the adequacy of the control. Detailed questions on a particular control technique should be answered only if that technique has been identified as a principal control. Furthermore, the answers should be given only for those transaction types controlled by that particular technique.

Evidence of Control. Except in the case of certain programmed procedures, the CICQ does not ask whether control procedures are evidenced, on the grounds that control cannot be adequate if it is not evidenced. If procedures are not evidenced, the control designer/reviewer should give a "no" answer and include the reason for that answer.

Disciplines Over Basic Controls. Internal controls consist of basic controls and disciplines over basic controls. Basic controls are those that are necessary for the reliability of the data and records. Disciplines over basic controls help ensure the continued and proper operation of basic controls and the safeguarding of assets. The CICQ has separate questions to assess disciplines over basic controls.

ORGANIZATION OF THE ICRM FOR COMPUTER SYSTEMS

The ICRM for computer systems consists of two volumes. The introduction and the common application control procedures found in one volume have been edited for inclusion in this chapter. Considerations relating to general controls comprise a separate volume, which is presented in Chapter 26.

Common Control Procedures

As discussed previously, it is convenient to classify controls in computer systems according to the particular aspect of processing that they cover, such as input, update, maintenance, validity, and so forth. Superimposed on this categorization of controls are the particular techniques that can be used to achieve control.

In order to facilitate reference to the CICQ, the discussion of common control procedures is structured in much the same way as the individual computer control objectives. The adequacy of individual control techniques is discussed within each aspect of control. Consequently, certain control techniques appear under more than one heading. For example, the use of batch totals is included under completeness of input and update, accuracy of input and update, and maintenance of data files.

Disciplines over user controls are not considered in detail in the ICRM, since the specific requirements for supervisory controls, custodial controls, and a proper segregation of duties vary with, and are adequately described in, each individual control objective in the ICQ.

STANDARD CONTROL OBJECTIVES FOR APPLICATIONS

Some of the common control objectives for widely used applications are discussed in the following sections.

Payment Cycle

Orders. Purchases should be initiated only on the basis of appropriate authorization. Records of commitments should be maintained as a basis for

- Determining that transactions are executed in accordance with authorization, and
- Establishing the amount of any provision required for losses arising from unfulfilled commitments.

Receipts. Control should be established over goods and services received as a basis for

- Determining and recording the liability for goods and services received but not entered as accounts payable, and
- Where required, posting the items to detailed inventory records.

Returns. Control should be established over goods returned to, and claims on, suppliers as a basis for

- Obtaining credit for all such items, and
- Where required, posting the items to detailed inventory records.

Approval. Invoices and related documentation should be properly checked and approved as being valid before being entered as accounts payable.

Posting. All valid accounts payable transactions, and only those transactions, should be accurately recorded as accounts payable.

Petty Cash. Reimbursements of imprest and similar funds (such as postage and other franking meters) should be made only for valid transactions.

Checks. Disbursements from bank accounts should be made only for valid transactions.

Raw Materials. Accurate detailed records should be maintained of materials and supplies inventories.

Fixed Asset Approval. Additions to and disposals of property, plant, and equipment should be properly authorized.

Fixed Asset Depreciation. Accurate records should be maintained of the cost and accumulated depreciation of property, plant, and equipment.

Account Distribution. General ledger entries arising from the payment cycle should be accurately determined.

Payroll. Payments with respect to wages and salaries should be

- Made only to company employees at authorized rates of pay;
- Where required, in accordance with records of work performed; and
- Accurately calculated.

Deductions. Payroll deductions should be correctly accounted for and paid to the third parties to whom they are due.

Production Cycle

Approval. Control should be established over

- Issues from inventories of materials and supplies to production and returns;
- Charges to production for labor and overheads; and
- Transfers from production to inventories of parts and finished products, as a basis, when required, for making the entries in the inventory records.

This control objective does not cover the controls over the receipt of materials and supplies from suppliers that are put directly into production or the shipment of finished products directly from production to customers. These are included within the scope of other control objectives.

Posting. Accurate inventory records should be maintained for work in progress.

Account Distribution. General ledger entires arising from the production cycle should be determined accurately. This control objective does not cover the general ledger entries for the receipt of raw materials and supplies that are put directly into production and the shipment to customers of finished products directly from production, which are included within the scope of other control objectives.

Revenue Cycle

Orders. Records should be maintained of unfulfilled sales commitments, as a basis for determining any provisions required for losses that may arise.

Shipments. Control should be established over goods shipped and services performed as a basis for

- Making charges to customers for all such sales.
- Determining the amount of the related revenues that have not been entered as accounts receivable.
- Making the related entries in the detailed inventory records, when required.

This control objective is not intended to cover sales in retail and similar businesses, where the invoices or similar documents are issued to customers at the same time the goods are supplied or returned.

Cash Sales. Control should be established over cash sales of goods and services as a basis for

- Accounting for all such sales, and
- When required, making the related entries in the detailed inventory records.

For this purpose "cash sales" should be regarded as including credit sales made under similar conditions, such as when the customer receives the goods or services on the vendor's premises and the sales invoice or similar document is issued to the customer simultaneously.

Returns. Control should be established over goods returned by and claims received from customers as a basis for

- Determining and recording the liability for goods returned and claims received but not entered in the accounts receivable records, and
- When required, making the related entries in the detailed inventory records.

Approval and Pricing. All charges and credits should be appropriately checked as being valid before being entered in the accounts receivable records.

Posting. All valid accounts receivable transactions, and only those transactions, should be accurately recorded as accounts receivable.

Cash Receipts. Control should be established over all cash and checks received, and they should be deposited promptly in the organization's bank accounts.

Finished Goods. Accurate, detailed records should be maintained of finished products.

- The procedure should normally cover inventories of finished products that have been manufactured by the company and are held in stock (either on the company's premises or in the hands of third parties). In some cases, it may also be appropriate to cover certain of the inventory categories covered by other controls, as when these are accounted for by the company as part of finished products, rather than materials and supplies inventories.
- If the inventories of finished products are recorded in the same records, and are subject to the same controls, as those for materials and supplies covered under other control objectives, there is no need to complete a separate questionnaire.

The inventory categories covered by the answers to the ICQ questions should be stated.

Account Distribution. General ledger entries arising from the revenue cycle should be determined accurately.

Time Cycle

Financial Reports. All financial reports (both internal and external) should be prepared accurately and submittted on a consistent and timely basis.

Inventory. Adequate procedures should be followed to confirm the physical existence of inventories recorded in the general ledger. When the physical existence of inventories is determined other than on a continuous basis, the compliance tests of the answers to the detailed ICQ questions are normally carried out as part of the substantive tests.

Inventory Costing. Costs attributable to inventories should be determined accurately.

Inventory Provisions. Adequate steps should be taken to identify all inventories for which provisions may be required.

Fixed Asset Counts. Adequate steps should be taken to confirm the physical existence of and, when appropriate, the titles to property, plant, and equipment.

Bad Debts. All doubtful accounts receivable should be identified, either individually or by category, as a basis for determining any provisions required for such accounts.

Bank Reconciliation. Adequate steps should be taken to confirm the accuracy of the bank balance shown in the general ledger.

Investments. Investments should be adequately safeguarded and accurately accounted for.

These ICQ questions relate to a company that does not have sufficient volume of trading in, or holdings of, securities to justify more detailed procedure for control over security transactions.

Accurate records should be maintained in respect to outstanding capital stock and debt obligations. Transactions relating to these should be considered under adequate accounting control, including appropriate segregation of duties.

General Ledger

All valid general ledger entries, and only those entries, should be accurately recorded in the general ledger.

COMPUTER INTERNAL CONTROL QUESTIONNAIRE FOR COMPUTER APPLICATION CONTROLS

The CICQ — Applications document is comprised of the following parts:

- List of standard control objectives
- Application control objectives with questions for computer-based systems
- Master file data controls
- Examples of functional tests

The information in this ICRM is structured to correspond to the CICQ.

Computer general controls are not addressed in this document. A separate CICQ for general or integrity controls is used to assist in evaluating those controls. (See Chapter 26.)

The computer application control objectives described previously correspond to the control objectives of the manual questionnaire. Certain control objectives in the manual ICQ are pertinent even when the accounting records are computer-based.

ADEQUACY OF CONTROLS OVER COMPLETENESS OF INPUT AND UPDATE

Obviously it is important that all transactions are recorded, input, and updated to the correct master file. This requirement is referred to as the completeness of input and update. It should not be confused with the accuracy of input and update. The reason for the distinction is that different techniques are often used to control completeness and accuracy. Completeness means simply that all the transactions were processed, whereas accuracy is concerned with information in the data fields making up each transaction.

Questions dealing with these procedures appear under many control objectives in the ICQ and CICQ. Adequacy of control is discussed here for convenience and to emphasize that similar control procedures may apply to different cycles and different control objectives.

Various techniques are available to establish completeness of input and update. For convenience, they can be considered under the following headings:

- One-for-one checking
- Agreement of manually established batch totals
- Computer sequence check of serially numbered documents
- Computer matching with a file of previous accepted data
- Run-to-run controls
- Rejections
- Reliance on controls over another application

Each of these techniques is discussed in detail in the following sections.

Some controls over completeness of input can also ensure completeness of update. In order to ensure completeness of update in this situation, the input control must be exercised at or after the update process. For example, input controls involving the checking of reports may ensure completeness of update, provided the output report is produced at, or after, update. If separate controls are used to achieve completeness of input and update, the update control must be established at the time, or before, the input control is exercised. Otherwise there will be a break in the control sequence and overall control will not be adequate.

ONE-FOR-ONE CHECKING

SITUATION 1:

The user department retains copies of all documents submitted for processing and checks these off individually against a report of transactions processed.

IMPACT ON ADEQUACY OF CONTROL. The extent of control achieved depends on the stage of processing at which the information on the report is gathered. If this is done during the input stage, control will be adequate to ensure that data is input completely. If the report shows data actually updated onto the master file at the time of update, control over completeness of both input and update will be assured.

EXAMPLE. Amendments to payroll master file data are prepared by the personnel office staff, who retain a copy of all documents submitted for processing. A report is received that shows data updated onto the payroll master file. This is checked on a one-for-one basis with the document copies retained in the personnel office.

SITUATION 2:

The user department agrees details on a printout, produced during either input or update, to input documents returned from data processing.

IMPACT ON ADEQUACY OF CONTROL. Control is not adequate unless there are additional procedures to ensure that all documents are returned from the EDP department. Adequate procedures would include a document count over data sent for processing or a manual sequence check over documents submitted for processing.

EXAMPLE. In the example for Situation 1, the personnel office does not retain copies of documents submitted for processing. Instead, all documents are serially prenumbered and the personnel office maintains a control list of the numbers of the documents submitted. Checking this list against the document reference number recorded on the update report ensures that all documents are updated to the master file.

SITUATION 3:

A one-for-one check of a computer report is to be considered an adequate control over completeness of update.

IMPACT ON ADEQUACY OF CONTROL. The programmed procedures must ensure that the information reported reflects data actually written to the master file and not just that accepted by the system.

EXAMPLE. In this example the report identifies not only data written to the master file but also the old data overwritten. This provides some assurance that the report is not produced at the data acceptance stage.

SITUATION 4:

User procedures relating to a one-for-one check are to be considered adequate.

IMPACT ON ADEQUACY OF CONTROL. The procedures should include procedures to ensure that a copy is retained of all documents and that the file of unprocessed documents is controlled for completeness; a regular review of retained source documents or missing documents (see preceding examples) to ensure that all transactions are processed; and an investigation of all differences disclosed by the checking procedure.

EXAMPLE. In the Situation 1 example, the personnel office notes on the update report any differences identified and the follow-up action taken. Once the report has been cleared, it is filed together with the appropriate source documents. The file of source documents is reviewed each week for any items not yet processed.

SITUATION 5:

The one-for-one check is only adequate to ensure completeness of input (because of the stage of processing at which the report is produced).

IMPACT ON ADEQUACY OF CONTROL. A separate control is required to ensure the completeness of update. If this involves the use of control totals, a total of accepted items must be generated by the computer during the run in which the report is produced.

EXAMPLE. Amendments to rate of pay are input to the computer, and retained copies of source documents are agreed to the input validation report, which lists all accepted amendments. During the input validation run, a hash total is produced of all rates of pay and this is agreed (by the user) to a similar total accumulated and reported during update of the master file.

BATCH TOTALS

SITUATION 1:

To ensure that all documents are included in a batch, sequentially prenumbered documents are used. In this case, the following conditions are met: Physical control is maintained over unissued documents, documents are issued in numerical order, and all series are controlled.

IMPACT ON ADEQUACY OF CONTROL. Control is adequate if periodically (at least monthly) the organization identifies missing documents by using a complete list of document numbers against which an appropriate cross-reference is made at the time batch totals are established. Voided documents should be so indicated on the list and retained intact by the organization. Another method is to use a numerical file of document copies on which appropriate cross-references are made at the time batch totals are established. Once missing numbers have been identified, they should be properly investigated and adjustments made as necessary.

EXAMPLE. Sequence numbers are indicated on a list of sales invoice numbers at the time the invoices are batched and totals established. Copies of receiving reports are filed numerically and the relevant batch number is noted on each document.

SITUATION 2:

As in Situation 1, but documents are numbered as they are prepared (internal documents) or received (external documents).

IMPACT ON ADEQUACY OF CONTROL. Control may be exercised as in Situation 1, but it is not as strong as when documents are prenumbered. Control may be adequate, however, if there are additional procedures to ensure that all documents are numbered immediately upon preparation or receipt; the documents are numbered sequentially; there are no duplicate or missing numbers; and the documents are only prepared/received in authorized locations.

EXAMPLE. Shipping advices are numbered sequentially when goods are transferred from the finished inventory warehouse. The shipping supervisor ensures that a shipping advice accompanies all goods shipped and that the numbers are sequential.

SITUATION 3:

Documents are numbered sometime after they are prepared or received.

IMPACT ON ADEQUACY OF CONTROL. Control is not adequate because documents may be lost or misplaced between the time of preparation or receipt and numbering. This may be compensated for by other controls.

EXAMPLE. Purchase invoices are not numbered until after matching with receiving reports. However, each month all recorded accounts payable balances are reconciled with supplier's statements.

SITUATION 4:

Documents are entered in a register immediately upon preparation or receipt.

IMPACT ON ADEQUACY OF CONTROL. Control is adequate if the appropriate cross-reference is indicated in the register when batch totals are established. In addition, procedures are required to ensure that the register is complete (no pages are missing) and unauthorized alterations cannot be made.

EXAMPLE. All purchase invoices are entered in a register when received in the mail office. The register is a loose-leaf book, but all pages are prenumbered and all entries are in ink. When invoices have been batched, the batch number is entered in the register. Any amendments must be initialled by the accounts payable supervisor.

SITUATION 5:

A numerical control list, register, or file is merely marked off when the document is batched; an actual cross-reference is not given.

IMPACT ON ADEQUACY OF CONTROL. Control is less effective because the control documents do not demonstrate that an item has actually been batched. The effectiveness of a supervisory review procedure is reduced because the supervisor cannot see that a valid batch has been prepared.

EXAMPLE. A check mark rather than a batch number is placed against the sales invoice number when that invoice is batched. A check mark can be made even if the invoice is not processed.

SITUATION 6:

No numerical control or register exists, but the organization maintains a file of documents not yet batched.

IMPACT ON ADEQUACY OF CONTROL. The file, by itself, is not an adequate control, since documents may be improperly added or removed without detection or may never be filed at all.

EXAMPLE. Shipping advices are removed to suppress production of an invoice.

SITUATION 7:

The cross-references referred to in any of the preceding controls are made before actual batch totals have been established.

IMPACT ON ADEQUACY OF CONTROL. Control is not adequate because documents may be lost or mislaid between the time of making the cross-reference and establishment of control totals. Control may be adequate if, for example, all batches must contain a fixed number of documents and this is checked at the time the batch totals are established.

EXAMPLE. Purchase invoices are batched each time a convenient number of documents has accumulated. At this stage a prenumbered batch header is attached and the batch number is entered in the invoice register. Value batch totals are not established until the end of each day.

SITUATION 8:

To ensure that all batches are submitted for processing, batch headers are prenumbered and the conditions specified in Situation 1 are met.

IMPACT ON ADEQUACY OF CONTROL. Control is adequate if the company periodically (such as daily) identifies missing batches not returned from EDP by one of the methods specified in Situation 1. Alternately, control may be exercised by a computer sequence check on batch numbers. Although such a procedure is unusual, control is adequate provided requirements similar to those specified subsequently for a sequence check on transaction documents are met.

EXAMPLE. Batch headers are prenumbered and a control list is maintained of all numbers used. As batches are returned from EDP, the date of return is noted on the control list.

The batch number is input to the computer and by reference to a table of permitted and used numbers, the input validation program identifies duplicate and missing batch numbers. These are separately reported at the end of each input run for investigation by the user department.

SITUATION 9:

Batch headers are numbered when prepared.

IMPACT ON ADEQUACY OF CONTROL. Control is adequate provided there are procedures to ensure that all batches are numbered, the numbers are sequential, and batch headers are only prepared in authorized locations. Frequently, these requirements are achieved by use of a register in which details of each batch are recorded. The register itself should be controlled as described in Situation 4.

EXAMPLE. A permanent bound batch register is maintained. As each batch is prepared, reference is made to the register to obtain the next number in sequence, and the batch details are recorded in the register. This includes batch number, batch total, and date returned from EDP.

SITUATION 10:

All batches are recorded in a register when they are prepared.

IMPACT ON ADEQUACY OF CONTROL. It is unlikely that entry in the register will not be accompanied by allocation of a batch number. The control is then identical to that in Situation 9.

SITUATION 11:

For agreement of totals, manually established batch totals are recorded in a register before batches are submitted for processing.

IMPACT ON ADEQUACY OF CONTROL. Control is adequate if these totals are subsequently agreed to batch totals based on the same variable as used manually, but accumulated and reported by the computer. It is probable that the computer totals will be produced early during input validation and, therefore, that control will only be effective over completeness of input. Additional run-to-run controls will be required to ensure completeness of update.

EXAMPLE. Batch totals over quantities of goods shipped are entered in a register. The input validation program accumulates and reports quantity batch totals that are agreed each day to those entered in the register. The check is evidenced by recording the computer total in the register.

SITUATION 12:

Manually established batch totals are accumulated and posted to a manual control account.

IMPACT ON ADEQUACY OF CONTROL. Control over completeness of both input and update is adequate if the organization periodically agrees the balance on the manual control account to that reported for the computer master file.

EXAMPLE. Dollar batch totals are calculated manually for all transaction types input to the accounts receivable file. Each day these totals are accumulated and posted to a manual control account that is agreed at the end of each week to the balance reported for the accounts receivable file.

SITUATION 13:

Batch totals are recorded on a batch header slip and entered into the computer, which independently accumulates the total of the details in the batch and compares it with the manual total input from the header slip.

IMPACT ON ADEQUACY OF CONTROL. Control over completeness of input is adequate provided there are procedures to ensure that all batches are input to the computer, such as by use of a register, and programmed procedures result in all out-of-balance batches being reported. This is likely to involve reliance on general controls, unless all batches input are printed for manual review; there is adequate evidence that the computer agreement of batch totals was satisfactory. Additional run-to-run controls (discussed subsequently) are required to ensure that update is satisfactory.

EXAMPLE. Batch totals are recorded on a prenumbered header slip and all batch numbers are entered in a register before batches are sent to EDP. The computer input validation procedures provide that a batch total is accumulated for each batch and compared to the manual total input. All out-of-balance batches are rejected and reported. Both manual and computer totals are printed to facilitate investigation; all accepted batches are separately listed at the end of the validation report. The user ensures that all batch numbers in the register are reported either as out of balance or accepted.

SITUATION 14:

Batch totaling is to be employed as an effective control over completeness.

IMPACT ON ADEQUACY OF CONTROL. The total used must be capable of demonstrating that all transactions have been processed (e.g., a document count over multiline documents does not ensure that all transactions are processed). Provided this requirement is met, the total may be established over any field that is meaningful within the context of the particular application.

EXAMPLES. Acceptable batch totals include gross dollar values on purchase invoices, hash totals over selling prices for amendments to sales master file data, or total of hours worked for employees' time records.

SITUATION 15:

Any of the reconciliation procedures discussed previously disclose differences.

IMPACT ON ADEQUACY OF CONTROL. Control is adequate provided there are procedures for investigation and correction of all differences by the user.

SITUATION 16:

Input and/or update procedures can result in rejection of data from the system.

IMPACT ON ADEQUACY OF CONTROL. Batch totals provide adequate control if there are procedures to adjust any manually established totals for rejected items and to ensure that rejected data is corrected and later re-input. (See the section "Rejections.")

COMPUTER SEQUENCE CHECK

SITUATION 1:

All transactions are recorded on serially prenumbered documents.

IMPACT ON ADEQUACY OF CONTROL. Control is satisfactory provided the issue of documents is controlled in such a way that the numbers of all documents in issue are known.

EXAMPLE. Details of goods received are recorded on serially prenumbered forms. Unissued pads of forms are held by the purchasing department, which issues them to the receiving areas on request. A register is maintained which records the number series of all pads of documents and the date of their issue to receiving areas. A documents issued report is sent to the EDP department daily.

SITUATION 2:

Transactions are recorded on forms that are numbered at the time or after they are completed.

IMPACT ON ADEQUACY OF CONTROL. It may be possible to establish adequate control if there are additional procedures to ensure that all documents are numbered, a proper number sequence is generated, and there are no missing or duplicate numbers. Control is not as strong as when prenumbered documents are used.

EXAMPLE. Shipping advices are numbered sequentially when goods are transferred from the finished inventory warehouse. The shipping supervisor ensures that a shipping advice accompanies all goods shipped and that the numbers are sequential.

SITUATION 3:

Programmed procedures are to be considered adequate.

IMPACT ON ADEQUACY OF CONTROL. The following factors must be considered: The sequence check must be logically sound. In this context, procedures are required to deal with more than one sequence of numbers running concurrently, changes or breaks in sequence, identification of missing numbers until the document is processed or the number is voided, and identification and rejection from further processing of duplicate numbers. All exceptions identified should be regularly reported in sufficient detail to permit proper investigation and follow-up by the user. General controls must ensure the continued and proper operation of the programmed procedures.

EXAMPLE. In Situation 1, the documents issued report is used to set the issued-numbers parameters for use by the sequence check program. The document number of all goods received forms is first compared with an index file that records all numbers previously accepted by the system. This step identifies duplicate numbers and rejects them from further processing. Accepted numbers are written to the index file, which is then compared with the issued-numbers parameters to identify any missing numbers. Any numbers falling outside the parameters are also identified and rejected from further processing. Rejections are reported immediately and all other exceptions are reported on a cumulative basis at the end of each week.

SITUATION 4:

Exception reports are not cumulative and data can be rejected by the system.

IMPACT ON ADEQUACY OF CONTROL. Additional user procedures are required to ensure that all rejections are investigated and reentered. (See the section "Rejections.")

EXAMPLE. In the preceding example, housekeeping procedures on the index file mean that once a number sequence has been in issue for three months, it is cleared from the file and the issued-numbers parameters are adjusted accordingly. This means that missing-numbers reports are cumulative only for number sequences issued within the last three months. However, any documents submitted that fall outside the current parameters are rejected and reported, and therefore must be investigated by the user department.

SITUATION 5:

User procedures described previously are to be considered adequate.

IMPACT ON ADEQUACY OF CONTROL. The following conditions should be met: The user must understand the nature of the programmed procedures on which the exception report is based and the extent to which general controls are relied on to ensure the continued and proper operation of the programmed procedures. All reports must be properly reviewed in a timely manner. All exceptions must be investigated and appropriate action taken.

EXAMPLE. In the preceding example, the user (purchasing department) approved the sequence check at the system implementation stage and has been provided with a manual describing the way in which exceptions will be identified and reported. Each week rejections are investigated and re-input; missing numbers are queried with the goods receiving area. The user ensures that all number sequences issued are completely accounted for within three months of their issue.

SITUATION 6:

A sequence check is relied on to ensure completeness of input.

IMPACT ON ADEQUACY OF CONTROL. A separate control is required over completeness of update. It is likely that this will involve the use of run-to-run totals. (See the section "Run-to-Run Controls.") In this situation, a total of accepted items must be produced at the time of, or before, the point at which the sequence check operates.

EXAMPLE. In the previous example, as each accepted number is written to the index file, the quantity of goods received for that transaction is added to an accumulator to produce a total for all accepted items. This total is reported at the end of the input validation report.

COMPUTER MATCHING

SITUATION 1:

Matching is to be acceptable as a control over completeness of input.

IMPACT ON ADEQUACY OF CONTROL. The relationship between input data and the reference data used in the matching process must be such that an input transaction is expected for each element of reference data. If this is not the case, a report of unmatched reference data cannot be used to ensure that all transactions are entered.

EXAMPLE. An employee master file is maintained and payroll transaction data is matched against the file. Transaction types processed include time records for each production worker (paid at an hourly rate) and overtime records for salaried staff. Matching can be used to ensure completeness of production time records, since a time record is expected for all production employees, who are identified separately on the employee master file. Since, however, not all salaried staff may work overtime during any one period, matching cannot be used to ensure that all overtime records are entered.

SITUATION 2:

Transaction data input is matched with a file of master file data or previously processed transaction data.

IMPACT ON ADEQUACY OF CONTROL. The matching procedures ensure completeness of input only if there are adequate controls over the file holding the master file reference data. Those controls must provide assurance that all reference data held on file is validated, the master file reference file is correctly maintained, and all amendments to the reference data are appropriately authorized. (The procedures necessary to achieve adequate control over validity of data and maintenance of data are discussed in subsequent sections of this chapter.)

EXAMPLE. Completeness of input of purchase invoices is achieved by matching against a file of goods received. All entries to this file are properly controlled for validity and for completeness and accuracy of input and update. Maintenance of the file is controlled by use of a total over the quantity field, which is agreed to a manual control account. Any adjustments to the file are printed separately for authorization by the purchasing supervisor.

SITUATION 3:

Programmed procedures are to be considered adequate.

IMPACT ON ADEQUACY OF CONTROL. The following condition should be met: The data fields matched must ensure that mismatches will be properly indentified and reported. This usually involves matching on more than one field to ensure that an erroneous match is not possible, and it is particularly important if matching is also used to ensure accuracy of input. (See the section "Adequacy of Controls Over Accuracy of Input and Update.")

EXAMPLE A. In the example in Situation 1, purchase invoices are matched with goods received on the following fields: goods received number, product code, supplier code, and quantity.

IMPACT ON ADEQUACY OF CONTROL. The matched records must be indicated appropriately on the reference file to permit production of a report of unmatched items.

EXAMPLE B. Any "matched" goods received record is deleted from file; consequently, only unmatched items are held on file.

IMPACT ON ADEQUACY OF CONTROL. Reports must be produced at regular intervals, listing outstanding items for user investigation. It may be appropriate to list only long outstanding items if there is a time lag associated with processing of master file reference data and processing of transactions.

EXAMPLE C. The company expects to receive suppliers' invoices within two weeks of receiving the goods. Consequently, the report of "unmatched" goods received does not list any items where the goods were received within the two weeks prior to the date of the report.

SITUATION 4:

User procedures relating to Situations 1, 2, and 3 are to be considered adequate.

IMPACT ON ADEQUACY OF CONTROL. The user should understand the principal programmed procedures on which the matching control relies and the fact that the continued and proper operation of these programmed procedures is ensured by general controls, and investigate and correct, as appropriate, all mismatches and reports of long outstanding items.

EXAMPLE. In the example in Situation 1, the purchase accounts department is responsible for following up all mismatches and unmatched goods received reports.

SITUATION 5:

Matching is used to ensure completeness of input.

IMPACT ON ADEQUACY OF CONTROL. A separate control is required to provide assurance that all data is updated to the computer file. This usually is achieved by use of run-to-run controls. (See the following section, "Run-to-Run Controls.") In order to be satisfied that there is no gap in control between the input and update stages, a total of accepted items should be generated during the run in which the matching control operates.

EXAMPLE. In the previous example, during the run in which purchase invoices are matched with the goods received file, whenever a match is achieved, the gross dollar value of the invoice is accumulated to produce a total of accepted items, which is reported at the end of the input run. This total is reconciled to the update report.

RUN-TO-RUN CONTROLS

SITUATION 1:

This type of control can be used only to ensure completeness of update. An additional control is required to ensure completeness of input when run-to-run totals are used to ensure completeness of update.

IMPACT ON ADEQUACY OF CONTROL. The total of accepted data must be established during the run in which the input control operates. A total established in this way automatically includes all data accepted into the application and ensures that there is no break in control between input and update stages.

EXAMPLE. During a computer sequence check of serially numbered documents, the reference number of each accepted transaction is written to an index file. At the same time, the quantity field for that transaction is added to an accumulator to produce a quantity total for all accepted transactions. This total is recorded at the end of the input validation report and is subsequently agreed to a total of updated transactions.

SITUATION 2:

The total of accepted items is manually agreed to the total of items actually updated onto the master file.

IMPACT ON ADEQUACY OF CONTROL. Control is adequate provided there are procedures to investigate any differences disclosed by the reconciliation and to take appropriate follow-up action. Reconciliation procedures may have to take account of summarization of totals, when input runs occur more than once during a day, but a single update (often overnight) is carried out. Rejection of data between input and update stages must be considered. This is more likely in a batch processing situation than in on-line/real-time systems, since the increased availability of master file reference data associated with on-line entry facilitates validation of data at the input stage. This usually eliminates the need for pre-update validation of data.

EXAMPLE. A company operates out of several locations, each of which has its own computer processing facilities. Inventory movements are entered at each location and updated to detailed inventory master files maintained (by quantity only) at each site. In addition, all accepted input is transmitted to the head office (via remote terminals at each site) where it is consolidated, evaluated, and updated to the company's financial inventory records. The head office receives input control totals from each site. These totals are summarized to produce a grand total of all accepted input data; adjusted to take account of rejections which may occur if financial information is not available for a particular inventory; and reconciled with the total of inventory movements reported as updated to the financial inventory records. The reconciliation is carried out by head office staff, who also ensure that all rejections are investigated and reentered.

SITUATION 3:

The total of accepted items is reconciled by the computer with the total of items updated onto the master file.

IMPACT ON ADEQUACY OF CONTROL. Control is adequate provided that programmed procedures take account, as appropriate, of summarization of totals, changes in totals, and rejections. Adequate evidence of the result of the reconciliation is printed and any differences are reported in sufficient detail to permit user investigation. The user department confirms that the reconciliation was satisfactory, investigates and acts on any differences reported, and ensures that all rejections are entered. General controls are sufficient to ensure the continued and proper operation of programmed procedures.

EXAMPLE. Details of shipments are entered to a sales accounting system; they are then evaluated and updated to the accounts receivable file. Control over completeness of input is assured by a computer sequence check and, during the sequence check run, a total over the quantity field is established for all accepted data. As each accepted item is evaluated, the computer accumulates totals over the quantity field and the value field, and at the end of the evaluation run, it agrees the total quantity evaluated to the total of accepted items. Evaluated shipments are then updated to the accounts receivable file, and the computer agrees the total value updated to the previous total. All totals are reported and the differences are evaluated and specified to assist in user follow-up procedures.

SITUATION 4:

Run-to-run controls are used to ensure the completeness of update in an on-line system.

IMPACT ON ADEQUACY OF CONTROL. Although the concept of a single program run total is no longer valid in an on-line system, it is still possible to accumulate totals at various stages in processing. The totals can then be reconciled to ensure that data is not lost during processing. For example, programmed procedures are designed to ensure that during any fixed time period, separate totals are accumulated for all accepted transactions and all transactions updated to the master files. Provided these requirements are met, the totals can subsequently be reconciled (see preceding situations), thereby ensuring that accepted data is completely updated onto the computer files.

EXAMPLE. In the system described previously, details of shipments are entered via on-line terminals situated in the shipping area. Data is validated on entry and, if accepted, immediately written to a transaction file, evaluated, and updated onto the accounts receivable file. Throughout the day, the following separate totals are accumulated for all transactions: the quantity field of all accepted items, quantity fields of all updated items, and the value fields of all updated items. These totals are subsequently reconciled in the way described previously.

SITUATION 5:

Run-to-run controls are used to ensure completeness of update in a data base system.

IMPACT ON ADEQUACY OF CONTROL. The totals used may only be item counts over data elements accepted and updated. In this case, system software is relied on to ensure that all necessary linkages are set up to establish the logical relationships between individual items of data. The function of systems software procedures should be ensured by appropriate general controls. Periodically, the completeness of the linkages should be tested by reconciling the various logical groupings with independent control accounts.

EXAMPLE. A company has a fully integrated, computerized accounting system that covers all accounting functions. Data is organized as a data base, and various control techniques are used to ensure that all items of data are written to the data base. In order to confirm the completeness of the logical linkages within the data base, each month value totals for each logical unit— accounts receivable, accounts payable, inventory—are reported and reconciled with control totals established independently by users using transaction reports produced during normal day-to-day processing.

REJECTIONS

SITUATION 1:

Data is rejected by the system at input and/or update stages and written to a suspense file.

IMPACT ON ADEQUACY OF CONTROL. Control is adequate if the following requirements are met: Programmed procedures are appropriate to ensure that all rejected items are completely and accurately written to the suspense file; the suspense file is subject to proper maintenance controls (discussed subsequently); programmed procedures are adequate to ensure that re-input of rejected data is identified by the system; data found to be correct is matched with the suspense file and the appropriate record is deleted from the suspense file; records still on the suspense file are reported regularly and the reports are investigated by the user. Corrective action taken should be noted on the report to facilitate a supervisory review of follow-up procedures. The function of appropriate programmed procedures is assured by adequate general controls.

EXAMPLE. Batch totals are entered in a register and the documents are entered to the sales invoicing system. Documents with invalid customer or inventory codes are rejected by the input validation program and written to a suspense file. The suspense file is controlled via totals over the quantity field. After each update, a report is produced showing totals for balance brought forward, additions, deletions, and balance carried forward. All rejections are listed as they arise, and the suspense file is then printed in full at the end of each week. The following procedures ensure that rejections are dealt with properly: Totals of rejected items are noted in the batch register during reconciliation of batch totals and are also posted to a manual suspense control account; rejections are investigated and corrected, and reinputs are rebatched, these batch numbers being prefixed with an "R." Reentered totals are posted to the suspense control account. If reentered data is correct, it is matched with the suspense file and the relevant suspense record is deleted; at the end of each week, the manual suspense balance is reconciled to that reported for the computer file, and the suspense listing is reviewed to ensure that there is no undue build-up of rejections.

SITUATION 2:

Data is rejected by the system at input and/or update stages but no suspense file is maintained.

IMPACT ON ADEQUACY OF CONTROL. Control is adequate if there are appropriate programmed and user procedures to ensure that all rejections are printed and investigated promptly, and that the appropriate corrective action is taken. The actual procedures depend in part on the input control used. When batch or control totals are used, a manual control total over rejections not yet resubmitted may be used.

EXAMPLE A. The example in Situation 1 demonstrates use of a manual control account. Control is not as good as in that example because there is no suspense file or related reports.

IMPACT ON ADEQUACY OF CONTROL. When other input control techniques are used (such as matching or sequence check), it is likely that the associated exception reports will be cumulative in nature. Therefore, a regular review of these reports to identify and investigate old items should ensure that rejections are all reentered eventually. If reports are not cumulative, manual procedures that ensure that all items on all reports have been cleared properly, plus an appropriate level of supervision, may be the only assurance that all rejections are dealt with properly.

EXAMPLE B. Data is rejected as in the example in Situation 1. However, the input control is a cumulative sequence check that produces regular reports of shipping advices not yet accepted by the system. Investigation of these reports on a regular basis ensures that all transactions are eventually accepted into the invoicing system.

IMPACT ON ADEQUACY OF CONTROL. In on-line systems, rejections are most likely to occur at the time of original input of data. Usually, corrections are made immediately. If checking reports, computer sequence check, or computer matching is used as a control over completeness of input, rejections are probably controlled as described previously. If these techniques are not used, pre-input or session control totals should be established manually. By reconciliation with accepted data totals, these are used to ensure that rejections are reentered.

EXAMPLE C. A company ships goods to its customers based on shipping advices that are output from the sales order processing system. A file is maintained of sales orders not yet shipped. Controls over the maintenance of this file are considered adequate. When goods are shipped, a copy of the shipping advice is reentered via on-line terminals in the shipping department and matched against the outstanding order file. Accepted shipping advices are valued, a sales invoice is produced, and the transaction is updated on the accounts receivable file. Any rejections are investigated and corrected in the shipping department and re-input. Each week an exception report of unshipped orders over one month old is produced. Proper investigation of this report ensures that all orders are completed and, therefore, that all shipments are entered to the invoicing system.

SITUATION 3:

Data is not actually rejected by the system. Unusual situations are reported and processing continues.

IMPACT ON ADEQUACY OF CONTROL. Control is adequate if there are procedures to ensure that all unusual situations are identified (by programmed procedure) and reported, all reports are investigated promptly, and all necessary adjustments are made. It is particularly important that reports are investigated and adjustments made promptly, since when the "unusual situation" is actually an error, the company's accounting records will be inaccurate until the adjustment is made. Similarly, the function of proper programmed procedures is essential to ensure that all possible error situations are identified.

EXAMPLE. Customer remittance advices are entered to the accounts receivable file, which is organized on an open-item basis. If the remittance cannot be matched accurately against an outstanding transaction, it is updated as a new unmatched item and coded as "unmatched cash." A cumulative report of all such items on the accounts receivable file is produced each week to permit manual matching. The accounts receivable supervisor reviews this report at the end of each month to ensure that all cash is matched and that therefore an accurate age analysis of outstanding accounts will be produced.

RELIANCE ON CONTROLS OVER ANOTHER APPLICATION

SITUATION:

Data input to one application system is updated to a different system.

IMPACT ON ADEQUACY OF CONTROL. Control over completeness of update of data to the second system is adequate if control over entry of data to the intitial system is satisfactory and programmed procedures are adequate to identify and extract all accepted data required for update within the second system. In particular, a total of data so identified should be accumulated during the extraction process. Adequate run-to-run controls are needed to ensure that all data extracted is actually updated to the relevant computer files and the function of proper programmed procedures is assured.

EXAMPLE. A company has computerized all of its inventory systems. All inventory movements (including scrappings, interstore transfers, perpetual inventory) are input via terminals located within the various inventory locations to an integrated data collection (IDC) system. Completeness of input is ensured by computer sequence checks. Data is then extracted for update to the various inventory and production control sytems. Item counts and quantity totals are accumulated during the extraction procedures. These are reported and reconciled, by an inventory control section, with the totals updated to the appropriate inventory sytems.

ADEQUACY OF CONTROLS OVER ACCURACY OF INPUT AND UPDATE

It is important that the transaction data is accurately entered and updated. For these purposes, input includes initial recording, transcription from source data to input documents, or the conversion of the data on documents into machine-readable form.

Questions dealing with these procedures appear under many control objectives. Adequacy of control is discussed here for convenience and to emphasize that similar control procedures may apply to different cycles and different control objectives.

Accuracy of input and update is concerned with individual data fields, as opposed to transactions. It can be achieved only if all significant data fields are adequately controlled. Consequently, it is necessary to identify those data fields that must be controlled and the level or standard of control that is required. Two other factors that must be considered are the following:

1. It may not be practical to establish a high standard of control over all important data fields.
2. Different control techniques may be applied to different data fields within the same transaction.

In general, all value and quantity fields are financially significant and should be subject to adequate control procedures. Certain reference data fields may also be important. Examples of these are

- *Reference numbers.* These include account numbers, general ledger codes, and inventory codes. The latter are important, for example, in ensuring that inventory is priced correctly.
- *Dates.* There are many instances where dates are of accounting significance. For example, dates may be used either to analyze data, as in aging of accounts receivable or inventory balances, or to initiate accounting procedures, such as due date of installment repayments.
- *Indicators.* These also may be of accounting significance. For example, in payroll systems, the distinction between new hires and terminations may be made by use of different indicators. Credit control procedures within an accounts receivable system also may rely heavily on the use of indicators. Failure to input and update these indicators accurately may result in a breakdown of control procedures and a loss of revenue to the company.

In order to achieve control over accuracy of update, procedures must ensure that

- The correct amount is updated to the correct account.
- The correct generation of the master file is updated.

Although user controls may be of some assistance in these areas, it is probable that considerable reliance will be placed on programmed procedures, particularly to ensure that data is updated to the correct account.

There are a wide variety of techniques available to establish accuracy of input and update. For this reason, it is not considered practical to list the various techniques in the CICQ, as is done for completeness. Instead, the questions asked are of a general nature. They are designed to ensure that

- There are adequate controls over data fields of accounting significance.
- There are adequate procedures to identify and investigate any differences.
- The programmed procedures are adequate to ensure that the correct account will be updated.

The following techniques can be used to achieve control over accuracy of input and update:

- Extension of the controls used to achieve completeness of input and update
- Programmed edit checks
- Review of output
- Use of prerecorded input
- Verification of data conversion

These techniques are discussed in more detail in following sections.

In practice, the auditor is likely to be confronted with a combination of these techniques. It is important to identify the principal controls on which to place reliance. In general, controls should be selected in the order just listed. As is discussed in more detail subsequently, verification of data conversion is not considered an adequate control for audit purposes.

EXTENSION OF CONTROLS OVER COMPLETENESS OF INPUT AND UPDATE

SITUATION 1:

Batch totals are used to control completeness of input via manual or computer agreement of pre-established totals.

IMPACT ON ADEQUACY OF CONTROL. Control over accuracy of input is adequate only with respect to the particular data field used to establish totals. It should also be noted that the use of batch totals does not guard against compensating errors in one or more individual items. Additional procedures are required to ensure that all entries are accurately updated to the correct computer files. The use of computer agreement of pre-established totals entered on a batch header does not provide any security protection over unauthorized change because it allows anyone who has access to the batch access to both the data (the transactions) and the control (the batch header).

EXAMPLE. Employees' time cards are entered into the payroll system. Batch totals are established over hours worked. These are manually agreed to similar batch totals accumulated and reported by the computer as part of the input validation system.

SITUATION 2:

Batch totals are posted to a manual control account that is reconciled periodically with the balance on the master file.

IMPACT ON ADEQUACY OF CONTROL. Controls are adequate to ensure that the particular field totaled is accurately updated in total to the correct generation of the master file. Additional controls are required to provide assurance that the correct individual account is updated accurately. This may be achieved by user controls, such as periodic reconciliation of accounts payable balances with suppliers' statements. However, in the absence of adequate user procedures, reliance is placed on programmed procedures, and therefore on general controls, to ensure that individual accounts are accurately updated.

EXAMPLE. All transactions types entered into the accounts receivable system are batched and totals are established over gross dollar values. These totals are posted to a manual control account that is reconciled each month with the total balance reported for the accounts receivable file. There are no specific user controls to ensure that individual accounts receivables balances are stated accurately, but the general controls are adequate.

SITUATION 3:

A one-for-one check is carried out, using retained copies of source documents.

IMPACT ON ADEQUACY OF CONTROL. Control is adequate to ensure accuracy either of input or both input and update, depending on the stage at which the output report is produced. (See the section "Adequacy of Controls Over Completeness of Input and Update.") This control is particularly effective, since it can cover all data fields of significance. It is, however, time-consuming and therefore relatively costly. It is usually encountered only when low volumes of financially sensitive data are being processed.

EXAMPLE. Following the example in Situation 1, the personnel department agrees all data fields on the source documents to the details reported on the report.

SITUATION 4:

A one-for-one check is carried out, using documents returned from data processing.

IMPACT ON ADEQUACY OF CONTROL. Control over accuracy of input and update is not adequate, since unauthorized amendments to data can be made while the documents are outside the user department's control.

EXAMPLE. In the payroll example of completeness controls, there is no control to ensure that data recorded on source documents (such as rates of pay) cannot be amended in an unauthorized manner while outside the control of the personnel department.

SITUATION 5:

Run-to-run totals are used to ensure completeness of update.

IMPACT ON ADEQUACY OF CONTROL. The control is also adequate to ensure that, for the particular field totaled, the computer file is accurately updated in total. This type of control does not, however, guard against compensating errors involving more than one individual account; neither can it ensure that the correct individual account has been updated.

EXAMPLE. Details of goods shipped are entered into a sales accounting system for evaluation and update to the accounts receivable file. Run-to-run totals are accumulated at each stage of processing, including data acceptance. The totals, which are printed, are as follows:

- During data acceptance, a total over the quantity field
- During evaluation, totals over both the quantity and the value fields
- During update, a total over the value field

The user deparment reconciles all totals and investigates differences, thereby ensuring that the accounts receivable file is accurately updated in total.

SITUATION 6:

Computer matching is used to ensure that data is completely entered.

IMPACT ON ADEQUACY OF CONTROL. Control is adequate to ensure that, with respect to those data fields matched, data is also entered accurately. The effectiveness of this control is determined by

- The availability of reference data to use in the match. For this reason, matching as a control over accuracy of input is most commonly used in on-line systems.
- The extent to which the reference data can be relied on. Controls should exist to ensure that only valid, authorized data is used in the matching process.
- The function of the appropriate programmed procedures that are relied on to ensure that
  a. Only matched data is accepted.
  b. All mismatches are reported.
- In on-line systems, the facility may exist to override a mismatch. If this is possible, programmed procedures should be appropriate to ensure that all such situations are reported.
- The diligence of the user department in investigating and following up all mismatches (and overrides, as just described for on-line systems).

EXAMPLE. Purchase invoices are entered into a purchase accounting system and, during input validation procedures, certain fields are matched with data held on a goods received suspense file. The following fields are matched:

- Supplier code
- Product code
- Quantity received
- Purchase price

All mismatches are rejected and investigated by the accounts payable staff.

SITUATION 7:

A transaction log is produced during processing of data in an on-line, real-time system.

IMPACT ON ADEQUACY OF CONTROL. It may be possible to ensure accuracy of update by using special programs and the transaction log to reperform processing and compare the results (on an item-by-item basis) with the original results of processing. In a large, complex computer installation where it is impractical, or even impossible, to rely on user procedures to ensure accuracy of processing, this method may be effective. It must be remembered, however, that controls of this nature rely heavily on programmed procedures, and therefore on the adequacy of general controls, for their effectiveness.

EXAMPLE. A company operates an on-line, computerized accounting system. Once accepted, all data is captured on a transaction log. At the end of each day's processing, security dumps are taken of all data files. Overnight, a set of programs reperforms the day's processing using the current day's transaction log and the file dumps from the previous evening. The results are then compared, on an item-by-item basis, with the original results of processing as per the most recent file dumps. All differences are printed and then investigated by a central data control section.

PROGRAMMED EDIT CHECKS

SITUATION 1:

Edit checks are to be considered adequate to ensure accuracy of input.

IMPACT ON ADEQUACY OF CONTROL. Edit checks are programmed procedures that usually result in the production of exception reports. If user controls do not ensure the function of the appropriate programmed procedures, the adequacy of general controls must be established.

- The effectiveness of edit checks in ensuring accuracy of data is determined by
  a. The extent to which possible error conditions were identified at the time the system was designed.
  b. The skill of the system analysts and programmers in incorporating into the systems and programs checking procedures capable of identifying and reporting the error conditions expected to occur.
- In many cases, edit checks cannot provide conclusive proof that only accurate data is accepted; however, a suitable combination of edit checks may be of considerable assistance in reducing the likelihood of error.

- In on-line systems, it may be possible to override edit checks. In these cases, the system should ensure that all instances of override are suitably reported for investigation.

EXAMPLE. Input validation programs often incorporate edit checks on data input to the system. Any data failing these checks is rejected and reported as an exception, but accepted data is not reported. Consequently, user procedures cannot ensure the function of the validation programs.

A company has set up a product coding structure that allows any number in the range 01 to 99 as a valid code. A programmed edit check can ensure that the code is valid (by checking whether if it is in the range 01 to 99), but cannot ensure that no errors of transposition have occurred, since any valid code transposes to another valid code. Protecting reference codes from transposition error is usually achieved by use of techniques such as check digits and alphanumeric combinations.

SITUATION 2:

Edit checks are identified as controls over accuracy.

IMPACT ON ADEQUACY OF CONTROL. The edit checks are likely to be from one of the following categories:

- *Format check.* This check ensures that data is in the correct format.

- *Reasonableness check.* This check compares the data with predetermined parameters that indicate the expected values of the data.

- *Dependency check.* This check presumes that there is a logical relationship between two or more data fields.

- *Existence check.* This check is the standard validity check and compares reference data with a table or master file of permitted codes.

- *Double matching check.* This method requires that the input includes both new data and the old data to be overwritten. By matching new input against data already on file, some assurance is obtained that the correct account is updated.

- *Document reconciliation.* This technique, which is common in on-line systems that permit individual entry of transactions, involves checking the mathematical accuracy of numeric data prior to entry. A hash total is established of all, or all important, numeric data fields on the document. The hash total is entered, as well as the transaction data, and the program totals the numeric fields and compares the result with the hash total. Transactions that do not balance are rejected.

EXAMPLES. The following examples are arranged in the same sequence as the preceding categories.

- Data field is checked as numeric.

- Quantities of goods shipped are checked as being within an average range. The average is determined by the sales department, based on sales over the past year.

- All employees coded as "production" should have an hourly rate of pay, whereas all "staff" should have an annual salary.

- All inventory product codes are checked against the product code master file to ensure that only valid codes are used. The codes should be set up so as to identify transposition errors. (See the example in Situation 1.)

- Adjustments to payroll master file data require that both old and new salaries are entered. The old salary is matched against that recorded on the master file for the particular employee.

- Multiline sales orders are entered into an on-line system. A hash total is calculated manually including all product codes, quantities, account numbers, and date. The hash total is also entered and compared by the computer program with a similar total that it computes from the data entered. Any out-of-balance orders are rejected.

SITUATION 3:

User procedures associated with programmed edit checks are to be considered satisfactory.

IMPACT ON ADEQUACY OF CONTROL. The procedures must comply with the following requirements:

- The user must fully understand
    a. The nature of both the programmed procedures involved and the exception reports produced.
    b. The fact that general controls are being relied on to ensure the continued and proper operation of the programmed procedures.
- All exceptions must be promptly investigated and corrected.

EXAMPLE. The user department approves all edit checks at the time of systems design and implementation. Investigation of exceptions and follow-up action is noted on the exception report for review by a responsible official.

SITUATION 4:

Edit checks rely on reference data or parameters.

IMPACT ON ADEQUACY OF CONTROL. Control is adequate only if there are procedures to ensure that all reference data and parameters are properly authorized and maintained. The reference data may be held in program tables or in master files.

EXAMPLE. All files of reference data should be properly maintained (see the section "Adequacy of Controls Over Maintenance of Data") and amendments should be properly authorized (see the section "Adequacy of Controls Over Validity of Data"). Parameters used in validation procedures should be printed on the validation report and checked by the user department.

REVIEW OF OUTPUT

SITUATION:

User review of output is used to ensure accuracy of processing.

IMPACT ON ADEQUACY OF CONTROL. It is unlikely that the review by itself will be adequate to achieve control unless it is actually a one-for-one check. (See the section "One-for-One Checking.") However, if the review is of selected output only — the selection being made by use of appropriate edit checks — the combined edit/review procedures may provide reasonable assurance that only accurate data has been processed.

EXAMPLE. A company expects that 90 percent of all credit given to customers will be for less than $3,000. All credit notes of a value greater than or equal to $3,000 are printed. A responsible official reviews the list to ensure that all such items are valid and correct.

PRERECORDED INPUT

SITUATION 1:

Data to be entered is prerecorded on the input document.

IMPACT ON ADEQUACY OF CONTROL. Control over accuracy of initial recording of prerecorded fields is adequate provided there are procedures to ensure the data so recorded is correct. This situation may be associated with a turn-around document, where information is output by the computer and is subsequently used as input during a later stage or processing. Procedures must ensure that if correct data values are different from those prerecorded, the correct value is recorded and entered in place of the prerecorded value. Separate controls are required to ensure the accuracy of input of altered data.

EXAMPLE. If data is rejected from processing, it is written to a suspense file and reported on an error correction turn-around document. The fields causing the error condition are asterisked. The user investigates and corrects these fields and resubmits the error correction form. A one-for-one check is used to ensure accuracy of input of the amended data.

SITUATION 2:

Turn-around documents are used to make amendments to master file data.

IMPACT ON ADEQUACY OF CONTROL. Control is adequate provided the user ensures that the correct input form is used by checking the relevant reference data.

EXAMPLE. Personnel history cards are printed by the computer. When a personnel change is necessary, the card is retrieved from the file, the name is checked to ensure that the correct card is pulled, and changes are indicated by amending the appropriate fields. (Output is checked one-for-one for these changed fields.)

SITUATION 3:

Prerecorded data is in one of the following machine-readable forms:

- Optical character recognition (OCR)
- Optical mark recognition (OMR)
- Magnetic ink character recognition (MICR)
- Punched card
- Bar code
- Magnetic stripe

IMPACT ON ADEQUACY OF CONTROL. Control over both initial recording and conversion to machine-readable form is adequate provided that

- The particular edit software used is appropriate to identify, report, and reject from further processing any incorrect input forms.
- General controls are adequate to ensure the function of proper programmed procedures.
- User procedures include the investigation, correction, and reentry of rejected data. If documents are damaged so that the particular input technique can no longer be used, alternate procedures and controls will be necessary to ensure that such data is accurately entered.

EXAMPLE. Remittance advices are sent to customers. The customer number and amount outstanding are recorded using OCR characters on the returnable remittance advice. The company need only key the amount paid if it differs from the amount due.

INTERACTIVE FEEDBACK CHECK

SITUATION:

Reference data is entered through a terminal and the system replies with descriptive information that can be used to check the data entered.

IMPACT ON ADEQUACY OF CONTROL. Control is adequate if the feedback data is actually used to check the accuracy of the input.

EXAMPLE. A sales clerk takes orders over the telephone. The customer number, product number, and quantity ordered are entered via a terminal. The customer's name, product name, quantity, price, and dollar value appear on the terminal screen. The clerk verifies the customer's name, product name, quantity, price, and dollar value with the customer before releasing the order to the system.

VERIFICATION OF DATA CONVERSION

SITUATION:

Verification of data conversion is the only control over accuracy of input.

IMPACT ON ADEQUACY OF CONTROL. It may be possible to rely on key verification to ensure that data is accurately converted to machine-readable form. Programmed procedures then have to be adequate to ensure that all data is accurately processed. This is a very weak control; it should not be relied on to control financially sensitive data.

EXAMPLE. Certain customer master file data (such as delivery address) is not financially significant, and therefore is not controlled for accuracy of input and update except by key verification and reliance on programmed procedures.

CORRECT GENERATION OF FILE

SITUATION 1:

Either batch totals or totals of accepted items are posted to a manual control account that is periodically agreed to the balance reported for the computer master file.

IMPACT ON ADEQUACY OF CONTROL. Control is adequate to ensure that the correct generation of the master file is updated. If this was not the case, manual and computer control totals would disagree. Any differences should be investigated and acted upon by the user responsible for maintaining the control account.

EXAMPLE. The following totals are posted to a manual accounts receivable control account in the general ledger:

- Invoice values as reported by the computer during the evaluation of goods shipped records
- Customer remittances as recorded in the cash book
- Adjustments, write-offs, and such as recorded in a batch register
- Credit note values as accumulated by the computer during input validation procedures

At each month-end the accounts supervisor reconciles the balance in the general ledger with that reported for the computer accounts receivable file.

SITUATION 2:

A manual control account is not maintained.

IMPACT ON ADEQUACY OF CONTROL. Control may be adequate to ensure that the correct generation of file is updated if either

- A user department ensures that the brought-forward total agrees with that carried forward after the last update, or
- Computer operations controls are adequate to ensure that the correct file is used.

EXAMPLE. Each time the accounts payable file is updated, a movements report is produced showing the following:

- Balance brought forward
- Movements by transaction type
- Balance carried forward

The accounts payable supervisor ensures that the balance brought forward is the same as that previously carried forward.

UPDATING CORRECT ACCOUNT

SITUATION:

Programmed procedures relating to update of individual accounts are to be considered appropriate.

IMPACT ON ADEQUACY OF CONTROL. Programmed procedures must ensure that if it is not possible to update the incorrect account (for example, because there is no corresponding master record on file), all relevant data will be reported and either rejected or written to a suspense account, as considered appropriate. User procedures must provide that all reports are investigated and the necessary adjustments made. (See the section "Rejections.") Since it is unlikely that user procedures will be adequate to ensure the continued and proper operation of the programmed update procedures, general controls should be adequate to provide assurance in this area.

EXAMPLE. Accepted inventory movements are updated to the financial inventory file, which reports inventory valued at a moving average price. The calculation of the average price requires that negative stock balances do not exist. Consequently, if outward movement would result in a negative inventory balance, it is not updated to the inventory master file but is posted to a suspense account until there is adequate inventory to cover the movement. Any movements of inventory for which a financial master record is not available are also reported and written to the suspense file. The suspense file is printed out in full after each update to permit user investigation.

ADEQUACY OF CONTROLS OVER VALIDITY OF DATA

An organization's procedures for ensuring that transactions are valid and are being executed in accordance with management's intentions are an important part of its internal control. Questions dealing with these procedures appear under many control objectives. Adequacy of control is discussed here for convenience and to emphasize that similar control procedures may apply to different cycles and different control objectives.

Computer systems rely on a highly structured environment for their effectiveness. The specific definition of standard procedures associated with such an environment usually results in increased requirements for authorization. For example, in addition to authorization of individual transactions, it may be necessary to authorize control reconciliations, treatment of rejections, overrides of normal procedures, and master file data amendments.

The procedures used to ensure that only valid data is processed usually take one of two forms:

1. Transactions are subject to a manual check and/or authorization by a responsible, supervisory official.
2. Transactions are checked by programmed procedures that examine the data by reference to criteria set by management.

Where applicable, the ICQ requires the auditor to identify whether the checks on validity are carried out manually or by the computer. Separate detailed questions are usually provided for each situation.

The term "validity," as used in this context, refers to the authorization of data. It should not be confused with the term "validation" as applied to the edit programs. The latter refers to an existence check against a table or file of valid numbers. (See the discussion of existence checks in the section "Programmed Edit Checks," Situation 2.)

One of the important aspects of authorizing data in computer systems is the timing of authorization. This refers to the fact that data frequently is authorized at the time it is first introduced into the system, rather than at the time the data is used. This is particularly true of master file data, but also occurs with transaction data. For authorization to be effective and to ensure that only authorized data is processed, it is necessary to structure procedures so that authorization is either

- Carried out or rechecked after control has been established over completeness and accuracy of input and update, or
- Carried out or rechecked after processing is complete.

The adequacy of control procedures is discussed in more detail in the following sections.

TIMING OF AUTHORIZATION

SITUATION 1:

Authorization is carried out or rechecked on documents after control has been established over completeness and accuracy.

IMPACT ON ADEQUACY OF CONTROL. Provided that the completeness and accuracy controls are satisfactory, control over authorization is adequate to ensure that

- Only authorized documents are processed.
- Only authorized amounts are processed.

EXAMPLE. Purchase invoices are posted to an accounts payable master file and check payments are generated automatically for all invoices on file. It is therefore important to ensure that all invoices on file have been properly authorized for payment. Control over completeness and accuracy of input and update of invoices is achieved by use of batch totals that are posted to a manual control account. All user procedures are considered to be satisfactory. Batched invoices are passed to the accounts payable supervisor after batch totals have been established and recorded on a header slip. The supervisor test-checks the batch totals, authorizes all invoices in the batch, and notes the batch total in a register. At the end of each day, the supervisor totals the register, thereby accumulating a figure of authorized purchase invoices for posting to the manual control account. Checking the agreement of manual and computer control accounts ensures that only authorized data is processed.

SITUATION 2:

Authorization is carried out or rechecked on reports after processing.

IMPACT ON ADEQUACY OF CONTROL. Control is adequate to ensure that only authorized data is processed provided that the organization is satisfied that all processed data is, in fact, reported on the printout. This can usually be ensured by appropriate programmed procedures and adequate general controls.

EXAMPLE. A company awards salary increases every six months. After the amendments have been processed, a full report of the employee master file is produced. Each person's salary is authorized by the personnel director. The completeness of the list is ensured by checking entries against a master list maintained by the personnel office.

SITUATION 3:

Data is authorized at the time a document is prepared.

IMPACT ON ADEQUACY OF CONTROL. The presence of an authorizing signature is not, in itself, adequate to ensure that only authorized data is processed. For authorization to be effective, it must be controlled in one of the ways described in Situations 1 and 2.

EXAMPLE. Selling price increases are authorized by the sales director. A copy of the relevant memo is sent to the sales department that is responsible for updating the sales price file. The sales director does not check subsequently that only amendments authorized personally are updated to the sales price file.

SITUATION 4:

Rejections occur.

IMPACT ON ADEQUACY OF CONTROL. It is necessary to ensure that unauthorized data cannot be introduced during correction and reentry of errors. This might be achieved in one of the following ways:

- Ensuring that any adjustments to previously authorized control totals are themselves subjected to authorization.
- Ensuring that all data reentered is controlled for authorization in one of the ways described in Situations 1 and 2 for original data.

EXAMPLES. In the example in Situation 1, insertion of unauthorized data would be identified during agreement of the control accounts.

In the example in Situation 2, if the master file report is not produced until all data has been accepted, the post-processing authorization is effective over both original and reentered data.

MANUAL VALIDITY CHECKS

Manual procedures for checking validity of data are not discussed here, since they are the same as those for noncomputer systems.

PROGRAMMED VALIDITY CHECKS

SITUATION:

The validity of data is checked by the computer.

IMPACT ON ADEQUACY OF CONTROL. Control is adequate if the following requirements are met:

- Programmed procedures can be relied on to ensure that all exceptions are reported in sufficient detail to permit adequate user investigation.
- All reference data items, or parameters, used by the validation procedures are themselves subject to adequate controls with respect to maintenance of data and authorization of amendments.
- All reference data items, or parameters, are set at levels that result in the production of meaningful exception reports.
- Any facility to override the validation procedures is subject to appropriate approval procedures.
- All exception reports are investigated and acted upon by user departments in a timely manner. To do this effectively, the user must understand the programmed procedures on which the reports are based.

EXAMPLES. The following examples are arranged in the same sequence as the requirements.

- General controls are adequate to ensure the functioning of proper programmed procedures.
- Credit limits used in validation of incoming sales orders are controlled satisfactorily for authorizations and maintenance. (See relevant sections of this chapter.)
- All credit memos over $1,000 are printed for manual authorization, but this results in 40 percent of all credits being printed. Clearly, the $1,000 limit is too low to produce a useful report.

- A separate validation report lists any instances of override and is distributed directly to the person responsible for approving these events.
- Exception reports are distributed directly to people responsible for investigating and authorizing the exception conditions.

ADEQUACY OF CONTROLS OVER MAINTENANCE OF DATA

An organization's procedures for ensuring that data is correctly maintained on computer files are an important part of its internal control. Questions dealing with these procedures appear under many control objectives. Adequacy of control is discussed here for convenience and to emphasize that similar control procedures may apply to different cycles and different control objectives.

The term "maintenance" is used in this context to describe those procedures intended to ensure the following:

- *Data remains correct.* It must be valid, accurate, and complete as input and updated to the file, until such time as it is deleted during authorized processing.
- *Data remains current.* All data requiring amendment is identified and the appropriate action taken.

In manual systems, all data is visible. As such, it is subject to scrutiny during normal day-to-day processing. This usually ensures that the data remains reliable. In computer systems, however, data is stored on magnetic media and may be erroneously changed without visible evidence of the change. Consequently, maintenance controls are required to ensure that the stored data is not altered, except in accordance with management's intentions.

The requirement to ensure that data remains correct applies to both transaction data and master file data. In theory, the fact that errors in master file data will be more far-reaching in effect than errors in transaction data means that master file data should be subject to a higher standard of control. However, in practice it is often found that

- Maintenance of transaction data is more secure than that of master file data.
- Maintenance controls are only adequate for particularly significant data fields, such as value fields. Maintenance of fields of lesser accounting significance are often dependent on the existence of adequate data file security controls in EDP. (See the discussion of general controls in Chapter 20, "General or Integrity Controls," and in Chapter 26.)

The term "maintenance" (also referred to as "continuity") as used here should not be confused with the term "maintenance" as applied to computer files. The latter term refers to the process used to amend data stored on files.

CORRECTNESS OF DATA

SITUATION 1:

Batch totals are posted to a manual control account that is periodically agreed to the balance reported for the computer master file.

IMPACT ON ADEQUACY OF CONTROL. Control is adequate to ensure that the particular data field used to generate the totals is properly maintained. It does not, however, identify compensating errors within one or more individual records on the file. This control technique is most commonly applied to transaction data held on master files. Usually the relevant value field is totaled. It also may be used to control master file reference data (by producing a hash total of the relevant field). However, since master file data requires more stringent control than transaction data (bearing in mind the problem of compensating errors inherent in the use of control totals), it is preferable to use a stronger maintenance control over master file data.

EXAMPLE. All transaction types entered into the accounts receivable system are batched and totals established over gross dollar values. These totals are posted to a manual control account that is reconciled each month with the total balance reported for the accounts receivable file. There are no specific user controls to ensure that individual accounts receivable balances are accurately stated.

SITUATION 2:

Computer-produced control totals (of accepted data) are posted to a manual control account that is periodically agreed to the balance reported for the computer master file.

IMPACT ON ADEQUACY OF CONTROL. Control over maintenance of data is adequate to the same extent as in Situation 1.

EXAMPLE. Control totals of accepted data are produced for all entries to an inventory master file. These totals are posted to a manual control account that is regularly reconciled to the balance reported for the inventory master file.

SITUATION 3:

A control account is used to ensure that data is correctly maintained.

IMPACT ON ADEQUACY OF CONTROL. The frequency of the reconciliation procedures should be sufficient to ensure that errors cannot accumulate to an extent where it is difficult to investigate and correct them. Within this basic requirement, it is likely that the frequency of reconciliation procedures will be affected by the method of processing used. For example, if the file is accessed sequentially, it is convenient to produce a total after each update. However, if the file is accessed directly, a special run is required to produce a total. It is therefore unlikely that this will be done after each update.

EXAMPLE. A company has an inventory recording system. The master file is held on disk and is on-line to several terminals situated in the major inventory locations. Each week, this direct access file is sorted to produce a sequential file used in the production statistics system. At the same time, a file total is accumulated. This is then reconciled to a manual control account, prepared each day from inventory movement totals.

SITUATION 4:

The computer reconciles the total of items on the master file with a control record on the same file.

IMPACT ON ADEQUACY OF CONTROL. Control is adequate if there are procedures to ensure that

- Programmed procedures are adequate and can be relied on to identify and report any differences arising; and either
- The total brought forward prior to update is manually agreed to that carried forward after the last update; or
- Controls over data file security are adequate to ensure that the correct file is used.

The latter two requirements mean that this control is not usually as strong as when a manual control account is used. The user must also ensure that either the reconciliation is reported as satisfactory or any differences reported are investigated and corrected.

EXAMPLE. An open-item accounts receivable file is updated twice a week from transaction files accumulated during the intervening period. After each update, the total of individual items on the file is reconciled with a header record that contains a control total for the file. The control total is itself updated directly from the transaction files. The movement report, produced after each update, records brought forward and carried forward totals, movements updated, and the results of the reconciliation procedure. This report is received by the accounts receivable supervisor who ensures that

- The total brought forward agrees with that carried forward on the previous report.

- The reconciliation is reported as satisfactory or any differences reported are investigated.

SITUATION 5:

The computer reconciles the total of items on the file with the total on a separate control file.

IMPACT ON ADEQUACY OF CONTROL. Control is adequate provided the same requirements specified previously are met. This control is usually stronger than using a control record because

- It requires the use of an independent set of programs, whereas the control record reconciliation is usually part of the update program.
- It can provide a check on the results of processing by many programs. Since, however, the effectiveness of the control is very dependent on the appropriate functioning of programmed procedures, strong general controls are necessary.

EXAMPLE. A large corporation has a multilevel divisional and departmental structure. It has developed a general ledger system that accumulates data from all of the various organizational levels, either by direct interface with their other accounting systems or by entry of journal vouchers. Output includes trial balances and financial statements at departmental, divisional, and corporate levels, and also management accounts at departmental and divisional levels. Before any update of the general ledger files can occur, all accepted data is written to a control file. The control file movement total is reconciled with the various accepted data totals. After each update of the general ledger files, a separate set of programs reconciles the control file with the general ledger files and produces a variety of reconciliation reports. These are reviewed by the user to ensure that both update and maintenance of the files are satisfactory.

SITUATION 6:

Neither manual nor computer control accounts are used.

IMPACT ON ADEQUACY OF CONTROL. Control over maintenance of data can be achieved by obtaining a full printout of the file and manually checking each item with source data. The work load can be spread by having the file printed out on a cyclical basis. In any case, the frequency of checking should take into account both the volume of data and its financial sensitivity. This is an effective but costly control procedure. As such, it is usually used only for low volumes of financially sensitive data.

EXAMPLE. A carpet manufacturer produces several different ranges of carpet in a variety of designs and colors. Selling prices reflect the quality and range of carpet. Consequently, there are relatively few standard selling prices. Volumes of turnover, however, are high. As a result, errors in selling prices would have far-reaching effects. The selling price file is therefore printed in full each month and a one-for-one check is carried out to ensure that prices remain correct.

SITUATION 7:

There are no application controls over the maintenance of data.

IMPACT ON ADEQUACY OF CONTROL. It may be possible to rely on strong general controls in the area of data file security to ensure that data is properly maintained.

CURRENCY OF DATA

SITUATION 1:

Data held on file is printed on a cyclical basis for review by the user department.

IMPACT ON ADEQUACY OF CONTROL. Control is adequate provided that

- All data on file is printed within an appropriate time span.
- The user reviews the data and ensures that all necessary amendments are made.

EXAMPLE. A company has an order processing accounts receivable system. Initial order entry includes validation against credit limits. In order to ensure that credit limits are set at reasonable levels, the customer file on which they are recorded is printed on a cyclical basis. Each month, 100 accounts are printed for checking. The accounts are selected for printing in order of account number. As well as reviewing the credit limits, the credit controller checks the accounts against a master list to ensure that all accounts are covered during a six-month period.

SITUATION 2:

The computer produces exception reports of data that has remained unchanged for a certain period of time.

IMPACT ON ADEQUACY OF CONTROL. Control is adequate if the following requirements are met:

- General controls are adequate to ensure the appropriate functioning of programmed procedures.
- Programmed procedures are appropriate to ensure that all exceptions will be identified and reported (such as interrogating each record and comparing the relevant data with predetermined limits or parameters).

- Parameters or limits used in the programmed procedures are set at reasonable levels and in accordance with management's intentions.

- All exceptions are investigated by the user and amendments are made when appropriate.

EXAMPLE. During a period of inflation, a company expects the cost of purchased inventories to increase at least once a year. Provided the appropriate data is maintained on file, it can be reviewed by the computer and any items where the cost has not changed in the last year can be reported for manual investigation.

The aging of inventory and accounts receivable balances to identify old items is another example of this type of review.

PART VI

Controlling Computers

Testing Techniques for Computer-Based Systems

INTRODUCTION

Special testing techniques are available to auditors of computer-based systems. In many instances these tests, performed using audit software tools, are the only efficient and effective way to evaluate computer-based systems. Audit tests fall into two general categories: (1) compliance tests of controls and (2) substantive procedures. To perform these tests, the auditor chooses a strategy and specific testing methods. In computer-based systems, the strategy usually includes audit software tools.

The methods an auditor can use to test the accuracy of data processing results and the adequacy of controls over that processing include the following:

- Manual tests
  a. Manual checking
  b. Manual simulation
- EDP testing methods
  a. Program code analysis
  b. Parallel simulation
  c. Test data and Integrated Test Facility

After a strategy has been developed and methods have been selected, the auditor can decide on the types of software to use. Among the audit software tools available are:

- Generalized audit software
- Application audit software
- Industry-related audit software
- Specialized audit software for systems activities
  a. Comparison programs
  b. Unexecuted code analysis
  c. Flowcharting programs
  d. System log analysis
  e. Data base analysis
- Time-sharing library and microcomputer programs
- System utility software and service aids
- Custom audit software

METHODS OF TESTING COMPUTER-BASED SYSTEMS

Due to the nature of computer system processing, the auditor cannot always carry out tests using conventional methods. As a result, a number of specific testing methods for computer-based systems have been developed. The basic techniques available to the auditor for testing computer-based systems and the circumstances in which they are commonly used are described in the following sections.

MANUAL TESTING

Many of the manual tests for computer-based systems are the same as those used to test manual systems, although the documents that are examined may be different. Customary manual audit testing techniques can be used whenever

- Adequate evidence is readily available;
- Information is presented in normal accounting terms; and
- Volumes of data are not too large to carry out the test.

Accordingly, many transaction review techniques, compliance tests, and substantive procedures do not change significantly in a computer-based system.
    Some manual audit tests require special EDP skills. For instance, general or integrity controls and program coding are usually described in data processing terminology. Review may require the assistance of a specialist, both to understand the evidence examined and to test the relevant processing functions. In those cases, some form of audit software can normally be used. Audit software is discussed later in this chapter.

Manual Checking

Manual checks that can be used to perform compliance tests generally include the following:

- *Examination* — For example, examining reports indicating that the numerical sequence of prenumbered documents is checked periodically and missing numbers are investigated by someone who does not normally work with these documents, or examination of program amendment forms to see that they have been approved by the appropriate people.

- *Reperformance* — For example, selecting items from the report of missing numbers and verifying that the correct follow-up action has been taken; selecting approved program amendment forms and confirming that the amendment forms and amendments have been adequately designed, tested, and documented.

- *Observation* — For example, attending physical inventories; observing the physical restrictions on access to the computer room.

User controls and many of the general controls can be tested in this conventional way. Therefore they present no major change in procedures for the auditor.

Similarly, substantive procedures, although likely to be carried out on computer printouts instead of on traditional lists of balances, can be performed by conventional manual tests in some instances.

Limitations on Manual Checking. The auditor should also test certain programmed procedures. These are checked as part of compliance tests on implementation controls or as substantive procedures to provide assurance that a particular programmed procedure is operating. Some evidence that the programmed procedure is functioning usually is available, but steps taken to produce those results by computer processing are rarely printed out in detail. In the absence of such a printout, the auditor cannot test the operation of programmed procedures by conventional means. There are two ways this difficulty can arise:

1. Totals and analyses are often printed out without supporting details, making it impossible for the auditor to check the method used to arrive at that total or analysis.

2. When exception reports and rejection listings are produced, it is often impossible to establish that all items that should have been reported or rejected have been. By examining the reports or listings themselves, the auditor only sees the ones that were reported. Another method of testing, obviously, is called for.

In both cases, there is a lack of visible evidence showing how the programmed procedure operates within the computer, since only the results of its operations are seen.

Manual Simulation Techniques

Manual tests can also be carried out when full visible evidence is not readily provided by the system, but can be re-created by special means. Methods for achieving this re-creation of evidence are known collectively as "manual simulation." They include

- Reassembling processed data so that it is in the same condition as it was when the programmed procedure was first applied. For example, reassembling batches of sales invoices to test the batch totals that were posted to the sales ledger control account.

- Working on current data before it is sent for processing by the computer. For example, checking the additions of batches before they are sent for conversion in order to test how a total, used to control subsequent processing, was reached.

- Selecting a small number of items from those submitted for processing and processing them in a separate run. For example, splitting a batch into two batches, one large and one small, and then processing the small batch separately to see whether the computer-produced totals agree with precalculated results.

- Simulating a condition that will produce a report if the programmed procedure is working properly. For example, altering a batch total to an incorrect figure so that the batch is rejected or withholding a document so that it is reported as missing. This approach requires careful planning, execution, and the agreement of a responsible user-department official.

- Requesting a special printout of items processed. For example, a listing of sales invoices included in a sales total produced by the computer.

When visible evidence of the operation of a programmed procedure neither exists nor can be created, and the appropriate condition cannot be simulated, it is not possible to carry out the kinds of manual tests described in the preceding section.

EDP TESTING TECHNIQUES

Program Code Analysis

Program code analysis is used by an auditor to confirm the existence of programmed procedures in a program or series of programs. The programmed procedures to be confirmed are those identified in the Computer Internal Control Questionnaire (see Chapter 25, "The Evaluation Process and How to Use Documents") or similar document. The technique may also be used by the auditor to obtain or confirm an understanding of the programs, or parts of programs, in the system.

For this technique to be effective, the auditor must either examine the code in object form (the machine language the computer uses internally), which is probably not practical, or confirm that the code examined in source statement form (the language programmers use) relates to the instructions in the executable programs (the programs in form the computer can run).

This confirmation usually can be obtained from the tests carried out on program security controls and computer operation controls. In more advanced installations, where the auditor is most likely to use program code analysis, system software may ensure that the source and executable programs are the same. The auditor can often rely on tests of these procedures. As an alternative, the auditor may be able to make special use of testing software. (Testing software is discussed more fully in the section "Comparison Programs"). This software can check a newly compiled version (the version of source program after conversion into machine code) of the source program in question against the executable program in use.

Program code analysis usually consists of three steps:

1. *Identifying the programs to be examined.* This can be done by referring to the company's system documentation, which should include block diagrams of programs and detailed specifications of individual programs.

2. *Selecting the form of code to be examined.* The auditor normally decides to examine the source statement program. This requires
   - A knowledge of the source (or high-level programming) language used, such as COBOL in many environments.
   - Care in selecting the version of the source statement program to be examined. It is usually preferable to compile the authorized source for the production program and check the compiled results against the production version that is actually in use. The software also may provide options such as cross-referenced data names and verb listings.

3. *Analyzing the selected code.* Understanding the logic of programs written by someone else is sometimes difficult. It is usually easier when the auditor is in an installation that adheres to certain standards for programming and program documentation. In any case, it is important to adopt a systematic approach to reviewing the code. Starting with the first program statement and following the code through line by line to the last statement is unlikely to be an efficient or effective way to proceed. The following approach is more practical:
   - Obtain an understanding of the data and files used by the programs being analyzed.
   - Analyze the logic of the relevant lines of code.
   - Ensure that the relevant lines of code analyzed are not bypassed or distorted by another part of the program or by an entirely different program.

To analyze the code, an auditor may use audit software packages to provide additional documentation and comparison programs to uncover changes made in programs during the period under investigation. Comparison programs are, therefore, particularly useful in subsequent years' audits.

Parallel Simulation

Parallel simulation tests the proper functioning of programmed procedures and the accuracy of the financial data processed. The method consists of taking real data that is being run through production programs and processing it through programs developed by the auditor. For this method to work, the test programs must perform some, but not necessarily all, of the same functions as the production programs being simulated.

Parallel simulation can check the following:

- Input validation procedures
- Data updating logic
- Processing logic and controls

In parallel simulation, all transactions chosen for the test are checked. Checking can take place at any time; the programs can be run whenever computer time is available.

The method of parallel simulation employed depends on the software tools selected. These can consist of generalized audit software, industry-oriented audit software, application audit software, or custom audit software developed for special circumstances.

To perform parallel simulation, all data and files processed by the auditor's programs must be exactly the same as those required to run the production programs. Additionally, reports should be generated for the same periods of time. Any and all documentation that refers to controls, or to reconciliations conducted, should be retained.

The parallel simulation programs used are usually less complex than the regular production programs they are simulating. Certain discrepancies can occur as a result of this difference. Rather than trying to amend the test program to conform exactly to the processing requirements of the production program, it may be far more cost-effective to reconcile the discrepancies manually. Most likely, the auditor will choose to use a program and compare the test processing results to detect any differences or discrepancies.

In all cases, exceptions and unexplained discrepancies should be documented fully. The auditor should then recommend corrective measures.

Parallel simulation can be repeated using the same testing programs provided the production programs have not changed in ways that have audit significance. To verify whether authorized programming changes have been made, the auditor should check the program change log and then test it by comparing the current version of the source program to a controlled version of this program. Unauthorized or unrecorded changes would probably show up as differences in the results between the simulation and the production run. Hence the importance of following up on discrepancies.

Test Data and Integrated Test Facility

Test data is one method used as an EDP audit technique to test processing and controls in application systems. In parallel simulation, test programs process real data; in the test data method, real programs process test data. The output of this processing is then compared to predefined results.

Audit test data should not be confused with the comprehensive test data prepared by the organization's data processing staff to test the operation of new programs. Audit test data is restricted to testing only the particular programmed procedures on which the auditor wishes to rely for the processing of financial transactions. It is designed to be as representative as possible of the actual data processed by the company. However, when it has been decided that audit test data will be used to test particular procedures, it is often efficient to include tests on other procedures that would otherwise be done manually.

Test data is used to check the following:

- Input validation routines, error detection, and transaction data control procedures integral to the programs
- Processing logic and controls on master file data
- Standard calculations, such as interest, taxes, or gross pay
- Program modifications
- Manual procedures in use

The test data method is applicable for the following:

- Acceptance testing of a new system or a system modification
- Compliance testing of a system already in use

The test data method therefore can be applied to program processing verification and evaluation. It is not a way to check completeness or accuracy of input and update of data or master files.

There are two methods of running test data:

1. Test data can be processed using the organization's operational programs, separately from the actual data, using copies of master files or dummy files specially designed and set up for the purpose.
2. Test data can be included with the organization's data for regular processing, with approval from a responsible department official.

The second method is called an Integrated Test Facility (ITF). (See Figure 28-1.) When specific records on the master files are reserved or created for this purpose and consistently processed for testing at regularly established milestones, the ITF is also referred to as the Base Case System Evaluation.

Test data can be created in three ways:

1. The simplest, although the most time-consuming, is to complete actual input forms in such a way that each condition specified in the test plan will be tested. This would include creation of master records, followed by running the transactions to test processing and controls.

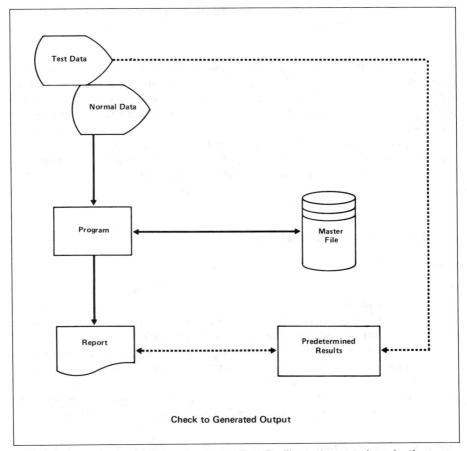

FIG. 28-1 The relationship of an Integrated Test Facility to generated production program output

2. A related method is to copy existing master file records onto a test master and then, as in the first method, to run transactions. When this is done, the auditor should be sure that each possible condition as described by the test plan is covered in the processing of master file records.

3. Auditors also make limited use of special computer programs called test data generators. Two examples are PRO TEST, owned by Synergetics, and DATAMACS, marketed by Management and Computer Services Inc. A test data generator assists in preparing test data sets. Although cost often becomes a consideration when deciding whether to use test data generators, their advantages

include (a) reduction of clerical effort and (b) increased thoroughness in testing input validation routines, error detection procedures, and calculations.

Test data transactions must be scheduled to be run on executable programs as they exist in the production library. The auditor should receive output that was either observed being run or was handled in such a way that it could not have been tampered with. Care should be taken that production files are not affected by the presence of test data. The output should then be compared to the expected results. Differences should be analyzed when possible; in these cases the test should be rerun to verify the results. Where differences in procedures do exist, documentation should be written.

AUDIT SOFTWARE TOOLS

Introduction

Auditors have been using computers as part of the audit process for many years. The use of computerized techniques affords access to the large amounts of data stored in electronic data processing systems. The audit software available can be particularly effective in accessing this information.

When complex, integrated computer systems are involved, the use of audit software tools is not only audit efficient; it is often a necessary ingredient of an effective audit. Audit software is not, however, a panacea for computer audit problems. This is an important technique, yet it is only one of many an auditor must master to audit complex business systems successfully.

What Is Audit Software?

Audit software is a special program or set of programs that can readily audit data stored on computer media. Audit software has functions similar to query facilities, report writers, utilities, computer languages, and other data processing software techniques. Indeed, the auditor may well use these standard data processing techniques to assist with the audit if they are more efficient. In most cases, special purpose audit software is more suitable.

The following are the principal features of audit software, as compared to other auditing techniques:

- Complete files can be read speedily and accurately, resulting in
  a. Examination of all data on file rather than a small sample.
  b. The ability to obtain information that would not be available otherwise.

   c. The ability to specify and identify data that meets a particular condition, such as all customer balances that are more than double their credit limits.

   d. The ability to quantify the extent of unusual or erroneous data on the file, such as the total number of customers with credit totals that exceed their limits and the total of the balances involved.

- Conventional audit time can be devoted to an examination of items identified as needing audit attention.

- The software can be made flexible by using parameters that can be altered each time the program is run.

- Once audit software is set up, subsequent running costs are reasonable and overall time savings are often considerable. The same program is used for each audit until there is a major change in the system.

- To run the program, computer resources must be obtained. These should be planned in advance, as should the procedures for capture and retention of the data to be examined.

What Data Is Available?

Modern decision-support systems contain much more data than traditional accounting systems. With proper design, large quantities of relevant data can be stored on computer media. Modern systems are designed to maintain the organization's data in forms that can satisfy most management demands, even those unanticipated when the system is designed. Data stored that is relevant to management and to the auditor includes the following:

- Accounting data
- Historical results
- Statistical information
- Computer programs
- Operational data (such as computer operating logs)

This data is not stored indefinitely. As soon as its usefulness has expired, data stored on computer media is regularly destroyed. The auditor may have to make a special request to ensure that the relevant data is retained for audit examination.

Audit Objectives

A critical part of using audit software effectively is to accurately translate audit objectives into actual computer processing functions.

To set the audit objectives, the auditor should have a knowledge of fundamental EDP concepts. If his or her knowledge of EDP is more comprehensive, the auditor can also prepare and execute the software. If not, the broad computer functions can be discussed with an EDP audit specialist or a data processing technician. The specialist or technician can then develop the automated application specifications and prepare the computer programs. The degree of technical ability needed depends on the technique used. In general, the more flexible the software is, the more the auditor needs to know to use it.

For example, a typical audit objective might be to determine that the general ledger control account balance agrees with the total of the individual account balances included in the subsidiary records. The corresponding computer function would be to total the amount in the dollar balance field of each record included in the file or data base and to print the total. To prepare for the computer specialist to do this, the auditor would

- Indicate the location of the relevant fields on the records in the file.
- Direct that the amounts in those fields are to be added.
- Specify the format of the report on which the totals are to be printed.

Although the previous example is simple, it demonstrates the basic, step-by-step thought process that is required. By following the same process, even complex audit objectives can be translated into specific computer functions. Figure 28-2 illustrates how some of the compound audit objectives relating to accounts receivable processing may be translated into basic computer functions and thus converted to a computer program.

For purposes of illustration, assume that EDP maintains a file containing each customer's balance-forward information. Typically, this file would include customer name, number, balance due, and the totals of the aging categories within which the amounts comprising the balance fall. In addition, a supporting transaction file is maintained, which shows customer number, invoice number, and amount of all items uncollected at the end of the month. To meet some of the audit objectives, the auditor would follow the procedures shown in Figure 28-2.

GENERALIZED AUDIT SOFTWARE

The examples of audit software tools discussed subsequently are representative of the ones currently available. With the staggering pace of technological EDP developments, auditors should always be prepared to learn new techniques and keep abreast of current audit developments.

The auditor who knows how to use standard data processing techniques, such as languages or utilities, may be able to use those techniques to satisfy some audit requirements. But when an audit department is using software

Audit Objectives	Computer Function
1. Determine that the total of the balances of individual customer accounts agrees with the general ledger account balance.	**1.** Add the balance due amount for each record on the balance forward file and print total.
2. a. Request confirmation of amounts due from customers on a given basis of selection.	**2. a.** Compare balance, customer name, or other relevant information on each record with established selection criteria and select those records that meet or exceed the criteria; print confirmation requests.
b. Test the aging calculations by selecting individual customer accounts on a given basis and check the aging of unpaid amounts by tracing to source documents.	**b.** Compare selection criteria with relevant information on each record and select those records that meet or exceed the criteria. For each of the accounts selected, print the customer number and the invoice number and amount for items comprising each aging category for manual comparison to source documents.

FIG. 28-2   How audit objectives can be translated into basic computer functions which can in turn be translated into computer programs that perform those functions

extensively, it is best to choose software aids specifically suited to the environment.

Generalized audit software exists because, in the normal course of events, many different audits require similar audit tasks (e.g., adding files, formatting reports) and this software can be adapted easily to carry out these tasks in different computer environments. This software can be adapted quickly to the specific goals of an audit. Generalized software is usually more cost effective than custom software, which is written specifically for a job.

The auditor uses generalized audit software to examine the information held on computer files and to

- Carry out audit tests, such as verification of calculations and totals or analyses produced. An example would be the evaluation and summation of aged inventory balances.
- Create and print additional analyses of data for audit purposes, such as the calculation of total inventory holdings in excess of current demand or total receivables that exceed credit limits.
- Critically examine the state of the data held on the file in order to
  a. Provide totals of unusual items, such as customers without any credit limit or inventory issues with invalid dates.

   b. Select and print data from the file for subsequent examination, either as a sample of normal data or because it falls within the auditor's definition of unusual, such as customer credit balances over $2,000 or unusual discount terms.

A good generalized audit software package is a software product specifically designed for audit use. It should make it easy for the auditor to translate audit objectives into program code. A package can perform varied data processing functions: reading data from computer files; selecting all or only certain records for processing; performing auditor-specified computations; sampling, sorting, and summarizing data; and printing reports in the form requested by the auditor.

For example, the AUDITPAK II package from Coopers & Lybrand is a preprocessor that generates a COBOL or RPG II program from a simple questionnaire that the auditor completes. The COBOL or RPG II program can then be compiled and executed in the normal way. It offers the auditor the following capabilities:

- Read and analyze information stored in a data file or match and analyze information stored in two separate but logically related files.
- Select items for review, stratify selected items or complete files, and analyze the resulting information.
- Apply interval sampling methods, beginning the analysis at any random start point and continuing the selection at fixed intervals.
- Summarize data files and analyze the data.
- Subtotal and develop column totals or column averages for different logical levels (for example, payroll by department, plant, and division).
- Develop statistics on any number of data elements in the file and calculate percentages for selected items in relation to the total population and control totals showing positive, negative, and zero constituents as well as net values.
- Assist substantive testing by sampling the data file and generating reports.
- Perform any number of mathematical calculations on an entire file or selected records.
- Format reports with descriptive headings, automatic horizontal columns, and page numbers.
- Produce multiple reports and machine-readable output files from a single pass of the file. Each report or output file may show details of up to nine logical levels and can summarize at any of these levels.
- AUDITPAK II reports:
  a. Initial edit for syntax errors

  b. Cross edit for relationship errors
  c. Summary of the total number of errors and number of COBOL source statements generated when there are no fatal errors
  d. Parameters entered for execution of the COBOL program
- Reports designed by the auditor, such as:
  a. Accounts with balances over credit limit
  b. Confirmation control
  c. Selected representative accounts
  d. Statistics for specific data
  e. Wrap-up report showing file statistics

APPLICATION AUDIT SOFTWARE

The increased use of purchased software packages has shown that data processing functions can be largely standardized to meet the needs of different organizations. Audit software tasks for common applications such as accounts receivable, accounts payable, general ledger, payroll, and inventory can be similarly standardized. These applications are described in Part III, "Accounting Systems."

Application audit software systems are developed to achieve common audit objectives. These functions are then precoded into the package and its associated documentation. The auditor saves time and effort, since audit functions are predefined. As an example, for accounts receivable: age analyze the ledger, select items for audit testing, produce confirmation letters, and match subsequent cash received. Of course, it may be necessary to alter the functions somewhat, depending on the particular audit concerns, but even this flexibility can be built into the software. To run the software, the auditor converts the data files into a format compatible with the software package, determines the appropriate parameters, and then executes the prepackaged software.

INDUSTRY-RELATED AUDIT SOFTWARE

Some audit tests are specific to particular industries. Among these are the insurance, health care, and financial services industries. Tests are also designed for applications within those industries, such as investment portfolio accounting. Because of the intricacy, and resultant cost, of designing the kinds of programs that are necessary to achieve common audit objectives, EDP auditing firms have produced standard software packages and routines to meet these special needs.

SPECIALIZED AUDIT SOFTWARE FOR SYSTEM ACTIVITIES

Comparison Programs

Comparison programs are used to compare the source or executable versions of operational programs with authorized copies that have been investigated and held by the auditor. They generally provide listings that set out the contents of the programs being compared and the differences (if any) between them. This technique is extremely useful to identify unauthorized changes, or to confirm a lack of changes, in programs. The software can also confirm that source programs are logically identical to their executable form.

Auditors — both internal and external — need to determine that once a program is properly implemented on a controlled basis, it is not changed on an unauthorized basis. To ensure this, the auditor reviews a controlled version of a source program and compares it to the production version. There are programs, such as Coopers & Lybrand's Source Compare Program, that can help the auditor identify additions, deletions, and changes in a program between two points in time.

This general or integrity control software package compares, line by line, two versions of a program's source code (the controlled and the production versions) and identifies any additions, deletions, or changes, along with their locations. When this information is available, it is easier to confirm, or strengthen, program security.

The Source Compare Program generates four reports:

1. A listing of the production version's input

2. A listing of the controlled version's input

3. Production version variations, including additions, deletions, and changes, and where they occur

4. Controlled version variations, including additions, deletions, and changes, and where they occur.

Typically, the auditor works with one pair of reports. If the focus is on the production program, the auditor reviews the controlled version's input and the production version's changes. If the focus is on the controlled program, the auditor reviews the changes, if any.

The variation reports are printed with the same number of lines per page, so they may be analyzed more easily. In addition, the auditor can choose to see only the revision totals first. Then detail reports can be printed if required. Knowing the magnitude of the changes before embarking on a complete review can speed up the review process.

This type of software is especially helpful during conversion efforts, to help ensure that programs used in the old and the new systems are the same. Additionally, when the EDP department wants to ensure that authorized

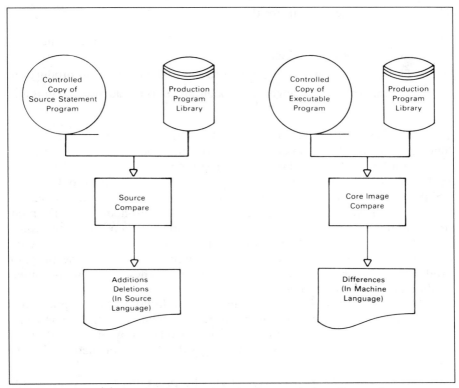

**FIG. 28-3 Flowchart showing the use of comparison programs: Source Compare
and Core Image Compare programs from Coopers & Lybrand**

program changes have actually been made in accordance with program change requests, the program can flag the changes.

The programs nearest the heart of the computer system, the load modules, are those that instruct the computer in the language it understands. Changes in these modules can be particularly hard to detect. There are software packages that can aid the auditor in determining whether the load module that was created from the source program is still unchanged. (The source program, one that can be read by the user, must go through a compiler to translate it into an object module before comparison.)

All of the object modules — programs in machine code — are brought together in a process called linkediting to create a load module. The load module is entered (loaded) into the computer for execution. Coopers & Lybrand's Core Image Compare Program is one example of a program that can compare the object module to the load module to determine if any changes have been made. (See Figure 28-3 for an overview of these two comparison programs.) The program can also be used to compare two load modules.

The package can help to ensure that

- A reviewed program produces the same executable code as the current production version.
- The source program corresponds to the current version in production.
- No unauthorized changes have been made to production programs between two points in time.

The program would not detect a change that was made at a particular point in time if, in the interim, the load module was changed back to its original status.

To understand how this particular program works, imagine that the auditor has identified significant programmed procedures and wants to determine whether they are operating properly. One of the techniques available to ensure that the program is being executed in accordance with management's intentions is to review the source code of the production program. Then the auditor must determine whether the version that has been checked is identical to the one that is actually in production. To facilitate this process, the program produces an exception report, which lists mismatches between the object module and the load module.

After the package is used, the auditor should note any exceptions and consider them when deciding whether to rely on general controls. For subsequent audits, the auditor should retain a controlled copy of the authorized program and use it to detect program changes that have been made within the period.

This kind of software is useful not only for programs and software developed in-house, but also for testing vendor-supplied software as well. Using this program, the auditor can compare the vendor-supplied modules with those used in production. If these tests are performed on vendor software, the auditor should first determine that the user has not already customized the software with the vendor's permission or has not made maintenance updates as prescribed by the vendor.

Another example of the need to use comparison programs occurred not long ago when a national company hired a consultant to upgrade its computer system. During his assignment, the consultant did some programming of his own. He modified the system so it would ignore the paid, returned checks written to fictitious people and cashed by him. It was not until the company lost $100,000 in money orders that the unauthorized financial drain was detected.

If appropriate controls had existed in the company's computer system, this unfortunate situation might not have occurred. Software can help detect whether program change controls are operating. One such package is Coopers & Lybrand's Special Linklib Analysis Program Series (SLAPS). This software package provides the auditor with a means of testing load libraries. It can also detect unauthorized changes in modules, as well as unauthorized programs placed in libraries.

Once a compile occurs (after no errors in program syntax have been detected by the compiler), a linkedit is executed. This process joins parts of programs together so that they function properly, in sequence. The linkedit combines the object program with the standard routines necessary to produce a machine-executable program.

The SLAPS audit software consists of programs that extract and print the date of compilation and linkedit, and report any changes that might bypass controls created by the compile and linkedit procedures. The reports include such information as the language that the program was written in, the date the program was compiled and linkedited into the library, and the number of modules (control sections) in the program.

The reports generated are:

- Parameter Card Edit Report, which prints the parameter card exactly as it was read. It also prints any errors or warnings regarding the parameters.

- Messages and Information Report, which specifies inconsistencies in information regarding the user's load modules.

- Serial Partitioned Data Set (PDS) List Report, which lists all load modules, with more recent data listed first.

- The Compile/Linkedit Report, which lists the program name, compiler name, date of compile, and the linkedit date. This information helps the auditor to trace all changes and implementations for the examination period.

- The ZAP Report, which lists ZAPs or SuperZAPs. (ZAPs are a series of programs that can change an object program or an executable program. ZAPs can be used to change programs or data files directly, thereby bypassing the procedures used to control programs or data file changes.) The report provides the control section, the linkedit date, the ZAP date, and the area where the ZAP occurred. It can be used to trace changes to proper documentation.

- The Change Report, which compares two examination periods and lists changed programs, new programs, and programs no longer used. When used in conjunction with source program comparison software (which detects what has been changed within the program), it allows the auditor to continue to rely on programmed procedures. (Programmed procedures include many accounting and control procedures that are executed by computer programs.)

Other categories of audit software packages are available, in addition to comparison programs, which provide the auditor with specialized capabilities for systems activities.

Unexecuted Code Analysis

Software is available that monitors the execution of a program and produces a report showing the number of times each line of source code was executed during processing. This report can be useful when performing code analysis, since it indicates any line of code that is not executed. Unexecuted code should be investigated to find out why it exists in a program. The investigation may make the auditor aware of code that is fraudulent, redundant, or erroneous.

Flowcharting Programs

Flowcharting programs document and analyze programmed procedures. The flowcharts produced by these programs are often too voluminous to be helpful in an audit. However, the verb listings and the cross-referenced data name listings also generated are normally quite worthwhile. Among other uses, they are often helpful in program code analysis. Job control language (JCL) flowchart programs can assist in understanding and confirming system flows.

System Log Analysis

Many installations automatically produce a log of all computer activity (such as IBM's System Management Facility (SMF) log for the OS system). Programs have been developed that analyze the systems log to report specific defined items. Using this software, the auditor can carry out tests to ensure that

- Only approved programs access sensitive data.
- Utilities or service aids that can alter data files and program libraries are used only for authorized purposes.
- Approved programs are being run only when scheduled; conversely, unauthorized runs are not taking place.
- The correct data file generation is being accessed for production purposes.
- Data files reported to be password-protected actually are protected.

System Management Facility

SMF software can be used by auditors, as is shown by the following example. A computer operator, unsupervised during the night shift, decided to make a change to a production program to increase his weekly pay by $1,000. The next day, the payroll was run under the normal supervised procedures; the third shift operator was not even there. The programmer's check was automatically deposited in his account at the bank. To cover his tracks, he then changed the program back to its original version, without the salary increase. Depending on the technique this operator had used to modify the production program, an activity log might have shown that the program was changed twice at irregular times without authorization.

Fortunately, there are operating systems with built-in reporting features that log such activity as system and data file accesses. SMF has a report feature, used in the IBM OS, SVS (single virtual storage), and MVS (multiple virtual storage) System Control Programs. SMF collects a variety of system- and job-related data. System-related data applies to the computer configuration, paging activity, and workload. Job-related data provides information about job set-up, jobs run, and time-sharing sessions.

The volume and variety of information in the SMF records enable an organization to produce many types of analyses and summaries. This data on accounting and system performance can aid installations in managing their computer resources. The information can be used for billing processing costs to users, and for adjusting hardware and system software configurations for optimal performance. This same information can be quite useful to the auditor.

Much of the information generated by SMF is not of financial audit significance. The auditor, sifting through a veritable mountain of SMF data, must glean only that data necessary to reach the audit objectives. Coopers & Lybrand's SMF Analyzer was developed as an audit tool for extracting SMF data that is pertinent to the audit. This package provides up to 13 different reports containing information on activity within the computer center.

The adaptability of the SMF Analyzer is what makes it a useful tool in the evaluation of general controls. By choosing the appropriate parameters, the auditor can select only those reports necessary for a particular situation. To run the Selected Program Report, for example, the auditor specifies the names of the programs to be reported on, thereby eliminating the necessity of going through extraneous data. The auditor can request this report for all executions of utilities that could have modified production data files. These reported executions can than be traced to records of authorizations for use of the utilities on the files.

The information generated in the reports can assist the auditor in addressing issues such as the following:

- Are modifications to production files authorized?
- What data files have been accessed?
- Are accesses to change control records authorized and documented?
- Have all the jobs on the production schedule been executed, and only those?

To assist in the process, the program's reports list information such as executions of specific programs, accesses to program libraries, all jobs and programs executed, all accesses to data files, and scratched and renamed data files.

An analysis program can help determine whether production data files are being accessed by production programs. For example, a large East Coast manufacturing installation uses standard naming conventions for production programs and data files. By scanning the analyzer's reports, the auditors can determine that only production data files are being accessed by production programs.

Data Base Analysis

Recently, a 19-year-old student at the University of California was arrested on charges of illegal entry and theft involving 14 computer systems. These systems included those at the Naval Research Laboratory in Washington, the Rand Corporation in Santa Monica, and Cornell University. This is only one of many recent instances in which data bases linked by telecommunications networks have been shown to be too readily accessible to a variety of users and thus more vulnerable to security breaches.

A data management system, if properly administered, can enhance controls over data and programs. Software aids can help the auditor understand a data base structure. Information Management System/Virtual Storage (IMS/VS) is an IBM program product designed to organize and maintain a large centralized information file for on-line and batch data processing applications. With IMS, data can be integrated and shared by different users. Individual data elements can be used in many applications, eliminating redundancy of information. In this type of system, the ability of the auditor to assess the adequacy of data base security is particularly important.

Coopers & Lybrand has developed a modularized software package specifically designed for use with IBM's IMS. Each of the three programs contained in the package produces easy-to-understand reports that assist in analyzing IMS controls over access to data. (See Chapter 10, "Data Base.")

In an IMS environment, it is usually possible to read the control program load library and the program specification block library to extract information describing the teleprocessing network. The network is described in terms of the transactions that can be entered, the programs that process the transactions, and the data base(s) that can be accessed.

Using the reports generated, the auditor can test the validity of the data base administrator's (DBA) documentation and determine that the control standards are operational and that the necessary security features are in place.

In addition, the data base management system library can be examined to extract information from the IMS communication security tables that can help in identifying resources (such as terminals, transactions, and data elements) that are supposed to be secured.

The reports generated by the analyzers can help the auditor determine whether the control standards that are documented are actually in place. They can furnish data to answer questions such as:

- What does the data base structure look like?
- How many data bases are there?
- Who can access the data base? What information is available to them?
- What is the interaction between the data bases?
- Which terminals can be used to enter certain types of transactions?
- Which on-line transactions can access certain data bases?

This information makes it easier to check on whether the data base security is actually implemented as documented.

SYSTEM SOFTWARE AND SERVICE AIDS

The auditor should know the abilities of the various system utilities and service aids provided by computer manufacturers and software vendors. These software tools are part of the software that is used in the running of the system. They can be very useful to the auditor for examining processing activity, developing data interrogation audit systems, and testing programs and operational procedures. For example, under IBM/OS, the utility IEBGENER can be used to copy and reblock sequential files. OS/DITTO can be used to extract particular records from one file, thus creating a subset file for audit examination. Similarly, Coopers & Lybrand's generalized audit software package, AUDITPAK II, has file reformatting capabilities that can be used in conjunction with either industry-specific packages or application audit software. Utility Coder, a software package owned by Cambridge Computers, is another such tool used for performing these functions.

TIME-SHARING LIBRARY AND MICROCOMPUTER PROGRAMS

Time-sharing library programs are used widely, since they offer the capabilities of large-scale computers to organizations that do not own them. For example, Coopers & Lybrand has written a library of financially oriented programs accessible through a major time-sharing network. Originally developed to support the firm's activities in the accounting, auditing, tax, and consulting areas, many of these well-received programs are now available to external users, and have also been redeveloped for use on microcomputers.

Many of these programs are listed in the *Catalog of Microcomputer Software*, available from Coopers & Lybrand. This catalog provides an idea of the kinds of software available to users of popular microcomputers. Some of the programs that provide reperformance capabilities and thus are commonly used in the audit field are listed here; many of these are available for lease or purchase for microcomputer use.

- *Lease Disclosures* — Produces the disclosure requirements put forth in Statement of Financial Accounting Standards No. 13, "Accounting for Leases," issued in November 1976.
- *Imputed Interest* — Computes and amortizes the discount or premium inherent in an obligation in accordance with Opinion 21 of the Accounting Principles Board.
- *Book and Tax Depreciation* — Produces asset depreciation and cost schedules summarized in a format compatible with Securities and Exchange Commission (SEC) Form 10-K.
- *Depreciation Analysis* — Produces depreciation schedules.
- *Multi-Level Financing Calculations* — Produces debt schedules.
- *Random Number Generator* — Provides the means to select random statistical samples.
- *Attribute Sampling Programs* — Permits the design and evaluation of samples to estimate population occurrence rates.
- *Sample Analysis for LIFO Studies* — Permits the estimation of inflation indices used in last in, first out (LIFO) inventory evaluations.
- *Inventory Analysis* — Based on a sample of inventory, provides guidance on the possible need for additional reserves, reclassification of certain inventory as noncurrent, or inventory write-offs.
- *Cost Allocation* — Allocates departmental costs to cost centers, using a matrix inversion method.
- *Multipurpose Accounting, Financial Analysis, and Reporting System* — In addition to providing the ability to produce financial reports and analyze data for trends and fluctuations, also performs multidivisional financial consolidations.
- *Pre-Audit* — A compilation and review package.

As shown by the programs just listed there are numerous programs in accounting, tax, financial planning, and related areas. They are available from many sources and are of interest and assistance to the auditor.

CUSTOM AUDIT SOFTWARE

In some circumstances, prepackaged audit software is unsuitable, usually because system constraints make it difficult or impossible to use. To use audit software in such a location, EDP audit specialists and computer programmers can write programs to order. These are sometimes referred to as "one-off" programs. However, the expense involved in designing and writing a program to meet particularly complex goals may be prohibitive.

Although prepackaged software is useful in the majority of file interrogation audit applications, the auditor normally must be able to develop software for special circumstances that may exceed the capabilities of the prepackaged software. This may be necessary because the package is not available for the particular computer, the output required is very specialized, or the computations and data handling are particularly intricate.

SUCCESSFUL IMPLEMENTATION: A SUMMARY

A great deal of the success of any audit software system is, of course, attributable to effective implementation. No system, however appropriate its capabilities, will meet auditor or organization needs without careful and comprehensive selection, preparation, and implementation strategies. The following list provides a summary outline of considerations for the successful integration of audit software to immediate and long-range operations.

To be successful, audit software should

- Be properly executed.
- Meet all of its intended audit objectives.
- Be completed within the approved budget.

The skills required to implement audit software effectively are

- Training in selected audit software.
- Skills in programming language (frequently COBOL).
- Strong knowledge of JCL.
- Ability to translate audit objectives into audit software procedures.
- Ability to function with user staff and data processing personnel.

Audit software solutions are dictated by the following data processing environment considerations:

- Available computer hardware
- Available generalized audit software
- The automated system being tested
- The abilities of the available data processing personnel
- Computer operations schedule

To implement audit software within the audit plan, time must be allocated for the following:

- Scoping of the program and gathering information
- Evaluating and estimating time required
- Learning from other auditors
- Coordination of efforts
- Participation of appropriate personnel
- Program development, including the following:
  a. Detailed program specifications
  b. Program coding
  c. JCL development and coding
  d. Obtaining an executable load module — compiling and linkediting
  e. Program testing
  f. Program processing
  g. Output results reconciliation
  h. Turnover of output for use
  i. Program documentation
  j. Completion report

Complicating considerations include the following:

- Limited or nonexistent on-site support
- Limited or nonexistent organizational support
- Incompatible hardware
- Limited computer time available
- Nonstandard data structure or data access
- External sort(s) required
- Large data volume input file(s)
- Extremely slow input/output (I/O) devices
- Complicated or extensive output reconciliation procedures required

When establishing budgets, many factors have to be considered. Some of the more important are listed following:

- Situation-related factors:
  a. Hardware type
  b. Generalized audit software type
  c. Extent of documentation
  d. Availability of technical support on site
  e. Amount of computer time available
  f. Program coding requirements and support

- Specific audit test factors:
  - a. Test file availability
  - b. Input file sizes
  - c. File access methods
  - d. Difficulty of calculation methodology
  - e. Existence and retention of all required files
  - f. Defined reconciliation report or information

Aside from knowing the exact audit objectives that audit software and its use are to achieve, few other implementation functions are as important as planning the scope of audit procedures. An overview of scoping procedures includes the following steps:

1. Gathering all necessary data on:
   - The EDP environment in which the audit software will be executed;
   - The exact results expected; and
   - The timing and performance of audit support.
2. Evaluating and estimating all of the accumulated data within specific guidelines:
   - Audit software should be able to be implemented within a certain reasonable time period. This base may be increased by any additional time needed to meet all conditions unique to the audit software and the software's processing environment.
   - The basic implementation time should be realistically estimated to include the preceding considerations.

Actual audit software development and processing can be divided into three distinct categories.

1. To develop programs:
   - Develop detailed program specifications.
   - Code the source program.
   - Develop JCL.
   - Prepare source program and JCL.
   - Obtain an executable program — compile and linkedit.
   - Test the executable program.
   - Reconcile the test results.
2. To process the tested program(s):
   - Confirm access to the computer.
   - Confirm the availability of required input data files.
   - Confirm that the proper version of the reconciliation report is the one on hand.
   - Keep a written record of any processing problems encountered.

3. To complete reconciliation of the audit software reports:
    - Reconcile all key items, noting any discrepancies.
    - Establish any discrepancies that could affect the audit (such as those that would require an adjustment to the financial statements).
    - Determine if audit software must be revised to obtain reconcilable results.

In summary, when using audit software the auditor should

- Plan what is to be done before beginning.
- Understand the environment in which he or she will be operating.
- Develop a clear-cut strategy.
- Pay attention to details and follow the plan.
- Reconcile all results and investigate discrepancies.
- Write appropriate documentation, letters, and reports.

CHAPTER **29**

Implementation Reviews

INTRODUCTION TO IMPLEMENTATION REVIEWS

One of the primary reasons for implementing a computerized information
system is to enhance the efficiency, integrity, and use of an organization's data.
Many technically sound systems may not function as anticipated and, in fact,
may fail to meet desired objectives because of inadequate controls. If proper
controls are not incorporated into the initial system design, significant costs
and additional losses can be incurred later on. Data and system auditability

can be essential to system control. Implementation reviews can monitor, review, and audit information systems at vital points in system development and implementation, thus ensuring that controls exist to protect programs, information, and system resources from unplanned or unauthorized modifications.

Implementation reviews include testing techniques employed by auditors to identify, review, and evaluate internal controls in an organization's computer-based system before and during operation.

Among the types of implementation review are the following:

- *Pre-implementation review* — An independent review and assessment of the internal controls and auditability of a proposed information system.

- *Software evaluation review* — An examination of software packages in order to determine the quality of controls, audit or information trails, documentation, and, when applicable, conformity with generally accepted accounting principals (GAAP) and generally accepted auditing standards (GAAS).

- *Third party review* — An examination of the general and applications controls of a service bureau's EDP environment.

- *Post-implementation review* — Identification, review, and evaluation of the internal controls in an information system after operation begins.

A comprehensive review evaluates the system according to an established set of control objectives that can be modified, if necessary, for a particular environment. Thus, discrepancies between existing controls and the control objectives can be identified, taking the costs and benefits into consideration. If certain controls are absent or need improvement, EDP auditors can offer specific recommendations. A review should incorporate four phases:

1. *Planning.* Control objectives and checklists are tailored to the particular environment.

2. *Fact gathering.* Existing system documentation, reports, and procedures are reviewed and personnel interviewed.

3. *Analysis.* Existing controls are compared with predefined control objectives, differences are identified, and findings are reviewed with staff.

4. *Reporting.* A written evaluation is developed of the major manual and automated control procedures, along with the findings and recommendations of the reviewers.

PRE-IMPLEMENTATION REVIEW

A pre-implementation review is the examination of a proposed computer system or set of programs performed by auditors during the system development phase to determine the extent of control over and the auditability of the proposed system. Management requests for pre-implementation reviews are increasing as organizations recognize the need to provide adequate controls over their computer environments. Frequently, this review uncovers potential inefficiencies in an organization's data processing operation or physical security risks.

The primary purpose of a pre-implementation review is to provide an independent evaluation of the controls designed into the system. The computer system stores data that represents an organization's customer or client and management information and financial records, two of its most valuable assets; therefore, it is critical to ensure that there are adequate controls in place when the system goes "live." The point is not to critique the basic design of the system, nor the selection of computer equipment, nor the methodologies employed by those responsible for its implementation. Rather, the auditor is interested in the system's ability to function properly with adequate controls.

If proper controls are not built in during initial system design, significant costs and additional losses can be incurred later. This applies to prepackaged software as well as software developed by the organization for internal use. The auditor may also review a system to ensure that it complies with management's standards for development, design, and processing. It is important to monitor or audit system design to ensure its adequacy and to evaluate its processing results.

In addition to evaluating the designed controls, a pre-implementation review includes evaluation of the following:

- The adequacy of testing
- Defined user responsibility
- The planned conversion procedures
- The adequacy of audit or information trails
- The recovery capability, that is, in the event that the new system fails, can the old system be put back into operation or is there an appropriate manual system that can be used?

When a pre-implementation review is complete, the auditor issues a detailed report outlining the scope of the review and the auditor's findings and recommendations to correct any weaknesses.

The system development phase is the best time to determine whether proper controls are in place to ensure that system data will be entered and processed completely and accurately, in accordance with management's intentions. The advantages of reviewing a new or modified system prior to its general use in daily production are

- Corrective action can be taken before the system is implemented if significant weaknesses are found. This avoids the problem of uncovering weaknesses during the annual review, which might adversely affect the degree of reliance that can be placed on controls.
- The user gets an objective review of the planned system.
- An EDP auditor can suggest conversion procedures and planning that will result in a controlled implementation.

A pre-implementation review may include evaluation of the following:

- Compliance with system development standards
- The system at a test site or during parallel processing
- Reporting and input features to ensure the adequacy of controls over completeness, accuracy, and authorization
- System design to ensure that reports provide an adequate audit or information trail
- Adequacy of documentation
- Design and implementation of appropriate control procedures
- Adequacy of control over access to information for only authorized personnel (who can manipulate the data, or permissions)
- Whether design includes controls for all major transaction types
- Whether user responsibilities are defined clearly
- Whether files created in other systems that will interface with this system meet the control requirements of both systems
- The plan for ensuring accurate conversion of data as the system is put into use
- Error resolution procedures, to ensure that errors are corrected and reviewed
- Provisions made to train user and data processing personnel
- Backup and recovery procedures

Pre-implementation reviews should involve a close working relationship between all members of the internal audit staff including EDP audit professionals. In this way, auditors can gain on-the-job knowledge in evaluating computerized controls.

Work Plan

The following outline presents the steps that are suggested for the auditor to perform a comprehensive pre-implementation review:

1. Review Planning:

☐ Plan the review, including determining system-specific scope and objectives, number of hours required, length and location of the review, and structure of the review team.

☐ Determine and complete any required training for members of the review team.

☐ Explain to system operations personnel and users the nature, scope, and extent of upcoming review.

2. Pre-Implementation Questionnaire:

☐ The EDP auditor conducting the review should formulate and complete a pre-implementation questionnaire, such as the Internal Control Questionnaire (ICQ), and the Record of Control Weaknesses (RCW) (see Chapter 25, "The Evaluation Process and How to Use Documents") identifying and obtaining information about any potential control weaknesses, conversion procedures, and user acceptance procedures.

☐ Complete a Program and Record of Tests (PRT) along with the RCW, focusing on the conversion and user acceptance testing procedures.

☐ Draft an interim review memo, identifying weaknesses or concerns for management.

☐ Organize, number, and index working papers that relate to the proposed system, including conversion and user acceptance.

☐ The EDP auditor should review working papers and interim memos.

☐ Prepare and clear review notes.

3. System Controls:

☐ EDP auditors should gain an understanding of the system under development. Activities include appropriate meetings with the management of EDP and user departments, interviewing users, and studying the project documentation.

☐ Record understanding of procedures and controls by using standard flowcharting techniques (see Chapter 23, "How to Document Systems and Use Flowcharts") including supporting narratives and exhibits.

☐ Confirm that the recorded understanding of the system is complete and accurate.

☐ Evaluate the controls that have been developed for the system. (EDP auditors may use the ICQ, RCW, and PRT process.)

☐ Draft interim audit memo describing weaknesses or concerns relating to the review of the proposed system of controls.

☐ Follow up on review comments about deficiencies until resolved.

☐ Organize, number, and index separate working papers; prepare review notes.

☐ Discuss any remaining control issues with the management of EDP and user departments.

☐ Draft and review audit report prior to its final issuance.

4. Review Requirements:

☐ EDP auditors should define computer-assisted procedures that are required for effective and efficient ongoing reviews of the implemented system.

☐ EDP auditors can develop a PRT for testing the system subsequent to implementation, maximizing the use of computer-assisted audit techniques and software.

☐ EDP auditors can help develop and document detailed program specifications for audit software required to support the PRT.

☐ Have PRT and specifications reviewed by management.

☐ EDP auditors should develop, test, and document audit software.

☐ Review test results; draft detailed working papers for entire review.

5. Conduct Detailed Presentation of New System for Internal Auditors and System Personnel; Coordinate Training Session.

6. Plan Post-Audit Evaluation.

Pre-Implementation Review of a Payroll/Personnel System

This section provides a brief sample of the contents of a pre-implementation review report regarding a planned payroll/personnel system, including the objectives as well as a summary of findings and recommendations. Of course, these assessments would be documented in detail in the audit report.

The objective of this pre-implementation review was to assess the adequacy of controls over the payroll/personnel system. The general work plan and specific findings and recommendations for the payroll/personnel system are given here to provide an example of this type of review.

The planned approach included a detailed review of all existing systems documentation:

- Flowcharts
- File layouts
- Transactions
- Output

The EDP auditor interviewed key individuals in data processing, payroll, and personnel departments to obtain an understanding of the system. The auditor documented the understanding in the form of process flowcharts and narrative descriptions. This understanding was confirmed with the appropriate user personnel prior to assessing identified controls. (Audit procedures for a payroll system are discussed in Chapter 13, "Disbursement Systems.")

With this detailed knowledge of the system, the EDP auditor developed a set of control objectives in order to review the quality of control provided by the proposed systems. These control objectives were based on the typical controls as identified using the ICQ on which the auditor relied in the course of audit work.

The EDP auditor compared the control objectives with the actual or planned methods and facilities and formulated assessments. In addition, where appropriate, the auditors made recommendations about how various controls could be strengthened and how the system could be enhanced to provide additional reporting capabilities for management purposes.

These recommendations and assessments were then reviewed informally with the payroll, personnel, and EDP departments prior to formal release of the report. Once formalized, these assessments and recommendations appeared in a detailed report.

Summary of Findings and Recommendations

In the review of the payroll/personnel system described here, the following recommendations were made:

1. Data Entry:

☐ Hourly payroll:
- Establish a manual batch control log book.
- Create an exception report of unreasonable overtime hours entered.
- Alter data entry procedures to provide system messages on a terminal when a batch is out of balance.

☐ Administrative payroll:
- The methods currently planned should be adopted (this was in relation to the changes in the particular system for processing administrative payroll as compared to processing hourly payroll).

2. Master Files:

☐ Hourly payroll:
- Clarify error messages reported on the edit report.
- Check one-for-one change transactions entered against the file maintenance report.
- Utilize the batch control log book to control update.
- Implement the planned payroll user manual.

☐ Administrative payroll:
- Implement the planned procedures; document them in the user manual currently under preparation.

3. Report Preparation/Reconciliation:

☐ Hourly payroll:
- Design a report distribution form.
- Specify report retention periods.
- Conduct a supervisory review of reports.

☐ Administrative payroll:
- Implement planned controls.

4. Computer File Access, Security, and Recovery:

☐ Lock the computer room when unattended.

☐ Change passwords periodically.

☐ Change the safe combination periodically.

☐ Review the system history log periodically.

☐ Review user capabilities periodically.

☐ Implement a source code change log.

☐ Consider moving backup diskettes to an off-site location.

☐ Develop a contingency plan.

☐ Review alternate compatible hardware installations for backup purposes.

5. System Implementation:

☐ Establish control totals for file conversion.

☐ Check data, using one-for-one technique, entered to computer during user training programs.

☐ Run the automated and manual hourly payroll systems in parallel for a test period.

Pre-Implementation Review of a Financial System

At the request of the management of a major corporation, a major public accounting firm and its computer audit assistance group conducted a pre-implementation review of three major systems that were being automated. The systems were the insurance processing system, the financial general ledger system, and the voucher payable system. The review is presented here to provide an example of a review of such systems.

Like the pre-implementation review in the previous section (payroll/personnel), the financial systems pre-implementation review is designed to assess the adequacy of controls in the systems. The pre-implementation review generates several reports that are to be included in the audit team's final report to management:

- The system descriptions
- Overview flowcharts
- Computer control matrices

Alternate approaches to satisfying internal control objectives may be discovered and also should be presented in the report to management. Ways to ensure continuing proper operation of the systems should be included in the report. For example, the audit procedures that could be computerized are illustrated in Figure 29-1.

Audit Concern	Audit Procedures	Manual	Computer
INSURANCE TRANSACTIONS			
Insurance transactions processed are documented and authorized.	Test accuracy and completeness of input by referring to supporting documentation, and review supervisory controls over such input.	X	
Programmed procedures used to edit and validate incoming insurance transactions are operating in accordance with management's understanding.	Reperform significant edit, validation, and authorization procedures through the use of test data.		X
			(continued)

FIG. 29-1 Audit procedures from a pre-implementation review of financial systems

Audit Concern	Audit Procedures	Manual	Computer
Rejects and corrections are resubmitted completely, accurately, and on a timely basis.	Review procedures and controls over resubmitting rejected insurance transactions.	X	
Programmed procedures used to generate voucher payable transfer entries are operating in accordance with management's understanding.	Reperform generation of voucher payable transfer file using daily insurance transactions.		X
Programmed procedures used to generate journal entries to the general ledger system are operating in accordance with management's understanding.	Reperform generation of general ledger journal entries using insurance transactions.		X
	Reconcile journal distribution back to source documents.	X	
VOUCHER TRANSACTIONS			
Voucher input transactions processed are documented and authorized.	Test accuracy and completeness of input by referring to supporting documentation, and review supervisory controls over such input.	X	
Programmed procedures used to edit and validate incoming voucher transactions are operating in accordance with management's understanding.	Reperform significant edit, validation, and authorization procedures through the use of test data.		X
Rejects and corrections are resubmitted completely, accurately, and on a timely basis.	Review procedures and controls over resubmitting rejected voucher transactions.	X	
Programmed procedures used to generate journal entries to the general ledger system are operating in accordance with management's understanding.	Reperform generation of general ledger journal entries using voucher transactions.		X
	Reconcile journal distribution back to source documents.	X	

FIG. 29-1 *(continued)*

THIRD-PARTY REVIEW: SERVICE BUREAUS

Many businesses find the computer service bureau to be an efficient and economical alternative to an in-house computer. However, while realizing savings in time and money, the user may suffer a loss of control. While it is obviously impractical to have group after group of outsiders — users and their representatives — observe the service bureau operations on site, users will want to be reassured that the service bureau has adequate internal controls.

How can the user be reasonably assured that the service bureau is processing data correctly and that the service bureau's controls address concerns that

- Applications systems and programs are developed, implemented, and maintained in accordance with management's intentions (or understanding)?
- Processing results are complete and accurate?
- Data is kept confidential?
- Service can be maintained in the event of a disaster, such as system failure, fire, or other event?

In the past, management may have been able to maintain control over data processed at the service bureau by using extensive manual control procedures, but, as systems become more complex, this may no longer be possible. An organization can have its external auditors review the service bureau, but this would be costly and may not produce the desired results because of constraints at the service bureau. Such constraints might include the service bureau's unwillingness to provide complete access to information at any time.

An effective solution to this problem is the third-party review, an objective appraisal of service bureau control policies and procedures by independent CPAs, independent auditors, or independent accountants. This review, performed in accordance with the auditing standards set forth in the guide published by the American Institute of Certified Public Accountants (AICPA), *Audits of Service-Center-Produced Records*, and in Federal Home Loan Bank Board bulletins, may incorporate both application and general data processing control concerns.

Findings and recommendations are discussed in a detailed report, which can be used by management to make decisions about the reliability of the service bureau's internal controls and by other auditors in their examinations. The ability to provide this type of documented evidence of the reliability of internal controls is often used as a major selling point by the service bureaus themselves once they have received a favorable review.

Reports cover matters such as:

- *The computer environment and general controls.* These include the service bureau's plan of organization, procedures for new system development, application programs and operating system maintenance, access to data files and program libraries, standardized procedures in computer operations, whether those procedures are actually followed, and physical security and contingency planning. They may also address the adequacy of new applications through the development life cycle, focusing on the definition of the system, feasibility study, general design and detailed specifications, program development and testing, system testing, and conversion and documentation.

- *Application controls.* These include controls over the system's input, processing, and output, with emphasis on existence of controls that provide for completeness and accuracy of input and update, proper authorization of data, and proper maintenance of data on the computer files.

The report normally describes the control objectives and the related controls that are in place at the service bureau and gives an overview of procedures used to confirm that controls are functioning properly. It also reports weaknesses and provides recommendations.

A report on the extent and effectiveness of the service bureau's internal and operational controls is the primary benefit that both service bureaus and users obtain from a third-party review. However, a number of additional benefits accrue to service bureau management, including:

- Ongoing discussions concerning the bureau's data processing systems and operations
- Identification of operational problems and opportunities
- Suggestions for enhanced marketability of the bureau's services

Work Plan

The following is a specimen work plan for a third-party review of a service bureau.

1. Organizational Review:

☐ Obtain and review service center organization chart.

☐ Examine contracts with customers:
- Review for consistency
- Review for completeness

☐ Examine coverage defined in insurance policies:
- Blanket bond
- Building and contents insurance

- Emergency flood insurance
- Data processing equipment insurance
- Errors and omissions insurance
- Business interruption insurance
- Other types of coverage that may exist

☐ Identify applications processed.

☐ Obtain list of all hardware.

☐ Obtain list of all software.

☐ Review physical and data security.

☐ Complete service bureau review questionnaire — background.

☐ Obtain and record an understanding of service bureau's general controls.

☐ Confirm understanding.

☐ Complete service bureau review questionnaire — general controls.

☐ Test the general controls, as required.

☐ Test application controls, as required.

☐ Discuss control weaknesses or deficiencies noted with appropriate user management personnel.

☐ Draft comments to be included in the report.

2. **Application Review.** Identify applications to be reviewed and for each application:

☐ Obtain an understanding by interviewing service organization personnel, examining application documentation, and observing processing procedures.

☐ Document understanding in flowchart or narrative form.

☐ Identify significant control procedures over the following:
- Completeness of input
- Completeness of update
- Accuracy of input
- Accuracy of update
- Authorization of transactions
- Maintenance of data on files

☐ Identify significant procedures being performed by the computer:
- Classification of data

- Summarization of data
- Arithmetic functions, calculations, and so forth
- Reporting of data

☐ Confirm the accuracy, correctness, and operation of the controls and procedures documented as being in effect.

☐ Identify control weaknesses or other deficiencies noted as a result of the application review.

☐ Draft comments to be discussed with service bureau management.

☐ Draft final report to user management or third-party report to the service bureau, as appropriate.

Service Bureau Review Questionnaire

The following questionnaire provides an example of the type that can be used to review a service bureau.

SECTION A — BACKGROUND

1. Name of the data processing organization _____

2. Address _____

3. D&B or other report on financial condition _____
_____

4. Describe major computer equipment:

Hardware

Mainframes _____

Storage capacity _____

Peripheral devices _____

_____

_____

_____

Software (include version number as well as name)

Operating system _____

Data base management system _____

Telecommunications software _____

Library software _____

Job accounting software _____

Application software _____

Utilities _____

_____

_____

5. List of applications being processed:

Name _____

Program language _____

Processing mode (e.g., batch, on-line, data capture, real-time, etc.) ___

_____

Documentation available:

System

Narrative _____

Flowcharts _____

Programs

Narrative _____

Listing _____

Record layouts _____

Report layouts _____

Control procedures _____

Operation run books _____

Job control language (JCL) listings _____

6. Review of service bureau contracts:

☐ Identify cost of the following:

- System design   _____
- Programming   _____
- Preparation of data   _____
- Computer time   _____
- Special reports   _____
- Materials   _____
- Transaction processing _____

☐ Identify user's responsibility regarding:

- Batching of source documents _____
- Balancing procedures _____
- Coding _____

☐ Identify the service bureau's responsibility for:

- Output or report preparation _____

- Schedules for above _____

☐ Identify responsibilities and liabilities for:

- Errors and irregularities _____

- Computer rerun charges _____

☐ Identify length of contract and terms of termination _____

☐ Does contract permit visit by the user's external auditors?

☐ Yes   ☐ No

Is a consulting fee involved?   ☐ Yes   ☐ No

7. Name and title of the person in the user organization responsible for liaison with the service bureau _____

8. Security of data

☐ Do the service bureau contract and procedures preclude the unauthorized disclosure of any user data?   ☐ Yes   ☐ No

☐ What procedures are in effect over error recovery and disaster recovery? _____

☐ How are the user's magnetic files protected and secured?

_____

SECTION B — GENERAL CONTROLS (only summary-level questions are included here; supplemental report, if any, contains details)

1. Is there an adequate separation of responsibilities within the data processing function?   ☐ Yes   ☐ No

2. Are there adequate controls over computer operations?

☐ Yes   ☐ No

3. Is there adequate supervision of computer operations?

☐ Yes   ☐ No

4. Are there adequate controls over systems maintenance:

☐ For application program modifications?   ☐ Yes   ☐ No

☐ For operating system modifications?   ☐ Yes   ☐ No

5. Is there adequate supervision of systems maintenance:

   ☐ For application program modifications?   ☐ Yes   ☐ No

   ☐ For operating system modifications?   ☐ Yes   ☐ No

6. Are there adequate controls over access to data files?

   ☐ Yes   ☐ No

Detailed questions on general controls, such as those found in an ICQ, should be used to provide adequate information about the general controls.

SECTION C — APPLICATION CONTROLS (only summary-level questions are included here; supplemental report, if any, contains details)

For each significant transaction processed by the application, identify the control technique or procedure that satisfies the specific application control objective.*

Controls Over	Transaction I.D.		
Completeness of input			
Accuracy of input			
Completeness of update			
Accuracy of update			
Authorization			
Maintenance			

Figure 29-2 shows a page of a report from a third-party review of a bank system.

SOFTWARE EVALUATION REVIEW

With more and more businesses turning to packaged software as an economical alternative to in-house system development, vendors are scrambling to meet the seemingly endless demand for various types of financial applications soft-

---

*The information supplied should be the reference to the application, flowchart, or narrative that describes the respective control procedure.

D. DATA FILE SECURITY

The bank utilizes magnetic tape data files as well as
on-line direct access (disk) data files.

The magnetic tape data files are stored on racks physically
located in the city data center. The suburban data center
has a separate tape library with fireproof walls. Tapes at
both sites are identified by two separate external labels:
one displays a permanent, unique volume serial number and
the other a description of the files contained on the tape.
A full-time tape librarian, utilizing a bank-developed tape
library system, is responsible for the management of the
tapes. Among the various reports produced daily are the
records of the back-up tapes stored in both locations, a
listing of scratch tapes available, and the current listings
of the tape data files stored in-house.

We conducted a test of the tape library records in the city
data center. The following elements were reviewed:

. Tapes recorded as being off-site were searched for
   throughout the tape racks.

. Tapes reported as being scratch tapes and available for
   use were checked to ensure that there were no external
   data labels.

. Tapes recorded as containing retained data files were
   reviewed to ensure that the external label properly
   reported the contents of the tape.

There were no exceptions found.

Operator intervention is required for the usage of all
data files. As DOS/VS is an operator controlled operating
system, a response is required through the operator's
console prior to the accessing of any data file. If the
operator is not provided with the proper authorization
for the use of a particular data file, the operator will
intervene and refuse the access request. The on-line
data files are identified by standard DOS labels and are
protected by operator intervention as well.

E. SYSTEM SOFTWARE CONTROLS

The bank uses the Standard IBM DOS/VS, release 34, operating
system, enhanced by IBM's POWER/VS spooling package. This
system is only modified by the implementation of IBM
supplied updates. During our review, testing was taking
place on a more current IBM operating system - DOS/VSE.
The bank plans to place DOS/VSE into production during
August, 1983.

**FIG. 29-2 A page of a report from a third-party review of correspondent computer
services for a major bank**

ware. In the 1980s, packaged software is the segment of the computer services industry that is growing most rapidly; this market has increased at an amazing rate. In 1979, the industry total was under $2 billion; in the mid-1980s, it will pass $10 billion and projections place it over $38 billion by 1990. The result of this phenomenal growth is twofold: Emerging software vendors face stiff competition that threatens their survival and purchasers of financial applications software are confused by the diversity of products on the market.

Assessing Controls

Software packages are receiving close scrutiny as buyers seek to maximize an often sizeable investment in software, especially since no mandatory standards for software development controls have been issued. (Development controls are procedures for developing, testing, and modifying software. They have a significant impact on the reliability of information generated by the software.)

Vendors' quality assurance programs usually deal with the proper operation of the software. Buyers are concerned initially about ease of installation, training, and accurate and efficient operation. Businesses that use a computer to process vital information, however, should consider another major issue: whether management can depend on the information that the software generates.

When businesses kept their financial records by hand, management — and auditors — could check "visible" evidence such as ledgers and invoices. But now, with financial records kept on tapes and disks, how does the user know that the information stored in these "invisible" records has been processed in accordance with management's intentions? How does the user know that the package that processes the information is auditable? In the process of acquiring financial applications software, business often overlook these questions. And yet, controls over the processing of financial data are critical.

Both users and vendors may be risking exposure to misstatements and the like if financial applications software is developed without an awareness of:

- Generally accepted accounting principles (GAAP)
- Generally accepted auditing standards (GAAS)
- The need for an independent review of control procedures and audit or information trails embodied in a package

Is there a way of ensuring that a software package encompasses controls that facilitate the proper processing of information? A software evaluation, performed by external EDP auditors and accompanied by a report attesting to the package's documentation and internal processing controls, can go a long way toward diminishing the uncertainty of potential users.

Firms have developed various approaches to software evaluation in order to meet the increasing need for assurance about the reliability of software products.

Software Evaluation Review of Financial Applications

In a software evaluation, the auditor reviews the controls and accounting procedures in a package. Tests are performed to ascertain how well these controls and accounting procedures actually function.

Reports about the package resulting from this type of review should answer the following questions. Does the package

- Provide adequate documentation to allow its intended users to understand the package?
- Provide internal processing controls, reports, and/or data files that are adequate to permit the performance of audits in accordance with GAAS?
- Process accounting information using procedures that produce reports that enable users to prepare financial statements in conformity with GAAP?

Limitations of Software Evaluation

When considering a software evaluation review, it is important to know its limitations. These include the following:

- A review normally relates only to the specific release level of the software reviewed. It does not extend to the installation or customization of the software package.
- As a normal part of a review, the reviewers do not accept responsibility for testing the functioning of the operating system(s) per se, even when the package is tested using the vendor-specified operating system.
- A software evaluation also does not involve the evaluation of the functional adequacy (such as whether a general ledger package provides enough subaccounts) or performance specifications (such as response time) of a package.
- Reviewers generally do not endorse the software product, they only evaluate it.

Therefore, an evaluation does not cover the following:

- The potential effectiveness of the system
- The suitability of the system for a specific user environment

- The relative efficiency or reliability of the system or its underlying hardware and software
- The ease with which the system can be installed
- The capabilities of vendor personnel

Stages of a Software Evaluation Review

The following list outlines the individual stages to complete a software evaluation review:

1. Environmental factors
2. Development controls
3. Application design and controls
4. Detailed application documentation
5. Technical design
6. Application test plan
7. Testing
8. Evaluation
9. Report

The possible steps involved in each phase of the review are discussed in the following sections.

Review of Environmental Factors. This stage assesses whether the vendor environment — its policies, procedures, and personnel — is conducive to developing reliable software products, encompassing the following:

- Project management plan (product development)
- Development and testing standards
- Documentation and documentation standards
- Automated testing support tools
- Software change/release control procedures
- Test plan and test document
- Competence of vendor personnel

This stage also includes tasks relating to reviewing, testing, and evaluating a software package in light of the standards, procedures, and controls in the vendor environment.

Review of Development Controls. This review covers procedures for developing, testing, and making changes in the package:

- Identifying how the development controls were applied to the package
- Considering whether it is more efficient to rely on and test the development controls than to apply extensive procedures in testing the application
- Evaluating the development controls if it is decided that reliance will be placed on them in establishing the scope of the application testing
- Testing whether the development controls to be relied on were operating during the period of reliance (such as the period during which the package was developed)

Review of Application Design and Controls. The activities involved in this task include:

- Verifying that implementation documentation adequately supports the applications
- Verifying that internal processing controls and reports and/or data files:
  a. Are described in the documentation of the package
  b. Are adequate to permit the performance of audits thereof in accordance with GAAS
- Verifying that procedures in the package for processing accounting information produce reports that enable users to prepare financial statements in conformity with GAAP

Review of Detailed Application Documentation. The elements of documentation to be reviewed include:

- All documentation that will be delivered to the customer with the software product
- System and program documentation, including system and program documentation delivered to the customer and proprietary documentation held by the vendor

This documentation review should

- Assure that the documentation is adequate to allow its intended users to understand the package.
- Assure that the documentation is adequate for the vendor to maintain the package.

Review of Technical Design. This procedure should determine

- The hardware, components, and features relied on by the application.
- The system software, releases, and version relied on by the application.
- Whether the system software has been modified.

Development of Application Test Plan. The purpose of this procedure is to determine the extent of application testing that is necessary. Emphasis is placed on controls, balancing procedures, and exception conditions. Test conditions include those relating to the accuracy and completeness of processing and to conformance with GAAP or another comprehensive basis of accounting, such as those prescribed by government regulations.

Testing. All tests are performed according to the application test plan and, where applicable, using the operating system software needed to operate the package.

Evaluation. The results of the preceding procedures are evaluated to determine whether the software package meets the specified objectives of the evaluation.

Report. A report on software evaluation is prepared. It should

- Identify the software package reviewed.
- Direct potential users to consider the internal controls included in the entire system of which the package is a part.
- Direct users to compare their particular requirements with the package documentation and the report.
- Describe the factors included in the review.
- Describe the factors excluded from the review.
- Describe the inherent limitations of a software evaluation (such as test limitations, human error, or subversive intent).
- State that the report is neither a warranty nor an expression of an opinion on a specific user's system of internal accounting control.
- Describe the conclusions.
- Include a restriction on the use of the report.
- Specify the date the review was completed and the version of the software reviewed.

IMPLEMENTATION REVIEW

In addition to systems that process financial data and transactions, many different types of computerized systems can be reviewed. This section presents a review of a kind of system that is frequently of particular concern to local or state governments — a computerized election system.

Computerized Election System Evaluation

A method is available to minimize problems that can undermine the reliability and credibility of a computerized election system that counts votes. It is a type of system review, the objectives of which are to identify and correct weaknesses that may exist in a computerized ballot system. This type of review encompasses performance of a quality review of the computerized election system and provision of comprehensive recommendations for improvement.

The following items are reviewed and tested:

- Accuracy of ballot processing
- Reliability of the system
- Ability of the system to detect and report on errors
- Software and hardware disaster recovery procedures
- Security of the data center, programs, and ballots data files, once they are transcribed to machine-readable media

Benefits of this evaluation include increased reliability of the computerized vote counting procedures, reducing

- The public's inherent skepticism about computers;
- Challenges by candidates regarding vote tabulation accuracy;
- Concerns regarding the county data processing staff's qualifications and experience; and
- Occasional delays and breakdowns in computer vote counting, by evaluating contingency procedures.

The objectives of an evaluation of this nature are to give reasonable assurance that

- The computerized election system is properly controlled.
- The computerized election system can accurately count the vote and resist unauthorized manipulation.
- The system's basic design complies with the established requirements (including, after consultation with attorneys, local election laws); in cases of noncompliance, the review should indicate changes needed.

To accomplish these objectives, a review and test of a computerized election system should focus on several characteristics:

- Accuracy
- Reliability
- Error detection
- Disaster recovery
- Security

The review and test include:

- Meeting with election officials and data processing management to discuss and coordinate testing and processing requirements
- Reviewing program code, flowcharts, and documentation to become familiar with the system's logic and operating characteristics
- Reviewing operating instructions, including recovery procedures
- Reviewing processing controls
- Developing computer audit software to test the computerized election system program procedures
- Observing and verifying logic and accuracy tests on election system equipment
- Evaluating source programs and election program parameter requirements
- Using test ballots to conduct tests of key programs and the system as a whole
- Evaluating hardware facilities and determining whether contingency and backup arrangements have been made for these facilities

A report evaluating the computerized election system is prepared as a result of the preceding process. It should note weaknesses and recommend a corrective action plan.

POST-IMPLEMENTATION REVIEW

A post-implementation review is similar in nature to a pre-implementation review, the basic difference being that the system is already in use. It employs the expertise of EDP auditors and automated testing techniques to identify, review, and evaluate the internal controls in a company's computer-based system once it is operational.

This type of review generally arises from management's desire to receive a special report, or a more in-depth review, of one or more of their applications outside of the normal audit review. This type of review may be performed in conjunction with a company's internal auditors or as an on-the-job training exercise for the staff.

Post-Implementation Review of a Tracking System

Whether it processes dollars or people, a computerized system should have controls over completeness, accuracy, maintenance, and authorization. Consider a computerized system that detains prisoners, even after the courts have released them. This was a real concern of jail officials after several complaints were filed against these officials by prisoners. The resulting adverse publicity, as well as the complaints themselves, led the county's board of commissioners to focus on two main issues:

1. Were prisoners held in jail after being ordered released by the courts?
2. Were there serious problems with the county's computerized prisoner tracking system?

To help address these concerns, the commissioners contacted a major accounting firm. It was decided that a physical inventory of prisoners would be taken to find out if, in fact, prisoners who should have been released were being detained.

To determine if there were any problems with the county's computerized prisoner tracking system, an EDP auditor was called in to perform a review of the system. The objective of the review was to identify and evaluate the manual and automated controls and recommend improvements to the existing system of controls. The EDP auditor was assisted by a criminal justice specialist from the firm's management consulting services staff.

The county's automated tracking system is still one of the most sophisticated systems in use in the United States today. It was implemented with the opening of the county jail in 1981 and was designed to record on-line all information pertaining to an individual, from the moment of entry into the criminal justice system until final release or transfer out of the facility.

This on-line, real-time data base system runs on two Honeywell large-scale mainframes. All data entry is done remotely through terminals located in the detention area, the courts, and several police precincts throughout the city.

Evaluating System Controls. To identify and evaluate the system controls, the EDP auditor

- Gained an understanding of the system;
- Reviewed computer operations, system design, and change procedures; and

- Reviewed data file control, disaster recovery, and contingency planning.

These reviews were conducted by interviewing key personnel, observing procedures, and reviewing documentation. In addition, transactions were submitted through the system to a test data base to confirm the understanding of system processing. A written report of findings and recommendations was provided to the commissioners.

A Better Audit or Information Trail. In addition to accounting for all prisoners who were physically in jail at the time of the inventory, there were several recommendations to improve the security and auditability of the system. Satisfactory application controls were found to be in place. However, in order to provide a better trail of transaction processing and to increase security over transaction input, the EDP auditor recommended that additional security codes be required for transaction input.

Virtually all transactions entered into the system are based on hard copy documents from law enforcement or the courts. To ensure that the computerized data base stays current with the paper flow, a comprehensive set of exception reports was recommended. Jail and court personnel could then control the input of information by monitoring these reports.

The report also recommended that the county develop and test a contingency plan to be put into effect should computer operations be disrupted for a significant period of time. Other recommendations concerned the review of attempted access violations and manual procedures to ensure the integrity of the data base.

The review pointed out several ways that the criminal justice system could improve the quality and timeliness of its information. As a result of the review, the county gained assurance that its automated tracking system operates in a controlled manner. Still, a computer system is only as useful and current as the data it processes.

CHAPTER 30

Microcomputers and How to Audit Them

INTRODUCTION TO MICROCOMPUTERS

Microcomputers were already finding a place in people's homes when IBM introduced the Personal Computer (PC) in 1981. The PC spearheaded the microcomputer invasion of organizations throughout the country. A simultaneous mushrooming of the software packages available for spreadsheet and other user-friendly applications occurred. In the future, there seems little doubt that the range and power of these small machines and associated software packages will continue to increase rapidly, at an ever-decreasing cost.

Today microcomputers are encountered in a variety of situations, the most common of which are:

- A large organization where department managers have purchased microcomputers (sometimes called decentralized or dispersed processing)
- A large organization with a series of microcomputers and minicomputers doing local processing but linked to a central mainframe or minicomputer (distributed processing), or linked together (local area network or LAN)
- A small business or individual using a microcomputer

Certain features of small computer environments present the auditor with some practical difficulties in determining the most appropriate audit strategy to adopt within the framework of a systems audit approach. Implementing that strategy at reasonable cost is another consideration.

The Environment

Small computers are bringing in-house computer processing within the range of small- and medium-sized businesses or individual departments in larger businesses which, in the past, would have relied on manual methods. For such organizations the change may become problematic: They may have little or no understanding of how to choose a computer, how to design computer systems or assess software packages, and how to control computers and computer systems in operation. Furthermore, particularly in smaller businesses where manual systems of control have traditionally been weak, there may be too few staff to enable adequate controls (such as division of duties) to be set up over a new small computer system, even when the need for controls is understood.

In some organizations, just finding out where all the microcomputers are located can be difficult for the auditor. To audit microcomputers, it helps to realize how many different kinds of microcomputers are available and how many different ways they can be used.

The general classes of microcomputer range from small to large portables, desktop, multistation, and the wide range of home computers. Current microcomputers equipped with hard disk drives surpass some minicomputers in size of memory and processing capabilities, so that the distinctions between the classes of machine are becoming harder to make.

Microcomputer's Effect on Program Integrity

In a small computer environment, programmers may use microcomputers for program development and testing. Hands-on testing is common in small installations and it is therefore difficult to control program integrity.

When interpretive languages are used, program integrity is further threatened since, as a program is executed, its source code is displayed and becomes available to the user. (See Chapter 5, "Computer Concepts.") Therefore, procedures must be developed for internally developed program documentation. In some locations, documentation is not even created.

Failure to provide proper documentation has always been a problem in conventional systems. Small computer systems share this problem and, in fact, the relatively shorter development cycles tend to encourage less attention to documentation. Short development times and ever-increasing use of purchased software packages make it imperative for the auditor to ensure that audit design requirements are made known early in the development cycle.

Knowledge Gap and Product Incompatibility

Small computers are being sold by a mass of vendors, usually supplying the operating system software. The vast variety of equipment and software makes it particularly difficult for auditors to maintain the requisite skills to cope with the evolving technology. Another audit problem that has evolved from the multivendor, multiproduct environment is incompatibility. The original concept held each microcomputer as belonging to one user or small group of users, and no efforts were made to enable microcomputers from different manufacturers to be able to interact. As it became evident that there was a need for such interaction, more vendors developed compatible systems. In machines that use the same operating system, for the most part, programs and data can be transferred easily from one machine to another. Auditing the data can sometimes be done by taking diskettes of data from a user's system and processing on a host computer where the auditor has the requisite skills and techniques available, when the diskettes can be read by the mainframe. The volume of data associated with a particular application on a microcomputer may not be sufficient to warrant computerized auditing of that data. Obviously, other techniques are required.

Turnkey Systems

The introduction of small computer turnkey systems has had an impact on the auditor. These ready-to-use systems include hardware and software offering many popular applications. They may be particularly complex, sometimes using on-line and data base technologies. The problem facing the auditor is that the time spent in gaining an understanding of the system and developing appropriate audit techniques is very likely to be disproportionate to the audit resource allocation. Packaged turnkey systems are relatively low in cost but, at the same time, can include many complex programs. Auditors face difficulties with these systems because the cost of an effective review may well exceed what a small business can pay, or go beyond the time or staff allocated by an internal audit department.

VALUE OF SMALL COMPUTERS TO A BUSINESS

Many microcomputers are acquired to use the general-purpose programs, such as spreadsheets and modeling, available as packaged software. Data base packages allow users to create their own data bases of business information. Microcomputers can also replace time-sharing by acquiring versions of programs that would be accessed in a time-sharing system. Other applications, which may have particular significance to the auditor, are in widespread use. These include:

- *Sales order processing* — For quicker deliveries and more accurate order statistics
- *Invoicing and sales accounting* — To provide faster routing, billing, and collection of debts
- *Inventory recording and control* — To help maintain reduced stock investment and improved purchasing terms
- *Purchasing accounting* — For better cash management and improved purchasing terms
- *Payroll* — To produce faster payroll and pay calculations and wider analysis of payroll costs
- *General ledger* — To give a small organization or business more timely management accounting summaries
- *Production planning and control* — To provide better utilization of labor and production facilities

Other applications that have become fairly common are the maintenance of shareholder records, subscription accounting and mailing lists, personnel records, and vehicle and machine scheduling.

Many new sources of information have developed that can be accessed by a microcomputer with a modem. Among these information utilities and services are:

- Access to public data bases and newswires (such as Dow Jones, Knowledge Index)
- Keyword search of periodicals and reference texts on law, medicine, engineering, taxes, and so forth (e.g., LEXIS and NEXIS)
- Services that include electronic mail, banking, shopping, and access to plane schedules and reservations (called videotex), such as CompuServe and the Source
- Personals, including want ads, program purchase, and download or sending of data and programs

Microcomputers can interact with each other or larger computers when they are linked into a network. Among these microcomputer communications possibilities are multistation microcomputers, local area networks, linking of microcomputers to each other via modems, linking microcomputers to mainframes, and the above-mentioned access to information utilities or services.

As microcomputers follow the pattern recently seen in electronic calculators of increasing miniaturization, complexity, and falling costs, the microcomputer market is splitting into two major segments — the business market and the home market — generally distinguishable by cost, memory, and capabilities.

The flexibility in use and availability of software are increasing all the time. An audit security question arises when employees might "borrow" software and diskettes for home use. Dedicated function terminals, such as those used to access public data bases, are becoming widespread as are programs called terminal emulators, which allow microcomputers to access data in these sources, creating multipurpose microcomputers. These create audit concerns, such as whether a home system can be used to dial up an organization's computer.

In the general business market, prices are continuing to drop. Functional integration is increasing as communications are becoming more flexible all the time. As programs and hardware become even more user-friendly, ease of use is constantly improving. In some larger organizations, multistation microcomputers are replacing some of the low-end minicomputers.

Microcomputer Hardware Limitations

Microcomputers have limitations that may become apparent with use, including the following:

- There may be limited size of main memory and disk storage; expansion is possible, such as adding an external hard disk, but there are some limits here as well.

- They may have relatively slow speed in calculations, moving data, and printing.
- Direct mainframe interface is available for the widely used business microcomputers, which becomes a problem in relation to data integrity and security in larger organizations.
- Microcomputers may not include printer and keyboard buffers, or temporary memory areas. (See Chapter 5.)
- Difficulties may be hard to track down beyond the built-in hardware self-test.
- Expansion slots and ports make it possible to expand the basic system, but they may be limited in number.

Incompatible hardware concerns surface when several different microcomputers and devices have already been purchased by one organization. These can include incompatibility between:

- Central processor and input/output (I/O) device (a parallel printer will not work when there is only a serial port)
- Peripheral board interactions (they may not be easily switched)
- Different models of the same equipment (a more advanced operating system may work only on the larger machines; the earlier releases may be upward compatible, but the later ones will not be downward compatible, i.e., they will not work on older machines)

Developing Hardware Trends

As technology advances, the trends are toward the following:

- Faster processing and longer word length: 8, 16, and 32 bits is the progression so far
- More internal memory and diskette storage
- Cheaper, more intelligent or built-in modems
- Easy-to-use color graphics
- Sound and voice output
- Faster input (hand-manipulated mouse to move cursor and make selections; voice response; touch-sensitive screens)
- Built-in hard disk drives
- Multitasking, multiprogramming environments

SOFTWARE CONSIDERATIONS

The system software, including the operating system, is a master director controlling the flow of programs and events. Software to be used on a microcomputer must be compatible with the operating system. There are dozens of microcomputer operating systems; some of the most widely used are Apple DOS and TRS/DOS for 8-bit microcomputers, and PC-DOS, MS/DOS, and a growing use of XENIX and UNIX™ for 16-bit microcomputers.

Each operating system has standard utility programs, which:

- Copy files to other disks, tape, or the printer
- Delete files
- Protect files
- Check free disk space
- Rename files
- Verify files
- Initialize or format diskettes
- Save and load files

Software applications (already mentioned) include spreadsheet calculations, which are probably the single software concept that most helped spread the use of microcomputers in business. They automate "what if" analysis and modeling to reduce the effort and improve accuracy in projections. Software applications can also integrate divisional information for optimization of report capabilities. Examples are VisiCalc or SuperCalc. Lotus 1-2-3 integrates a spreadsheet, graphics, and data base management in one package. Since management reports are used in decision making, these applications can be critical. Data base packages allow storage and retrieval of data, search by criteria and report of results, and information access control. Data bases also allow modification of control and structure to include new data elements. Popular examples are Condor, dBase II, and DB Master. Word-processing is so popular because it eliminates repetitive typing and reduces the cost of form letters and boilerplate preparation. Usually, these packages allow global word changes, moving paragraphs within a text, mailmerge or computerized joining of two documents (e.g., a mailing list and a form letter), and spelling check. Examples of these packages are WordStar, Displaywriter II, and Multimate. Packages such as Symphony include several applications: spreadsheet, graphics, data base, and word processing. As these packages require more memory, larger machines are being used.

Application software can be off-the-shelf, customized, or do-it-yourself. Some of the popular microcomputer programming languages are BASIC,

PASCAL, COBOL, FORTRAN, and C. These are used for internal program development.

Desirable Software Features

Much software can be run on different computers; for example, when they are all MS-DOS machines, the same software should run on them successfully. Well-written software takes advantage of a computer's special features. User-friendly menus include single-key, easy-to-remember commands. Good software should request confirmation of dangerous operations; for example, when exiting a program without saving new data, the software should require affirmation that the user does not want to save the new data. "Help" should be available to describe commands on-screen. The software should trap errors and give clear error messages. It should also provide choice of input source and output disposition.

Microcomputer Software Limitations

The limitations of microcomputer software include operating system differences, such as those found between two release versions. The newer release may include desirable enhancements, yet may not be able to be implemented in place of the existing release for a smaller microcomputer. There may be disk format differences within a family of operating systems. The following are some limitations of microcomputer software:

- Microcomputer programming languages often use a subset of the full language and therefore have fewer capabilities.
- Users may find that there are frequent compiler revisions.
- Microcomputer core limitations can cause problems when handling extremely large numbers and rounding.
- It is not possible to move software from copy-protected diskettes to hard disk.

Good Microcomputer Software Documentation

Good documentation should be included with purchased software and include the hardware and operating system requirements. The installation instructions are very important and user manuals should include the meaning of all menu choices and error messages. It is also helpful to see samples of all output reports with explanations of all columns, totals, and breaks. New users should receive tutorial examples of typical operations. Definition of formulas and calculations can also be extremely useful.

Software and Hardware Obsolescence

Software can be rendered obsolete when the user outgrows the maximum space in a particular microcomputer, and processing speeds become too slow when a system receives heavy demands. Hardware becomes obsolete as technological evolution continues; more flexible, integrated, or specialized software packages become available; and users cannot run them due to memory limitations unless they replace the existing equipment. Business environment changes often require new software. As more applications are employed, the user needs to integrate functions so that repetitive entry and data redundancy are lessened. This integration of functions may not be possible within the existing configuration.

Customized Software Concerns

High development costs tend to keep the use of customized software out of reach of many organizations. There is also a great risk of customization failure, even after great expense, and, unfortunately, it is often the user who discovers all the errors. Users then must also maintain the programs, not the software vendors who normally maintain the packages. The user must document the software, which may only work on the existing computer that it was written for. Documentation of source code and technical documentation may not be adequately developed, making maintenance of the software difficult if the original programmer is no longer available.

Some Operational Concerns

Microcomputers can create the same concerns as a mainframe computer. In addition to being sensitive to power fluctuations and static electricity, they are portable and easily stolen. For comfortable use, microcomputers require appropriate furniture (ergonomics). Diskettes and hard disks are sensitive to the dust and cigarette smoke found in office environments. Compounding these difficulties, when a microcomputer is composed of hardware and software from different vendors, the source of a problem may be difficult to find and even more difficult to resolve.

Typical microcomputer problems become evident long after first use and are thus called "time bombs." Some of the problems that occur are due to power surges and dust problems, which take their toll slowly; intermittent failures or errors may appear randomly; failure of semiconductor chips might be indicated by increasingly frequent random errors (such chips are said to "go sour").

Special Diskette Concerns. Diskette quality is important; careful handling of diskettes is even more important. Frequently, backup is overlooked or ignored, and yet diskette backup is essential to maintaining data. When mailing, diskettes should be placed between layers of corrugated cardboard at right angles or in special mailers made specifically for that purpose. When traveling, airport x-rays may or may not be harmless, and the electromagnetic coils around the machine are dangerous to diskettes.

Diskette Error Types. Diskettes can fail for several reasons. Dropouts, which are bits missing from the data, can occur and can stem from various causes. Diskettes may have surface defects, which indicate poor manufacturing quality control. A weak read/write signal is a problem that may be caused by the computer program, whereas a dirty read/write head is a drive problem that can cause errors. Drop-ins, which are bits that are added randomly, can be added by electromagnetic interference (EMI), a malfunctioning disk drive, or bad software. Bit shifts are bits moved to incorrect locations, due to physical distortion of the diskette, EMI, normal wear, or, possibly, high temperatures.

Backup. At all times there should be backup copies or duplicates of programs, data, and equipment. When it comes to microcomputer use, backup is the only certain protection.

USE AND AUDIT OF MICROCOMPUTERS

The role of microcomputers within the organization should be formalized. Accordingly, a microcomputer steering committee or another such function should be assigned overall responsibility for microcomputers, including planning their implementation within the organization.

A formal link to EDP should be established for ongoing microcomputer user support. The committee should make decisions regarding centralization and decentralization, as appropriate, and assignment of responsibility for functions such as:

- Justification for purchase
- Selection, purchase, testing, and acquisition of hardware and software
- Programming microcomputers (new programs and changes to existing ones)
- Installation of hardware

- Implementation of software
- Documentation
- Maintenance of equipment and supplies purchases
- User training and technical support

The roles of security administration and internal audit must be considered in applying procedures and standards. Auditors should be responsible for monitoring ongoing situations.

A policy for on-site use of employee-owned microcomputers should be set and issued. Employees' use of microcomputers for personal purposes must be similarly controlled.

Another important step is to review who will approve the organizational structure. There should be executive management support and involvement to ensure a system that functions effectively.

Reporting

There are numerous methods of reporting various aspects of microcomputers, and there should be carefully defined reporting standards covering:

- EDP steering committee
- Microcomputer steering committee
- Selection and implementation committee
- EDP department involvement with end-user microcomputers
- End users' training and ongoing education in use of microcomputers
- Auditors' role in relation to microcomputers
- Legal department, when required
- General newsletters to provide up-to-date microcomputer information

Adequate audit or information trails should exist when data processed by microcomputers is being relied on for financial figures that are audited. The retention of data must be appropriately scheduled to satisfy taxation and Securities and Exchange Commission requirements, where necessary. A policy of ownership of programs and data files on software developed by employees should be issued.

Copying of software by employees that may violate copyright laws should be guarded against by issuing appropriate policies. Major software houses in some cases have begun formal actions against large organizations that they suspect of violating copy-protected software. Organizational policies and user education should prevent such possibilities.

AUDITOR'S ROLE IN SELECTING, PURCHASING, TESTING, AND IMPLEMENTING HARDWARE AND SOFTWARE

An EDP auditor can be of invaluable assistance when establishing and issuing policies. Whether there is a centralized or decentralized approach to the selection, purchase, testing, and implementation of microcomputer hardware and software, this advice should be sought.

The auditor may recommend the formation of a task force or selection committee to evaluate and select hardware and software, with specific responsibilities, authority, and schedules. The auditor can then monitor the performance and review the reports produced by such a committee.

The auditors should consider and decide the following points consistent with the level of investment in microcomputers and the degree of risk to the organization:

- Identify microcomputer users that exist in the organization
- Decide on possible uses that can be justified
- Identify microcomputer applications or interest and availability
- Develop specifications of needs or requirements
- Learn about vendor product capabilities and how they address the requirements specified
- Identify microcomputer hardware that fits the software
- Always insist on and check vendor references before purchase, possibly through interview of current users
- Review the vendor backing, including the structure of the organization, financial status, obligations to customers, and maintenance support
- Ensure that all purchase order requirements are fulfilled
- Review documentation
- Review software for provision of audit trails
- Review implementation schedules and actual dates
- Review data conversion for new systems
- Identify whether the software vendor has a charge for user documentation, offers user training, and provides assistance in converting files

A commitment to evaluation and testing is essential for both hardware and software in a suitable environment. This should be done by knowledgeable staff within a reasonable time period.

Any contracts signed with vendors should be filed and recorded centrally, so that they are always available for reference. Service contracts should be reviewed to ensure that they provide what the users require.

Software: In-House Change or Development

A decision must be made regarding programming for microcomputers, both for in-house development and existing software modifications. Auditor and end-user involvement should be specified, as they would be for any EDP system.

In-house software development and modifications should conform to standards specified by the organization. A register of software developed should be maintained, preferably on a centralized basis, helping avoid duplication of efforts.

Audit and EDP involvement in the microcomputer software development cycle should be described and the procedures should be followed. There is a tendency to skip many normal EDP procedures when microcomputers are involved; this should not occur.

Staff Education and Training

It is important to consider carefully the training of staff who will be using microcomputers. The type, degree, and method of training will obviously vary, depending on factors such as the functions the staff will be performing on the microcomputers, the applications processed, and so forth.

The following types of training should be considered for recommendation in the organization's education and training of staff:

- General background in computer concepts
- Orientation session covering:
  a. Goals
  b. Uses of microcomputers
  c. Expectations
  d. Operational changes
  e. Standards (covering all the areas mentioned)
- Specific training on the system explaining:
  a. Basic operation
  b. Procedures
  c. Documentation
- Learning to use software packages that are installed (procedures, controls, and documentation)
- Maintaining (cleaning) equipment

- Computer application controls, especially user controls for completeness, accuracy, validity, and maintenance of transactions, data, and files

Documentation

Documentation is an important and often neglected area in any microcomputer installation. Recommendations from the EDP auditor on documentation standards will vary depending on how microcomputers are being used. However, the following items should be considered, conveniently available, and kept up-to-date. Programs and packages developed in-house should be documented with:

- Narratives
- Flowcharts
- Input/output
- Backup procedures
- Sample reports

Software package manuals should be readily available and maintained to include any revisions issued. Other documentation that should be required is various logs, including problem logs, computer usage logs, maintenance calls, and user maintenance schedules and performance.

It is often useful to establish a central library for maintaining an inventory of computers and peripherals, and all software developed in-house and purchased. Inventories of the backup diskettes (systematically labeled), general-use diskettes (systematically labeled), and any other disks should also be maintained locally. The actual operating procedures should also be documented including the computer operation, data entry, and user procedures.

SECURITY

One area where the EDP auditor is often requested to provide assistance is in the provisions required for security over microcomputer use. Although seemingly small investments to begin, microcomputer hardware and software can become considerable assets when they exist in quantity, and the data they contain may be irreplaceable.

Hardware Security

Because the hardware is portable, easy to steal, and accessible when kept in the area, stringent security controls must exist. At a minimum, locked doors or devices for microcomputers, a system of identification of machines and their users, the availability of backup hardware for use when other equipment fails, and other hardware security and related procedures should be developed.

Software Security

Utilities that change data, and the data itself, are accessible. Security software packages that provide passwords and other access controls are available for most microcomputers. Other solutions include hidden characters in file names, electronic locks, and encryption boards. Another software concern is that source code is available if programming is done with an interpreter. (See Chapter 5.) Also, access to compilers by many people enables programs to be amended and recompiled. Access to corporate data bases with edit and update capabilities causes synchronization and consistency problems.

Purchased software is usually insurable against theft. Its physical security should be ensured through suitable locked storage facilities and other procedures.

Another problem area is that employees, out of idle curiosity, may abuse information utility and public data bank access. They may also enjoy playing computer games available through some services, and poor accounting by the utility may make such use hard to track. Sound controls require time recording and reconciliation and password control.

Application Programs Security

Measures for application programs security can run into problems of in-house development and maintenance, since there may be unrealistic time/cost expectations or limited staff knowledge and experience. Simple programming languages and operating systems allow novices to program, sometimes with disastrous results, and insufficient initial system analysis may make programs difficult to maintain. Application programs developed in-house require adequate procedures to protect them from unauthorized changes. Purchased programs require maintenance by vendors, and should be protected from unauthorized copying and use. Backup copies of all application programs should exist.

Operations

There are many problems due to a small operating environment: There may be no formal operating documentation or procedures; systems may provide little audit or information trail; systems may provide few audit reports; systems may not track on-line rejects; and even more difficult, there may be unknown update status.

Frequently, organizations have no formal backup and contingency procedures; as a result, the staff is ill-informed. In small organizations, it may be difficult to resolve this problem because of a lack of resources.

TYPICAL MISTAKES OF MICROCOMPUTER IMPLEMENTATION

The following is a sample of commonly observed errors:

- Unnecessary duplication of resources on the company mainframe and the local department
- Poor project control
- If each user selects its own microcomputer without consulting central purchasing, discounts for hardware and software may be missed
- No or inadequate documentation
- Inexperienced buyers make mistakes by using unknown vendors, who may not be in business when problems or questions arise
- Exaggerating the benefits and underestimating the costs
- Selecting incompatible systems
- Spending excessive management time for implementation
- Lack of controls over accuracy, completeness, and currency of data
- Underestimating growth; buying to meet only today's needs
- Having only one of anything (computer, operator, software), so that no work can be done when it is not functional

Solutions to Implementation Problems

Most implementation problems can be resolved by formal selection procedures, with risk analysis by experienced EDP personnel.

Staff training in operation of hardware and software, programming, and systems analysis and "good housekeeping" practices help tremendously. Physical solutions (see later section entitled "Auditing Physical Security") can include locked doors in office areas, secure storage of files, and proper custody and recording of files. Documentation should be maintained of:

- Files and programs
- Backup and retention policies
- Codes and naming conventions

- Procedures
    a. Accounting
    b. Job descriptions
    c. Adding, deleting, and setting levels of authority for users

Among the control criteria (see later section entitled "Auditing Data File Security") are the controls over the amendment and use of compiled code and the controls over access to program libraries, data files, and in-memory programs. An effort should be made to select and use software packages that allow full edit, have duplicate and missing record checks, use passwords, and provide control totals.

Among the solutions auditors can help implement for large organizations is the development of internal support groups. Auditors can help control purchases by evaluating and advising on hardware, software, and supplies. They can also advise on training, manuals, and publications to help meet internal audit requirements and assist communications.

AUDITING PHYSICAL SECURITY

Physical security in a microcomputer environment is important due to the lack of sophisticated software protection of files and programs and the easy transportability of microcomputers and peripherals.

Physical security aspects that should be considered include securing and restricting access to the locations housing the machines. Procedures should be established so that only authorized personnel use the microcomputers. Terminal locking devices can be used.

Effective procedures should be developed to identify, maintain, and store reports and diskettes in user locations, such as using locked cabinets, labeling reports and disks, and numerical logging for control.

AUDITING DATA FILE SECURITY

Responsibility for security over data files should be established. Where possible, software (both application and system) should be reviewed for provision of user identification and password security over data file access. Security software packages are available for use when access controls, such as passwords, are not built into the system.

Critical and sensitive data, such as personnel-related information, should be protected. The encryption and password security features that are available should be reviewed and applied wherever possible. Electronic hardware locks are also available.

Passwords should be changed regularly. Lists of passwords and user IDs should be confidential and secured. Passwords should not be displayed on the terminal screen as they are input, nor should they be printed and kept on the machine. When employees leave the organization, their passwords should be disabled immediately. These procedures are particularly important when microcomputers are networked through telecommunications and other links. When they can access other organizational data, controls should be in place to protect that data from unauthorized access, such as association of resources with the user ID.

AUDITING PROGRAM SECURITY

The password-related controls discussed for data file security should be applied to program files, where applicable. Only authorized users should access programs.

Policies must be issued declaring whether, if possible, software packages are issued in object form together with the source code listing, and whether user-developed software is maintained in source code listing or object form. (See Chapter 5.) These are needed so that versions in use can be controlled.

Review of the potential to restrict programming on microcomputers by disabling compilers should also be done, making it possible to control unauthorized amendments to some extent. Programs should also be tested to ensure that they do not have a negative effect on other programs and data.

AUDITING APPLICATION CONTROLS

Policies should be issued to define responsibility for controlling the completeness, accuracy, validity, and maintenance of data on the microcomputer and in the hands of users. These user controls can be the only way to provide a controlled microcomputer environment. They should include error correction and follow-up procedures.

Software packages, whether purchased or developed in-house, should be reviewed to determine whether

- Data is verified and balanced on entry.
- Programmed edit checks exist, when possible.
- Input is formatted to reduce input error.
- Output records are reviewed for reasonableness.

Output report distribution and user procedures should be reviewed and implemented where necessary, much as they would be for any computer use.

It is important that the following types of standards be introduced for problems that may occur during processing: Document the circumstance, including the error message received, the contents of each disk, and which operation was being performed. Then, document the action taken to correct the problem and results (e.g., retries, reload of software, execution of hardware self-test, or use of diagnostic software). In this way, common errors in processing can be controlled through user re-education.

Backup and Recovery

Backup is the best way to ensure the constant functioning and reliability of a system. It provides resources to fall back on if something goes wrong. Some businesses, for example, keep the same data on three different diskettes that are rotated every week or so: one is kept for use on the microcomputer, another stored in the office, and a third kept off-site (perhaps in a safe-deposit box). Storing printed copies of important information offers additional insurance against loss of data. Backup diskettes should be created whenever data critical to the operation of a business is altered. Backup diskettes should be distinguishable from the masters, perhaps by using color-coded labels.

Backing up important programs and data to diskette or tape (especially important when using a hard disk) is crucial. It is the only absolutely certain protection there is in microcomputer use. The following backup standards should be considered:

- Always maintain one (or preferably two) extra copies of all important programs and data files.
- Always have at least one backup copy (especially when running a program or data from the backup copy, another copy should first be made).
- Duplicate equipment (depending on the risk).
- Always have a manual or automated control list of backup diskettes, names, and numbers.

When entering data into the microcomputer, users should transfer it to a disk at reasonable intervals — at least every 30 minutes. The reason for this is that data in the microcomputer's temporary (random access) memory depends on a constant current of electricity to remain accessible. A surge or spike in electrical current could obliterate the contents of the microcomputer's memory. This may be inconsequential if data diskettes for backup exist, but very important if new data that has taken hours to prepare is eliminated. When data is saved at intervals, a power surge or brownout will result in the loss of minutes rather than hours of work. Some microcomputers have battery protection from power failure, and surge protectors can smooth out spikes in power, but it is still a good idea to save data frequently.

Consideration should also be given to developing narratives describing the source of data for important reports and the various steps required to complete the report or provide the completed data. This type of narrative should be in sufficient detail to ensure that another employee with a reasonable understanding of the department's area of responsibility can reproduce the required report or data.

Contingency plans should be considered and implemented where necessary, or microcomputers should be included as part of the overall organizational contingency plan.

Diskettes should be monitored when they hold critical data. After 40 hours of use, there may be signs of deterioration, in which case diskettes should be replaced. This number varies according to the disk and its use, but can be used as a rough guide for replacement. If data starts becoming garbled or there are frequent write errors, disks should be copied and replaced.

AUDIT STRATEGY

It is apparent that the features described previously give rise to a number of practical considerations in relation to the audit and control of small machine environments. These features affect the determination of audit strategy. The small computer environment often restricts the nature, extent, and timing of the audit procedures that can be employed. None of these features, however, is such that a fundamental change in audit approach is required; the systems audit approach is appropriate in small computer environments.

The following paragraphs discuss the features of the small computer environment as they affect both large and small companies. Likely audit strategies are described.

Large Organizations

The auditor of a large organization using small computers is likely to be confronted with varying environments, depending on the conditions under which the small computers were purchased and installed. A large organization can use small computers in either stand-alone mode or as part of a network or distributed system. Computer processing and related control concepts that one can expect to find are:

- Significant programmed procedures
- Comprehensive user controls, including disciplines
- Adequate general controls (may not exist in some cases)

In these circumstances, the auditor may not have the usual options open in determining the audit strategy. Evaluating and testing user controls and substantiating the programmed procedures themselves may be the only logical way to audit microcomputers.

The auditor can determine a strategy on the grounds of efficiency. The control reliance strategy may still be available in large organizations where the microcomputers are part of the overall EDP environment and are similarly controlled.

Systems can be flowcharted, transaction reviews can be carried out, and internal control questionnaires can be used. Compliance tests of user controls, together with any additional tests springing from the assessment of programmed procedures, should be conducted. Substantive tests for the testing of programmed procedures should take into account the results of any compliance tests.

When a large organization uses small computers, departments or divisions may have purchased their own machines. There may have been little or no control and advice given institutionally. It is likely that the auditor will be placed in a situation similar to that described subsequently for small organizations. The only major distinction should be in the size of the user staff, which may be sufficient to implement adequate division of duties and user controls. It is still unlikely, however, that there will be adequate general controls. The department or division may have little or no experience or understanding of how to control computers and computer systems. A sound audit strategy in this situation is likely to be similar to that described previously, wherein user controls are evaluated and tested, and substantive tests are performed on the data manipulated by programmed procedures.

Audit or Information Trail

The following situations may be encountered more often in large organizations using microcomputers than in mainframe environments:

- History files do not exist.
- Printed output is incomplete.
- The system does not have an internal clock/calender (e.g., dates of logs, output, and program changes may not be accurately recorded).
- It is very common to have destructive updates (e.g., where the previous version is overwritten) of both programs and data files.

Each of the preceding points can place considerable restrictions on the nature and timing of the audit procedures adopted. To assist in overcoming these problems, it is essential to start planning early. Where it can be used, audit software should be developed, and run times should be established well in advance so that software may be executed when live files become available.

Distributed Processing

As discussed previously, the small computer system typically presents the auditor with a situation where there is a small EDP staff and poor general controls. Distributed processing tends to create a related problem because it offloads EDP responsibility onto the shoulders of local line management. Often the line management has had little experience with system implementation and EDP operations and may not understand the need for EDP controls.

Distributed processing disperses an organization's overall risk of EDP failure, since a microcomputer failure usually affects only one application or department. Further, having a number of subsystems with similar configurations provides a ready source of backup. In some cases, however, this may create a false sense of security: Configuration or software differences may limit compatibility, and it is often both difficult and costly to resolve this situation.

Small Organizations

In smaller organizations (businesses or departments) the auditor is likely to find a more restricted position. Often there may be a significant number of programmed procedures. The microcomputer may be able to handle quite sophisticated systems or be geared to on-line processing. However, there will almost certainly be a lack of adequate general controls, to the extent that reliance cannot be placed on them for the consistent and proper operation of the programmed procedures. In a small business, there may be limited user controls and, in particular, a lack of disciplines over basic controls. This lack of general controls and limited user controls may significantly increase the risk of possible misuse or unauthorized disclosure of data.

These weaknesses in internal control directly affect the audit strategy adopted. Additionally, there are environmental factors that the auditor has to consider to determine the most efficient audit strategy.

Consequently, a substantive approach combined with evaluating and testing user controls is usually adopted. The EDP auditor is required to assist in the substantiation audit in the usual way, by making recommendations for use of audit software or other EDP audit techniques and assisting in the formulation of audit strategy. Among these are the large number of microcomputers that may exist, the time it would take to review them all, and so forth.

Audit Report

The audit report and recommendations must be drafted with the size of the organization in mind. Very often, recognition of this fact in a preface or paragraph assures the reader that the auditor is providing a meaningful service tailored to the organization's needs instead of an "idealistic" approach. There is a need to focus attention on the importance of user controls as the only effective controls in these systems.

A Control Matrix (see Chapter 25, "The Evaluation Process and How to Use Documents" and Chapter 26, "*Internal Control Reference Manual —* General Controls") and preliminary evaluation of user controls can be used for auditing microcomputer environments. The following are points to consider as guidelines for such use:

- Implementation controls
  a. New systems may be either purchased or developed, tested, and implemented by independent contractors. This makes the internal documentation of initial specifications, test results, and user approval of these packages very important.
  b. It is not that difficult to develop and implement the necessary review and approval procedures.
  c. System and program documentation is a key element in any package because of the potential lack of in-house technical expertise.
  d. Program and system changes should be implemented in the same way as new systems development.
  e. To answer control questions about the responsible officials in EDP and user departments, the organizational structure should be considered. Very often the person responsible for microcomputer data processing is a user department head.
- Program security controls
  a. On-line programs — Generally, there are no system software controls to ensure security of on-line programs. (Single-station microcomputers are considered on-line when they access other computers via communications links.)
  b. Authorization — Manual authorization of jobs before processing is effectively a user control in the small-system environment.
  c. Utilities — These may be password-protected and usually leave no discernible evidence of use.
  d. Physical library procedures — The physical size of data files containing libraries (diskettes, tapes, and such) and their resulting portability, as well as easy concealment, should be considered.
- Computer operations controls
  a. System software controls are often limited in this environment; manual controls must supplement them.
  b. Job set-up can be menu driven. Examine user instructions. Approvals of job set-ups are usually conducted by user department heads.
  c. Logs are usually manual and must be adequately maintained.
  d. Recovery from processing failure is the same as in larger systems.
- Data file security controls
  a. Menus and password protection should be examined, or implemented when possible.

    b. Encryption capabilities for sensitive data files should be evaluated.

    c. As in any EDP department, data files should be backed up and stored in a secure area with a record of removal and replacement.

- Password security files should contain a profile of each person authorized to use the system.
- Password profiles should contain user IDs, passwords, and user authorization for access to data files and programs.
- Procedures for adding and deleting users and for changing levels of authorization should be examined.

Communications

Recommendations on standards to be established for the use of microcomputers within the organization to communicate with the outside, with in-house microcomputers, and with other in-house computers should cover the downloading and uploading of data and programs.

The methods of restriction of access via communications must be considered and implemented. If possible, communication security software should be reviewed. It may be possible to automatically log off microcomputers if unused for a predetermined time period. Another useful device is periodic reverification of user IDs and passwords for microcomputers in use. A log should be maintained of successful and invalid log-on attempts. A call-back feature may be implemented for dial-up verification.

Other considerations regarding microcomputers that communicate include:

- Password security is effective only when computers are signed off when not in use.
- Menu choices can be based on user ID:
  - a. Users can perform only the functions in the restricted menu
  - b. Password control must be properly maintained
- Resource restriction based on user ID:
  - a. Defines access to files and programs according to user classification
  - b. Levels of authority can be predefined:
    - — *Change or write:* Can read, display, delete, or change file or library
    - — *Read:* Can read or display file or library
    - — *Execute:* Can execute members in a library
  - c. Password control must be properly maintained
- Communications may allow microcomputers to interact with other different systems or other same systems.
- Backup and recovery protects against loss of data files and programs.

ADDITIONAL PROCEDURES AND CONTROLS TO CONSIDER

Microcomputer technology is becoming so sophisticated that it needs to be protected; computer frauds have been committed by people who were not technically sophisticated. The best protection does not necessarily result from installing a better lock; good security comes from management policies and procedures that encourage employees to understand why they should use the locks. Controls, however, are of little use if they are not used or periodically reexamined. Unless the accuracy of the information stored in a computer is continually checked, any breaches of security will never be detected. Generally, any decrease in the number of manual control procedures in a computerized environment results in data receiving less manual scrutiny and review.

Security is another important consideration that includes data integrity, or the extent of control over the accuracy of information; the system's physical security; the vulnerability of business and operations information (including the microcomputer itself) to destruction or loss; and the risks of unauthorized use or disclosure of data.

A microcomputer makes mistakes in about the same way a typewriter makes typographical errors: with the assistance of the operator. Although some errors result from hardware or software errors ("bugs" in the chips or programs), most result from operator errors, especially when entering new data. The possibility for error can be significantly reduced if software has "error catching" controls. These controls can call attention to potential errors. The best way to ensure data integrity is to train users as thoroughly as possible.

The physical security of a system should receive the attention it deserves. First, control access to the equipment and software by locking any cabinets in which such items are stored. It is also important to ensure that the microcomputer itself is protected from physical abuse or damage, vandalism, environmental damage, and unauthorized use when unattended. These concerns may be addressed by securing a separate room for the microcomputer or by using special locking devices within or around the microcomputer.

It is important to protect against accidental destruction of data; the data contained on floppy disks may be the most valuable part of a system. Whatever the application — bookkeeping or word processing — reliability is essential. With considerate handling and maintenance, diskettes can give reliable service. When an organization loses data because of a faulty diskette, information that the organization was counting on is gone and it takes additional time and money to replace it. A diskette problem can sometimes be mistaken for a hardware problem, and personnel might not realize where the trouble lies. By following established procedures, it is possible to ensure that a defective floppy disk is not causing the problem.

In addition to the physical protection of data through backups and physically separate storage, backup personnel should be available; more than one person should know how to access data if needed. Otherwise, the absence of key operators or people with primary responsibility over the data could mean inaccessible data. It is critical that no one person be the exclusive user or have control over significant functions of the microcomputer. Guidelines on procedures and controls should ensure adherence to policies and procedures.

Attention must be given to the issue of information "gatekeepers" and backup personnel. In a business environment, an important issue is whether computerization is personal or institutional. There is grave danger in having the driving force behind the microcomputer reside in one person, and also in having the microcomputer regarded as "Jack's" or "Mary's." The risk, of course, is that if the person leaves, use of the microcomputer could be disrupted or even lost entirely.

The saying that "information is power" is highly relevant when a business computerizes. Care should be taken that no one individual moves into a position of total control over major parts of the information contained in the computerized system. At least two people should be sufficiently familiar with each major application so that one can take over for the other in the event of vacation, illness or injury, or personnel transfer. Failing to provide for backup personnel raises the spectre of the business being paralyzed in major areas of its operations.

Controls

In larger computer environments, input is balanced before it is processed; edit checks are performed in the data entry process; and systems controls that perform logic and range-boundary tests are built in. In addition, these controls check for characters in numeric fields and vice versa, produce error warning and exception lists, and reconcile output. In other words, errors are expected and anticipated and systems controls are an integral part of the system.

Information in a microcomputer, however, often cannot be subject to these types of control, since to perform edit checks the computer needs access to table files and other information that is not available to a microcomputer. The data may also be changed without leaving any trace. Not all microcomputer software provides the kind of information trails to control security and data integrity that are found in larger computer software. Therefore, anticipate errors. Controls are essential in three areas: (1) software verification, (2) parallel testing during installation, and (3) written documentation. Beyond the mechanical or electrical sources of error, the microcomputer program itself may contain "bugs" or inaccurate instructions that cause flaws in the way the microcomputer handles information. For these reasons, several operational procedures are critically important to ensure the accuracy of a microcomputer system.

- When a microcomputer is first installed, it is critical to test it side-by-side with previous manual or other systems. This parallel test should continue until personnel are satisfied that the new system handles requirements accurately and can be relied on to replace the previous system.

- When software is first received, a duplicate of the original should be made, and then the original should be stored in a secure place. The duplicate should be used in the microcomputer.

- Reports should be immediately spotchecked, item by item, if the accuracy of information is critical.

- Underlying all of these procedures is the need for documentation — thorough and detailed references on how the system is organized, step-by-step procedures for entering and retrieving data, and procedures for correcting errors if the system does not work as it should. Documentation should cover operation of both software and hardware and any changes made to the system. Inadequate documentation, or no documentation at all, makes the troubleshooting of problems difficult or impossible. It also makes system operation heavily dependent on the abilities and memories of current users. If those personnel leave, the system may collapse.

- Adequate user controls must be developed around the system; once it is ascertained that the programmed procedures function properly, user controls can ensure that the data entered is complete, accurate, valid, and current.

Maintenance and Review

Once the microcomputer is running successfully, users become aware of limitations in its responsiveness or capabilities. Of course, if something does go wrong, a good service contract should be there to assume responsibility. Nonetheless, it is possible to reduce or even eliminate many causes of microcomputer failure by taking a few simple precautions. Whether or not problems surface, microcomputer performance and adequacy should be evaluated periodically.

Maintenance. The microcomputer itself (the central processing unit and main memory) is actually the least delicate component in a system. Its integrated circuits have no moving parts and are as rugged as those in a transistor radio. Heavy and prolonged vibration may cause chips to unseat from their sockets, but this is highly unlikely (a microcomputer operated without a hitch on the space shuttle's first flight). Still, even the most reputable microcomputers are known to "crash" now and then. Printers and disk drives are mechanical and can have problems, as can on/off switches, keyboards, sockets that are frequently unplugged, and other mechanisms that have moving parts.

Breakdowns are inevitable, even with a microcomputer that has been well-maintained. Normal wear and tear takes its toll on a microcomputer, as it does on any other machine. Microcomputers are sophisticated machines, so virtually every one of them will need help sometime.

What if a microcomputer or a vital peripheral like a printer or monitor breaks down? How quickly can the microcomputer be operating again? If it is down for more than a few days, can a substitute be acquired with reasonable speed? What happens if the dealer now no longer carries a spare, or if the spare has been loaned to someone else? Obviously, it is important to have a contingency plan, so check with the computer dealer. Find out what provisions can be made when a microcomputer needs service. Substitutes may be needed in an emergency, so do not rely on a dealer's oral promise for too long: The salesperson who promised to lend a substitute microcomputer a year ago may have left.

Review. Installing a microcomputer is not the last chapter in the process of computerization; for most businesses, it is merely the preface. As a microcomputer is put into actual use, any limitations in the original requirements study and the limitations in the responsiveness or capability of the microcomputer come to the surface. Whether or not these problems surface, it is good business practice to evaluate periodically the performance and adequacy of a microcomputer.

Proper evaluation and review require ongoing management of the microcomputer; it cannot simply be plugged in and left alone. Once a microcomputer is installed, greater demand may surface among users. There is a tendency for users to need additional terminals and to want additional applications, once they have been exposed to the microcomputer's initial capabilities: a classic case of rising expectations. It is easier, of course, to anticipate this demand before the microcomputer is acquired; but in most cases, the demand must be accommodated after the microcomputer is installed. Realize that as more applications are added, an area may need a new computer.

Beware of Glitches

These days, microcomputers have become almost routine pieces of office equipment, hardly more mysterious or demanding than typewriters and copiers. As a result, a microcomputer is often treated with the same degree of benign neglect accorded to other office equipment. Such casual treatment is a mistake. A broken typewriter or failed copier is a minor irritation in most businesses, but a microcomputer failure can destroy records and bring important procedures such as billing to a complete halt.

Even properly maintained microcomputers are occasionally subject to mysterious ailments known in computer jargon as "glitches." A glitch is a temporary malfunction in the microcomputer's circuitry and is usually caused by static electricity or an erratic power line. Although glitches do not necessarily stop a microcomputer from operating, they can destroy data and programs. Fortunately, many of the causes of glitches and other computer failures can be reduced or eliminated by taking a few simple and inexpensive precautions: Protect the computer from overheating, static electricity, dirt and dust, voltage fluctuations, mishandled diskettes, and inexperienced users.

Upgrading

An upgrade in microcomputer capabilities may be needed after the first few months of operation or may not arise for two or three years. The following are some symptoms of a need to upgrade microcomputer capacity:

- Insufficient number of terminals available for those requiring terminal access
- Need to install applications that are beyond the system's current capabilities
- All ports for peripherals and other devices have been used, but more are required
- Expansion slots have been used for additional boards, but more capability is still required
- Lack of storage space on diskette or hard disk systems
- Need to undertake several processing steps in handling large files because of the system's inability to process all of the information on one storage device

It is important to assess upgrading needs in the same systematic way that the original microcomputer requirements were addressed. This type of approach is needed so that an upgrade decision will include all current and anticipated needs and not just respond to a specific capacity or application problem. In fact, an upgrading decision represents a good opportunity to recover from any mistakes in the original microcomputer requirement definition and selection process.

Before undertaking upgrading as the means to increase capacity, consider other, more immediate, alternatives:

- Better file management procedures to reduce the disk storage requirements
- Work-scheduling improvements to better utilize the available equipment and user time

- Low-cost additions to the current installation, including terminals and some upgrades in peripherals, such as higher speed printers, larger capacity disk drives, hard disk external drives, or additional circuit boards to increase capacity.

Finally, equipment and software compatibility is an important consideration when upgrading a system. If practical, new equipment should be compatible with existing equipment in order to preserve prior investment costs. A second compatible system also solves the problem of equipment backup.

Computer Abuse

INTRODUCTION

As computerization increases, the potential for an organization to suffer from disrupted operations — due in part to the difficulties of restricting access to computers and data — increases. This threat has grown in recent years as rapidly advancing technology has brought about a proliferation of computers and users. Developments in the computerized environment that exacerbate this situation are:

- A growing need to control computer use and access to data files that is often overlooked by management

- Organizational controls that are insufficient or can be circumvented

- On-line systems that make it even more difficult to control remote users in multiple locations

- Sensitive data may be concentrated at key sites
- Lack of contingency plans for alternative processing
- Lack of visible records and evidence of processing
- Lack of systems to record and/or report abuse

Intentional interruptions obviously interfere with the smooth and proper operation of a computer system; computer abuse is generally thought of as an intentional act ranging from fraud to espionage to misuse of software and hardware. Deliberate disruption can range from terrorist attacks on computer centers or automated teller machines to unauthorized changes made in programs and data the system contains.

Accidents, such as fires, floods, and earthquakes, and more localized events such as power supply failure, hardware malfunction, and operator and software errors, can create major unintentional disruptions. (See Chapter 32, "Security.")

DEFINITION OF COMPUTER ABUSE

One of the difficulties that arises when attempting to deal with the problems of computer abuse and computer crime is that there is no one precise definition for either term. While distinctions may be made, the terms are used interchangeably by many people, and their use varies from one organization to the next. It is perhaps easier to develop a working definition by distinguishing two broad categories: (1) abuse being actions against computers and related software, making the computer the object of the crime, and (2) crime where the computer is used as a tool or instrument to commit a crime.

Donn B. Parker, who is considered one of the foremost researchers of computer abuse and is a computer criminologist at SRI International, a leading research institute, defines computer crime as "any illegal act for which knowledge of computer technology is essential for successful perpetration." On the other hand, he defines computer abuse as "any intentional act involving a computer where one or more perpetrators made or could have made a gain and one or more victims suffered or could have suffered a loss."

When analyzing the kinds of abuse that can occur, it is helpful to place computer abuse in its proper context. It is rarely the chief reason for financial loss in an organization; researchers have found that the financial loss involving computers results mainly from errors and omissions. The second largest cause is natural disaster; computer abuse is only third on the list. Yet, many incidences of computer crime are undetected; fewer still are reported to law enforcement agencies. These findings may, as a result, provide an inaccurate accounting.

EXTENT OF COMPUTER ABUSE

Instances of computer abuse were first documented in the late 1950s and prosecuted for the first time during the following decade. Since those early days, the problem seems to have grown as rapidly as computer technology itself.

Collecting data on computer abuse in the private sector is usually quite difficult, in part because such abuse frequently goes unreported. There are several generally acknowledged reasons for this:

- The resulting adverse publicity might hurt the company's business.
- The difficulties in prosecution make convictions for such crimes somewhat unlikely, even when they have been reported.
- Widespread publicity greatly increases the possibility that the abuse will be repeated, especially when the organization concerned finds that computer security cannot be improved and controls cannot be strengthened cost-effectively or in a manner that secures the entire system.

Estimates of percentages of computer crime detected and the amount that is reported to law enforcement agencies also vary considerably. In a recent survey, only 16 percent of all respondents (officials from major corporations in the United States) stated that all such incidents were reported; 5 percent said that most were, 18 percent that some were, and 20 percent that none were.[1]

The situation regarding computer abuse in government is thought to be somewhat different:

- About twice as many computer crimes against government systems are reported as in private organizations.
- The average loss is estimated to be one tenth the loss experienced by the private sector.

A recent survey of 12 U.S. government agencies, which documented 172 instances of computer crime over a four-year period, concluded that the government was also greatly underestimating its losses.

Since 1979, when the following figures were first published, statistics on losses from computer crime have increased. But these figures, published by Brandt Allen and based on Donn Parker's studies of 150 major computer fraud cases, suggest the scope of the problem:

---

[1] From the *Report on Computer Crime*, Task Force on Computer Crime, Section of Criminal Justice, American Bar Association, June 1984.

Crime Against:	Average Loss
Corporations	$621,000
Banks and savings and loans	193,000
State and local government	329,000
Federal government	45,000

Crime Involving:	Average Loss
Account, transactions, inventory	$1,300,000
Payment to creditors	324,000
Payment to employees	139,000
Office managers	274,000
Other staff	48,000
Clerks or tellers	37,000
Computer operators	33,000
Computer programmers	20,000
Data entry personnel	8,000

More recent findings include far greater sums but again vary widely. In the survey of corporations by the ABA already cited, the "known and verifiable losses" of 72 respondents who had this information ranged from $145 million to $730 million. This placed the average loss per organization at somewhere between $2 and $10 million per year. And this was based on a small sample in that one survey.

In April 1982, *Technology Review* estimated nationwide losses of $300 million to $5 billion yearly. In June 1983, *Police Chief* put yearly losses at a more conservative $20 to $100 million a year. While these figures continue to be compiled, it is obvious that the amount of money being consumed by computer-related crime is staggering.

The Computer Criminal

The typical computer criminal appears to be indistinguishable from the white-collar population as a whole. However, a team of researchers recently identified a combination of factors that seem to characterize individuals who are likely to commit computer crimes. These factors are situational pressure, opportunity to commit crimes without feeling fear of being caught, and certain character traits, as described in the following paragraphs.

By occupation, researchers have found that among those within the organization who pose the greatest threat to systems are security officers, computer operators, data entry and update clerks, operations managers, and computer programmers. These are all occupations that provide somewhat free access to the system. In one study, computer system engineers and programming managers were thought to pose only moderate risks to systems. Executives and managers outside of computer operations were found to have actually committed such crimes in 21 percent of known incidents in a recent survey; those outside of an organization included consultants, competitors, clients and customers of the organization, and individuals with no connection to the organization at all.

According to one profile, the computer criminal is likely to be a married male, between the ages of 25 and 40, the father of two children, highly intelligent, with well-defined career goals. He commits the computer crime for himself (either for material gain or to "beat the system"), for benefit of family and friends, or to gain the approval of an outsider. In the latter instance, the so-called computer mystique contributes to the impression the person is trying to create: that he is quite knowledgeable and enjoys a high degree of professional prestige.

In general, it has been found that most people involved in computer crimes have never been part of anything seriously illegal before. They often see themselves as using or borrowing, rather than stealing, thus avoiding any difficult moral implications. Some fear exposure, while others are fearless; many intend to repay their victims at some later time and rarely do so.

The majority of computer criminals view their manipulation of the computer not as a crime but as a clever personal, intellectual response to a technological challenge. This can also be in response to peer pressure. They are often trusted employees who perceive a vast difference between stealing from people and stealing from huge, impersonal organizations (which is sometimes called the Robin Hood syndrome). In fact, computer criminals often go to great lengths to avoid hurting people.

Categories of Computer Abuse

Senator Abraham Ribicoff introduced the Federal Computer Systems Protection Act, the first national computer-related crime bill, in 1977. (See later section entitled "Legal Aspects.") The Act identified four major categories of computer crime:

1. Introduction of fraudulent records or data into a computer
2. Unauthorized use of a computer and facilities
3. Alteration or destruction of information or files
4. Theft by electronic or other means of money, financial tools, property, services, and/or data

A subsequent study done for the Department of Justice in 1979 showed that specific methods of computer-related abuse fall into the following categories:

- *Data diddling.* Perhaps the most widespread abuse, this involves changing data before or during its input.

- *Trojan horse.* This consists of writing unauthorized, hidden instructions into a computer program so that the computer performs these unauthorized functions in addition to its regular activities.

- *Salami technique.* This method is the siphoning or "slicing" off of small, almost undetectable amounts of money from a number of larger transactions, so that the quantity taken is not readily apparent. The totals obtained in this way can add up to a large sum. One salami technique, called "rounding down," is used to round fractional remainders down to the nearest whole, placing those tiny fractions into an unauthorized account. When this operation is performed repeatedly on numerous transactions, the fractions in the unauthorized account can grow into considerable sums of money.

- *Superzapping.* This involves using a utility ZAP program, which can modify programs bypassing controls, to change programs or data stored in the computer. ZAP programs have legitimate uses, but they can easily be misused, since their use leaves few traces.

- *Trap doors.* Trap doors are breaks in the program code that make it possible to insert additional instructions and intermediate output capabilities. A useful tool for programmers trying to debug a system, they also make it possible to insert unauthorized program procedures to facilitate abuse. Trap doors, like ZAP programs, are useful in getting a system to function properly but are easily misused to compromise programs by those who know how to work with them.

- *Logic bombs.* These are unauthorized programs that trigger a computer action based on a certain prespecified condition. For example, one employee inserted a logic bomb in his company's personnel file that specified that the whole file would be erased if the particular employee's name were ever deleted from the file. (A similar technique is called a "worm" and works in much the same way.)

- *Asynchronous attacks.* These are ways of confusing the operating system by inserting instructions that contradict the computer's programmed logic.

- *Scavenging.* Scavenging is searching for leftover information after an authorized job has been executed.

- *Data leakage.* This is the removal of data from a computer or a computer facility, taking printouts or other seemingly innocuous data, such as scratched tapes scheduled for reuse but then rerouted improperly to take the data they still contain.

- *Piggybacking and impersonation.* Both of these methods are used physically as well as electronically. Piggybacking is a way to gain access to controlled areas, such as by walking in behind an authorized entrant. It also refers to intercepting messages to add to or alter them, or to a hidden terminal attached to a line that is used to access the system when it is not otherwise in operation. Impersonation is when one person assumes the identity of another, either for physical access or to access the system, such as using another's password.

- *Wiretapping.* Much like wiretapping telephone lines to listen to conversations, this involves tapping into data transmission lines to collect information. A great deal of superfluous data must usually be collected before the sought-after information is located.

- *Simulation and modeling.* Simulating is copying a computer process to learn it, here, in order to be able to alter it; modeling is a type of planning using a computer program, here, to plan a crime.

The preceding list is of specific ways to manipulate data, programs, or computers.

Most computer abuse falls into one of two broad categories: (1) using the computer to commit a crime or (2) crimes directed against the computer itself. Within these categories of computer abuse, there are general overall categories:

- Using a computer to steal assets or embezzle funds
- Using a computer to commit fraud
- Espionage
- Sabotage
- Unauthorized access
- Unauthorized computer use
- Destruction, interception, or alteration of data and software
- Theft of hardware, software, or data

In this context, the first three items are usually crimes committed by use of a computer; the last five are crimes against a computer (although sabotage can fall in either category).

Using a Computer to Steal Assets or Embezzle Funds. Accountants, auditors, and managers probably consider this the most serious crime, in part because it is so difficult to detect and in part because it is possible to appropriate huge amounts of money. The widespread use of electronic funds transfer (EFT) systems shows one aspect of this category of computer-related crime. EFT crime is taking place in both corporate and consumer EFT systems, including cash management services, automated clearinghouses, point-of-sale terminals, telephone banking services, and automated teller machines (ATMs). A recent example occurred when a university instructor joined forces with two former employees of a South American bank. They transferred nearly $200,000 of the bank's deposits electronically into the account of a dummy corporation in the names of three conspirators. Armed with the foreign bank's account number, identification codes, and the knowledge that there was a new clerk at the depositor's bank, the trio requested electronic transfer of the foreign bank's deposits to their phony company. The new clerk transferred the money without a follow-up call to the new bank. The theft was uncovered during an audit of the South American bank, and the money was traced to the dummy corporation. An audit of the dummy corporation's books revealed that there had been an earlier transfer of nearly $100,000 from the same bank.

Often this type of computer crime involves stealing assets (tangible or intangible) through use of a computer, as a recently prosecuted case illustrated. A computer expert was called in by a major league baseball team to design a computer system to print out and issue tickets for games. Once the system was designed, installed, and operational, the expert used his knowledge of the process to print more than 1,000 tickets from the same machine. This crime went unnoticed until the beginning of the next baseball season, when officials of the team compared their accounts with tickets purchased. They discovered that three accounts belonged to nonexistent companies. The officials then traced the companies back to the computer expert, who, it turned out, had sold most of the tickets to a ticket service for over $15,000. The expert was fined, put on probation, and ordered to make restitution to the baseball team.

Embezzlement usually takes place from within an organization by its employees, who are now beginning to use computers to help commit this crime. In a recent case, the head of a European bank's foreign transfer department and his assistant were arrested on forgery and embezzlement charges. During a two-year period, they had channeled over $60 million to outside accounts in their own names. They were able to transfer the funds electronically because they had cracked the bank's computer access code. An audit uncovered the crime.

In another case a few years ago, a member of an alleged organized crime family used an EFT system to embezzle millions of dollars from a large bank. In an attempt to launder the stolen money, the funds were transferred through a maze of foreign and domestic banks. Although the thief was eventually caught and sent to jail, this offense is significant in that it marks what may be the first documented instance of organized crime getting involved in illegal computer activities.

Traditional manual recordkeeping has usually been employed by criminals to follow their activities. Recent raids have shown that computer applications exist to track operations as diverse as racketeering, prostitution, drug trafficking, and bookmaking, and that their use is increasing. Some computer industry experts believe that once members of organized crime syndicates develop their own knowledge of computerized technology, crime will be re-defined. The same experts agree that this new type of crime will be much harder to trace.

Using a Computer to Commit Fraud. This is a broad category of computer crime, whereby computer records or data are manipulated for illegal gains or similar purposes.

A recent example of such manipulation to commit fraud was seen when several members of a midwestern family pleaded guilty to conspiracy to commit mail fraud after an internal audit showed that an insurance company's computers had been used to issue false benefit checks. Two members of the family, who worked for the insurance company's customer claims division and who had clearance to process claims with the company computer, were charged, as were one employee's sons. The two family members had authorized payments to themselves and to their children; after receiving the checks they would delete the transactions from the files.

Four years after the scheme began, and after both people had left the company, an internal audit revealed that there were no claims to justify numerous expenditures. By the time authorities caught up with the pair, one was working for another insurance company and was already involved in a similar scheme at the new location.

Another recent case of fraud through a computer occurred on the West Coast, where two county welfare employees defrauded a county of over half a million dollars. Their far-reaching scheme involved dozens of accomplices.

The pair worked in the welfare department's compliance unit, which authorizes payments after arbitration. They approached former recipients and offered them kickbacks for cooperation. Then they would reactivate the dormant files, substituting the name of a friend who had the same last name, but a different first name, as the former recipient. To complete the process, they forged authorizations of the transactions.

When a check came with the slightly altered name, the former recipient would notify the pair, who in turn would notify the friend or relative whose name was on the check. Then, armed with proper identification, the friend or relative would claim the check at the bureau, and everyone involved would split the proceeds.

An alert coworker unearthed the scheme when he questioned various omissions on an input document. He asked the person who allegedly authorized the payment about the document and discovered that it had been forged. They notified superiors, who began an investigation that uncovered the entire scheme.

Espionage. Another crime that can be computer-related is espionage. It is readily understood in the traditional sense; when it is computer-related, espionage can either be the passive collecting of information or the active destruction of data. Foreign agents may approach those with access to computers and the sensitive information they contain in some of the following ways:

- *Hope of financial gain.* Perhaps the most common approach, a spy exploits need or greed by offering money or gifts in exchange for seemingly innocuous information. As time passes, the amount of money is gradually increased, along with the sensitivity and damaging nature of the information requested.
- *Blackmail.* This technique is one frequently used against Americans visiting certain foreign countries. The blackmailer exaggerates and plays on visitors' fears by threatening harm to relatives in these countries.
- *False flags.* Here, the agent pretends to be working for the same cause, misrepresenting himself and his purpose to dupe the victim out of information, while seeming to support a common goal.
- *Beliefs.* Playing on an unsuspecting person's ideological beliefs is another way to obtain classified information. Phrases such as "for the good of mankind" or "for world peace" are abused by those seeking information.
- *Naiveté.* The spy may pretend to be interested in the same cause while building the victim's confidence in himself and counting on the victim's ignorance about the value of the information.

To obtain the desired information, the techniques for unauthorized access to data that are frequently used include eavesdropping, impersonation, piggybacking, and line-grabbing or intercepting an authorized sign-off signal and sending a responsive sign-off, leaving the intercepted line available for unauthorized use.

Sabotage. Sabotage can range from terrorist bombings of computer centers to malicious reprogramming. In the early 1970s, angry students attacked computer installations on various college campuses throughout the United States to protest the Vietnam War. In one incident, a person was killed and $16 million worth of data and equipment was lost. In the mid-1970s, radicals identified U.S. multinational companies as enemies of the state and began a campaign of bombings throughout Europe. Such terrorism varies in intensity of activity over the years, but recent attacks have been directed against American corporations in Italy, France, and Germany. Some observers believe that other terrorist acts may be planned, directed at companies involved in arms production and defense-related work.

Experts predict that other forms of computer-related sabotage may be on the rise. The horrible possibilities were demonstrated in 1979, when a New

Zealand airliner crashed into a mountain, killing 250 people. Investigators sifting through the wreckage of the plane located its computers. On examination, it was discovered that the computers had been reprogrammed. The pilot believed he was flying toward a body of water when he was actually headed directly into the mountain.

Unauthorized Access. Unauthorized access to computer installations and networks via phone lines is on the rise. Such "hacking" was originally considered relatively harmless; hackers were even admired for their ingenuity, although this is no longer the case. Typically, hackers are young people who like working with computers and extend that enjoyment by the perceived challenge of breaking into someone else's system. Some think of it as a hobby, pursued for excitement or adventure. A microcomputer with a modem can connect with many of the telecommunications networks that link thousands of computers across the country using telephone access numbers. These numbers can be obtained through electronic bulletin boards or by trial and error.

In one widely reported case in 1983, a group of Milwaukee youths — named "414s" after their city's telephone area code — broke into numerous business and government computers, including installations at Los Alamos National Laboratory, Security Pacific National Bank in Los Angeles, and New York's Memorial Sloan-Kettering Cancer Center. Although no apparent damage was done, files and records were deleted during access to the computer at the Milwaukee School of Engineering.

Hackers have also broken into the huge TRW computer system, which contains credit histories of over 90 million people, one of the largest confidential data files anywhere.

Unauthorized Computer Use. There are numerous ways in which unauthorized use occurs, some as seemingly harmless as using a business computer to do personal processing. An example of such a case on the East Coast was seen when a programmer for a large city was brought to trial. He had used his employer's computers to create a betting system and to trace the genealogies of horses in which he had an interest. The presiding judge ruled that the employee had not broken the state's computer crime law because the law specified that it was illegal to make unauthorized use of leased equipment. It did not mention unauthorized use of nonleased equipment to which an employee had legitimate access. In commenting on the judge's decision, the programmer's lawyer likened his client's actions to those of a secretary who uses an office typewriter to write personal letters.

Using a computer in ways not authorized or intended by its owners can obviously occur on a larger scale. For example, two computer programmers were charged with fraud and grand theft when they used their employer's computers to run programs for the company's chief competitor. The pair had been hired as programmers for a local wholesaler who was unaware that they had a burgeoning programming business on the side. When another local wholesaler offloaded part of his programming to the duo, they used their employer's equipment and time to do the work. Coworkers became suspicious when the pair refused them access to the computer room. The coworkers notified their superiors, who uncovered the situation.

Destruction, Interception, or Alteration of Data or Software. These acts can take place in many ways, as described previously. A case of interception of data occurred when an economist for a major brokerage house was accused of tapping into his former employer's computer. He did this because he wanted to obtain confidential information on money supply trends that he hoped would give him an edge in his new job. The accused worker's former supervisor became suspicious when she received an automatic printout of all data that had been requested. She then realized that an access code used belonged to a former employee. Authorities traced subsequent outside calls to the computer and eventually arrested the former employee, who faced up to five years in prison and a $1,000 fine.

In another recent incident, unauthorized users accessed the computer of a thoroughbred horse-listing service. The FBI was called in to uncover who had tampered with data on pedigrees, breeding records, and racing statistics of thoroughbred horses throughout North America. During the investigation, the horse-listing service was forced to shut down some of its services and eventually lost over $100,000 in revenues. But the implications of this interference were far greater. The company's owner explained that all they had was information about horses on their computer, but if that had been totally destroyed, the jobs of 40 people who work for the service would have been grossly affected.

Theft of Hardware, Software, or Data. An obvious crime that is usually easy to recognize is the theft of hardware. When a portable or desktop computer disappears, it is usually safe to assume that someone stole it. But when a copy of a software program is made — with the original left in place, intact — how easily can that be traced? Or, when traced, in what manner is it prosecuted? Bringing the writing of programs under Federal Copyright Act protection may ease some aspects of this situation, but unauthorized copying is still extremely difficult to detect. When data itself is stolen, in the form of a diskette, for example, in many areas the only crime that can be prosecuted is the theft of the diskette itself. This is hard to reconcile with the actual monetary losses incurred on consideration that the data can sometimes be irreplaceable; even when it can be put back in, it might involve days or weeks of work.

A recent example of theft of output/data involved a case where a computer executive obtained a great deal of classified information about U.S.

energy sources and resources via a remote terminal and a telephone. The man, an employee of a large company that provided computer services, was convicted of fraud. His employer, who had no knowledge of the crime, said the printouts were not valuable because of the data they contained. However, they could demonstrate the system devised to store the information — knowledge of which could give an unfair advantage to many related industry competitors.

PRIVACY AND CONFIDENTIALITY

Privacy and confidentiality are two issues that are becoming related to abuse of computerized information. Privacy is an individual's right to limit the recording and dissemination of personal information. Since much of this information is now kept on computer, abuse can occur when such records are accessed on an unauthorized basis.

Confidentiality is the right to limit access to sensitive data. This confidential information is the kind of material which, if revealed about an organization, might diminish that company's competitive edge in the marketplace or lead to a rival company's gaining an advantage. Examples of such confidential information are customer, supplier, shareholder, and personnel data; development, sales, and marketing strategies; security measures; research findings and other proprietary information.

The balance between the issues of privacy and confidentiality is of concern to organizations, government, associations, and private individuals. Formal protection, and legislation to protect all concerned, including a comprehensive definition, has been sought.

During the 1970s, efforts were made to collect guidelines protecting individual and organizational rights to privacy, based on generally accepted principles and existing laws under "fair information practices" rules, directed toward

- Limiting the kind of data that business or government organizations may maintain on individuals.
- Limiting access to that data.
- Limiting the length of time certain data may be maintained (such as criminal and/or credit histories).
- Allowing individuals to know who maintains data about them.
- Allowing individuals to review and change data gathered and maintained about themselves.

As a result, organizations that gather and maintain data, especially those with extensive electronic data processing (EDP) facilities, should make sure that they do the following:

- Maintain the validity of data
- Control access to the data
- Monitor accesses to the data

Privacy protection is similarly a concern, relating to credit reporting agencies, employment and insurance investigations, law enforcement agencies, education and medical records, and computer and program design.

Limiting Access to Data

Traditionally, access to data was restricted by retaining confidential data and records in user departments under suitable physical security arrangements. The proliferation of computerized systems has concentrated data in the EDP department, resulting in growing concerns about security arrangements for computer operations, data files, and distribution of reports. When data can be accessed on-line from a terminal outside the EDP department, controls are needed to ensure that terminal use is restricted to authorized users and that access to data is restricted outside of authorized functions.

Controls in use for restriction of access to computers and data include physical security; software checks, such as passwords; terminals dedicated only to certain processing functions; automatic disconnect of terminals unused for a given time or after a specified number of unsuccessful password entries for attempted access; and controls over the master terminal that controls other terminals and the passwords used. (See Chapter 32.)

The problems inherent in controlling access to data have been complicated by the phenomenal growth of microcomputer use by general office personnel. Controls and standards for these new uses rarely exist, since organizations are just becoming aware of the need to control and audit microcomputer use. Other issues over growing use are the data gathered and how it is used, how such recordkeeping may affect compliance with legislation, and controlling and protecting messaging systems.

A survey conducted by a computer industry publication found that as computers move out of a strictly EDP environment, their new users inadvertently circumvent controls, ignore procedures, or violate standards of privacy because they do not know the principles involved. Microcomputer users may handle very sensitive data, since they frequently work with whole documents, not unassembled data as in an EDP department.

The information contained in personnel files is a particular case in point. This data can be obtained all too easily by unauthorized people in many organizations. Management should act to rectify such control deficiencies, auditing operations to see how data is handled and accessed. Standards applicable to all employees should be developed and enforced, and the personnel educated. Many companies have designated a compliance manager, whose duties include monitoring activities and keeping up to date on trends and legislation to help ensure that corporate policy conforms with evolving control standards.

LEGAL ASPECTS

Congress has recently passed a measure on computer crime. It took many years, for a variety of reasons, including debate about a definition of the problem, a preference by many that the problem be dealt with at the state level, general lack of consensus in the EDP community, and the absence of a strong drive from the other branches of government in support of such proposed legislation. As of October 1984, the President had not signed the measure.

Consider a couple of examples that demonstrate the difficulties of legally defining computer crime:

- If a man takes paper securities, he is a thief. If he takes a magnetic tape whose electronic impulses represent those papers, is he a thief stealing a magnetic tape, or is he accountable for what the data on that tape represents as well?
- If someone duplicates an original computer program without authorization, is that person stealing the program or not?

Proposed Federal Legislation

Since 1977, when Senator Ribicoff first introduced the Federal Computer Systems Protection Act, a proposal for comprehensive computer crime legislation, Congress has considered a number of different measures.

In the House of Representatives, the Counterfeit Access Device and Computer Fraud and Abuse Act (H.R. 5616) passed by unanimous vote in July 1984. Sponsored by Subcommittee Chairman Bill Hughes and Congressman Bill Nelson, it includes many of the provisions of the Federal Computer Systems Protection Act, one of the original measures introduced on computer crime, also sponsored by Congressman Nelson.

The Computer Fraud and Abuse Act combines the possible penalties for computer crime and abuse of credit cards. In the computer area, these penalties would include fines from $5,000 to $100,000, and up to 20 years of imprisonment, for those who "knowingly access a computer (which affects interstate or foreign commerce) without authorization" and obtain anything of over $5,000 value within one year.

The bill would mandate penalties against system abusers, who "use, modify, destroy, disclose information in, or prevent authorized use" of computers operating on behalf of the U.S. government. It specifically includes protection for classified information. An amendment imposes penalties (misdemeanor) for unauthorized access of records protected by the Right to Financial Privacy Act of 1978 or the Fair Credit Reporting Act. The U.S. Senate is considering similar measures.

The Federal Computer Systems Protection Act of 1984 was proposed by the U.S. Department of Justice in August 1984. It differs from the House bill in some respects. Other related measures are also under consideration.

Legal Protection

Protection of privacy and confidentiality is a concern of individuals and a growing concern of business and government. Usually, privacy and confidentiality statutes are not computer-specific; much of the legislation in this area has been enacted recently and is in regard to the general protection of information. Such statutes impose penalties for unlawful access or disclosure of information to safeguard confidential information. Some enable law enforcement groups to access confidential information following certain requirements.

Statutes Relating to Access or Disclosure of Information. The 1974 Privacy Act makes it illegal to gather, maintain, use, and disseminate information held in federal computer systems. Since the government's computers have been estimated to store 4 billion records on individuals, the Privacy Act was important legislation. The Espionage Act makes it illegal to obtain information for use against the United States (relating to espionage per se, not industrial espionage). The Wire Fraud Statute makes it a crime to obtain money or property via wire fraudulently. There is some concern in the computer community about the Wire Fraud Statute definition of wiretapping as "aural acquisition," which might exclude tapping lines into computers to acquire the data transmitted.

Other provisions sometimes used against computer abusers are the Soliciting Federal Tax Information provision of the Tax Code; the Fair Credit Reporting Act, which imposes penalties for those who obtain information from credit agencies under false pretenses; and the Electronic Funds Transfer Act, which makes it a crime to use fictitious, altered, lost, stolen, or fraudulently obtained debit instruments. There are other statutes that apply to privacy of federal, state, and industry information.

Several of the preceding statutes also cover unlawful disclosure of information, including the Privacy Act, the Espionage Act, and the Fair Credit Reporting Act. Other relevant statutes are the Trade Secrets Act, which makes it illegal for federal employees to release such information; the Disclosing Federal Tax Return Information provision; the Redisclosure of Privileged Information provision; and the Disclosure of Prepared Income Tax Data provision.

Additional provisions protecting confidentiality and privacy that have been related to computer abuse include the Executive Order on the Disclosure of Classified Information, the Right to Financial Privacy Act, the Family Education Rights and Privacy Act, and various provisions attached to the Internal Revenue Code.

Computer Abuse or Crime Laws

A variety of statutes impose penalties for violations of privacy and confidentiality, as just discussed. In prosecuting computer crime, problems exist when attempting to apply traditional laws to what are thought of as nontraditional crimes. For example, in most areas computer programs are not currently defined as property, and the larceny laws relate to theft of property with the intent to deprive the owner of its use. If a program is copied, then such laws may not apply by definition.

Investigatory Problems. Investigation of computer abuse by law enforcement units is a troublesome area, since highly technical knowledge is needed to collect the kind of evidence found in computer abuse situations. And, of course, the crime must first be detected and reported, both of which rarely happen. There is a general perception, as reported in various surveys, that law enforcement agencies do not understand the problem, and that in addition to this, there is a lack of management awareness and concern about dealing with such situations.

Prosecutors, like their law enforcement counterparts, may not have sufficient technical knowledge of computers to prepare effective cases against computer criminals and may not even be able to do so when that knowledge is present because of the lack of applicable laws.

Crimes committed using a computer as an instrument can be prosecuted under existing statutes that apply to the crime itself, such as those on theft of trade secrets, embezzlement, receipt of stolen property, theft of services, conspiracy, forgery, and the like. To apply traditional laws to crimes against computers, prosecutors have tried to extend the standard definitions of the elements of a crime and definitions of property, particularly in relation to software and data.

On the federal level, the Privacy Act, the Financial Institutions and Interest Rate Control Act of 1978, and the U.S. Copyright Law of 1976, as well as others, have been used to prosecute computer crime.

The following areas have caused concern in prosecuting computer crime in general:

- *Procedural problems.* Computer-based evidence, stored in electronic form, becomes a problem in itself. It is obtained in a variety of standard ways, including administrative searches and subpoenas, but to apply these techniques can be difficult. Requirements and narrowly defined parameters on what is being searched for and where need technical expertise, since, for example, search warrants must be very specific. In some instances, potential defendants can easily destroy possible evidence in milliseconds, or can manage to commit the crime so that no evidence is available.

- *Evidentiary problems.* Relating computer-based evidence to traditional evidentiary rules can also be difficult. Computerized books and records may be intelligible only after translation into hard-copy reports or output. Frequently, component transactions can only be checked by combining them with existing data and producing totals. As a result, it has been hard for prosecutors to satisfy the basic conditions that are necessary for admission of documents. Naturally, computer-based evidence must meet the same requirements of the best evidence rule and the hearsay rule as any evidence does to be admitted.

  a. *Best Evidence Rule.* Under the best evidence rule, the original document or writing must be submitted as evidence. In the case of computer-generated evidence, the originals may no longer exist or, for that matter, may never have existed to begin with, so courts would have to redefine their concept of "original." The voluminous writings exception allows submission of summaries of writings that are too voluminous to be brought into court. The opponent has to have had the opportunity to examine the underlying data. The competency of the person who creates the summaries must also be established.[2]

  b. *The Hearsay Rule.* Hearsay evidence is normally inadmissible, but through various exceptions to the hearsay rule prosecutors can admit it in certain circumstances. Reliability of the evidence is the key. Some of the exceptions to the hearsay rule may allow for admission of reliable computerized evidence.

    — The business records exception allows for admission into evidence of records made in the regular course of business at the same time as the events they record. It is the most common exception used to introduce computerized evidence. Rule 8036 of the Federal Rules of Evidence has been amended to include "data compilations," which can be entered as evidence when the computer system that produced them is demonstrably reliable.

---

[2]Federal Rules of Evidence § 1001(3).

State Laws

The following states (as of mid-1984) have specific computer crime laws:

Alaska	Iowa[3]	Ohio
Arizona	Maryland[4]	Oklahoma
California	Massachusetts	Pennsylvania
Colorado	Michigan	Rhode Island
Connecticut	Minnesota	South Dakota
Delaware	Missouri	Tennessee
Florida	Montana	Utah
Georgia	Nevada	Virginia
Hawaii	New Mexico	Wisconsin
Idaho	New York	
Illinois	North Carolina	

Many states have also passed privacy legislation, relevant to computerized information, similar to federal provisions on privacy. There are also a number of administrative guidelines related to invasion of privacy via computers, where, unfortunately, compliance may not be mandatory.

AUDIT IMPLICATIONS

As has been discussed, the growing use of on-line facilities and data bases has affected the ease of access to information. These environments, if uncontrolled, may allow unauthorized access to data, procedures, and possibly permit learning how to circumvent the controls over the environment. Susceptibility to unauthorized access of sensitive records, such as salary information, may be greatly increased. As part of auditing such systems, the internal or EDP auditor frequently recommends additional or improved controls.

Included in audit assessments may be the sharing of data by different organizations, a possible infringement of individual privacy or confidentiality. As a result, it is important to ensure that adequate controls are in place or are implemented over data transfer and the sharing of data.

As an auditor tests the continued existence of controls, they may also affect the auditor's procedures. For example, when strict confidentiality controls are in place it may actually become more difficult to obtain the data and other information needed for the audit. Naturally, the auditor also checks

---

[3]Passed in legislature, awaiting governer's signature.
[4]Limited to computerized public records.

controls over access to data. Audit tests to ensure the security of the files, data elements, and systems operations as a whole are discussed in Part IV, "Controls" (Chapters 16–22), and in Part VI, "Controlling Computers" (Chapters 28–32).

Another of the auditor's responsibilities is to ensure that controls comply with applicable federal, state, and local regulations. Therefore, the auditor needs to be well-versed in such rulings and interpretations to relate this information to the computer system under audit, as required.

Auditor's Role

An EDP auditor's primary task is not to assume that computer abuse or crime has already happened and to go into an area to try to uncover it. Instead, an auditor can focus on performing audits of systems throughout the year, suggesting ways to improve controls, watching the behavior of EDP personnel, noting changes in established patterns, conducting periodic surprise audits, and broadening the scope of audit support to include review of implementation of applications and user and supervisory controls. Of course, management must sanction such procedures. High visibility of the EDP auditor may be an effective deterrent to computer abuse in itself.

Computer abuse may be discovered during the regular course of an audit. When fraud or other computer crime is uncovered, an EDP auditor can help with the investigation and subsequently provide litigation support for prosecution. An audit committee may also request an investigation when computer crime or fraud is suspected. Proceeding on such assignments requires a high degree of tact, knowledge, and discretion.

One of the auditor's first tasks might be to determine whether the situation was a one-time occurrence or part of an ongoing process. Where the abuse is part of an ongoing scheme, obviously the auditor has to try to find out when it started. Once the full extent of the problem is uncovered, if that is possible, the auditor reports his or her findings to management. Management can then decide how they want the situation to be handled. That decision can include attempting to recover lost money, goods, or services; bringing the incident to the attention of legal authorities; and recommending improved controls to avoid having the situation, or a similar one, recur.

Performing a regular or an investigatory audit, the auditor is naturally aware that auditing procedures followed are subject to outside scrutiny, such as from the Securities and Exchange Commission. This has been particularly true since the 1970s, when landmark court cases established that an auditor is liable for prosecution if an unreported situation that materially affects a company's financial records has not been discovered and properly reported. Obviously, one way to preclude unanswerable questions is for an auditor to carefully document audit strategy, each procedure performed during an audit, and principles applied.

Preventing Computer Abuse

Without definitive laws, established organizational procedures, and detection/ reporting systems, the problems of detecting and prosecuting computer crime and abuse will continue to plague owners and users of computers systems. Managements' growing concerns in the area have led many to realize how important it is for an organization to protect its systems so that the opportunities for abuse are lessened. To help develop workable plans, the following checklist asks some essential questions about computer abuse prevention:

- Does the organization have a contingency plan to put into effect once computer abuse is suspected?
- If confirmed abuse occurs in the organization, would notification of the proper officials be timely?
- Does the organization have insurance coverage commensurate with the increased risks due to modern computer technology?

If computer abuse is suspected:

- Does the organization know its responsibilities to its insurance carrier, and vice versa?
- Is the organization aware of responsibilities to investors, stockholders, and reporting agencies?
- Has the organization ever had a comprehensive diagnostic security study conducted?
- Has the organization had a review of computer integrity controls within the last year? Were all recommendations and directives implemented?
- Is there assurance that the organization's internal audit program is comprehensive?
- Do relevant personnel know the legal limitations regarding questioning individuals, discharging employees, or discussing suspected events with third parties?
- Has the organization embraced an overall corporate security plan or philosophy?

The article, "Computer Logs Can Pinpoint Illegal Transactions," written by Pamela Pfau and James Keane (*Legal Times*, May 14, 1984), indicates some of the ways organizations can detect computer abuse. It is reprinted in Figure 31-1.

Computer crime is a growth industry. Rising numbers of computers exist in uncontrolled environments, and our society has become more trusting of automated accuracy. Indeed, since computer literacy has grown faster than a proper awareness of computer security, systems increasingly are accessed illegally to enter phony mistakes, to create bogus transactions, or to subtly change computer programs for illicit ends.

To date, the bogus transactions most easily turn a profit for the perpetrator. Bogus transactions need not involve the receipt of tangible assets. In some organizations, middle management is closely scrutinized to ensure that it is not manipulating computer data to reflect a rosier picture than actually exists.

Since a computer reports only what it is told and makes no unprogrammed judgment, it becomes an easy means of distorting the real financial information. If someone catches on, the perpetrator always has the alibi, "It was a computer error," or the defense, "Prove that I did it."

Management is not defenseless, however — a misconception that is all too prevalent among the newly computer literate. Computers *can* monitor their own use. Unlike such other forms of physical evidence as guns, computers can keep track of individual users and other identifying data. Imagine a gun that logs every instance it is fired or even handled, and shows the date, time, and activity. Recovery of such a weapon would be essential to the prosecution.

Most computers long have had built-in logging capabilities. Unfortunately, few standalone minicomputers have this feature, and even fewer of the new generation of microcomputers. The log function was designed to facilitate billing for use of computer resources rather than to assist crime detection. To the extent that the owner of a smaller computer does not charge for its use, he or she has no incentive to purchase a self-executing log. Still, such logs keep surprisingly accurate records of who is using the computer.

Any log data provides a resource for investigating perpetrators. Suppose a building's security guard keeps a log of who has entered a building between 7 p.m. Friday and 8 a.m. Monday. If the facility was totally secured during the hours illegal activity occurred, any investigator would check the log entries to identify suspects.

This same concept applies to the computer's log data. Of course, it's not quite as easy as checking the entry log. First and foremost, the crime must be detected. A major problem with many computer crimes is that the perpetrator enters a number of bogus transactions over a period of time, none of which is significant enough to warrant suspicion or rejection by the system. No one thinks to look at the log.

Computer crimes such as these often start out small, with the perpetrator planning to pay it all back. In several cases, however, individuals insouciantly and clandestinely enter large and undetected bogus transactions.

What type of computer misuse would analysis of the log file uncover? Unauthorized execution of a normally scheduled production job may reveal a payroll crime. A computer operator who knows how to program is unsupervised during the third shift. He decides to change the program to increase his pay by $1,000.

The next day, the payroll runs under the normal supervised procedures; the third shift operator isn't even around. His check is automatically deposited in his account at the bank. (He never signs it and can easily play innocent if someone discovers that he was overpaid by $1,000.) To cover his tracks, he then changes the program back to its original version, sans salary increase.

FIG. 31-1 Using a computer log to detect computer abuses

In this example, the computer log file would show that someone changed the program twice at irregular times without authorization. The procedures used to protect a computer center from this type of misuse are called "program change control procedures."

These procedures exist, not to protect against misuse, but to ensure that programs operate properly. Computer centers that allow anyone to change production programs cannot exist for long. This would be equivalent to letting a production worker modify the assembly line process. While it might work for the moment, serious repercussions could arise later.

You can change program procedures in several ways:

- Change the source code. If the program were written in COBOL (an English-like language), the change might look like this:

   IF EMPLOYEE-NO EQUALS 12891 ADD 1000 TO CHECK-AMOUNT

   The next step would be to compile the source code into the object code so the computer could execute the program as a production job. Thus, the log file would show the change to the program and the compile of the program.

- A more obscure method exists. You can directly change the object code by using a ZAP to the object program. This method eliminates the compile step and is more difficult to detect. Many computer centers have restricted the use of the ZAP capability in production program libraries — not out of fear of misuse, but because a ZAP leaves no record of the change to the source program. Since the source program will not match the object program, this is especially problematic for program maintenance.

   To detect this, search the log data for the execution of all ZAPs. Don't think you have to do this yourself. You can program the computer to report all ZAPs to production libraries. To make the task even easier, request a report of these activities during the time period under investigation.

This is a simple example. You may question the likelihood of these actions going undetected, but remember, in our relatively paperless society, no traceable source document of the intermediate transaction ever would have existed.

Furthermore, controls do not always function, especially when performed by people. That's why a round number of a one-digit increment will go undetected. A $1,000 error easily can fall into the category of an arithmetic error. But even if the changes in the source and object program libraries are removed, a trace will remain that indicates the activity took place. From this trace, you can identify suspects.

Given the neutrality of log information, you must demonstrate the corpus delecti: A suspect perpetrated a wrongful act — i.e., it wasn't a computer mistake.

Try the same case with a slight modification: The computer operator decides to enter a bogus transaction by duplicating an authorized valid record. The computer operator gets paid double and still calls it a computer mistake.

This all can be done without changing the source documents or the program. The operator needs only to use a standard utility software package called COPY to duplicate the pay record. Using the log file, you can isolate the use of the COPY program and determine which terminals accessed the data file in which the payroll transaction records were stored.

The case should be modified further, for what savvy computer operator would take such an obvious risk? After all, as the one closest to the computer, he or she could be under surveillance.

It might be the payroll clerk, who has a yen for computers and worked closely with the computer center during implementation of the payroll system. The payroll clerk even has a remote on-line terminal to more effectively process the payroll. A remote terminal with access by direct connect line or a dial-up telephone can just as easily perform the procedures described in the other examples. But it will leave the same evidence on the log file. In fact, when certain types of computers are involved, you can easily determine the remote terminal that entered the information.

The auditing profession developed EDP auditors who review controls and extract data from the computers clients use to run their businesses. The legal profession also should harness the computer power at hand to assist in investigations and case preparation.

During a fraud audit or an investigation, take advantage of the data on the computer log file. Begin by asking these questions:

- What type of computer is involved?
- Does the operating system maintain a log?
- Is some or all of the suspected activity recorded on a log file?
- What program was run without authorized approval?
- How long is the log data available? (Sometimes this information is kept no longer than 10 days.)
- Is the log file data to be compared — e.g., a list of the programs scheduled for approved production — maintained in the form of standardized records that will make analysis easier?

Computer crime is a growing problem, but its incidence can be detected and its perpetrators prosecuted. Prosecutors and trial lawyers can use the computer's own "fingerprints" to secure the evidence necessary for an effective investigation or trial presentation.

FIG. 31-1   *(continued)*

Security

INTRODUCTION TO COMPUTER SECURITY

This chapter discusses various aspects of EDP security and the methods and planning tools that can be used to conduct a security review. Security objectives are identified and discussed, and methods for achieving those objectives are described. While 100 percent security cannot be achieved, the goal is to achieve the highest possible security protection commensurate with business demands and cost considerations.

The increasing use of automated systems to communicate, process, and store data has concentrated the information of many organizations into their EDP and information systems. Data is a vital resource, common to the organization, and its exposure through neglect, carelessness, catastrophe, or an overt act (anything from improper data manipulation to divulgence of confidential information to competitors) could seriously impair the entire organization and result in a loss of assets, possibly of catastrophic proportions if the EDP facility became inoperable. Providing adequate security has become all the more challenging with the introduction of decentralized processing, microcomputers, micro-to-mainframe links, and such.

Information systems are key components of an organization's operation, and it is therefore essential that the processing capability as well as the data be safeguarded and protected. It is the responsibility of management to implement safeguards that will protect these assets. Figure 32-1 shows some of the security threats to computer systems.

OVERVIEW OF SECURITY

During the past three decades the use of EDP equipment in business and government has grown at an enormous rate. While developing EDP installations and applications, few designers included sufficient security or auditability features. Future developments, such as the ability of outsiders to break into the system using small computers and modems, were not anticipated. As a consequence, many processing systems can be violated, exposing corporate assets and trade information to theft or misstatement and business disruption.

As automated business systems become larger and more complex, additional control is required to ensure that sensitive information and vital assets are not unnecessarily exposed. In most organizations, data has become recognized as a vital resource that is especially vulnerable to security breaches because of the increased use of automated data communications, processing, and storage functions. Management awareness of these possibilities has increased the concern for establishing and maintaining proper EDP security. The current need is to perform reviews today to set minimum standards for tomorrow's real exposures, likely to exist due to growing use of telecommunications, relational data bases, and the like.

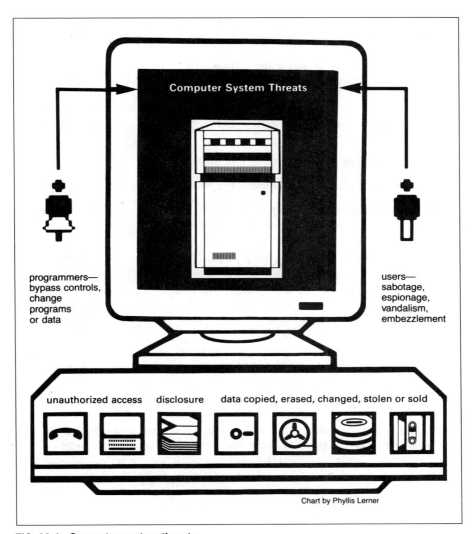

FIG. 32-1   Computer system threats

OBJECTIVES OF THE REVIEW

When EDP systems are introduced to assist in the conduct of an organization's business, management is responsible for ensuring that those systems are controlled and used effectively. The EDP auditor is responsible for ensuring that management knows what needs to be done.

The security review is designed to provide management with an independent assessment of the controls over and security structure of their current EDP systems.

A security review should address four major issues:

1. Ability to deliver uninterrupted service
2. Quality and timeliness of information processed and produced
3. Impact of, and the ability to make timely recovery from, disruptive events
4. Preservation of confidentiality of information

The review is designed to achieve the following objectives:

- Provide management with an assessment of their current position as it relates to the security and control exercised over their computer system
- Identify for management the potential exposures that result from deficiencies in current control or operating practices
- Provide management with practical recommendations for improvement (i.e., it might be good security to implement data encryption, but the costs of doing so, for example in a satellite network, might be prohibitive)
- Provide management with a plan to correct identified deficiencies and the associated costs for the implementation of recommendations

To achieve these objectives, the following areas require detailed examination and evaluation:

- The EDP environment, including the arrangement of physical facilities, access to equipment and storage media, and physical security devices installed (fire detection, suppression systems, etc.)
- The computer department operations including procedures, documentation, and controls used in:
  a. Operating and maintaining equipment
  b. Developing and modifying programs
  c. Security data files and program libraries
  d. Backup and recovery of programs and data files
- The administrative practices such as policies and procedures that govern personnel matters, insurance protection, and the interaction between system users, the EDP resources, and support services personnel

The information gathered throughout the examination and evaluation should be sufficiently detailed to assess accurately the areas of exposure and their potential impact on the operation. This assessment should identify for management those areas in the operation where improvement should be considered and recommend strategies for correcting those deficiencies.

Scope of a Security Review

A security review is normally undertaken as a result of management recognition that security needs to be improved, or to evaluate existing security to determine if it is sufficient. In both situations, it is critical to determine the extent of examination required. Development of a security-scoping information sheet or similar document assists in gathering information and determining the areas of concern to management. In the future, security reviews may be performed on a somewhat continuous basis.

The areas to be reviewed should be selected and presented to management for agreement. Once all of the people concerned have agreed which areas are to be included in the review, detailed work plans should be prepared and the appropriate EDP and other audit staff assigned.

Security reviews are frequently performed by third-party reviewers to provide the objectivity of an independent evaluation.

SECURITY REVIEW APPROACH

The security review can be conducted in a series of discrete phases. The work in each phase depends on the accuracy of the findings from the previous phase. Therefore, it is essential that the findings for each phase be confirmed before beginning the next phase. This verification process includes meetings with appropriate line management, EDP staff, and audit staff. These meetings also enable management to keep abreast of the progress of the review.

The four phases of the review are:

Phase I — Review and Evaluation of Current Operations
Phase II — Exposure Assessment
Phase III — Preparation of Recommendations
Phase IV — Implementation Plan

Each of these phases is outlined below, together with a description of the tasks to be performed.

Phase I — Review and Evaluation of Current Operations

The first phase is designed to review, document, and evaluate current EDP operations to determine the strengths and weaknesses of the existing security and control structure within the organization.

To gather the information necessary for the evaluation process, the following tasks are performed by the EDP auditor and other audit staff members:

- Inspecting sites
- Conducting interviews
- Completing detailed control questionnaires
- Observing operations
- Examining previous audit reports
- Examining available system documentation
- Examining relevant correspondence, insurance policies, and contracts
- Examining computer access controls and listings, such as use of security software or access reports based on system logs

Current security procedures, policies, and practices should be evaluated to determine their completeness, intent, and effectiveness.

For each area selected for review, the auditor needs to identify the controls in place, assess their effectiveness, and identify where additional control mechanisms should be employed. Work plans and checklists should be used to guide the review process. The special skills of the EDP auditor should be of particular help in this process.

This phase is critical to the overall success of the project, since it establishes the current security structure and related exposures, and leads to the development of recommendations.

Phase II — Exposure Assessment

Risk can be defined as the possibility of loss or injury. Exposure is the deprivation of protection, shelter, or care provided to an asset that may have the effect of increasing risk. Phase II identifies the risks to which the organization is exposed as a result of the specific weaknesses identified in Phase I. Risks can include both loss of assets and public embarrassment to an organization. For example, if confidential business information is revealed, the consequences could include stockholders' loss of confidence in management.

There are five major risk classifications that can affect information processing and place the assets of the organization in jeopardy. These risks can arise either accidentally or deliberately (accidents may be an act of God, such as a fire; deliberate events may be someone taking advantage of a weak control over system access) and are as follows:

1. Destruction of physical assets or information
2. Disclosure of confidential information

3. Removal of physical assets or information
4. Corruption of data or programs
5. Interruption of service

A weakness may expose an asset to one or more of these risks. The impact of any event can be determined using two factors: (1) the frequency of occurrence and (2) the amount of the potential loss. These two factors are considered to ascertain the priorities for addressing any identified weaknesses. It is important to note that the loss of an asset cannot be determined by replacement value alone. Consideration must also be given to additional loss that may result if the asset is no longer available. For example, accidental damage to a disk would not only result in the loss of the physical component, but also the loss of the information on the disk and system disruption until the information is restored.

At the completion of Phase II, exposures will have been identified and ranked in a practical, logical manner consistent with the company's business environment. The auditor should discuss the assessment of dangers resulting from exposures in the organization's current procedures with management before proceeding to Phase III.

Phase III — Preparation of Recommendations

Recommendations can be prepared based on the assessment of exposures. These recommendations should include procedures that should be implemented to mitigate the exposure and its potential impact on the organization. In many situations, more than one solution may be available, in which case the alternatives should be presented for consideration.

Although the specific recommendations vary from one situation to the next, normally they fall within the following broad categories:

• Additional hardware and software requirements
• Software modifications
• Manual controls
• Writing of procedures and guidelines
• Contractual agreements
• Preventive maintenance
• Management review

At the completion of Phase III, the auditors should discuss the recommendations with management to ensure that the solutions presented are the most practical for the organization.

Phase IV — Implementation Plan

Phase IV work results in a plan for implementation of the recommendations developed in Phase III. The sequence and timing of implementation depends on:

- Urgency for improvement
- Availability of company personnel with the appropriate skills to implement improvements; alternately, using an independent organization to assist with the implementation
- Availability of software tools and other products in the market to quickly address the issues
- The organization's future development plans

For example, some high-priority recommendations may not be implemented first because they can logically be incorporated into future system development activities and will thereby be implemented on a more cost-effective basis.

The implementation plan consists of identifying the sequence and timing of activities, the nature and extent of the resources required, and the estimated costs of implementation. In addition, those recommendations that are independent of others are identified. These can then be implemented concurrently with other recommendations, delayed, or brought forward, as need dictates.

The auditors should review the implementation plan in detail with management to ensure that the plan is clear and the timing of events is agreeable to them.

STAFFING REQUIREMENTS

A security review should be staffed with experienced EDP auditors, other senior personnel with a background in security and exposure analysis, and information technology specialists. Since it is not always easy to find personnel with enough technical depth and breadth to conduct a review of all areas, the use of such a group of people should be considered. Some areas require specialized technical skills. For example, system software integrity evaluation requires experience in the use and design of operating systems.

INFORMATION SECURITY EXPOSURES

All organizations face possible information security exposures. The potential seriousness of a breach in security can be evaluated according to the function of the organization's business, dependence on the information, and sensitivity to the potential loss.

Risks can be classified into five categories. The events in these categories can occur either accidentally or deliberately and are:

1. *Information disclosure.* Unauthorized disclosure can affect an organization's profitability, impair customer relations, be used for personal gain or for malicious purposes.

2. *Corruption of data or programs.* Modified or altered documents, computer programs, data files, transactions, or reports can result in misstated assets, erroneous management planning and control data, or be used to conceal possible fraud or defalcation.

3. *Destruction of physical assets or information.* Business can be seriously interrupted or indefinitely curtailed depending on the degree of information or processing dependency, the target, and extent of destruction.

4. *Interruption of service.* Interruption of processing schedules can impair or curtail basic service and product delivery.

5. *Removal of physical assets or information.* Unauthorized or accidental removal of hardware components or storage media can seriously disrupt an organization's ability to continue normal business operations.

Security safeguards should be tailored to meet each organization's specific needs. They are effective to the extent that the costs of implementing safeguards are properly balanced against the potential losses.

SECURITY BREACH CAUSES

Other than natural hazards, the integrity of any security system is ultimately vested in personnel and depends on the integrity of individuals.

Generally, data processing is exposed to physical disaster, fraud, vandalism, mischief, and human error. During a security review, each area of data processing is evaluated to determine what security measures are being used to prevent, detect, and control the potential for abuse and to identify areas where additional control mechanisms should be employed.

Physical Disaster

Disaster-causing events occur in many different ways, and the end result could be a discontinuance of business. Recovery time varies depending on the cause of the disturbance; in some cases, the damage is irreparable. Disaster-causing events can be intentional (e.g., bombings, fires), natural hazards (e.g., hurricanes, tornadoes, floods, and earthquakes), or acts of negligence (e.g., dropping a disk pack).

The primary concern is to determine what and how data and assets should be protected or duplicated to ensure that the business can recover. The type of protection required depends on the nature of the business and, because even similar businesses do not operate identically, the unique protection methods available for that environment.

Analysis of probable occurrence is done by examining disaster vulnerabilities. Cost-effectiveness is then determined after rating alternative protection techniques. For example, a fire suppression system may not be cost-justified for a small retail establishment with a computer operator in attendance during all processing, but a system of fire extinguishers and smoke alarms could be a sufficient substitute.

Fraud

When system designers initially developed automated systems, few realized the potential for criminal abuse by embezzlement, fraud, or theft of organizational assets. Protection or detection techniques were generally not included in early systems and the complexity of new systems has made defalcation even more difficult to detect. Data previously maintained within different departments has been compressed and centralized for faster and easier use. Often organizations were restructured and manual document processing procedures, which allowed many people to observe how data was being handled, were replaced by automated processing without accompanying security measures.

These automated processing systems were designed to require fewer people with more authority to handle transactions at a faster rate. In fact, fewer people were familiar with the new processes and not many questioned their use. Even fewer understood that data could be fraudulently entered or processed. As a result, authorized individuals who wished to do so had a vehicle for perpetrating crime through unauthorized use of the computer. There were fewer methods of detecting fraud by those select individuals who had access to vast amounts of information.

Elaborate schemes can be developed to defraud an organization for personal gain. Computer-related crimes over the past decade substantiate this, as in the Equity Funding scandal (discussed in the opening of Chapter 19, "Controls for Validity, Maintenance and Operations"). Such crimes may occur because security controls are either missing or lax, and personnel have enough knowledge of the system to use it for their own advantage. When weak controls are in place, they can be circumvented. Very few systems have sufficient controls to detect fraud as it is occurring. Typically, the crime is detected only after it has been committed, and it is usually detected because the perpetrator makes a mistake, or an inconsistency is accidentally discovered. (See Chapter 31, "Computer Abuse.")

Many systems do not have adequate audit trails to indicate how a transaction has been processed and the personnel who were involved. Methods commonly used in manual systems, such as journals, ledgers, receipts, and other documents, are now automated. Reports are printed, but source documents used to create these reports are often destroyed. Those with access authority can manipulate data for fraudulent purposes by falsifying transactions and records.

To reduce the opportunities and instances of fraud, adequate controls with prescribed audit checkpoints should exist. The complete processing of a transaction must be traceable from creation to disposition. Cross-checking involving more than one individual should exist, but may serve only as a deterrent rather than an absolute means of fraud prevention.

Vandalism

Vandalism takes many forms. It can be planned or "spur of the moment" and can arise from external or internal sources. For example, children can use windows as targets for rocks or a disgruntled employee may destroy data. Neither of these events is predictable.

Vandalism has long been a method used by disgruntled employees seeking revenge against an employer they believe to be unjust. Such employees are tempted to destroy resources needed by the employer, such as computer hardware or programs and essential data. Destruction is usually camouflaged and not detected until much later; often it is untraceable. Unprotected storage media, such as tapes, are prime targets; if backup copies do not exist at some secure location, it may be virtually impossible to recreate the contents of the tapes. Program modification is another method of revenge: Modifying a program by introducing destruct instructions or illogical processing instructions can cause a system to fail or to create invalid data.

Mischief

Mischievous acts, unlike vandalism, are usually nondestructive. Although those involved usually do not realize it, the disruption caused is often serious. The acts are generally pranks, such as hiding or purposely misplacing media.

Human Error

The greatest ongoing cause of disruption within an EDP installation is human error. For example, computer operators may accidentally damage equipment and storage media; incorrectly coded programs may be entered into production without adequate testing or quality control; or sensitive information may be publicly disclosed through inappropriate procedures.

Human error cannot be completely eliminated, but the security and control techniques used to reduce the risk of other exposures also reduce the frequency of errors.

DISASTER RECOVERY AND CONTINGENCY PLANNING

A security review describes the security deficiencies and potential problems that may result. Some events that can disrupt EDP activities are not security breaches but are unlikely operational events that merit contingency planning. Contingency planning is frequently a forgotten function, but is perhaps one of the most important in running an EDP facility. Many businesses are so highly dependent on their computers that contingency plans exist to ensure that business operations will continue in the event computer service is disrupted. Equal care and planning must be expended to ensure that adequate security measures and controls are maintained both during and following a disruption. These plans are often reviewed as part of an operational audit.

The best way to ensure a rapid recovery from either short interruptions or a catastrophe is to have a written plan. The vague ideas of a few people do not constitute a viable recovery plan. When they are not available or cannot remember the details of a complex system, an undocumented plan is ineffective. Figures 32-2, 32-3, and 32-4 show sample checklists used to evaluate and review a contingency plan.

For a business to continue operating following a disaster, a recovery manual should be prepared to

- Identify the critical applications.
- Provide a step-by-step plan defining the responsibilities of each organizational unit.
- Identify locations where EDP operations may continue.
- Specify the security controls needed during recovery.

Some organizations are large enough to have both decentralized EDP facilities and centralized EDP activities. If such an organization plans to maintain continuity of processing by switching from one site to another in a disaster situation, it must be supported by a detailed recovery plan. Procedures must be established to communicate hardware and software changes at one location to all other sites that are relying on that one for recovery, while ensuring that appropriate levels of security over the systems exist.

Plan Status	Workpaper Reference	Yes	No	RCW	CC
1. Is a contingency or disaster recovery plan written?	. . . .	☐	☐	. . . .	. . . .
2. Has plan been updated in the last 6 months?	. . . .	☐	☐	. . . .	. . . .
3. Have all current systems been evaluated?	. . . .	☐	☐	. . . .	. . . .
4. Has plan been distributed to all concerned staff?	. . . .	☐	☐	. . . .	. . . .
5. Has plan been approved and resources budgeted?	. . . .	☐	☐	. . . .	. . . .
6. Are recovery staff identified?	. . . .	☐	☐	. . . .	. . . .
7. Are staff familiar with their responsibilities?	. . . .	☐	☐	. . . .	. . . .
8. Are potential disasters identified?	. . . .	☐	☐	. . . .	. . . .
9. Are potential disasters not covered under the plan identified?	. . . .	☐	☐	. . . .	. . . .

FIG. 32-2   Partial security review checklist: Contingency planning — Plan status (RCW = Record of Control Weaknesses; CC = Compensating Controls)

Plan Requirements	Workpaper Reference	Yes	No	RCW	CC
1. Have all functions of data processing been considered in contingency planning?	. . . .	☐	☐	. . . .	. . . .
2. Has a checklist of requirements and supplies been compiled?	. . . .	☐	☐	. . . .	. . . .
3. Have business functions not covered been identified?	. . . .	☐	☐	. . . .	. . . .
4. Have meeting places been identified?	. . . .	☐	☐	. . . .	. . . .
5. Have necessary supplier contacts been established?	. . . .	☐	☐	. . . .	. . . .
6. Are non-EDP departments aware of their individual requirements?	. . . .	☐	☐	. . . .	. . . .
7. Do non-EDP departments have their own action plans?	. . . .	☐	☐	. . . .	. . . .
8. Is alternative processing required?	. . . .	☐	☐	. . . .	. . . .

FIG. 32-3   Partial security review checklist: Contingency planning — Plan requirements (RCW = Record of Control Weaknesses; CC = Compensating Controls)

	Workpaper Reference	Yes	No	RCW	CC
Plan Implementation					
1. Has contingency plan been fully implemented?	. . . .	☐	☐	. . . .	. . . .
2. Have the following areas been checked for availability, compatibility, and readiness:					
a. EDP equipment and facilities?	. . . .	☐	☐	. . . .	. . . .
b. System and data base management software?	. . . .	☐	☐	. . . .	. . . .
c. Special software and utilities?	. . . .	☐	☐	. . . .	. . . .
d. Communication services?	. . . .	☐	☐	. . . .	. . . .
e. Programs and files?	. . . .	☐	☐	. . . .	. . . .
f. Procedures?	. . . .	☐	☐	. . . .	. . . .
3. Is there a test cycle for the plan?	. . . .	☐	☐	. . . .	. . . .
4. Has the plan been tested?	. . . .	☐	☐	. . . .	. . . .
5. Has a procedure for updating the plan been identified?	. . . .	☐	☐	. . . .	. . . .

FIG. 32-4 Partial security review checklist: Contingency planning — Plan implementation (RCW = Record of Control Weaknesses; CC = Compensating Controls)

CONTROL MEASURES

Control measures to protect assets are designed according to the asset type, location, and value. Careful analysis of the environment is required to determine the degree of protection necessary to ensure a secure facility. There are a variety of controls and protection methods available. Usually, a combination of control mechanisms is employed to provide an effective level of security.

Access Control

Access control systems are normally composed of two types: (1) physical controls and (2) logical controls. Physical systems control access to specific areas, whereas logical systems control access to the computer systems and the information stored in them. Both systems are intended to restrict the use of the computer's resources to authorized persons.

Physical Access Control

A variety of physical access control systems are used to regulate an individual's movement within a complex or structure. In some instances, security requirements demand concurrent use of several methods for restricting access to an area. Access systems other than guards are categorized as:

- Mechanical
- Electronic
- Electromechanical
- Digital
- Computerized

Mechanical

Mechanical controls are padlocks, combination locks, key locks, and deadbolts and are used either individually or jointly to secure an area. These are usually the least costly security controls but provide no trace of an individual's movement within the building. As a result, the level of security is low because duplicate keys can be made for key locks and combinations can be discovered.

Electronic

Electronic devices usually consist of an electronic control box used with a plastic card, which acts as a key. A special code is stored on the card, and if the code matches the one required, it activates the electronic component which, in turn, operates the mechanical device that unlocks the door. Cards are read either optically or electronically when inserted. Decoders read the encoded geometry or unique code and, if is correct, allow access. Silent or audible alarms can be installed that will alert security personnel to unauthorized access attempts. These devices are not easily manipulated and are virtually tamper-proof because they cannot be readily duplicated or deciphered. However, if a card is lost and goes unreported, unauthorized individuals could find and use the card to gain access. If an effective reporting procedure for lost cards is implemented, new cards can be prepared with new codes, rendering the lost card useless and maintaining the facility's security.

Electromechanical

Electromechanical devices require some manual effort. They are usually push-button or rotary combination devices that work independently with an electronic card reader to activate and open the lock. This system is more secure than the electronic system, since only having either the code or the card is not sufficient to gain entry.

Digital

Digital devices enable the user to set any combination, thus providing an easy means of changing the combination on a regular basis to reduce the potential for unauthorized use. However, there is no assurance that entry of the number code will not be observed by a bystander. Authorized users should be made aware of this risk and exercise proper care when using the number code.

Computerized

Computerized systems provide the most automatic, advantageous, and sophisticated means of controlling access to a facility. They offer the most complete method for capturing entry and exit data and for tracing an individual's movement within a facility. By continually monitoring an access path, they ensure that only properly identified and authorized individuals are permitted to enter or leave.

Computerized systems can be equipped to sound alarms when an unauthorized access is attempted or the environment changes, such as changes in temperature, humidity, or air flow. In addition, these systems can record data for employee attendance, payroll hours, current employee location, time reports by entry and exit, as well as operational control reports.

Logical Access Control

On-line information includes both data and software. Modern EDP technology has been made easier to use, but also easier to destroy. To protect information from deliberate or accidental destruction and unauthorized use, logical access methods are implemented.

Effective logical access methods restrict the EDP resources each user may access and how they can access them. These controls are implemented within computer hardware and software and generally consist of passwords, user identification, and logical mapping between physical devices and data files.

The use of a communication network and public carriers further complicates the access issues. Communication networks may be secured against penetration by foreign terminals and wiretapping by using identifiers and encryption methods. When identifiers are used, each connected terminal "signs on" with an identity code. Identifiers can be passwords with additional unique codes that identify each terminal and user. When a disruption in communications is detected, the terminal is required to identify itself again. This prohibits substitute terminals from switching into the network. Figure 32-5 shows a sample set of questions used to review access security for a communications network.

Data encryption is used to prevent data theft by wiretapping. Installing hardware scrambling devices at both ends of the communications line, or

Access Protection	Workpaper Reference	Yes	No	RCW	CC
Access Security Communications Network					
1. Are terminals equipped with physical key locks?	....	☐	☐	....	....
2. Are terminals identified and verified by software?	....	☐	☐	....	....
3. Are operators required to supply a user identification?	....	☐	☐	....	....
4. Are user identification and terminal identification cross-referenced?	....	☐	☐	....	....
5. Are user identification and time cross-referenced?	....	☐	☐	....	....
6. Are passwords required for:					
a. System access?	....	☐	☐	....	....
b. Program access?	....	☐	☐	....	....
c. File access?	....	☐	☐	....	....
d. Data field access?	....	☐	☐	....	....
7. Are passwords required to be at least five characters in length?	....	☐	☐	....	....

FIG. 32-5 Partial security review checklist: Communications security — Access protection (RCW = Record of Control Weaknesses; CC = Compensating Controls)

implementing a complex data coding algorithm within the computer program, makes the transmitted data uninterpretable to the wiretapper.

Fire Protection

Fire-suppression and alarm systems are essential if areas with valuable contents, important equipment, or vital functions are to be protected. They are designed to detect and suppress fire within the first few seconds and reduce the need for manual fire-fighting techniques, which may prove unsatisfactory or late in arriving.

Fire-suppression systems can also provide a variety of significant support functions automatically, such as opening fire exits and smoke doors, controlling elevators and shutting off equipment fans, in addition to warning the fire department through a municipal communication link. Fire control systems usually use Halcon 1301 as the fire-extinguishing agent.

Where sophisticated and costly suppression systems are inappropriate, water sprinkler systems, self-contained smoke alarms, and fire extinguishers should be used.

Movement Detection

Intrusion detectors and closed circuit television cameras and monitors are the foundation of most systems that observe and detect movement (e.g., the electronic eyes or infra alarms). Electronic eyes are photoelectric devices, which detect movement and sound an alarm. Infra alarms are sensing devices that measure the change in thermal radiation within the environment. When an intruder is present, heat emitted from the moving body generates a change in the thermal radiation and triggers an alarm.

Closed-circuit television is used wherever constant surveillance is required. It provides continual coverage of remote locations and deters potential intruders who would be wary of entering an area under surveillance.

Documentation Control

Implemented systems and their operational features must be documented and protected. In addition to being required for maintenance or system modifications, the documentation is also needed for recovery purposes.

To provide a satisfactory level of control, documentation may be classified by sensitivity, such as restricted confidential, confidential, and unclassified or public, as may be the case with vendor manuals.

Retention cycles should be prepared for all documentation, reports, and data, and procedures should be established in accordance with applicable laws, rules, and regulations to control access/return and disposal.

Installations usually maintain protected documentation libraries, which are housed in special cabinets with access controlled by a librarian. Documentation is normally also stored off-site to ensure that backup copies of critical documents are available if the library copy is destroyed.

Distribution of confidential or sensitive reports/output requires a special data control area with strict procedures to limit distribution to the proper individuals. Similar control is essential for destroying unnecessary or outdated reports. Special equipment, such as paper shredders and compacters, is used to ensure total destruction.

Audit Controls

Information is protected against unauthorized penetration by installing a control system capable of identifying and logging attempts at unauthorized use and notifying security for immediate investigation.

Users can gain access to computerized information from terminals only through established recognition and authorization procedures. Attempts to gain access by entering invalid codes or passwords are logged and either the terminal is disconnected or the keyboard is locked to prevent entry until the violation is resolved. Jobs submitted for execution are monitored, so that any unauthorized attempt to access files is detected and logged and the offending job is canceled. Performance measurement logs and accounting information are also used to detect problems that can invalidate the computerized results or data files. Any significant changes that the auditor detects in the performance of the operating environment can alert management that unauthorized access attempts may have been made.

Logs and procedures, whether automatic or manual, provide an audit or information trail of all transactions inside and outside the EDP facility. They identify all data movement, security violations, errors, and changes that have occurred. Internally implemented program controls complement external controls, detect and account for input errors, maintain intermediate results and file control balances, and reconcile controls to results. Circumvention of controls, security procedures, logs, and audit trails should never be permitted.

Legal Obligations and Insurance

Organizations must be aware of any privacy legislation that has been enacted, or that is being considered, that sets out the measures a business must follow to prevent the disclosure of sensitive data about its employees or customers. (See Chapter 31.) Legislation of this kind usually refers to information on credit, mailing lists, employment, medical care, and other personal information. Security procedures and policies must protect this data from improper disclosure and use.

Improper disclosure of data or technology can also affect a business' position in the marketplace. A business uses contracts, insurance policies, copyrights, patents, licenses, and other agreements to establish protection and ensure that it will have legal recourse against any unwarranted disclosure. Legal action can normally only be taken if the organization has exercised due care in protecting its interests.

Insurance can be purchased to cover loss related to EDP activities; however, the coverage must be specific and comprehensive. Most policies only cover the replacement of physical equipment unless specific riders or additional insurance is obtained to cover such things as:

- Valuable records
- Program and data reconstruction
- Extra expense
- Business interruption
- Employee infidelity

PHYSICAL LAYOUT AND INFORMATION HANDLING

The auditors also evaluate the physical layout of all equipment used by the business for data processing in a security review. Figure 32-6 shows a sample set of questions used to evaluate physical security during a security review.

	Workpaper Reference	Yes	No	RCW	CC
Access Protection					
1. Is prior approval of off-hour entry by employees required?	. . . .	☐	☐	. . . .	. . . .
2. Are programmers prohibited from all processing areas?	. . . .	☐	☐	. . . .	. . . .
3. Are movement detection devices used during unstaffed hours?	. . . .	☐	☐	. . . .	. . . .
4. Is video surveillance used?	. . . .	☐	☐	. . . .	. . . .
5. Are locks and combinations changed regularly?	. . . .	☐	☐	. . . .	. . . .
6. Is employee entry/exit controlled and logged?	. . . .	☐	☐	. . . .	. . . .
7. Are electronic access control devices equipped with backup power supply?	. . . .	☐	☐	. . . .	. . . .
8. Are all external windows in the data center reinforced and barred?	. . . .	☐	☐	. . . .	. . . .
9. Do employee identification badges bear a photograph of the owner?	. . . .	☐	☐	. . . .	. . . .
10. Are badges used to identify areas of access?	. . . .	☐	☐	. . . .	. . . .

FIG. 32-6 Partial security review checklist: Physical security, internal — Access protection (RCW = Record of Control Weaknesses; CC = Compensating Controls)

Computer Room

The computer room contains the EDP equipment required for running the computer programs. An installation should have security measures and procedures that control all access and observe movement throughout the facility. These can be automated, using access control and television systems that

- Verify the identify of the person requesting entry.
- Log all requests for access.
- Alert security to unauthorized access attempts.
- Identify movement in areas at restricted hours.
- Detect unauthorized removal of items.

Some systems are also designed to trap violators either by locking or sealing off the area involved. The violator's movement can be observed through television cameras to determine the proper action to be taken.

Terminal Room

All terminals should be protected against damage or misuse by having separate areas, either independent rooms or sections of rooms that control access. This eliminates the possibility that sensitive data will be observed when it is entered or requested. Each room or section should be arranged by specific business function, such as credit authorization, order processing, and customer service.

The use of terminals should be regulated by system authorization controls that verify the identity of the user before permitting access. In addition, terminals can be equipped with mechanical locks.

Source Document Control

Source documents are the original documents used to record information required by the organization. Their movement among departments that need to use them should be safeguarded. Central or locally controlled storage areas should be available, and document storing, handling, and retaining procedures should be implemented.

Data Entry

Data entry systems vary from full on-line terminal systems performing key-to-tape or key-to-disk operations to off-line key-entry diskette recorders and/or keypunches. Whatever the mode of operation, the equipment involved should be protected in a controlled, secured area. Documents received should be safeguarded, and all sensitive data should be secured in locked cabinets.

Input/Output Control

Input/output (I/O) control functions include source document receipt and logging, batch control posting, job scheduling, job set-up, and output logging and distribution. Because information received or distributed is sometimes sensitive and confidential, precautions should be taken to ensure that all data handled is safe from modification, loss, or theft. Only authorized employees should handle the documents.

I/O control should be in a separate area that is accessible only by authorized employees. Procedures should be established that describe job submission and output distribution methods.

Data Communication Facilities

Safeguarding and controlling access to the location where communication lines terminate can be difficult where more than one tenant resides in a building.

Generally, the location of communication line entry is under the physical control of building management. It is, therefore, important that the property manager understand the necessity to protect these facilities from damage and provide for their security. Tenants might assume responsibility for providing a fair share of the cost of securing the area. Common carrier facilities are beyond the user's physical control. The carrier's responsibility to provide protection from penetration may not be specified.

Communication lines should not terminate on a hallway wall where access is unrestricted. A separate room or area with access control should be used. In many instances the communication facilities should be combined with the computer room's communication area, which houses the modems, line-switching facilities, line test equipment, and modem racks.

Power Sources

Power is terminated at breaker junction boxes that are not usually on the tenant's site. (These boxes may be located in the basement or elsewhere in the building.) They, too, should be protected against tampering, since power disruptions can curtail use of the facility. Power interruption systems and generators may be used to power the equipment and building so that operations can be sustained for a short term.

Duplicating Facilities

Most organizations have duplicating facilities. They may consist of copying machines, computer equipment, photography equipment, output microfiche equipment, or other devices capable of duplicating information. Access to and use of this equipment should be controlled, especially when confidential documents are nearby.

Programs

The programs that comprise the system are assets. They define the technology and methodology required for processing essential business functions. Program safeguards include control and authorization of access, use, and modification. Safeguards from destruction include keeping backup copies available at a secured site that are retrievable when necessary and updated regularly.

Data Files

Securing data files against unauthorized changes or use is essential: Backup copies of data files should be stored at a secured site. Procedures should describe replacement frequency, retention cycles, and methods to be used if recovery becomes necessary.

PERSONNEL

Competence is the primary characteristic used to judge candidates for employment. Honesty and loyalty are sometimes overlooked, although these attributes are equally important. The damage done by a dishonest or disloyal employee is potentially more devastating than damage from external sources or incompetent staff. Careful hiring practices should be followed to provide reasonable assurance of employee integrity.

Employees should be given job descriptions that fully outline their responsibilities with respect to security issues. The consequences of their failure to follow security policies should be clearly communicated. To ensure that there is no misunderstanding of these matters, particularly when employees hold senior positions, specific requirements or limitations should be stated in an employment contract.

If for any reason employees involved in EDP activities require termination, they should be immediately removed from their responsibilities and escorted from the premises. Procedures should include immediate notification of building security and changes in appropriate password and access systems.

Rules and Regulations

Any security program must be based on rules and regulations employees are expected to observe. These rules are derived from policies and guidelines set forth by management and should include all facets of the employer/employee relationship. Rules and regulations most important to an EDP facility deal with control and access to the computer and related resources and disaster-related activities. They include which personnel are permitted in certain areas, "need-to-know" criteria, distribution and destruction of sensitive reports, program submission procedures, and other security measures within the installation, such as emergency evacuation of the premises.

Procedures should exist to describe the proper interface with temporary personnel, delivery people, repairmen, and vendors who may come on-site.

APPENDIX

Questionnaires, Forms and Charts

INTRODUCTION

Throughout this book, reference is made to the use of various questionnaires, forms, and charts that provide assistance to the auditor in stucturing and organizing audit work. This appendix consists entirely of samples of those documents. The documents shown here are among those developed and used by Coopers & Lybrand (C&L) in its computer audit work. They are representative of the kinds of documents that can be used, and are presented here since they have proven their effectiveness in many situations.

In the case of questionnaires that are too lengthy to include in their entirety, a representative portion is shown. The volumes of the *Internal Control*

A-1

Reference Manual for general controls and application controls, also developed by C&L, are presented in Chapters 26 and 27, respectively.

The documents are presented in the following sequence: the Conditions of Control Questionnaire; the Record of Flowchart Preparation and Transaction Reviews; the Flowcharting Worksheet Form; the Computer Application Control Matrix; the Record of Control Weaknesses (RCW); the Program and Record of Functional (Compliance) Tests and Operational Reviews (PRT) — Summary Sheet; the Program and Record of Functional (Compliance) Tests and Operational Reviews (PRT); the Computer Internal Control Questionnaire (CICQ); and the Integrity (General) Controls Internal Control Questionnaire (ICQ).

CONDITIONS OF CONTROL QUESTIONNAIRE
(Complete)

Location _____

	19__	19__	19__	19__	19__
Completed/updated by evaluator in charge of location					
Approved by supervisor of evaluator					

PART I — Completion / Updating of Conditions of Control Questionnaire

1. The Conditions of Control Questionnaire should be completed or reviewed whenever the Internal Control Questionnaire is completed or reviewed. Similarly, it is preferable to renew the Conditions of Control Questionnaire completely once every three years.

2. The Conditions of Control Questionnaire should be completed and reviewed before the completion or review of the flowcharts and the ICQ.

3. Because of the information sought, the Conditions of Control Questionnaire should normally be completed by the evaluator in charge of the particular location on the basis of discussions with and inquiries of senior management (especially financial management) at each location. Space is provided on the cover sheet for the name or initials of the evaluator completing it.

4. For many of the questions, the end product (e.g., internal financial statement) is in itself evidence of the control operation. Because the evaluator will not be placing direct reliance on the operation of such controls, it is not always necessary for him to see evidence of the operation of the controls before recording a "Yes" answer. Nevertheless, it will frequently be helpful for him to review the documentation at the time of completion of the Conditions of Control Questionnaire to facilitate his evaluation. Where useful and practicable, filled-in copies or samples of documents referred to in the Conditions of Control Questionnaire should be obtained and placed on file and the filing location indicated in the column provided in the Questionnaire. Alternatively, a note may be placed in the column as to where such documents may be obtained. Documents would include, for example, copies of organization charts, accounting department job descriptions, accounting policy and procedures manuals, sample internal financial statements and sample budgets. Items marked "(S)" refer to supervisory controls.

PART II — Review and Approval

5. The supervisor of the evaluator should review the Conditions of Control Questionnaire. The cover sheet provides a place for the supervisor's name or initials as evidence of such a review.

	Reference	Yes	No	"No" Answers Reported to Senior Management? Yes (Date)	No
A. Overall Organization of Business					
1. Is the overall management and departmental structure of the company, including the duties, lines of responsibility, and accountability of its key employees, defined in:					
a. Organization charts?	. . . .	☐	☐	☐	☐
b. Written job descriptions?	. . . .	☐	☐	☐	☐
2. Are the organization charts and written job descriptions:					
a. Reviewed periodically to determine whether they are appropriate and up-to-date?	. . . .	☐	☐	☐	☐
b. Approved by appropriate levels of management? (S)	. . . .	☐	☐	☐	☐
3. With regard to financial interests of officers and key employees in vendors, customers, and the like:					
a. Does the company have a well-defined policy as to the extent (if any) to which such investments are permitted?	. . . .	☐	☐	☐	☐

(continued)

	Reference	Yes	No	"No" Answers Reported to Senior Management? Yes (Date)	No
b. Do officers and key employees report periodically on their compliance with that policy?	....	☐	☐	☐	☐
4. With regard to possibly questionable payments, political contributions, and the like:					
a. Is there a well-defined corporate conduct policy?	....	☐	☐	☐	☐
b. Has the policy been distributed to all corporate persons?	....	☐	☐	☐	☐
c. Are there adequate procedures for monitoring compliance with the policy?	....	☐	☐	☐	☐
B. Organization of the Accounting Department					
5. Are the duties, lines of responsibility, and accountability of the accounting department staff adequately defined in:					
a. Organization charts?	....	☐	☐	☐	☐
b. Written job descriptions?	....	☐	☐	☐	☐
6. Are the organization charts and written job descriptions:					
a. Reviewed periodically to determine whether they are appropriate and up-to-date?	....	☐	☐	☐	☐
b. Approved by appropriate levels of management? (S)	....	☐	☐	☐	☐
7. Are there written policies in respect of accounting department staff relating to:					
a. Delegation of duties when staff are absent?	....	☐	☐	☐	☐
b. Annual vacations for all staff?	....	☐	☐	☐	☐
c. Obtaining references for new staff?	....	☐	☐	☐	☐

	Reference	Yes	No	"No" Answers Reported to Senior Management? Yes (Date)	No

C. Accounting Policies and Procedures

8. Has the company written policies relating to:

	Reference	Yes	No	Yes (Date)	No
a. Distinguishing capital expenditures from charges to expense?	. . . .	☐	☐	☐	☐
b. Depreciation rates to be used for each type of property, plant, and equipment?	. . . .	☐	☐	☐	☐
c. Depreciation calculations in the year of acquisition or disposal of capital assets?	. . . .	☐	☐	☐	☐
d. Accounting treatment of gains and losses on the disposal of capital assets?	. . . .	☐	☐	☐	☐
e. Accounting for amortization of deferred expenditures and intangible assets?	. . . .	☐	☐	☐	☐
f. Basis of calculation of provisions for doubtful accounts, obsolete and slow-moving inventory, warranties and guarantees, and similar provisions?	. . . .	☐	☐	☐	☐
g. Where required, the timing of profit recognition on sales?	. . . .	☐	☐	☐	☐
h. The disposition in the accounts of variances from standard costs and/or under and over absorptions of overhead costs?	. . . .	☐	☐	☐	☐
i. Basis of establishing costs for inventories?	. . . .	☐	☐	☐	☐
j. Other accounting matters of particular significance to the business (specify)?	. . . .	☐	☐	☐	☐

(continued)

	Reference	Yes	No	"No" Answers Reported to Senior Management? Yes (Date)	No
9. Are the policies in 8 above:				·	
a. Reviewed periodically to determine whether they are appropriate?	. . . .	☐	☐	☐	☐
b. Approved by appropriate levels of management?(S)	. . . .	☐	☐	☐	☐
c. Distributed to appropriate accounting personnel?	. . . .	☐	☐	☐	☐
10. Has the company prepared:					
a. Manuals of accounting procedures?	. . . .	☐	☐	☐	☐
b. A list of accounts codes (chart of accounts)?	. . . .	☐	☐	☐	☐
c. Accounting instructions for the preparation of the financial statement?	. . . .	☐	☐	☐	☐
11. Does the company review accounting documents and forms on a pre-issuance basis to ensure that they are:					
a. Understandable?	. . . .	☐	☐	☐	☐
b. Easy to use?	. . . .	☐	☐	☐	☐
12. Are there written policies relating to:					
a. Physical safeguarding of critical accounting forms, records, transaction processing areas, and procedural manuals?	. . . .	☐	☐	☐	☐
b. Record retention criteria that meet corporate needs and legal requirements?	. . . .	☐	☐	☐	☐
13. Is the documentation in 10 to 12 above:					
a. Reviewed periodically to determine whether it is appropriate?	. . . .	☐	☐	☐	☐
b. Approved by appropriate levels of management?(S)	. . . .	☐	☐	☐	☐

	Reference	Yes	No	"No" Answers Reported to Senior Management? Yes (Date)	No
c. Distributed to appropriate accounting personnel?	. . . .	☐	☐	☐	☐
14. Are the following prohibited as a matter of written policy:					
a. Checks issued in blank?	. . . .	☐	☐	☐	☐
b. Checks issued to "cash" or "bearer"?	. . . .	☐	☐	☐	☐
c. Alteration of checks or bank transfers?	. . . .	☐	☐	☐	☐
15. Are the following used in the preparation of checks:					
a. Check protection machines (where appropriate)?	. . . .	☐	☐	☐	☐
b. Protective paper?	. . . .	☐	☐	☐	☐
D. Computer Department					
16. Are the duties, lines of responsibility, and accountability of the computer department staff adequately defined in:					
a. Organization charts?	. . . .	☐	☐	☐	☐
b. Written job descriptions?	. . . .	☐	☐	☐	☐
17. Are the organization charts and written job descriptions:					
a. Reviewed periodically to determine whether they are appropriate and up-to-date?	. . . .	☐	☐	☐	☐
b. Approved by appropriate levels of management?	. . . .	☐	☐	☐	☐
18. Are there written policies in respect of computer department staff relating to:					
a. Delegation of duties when staff are absent?	. . . .	☐	☐	☐	☐

(continued)

	Reference	Yes	No	"No" Answers Reported to Senior Management? Yes (Date)	No
b. Annual vacations for all staff?	. . . .	☐	☐	☐	☐
c. Obtaining references for new staff?	. . . .	☐	☐	☐	☐
19. Are there written policies with respect to:					
a. Development and maintenance of systems?	. . . .	☐	☐	☐	☐
b. Selection of purchased hardware, software, and other computer services?	. . . .	☐	☐	☐	☐
c. Security of important software and data stored on computer media?	. . . .	☐	☐	☐	☐
d. Privacy and confidentiality of information stored in computer files, output, and documentation?	. . . .	☐	☐	☐	☐
e. Physical safeguarding of equipment, documentation, and computer files?	. . . .	☐	☐	☐	☐
20. Does the company review input forms, output formats, and CRT terminal screen formats on a pre-implementation basis to ensure that they are understandable and easy to use?	. . . .	☐	☐	☐	☐
21. Does the company have adequate backup arrangements or plans covering:					
a. Processing and transmission equipment?	. . . .	☐	☐	☐	☐
b. Data files, program files, and systems files stored on computer media?	. . . .	☐	☐	☐	☐
c. Documentation and instructions?	. . . .	☐	☐	☐	☐

	Reference	Yes	No	"No" Answers Reported to Senior Management? Yes (Date)	No

E. Preparation of Budgets

Note: These questions need not be answered where it is apparent that there are no effective budgeting (short-term planning) procedures.

	Reference	Yes	No	Yes (Date)	No
22. Are budgets prepared for the current or impending fiscal period for each significant function or activity within the company following the organization structure of the company as a basis for responsibility reporting?	. . . .	☐	☐	☐	☐
23. With respect to the budgeting system:					
a. Is there a written statement of assumptions supporting the budget?	. . . .	☐	☐	☐	☐
b. Are the programs of the various functional areas (e.g., research, marketing, production) integrated and related to long-term plans?	. . . .	☐	☐	☐	☐
c. Is a senior officer responsible for the preparation of operating budgets?	. . . .	☐	☐	☐	☐
d. Are budgets approved by the board of directors or an appropriate committee thereof?	. . . .	☐	☐	☐	☐
e. If budgets are revised during the year, are the revisions subject to the controls in (a) to (d) above?	. . . .	☐	☐	☐	☐
24. Are sales and cost of sales budgets:					
a. Based on both budgeted quantities and prices?	. . . .	☐	☐	☐	☐

(continued)

	Reference	Yes	No	"No" Answers Reported to Senior Management? Yes (Date)	No
b. Detailed by product line, sales manager, or other appropriate category?	. . . .	☐	☐	☐	☐
c. Approved at departmental levels by department heads?	. . . .	☐	☐	☐	☐
Are actual results analyzed by the same categories used in preparation?	. . . .	☐	☐	☐	☐
25. Are operating expense budgets:					
a. Based on individual expense captions (as opposed to broad, general categories)?	. . . .	☐	☐	☐	☐
b. Approved at departmental levels by department heads?	. . . .	☐	☐	☐	☐
Are actual results analyzed by the same captions used in preparation?	. . . .	☐	☐	☐	☐
26. Do budgets include:					
a. "Other income"?	. . . .	☐	☐	☐	☐
b. Provisions for known contingencies?	. . . .	☐	☐	☐	☐
c. Forecast balance sheets at the end of the periods covered?	. . . .	☐	☐	☐	☐
d. Cash flow?	. . . .	☐	☐	☐	☐
27. Are the original and/or revised budgets compared with subsequent actual performance?	. . . .	☐	☐	☐	☐
F. Authority for Transactions					
28. Does an appropriate level of management establish policy for the authorization of transactions?	. . . .	☐	☐	☐	☐

	Reference	Yes	No	"No" Answers Reported to Senior Management? Yes (Date)	No
29. Is there a policy concerning maintaining records of the names and/or specimen signatures/initials of all persons who are authorized to approve specific transactions?	. . . .	☐	☐	☐	☐
30. Are there clearly defined authority limits as to approval and execution of significant contracts and other agreements, not in the ordinary course of business (e.g., approval by board of directors or designated officials)?	. . . .	☐	☐	☐	☐
31. Are minutes kept of decisions made at meetings of the board of directors, committees thereof, and senior management committees?	. . . .	☐	☐	☐	☐

G. Insurance Coverage and Employee Fidelity

	Reference	Yes	No	"No" Answers Reported to Senior Management? Yes (Date)	No
32. Does the company take appropriate steps to conform the adequacy of its insurance coverage (e.g., by ensuring that the coverage is regularly reviewed by a knowledgeable person who strives to make a professional-type evaluation)?	. . . .	☐	☐	☐	☐
33. Does the company carry fidelity bond coverage? What is the type and amount of coverage?	. . . .	☐	☐	☐	☐

RECORD OF FLOWCHART PREPARATION AND TRANSACTION REVIEWS

Location _____

Preparation/updating of flowcharts (F) and performance of transaction reviews (TR)

NO.	DESCRIPTION OF SYSTEM	19				19				19			
		Prepared/Updated*				Prepared/Updated*				Prepared/Updated*			
		F	TR	Done By	Reviewed By	F	TR	Done By	Reviewed By	F	TR	Done By	Reviewed By

*Place ticks (√) in columns provided.

FLOWCHARTING WORKSHEET FORM

Location _____ Flowchart No. _____ Page _____ of _____
Date _____
Flowchart   Preparer _____
Description _____ Reviewer _____

Description	Oper. No.	

COMPUTER APPLICATION CONTROL MATRIX
(Two Versions — Internal Auditor, External Auditor)

Application _____

Location _____

Date _____

Prepared By _____

Reviewed By _____

Transaction (Document)	COMPLETENESS		ACCURACY*		Validity (Authorization)	Maintenance†	Timing (Establishment and Exercise)	Effectiveness and Efficiency	Programmed Procedures
	Input	Update†	Input	Update†					

†Specify file or data base.   *Specify significant fields.

Developed for internal audit use.

Application _____

Client _____

Date _____

Prepared By _____

Reviewed By _____

Transaction (Document)	COMPLETENESS		ACCURACY*		Validity (Authorization)	Maintenance†	Programmed Procedures
	Input	Update†	Input	Update†			

*Specify significant fields.   †Specify file or data base.

Developed for external audit use.

RECORD OF CONTROL WEAKNESSES (RCW)
(Two Versions — Internal Auditor, External Auditor)

Function _____
Location _____

Date _____
Prepared By _____   Reviewed By _____

Workpaper Reference # (1)	Nature of weakness and possible effect on internal accounting control and/or on efficiency of operations (2)	COULD SUBSTANTIAL ERROR ARISE?		Audit Program Reference # (5)	EFFECT ON NATURE, EXTENT AND/OR TIMING OF AUDIT PROCEDURES	NOTIFICATION OF WEAKNESS TO RESPONSIBLE MANAGEMENT		
		Yes/No (3)	Justification (4)		Nature of Amendment Required (6)	Informal discussion with Site Management (Date) (7)	Formal Report to Senior Management Yes (Date) No (8)	Management Response/Comments (If Applicable) (9)

Developed for internal audit use.

Client _____ Date _____

Application _____ Prepared By _____

ICQ Reference (1)	Nature of Weakness and Possible Effect on Financial Statements (2)	Comments of Client (Note With Whom Discussed Name and Position -- and Date) (3)	Could Material Error Arise?		Effect on Nature, Extent and/or Timing of Audit Procedures		Was Weakness Formally Notified to Client?	Weakness Rectified	
			Yes/No (4)	Justification (5)	Nature of Amendment Required (6)	Audit Program Reference (7)	Yes/No and Date (8)	Date (9)	Audit Program Revised or N/A (10)

Developed for external audit use.

PROGRAM AND RECORD OF FUNCTIONAL (COMPLIANCE) TESTS AND OPERATIONAL REVIEWS (PRT) — SUMMARY SHEET

Location _____

COMPLETION OF PRT

INDEX		COMPLETION OF PROGRAM	
Control Objective No.	File Reference	SIGNATURE	DATE

REVIEW AND APPROVAL

Preparation/updating of program

Completion of program

PROGRAM AND RECORD OF FUNCTIONAL (COMPLIANCE) TESTS AND OPERATIONAL REVIEWS (PRT)

Location _____

Control Objective No. _____

ICQ Ref. (1)	Details of Test or Reason for Omitting Test (2)	Level of Test (3)	Program Update (√) (4)	Evidence Seen, Period(s) Selected (or Workpaper Reference) (5)	EXCEPTIONS			Signature and Date (9)
					Yes/No (6)	Cleared (7)	W.P.Ref. (8)	

COMPUTER INTERNAL CONTROL QUESTIONNAIRE (CICQ)
(Partial)

Items are distinguished as follows: "(S)" refers to supervisory controls; "(C)" refers to custodial controls; "(D)" refers to division of duties.

CONTROL OBJECTIVE

35. All valid accounts receivable transactions, and only those transactions, should be accurately recorded as accounts receivable.

	Flowchart Reference	Yes	No	"Yes" Answers PRT Reference	"No" Answers CC	RCW
Accounting for and Control Over Processing of All Transactions. Specify below which of the following are input to update the accounts receivable file:						
a. File of evaluated sales invoices	. . . .	☐	☐	. . . .	. . . .	. . . .
b. Manually prepared invoices	. . . .	☐	☐	. . . .	. . . .	. . . .
c. Manually prepared credit memoranda	. . . .	☐	☐	. . . .	. . . .	. . . .
d. Details of cash received	. . . .	☐	☐	. . . .	. . . .	. . . .
e. Adjustments (including requests for credit)	. . . .	☐	☐	. . . .	. . . .	. . . .
f. Other (specify)	. . . .	☐	☐	. . . .	. . . .	. . . .

Input of Evaluated Invoices

35.1   If a file of evaluated invoices is input, are the totals of items accumulated by the computer during the evaluation run agreed to the total of items written to the accounts receivable file or, alternatively, are such totals carried through intermediate processing (including summarization of totals or changes in the totals used) so that it is established that all accepted input items are updated to the accounts receivable file?   . . . .   ☐ ☐   . . . .

	Flowchart Reference	Yes	No	"Yes" Answers PRT Reference	"No" Answers CC	RCW

35.2 Is the reconciliation of totals in 35.1 carried out manually or, alternatively, is the reconciliation carried out by the computer with adequate evidence of this check being printed out? . . . . ☐ ☐ . . . .

35.3 Are there adequate procedures for the investigation and correction of differences disclosed by the update reconciliations (35.2)? . . . . ☐ ☐ . . . .

Completeness of Input and Update. Specify below for each type of input the principal control that all documents in (b) to (f) above are input to the computer and updated. If the principal control is

a. Agreement of manually established batch totals (specify totals used), answer questions 35.4 to 35.8. . . . . ☐ ☐ . . . .

b. Computer sequence check of serially numbered input documents, answer questions 35.9 to 35.14. . . . . ☐ ☐ . . . .

c. Checking of printouts of items written to the accounts receivable file, answer questions 35.15 to 35.18. . . . . ☐ ☐ . . . .

Batch Totals

35.4 Are there adequate controls to ensure that

a. A document is raised for each transaction? . . . . ☐ ☐ . . . .

b. All documents are included in a batch? . . . . ☐ ☐ . . . .

c. All batches are submitted for processing? . . . . ☐ ☐ . . . .

(continued)

	Flowchart Reference	Yes	No	"Yes" Answers PRT Reference	"No" Answers	
					CC	RCW

35.5   Are the totals of individual items accepted by the computer compared manually to predetermined control totals or, alternatively, is such a comparison made by the computer with adequate evidence of the check being printed out?   . . . . ☐ ☐   . . . .

35.6   Are the totals in 35.5 agreed to the total of items written to the accounts receivable file, or alternatively, are such totals carried through intermediate processing (including summarization of totals or changes in the totals used) so that it is established that all accepted input items are updated to the accounts receivable file?   . . . . ☐ ☐   . . . .

35.7   Is the reconciliation of totals in 35.6 carried out manually or, alternatively, is the reconciliation carried out by the computer with adequate evidence of this check being printed out?   . . . . ☐ ☐   . . . .

35.8   Are there adequate procedures for:

a. Investigation and correction of differences disclosed by the input reconciliations (35.5)?   . . . . ☐ ☐   . . . .

b. Resubmission of all rejections?   . . . . ☐ ☐   . . . .

c. Investigation and correction of differences disclosed by the update reconciliations (35.7)?   . . . . ☐ ☐   . . . .

Computer Sequence Check

35.9   Are there adequate controls to ensure that all transactions are recorded on a serially numbered document?   . . . . ☐ ☐   . . . .

	Flowchart Reference	Yes	No	"Yes" Answers PRT Reference	"No" Answers CC	RCW
35.10 Is the method used in the program for the checking of numerical sequence appropriate (e.g., does it cater for changes in sequence and more than one sequence running at a time)?	....	☐	☐	*	....	....
35.11 Is a printout of missing documents produced at regular intervals (e.g., weekly)?	....	☐	☐	....	....	....
35.12 Is a total of accepted items accumulated by the computer during the sequence check run agreed to the total of items written to the accounts receivable file or, alternatively, are such totals carried through intermediate processing (including summarization of totals or changes in the totals used) so that it is established that all accepted input items are updated to the accounts receivable file?	....	☐	☐	....	....	....
35.13 Is the reconciliation of totals in 35.12 carried out manually or, alternatively, is the reconciliation carried out by the computer with adequate evidence of this check being printed out?	....	☐	☐	....	....	....
35.14 Are there adequate procedures for:						
a. Investigation of missing documents (35.11)?	....	☐	☐	....	....	....
b. Investigation and correction of differences disclosed by the update reconciliations (35.13)?	....	☐	☐	....	....	....

*Programmed procedure, see substantive tests or computer audit program

(continued)

	Flowchart Reference	Yes	No	"Yes" Answers PRT Reference	"No" Answers CC	RCW

Checking of Printouts

35.15 Are there adequate controls to ensure that all documents are submitted for processing (e.g., by checking against retained copy, by manual sequence check)?

. . . .   ☐ ☐   . . . .

35.16 Is there a regular (e.g., monthly) review of source documents for unprocessed items?

. . . .   ☐ ☐   . . . .

35.17 Is the method used in the program for the production of the printout appropriate (e.g., does it contain details of items that have been written to the accounts receivable file)?

. . . .   ☐ ☐   *   . . . .

35.18 Are there adequate procedures for investigation and correction of differences disclosed by the checking?

. . . .   ☐ ☐   . . . .

Disciplines Over Basic Input Completeness and Updating Controls

35.19 Are the procedures in (i) to (viii) below either performed or checked by persons other than those who

   a. Are involved in computer operations; (C)

. . . .   ☐ ☐   . . . .

   b. Prepare invoices; (C)

. . . .   ☐ ☐   . . . .

   c. Record shipments; (C)

. . . .   ☐ ☐   . . . .

   d. Prepare credit memoranda; (C)

. . . .   ☐ ☐   . . . .

   e. Record goods returned and claims made by customers; (C)

. . . .   ☐ ☐   . . . .

   f. Process accounts receivable adjustments; (C)

. . . .   ☐ ☐   . . . .

   g. Deal with cash receipts functions; or (C)

. . . .   ☐ ☐   . . . .

*Programmed procedure, see substantive tests or computer audit program

	Flowchart Reference	Yes	No	"Yes" Answers PRT Reference	"No" Answers	
					CC	RCW
h. Authorize the voiding of accountable invoices? (C)	. . . .	☐	☐	. . . .	. . . .
i. Manual agreement of input totals (35.5)	. . . .	☐	☐	. . . .	. . . .
ii. Investigation and correction of differences disclosed by the input reconciliations (35.8(a))	. . . .	☐	☐	. . . .	. . . .
iii. Resubmission of all rejections (35.8(b))	. . . .	☐	☐	. . . .	. . . .
iv. Investigation of missing documents (35.14(a))	. . . .	☐	☐	. . . .	. . . .
v. Regular (e.g., monthly) review of source documents for unprocessed items (35.16)	. . . .	☐	☐	. . . .	. . . .
vi. Investigation and correction of differences disclosed by the checking of printouts (35.18)	. . . .	☐	☐	. . . .	. . . .
vii. Manual agreement of update totals (35.2, 35.7, 35.13)	. . . .	☐	☐	. . . .	. . . .
viii. Investigation and correction of differences disclosed by update reconciliations (35.3, 35.8(c), 35.14(b))	. . . .	☐	☐	. . . .	. . . .
35.20 Are the results of the following procedures reviewed and approved by a responsible official:					
a. Manual agreement of input totals (35.5)? (S)	. . . .	☐	☐	. . . .	. . . .
b. Investigation and correction of differences disclosed by the input reconciliations (35.8(a))? (S)	. . . .	☐	☐	. . . .	. . . .

(continued)

	Flowchart Reference	Yes	No	"Yes" Answers PRT Reference	"No" Answers CC	RCW
c. Resubmission of all rejections (35.8(b))? (S)	....	☐	☐	....	....	....
d. Investigation of missing documents (35.14(a))? (S)	....	☐	☐	....	....	....
e. Regular (e.g., monthly) review of source documents for unprocessed items (35.16)? (S)	....	☐	☐	....	....	....
f. Investigation and correction of differences disclosed by the checking of printouts (35.18)? (S)	....	☐	☐	....	....	....
g. Manual agreement of update totals (35.2, 35.7, 35.13)? (S)	....	☐	☐	....	....	....
h. Investigation and correction of differences disclosed by update reconciliations (35.3, 35.8(c), 35.14(b))? (S)	....	☐	☐	....	....	....

Accuracy of Input and Update

35.21 Are there adequate controls to ensure that the following fields are accurately input and updated (e.g., batch totals, edit checks in program, reporting of non-matched items):

a. Value?	....	☐	☐	....	....	....
b. Customer reference?	....	☐	☐	....	....	....

35.22 Are there adequate procedures for:

a. The agreement of totals, where applicable?	....	☐	☐	....	....	....
b. Investigation and correction of differences or exceptions (35.21)?	....	☐	☐	....	....	....
35.23 Is the method used in the program for the updating of individual accounts appropriate?	....	☐	☐	*	....	....

*Programmed procedure, see substantive tests or computer audit program

	Flowchart Reference	Yes	No	"Yes" Answers PRT Reference	"No" Answers CC	RCW
35.24 Are the agreement of totals, where applicable (35.22(a)), and the investigation and correction of differences (35.22(b)) either performed or checked by persons other than those who:						
a. Are involved in computer operations; (C)	....	☐	☐	....	....	....
b. Prepare invoices; (C)	....	☐	☐	....	....	....
c. Record shipments; (C)	....	☐	☐	....	....	....
d. Prepare credit memoranda; (C)	....	☐	☐	....	....	....
e. Record goods returned and claims made by customers; (C)	....	☐	☐	....	....	....
f. Process accounts receivable adjustments; (C)	....	☐	☐	....	....	....
g. Deal with cash receipts functions; (C) or	....	☐	☐	....	....	....
h. Authorize the voiding of accountable invoices? (C)	....	☐	☐	....	....	....
35.25 Are the results of the following procedures reviewed and approved by a responsible official:						
a. Agreement of totals, where applicable (35.22(a))? (S)	....	☐	☐	....	....	....
b. Investigation and correction of differences or exceptions (35.22(b))? (S)	....	☐	☐	....	....	....

Authorization

35.26 If data is authorized prior to the establishment of the controls for completeness and accuracy of input (e.g., prior to establishment of batch control totals or recording on a sequentially numbered document), are there adequate

(continued)

	Flowchart Reference	Yes	No	"Yes" Answers PRT Reference	"No" Answers CC	RCW

controls (e.g., checking authorization after batch control totals are established or sequentially numbered documents raised) to ensure that

   a. No unauthorized alterations are made to authorized data during subsequent processing?   . . . . ☐ ☐ . . . .

   b. Unauthorized data is not added?   . . . . ☐ ☐ . . . .

   c. All authorized items are included in subsequent processing?   . . . . ☐ ☐ . . . .

Computer Generated Data

35.27 Are the methods used in the programs to generate the data and related control record appropriate (e.g., automatic write-offs, service charges)?   . . . . ☐ ☐   * . . . .

35.28 Is there an adequate check over the accuracy of the data generated (e.g., reasonableness check)?   . . . . ☐ ☐ . . . .

35.29 Are the results of the check (35.28) reviewed and approved by a responsible official? (S)   . . . . ☐ ☐ . . . .

35.30 Is a total (specify total used) of generated items accumulated by the computer and agreed manually with a total of items written off/to the accounts receivable file or, alternatively, are the totals agreed by the computer with adequate evidence of this check being printed out?   . . . . ☐ ☐ . . . .

35.31 Are there adequate procedures for investigation and correction of differences disclosed by the update reconciliation?   . . . . ☐ ☐ . . . .

*Programmed procedure, see substantive tests or computer audit program

	Flowchart Reference	Yes	No	"Yes" Answers PRT Reference	"No" Answers	
					CC	RCW
35.32 Are the following procedures either performed or checked by persons other than those involved in computer operations or in maintaining a manual accounts receivable control account:						
a. Manual agreement of update totals (35.30)? (D)	. . . .	☐	☐	. . . .	. . . .
b. Investigation and correction of differences disclosed by the update reconciliation (35.31)? (D)	. . . .	☐	☐	. . . .	. . . .
35.33 Are the results of the following procedures reviewed and approved by a responsible official:						
a. Manual agreement of update totals (35.30)? (S)	. . . .	☐	☐	. . . .	. . . .
b. Investigation and correction of differences disclosed by the update reconciliation (35.31)? (S)	. . . .	☐	☐	. . . .	. . . .
Maintenance of the Accounts Receivable File						
35.34 Is an accumulation of the items on file regularly reconciled with a manual control account maintained by a user department or, alternatively, reconciled with a control record on file with adequate evidence of reconciliation being printed out?	. . . .	☐	☐	. . . .	. . . .
35.35 Where the reconciliation is carried out by the computer, is the brought forward total checked or, alternatively, are there adequate controls over access to data files (review the answers to section 4 of the integrity control questions)?	. . . .	☐	☐	. . . .	. . . .

(continued)

	Flowchart Reference	Yes	No	"Yes" Answers PRT Reference	"No" Answers CC	RCW

35.36 Are there adequate procedures for investigating differences disclosed by the reconciliations (35.34, 35.35) before any adjustments are made? .... □ □ ....

35.37 Are the following procedures either performed or checked by persons other than those involved in computer operations (D), in maintaining a manual accounts receivable control account (D), in dealing with the cash receipts function (C), or in controlling input to the accounts receivable system (C):

   a. Manual agreement of totals (35.34)? .... □ □ ....

   b. Checking of brought forward total (35.35)? .... □ □ ....

   c. Investigation and correction of differences disclosed by the reconciliation (35.36)? .... □ □ ....

35.38 Are the results of the following procedures reviewed and approved by a responsible official:

   a. Manual agreement of totals (35.34)? (S) .... □ □ ....

   b. Checking of brought forward total (35.35)? (S) .... □ □ ....

   c. Investigation and correction of differences disclosed by the reconciliation (35.36)? (S) .... □ □ ....

Agreement With Customer's Records

35.39 Are the accounts receivable subsidiary records periodically reconciled to customer's records (e.g., by sending statements to customers)? .... □ □ ....

	Flowchart Reference	Yes	No	"Yes" Answers PRT Reference	"No" Answers	
					CC	RCW
35.40 Is the procedure in 35.39 either performed or checked by persons other than those who						
a. Deal with cash receipts? (C)	....	☐	☐	....	....	....
b. Are involved in computer operations? (D)	....	☐	☐	....	....	....
c. Control input to the accounts receivable system? (C)	....	☐	☐	....	....	....
Programmed Procedures						
35.41 List below the programmed procedures whose continued and proper operation is not assured by user controls.						
....						
In respect of the items listed above, review the answers to the integrity control section. Are there adequate controls to ensure that						
a. Appropriate programmed procedures are implemented in respect of:						
i. Where applicable, new systems (questions 1.1 to 1.4 and questions 1.11 to 1.20)?	....	☐	☐	....	....	....
ii. Program changes (questions 1.5 to 1.10 and questions 1.11 to 1.20)?	....	☐	☐	....	....	....
b. Unauthorized changes cannot be made to production programs (questions 2.1 to 2.15)?	....	☐	☐	....	....	....
c. Programmed procedures are consistently applied (questions 3.1 to 3.24)?	....	☐	☐	....	....	....

	Flowchart Reference	PRT Reference
Compensating Controls		

If any "no" answers are compensated by alternative
controls, identify such controls below.

. . . .	. . . .	. . . .
. . . .	. . . .	. . . .
. . . .	. . . .	. . . .
. . . .	. . . .	. . . .
. . . .	. . . .	. . . .

INTEGRITY (GENERAL) CONTROLS
INTERNAL CONTROL QUESTIONNAIRE (ICQ)
(Partial, for Implementation Controls)

INTEGRITY CONTROL QUESTIONNAIRE —
CONTROL OBJECTIVES

A. Implementation Controls. Appropriate procedures should be effectively included in production programs, both when the system originally becomes operational and when changes are subsequently made.

Note: This control objective should also be answered in respect of new system software developed by the company (see Control Objective E).

B. Program Security Controls. Adequate steps should be taken to ensure the security of programs. (This control objective does not cover the controls over the authorization of program modifications which are included within the scope of control objective A).

C. Computer Operations Controls. Computer operations procedures should be adequate to ensure that

    1. Authorized programmed procedures are consistently applied; and

    2. The correct data files are used.

D. Data File Security Controls. Adequate steps should be taken to ensure the security of data files.

E. System Software. Controls should be established over system software to ensure that

    1. System software procedures are properly checked and approved as being appropriate before being implemented;

    2. All appropriate modifications are properly implemented; and

    3. System software is adequately safeguarded.

IMPLEMENTATION CONTROLS

CONTROL OBJECTIVE

A. Appropriate procedures should be effectively included in production programs, both when the system originally becomes operational and when changes are subsequently made.

Note: This control objective should also be answered in respect of new system software developed by the company (see Control Objective E).

Items marked "(S)" refer to supervisory controls; items marked "(D)" refer to division of duties.

	Flowchart Reference	Yes	No	"Yes" Answers PRT Reference	"No" Answers CC/I	RCW
New Systems						
A.1 Are new systems reviewed and approved by responsible officials:						
a. In the user departments?	....	☐	☐	....	....	....
b. In the data processing function?	....	☐	☐	....	....	....
A.2 Are new systems adequately tested to ensure the proper operation of programmed procedures?	....	☐	☐	....	....	....
A.3 Are the testing procedures either performed or checked by persons other than those involved in writing the programs? (D)	....	☐	☐	....	....	....
Systems and Program Changes						
A.4 Are all systems and program changes, including immediate modifications, supported by appropriate written authorizations?	....	☐	☐	....	....	....
A.5 Are program changes, including immediate modifications, adequately tested to ensure:						
a. The proper operation of changed programmed procedures?	....	☐	☐	....	....	....

(continued)

	Flowchart Reference	Yes	No	"Yes" Answers PRT Reference	"No" Answers CC/I	RCW
b. The proper effect of the changes on unchanged programmed procedures?	....	☐	☐	....	....	
A.6 Are the testing procedures either performed or checked by persons other than those involved in writing the program changes? (D)	....	☐	☐	....	....	
Cataloging of New Systems and Programs Changes						
A.7 Is the following documentation prepared prior to final acceptance of programs and program changes:						
a. Instructions for setting up and running the job?	....	☐	☐	....	....	
b. Instructions for user procedures?	....	☐	☐	....	....	
A.8 As part of the final acceptance procedures, does a responsible official review and approve:						
a. The appropriateness and results of testing procedures? (S)	....	☐	☐	....	....	
b. The instructions for setting up and running the job?	....	☐	☐	....	....	
c. Instructions for user procedures? (S)	....	☐	☐	....	....	
d. The date of implementation?	....	☐	☐	....	....	
A.9 Are there adequate controls to ensure that tested and approved programs are properly taken into production?	....	☐	☐	....	....	
A.10 Are the results of the cataloging (A.9) reviewed and approved by a responsible official? (S)	....	☐	☐	....	....	

	Flowchart Reference	Yes	No	"Yes" Answers PRT Reference	"No" Answers	
					CC/I	RCW

System Software

A.11 In respect of the system software procedures relied on for the purposes of this control objective:

   a. Are the system software procedures appropriate?   . . . .   ☐   ☐   . . . .

   b. Review the answer to control objective E. Are there adequate controls to ensure that

      i. Appropriate system software is properly implemented?   . . . .   ☐   ☐   . . . .

      ii. Unauthorized changes cannot be made to system software?   . . . .   ☐   ☐   . . . .

	Flowchart Reference	PRT Reference

Compensating Controls
- If any "no" answers are compensated by alternative controls, identify such controls below.

. . . .

. . . .

. . . .

. . . .

. . . .

- If any "no" answers are inconsequential, set out the reasons below.

. . . .

. . . .

. . . .

. . . .

. . . .

GLOSSARY

A Programming Language   *See* APL.

AAA   American Accounting Association.

abend   *Ab*normal *end* of task. Early termination of a computer processing task when an error state prohibits resolution during the performance of that task.

abort   In a computer system, controlled termination of a processing activity when it cannot or should not continue.

ACB   Application control block.

accelerated depreciation   A depreciation accounting method where depreciable costs are deducted in greater amounts during the beginning years of an asset's economic life and decreased each year thereafter.

access   The way the computer refers to data so that particular data can be located within the system and made available for processing.

access method   System techniques to move data from storage to the specific data bases and to input/output devices. For example, IBM's Information Management System (IMS) uses (among other IBM system products) virtual storage access method (VSAM) to create the IMS accesses to data bases including hierarchic indexed direct access method (HIDAM) and hierarchic indexed sequential access method (HISAM).

account balance   The difference in dollars between the total debits and the total credits in an account.

accounting cycle   The complete sequence of reporting and summarizing procedures performed on financial data.

accounting equation   Assets equal liabilities plus owner's equity (A = L + OE).

accounting period   The time covered by an operating statement. One year is the accounting period for much financial reporting; financial statements are prepared by many organizations for each quarter of the year as well as for each month.

accounting system   A set of forms, records, instruction manuals, flowcharts, equipment, and programs that reports the financial activities of an organization.

accounts payable   Amounts that a company owes its creditors for goods and services purchased on open account.

accounts receivable   Amounts that a company expects to collect from its customers for goods and services sold on open account.

accounts receivable ledger   A listing of accounts that includes a detailed summary of activities for each customer. The total of this subsidiary ledger agrees with the general ledger controlling account, accounts receivable.

accrual basis   A method of accounting where revenue is recorded in the period it is earned and expenses are recorded in the period incurred, regardless of when cash is received or disbursed.

accrued expenses   Expenses that have accumulated at the end of the accounting period but are payable at a future date.

accrued revenue (unrecorded revenue)   Revenue earned in the current accounting period but not yet received.

accumulated depreciation   A contra-asset (liability) account shown as a deduction from the related fixed asset account in the balance sheet. Depreciation charged throughout the useful life of an asset is recorded in this account.

acoustic coupler   A simple kind of modem that uses sound waves to transmit data over the public telephone network via a conventional telephone handset and a cradle the handset fits into.

active file   A fixed and related group of computerized records whose expiration date falls after its processing date.

address, disk   Specifies physical location of machine-readable data on the magnetic storage device.

address, memory   The location of a particular byte stored within the computer's memory.

adjusted trial balance   A listing of all ledger account balances after the amounts have been changed to include the adjusting entries made at the end of the period.

adjusting entries   Journal postings required at the end of the period to update the accounts before financial statements are prepared. Primarily, adjusting entries serve to apportion transactions properly between the accounting periods affected and to record any revenue earned or expenses incurred that have not been recorded before the end of the period.

after-closing trial balance   A trial balance prepared after all closing entries have been made. Consists of accounts for assets, liabilities, and owner's equity.

aging of accounts receivable   An analysis of individual customer's uncollected account records according to the length of time amounts due are outstanding. Groups are usually formulated as follows: current, past due 1−30 days, past due 31−60 days, past due 61−90 days, more than 90 days past due. A step in estimating the total uncollectible portion of accounts receivable.

AICPA   American Institute of Certified Public Accountants.

algebra, Boolean   *See* Boolean algebra.

ALGOL   A high-level programming language, most often used in nonbusiness applications, that expresses programs by algorithms.

algorithm   A step-by-step process designed for problem solving. Governing rules, as well as the steps themselves, are finite in number.

ALI   American Law Institute.

allocate   To grant a resource to, or reserve it for, a job or task, such as allocated disk space for data to be stored on as it is updated.

allowance for doubtful accounts   An asset valuation account that compares the total number of receivables with that portion estimated to be uncollectible.

alphanumeric (also called **alphameric**) The alphabetic, numeric, and symbolic character elements used by computers to describe data.

alternate routing In a computer system, another communications path used if the primary path is not available. There may be one or more possible paths.

ALU Arithmetic logic unit. A basic part of the central processing unit of the computer.

American Standard Code for Information Interchange *See* ASCII.

amortization The systematic write-off, to expense, of the cost of an intangible asset over the period of its economic usefulness.

amplitude modulation With respect to communications techniques, one of three ways of modifying a sine wave signal so it can carry data information. The sine wave, or carrier, is modified in accordance with the information to be transmitted.

analog computer Processes data that is represented as measures of physical variables.

analog transmission Sending a continuously variable signal over communication lines as opposed to sending the discretely variable signal of digital.

analytical engine The machine designed by Charles Babbage in 1830 to calculate mathematical processes automatically while storing their intermediate results. Essentially a precursor to the modern computer.

analytical review A type of accounting survey intended to corroborate the logical interrelationship among accounts and to identify and explain all significant changes and abnormalities.

ANSI American National Standards Institute.

APF Authorized program facility. A system facility whereby access to restricted system functions is controlled by maintenance of a list. The list identifies modules that are permitted to use restricted functions.

APL A Programming Language. A high-level programming language used for mathematical applications.

application program A specific task-oriented program, such as an accounts payable processing program, supplied or designed to suit individual user needs. In IBM's Information Management System (IMS), application programs interface with DL/1 to process a data base.

appropriation of retained earnings The transfer of a portion of earned surplus to a separate account by order of the board of directors to indicate that portion's unavailability for dividends.

arithmetic logic unit. *See* ALU.

ARQ *A*utomatic *ReQ*uest for repetition. A system employing an error-detecting code, structured so that any transmission error included in a signal initiates a retransmission of the character incorrectly received.

Artifical Intelligence (AI) A broad term identifying the study of advanced computer systems that includes research in the development of natural languages for programming and addressing computers, and systems that can simulate human capabilities such as learning and analysis, and alphanumeric character and voice recognition.

ASB Auditing Standards Board.

ASCII   American Standard Code for Information Interchange. An eight-bit code for data transfer adopted by the American Standards Association to achieve compatibility between data devices.

Assembler (also called **Assembly**)   A low-level programming language, designed for a particular computer model or type, in which instructions are written alphanumerically and represent specific machine and memory functions.

asset turnover   Sales divided by total assets.

assets   Economic resources (things of value) owned by a business that are expected to benefit future operations. Current assets are cash and other assets expected to be converted into cash within one year or the current operating cycle (whichever is longer).

asynchronous transmission (also called **start-stop transmission**)   Transmission in which each data character is individually synchronized, usually by the use of start and stop elements. The intervals between transmitted characters may not be of equal length.

ATM   Automated teller machine.

audit equation   Knowledge plus corroboration equals understanding of the subject matter.

audit opinion   The report issued by certified public accountants after an audit, or examination of the financial statements, of an organization. Expresses a judgment on the fairness and accuracy of the financial statements and indicates the nature and limits of the responsibility being assumed by the independent auditors.

audit program   A list of steps to be performed during an examination. It controls the nature, extent, and timing of procedures performed during the examination.

audit report   A written declaration issued by a certified public accountant that expresses an independent professional opinion on the fairness and reliability of the financial statements of a business.

audit risk   The chance that the auditor will issue an unqualified opinion on financial statements that are materially misstated.

audit trail   In computer systems, a step-by-step history of a transaction, especially a transaction with security sensitivity. Includes source documents, electronic logs, and records of accesses to restricted files.

auditing   The principal activity of a certified public accountant (CPA). An independent examination of the accounting records and other business-related evidence to support the expression of an impartial, informed opinion about the reliability of the financial statements.

AudSEC   Auditing Standards Executive Committee.

authorization   The act of first comparing a proposed transaction with plans, conditions, constraints, or general knowledge of what constitutes propriety and then deciding whether or not the transaction is valid and in accord with management intentions.

authorized program facility   *See* APF.

automatic request for repetition   *See* ARQ.

average-cost   Total cost of goods available for sale divided by the number of units available for sale. A method of inventory valuation.

background Processing lower priority jobs or tasks when computer resources are not otherwise needed for higher priority jobs.

backup Any duplicate of a primary resource function, such as a copy of a computer program or a data file. This standby is used in case of loss or failure of the primary resource.

bad debt A receivable (or a portion thereof) that has been determined to be uncollectible and is charged as an expense of the accounting period.

BAL Basic Assembler Language. An assembly language used to write computer programs.

balance sheet An organization's statement of financial position, presenting assets, liabilities, and owner's equity as they exist on a specific date.

bandwidth The range of frequencies available for signaling. The differences are expressed in cycles per second (hertz) between the highest and lowest frequencies of a band.

bar code The arrangement of black stripes and spaces on products that is read by an optical scanner to identify the products and/or their prices.

baseband signaling A communications transmission technique where digitally encoded information remains in its original frequency (such as amplitude) during transmission over a communications channel.

BASIC Beginner's All-purpose Symbolic Instruction Code. A high-level procedure-oriented programming language. Developed as a teaching tool at Dartmouth University, BASIC is easy to learn and use.

Basic Assembler Language *See* BAL.

batch In computer operations, the processing of a group of related transactions or other items at planned intervals. Large cyclic processing needs, such as payroll and inventory, benefit from this individual processing of application programs. In many systems, batches are processed overnight or during periods of off-peak usage.

baud Unit of signaling speed for data transmission. If each signal event represents only one bit condition, baud rate is the same as bits per second. When each signal event represents an amount other than one bit, then baud rate does not equal bits per second. A 300 baud rate transmits 30 characters per second. A 9,600 baud rate can send a full data screen in two seconds.

Beginner's All-purpose Symbolic Instruction Code *See* BASIC.

beginning inventory Goods on hand and available for sale at the start of the accounting period.

bidirectional logical relationship In a data base, when the two possible paths between the structural element connection of a data base are defined. For example, in IBM's Information Management System (IMS), definition of the logical relationship of both paths can be from the physical parent through the logical child to the logical parent and from the logical parent through the logical child to the physical parent. (Differs from a unidirectional logical relationship in that both paths are defined.)

binary digit The smallest unit of information in a two-part system, the binary digit represents either the mark or space of an on or off (1 or 0) condition. The way in which data is stored in a computer system.

binary synchronous transmission (BISYNC)   A uniform discipline using a defined set of control characters and control character sequences for synchronized transmission of binary coded data between stations in a data communications system.

bit (b)   Contraction of binary digit.

BLP   *See* bypass label processing.

board   A printed circuit board that is a subcomponent of computer hardware.

book value   The net amount at which an asset is shown in the accounting periods. For depreciable assets, book value equals cost minus accumulated depreciation.

Boolean algebra   A set of logical rules that establishes relationships between statements. Those statements form a binary system where their combination of statements is either true or false.

Boolean search capability   In IBM's Information Management System (IMS) data base software packages, portions of information can be labeled and retrieved using the logic capabilities of Boolean algebra.

bootstrap (boot)   A program that brings another program (often the operating system) into operation to run the computer. May be called the initial program load (IPL).

bpi   Bits per inch. Relates to the density of data on a magnetic storage medium like tape.

BPI   Bytes per inch (equal to 8 bpi).

bps   Bits per second. Relates to the speed of data transfer.

BPS   Bytes per second (equal to 8 bps).

branch   A decision location in the computer's processing flow or a departure from the normal processing route within a program. A branch may occur as the result of a condition test, depending on the results of that test (*see* test).

broadband   With respect to communications, a subdividable portion of the data transfer frequency spectrum.

budget   With respect to capital assets, used in evaluating proposed investments in capital assets and the financing of these investments. With respect to cash accounting, a forecast of cash receipts and cash disbursements expected for a future period, as well as cash balances and cash requirements within future periods.

buffer   The computer's temporary storage area used to compensate for a difference in rate of data flow when transmitting data from one device to another, such as from a computer to a printer.

bug   A mistake or error in a computer program.

burst   To separate on the perforated line the continuous multi-part stationery of computer printers into separate sheets after printing.

bus   An information path used as a common connection between several similar or different devices. Used frequently in microprocessors as a simple path for transferring data, control, and addressing information.

business entity   A group of people that enters into economic activity whose transactions must be recorded, summarized, and reported as separate functions in the community.

bypass label processing (BLP) An option used in job control language statements to locate a file, so that volume and data set labels (header information) on a magnetic tape are not checked for existing volumes or created for new ones.

call An internal computer communication interface, as when a program is called into use. In IBM's Information Management System (IMS) data base, calls are between DL/1 and user programs. Related in function to: function code, Boolean search capability.

capital assets Stocks, bonds, and rental property not used in a trade or business.

card reader A computer input device that identifies the hole pattern in punched cards and translates the characters represented by those holes into an electronic form understood by the computer.

carrier, communications common A company that furnishes communications services to the general public, regulated by appropriate local, state, or federal agencies. The term includes truckers and movers, bus lines, and airlines but is also used to refer to telecommunications companies.

carrier system With respect to communications, a way to obtain a number of channels over a single path by first modulating each channel on a different frequency and then demodulating at the receiving point to restore the signals to their original form.

cash basis An accounting system in which revenue and expenses are recorded when received and paid, regardless of the period they apply to. This system fails to match revenue with related expenses and does not meet generally accepted accounting principles (GAAP). Used for individual income tax returns and in accounting records of many professional firms and small service-type enterprises.

cash flow statement A statement showing the sources of cash receipts and the purpose of cash payments during an accounting period. This information is useful for explaining changes in the balance of the cash account, but it is not a substitute for an income statement.

catalog The collection of data set indexes (data set name, I/O unit, and volume serial number) maintained by data management. One way a computer system keeps track of stored data.

cathode ray tube *See* CRT.

central processing unit *See* CPU.

centralization In a computer system, when the main processing activity is done in one geographic location (often called the home office or the computer center).

centralized accounting A technique in which the branches of a company send information on transactions to the home office, which maintains the financial records for the entire company.

certified information systems auditor (CISA) A professional certification sponsored by the EDP Auditors Association.

certified public accountant (CPA) An independent professional accountant registered and licensed by a state to offer auditing and accounting services to clients.

change accumulation log   A system-created computerized log. In IBM's Information Management System (IMS), all changes to a data base in a given run are recorded on this data set.

channel   A path for electrical transmission between two or more points. Also referred to as a circuit, line, or link.

channel, analog   A channel on which the information transmitted can take any value between the limits defined by the channel. Most voice channels are analog channels.

channel, voice-grade   A channel suitable for transmission of speech, digital or analog data, or facsimile, generally with a frequency range of about 300 to 3,400 cycles per second.

channel to channel   *See* CTC.

character   Letter, number, punctuation, or other sign contained in a message. There may be characters for special symbols and some control functions in a computer system.

character distortion   With respect to data communications, distortion caused by transients that, as a result of the modulation, are present in the data transmission channel. Depending on transmission qualities, unreliable data may be transmitted.

chart of accounts   A systematic listing of account names and numbers that applies to a specific accounting concern.

check digit   In computerized data, a numeric value added to provide assurance that the original value has not been altered (and is, therefore, possibly erroneous) in storage, construction, or transmission.

check register   A simplified version of the cash payments journal used for recording cash payments when a voucher is being used.

child   In a data base, a dependent segment (lower level, as a child of its parent). Can have a physical parent and/or a logical parent. A logical child has both a physical and a logical parent. This segment data, which physically exists and is retrievable in a physical data base, can be logically processed using a data base definition (DBD) and program specification blocks (PSBs) that define a logical view.

chip   The miniature wafer on which circuit elements, which carry electronic impulses understood by the computer, have been imprinted.

CICS   Customer Information Control System. An IBM communications system used for production applications in a mainframe environment.

circuit   A conducting path through which an electronic current passes. With respect to two-wire circuitry, where a circuit is formed by two conductors that are insulated from each other. The two conductors can be used as either a one-way transmission path, a half-duplex path, or a duplex path. With respect to four-wire circuitry, where a communication path with four wires (two for each direction of transmission) links separated sending and receiving devices.

CISA   *See* certified information systems auditor.

closing entries   Journal postings made at the end of the period to close temporary accounts (revenue, expense, and drawing accounts) and transfer balances to a capital account.

CMS   Conversational Monitor System. An IBM on-line interactive system product used for application development.

COBOL Common Business Oriented Language. A high-level procedure-oriented programming language used for many business applications.

code A system of symbols representing words or instructions to the computer and used to convert, transmit, or store data. As a verb, to write a program. With respect to command codes in data base applications, may be used to modify the function code of a call, the segment qualification, and the establishment of parentage (*see* parentage).

command A job control statement or a message, sent to the computer system, that initiates a processing task.

Common Business Oriented Language *See* COBOL.

communications Transmitting data or information between locations, often between two or more computers.

comparative financial statement Financial statement data that covers two or more successive periods and is placed in adjacent columns to facilitate a study of changes.

compare In a computer program, a function where two or more items are examined to reveal their relationship.

compile The act of translating a high-level language source program into an object module or program written in machine language. A compiler is a program that translates a source program into an object module after checking its syntax and produces a listing of the source program with diagnostics that may affect the source program's execution.

component percentage The relationship of any financial statement item to a total including that item. For example, each type of asset as a percentage of total assets.

concatenated fields A string of fields. Data sets can also be concatenated, or run together.

conditioning With respect to data communications, the addition of equipment to a leased voice-grade communications channel to reduce distortion.

confidentiality In general, the concept that confidential computerized files or information will remain so. In an audit, assuring the client that, except for disclosure required by law and custom, information shared with the auditor will go no further without the client's permission.

consolidated financial statements Reports that present the economic position and operating results of a group of affiliated corporations as if the group represented a single unified business.

constant With respect to computer systems, a value that does not change during program execution.

contention With respect to computer systems, when different users try to access the same system resources. With respect to communications, a method of line control in which the terminals request to transmit. If the channel in question is free, transmission goes ahead; if it is not free, the terminal waits until it is free. A queue of contention requests may be built up by the computer in a set sequence or in the same sequence in which requests are made.

contingency plan Management policy of procedures designed to maintain or restore computer operations, possibly at an alternate data center, in the event of emergencies, system failure, or disaster.

contingent liabilities   Recorded obligations that relate to past events but may arise on occurrence of a future event deemed possible but not probable.

contra-account   A ledger account that is deducted from, or offset against, a related account in the financial statement, such as allowance for doubtful accounts. A contra-asset account is one with a credit balance that is offset against, or deducted from, an asset account to produce the proper balance sheet valuation for the asset.

contribution margin   Sales less variable costs.

contribution margin ratio   The percentage of sales available to cover fixed expenses and yield a net income.

control (or controlling) account   A general ledger account supported by detailed information in a subsidiary ledger.

control character   In computerized data, an alphanumeric character whose occurrence in a particular context initiates, modifies, or stops a control operation, such as "carriage return" or "enter."

control logic (or structure)   The order of the computer's processing functions.

control program (CP)   The independent program that operates to schedule and supervise the execution of programs in the computer system.

control read-only memory   *See* CROM.

control section (CSECT)   The part of a computer program specified by the programmer to be a relocatable unit, all elements of which are to be loaded into adjoining storage locations for execution. Usually given a name; if not, it is known as a private code. A CSECT is sometimes called a section definition.

control statement   In computer programming, a command that directs the logical sequence of processing operations.

control total   A total, generated manually or by computer, used to check the processing results.

control unit   The part of the central processing unit that holds computer instruction codes and whose functions include decoding instructions, initiating operations, and monitoring system operations.

controls   The methods, policies, and procedures adopted within an organization to ensure the safeguarding of assets, the accuracy and reliability of data, the promotion of administrative efficiency, and the adherence to management standards and intentions.

controls, application (also called **input, processing, output**)   Methods of ensuring that only complete, accurate, and valid data is entered and updated in a computer system; that processing accomplishes the correct task; that processing results meet expectations; and that data is maintained.

controls, general (also called **integrity controls**)   Controls over the EDP system operations as a whole, including the design, security, and use of computer programs; the security of data files; and controls over access. Consists of system software and related manual procedures.

conversational mode (also called **interactive**)   A computer processing technique that involves step-by-step interaction between the user at a terminal, by means of keyboard and display, and a computer.

Conversational Monitor System *See* CMS.

copyright An exclusive right inferred by authorship and ensured by the federal government (Copyright Act of 1977) to protect the production and sale of literary or artistic material for a certain period of years. Can also refer to software.

core Main memory within the computer.

cost accounting A specialized field of accounting concerned with determining and controlling the cost of particular products or processes.

cost center An organizational unit, such as the personnel department, that incurs expenses or costs but does not directly generate revenue.

cost of goods manufactured Cost of units of finished product completed during a period. Beginning inventory of goods in process, plus cost of raw material used, plus direct labor and factory overhead, minus ending inventory of goods in process equals cost of goods manufactured.

cost of goods sold A computation appearing as a separate section of an income statement showing the cost of goods sold during the period. Computed by first adding net delivered cost of merchandise purchased to beginning inventory (to obtain cost of goods available for sale) and then deducting the amount of the ending inventory from this total.

cost of inventory The price paid for the inventory plus the cost of bringing the goods to the point where they are offered for sale.

cost principle (historic cost) An accounting policy whereby assets are recorded at their original cost to the organization.

cost revenue analysis A method of studying the response of revenue and costs to variations in business volume.

CP *See* control program.

CPA *See* certified public accountant.

CP/M Control program/microcomputers.

CPU Central processing unit. The part of the computer housing the electronic circuits that control the hardware, arithmetic logic unit, and main memory. Functions include decoding the instructions that control the electronic circuits, performing arithmetic and logic operations, and monitoring machine performance.

CRC *See* cyclic redundancy check.

credit An amount entered on the right-hand side of an account. A credit is used to record a decrease in an asset and an increase in a liability or in owner's equity.

credit agency An organization, such as Dun & Bradstreet, Inc. or TRW Credit, that gathers credit data on individuals and business concerns and distributes the information to its clients for a fee.

credit memorandum A document issued to show a reduction in the amount owed by a customer because of goods returned, a defect in the goods or services provided, or an error.

CROM Control read-only memory. The programming embodied in the read-only memory (ROM) is used to control the processing of operations or the function of a microprocessor.

cross-foot   To add footed columns across to obtain a total. This total is checked against the accumulated total for a column.

CRT   Cathode ray tube. A television-like vacuum tube unit used for information entry and display. Terminals including such displays are frequently called CRTs. This is an I/O device.

CSECT   *See* control section.

CTC   Channel to channel. A communications term relating to data transmission.

current ratio   Current assets divided by current liabilities. A measure of short-run debt-paying ability.

current-value accounting   The valuation of assets and measurement of income in terms of current values rather than historical cost. An approach designed to avoid the distortion of financial statements by inflation.

cursor   A moveable shape (often a bar or rectangle) that marks the place on a computer terminal screen where the next character entered will be displayed.

Customer Information Control System   *See* CICS.

cycle billing   A system of billing customers at various dates during the month to avoid concentration of work at month-end.

cyclic redundancy check (CRC)   An error detection scheme for computer systems in which a check character is generated by first dividing all the serialized bits in a block of data by a predetermined binary number and then using the remainder as the check character.

cylinder   A unit of storage on a disk, composed of tracks. In a disk pack, the set of all tracks with the same nominal distance from the center of the axis of rotation.

data   Facts and information that can be communicated and manipulated. In relation to a computer program, the input that a program and its instructions perform on and that determines the results of processing.

data base   A computerized systematic collection of data elements organized according to a specific design that can be hierarchical or relational.

data base administrator (DBA)   The individual responsible for both the design of the data base, including the structure and contents, and the access capabilities of application programs and users to the data base. Additional responsibilities include operation, performance, integrity, and security of the data base.

data base definition (DBD)   Describes structure (hierarchy), sequence, key fields, update rules, and so forth of a computerized data base. In IBM's Information Management System (IMS), the DBD can describe a physical or a logical data base.

data base management system (DBMS)   A system software product that aids in controlling and using the data needed by application programs. A DBMS can help create and maintain a well-organized data base.

data base record   The single occurrence of a root segment and all its dependent segments arranged in a particular sequence.

data communications   The movement of data between geographically separated locations via public and/or private electrical transmission systems.

data definition statement (DD statement) An IBM operating system job control statement that describes the data set to be associated with a particular job step; the data required for that job.

data dictionary A data structure listing and defining the contents of the data base.

data element The smallest unit of addressable information in a data base. A field in a data base segment.

data element dictionary (DED) A file listing data element specifications, definitions, descriptions, and other information as developed for a particular application.

data entry Placing data into a computer system through a data input device such as a keyboard, a diskette, or a card reader.

Data Language/1 *See* DL/1.

data processing The computerized preparation of documents and the flow of data contained in these documents through the major steps of recording, classifying, and summarizing.

data set A group of related computerized records.

data set group In IBM's Information Management System (IMS), the partitioning of the data base record type into subtrees of segment types, and the storing of instances of each subtree in a separate group.

data set name (DSNAME, DSN) The DSNAME is a naming convention used to uniquely designate a group of related computerized records (a file in a data base). In job control language, the DSN must be specified in the data definition (DD) statement.

data transmissions The technique, and its related technology, used in sending data between geographically separated locations or devices over a communications channel.

dataphone The communications equipment furnished by AT&T for data communication services.

DBA *See* data base administrator.

DBD *See* data base definition.

DBMS *See* data base management system.

DD statement *See* data definition statement.

debit An amount entered on the left-hand side of an account. A debit is used to record an increase in an asset and a decrease in a liability or in owner's equity.

debit memorandum A document issued by a buyer to show a decrease in the amount previously recorded as owed to a seller. May also be issued by a seller to increase the amount previously recorded as receivable from a customer.

debug To find and eliminate program errors or computer system malfunctions. Debugging programs means locating logic errors.

decentralization Distributing computer processing among the different data centers of a geographically diversified organization.

decentralized accounting system A system in which each branch of a company maintains its own complete set of accounting records.

deck A group of related punch cards; it is analogous to a file.

DED   *See* data element dictionary.

default   Failure to pay interest on, or principle of, a promissory note at the due date. In a computer system, a default or a default value is automatically chosen by the program from the alternatives when the user does not specify a choice.

deferred charge   An expenditure expected to yield benefits for several accounting periods and therefore be capitalized and written off during the periods benefited.

deferred revenue   An obligation to render services or deliver goods in the future because of advance receipt of payment.

density   With respect to data storage, the number of elements per unit length, area, or volume, such as characters or bits per inch on magnetic tape.

depletion   Allocating the cost of a natural resource to the units removed as the resource is mined, pumped, cut, or otherwise consumed.

depreciable cost   The cost of an asset minus the estimated residual or salvage value.

depreciation   The systematic allocation of the cost of an asset to expense during the periods of its useful life.

dial-up terminal   A remote terminal that is connected to a telecommunications line where the connection between the terminal and the computer is initiated at the remote terminal. Several remote terminals may share the single telecommunications line connected to the computer.

dibit   A set of two bits. In four-phase modulation, each possible dibit is encoded as one of four possible states: 00, 01, 10, 11.

digit   In the binary system, a numeric character representing the integers 1 or 0.

digit portion (byte)   The four right-most bit positions in a byte.

digital computer   A device that processes data, represented in discrete form, in the on/off, 1/0 condition. Generically, computer usually refers to a digital computer.

digital data   Information represented by a code or characters, such as numbers or letters, consisting of a sequence of discrete elements, rather than the continuous wave-like sequence of analog data.

digital signal   A discontinuous signal where the various states come at discrete intervals. *Compare with* analog transmission.

direct access device (also called **direct access storage device — DASD**)   A peripheral hardware unit that provides the capability to access and/or manipulate data as required without having to access all preceding records to reach it. (In sequential access, as in tape, all records must be read to reach the one required.)

direct address pointer   Contains the address of the physical storage location of a related segment in a computer system data base. A component of the segment prefix.

direct charge-off method   A method of accounting for uncollectible receivables in which no expense is recognized until individual accounts are determined to be worthless. At that point the account receivable is written off with an offsetting debit to uncollectible accounts expense. Fails to match revenue and related expenses.

direct labor   Employees' wages directly related to production.

directory   A computerized index of all system and user files currently maintained by the computer system.

disclosure principle   Financial statements should disclose all material and relevant information about the financial position and operating results of a business. The notes accompanying financial statements are an important means of disclosure.

discontinued operations   The operations (revenue and expenses) of a company segment that has been eliminated, rendered obsolete, or sold.

discount   With respect to cash sales accounting, a price reduction offered by manufacturers and wholesalers to encourage customers to pay invoices within a specified discount period.

discount rate   The required rate of return used by an investor to discount future cash flows to their present value.

discounted cash flows   The present value of expected future cash flow.

disk   *See* magnetic disk.

disk drive   A type of direct access storage device that uses magnetic disks as the storage medium, and physically reads from, or writes to, the data stored on the magnetic disk.

disk operating system   *See* DOS.

diskette (also called **floppy disk**)   A flexible magnetic storage medium. The flexible plastic disk is housed in a rigid protective cardboard or plastic cover. Most microcomputers use diskettes.

distributed processing   A computer system whose processing is spread among the different data centers of an organization.

DL/1   Data Language/1. The interface between the user program and IBM's Information Management System (IMS).

documentation   All the charts, forms, tapes, reports, and other business papers that guide and describe the working of a company's system of accounting and internal control. A complete and accurate description and authorization of a transaction and each operation a transaction passes through. In computer terminology, the written description of a system or program and how it operates.

DOS   Disk operating system. A disk-resident operating system that provides operating system capabilities for computing systems of 16K and larger.

dot-matrix   A two-dimensional representation of characters that is arranged by combining dots into rows and columns. A dot-matrix that represents graphic characters is used for a computer terminal and can be reproduced on hard copy using a dot-matrix printer.

double declining balance depreciation   The most widely used version of declining balance depreciation. The rate is double the straight-line rate.

double-entry method   In recording financial transactions, the total dollar amount of debits must equal the total dollar amount of credits.

down time   The time that the computer system is unavailable for processing, usually calculated as a percentage of total time available for processing.

DSN   *See* data set name.

DSNAME   *See* data set name.

dump (also called **file dump, core dump,** or **memory dump**)   To write, in a condensed manner, the contents of a computer file or memory location. A process often used to find problems (bugs).

duplex transmission (also called **full-duplex transmission**)   With respect to communications, simultaneous two-way independent transmission in both directions. *Compare with* half-duplex transmission.

dynamic processing   In a multiprogramming system, swapping jobs among different system resources (memory locations and peripherals) according to priorities during execution.

EBCDIC   Extended Binary-Coded Decimal Interchange Code. An eight-bit coded set of characters used for data representation.

edit   To prepare data for future computer operations including programmed procedures that inspect data for accuracy, add or delete items, and do format checks on data contents.

EDP Auditors Association/EDP Auditors Foundation (EDPAA/EDPAF)   Founded in 1969, these professional associations established the CISA (certified information systems auditor) designation and examination.

electronic journal   A chronological file that records the processing activities of a computer system and is maintained and stored by the system.

electronic mail   Written messages, such as letters or memos, sent and delivered by computer communications links from person to person.

employee's individual earnings record   A record maintained for each employee summarizing gross earnings, deductions, net pay, and other payroll information.

employee's withholding exemption certificate (W-4)   A federal form prepared by the employee and given to the employer stating the number of withholding exemptions claimed. Used in determining the amount of income tax to be withheld from the employee's pay.

employer's quarterly federal tax return (941)   A report prepared every three months by the employer to provide the federal government with a record of all wages paid, amounts withheld, and amounts of tax on both employees and employer.

encryption   Scrambling computerized information to secure data by using special algorithms for transmission or other purposes. Passwords are stored within the system and are often encrypted, so that even when unauthorized access of their file takes place, they cannot be read or understood.

ending inventory   Goods still on hand and available for sale to customers at the close of the accounting period.

equity method   An accounting method used when one corporation's investment in another is large enough to influence the policies of the investee. The investor recognizes as investment income its proportionate share of the investee's net income, rather than considering dividends received as income.

execute   When the computer system performs operations it is directed to do by the program instructions.

expenditure With respect to capital, the amount of cash or property paid for assets incurred for the benefit of future periods.

expenses The cost of the goods and services used up in obtaining revenue. Sometimes referred to as expired costs.

expiration date With respect to a computer file, the date after which the computer system no longer automatically protects the file from being overwritten by other data.

Extended Binary-Coded Decimal Interchange Code *See* EBCDIC.

extraordinary items Transactions and events that are both unusual and infrequent, such as a sale of a major asset, noted in financial statements.

factory overhead All costs incurred in the manufacturing process other than the cost of raw material and direct labor, such as insurance, depreciation of machinery, and supervisors' salaries.

FASB *See* Financial Accounting Standards Board.

federal employment compensation tax A tax imposed on the employer by the Federal Unemployment Tax Act (FUTA) and based on the amount of payrolls. Designed to provide temporary payments to unemployed persons.

Federal Insurance Contribution Act tax *See* FICA tax.

feedback System output. Includes control operations' output returned to the input side of computer processing to evaluate the system conformation's effectiveness.

FICA tax A tax imposed by the Federal Insurance Contribution Act on both employer and employees. Used to finance the social security program.

field In a data base, the smallest unit of data that can be named and directed. A string of fields is a concatenated field or a record. In a record, such as an invoice, the physical area assigned to categorized data, such as a customer account number.

field signature In a data base, defines the interpretation of a unique data unit according to application program specifications.

FIFO *See* first-in, first-out.

file A collection of records stored in computerized form, often on magnetic storage media. Files may be created, located, queried, updated, displayed, scratched, backed up, printed, named, and classified by type.

Financial Accounting Standards Board (FASB) An independent group that conducts research in accounting and that issues authoritative statements as to proper reporting of financial information. Formerly the Accounting Principles Board (APB).

financial forecast A plan of operations for a future period with expected results expressed in dollars.

financial statement order Sequence of accounts in the ledger: balance sheet accounts first (assets, liabilities, and owner's equity), followed by income statement accounts (revenue and expenses).

financial statements Reports that summarize the financial position and operating results of a business (balance sheet and income statement).

finished goods inventory Completed manufactured products that are available for sale.

firmware   Permanent computer instructions encoded into the circuits of semiconductor chips. A type of read-only memory.

first-in, first-out (FIFO)   In inventory accounting, the cost of goods sold based on the assumption that the first merchandise acquired is the first merchandise sold, and that the ending inventory consists of the most recently acquired goods. In data processing, a queuing technique where the next item to be handled is the item that has been in the queue the longest.

fiscal year   Any 12-month accounting period adopted by a business.

fixed costs   A cost that does not change with variations in the level of output.

flag   In programming, a predetermined piece of data that marks an expected or special event during processing.

flexible budget   A budget or series of budgets that cover a variety of production levels.

floppy disk   *See* diskette.

flowchart   A diagram of the movement of transactions, computer functions, media, and/or operations within a system. The processing flow is represented by symbolic shapes for operation, device, data file, and so on to depict the system or program.

FOB   Free on board. With respect to FOB destination, when the seller incurs the cost of shipping the goods to the buyer and retains title to the goods while they are en route. With respect to FOB shipping point, when the buyer incurs the cost of shipping the goods, and title to the goods passes to the buyer at the time of shipment.

footing   The total of amounts in a column.

format   The spatial organization of data (characters, fields, records, files) whether they may be printed, displayed, or stored.

FORTRAN   *FOR*mula *TRAN*slation. A high-level programming language that uses arithmetic formulas to express computer programs.

fraud   Dishonest acts intended to deceive. May involve the theft of assets and falsification of records and statements.

free on board   *See* FOB.

frequency-division multiplex   With respect to communications, a multiplex system in which the available transmission frequency range is divided into narrower bands, each used for a separate channel.

frequency modulation   With respect to communications, one of three ways of modifying a sine wave signal to make it carry information. The sine wave, or carrier, is modified in accordance with the information to be transmitted.

full (absorption) costing   The traditional method of product costing in which both fixed and variable manufacturing costs are treated as product costs and charged to inventories.

full-duplex transmission   *See* duplex transmission.

function   The special activity or purpose of a task; a processing operation for which a computer has hardware and/or software facilities.

function code   A data base call element that specifies the action to be taken on the data base.

GAAP   *See* generally accepted accounting principles.

GAAS *See* generally accepted auditing standards.

gain With respect to capital, the amount of excess proceeds realized in the sale or exchange of a capital asset over its book value.

general and administrative expenses Expenses of the general offices, accounting department, personnel office, credit and collection department, and activities other than the selling of goods. A subdivision of operating expenses.

general ledger The recorded collection of accounts where all of an organization's financial transactions are classified, either in detail or in summary form from a subsidiary ledger.

generally accepted accounting principles (GAAP) Standards or guidelines for the preparation of financial statements to achieve the objectives of understandability, reliability, and comparability. Also used as criteria for judging acceptability of accounting methods. Those accounting principles that have received substantial authoritative support, such as the approval of the Financial Accounting Standards Board, the American Institute of Certified Public Accountants, or the Securities and Exchange Commission.

generally accepted auditing standards (GAAS) Quality guidelines issued by the American Institute of Accountants regarding the conduct and report of the field work and audit of a public accountant.

goods in process (work in process) inventory Inventory consisting of partially finished products at various stages of completion in the manufacturing process.

gross earnings Total amount earned by an employee before deductions such as social security taxes, federal income tax withheld, and any voluntary deductions.

gross income All income and gains from whatever source derived unless specifically excluded by law, such as interest on state and municipal bonds.

gross price method A policy of recording invoices at the gross amount before cash discounts and of recording cash discounts taken in accounts called Purchase Discounts and Sales Discounts.

gross profit method A way to estimate the cost of ending inventory, based on the assumption that the rate of gross profit remains approximately the same from year to year.

gross profit on sales Revenue from sales minus cost of goods sold.

half-duplex transmission With respect to communications, an independent transmission that may flow in either direction but in only one direction at a time. *Compare with* duplex transmission.

hard copy Computer reports, files, and documents printed on paper and visually readable.

hardware The actual equipment of a computer system. Describes components of the machine including electronic circuitry, peripherals, and processor.

hash totals The addition of any numeric data existing for all documents in the batch, that can be checked against the total of the same numeric data fields for items processed.

HASP   Houston Automatic Spooling Program. A computer program that provides supplementary management functions, such as the control of job flow that is part of job management, ordering of task processing that is part of task management, as well as data management and spooling.

HDAM   Hierarchic direct access method. A data access technique for storing or retrieving data in a continuous sequence; the data may be stored on a direct access device.

Hertz   A unit of frequency equal to one cycle per second.

HIDAM   Hierarchic indexed direct access method. *See* HDAM.

hierarchic direct access method   *See* HDAM.

hierarchic indexed direct access method (HIDAM)   *See* HDAM.

hierarchic indexed sequential access method (HISAM)   *See* HDAM.

hierarchy   A structured set of computerized data.

Hierarchy: Input-Processing-Output   *See* HIPO.

high-level language   Programming language closely related to the English language or human mathematical expressions. High-level languages do not reflect the structure of a specific computer. COBOL, FORTRAN, BASIC, ALGOL, and PL/1 are high-level languages.

HIPO   Hierarchy: Input-Processing-Output. A flowcharting technique used during program design and development; also used to document program function.

historical cost   An asset's cost at its acquisition. Includes actual cost and associated costs, such as shipping and installation.

holding gains   The change in an asset's current value (whether an increase or a decrease) during the current period.

host computer   The primary computer in a distributed or multiple computer system. Data base access and access to the network is controlled by the host computer. Synonymous with host processor.

host language   The programming mechanism that functions with DL/1 to access IBM's Information Management System (IMS) data bases.

Houston Automatic Spooling Program   *See* HASP.

hybrid computer   Using digital and analog technology, can process discrete and variable data in the same machine.

IAPC   *See* International Auditing Practices Committee.

IBG   *See* interblock gap.

IC   *See* integrated circuit.

IFAC   *See* International Federation of Accountants.

IIA   *See* Institute of Internal Auditors; Insurance Institute of America.

IMS   *See* Information Management System.

income statement   A report used to evaluate the performance of a business by matching its revenue and related expenses for a particular accounting period. Shows the net income or net loss.

income summary account   The summary account in the ledger to which revenue and expense accounts are posted for closing at the end of the period. The balance (credit balance for a net income, debit balance for a net loss) is transferred to the owner's capital account.

index   Area containing master and cylinder indexes associated with a data set. An index exists for any indexed sequential data set that has a prime area occupying more than one cylinder. Indexed sequential data sets reside on direct access volumes.

index data base   Contains HIDAM (hierarchic indexed direct access method) root segment keys, which are used to index the retrieval of the physical HIDAM root segment.

indexed sequential access method (ISAM)   *See* HDAM.

indirect labor   Employee wages that are not directly related to production.

Information Management System (IMS)   A general purpose IBM system product that allows users to access a computer-maintained data base through remote terminals.

initial program load (IPL) (also called a **bootstrap** or **boot program**)   A program that brings another program (often the operating system) into operation to run the computer.

initialize   With respect to a magnetic disk, the process of establishing the disk areas that will store files.

input   Information/data received by the computer environment from the external environment or another area within the computer environment. The process of entering information to the computer.

input device   Equipment, such as a tape drive or a disk drive, used to enter data/information to the magnetic storage of a computer system.

input media   The physical tool that data can be recorded on in machine-readable format for entry into a computer system.

input/output   *See* I/O.

input, processing, output   *See* controls, applications.

inquiry processing   Direct, on-line access to a computer file, providing immediate reference to its contents and resulting in a response to the requested information.

installment basis of accounting   A method of recognizing income from installment sales that is based on collections rather than date of sale. Acceptable for income tax purposes but ordinarily not for other accounting purposes.

Institute of Internal Auditors (IIA)   Formed in 1941 to promote professionalism and education. Activities include sponsoring seminars, conferences, research, and *The Internal Auditor*, a monthly professional journal.

Insurance Institute of America (IIA)   Founded in 1909, the IIA offers educational programs and professional certification for the property-liability insurance business.

intangible assets   Those assets used in the operation of a business that have no physical substance and are noncurrent.

integrated circuit (IC)   A combination of interconnected electronic circuit elements, components that are manufactured together and otherwise inseparable, on a single unit.

integrity   With respect to data, its accuracy, quality, validity, and safety from unauthorized use.

integrity controls   *See* controls, general.

interactive   A computer system that involves responses or prompts between the user and the computer, such as an automated teller machine. Often called a conversational system.

interblock gap (IBG)   The space between units of data on magnetic storage media where no data is recorded.

interest   A charge made for the use of money. The formula for computing interest is: principle $\times$ rate of interest $\times$ time = interest (P $\times$ R $\times$ T = I).

interface   The place, or boundary, of two or more computer systems, devices, or processes that permits this interaction to occur.

interim statements   Financial reports prepared at intervals of less than one year, such as quarterly and monthly statements.

internal auditing   An activity carried on in organizations by an in-house professional staff to investigate and evaluate the system of internal controls on a year-round basis. Also, evaluating the efficiency of individual departments within the organization.

internal control   All measures used by a business to guard against errors, waste, or fraud and to assure the reliability of accounting data. Designed to aid in the efficient operation of a business and to encourage compliance with company policies.

International Auditing Practices Committee (IAPC)   Established by the International Federation of Accountants to develop guidelines regarding generally accepted auditing practices and audit responses.

International Federation of Accountants (IFAC)   Serves to promote a coordinated worldwide accounting profession, including coordinated auditing standards.

interpreter   A programming language processor that translates and executes source code into machine code serially (that is, one instruction at a time with instructions processed immediately).

intersection data   With respect to the hierarchical relationship of data in a data base, when a logical child is retrieved, the data returned into the I/O area can include the logical parent concatenated key, physical segment data, and logical parent data, in that order. The physical segment data is said to be intersection data.

inventory   Goods acquired or produced for sale in the regular operation of a business. Goods in which a business deals.

inverted data base   A logical data base that permits the processing of segments in a physical hierarchy in an "upward" fashion.

invoice   An itemized statement of goods being bought or sold. Shows quantities, prices, and credit terms. Serves as the basis for an entry in the accounting records of both seller and buyer because it evidences the transfer of ownership of goods.

I/O   Input/output. Devices that can be used for input and/or output.

I/O area (segment I/O area) As a result of a call, this area can contain the segment(s) retrieved, the segment(s) to be replaced, the segment(s) to be inserted, or the segment(s) to be deleted.

IPL *See* initial program load.

ISAM Indexed sequential access method. *See* HDAM.

JCL *See* job control language.

JES Job entry subsystem. A system facility that provides I/O spooling functions, job class scheduling, remote job entry capability, and managing. The primary job entry subsystem is Multiple Virtual Storage (MVS).

job A set of data that completely defines a unit of work for a computer. A job usually includes programs, linkages, files, and instructions to the operating system.

job control language (JCL) Any one of the control statements in the input job stream that identifies a job or defines its requirements.

job entry subsystem *See* JES.

job-order costing system An accounting method that assigns the costs of raw material, direct labor, and factory overhead to a specific job.

job step In a computer system, a unit of work associated with one processing program. A job consists of one or more job steps.

journal A chronological record of transactions, showing for each transaction the debits and credits to be entered in specific ledger accounts. With respect to cash receipts, used only to record all cash received. With respect to cash payments, a special journal used to record all payments of cash. With respect to computer systems, the logging of data for an information trail.

journal entry A financial transaction translated into its debit and credit components, and an explanation of the transaction. In systems, can be computerized.

journalize To state a transaction and enter it in a journal.

K Stands for 1,024; in computers, usually bytes.

key entry *See* data entry.

key field A field used by the computer to locate data.

labor rate variance The difference between the standard labor rate and the actual rate, multiplied by the actual hours.

language In the computer environment, a set of alphabetic, numeric, and symbolic character elements used with a rule structure to communicate between people and machines.

language translator A computer program that changes the source code of one computer language into the source code of another.

last-in, first-out (LIFO) A method of computing the cost of goods sold by using the prices paid for the most recently acquired units. Ending inventory is valued on the basis of prices paid for the units first acquired.

ledger   A book, file, or other record containing all the separate accounts of a business. In systems, can be computerized.

level   A number representing the vertical position at which segments are contained within a data base. It also represents the level of dependency.

liabilities   Debts or obligations of a business. The claims of creditors against its assets.

library   In computer terms, a library is a collection of similar files, such as data sets contained on tape and/or disks, stored together in a common area. Typical uses are to store a group of source programs or a group of load modules. In a library, each program is called a member. Libraries are also called partitioned data sets (PDS).

LIFO   *See* last-in, first-out.

linkage editor   A utility program that takes as its input object modules from a compiler and produces a machine language load module.

linkedit   The act of combining an object program with needed read/write or other specialized functions to create a computer-executable program (or load module). This procedure is performed by a computer program called a linkage editor.

load   Moving data or programs from a storage device to the computer's memory for processing.

load library   A partitioned data set used for storing load modules for later retrieval.

load module   The results of the linkedit process. The load module is fully executable by the computer.

log   With respect to computer systems, to record an event or a transaction. May include the time and duration of the event; often a log is recorded on a computerized journal.

log-in (logon)   To begin a session, usually in a mainframe or minicomputer environment, by identifying an authorized user and a password that permits access to the computer's resources.

log-out (logoff)   To end a session, usually in a mainframe or minicomputer environment, when the authorized user has finished working with the computer's resources.

logic error   In computer programming, when an error in processing occurs even though the program is syntactically correct.

logical data base   A data base containing segments that are involved in logical relationships. Many logical data bases (representing different hierarchical views) can be defined for one physical data base. One logical data base can be defined to view several physical data bases. The segments in a logical data base must be defined in at least one physical data base. A logical data base must have a corresponding logical data base definition.

logical terminal   A name that is related to a physical terminal. One physical terminal can have one or more logical terminals associated with it. The user can reference the logical terminal in the construction and transmission of messages without concern for such things as physical terminal address. If the physical terminal becomes inoperative, the logical terminals associated with it can be dynamically reassigned to another physical terminal.

long-term capital gains and losses   Gains and losses resulting from sale of capital assets owned for more than a specific period (nine months in 1977 and one year thereafter). A net long-term capital gain qualifies for a special tax rate.

longitudinal redundancy check (LRC)   A system of error control based on the formation of a block check using a preset formula. The formula is applied in the same manner to each character. In a simple case, the LRC is created by forming a parity check on each bit position of all the characters in the block, for example, the first bit of the LRC character creates odd parity among the one-bit positions of the characters in the block.

loop checking   A method of checking the accuracy of data transmission. The received data is returned to the sending unit for comparison with the original data, which has been stored there for this purpose. May be referred to as message and/or information feedback.

loss   With respect to capital, the deficit resulting from the sale or exchange of a capital asset for less than its cost.

low-level language   Computer programming language designed to reflect the structure of a specific computer. Provides each object code instruction with a source code instruction. Assembly is a low-level language.

lower of aggregate cost or market   The total cost of marketable securities owned is compared with the market value determined at the balance sheet date. The lower of these two aggregate figures is the amount used to value the asset in the balance sheet. The method presently required by Financial Accounting Standards Board rules for valuation of marketable securities.

lower-of-cost-or-market   A method of inventory pricing in which goods are valued at original cost or replacement cost (market), whichever is lower.

LRC   *See* longitudinal redundancy check.

machine language   A code that is understood and used directly by a computer. Written in instructions (sets of bit patterns) understood by a computer. ZAPs are written in machine language. A load module is in machine language.

macro instruction   A general term used to collectively describe a macro instruction statement, the corresponding macro instruction definition, the resulting assembly language statements, the machine language instructions, and other data produced from the assembly language statements. Representation of a sequence of machine language instructions.

magnetic disk   With respect to computer storage, the rotating platters that data is written to and read from. The data is recorded on the magnetic surface in bit patterns that run in the tracks within cylinders on the surface of the disk.

magnetic ink character recognition (MICR)   A computer input technique that translates characters printed in magnetic ink into bit patterns understood by the computer.

magnetic tape   With respect to computer storage, the magnetically coated plastic ribbon that data is written to and read from. The data is recorded in bit patterns that correspond to the channels on the tape's surface.

mainframe   In reference to a computer environment, a large general purpose computer consisting of control unit, arithmetic unit, and main storage. Because of its size, this hardware unit can process and store tremendous amounts of data.

maintenance, file Altering computerized records by updating them to keep their contents current, adding new records, and adjusting storage organization as required and indexes as changes occur.

maintenance, program Altering computer programs to reflect new processing requirements or fluctuating processing requirements, and documenting these changes.

management information system *See* MIS.

manual processing Noncomputerized, nonautomated manipulation of data.

manufacturing account A summary account used in closing the accounts of a manufacturing business. All costs used in computing the cost of goods manufactured are transferred into the account, which is then closed to the income summary.

margin of safety Amount by which actual sales exceed the break-even point.

master budget A report that combines the overall financial and operating plan of an organization.

master file In a computer, the most currently accurate and authoritative permanent or semi-permanent computerized record of information maintained over an extended period. Standing data is a term (sometimes) used to refer to the master file data.

master terminal A logical terminal that has complete control of the IBM Information Management System (IMS) communications facilities, message scheduling, and data base operation.

matching principle To measure income, the revenue earned during an accounting period is compared with the expenses incurred in generating this revenue.

material price variance The difference between the standard price and the actual price of material used, multiplied by the standard quantity.

materiality An auditing concept regarding the relative importance of an amount or item. An item is considered as not material when it is neither important nor significant enough to influence decisions or have an effect on the financial statements.

member The generic name for a computerized file in a computer system's library.

memory The unit or component of a computer that can receive, contain, and output data. Main memory stores programs during program execution. Secondary memory, or storage, is usually held on a peripheral device.

menu A list of options, or items, displayed on a terminal from which a user can choose. The selection initiates the next task performed by the computer.

menu driven A program, usually in an interactive computer system, controlled by the selections made by the user from a menu.

message switching With respect to communications, the technique of receiving a message, storing it until the proper outgoing line is available, and then re-transmitting. No direct connection between the incoming and outgoing lines is set up, as it is in line-switching.

microcomputer A small computer built around a microprocessor. The relatively small expense of a microcomputer allows home users and business professionals access to low-cost computer resources.

microprocessor   An integrated circuit device that contains the miniaturized circuitry to perform arithmetic, logic, and control operations. Popularly called a "computer on a chip."

microwave   Any electromagnetic wave in the radio-frequency spectrum above 890 megacycles per second.

million instructions per second   *See* MIPS.

minicomputer   General all-purpose computer designed for an office environment and ranging in price from $20,000 to more than $200,000. Memory size and processing speed fall between a microcomputer and a medium-sized mainframe.

MIPS   Million instructions per second. Used when describing the computing speed of some computers.

MIS   Management information system. Computer applications designed to support management with appropriate and timely information for analysis and to support their control function.

mnemonic   With respect to computer systems, programming language symbols that represent computer operations and memory addresses.

modem   A contraction of modulator-demodulator. A hardware peripheral device. The term may be used when the modulator and the demodulator are associated in the same signal-conversion equipment. *See* modulation.

modulation   The process by which some characteristic of one wave is varied in accordance with another wave or signal. This technique is used in data sets and modems to make business machine signals compatible with communications facilities.

module   A separate independent subset of instructions within a computer program, a module can be written, compiled, and tested before being linked with the remaining parts of the program.

monetary items   With respect to changes in price levels, monetary items include assets representing claims to a fixed number of dollars, such as cash and receivables, and all liabilities. Monetary items are not restated when preparing general purchasing power financial statements.

multidrop line (also called **multipoint**)   With respect to communications, a line or a circuit interconnecting several computer stations within a network.

multiple occurrence of a segment   In IBM's Information Management System (IMS), when more than one segment with the same name exists within the same data base record.

multiplex, multichannel   Use of a common communications channel to make two or more channels. This is achieved either by splitting the frequency band transmitted by the common channel into narrower bands, each of which is used to constitute a distinct channel (frequency-division multiplex) or by allocating the common channel in turn to constitute different intermittent channels (time-division multiplex).

multiplexer   A device that uses several communication channels at the same time, a multiplexer can transmit and receive messages and control the communication lines so that multiple users can access a system.

multiprocessing (also called **parallel processing**)   In a computer system, two or more processors linked by an operating system that share data and peripheral devices and can execute multiple programs simultaneously.

multiprogramming   A computer operation that provides for two or more application programs to execute simultaneously from a single computer resource. A typical multiprogramming operation is a time-sharing system.

negative confirmation   With respect to data communications, a type of confirmation that requests the recipient to respond only if in disagreement with the information provided.

net assets   Assets minus liabilities. Equal to owner's equity.

net income   Revenue earned above the related expenses for a given period.

net present value   The excess of the present value of the net cash flows expected from an investment over the amount to be invested.

net price method   A policy of recording purchase invoices at amounts net of (reduced by) cash discounts.

net realizable value   The prospective selling price minus anticipated selling expenses. Inventory should not be carried at more than net realizable value.

net tangible assets   Total of all assets (except the intangibles) minus liabilities.

network   Linking two or more computers, at different geographical locations, with data communications technology to provide the sharing of computer resources.

noise   Random electrical signals, introduced by circuit components or natural disturbances, that tend to degrade the performance of a communications channel.

noncurrent account   Any balance sheet account other than a current asset or a current liability. Noncurrent accounts include long-term investments, plant assets, intangible assets, long-term liabilities, and stockholder's equity accounts.

notes payable   Formal written obligations to pay a stipulated amount of money, usually with interest, at a specific future date.

notes receivable   Receivables (assets) evidenced by a formal written promise to pay a certain amount of money, usually with interest, at a future date.

object program (also called **object module**)   The result of compiling a source program. Not a fully executable program, an object program is used by the linkedit program to create a load module.

obsolescence   The process of becoming out of date and less efficient than newer types of equipment. In accounting, a major factor limiting the useful life of most depreciable assets.

OCR   Optical character recognition. A computer input technique that translates printed graphic characters (may be handwritten) into bit patterns. The newer bit patterns are compared with bit patterns held in memory to determine which known character the graphic character resembles.

OEM   Original equipment manufacturer. Describes a purchaser, or customer, who buys a product from another manufacturer to be used as an element in the purchaser's own saleable product. For example, an organization that gathers the hardware and software resources that compose a ready-to-perform computer system and then sells the complete system as a single package.

off-line   Computer operations and devices not directly and continually controlled by a system's CPU. Types of input such as punched cards are considered elements of an off-line system because a manual operation is required between initial recording of data on the card and actual processing of data.

office automation   As computer resources become increasingly affordable, the concept of a paperless office that relies on computer technology to store records in machine-readable form, manipulate documents through word processors, and transfer data through communications carriers.

on-line   A processing term that categorizes operations under direct, immediate control of the CPU. Interactive and real-time systems are among those classified as on-line systems.

operand   A basic unit of data in a computer instruction, an operand contains the memory address of an item of data to be processed.

operating cycle   The average period from the purchase of merchandise to its sale and conversion back to cash.

operating expenses   Includes selling, general, and administrative expenses. Deducted from gross profit on sales to determine net income.

operating system   Software that controls the execution of computer programs and that may provide scheduling, debugging, input/output control, accounting, compilation, storage assignment, data management, and related services. *See also* DOS.

opinion, adverse   A judgment that the financial statements do not present fairly what they purport to present. It is required when the auditor has sufficient evidence for believing that the statements are misleading.

opinion, disclaimed   Used if the auditor does not have enough evidence to form an opinion either because the scope of the auditor's examination was seriously limited or because there are major and pervasive uncertainties that cannot be resolved.

opinion, piecemeal   The complement of a qualified opinion, that is, a qualified opinion gives an opinion on the financial statements as a whole and makes exceptions for certain items, while a piecemeal opinion disclaims or is adverse on the financial statements as a whole and gives an opinion on certain items.

opinion, qualified   An opinion containing a modifying phrase for one of four basic reasons: departures from generally accepted accounting principles, departure from consistent application of accounting principles, limitations on the scope of the examination, and uncertainties affecting the financial statements that cannot be resolved. The first three use the term "except for"; the fourth, "subject to."

optical character recognition   *See* OCR.

original equipment manufacturer   *See* OEM.

output   Data/information produced by computer processing, such as graphic display on a terminal and hard copy.

output device   Peripheral equipment, such as a printer or tape drive, that translates the machine code produced by a computer system into a form that can be used outside the system.

output media   The form on which data is displayed, printed, or punched, including terminal display and microfilm.

owned data   Data base information that can be accessed — through data base definitions and program specification block (PSB) specifications — only by a given application or group of applications.

owner's equity   The excess of assets over liabilities. The amount of an owner's net investment in a business plus profits from successful operations that have been retained in the business.

package   With respect to computer software, an application-specific program or set of programs that is mass-marketed and usually mass-produced.

packet switching   A method of transmitting data where messages are broken up into a number of packets that are transmitted independently and subsequently regrouped at a receiving point.

page   That portion of a program swapped between secondary computer storage and primary computer storage (memory) during program execution.

paging   The interchange of a page between primary and secondary computer storage. Since main memory cannot hold the larger quantity of data that a storage device can, paging maximizes memory storage space by keeping on hand only the data currently required.

par value   The legal capital of a corporation. Also the face amount of a share of capital stock. Represents the minimum amount per share to be invested in the corporation when shares are originally issued.

parallel conversion   An installment technique whereby a new computer system is run concurrently with the old system until the new system has been proven.

parallel processing   *See* multiprocessing.

parallel transmission   Simultaneous transmission of the bits making up a character or byte, either over separate communications channels or on different carrier frequencies on the channel.

parameter (PARM)   A variable that is given a constant value for a specified computer application and that may denote the application. A parameter establishes limits, selects options, or otherwise controls the behavior of a computer system.

parent   Any data base segment that has physical or logical children.

parent company   A corporation that owns a controlling interest in another company.

parentage   In a data base, a state of positioning that allows the user to control the processing of dependent (lower level) segments.

parity bit   Addition of noninformation bits to data, making the sum in a grouping of bits either always even or always odd. This permits detection of bit groupings that contain errors. It may be applied to characters, blocks, or any convenient bit grouping.

parity check   A horizontal parity check exists when a parity check is applied to the group of certain bits from every character in a block (also called longitudinal redundancy check). A vertical parity check exists when a parity check is applied to the group that is all bits in one character (also called vertical redundancy check). An even or odd parity check tests whether the value of digits in a group of binary digits is even (even parity check) or odd (odd parity check).

PARM *See* parameter.

PARM field The parameter or PARM field on the JCL execute statement for a DL/1 program. Specifies the program specification block (PSB) to be used and tells DL/1 how to obtain the control blocks.

partition That part of computer memory assigned to a program during execution.

partitioned data set *See* PDS.

partnership An association of two or more persons to carry on, as co-owners, a business for profit.

Pascal A high-level programming language, rigidly structured.

password A key word (known only to an authorized user) that permits access to the computer's resources when presented to the system.

path Any hierarchical path in a data base.

payback period The length of time necessary to recover the cost of an investment through the cash flows generated by that investment. Payback period is one criterion used in making capital budgeting decisions.

payroll record A record listing the names of employees during a given pay period, the rates of pay, time worked, gross earnings, deductions for taxes and any other amounts withheld, and net pay.

payroll register A form of payroll record showing, for each pay period, all payroll information for employees (individually and in total).

PCB Program communication block. A part of a program specification block (PSB), the PCB communicates a data base definition name to DL/1 and specifies processing options that can be performed on the data base by an application program. Also indicates the segments that can be affected by the specified processing options. Segments in a data base can be masked from application program view by not specifying them in the PCB.

PCB mask An interface between DL/1 and the application program. Exists in the linkage or protected areas of an application program and contains data base definition name, segment level retrieved, status code, processing options, segment name, key length, number of sensitive segments, and the key feedback area.

PDS Partitioned data set. Independent groups of sequentially organized data sets (called members), each identified by a name in the dictionary.

percentage of completion method An accounting method for long-term contracts, when the percentage of costs incurred to the estimate of total costs is multiplied by the estimate of total profit. This process determines an amount of revenue earned to date for recognition in the current accounting period.

performance monitor With respect to system software, a program that tracks and records the speed, reliability, and other service levels delivered by a computer system.

period costs Costs that are charged to expense during the period in which they are incurred. Generally include costs associated with selling and administrative functions.

periodic inventory system A method of accounting whereby a physical count is taken and the goods on hand are priced at regular intervals.

peripheral   A hardware unit that is separated from the CPU and provides input, output, or storage capabilities when used in conjunction with a computer.

perpetual inventory system   A system of accounting for merchandise, it provides a continuous record showing the quantity and cost of all goods on hand.

phase modulation   With respect to communications, one of three ways of modifying a sine wave signal to make it carry information. The sine wave, or carrier, is changed in accordance with the information to be transmitted.

physical inventory   The process of counting and pricing the merchandise on hand at a given date, usually the end of the accounting period.

physical terminal   A hardware device used to enter or record messages being sent or received over communications lines. A physical terminal can be defined as many logical terminals.

PL/1   Programming Language/1 A high-level programming language. Versatile enough for both novice and experienced programmers.

plant and equipment (fixed assets)   Long-lived assets used in the operation of a business.

plug compatible   With respect to computer equipment, hardware designed and distributed by one manufacturer that can be connected to, and operate with, the hardware of a different manufacturer to create one integrated computer system.

pointer   With respect to a data base, indicates the location of an item of data.

polling   A means of controlling communication lines. The communication control device calls the terminals under its control as a means of permitting them to transmit information. Polling is an alternative to contention; it makes sure that no terminal is kept waiting for a long time.

polling list   The polling signal is usually sent under program control. The program refers to a polling list that exists for each channel and tells the sequence in which the terminals are to be polled.

polynomial checking   An error detection code designed to discover if any data has been altered during transmission, thereby causing the receiving end to have erroneous data. A mathematical operation is performed on the data by the sender and repeated by the receiver. If the results are the same, then the data is unaltered.

port   An interface between a peripheral device and the CPU. Usually a physical connection point such as a multiple-pin electrical connector or a cable ending that data passes through when entering or exiting the CPU.

positive confirmation   A type of confirmation that requests the recipient to respond in any event.

posting   The process of transferring information from the journal to individual accounts in the ledger.

prefix   With respect to data base processing, the control portion of a segment.

prepaid expenses   Payments that are made in the current accounting period and benefit the current and future accounting periods. The amount applicable to future periods is classified as an asset on the balance sheet.

present value   The amount of money today that is considered equivalent to a cash inflow or outflow expected to take place in the future. The present value of money is always less than the future amount, since money on hand today can be invested to become the equivalent of a larger amount in the future.

price/earnings ratio   Market price of a share of common stock divided by annual earnings per share.

pricing the inventory   The assignment of an appropriate dollar value to each item of merchandise determined to be on hand at the time of taking a physical count of inventory.

primary data   The data base information that is not stored in the overflow area and is therefore more quickly accessed.

prime   An area containing data and related track indexes. Prime areas exist for all indexed sequential data sets.

printed circuit board   The plastic and bonded copper board that has etched electrical conductor patterns, integrated circuitry soldered and mounted in place, and edge connectors lined up along one side of the board to connect with external circuitry. Most modern technology has all electronic circuitry on printed circuit boards.

printer   A peripheral output device that records on paper the information from computer systems.

prior period adjustments   Gains or losses of material amounts that constitute adjustment of prior years' reported earnings and are recorded directly in the retained earnings account.

pro forma statement   A statement that presents the effects of specific hypothetical conditions or prospective transactions on historical financial statements.

process cost system   A method of cost accounting, used mainly in continuous mass production, in which costs are assigned to processes or operations and averaged over units produced.

processing options   Specified in program specifications block (PSB) generation to indicate the processing that an application can perform on a segment in IBM's Information Management System (IMS).

processing regions   In IBM's Information Management System (IMS) the four processing regions are Control Region, Batch Processing Region, Batch Message Processing Region, and Message Processing Region.

product costs   Costs that are directly related to work in process and finished goods inventory, such as costs of direct material, direct labor, and overhead.

profit center   A unit of a business that produces revenue that can be identified with the unit.

profit-volume formula   Sales equal variable expenses plus fixed expenses plus net income.

program   A set of related instructions that, when followed and executed by a computer, perform operations or tasks. Application programs, user programs, system programs, source programs, and object programs are all software programs.

program communication block   *See* PCB.

program development   The activities involved in creating workable, applicable programs. Includes writing, coding, debugging, and testing.

program specification block   *See* PSB.

program temporary fix   *See* PTF.

programmable read-only memory   *See* PROM.

Programming Language/1   *See* PL/1.

programming specification   The phase during program design that describes the function, structure, input, output, and storage requirements of the program.

PROM   Programmable read-only memory. Typically, a semiconductor memory chip that is programmed after it is manufactured. The programming is normally accomplished through physical or electrical techniques.

prompt   With respect to an interactive computer system, a message sent to the user from the computer system and displayed on a video peripheral unit. The message is usually a question, the response to which initiates the computer's next task.

PSB   Program specification block. With respect to an Information Management System (IMS) data base, contains one or more (or possibly no) program communication blocks (PCBs) that indicate segments and how data can be processed by an application program.

PTF   Program temporary fix. When a problem is identified in vendor-provided programs, the vendor, such as IBM, first provides a PTF to temporarily overcome the problem. These PTFs are often implemented using a ZAP with a PTF serial number for identification. Most vendors distribute their software in object code format.

public switched network   With respect to communications, any switching system that provides circuit switching to many customers. It includes these four networks: Telex, TWX, telephone, and Broadband Exchange.

punched card   A rectangle of cardboard in which holes can be placed in specific patterns that represent data. These hole patterns are read by a device that translates a pattern into information understood by the computer. The holes can also be punched by a computer for subsequent input, as they are for utility bills.

purchase journal   A special journal used exclusively to record purchases for merchandise on credit.

purchase method   Accounting for a business combination by recording assets at current market values as indicated by the price paid in the acquisition.

purchase order   A serially numbered document sent by the purchasing department of a business to a supplier or vendor for ordering material or services.

purchase returns and allowances   An account used by the buying company to record the cost of unsatisfactory merchandise returned to the supplier. Also used for a downward adjustment of the purchase price of merchandise because of some defect in the goods.

purchases   An account used to record the cost of merchandise purchased for sale to customers.

query   A message that requests a programmed search of available data for a specific item when sent to a computer system. Also may be the facility in a data base that allows data to be viewed by a user but not manipulated and therefore changed.

queue   With respect to computer systems, the first in, first out waiting line that prioritizes programs awaiting processing, including files and records.

RAM   Random access memory. An internal memory component, usually a semiconductor, that data can be read from and written to. Data is transferred from a disk or diskette to RAM during processing. Since a semiconductor is volatile, data can be lost from RAM if electrical power is interrupted during processing.

randomizing module   A user-supplied routine that converts a root segment key to a root segment address. Required for hierarchic direct access method (HDAM) data bases only.

rate of corporate earnings   Usually expressed as the percentage relationship of net income to sales. Can also be reflected by comparing net income with total assets or stockholder's equity.

rate of return on investment   The overall test of management's ability to earn a satisfactory return on the assets under its control. Numerous variations of the return on investment (ROI) concept are used, such as return on total assets and return on total equities.

raw (direct) material inventory   Raw material or purchased components that are available for production and will become part of the finished product.

read-only memory   *See* ROM.

read/write head   With respect to magnetic tape and disk drive units, the mechanism that reads data from the tape or disk and/or writes data to the tape or disk.

real-time processing   An interactive on-line computer system that produces results, initiated by an operator at a terminal, in a very short time to allow tasks to be started and finished almost immediately, with immediate update of files concerned.

realization   Income recognition when both the earning process is virtually complete and goods and services have been exchanged.

receiving report   An internal form that is prepared by the receiving department for each incoming shipment and shows the quantity and condition of goods received.

reciprocal accounts   Offsetting accounts maintained by the home office and a branch. The home office maintains an account (with a debit balance) summarizing its investment in the branch. The branch maintains a home office account (with a credit balance).

record   A unit of related data items. The group of data fields that can be accessed by a program and contains the complete set of information on a particular item, such as a payroll master file record that would contain employee name, number, address, rate of pay, etc.

recovery of accounts receivable   The collection of accounts receivable previously written off as worthless.

referback   A job control language (JCL) statement that refers back to a previous step/statement for information, such as a program name, to be used at a new point in the processing sequence.

remote job entry   *See* RJE.

replacement cost   The estimated current cost of replacing goods in inventory or goods sold during the period. In financial statements, large corporations must disclose historical and current replacement costs of inventories and cost of goods sold.

report   Computer processing output formatted to be easily read and understood by the user.

Report Program Generator   *See* RPG.

research and development (R&D) expenses   Expenditures intended to lead to new products or to improve existing products.

residual (salvage) value   The portion of an asset's cost expected to be recovered through sale or trade-in of the asset at the end of its useful life.

responsibility accounting   A cost accounting system that establishes centers of responsibility through an organization by allocating costs and revenue to each center. This approach provides the organization with information on the performance of each center and the proficiency of the person to whom authority for the center has been assigned.

retail method   A way of estimating inventory in a retail store. The method is based on the assumption that the cost of goods on hand bears the same percentage relationship to retail prices as does the cost of all goods available for sale to the original retail prices.

retained earnings   That portion of stockholder's equity resulting from profits earned and retained in the business.

return on investment (ROI)   A percentage that expresses the relationship between investment and profit. Computed by dividing the organization's net income by investment or owner's equity.

revenue   The price of goods sold and services rendered by a business. Equal to the inflow of cash and receivables in exchange for services rendered or goods delivered during the period.

RJE   Remote job entry. With respect to computer systems with locations geographically separate from the main computer center, submitting batch processing jobs via a data communications link.

robotics   A general term that includes the design and construction of automated, programmable equipment that can perform physical operations (such as production work and mechanical tasks) involving three-dimensional movement.

ROI   *See* return on investment.

ROM   Read-only memory. Preprogrammed memory circuitry that can be read from, but not written to (altered). Usually programmed during manufacturing, routines such as loading the computer and language translators are stored in this form.

root segments   The highest level, or topmost segment, of data base system hierarchy. Always a parent in Information Management System (IMS).

routing   The assignment of the communications path by which a message or telephone call reaches its destination.

routing indicator   An address, or group of characters, in the heading of a message, the routing indicator defines the final circuit or terminal to which the message has to be delivered.

RPG   Report Program Generator. A high-level, commercially oriented programming language specifically designed for writing application programs that meet business data processing requirements, such as management reports.

rules   A data base definition specification that controls inserting, replacing, and deleting segments involved in logical relationships.

run   A popular, idiomatic expression for program execution.

sales   The revenue account credited with the sales price of goods sold during the accounting period.

sales journal   A special journal used exclusively to record sales of merchandise on credit.

sales returns and allowance   An account used by the selling company to record the sales price of goods returned by customers. Also used for a downward adjustment of the sales price allowed to the customer because of some defect in the goods.

sample   With respect to auditing, choosing a portion of available data to represent or reflect the validity, accuracy, etc. of financial statements to be reported in the audit report.

SAP   Statements of Auditing Procedures. Now called Statements on Auditing Standards. *See* SAS.

SAS   Statements on Auditing Standards. Released by the American Institute of Certified Public Accountants to guide external audits conducted by public accountants.

save   In a computer system, a command or operation that moves recently entered data from temporary memory storage to a permanent file or storage medium such as a disk or tape.

scoresheet   A listing of all items, large and small, that the auditor believes could or should be adjusted.

scratch   With respect to a computer file, to delete or make unavailable.

SDLC   *See* Synchronous Data Link Control; system development life cycle.

search field   A search field defined in a data base definition is used to access a data base through segment search arguments to qualify non-key fields.

Securities and Exchange Commission (SEC)   A government agency that reviews various financial reports of corporations that offer securities for sale to the public. Works closely with the Financial Accounting Standards Board and the American Institute of Certified Public Accountants to improve financial reporting practices.

segment   The primary unit of information in a data base. In Information Management System (IMS), composed of a prefix and data element (possibly key fields, intersection data, and concatenated information). A dependent segment in a data base is one that has a parent (*see* parent; child) and is independent of the parent segment as well as of any higher level segments in its hierarchical path. All segments are considered logical segments in a logical data base definition (DBD). A physical segment is any segment defined in a physical DBD except for a virtual segment.

segment key field   Defined in a data base definition and used to communicate with other data base facilities, such as IBM's Information Management System DL/1; a means to process data base segments.

segment level   In IBM's Information Management System (IMS), data base structure can have up to 15 levels in a hierarchical structure. Segment level 1 is the root or base level; segment levels 2–15 are for lower level segments.

segment name   Defined by the SEGM statement in an IBM Information Management System (IMS) data base definition generation (DBDGEN). References a logical relationship in a logical data base definition.

segment pairing   When the same segment data in a data base exists or is available in more than one logical view, the segments are said to be paired.

segment search argument   *See* SSA.

segment sensitivity   Described by a SENSEG statement of the program communication block (PCB) in IBM's Information Management System (IMS). Indicates which segments are available to an application program. Segment data that is available to one application or group of applications but not available to other applications is said to be owned data.

segment type   *See* segment name.

selling expenses   Expenses of marketing the product, such as advertising, salaries, and delivery of merchandise to customers. A subdivision of operating expenses.

semiconductor   An electronic device that conducts electricity by utilizing the atomic instability of silicon when combined with phosphorous. A semiconductor can limit the flow of electricity to one direction. Circuitry that uses semiconductors is called solid state.

semivariable costs   Costs that respond to changes in volume of output by less than a proportionate amount.

serial numbering of documents   The assignment of an unbroken sequence of numbers to a given class of documents, such as checks or invoices, so that the omission or loss of a document will be readily apparent.

SFAS   Statements of Financial Accounting Standards. Issued by the Financial Accounting Standards Board, statements of standards governing the preparation of financial reports.

sign-on   The procedure performed at a computer terminal while it is in initial mode. This procedure may include the sign-on commands (or command) and a password only, or it may include other user-specified security data.

silicon-on-sapphire   *See* SOS.

simplex mode   Operation of a communication channel in one direction only, with no capability for reversing.

simulation   With respect to mathematics, a model of a future event created by using current and historical data. In regard to computer systems, a programming technique whereby one computer system's operation can be imitated by a different computer.

SMF   System Management Facility. An IBM control program that provides the means for gathering and recording information that can be used to evaluate the extent of computer system usage.

SMP   System Modification Program. An IBM service aid for controlling modifications to an operating system.

SNA Systems Network Architecture. Both an IBM system product and a concept that defines the internal architecture of a computer's communications system.

Social Security taxes FICA and FUTA taxes based on payrolls and intended to provide funds for operating benefit programs in which monthly retirement payments and Medicare benefits are paid to qualified workers in covered industries, as well as benefits to the family of a worker who dies before reaching retirement age.

software Computer programs that direct computer processing and can be stored and manipulated by a computer system.

SOP Statement of Position.

sort The rearrangement of computerized data into groups according to specific criteria, such as ascending, descending, numeric, or alphabetic sequence.

SOS Silicon-on-sapphire. An integrated circuit fabrication technology that uses a sapphire substrate or base on which to build silicon based semiconductors/integrated circuits.

source and allocation of funds *See* statement of changes in financial position.

source document The initial, or original, recording of data before it is introduced to a computer system.

source program A version of a computer program written in human-readable statements. In this state, a program can be reviewed, analyzed, updated, and read by a compiler. It must be compiled and linkedited before it can be executed by the computer.

specific identification method A method of pricing inventory by identifying the units in the ending inventory in terms of specific purchases.

spool Sending data from one computer storage area to another storage area with a different speed capability, such as from a high-speed device to a slow-speed device, where an intermediate device, such as a buffer, exists between the transfer source and the destination.

SSA Segment search argument. In IBM's Information Management System (IMS) data base structure, SSAs are a component of a call and are used (through Boolean logic, relational values) to obtain a desired position in a data base. Can be qualified by specifying only a segment name.

standard cost A formulated estimate of future cost that should be incurred under conditions expected to prevail. It establishes a measure from which current results can be compared and deviations and inefficiencies can be observed. Standard cost is usually expressed per unit.

standing data (also called **master file data**) In a computer system, the most currently accurate and authoritative permanent or semi-permanent computerized record of information maintained over an extended period.

start element With respect to data communications, the first element of a character used to permit synchronization in certain serial transmissions.

statement A computer operation command written in a high-level programming language that translates into a low-level language instruction and initiates the processing operation.

statement of account   A monthly statement, sent by a company to a customer, showing charges for sales during the month, credits for payments received on goods returned, and the balance receivable from the customer at the end of the month.

statement of changes in financial position (also called **source and allocation of funds**) A financial statement showing the sources and uses of working capital during the accounting period. In addition, this statement shows financing and investing activities, such as exchange transactions, that do not directly affect working capital.

statement of retained earnings   A financial statement that presents the variation in retained earnings for the year being reported on.

Statements of Auditing Procedure   Now called Statements on Auditing Standards. *See* SAS.

Statements on Auditing Standards   *See* SAS.

status code   A code that can be used by an application program to discover any possibly invalid results. The code may be found in the program communication block mask (PCB mask). In IBM's Information Management System (IMS), DL/1 operates in association with the application program when using a status code.

steplib   A data definition statement in job control language in which a private library (where a program resides) is specified.

stock   Transferable units of ownership in a corporation. Refers to both common and preferred stock.

storage   An area in a computer system where the bit patterns that represent data are held before, during, and after processing. Primary storage is considered main memory.

storage device   A hardware unit that can receive, retain, and output data.

store and forward   With respect to communications, the process of message handling used in a message switching system. (*See* message switching.)

straight-line depreciation   A method of depreciation that allocates the cost of an asset (minus any residual value) equally to each year of its useful life.

subroutine   A sequenced set of statements or a short program that may be used in one or more computer programs and at one or more points in a computer program. Subroutines can be referenced by a program, so that they do not have to be written in full within the program each time they are used.

subsidiary company   A corporation in which a controlling stock interest is held by another corporation.

subsidiary ledger   A supplementary record used to provide detailed information for a control account in the general ledger. The total of accounts in a subsidiary ledger equals the balance of the related control account in the general ledger.

substantiation   *See* validation.

sum-of-the-years'-digits depreciation   An accelerated method of depreciation. The depreciable cost is multiplied each year by a fraction, the numerator of which is the remaining years of useful life (as of the beginning of the current year) and the denominator of which is the sum of the years of useful life.

supervisor   As applied to the computer operating system, a routine executed either in response to a requirement for altering or interrupting the flow of operations through the CPU, or for performance of input/output operations. Also may be the medium through which the use of resources is coordinated and the flow of operations through the CPU is maintained.

SVC Routine   In Coopers & Lybrand's Integrity Control Software, a control program routine that performs or initiates a control program service specified by a supervisor call.

symbolic language   A programming language that uses numeric words or symbols to represent operations and memory addresses. High-level and low-level languages as we know them are virtually all symbolic languages.

symbolic pointer   Used mainly to construct logical relationships in a HISAM data base or between HDAM or HIDAM and HISAM. These pointers are user data fields and do not exist in a prefix. The fields must, however, be physically concatenated at the beginning of the segment data. This type of pointer is required for HISAM logical relationships because DL/1 must use ISAM to index through the data base, beginning at the root level (thus, the concatenated key). Symbolic pointers are optional in HDAM or HIDAM.

Synchronous Data Link Control (SDLC)   A uniform data communications discipline using synchronous data transmission techniques for the transfer of data between stations in a point-to-point, multipoint, or loop arrangement.

synchronous transmission   With respect to data communications, transmission in which data characters and bits are transmitted at a fixed rate with the transmitter and receiver synchronized, This method eliminates the need for start-stop elements, providing greater efficiency.

syntactical error   A violation of the rules governing statement formats of computer programming. A syntactical error in a program prevents the program from executing correctly, if it executes at all.

sysout   With respect to IBM's job control language (JCL) an indicator used in data definition statements to signify that a data set is to be written to a system output unit.

system   An integrated set of elements designed to direct, cooperatively, the control and management of computer processing functions.

system development life cycle (SDLC)   The organizational arrangements and procedures involved in developing new computer applications or modifying existing systems or programs.

System Management Facility   *See* SMF.

System Modification Program   *See* SMP.

system software   Computer programs and related routines that control the processing of computer hardware and non-user-related functions.

Systems Network Architecture   *See* SNA.

table   With respect to computer programs, a table, like a dictionary, is a collection of data items where an item can be identified by an assigned label, by its positional relationship to other items in the collection, or by other elements that unambiguously identify that item.

tangible plant assets   Long-lived assets used in the operation of the business and possessing physical substance, such as land and buildings.

tape   *See* magnetic tape.

tape management system (TMS)   A specialized system software tool that lists the computer resource allocations needed in a specified job run, including individual reels of tape.

target segment   In IBM's Information Management System Virtual Storage (IMS/VS), the segment that the secondary index points to. *See* index data base.

task   A unit of work or an instruction performed by a computer. May include larger functions, such as payroll processing, or an operation, such as data input/output.

telecommunications (TC)   With respect to data communications, a general term applied to data that is transmitted by electrical, optical, or acoustical means between separate computing facilities.

teleprocessing (TP)   A form of information handling in which a data processing system utilizes communications facilities. (Originally, but no longer, an IBM trademark.)

Teletype   Trademark of Teletype Corporation, usually referring to a series of different types of teleprinter equipment, such as tape punches, reperforators, and page printers, utilized for communications systems.

terminal   Any device capable of sending and/or receiving information over a communications channel. CRTs are often used as operator terminals.

test   With respect to data accuracy, the comparison of data values during program processing to determine their "truthfulness."

text processing   *See* word processing.

tie line   A private-line communications channel of the kind provided by communications common carriers for linking two or more points together.

time-sharing   A multiprogramming system that provides multiple users, at different geographic locations, on-line access to a central computer resource. The computer's resources are divided among the users in individual slices of time.

time slice   In a multiprogramming system, the amount of processing time devoted to a job or specific processing resource in relation to the entire duration of all computer processing activities.

total manufacturing costs   The total cost of raw material used, direct labor, and factory overhead cost for a given period without regard to whether products are completed.

TP   *See* teleprocessing.

track   The path on a magnetic storage medium, tape or disk, that data is recorded on. On a magnetic tape, parallel tracks run the length of the tape; on a magnetic disk, these tracks circle the area of the disk.

transaction file   A group of one or more computerized records, usually transient in nature, containing current business activity and processed with an associated master file. Transaction files are sometimes accumulated during the day and processed in batch production overnight or during off-peak processing periods.

transactions   Business events that can be measured in money and are entered in the accounting records.

transcription   The translated copy of human-readable source documents to machine-readable tape, disk, diskette, or punched cards.

transistor   A semiconductor device that, for computer applications, can serve as a logic device for Boolean functions and as a switching device in communications applications.

transmit   To send data from one location to one or more receiving locations, often over public telephone lines.

turnaround time   The elapsed time between input and output results during which computer processing takes place.

turnkey   A computer system delivered to the purchaser by the vendor ready to begin operations by installing the equipment with its software in the prepared environment and turning it on.

twin (also called **physical twin**)   In a data base, the multiple occurrences of physical segments within the same physical parent. All root segments in a data base are physical twins.

uncollectible accounts expense   The expense caused by failure of customers to pay amounts owed to the company. Also, the ledger account used to show the estimated uncollectible credit sales for the year.

unidirectional logical relationship   In IBM's Information Management System (IMS), only one path of a logical relationship is defined: from the physical parent through the logical child to the logical parent. There is no segment pairing involved. *See* bidirectional logical relationship; segment pairing.

units-of-output depreciation   A depreciation method in which cost (minus residual value) is divided by the estimated units of lifetime output. The unit depreciation cost is multiplied by the actual units of output each year to compute the annual depreciation expenses.

universal product code   A type of bar code used in marking merchandise for identification in pricing and description at point-of-sale equipment.

UNIX™   A real-time, multitasking, multiuser operating system. A registered trademark of AT&T Information Systems.

unrealized losses and gains   An unrealized loss results from writing down marketable securities to a market value below cost. An unrealized gain results from restoring a former write-down because of a recovery in market price. Securities cannot be written up above aggregate cost. Unrealized losses and gains on marketable securities classified as current assets are included in determining the year's net income.

update   A computer processing activity whose function is to incorporate new versions of data into current data; includes adding, deleting, and replacing data.

useful life   Normal life of an asset, determined by its usefulness to its owner.

user friendly   Describes computer products that are conversational, free of technical jargon, and easy to use and learn.

USERID   User identification. A unique identifier assigned to each authorized computer user.

utilities   A type of system software function; usually routines that are frequently required by the system during normal processing operations. Sort programs are considered utilities, for one example.

utility program   A function-specific program that defines the routine performed during a computer processing procedure.

validation (also called **substantiation**)   The act of establishing the truth, accuracy, or relevance of an amount or fact by corroborating it through reperformance, vouching, confirmation, or reconciliation. In computer programs, procedures or routines can validate data as it is entered.

valuation account   An account, such as allowance for doubtful accounts, with a credit balance, which is offset against an asset account to produce the proper balance sheet value for an asset.

valuation allowance for marketable securities   Used to reduce the carrying value of marketable securities from cost to a market value below cost. Adjusted at each balance sheet date.

value added networks   Federal Communication Commission (FCC) term for packet switching network services, such as Telenet and Tymnet, deemed to have offered a communication facility not previously available.

variable (direct) costing   A method of cost accounting that treats only raw material, direct labor, and overhead that varies directly with the level of production as product costs. These are charged to inventory. The fixed component of overhead is recognized as a period cost.

variable costs   Costs that vary proportionately with volume of output.

variable length segment   IBM's Information Management System Virtual Storage (IMS/VS) capability that allows a segment to vary in length between a minimum and maximum specified in the data base definition.

verify   To check that data has been entered into the computer system accurately. For example, data entered through the keyboard, or keyed, is checked for correctness.

videotex   A interactive, transactional computer system used to receive information, send electronic mail, order goods and services from on-line catalogs, and do banking through a central computer containing complex data bases. Access is via a videotex terminal or a personal or home computer with a modem.

view   The appearance of a hierarchy to an application program. The data base definition and program specification block define the way the data looks and is structured.

Virtual Machine   *See* VM.

virtual storage access method (VSAM)   *See* HDAM.

VM   Virtual Machine. An IBM system product for on-line time-sharing applications, where multiple users, including remote users, access a functional simulation of a complete computing system and its related devices.

voice synthesizer   A computer output device that translates data in digital form to human-audible form, similar to that of a human voice.

volume   A method of naming or defining a single computer disk or reel of magnetic tape. For tape, a volume defines a single reel of tape and the volume name is usually a serial number. For disk storage, the volume is a single unit (logically and sometimes physically).

volume header   The label that names the data files on the volume or a subsection of the volume.

voucher   A document prepared to authorize and describe an expenditure.

voucher register   A special journal used to record all liabilities that have been approved for payment.

voucher system   A method of controlling expenditures and the payment of liabilities. Requires that every liability be recorded as soon as it is incurred, and that checks be issued only in payment of approved liabilities.

VSAM   Virtual storage access method. *See* HDAM.

weakness   With respect to a control, the inconsistent or improper operation of that control, rendering it deficient.

word processing (also called **text processing**)   Using computer technology, such as a keyboard, terminal, and software, to facilitate the storage, input, editing, and revision of printed documentation.

working capital   The difference between current assets and current liabilities. This amount represents the net amount of capital available for current use in a business.

working papers (also called **work papers**)   With respect to auditing, the forms, schedules, flowcharts, analyses, and correspondence, prepared and collected during an examination, that serve as the basis for the audit report.

worksheet   A large columnar sheet designed to arrange all the accounting data required at the end of the period in convenient form. Facilitates preparation of financial statements.

writing off an account receivable   The removal of an account receivable from the accounting records because it is considered uncollectible and therefore is no longer regarded as an asset. The offsetting debit is to the allowance for doubtful accounts.

Xenix   A licensed version of the AT&T Information Systems' operating system, UNIX™.

XMT   In computer systems, the abbreviation for transmit.

year-end adjustment   At the close of a fiscal period, modifications made to add any unrecorded or nonroutine transactions, such as accruals, inventory changes, policy changes, or reclassification, to a ledger account. Not usually a correction.

ZAP   A generic term used to define a type of program that can alter data and programs directly, bypassing controls. Because of this ability, the ZAP and SuperZAP programs must be secured from casual or unauthorized use.

zone portion   The four left-most positions in a byte.

BIBLIOGRAPHY

Abbot, J. *On-Line Programming: A Management Guide*. New York: John Wiley & Sons, 1981.

Ahituv, Niv, and Seev Neumann. *Principles of Information Systems for Management*. Dubuque, Iowa: William C. Brown Co., 1982.

American Bar Association. *Report on Computer Crime*. Washington, D.C.: Section on Criminal Justice, 1984.

American Institute of Certified Public Accountants. *Audit Guide: Audits of Service-Center-Produced Records*. Rev. ed. New York: American Institute of Certified Public Accountants, 1985.

—————. *Statement on Auditing Standards No. 48, The Effects of Computer Processing on the Examination of Financial Statements*. New York: American Institute of Certified Public Accountants, 1984.

—————. *Audit Approaches for a Computerized Inventory System*. New York: American Institute of Certified Public Accountants, 1980.

—————. *Guidelines to Assess Computerized General Ledger and Financial Reporting Systems for Use in CPA Firms*. New York: American Institute of Certified Public Accountants, 1979.

—————. *Audit Considerations in Electronic Fund Transfer Systems*. New York: American Institute of Certified Public Accountants, 1978.

—————. *The Auditor's Study and Evaluation of Internal Control in EDP System*. New York: American Institute of Certified Public Accountants, 1977.

—————. *Codification of Statements on Auditing Standards*. New York: American Institute of Certified Public Accountants, 1977.

American National Standards, Inc. *Flowchart Symbols and Their Usage in Information Processing*. New York: American National Standards Institute, 1971.

American Society of Certified Public Accountants. *Codification of Auditing Standards and Procedures*. New York: American Society of Certified Public Accountants, 1973.

Arthur Anderson & Co. *A Guide for Studying and Evaluating Internal Accounting Controls*. Chicago: Arthur Anderson & Co., 1978.

Andriole, Stephen J. *Interactive Computer-Based Systems*. Princeton, N.J.: Petrocelli Books, 1983.

Arens, Alvin, and James K. Loebbecke. *Auditing: An Integrated Approach*. Englewood Cliffs, N.J.: Prentice-Hall, 1976.

Arkins, Herbert. *Handbook of Sampling for Auditing and Accounting.* 2nd ed. New York: McGraw-Hill Book Co., 1974.

Arsenault, J. E., and J. A. Roberts, eds. *Reliability and Maintainability of Electronic Systems.* Rockville, Md.: Computer Science Press, 1980.

Atre, Shakuntala. *DBMS for the Eighties.* Wellesley, Mass.: QED Information Sciences, 1983.

————. *Structured Techniques for Design, Performance, and Management: With Case Studies.* New York: John Wiley & Sons, 1980.

Auerbach Publishers, Inc. *Practical Data Base Management.* Reston, Va.: Reston Publishing Co., 1982.

————. *EDP Auditing.* Pennsauken, N.J.: Auerbach Publishers, 1978.

Aumiaux, M. *Microprocessor Systems.* New York: John Wiley & Sons, 1982.

Banahan, Mike, and Andy Rutter. *The Unix™ Operating System Book.* New York: John Wiley & Sons, 1983.

Bank Administration Institute. *Statement of Principle and Standards for Internal Auditing in the Banking Industry.* Park Ridge, Ill.: Bank Administration Institute (undated).

Becker, Jay. *Operations Guide to White-Collar Crime Enforcement, on the Investigation of Computer Crime.* Seattle, Wash.: Battelles Law and Justice Center, 1978.

Beizer, Boris. *Software Testing Techniques.* New York: Van Nostrand Reinhold (Electrical-Computer Science and Engineering Series), 1982.

Belzer, Jack, ed. *Encyclopedia of Computer Science and Technology.* New York: Marcel Dekker, Inc., 1980.

Bently, T., and I. Forkner. *Making Information Systems Work for You: An MIS Guide for Business and Professional People.* Old Tappan, N.J.: Prentice-Hall, 1983.

Benton, C. *The Database Guide: How to Select, Organize and Implement Database Systems for Microcomputers.* Bowie, Md.: Robert J. Brady Co., 1984.

Bigelow, R., and S. Nycum. *Your Computer and the Law.* 2nd ed. Reston, Va.: Reston Publishing Co., 1984.

Birkle, J., and R. Yearsley. *Computer Applications in Management.* New York: John Wiley & Sons, 1976.

Bjorner and Jones. *Formal Specification and Software Development.* Englewood Cliffs, N.J.: Prentice-Hall, 1982.

Bohl, Marilyn. *Information Processing.* Chicago: Science Research Associates, 1976.

Boutell, Wayne S. *Computer-Oriented Business Systems.* Englewood Cliffs, N.J.: Prentice-Hall, 1968.

Bradley, J. *Introduction to Data Base Management in Business.* New York: Holt, Rinehart and Winston, 1983.

Braiotta, Jr., Louis. *The Audit Director's Guide: How to Serve Effectively on the Corporate Audit Committee.* New York: John Wiley & Sons, 1981.

Brill, Alan E. *Building Controls into Structured Systems*. New York: Yourdon, Inc., 1983.

Brink, Victor Z., and Herbert Witt. *Modern Internal Auditing: Appraising Operations and Controls*. 4th ed. New York: John Wiley & Sons, 1982.

British Computer Society. *Control and Audit of Minicomputer Systems: A Report of British Computer Society Auditing by Computer Specialist Group*. New York: John Wiley & Sons, 1981.

—————. *Audit and Control of Database Systems*. New York: John Wiley & Sons, 1977.

—————. *Privacy and the Computer — Steps to Practicality*. 2nd ed. New York: John Wiley & Sons, 1972.

Broadbent, D. *Contingency Planning*. New York: John Wiley & Sons, 1979.

Brooner, Ernie. *Microcomputer Data-Base Management*. Indianapolis, Ind.: Sams & Co., 1982.

Bruce, Phillip, and Sam M. Pederson. *The Software Development Project: Planning and Management*. New York: John Wiley & Sons, 1982.

Burch, Jr., John G., and Nathan Hod. *Information Systems: A Case Workbook Approach*. Santa Barbara, Cal.: Wiley/Hamilton, 1975.

Burch, Jr., John G., and Felix R. Strater. *Information Systems, Theory and Practice*. Santa Barbara, Cal.: Hamilton Publishing Co., 1974.

Burton, John C., Russell E. Palmer, and Robert S. Kay, ed. *Handbook of Accounting and Auditing*. Boston, Mass.: Warren, Gorham, & Lamont, 1981.

Byers, Robert A. *Everyman's Database Primer*. Reston, Va.: Reston Publishing Co., 1983.

California Society of Certified Public Accountants. *A Computer Impact Series Report Prepared by the Committee on Electronic Data Processing*. Palo Alto, Cal.: California Society of Certified Public Accountants (undated).

Canadian Institute of Chartered Accountants. *Computer Audit Guidelines*. Toronto, Ontario, Canada: Canadian Institute of Chartered Accountants, 1975.

Carroll, Harry. *OS Data Processing*. New York: John Wiley & Sons, 1974.

Chereb, D. *Business Simulation: Forecasting with Microcomputers*. Old Tappan, N.J.: Prentice-Hall, 1983.

Chorafas, Dimitris N. *Databases for Networks and Minicomputers*. Princeton, N.J.: Petrocelli Books, 1982.

—————. *Data Communications for Distributed Information Systems*. Princeton, N.J.: Petrocelli Books, 1980.

Christian, Kaare. *The UNIX™ Operating System*. New York: John Wiley & Sons, 1983.

Christie, L., and L. Christie. *The Encyclopedia of Microcomputer Terminology: A Sourcebook for Business and Professional People*. Old Tappan, N.J.: Prentice-Hall, 1984.

Cohen, Leo J. *Creating and Planning the Corporate Data Base System Project.* Wellesley, Mass.: QED Information Sciences, 1981.

Collins, G., and G. Blay. *Structured Systems Development Techniques: Strategic Planning to System Testing.* New York: John Wiley & Sons, 1983.

The Computer and Business Equipment Manufacturers Association. *Privacy and Security: A Bibliography.* Washington, D.C.: The Computer and Business Equipment Manufacturers Association, 1982.

Condon, R. *Data Processing Systems Analysis and Design.* 3rd ed. Reston, Va.: Reston Publishing Co., 1982.

Connor, Joseph E., and Burnel H. Devos, Jr., eds. *Guide to Accounting Controls.* Boston, Mass.: Warren, Gorham & Lamont, 1979.

Cornick, Delroy L. *Auditing in the Electronic Environment: Theory, Practice and Literature.* Mt. Airy, Md.: Lomond Publications, 1981.

Cortada, James W. *An Annotated Bibliography on the History of Data Processing.* Westport, Conn.: Greenwood Press, 1983.

Cushing, Barry E. *Accounting Information Systems and Business Organizations.* Reading, Mass.: Addison-Wesley Publishing Co., 1978.

Daniels, Alan, and Don Yeates. *Design and Analysis of Software Systems.* Princeton, N.J.: Petrocelli Books, 1983.

Danning, Dorothy E. *Cryptography and Protection.* Reading, Mass.: Addison-Wesley Publishing Co. (Computer Science Series), 1982.

Date, C. J. *Database: A User's Guide.* Reading, Mass.: Addison-Wesley Publishing Co., 1983.

Davis, B. *Database in Perspective.* New York: John Wiley & Sons, 1980.

Davis, Gordon B. *Management Information Systems: Conceptual Foundations, Structure, and Development.* New York: McGraw-Hill, 1974.

―――. *Auditing and EDP.* New York: American Institute of Certified Public Accountants, 1968.

Davis, James R., and Barry E. Cushing. *Accounting Information Systems: A Book of Readings.* Reading, Mass.: Addison-Wesley, 1982.

Davis, Keagle W., and William E. Perry. *Auditing Computer Applications: A Basic Systematic Approach.* New York: John Wiley & Sons, 1982.

Davis, William S. *Operating Systems — A Systematic View.* Reading, Mass.: Addison-Wesley Publishing Co., 1977.

Defliese, P. L., H. R. Jaenicke, J. D. Sullivan, and R. A. Gnospelius. *Montgomery's Auditing.* 10th ed. New York: John Wiley & Sons, 1985.

Delobel, C., and W. Litwin, eds. *Distributed Data Bases.* New York: Elsevier North-Holland Publishing Co., 1980.

DeMarco, Tom. *Controlling Software Projects: Management Measurement and Estimation.* New York: Yourdon, Inc., 1982.

Deutsch, Michael S. *Software Verification and Validation: Realistic Project Approaches*. Englewood Cliffs, N.J.: Prentice-Hall, 1982.

Dickinson, Brian. *Developing Structured Systems: A Methodology Using Structured Techniques*. New York: Yourdon, Inc., 1981.

Doll, Dixon R. *Data Communications: Facilities, Networks and Systems Design*. New York: John Wiley & Sons, 1978.

Donaldson, H. *A Guide to the Successful Management of Computer Projects*. New York: John Wiley & Sons, 1978.

Duffy, Neil, and Mike Assad. *Information Management: An Executive Approach*. New York: Oxford University Press, 1980.

Eaton, J., and J. Snithers. *This Is It: A Manager's Guide to Information Technology*. London, England: Philip Allan Publishers, Ltd., 1982.

EDP Auditors Foundation. *Certification Program for EDP Auditors*. Hanover Park, Ill. EDP Auditors Foundation, (undated).

————. *Control Objectives*. Steamwood, Ill.: EDP Auditors Foundation, 1980.

Edwards, Chris. *Developing Microcomputerbased Business Systems*. Englewood Cliffs, N.J.: Prentice-Hall, 1983.

Elbert, R., and J. Luggar, eds. *Practice in Software Adaption and Maintenance*. New York: Elsevier North-Holland Publishing Co., 1980.

Enger, Norman L. *Management Standards for Developing Information Systems*. New York: American Management Associations, 1980.

Enger, Norman L., and Paul W. Howerton. *Computer Security: A Management Audit Approach*. New York: American Management Associations, 1980.

Fernandez, Eduardo B., et al. *Database Security and Integrity*. Reading, Mass.: Addison-Wesley Publishing Co. (International Business Machines Systems Programming Series), 1981.

Ferngold, Carl. *Introduction to Data Processing*. Dubuque, Iowa: William C. Brown, 1975.

Fick, G., and R. H. Sprague, Jr., eds. *Decision Support Systems — Issues and Challenges: Proceedings of an International Task Force Meeting*. Elmsford, N.Y.: Pergamon Press, 1980.

Flavin, Matt. *Fundamental Concepts of Information Modeling*. New York: Yourdon, Inc., 1981.

Franta, W. R., et al. *Formal Methods of Program Verification and Specification*. Englewood Cliffs, N.J.: Prentice-Hall, 1982.

Fried, L. *Practical Data Processing Management*. Reston, Va.: Reston Publishing Co., 1979.

Froehlich, Allan F. *Managing the Data Center*. Belmont, Cal.: Lifetime Learning Publications, 1982.

Galland, Frank J. *Dictionary of Computering: Data Communications, Hardware and Software Basics*. New York: John Wiley & Sons, 1982.

Gaydasch, A. *Principles of Electronic Data Processing Management*. Reston, Va.: Reston Publishing Co., 1981.

Gemignam, Michael. *Law and the Computer*. Boston, Mass.: CBI Publishing Co., 1981.

Glass, Ronald A., and Robert L. Noiseux. *Software Maintenance Guidebook*. Englewood Cliffs, N.J.: Prentice-Hall, 1981.

Goldberg, Robert, and Harold Lorin. *The Economics of Information Processing (Volume I: Management Perspectives; Volume II: Operation, Programming and Software Models)*. New York: John Wiley & Sons, 1982.

Goodman, S. and Prentice-Hall editorial staff. *Corporate Treasurer's and Controller's Encyclopedia*. 2 vols., rev. Old Tappan, N.J.: Prentice-Hall, 1975.

Green, Jr., Paul E., and Robert W. Lucky, eds. *Computer Communications*. New York: John Wiley & Sons, 1975.

Gremillion, Lee L. *Managing MIS Implementation*. Ann Arbor, Mich.: University Microfilms International Res Press, 1982.

Hampton, J. *Financial Management Concepts Using Spreadsheet Applications*. Reston, Va.: Reston Publishing Co., 1984.

Harper, William. *Data Processing Documentation: Standards, Procedures and Applications*. Englewood Cliffs, N.J.: Prentice-Hall, 1973.

Harris, Martin L., and Nancy B. Stern. *Introduction to Data Processing,* 2nd ed. New York: John Wiley & Sons, 1979.

Harvard Business Review. *Catching Up With the Computer Revolution*. New York: John Wiley & Sons, 1983.

Heany, Donald F. *Development of Information Systems: What Management Needs to Know*. New York: Ronald Press, 1968.

Hicks, Jr., James O., and Wayne E. Leininger. *Accounting Information Systems*. St. Paul, Minn.: West Publishing Co., 1981.

Hodge, B., R. Fleck, and C. Honess. *Management Information Systems*. Reston, Va.: Reston Publishing Co., 1984.

Hoffman, Lance J. *Security and Privacy in Computer Systems*. New York: John Wiley & Sons, 1973.

Horton, F. *Information Resources Management*. Old Tappan, N.J.: Prentice-Hall, 1984.

House, William C., ed. *Decision Support Systems*. Princeton, N.J.: Petrocelli Books, 1983.

Hoyle, J., and R. Scott. *Practical Case to Auditing: A Systems Approach*. Reston, Va.: Reston Publishing Co., 1982.

Inmon, William H. *Management Control of Data Processing: Preventing Management-by-Crisis*. Englewood Cliffs, N.J.: Prentice-Hall, 1983.

Inmon, William H., and L. Jeanne Friedman. *Design Review Methodology for a Database Environment*. Englewood Cliffs, N.J.: Prentice-Hall, 1982.

Institute of Electrical and Electronic Engineers. *Advances in Software Technology.* New York: Institute of Electrical and Electronic Engineers, 1981.

Institute of Internal Auditors. *Common Body of Knowledge for Internal Auditors.* Altamonte Springs, Fla.: Institute of Internal Auditors, 1984.

―――――. *How to Acquire and Use Generalized Audit Software.* Altamonte Springs, Fla.: Institute of Internal Auditors, 1979.

―――――. *Standards for the Professional Practice of Internal Auditing.* Altamonte Springs, Fla.: Institute of Internal Auditors, 1978.

―――――. *Systems Auditability and Control Study.* 3 vols. Altamonte Springs, Fla.: Institute of Internal Auditors, 1978.

―――――. *Systems Auditability and Control — Audit Practices.* Altamonte Springs, Fla.: Institute of Internal Auditors, 1977.

―――――. *Systems Auditability and Control — Control Practices.* Altamonte Springs, Fla.: Institute of Internal Auditors, 1977.

―――――. *Modern Concepts of Internal Auditing, Establishing the Internal Audit Function DEP-JOB Descriptions.* Orlando, Fla.: Institute of Internal Auditors, 1974.

International Business Machines Corporation. *Managing the Data Processing Organization.* Pub. No. GE19-5208. White Plains, N.Y.: International Business Machines, 1976.

―――――. *Data Security Controls and Procedures: A Philosophy for DP Installations.* Pub. No. G320-5649. White Plains, N.Y.: International Business Machines, 1977.

―――――. *Systems Auditability and Control — Audit Practices.* Pub. No. G320-5790. White Plains, N.Y.: International Business Machines, 1977.

―――――. *Systems Auditability and Control — Control Practices.* Pub. No. G320-5792. White Plains, N.Y.: International Business Machines, 1977.

―――――. *Systems Auditability and Control — Executive Report.* Pub. No. G320-5791. White Plains, N.Y.: International Business Machines, 1977.

―――――. *Management Controls for Data Processing.* Pub. No. GF20-0006. White Plains, N.Y.: International Business Machines, 1976.

―――――. *Auditability Information Catalog.* Pub. No. GB21-9883. White Plains, N.Y.: International Business Machines, 1975.

―――――. *The Considerations of Physical Security in a Computer Environment.* Pub. No. GB20-2700. White Plains, N.Y.: International Business Machines, 1972.

Jancura, Elise, and Arnold Berger, eds. *Computers: Auditing and Control.* Philadelphia, Pa.: Auerbach Publishers, 1973.

Johnson, K. P., and H. R. Jaenicke. *Evaluating Internal Control: Concepts, Guidelines, Procedures, Documentation.* New York: John Wiley & Sons, 1980.

Jones, Seymore, and M. Bruce Cohen. *The Emerging Business: Managing for Growth.* New York: John Wiley & Sons, 1983.

Kacmar, C. *On-Line Systems Design and Implementation (Using ANS COBOL and Command Level CICS).* Reston, Va.: Reston Publishing Co., 1984.

Katzan, Jr., Harry. *An Introduction to Distributed DP*. Princeton, N.J.: Petrocelli Books, 1979.'

Keen, Jeffrey S. *Managing Systems Development*. New York: John Wiley & Sons, 1981.

Klien, M. *Data Communications With IBM Microcomputers*. Bowie, Md.: Robert J. Brady Co., 1984.

Koshy, G. *Local Area Computer Networks*. Reston, Va.: Reston Publishing Co., 1984.

Krause, L., and E. MacGahan. *Computer Fraud and Counter-measures*. Englewood Cliffs, N.J.: Prentice-Hall, 1979.

Kuong, Javier F. *Computer Security, Auditing and Controls: Text and Readings*. Wellesley Hills, Mass.: Management Advisory Publications, 1974.

Kurshan, B., and B. Healy. *Computer Fundamentals*. Reston, Va.: Reston Publishing Co., 1984.

Lane, J. E. *Operating Systems for Microcomputers*. New York: John Wiley & Sons, 1981.

————. *Communicating With Microcomputers*. New York: John Wiley & Sons, 1980.

Lano, R. J. *Technique for Software and Systems Design*. New York: Elsevier North-Holland Publishing Co., 1979.

Larsen, Kent S. *A Public Concern: A Resource Document Based on the Proceedings of a Seminar on Privacy Sponsored by the Domestic Council Committee on the Right of Privacy and the Council of State Governments*. Washington, D.C.: Government Printing Office, August 1975.

Larson, ed. *Distributed Control*. New York: Institute of Electrical and Electronic Engineering, 1981.

Law Enforcement Assistance Administration. *Criminal Justice Resource Manual on Computer Crime*. Washington, D.C.: Office of Justice Assistance, Research, and Statistics, U.S. Department of Justice, 1979.

Leibholz, Stephen W., and Louis D. Wilson. *User's Guide to Computer Crime: Its Commission, Detection and Prevention*. Radnor, Pa.: Chilton Book Co., 1974.

Leiss, Ernst L. *Principles of Data Security*. New York: Plenum Publishing Corp., 1982.

Lewin, Douglas. *Theory and Design of Digital Computer Systems*. 2nd ed. New York: John Wiley & Sons, 1980.

Lientz, Bennet P. *An Introduction to Distributed Systems: Contract Title: Network Services — Managerial Evaluation*. Reading, Mass.: Addison-Wesley Publishing Co., 1981.

Lientz, Bennet P., and E. Burton Swanson. *Software Maintenance Management*. Reading, Mass.: Addison-Wesley Publishing Co., 1980.

Lindhe, Richard, and Steven D. Grossman. *Accounting Information Systems*. Houston, Texas: Dame Publications, Inc., 1980.

Long, L. *Managers Guide to Computers and Information Systems*. Englewood Cliffs, N.J.: Prentice-Hall, 1983.

————. *Data Processing Documentation and Procedures Manual*. Reston, Va.: Reston Publishing Co., 1982.

Longworth, G. *Management Handbook of Computer Operations*. New York: John Wiley & Sons, 1982.

Lorin, Harold. *Aspects of Distributed Computer Systems*. John Wiley & Sons, 1980.

Loscalzo, Margaret A., and Paul J. Wendell, eds. *Modern Accounting and Auditing Checklists*. Boston, Mass.: Warren, Gorham & Lamont, 1981.

Lucas, Henry, and Cyrus F. Gibson. *A Casebook for Management Information Systems*. 2nd ed. New York: McGraw-Hill Book Co., 1981.

Lyon, John K. *The Database Administrator*. New York: John Wiley & Sons, 1976.

Macron, T. *Microcomputers in Large Organizations*. Old Tappan, N.J.: Prentice-Hall, 1983.

Mair, William C., Keagle W. Davis, and Donald Wood. *Computer Control and Audit*. 2nd ed. Altamonte Springs, Fla.: Institute of Internal Auditors, 1978.

————. *EDP Controls and Audit*. Altamonte Springs, Fla.: Institute of Internal Auditors, 1976.

Martin, James. *Managing the Database Environment*. Englewood Cliffs, N.J.: Prentice-Hall, 1983.

————. *Strategic Data Planning Methodologies*. Englewood Cliffs, N.J.: Prentice-Hall, 1982.

————. *Computer Networks and Distributed Processing: Software, Techniques and Architecture*. Englewood Cliffs, N.J.: Prentice-Hall, 1981.

————. *Design and Strategy for Distributed DP*. Englewood Cliffs, N.J.: Prentice-Hall, 1981.

————. *Security, Accuracy and Privacy in Computer Systems*. Englewood Cliffs, N.J.: Prentice-Hall, 1973.

Matthews, Don Q. *The Design of the Management Information System*. New York: Moffat Publishing Co., 1981.

McClure, Carma. *Managing Software Development and Maintenance*. New York: Van Nostrand Reinhold, 1981.

McCosh, Andrew, Mawdudr Rahman, and Michael J. Earl. *Developing Managerial Information Systems*. New York: John Wiley & Sons, 1981.

McCosh, Andrew, and Michael Scott-Morton. *Management Decision Support Systems*. New York: John Wiley & Sons, 1978.

McElreath, T. Jack. *IMS Design and Implementation Techniques*. Wellesley, Mass.: QED Information Sciences, Inc., 1979.

McLean, Ephraim R., and John V. Soden. *Strategic Planning for MIS*. New York: John Wiley & Sons, 1977.

McLeod, Raymond, and Irvine Forkner. *Computerized Business Information Systems: An Introduction to Data Processing*, 2nd ed. New York: John Wiley & Sons, 1982.

McNichols, C. *Microcomputer-Based Data Analysis*. Reston, Va.: Reston Publishing Co., 1984.

————. *Microcomputer-Based Information and Decision Support Systems*. Reston, Va.: Reston Publishing Co., 1983.

McRae, T. W. *Statistical Sampling for Audit and Control*. New York: John Wiley & Sons, 1974.

Meigs, Walter, John Larsen, and Robert F. Meigs. *Principles of Auditing*. 8th ed. Homewood, Ill.: Richard D. Irwin, 1985.

Metropolis, Edby N., et al. *A History of Computing in the 20th Century*. New York: Academic Press, Harcourt Brace Jovanovich, 1980.

Morris, Michael F., and Paul Roth. *Computer Performance Evaluation: Tools and Techniques for Effective Analysis*. New York: Van Nostrand Reinhold Co., 1981.

Moscove, Steven A., and Mark G. Simkin. *Accounting Information Systems: Concepts and Practice for Effective Decision Making Systems*. New York: John Wiley & Sons, 1981.

Muchnik, Steven, and Neil D. Jones. *Program Flow Analysis: Theory and Application*. Englewood Cliffs, N.J.: Prentice-Hall, 1981.

Mullins, C., and T. West. *Harnessing Information Technologies*. Old Tappan, N.J.: Prentice-Hall, 1984.

Mumford, Enid, and Don Henshall. *A Participative Approach to Computer Systems Design: A Case Study of the Introduction of a New Computer System*. New York: John Wiley & Sons, 1978.

Murdick, Robert G., and Thomas C. Fuller. *Accounting Information Systems*. Englewood Cliffs, N.J.: Prentice-Hall, 1978.

Myers, Glenford J. *Software Reliability: Principles and Practices*. New York: John Wiley & Sons, 1976.

National Bureau of Standards. *Software Documentation*. Washington, D.C.: Government Printing Office, 1982.

————. *An Analysis of Computer Security Safeguards for Detecting and Preventing Intentional Computer Misuse*. National Bureau of Standards Special Publication 500-25. Washington, D.C.: Government Printing Office, 1978. (Check with National Bureau of Standards for availability.)

————. *Data Encryption Standard*. FIPS Pub. No. 46. Washington, D.C.: National Technical Information Services, 1978.

————. *Automatic Data Processing Risk Assessment*. NBSIR 77-1228. Washington, D.C.: Government Printing Office, 1977. (Check with National Bureau of Standards for availability.)

————. *EFT in the United States: The Final Report of the National Commission on Electronic Funds Transfer, October 28, 1977, Washington, DC*. 052-003-00475-5. Washington, D.C.: Government Printing Office, 1977.

————. *The Use of Passwords for Controlled Access to Computer Resources*. Washington, D.C.: Government Printing Office, 1977. (Check with National Bureau of Standards for availability.)

————. *Glossary for Computer Systems Security*. FIPS Pub. No. 39. Washington, D.C.: National Technical Information Services, 1976.

————. *Computer Security Guidelines for Implementing the Privacy Act of 1974.* FIPS Pub. No. 41. Washington, D.C.: National Technical Information Services, 1975.

————. *Approaches to Privacy and Security in Computer Systems.* SD Catalog No. C13, 10:404. Washington, D.C.: Government Printing Office, 1974. (Check with National Bureau of Standards for availability.)

————. *Guidelines for ADP Physical Security and Risk Management.* FIPS Pub. No. 31. Washington, D.C.: National Technical Information Services, 1974.

National Computing Centre (Manchester). *Computing Practice: Security Aspects.* New York: John Wiley & Sons, 1979.

Newman, Maurice S. *Accounting Estimates by Computer Sampling.* New York: John Wiley & Sons, 1982.

Nilles, J. *Micros and Modems: Telecommunicating With Personal Computers.* Reston, Va.: Reston Publishing Co., 1983.

Page, John, and Paul Hooper. *Accounting and Information Systems.* 2nd ed. Reston, Va.: Reston Publishing Co., 1982.

Parikh, Girish. *Techniques of Program and System Maintenance.* Boston, Mass.: Little, Brown & Co., 1982.

Parker, Donn B. *Manager's Guide to Computer Security.* Reston, Va.: Reston Publishing Co., 1983.

————. *Computer Security.* Reston, Va.: Reston Publishing Co., 1981.

————. *Computer Security Management.* Reston, Va.: Reston Publishing Co., 1981.

————. *Computer Abuse Assessment and Control Study Final Report.* Menlo Park, Cal.: SRI International, March 1979.

————. *Ethical Conflicts in Computer Science and Technology.* Arlington, Va. AFIPS Press, 1979.

————. *Crime by Computer.* New York: Charles Scribner's Sons, 1976.

Passen, Barry J. *Program Flowcharting for Business Data Processing.* New York: John Wiley & Sons, 1978.

Perry, William E. *Ensuring Database Integrity.* New York: John Wiley & Sons, 1983.

————. *Managing Systems Maintenance.* Wellesley, Mass.: QED Information Sciences, 1983.

————. *The Accountant's Guide to Computer Systems.* New York: John Wiley & Sons, 1982.

————. *Computer Control and Security: A Guide for Managers and Systems Analysts.* New York: John Wiley & Sons, 1981.

————. *Planning EDP Audits.* Carol Stream, Ill.: EDP Auditors Foundation, 1981.

————. *Selecting EDP Audit Areas.* Carol Stream, Ill.: Auditors Foundation, 1980.

Peters, Paul, and Anton Meijer. *Computer Network Architectures.* Rockville, Md.: Computer Science Press, 1983.

Pfleeger, Charles P. *Machine Organization: An Introduction to the Structure and Programming of Computing Systems*. New York: John Wiley & Sons, 1982.

Porter, Thomas, and John Burton. *Auditing: A Conceptual Approach*. Belmont, Cal.: Wadsworth Publishing Co., 1971.

Porter, Thomas W. *EDP Controls and Auditing*. Belmont, Cal.: Wadsworth Publishing Co., 1974.

Pritchard, J. A. T. *Computer Security: Facts and Figures*. New York: John Wiley & Sons, 1981.

Puzman, Josef, and Radoslav Porizek. *Communications Control in Computer Networks*. New York: John Wiley & Sons, 1980.

Radford, K. *Information Systems for Strategic Decisions*. Reston, Va.: Reston Publishing Co., 1978.

Ralston, Anthony, ed. *Encyclopedia of Computer Science and Engineering*. 2nd ed. New York: Van Nostrand Reinhold, 1982.

Randall, R. *Microcomputers in Small Business*. Old Tappan, N.J.: Prentice-Hall, 1982.

Rasmussen, J., and W. B. Rouse, eds. *Human Detection and Diagnosis of System Failures*. New York: Plenum Publishing Corp., 1981.

Riley, M. J. *Management Information Systems*. San Francisco, Cal.: Holden-Day, Inc., 1981.

Rosenthal, S. *Rosenthal's Computer Glossary*. Old Tappan, N.J.: Prentice-Hall, 1984.

Ross, J. *Modern Management and Information Systems*. Reston, Va.: Reston Publishing Co., 1976.

Rotch, W., and B. Allen. *Cases in Management Accounting and Control Systems*. Reston, Va.: Reston Publishing Co., 1983.

Rullo, Thomas A. *Advances in Computer Security Management*. New York: John Wiley & Sons, 1980.

————. *The Heyden Advances Library in EDP Management*. New York: John Wiley & Sons, 1980.

Salton, G., and M. McGill. *Introduction to Modern Information Retrieval*. New York: McGraw-Hill Book Co., 1983.

Sanders, Donald H. *Computers in Business: An Introduction*. New York: McGraw-Hill Book Co., 1968.

Sardinas, Joseph, and John G. Burch. *EDP Auditing: A Primer*. New York: John Wiley & Sons, 1981.

Sawyer, Lawrence B. *The Practice of Modern Internal Auditing, Appraising Operations for Management*. New York: Institute of Internal Auditors, 1973.

Schmittroth, Jr., John, ed. *Encyclopedia of Information Systems and Services*. Detroit: Gale Research Co., 1982.

Schoderbek, Peter P., Asterios G. Kafalas, and Charles G. Schoderbek. *Management Systems: Conceptual Considerations*. Dallas, Texas: Business Publications, 1975.

Schweitzer, J. *Protecting Information in the Electronic Workplace: A Guide for Managers*. Reston, Va.: Reston Publishing Co., 1983.

Scott, R., et al. *Auditing: A Systems Approach*. Reston, Va.: Reston Publishing Co., 1982.

Seidler, Lee L., and Douglas R. Carmichael. *The Accountants' Handbook*. New York: John Wiley & Sons, 1981.

Seitz, N. *Business Forecasting: Concepts and Microcomputer Applications*. Reston, Va.: Reston Publishing Co., 1984.

Sharma, Rosham L., et al. *Network Systems*. New York: Van Nostrand Reinhold, 1981.

Sippl, Charles J., and Roger J. Sippl. *Computer Dictionary and Handbook*. 3rd ed. Indianapolis, Ind.: Sams & Co., 1980.

Squires, T. *Security in Systems Design*. New York: John Wiley & Sons, 1981.

————. *Computer Security: The Personal Aspect*. New York: John Wiley & Sons, 1980.

Stern, Nancy. *Flowcharting: A Tool for Understanding Computer Logic*. New York: John Wiley & Sons, 1975.

Stokes, Adrian V. *Concise Encyclopedia of Computer Terminology*. Brookfield, Vt.: Gower Publishing Ltd., 1980.

Sundburg, M., and G. Goldkuhl. *Information Systems Development: A Systematic Approach*. Englewood Cliffs, N.J.: Prentice-Hall, 1981.

Talbot, James Reid. *Computer Security*. New York: John Wiley & Sons, 1981.

————. *Management Guide to Computer Security*. New York: John Wiley & Sons, 1979.

Taylor, D. H., and G. W. Glezen. *Auditing: Integrated Concepts and Procedures*. New York: John Wiley & Sons, 1982.

Techo, Robert. *Data Communications: An Introduction to Concepts and Design*. New York: Plenum Publishing Corp., 1980.

Thomas, A. J., and I. J. Douglas. *Audit of Computer Systems*. New York: John Wiley & Sons, 1981.

Tricker, R. I., and Richard Boland. *Management Information and Control Systems*. 2nd ed. New York: John Wiley & Sons, 1982.

Tyran, M. *Computerized Accounting Methods and Controls*. 2nd ed. Old Tappan, N.J.: Prentice-Hall, 1978.

U.S. Senate Committee on Government Operations. *Problems Associated With Computer Technology in Federal Programs and Private Industry*. Washington, D.C.: Government Printing Office, June 1976.

Vaillancourt, Pauline M. *International Directory of Acronyms in Library, Information and Computer Sciences*. New York: R. R. Bowker Co., 1980.

Van Dyyn, J. *Practical Systems and Procedures Manual*. Reston, Va.: Reston Publishing Co., 1975.

Walsh, M. *Database and Data Communications Systems: A Guide for Managers*. Reston, Va.: Reston Publishing Co., 1983.

—————. *Information Management Systems/Virtual Storage*. Reston, Va.: Reston Publishing Co., 1983.

—————. *Understanding Computers: What Managers and Users Need to Know*. New York: John Wiley & Sons, 1981.

Warnier, Jean-Dominique. *Logical Construction of Systems*. New York: Van Nostrand Reinhold, 1981.

Watson, Hugh J., and Archie B. Carrol, eds. *Computers for Business*. Plano, Texas: Business Publications, 1980.

Weber, R. *EDP Auditing: Conceptual Foundations and Practice*. New York: McGraw-Hill Book Co., 1982.

Weil, Ulric. *Information Systems in the Eighties: Products, Markets and Vendors*. Englewood Cliffs, N.J.: Prentice-Hall, 1982.

Weis, S. *Computer Applications Guide for Accountants*. Reston, Va.: Reston Publishing Co., 1984.

Weldon, Jay-Louise. *Database Administration*. New York: Plenum Publishing Corp., 1981.

Wendell, Paul J., et al. *Corporate Controller's Manual*. Boston, Mass.: Warren, Gorham & Lamont, 1981.

Wendell, Paul J., ed. *Modern Accounting and Auditing Forms*. Boston, Mass.: Warren, Gorham & Lamont, 1978.

Wessel, A. E. *The Implementation of Complex Information Systems*. New York: John Wiley & Sons, 1979.

Westermeier, ed. *EDP and the Law*. Parkridge, Ill.: Data Processing Management Association, 1981.

Wetherbe, James C. *Executive's Guide to Computer-Based Information Systems*. Englewood Cliffs, N.J.: Prentice-Hall, 1983.

Wilkins, Barry J. *The Internal Auditor's Information Security Handbook*. Altamonte Springs, Fla.: Institute of Internal Auditors, 1979.

Wilkinson, Joseph W. *Accounting and Information Systems*. New York: John Wiley & Sons, 1982.

Wood, M. B. *Introducing Computer Security*. New York: John Wiley & Sons, 1982.

Woolfe, Roger. *Videotex: The New Television-Telephone Information Services*. New York: John Wiley & Sons, 1980.

INDEX

[*Chapter numbers are boldface and are followed by a colon; lightface numbers after the colon refer to pages within the chapter.*]

[Chapter numbers are boldface and are followed by a colon; lightface numbers after the colon refer to pages within the chapter.]

[Chapter numbers are boldface and are followed by a colon; lightface numbers after the colon refer to pages within the chapter.]

*[Chapter numbers are boldface and are followed by a colon; lightface
numbers after the colon refer to pages within the chapter.]*

[Chapter numbers are boldface and are followed by a colon; lightface numbers after the colon refer to pages within the chapter.]

[Chapter numbers are boldface and are followed by a colon; lightface numbers after the colon refer to pages within the chapter.]

[Chapter numbers are boldface and are followed by a colon; lightface numbers after the colon refer to pages within the chapter.]

*[Chapter numbers are boldface and are followed by a colon; lightface
numbers after the colon refer to pages within the chapter.]*

[*Chapter numbers are boldface and are followed by a colon; lightface numbers after the colon refer to pages within the chapter.*]

[Chapter numbers are boldface and are followed by a colon; lightface numbers after the colon refer to pages within the chapter.]

[Chapter numbers are boldface and are followed by a colon; lightface numbers after the colon refer to pages within the chapter.]

[Chapter numbers are boldface and are followed by a colon; lightface numbers after the colon refer to pages within the chapter.]

[Chapter numbers are boldface and are followed by a colon; lightface numbers after the colon refer to pages within the chapter.]

[Chapter numbers are boldface and are followed by a colon; lightface numbers after the colon refer to pages within the chapter.]

[Chapter numbers are boldface and are followed by a colon; lightface numbers after the colon refer to pages within the chapter.]

*[Chapter numbers are boldface and are followed by a colon; lightface
numbers after the colon refer to pages within the chapter.]*

[Chapter numbers are boldface and are followed by a colon; lightface numbers after the colon refer to pages within the chapter.]

[Chapter numbers are boldface and are followed by a colon; lightface numbers after the colon refer to pages within the chapter.]

[*Chapter numbers are boldface and are followed by a colon; lightface numbers after the colon refer to pages within the chapter.*]

[Chapter numbers are boldface and are followed by a colon; lightface numbers after the colon refer to pages within the chapter.]

[Chapter numbers are boldface and are followed by a colon; lightface numbers after the colon refer to pages within the chapter.]

[Chapter numbers are boldface and are followed by a colon; lightface numbers after the colon refer to pages within the chapter.]

[Chapter numbers are boldface and are followed by a colon; lightface numbers after the colon refer to pages within the chapter.]

[Chapter numbers are boldface and are followed by a colon; lightface numbers after the colon refer to pages within the chapter.]

*[Chapter numbers are boldface and are followed by a colon; lightface
numbers after the colon refer to pages within the chapter.]*

[Chapter numbers are boldface and are followed by a colon; lightface numbers after the colon refer to pages within the chapter.]

[Chapter numbers are boldface and are followed by a colon; lightface numbers after the colon refer to pages within the chapter.]

[Chapter numbers are boldface and are followed by a colon; lightface numbers after the colon refer to pages within the chapter.]

[Chapter numbers are boldface and are followed by a colon; lightface numbers after the colon refer to pages within the chapter.]

[Chapter numbers are boldface and are followed by a colon; lightface numbers after the colon refer to pages within the chapter.]

[*Chapter numbers are boldface and are followed by a colon; lightface
numbers after the colon refer to pages within the chapter.*]

[Chapter numbers are boldface and are followed by a colon; lightface numbers after the colon refer to pages within the chapter.]